The Ultimate Guide to

U.S. Army Combat

Skills, Tactics, and Techniques

The Ultimate Guide to

U.S. Army Combat

Skills, Tactics, and Techniques

Edited by
Jay McCullough

Skyhorse Publishing

Skyhorse Publishing books may be purchased in bulk at special discounts for sales promotion, corporate gifts, fund-raising, or educational purposes. Special editions can also be created to specifications. For details, contact the Special Sales Department, Skyhorse Publishing, 555 Eighth Avenue, Suite 903, New York, NY 10018 or info@skyhorsepublishing.com.

www.skyhorsepublishing.com

10 9 8 7 6 5 4 3 2 1

Library of Congress Cataloging-in-Publication Data

The ultimate guide to U.S. Army combat skills, tactics, and techniques / edited by Jay McCullough.
p. cm.
ISBN 978-1-61608-010-5 (pbk. : alk. paper)
1. Combat--Handbooks, manuals, etc. 2. Combat survival--Handbooks, manuals, etc. 3. Hand-to-hand fighting--Handbooks, manuals, etc. 4. United States. Army--Handbooks, manuals, etc. I. McCullough, Jay.
U260.U47 2010
355.40973--dc22

2010019496

Printed in Canada

CONTENTS

INTRODUCTION

The U.S. has the best-equipped and well-trained Army in the world. Barring unforeseen political considerations or a catastrophic act of nature, it can deploy nearly anywhere and accomplish almost any reasonable mission. This is due in large part to the Army's experience as an institution in a variety of wartime environments. Its hard-earned wisdom about how to cope with almost every imaginable scenario, on a soldier-by-soldier basis, distinguishes it as a service of excellence whose individuals are highly adaptable. They are well prepared, they accomplish the mission, and when the circumstances are truly unfavorable to life itself, they are survivors.

The keys to this preparation are contained in the Army's many sensible, well-written, voluminous, and scattered publications. They address nearly every aspect of running, provisioning, or being in the Army, and include what constitutes really the best information on combat operations available anywhere. With the exception of being a professional soldier, I can think of no better way to learn about combat than from these many volumes. The task of culling every bit of useful information about combat from every U.S. Army publication would take months however, so I've done it here for you in *The Ultimate U.S. Army Guide to Combat Skills, Tactics, and Techniques*. You could say, it practically wrote itself. Anything useful you find within these pages is due to hard working and dedicated Army personnel who took the time to research and assemble this valuable information. Anything incorrect or inconsequential is my fault for including it.

I've tried to make the selections useful to a general reader who may find him- or herself in a combat situation, whether they are alone or in a small group. Here you will find information on how to defend yourself with your bare hands, how to pick through an urban battlefield, learn how to draw a bead on someone or something, and how to avoid having sniper get the best of you. On a battlefield you may need to recognize grenades, boobytraps, and natural defensive locations, and they are all discussed here. Since you may have occasion to find a machine gun, there are also sections about the tactical considerations of using one. Alas, since you are unlikely to become a tank commander, or forge a tank in your back yard (and because the stingy publisher would give me only a thousand pages), you will find no information on how to conduct a classic set-piece tank battle on the plains of central Europe. But, you will discover the weaker points of Soviet-era and modern Russian tanks. Useful stuff when you need it!

As a final note, I'd like to suggest some of what I'd consider the best advice about combat I can give. Just as hospitals are excellent places to get sick, battlegrounds are excellent places to get dead. War is a conflagration; it does not seek peace, rather, like many human institutions, it seeks its own continuance, jumping from country to country like a wildfire or a pestilence, and it ceases only when it has destroyed everything in its path and utterly exhausted all a people's political oxygen, ruins or expends all their resources, and has crippled or killed all their children. So, it's probably best to avoid combat situations for reasons large and small. But some wars are unavoidable, and for those times, the ability to survive, and yes, even thrive belongs to those who are best trained, properly equipped, and who are adaptable to rapidly changing conditions. Your training starts here.

Jay Mccullough
December 2009
North Haven, Connecticut

PART I

Hand-to-Hand Combat

Introduction to Combatives

Very few people have ever been killed with the bayonet or saber, but the fear of having their guts explored with cold steel in the hands of battle-maddened men has won many a fight.

–PATTON

DEFINITION OF COMBATIVES

Hand-to-hand combat is an engagement between two or more persons in an empty-handed struggle or with hand-held weapons such as knives, sticks, or projectile weapons that cannot be fired. Proficiency in hand-to-hand combat is one of the fundamental building blocks for training the modern soldier.

PURPOSES OF COMBATIVES TRAINING

Soldiers must be prepared to use different levels of force in an environment where conflict may change from low intensity to high intensity over a matter of hours. Many military operations, such as peacekeeping missions or non-combatant evacuation, may restrict the use of deadly weapons. Hand-to-hand combatives training will save lives when an unexpected confrontation occurs.

More importantly, combatives training helps to instill courage and self-confidence. With competence comes the understanding of controlled aggression and the ability to remain focused while under duress. Training in combatives includes hard and arduous physical training that is, at the same time, mentally demanding and carries over to other military pursuits. The overall effect of combatives training is—

- The culmination of a successful physical fitness program, enhancing individual and unit strength, flexibility, balance, and cardiorespiratory fitness.
- Building personal courage, self-confidence, self-discipline, and esprit de corps.

BASIC PRINCIPLES

Underlying all combatives techniques are principles the hand-to-hand fighter must apply to successfully defeat an opponent. The natural progression of techniques, as presented in this manual, will instill these principles into the soldier.

a. **Mental Calm.** During a fight a soldier must keep his ability to think. He must not allow fear or anger to control his actions.

b. **Situational Awareness.** Things are often going on around the fighters that could have a direct impact on the outcome of the fight such as opportunity weapons or other personnel joining the fight.

c. **Suppleness.** A soldier cannot always count on being bigger and stronger than the enemy. He should, therefore, never try to oppose the enemy in a direct test of strength. Supple misdirection of the enemy's strength allows superior technique and fight strategy to overcome superior strength.

d. **Base.** Base refers to the posture that allows a soldier to gain leverage from the ground. Generally, a soldier must keep his center of gravity low and his base wide—much like a pyramid.

e. **Dominant Body Position.** Position refers to the location of the fighter's body in relation to his opponent's. A vital principle when fighting is to gain control of the enemy by controlling this relationship. Before any killing or disabling technique can be applied, the soldier must first gain and maintain one of the dominant body positions.

f. **Distance.** Each technique has a window of effectiveness based upon the amount of space between the two combatants. The fighter must control the distance between himself and the enemy in order to control the fight.
g. **Physical Balance.** Balance refers to the ability to maintain equilibrium and to remain in a stable upright position.
h. **Leverage.** A fighter uses the parts of his body to create a natural mechanical advantage over the parts of the enemy's body. By using leverage, a fighter can have a greater effect on a much larger enemy.

SAFETY

The Army's combatives program has been specifically designed to train the most competent fighters in the shortest possible time in the safest possible manner.

a. **General Safety Precautions.** The techniques of Army combatives should be taught in the order presented in this manual. They are arranged to not only give the natural progression of techniques, but to present the more dangerous techniques after the soldiers have established a familiarity with the dynamics of combative techniques in general. This will result in fewer serious injuries from the more dynamic moves.
b. **Supervision.** The most important safety consideration is proper supervision. Because of the potentially dangerous nature of the techniques involved, combatives training must always be conducted under the supervision of qualified leaders.
c. **Training Areas.** Most training should be conducted in an area with soft footing such as a grassy or sandy area. If training mats are available, they should be used. A hard surface area is not appropriate for combatives training.
d. **Chokes.** Chokes are the best way to end a fight. They are the most effective way to incapacitate an enemy and, with supervision, are also safe enough to apply in training exactly as on the battlefield.
e. **Joint Locks.** In order to incapacitate an enemy, attacks should be directed against large joints such as the elbow, shoulder, or knee. Attacks on most of these joints are very painful long before causing any injury, which allows full-force training to be conducted without significant risk of injury. The exceptions are wrist attacks and twisting knee attacks. The wrist is very easily damaged, and twisting the knee does not become painful until it is too late. Therefore, these attacks should be taught with great care and should not be allowed in sparring or competitions.
f. **Striking.** Striking is an inefficient way to incapacitate an enemy. Strikes are, however, an important part of an overall fight strategy and can be very effective in manipulating the opponent into unfavorable positions. Striking can be practiced with various types of protective padding such as boxing gloves. Defense can be practiced using reduced force blows. Training should be continuously focused on the realities of fighting.

CHAPTER 1

Basic Ground-Fighting Techniques

Basic ground-fighting techniques build a fundamental understanding of dominant body position, which should be the focus of most combatives training before moving on to the more difficult standing techniques. Ground fighting is also where technique can most easily be used to overcome size and strength.

SECTION I. DOMINANT BODY POSITION

Before any killing or disabling technique can be applied, the soldier must first gain and maintain dominant body position. The leverage gained from dominant body position allows the fighter to defeat a stronger opponent. An appreciation for dominant position is fundamental to becoming a proficient fighter because it ties together what would otherwise be a long confusing list of unrelated techniques. If a finishing technique is attempted from dominant position and fails, the fighter can simply try again. If, on the other hand, a finishing technique is attempted from other than dominant position and fails, it will usually mean defeat. The dominant body positions will be introduced in order of precedence.

1-1. BACK MOUNT

The back mount gives the fighter the best control of the fight (Figure 1-1, page 1-2). From this position it is very difficult for the enemy to either defend himself or counterattack. Both legs should be wrapped around the enemy with the heels "hooked" inside his legs. One arm is under an armpit and the other is around the neck and the hands are clasped. Even though a fighter may find himself with his own back on the ground this is still the back mount.

> ⚠ **CAUTION**
>
> While in the back mount, the fighter's feet should never be crossed because this would provide the enemy an opportunity for an ankle break.

Figure 1-1: Back mount.

1-2. FRONT MOUNT

The front mount (Figure 1-2) is dominant because it allows the fighter to strike the enemy with punches without the danger of effective return punches, and also provides the leverage to attack the enemy's upper body with joint attacks. Knees are as high as possible toward the enemy's armpits. This position should be held loosely to allow the enemy to turn over if he should try.

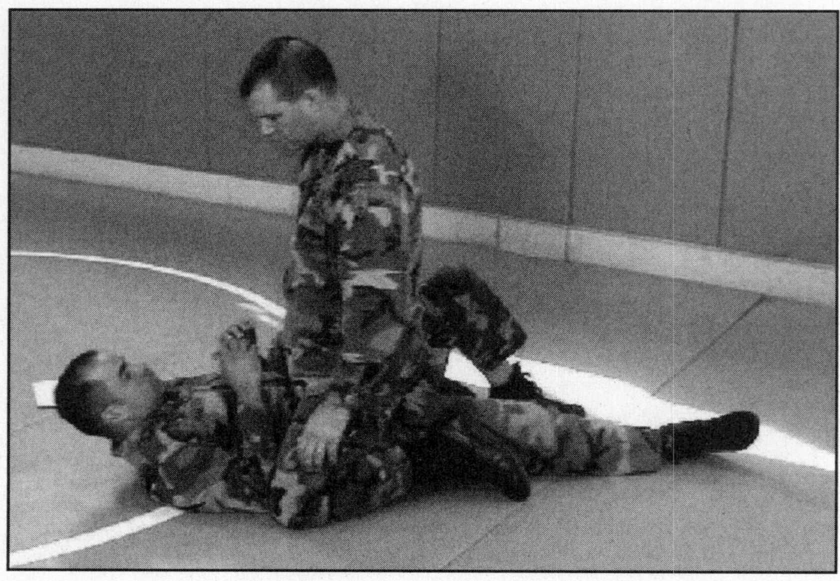

Figure 1-2: Front mount.

1-3. GUARD

If the fighter must be on the bottom, the guard position (Figure 1-3) allows the best defense and the only chance of offense. It is important initially for the fighter to lock his feet together behind the enemy's back to prevent him from simply pushing the fighter's knees down and stepping over them.

Figure 1-3: Guard.

1-4. SIDE CONTROL

Although side control (Figure 1-4) is not a dominant position, many times a fighter will find himself in this position, and he must be able to counter the enemy's defensive techniques. The fighter should place his elbow on the ground in the notch created by the enemy's head and shoulder. His other hand should be palm down on the ground on the near side of the enemy. The leg closest to the enemy's head should be straight and the other one bent so that the knee is near the enemy's hip. He should keep his head down to avoid knee strikes.

Figure 1-4: Side control.

SECTION II. BASIC TECHNIQUES

These basic techniques not only teach a fighter to understand dominant body position, but also provide an introduction to a systematic way of fighting on the ground. Almost all types of finishing moves are represented by the simplest and, at the same time, most effective example of the type. Before any time is spent on the more complex and harder to learn techniques presented later in this manual, the fighter must master these basics.

1-5. BODY POSITIONING MOVES

The key to developing good ground fighters is ingraining a feel for the dominant body positions and how they relate to each other.

a. **Stand up in Base.** This is the most basic technique. It allows the fighter to stand up in the presence of an enemy or potential enemy without compromising his base and thus making himself vulnerable to attack. The principles of body movement inherent in this technique make it so important that leaders should reinforce it every time a fighter stands up.

(1) ***Step 1*** (Figure 1-5). The fighter assumes a seated posture resting on his strong side hand with his weak side arm resting comfortably on his bent knee. His feet should not be crossed.

Figure 1-5: Stand up in base, step 1.

(2) ***Step 2*** (Figure 1-6). Placing his weight on his strong side hand and weak side foot, the fighter picks up the rest of his body and swings his leg between his two posts, placing his foot behind his strong side hand. It is important that the knee should be behind the same side arm as shown.

Figure 1-6: Stand up in base, step 2.

(3) ***Step 3*** (Figure 1-7). After placing his weight on both feet, the fighter lifts his hand from the ground and assumes a fighter's stance. He holds his hands high to protect his head and face. His fists are clenched, but relaxed. His elbows are close to his body, and his weight is evenly distributed on both feet, creating a stable base. He is light on his feet with his knees slightly flexed to allow quick movement in any direction.

Figure 1-7: The fighter's stance.

b. **Escape the Mount, Trap, and Roll.** This move starts with the fighter on his back and the enemy mounted on his chest.

(1) ***Step 1*** (Figure 1-8). Using both hands the fighter secures one of the enemy's arms and places his foot over the same side foot of the enemy, keeping his elbows tucked in as much as possible.

Figure 1-8: Escape the mount, trap, and roll, step 1.

(2) ***Step 2*** (Figure 1-9). The fighter now lifts the enemy straight up with his hips and, because the enemy has neither a hand nor a foot to stop him, he will topple over.

Figure 1-9: Escape the mount, trap, and roll, step 2.

(3) ***Step 3*** (Figure 1-10). As the enemy begins to fall, the fighter turns over, ending within the enemy's guard.

Figure 1-10: Escape the mount, trap, and roll, step 3.

c. **Escape the Mount, Shrimp to the Guard.** This move also starts with the fighter on his back and the enemy mounted on his chest. While the fighter is attempting to escape the mount, trap, and roll, he may be unable to capture the enemy's leg. This occurs when the enemy moves his leg away. This movement, however, creates an opening under the same leg. The term shrimp refers to the action of moving the hips away, which is crucial to the success of this technique.

(1) ***Step 1*** (Figure 1-11). The fighter turns on his side and faces toward the opening created by the enemy, ensuring that his leg is flat on the ground.

Figure 1-11: Escape the mount, shrimp to the guard, step 1.

(2) ***Step 2*** (Figure 1-12). The fighter now uses either his elbow or hand to hold the enemy's leg in place and brings his knee through the opening.

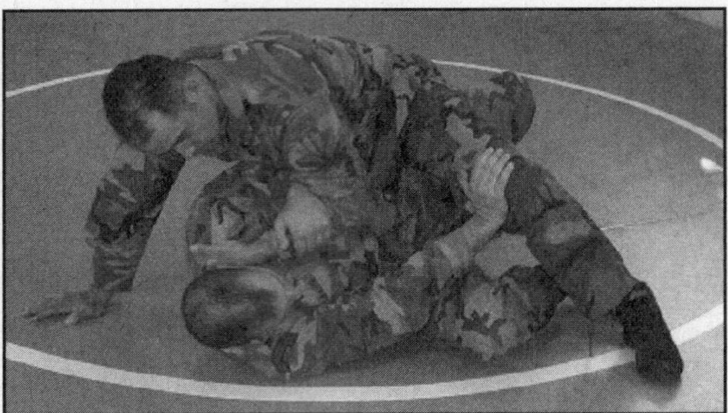

Figure 1-12: Escape the mount, shrimp to the guard, step 2.

(3) ***Step 3*** (Figure 1-13). When his knee gets past the enemy's leg, the fighter places his weight on the same leg and turns towards the other side. This action will bring his knee up and create enough space to pull the leg out and place it over the enemy's leg.

Figure 1-13: Escape the mount, shrimp to the guard, step 3.

(4) ***Step 4*** (Figure 1-14). The fighter now uses his hands to hold the enemy's other leg in place to repeat the actions from the first side.

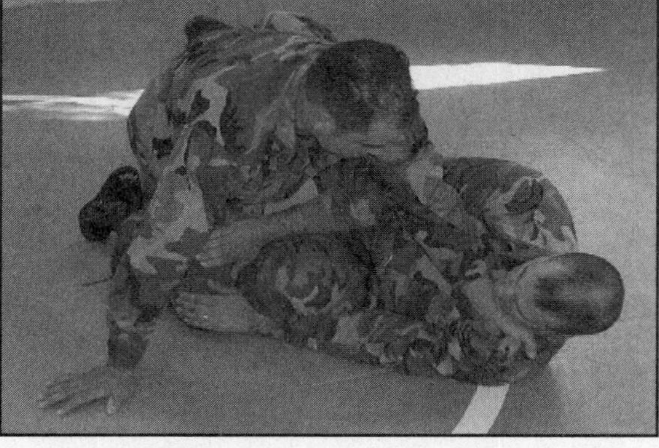

Figure 1-14: Escape the mount, shrimp to the guard, step 4.

(5) ***Step 5*** (Figure 1-15). It is important that the fighter lock his feet together around the enemy, placing him in the open guard.

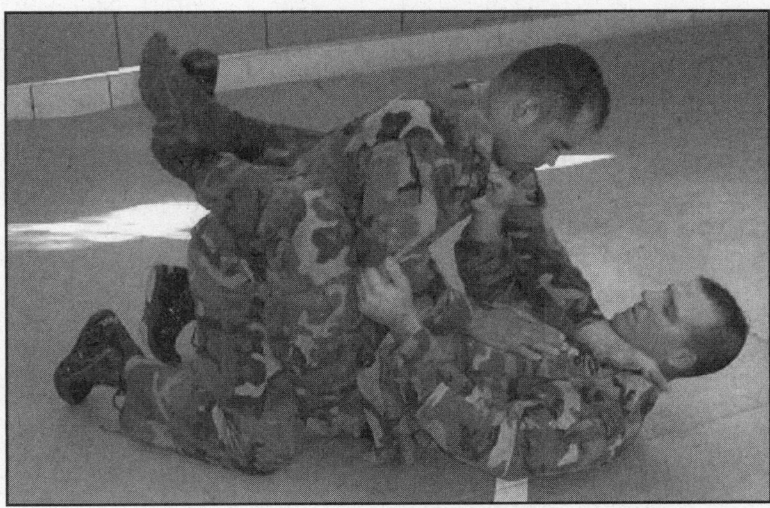

Figure 1-15: Escape the mount, shrimp to the guard, step 5.

d. **Pass the Guard and Achieve the Mount.** The fighter is in base within the enemy's guard. From this position, the fighter must escape from within the enemy's legs. This action is called passing the guard.

(1) ***Step 1*** (Figure 1-16). The first thing the fighter must do is defend against the front choke by using one hand to pin one of the enemy's arms to the ground at the biceps. He also keeps an upright posture.

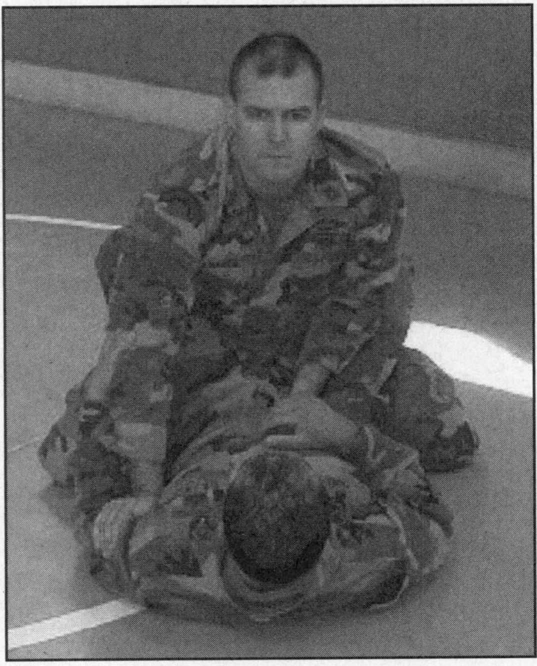

Figure 1-16: Pass the guard and achieve the mount, step 1.

(2) ***Step 2*** (Figure 1-17). The fighter then raises his opposite side foot and places it on the ground just out of reach of the enemy's hand. He turns his hips, creating an opening, and pushes his hand through, fingertips first.

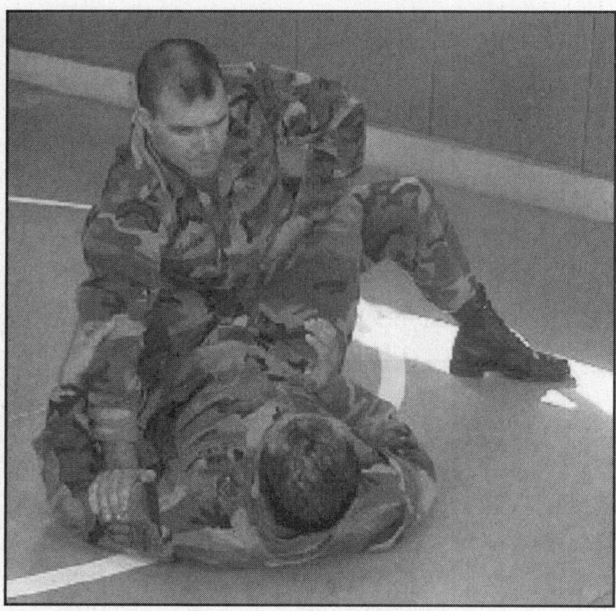

Figure 1-17: Pass the guard and achieve the mount, step 2.

(3) ***Step 3*** (Figure 1-18). The fighter then slides down and back until the enemy's leg is on his shoulder.

Figure 1-18: Pass the guard and achieve the mount, step 3.

(4) ***Step 4*** (Figure 1-19). With the same hand, the fighter grasps the enemy's collar with his thumb on the inside and drives the enemy's knee straight past his head. Pressure on the enemy's spine forces him to release his legs.

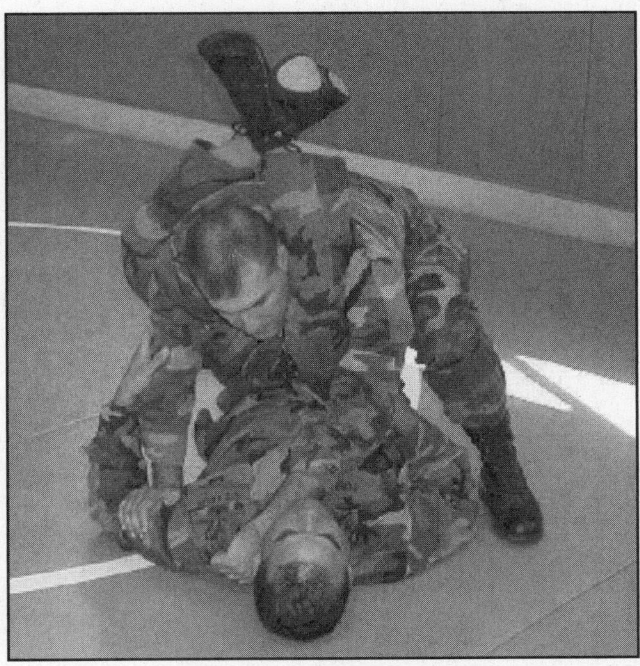

Figure 1-19: Pass the guard and achieve the mount, step 4.

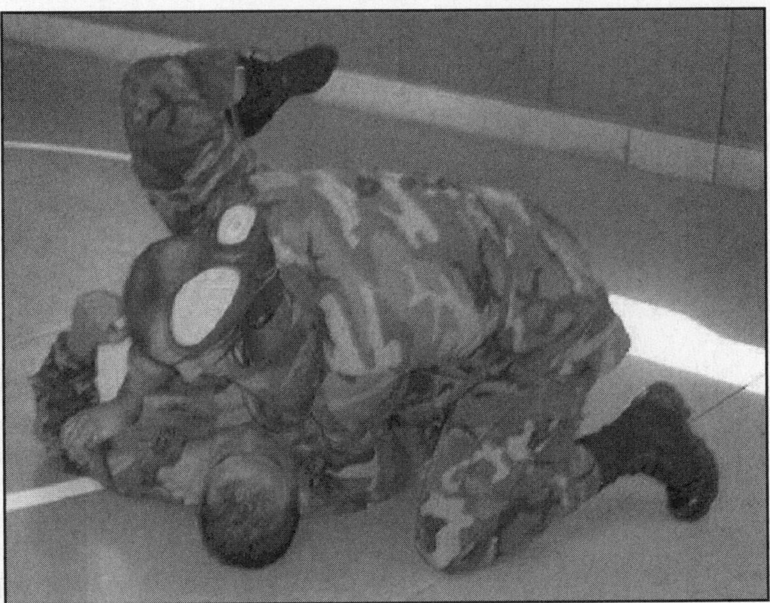

Figure 1-19: Pass the guard and achieve the mount, step 4. *(Continued)*

(5) ***Step 5*** (Figure 1-20). The fighter rides the enemy down into side control.

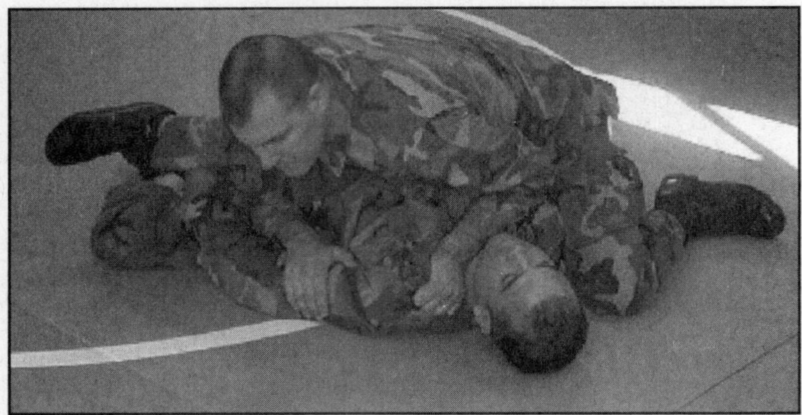

Figure 1-20: Pass the guard and achieve the mount, step 5.

Figure 1-20: Pass the guard and achieve the mount, step 5. ***(Continued)***

(6) ***Step 6*** (Figure 1-21). The fighter faces toward the enemy's legs and changes his hips, ensuring that his knee is controlling the enemy's hip, and that his legs are spread out to avoid a reversal.

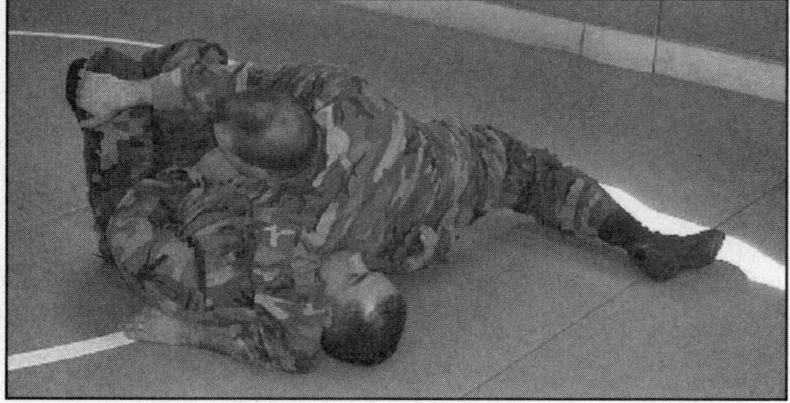

Figure 1-21: Pass the guard and achieve the mount, step 6.

(7) ***Step 7*** (Figure 1-22). The fighter uses his free hand to control the enemy's legs, and swings his leg over into the mount.

Figure 1-22: Pass the guard and achieve the mount, step 7.

e. **Escape the Half Guard.** Frequently the enemy will wrap his legs around one of fighter's from the bottom. This is called the half guard.

(1) ***Step 1*** (Figure 1-23). The fighter must prevent the enemy from either regaining the guard, or rolling him over. To do this, the fighter must assume a strong position. He should ensure that his elbow is against the side of the enemy's neck, and he is blocking the enemy from placing his leg under him with his bottom knee.

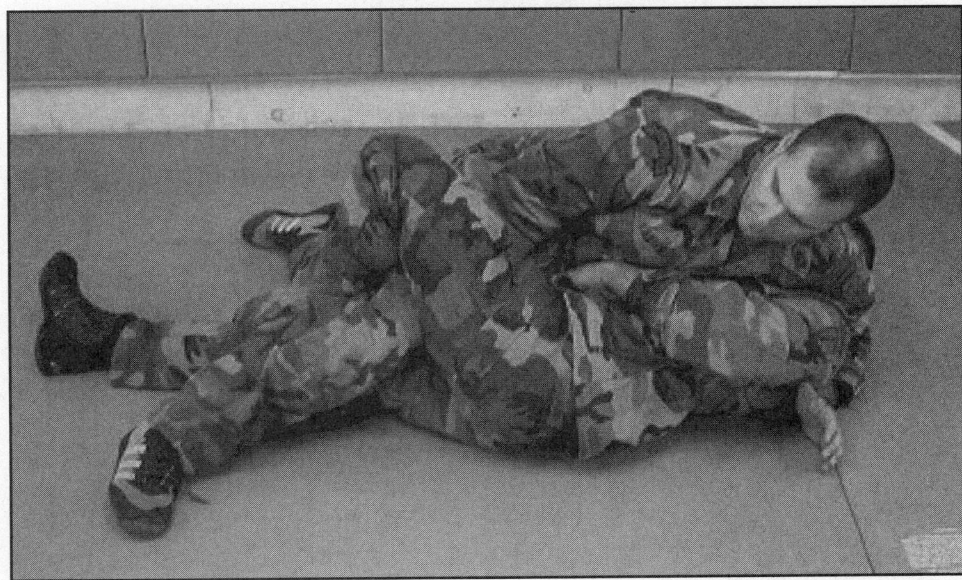

Figure 1-23: Escape the half guard, step 1.

(2) ***Step 2*** (Figure 1-24). By moving first the toe and then the heel of the captured foot, the fighter "walks" it closer to the enemy's buttocks.

Figure 1-24: Escape the half guard, step 2.

(3) ***Step 3*** (Figure 1-25). The fighter uses his free hand to push the enemy's knee until the fighter's knee is exposed, and then drives it over the enemy until it is on the ground.

Figure 1-25: Escape the half guard, step 3.

(4) ***Step 4*** (Figure 1-26). If the enemy attempts to push against the fighter's knee with his hand, the fighter places his hand under the enemy's arm at the bend in his elbow and pushes it upward towards his head.

Figure 1-26: Escape the half guard, step 4.

f. **Arm Push and Roll to the Rear Mount.** The fighter starts this technique in the front mount.

(1) ***Step 1*** (Figure 1-27). When the enemy attempts to protect his face from punches by crossing his arms over it, the fighter uses both hands to push one arm farther across and captures it in place by using his body weight.

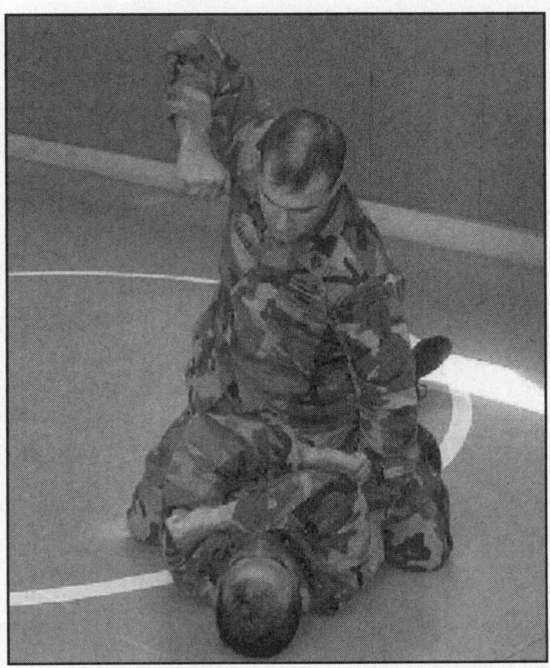

Figure 1-27: Arm push and roll to the rear mount, step 1.

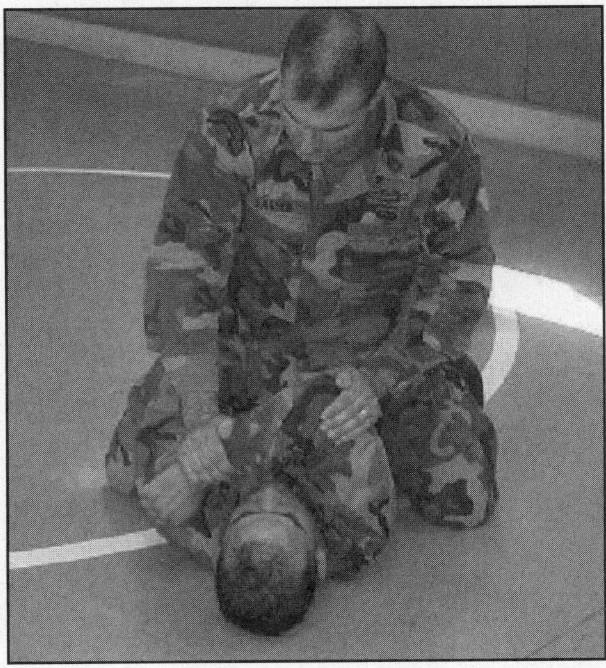

Figure 1-27: Arm push and roll to the rear mount, step 1. *(Continued)*

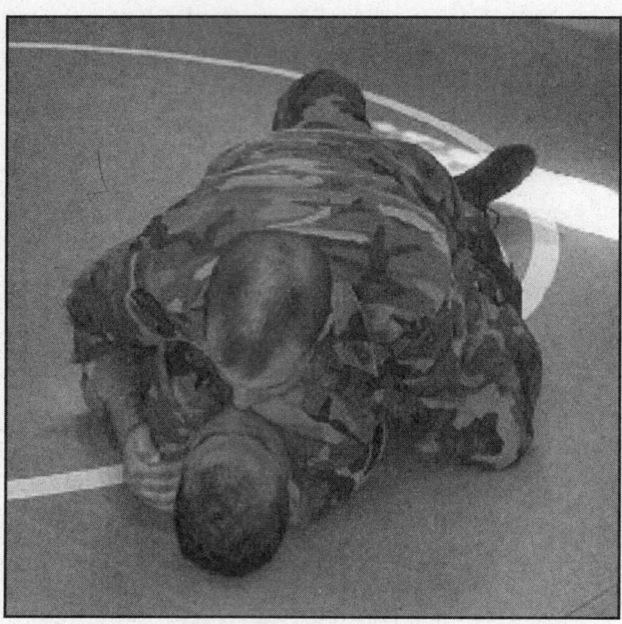

Figure 1-27: Arm push and roll to the rear mount, step 1. *(Continued)*

(2) ***Step 2*** (Figure 1-28). While keeping control with one hand, the fighter uses the other hand to reach around the enemy's head and grasp the wrist of the captured hand.

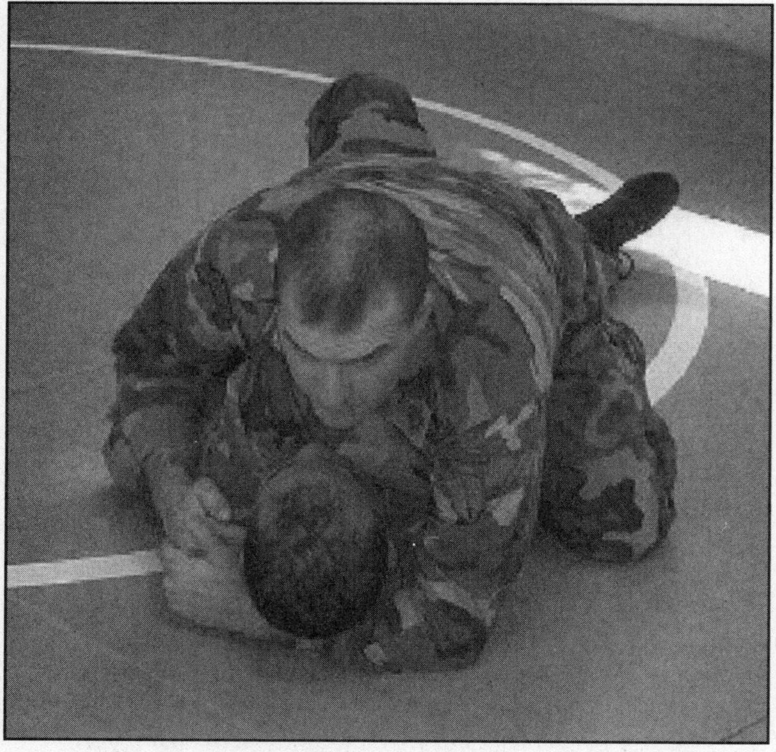

Figure 1-28: Arm push and roll to the rear mount, step 2.

(3) ***Step 3*** (Figure 1-29). The fighter now places the first hand on the enemy's elbow and, by pushing with his chest, turns the enemy onto his stomach. The hand on the elbow is used to hold the enemy in place while the fighter repositions his chest for further pushing.

Figure 1-29: Arm push and roll to the rear mount, step 3.

(4) ***Step 4*** (Figure 1-30). The enemy will sometimes use his elbow as a post to avoid being turned to his stomach. When this happens, the fighter brings his weight slightly off of the enemy and uses his hand to pull the elbow under the enemy, pushing him forward onto his stomach.

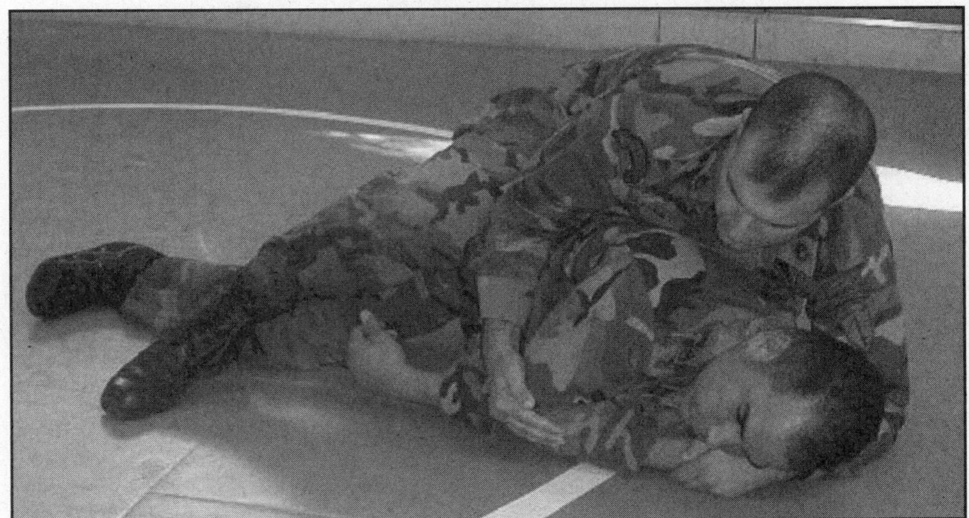

Figure 1-30: Arm push and roll to the rear mount, step 4.

(5) ***Step 5*** (Figure 1-31). From this position the enemy normally tries to rise up and get his knees under him. When he attempts this, the fighter sits up and brings both legs around, "hooking" them inside of the enemy's legs, and grasps his hands together around the enemy's chest. One arm should be over the enemy's shoulder and the other should be under his arm.

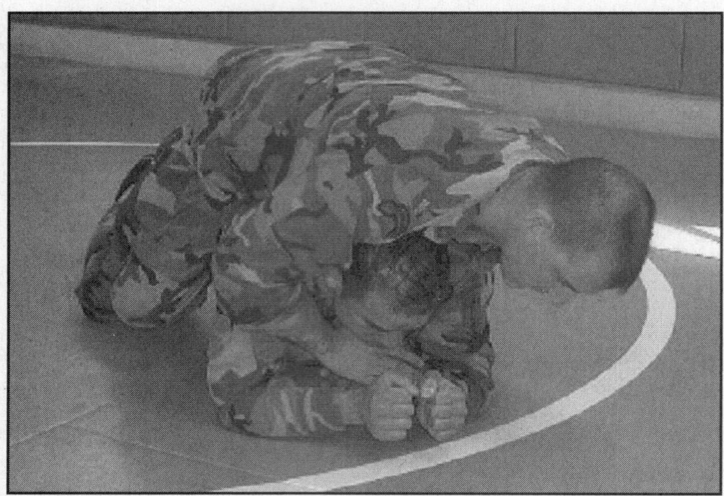

Figure 1-31: Arm push and roll to the rear mount, step 5.

g. **Escape the Rear Mount.** This technique begins with the fighter face down and the enemy on the fighter's back in the rear mount.

(1) ***Step 1*** (Figure 1-32). The fighter must first roll over one shoulder so the enemy ends up underneath him, both facing skyward.

Figure 1-32: Escape the rear mount, step 1.

(2) ***Step 2*** (Figure 1-33). He now places one arm beside his own ear as shown and the other across his body in his armpit. This will prevent the enemy from securing a choke.

Figure 1-33: Escape the rear mount, step 2.

(3) ***Step 3*** (Figure 1-34). Falling toward the side of his own raised arm, the fighter pushes himself toward his own shoulders using the ground to "scrape" the enemy off his back.

Figure 1-34: Escape the rear mount, step 3.

(4) ***Step 4*** (Figure 1-35). Once his back is on the ground, the fighter uses his arms and legs to step over and gain the mount.

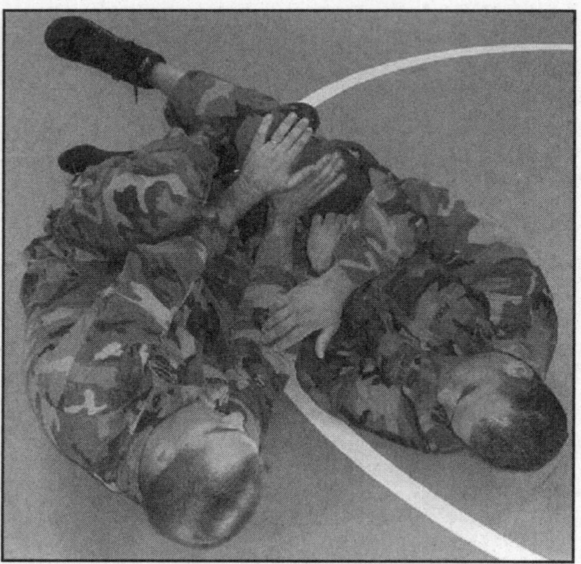

Figure 1-35: Escape the rear mount, step 4.

Figure 1-35: Escape the rear mount, step 4. *(Continued)*

1-6. FINISHING MOVES

When dominant body position has been achieved the fighter can attempt to finish the fight secure in the knowledge that if an attempt fails, as long as he maintains dominant position, he may simply try again.

a. **Rear Naked Choke.** Chokes are the most effective method of disabling an enemy. This technique should only be executed from the back mount after both leg hooks are in place.
   (1) ***Step 1*** (Figure 1-36). Leaving the weak hand in place, the fighter reaches around the enemy's neck and under his chin with the strong hand.

Figure 1-36: Rear naked choke, step 1.

(2) ***Step 2*** (Figure 1-37). The fighter now places the biceps of the weak hand under the strong hand, moves the weak hand to the back of the enemy's head, and completes the choke by expanding his chest.

Figure 1-37: Rear naked choke, step 2.

b. **Cross Collar Choke from the Mount and Guard.** This technique can only be executed from the guard or the mount.

(1) ***Step 1*** (Figure 1-38). With the weak hand, the fighter grasps the enemy's collar and pulls it open.

Figure 1-38: Cross collar choke from the mount, step 1.

(2) ***Step 2*** (Figure 1-39). While keeping a hold with the weak hand, the fighter now inserts his strong hand, fingers first, onto the collar. The hand should be relaxed and reach around to the back of the neck grasping the collar.

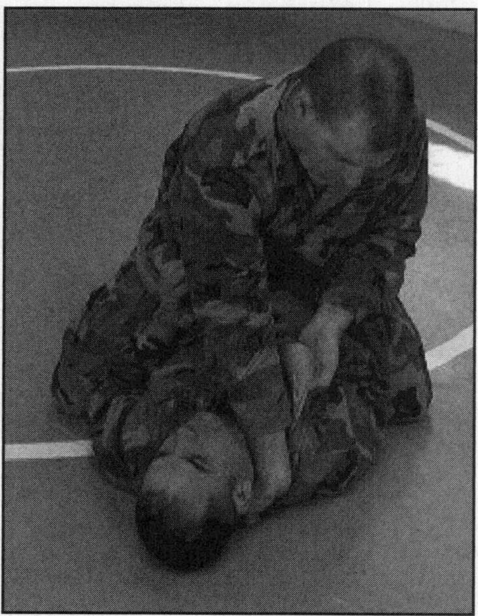

Figure 1-39: Cross collar choke from the mount, step 2.

(3) ***Step 3*** (Figure 1-40). After grasping the back of the enemy's collar, the fighter inserts the weak hand under the strong hand and into the collar, fingers first, touching or very close to the first hand.

Figure 1-40: Cross collar choke from the mount, step 3.

(4) ***Step 4*** (Figure 1-41). The fighter turns his wrists so that the palms face toward him, and brings his elbows to his side. He will complete the choke by expanding his chest and pulling with the muscles of his back.

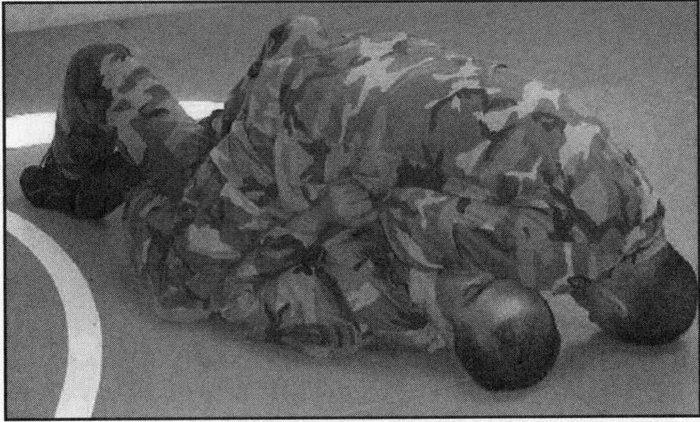

Figure 1-41: Cross collar choke from the mount, step 4.

> ✍ NOTE
>
> If the fighter is applying this choke from the mount, he should put his head on the ground on the side of the top hand and relax into the choke.

c. **Front Guillotine Choke.** Many times this technique may be used as a counter to the double leg takedown.

(1) ***Step 1*** (Figure 1-42). As the enemy shoots in toward the fighter's legs, the fighter should ensure that the enemy's head goes underneath one of his arms. The fighter wraps his arm around the enemy's head and under his neck. The fighter's palm should be facing his own chest.

Figure 1-42: Front guillotine choke, step 1.

(2) ***Step 2*** (Figure 1-43). With the other hand, the fighter grasps the first hand, ensuring that he has not reached around the enemy's arm, and pulls upward with both hands.

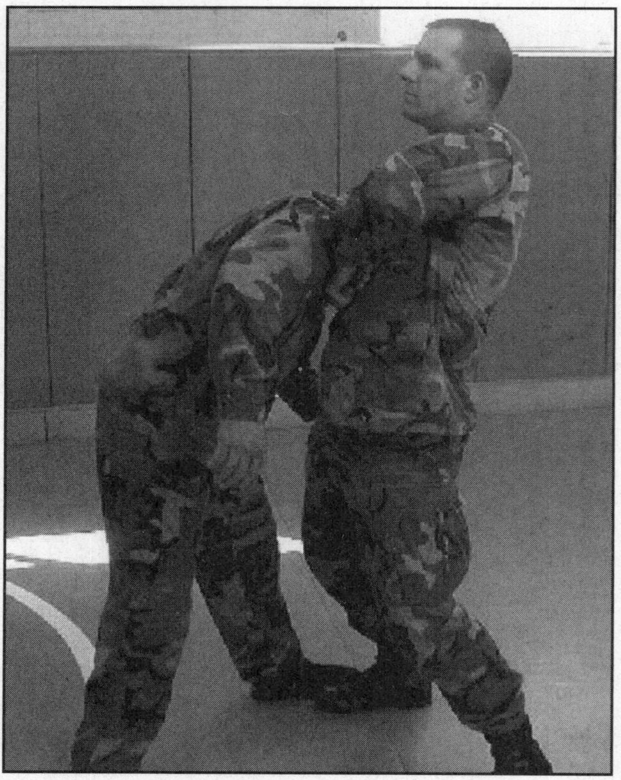

Figure 1-43: Front guillotine choke, step 2.

(3) ***Step 3*** (Figure 1-44). He now sits down and places the enemy within his guard, and finishes the choke by pulling with his arms and pushing with his legs.

Figure 1-44: Front guillotine choke, step 3.

d. **Bent Arm Bar from the Mount and Cross Mount.**

(1) ***Step 1*** (Figure 1-45). When the fighter has mounted the enemy, the enemy may try to cover his face by putting both arms up. Using the heel of his hand, the fighter drives the enemy's wrist to the ground ensuring that his elbow goes to the elbow notch (elbow between collarbone and the head with pressure against the neck).

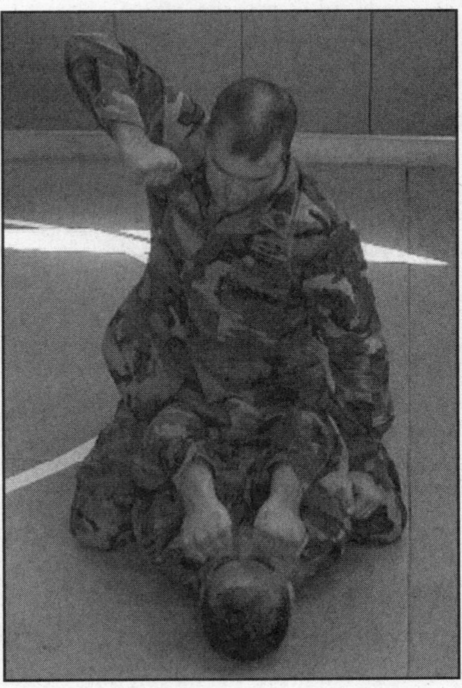

Figure 1-45: Bent arm bar from the mount and cross mount, step 1.

Figure 1-45: Bent arm bar from the mount and cross mount, step 1. *(Continued)*

(2) ***Step 2*** (Figure 1-46). With the other hand, the fighter reaches under the enemy's bent arm and grasps his own wrist.

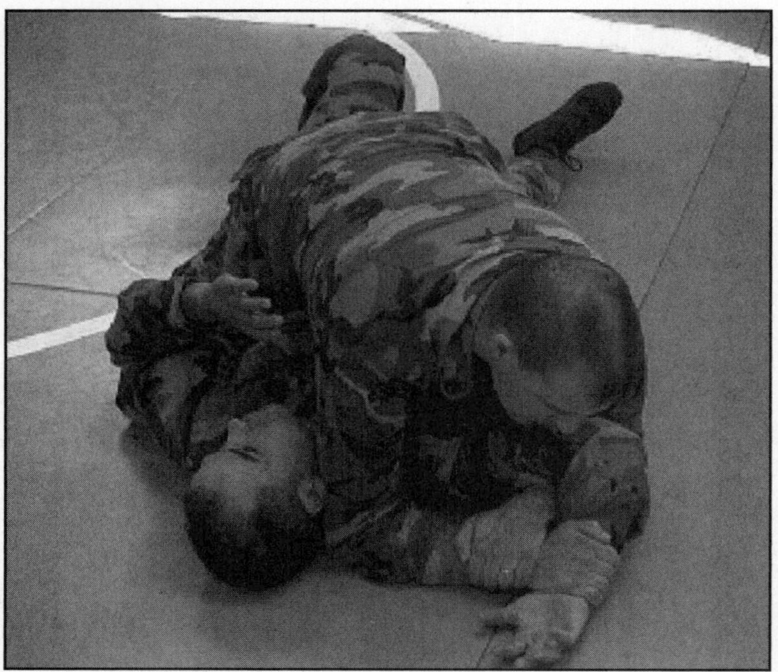

Figure 1-46: Bent arm bar from the mount and cross mount, step 2.

(3) ***Step 3*** (Figure 1-47). The fighter raises the enemy's elbow and at the same time drags the back of his hand along the ground like a paint brush, breaking the enemy's arm at the shoulder.

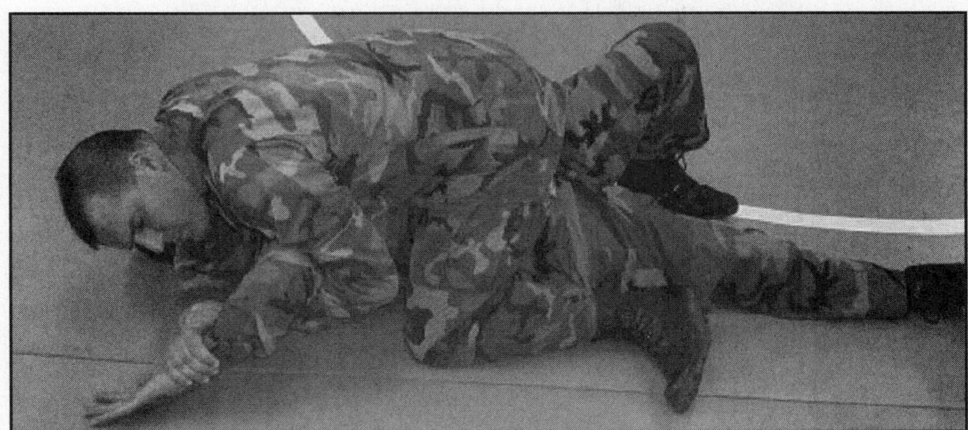

Figure 1-47: Bent arm bar from the mount and cross mount, step 3.

e. **Straight Arm Bar from the Mount.**

(1) ***Step 1*** (Figure 1-48). From the mount, the enemy may attempt to push the fighter off with his arms. The fighter places both of his arms on the enemy's chest ensuring that his arm goes over the targeted arm.

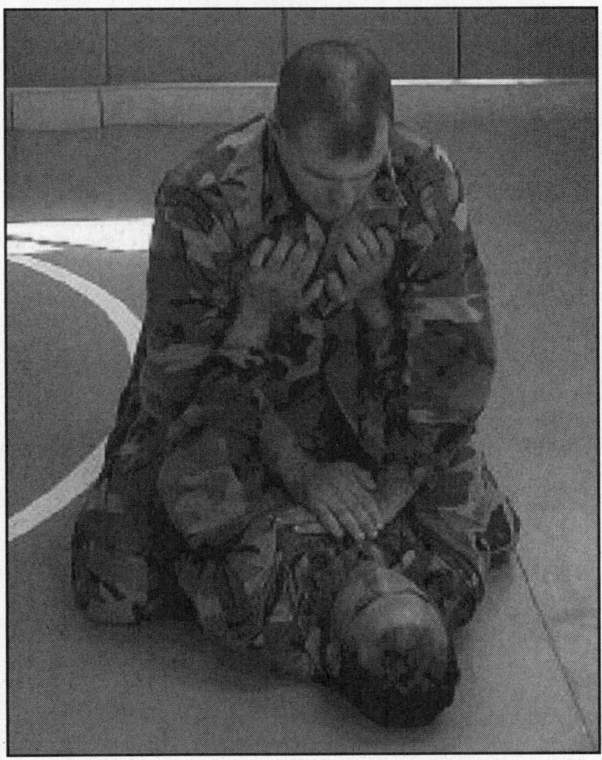

Figure 1-48: Straight arm bar from the mount, step 1.

(2) ***Step 2*** (Figure 1-49). Placing all of his weight on the enemy's chest, the fighter pops up and places his feet under him, ensuring that he keeps his butt low.

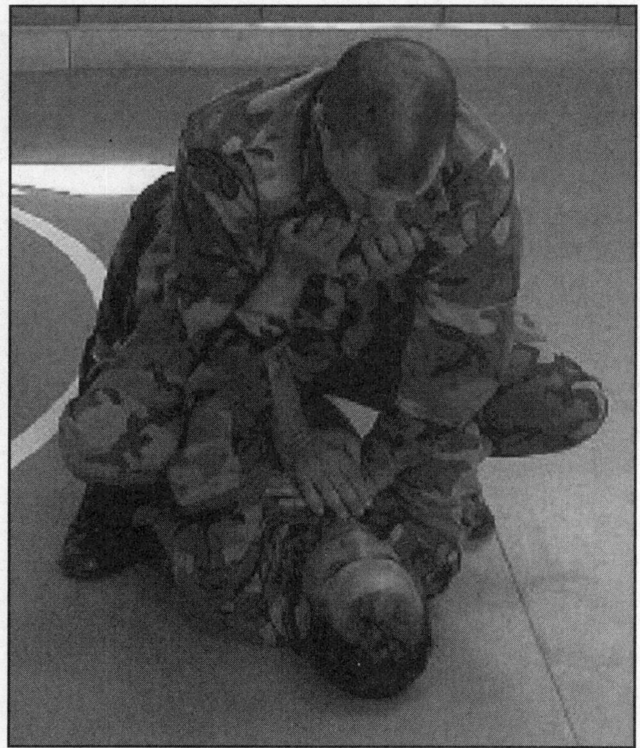

Figure 1-49: Straight arm bar from the mount, step 2.

(3) ***Step 3*** (Figure 1-50). Keeping his weight on the enemy's chest, he now swings his leg around and over the enemy's head and slides down the arm.

Figure 1-50: Straight arm bar from the mount, step 3.

(4) ***Step 4*** (Figure 1-51). The fighter now pinches the enemy's arm between his legs, grasps the arm at the wrist, and falls back extending the arm. The breaking action is hip pressure against the elbow joint.

Figure 1-51: Straight arm bar from the mount, step 4.

f. **Straight Arm Bar from the Guard.**

(1) ***Step 1*** (Figure 1-52). When the fighter is on his back with the enemy in his guard, the enemy will sometimes present a straight arm such as when trying to choke. The fighter should secure the target arm above the shoulder.

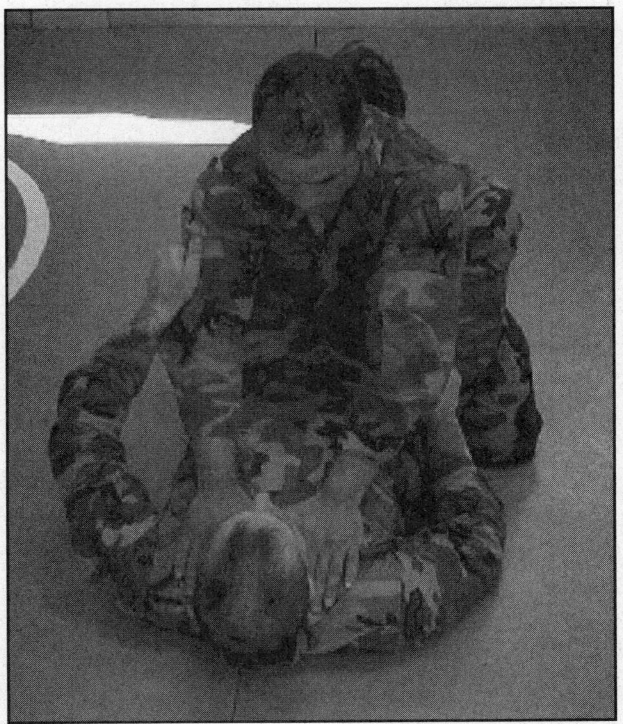

Figure 1-52: Straight arm bar from the guard, step 1.

(2) ***Step 2*** (Figure 1-53). The fighter inserts his other hand under the enemy's leg on the side opposite the targeted arm. The hand should be palm up.

Figure 1-53: Straight arm bar from the guard, step 2.

(3) ***Step 3*** (Figure 1-54). By releasing his legs from around the enemy's waist and raising them above him, the fighter changes his center of gravity.

Figure 1-54: Straight arm bar from the guard, step 3.

(4) ***Step 4*** (Figure 1-55). He now curls his back to give himself a point on which to spin, and by pulling with the arm on the side opposite the targeted arm, he spins around and places his leg over the enemy's head, capturing the target arm between his legs.

Figure 1-55: Straight arm bar from the guard, step 4.

(5) ***Step 5*** (Figure 1-56). The fighter now brings his hand from under the enemy's leg and secures the wrist of the targeted arm, completing the move by breaking the targeted arm with pressure from his hips.

Figure 1-56: Straight arm bar from the guard, step 5.

g. **Sweep from the Attempted Straight Arm Bar.**

(1) ***Step 1*** (Figure 1-57). If the enemy tucks his head in to avoid the arm bar, the fighter maintains his grip on the enemy's leg and swings his own leg down to gain momentum. The fighter ensures that he curls his leg under after swinging it down.

Figure 1-57: Sweep from the attempted straight arm bar, step 1.

(2) ***Step 2*** (Figure 1-58). The fighter pushes the enemy straight over with his other leg and finishes mounted.

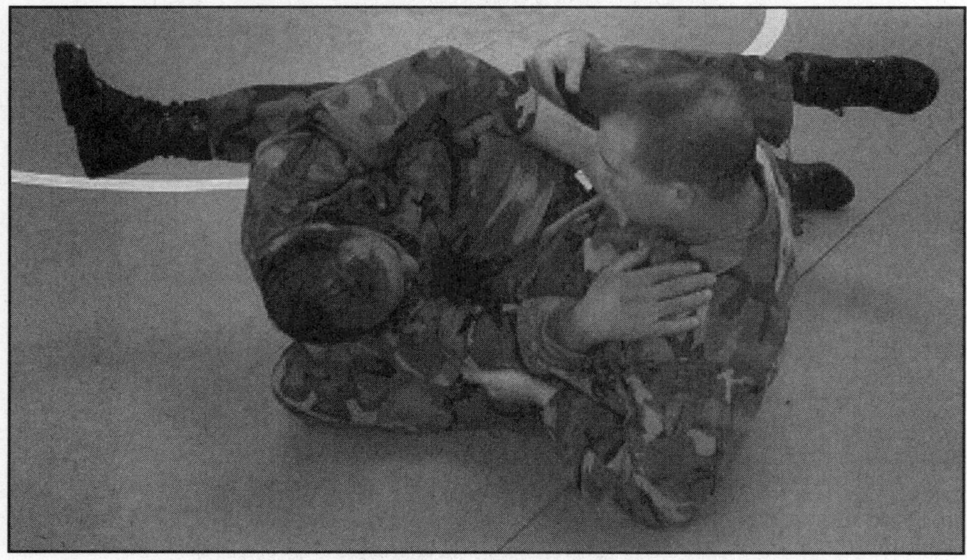

Figure 1-58: Sweep from the attempted straight arm bar, step 2.

Figure 1-58: Sweep from the attempted straight arm bar, step 2. ***(Continued)***

1-7. DRILLS

Drills are used as a portion of the warm-up, which allows the maximum use of training time, stresses the importance of position, and also keeps training focused on perfecting the basic moves. Different details can be taught or emphasized during each training session. This will result in a deeper understanding of the techniques, as well as building muscle memory, teaching the soldiers to move in the most efficient ways naturally. More advanced techniques can be substituted within the framework of the drill after sufficient skill level is shown in the basics.

a. **Drill 1 (Basic Drill).** This drill begins with one soldier mounted.
   (1) ***Step 1.*** The soldier on the bottom escapes the mount using the trap and roll technique.
   (2) ***Step 2.*** The same soldier passes the guard and achieves the mount.
   (3) ***Step 3.*** The roles now reverse and the second soldier goes through steps one and two.

b. **Drill 2.** This drill also begins with one soldier mounted.
   (1) ***Step 1.*** Using the arm trap and roll technique, the soldier on top gains the back mount.
   (2) ***Step 2.*** As soon as the first soldier sets the hooks in, the second soldier rolls over one shoulder and escapes the back mount.
   (3) ***Step 3.*** When the second soldier is mounted, the roles will reverse, and they will go back through steps one and two.

1-8. DEFENSE AGAINST HEADLOCKS

The headlock is a very poor technique for anything more than immobilizing an enemy. It is, however, a very common technique in actual fighting; therefore, knowing how to escape is very important for a soldier. The techniques are progressive, and should be attempted in the order taught.

a. **Form the Frame.**
   (1) ***Step 1*** (Figure 1-59). The fighter's first step in escaping from a headlock is to ensure that his arm is not captured. With a short jerky motion, the fighter pulls his elbow in and turns on his side.

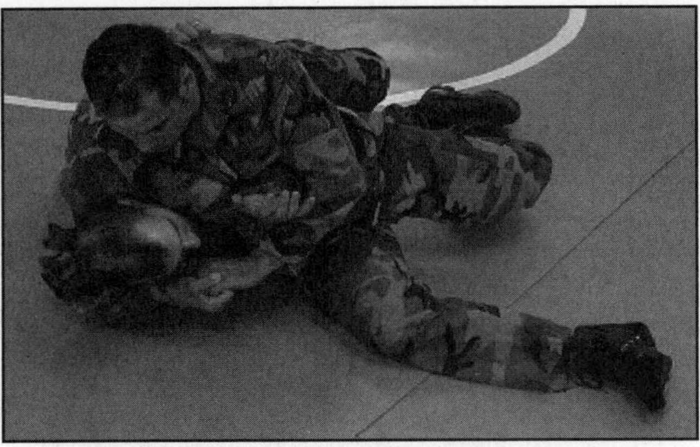

Figure 1-59: Form the frame, step 1.

(2) ***Step 2*** (Figure 1-60). If able, the fighter forms a frame under the enemy's chin. The fighter's top arm should be under the enemy's jawbone, and his top hand should rest comfortably in the grasp of the other hand. At this point, the fighter's bone structure should be supporting the enemy's weight.

Figure 1-60: Form the frame, step 2.

(3) ***Step 3*** (Figure 1-61). By pushing with the top leg, the fighter moves his hips back away from the enemy.

Figure 1-61: Form the frame, step 3.

(4) ***Step 4*** (Figure 1-62). The fighter reaches with both legs to grasp the enemy's head. If the enemy lets go of his headlock, the fighter squeezes the enemy's neck with his legs.

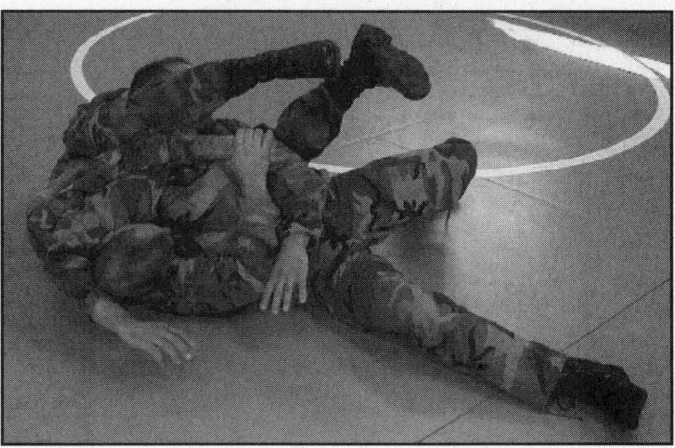

Figure 1-62: Form the frame, step 4.

(5) ***Step 5*** (Figure 1-63). If the enemy does not release the headlock, the fighter rotates around until he is on both of his knees behind the enemy's back.

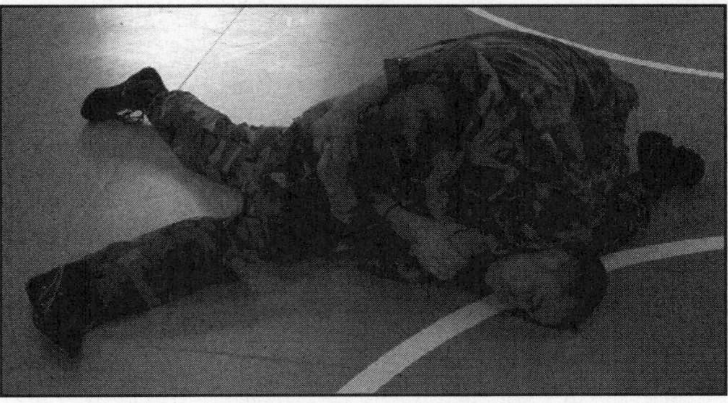

Figure 1-63: Form the frame, step 5.

(6) ***Step 6*** (Figure 1-64). The fighter uses his top hand to clear the enemy's legs out of the way and steps over, bringing his foot in tight against the enemy's hip. The fighter establishes his base by putting both hands on the ground.

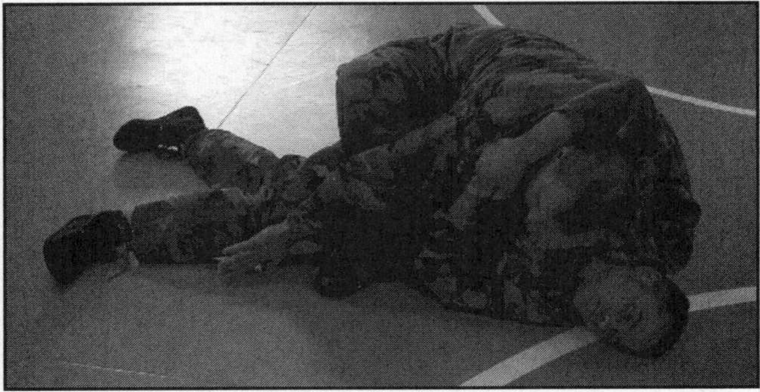

Figure 1-64: Form the frame, step 6.

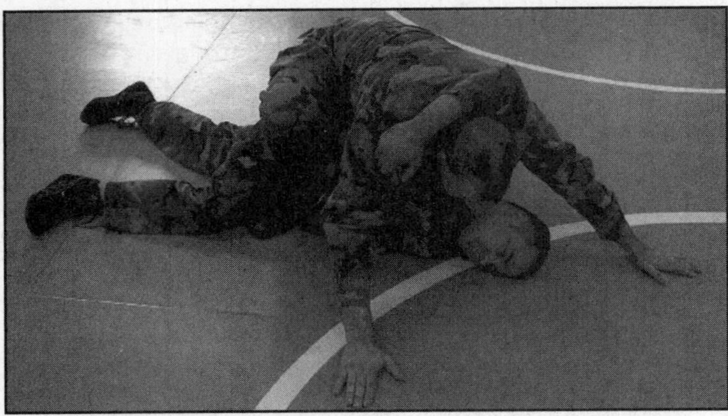

Figure 1-64: Form the frame, step 6. ***(Continued)***

(7) ***Step 7*** (Figure 1-65). The fighter forces the enemy to release his grip on the fighter's neck by forming the frame and leaning toward the enemy's head, driving the bone of his upper arm under the enemy's jawbone.

Figure 1-65: Form the frame, step 7.

b. **Follow the Leg.** Although the fighter should always try to form the frame, sometimes the enemy will tuck his head in making it impossible.

(1) ***Step 1*** (Figure 1-66). After ensuring that his arm is not captured as in the first technique, the fighter moves as close to the enemy as possible and places his leg over him. The fighter's heel should find the crease at the enemy's hip formed by his leg.

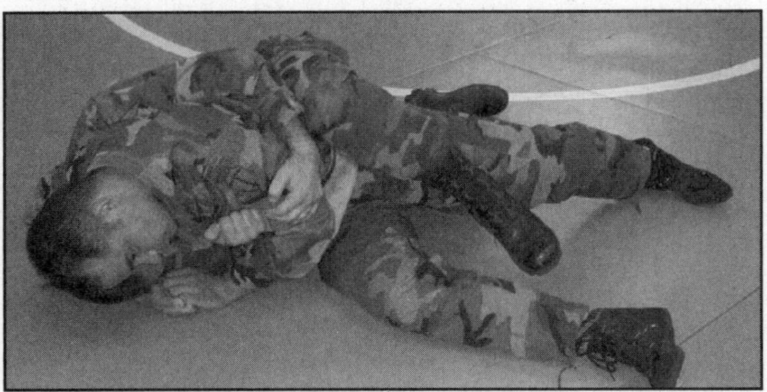

Figure 1-66: Follow the leg, step 1.

(2) ***Step 2*** (Figure 1-67). The fighter pulls his bottom arm free and places his weight on it. Holding the enemy tightly at the other shoulder, the fighter crawls over him using his own leg as a guide.

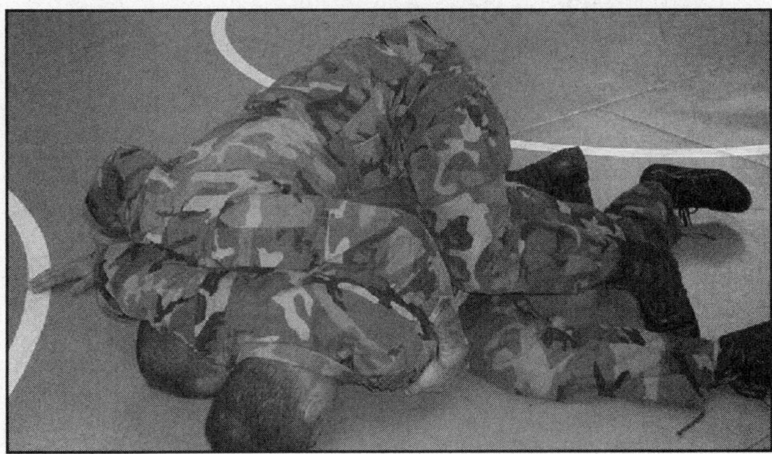

Figure 1-67: Follow the leg, step 2.

(3) ***Step 3*** (Figure 1-68). At this point the enemy has the option to either roll with the fighter or not. If he does not, the fighter uses all of his body to apply pressure to the enemy's shoulder. This will break the enemy's grip and leave the fighter behind the enemy. If the enemy rolls with the fighter, the fighter brings his foot into the enemy's hip as before and breaks his grip by forming the frame and applying pressure toward his head.

Figure 1-68: Follow the leg, step 3.

c. **Roll Toward the Head** (Figure 1-69). If the enemy should succeed in capturing the fighter's arm, the fighter can use the enemy's reaction to his attempts to free it to his advantage. With short jerky motions, the fighter attempts to pull his arm free. The enemy will have to adjust his position by leaning toward the fighter. Immediately after the fighter attempts to pull his arm free and feels the enemy pushing, the fighter arches toward his head and then over his opposite shoulder, taking the enemy over.

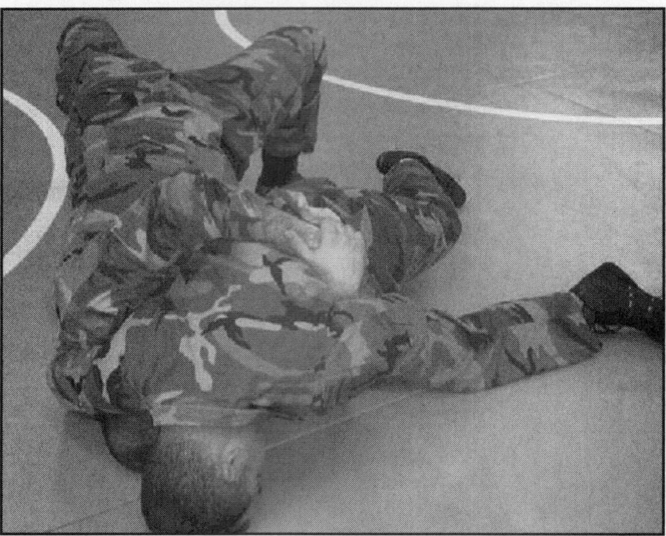

Figure 1-69: Roll toward the head.

Figure 1-69: Roll toward the head. ***(Continued)***

> ✍ NOTE
> The roll must be timed correctly and must be toward the fighter's head and not straight over his body.

CHAPTER 2

Advanced Ground-Fighting Techniques

After achieving an understanding of the basics of ground fighting, other elements of fighting on the ground are added. These techniques, however, are dependent on a thorough grasp of the basics. Being systematic is important in building competent fighters. Staying with the program will not only produce competent fighters quickly, but will produce the most competent fighters over time as well.

SECTION I. ADVANCED ATTACKS

Concentrating on offensive techniques is preferable when developing a training plan. The best defense is simply knowing that the technique exists. If defenses are to be taught, there should be ample time between teaching the offense and teaching the defense to allow time for the students to master the offensive skills first. Training the defense prematurely will hinder development.

2-1. ADVANCED BODY POSITIONS

a. **North-South Position** (Figure 2-1). This position allows many possible attacks and is very difficult for the enemy to escape from. You should attempt to control the enemy's arms by placing your elbows on the ground in his arm pits. You will also need to shift your weight in order to prevent him from rolling you over.

Figure 2-1: North-south position.

b. **Knee in the Stomach** (Figure 2-2). Another very important dominant body position is the knee mount. When in the knee mount, the knee should be in the middle of the enemy's chest. The foot should be hooked around his hip. The opposite knee should be off of the ground and back away from the enemy's head, and the hips should be set forward to maintain balance.

Figure 2-2: Knee in the stomach.

2-2. PASS THE GUARD

When you are inside of the enemy's guard, he has many options to attack you or reverse the positions. Therefore, you will need several possible techniques to pass.

a. **Closed Guard.** In the closed guard, the enemy has his legs locked together behind your back.

(1) ***Knee in the Tailbone.***

(a) ***Step 1*** (Figure 2-3). Moving one hand at a time, grasp the enemy at the belt with both hands. Keep pressure on him to prevent him from sitting up.

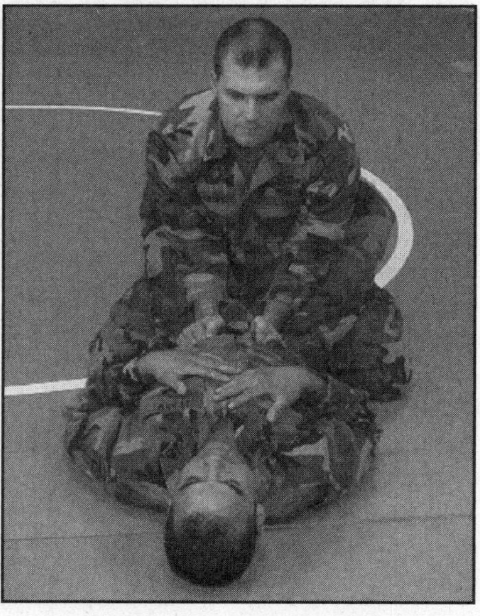

Figure 2-3: Knee in the tailbone, step 1.

(b) ***Step 2*** (Figure 2-4). Place one of your knees in the enemy's tailbone. You will need to lean toward the other side to prevent him from compromising your balance.

Figure 2-4: Knee in the tailbone, step 2.

(c) ***Step 3*** (Figure 2-5). Push with both hands, and move your other knee back away from him. This should create a 90 degree angle from the knee in the tailbone. This action will also create more distance between the knee in the tailbone and your hip, forcing him to loosen the grip with his legs.

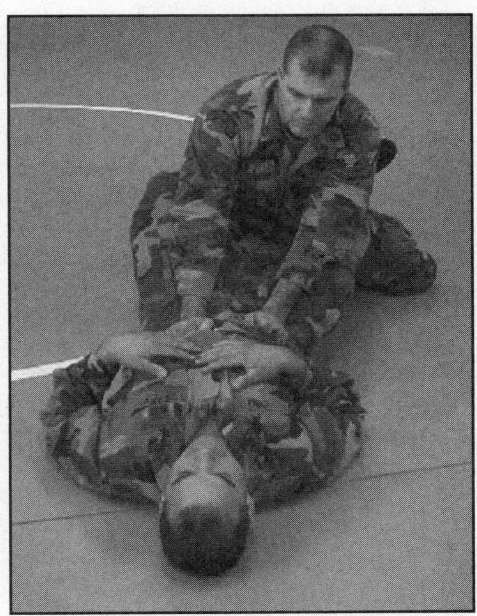

Figure 2-5: Knee in the tailbone, step 3.

(d) ***Step 4*** (Figure 2-6). Release your grip with the hand on the side you are facing and move it under the enemy's leg on the same side. You will then lift his leg, pulling it to you to gain control, and pass normally.

Figure 2-6: Knee in the tailbone, step 4.

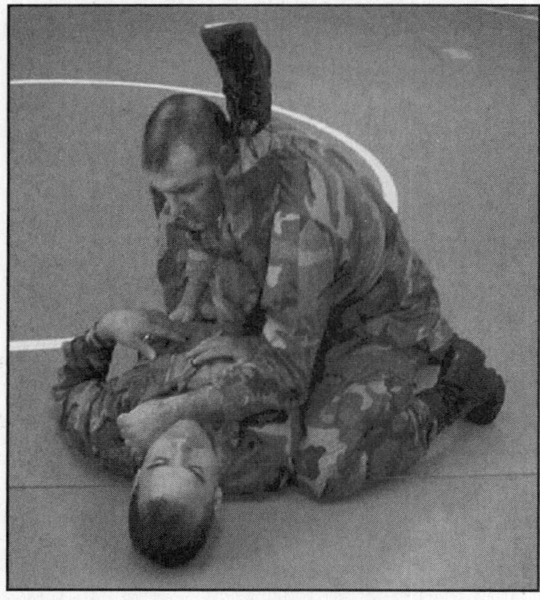

Figure 2-6: Knee in the tailbone, step 4. *(Continued)*

(e) ***Step*** **5** (Figure 2-7). Pull your remaining hand out from between his legs at the earliest possible time to avoid the arm bar, and secure a grip at his waist.

Figure 2-7: Knee in the tailbone, step 5.

(2) ***Stand Up With One Sleeve.***

(a) ***Step 1*** (Figure 2-8). Gain control of one of the enemy's sleeves near the wrist, and with the other hand grasp his jacket in the center to keep him from sitting up.

Figure 2-8: Stand up with one sleeve, step 1.

(b) ***Step 2*** (Figure 2-9). Stand up with the leg closest to the arm you are controlling first and arch your back slightly, pulling on the sleeve that you control.

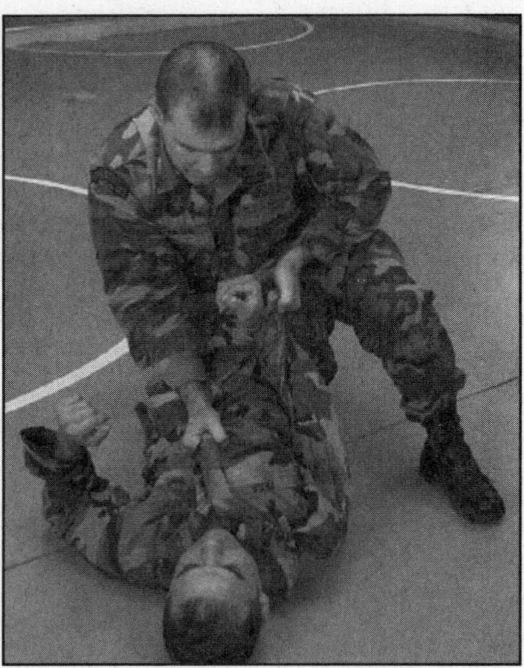

Figure 2-9: Stand up with one sleeve, step 2.

Figure 2-9: Stand up with one sleeve, step 2. ***(Continued)***

(c) ***Step 3*** (Figure 2-10). Switch control of his sleeve to your other hand and use the original hand to push downward on his legs to break his grip. It is helpful to step slightly back with the leg on the side you are attempting to open.

Figure 2-10: Stand up with one sleeve, step 3.

(d) ***Step 4*** (Figure 2-11). When his grip breaks, reach under the leg and pull it to you, tightening up to gain control and pass like before. It is important to control the leg below his knee so that he cannot bend it to escape and regain the guard.

Figure 2-11: Stand up with one sleeve, step 3.

(3) ***Hands in the Arm Pits.***

(a) ***Step 1*** (Figure 2-12). Pin the enemy's shoulders to the ground by either placing the fingers of your hands in both of his armpits, or placing both hands around his neck.

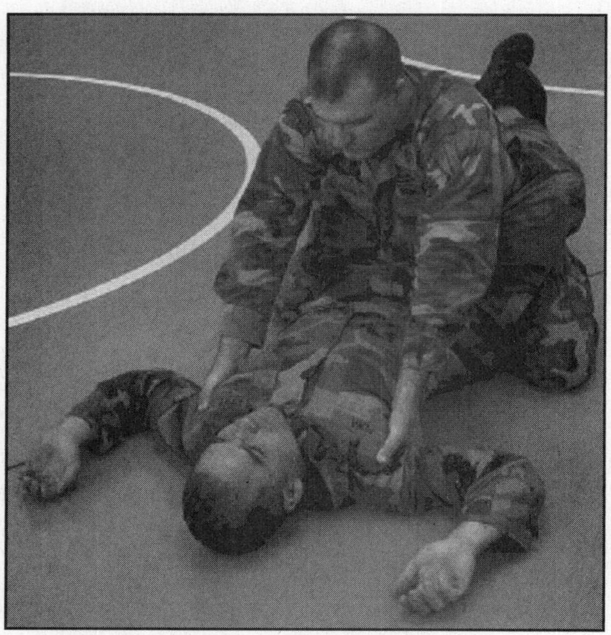

Figure 2-12: Hands in the arm pits, step 1.

Figure 2-12: Hands in the arm pits, step 1. *(Continued)*

(b) ***Step 2*** (Figure 2-13). Stand up one leg at a time, placing one of your knees in his tailbone and stepping back with the other. The heal of your foot must be planted on the ground.

Figure 2-13: Hands in the arm pits, step 2.

(c) ***Step 3*** (Figure 2-14). Sit down so that your knee is driven upward between the enemy's legs. This will break the grip of his legs behind your back.

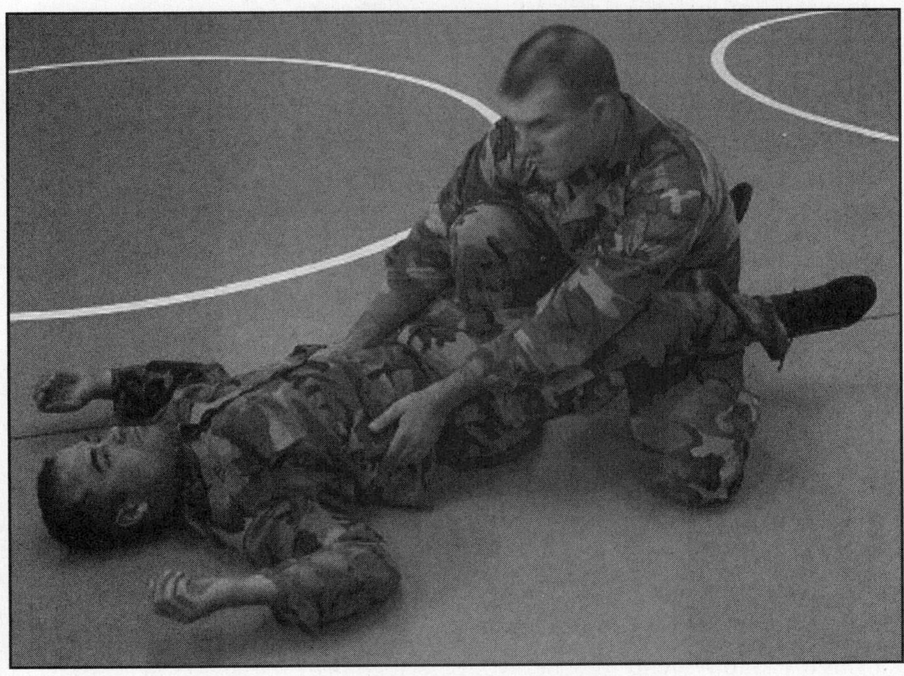

Figure 2-14: Hands in the arm pits, step 3.

(d) ***Step 4*** (Figure 2-15). Drive your knee over his leg on the opposite side. This will immobilize the leg so that you can bring both legs over into side control.

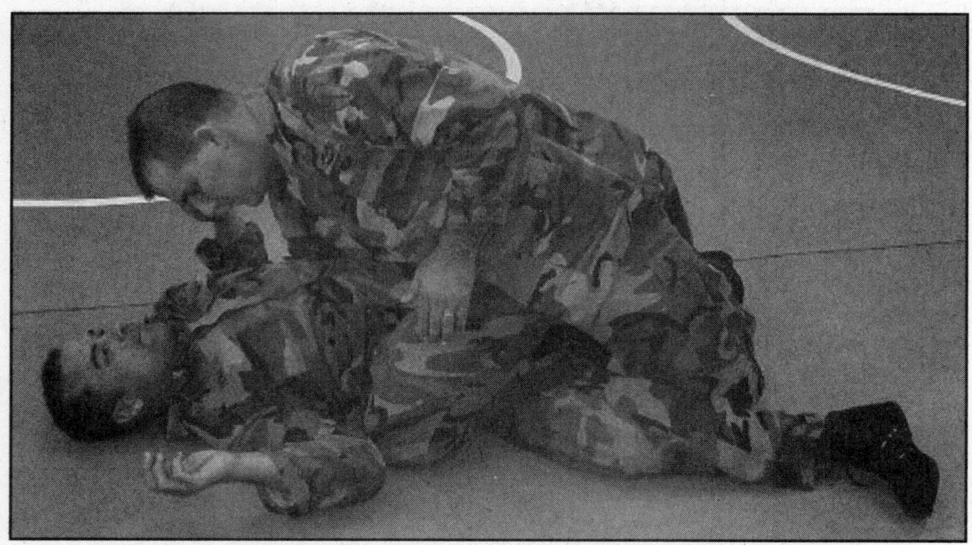

Figure 2-15: Hands in the arm pits, step 4.

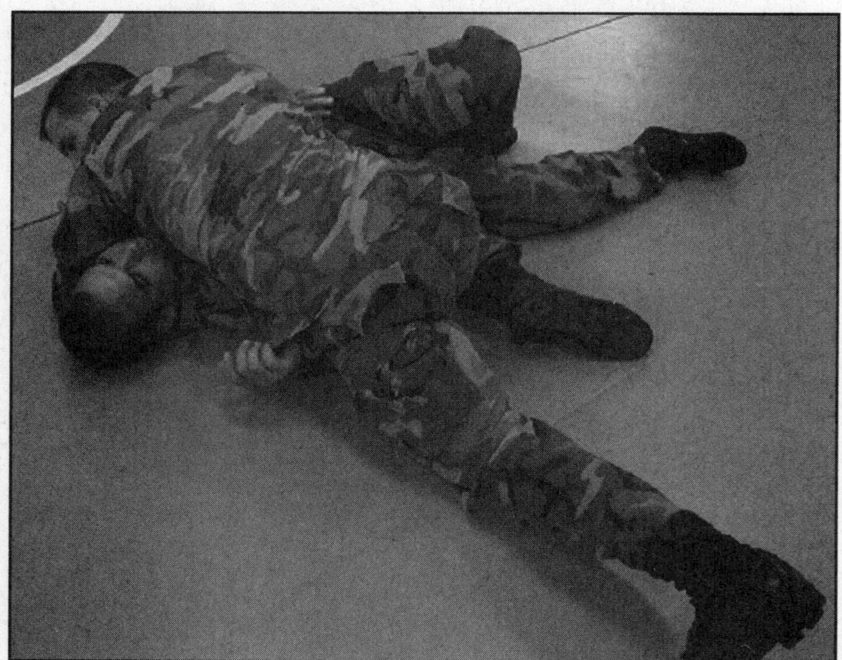

Figure 2-15: Hands in the arm pits, step 4. ***(Continued)***

b. **Open Guard.** Once you have opened the enemy's guard, he may block your passing by controlling you with his legs. You must gain control of his legs before you can pass.

(1) ***Throw the Legs.***

(a) ***Step 1*** (Figure 2-16). Grasp the enemy's pant legs near the ankles with a firm grasp and stand up, pulling him slightly toward you.

Figure 2-16: Throw the legs, step 1.

(b) ***Step 2*** (Figure 2-17). Swing both legs from side to side and then throw them forcefully to one side.

Figure 2-17: Throw the legs, step 2.

(c) ***Step 3*** (Figure 2-18). Close the distance and gain control in either the side control or knee mount position.

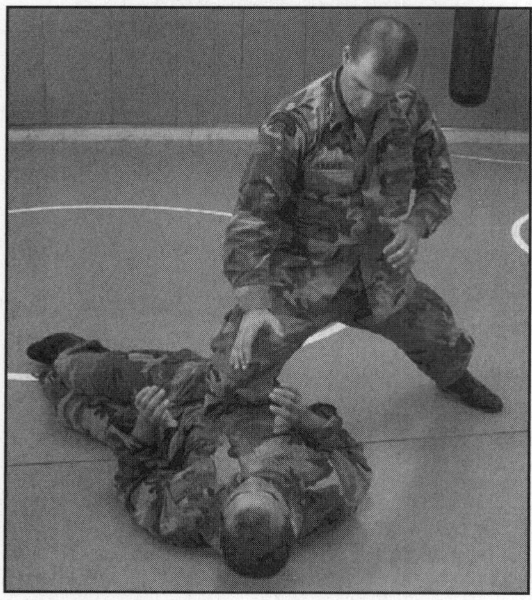

Figure 2-18: Throw the legs, step 3.

(2) ***Push the Knees.***

(a) ***Step 1*** (Figure 2-19). Gain control of the enemy's pant legs on top of each knee.

Figure 2-19: Push the knees, step 1.

(b) ***Step 2*** (Figure 2-20). Step back and drive both knees downward.

Figure 2-20: Push the knees, step 2.

(c) ***Step 3*** (Figure 2-21). While still holding the enemy's knees down, jump forward with both legs into the mounted position.

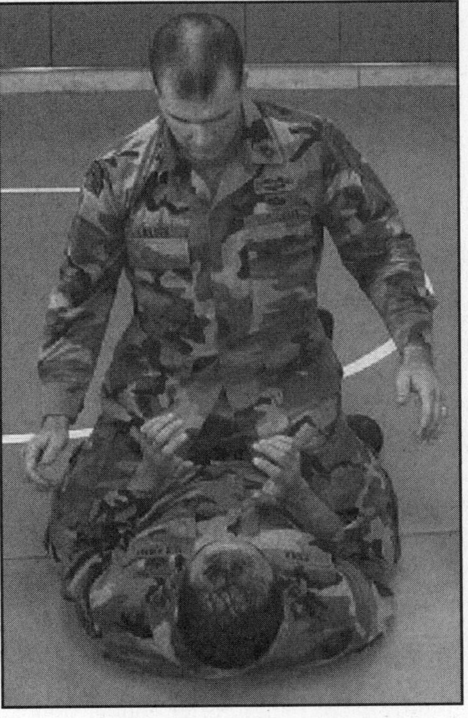

Figure 2-21: Push the knees, step 3.

2-3. ATTACKS FROM THE MOUNT

After the mount has been achieved, there are many options on how to attack. The first is to throw punches into the enemy's face and force him to turn over, giving up his back. If he does not turn over he will most likely give an opening, making the following attacks easier.

a. **Chokes.** The most efficient way to incapacitate an enemy is to choke him into unconsciousness. An advantage of prioritizing chokes in training is that they can be applied in training exactly as applied in combat.

(1) ***Paper Cutter Choke.***

(a) ***Step 1*** (Figure 2-22). Start by opening the collar with the weak hand, as in the cross collar choke. With the strong hand grasp deep into the collar, inserting the thumb on the inside.

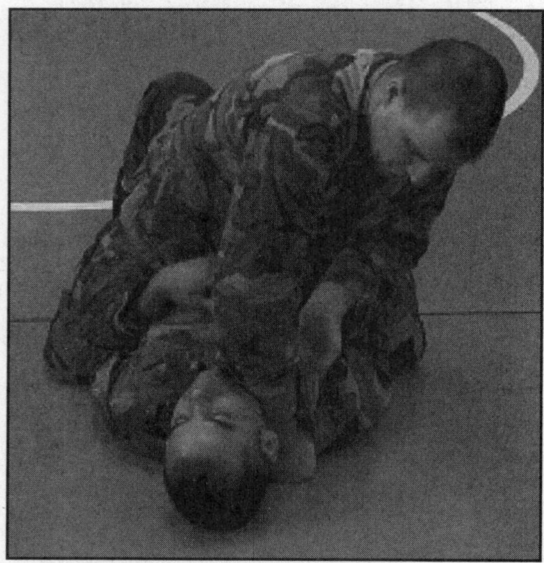

Figure 2-22: Paper cutter choke, step 1.

(b) ***Step 2*** (Figure 2-23). Release the grip of the first hand and grasp the opposite side of the enemy's jacket, pulling it tight against the back of his neck.

Figure 2-23: Paper cutter choke, step 2.

(c) ***Step 3*** (Figure 2-24). Drive the elbow of the other hand across the enemy's neck to complete the choke.

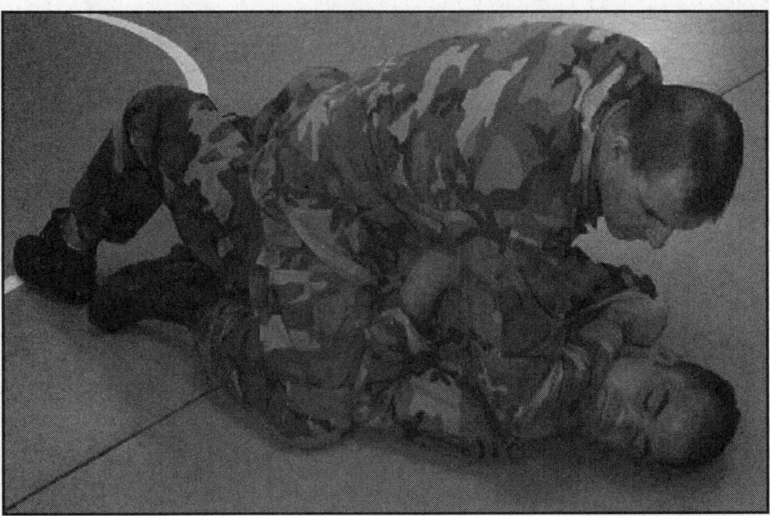

Figure 2-24: Paper cutter choke, step 3.

(2) ***Leaning Choke.***

(a) ***Step 1*** (Figure 2-25). Grasp both sides of the collar. The knuckles should be pointed inward and there should be three or four inches of slack.

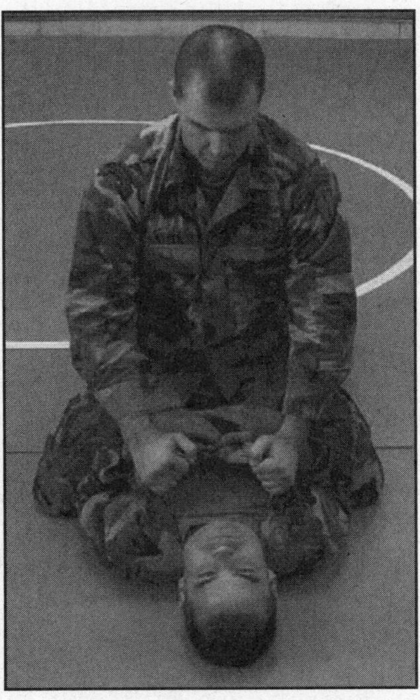

Figure 2-25: Leaning choke, step 1.

(b) ***Step 2*** (Figure 2-26). Pull one side of the collar across the enemy's neck so the pinky knuckle is just past the Adam's apple where the blood vessels are located. Pull the other hand tight as you drive this hand into the enemy's neck.

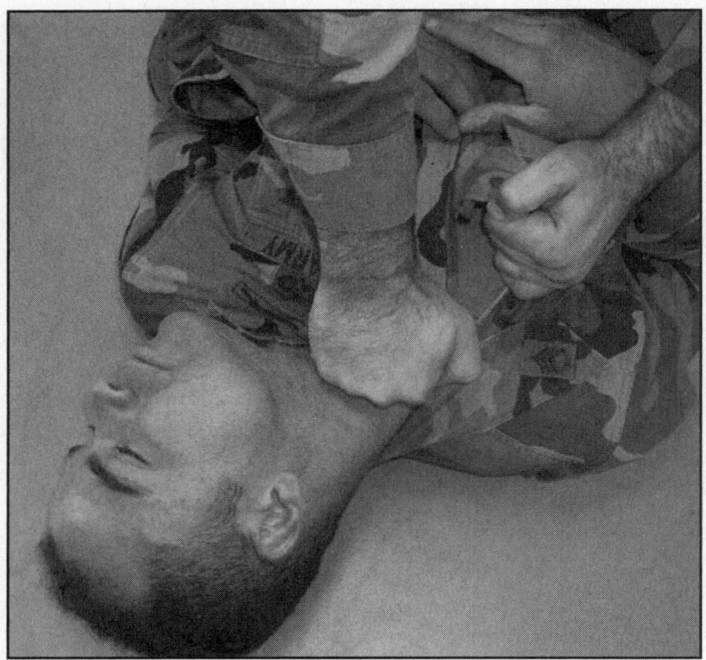

Figure 2-26: Leaning choke, step 2.

(3) ***Nutcracker Choke.***

(a) ***Step 1*** (Figure 2-27). Grasp the collar with both hands at the sides of the enemy's neck. Knuckles should be pointed in against the neck.

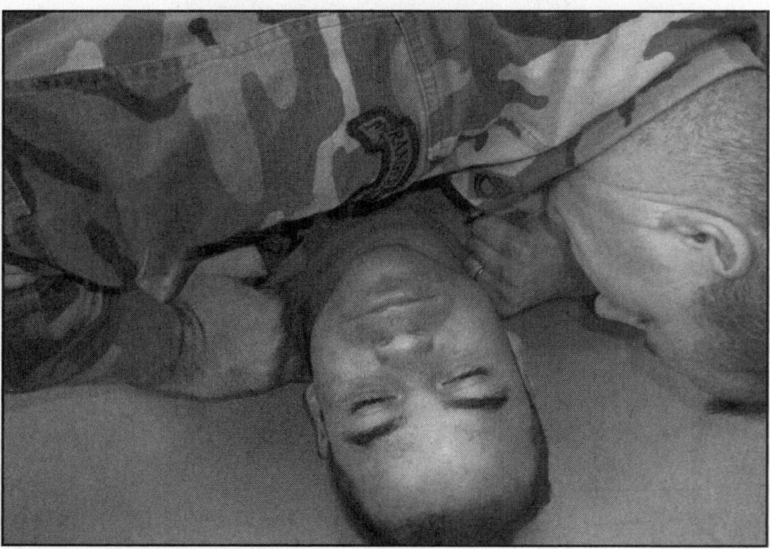

Figure 2-27: Nutcracker choke, step 1.

(b) ***Step 2*** (Figure 2-28). Pull the collar tight against the back of the enemy's neck with both hands and, with the pinkies acting as the base, drive the pointer finger knuckles of both hands into the enemy's neck on either side of the Adam's apple.

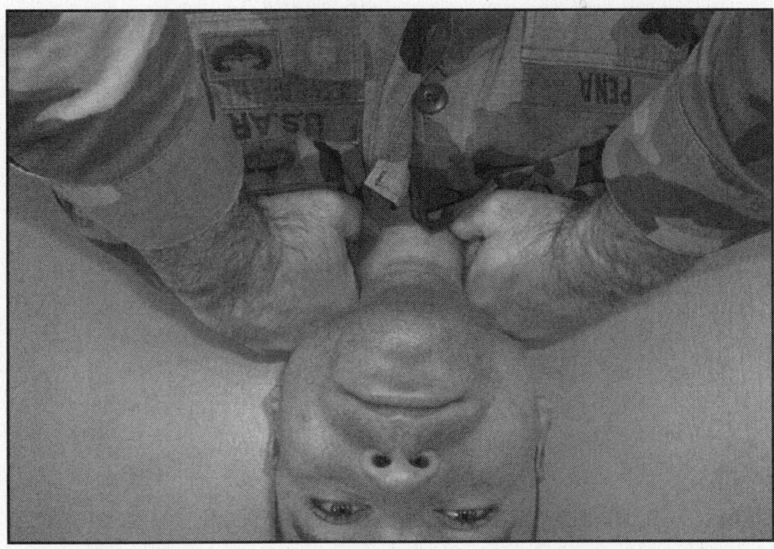

Figure 2-28: Nutcracker choke, step 2.

(4) ***Sleeve Choke.***

(a) ***Step 1*** (Figure 2-29). Place the fingers of one hand inside the sleeve cuff of the other with a firm grip.

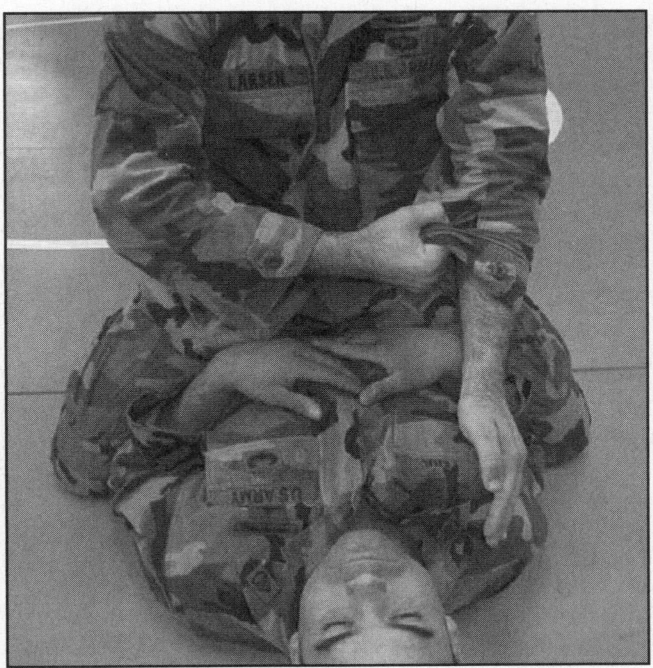

Figure 2-29: Sleeve choke, step 1.

(b) ***Step 2*** (Figure 2-30). Drive the other hand behind the enemy's head so the forearm of the first hand goes across the neck.

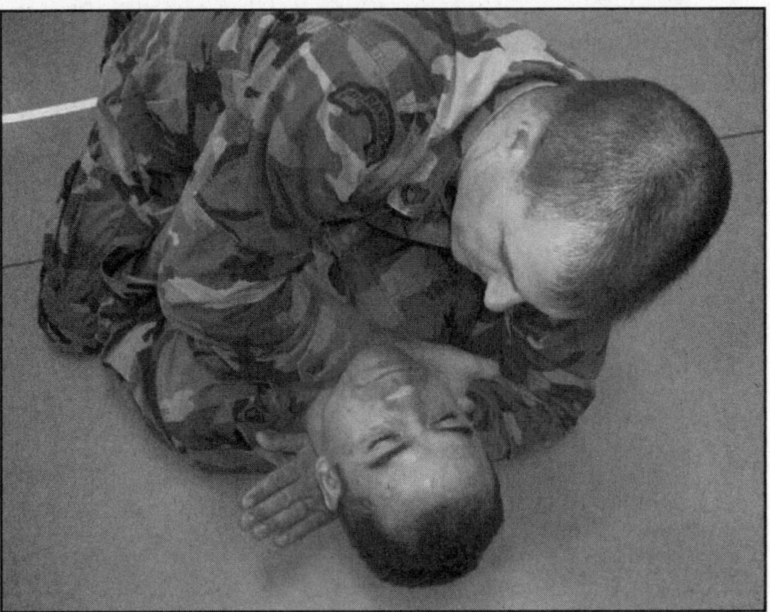

Figure 2-30: Sleeve choke, step 2.

(c) ***Step 3*** (Figure 2-31). Drive the elbow across the enemy's neck toward the back while pulling with the other hand.

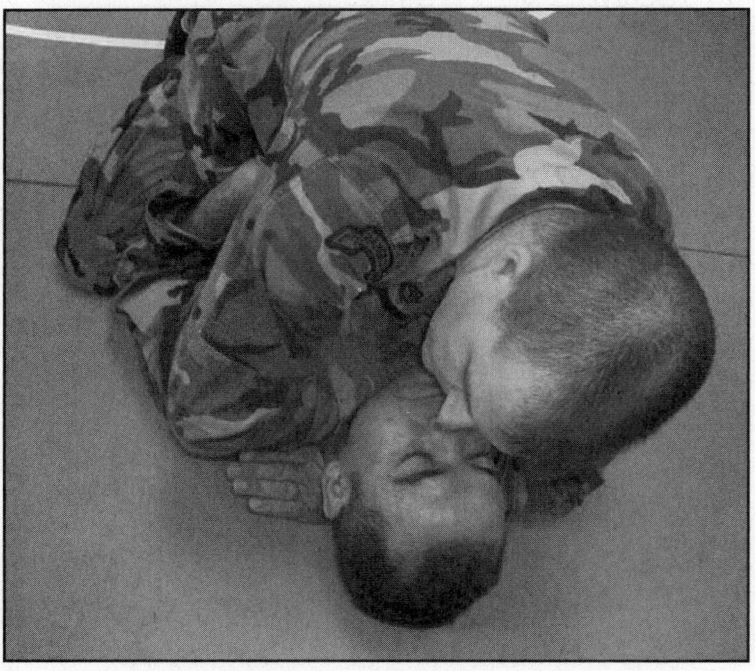

Figure 2-31: Sleeve choke, step 3.

b. **Triple Attack.** When the enemy tries to escape the mount using the trap and roll technique, he can be moved into the position shown by sliding the trapped foot forward and lifting on the enemy's opposite shoulder. This position presents several attack opportunities.

(1) ***Lapel Choke.***

(a) ***Step 1*** (Figure 2-32). With the hand that corresponds to the side the enemy is facing, place the fingers inside of the enemy's collar and pull it open.

Figure 2-32: Lapel choke, step 1.

(b) ***Step 2*** (Figure 2-33). Reach under his head with the other hand and insert the thumb as deep as possible into the collar.

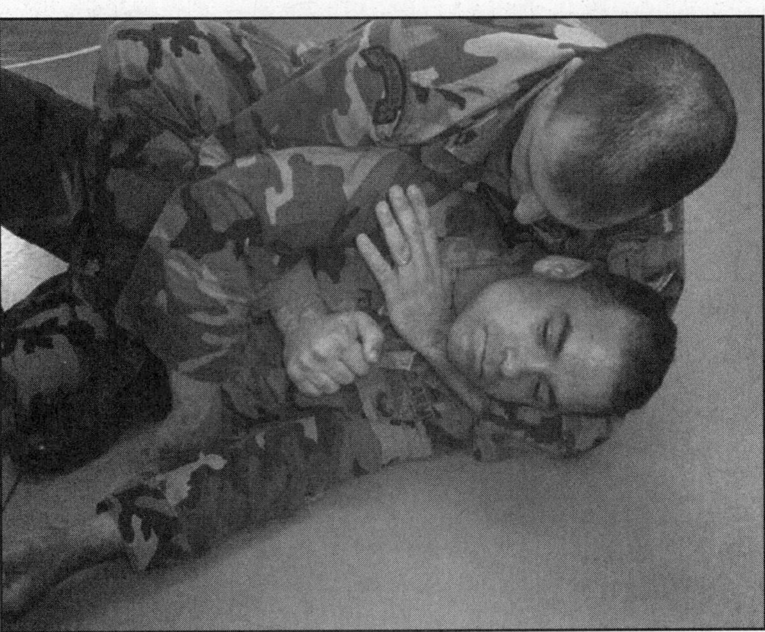

Figure 2-33: Lapel choke, step 2.

(c) ***Step 3*** (Figure 2-34). Change the grip of the first hand to the opposite side of his lapel to tighten the collar against the back of his neck.

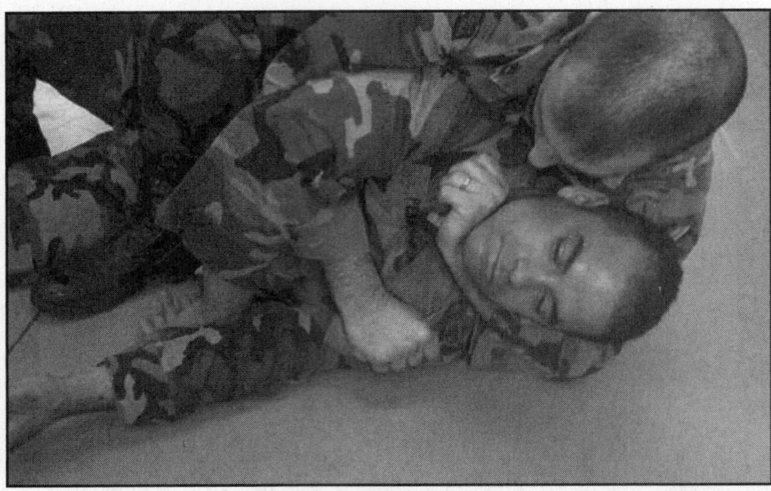

Figure 2-34: Lapel choke, step 3.

(d) ***Step 4*** (Figure 2-35). Tighten by extending both arms.

Figure 2-35: Lapel choke, step 4.

(2) ***Straight Arm Bar.*** The enemy may attempt to block the choke with his hands.

(a) ***Step 1*** (Figure 2-36). Ensuring that your arm is under the enemy's arm, push his elbow forward and hold it in place by grasping your own collar.

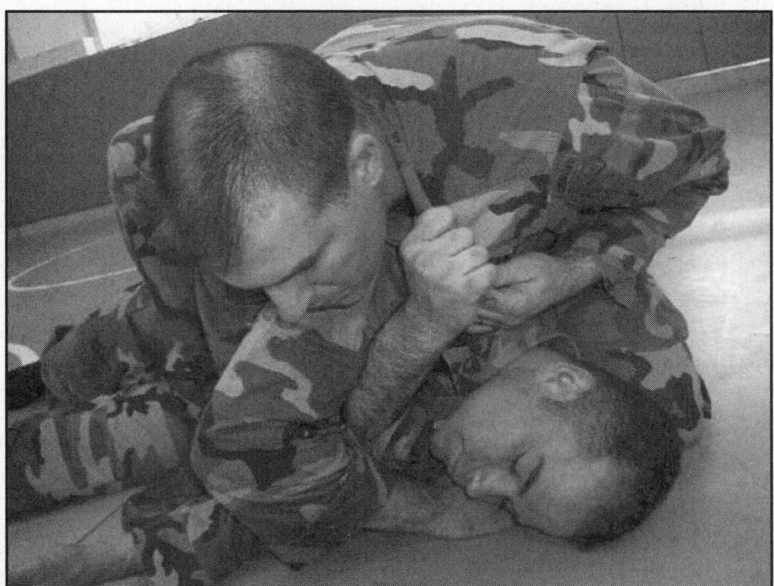

Figure 2-36: Straight arm bar, step 1.

(b) ***Step 2*** (Figure 2-37). Place your other hand on the enemy's head.

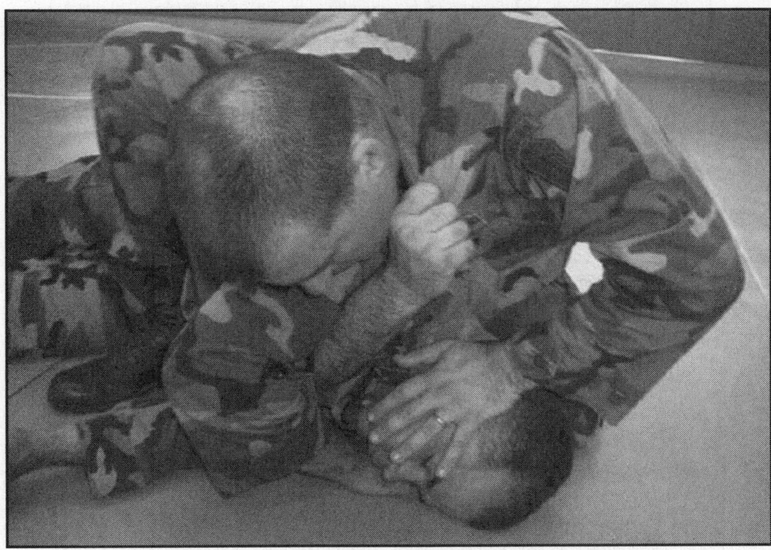

Figure 2-37: Straight arm bar, step 2.

(c) ***Step 3*** (Figure 2-38). Rest all of your weight on the enemy's head, and point your toe straight back.

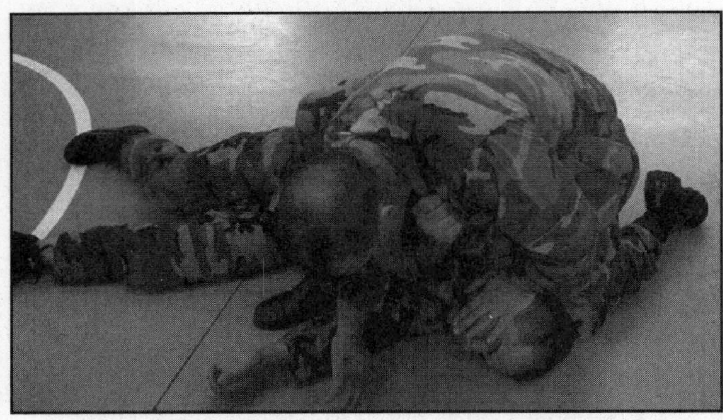

Figure 2-38: Straight arm bar, step 3.

(d) ***Step 4*** (Figure 2-39). Swing your leg around on top of his head and sit back into the straight arm bar.

Figure 2-39: Straight arm bar, step 4.

(3) ***Gain the Back Mount.*** If the enemy defends both the choke and the arm bar, you still have another option.

(a) ***Step 1*** (Figure 2-40). Push the enemy toward his stomach with chest pressure, and at the same time bring your foot close to the enemy's back.

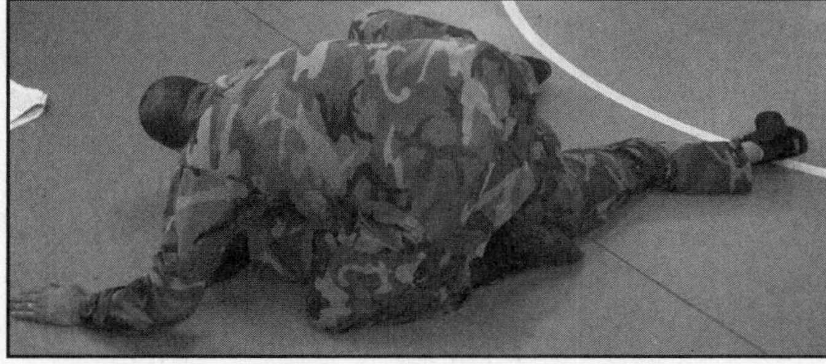

Figure 2-40: Gain the back mount, step 1.

(b) ***Step 2*** (Figure 2-41). Sit back, pulling the enemy on top of you, ensuring you give yourself room to swing your foot around to sink in your hook. You will finish in the back mount.

Figure 2-41: Gain the back mount, step 2.

2-4. ATTACKS FROM THE BACK MOUNT

Once the back mount has been achieved, keeping it is the most important goal. The position learned earlier of one hand in the armpit and the other over the opposite shoulder allows the most possible attacks.

a. **Collar Choke.**

(1) ***Step 1*** (Figure 2-42). Grasp the collar with the hand in the armpit, pulling it open to insert the thumb of the other hand deep into the collar. Secure a firm grip.

Figure 2-42: Collar choke, step 1.

(2) ***Step 2*** (Figure 2-43). Change the grip of the hand under the armpit to grasp the opposite lapel, pulling down to tighten the collar against the back of the enemy's neck.

Figure 2-43: Collar choke, step 2.

(3) ***Step 3*** (Figure 2-44). Set the choke by pushing outward with both hands.

Figure 2-44: Collar choke, step 3.

b. **Single Wing Choke.**

(1) ***Step 1*** (Figure 2-45). Open the collar and secure a grip the same as in the collar choke.

Figure 2-45: Single wing choke, step 1.

(2) ***Step 2*** (Figure 2-46). With the hand that is under the enemy's armpit, pull his arm out at the elbow.

Figure 2-46: Single wing choke, step 2.

(3) ***Step 3*** (Figure 2-47). Bring your hand around behind his head and finish the choke by pushing out with both hands.

Figure 2-47: Single wing choke, step 3.

c. **Straight Arm Bar.**

(1) ***Step 1*** (Figure 2-48). If the enemy is protecting his collar effectively, push your arm further through his armpit, pulling your own collar open with the other hand. Grasp your collar with the hand that is through his armpit.

Figure 2-48: Straight arm bar, step 1.

(2) ***Step 2*** (Figure 2-49). With the palm of your other hand, push his head away and step your leg over it. Break his grip by pushing with your legs and extending your body.

Figure 2-49: Straight arm bar, step 2.

(3) ***Step 3*** (Figure 2-50). Finish with hip pressure against his elbow as in the basic straight arm bar.

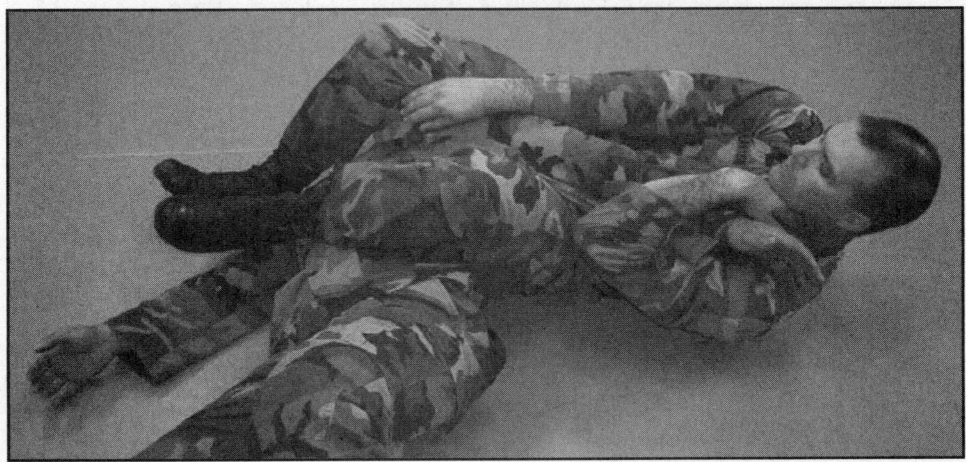

Figure 2-50: Straight arm bar, step 3.

2-5. ATTACKS FROM THE GUARD

a. **Arm Lock.**

(1) ***Step 1*** (Figure 2-51). If the enemy places his hand on the ground, grasp it around the wrist.

Figure 2-51: Arm lock, step 1.

(2) ***Step 2*** (Figure 2-52). Release your legs and sit up. Reach over and around his arm grasping your own wrist.

Figure 2-52: Arm lock, step 2.

(3) ***Step 3*** (Figure 2-53). Keep your legs tight against his sides to prevent him from stepping over them, and sit back.

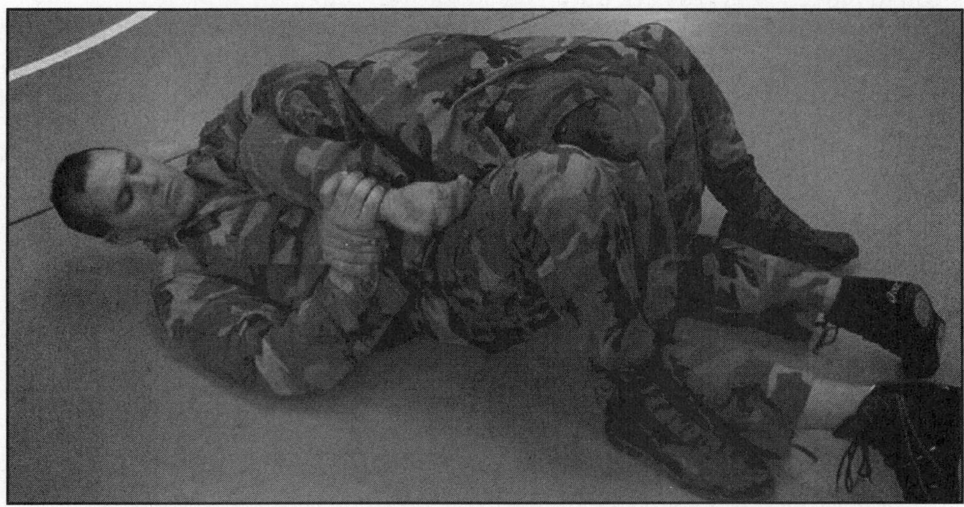

Figure 2-53: Arm lock, step 3.

(4) ***Step 4*** (Figure 2-54). Move your hips out from under him and finish by rotating your torso to attack his shoulder joint. Ensure that his arm is held at 90 degrees and not up behind his back.

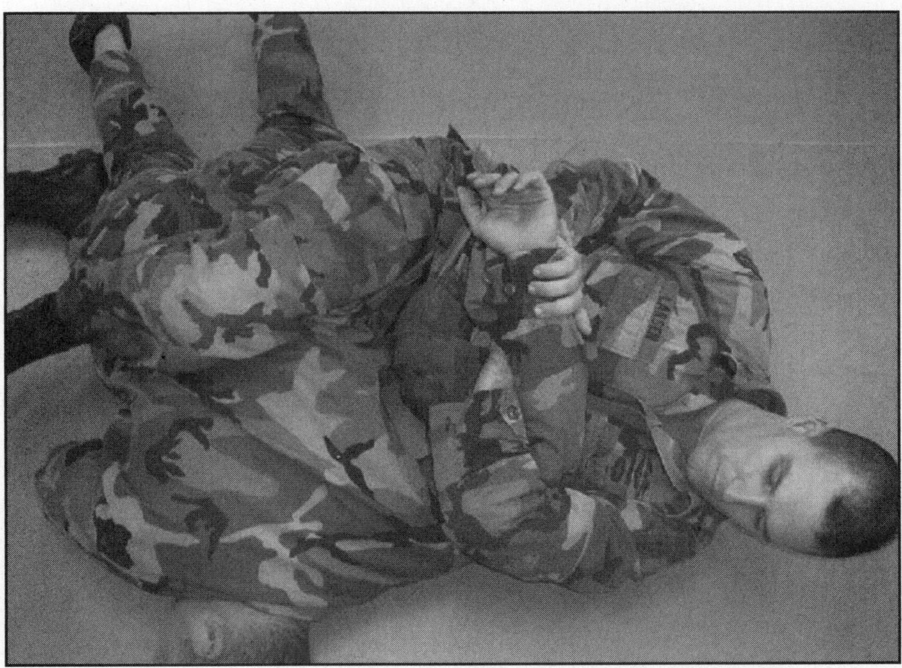

Figure 2-54: Arm lock, step 4.

b. **Guillotine Choke.** When you are attempting the arm bar, the enemy may try to counter by grasping you around the waist.

(1) ***Step 1*** (Figure 2-55). Release your grasp of his wrist and place your hand on the ground behind you. This allows you to move your hips back until you are sitting straight up.

Figure 2-55: Guillotine choke, step 1.

(2) ***Step 2*** (Figure 2-56). Wrap your other hand around the enemy's neck and under his chin. Grasp his chin with the hand that was on the ground. Both palms should be facing your body.

Figure 2-56: Guillotine choke, step 2.

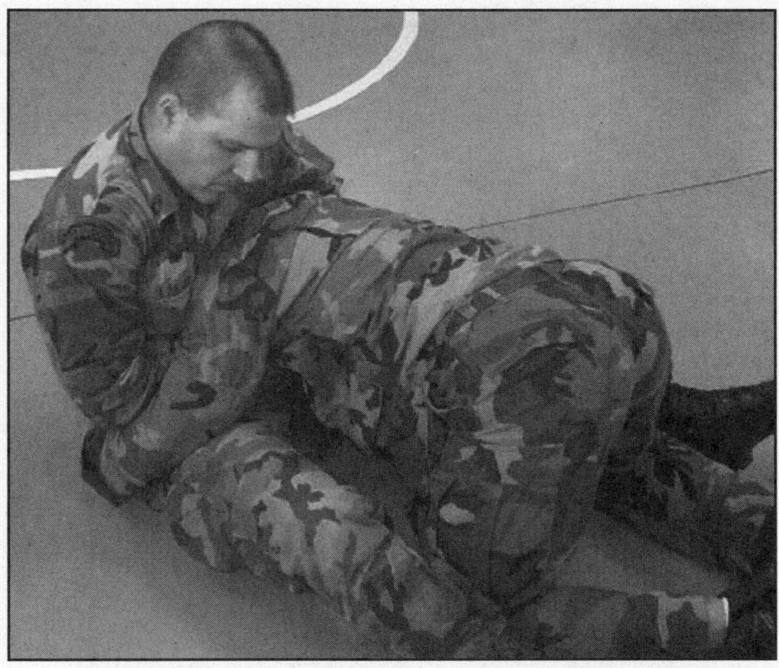

Figure 2-56: Guillotine choke, step 2. *(Continued)*

(3) ***Step 3*** (Figure 2-57). Pull upward with both hands and finish the choke by leaning backwards and wrapping your legs around him, pull with your arms and push with your legs.

Figure 2-57: Guillotine choke, step 3.

c. **Sweeps.** When you have the enemy within your guard, he may provide the chance to reverse the positions.

(1) ***Scissors Sweep.***

(a) ***Step 1*** (Figure 2-58). When the enemy raises one leg while attempting to pass the guard, you should place your weight on the calf on that side and swing your hips out from underneath him. Your leg should go along his belt line with your foot hooked around his waist.

Figure 2-58: Scissors sweep, step 1.

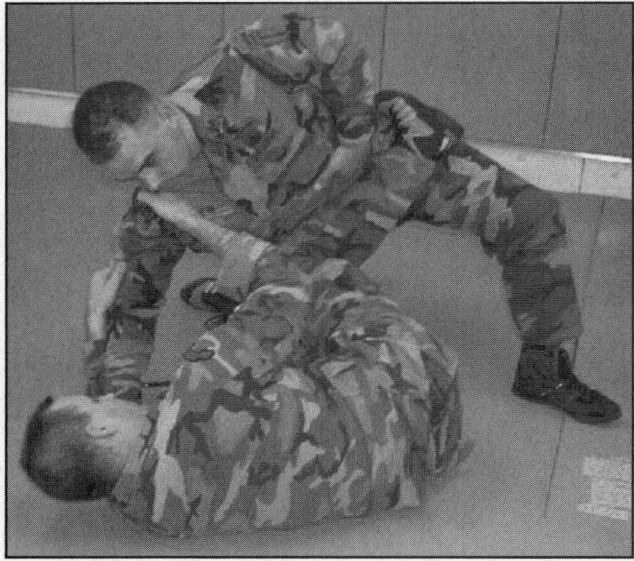

Figure 2-58: Scissors sweep, step 1. ***(Continued)***

(b) ***Step 2*** (Figure 2-59). Move your chest away and kick him over with a scissors action from your legs, ending up mounted.

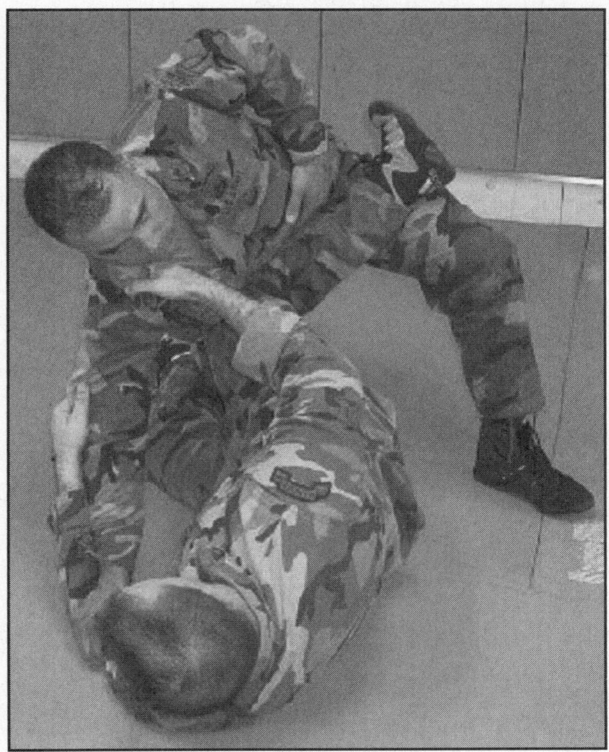

Figure 2-59: Scissors sweep, step 2.

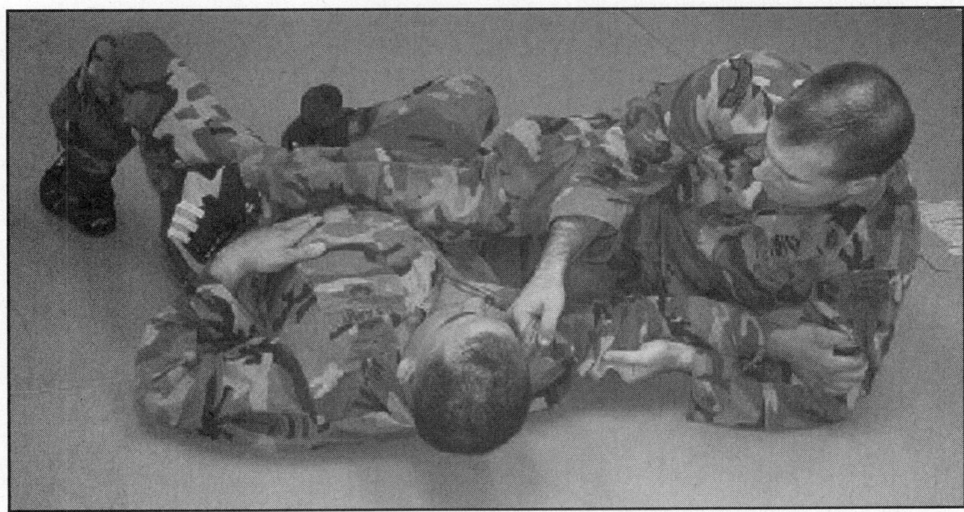

Figure 2-59: Scissors sweep, step 2. *(Continued)*

(2) ***Captain Kirk.*** The enemy may attempt to pass by standing up. When he does he is very susceptible to being swept.

(a) ***Step 1*** (Figure 2-60). When the enemy stands up, maintain control with your arms and let your feet slide naturally down until they are on his hips.

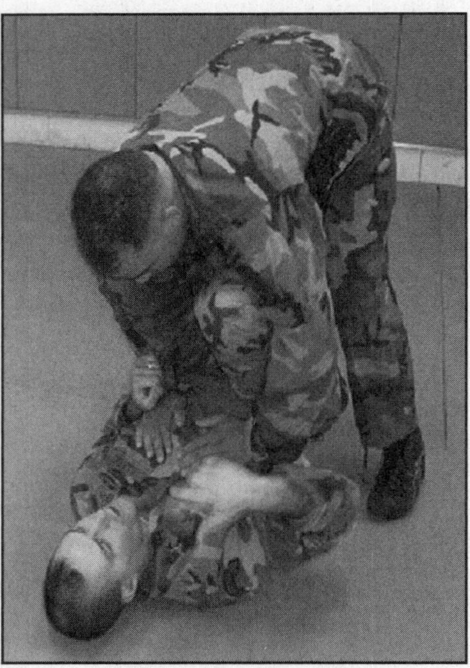

Figure 2-60: Captain Kirk, step 1.

(b) ***Step 2*** (Figure 2-61). If his weight gets too far forward, pick him up with your legs and throw him over one of your shoulders. Ensure that you move your head to the opposite side to prevent him landing on you. Finish mounted.

Figure 2-61: Captain Kirk, step 2.

(3) ***Ankle Grab/Knee Push.***

(a) ***Step 1*** (Figure 2-62). When the enemy stands up, maintain control with your arms and let your feet slide to his hips as in the previous move.

Figure 2-62: Ankle grab/knee push, step 1.

(b) ***Step 2*** (Figure 2-63). If his weight gets too far back, let go with your arms and grasp both of his ankles. Push your knees upward causing him to fall backwards.

Figure 2-63: Ankle grab/knee push, step 2.

Figure 2-63: Ankle grab/knee push, step 2. *(Continued)*

(c) ***Step 3*** (Figure 2-64). Drive one of your knees to the ground and grasp the back of his neck with the other hand to pull yourself to the mount.

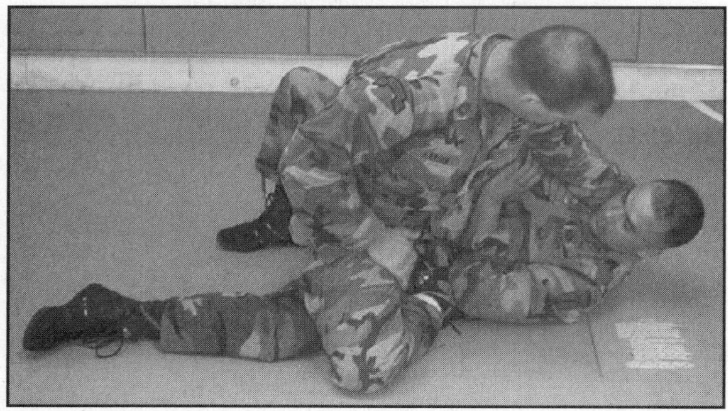

Figure 2-64: Ankle grab/knee push, step 3.

(d) **Triangle Choke.** If the enemy gets his hand through and begins to pass your guard, you still have a chance to apply a choke.

(1) ***Step 1*** (Figure 2-65). Post your leg on the ground and turn your body perpendicular to the enemy's. Your leg should be around the back of his neck.

Figure 2-65: Triangle choke, step 1.

(2) ***Step 2*** (Figure 2-66). Place the inside of your knee over your own foot. You may assist yourself by grasping your foot with your hand.

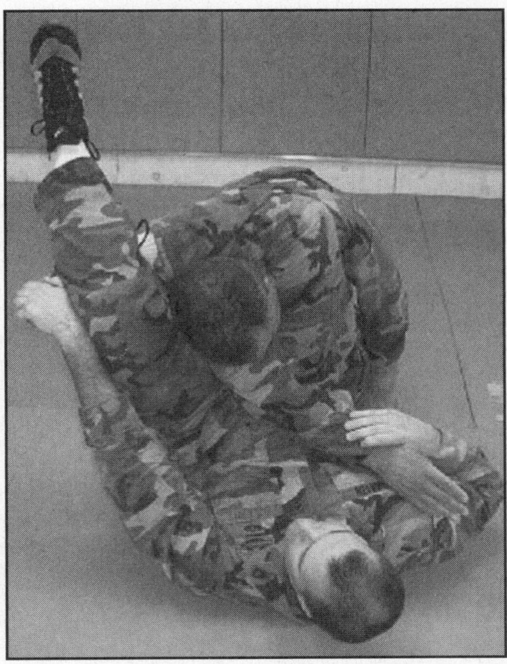

Figure 2-66: Triangle choke, step 2.

(3) ***Step 3*** (Figure 2-67). Place both of your hands on the back of the enemy's head and push upward with your hips.

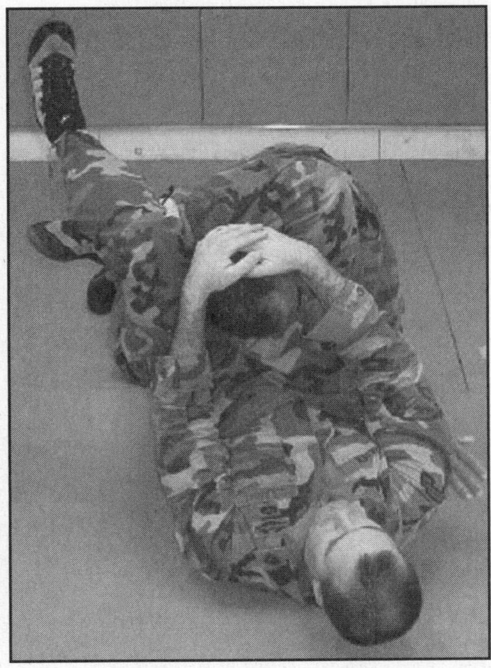

Figure 2-67: Triangle choke, step 3.

2-6. KNEE MOUNT

When the enemy is defending well from side control, a good option is to go to the knee mount.

a. Achieve the knee mount from standard side control.

(1) ***Step 1*** (Figure 2-68). With the hand closest to the enemy's head, grasp the collar on either side of his head.

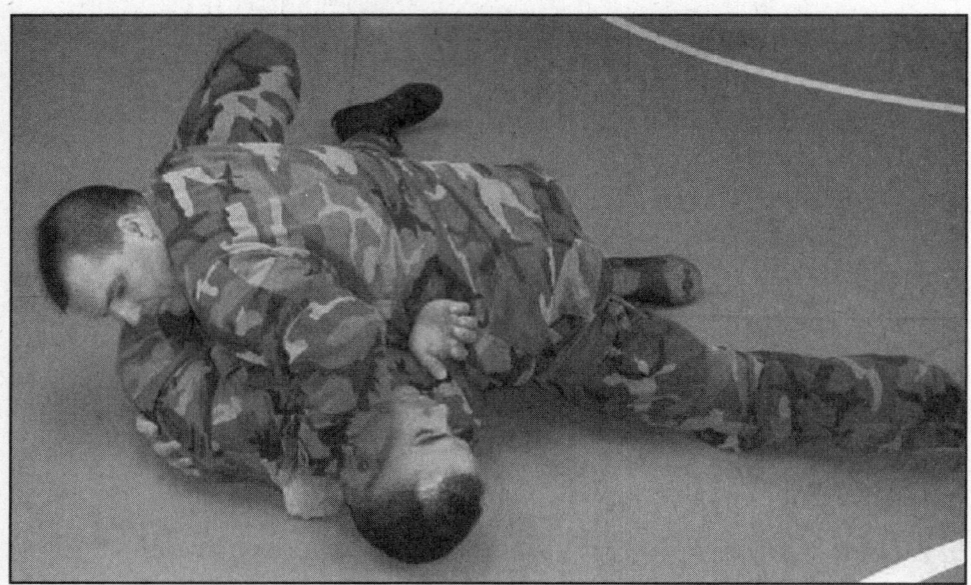

Figure 2-68: Knee mount from standard side control, step 1.

(2) ***Step 2*** (Figure 2-69). With the other hand, grasp his belt or his uniform over his hip.

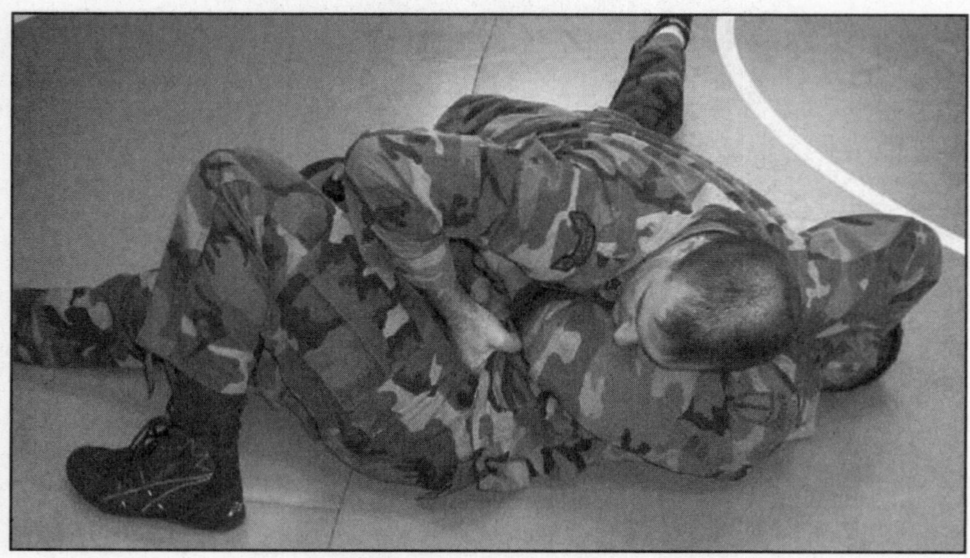

Figure 2-69: Knee mount from standard side control, step 2.

(3) ***Step 3*** (Figure 2-70). Pushing up with both hands, pop up into the knee mount with one swift movement.

Figure 2-70: Knee mount from standard side control, step 3.

b. Achieve the knee mount with control of the far side arm.
   (1) ***Step 1*** (Figure 2-71). From side control, move your arm through the enemy's armpit.

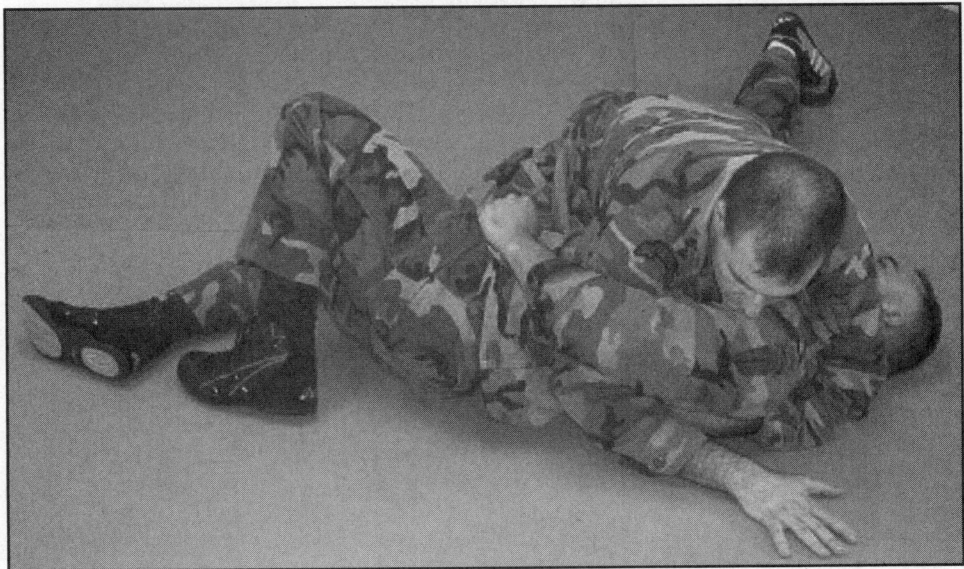

Figure 2-71: Achieve knee mount with control of far side arm, step 1.

(2) ***Step 2*** (Figure 2-72). With the other arm, reach back and gain control of his elbow. Pulling the arm upwards as you change your hips, sit through to the position shown.

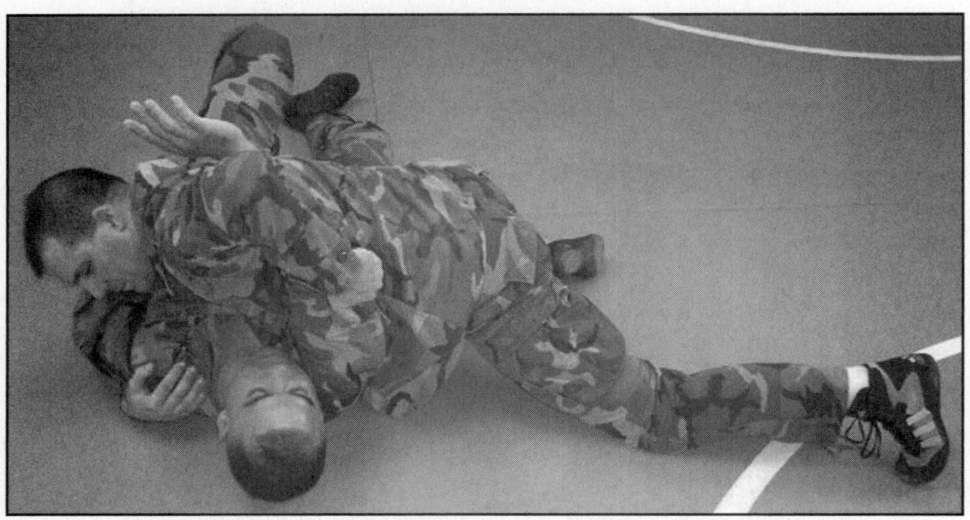

Figure 2-72: Achieve knee mount with control of far side arm, step 2.

Figure 2-72: Achieve knee mount with control of far side arm, step 2. *(Continued)*

(3) ***Step 3*** (Figure 2-73). Place the foot of the leg closest to the enemy underneath the other leg. With your weight on the hand in the enemy's armpit and your outside leg, swing your inside leg up into the knee mount. Ensure that you maintain control of the enemy's near side arm.

Figure 2-73: Achieve knee mount with control of far side arm, step 3.

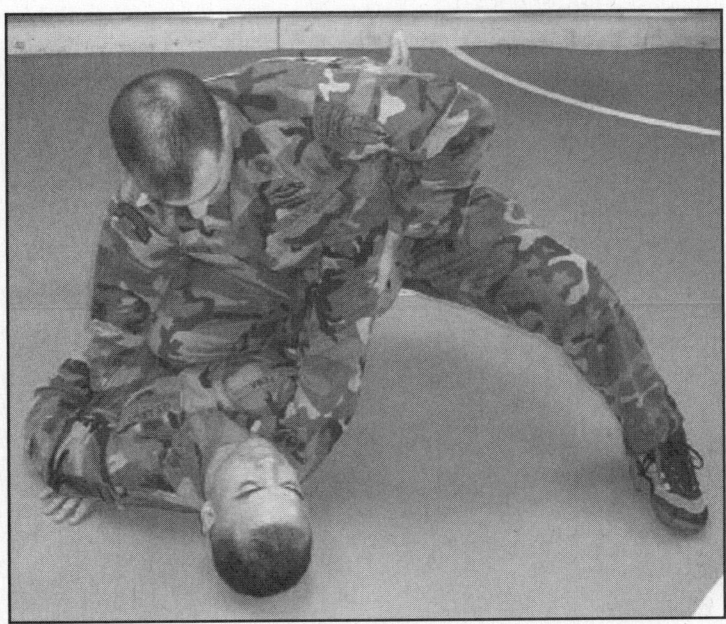

Figure 2-73: Achieve knee mount with control of far side arm, step 3. *(Continued)*

c. **Attacks from the Knee Mount.**

(1) ***Chokes with Hand on the Far Side of the Enemy's Neck.***

(a) ***Step 1*** (Figure 2-74). If the enemy does not defend against chokes, reach under the first arm and grasp well down into the collar with your fingers inside the collar.

Figure 2-74: Choke from the knee mount with hand on far side of enemy's neck, step 1.

(b) ***Step 2*** (Figure 2-75). Bring your knee back off of the enemy's chest, placing it to control his hip, and finish as in the paper cutter choke.

Figure 2-75: Choke from the knee mount with hand on far side of enemy's neck, step 2.

(2) ***Chokes with Hand on the Near Side of the Enemy's Neck.***

(a) ***Step 1*** (Figure 2-76). Reach into the far side of the enemy's collar with your fingers on the inside of the collar.

Figure 2-76: Choke from the knee mount with hand on near side of enemy's neck, step 1.

(b) ***Step 2*** (Figure 2-77). With your weight on the leg closest to his head, sit through and drive your elbow across his neck.

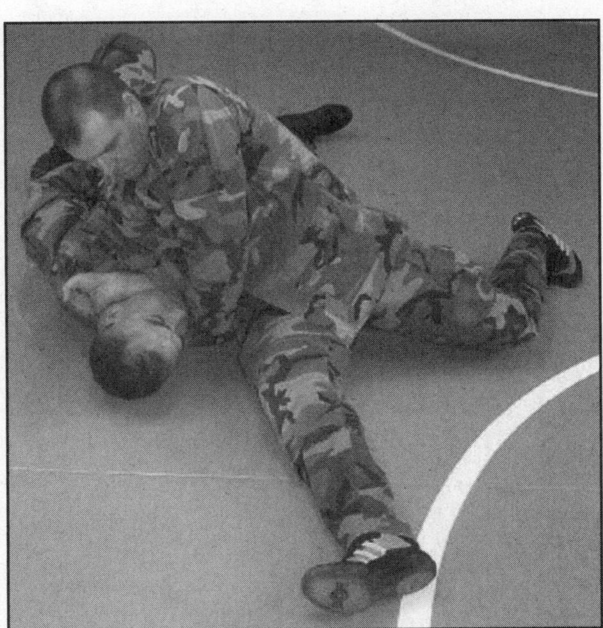

Figure 2-77: Choke from the knee mount with hand on near side of enemy's neck, step 2.

(3) ***Straight Arm Bar from the Knee Mount.***

(a) ***Step 1*** (Figure 2-78). If the enemy pushes up with his near side arm, grasp it at the elbow with your arm closest to the enemy's head. Step over his head with the same side leg.

Figure 2-78: Straight arm bar from the knee mount, step 1.

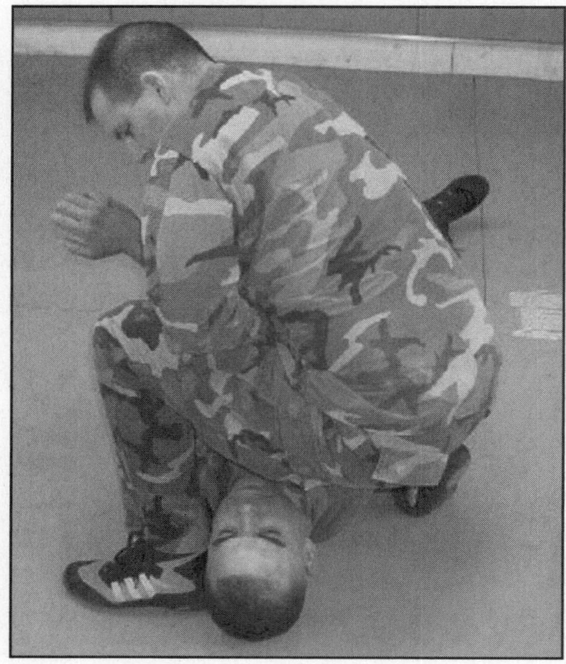

Figure 2-78: Straight arm bar from the knee mount, step 1. *(Continued)*

(b) ***Step 2*** (Figure 2-79). Sit down as close to his shoulder as possible and lay back into the straight arm bar. You may need to twist slightly toward his legs because the change in your leg position allows him an opportunity to roll out of the technique. You do not need to bring your other leg across his body.

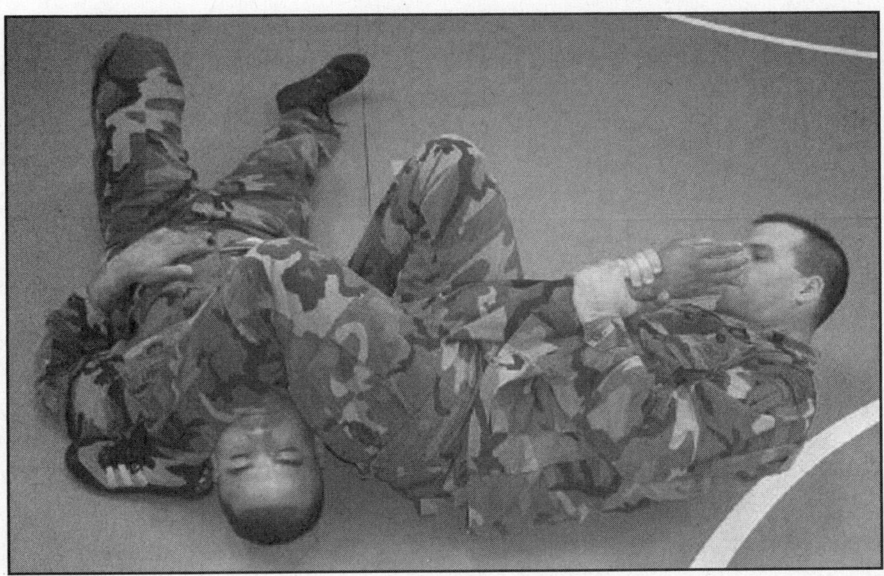

Figure 2-79: Straight arm bar from the knee mount, step 2.

(4) ***Bent Arm Bar from the Knee Mount.***

(a) ***Step 1*** (Figure 2-80). If the enemy tries to push your knee off, grasp his wrist with the hand closest to his legs.

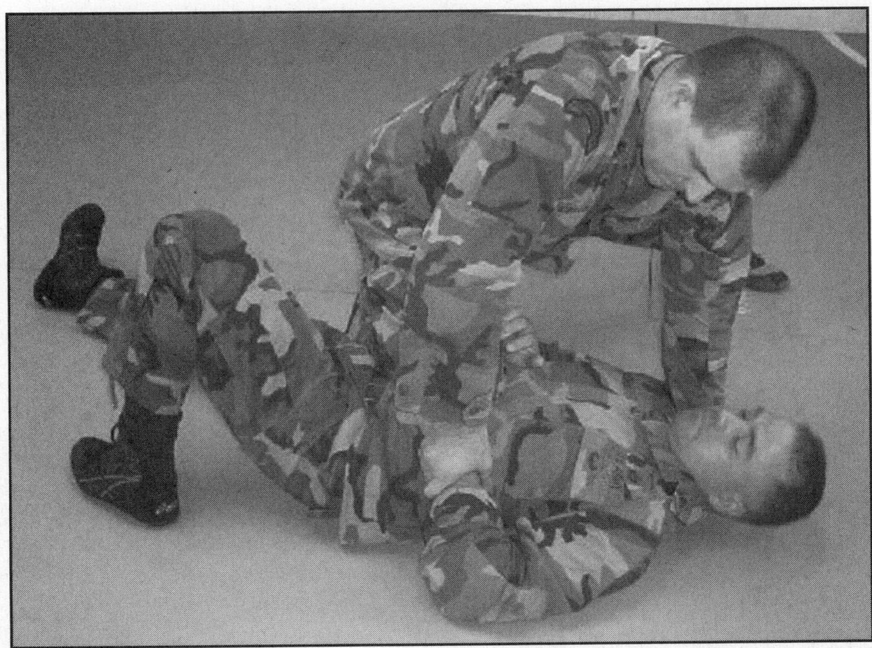

Figure 2-80: Bent arm bar from the knee mount, step 1.

(b) ***Step 2*** (Figure 2-81). Back your knee off of his chest and reach over his arm with the other hand, grasping your own wrist. Your second hand should be wrapped completely around his arm at this time.

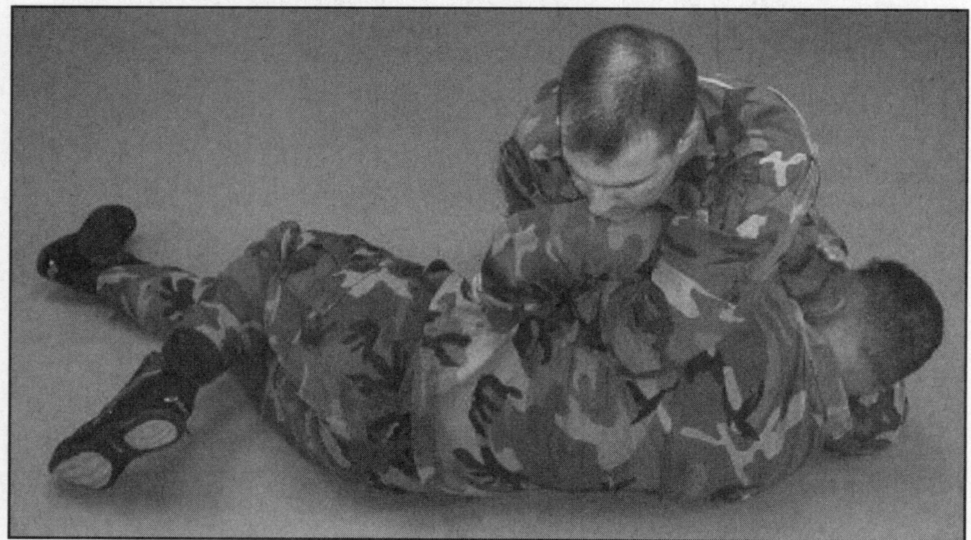

Figure 2-81: Bent arm bar from the knee mount, step 2.

(c) ***Step 3*** (Figure 2-82). Move around until his head is between your knees, and pull him up onto his side.

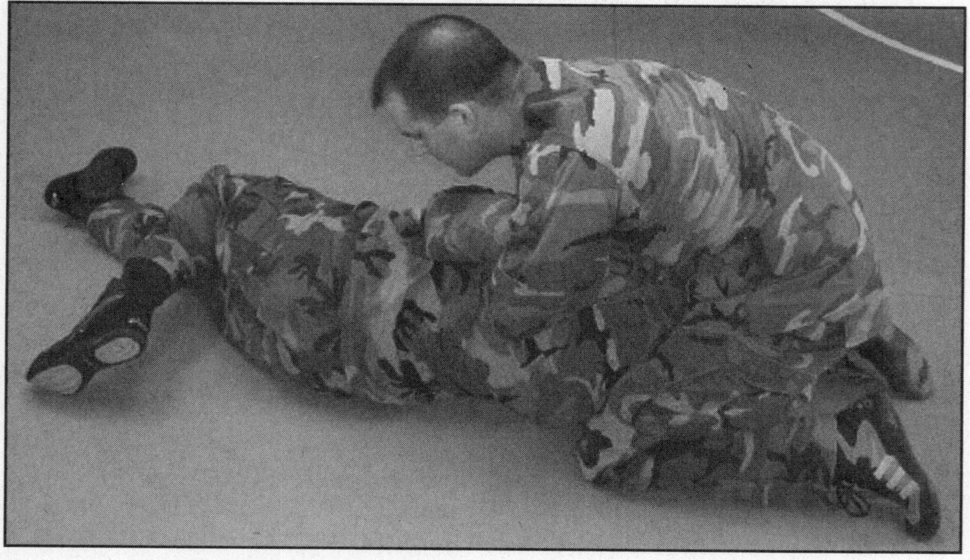

Figure 2-82: Bent arm bar from the knee mount, step 3.

(d) ***Step 4*** (Figure 2-83). Break his grip by pulling his arm quickly toward his head.

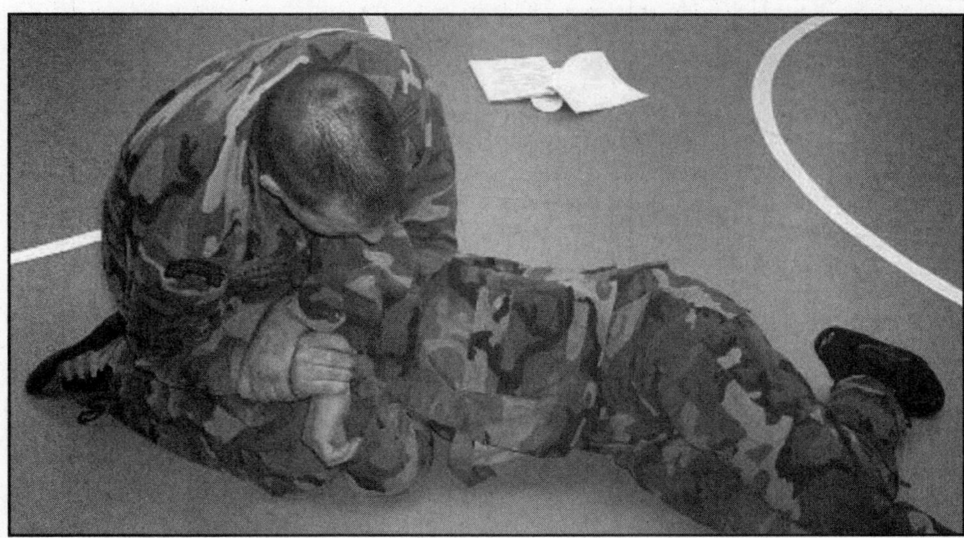

Figure 2-83: Bent arm bar from the knee mount, step 4.

(e) ***Step 5*** (Figure 2-84). Step your foot into the small of his back, and break his shoulder by rotating your torso towards his back.

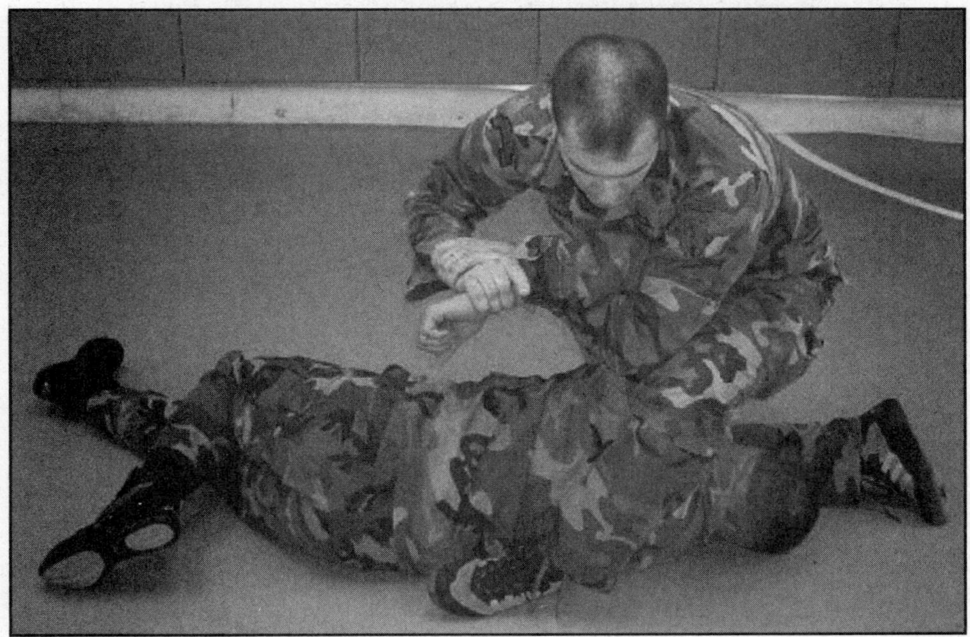

Figure 2-84: Bent arm bar from the knee mount, step 5.

> ✍ NOTE
> It is important to keep the enemy's elbow tight to your chest to keep him from escaping.

(5) ***Variation of Straight Arm Bar from the Knee Mount.***

(a) ***Step 1*** (Figure 2-85). If the enemy has a firm grip and you cannot get the bent arm bar, push your arm farther through and grasp your own lapel.

Figure 2-85: Variation of the straight arm bar from the knee mount, step 1.

(b) ***Step 2*** (Figure 2-86). Stand up and place your foot over his head and in front of his chin.

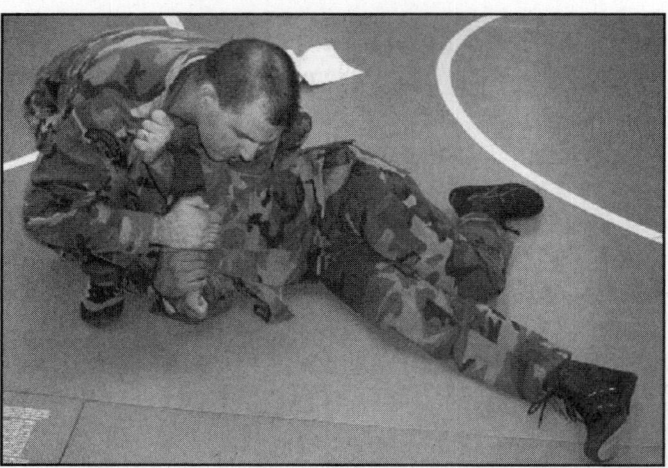

Figure 2-86: Variation of the straight arm bar from the knee mount, step 2.

2-7. LEG ATTACKS

Leg attacks, although very effective, have the drawback of giving up dominant body position. Therefore, they are not the preferred method of attack. Soldiers must be familiar with them or they will fall easy prey to them. As in all attacks, knowing the technique exists is the primary defense.

a. **Straight Ankle Lock.**

(1) ***Step 1*** (Figure 2-87). When you are trying to pass the enemy's open guard, you may catch his foot in your armpit. Wrap your arm around his leg and squat down, ensuring that your opposite side knee comes up between his legs.

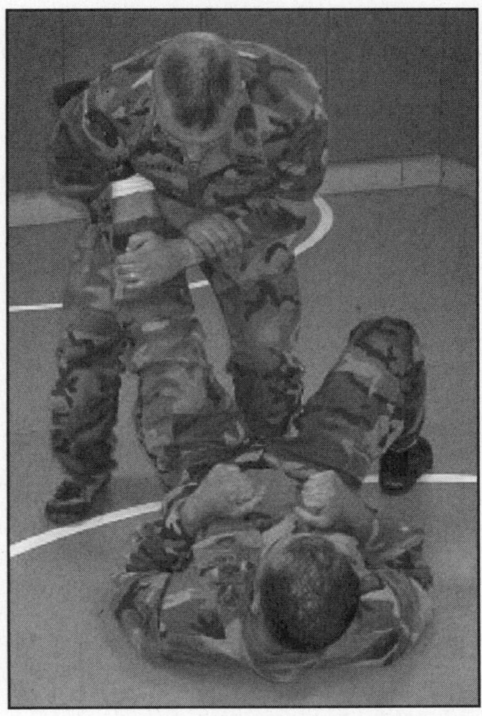

Figure 2-87: Straight ankle lock, step 1.

(2) ***Step 2*** (Figure 2-88). Push away from the enemy, ensuring that you allow his leg to slide through your grip until you are holding around his ankle.

Figure 2-88: Straight ankle lock, step 2.

(3) ***Step 3*** (Figure 2-89). Bring your outside foot up to push the enemy's torso back, preventing him from sitting up to counter the lock. Form a figure four on his ankle and finish the break by arching your back.

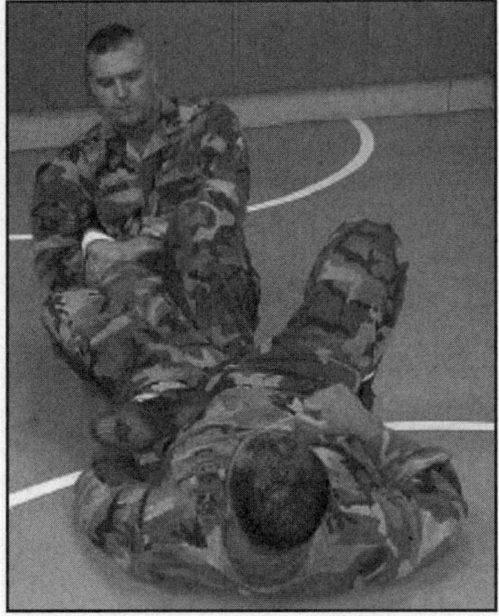

Figure 2-89: Straight ankle lock, step 3.

b. **Figure-Four Ankle Lock** (Figure 2-90). You are on top of the enemy in the north-south position. The enemy may bring his knee up in order to defend against your attacks or attempt to strike you. When he does, reach under his leg from the outside, near the ankle. With the other hand, grasp his foot and form the figure four as shown with the first hand. Apply pressure to break the enemy's foot.

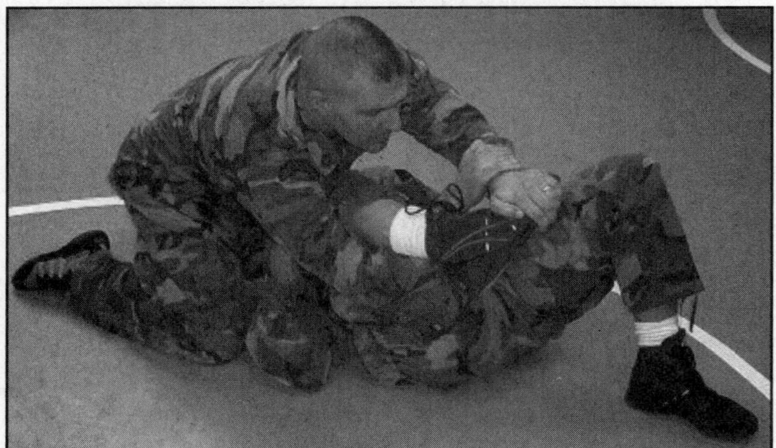

Figure 2-90: Figure-four ankle lock.

c. **Straight Knee Bar.**

(1) ***Step 1*** (Figure 2-91). The enemy is beneath you and has one of your legs between his. Reach your arm under his far side leg, stand up, and step over his body with your other leg.

Figure 2-91: Straight knee bar, step 1.

Figure 2-91: Straight knee bar, step 1. ***(Continued)***

(2) ***Step 2*** (Figure 2-92). Keep your hips as close to the enemy's as possible and lock your legs behind his buttocks. Break the knee with hip pressure just as in a straight arm bar. You may also place his leg into your armpit to increase the pressure, or switch to the figure-four ankle lock at any time.

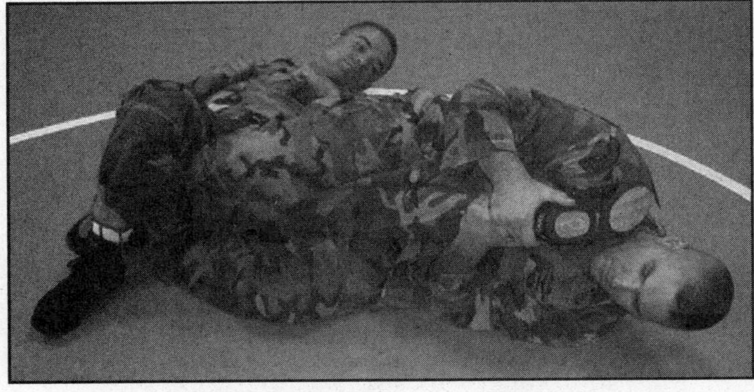

Figure 2-92: Straight knee bar, step 2.

Figure 2-92: Straight knee bar, step 2. ***(Continued)***

SECTION II. STRIKES

Striking is an integral part of all actual fighting. Practicing ground-fighting techniques exclusively without strikes is a common mistake.

2-8. PASS THE GUARD WITH STRIKES

a. ***Step 1*** (Figure 2-93). Keeping your head close to the enemy's chest, drive both hands up the center of his body and then out to control his arms at the biceps.

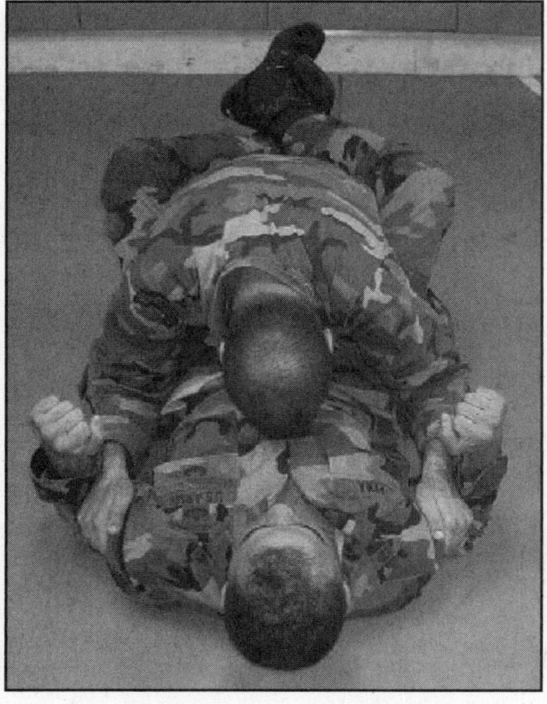

Figure 2-93: Pass the guard with strikes, step 1.

b. ***Step 2*** (Figure 2-94). Give the enemy a couple of head butts.

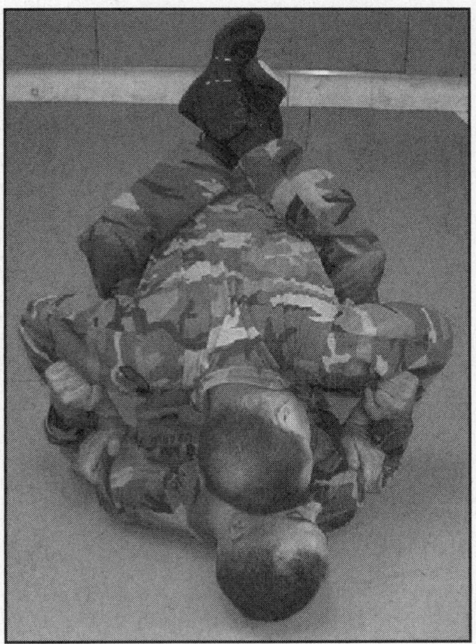

Figure 2-94: Pass the guard with strikes, step 2.

> ✍ NOTE
>
> Ensure that head butts are not given with the center of the forehead, which could result in injuring your own nose.

c. ***Step 3*** (Figure 2-95). Stand up one leg at a time, and change your grip to one hand on the jacket. Your hips should be pushed slightly forward.

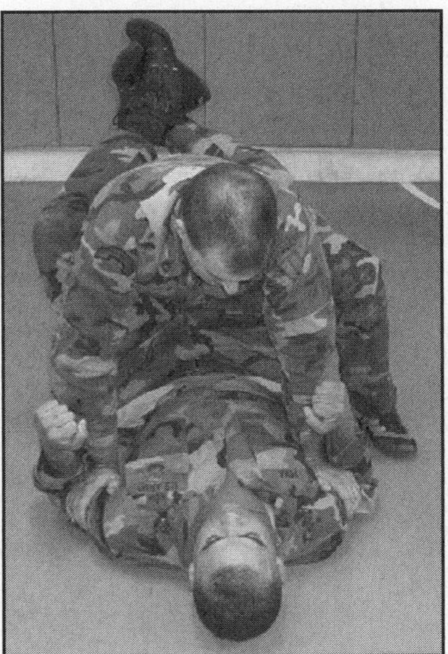

Figure 2-95: Pass the guard with strikes, step 3.

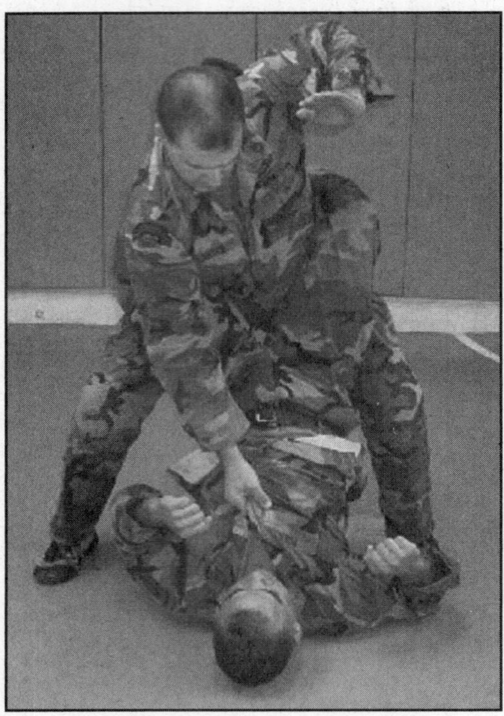

Figure 2-95: Pass the guard with strikes, step 3. ***(Continued)***

d. ***Step 4*** (Figure 2-96). With your free hand, strike the enemy a couple of times in the head.

Figure 2-96: Pass the guard with strikes, step 4.

(At this point the enemy may release the grip with his legs. If he does, step 5 is as follows.)

e. ***Step 5*** (Figure 2-97). Press inward with your knees. This will cause his legs to stick out so that you can reach behind one of them. Gain control of the leg and pass normally.

Figure 2-97: Pass the guard with strikes, step 5.

Figure 2-97: Pass the guard with strikes, step 5. *(Continued)*

(If he does not release his legs, step 5 is as follows.)

f. ***Step 5* (Alternate)** (Figure 2-98). While he is distracted by your strikes, step back with one leg and push your hand through the opening. Place your hand on your own knee and squat down to break the grip of his legs. Gain control of his leg and pass normally.

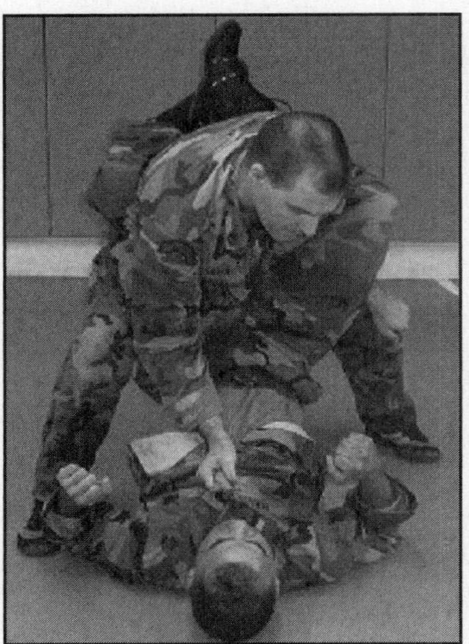

Figure 2-98: Pass the guard with strikes, step 5 (alternate).

Figure 2-98: Pass the guard with strikes, step 5 (alternate). ***(Continued)***

2-9. STRIKING FROM SIDE CONTROL

The goal of striking while ground fighting is to improve your position or create an opening for a better attack. In this case you would most likely be trying to mount.

a. ***Step 1*** (Figure 2-99). Keeping your head low so that the enemy will not be able to knee you in the head, move your hand that is closest to the enemy's legs into his armpit.

Figure 2-99: Striking from side control, step 1.

b. ***Step 2*** (Figure 2-100). Move your other arm around his head and clasp your hands together. Lean your shoulder onto his head to keep his chin pointed away from you. This will make it more difficult for him to turn his body toward you to regain the guard.

Figure 2-100: Striking from side control, step 2.

c. ***Step 3*** (Figure 2-101). Move your leg that is closer to his head into his armpit, driving his arm upwards until it is pinched against his head between your arm and leg.

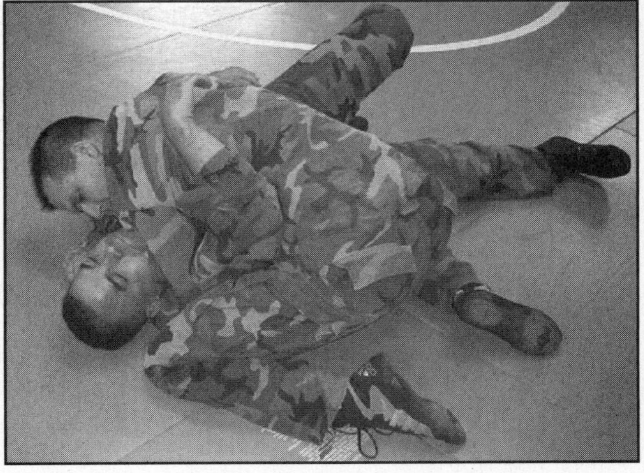

Figure 2-101: Striking from side control, step 3.

d. ***Step 4*** (Figure 2-102). Point the toes of your other foot toward the sky and drive your knee into his ribs.

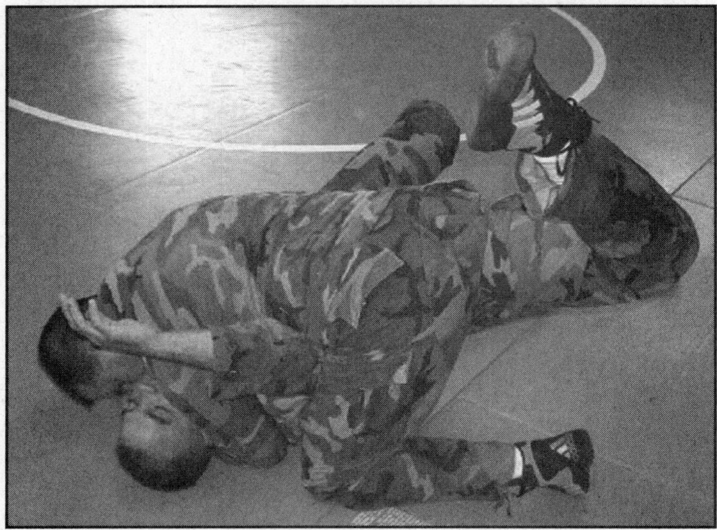

Figure 2-102: Striking from side control, step 4.

e. ***Step 5*** (Figure 2-103). When he changes his position to defend against your strikes, step over and gain the mounted position.

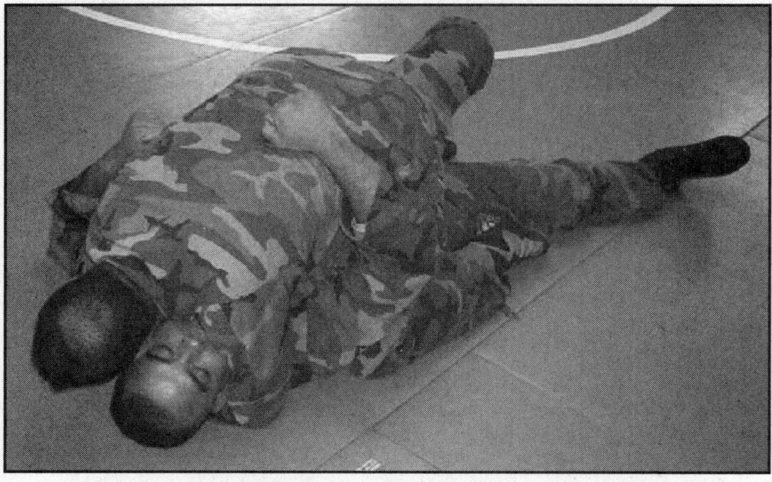

Figure 2-103: Striking from side control, step 5.

2-10. DEFENDING AGAINST STRIKES IN THE GUARD

As with standup fighting, the best method to avoid punches is to stay very close to the enemy. Controlling the range is the key.

a. ***Step 1*** (Figure 2-104). Pull the enemy into your closed guard and grasp him around the neck. One hand should be pushing his head and the other should be pulling it to defend against head butts and punches. Tuck your head in and control his punches with your elbows.

Figure 2-104: Defending against strikes in the guard, step 1.

b. ***Step 2*** (Figure 2-105). The enemy will eventually become frustrated by his inability to land solid blows and will attempt to pull away. When he does so, slide your arms over his triceps and your feet to his hips. Control his punches with your knees. As he struggles to gain a position to strike from, you will have to continuously regain this position.

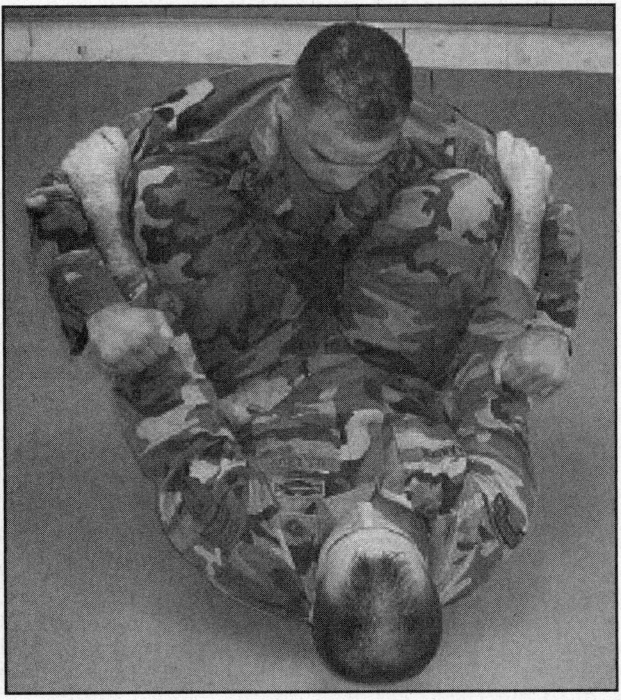

Figure 2-105: Defending against strikes in the guard, step 2.

c. ***Step 3*** (Figure 2-106). Your hands are placed over the enemy's triceps to keep him from getting his arms loose for big punches. He may, however, be able to free one of his arms. If he does so and attempts to land a big punch, push your knee toward the loose arm to extend the distance and reach to the inside of his punching arm. This will avoid the strike and allow you to regain control of his arm.

Figure 2-106: Defending against strikes in the guard, step 3.

d. ***Step 4*** (Figure 2-107). The enemy may attempt to stand up. When he does you should sit up toward him, and when you have enough space to do so safely, stand up in base. You may need to use a kick with your bottom leg to create enough space.

Figure 2-107: Defending against strikes in the guard, step 4.

CHAPTER 3

Takedowns and Throws

Before progressing into takedowns and throws, soldiers must learn how to fall to the ground without getting hurt, both during training and during combat. Each practice repetition of a throw or takedown is a chance for the training partner to perfect his breakfalls.

3-1. BREAKFALLS

The most important point during breakfall training is to not try to catch yourself by reaching out with your arms, but to take the impact of the fall on the meaty portions of the body. After initial training on breakfalls has been conducted, it must be followed up with refresher breakfall training before training on throws and takedowns. This can be accomplished easily by making it part of your warm-up.

a. **Side Breakfall Position** (Figure 3-1). Before training on breakfalls can take place, soldiers must understand the basic breakfall position. Laying on his left side, the soldier extends his left leg and bends his right leg, raising his right leg off the ground. His left arm is extended, palm down, slightly away from his side. His right arm is bent in front of his face to defend against attacks. This should be practiced on both sides.

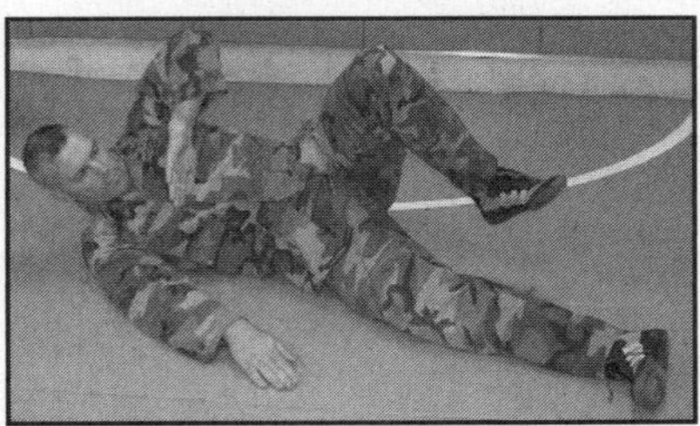

Figure 3-1: Side breakfall position.

b. **Forward Rolling Breakfall from the Kneeling Position.** After soldiers are familiar with the side breakfall position, the best way to introduce them to the mechanics of falling is by starting them on their knees.
   (1) ***Step 1*** (Figure 3-2). The fighter assumes a kneeling posture with his left arm raised in the air. He places his left arm across the front of his body, palm down, outside of his right knee.

Figure 3-2: Forward rolling breakfall from the kneeling position, step 1.

Figure 3-2: Forward rolling breakfall from the kneeling position, step 1. *(Continued)*

(2) ***Step 2*** (Figure 3-3). He rolls over his left shoulder, along his arm, landing on his right side with his right leg extended in the right side breakfall position.

Figure 3-3: Forward rolling breakfall from the kneeling position, step 2.

c. **Forward Rolling Breakfall** (Figure 3-4). When soldiers have mastered the forward rolling breakfall from the kneeling position, they will progress to the standing position.
(1) ***Step 1.*** The soldier starts the fall from the standing position. He raises one arm to expose his entire side, places both hands on the ground, and bends both knees.
(2) ***Step 2.*** He rolls forward across the body along the hand, arm, and back to the opposite hip.
(3) ***Step 3.*** He ends in a good side breakfall position.

Figure 3-4: Forward rolling fall.

d. **Rear Breakfall** (Figure 3-5). There are also many times when a fighter will take a fall straight down to his back.

(1) ***Step 1.*** The fighter starts the fall from the standing position and keeps his head forward to reduce the chance of head and neck injuries.

(2) ***Step 2.*** He then falls backward and lowers his center of gravity by bending both knees. As his buttocks touch the ground, he rolls backward to absorb the momentum of the fall.

(3) ***Step 3.*** He keeps his hands cupped and slaps his hands and arms down to help absorb the shock of impact and to stabilize his body.

Figure 3-5: Rear breakfall.

3-2. CLOSING THE DISTANCE AND ACHIEVING THE CLINCH

Controlling a standup fight means controlling the range between fighters. The untrained fighter is primarily dangerous at punching range. The goal is to avoid that range. Even if you are the superior striker, the most dangerous thing you can do is to spend time at the range where the enemy has the highest probability of victory. When training soldiers, the primary goal should be instilling the courage to close the distance. Recognizing that standup fighting skills are difficult to master in a short amount of time, compare takedowns to the basic tackle. The following techniques are essentially a more sophisticated way to tackle the enemy.

a. **The Clinch.** The clinch position is the optimum way to hold an enemy after you have successfully closed the distance, but have not yet executed a successful takedown. While in the clinch, you have control of the enemy's far side arm at the elbow, with the arm also tucked into your armpit. Your head is tucked into the enemy's chest, and your hand is around his waist, controlling his hip. Your legs are sufficiently back to prevent him from getting his hips under you to attempt a throw. There are two ranges where confrontations start.

(1) ***Close Range.*** This occurs when the enemy is within striking range.

(a) ***Step 1*** (Figure 3-6). When a confrontation seems likely, you will face the potential enemy and bring your hands up in a non-threatening manner.

(b) ***Step 2*** (Figure 3-7). When the enemy attacks, change levels by pulling both feet up and placing them out in a broad stance. Simultaneously bring both arms up to cover the most dangerous possible attacks. It is important not to anticipate the means of attack, but to cover for the most dangerous potential attacks. Therefore, both arms should come up every time.

Figure 3-6: The clinch, step 1.

Figure 3-7: The clinch, step 2.

(c) ***Step 3*** (Figure 3-8). To clinch, reach over the far side arm and pull it down into your armpit, controlling it at the elbow. Simultaneously step around to the other side and drive your other elbow under his arm until you can reach around his waist and achieve the clinch.

Figure 3-8: The clinch, step 3.

(2) ***Long Range.*** It is more common for a confrontation to start outside of striking range. Having the courage to close the distance is the principle training goal.

(a) *Basic Long Range.* From a fighter's stance, at an opportune moment, drive into the enemy. Try to place your forehead on his chest. You should keep your head up so that your forehead is pointed at the enemy and your hands should go just over his biceps. From this position, achieve the clinch as before.

(b) *Long Range when the Enemy Attacks.* If the enemy tries to initiate the attack with punches, use this opportunity to close the distance. He will be closing the distance to get into punching range, and therefore clinching will be that much easier.

(c) *Long Range with a Kick.* If the enemy is content to stand back and await your attack, you will need to gain some form of advantage before closing the distance. One way to do this is with a kick. The kick should be with the front leg, and should be aimed at the enemy's thigh. It is important that if you miss the kick, your leg should fall in front of the enemy so that you do not give up your back.

3-3. THROWS AND TAKEDOWNS

All of the throws and takedowns in this section assume that you have already achieved the clinch. It is important to remember that most sport-type throws are executed at what, in a real fight, would be striking range.

a. **Basic Takedown.** This is the basic tackle.

(1) ***Step 1*** (Figure 3-9). From the clinch, step slightly to the front of the enemy and change your grip. Both palms are pointed down and your hands are at the enemy's kidneys.

Figure 3-9: Basic takedown, step 1.

(2) ***Step 2*** (Figure 3-10). Pulling with your hands and pushing with your head and shoulder, break the enemy's balance to the rear.

Figure 3-10: Basic takedown, step 2.

(3) ***Step 3*** (Figure 3-11). Step over the enemy and release your grip, ending in the mounted position.

Figure 3-11: Basic takedown, step 3.

> ✍ **NOTE**
> It is very important to release your hands to avoid landing on them.

b. **Hook the Leg** (Figure 3-12). If the enemy attempts to pull away, use your leg closest to his back to hook his leg. When he begins to fall, release the leg and finish as before.

Figure 3-12: Hook the leg.

c. **Hip Throw.** The enemy may attempt to avoid the tackle by leaning forward.

(1) ***Step 1*** (Figure 3-13). With the leg that is behind the enemy, step through until you are standing in front of him with your legs inside of his. Your hip should be pushed well through.

Figure 3-13: Hip throw, step 1.

(2) ***Step 2*** (Figure 3-14). Using a scooping motion with your hips, lift the enemy and throw him over your hip. You should land in the knee mount or side control.

Figure 3-14: Hip throw, step 2.

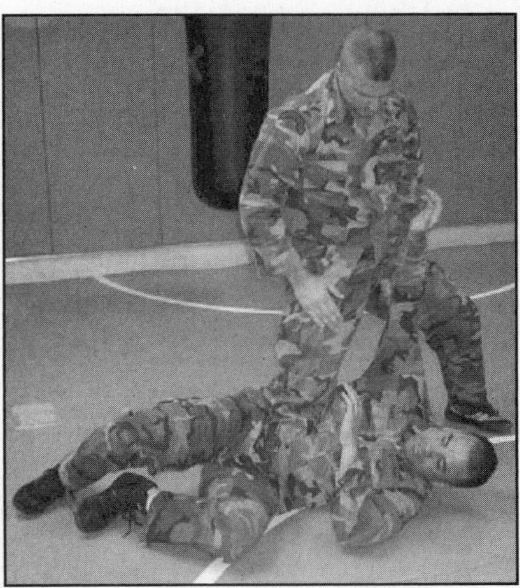

Figure 3-14: Hip throw, step 2 . ***(Continued)***

d. **Rear Takedown** (Figure 3-15). Frequently, you will end up after the clinch with your head behind the enemy's arm. When this happens, you grasp your hands together around his waist by interlocking your fingers, and place your forehead in the middle of the small of his back to avoid strikes. From this secure position, you can attempt to take the enemy down.

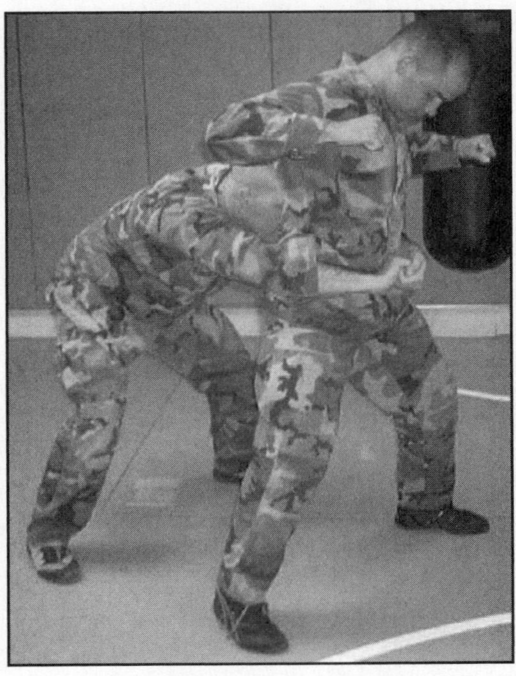

Figure 3-15: Rear takedown.

(1) ***Step 1*** (Figure 3-16). Step to one side so that you are behind the enemy at an angle.

Figure 3-16: Rear takedown, step 1.

(2) ***Step 2*** (Figure 3-17). With the leg that is behind the enemy, reach out and place the instep of your foot behind the enemy's far side foot so that he cannot step backward. Sit down as close to your other foot as possible and hang your weight from the enemy's waist.

Figure 3-17: Rear takedown, step 2.

(3) ***Step 3*** (Figure 3-18). The enemy will fall backwards over your extended leg. As he does so, tuck your elbow in to avoid falling on it, and rotate up into the mounted position.

Figure 3-18: Rear takedown, step 3.

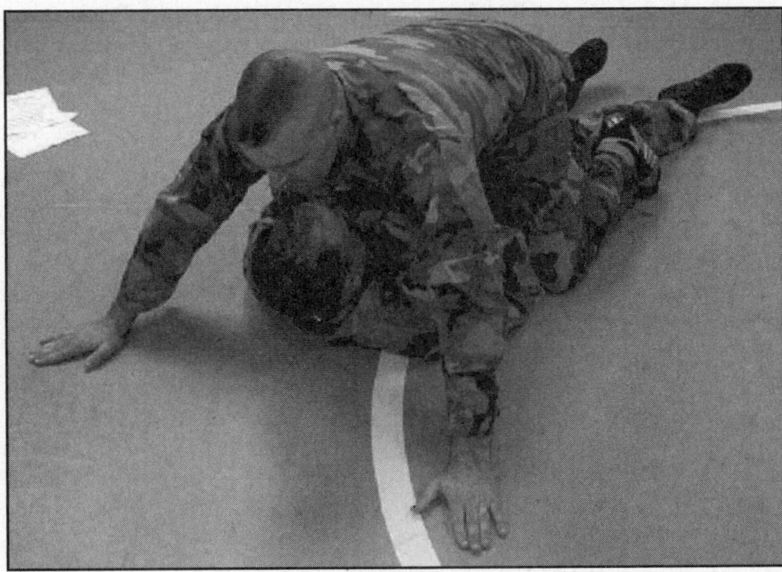

Figure 3-18: Rear takedown, step 3. ***(Continued)***

3-4. DEFENDING AGAINST HEADLOCKS

a. **Defend the Guillotine.**

(1) ***Step 1*** (Figure 3-19). When you find yourself caught in the guillotine choke, reach over the enemy's opposite shoulder with your arm. Turn your head slightly inward and grasp the enemy's wrist to help alleviate the pressure. You should also relax and hang as dead weight. If the enemy is taller than you, place your knees on his thighs to support you.

Figure 3-19: Defend the guillotine, step 1.

(2) ***Step 2*** (Figure 3-20). As the enemy tries to pick you up to choke you, bounce around to the opposite side from the choke. Break his base by bumping the back of his knee with your knee, and lower him carefully to the ground. Ensure that you are in side control as you set him down.

Figure 3-20: Defend the guillotine, step 2.

Figure 3-20: Defend the guillotine, step 2. ***(Continued)***

Figure 3-20: Defend the guillotine, step 2. ***(Continued)***

(3) ***Step 3*** (Figure 3-21). With the hand that is closest to his head, grasp his far side shoulder and drive the bony portion of your forearm under his chin until you can pull your head free.

Figure 3-21: Defend the guillotine, step 3.

b. **Defend the Guillotine with Knee Strikes.** When the enemy has secured the guillotine choke, he may attempt to direct knee strikes to your head.

(1) ***Step 1*** (Figure 3-22). With both arms locked out at the elbows, and the heels of the hands together, block the enemy's knee strikes just above the knee. It is very important that your thumbs be alongside your hands so that they are not broken by the enemy's knee strikes. Your leg that is on the side corresponding with the side of the enemy that your head is on, should be forward, and the other leg back. Your leg that is on the same side of the enemy as your head should be forward, and your other leg back.

Figure 3-22: Defend the guillotine with knee strikes, step 1.

(2) ***Step 2*** (Figure 3-23). Swing your back leg forward, between the enemy's legs, and sit down on your other heel. This dropping action will send the enemy over your head, driving his head into the ground.

Figure 3-23: Defend the guillotine with knee strikes, step 2.

Figure 3-23: Defend the guillotine with knee strikes, step 2. *(Continued)*

⚠ CAUTION

This technique can be very dangerous to practice. It should always be practiced with the enemy's outside hand free, allowing him to roll out. Soldiers should be proficient in rolling breakfalls, and great care must be taken to ensure they know how to properly roll out while practicing (Figure 3-24).

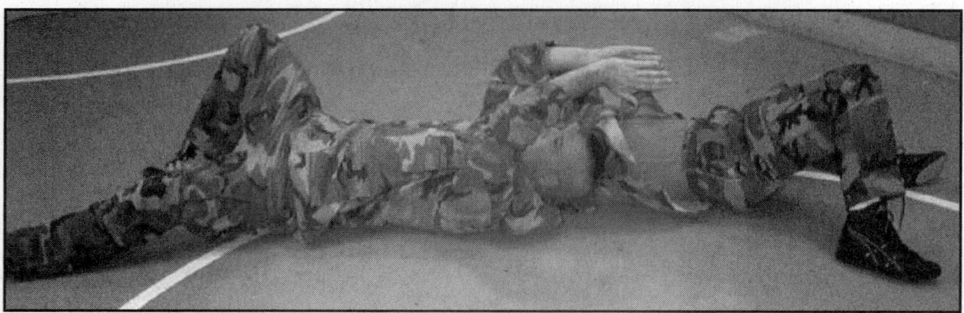

Figure 3-24: Defend the guillotine with knee strikes, caution.

c. **Headlock with Punches.** When you are behind the enemy and he has control of your head, he must release one of his hands in order to punch.
   (1) ***Step 1*** (Figure 3-25). With your front arm, attempt to grasp the enemy's punching arm and push it back, feeding it to your other arm. Grasp it from behind his back at the elbow.

Figure 3-25: Headlock with punches, step 1.

(2) ***Step 2*** (Figure 3-26). When the punching arm has been controlled, secure a grip on the top of the hand that is around your head, and place your hip against the enemy's side. At the same time, step and look away from the enemy, extending your body to break his grip. Hip pressure will keep him from following.

Figure 3-26: Headlock with punches, step 2.

(3) ***Step 3*** (Figure 3-27). Keep his hand pressed tightly against your chest, and with the foot closest to him, step backwards to place yourself standing behind him with his hand still captured against your chest.

Figure 3-27: Headlock with punches, step 3.

Figure 3-27: Headlock with punches, step 3. ***(Continued)***

d. **Headlock Without Punches.** When the enemy has control of your head, he will normally try to hold on with both hands.
   (1) ***Step 1*** (Figure 3-28). Block potential knee strikes by placing the heel of one hand just above the opposite side knee. Reach the other hand around the enemy's back and secure a grip at the far side of his hip bone. Your legs should be back so that he cannot get his hip under you.

Figure 3-28: Headlock without punches, step 1.

(2) ***Step 2*** (Figure 3-29). Step slightly in front of the enemy, and then with your outside foot, step between the enemy's legs and sit down on your heel. This should be a spinning action, and as you drop between his legs, pull him with the hand that was on his hip. He will fall over you so that you can roll up into the mount.

Figure 3-29: Headlock without punches, step 2.

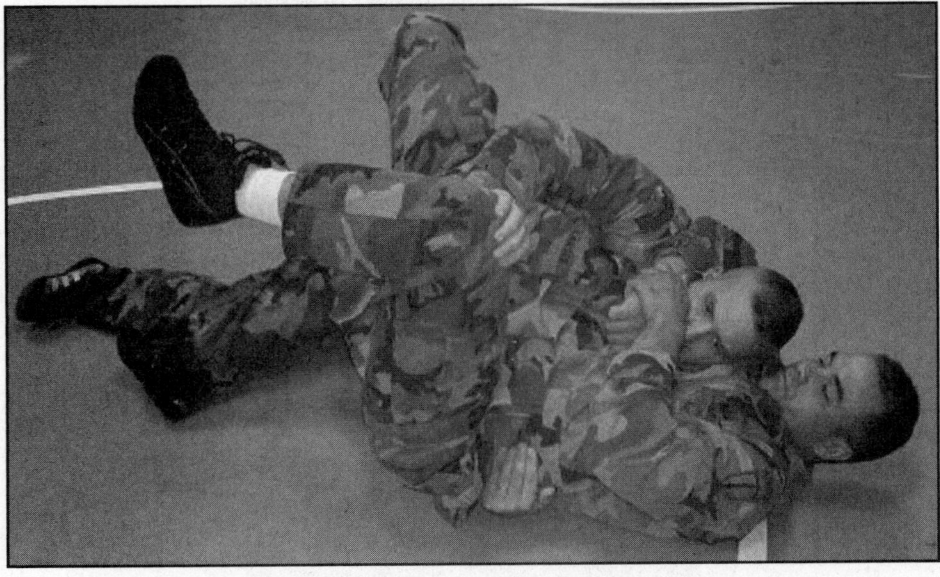

Figure 3-29: Headlock without punches, step 2. *(Continued)*

> ✍ NOTE
>
> Ensure that you tuck your elbow in as he falls to avoid landing on it.

3-5. TAKEDOWNS FROM AGAINST A WALL

If you are having difficulty gaining control of the enemy, a good technique is to push him against a wall.

a. **Position and Strikes** (Figure 3-30). Push him against the wall with one shoulder. One arm should be around his waist, and the other one should be on the inside of his knee to deflect knee strikes to your groin. One of your legs should be back to push, and the other one should be inside of the enemy's knee to deflect knee strikes. From this position, you can deliver strikes to the enemy's ribs by turning your hand over and attacking with the knuckles. When he attempts to cover his ribs, with a sharp movement, push your shoulder into him to gain enough space to strike his head.

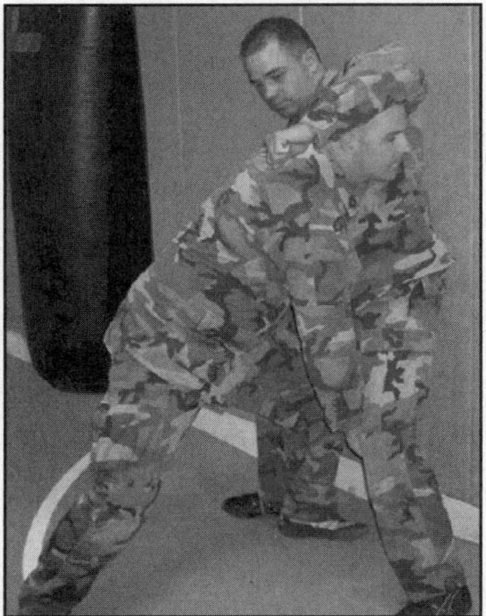

Figure 3-30: Position and strikes against the wall.

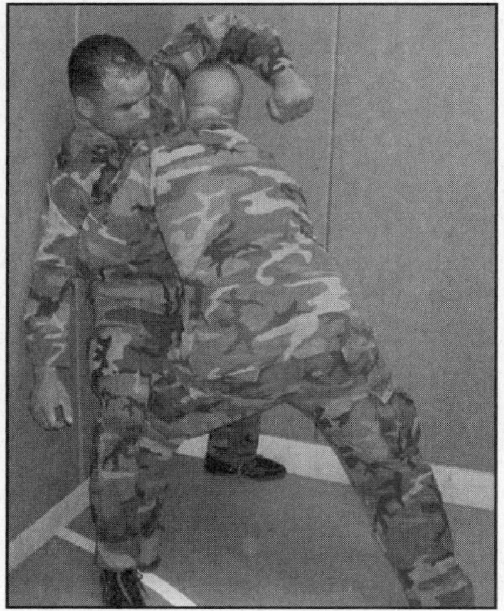

Figure 3-30: Position and strikes against the wall. ***(Continued)***

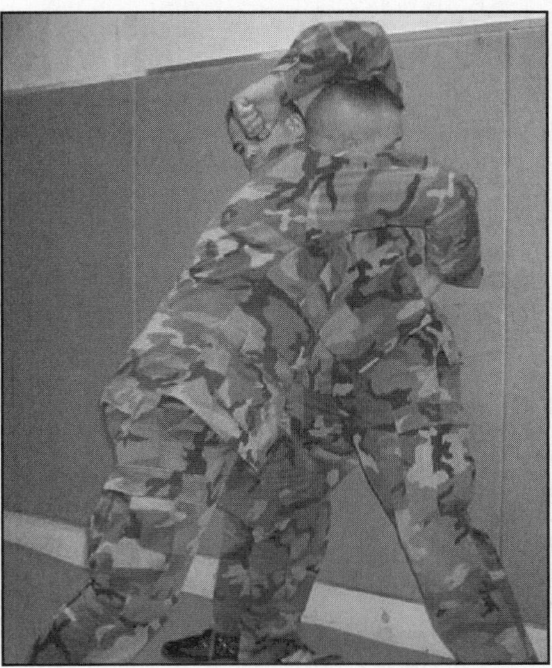

Figure 3-30: Position and strikes against the wall. ***(Continued)***

Figure 3-30: Position and strikes against the wall. ***(Continued)***

Figure 3-30: Position and strikes against the wall. ***(Continued)***

b. **Leg Drag** (Figure 3-31). When the enemy attempts a knee strike on the side you are facing, capture his leg. Step back with the foot on the same side pulling him from the wall.

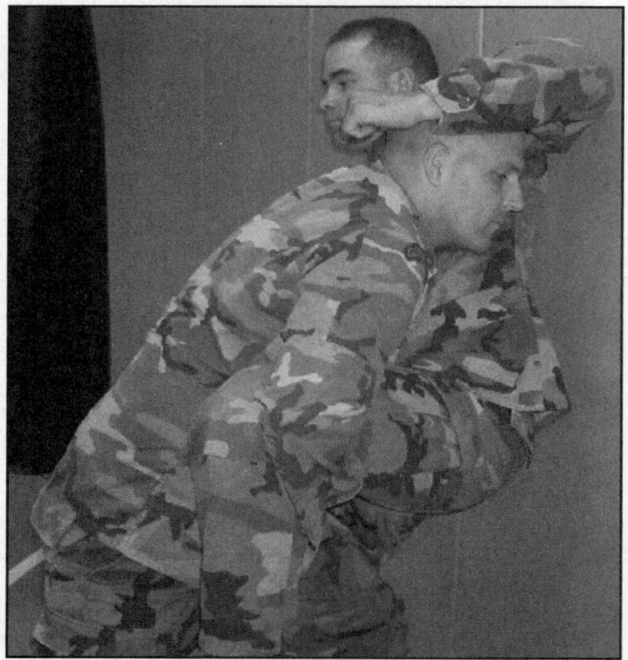

Figure 3-31: Leg drag.

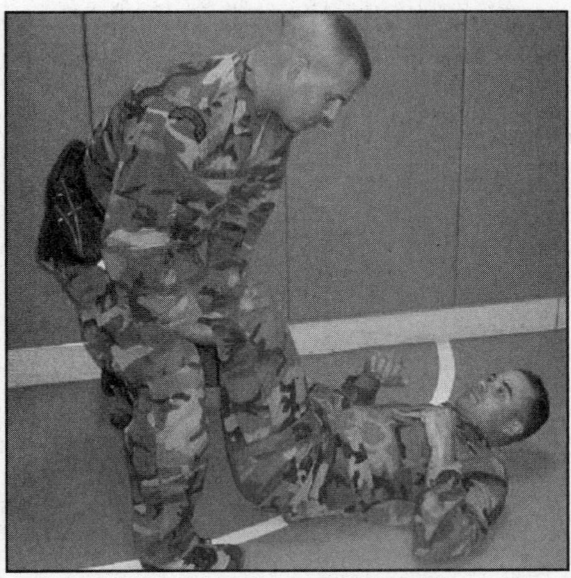

Figure 3-31: Leg drag. ***(Continued)***

3-6. DOUBLE LEG ATTACKS

Going under the enemy's arms and straight to the legs is a very useful type of attack. There are several ways to finish depending on the enemy's actions, but the initial attack is the same. When you find yourself relatively close to the enemy, change your level by bending both of your knees and drive into his midsection with your shoulder (Figure 3-32). One of your feet should penetrate as deep as the enemy's feet. Continue to drive and control the legs to end in side control.

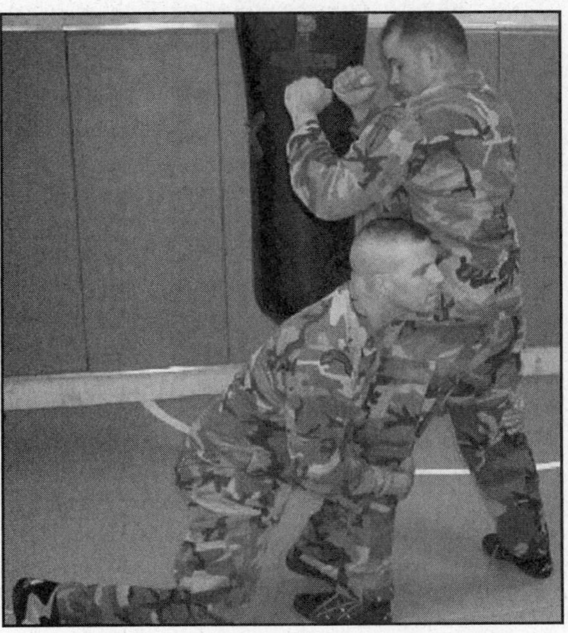

Figure 3-32: Double leg attack.

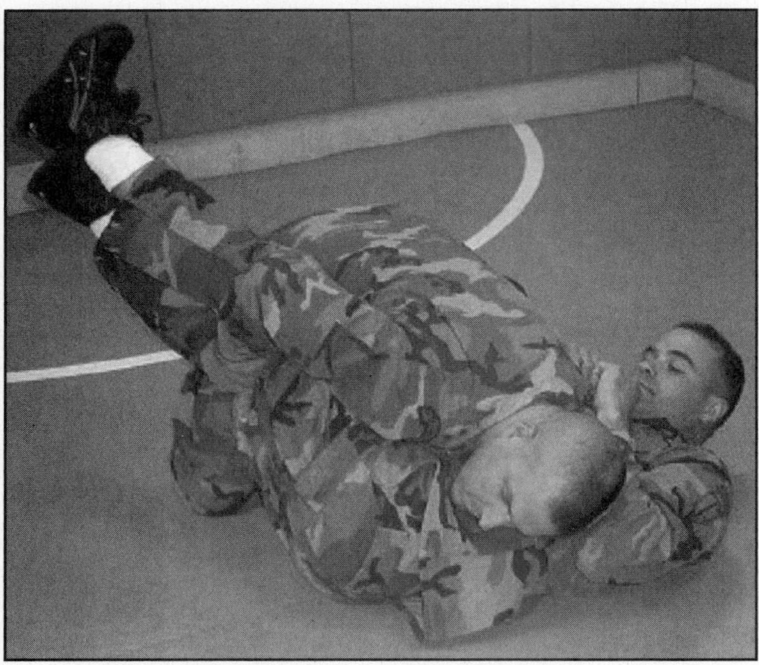

Figure 3-32: Double leg attack. ***(Continued)***

a. **Finishes from the Double Leg Attack.**

(1) ***Lift*** (Figure 3-33). By driving your hips under him and arching your back, lift the enemy up. Push up with your head and, by controlling his legs with your arms, gain side control.

Figure 3-33: Lift.

Figure 3-33: Lift. ***(Continued)***

Figure 3-33: Lift. ***(Continued)***

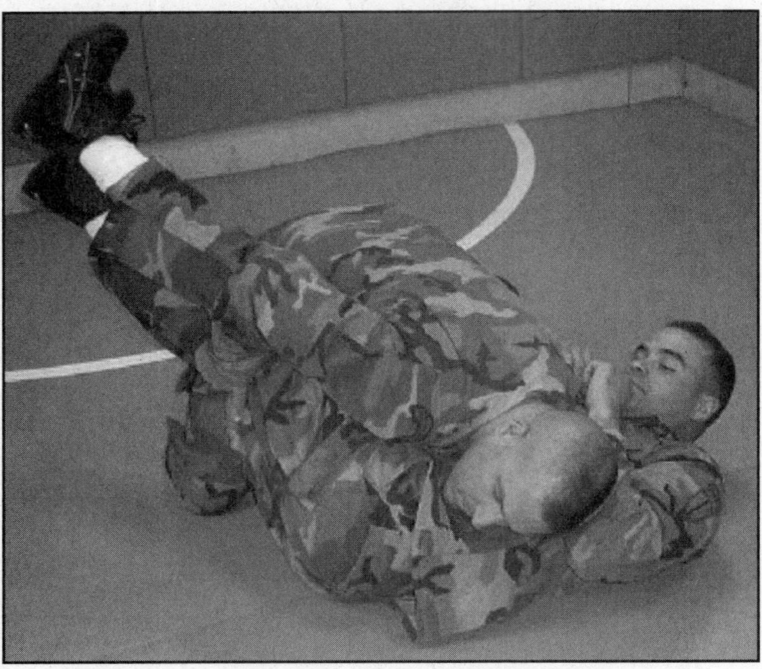

Figure 3-33: Lift. ***(Continued)***

b. **Hook the Leg** (Figure 3-34). Hook the enemy's heel with your outside leg and continue to drive through him.

Figure 3-34: Hook the leg.

3-7. SINGLE LEG ATTACKS

You may also choose to attack only one leg (Figure 3-35). Making a deep step with the inside leg, and reaching with the same side arm to the enemy's opposite knee, step to the outside and grasp your hands together behind his knee. Your head and shoulder should be tight against his thigh. Moves to finish a single leg attack include the dump, block the opposite knee, and the leg sweep.

Figure 3-35: Single leg attack.

Figure 3-35: Single leg attack. ***(Continued)***

a. **Dump** (Figure 3-36). From the single leg position, with your shoulder tight against his thigh, take a short step in front of him, and then a longer step backward with your trail foot. Pressure from your head and shoulder will "dump" him on to his buttocks.

Figure 3-36: Dump.

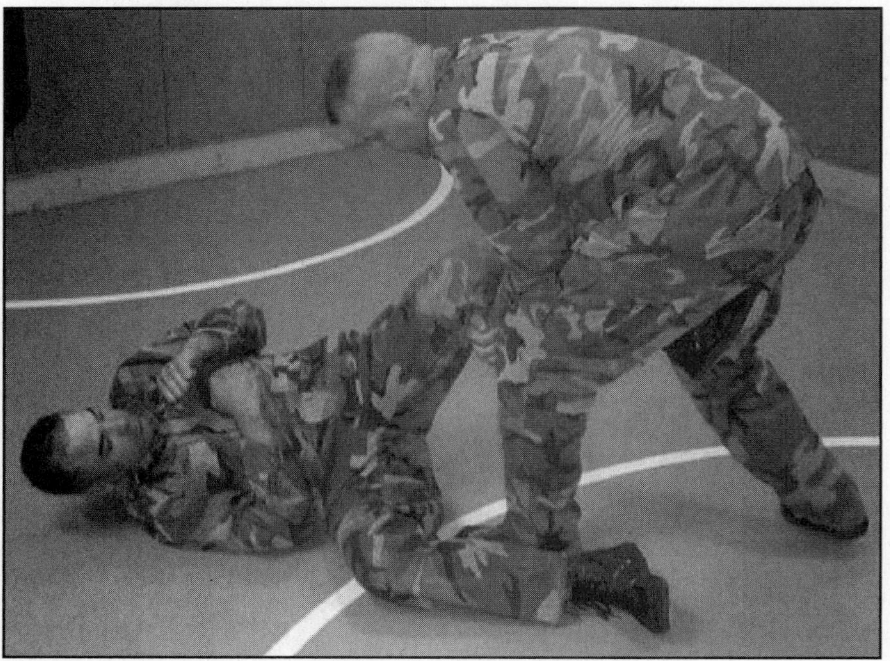

Figure 3-36: Dump. ***(Continued)***

b. **Block the Opposite Knee** (Figure 3-37). If the enemy turns away from you, maintain control of his leg and reach between his legs to block his opposite leg. Use pressure with your shoulder on the back of his leg to bring him face down on the ground.

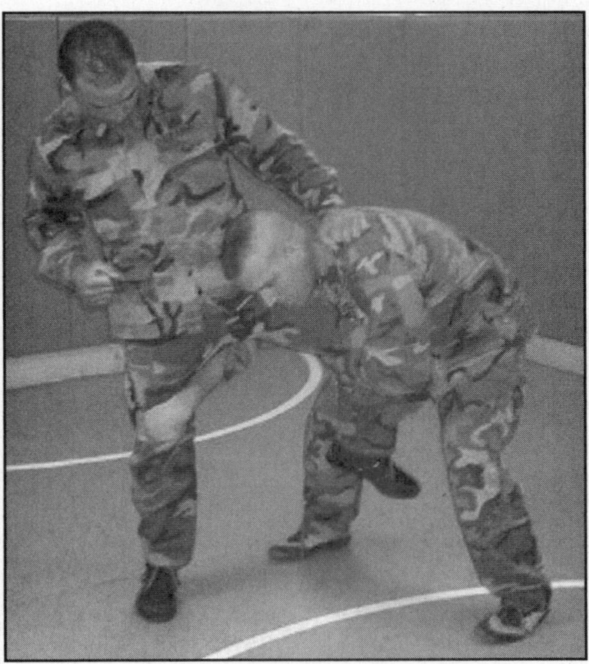

Figure 3-37: Block the opposite knee.

c. **Leg Sweep** (Figure 3-38). Reach your outside arm under his leg, and with your outside hand, reach down and gain control of his ankle. Pull his leg up with both of your arms and use your foot to sweep his post leg.

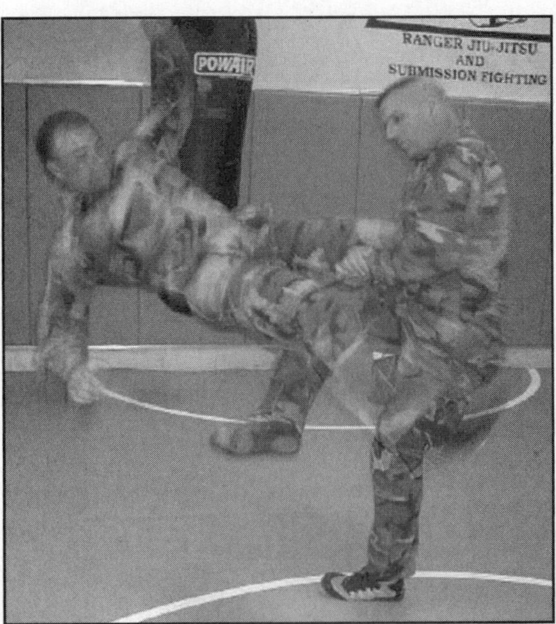

Figure 3-38: Leg sweep.

3-8. ATTACK FROM THE REAR

In the rear attack, the unsuspecting is knocked to the ground and kicked in the groin, or rear mounted. The soldier can then kill the sentry by any proper means. Since surprise is the essential element of this technique, the soldier must use effective stalking techniques (Figure 3-39, Step 1). To initiate his attack, he grabs both of the sentry's ankles (Figure 3-39, Step 2). Then he heaves his body weight into the hips of the sentry while pulling up on the ankles. This technique slams the sentry to the ground on his face. Then, the soldier may follow with a kick to the groin (Figure 3-39, Step 3) or by achieving the rear mount.

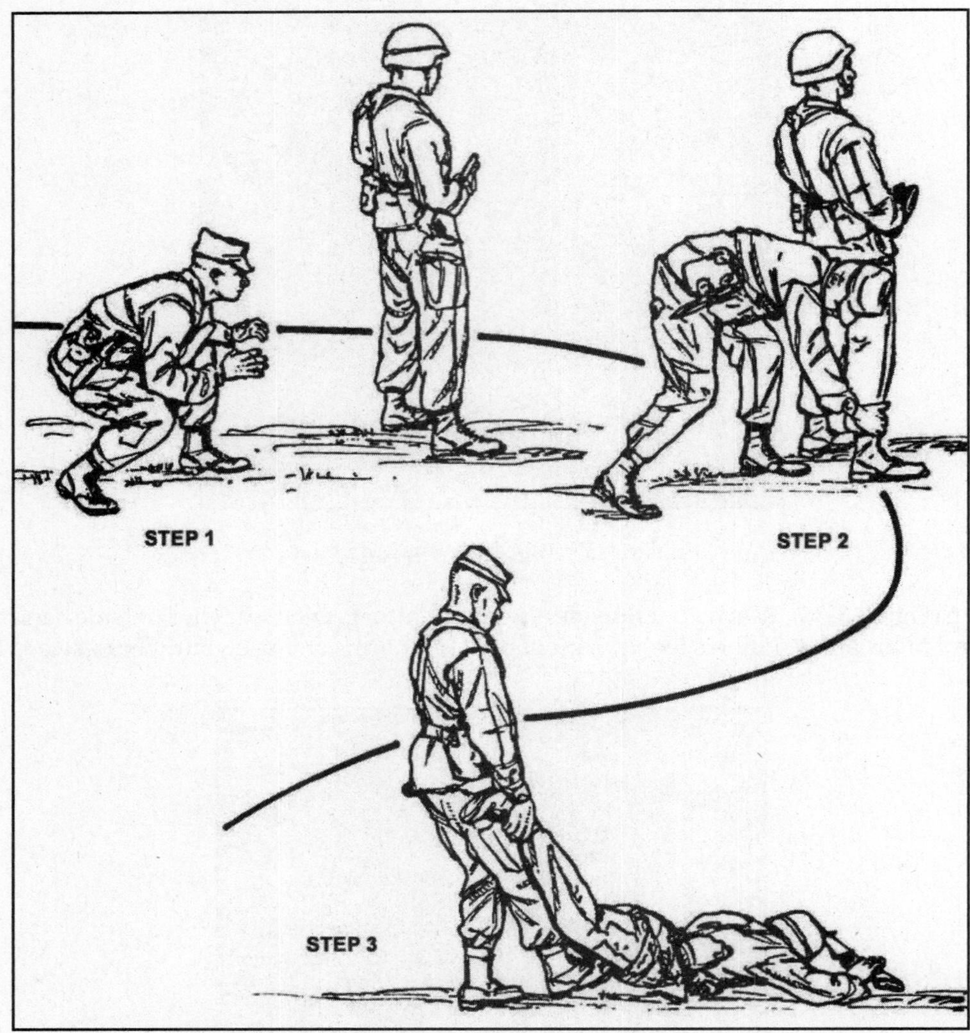

Figure 3-39: Attack from the rear.

CHAPTER 4

Strikes

Strikes are an inefficient method of ending a fight. However, they are a significant part of most fights, and a soldier must have an understanding of fighting at striking range. It is important to note that while at striking range, you are open to being struck. For this reason, it is often better to avoid striking range.

SECTION I. NATURAL WEAPONS

The key to developing effective striking skills is understanding range and knowing what techniques are effective at what range and controlling the transition between ranges. Techniques are taught individually, but they must be approached as a part of an overall fighting strategy. Effective striking is not something that can be taught overnight. This section describes natural weapon techniques of various punches, strikes, and kicks and addresses the ranges from which they are effective.

4-1. ARM STRIKES

The strikes in this section are presented individually. It is important to know that they will almost never be used this way. Follow-up sections will address combinations and how strikes fit into an overall fight strategy. Remember to keep your guard up with the non-punching arm when learning each of the following strikes.

a. **Jab** (Figure 4-l). The jab is thrown with the lead hand and is used for controlling the range, and setting up further techniques. From the basic stance, snap your lead arm out with a slight pivot of your hip and shoulder. You should rotate your shoulder so that the punch lands with your palm down and quickly snap your arm back into the ready position. Your punch should travel in a straight line, and your elbow should never stick out away from your body at any time during the punch.

Figure 4-1: Jab.

> ✍ NOTE
> To step into your jab, drive off of your trail leg as you punch and slide your trail leg forward as you withdraw your punching arm.

b. **Reverse Punch** (Figure 4-2). The reverse punch is a power punch thrown from the rear arm. It can be a fight ender by itself, but it is also very useful to set up takedowns. From the basic stance, turn on the ball of your trail foot as if you were putting out a cigarette so that your hips and shoulders are facing toward the enemy. As you extend your punch, rotate your arm so that you strike with your knuckles up and palm facing down. You should extend your punch as if to go through your opponent and then snap back into the ready position.

Figure 4-2: Reverse punch.

> ✍ **NOTE**
> Ensure that you do not lock your elbow when your punch is fully extended.

c. **Hook** (Figure 4-3). The hook is a power punch that is usually thrown from the front arm. It is very powerful and works well in combinations. One of its main advantages is that it can be fully executed outside of the enemy's field of vision. The common mistake is to think of it as a looping arm punch. In reality, a powerful hook does not involve very much arm movement, generating its power from your leg hip and shoulder movement. From the basic stance, turn on your lead foot as if you were putting out a cigarette, turning your hips and shoulders toward the inside. Raise your elbow as you turn so that your punch lands with your arm parallel with the ground, and your palm facing toward your chest. Your trail foot should remain planted. You should then smoothly tuck your elbow back in to your side and turn your shoulders to return to the ready position.

Figure 4-3: Hook.

d. **Uppercut.** The uppercut can be thrown with either hand and is particularly effective against an opponent who is crouching or trying to avoid a clinch.

(1) ***Lead Hand Uppercut.***

(a) ***Step 1*** (Figure 4-4). From the basic stance, turn your hips and shoulders slightly to face the enemy, and dip your lead shoulder downward. You should be changing your level slightly by bending your knees.

Figure 4-4: Lead hand uppercut, step 1.

(b) ***Step 2*** (Figure 4-5). Keep your elbow tucked in and drive off of your lead leg to land your punch, palm facing up with your wrist firm and straight.

Figure 4-5: Lead hand uppercut, step 2.

(c) ***Step 3.*** Turn your shoulders and snap back into the ready position.

(2) ***Trail Hand Uppercut.***

(a) ***Step 1*** (Figure 4-6). From the basic stance, turn your hips and shoulders slightly to face the enemy, and dip your rear shoulder downward. You should be changing your level slightly by bending your knees.

Figure 4-6: Trail hand uppercut, step 1.

(b) ***Step 2*** (Figure 4-7). Drive off of your trail leg through your hip to land your punch, palm facing up with your wrist straight and firm. Your arm will be slightly more extended than the lead hand punch.

Figure 4-7: Trail hand uppercut, step 2.

(c) *Step 3.* Snap back into the ready position.

e. **Elbow Strikes.** Elbow strikes can be devastating blows and are very useful at close range. You should remember that they gain their power from the hips and legs.

(1) ***Horizontal Elbow Strike*** (Figure 4-8). A horizontal elbow strike is thrown almost exactly like a hook, with the exceptions that at the moment of impact the palm should be facing the ground.

Figure 4-8: Horizontal elbow strike.

(2) ***Upward Elbow Strike*** (Figure 4-9). The upward elbow strike is thrown almost exactly like an uppercut, with the exception that at the moment of impact the palm should be facing inward toward your head.

Figure 4-9: Upward elbow strike.

4-2. PUNCHING COMBINATIONS

Strikes must be thrown in combinations to be effective—"bunches of punches" as the old boxing saying goes. Combination punching must be practiced in order to come naturally while under the stress of combat. After the basic punches are learned individually, they should be practiced in combination. Particular attention should be paid to snapping each hand back into a defensive posture after it is used. Remember that when you are in punching range, so is the enemy. You must make a good defense an integral part of your offense. Some combination punches are:

- Jab—reverse punch.
- Jab—reverse punch—hook.
- Jab—hook.
- Jab—hook—reverse punch.
- Lead hand uppercut to the body—trail hand uppercut to the body—hook to the head.
- Lead hand uppercut to the body—trail hand uppercut to the body—lead hand horizontal elbow strike—trail hand upward elbow strike.

4-3. KICKS

Kicks during hand-to-hand combat are best directed at low targets and should be simple but effective. Combat soldiers are usually burdened with combat boots and LCE. His flexibility level is usually low during combat, and if engaged in hand-to-hand combat, he will be under high stress. He must rely on gross motor skills and kicks that do not require complicated movement or much training and practice to execute.

a. **Lead Leg Front Kick** (Figure 4-10). The lead leg front kick is not a very powerful kick, but it can be a very good tool to help control the range. The target should be the enemy's thigh, just above the knee. The striking surface is the sole of the foot. It is very important that if the kick does not land, your foot should not slide off toward the enemy's back. This would present your back to him.

Figure 4-10: Lead leg front kick.

b. **Rear Leg Front Kick** (Figure 4-11). The rear leg front kick is a much more powerful kick. The best target is the abdomen. The striking surface should be either the ball of the foot or the entire sole of the foot.

Figure 4-11: Rear leg front kick.

c. **Shin Kick.** The shin kick is a powerful kick, and it is easily performed with little training. When the legs are targeted, the kick is hard to defend against (Figure 4-12), and an opponent can be dropped by it.

Figure 4-12: Shin kick to the outer thigh.

d. **Stepping Side Kick** (Figure 4-13). A soldier starts a stepping side kick (Step 1) by stepping either behind or in front of his other foot to close the distance between him and his opponent. The movement is like that in a skip. The soldier now brings the knee of his kicking foot up and thrusts out a sidekick (Step 2). Tremendous power and momentum can be developed in this kick.

Figure 4-13: Stepping side kick.

e. **Knee Strike** (Figure 4-14). A knee strike can be a devastating weapon. It is best used when in the clinch, at very close range, or when the enemy is against a wall. The best target is the head, but the thigh or body may also be targeted under certain conditions.

Figure 4-14: Knee strike.

4-4. TRANSITION BETWEEN RANGES

In order to dominate the standup fight, you must be able to control the range between you and the enemy, and to operate effectively at the various ranges, keeping the enemy reacting to your techniques, and setting the pace of the fight. The ability to keep your head and continue to execute effective techniques requires practice. This is the heart of standup fighting. To transition between ranges, use a combination of techniques such as:

- Jab—reverse punch—shin kick to the outer thigh.
- Jab—reverse punch—shin kick to the outer thigh—high single leg takedown.

CHAPTER 5

Handheld Weapons

Handheld weapons provide a significant advantage during a fight. For soldiers to be well trained in their use there must be connectivity between the techniques of armed and unarmed fighting. As soldiers progress in their training, bayonet fighting techniques that are taught in initial entry training will merge with the other elements of hand-to-hand fighting to produce a soldier who is capable of operating across the full range of force.

SECTION I. OFFENSIVE TECHNIQUES

In most combat situations, small arms and grenades are the weapons of choice. However, in some scenarios, soldiers must engage the enemy in confined areas, such as trench clearing or room clearing or where noncombatants are present. In these instances, or when your primary weapon fails, the bayonet or knife may be the ideal weapon to dispatch the enemy. Soldiers must transition immediately and instinctively into the appropriate techniques based on the situation and the weapons at hand.

5-1. ANGLES OF ATTACK

Any attack, regardless of the type weapon, can be directed along one of nine angles of attack (Figure 5-1).

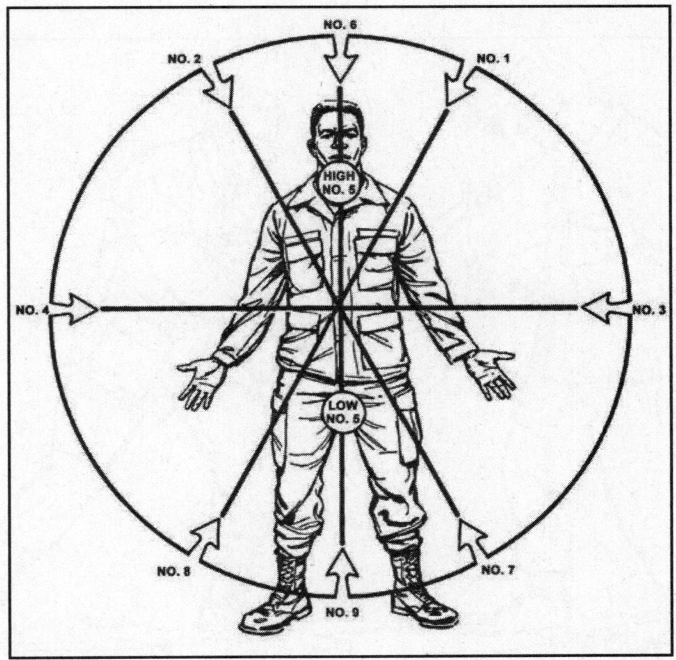

Figure 5-1: Angles of attack.

a. **No. 1 Angle of Attack.** A downward diagonal slash, stab, or strike toward the left side of the defender's head, neck, or torso.
b. **No. 2 Angle of Attack.** A downward diagonal slash, stab, or strike toward the right side of the defender's head, neck, or torso.
c. **No. 3 Angle of Attack.** A horizontal attack to the left side of the defender's torso in the ribs, side, or hip region.
d. **No. 4 Angle of Attack.** The same as No. 3 angle, but to the right side.
e. **No. 5 Angle of Attack.** A jabbing, lunging, or punching attack directed straight toward the defender's front.
f. **No. 6 Angle of Attack.** An attack directed straight down upon the defender.
g. **No. 7 Angle of Attack.** An upward diagonal attack toward the defender's lower-left side.
h. **No. 8 Angle of Attack.** An upward diagonal attack toward the defender's lower-right side.
i. **No. 9 Angle of Attack.** An attack directed straight up—for example, to the defender's groin.

5-2. RIFLE WITH FIXED BAYONET

The principles used in fighting with the rifle and fixed bayonet are the same as when knife fighting. Use the same angles of attack and similar body movements. The principles of timing and distance remain paramount; the main difference is the extended distance provided by the length of the weapon. It is imperative that the soldier fighting with rifle and fixed bayonet use the movement of his entire body behind all of his fighting techniques—not just upper-body strength. Unit trainers should be especially conscious of stressing full body mass in motion for power and correcting all deficiencies during training. Whether the enemy is armed or unarmed, a soldier fighting with rifle and fixed bayonet must develop the mental attitude that he will survive the fight. He must continuously evaluate each moment in a fight to determine his advantages or options, as well as the enemy's. He should base his defenses on keeping his body moving and off the line of any attacks from his opponent. The soldier seeks openings in the enemy's defenses and starts his own attacks, using all available body weapons and angles of attack. The angles of attack with rifle and fixed bayonet are shown in Figures 5-2 through 5-8.

Figure 5-2: No. 1 angle of attack with rifle and fixed bayonet.

Figure 5-3: No. 2 angle of attack with rifle and fixed bayonet.

Figure 5-4: No. 3 angle of attack with rifle and fixed bayonet.

Figure 5-5: No. 4 angle of attack with rifle and fixed bayonet.

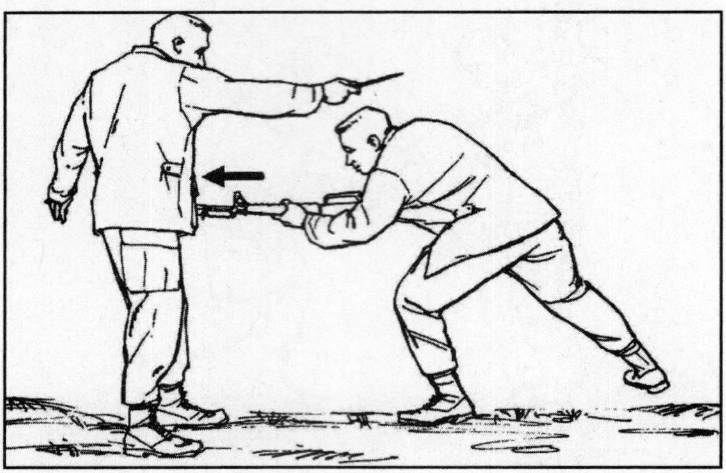

Figure 5-6: Low No. 5 angle of attack with rifle and fixed bayonet.

Figure 5-7: High No. 5 angle of attack with rifle and fixed bayonet.

Figure 5-8: No. 6 angle of attack with rifle and fixed bayonet.

a. **Fighting Techniques.** New weapons, improved equipment, and new tactics are always being introduced; however, firepower alone will not always drive a determined enemy from his position. He will often remain in defensive emplacements until driven out by close combat. The role of the soldier, particularly in the final phase of the assault, remains relatively unchanged: His mission is to close with and kill, disable, or capture the enemy. This mission remains the ultimate goal of all individual training. The rifle with fixed bayonet is one of the final means of defeating an opponent in an assault.
   (1) During infiltration missions at night or when secrecy must be maintained, the bayonet is an excellent silent weapon.
   (2) When close-in fighting determines the use of small-arms fire or grenades to be impractical, or when the situation does not permit the loading or reloading of the rifle, the bayonet is still the weapon available to the soldier.
   (3) The bayonet serves as a secondary weapon should the rifle develop a stoppage.
   (4) In hand-to-hand encounters, the detached bayonet may be used as a handheld weapon.
   (5) The bayonet has many nonfighting uses, such as to probe for mines, to cut vegetation, and to use for other tasks where a pointed or cutting tool is needed.

b. **Development.** To become a successful rifle-bayonet fighter, a soldier must be physically fit and mentally alert. A well-rounded physical training program will increase his chances of survival in a bayonet encounter. Mental alertness entails being able to quickly detect and meet an opponent's attack from any direction. Aggressiveness, accuracy, balance, and speed are essential in training as well as in combat situations. These traits lead to confidence, coordination, strength, and endurance, which characterize the rifle-bayonet fighter. Differences in individual body physique may require slight changes from the described rifle-bayonet techniques. These variations will be allowed if the individual's attack is effective.

c. **Principles.** The bayonet is an effective weapon to be used aggressively; hesitation may mean sudden death. The soldier must attack in a relentless assault until his opponent is disabled or captured. He should be alert to take advantage of any opening. If the opponent fails to present an opening, the bayonet fighter must make one by parrying his opponent's weapon and driving his blade or rifle butt into the opponent with force.
   (1) The attack should be made to a vulnerable part of the body: face, throat, chest, abdomen, or groin.
   (2) In both training and combat, the rifle-bayonet fighter displays spirit by sounding off with a low and aggressive growl. This instills a feeling of confidence in his ability to close with and disable or capture the enemy.
   (3) The instinctive rifle-bayonet fighting system is designed to capitalize on the natural agility and combative movements of the soldier. It must be emphasized that precise learned movements will NOT be stressed during training.

d. **Positions.** The soldier holds the rifle firmly but not rigidly. He relaxes all muscles not used in a specific position; tense muscles cause fatigue and may slow him down. After proper training and thorough practice, the soldier instinctively assumes the basic positions. All positions and movements described in this manual are for right-handed men. A left-handed man, or a man who desires to learn left-handed techniques, must use the opposite hand and foot for each phase of the movement described. All positions and movements can be executed with or without the magazine and with or without the sling attached.
   (1) ***Attack Position.*** This is the basic starting position (A and B, Figure 5-9) from which all attack movements originate. It generally parallels a boxer's stance. The soldier assumes this position when running or hurdling obstacles. The instructor explains and demonstrates each move.
      (a) Take a step forward and to the side with your left foot so that your feet are a comfortable distance apart.
      (b) Hold your body erect or bend slightly forward at the waist. Flex your knees and balance your body weight on the balls of your feet. Your right forearm is roughly parallel to the ground. Hold the left arm high, generally in front of the left shoulder. Maintain eye-to-eye contact with your opponent, watching his weapon and body through peripheral vision.
      (c) Hold your rifle diagonally across your body at a sufficient distance from the body to add balance and protect you from enemy blows. Grasp the weapon in your left hand just below the upper sling swivel, and place the right hand at the small of the stock. Keep the sling facing outward and the cutting edge of the bayonet toward your opponent. The command is, ATTACK POSITION, MOVE. The instructor gives the command, and the soldiers perform the movement.

Figure 5-9: Attack position.

(2) ***Relaxed Position.*** The relaxed position (Figure 5-10) gives the soldier a chance to rest during training. It also allows him to direct his attention toward the instructor as he discusses and demonstrates the positions and movements. To assume the relaxed position from the attack position, straighten the waist and knees and lower the rifle across the front of your body by extending the arms downward. The command is, RELAX. The instructor gives the command, and the soldiers perform the movement.

e. ***Movements.*** The soldier will instinctively strike at openings and become aggressive in his attack once he has learned to relax and has developed instinctive reflexes. His movements do not have to be executed in any prescribed order. He will achieve balance in his movements, be ready to strike in any direction, and keep striking until he has disabled his opponent. There are two basic movements used throughout bayonet instruction: the whirl and the crossover. These movements develop instant reaction to commands and afford the instructor maximum control of the training formation while on the training field.

(1) ***Whirl Movement.*** The whirl (Figure 5-11, Steps 1, 2, and 3), properly executed, allows the rifle-bayonet fighter to meet a challenge from an opponent attacking him from the rear. At the completion of a whirl,

Figure 5-10: Relaxed position.

Figure 5-11: Whirl movement.

the rifle remains in the attack position. The instructor explains and demonstrates how to spin your body around by pivoting on the ball of the leading foot in the direction of the leading foot, thus facing completely about. The command is, WHIRL. The instructor gives the command, and the soldiers perform the movement.

(2) ***Crossover Movement.*** While performing certain movements in rifle-bayonet training, two ranks will be moving toward each other. When the soldiers in ranks come too close to each other to safely execute additional movements, the crossover is used to separate the ranks a safe distance apart. The instructor explains and demonstrates how to move straight forward and pass your opponent so that your right shoulder passes his right shoulder, continue moving forward about six steps, halt, and without command, execute the whirl. Remain in the attack position and wait for further commands. The command is, CROSSOVER. The instructor gives the command, and the soldiers perform the movement.

> ✍ **NOTE**
> Left-handed personnel cross left shoulder to left shoulder.

(3) ***Attack Movements.*** There are four attack movements designed to disable or capture the opponent: thrust, butt stroke, slash, and smash. Each of these movements may be used for the initial attack or as a follow-up should the initial movement fail to find its mark. The soldiers learn these movements separately. They will learn to execute these movements in a swift and continuous series during subsequent training. During all training, the emphasis will be on conducting natural, balanced movements to effectively damage the target. Precise, learned movements will not be stressed.

(a) *Thrust.* The objective is to disable or capture an opponent by thrusting the bayonet blade into a vulnerable part of his body. The thrust is especially effective in areas where movement is restricted—for example, trenches, wooded areas, or built-up areas. It is also effective when an opponent is lying on the ground or in a fighting position. The instructor explains and demonstrates how to lunge forward on your leading foot without losing your balance (Figure 5-12, Step 1) and, at the same time, drive the bayonet with great force into any unguarded part of your opponent's body.

- To accomplish this, grasp the rifle firmly with both hands and pull the stock in close to the right hip; partially extend the left arm, guiding the point of the bayonet in the general direction of the opponent's body (Figure 5-12, Step 2).
- Quickly complete the extension of the arms and body as the leading foot strikes the ground so that the bayonet penetrates the target (Figure 5-12, Step 3).
- To withdraw the bayonet, keep your feet in place, shift your body weight to the rear, and pull rearward along the same line of penetration (Figure 5-12, Step 4).
- Next, assume the attack position in preparation to continue the assault (Figure 5-12, Step 5). This movement is taught by the numbers in three phases:

1. **THRUST AND HOLD, MOVE.**
2. **WITHDRAW AND HOLD, MOVE.**
3. **ATTACK POSITION, MOVE.**

- At combat speed, the command is, THRUST SERIES, MOVE. Training emphasis will be placed on movement at combat speed. The instructor gives the commands, and the soldiers perform the movements.

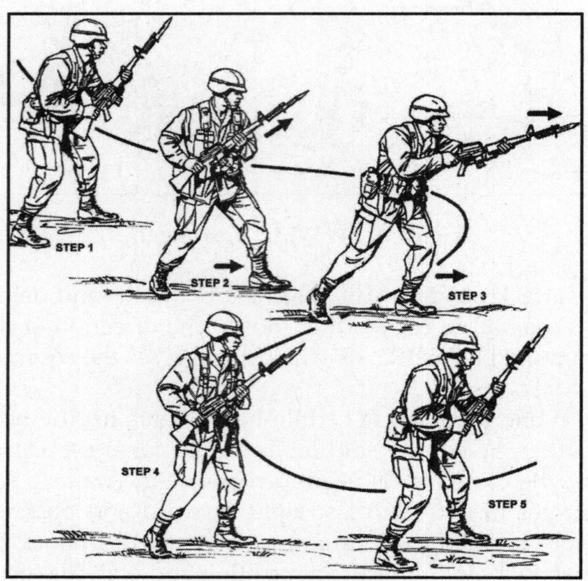

Figure 5-12: Thrust movement.

(b) *Butt Stroke.* The objective is to disable or capture an opponent by delivering a forceful blow to his body with the rifle butt (Figure 5-13, Steps 1, 2, 3, and 4, and Figure 5-14, Steps 1, 2, 3, and 4). The aim of the butt stroke may be the opponent's weapon or a vulnerable portion of his body. The butt stroke may be vertical, horizontal, or somewhere between the two planes. The instructor explains and demonstrates how to step forward with your trailing foot and, at the same time using your left hand as a pivot, swing the rifle in an arc and drive the rifle butt into your opponent. To recover, bring your trailing foot forward and assume the attack position. The movement is taught by the numbers in two phases:

1. **BUTT STROKE TO THE** (head, groin, kidney) **AND HOLD, MOVE.**
2. **ATTACK POSITION, MOVE.**

Figure 5-13: Butt stroke to the head.

Figure 5-14: Butt stroke to the groin.

At combat speed, the command is, BUTT STROKE TO THE (head, groin, kidney) SERIES, MOVE. Training emphasis will be placed on movement at combat speed. The instructor gives the commands, and the soldiers perform the movement.

(c) *Slash.* The objective is to disable or capture the opponent by cutting him with the blade of the bayonet. The instructor explains and demonstrates how to step forward with your lead foot (Figure 5-15, Step 1).

- At the same time, extend your left arm and swing the knife edge of your bayonet forward and down in a slashing arc (Figure 5-15, Steps 2 and 3).
- To recover, bring your trailing foot forward and assume the attack position (Figure 5-15, Step 4). This movement is taught by the number in two phases:
  1. **SLASH AND HOLD, MOVE.**
  2. **ATTACK POSITION, MOVE.**
- At combat speed, the command is, SLASH SERIES, MOVE. Training emphasis will be placed on movement at combat speed. The instructor gives the commands, and the soldiers perform the movements.

Figure 5-15: Slash movement.

(d) *Smash.* The objective is to disable or capture an opponent by smashing the rifle butt into a vulnerable part of his body. The smash is often used as a follow-up to a butt stroke and is also effective in wooded areas and trenches when movement is restricted. The instructor explains and demonstrates how to push the butt of the rifle upward until horizontal (Figure 5-16, Step 1) and above the left shoulder with the bayonet pointing to the rear, sling up (Figure 5-16, Step 2). The weapon is almost horizontal to the ground at this time.

- Step forward with the trailing foot, as in the butt stroke, and forcefully extend both arms, slamming the rifle butt into the opponent (Figure 5-16, Step 3).

Figure 5-16: Smash movement.

- To recover, bring your trailing foot forward (Figure 5-16, Step 4) and assume the attack position (Figure 5-16, Step 5). This movement is taught by the numbers in two phases:
  1. **SMASH AND HOLD, MOVE.**
  2. **ATTACK POSITION, MOVE.**
- At combat speed, the command is, SMASH SERIES, MOVE. Training emphasis will be placed on movement at combat speed. The instructor gives the commands, and the soldiers perform the movements.

(4) ***Defensive Movements.*** At times, the soldier may lose the initiative and be forced to defend himself. He may also meet an opponent who does not present a vulnerable area to attack. Therefore, he must make an opening by initiating a parry or block movement, then follow up with a vicious attack. The follow-up attack is immediate and violent.

⚠ CAUTION

To minimize weapon damage while using blocks and parries, limit weapon-to-weapon contact to half speed during training.

(a) *Parry Movement.* The objective is to counter a thrust, throw the opponent off balance, and hit a vulnerable area of his body. Timing, speed, and judgment are essential factors in these movements. The instructor explains and demonstrates how to—

- Parry right. If your opponent carries his weapon on his left hip (left-handed), you will parry it to your right. In execution, step forward with your leading foot (Figure 5-17, Step 1), strike the opponent's rifle (Figure 5-17, Step 2), deflecting it to your right (Figure 5-17, Step 3), and follow up with a thrust, slash, or butt stroke.

Figure 5-17: Parry right.

- Parry left. If your opponent carries his weapon on his right hip (right-handed), you will parry it to your left. In execution, step forward with your leading foot (Figure 5-18, Step 1), strike the opponent's rifle (Figure 5-18, Step 2), deflecting it to your left (Figure 5-18, Step 3), and follow up with a thrust, slash, or butt stroke. A supplementary parry left is the follow-up attack (Figure 5-19, Steps 1, 2, 3, 4, and 5).
- Recovery. Immediately return to the attack position after completing each parry and follow-up attack. The movement is taught by the numbers in three phases:
  1. **PARRY RIGHT (OR LEFT), MOVE.**
  2. **THRUST, MOVE.**
  3. **ATTACK POSITION, MOVE.**
- At combat speed, the command is, PARRY RIGHT (LEFT) or PARRY (RIGHT OR LEFT) WITH FOLLOW-UP ATTACK. The instructor gives the commands, and the soldiers perform the movements.

Figure 5-18: Parry left.

Figure 5-19. Parry left, slash, with follow-up butt stroke to kidney region.

(b) *Block.* When surprised by an opponent, the block is used to cut off the path of his attack by making weapon-to-weapon contact. A block must always be followed immediately with a vicious attack. The instructor explains and demonstrates how to extend your arms using the center part of your rifle as the strike area, and cut off the opponent's attack by making weapon-to-weapon contact. Strike the opponent's weapon with enough power to throw him off balance. Blocks are taught by the numbers in two phases:

1. **HIGH (LOW) or (SIDE) BLOCK.**
2. **ATTACK POSITION, MOVE.**

- High block (Figure 5-20, Steps 1, 2, and 3). Extend your arms upward and forward at a 45-degree angle. This action deflects an opponent's slash movement by causing his bayonet or upper part of his rifle to strike against the center part of your rifle.

Figure 5-20: High block against slash.

- Low block (Figure 5-21, Steps 1, 2, and 3). Extend your arms downward and forward about 15 degrees from your body. This action deflects an opponent's butt stroke aimed at the groin by causing the lower part of his rifle stock to strike against the center part of your rifle.
- Side block (Figure 5-22, Steps 1 and 2). Extend your arms with the left hand high and right hand low, thus holding the rifle vertical. This block is designed to stop a butt stroke aimed at your upper body or head. Push the rifle to your left to cause the butt of the opponent's rifle to strike the center portion of your rifle.

Figure 5-21: Low block against butt stroke to groin.

Figure 5-22: Side block against butt stroke.

- Recovery. Counterattack each block with a thrust, butt stroke, smash, or slash.
- At combat speed, the command is the same. The instructor gives the commands, and the soldiers perform the movement.

(5) ***Modified Movements.*** Two attack movements have been modified to allow the rifle-bayonet fighter to slash or thrust an opponent without removing his hand from the pistol grip of the M16 rifle should the situation dictate.

(a) The modified thrust (Figure 5-23, Steps 1 and 2) is identical to the thrust with the exception of the right hand grasping the pistol grip.

(b) The modified slash (Figure 5-24, Steps 1, 2, 3, and 4) is identical to the slash with the exception of the right hand grasping the pistol grip.

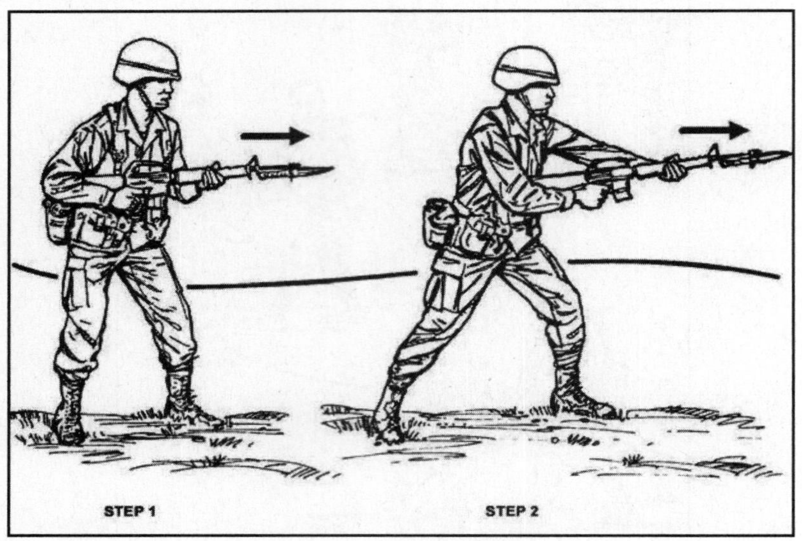

Figure 5-23: Modified thrust.

Figure 5-24: Modified slash.

(6) ***Follow-up Movements.*** Follow-up movements are attack movements that naturally follow from the completed position of the previous movement. If the initial thrust, butt stroke, smash, or slash fails to make contact with the opponent's body, the soldier should instinctively follow up with additional movements until he has disabled or captured the opponent. It is important to follow-up the initial attack with another aggressive action so the initiative is not lost. The instructor explains and demonstrates how instinct should govern your selection of a specific follow-up movement. For example—

- **PARRY LEFT, BUTT STROKE TO THE HEAD, SMASH, SLASH, ATTACK POSITION.**
- **PARRY LEFT, SLASH, BUTT STROKE TO THE KIDNEY, ATTACK POSITION.**
- **PARRY RIGHT, THRUST, BUTT STROKE TO THE GROIN, SLASH, ATTACK POSITION.**

Two examples of commands using follow-up movements are:

- **PARRY LEFT** (soldier executes), **THRUST** (soldier executes), **BUTT STROKE TO THE HEAD** (soldier executes), **SMASH** (soldier executes), **SLASH** (soldier executes), **ATTACK POSITION** (soldier assumes the attack position).
- **THRUST** (soldier executes), **THRUST** (soldier executes), **THRUST** (soldier executes), **BUTT STROKE TO THE GROIN** (soldier executes), **SLASH** (soldier executes), **ATTACK POSITION** (soldier assumes the attack position).

All training will stress damage to the target and violent action, using natural movements as opposed to precise, stereotyped movements. Instinctive, aggressive action and balance are the keys to offense with the rifle and bayonet.

✍ NOTE

For training purposes, the instructor may and should mix up the series of movements.

5-3. BAYONET/KNIFE

As the bayonet is an integral part of the combat soldier's equipment, it is readily available for use as a multipurpose weapon. The bayonet produces a terrifying mental effect on the enemy when in the hands of a well-trained and confident soldier. The soldier skilled in the use of the knife also increases his ability to defend against larger opponents and multiple attackers. Both these skills increase his chances of surviving and accomplishing the mission. (Although the following paragraphs say "knife," the information also applies to bayonets.)

a. **Grips.** The best way to hold the knife is either with the straight grip or the reverse grip.

(1) ***Straight Grip.*** Grip the knife in the strong hand by forming a "vee" and by allowing the knife to fit naturally, as in gripping for a handshake. The handle should lay diagonally across the palm. Point the blade toward the enemy, usually with the cutting edge down. The cutting edge can also be held vertically or horizontally to the ground. Use the straight grip when thrusting and slashing.

(2) ***Reverse Grip.*** Grip the knife with the blade held parallel with the forearm, cutting edge facing outward. This grip conceals the knife from the enemy's view. The reverse grip also affords the most power for lethal insertion. Use this grip for slashing, stabbing, and tearing.

b. **Stances.** The primary stances are the knife fighter's stance and the modified stance.

(1) ***Knife Fighter's Stance.*** In this stance, the fighter stands with his feet about shoulder-width apart, dominant foot toward the rear. About 70 percent of his weight is on the front foot and 30 percent on the rear foot. He stands on the balls of both feet and holds the knife with the straight grip. The other hand is held close to his body where it is ready to use, but protected (Figure 5-25).

(2) ***Modified Stance.*** The difference in the modified stance is the knife is held close to the body with the other hand held close over the knife hand to help conceal it (Figure 5-26).

c. **Range.** The two primary ranges in knife fighting are long range and medium range. In long-range knife fighting, attacks consist of figure-eight slashes along the No. 1, No. 2, No. 7, and No. 8 angles of attack; horizontal slashes along the No. 3 and No. 4 angles of attack; and lunging thrusts to vital areas on the No. 5 angle of attack. Usually, the straight grip is used. In medium-range knife fighting, the reverse grip provides greater power. It is used to thrust, slash, and tear along all angles of attack.

Figure 5-25: Knife fighter's stance.

Figure 5-26: Modified stance.

5-4. KNIFE-AGAINST-KNIFE SEQUENCE

The knife fighter must learn to use all available weapons of his body and not limit himself to the knife. The free hand can be used to trap the enemy's hands to create openings in his defense. The enemy's attention will be focused on the weapon; therefore, low kicks and knee strikes will seemingly come from nowhere. The knife fighter's priority of targets are the eyes, throat, abdominal region, and extended limbs. The following knife attack sequences can be used in training to help develop soldiers' knowledge of movements, principles, and techniques in knife fighting.

a. **Nos. 1 and 4 Angles.** Two opponents assume the knife fighter's stance (Figure 5-27, Step 1). The attacker starts with a diagonal slash along the No. 1 angle of attack to the throat (Figure 5-27, Step 2). He then follows through with a slash and continues with a horizontal slash back across the abdomen along the No. 4 angle of attack (Figure 5-27, Step 3). He finishes the attack by using his entire body mass behind a lunging stab into the opponent's solar plexus (Figure 5-27, Step 4).

Figure 5-27: Nos. 1 and 4 angles.

b. **Nos. 5, 3, and 2 Angles.** In this sequence, one opponent (attacker) starts an attack with a lunge along the No. 5 angle of attack. At the same time, the other opponent (defender) on the left moves his body off the line of attack, parries the attacking arm, and slices the biceps of his opponent (Figure 5-28, Step 1). The defender slashes back across the groin along the No. 3 angle of attack (Figure 5-28, Step 2). He finishes the attacker by continuing with an upward stroke into the armpit or throat along the No. 2 angle of attack (Figure 5-28, Step 3). Throughout this sequence, the attacker's weapon hand is controlled with the defenders left hand as he attacks with his own knife hand.

c. **Low No. 5 Angle.** In the next sequence, the attacker on the right lunges to the stomach along a low No. 5 angle of attack. The defender on the left moves his body off the line of attack while parrying and slashing the wrist of the attacking knife hand as he redirects the arm (Figure 5-29, Step 1). After he slashes the wrist of his attacker, the defender continues to move around the outside and stabs the attacker's armpit (Figure 5-29, Step 2). He retracts his knife from the armpit, continues his movement around the attacker, and slices his hamstring (Figure 5-29, Step 3).

d. **Optional Low No. 5 Angle.** The attacker on the right lunges to the stomach of his opponent (the defender) along the low No. 5 angle of attack. The defender moves his body off the line of attack of the knife. Then he turns and, at the same time, delivers a slash to the attacker's throat along the No. 1 angle of attack (Figure 5-30, Step 1). The defender immediately follows with another slash to the opposite side of the attacker's throat along the No. 2 angle of attack (Figure 5-30, Step 2). The attacker is finished as the opponent on the left (defender) continues to slice across the abdomen with a stroke along the No. 3 angle (Figure 5-30, Step 3).

Figure 5-28: Nos. 5, 3, and 2 angles.

Figure 5-29: Low No. 5 angle.

5-5. ADVANCED WEAPONS TECHNIQUES AND TRAINING

For advanced training in weapons techniques, training partners should have the same skill level. Attackers can execute attacks along multiple angles of attack in combinations. The attacker must attack with a speed that offers the defender a challenge, but does not overwhelm him. It should not be a contest to see who can win, but a training exercise for both individuals.

a. Continued training in weapons techniques will lead to the partners' ability to engage in free-response fighting or sparring—that is, the individuals become adept enough to understand the principles of weapons attacks, defense, and movements so they can respond freely when attacking or defending from any angle.

Figure 5-30: Optional low No. 5 angle.

b. Instructors must closely monitor training partners to ensure that the speed and control of the individuals does not become dangerous during advanced training practice. Proper eye protection and padding should be used, when applicable. The instructor should stress the golden rule in free-response fighting—Do unto others as you would have them do unto you.

SECTION II. FIELD-EXPEDIENT WEAPONS

To survive, the soldier in combat must be able to deal with any situation that develops. His ability to adapt any nearby object for use as a weapon in a win-or-die situation is limited only by his ingenuity and resourcefulness. Possible weapons, although not discussed herein, include ink pens or pencils; canteens tied to string to be swung; snap links at the end of sections of rope; kevlar helmets; sand, rocks, or liquids thrown into the enemy's eyes; or radio antennas. The following techniques demonstrate a few expedient weapons that are readily available to most soldiers for defense and counterattack against the bayonet and rifle with fixed bayonet.

5-6. ENTRENCHING TOOL

Almost all soldiers carry the entrenching tool. It is a versatile and formidable weapon when used by a soldier with some training. It can be used in its straight position—locked out and fully extended—or with its blade bent in a 90-degree configuration.

a. To use the entrenching tool against a rifle with fixed bayonet, the attacker lunges with a thrust to the stomach of the defender along a low No. 5 angle of attack (Figure 5-31, Step 1).
   (1) The defender moves just outside to avoid the lunge and meets the attacker's arm with the blade of the fully extended entrenching tool (Figure 5-31, Step 2).
   (2) The defender gashes all the way up the attacker's arm with the force of both body masses coming together. The hand gripping the entrenching tool is given natural protection from the shape of the handle. The defender continues pushing the blade of the entrenching tool up and into the throat of the attacker, driving him backward and downward (Figure 5-31, Step 3).

b. An optional use of entrenching tool against a rifle with fixed bayonet is for the attacker to lunge to the stomach of the defender (Figure 5-32, Step 1).
   (1) The defender steps to the outside of the line of attack at 45 degrees to avoid the weapon. He then turns his body and strikes downward onto the attacking arm (on the radial nerve) with the blade of the entrenching tool (Figure 5-32, Step 2).

Figure 5-31: Entrenching tool against rifle with fixed bayonet.

Figure 5-32: Optional use of the entrenching tool against rifle with fixed bayonet.

(2) He drops his full body weight down with the strike, and the force causes the attacker to collapse forward. The defender then strikes the point of the entrenching tool into the jugular notch, driving it deeply into the attacker (Figure 5-32, Step 3).

c. In the next two sequences, the entrenching tool is used in the bent configuration—that is, the blade is bent 90 degrees to the handle and locked into place.

(1) The attacker tries to stick the bayonet into the chest of the defender (Figure 5-33, Step 1).
 (a) When the attack comes, the defender moves his body off the line of attack by stepping to the outside. He allows his weight to shift forward and uses the blade of the entrenching tool to drag along the length of the weapon, scraping the attacker's arm and hand (Figure 5-33, Step 2). The defender's hand is protected by the handle's natural design.
 (b) He continues to move forward into the attacker, strikes the point of the blade into the jugular notch, and drives it downward (Figure 5-33, Step 3).

(2) The attacker lunges with a fixed bayonet along the No. 5 angle of attack (Figure 5-34, Step 1). The defender then steps to the outside to move off the line of attack and turns; he strikes the point of the blade of the entrenching tool into the side of the attacker's throat (Figure 5-34, Step 2).

Figure 5-33: Entrenching tool in bent configuration.

Figure 5-34: Optional use of entrenching tool in bent configuration.

5-7. THREE-FOOT STICK

Since a stick can be found almost anywhere, a soldier should know its uses as a field-expedient weapon. The stick is a versatile weapon; its capability ranges from simple prisoner control to lethal combat.

a. Use a stick about 3 feet long and grip it by placing it in the "vee" formed between the thumb and index finger, as in a handshake. It may also be grasped by two hands and used in an unlimited number of techniques. The stick is not held at the end, but at a comfortable distance from the butt end.

b. When striking with the stick, achieve maximum power by using the entire body weight behind each blow. The desired point of contact of the weapon is the last 2 inches at the tip of the stick. The primary targets for striking with the stick are the vital body points in Chapter 4. Effective striking points are usually the wrist, hand, knees, and other bony protuberances. Soft targets include the side of the neck, jugular notch, solar plexus, and various nerve motor points. Attack soft targets by striking or thrusting the tip of the stick into the area. Three basic methods of striking are—

(1) ***Thrusting.*** Grip the stick with both hands and thrust straight into a target with the full body mass behind it.

(2) ***Whipping.*** Hold the stick in one hand and whip it in a circular motion; use the whole body mass in motion to generate power.

(3) ***Snapping.*** Snap the stick in short, shocking blows, again with the body mass behind each strike.

(a) When the attacker thrusts with a knife to the stomach of the defender with a low No. 5 angle of attack, the defender moves off the line of attack to the outside and strikes vigorously downward onto the attacking wrist, hand, or arm (Figure 5-35, Step 1).

(b) The defender then moves forward, thrusts the tip of the stick into the jugular notch of the attacker (Figure 5-35, Step 2), and drives him to the ground with his body weight—not his upper body strength (Figure 5-35, Step 3).

Figure 5-35: Three-foot stick against knife.

c. When using a three-foot stick against a rifle with fixed bayonet, the defender grasps the stick with two hands, one at each end, as the attacker thrusts forward to the chest (Figure 5-36, Step 1).

(1) He steps off the line of attack to the outside and redirects the weapon with the stick (Figure 5-36, Step 2).

(2) He then strikes forward with the forearm into the attacker's throat (Figure 5-36, Step 3). The force of the two body weights coming together is devastating. The attacker's neck is trapped in the notch formed by the stick and the defender's forearm.

(3) Using the free end of the stick as a lever, the defender steps back and uses his body weight to drive the attacker to the ground. The leverage provided by the stick against the neck creates a tremendous choke with the forearm, and the attacker loses control completely (Figure 5-36, Step 4).

Figure 5-36: Three-foot stick against rifle with fixed bayonet.

5-8. SIX-FOOT POLE

Another field-expedient weapon that can mean the difference between life and death for a soldier in an unarmed conflict is a pole about 6 feet long. Examples of poles suitable for use are mop handles, pry bars, track tools, tent poles, and small trees or limbs cut to form a pole. A soldier skilled in the use of a pole as a weapon is a formidable opponent. The size and weight of the pole requires him to move his whole body to use it effectively. Its length gives the soldier an advantage of distance in most unarmed situations. There are two methods usually used in striking with a pole:

a. **Swinging.** Becoming effective in swinging the pole requires skilled body movement and practice. The greatest power is developed by striking with the last 2 inches of the pole.

b. **Thrusting.** The pole is thrust straight along its axis with the user's body mass firmly behind it.

(1) An attacker tries to thrust forward with a fixed bayonet (Figure 5-37, Step 1). The defender moves his body off the line of attack; he holds the tip of the pole so that the attacker runs into it from his own momentum. He then aims for the jugular notch and anchors his body firmly in place so that the full force of the attack is felt at the attacker's throat (Figure 5-37, Step 2).

(2) The defender then shifts his entire body weight forward over his lead foot and drives the attacker off his feet (Figure 5-37, Step 3).

> ✍ **NOTE**
>
> During high stress, small targets, such as the throat, may be difficult to hit. Good, large targets include the solar plexus and hip/thigh joint.

Figure 5-37: Thrusting with 6-foot pole.

CHAPTER 6

Standing Defense

A soldier cannot count on starting every encounter in a superior position. To survive, he must have simple techniques that will bring him back into his fight plan.

SECTION I. UNARMED OPPONENT

Most grasping type attacks will leave the enemy in striking range. Therefore, elaborate defenses are not necessary. You should simply attack with strikes and force the enemy to either close with you, or when he attempts to respond with strikes, take the opportunity to close or escape yourself. The techniques in this section are directed at escaping from positions that are more difficult.

6-1. DEFENSE AGAINST CHOKES

a. **Standing Rear Naked** (Figure 6-1). At the moment you feel the enemy's arm around your neck, your hands should immediately grasp it to keep him from tightening the choke, and you should hang your weight on his arm to feel where his weight is. If he is close to your back, simply lean forward at the waist and, using your hips to lift, throw him straight over your back.

Figure 6-1: Defense against the standing rear naked choke.

Figure 6-1: Defense against the standing rear naked choke. ***(Continued)***

Figure 6-1: Defense against the standing rear naked choke. ***(Continued)***

b. **Standing Rear Naked Pulling Back** (Figure 6-2). If, when you hang your weight on the enemy's arm, you feel that he is pulling you back over one of his legs, you should reach back with your leg and wrap it around the outside of the enemy's leg on the same side as the choking arm. As he tires from holding you up, use your leg as a guide and work your way around to the position shown. Your leg must be behind his, and you must be leaning forward, controlling his arm. Twisting your body, throw him to the ground.

Figure 6-2: Defense against the standing rear naked choke leaning back.

Figure 6-2: Defense against the standing rear naked choke leaning back. ***(Continued)***

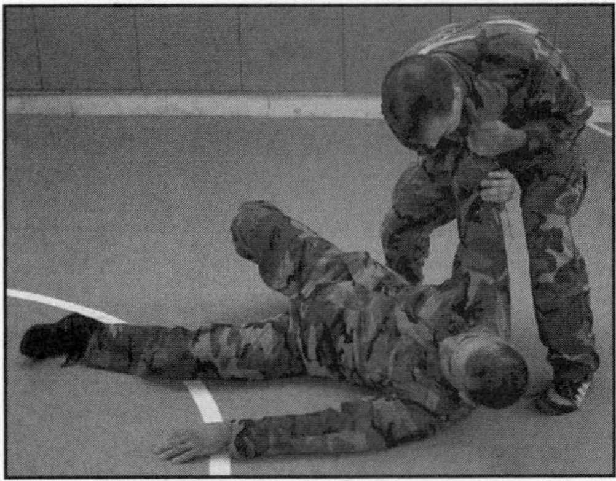

Figure 6-2: Defense against the standing rear naked choke leaning back. ***(Continued)***

c. **One-Hand Neck Press Against the Wall** (Figure 6-3). If the enemy pins you against the wall with one hand, strike his arm with the palm of your hand on the side where his thumb is pushing toward his fingers. This will make his arm slide off of your neck. Follow through with your strike and when your arm is in position, strike with a backward elbow strike to the head.

Figure 6-3: Defense against one-hand neck press against a wall.

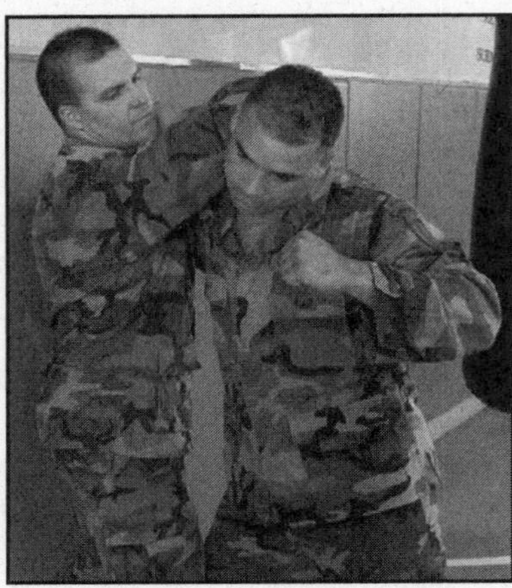

Figure 6-3: Defense against one-hand neck press against a wall. ***(Continued)***

d. **Two-Hand Neck Press While Pinned Against the Wall** (Figure 6-4). If the enemy uses both hands against your neck to press you into the wall, grasp under his elbows with both hands. Step out to either side and throw him against the wall. Finish with a knee strike.

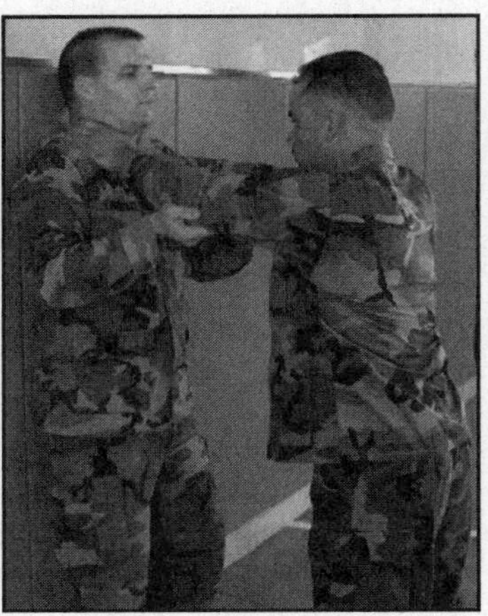

Figure 6-4: Defense against the two-hand neck press against a wall.

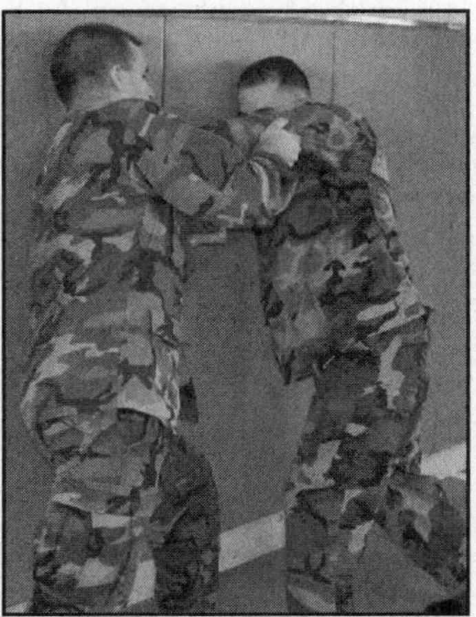

Figure 6-4: Defense against the two-hand neck press against a wall. ***(Continued)***

Figure 6-4: Defense against the two-hand neck press against a wall. ***(Continued)***

6-2. DEFENSE AGAINST BEAR HUGS

a. **Front Bear Hug Over Your Arms** (Figure 6-5). If the enemy attempts to grasp you in a bear hug from the front over your arms, move your hips back and use your arms as a brace between his hips and yours. Your hands should be on his hip bones, and your elbows should be braced against your hips. Keeping one arm as a brace, step to the opposite side to achieve the clinch. Finish with a takedown.

Figure 6-5: Defense against the front bear hug over your arms.

Figure 6-5: Defense against the front bear hug over your arms. ***(Continued)***

b. **Front Bear Hug Under Your Arms** (Figure 6-6). If the enemy attempts to grasp you under your arms, step back into a strong base and use both hands to push his chin upwards to break his grasp. Finish with a knee strike. If he is exceptionally strong, push upwards against his nose.

Figure 6-6: Defense against the front bear hug under your arms.

Figure 6-6: Defense against the front bear hug under your arms. ***(Continued)***

c. **Bear Hug From the Rear, Over the Arms** (Figure 6-7). When the enemy attempts to grab you from behind over your arms, drop down into a strong stance and bring your arms up to prevent him from controlling them. Step to the outside and then around his hip so that your legs are behind him. At this point you may attack his groin, or you may lift him with your hips and throw him.

Figure 6-7: Defense against the bear hug from the rear, over the arms.

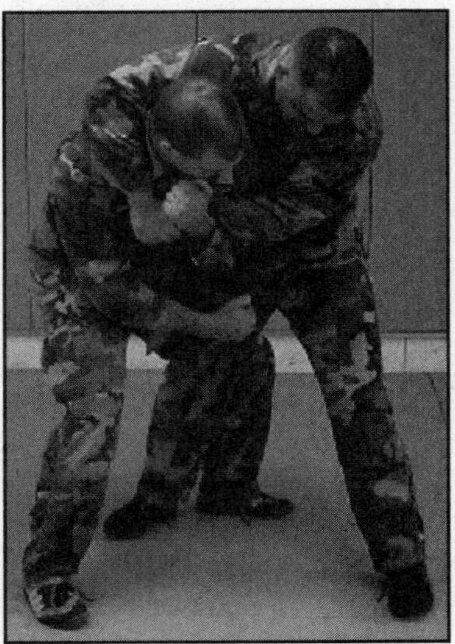

Figure 6-7: Defense against the bear hug from the rear, over the arms. ***(Continued)***

d. **Bear Hug from the Rear Under Your Arms** (Figure 6-8). When the enemy grasps you from the rear under your arms, he will probably try to lift you for a throw. If he does so, wrap your leg around his so that you are harder to maneuver for the throw. When he sets you down, or if he did not lift you in the first place, lean your weight forward and place your hands on the ground. Move to one side until one of his legs is between yours. Push backward slightly and reach one hand back to grasp his heel. When you have a good grip, reach back with the other hand. Pull forward with your hands, and when he falls, break his knee by sitting on it as you pull on his leg.

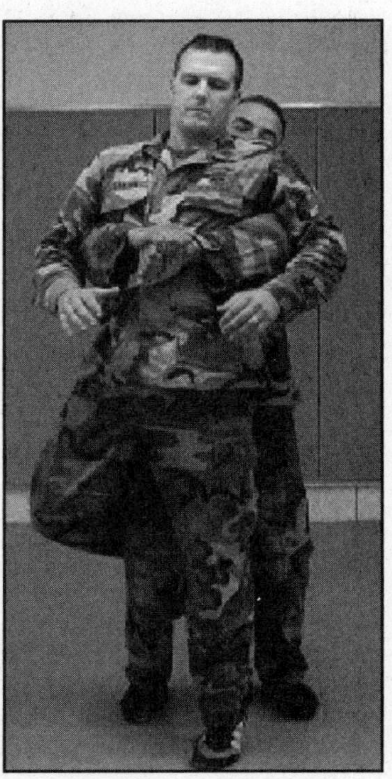

Figure 6-8: Defense against the bear hug from the rear, under the arms.

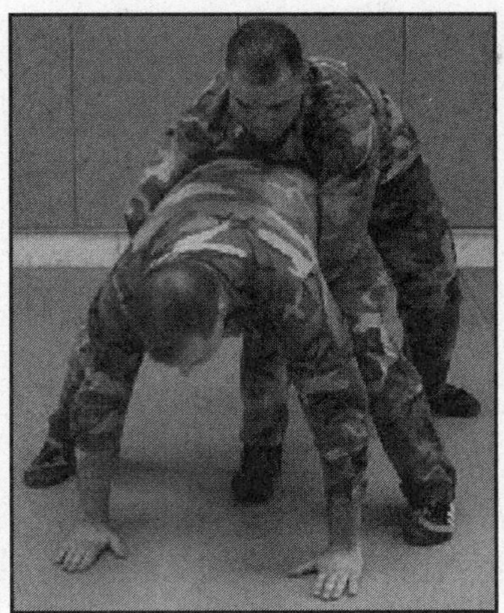

Figure 6-8: Defense against the bear hug from the rear, under the arms. ***(Continued)***

Figure 6-8: Defense against the bear hug from the rear, under the arms. ***(Continued)***

Figure 6-8: Defense against the bear hug from the rear, under the arms. ***(Continued)***

⚠ CAUTION
Care must be taken when practicing this technique to avoid accidental injury.

SECTION II. ARMED OPPONENT

A knife (or bayonet), properly employed, is a deadly weapon; however, using defensive techniques, such as maintaining separation, will greatly enhance the soldier's ability to fight and win.

6-3. DEFENSE AGAINST AN ARMED OPPONENT

An unarmed defender is always at a distinct disadvantage when facing an armed opponent. It is imperative, therefore, that the unarmed defender understands and uses the following principles to survive.

a. **Separation.** Maintain a separation of at least 10 feet plus the length of the weapon from the attacker. This distance gives the defender time to react to any attempt by the attacker to close the gap and be upon the defender. The defender should also try to place stationary objects between himself and the attacker.
b. **Unarmed Defense.** Unarmed defense against an armed opponent should be a last resort. If it is necessary, the defender's course of action includes:
   (1) ***Move the body out of the line of attack of the weapon.*** Step off the line of attack or redirect the attack of the weapon so that it clears the body.
   (2) ***Control the weapon.*** Maintain control of the attacking arm by securing the weapon, hand, wrist, elbow, or arm by using joint locks, if possible.
   (3) ***Stun the attacker with an effective counterattack.*** Counterattack should be swift and devastating. Take the vigor out of the attacker with a low, unexpected kick, or break a locked joint of the attacking arm. Strikes to motor nerve centers are effective stuns, as are skin tearing, eye gouging, and attacking of the throat. The defender can also take away the attacker's balance.
   (4) ***Ground the attacker.*** Take the attacker to the ground where the defender can continue to disarm or further disable him.
   (5) ***Disarm the attacker.*** Break the attacker's locked joints. Use leverage or induce pain to disarm the attacker and finish him or to maintain physical control.
c. **Precaution.** Do not focus full attention on the weapon because the attacker has other body weapons to use. There may even be other attackers that you have not seen.
d. **Expedient Aids.** Anything available can become an expedient aid to defend against an armed attack. The Kevlar helmet can be used as a shield; similarly, the LCE and shirt jacket can be used to protect the defender against a weapon. The defender can also throw dirt in the attacker's eyes as a distraction.

6-4 DEFENSE AGAINST A KNIFE

When an unarmed soldier is faced with an enemy armed with a knife, he must be mentally prepared to be cut. The likelihood of being cut severely is less if the fighter is well trained in knife defense and if the principles of weapon defense are followed. A slash wound is not usually lethal or shock inducing; however, a stab wound risks injury to vital organs, arteries, and veins and may also cause instant shock or unconsciousness.

a. **Types of Knife Attacks.** The first line of defense against an opponent armed with a knife is to avoid close contact. The different types of knife attacks are:
   (1) ***Thrust.*** The thrust is the most common and most dangerous type of knife attack. It is a strike directed straight into the target by jabbing or lunging.
   (2) ***Slash.*** The slash is a sweeping surface cut or circular slash. The wound is usually a long cut, varying from a slight surface cut to a deep gash.
   (3) ***Tear.*** The tear is a cut made by dragging the tip of the blade across the body to create a ripping-type cut.
   (4) ***Hack.*** The hack is delivered by using the knife to block or chop with.
   (5) ***Butt.*** The butt is a strike with the knife handle.

b. **Knife Defense Drills.** Knife defense drills are used to familiarize soldiers with defense movement techniques for various angles of attack. For training, the soldiers should be paired off; one partner is named as the attacker and one is the defender. It is important that the attacker make his attack realistic in terms of distance and angling during training. His strikes must be accurate in hitting the defender at the intended target if the defender does not defend himself or move off the line of attack. For safety, the attacks are delivered first at one-quarter and one-half speed, and then at three-quarter speed as the defender becomes more skilled. Variations can be added by changing grips, stances, and attacks.

(1) ***No. 1 Angle of Defense—Check and Lift*** (Figure 6-9). The attacker delivers a slash along the No. 1 angle of attack. The defender meets and checks the movement with his left forearm bone, striking the inside forearm of the attacker (Step 1). The defender's right hand immediately follows behind the strike to lift, redirect, and take control of the attacker's knife arm (Step 2). The defender brings the attacking arm around to his right side where he can use an arm bar, wrist lock, and so forth, to disarm the attacker (Step 3). He will have better control by keeping the knife hand as close to his body as possible (Step 4).

Figure 6-9: No. 1 angle of defense—check and lift.

(2) ***No. 2 Angle of Defense—Check and Ride*** (Figure 6-10). The attacker slashes with a No. 2 angle of attack. The defender meets the attacking arm with a strike from both forearms against the outside forearm, his bone against the attacker's muscle tissue (Step 1). The strike checks the forward momentum of the attacking arm. The defender's right hand is then used to ride the attacking arm clear of his body (Step 2). He redirects the attacker's energy with strength starting from the right elbow (Step 3).

(3) ***No. 3 Angle of Defense—Check and Lift*** (Figure 6-11). The attacker delivers a horizontal slash to the defender's ribs, kidneys, or hip on the left side (Step 1). The defender meets and checks the attacking arm on the left side of his body with a downward circular motion across the front of his own body. At the same time, he moves his body off the line of attack. He should meet the attacker's forearm with a strike forceful enough to check its momentum (Step 2). The defender then rides the energy of the attacking arm by wiping downward along the outside of his own left forearm with his right hand. He then redirects the knife hand around to his right side where he can control or disarm the weapon (Step 3).

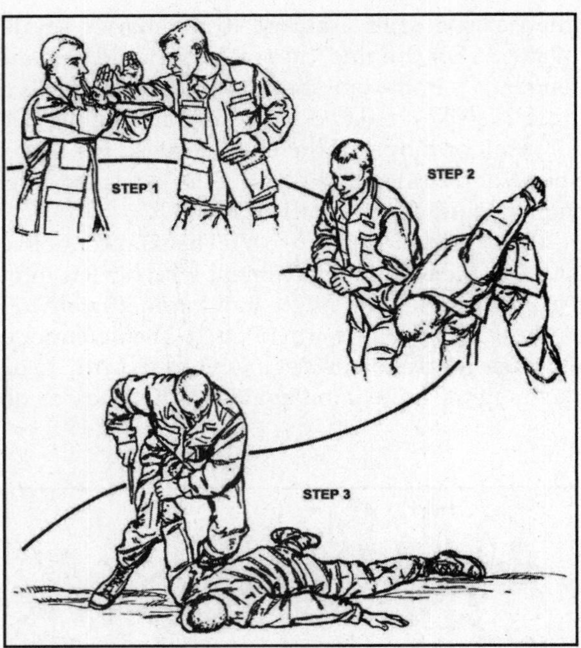

Figure 6-10: No. 2 angle of defense—check and ride.

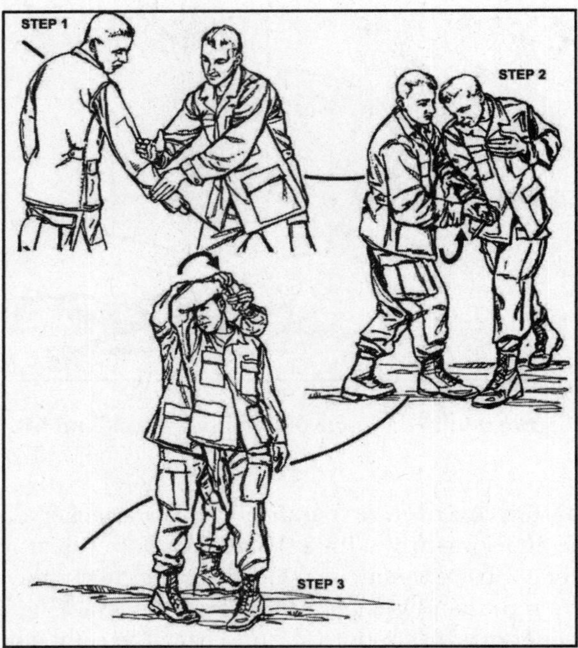

Figure 6-11: No. 3 angle of defense—check and lift.

(4) ***No. 4 Angle of Defense—Check*** (Figure 6-12). The attacker slashes the defender with a backhand slashing motion to the right side at the ribs, kidneys, or hips. The defender moves his right arm in a downward circular motion and strikes the attacking arm on the outside of the body (Step 1). At the same time, he moves off the line of attack (Step 2). The strike must be forceful enough to check the attack. The left arm is held in a higher guard position to protect from a redirected attack or to assist in checking (Step 3). The defender moves his body to a position where he can choose a proper disarming maneuver (Step 4).

Figure 6-12: No. 4 angle of defense—check.

(5) ***Low No. 5 Angle of Defense—Parry*** (Figure 6-13). A lunging thrust to the stomach is made by the attacker along the No. 5 angle of attack (Step 1). The defender moves his body off the line of attack and deflects the attacking arm by parrying with his left hand (Step 2). He deflects the attacking hand toward his right side by redirecting it with his right hand. As he does this, the defender can strike downward with the left forearm or the wrist onto the forearm or wrist of the attacker (Step 3). The defender ends up in a position to lock the elbow of the attacking arm across his body if he steps off the line of attack properly (Step 4).

Figure 6-13: Low No. 5 angle of defense—parry.

(6) ***High No. 5 Angle of Defense*** (Figure 6-14). The attacker lunges with a thrust to the face, throat, or solar plexus (Step 1). The defender moves his body off the line of attack while parrying with either hand. He redirects the attacking arm so that the knife clears his body (Step 2). He maintains control of the weapon hand or arm and gouges the eyes of the attacker, driving him backward and off balance (Step 3). If the attacker is much taller than the defender, it may be a more natural movement for the defender to raise his left hand to strike and deflect the attacking arm. He can then gouge his thumb or fingers into the jugular

notch of the attacker and force him to the ground. Still another possibility for a high No. 5 angle of attack is for the defender to move his body off the line of attack while parrying. He can then turn his body, rotate his shoulder under the elbow joint of the attacker, and lock it out (Step 4).

Figure 6-14: High No. 5 angle of defense.

(7) ***No. 6 Angle of Defense*** (Figure 6-15). The attacker strikes straight downward onto the defender with a stab (Step 1). The defender reacts by moving his body out of the weapon's path and by parrying or checking and redirecting the attacking arm, as the movement in the high No. 5 angle of defense (Step 2). The reactions may vary as to what is natural for the defender. The defender then takes control of the weapon and disarms the attacker (Step 3).

Figure 6-15: No. 6 angle of defense.

c. **Follow-Up Techniques.** Once the instructor believes the soldiers are skilled in these basic reactions to attack, follow-up techniques may be introduced and practiced. These drills make up the defense possibilities against the various angles of attack. They also enable the soldier to apply the principles of defense against weapons and allow him to feel the movements. Through repetition, the reactions become natural, and the soldier instinctively reacts to a knife attack with the proper defense. It is important not to associate specific movements or techniques with certain types of attack. The knife fighter must rely on his knowledge of principles and his training experience in reacting to a knife attack. No two attacks or reactions will be the same; thus, memorizing techniques will not ensure a soldier's survival.

(1) ***Defend and Clear.*** When the defender has performed a defensive maneuver and avoided an attack, he can push the attacker away and move out of the attacker's reach.

(2) ***Defend and Stun.*** After the defender performs his first defensive maneuver to a safer position, he can deliver a stunning blow as an immediate counterattack. Strikes to motor nerve points or attacker's limbs, low kicks, and elbow strikes are especially effective stunning techniques.

(3) ***Defend and Disarm.*** The defender also follows up his first defensive maneuver by maintaining control of the attacker's weapon arm, executing a stunning technique, and disarming the attacker. The stun distracts the attacker and also gives the defender some time to gain possession of the weapon and to execute his disarming technique.

6-5. UNARMED DEFENSE AGAINST A RIFLE WITH FIXED BAYONET

Defense against a rifle with a fixed bayonet involves the same principles as knife defense. The soldier considers the same angles of attack and the proper response for any attack along each angle.

a. Regardless of the type weapon used by the enemy, his attack will always be along one of the nine angles of attack at any one time. The soldier must get his entire body off the line of attack by moving to a safe position. A rifle with a fixed bayonet has two weapons: a knife at one end and a butt stock at the other end. The soldier will be safe as long as he is not in a position where he can be struck by either end during the attack.

b. Usually, he is in a more advantageous position if he moves inside the length of the weapon. He can then counterattack to gain control of the situation as soon as possible. The following counterattacks can be used as defenses against a rifle with a fixed bayonet; they also provide a good basis for training.

(1) ***Unarmed Defense Against No. 1 Angle of Attack*** (Figure 6-16). The attacker prepares to slash along the No. 1 angle of attack (Step 1). The defender waits until the last possible moment before moving so he is certain of the angle along which the attack is directed (Step 2). This way, the attacker cannot change his attack in response to movement by the defender. When the defender is certain that the attack is committed along a specific angle (No. 1, in this case), he moves to the inside of the attacker and gouges his eyes (Step 2) while the other hand redirects and controls the weapon. He maintains control of the weapon and lunges his entire body weight into the eye gouge to drive the attacker backward and off balance. The defender now ends up with the weapon, and the attacker is in a poor recovery position (Step 3).

Figure 6-16: Unarmed defense against No. 1 angle of attack.

(2) ***Unarmed Defense Against No. 2 Angle of Attack*** (Figure 6-17). The attacker makes a diagonal slash along the No. 2 angle of attack (Step 1). Again, the defender waits until he is sure of the attack before moving. The defender then moves to the outside of the attacker and counterattacks with a thumb jab into the right armpit (Step 2). He receives the momentum of the attacking weapon and controls it with his free hand. He uses the attacker's momentum against him by pulling the weapon in the direction it is going with one hand and pushing with his thumb of the other hand (Step 3). The attacker is completely off balance, and the defender can gain control of the weapon.

Figure 6-17: Unarmed defense against No. 2 angle of attack.

(3) ***Unarmed Defense Against No. 3 Angle of Attack*** (Figure 6-18). The attacker directs a horizontal slash along the No. 3 angle of attack (Step 1). The defender turns and moves to the inside of the attacker; he then strikes with his thumb into the jugular notch (Step 2). His entire body mass is behind the thumb strike and, coupled with the incoming momentum of the attacker, the strike drives the attacker's head backward and takes his balance (Step 3). The defender turns his body with the momentum of the weapon's attack to strip the weapon from the attacker's grip (Step 4).

Figure 6-18: Unarmed defense against No. 3 angle of attack.

(4) ***Unarmed Defense Against No. 4 Angle of Attack*** (Figure 6-19). The attack is a horizontal slash along the No. 4 angle of attack (Step 1). The defender moves in to the outside of the attacker (Step 2). He then turns with the attack, delivering an elbow strike to the throat (Step 3). At the same time, the defender's free hand controls the weapon and pulls it from the attacker as he is knocked off balance from the elbow strike.

Figure 6-19: Unarmed defense against No. 4 angle of attack.

(5) ***Unarmed Defense Against Low No. 5 Angle of Attack.*** (Figure 6-20). The attacker thrusts the bayonet at the stomach of the defender (Step 1). The defender shifts his body to the side to avoid the attack and to gouge the eyes of the attacker (Step 2). The defender's free hand maintains control of and strips the weapon from the attacker as he is driven backward with the eye gouge (Step 3).

Figure 6-20: Unarmed defense against low No. 5 angle of attack.

(6) ***Unarmed Defense Against High No. 5 Angle of Attack*** (Figure 6-21). The attacker delivers a thrust to the throat of the defender (Step 1). The defender then shifts to the side to avoid the attack, parries the thrust, and controls the weapon with his trail hand (Step 2). He then shifts his entire body mass forward over the lead foot, slamming a forearm strike into the attacker's throat (Step 3).

Figure 6-21: Unarmed defense against high No. 5 angle of attack.

(7) ***Unarmed Defense Against No. 6 Angle of Attack*** (Figure 6-22). The attacker delivers a downward stroke along the No. 6 angle of attack. The defender shifts to the outside to get off the line of attack and he grabs the weapon (Step 1). Then, he pulls the attacker off balance by causing him to overextend himself (Step 2). The defender shifts his weight backward and causes the attacker to fall, as he strips the weapon from him (Step 3).

Figure 6-22: Unarmed defense against No. 6 angle of attack.

CHAPTER 7

Group Tactics

Most hand-to-hand situations on the battlefield will involve several people. Varying levels of force will be appropriate based on the situation and rules of engagement. Whether there are more friendlies or enemies, or whether or not some of the parties are armed, soldiers should enter a fight with a well-rehearsed plan and an overall fight strategy.

SECTION I. LETHAL FORCE SCENARIOS

The fundamental truth of hand-to-hand fighting is that the winner will be the one whose buddies show up first with a weapon. Given modern equipment, complicated scenarios, and the split seconds available to make life and death decisions, soldiers must be armed with practical and workable solutions.

7-1. RANGE

You will usually find yourself in a hand-to-hand situation unexpectedly; for example, your weapon jams when entering a room during MOUT. The first thing you must do is determine the appropriate actions to take, which will primarily be based on the range to the enemy. Against an armed enemy, the deciding factor of range is whether or not you can close the gap before the enemy can bring his weapon to bear.

a. **Close Range.** If you are near enough to the enemy to close before he can bring his weapon to bear, you should immediately close the distance and gain control of him.

b. **Long Range.** If the range is too great, or the enemy has sufficient time to bring his weapon to bear, the only options are to escape or take cover. Give your buddy a clear shot or get where you can clear your weapon to get yourself back in the fight.

7-2. CONTROL

If you have closed the distance, your primary goal is to control the enemy. This means controlling his ability to influence the rest of the fight, and controlling his ability to damage you. You are essentially stalling until someone can come to your aid.

a. **Body Control.** You must control the enemy's ability to move, which can be done by gaining and maintaining a dominant body position. This can also be accomplished by pinning the enemy in place (for example, against the wall).

b. **Weapon Control.** You must immobilize the enemy's weapon. For example, use your weight to pin his rifle to his chest while you are mounted, or keep him from drawing a side arm by controlling it in the holster. You must also keep your weapons away from the enemy. It does you no good to immobilize the enemy if he can reach your side arm.

7-3. FINISHING

A very conservative approach should be taken to finishing moves. You must remember that the primary means of winning the fight is with the aid of your buddy. Any move that, if unsuccessful, would compromise your ability to control the situation should not be attempted.

SECTION II. RESTRICTIVE FORCE SCENARIOS

The most common error when fighting in groups is to enter the fight without a plan. This results in uncoordinated actions, and often in working against each other. Only practice gives soldiers the necessary confidence in themselves and their comrades and the ability to think and act together under the stress of hand-to-hand combat.

7-4. TWO AGAINST ONE

When fighting two against one, use the following procedures.

a. **Angles of Attack.** The fighters should advance together, spreading out so that if the enemy turns to face either soldier he will expose his flank to the other.
b. **Communication.** One soldier should attack the enemy's legs and the other should concentrate on his upper body. This can be done by signal, or the soldier attacking the flank can automatically go low. After the enemy is on the ground, good communication is necessary so that you can control and then finish him.

7-5. THREE AGAINST TWO

When fighting three against two, use the following procedures.

a. **Angles of Attack.** The fighters should advance so that the outside two are outside of the enemy. One of the enemies will have to make a choice to face either the outside or inside man. When he does, he will expose his flank to the other one. The fighter who is facing his opponent alone will stall until the other two have finished and can come to his aid.
b. **Communication.** Not only must the two who are fighting the same opponent communicate with each other, but also the fighter who is alone must keep them abreast of his situation. If he is in trouble, it may be necessary for one of them to disengage and come to his aid.

7-6. PARITY

If both groups have the same number of fighters, one fighter stays in reserve until the enemy has committed their entire force. When they have committed, the reserved fighter will attack the exposed back of the enemy.

7-7. ONE AGAINST TWO

When fighting one against two, use the following procedures.

a. **Remain Standing.** Defeating two opponents simultaneously is very difficult. When outnumbered, you should usually try to remain standing—mobility is critical to an effective defense or escape. It is very important not to expose your back. You must use the obstacles around you to restrict the enemies' movements so that you face only one at a time, or maneuver yourself to the flank of the one nearest to you and use him to block the other one. Attack the first enemy using strikes or field-expedient weapons, and then deal with the remaining one.
b. **Defense on the Ground.** If you should lose your footing or be taken to the ground, you must protect your back. Your best defense is to move into a corner or against a wall. Use a modified guard, so that your legs are not exposed, to limit the enemies' ability to attack simultaneously.

7-8. TWO AGAINST THREE

When fighting two against three, you should maneuver to the flanks either together or separately.

a. **Together.** If you can get to one flank together, with the help of restrictive terrain if possible, use strikes to attack one opponent at a time until you have defeated all three.
b. **Separately.** If you are separated, one of you defends as in one against two while the other attacks the remaining enemy with strikes and then comes to the aid of the first.

PART II

Combat Weapons

The Army Combat Rifle

CHAPTER 1

Introduction to the Army Combat Rifle

The procedures and methods used in the Army rifle marksmanship program are based on the concept that soldiers must be skilled marksmen who can effectively apply their firing skills in combat. FM 25-100 stresses marksmanship as a paramount soldier skill. The basic firing skills and exercises outlined in this manual must be a part of every unit's marksmanship training program. Unit commanders must gear their advanced marksmanship training programs to their respective METLs. The proficiency attained by a soldier depends on the proper training and application of basic marksmanship fundamentals. During initial marksmanship training, emphasis is on learning the firing fundamentals, which are taught in a progressive program to prepare soldiers for combat-type exercises.

TRAINING STRATEGY

Training strategy is the overall concept for integrating resources into a program to train individual and collective skills needed to perform a unit's wartime mission.

Training strategies for rifle marksmanship are implemented in TRADOC institutions (IET, NCOES, basic and advanced officer's courses) and in units. The overall training strategy is multifaceted and is inclusive of the specific strategies used in institution and unit programs. Also included are the supporting strategies that use resources such as publications, ranges, ammunition, training aids, devices, simulators, and simulations. These strategies focus on developing critical soldier skills, and on leader skills that are required for success in combat.

Two primary components compose the training strategies: **initial training** and **sustainment training**. Both may include individual and collective skills. Initial training is critical. A task that is taught correctly and learned well is retained longer and skills can be quickly regained and sustained. Therefore, initial training must be taught correctly the first time. However, eventually an individual or unit loses skill proficiency. This learning decay depends on many factors such as the difficulty and complexity of the task. Personnel turnover is a main factor in decay of collective skills, since the loss of critical team members requires retraining to regain proficiency. If a long period elapses between initial and sustainment training sessions or training doctrine is altered, retraining may be required.

The training strategy for rifle marksmanship begins in IET and continues in the unit. An example of this overall process is illustrated in Figure 1-1 and provides a concept of the flow of unit sustainment training. IET provides field units with soldiers who have been trained and who have demonstrated proficiency to standard in basic marksmanship tasks. The soldier graduating from these courses has been trained to maintain the rifle and to hit a point target. He has learned target detection, application of marksmanship fundamentals, and other skills needed to engage a target.

Training continues in units on the basic skills taught in IET. Additional skills such as area fire are trained and then integrated into collective training exercises, which include platoon and squad live-fire STXs. The strategy for sustaining the basic marksmanship skills taught in IET is periodic preliminary rifle instruction, followed by instructional and qualification range firing. However, a unit must set up a year-round program to sustain skills. Key elements include training of trainers, refresher training of nonfiring skills, and use of the Weaponeer or other devices for remedial training. Additional skills trained in the unit include semiautomatic and automatic area fires, night fire, MOPP firing, and moving target training techniques.

In the unit, individual and leader proficiency of marksmanship tasks are integrated into collective training to include squad, section, and platoon drills and STXs; and for the collective tasks in these exercises, and how they are planned and conducted, are in the MTP and battle drills books for each organization. Based on the type organization, collective tasks are evaluated to standard and discussed during leader and trainer after-action reviews. Objective evaluations of both individual and unit proficiency provide readiness indicators and future training requirements.

A critical step in the Army's overall marksmanship training strategy is to train the trainers and leaders first. Leader courses and unit publications develop officer and NCO proficiencies necessary to plan and conduct marksmanship

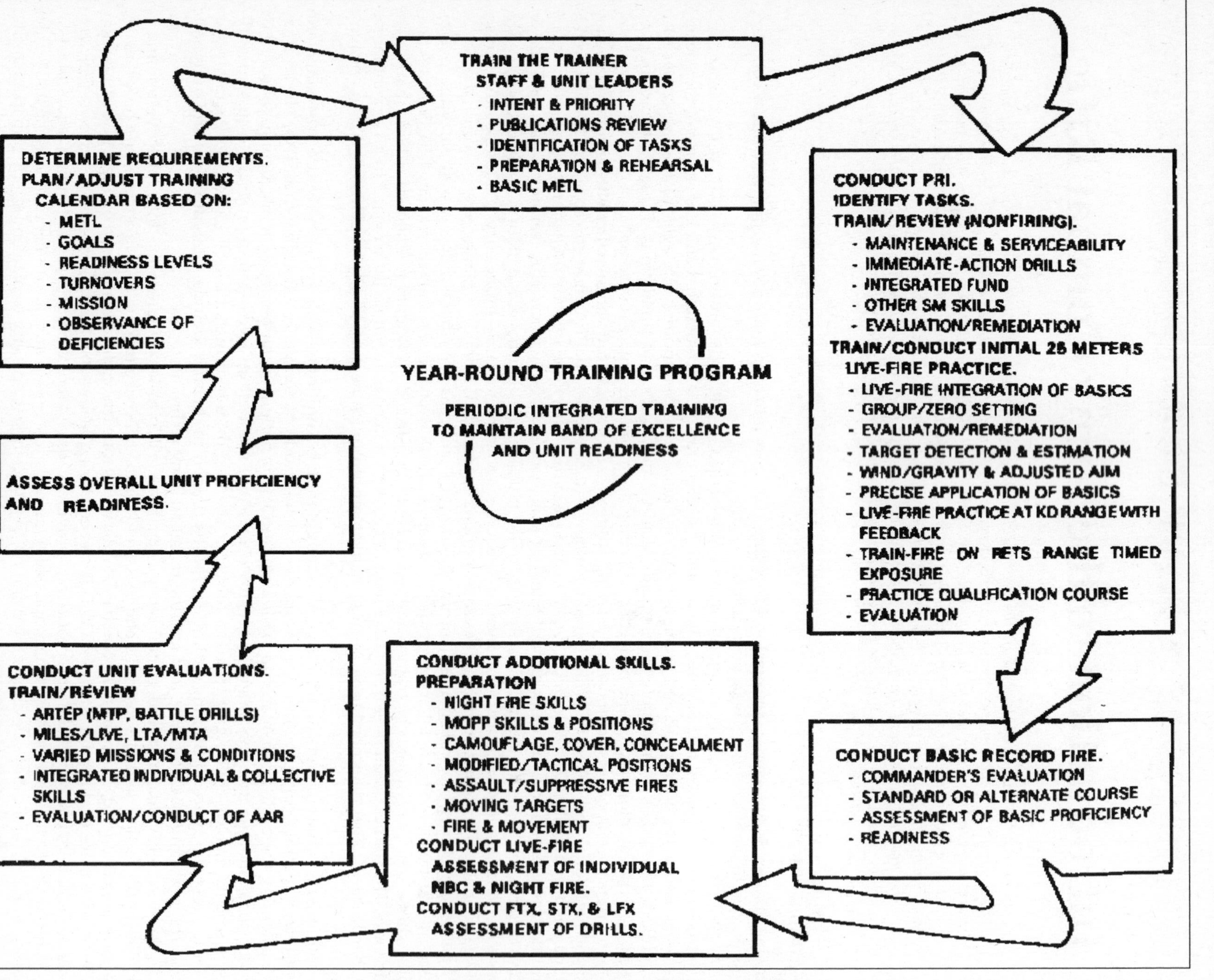

Figure 1-1: Unit marksmanship sustainment strategy.

training and to evaluate the effectiveness of unit marksmanship programs. Training support materials are provided by the proponent schools to include field manuals, training aids, devices, simulators, and programs that are doctrinal foundations and guidance for training the force.

Once the soldier understands the weapon and has demonstrated skill in zeroing, additional live-fire training and a target acquisition exercise at various ranges are conducted. Target types and scenarios of increasing difficulty must be mastered to develop proficiency.

Initial individual training culminates in the soldier's proficiency assessment, which is conducted on the standard record fire range or approved alternates. This evaluation also provides an overview of unit proficiency and training effectiveness.

General marksmanship training knowledge and firing well are acquired skills, which perish easily. Skill practice should be conducted for short periods throughout the year. Most units have a readiness requirement that all soldiers must zero their rifles within a certain time after unit assignment. Also, soldiers must confirm the zeros of their assigned rifles before conducting a qualification firing. Units should conduct preliminary training and practice firing throughout the year due to personnel turnover. A year-round marksmanship sustainment program is needed for the unit to maintain the individual and collective firing proficiency requirements to accomplish its mission.

COMBAT FACTORS

The ultimate goal of a unit rifle marksmanship program is well-trained marksmen. In order for a unit to survive and win on the battlefield, the trainer must realize that rifle qualification is not an end but a step toward reaching this combat requirement. To reach this goal, the soldier should consider some of the factors of combat conditions.

- Enemy personnel are seldom visible except when assaulting.
- Most combat fire must be directed at an area where the enemy has been detected or where he is suspected of being located but cannot be seen. Area targets consist of objects or outlines of men irregularly spaced along covered and concealed areas (ground folds, hedges, borders of woods).
- Most combat targets can be detected by smoke, flash, dust, noise, or movement and are visible only for a moment.
- Some combat targets can be engaged by using nearby objects as reference points.
- The range at which enemy soldiers can be detected and effectively engaged rarely exceeds 300 meters.
- The nature of the target and irregularities of terrain and vegetation may require a firer to use a variety of positions in addition to the prone or supported position to fire effectively on the target. In a defensive situation, the firer usually fires from a supported position.
- Choosing an aiming point in elevation is difficult due to the low contrast outline and obscurity of most combat targets.
- Time-stressed fire in combat can be divided into three types:
  - A single, fleeing target that must be engaged quickly.
  - Area targets that must be engaged with distributed fires that cover the entire area. The firer must maintain sustained fire on the sector he is assigned.
  - A surprise target that must be engaged at once with accurate, instinctive fire.

CHAPTER 2

Operation and Function

The procedures and techniques described in this chapter provide commanders, planners, and trainers information on the M16A1 and M16A2 rifles. These include mechanical training, operation, functioning, preventive maintenance, and common malfunctions. Technical data are presented in a logical sequence from basic to the more complex. Additional information is provided in technical manuals for the rifle.

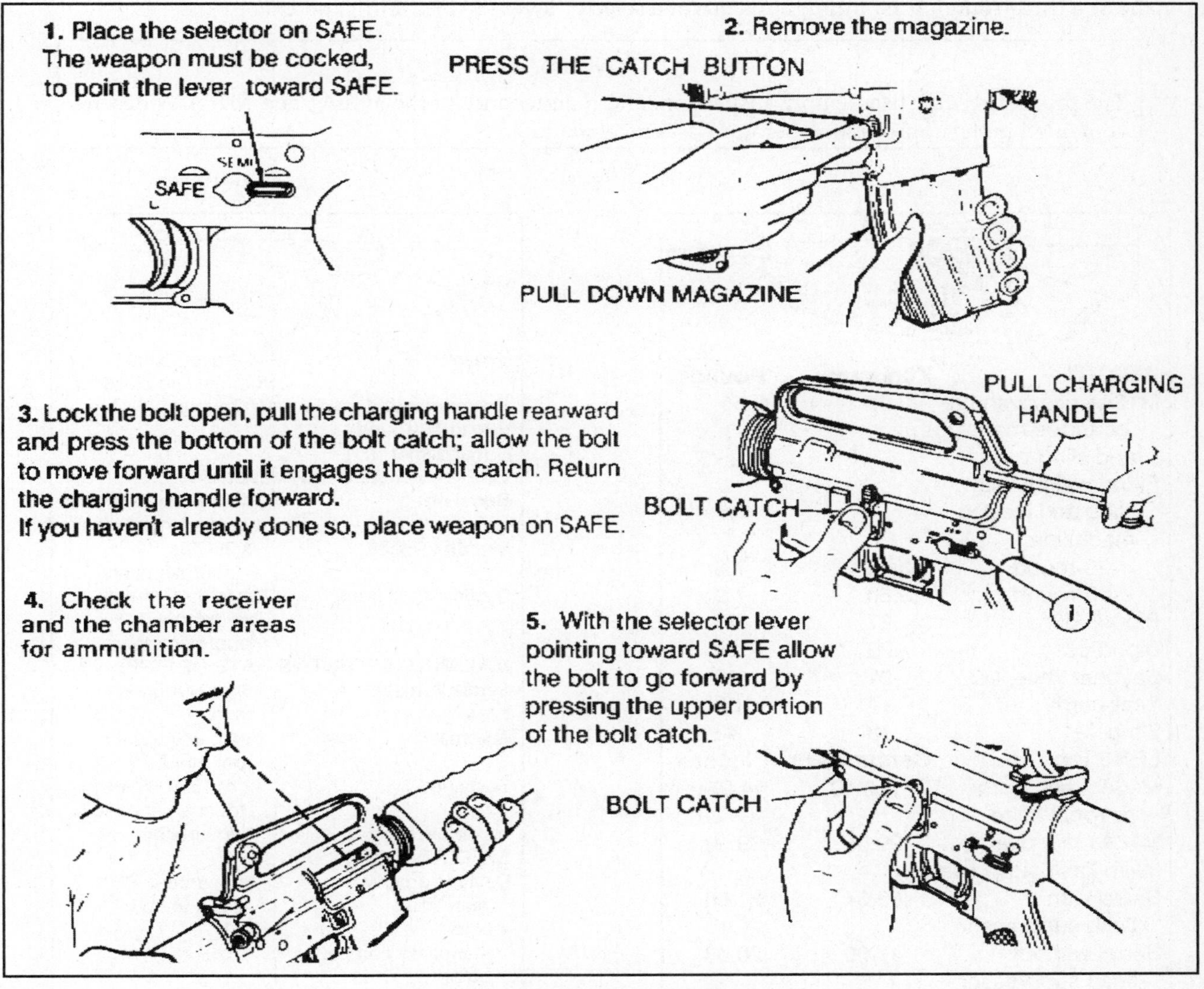

Figure 2-1: Clearing the Rifle.

SECTION I. OPERATIONAL CHARACTERISTICS

This section describes general characteristics of the M16A1 and M16A2 rifles.

M16A1 RIFLE

The M16A1 rifle (Figure 2-2) is a 5.56-mm, magazine-fed, gas-operated, shoulder-fired weapon. It is designed for either semiautomatic or automatic fire through the use of a selector lever (SAFE, SEMI, and AUTO).

M16A2 RIFLE

The M16A2 rifle features several product improvements illustrated in this chapter and the operator's manual. The rifle (Figure 2-3) is a 5.56-mm, magazine-fed, gas-operated, shoulder-fired weapon. It is designed to fire either semiautomatic or a three-round burst through the use of a selector lever (SAFE, SEMI, and BURST).

> ✍ **NOTE**
>
> The procedures for disassembly, inspection, and maintenance of the M16A1 and M16A2 rifles are contained in the appropriate operator's technical manual.

WEIGHT:	**Kilograms**	**Pounds**
M16A1 rifle, without cartridge magazine and sling	2.97	6.55
Firing weight with sling and loaded magazine:		
20-round	3.45	7.6
30-round	3.60	7.9
Bipod, M3	.27	.60
Bipod case	.09	.20
Bayonet knife, M7	.27	.60
Scabbard	.14	.30
Sling, M1	.18	.40
LENGTH:	**Centimeters**	**Inches**
M16A1 rifle with bayonet knife	112.40	44.25
M16A1 rifle overall with flash suppressor	99.06	39.00
Barrel with flash suppressor	53.34	21.00
Barrel without flash suppressor	41.80	20.00
AMMUNITION:		
M16A1, M193		
Complete round	179 grains	
Projectile	.55 grains	

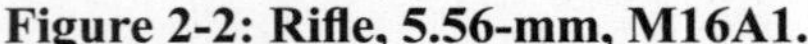
Figure 2-2: Rifle, 5.56-mm, M16A1.

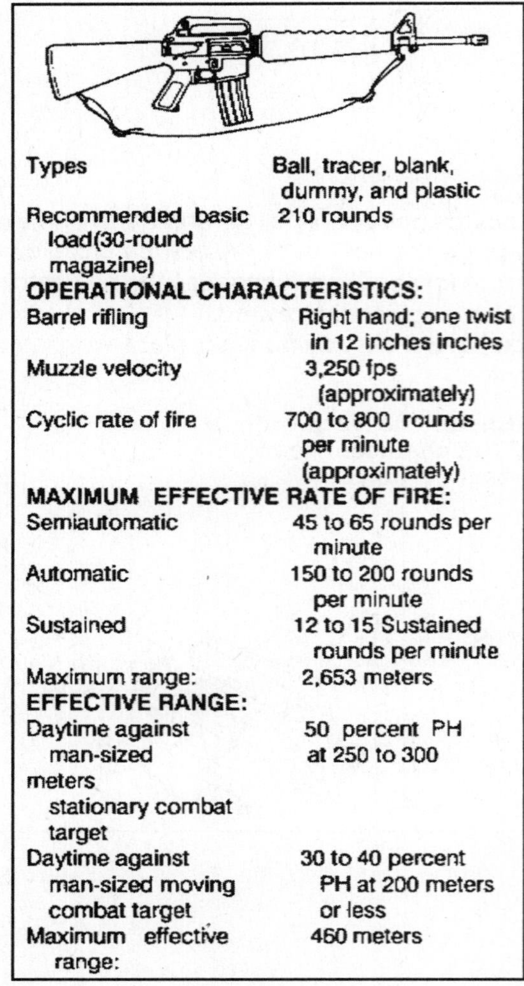

Types	Ball, tracer, blank, dummy, and plastic
Recommended basic load(30-round magazine)	210 rounds
OPERATIONAL CHARACTERISTICS:	
Barrel rifling	Right hand; one twist in 12 inches inches
Muzzle velocity	3,250 fps (approximately)
Cyclic rate of fire	700 to 800 rounds per minute (approximately)
MAXIMUM EFFECTIVE RATE OF FIRE:	
Semiautomatic	45 to 65 rounds per minute
Automatic	150 to 200 rounds per minute
Sustained	12 to 15 Sustained rounds per minute
Maximum range:	2,653 meters
EFFECTIVE RANGE:	
Daytime against man-sized meters stationary combat target	50 percent PH at 250 to 300
Daytime against man-sized moving combat target	30 to 40 percent PH at 200 meters or less
Maximum effective range:	460 meters

Figure 2-2: Rifle, 5.56-mm, M16A1. *(Continued)*

WEIGHT:	Kilograms	Pounds
M16A2 rifle, without cartridge magazine and sling	3.53	7.78
Firing weight with sling and loaded magazine:		
20-round	3.85	8.48
30-round	3.99	8.79
Bipod, M3	.27	.60
Bipod case	.09	.20
Bayonet knife, M9	.68	1.50
Scabbard	.14	.30
Sling, M1	.18	.40
LENGTH:	**Centimeters**	**Inches**
M16A2 rifle with bayonet knife,	113.99	44.88
M16A2 rifle overall with compensator	100.66	39.63
Barrel with compensator	53.34	21.00
Barrel without compensator	41.80	20.00
AMMUNITION:		
M16A2, M855		
Complete round	190 grains	
Projectile	.62 grains	

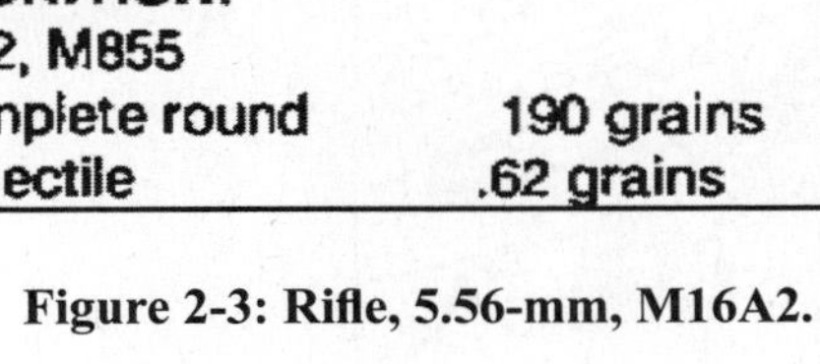

Figure 2-3: Rifle, 5.56-mm, M16A2.

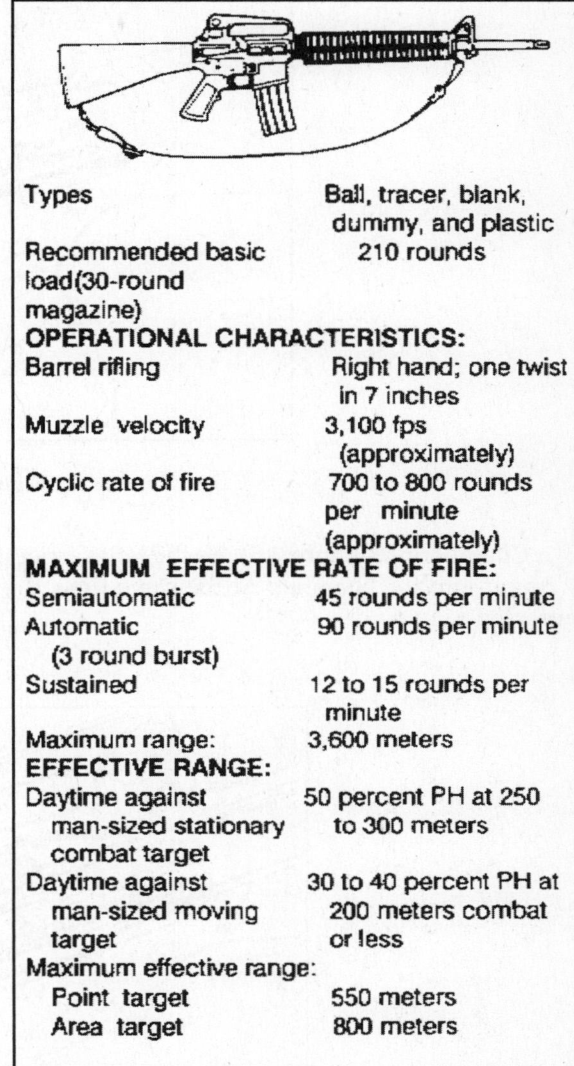

Types	Ball, tracer, blank, dummy, and plastic
Recommended basic load(30-round magazine)	210 rounds
OPERATIONAL CHARACTERISTICS:	
Barrel rifling	Right hand; one twist in 7 inches
Muzzle velocity	3,100 fps (approximately)
Cyclic rate of fire	700 to 800 rounds per minute (approximately)
MAXIMUM EFFECTIVE RATE OF FIRE:	
Semiautomatic	45 rounds per minute
Automatic (3 round burst)	90 rounds per minute
Sustained	12 to 15 rounds per minute
Maximum range:	3,600 meters
EFFECTIVE RANGE:	
Daytime against man-sized stationary combat target	50 percent PH at 250 to 300 meters
Daytime against man-sized moving target	30 to 40 percent PH at 200 meters combat or less
Maximum effective range:	
Point target	550 meters
Area target	800 meters

Figure 2-3: Rifle, 5.56-mm, M16A2. (*Continued*)

SECTION II. FUNCTION

The soldier must understand the rifles' components and the mechanical sequence of events during the firing cycle. The M16A1 rifle is designed to function in either the semiautomatic or automatic mode. The M16A2 is designed to function in either the semiautomatic or three-round burst mode.

STEPS OF FUNCTIONING

The eight steps of functioning (feeding, chambering, locking, firing, unlocking, extracting, ejecting, and cocking) begin after the loaded magazine has been inserted into the weapon.

Step 1: Feeding (Figure 2-4). As the bolt carrier group moves rearward, it engages the buffer assembly and compresses the action spring into the lower receiver extension. When the bolt carrier group clears the top of the magazine, the expansion of the magazine spring forces the follower and a new round up into the path of the forward movement of the bolt. The expansion of the action spring sends the buffer assembly and bolt carrier group forward with enough force to strip a new round from the magazine.

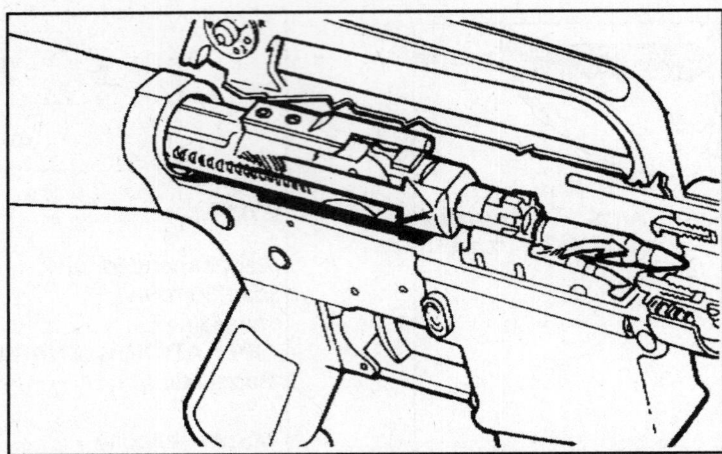

Figure 2-4: Feeding.

Step 2: Chambering (Figure 2-5). As the bolt carrier group continues to move forward, the face of the bolt thrusts the new round into the chamber. At the same time, the extractor claw grips the rim of the cartridge, and the ejector is compressed.

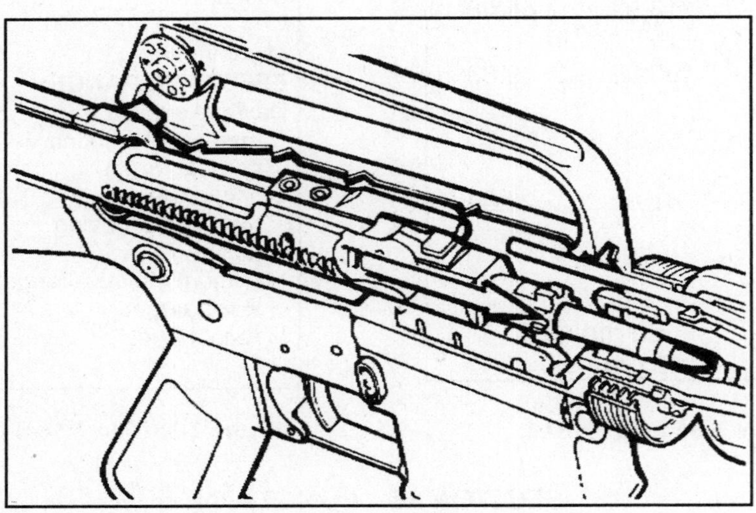

Figure 2-5: Chambering.

Step 3: Locking (Figure 2-6). As the bolt carrier group moves forward, the bolt is kept in its most forward position by the bolt cam pin riding in the guide channel in the upper receiver. Just before the bolt locking lugs make contact with the barrel extension, the bolt cam pin emerges from the guide channel. The pressure exerted by the contact of the bolt locking lugs and barrel extension causes the bolt cam pin to move along the cam track (located in the bolt carrier) in a counterclockwise direction, rotating the bolt locking lugs in line behind the barrel extension locking lugs. The rifle is then ready to fire.

Step 4: Firing (Figure 2-7). With a round in the chamber, the hammer cocked, and the selector on SEMI, the firer squeezes the trigger. The trigger rotates on the trigger pin, depressing the nose of the trigger and disengaging the notch on the bottom on the hammer. The hammer spring drives the hammer forward. The hammer strikes the head of the firing pin, driving the firing pin through the bolt into the primer of the round.

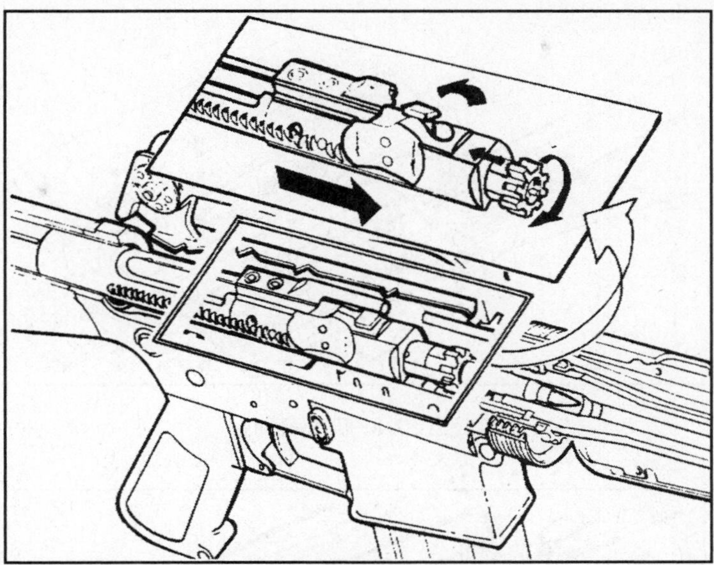

Figure 2-6: Locking.

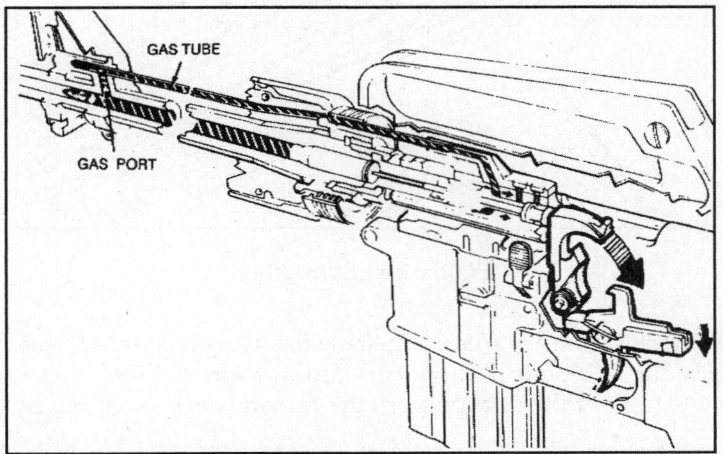

Figure 2-7: Firing.

When the primer is struck by the firing pin, it ignites and causes the powder in the cartridge to ignite. The gas generated by the rapid burning of the powder forces the projectile from the cartridge and propels it through the barrel. After the projectile has passed the gas port (located on the upper surface of the barrel under the front sight) and before it leaves the barrel, some gas enters the gas port and moves into the gas tube. The gas tube directs the gas into the bolt carrier key and then into the cylinder between the bolt and bolt carrier, causing the carrier to move rearward.

Step 5: Unlocking (Figure 2-8). As the bolt carrier moves to the rear, the bolt cam pin follows the path of the cam track (located in the bolt carrier). This action causes the cam pin and bolt assembly to rotate at the same time until the locking lugs of the bolt are no longer in line behind the locking lugs of the barrel extension.

STEP 6: EXTRACTING

(Figure 2-9). The bolt carrier group continues to move to the rear. The extractor (which is attached to the bolt) grips the rim of the cartridge case, holds it firmly against the face of the bolt, and withdraws the cartridge case from the chamber.

Figure 2-8: Unlocking.

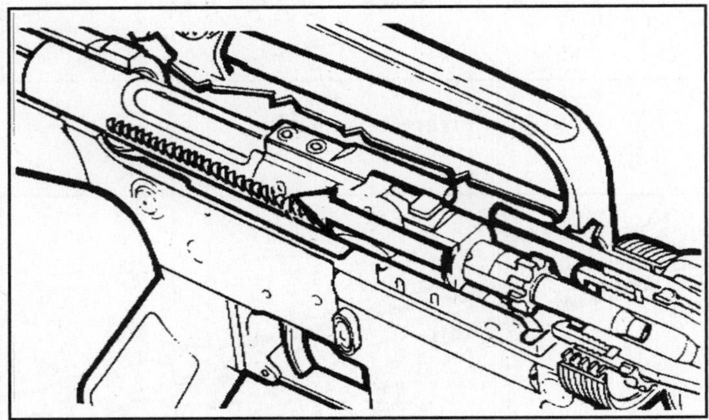

Figure 2-9: Extracting.

Step 7: Ejecting (Figure 2-10). With the base of a cartridge case firmly against the face of the bolt, the ejector and ejector spring are compressed into the bolt body. As the rearward movement of the bolt carrier group allows the nose of the cartridge case to clear the front of the ejection port, the cartridge is pushed out by the action of the ejector and spring.

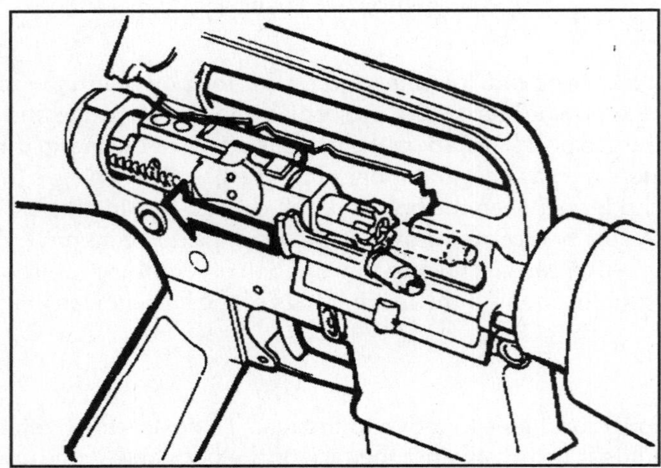

Figure 2-10: Ejecting.

Step 8: Cocking (Figure 2-11). The rearward movement of the bolt carrier overrides the hammer, forcing it down into the receiver and compressing the hammer spring, cocking the hammer in the firing position. The action of the rifle is much faster than human reaction; therefore, the firer cannot release the trigger fast enough to prevent multiple firing.

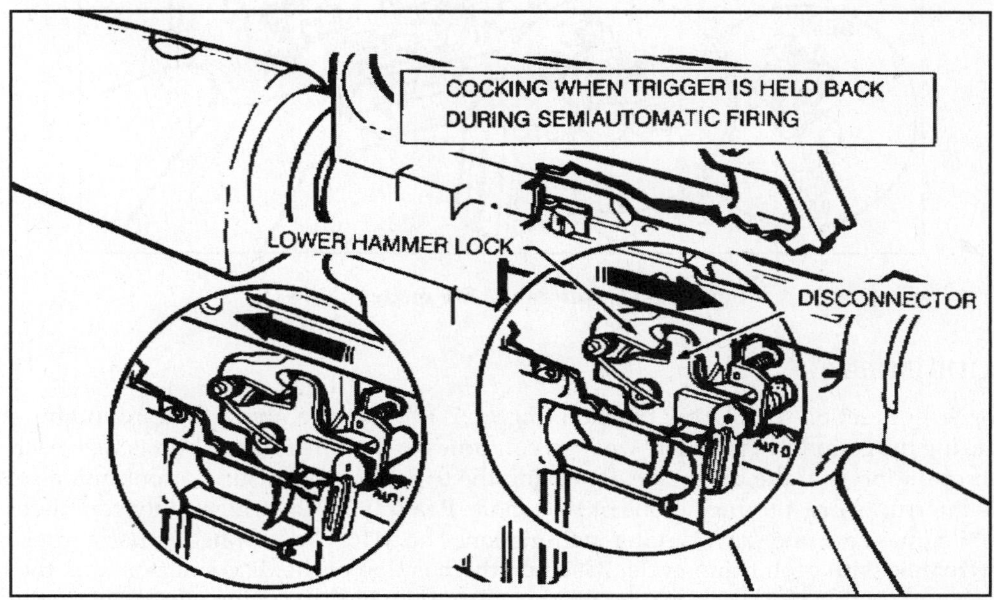

Figure 2-11: Cocking.

SEMIAUTOMATIC MODE (M16A1 AND M16A2)

The disconnector is mechanism installed so that the firer can fire single rounds in the M16A1 and M16A2 rifles. It is attached to the trigger and is rotated forward by action of the disconnector spring. When the hammer is cocked by the recoil of the bolt carrier, the disconnector engages the lower hook of the hammer and holds it until the trigger is released. Then the disconnector rotates to the rear and down, disengaging the hammer and allowing it to rotate forward until caught by the nose of the trigger. This prevents the hammer from following the bolt carrier forward and causing multiple firing. The trigger must be squeezed again before the next round will fire.

AUTOMATIC FIRE MODE (M16A1)

When the selector lever (Figure 2-12) is set on the AUTO position, the rifle continues to fire as long as the trigger is held back and ammunition is in the magazine. The functioning of certain parts of the rifle changes when firing automatically.

Once the trigger is squeezed and the round is fired, the bolt carrier group moves to the rear and the hammer is cocked. The center cam of the selector depresses the rear of the disconnector and prevents the nose of the disconnector from engaging the lower hammer hook. The bottom part of the automatic sear catches the upper hammer hook and holds it until the bolt carrier group moves forward. The bottom part strikes the top of the sear and releases the hammer, causing the rifle to fire automatically.

If the trigger is released, the hammer moves forward and is caught by the nose of the trigger. This ends the automatic cycle of fire until the trigger is squeezed again.

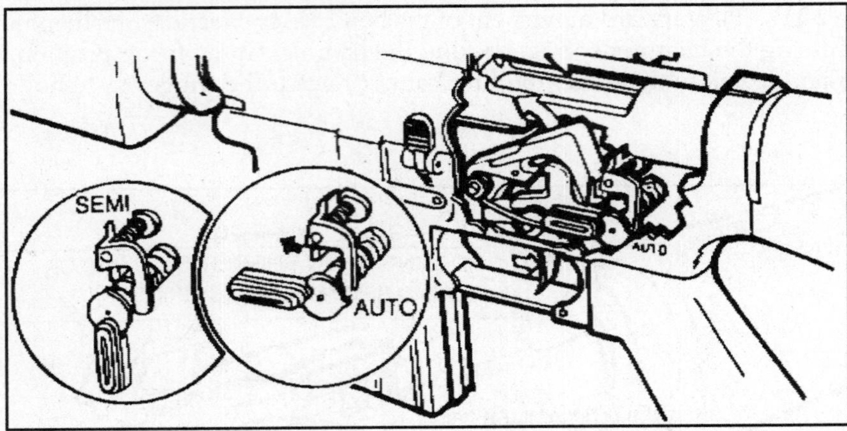

Figure 2-12: Automatic fire mode (M16A1).

BURST FIRE MODE (M16A2)

When the selector lever is set on the BURST position (Figure 2-13), the rifle fires a three-round burst if the trigger is held to the rear during the complete cycle. The weapon continues to fire three-round bursts with each separate trigger pull as long as ammunition is in the magazine. Releasing the trigger or exhausting ammunition at any point in the three-round cycle interrupts fire, producing one or two shots. Reapplying the trigger only completes the interrupted cycle—it does not begin a new one. This is not a malfunction. The M16A2 disconnector has a three-cam mechanism that continuously rotates with each firing cycle. Based on the position of the disconnector cam, the first trigger pull (after initial selection of the BURST position) can produce one, two, or three firing cycles before the trigger must be pulled again. The burst cam rotates until it reaches the stop notch.

> ✍ **NOTE**
> See the operator's manual for a detailed discussion on the burst position.

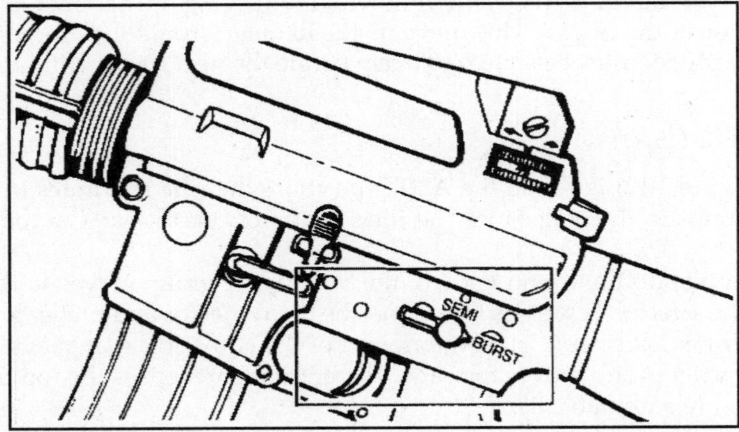

Figure 2-13: Burst fire mode (M16A2).

TROUBLESHOOTING AND DESTRUCTION

Commanders and unit armorers are responsible for the organizational and direct support maintenance of weapons and for the destruction of weapons when necessary. Soldiers are responsible for always keeping their weapons clean and operational in training and in combat and, therefore, should be issued an operator's technical manual and cleaning equipment for their assigned weapons.

Stoppages

A stoppage is a failure of an automatic or semiautomatic firearm to complete the cycle of operation. The firer can apply immediate or remedial action to clear the stoppage. Some stoppages cannot be cleared by immediate or remedial action and may require weapon repair to correct the problem. A complete understanding of how the weapon functions is an integral part of applying immediate action procedures.

a. ***Immediate Action.*** Immediate action involves quickly applying a possible correction to reduce a stoppage without performing troubleshooting procedures to determine the actual cause. The key word **SPORTS** will help the firer remember the steps in order during a live-fire exercise. To apply immediate action, the soldier:

- **S**laps gently upward on the magazine to ensure it is fully seated, and the magazine follower is not jammed (see note).
- **P**ulls the charging handle fully to the rear.
- **O**bserves for the ejection of a live round or expended cartridge. (If the weapon fails to eject a cartridge, perform remedial action.)
- **R**eleases the charging handle (do not ride it forward).
- **T**aps the forward assist assembly to ensure bolt closure.
- **S**queezes the trigger and tries to fire the rifle.

Only apply immediate action once for a stoppage. If the rifle fails to fire a second time for the same malfunction inspect the weapon to determine the cause of the stoppage or malfunction and take the appropriate remedial action outlined below.

> ✍ **NOTE**
> When slapping up on the magazine, be careful not to knock a round out of the magazine into the line of the bolt carrier, causing more problems. Slap only hard enough to ensure the magazine is fully seated. Ensure that the magazine is locked into place by quickly pulling down on the magazine.

b. ***Remedial Action.*** Remedial action is the continuing effort to determine the cause for a stoppage or malfunction and to try to clear the stoppage once it has been identified. To apply the corrective steps for remedial action, first try to place the weapon on SAFE, then remove the magazine, lock the bolt to the rear, and place the weapon on safe (if not already done).

> ✍ **NOTE**
> A bolt override may not allow the weapon to be placed on SAFE.

Malfunctions

Malfunctions are caused by procedural or mechanical failures of the rifle, magazine, or ammunition. Pre-firing checks and serviceability inspections identify potential problems before they become malfunctions. This paragraph describes the primary categories of malfunctions.

1. Failure to Feed, Chamber, or Lock.

A malfunction can occur when loading the rifle or during the cycle of operation. Once the magazine has been loaded into the rifle, the forward movement of the bolt carrier group could lack enough force (generated by the expansion of the action spring) to feed, chamber, or lock the bolt (Figure 2-14).

Probable Causes. The cause could be the result of one or more of the following:

- Excess accumulation of dirt or fouling in and around the bolt and bolt carrier.
- Defective magazine (dented, bulged, or a weak magazine spring).

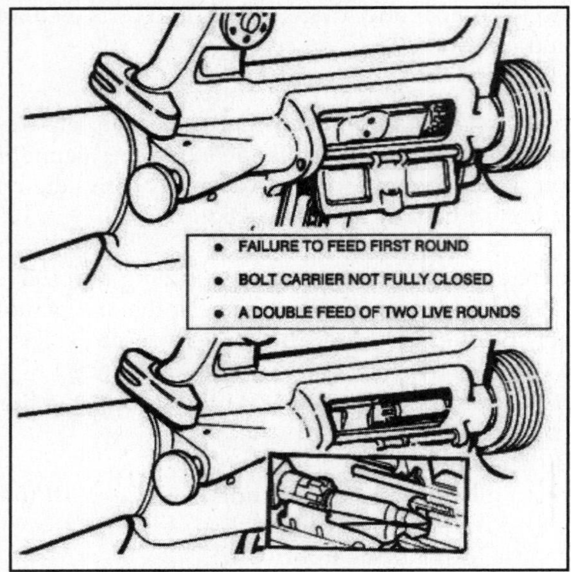

Figure 2-14: Failure to feed, chamber, or lock.

- Improperly loaded magazine.
- Defective round (projectile forced back into the cartridge case, which could result in a stubbed round or the base of the previous cartridge could be separated, leaving the remainder in the chamber).
- Damaged or broken action spring.
- Exterior accumulation of dirt in the lower receiver extension.
- Fouled gas tube resulting in short recoil.
- A magazine resting on the ground or pushed forward could cause an improper lock.

Corrective action. Applying immediate action usually corrects the malfunction. However, to avoid the risk of further jamming, the firer should watch for ejection of a cartridge and ensure that the upper receiver is free of any loose rounds. If immediate action fails to clear the malfunction, remedial action must be taken. The carrier should not be forced. If resistance is encountered, which can occur with an unserviceable round, the bolt should be locked to the rear, magazine removed, and malfunction cleared—for example, a bolt override is when a cartridge has wedged itself between the bolt and charging handle. The best way to relieve this problem is by —

- Ensuring that the charging handle is pushed forward and locked in place.
- Holding the rifle securely and pulling the bolt to the rear until the bolt seats completely into the buffer well.
- Turning the rifle upright and allowing the overridden cartridge to fall out.

2. Failure to Fire Cartridge.

Description. Failure of a cartridge to fire despite the fact that a round has been chambered, the trigger is pulled, and the sear has released the hammer. This occurs when the firing pin fails to strike the primer with enough force or when the ammunition is bad.

Probable causes. Excessive carbon buildup on the firing pin (Figure 2-15A) is often the cause, because the full forward travel of the firing pin is restricted. However, a defective or worn firing pin can give the same results. Inspection of the ammunition could reveal a shallow indentation or no mark on the primer, indicating a firing pin problem (Figure 2-15B). Cartridges that show a normal indentation on the primer but did not fire indicate bad ammunition.

Corrective action. If the malfunction continues, the firing pin, bolt, carrier, and locking lug recesses of the barrel extension should be inspected, and any accumulation of excessive carbon or fouling should be removed. The firing pin should also be inspected for damage. Cartridges that show a normal indentation on the primer but failed to fire could indicate a bad ammunition lot. Those that show a complete penetration of the primer by the firing pin could also indicate a bad ammunition lot or a failure of the cartridge to fully seat in the chamber.

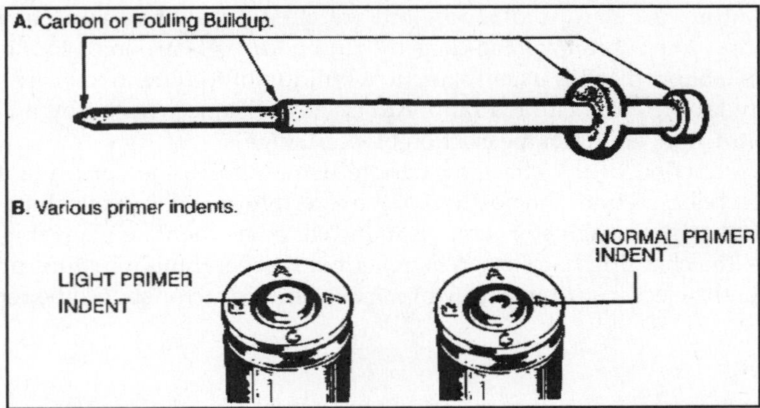

Figure 2-15: Failure to fire.

> **NOTE**
> If the round is suspected to be faulty, it is reported and returned to the agency responsible for issuing ammunition

3. **Failure to Extract and Eject.**

Failure to extract. The cartridge must extract before it can eject.

Description. A failure to extract results when the cartridge case remains in the rifle chamber. While the bolt and bolt carrier could move rearward only a short distance, more commonly the bolt and bolt carrier recoil fully to the rear, leaving the cartridge case in the chamber. A live round is then forced into the base of the cartridge case as the bolt returns in the next feed cycle. This malfunction is one of the hardest to clear.

> **NOTE**
> Short recoil can also be caused by a fouled or obstructed gas tube.

> **WARNING**
> A failure to extract is considered to be an extremely serious malfunction, requiring the use of tools to clear. A live round could be left in the chamber and be accidentally discharged. If a second live round is fed into the primer of the chambered live round, the rifle could explode and cause personal injury. This malfunction must be properly identified and reported. Failures to eject should not be reported as extraction failures.

Probable cause. Short recoil cycles and fouled or corroded rifle chambers are the most common causes of failures to extract. A damaged extractor or weak/broken extractor spring can also cause this malfunction.

Corrective action. The severity of a failure to extract determines the corrective action procedures. If the bolt has moved rearward far enough so that it strips a live round from the magazine in its forward motion, the bolt and carrier must be locked to the rear.

The magazine and all loose rounds must be removed before clearing the stoppage. Usually, tapping the butt of the rifle on a hard surface causes the cartridge to fall out of the chamber. However, if the cartridge case is ruptured, it can be seized. When this occurs, a cleaning rod can be inserted into the bore from the muzzle end. The cartridge case can be forced from the chamber by tapping the cleaning rod against the inside base of the fired cartridge. When cleaning and inspecting the mechanism and chamber reveal no defects but failures to extract persist, the extractor and extractor spring should be replaced. If the chamber surface is damaged, the entire barrel must be replaced.

Failure to Eject. A failure to eject a cartridge is an element in the cycle of functioning of the rifle, regardless of the mode of fire. A malfunction occurs when the cartridge is not ejected through the ejection port and either remains partly in the chamber or becomes jammed in the upper receiver as the bolt closes. When the firer initially clears the rifle, the cartridge could strike an inside surface of the receiver and bounce back into the path of the bolt.

Probable cause. Ejection failures are hard to diagnose but are often related to a weak or damaged extractor spring and/or ejector spring. Failures to eject can also be caused by a buildup of carbon or fouling on the ejector spring or extractor, or from short recoil. Short recoil is usually due to a buildup of fouling in the carrier mechanism or gas tube, which could result in many failures to include a failure to eject. Resistance caused by a carbon-coated or corroded chamber can impede the extraction, and then the ejection of a cartridge.

Corrective action. While retraction of the charging handle usually frees the cartridge and permits removal, the charging handle must not be released until the position of the next live round is determined. If another live round has been sufficiently stripped from the magazine or remains in the chamber, then the magazine and all live rounds could also require removal before the charging handle can be released. If several malfunctions occur and are not corrected by cleaning and lubricating, the ejector spring, extractor spring, and extractor should be replaced.

OTHER MALFUNCTIONS

Some other malfunctions that can occur are as follows.

- Failure of the bolt to remain in a rearward position after the last round in the magazine is fired. Check for a bad magazine or short recoil.
- Failure of the bolt to lock in the rearward position when the bolt catch has been engaged. Check bolt catch; replace as required.
- Firing two or more rounds when the trigger is pulled and the selection lever is in the SEMI position. This indicates a worn sear, cam, or disconnector. Turn in to armorer to repair and replace trigger group parts as required.
- Trigger will not pull or return after release with the selector set in a firing position. This indicates that the trigger pin (Figure 2-16A) has backed out of the receiver or the hammer spring is broken. Turn in to armorer to replace or repair.
- Failure of the magazine to lock into the rifle (Figure 2-16B). Check the magazine and check magazine catch for damage. Turn in to armorer to adjust the catch; replace as required.
- Failure of any part of the bolt carrier group to function (Figure 2-16C). Check for incorrect assembly of components. Correctly clean and assemble the bolt carrier group, or replace damaged parts.
- Failure of the ammunition to feed from the magazine (Figure 2-16D). Check for damaged magazine. A damaged magazine could cause repeated feeding failures and should be turned in to armorer or exchanged.

> ✍ **NOTE**
> Additional technical information on troubleshooting malfunctions and repairing components is contained in the organizational and DS maintenance publications and manuals.

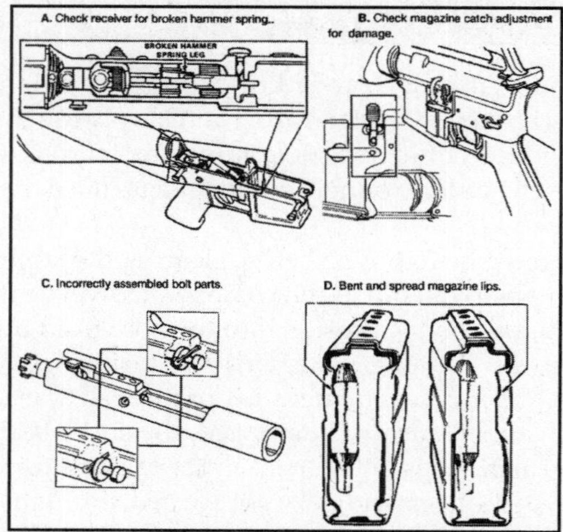

Figure 2-16: Other Possible Malfunctions.

SECTION IV. AMMUNITION

This section contains information on different types of standard military ammunition used in the M16A1 and M16A2 rifles. Use only authorized ammunition that is manufactured to U.S. and NATO specifications.

TYPES AND CHARACTERISTICS

The characteristics of the M16 family of ammunition are described in this paragraph.

Cartridge, 5.56-mm, Dummy, M199. (Used in both rifles.) The M199 dummy cartridge is used during dry fire and other training (see 3, Figure 2-17). This cartridge can be identified by the six grooves along the side of the case beginning about 1/2 inch from its head. It contains no propellent or primer. The primer well is open to prevent damage to the firing pin.

Cartridge, 5.56-mm, Blank, M200. (Used in the M16A1 or M16A2 rifle.) The M200 blank cartridge has no projectile. The case mouth is closed with a seven-petal rosette crimp and shows a violet tip (see 4, Figure 2-17). (See Appendix C for use of the blank firing attachment.). The original M200 blank cartridge had a white tip. Field use of this cartridge resulted in residue buildup, which caused several malfunctions. Only the violet-tipped M200 cartridge should be used.

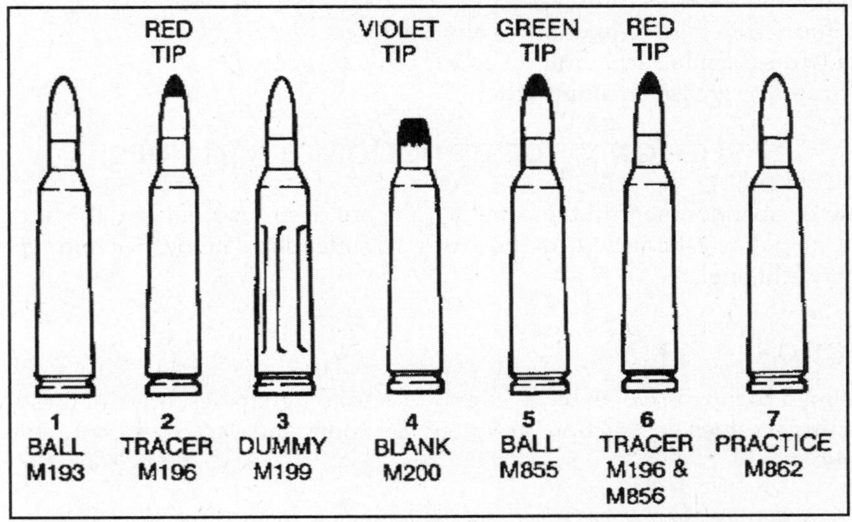

Figure 2-17: Ammunition (5.56-mm) for the M16A1 and M16A2.

Cartridge, 5.56-mm, Plastic Practice Ammunition, M862. (Used in the M16A1 and M16A2 rifles.) The M862 PPA is designed exclusively for training. It can be used in lieu of service ammunition on indoor ranges, and by units that have a limited range fan that does not allow the firing of service ammunition. It is used with the M2 training bolt.

Although PPA (see 7, Figure 2-17) closely replicates the trajectory and characteristics of service ammunition out to 25 meters, it should not be used to set the combat battlesight zero of weapons to fire service ammunition. The setting that is placed on the sights for a weapon firing PPA could be different for service ammunition.

If adequate range facilities are not available for sustainment (particularly Reserve Components), PPA can be used for any firing exercises of 25 meters or less. This includes the 25-meter scaled silhouette, 25-meter alternate qualification course, and quick-fire training. Units that have an indoor range with adequate ventilation or MOUT site could use PPA. (See Appendix C for use in training.)

Cartridge, 5.56-mm, Ball, M193. The M193 cartridge is a center-fire cartridge with a 55-grain, gilding-metal, jacketed, lead alloy core bullet. The primer and case are waterproof. The M193 round is the standard cartridge for field use with the M16A1 rifle and has no identifying marks (see 1, Figure 2-17). This cartridge has a projectile weight of 55 grains and is 1.9 cm long, with a solid lead core.

Figure 2-21. Ammunition for 5.56-mm M16A1 (1 through 4 and 7) and M16A2 (3 through 7).

Cartridge, 5.56-mm, Tracer, M196. (Used in the M16A1 rifle.) The M196 cartridge is identified by a red- or orange-painted tip (see 2, Figure 2-17). Its main uses are for observation of fire, incendiary effect, and signaling. Soldiers should avoid long-term use of 100-percent tracer rounds. This could cause deposits of incendiary material / chemical compounds that could cause damage to the barrel. Therefore, when tracer rounds are fired, they are mixed with ball ammunition in a ratio no greater than one-to-one with a preferred ratio of three or four ball rounds to one tracer round.

Cartridge, 5.56-mm, Ball, M855. The M855 cartridge has a 62-grain, gilding-metal, jacketed, lead alloy core bullet with a steel penetrator. The primer and case are waterproof. This is the NATO standard round for the M16A2 rifle (also used in the M249 SAW). It is identified by a green tip (see 5, Figure 2-17). This cartridge has a projectile weight of 62 grains and is 2.3 cm long, with a steel penetrator in the nose.

Cartridge, 5.56-mm, Tracer, M856. (Used in the M16A2 rifle.) The M856 tracer cartridge has similar characteristics as the M196 but has a slightly longer tracer burnout distance. This cartridge has a 63.7-grain bullet. The M856 does not have a steel penetrator. It is also identified by a red tip (orange when linked 4 and 1) (6, Figure 2-17).

CARE AND HANDLING

When necessary to store ammunition in the open, it must be raised on dunnage at least 6 inches from the ground and protected with a cover, leaving enough space for air circulation. Since ammunition and explosives are adversely affected by moisture and high temperatures, the following must be adhered to:

- Do not open ammunition boxes until ready to use.
- Protect ammunition from high temperatures and the direct rays of the sun.
- Do not attempt to disassemble ammunition or any of its components.
- Never use lubricants or grease on ammunition.

SECTION V. DESTRUCTION OF MATERIEL

Rifles subject to capture or abandonment in the combat zone are destroyed only by the authority of the unit commander IAW orders of or policy established by the Army commander. The destruction of equipment is reported through regular command channels.

MEANS OF DESTRUCTION

Certain procedures outlined require use of explosives and incendiary grenades. Issue of these and related principles, and specific conditions under which destruction is effected, are command decisions. Of the several means of destruction, the following apply:

- **Mechanical.** Requires axe, pick mattock, sledge, crowbar, or other heavy implement.
- **Burning.** Requires gasoline, oil, incendiary grenades, and other flammables, or welding or cutting torch.
- **Demolition.** Requires suitable explosives or ammunition. Under some circumstances, hand grenades can be used.
- **Disposal.** Requires burying in the ground, dumping in streams or marshes, or scattering so widely as to preclude recovery of essential parts.

It is important that the same parts be destroyed on all like material, including spare parts, so that the enemy cannot rebuild one complete unit from several damaged units. If destruction is directed, appropriate safety precautions must be observed.

FIELD-EXPEDIENT METHODS

If destruction of the individual rifle must be performed to prevent enemy use, the rifle must be damaged so it cannot be restored to a usable condition. Expedient destruction requires that key operational parts be separated from the rifle or damaged beyond repair. Priority is given in the following order:

FIRST: Bolt carrier group; removed and discarded or hidden.
SECOND: Upper receiver group; separated and discarded or hidden.
THIRD: Lower receiver group; separated and discarded or hidden.

CHAPTER 3

Rifle Marksmanship Training

The procedures and techniques for implementing the Army rifle marksmanship training program are based on the concept that all soldiers must understand common firing principles, be proficient marksmen, and be confident in applying their firing skills in combat. This depends on their understanding of the rifle and correct application of marksmanship fundamentals. Proficiency is accomplished through practice that is supervised by qualified instructors/trainers and through objective performance assessments by unit leaders. During preliminary training, instructors/trainers emphasize initial learning, reviewing, reinforcing, and practicing of the basics. Soldiers must master weapon maintenance, functions checks, and firing fundamentals before progressing to advanced skills and firing exercises under tactical conditions. The skills the soldier must learn are developed in the following four phases:

- *PHASE I. Preliminary Rifle Instruction.*
- *PHASE II. Downrange Feedback Range Firing.*
- *PHASE III. Field Firing on Train-Fire Ranges.*
- *PHASE IV. Advanced and Collective Firing Exercises.*

Each soldier progresses through these phases to meet the objective of rifle marksmanship training and sustainment. The accomplishment of these phases are basic and necessary in mastering the correct techniques of marksmanship and when functioning as a soldier in a combat area. (See Chapter 1 and Appendix A.)

SECTION I. BASIC PROGRAM IMPLEMENTATION

Knowledgeable instructors/cadre are the key to marksmanship performance. All commanders must be aware of maintaining expertise in marksmanship instruction/training. (See Appendix D.)

INSTRUCTOR/TRAINER SELECTION

Institutional and unit instructors/trainers are selected and assigned from the most highly qualified soldiers. These soldiers must have an impressive background in rifle marksmanship; be proficient in applying these fundamentals; know the importance of marksmanship training; and have a competent and professional attitude. The commander must ensure that selected instructors/trainers can effectively train other soldiers. Local instructor/trainer training courses and marksmanship certification programs must be established to ensure that instructor/trainer skills are developed.

Cadre/trainer refers to a marksmanship instructor/trainer that has more experience and expertise than the firer. He trains soldiers in the effective use of the rifle by maintaining strict discipline on the firing line, insisting on compliance with range procedures and program objectives, and enforcing safety regulations. A good instructor/trainer must understand the training phases and techniques for developing marksmanship skills, and he must possess the following qualifications:

Knowledge. The main qualifications for an effective instructor/trainer are thorough knowledge of the rifle, proficiency in firing, and understanding supporting marksmanship manuals.

Patience. The instructor/trainer must relate to the soldier calmly, persistently, and patiently.

Understanding. The instructor/trainer can enhance success and understanding by emphasizing close observance of rules and instructions.

Consideration. Most soldiers enjoy firing regardless of their performance and begin with great enthusiasm. The instructor/trainer can enhance this enthusiasm by being considerate of his soldiers feelings and by encouraging firing abilities throughout training, which can also make teaching a rewarding experience.

Respect. An experienced cadre is assigned the duties of instructor/trainer, which classifies him as a technical expert and authority. The good instructor/trainer is alert for mistakes and patiently makes needed corrections.

Encouragement. The instructor/trainer can encourage his soldiers by convincing them to achieve good firing performance through practice. His job is to impart knowledge and to assist the soldier so he can gain the practical experience needed to become a good firer.

DUTIES OF THE INSTRUCTOR/TRAINER

The instructor/trainer helps the firer master the fundamentals of rifle marksmanship. He ensures that the firer consistently applies what he has learned. Then, it is a matter of practice, and the firer soon acquires good firing skills. When training the beginner, the instructor/trainer could confront problems such as fear, nervousness, forgetfulness, failure to understand, and a lack of coordination or determination. An expert firer is often unaware that some problems are complicated by arrogance and carelessness. With all types of firers, the instructor/trainer must ensure that firers are aware of their firing errors, understand the causes, and apply remedies. Sometimes errors are not evident. The instructor/trainer must isolate errors, explain them, and help the firer concentrate on correcting them.

Observing the Firer. The instructor/trainer observes the firer during drills and in the act of firing to pinpoint errors. If there is no indication of probable error, then the firer's position, breath control, shot anticipation, and trigger squeeze are closely observed.

Questioning the Firer. The firer is asked to detect his errors and to explain his firing procedure to include position, aiming, breath control, and trigger squeeze.

Analyzing the Shot Group. This is an important step in detecting and correcting errors. When analyzing a target, the instructor/trainer critiques and correlates observations of the firer to probable errors in performance, according to the shape and size of shot groups. A poor shot group is usually caused by more than one observable error.

SECTION II. CONDUCT OF TRAINING

In the conduct of marksmanship training, the instructor/trainer first discusses an overview of the program to include the progression and step-by-step process in developing firing skills. Once the soldier realizes the tasks and skills involved, he is ready to begin. He receives preliminary rifle instruction before firing any course. Also during this initial phase, an understanding of the service rifle develops through review.

MECHANICAL TRAINING

Mechanical training includes characteristics and capabilities, disassembly and assembly, operations and functioning, serviceability checks, and weapons maintenance. It also stresses the performance of immediate action to clear or reduce a stoppage, and the safe handling of rifles and ammunition (see Chapter 2). Examples of mechanical training drills, along with tasks, conditions, and standards, are provided in Appendix A. These examples are also used for initial entry training at the Army training centers. Mechanical training must encompass all related tasks contained in the soldier's manual of common tasks (SMCT) to include the correct procedures for disassembly, cleaning, inspection, and reassembly of the rifle and magazine (Figure 3-1).

Serviceability inspections and preventive maintenance checks must be practiced to ensure soldiers have reliable weapons systems during training and in combat. Technical information necessary to conduct mechanical training is contained in the soldier's operator's manual (M16A1 – TM 9-1005-249-10; M16A2 – TM 9-1005-319-10). Once the basic procedures have been demonstrated, soldiers should practice the mechanical training skills under varied conditions to include during nighttime, and in MOPP and arctic clothing.

As part of mechanical training, soldiers must be taught and must practice procedures for properly loading ammunition into magazines to include both single loose rounds and speed loading of 10-round clips (Figure 3-2).

Emphasis on maintenance and understanding of the rifle can prevent most problems and malfunctions. However, a soldier could encounter a stoppage or malfunction. The soldier must quickly correct the problem by applying immediate action and continue to place effective fire on the target.

Immediate-action procedures contained in Chapter 2 and the operator's technical manual should be taught and practiced as part of preliminary dry-fire exercises, and should be reinforced during live-fire exercises.

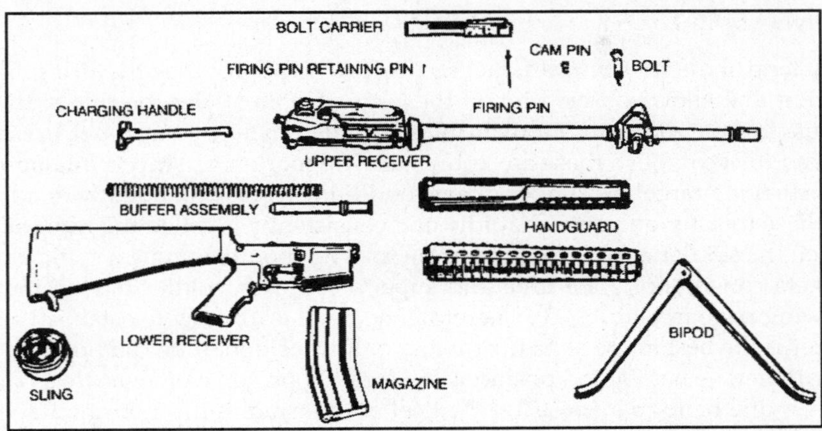

Figure 3-1: M16A2 field-stripped.

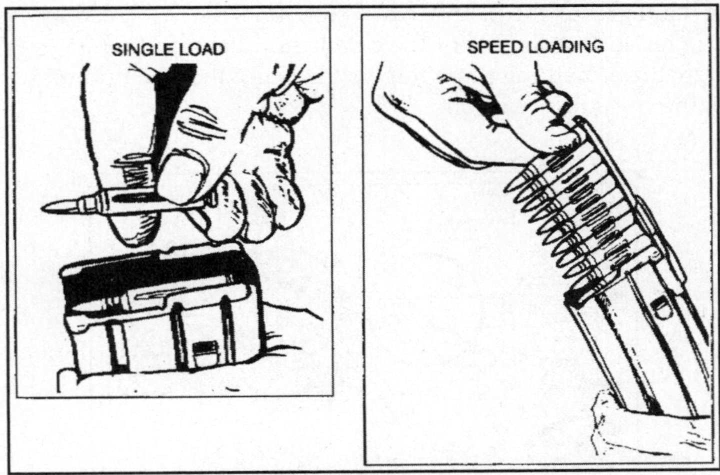

Figure 3-2: Loading and unloading magazine.

Immediate-action drills should be conducted using dummy ammunition (M199) loaded into the magazine. The soldier chambers the first dummy round and assumes a firing position. When he squeezes the trigger and the hammer falls with no recoil, this is the cue to apply the correct immediate-action procedure and to refire. Drill should continue until soldiers can perform the task in three to five seconds.

The word **SPORTS** is a technique for assisting the soldier in learning the proper procedures for applying immediate action to the M16A1 and M16A2 rifles.

First, **THINK,** then:

Slap up on the bottom of the magazine.
Pull the charging handle to the rear.
Observe the chamber for an ejection of the round.
Release the charging handle.
Tap the forward assist.
Squeeze the trigger again.

> ✍ **NOTE**
> When slapping up on the magazine, be careful not to knock a round out of the magazine into the line of the bolt carrier, causing more problems. Slap hard enough only to ensure the magazine is fully seated.

MARKSMANSHIP FUNDAMENTALS

The soldier must understand the four key fundamentals before he approaches the firing line. He must be able to establish a **steady position** that allows observation of the target. He must **aim** the rifle at the target by aligning the sight system, and he must fire the rifle without disturbing this alignment by improper **breathing** or during **trigger squeeze.** The skills needed to accomplish these are known as **rifle marksmanship fundamentals.** These simple procedures aid the firer in achieving target hits under many conditions when expanded with additional techniques and information. Applying these four fundamentals rapidly and consistently is called the **integrated act of firing.**

Steady Position. When the soldier approaches the firing line, he should assume a comfortable, steady firing position in order to hit targets consistently. The time and supervision each soldier has on the firing line are limited (illustrated on the following page in Figure 3-3). Therefore, he must learn how to establish a steady position during dry-fire training. The firer is the best judge as to the quality of his position. If he can hold the front sight post steady through the fall of the hammer, he has a good position. The steady position elements are as follows:

Nonfiring hand grip. The rifle handguard rests on the heel of the hand in the V formed by the thumb and fingers. The grip of the nonfiring hand is light, and slight rearward pressure is exerted.

Rifle butt position. The butt of the stock is placed in the pocket of the firing shoulder. This reduces the effect of recoil and helps ensure a steady position.

Firing hand grip. The firing hand grasps the pistol grip so that it fits the V formed by the thumb and forefinger. The forefinger is placed on the trigger so that the lay of the rifle is not disturbed when the trigger is squeezed. A slight rearward pressure is exerted by the remaining three fingers to ensure that the butt of the stock remains in the pocket of the shoulder, thus minimizing the effect of recoil.

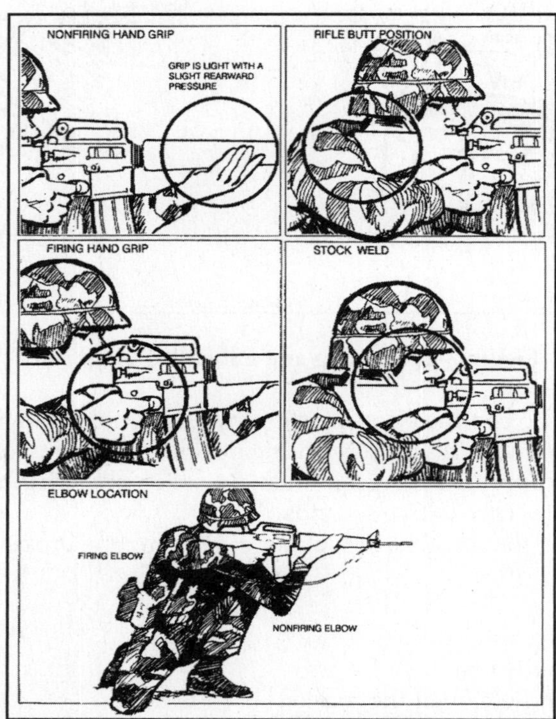

Figure 3-3: Steady position.

Firing elbow placement. The location of the firing elbow is important in providing balance. The exact location, however, depends on the firing/fighting position used—for example, kneeling, prone, or standing. Placement should allow shoulders to remain level.

Nonfiring elbow. The nonfiring elbow is positioned firmly under the rifle to allow for a comfortable and stable position. When the soldier engages a wide sector of fire, moving targets, and targets at various elevations, his nonfiring elbow should remain free from support.

Stock weld. The stock weld is taught as an integral part of various positions. Two key factors emphasized are that the stock weld should provide for a natural line of sight through the center of the rear sight aperture to the front sight post and to the target. The firer's neck should be relaxed, allowing his cheek to fall naturally onto the stock. Through dry-fire training, the soldier is encouraged to practice this position until he assumes the same stock weld each time he assumes a given position. This provides consistency in aiming, which is the purpose of obtaining a correct stock weld. Proper eye relief is obtained when a soldier establishes a good stock weld. There is normally a small change in eye relief each time he assumes a different firing position. Soldiers should begin by trying to touch his nose close to the charging handle when assuming a firing position.

Support. If artificial support (sandbags, logs, stumps) is available, it should be used to steady the position and to support the rifle. If it is not available, then the bones, not the muscles, in the firer's upper body must support the rifle.

Muscle relaxation. If support is properly used, the soldier should be able to relax most of his muscles. Using artificial support or bones in the upper body as support allows him to relax and settle into position. Using muscles to support the rifle can cause it to move.

Natural point of aim. When the soldier first assumes his firing position, he orients his rifle in the general direction of his target. Then he adjusts his body to bring the rifle and sights exactly in line with the desired aiming point. When using proper support and consistent stock weld, the soldier should have his rifle and sights aligned naturally on the target. When this correct body-rifle-target alignment is achieved, the front sight post must be held on target, using muscular support and effort. As the rifle fires, the muscles tend to relax, causing the front sight to move away from the target toward the natural point of aim. Adjusting this point to the desired point of aim eliminates this movement. When multiple target exposures are expected (or a sector of fire must be covered), the soldier should adjust his natural point of aim to the center of the expected target exposure area (or center of sector).

Aiming. Focusing on the front sight post is a vital skill the firer must acquire during practice. Having mastered the task of holding the rifle steady, the soldier must align the rifle with the target in exactly the same way for each firing. The firer is the final judge as to where his eye is focused. The instructor/trainer emphasizes this point by having the firer focus on the target and then focus back on the front sight post. He checks the position of the firing eye to ensure it is in line with the rear sight aperture. He uses the M16 sighting device to see what the firer sees through the sights. (See Appendix C.)

Rifle sight alignment. Alignment of the rifle with the target is critical. It involves placing the tip of the front sight post in the center of the rear sight aperture. (Figure 3-4.) Any alignment error between the front and rear sights repeats itself for every 1/2 meter the bullet travels. For example, at the 25-meter line, any error in rifle alignment is multiplied 50 times. If the rifle is misaligned by 1/10 inch, it causes a target at 300 meters to be missed by 5 feet.

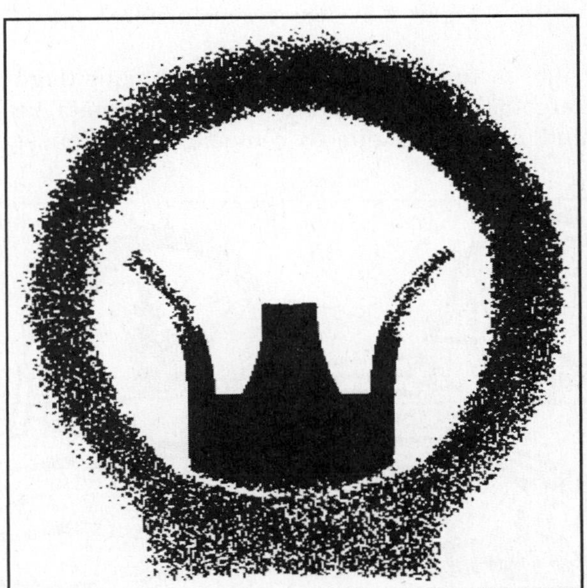

Figure 3-4: Correct sight alignment.

Focus of the eye. A proper firing position places the eye directly on line with the center of the rear sight. When the eye is focused on the front sight post, the natural ability of the eye to center objects in a circle and to seek the point of greatest light (center of the aperture) aid in providing correct sight alignment. For the average soldier firing at combat-type targets, the natural ability of the eye can accurately align the sights. Therefore, the firer can place the tip of the front sight post on the aiming point, but the eye must be focused on the tip of the front sight post. This causes the target to appear blurry, while the front sight post is seen clearly. Two reasons for focusing on the tip of the front sight post are:

- Only a minor aiming error should occur since the error reflects only as much as the soldier fails to determine the target center. A greater aiming error can result if the front sight post is blurry due to focusing on the target or other objects.
- Focusing on the tip of the front sight post aids the firer in maintaining proper sight alignment (Figure 3-4).

Sight picture. Once the soldier can correctly align his sights, he can obtain a sight picture. A correct sight picture has the target, front sight post, and rear sight aligned. The sight picture includes two basic elements: sight alignment and placement of the aiming point.

Placement of the aiming point varies, depending on the engagement range. For example, Figure 3-5 shows a silhouette at 250 meters—the aiming point is the center of mass, and the sights are in perfect alignment; this is a correct sight picture.

Figure 3-5: Correct sight picture.

A technique to obtain a good sight picture is the side aiming technique (Figure 3-6). It involves positioning the front sight post to the side of the target in line with the vertical center of mass, keeping the sights aligned. The front sight post is moved horizontally until the target is directly centered on the front sight post.

Figure 3-6: Side aiming technique.

Front sight. The front sight post is vital to proper firing and should be replaced when damaged. Two techniques that can be used are the carbide lamp and the burning plastic spoon. The post should be blackened anytime it is shiny since precise focusing on the tip of the front sight post cannot be done otherwise.

Aiming practice. Aiming practice is conducted before firing live rounds. During day firing, the soldier should practice sight alignment and placement of the aiming point. This can be done by using training aids such as the M15A1 aiming card and the Riddle sighting device.

Breath Control. As the firer's skills improve and as timed or multiple targets are presented, he must learn to hold his breath at any part of the breathing cycle. Two types of breath control techniques are practiced during dry fire.

- The first is the technique used during zeroing (and when time is available to fire a shot) (Figure 3-7A. There is a moment of natural respiratory pause while breathing when most of the air has been exhaled from the lungs and before inhaling. Breathing should stop after most of the air has been exhaled during the normal breathing cycle. The shot must be fired before the soldier feels any discomfort.
- The second breath control technique is employed during rapid fire (short-exposure targets) (Figure 3-7B). Using this technique, the soldier holds his breath when he is about to squeeze the trigger.

The coach/trainer ensures that the firer uses two breathing techniques and understands them by instructing him to exaggerate his breathing. Also, the firer must be aware of the rifle's movement (while sighted on a target) as a result of breathing.

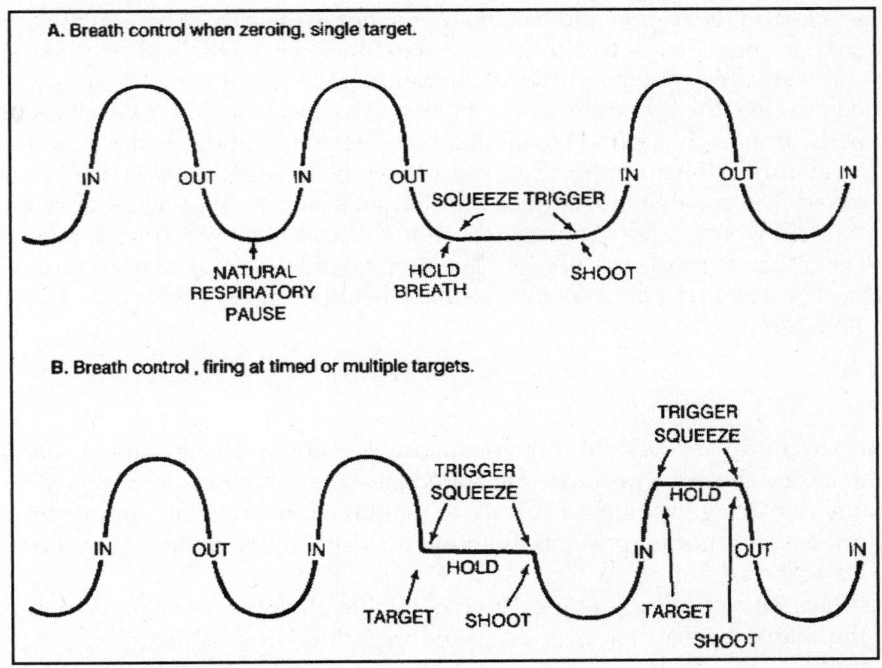

Figure 3-7: Breath control.

Trigger Squeeze. A novice firer can learn to place the rifle in a steady position and to correctly aim at the target if he follows basic principles. If the trigger is not properly squeezed, the rifle is misaligned with the target at the moment of firing.

Rifle movement. Trigger squeeze is important for two reasons:

- First, any sudden movement of the finger on the trigger can disturb the lay of the rifle and cause the shot to miss the target.
- Second, the precise instant of firing should be a surprise to the soldier.

The soldier's natural reflex to compensate for the noise and slight punch in the shoulder can cause him to miss the target if he knows the exact instant the rifle will fire. The soldier usually tenses his shoulders when expecting the rifle to fire, but it is difficult to detect since he does not realize he is flinching. When the hammer drops on a dummy round and does not fire, the soldier's natural reflexes demonstrate that he is improperly squeezing the trigger.

> ✍ **NOTE**
> See Appendix C for the Weaponeer and ball-and-dummy exercise. They are good training devices in detecting improper trigger squeeze.

Trigger finger. The trigger finger (index finger on the firing hand) is placed on the trigger between the first joint and the tip of the finger (not the extreme end) and is adjusted depending on hand size, grip, and so on. The trigger finger must squeeze the trigger to the rear so that the hammer falls without disturbing the lay of the rifle. When a live round is fired, it is difficult to see what affect trigger pull had on the lay of the rifle. Therefore, it is important to experiment with many finger positions during dry-fire training to ensure the hammer is falling with little disturbance to the aiming process.

As the firer's skills increase with practice, he needs less time to spend on trigger squeeze. Novice firers can take five seconds to perform an adequate trigger squeeze, but, as skills improve, he can squeeze the trigger in a second or less. The proper trigger squeeze should start with slight pressure on the trigger during the initial aiming process. The firer applies more pressure after the front sight post is steady on the target and he is holding his breath.

The coach/trainer observes the trigger squeeze, emphasizes the correct procedure, and checks the firer's applied pressure. He places his finger on the trigger and has the firer squeeze the trigger by applying pressure to the coach/trainer's finger. The coach/trainer ensures that the firer squeezes straight to the rear on the trigger avoiding a left or right twisting movement. A steady position reduces disturbance of the rifle during trigger squeeze.

From an unsupported position, the firer experiences a greater wobble area than from a supported position. Wobble area is the movement of the front sight around the aiming point when the rifle is in the steadiest position. If the front sight strays from the target during the firing process, pressure on the trigger should be held constant and resumed as soon as sighting is corrected. The position must provide for the smallest possible wobble area. From a supported position, there should be minimal wobble area and little reason to detect movement. If movement of the rifle causes the front sight to leave the target, more practice is needed. The firer should never try to quickly squeeze the trigger while the sight is on the target. The best firing performance results when the trigger is squeezed continuously, and the rifle is fired without disturbing its lay.

FIRING POSITIONS

All firing positions are taught during basic rifle marksmanship training. During initial fundamental training, the basic firing positions are used. The other positions are added later in training to support tactical conditions.

Basic Firing Positions. Two firing positions are used during initial fundamental training: the individual supported fighting position and prone unsupported position. Both offer a stable platform for firing the rifle. They are also the positions used during basic record fire.

Supported fighting position. This position provides the most stable platform for engaging targets (Figure 3-8). Upon entering the position, the soldier adds or removes dirt, sandbags, or other supports to adjust for his height. He then faces the target, executes a half-face to his firing side, and leans forward until his chest is against the firing-hand corner of the position. He places the rifle handguard in a V formed by the thumb and fingers of his nonfiring hand, and rests the nonfiring hand on the material (sandbags or berm) to the front of the position. The soldier places the stock butt in the pocket of his firing shoulder and rests his firing elbow on the ground outside the position. (When prepared positions are not available, the prone supported position can be substituted.)

Once the supported fighting position has been mastered, the firer should practice various unsupported positions to obtain the smallest possible wobble area during final aiming and hammer fall. The coach/trainer can check the steadiness of the position by observing movement at the forward part of the rifle, by looking through the M16 sighting device, or by checking to see that support is being used.

Figure 3-8: Supported fighting position.

> ✍ NOTE
> The objective is to establish a steady position under various conditions. The ultimate performance of this task is in a combat environment. Although the firer must be positioned high enough to observe all targets, he must remain as low as possible to provide added protection from enemy fire.

Prone unsupported position. This firing position (Figure 3-9) offers another stable firing platform for engaging targets. To assume this position, the soldier faces his target, spreads his feet a comfortable distance apart, and drops to his knees. Using the butt of the rifle as a pivot, the firer rolls onto his nonfiring side, placing the nonfiring elbow close to the side of the magazine. He places the rifle butt in the pocket formed by the firing shoulder, grasps the pistol grip with his firing hand, and lowers the firing elbow to the ground. The rifle rests in the V formed by the thumb and fingers of the nonfiring hand. The soldier adjusts the position of his firing elbow until his shoulders are about level, and pulls back firmly on the rifle with both hands. To complete the position, he obtains a stock weld and relaxes, keeping his heels close to the ground.

Advanced Positions. After mastering the four marksmanship fundamentals in the two basic firing positions, the soldier is taught the advanced positions. He is trained to assume different positions to adapt to the combat situation.

Figure 3-9: Prone unsupported position.

Alternate prone position (Figure 3-10). This position is an alternative to both prone supported and unsupported fighting positions, allowing the firer to cock his firing leg. The firer can assume a comfortable position while maintaining the same relationship between his body and the axis of the rifle. This position relaxes the stomach muscles and allows the firer to breathe naturally.

Figure 3-10: Alternate prone position.

Kneeling supported position (Figure 3-11). This position allows the soldier to obtain the height necessary to better observe many target areas, taking advantage of available cover. Solid cover that can support any part of the body or rifle assists in firing accuracy.

Figure 3-11: Kneeling supported position.

Kneeling unsupported position (Figure 3-12). This position is assumed quickly, places the soldier high enough to see over small brush, and provides for a stable firing position. The nonfiring elbow should be pushed forward of the knee so that the upper arm is resting on a flat portion of the knee to provide stability. The trailing foot can be placed in a comfortable position.

Figure 3-12: Kneeling unsupported position.

Standing position (Figure 3-13). To assume the standing position, the soldier faces his target, executes a facing movement to his firing side, and spreads his feet a comfortable distance apart. With his firing hand on the pistol grip and his nonfiring hand on either the upper handguard or the bottom of the magazine, the soldier places the butt of the rifle in the pocket formed by his firing shoulder so that the sights are level with his eyes. The weight of the rifle is supported by the firing shoulder pocket and nonfiring hand. The soldier shifts his feet until he is aiming naturally at the target and his weight is evenly distributed on both feet. The standing position provides the least stability but could be needed for observing the target area since it can be assumed quickly while moving. Support for any portion of the body or rifle improves stability. More stability can be obtained by adjusting the ammunition pouch to support the nonfiring elbow, allowing the rifle magazine to rest in the nonfiring hand.

Modified Firing Positions. Once the basic firing skills have been mastered during initial training, the soldier should be encouraged to modify positions, to take advantage of available cover, to use anything that helps to steady the rifle, or to make any change that allows him to hit more combat targets. The position shown in Figure 3-14 uses sandbags to support the handguard and frees the nonfiring hand to be used on any part of the rifle to hold it steady.

Figure 3-13: Standing position.

Figure 3-14: Modified firing position.

> ✍ **NOTE**
> Modified positions can result in small zero changes due to shifting pressure and grip on the rifle.

MOUT Firing Positions. Although the same principles of rifle marksmanship apply, the selection and use of firing positions during MOUT requires some special considerations. Firing from around corners could require the soldier to fire from the opposite shoulder to avoid exposing himself to enemy fire.

The requirement for long-range observation can dictate that positions be occupied that are high above ground. Figure 3-15 shows a soldier firing over rooftops, exposing only the parts of his body necessary to engage a target. Figure 3-16 shows a soldier firing around obstacles. Figure 3-17 highlights the need to stay in the shadows while firing from windows, and the requirements for cover and rifle support.

Figure 3-15: Firing over rooftops.

Figure 3-16: Firing around obstacles.

Figure 3-17: Firing from windows.

SECTION III. DRY-FIRE

Dry-fire exercises are conducted as they relate to each of the fundamentals of rifle marksmanship. The standard 25-meter zero targets (Figures 3-18 and 3-19) are mounted as illustrated, because they provide the consistent aiming point the soldier must use throughout preparatory marksmanship training.

CONDUCT OF DRY-FIRE TRAINING

A skilled instructor/trainer should supervise soldiers on dry-fire training. Once an explanation and demonstration are provided, soldiers should be allowed to work at their own pace, receiving assistance as needed. The peer coach-and-pupil technique can be effectively used during dry-fire training with the coach observing performance and offering suggestions. Several training aids are available to correctly conduct initial dry-fire training of the four fundamentals.

A supported firing position should be used to begin dry-fire training. Sandbags and chest-high support are used to effectively teach this position. While any targets at any range can be used, the primary aim point should be a standard silhouette zeroing target placed at a distance of 25 meters from the firing position. The other scaled-silhouette targets—slow fire and timed fire—are also excellent for advanced dry-fire training.

After the soldier understands and has practiced the four fundamentals, he proceeds to integrated dry-fire exercises. The objective of integrated dry-fire is to master the four fundamentals of marksmanship in a complete firing environment. With proper dry-fire training, a soldier can assume a good, comfortable, steady firing position when he moves to the firing line. He must understand the aiming process, breath control is second nature, and correct trigger squeeze has been practiced many times. Also, by adding dummy ammunition to the soldier's magazine, other skills can be integrated into the dry-fire exercise to include practicing loading and unloading, reinforcing immediate-action drills, and using the dime (washer) exercise.

When correctly integrated, dry-fire is an effective procedure to use before firing live bullets for grouping and zeroing, scaled silhouettes, field firing, or practice record fire. It can be used for remedial training or opportunity training, or as a primary training technique to maintain marksmanship proficiency.

PEER COACHING

Peer coaching is using two soldiers of equal firing proficiency and experience to assist (coach) each other during marksmanship training. Some problems exist with peer coaching. If the new soldier does not have adequate guidance, a "blind-leading-the-blind" situation results, which can lead to negative training and safety violations. However, when adequate instruction is provided, peer coaching can be helpful even in the IET environment. Since all soldiers in units have completed BRM, peer coaching should yield better results.

Benefits. The pairing of soldiers can enhance learning for both of them. The coach learns what to look for and what to check as he provides guidance to the firer. Communication between peers is different than communication between a firer and drill sergeant or senior NCO. Peers have the chance to ask simple questions and to discuss areas that are not understood. Pairing soldiers who have demonstrated good firing proficiency with those who have firing problems can improve the performance of problem firers.

Duties. The peer coach assists the firer in obtaining a good position and in adjusting sandbags. He watches the firer—**not the target**—to see that the firer maintains a proper, relaxed, steady position; that he holds his breath before the final trigger squeeze; that he applies initial pressure to the trigger; and that no noticeable trigger jerk, flinch, eye blink, or other reaction can be observed in anticipating the rifle firing. The peer coach can use an M16 sighting device, allowing him to see what the firer sees through the sights.

The peer coach can load magazines, providing a chance to use ball and dummy. At other times, he could be required to observe the target area—for example, when field-fire targets are being engaged and the firer cannot see where he is missing targets. The peer coach can add to range safety procedures by helping safety personnel with preliminary rifle checks.

> ✍ **NOTE**
> When a peer coach is used during M16A1 live-fire exercises, a brass deflector should be attached to the rifle and eye protection should be worn.

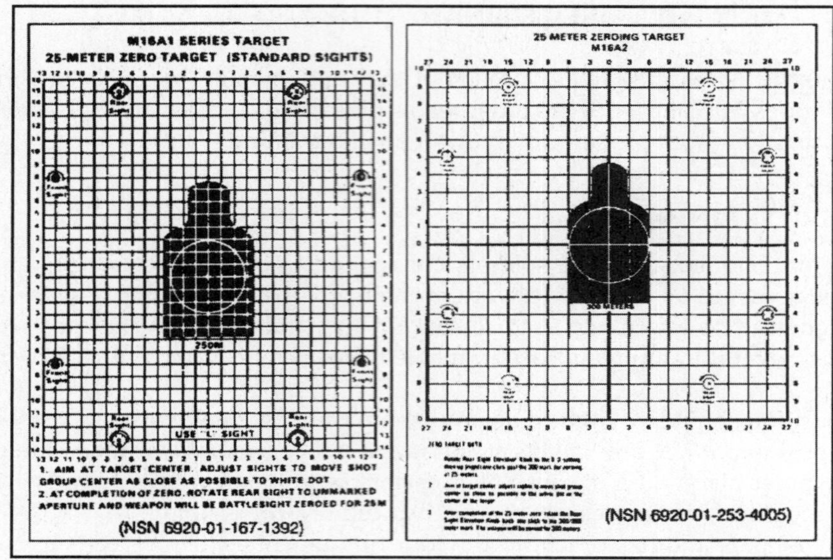

Figure 3-18: The M16A1 and M16A2 zero targets.

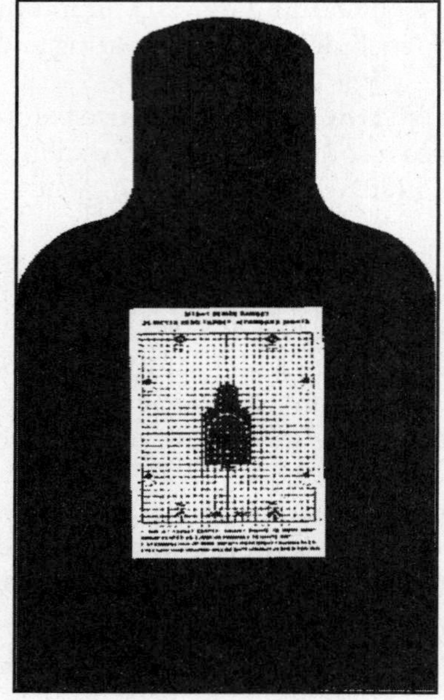

Figure 3-19: Zero target placed in the center of an E-type silhouette.

CHECKLIST FOR THE COACH

The procedures to determine and eliminate rifle and firer deficiencies follows.

The coach checks to see that the—

- Rifle is cleared and defective parts have been replaced.
- Ammunition is clean, and the magazine is properly placed in the pouch.
- Sights are blackened and set correctly for long/short range.

The coach observes the firer to see that he—

- Uses the correct position and properly applies the steady-position elements.
- Properly loads the rifle.

- Obtains the correct sight alignment (with the aid of an M16 sighting device).
- Holds his breath correctly (by watching his back at times).
- Applies proper trigger squeeze; determines whether he flinches or jerks by watching his head, shoulders, trigger finger, and firing hand and arm.
- Is tense and nervous. If the firer is nervous, the coach has the firer breathe deeply several times to relax.

Supervisory personnel and peer coaches correct errors as they are detected. If many common errors are observed, it is appropriate to call the group together for more discussion and demonstration of proper procedures and to provide feedback.

POSITION OF THE COACH

The coach constantly checks and assists the firer in applying marksmanship fundamentals during firing. He observes the firer's position and his application of the steady position elements. The coach is valuable in checking factors the firer is unable to observe for himself and in preventing the firer from repeating errors.

During an exercise, the coach should be positioned where he can best observe the firer when he assumes position. He then moves to various points around the firer (sides and rear) to check the correctness of the firer's position. The coach requires the firer to make adjustments until the firer obtains a correct position.

When the coach is satisfied with the firing position, he assumes a coaching position alongside the firer. The coach usually assumes a position like that of the firer (Figure 3-20), which is on the firing side of the soldier.

Figure 3-20: Prone position of coach (right-handed firer).

GROUPING

Shot grouping is a form of practice firing with two primary objectives: firing tight shot groups and consistently placing those groups in the same location. Shot grouping should be conducted between dry-fire training and zeroing. The initial live-fire training should be a grouping exercise with the purpose of practicing and refining marksmanship fundamentals. Since this is not a zeroing exercise, few sight changes are made. Grouping exercises can be conducted on a live-fire range that provides precise location of bullet hits and misses such as a 25-meter zeroing range or KD range.

CONCEPT OF ZEROING

The purpose of battlesight zeroing is to align the **fire control system** (sights) with the rifle barrel, considering the given ammunition ballistics. When this is accomplished **correctly**, the fire control and point of aim are point of impact at a **standard battlesight zero range** such as 250 (300) meters.

When a rifle is zeroed, the sights are adjusted so that bullet strike is the same as point of aim at some given range. A battlesight zero (250 meters, M16A1; 300 meters, M16A2) is the sight setting that provides the highest hit probability for most combat targets with minimum adjustment to the aiming point.

When standard zeroing procedures are followed, a rifle that is properly zeroed for one soldier is close to the zero for another soldier. When a straight line is drawn from target center to the tip of the front sight post and through the center of the rear aperture, it makes little difference whose eye is looking along this line. There are many subtle factors that result in differences among individual zeros; however, the similarity of individual zeros should be emphasized instead of the differences.

Most firers can fire with the same zeroed rifle if they are properly applying marksmanship fundamentals. If a soldier is having difficulty zeroing and the problem cannot be diagnosed, having a good firer zero the rifle could find the problem. When a soldier must fire another soldier's rifle without opportunity to verify the zero by firing—for example, picking up another man's rifle on the battlefield—it is closer to actual zero if the rifle sights are left unchanged. This information is useful in deciding initial sight settings and recording of zeros. All rifles in the arms room, even those not assigned, should have their sights aligned (zeroed) for battlesight zero.

There is no relationship between the specific sight setting a soldier uses on one rifle (his zero) to the sight setting he needs on another rifle. For example, a soldier could be required to move the rear sight of his assigned rifle 10 clicks left of center for zero, and the next rifle he is assigned could be adjusted 10 clicks right of center for zero. This is due to the inherent variability from rifle to rifle, which makes it essential that each soldier is assigned a permanent rifle on which all marksmanship training is conducted. Therefore, all newly assigned personnel should be required to fire their rifle for zero as soon as possible after assignment to the unit. The same rule must apply anytime a soldier is assigned a new rifle, a rifle is returned from DS or GS maintenance, or the zero is in question.

M16A1 STANDARD SIGHTS AND ZEROING

To battlesight zero the rifle, the soldier must understand sight adjustment procedures. The best possible zero is obtained by zeroing at actual range. Because facilities normally do not exist for zeroing at 250 meters, most zeroing is conducted at 25 meters. By pushing the rear sight forward so the L is exposed, the bullet crosses line of sight at 25 meters, reaches a maximum height above line of sight of about 11 inches at 225 meters, and crosses line of sight again at 375 meters (Figure 3-21).

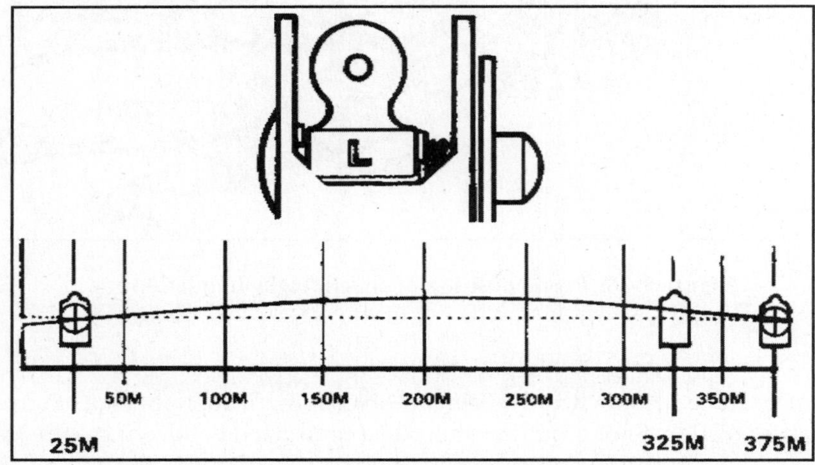

Figure 3-21: M16A1 zero trajectory.

To gain the many benefits associated with having bullets hit exactly where the rifle is aimed during 25-meter firing, the long-range sight is used on the zero range. Therefore, when bullets are adjusted to hit the same place the rifle is aimed at 25 meters, the bullet also hits where the rifle is aimed at 375 meters. After making this adjustment and flipping back to the short-range sight and aiming center of mass at a 42-meter target, the bullet crosses the line of sight at 42 meters and again at 250 meters as shown in Figure 3-22.

Most combat targets are expected to be engaged in the ranges from 0 to 300 meters; therefore, the 250-meter battlesight zero is the setting that remains on the rifle. At 25 meters, the bullet is about 1 inch below line of sight, crossing line of sight at 42 meters. It reaches its highest point above the line of sight (about 5 inches) at a range of about 175 meters, crosses line of sight again at 250 meters, and is about 7 inches below line of sight at 300 meters. Targets

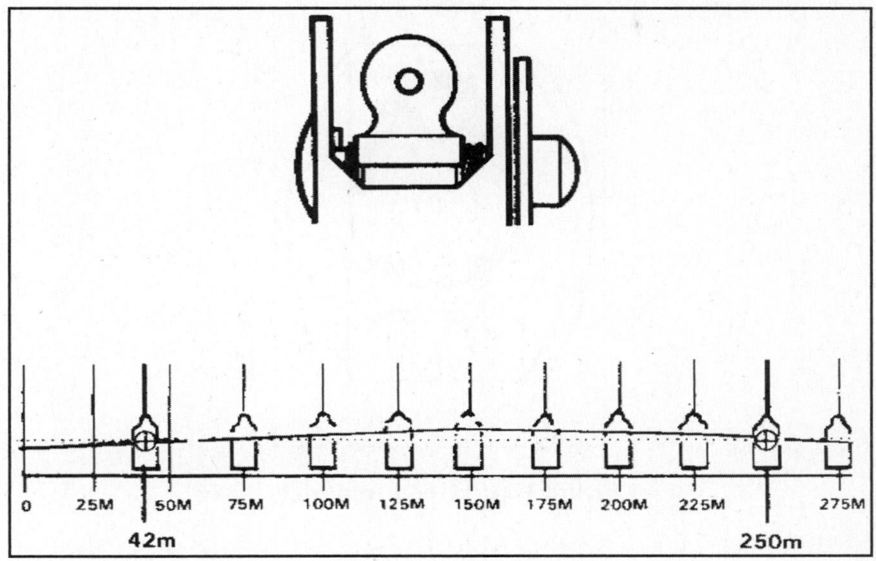

Figure 3-22: M16A1 250-meter trajectory.

can be hit out to a range of 300 meters with no adjustments to point of aim. (A somewhat higher hit probability results with minor adjustments to the aiming point.)

Sights. The sights are adjustable for both elevation and windage. Windage adjustments are made on the rear sight; elevation adjustments on the front sight.

Rear sight. The rear sight consists of two apertures and a windage drum with a spring-loaded detent (Figure 3-23). The aperture marked L is used for ranges beyond 300 meters, and the unmarked or short-range aperture is used for ranges up to 300 meters. Adjustments for windage are made by pressing in on the spring-loaded detent with a sharp instrument (or the tip of a cartridge) and rotating the windage drum in the desired direction of change (right or left) in the strike of the bullet.

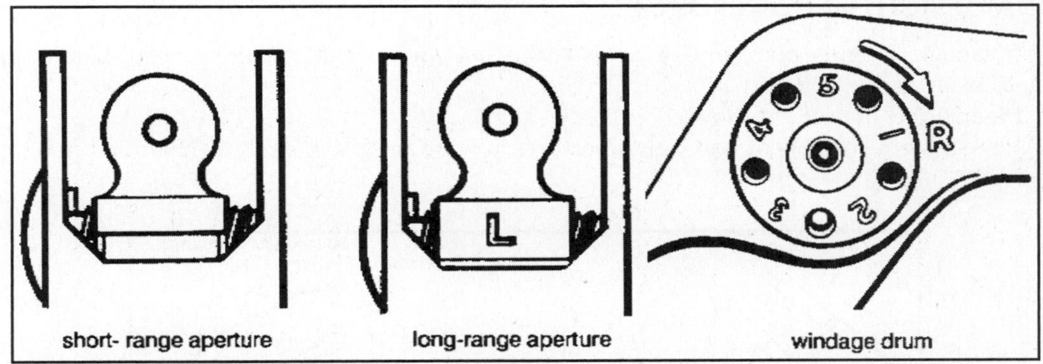

Figure 3-23: M16A1 rear sight apertures and windage drum.

Front sight. The front sight consists of a round rotating sight post with a five-position, spring-loaded detent (Figure 3-24). Adjustments are made by using a sharp instrument (or the tip of a cartridge). To move the front sight post, the spring-loaded detent is depressed, and the post is rotated in the desired direction of change (up or down) in the strike of the bullet.

Sight Changes. To make sight changes, the firer first locates the center of his three-round shot group and then determines the distance between it and the desired location. An error in elevation is measured vertically, while a windage error is measured horizontally. When using standard zero targets or downrange feedback targets, sight adjustment guidance on the target is provided. (See Appendix F for the elevation and windage rule.)

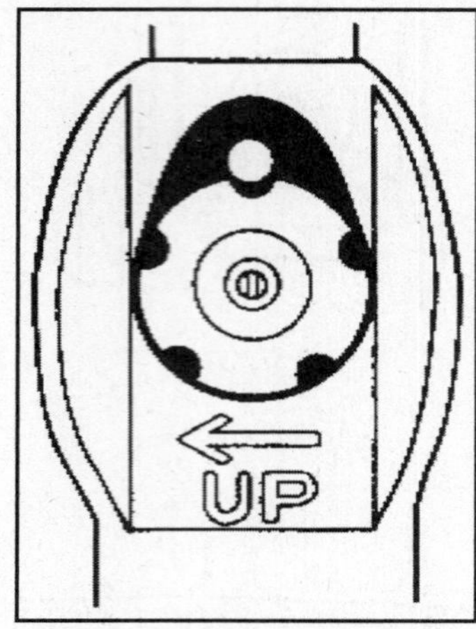

Figure 3-24: M16A1 front sight.

To raise the strike of the bullet, the firer rotates the front sight post the desired number of clicks clockwise (in the direction of the arrow marked UP in Figure 3-24). Thus, the strike of the bullet is raised but the post is lowered. He reverses the direction of rotation to move the strike of the bullet down.

To move the strike of the bullet to the right, the windage drum is rotated the desired number of clicks clockwise (in the direction of the arrow marked R, Figure 3-23). The firer reverses the direction of rotation to move the strike of the bullet to the left.

> ✍ **NOTE**
> Before making any sight changes, the firer should make a serviceability check of the sights, looking for any bent, broken, or loose parts. The firer must also be able to consistently fire 4-cm shot groups.

M16A2 STANDARD SIGHTS AND ZEROING

When the soldier can consistently place three rounds within a 4-cm circle at 25 meters, regardless of group location, he is ready to zero his rifle.

The front and rear sights are set as follows:

Rear sight. The rear sight consists of two sight apertures, a windage knob, and an elevation knob (Figure 3-25).

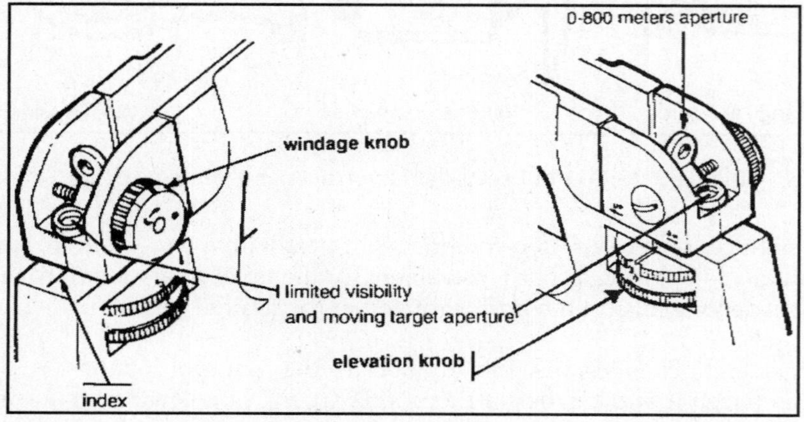

Figure 3-25: M16A2 rear sight.

The larger aperture, marked 0–2, is used for moving target engagement and during limited visibility. The unmarked aperture is used for normal firing situations, zeroing, and with the elevation knob for target distances up to 800 meters. The unmarked aperture is used to establish the battlesight zero.

After the elevation knob is set, adjustments for elevation are made by moving the front sight post up or down to complete zeroing the rifle. Adjustments for windage are made by turning the windage knob.

The rear windage knob start point is when the index mark on the 0–2 sight is aligned with the rear sight base index (Figure 3-26).

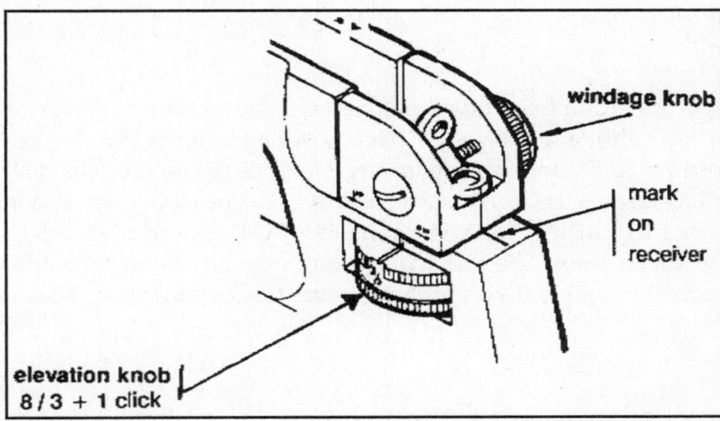

Figure 3-26: Initial rear sight adjustment.

Front sight. The front sight is adjusted the same as the front sight of the M16A1. It consists of a square, rotating sight post with a four-position, spring-loaded detent (Figure 3-27). Adjustments are made by using a sharp instrument or the tip of a cartridge. To raise or lower the front sight post, the spring-loaded detent is depressed, and the post is rotated in the desired direction of change (Figure 3-28).

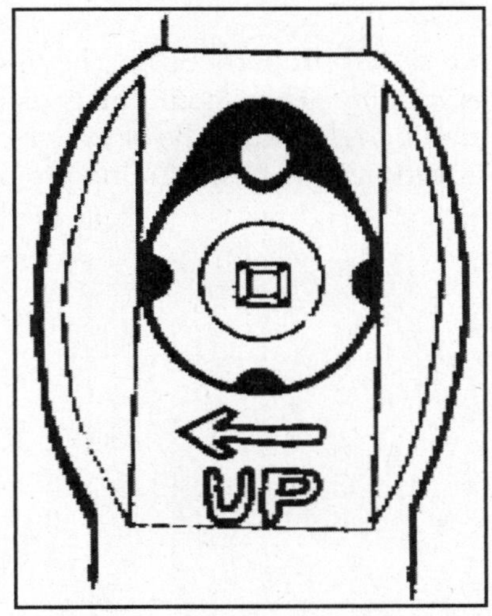

Figure 3-27: M16A2 four detent front sight.

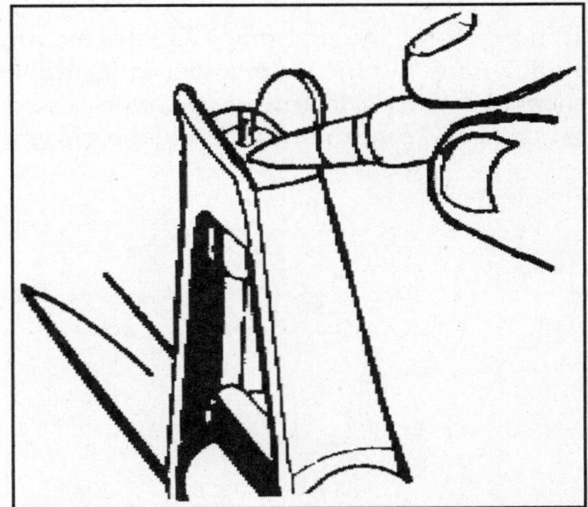

Figure 3-28: Front sight adjustment.

DOWNRANGE FEEDBACK TRAINING

The term downrange feedback describes any training method that provides precise knowledge of bullet strike (exactly where bullets hit or miss the intended target) at ranges beyond 25 meters. The soldier gains confidence in his firing abilities by knowing what happens to bullets at range. The inclusion of downrange feedback during the initial learning process and during refresher training improves the soldier's firing proficiency and record fire scores. Downrange feedback can be incorporated into any part of a unit's marksmanship program. However, an ideal sequence is to conduct downrange feedback following 25-meter firing and before firing on the field fire range.

The use of a KD firing range is an excellent way of providing downrange feedback. Also a good way to obtain downrange feedback is to modify existing field fire ranges by constructing target-holding frames, which requires the soldier to walk from the firing line to the target to locate bullet strike.

Units can design their own downrange feedback training to accommodate available facilities. Any silhouette target with a backing large enough to catch all bullet misses can be set up at any range. For example, it would be ideal if the confirmation of weapon zero could be conducted at the actual zero range of 250 meters/300 meters.

FIELD FIRE TRAINING

Field fire training provides the transition from unstressed slow firing at known-distance/feedback targets to engaging fleeting combat-type pop-up silhouettes. Two basic types of field firing exercises are single-target and multiple-target engagements, which use 75-, 175-, and 300-meter targets. Once the soldier has developed the unstressed firing skills necessary to hit single KD targets, he must learn to detect and quickly engage combat-type targets at various ranges. Time standards are provided during this instruction to add stress and to simulate the short exposure times of combat targets. The soldier must, therefore, detect, acquire, and engage the target before the exposure ends. During field fire training, the firer learns to quickly detect and apply the fundamentals at the same time.

PRACTICE RECORD FIRE

Practice record fire is a training exercise designed to progressively develop and refine the soldiers combat firing skills. During this exercise, the soldier is exposed to a more difficult course of fire with increased time stress to include single and multiple target engagements at six distances ranging from 50 to 300 meters. This exercise also provides the opportunity to practice and demonstrate skills learned during target detection. To perform well, a soldier must integrate all the tasks learned from previous training. When firing exercises are properly organized, conducted, and critiqued, the soldier gains knowledge and confidence in his firing performance. Through close observation, coaching, and critiquing, instructors/trainers can base remedial training on specific needs.

RECORD FIRE

Qualification ratings and first-time GO rates are important during record fire, if properly used. They provide goals for the soldier and aid the commander in identifying the quality of his training. This should be considered in the assignment of priorities, instructor personnel, and obtaining valuable training resources. The objective of record firing is to access and confirm the individual proficiency of firers and the effectiveness of the training program.

CHAPTER 4

Combat Fire Techniques

The test of a soldier's training is applying the fundamentals of marksmanship and firing skills in combat. The marksmanship skills mastered during training, practice, and record fire exercises must be applied to many combat situations (attack, assault, ambush, MOUT). Although these situations present problems, only two modifications of the basic techniques and fundamentals are necessary (see Chapter 3): changes to the rate of fire and alterations in weapon/target alignment. The necessary changes are significant and must be thoroughly taught and practiced before discussing live-fire exercises.

> ✍ **NOTE**
>
> For tactical applications of fire see FM 7–8.

SECTION I. SUPPRESSIVE FIRE

In many tactical situations, combat rifle fire will be directed to suppress enemy personnel or weapons positions. Rifle fire, which is precisely aimed at a definite point or area target, is suppressive fire. Some situations may require a soldier to place suppressive fire into a wide area such as a wood line, hedgerow, or small building. While at other times, the target may be a bunker or window. Suppressive fire is used to control the enemy and the area he occupies. Suppressive fire is employed to kill the enemy or to prevent him from observing the battlefield or effectively using his weapons. When a sustained volume of accurate suppressive fire is placed on enemy locations to contain him, it can be effective even though he cannot be seen. When the enemy is effectively pinned down behind cover, this reduces his ability to deliver fire and allows friendly forces to move.

NATURE OF THE TARGET

Many soldiers have difficulty delivering effective suppressive fire when they cannot see a definite target. They must fire at likely locations or in a general area where the enemy is known to exist. Even though definite targets cannot be seen, most suppressive fire should be well aimed. Figure 4-1, page 4–2, shows a landscape target suitable for suppressive fire training. When this type target is used, trainers must develop a firing program to include areas of engagement and designated target areas that will be credited as sustained effective suppressive fire. At 25 meters, this target provides the firer with an area to suppress without definite targets to engage.

POINT OF AIM

Suppressive fire should be well-aimed, sustained, semiautomatic fire. Although lacking a definite target, the soldier must be taught to control and accurately deliver fire within the limits of the suppressed area. The sights are used as when engaging a point-type target—with the front sight post placed so that each shot impacts within the desired area (window, firing portal, tree line).

RATE OF FIRE

During most phases of live fire (grouping, zeroing, qualifying), shots are delivered using the slow semiautomatic rate of fire (one round every 3 to 10 seconds). During training, this allows for a slow and precise application of the fundamentals. Successful suppressive fire requires that a faster but sustained rate of fire be used. Sometimes firing full automatic bursts (13 rounds per second) for a few seconds may be necessary to gain initial fire superiority. Rapid

Figure 4-1: Landscape target.

semiautomatic fire (one round every one or two seconds) allows the firer to sustain a large volume of accurate fire while conserving ammunition. The tactical situation dictates the most useful rate of fire, but the following must be considered:

Applying Fundamentals. As the stress of combat increases, some soldiers may fail to apply the fundamentals of marksmanship. This factor contributes to soldiers firing less accurately and without obtaining the intended results. While some modifications are appropriate, the basic fundamentals should be applied and emphasized regardless of the rate of fire or combat stress.

Making Rapid Magazine Changes. One of the keys to sustained suppressive fire is rapidly reloading the rifle. Rapid magazine changes must be correctly taught and practiced during dry-fire and live-fire exercises until the soldier becomes proficient. Small-unit training exercises must be conducted so that soldiers who are providing suppressive fire practice magazine changes that are staggered. Firing is, therefore, controlled and coordinated so that a continuous volume of accurate suppressive fire is delivered to the target area.

Conserving Ammunition. Soldiers must be taught to make each round count. Automatic fire should be used sparingly and only to gain initial fire superiority. Depending on the tactical situation, the rate of fire should be adjusted so that a minimum number of rounds are expended. Accurate fire conserves ammunition, while preventing the enemy from placing effective fire on friendly positions.

SECTION II. RAPID SEMIAUTOMATIC FIRE

Rapid semiautomatic fire delivers a large volume of accurate fire into a target or target area. Increases in speed and volume should be sought only after the soldier has demonstrated expertise and accuracy during slow semiautomatic fire. The rapid application of the four fundamentals will result in a well-aimed shot every one or two seconds. This technique of fire allows a unit to place the most effective volume of fire in a target area while conserving ammunition. It is the most accurate means of delivering suppressive fire.

EFFECTIVENESS OF RAPID FIRE

When a soldier uses rapid semiautomatic fire, he is sacrificing accuracy to deliver a greater volume of fire. The difference in accuracy between slow and rapid semiautomatic fire diminishes with proper training and repeated practice. Training and practice improve the soldier's marksmanship skills to the point that accuracy differences become minimal. There is little difference in the volume of effective fire that would be delivered by units using much less accurate automatic fire.

> ✍ **NOTE**
>
> Learning rapid fire techniques also improves the soldier's response time to short-exposure, multiple, and moving targets.

MODIFICATIONS FOR RAPID FIRE

Trainers must consider the impact of the increased rate of fire on the soldier's ability to properly apply the fundamentals of marksmanship and other combat firing skills. These fundamentals/skills include:

Immediate Action. To maintain an increased rate of suppressive fire, immediate action must be applied quickly. The firer must identify the problem and correct the stoppage immediately. Repeated dry-fire practice, using blanks or dummy rounds, followed by live-fire training and evaluation ensures that soldiers can rapidly apply immediate action while other soldiers initiate fire.

Marksmanship Fundamentals. The four fundamentals are used when firing in the rapid semiautomatic mode. The following differences apply:

Steady position. Good support improves accuracy and reduces recovery time between shots, somewhat tighter grip on the handguards assists in recovery time and in rapidly shifting or distributing fire to subsequent targets. When possible, the rifle should pivot at the point where the nonfiring hand meets the support. The soldier should avoid changing the position of the nonfiring hand on the support, because it is awkward and time-consuming when rapidly firing a series of shots.

Aiming. The aiming process does not change during rapid semiautomatic fire. The firer's head remains on the stock, his firing eye is aligned with the rear aperture, and his focus is on the front sight post.

Breath control. Breath control must be modified because the soldier does not have time to take a complete breath between shots. He must hold his breath at some point in the firing process and take shallow breaths between shots.

Trigger squeeze. To maintain the desired rate of fire, the soldier has only a short period to squeeze the trigger (one well-aimed shot every one or two seconds).

The firer must cause the rifle to fire in a period of about one-half of a second or less and still not anticipate the precise instant of firing. Rapid semiautomatic trigger squeeze is difficult to master. It is important that initial trigger pressure be applied as soon as a target is identified and while the front sight post is being brought to the desired point of aim. When the post reaches the point of aim, final pressure must be applied to cause the rifle to fire almost at once. This added pressure, or final trigger squeeze, must be applied without disturbing the lay of the rifle.

Repeated dry-fire training, using the Weaponeer device, and live-fire practice ensure the soldier can squeeze the trigger and maintain a rapid rate of fire consistently and accurately.

> ✍ **NOTE**
>
> When presented with multiple targets, the soldier may fire the first round, release pressure on the trigger to reset the sear, then reapply more pressure to fire the next shot. This technique eliminates the time used in releasing all the trigger pressure. It allows the firer to rapidly deliver subsequent rounds. Training and practice sessions are required for soldiers to become proficient in the technique of rapid trigger squeeze.

Magazine Changes. Rapid magazine changes are an integral part of sustaining rapid semiautomatic suppressive fire. Soldiers must quickly reload their rifles and resume accurate firing.

Magazine handling. Most units establish the soldier's basic load of ammunition and loaded magazines. The number of magazines vary based on the mission and tactical situation. During combat, some magazines are lost, but it is the soldier's responsibility to keep this loss to a minimum. While training a soldier to reload his magazines, the trainer must emphasize the need to account for these magazines.

The sequence for magazine handling during rapid changes is illustrated for right- and left-handed firers in Figure 4-2.

Rifle loading. Removing a magazine from the firing side ammunition pouch is the same for both right- and left-handed firers. Empty magazines must be removed from the rifle before performing the following.

To remove a magazine from the pouch, the magazine is grasped on the long edge with the thumb, and the first and second fingers are placed on the short edge.

The magazine is withdrawn from the ammunition pouch, and the arm is extended forward, rotating the hand and wrist so that the magazine is in position (open end up and long edge to the rear) to load into the rifle. It is loaded into the rifle by inserting the magazine straight up into the magazine well until it is seated. The base of the magazine is tapped with the heel of the hand to ensure the magazine is fully seated.

Removing a magazine from the nonfiring side of the ammunition pouch requires the firer to support the rifle with his firing hand. His nonfiring hand grasps the magazine and loads it into the rifle.

Rapid magazine changing. Training and repeated practice in this procedure improves soldier proficiency. The firer does not move the selector lever to SAFE during a rapid magazine change, but he must maintain a safe posture during the change.

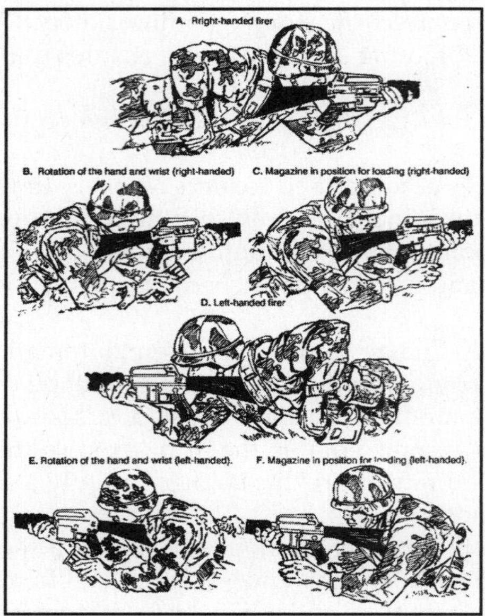

Figure 4-2: Rapid magazine changing.

The following is a step-by-step sequence for rapid magazine changing.

- *Right-handed firer.* Remove the index finger from the trigger and depress the magazine catch button while keeping a secure grip on the rifle with the nonfiring hand (Figure 4-3). Release the pistol grip, grasp and remove the empty magazine with the right (firing) hand, and secure it. Grasp the loaded magazine with the right hand (rounds up and forward). Insert the loaded magazine into the magazine well and tap upward with the palm of the right hand. This ensures that the magazine is fully seated and locked into the rifle. Depress the upper half of the bolt catch with the fingers of the right hand. This allows the bolt to go forward, chambering the first round. If necessary, use the right hand to tap the forward assist to fully chamber the first round. Return the right hand to its original firing position on the pistol grip. Return the index finger to the trigger.
- *Left-handed firer.* Remove the index finger from the trigger and release the pistol grip. Depress the magazine catch button with the index finger of the left (firing) hand. Remove the empty magazine with the left hand and secure it. Grasp the loaded magazine with the left hand (rounds up, bullets forward). Insert the loaded

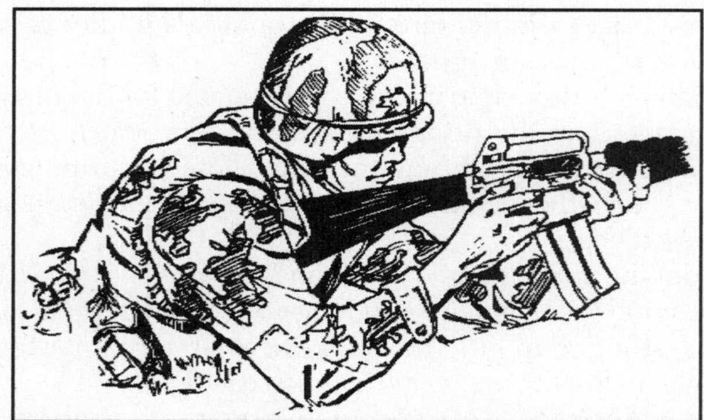

Figure 4-3: Magazine release catch button being depressed (right-handed firer).

magazine into the magazine well and tap upward with the palm of the left hand. This ensures that the magazine is fully seated and locked into the rifle. Depress the upper half of the bolt catch with a finger of the left hand. This allows the bolt to go forward, chambering the first round. If necessary, use the right hand to tap the forward assist to fully chamber the first round. Return the left hand to its original firing position on the pistol grip. Return the index finger to the trigger. The firer must maintain a safe posture during the change.

When loading from the nonfiring side, the previous steps are followed with with this exception: the loaded magazine is secured and inserted into the magazine well with the nonfiring hand. The firing hand supports the rifle at the pistol grip. After the magazine is inserted, the firer should shift the rifle's weight to his nonfiring hand and continue with the recommended sequence.

RAPID-FIRE TRAINING

Soldiers should be well trained in all aspects of slow semiautomatic firing before attempting any rapid-fire training. Those who display a lack of knowledge of the fundamental skills should not advance to rapid semiautomatic training until these skills are learned. Initial training should focus on the modifications to the fundamentals and other basic combat skills necessary during rapid semiautomatic firing.

Dry-Fire Exercises. Repeated dry-fire exercises are the most efficient means available to ensure soldiers can apply modifications to the fundamentals. Multiple dry-fire exercises are needed, emphasizing a rapid shift in position and point of aim, followed by breath control and fast trigger squeeze. Blanks or dummy rounds may be used to train rapid magazine changes and the application of immediate action. The soldier should display knowledge and skill during these dry-fire exercises before attempting live fire.

Live-Fire Exercises. There are two types of live-fire exercises.

Individual. Emphasis is on each soldier maintaining a heavy volume of accurate fire. Weapon down time (during immediate action and rapid magazine changes) is kept to a minimum. Firing should begin at shorter ranges, progressing to longer ranges as soldiers display increased proficiency. Exposure or engagement times are shortened and the number of rounds increased to simulate the need for a heavy volume of fire. Downrange feedback is necessary to determine accuracy of fire.

Unit. Rapid semiautomatic fire should be the primary means of delivering fire during a unit LFX. It is the most accurate technique of placing a large volume of fire on poorly defined targets or target areas. Emphasis should be on staggered rapid magazine changes, maintaining a continuous volume of fire and conserving ammunition.

SECTION III. AUTOMATIC FIRE

Automatic fire delivers the maximum amount of rounds into a target area. It should be trained only after the soldier has demonstrated expertise during slow and rapid semiautomatic fire. Automatic fire involves the rapid application of the four fundamentals while delivering from 3 to 13 rounds per second into a designated area. This technique of fire allows a unit to place the most fire in a target area (when conserving ammunition is not a consideration). It is a specialized technique of delivering suppressive fire and may not apply to most combat engagements. The M16A1 rifle has a full automatic setting. (The M16A2 uses a three-round burst capability.) Soldiers must be taught the advantages and disadvantages of automatic firing so they know when it should be used. Without this knowledge, in a life-threatening situation the soldier will tend to switch to the automatic/burst mode. This fire can be effective in some situations. It is vital for the unit to train and practice the appropriate use of automatic fire.

EFFECTIVENESS OF AUTOMATIC FIRE

Automatic fire is inherently less accurate than semiautomatic fire. The first automatic shot fired may be on target, but recoil and high-cyclic rate of fire often combine to place subsequent rounds far from the desired point of impact. Even controlled (three-round burst) automatic fire may place only one round on the target. Because of these inaccuracies, it is difficult to evaluate the effectiveness of automatic fire, and even more difficult to establish absolute guidelines for its use.

Closely spaced multiple targets, appearing at the same time at 50 meters or closer, may be engaged effectively with automatic/burst fire. More widely spaced targets appearing at greater distances should be engaged with semiautomatic fire.

The M16A1 and M16A2 rifles should normally be employed in the semiautomatic mode. Depending on the tactical situation, the following conditions would be factors against the use of automatic fire:

- Ammunition is in short supply or resupply may be difficult.
- Single targets are being engaged.
- Widely spaced multiple targets are being engaged.
- The distance to the target is beyond 50 meters.
- The effect of bullets on the target cannot be observed.
- Artificial support is not available.
- Targets may be effectively engaged using semiautomatic fire.

In some combat situations, the use of automatic fire can improve survivability and enhance mission accomplishment. Clearing buildings, final assaults, FPF, and ambushes may require the limited use of automatic fire. Depending on the tactical situation, the following conditions may favor the use of automatic fire:

- Enough available ammunition. Problems are not anticipated with resupply.
- Closely spaced multiple targets appear at 50 meters or less.
- Maximum fire is immediately required at an area target.
- Tracers or some other means can be used to observe the effect of bullets on the target.
- Leaders can maintain adequate control over rifles firing on automatic.
- Good artificial support is available.
- The initial sound of gunfire disperses closely spaced targets.

Trainers must ensure soldiers understand the capabilities and limitations of automatic fire. They must know when it should and should not be used.

MODIFICATIONS FOR AUTOMATIC FIRE POSITIONS

Trainers must consider the impact of the greatly increased rate of fire on the soldier's ability to properly apply the fundamentals of marksmanship and other combat firing skills. These fundamentals/skills include:

Immediate Action. To maintain automatic fire, immediate action must be applied quickly. The firer must identify the problem and correct it immediately. Repeated dry-fire practice, using blanks or dummy rounds, followed by live-fire training and evaluation ensures that soldiers can rapidly apply immediate action.

Marksmanship Fundamentals. The four fundamentals are used when firing in the automatic mode. The following differences apply:

Steady position (Figure 4-4). Maximum use of available artificial support is necessary during automatic fire. The rifle should be gripped more firmly and pulled into the shoulder more securely than when firing in the semiautomatic mode. This support and increased grip help to offset the progressive displacement of weapon/target alignment caused by recoil. To provide maximum stability, prone and supported positions are best. One possible modification involves forming a 5-inch loop with the sling at the upper sling swivel, grasping this loop with the nonfiring hand, and pulling down and to the rear while firing. Another modification involves grasping the small of the stock with the nonfiring hand, and applying pressure down and to the rear while firing. If a bipod is not available, sandbags may be used to support the rifle. The nonfiring hand may be positioned on the rifle wherever it provides the most stability and flexibility. The goal is to maintain weapon stability and minimize recoil.

Aiming. The aiming process does not change during automatic fire. The firer's head remains on the stock, his firing eye stays aligned with the rear sight aperture, and his focus is on the front sight post. Although recoil may disrupt this process, the firer must try to apply the aiming techniques throughout recoil.

Breath control. Breath control must be modified because the firer will not have the time to breathe between shots. He must hold his breath for each burst and adapt his breathing cycle, taking breaths between bursts.

Trigger squeeze. Training and repeated dry-fire practice will aid the soldier in applying proper trigger squeeze during automatic firing. Live-fire exercises will enable him to improve this skill.

✍ NOTE

The trigger is not slapped or jerked. It is squeezed and pressure is quickly released.

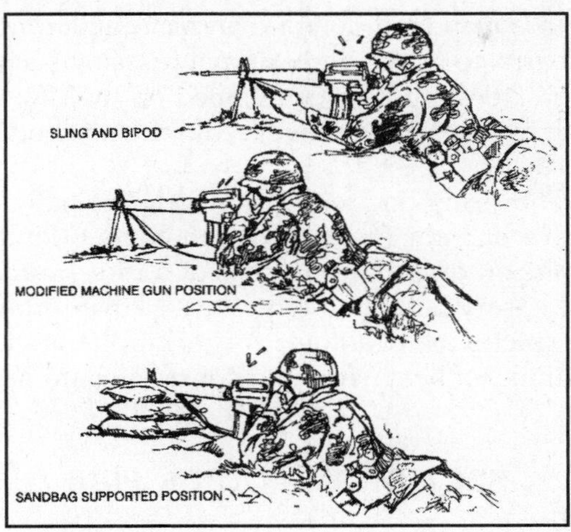

Figure 4-4: Steady positions.

- **M16A1.** Trigger squeeze is applied in the normal manner up to the instant the rifle fires. Because three-round bursts are the most effective rate of fire, pressure on the trigger should be released as soon as possible. The index finger should remain on the trigger, but a quick release of pressure is necessary to prevent an excessive amount of rounds from being fired in one burst. With much dry-fire practice, the soldier can become proficient at delivering three-round bursts with the squeeze / release technique.
- **M16A2.** Trigger squeeze is applied in the normal manner up to the instant the rifle fires. Using the burst-mode, the firer holds the trigger to the rear until three rounds are fired. He then releases pressure on the trigger until it resets, then reapplies pressure for the next three-round burst.

> ✍ **NOTE**
> Depending on the position of the burst cam when the selector is moved to the burst mode, the rifle may fire one, two, or three rounds when the trigger is held to the rear the first time. If the rifle fires only one or two rounds, the firer must quickly release pressure on the trigger and squeeze again, holding it to the rear until a three-round burst is completed.

Magazine Changes. Rapid magazine changes are vital in maintaining automatic fire. (See SECTION II. RAPID SEMIAUTOMATIC FIRE, Magazine Handling, for detailed information on rapid magazine changes.)

TRAINING OF AUTOMATIC FIRE TECHNIQUES

Soldiers should be well trained in all aspects of slow semiautomatic firing before attempting any automatic training. Those who display a lack of knowledge of the fundamental skills should not advance to automatic fire training until these skills are learned. Initial training should focus on the modifications to the fundamentals and other basic combat skills necessary during automatic firing.

Dry-Fire Exercises. Repeated dry-fire exercises are the most efficient means available to ensure soldiers can apply these modifications. Multiple dry-fire exercises are needed, emphasizing a stable position and point of aim, followed by breath control and the appropriate trigger squeeze. Blanks or dummy rounds may be used to train trigger squeeze, rapid magazine changes, and application of immediate action. The soldier should display knowledge and skill during these exercises before attempting live-fire.

Live-Fire Exercises. There are two types of live-fire exercises.

Individual. Emphasis is on each individual maintaining a heavy volume of fire. Weapon down time (during immediate action and rapid magazine changes) is held to a minimum. Firing can begin at 25 meters, progressing to 50 meters as soldiers display increased proficiency. Exposure or engagement times, as well as ranges, are varied to best simulate the need for a heavy volume of fire. Downrange feedback is necessary to determine effectiveness of fire. The course of fire should allow the soldier to decide whether he should engage a given target or area with automatic or semiautomatic fire.

A soldier's zero during automatic fire may be different than his semiautomatic (battlesight) zero. This is due to the tendency of the lightweight M16 barrel to respond to external pressure such as the bipod or pulling on the sling. However, it is recommended that the battlesight zero be retained on the rifle and holdoff used to place automatic fire on the target. This holdoff training requires downrange feedback and should be conducted before other live-fire exercises.

The soldier can begin by loading and firing one round from an automatic fire position. Three of these rounds, treated as a single group, can establish where the first shot of a three-round burst will probably strike. Loading and firing two rounds simulates the dispersion of the second shot of a three-round burst. Finally, several three-round bursts should be fired to refine any necessary holdoff to center these larger groups on the desired point of impact.

Unit. Unit LFXs should include the careful use of automatic fire. Emphasis should be on staggered rapid magazine changes, maintaining a continuous volume of heavy fire, and conserving ammunition.

SECTION IV. QUICK-FIRE

The two main techniques of directing fire with a rifle are to aim using the sights; and to use weapon alignment, instinct, bullet strike, or tracers to direct the fire. The preferred technique is to use the sights, but sometimes quick reflex action is needed to survive. Quick-fire is a technique used to deliver fast, effective fire on surprise personnel targets at close ranges (25 meters or less). Quick-fire procedures have also been referred to as "instinct firing" or "quick kill."

EFFECTIVENESS OF QUICK FIRE

Quick-fire techniques are appropriate for soldiers who are presented with close, suddenly appearing, surprise enemy targets; or when close engagement is imminent. Fire may be delivered in the SEMIAUTO or BURST/AUTO mode. For example, a point man in a patrol may carry the weapon on BURST/AUTO. This may also be required when clearing a room or bunker. Initial training should be in the SEMI mode. Two techniques of delivering quick-fire are —

Aimed. When presented with a target, the soldier brings the rifle up to his shoulder and quickly fires a single shot. His firing eye looks through or just over the rear sight aperture, and he uses the front sight post to aim at the target (Figure 4-5). Using this technique, a target at 25 meters or less may be accurately engaged in one second or less.

Pointed. When presented with a target, the soldier keeps the rifle at his side and quickly fires a single shot or burst. He keeps both eyes open and uses his instinct and peripheral vision to line up the rifle with the target (Figure 4-6). Using this technique, a target at 15 meters or less may be engaged in less than one second.

The difference in speed of delivery between these two techniques is small. Pointed quick fire can be used to fire a shot about one-tenth of a second faster than aimed quick-fire. The difference in accuracy, however, is more pronounced. A soldier well trained in pointed quick fire can hit an E-type silhouette target at 15 meters, although the

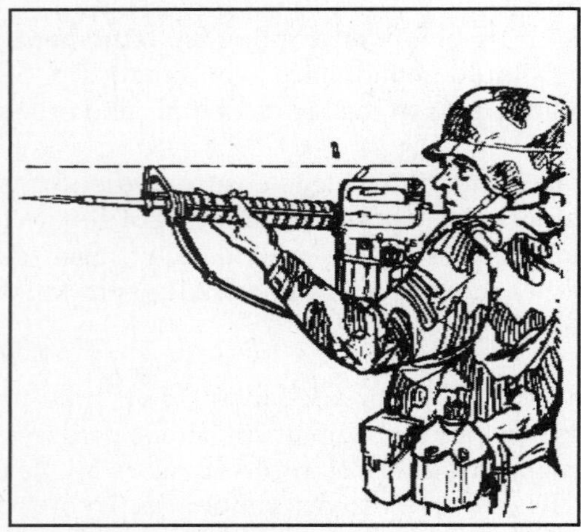

Figure 4-5: Aimed quick-fire.

Figure 4-6: Pointed quick-fire.

shot may strike anywhere on the target. A soldier well trained in aimed quick fire can hit an E-type silhouette target at 25 meters, with the shot or burst striking 5 inches from the center of mass.

The key to the successful employment of either technique is practice. Both pointed and aimed quick-fire must be repeatedly practiced during dry-fire training. Live-fire exercises provide further skill enhancement and illustrate the difference in accuracy between the two techniques. Tactical considerations dictate which technique is most effective in a given situation, and when single shot versus burst fire is used.

Pointed and aimed quick fire should be used only when a target cannot be engaged fast enough using the sights in a normal manner. These techniques should be limited to targets appearing at 25 meters or less.

MODIFICATIONS FOR QUICK- FIRE TECHNIQUES

Quick-fire techniques require major modifications to the four fundamentals of marksmanship. These modifications represent a significant departure from the normal applications of the four fundamentals. Initial training in these differences, followed by repeated dry-fire exercises, will be necessary to prepare the soldier for live-fire.

Steady Position. The quickness of shot delivery prevents the soldier from assuming a stable firing position. He must fire from his present position when the target appears. If the soldier is moving, he must stop. Adjustments for stability and support cannot be made before the round being fired.

Aimed. The butt of the rifle is pulled into the pocket of the shoulder as the cheek comes in contact with the stock. Both hands firmly grip the rifle, applying rearward pressure. The firing eye looks through or just over the rear sight aperture (Figure 4-5, page 4–12). The firer's sight is in focus and placed on the target.

Pointed. The rifle is pulled into the soldier's side and both hands firmly grip the rifle, applying rearward pressure (Figure 4-6, page 4–12).

Aiming. This fundamental must be highly modified because the soldier may not have time to look through the rear sight, find the front sight, and align it with the target.

Aimed. The soldier's initial focus is on the target. As the rifle is brought up, the firing eye looks through or just over the rear sight aperture at the target. Using his peripheral vision, the soldier locates the front sight post and brings it to the center of the target. When the front sight post is in focus, the shot is fired. Focus remains on the front sight post throughout the aiming process.

Pointed. The soldier's focus is placed on the center or slightly below the center of the target as the rifle is aligned with it and is fired. The soldier's instinctive pointing ability and peripheral vision are used to aid in proper alignment.

> ✍ **NOTE**
> When using either aiming technique, bullets may tend to impact above the desired location. Repeated live-fire practice is necessary to determine the best aim point on the target or the best focus. Such practice should begin with the soldier using a center mass arms/focus.

Breath Control. This fundamental has little application to the first shot of quick-fire. The round must be fired before a conscious decision can be made about breathing. If subsequent shots are necessary, breathing must not interfere with the necessity to fire quickly. When possible, use short, shallow breaths.

Trigger Squeeze. Initial pressure is applied as weapon alignment is moved toward the target. Trigger squeeze is exerted so that when weapon/target alignment is achieved, the round is fired at once. The soldier requires much training and practice to perfect this rapid squeezing of the trigger.

TRAINING OF QUICK- FIRE TECHNIQUES

Initial training should focus on the major modifications to the fundamentals during quick-fire.

Dry-Fire Exercises. This dry-fire exercise requires no elaborate preparations or range facilities, yet it provides the soldier with an opportunity to learn and practice quick-fire techniques. Repeated dry-fire exercises ensure soldiers can apply the modifications to the fundamentals. Multiple dry-fire exercises are needed, emphasizing a consistent firing position and weapon alignment with the target, followed by rapid trigger squeeze. No more than one second should elapse between the appearance of the target and a bullet striking it. One example of a dry-fire exercise is:

The trainer/coach places an E-type silhouette target 15 meters in front of the soldier. The soldier stands facing the general direction of the target (vary direction to simulate targets appearing at different locations), holding his rifle at or above waist level. His firing hand should be on the pistol grip; the nonfiring hand cradling the rifle under the handguards.

The trainer/coach should stand slightly behind the soldier, out of his field of view. The trainer/coach claps his hands, signaling target appearance. Immediately after clapping his hands, the trainer/coach counts out loud "one thousand one."

The soldier must either point or aim, squeeze the trigger, and hear the hammer fall before the trainer/coach finishes speaking (about one second or less).

> ✍ **NOTE**
> When using the aiming technique, the soldier holds his aim and confirms alignment of the rifle with the target. He keeps the rifle pointed toward the target after the hammer falls and looks through the sights to check his actual point of aim for that shot.

Live-Fire Exercises. There are two types of live-fire exercises.

Individual. Emphasis is on engaging each target in one second or less. The previously described timing technique may be used, or pop-up targets set to lock in the full upright position may be used. Pop-up targets require about one second to move from the down to the full up position. Targets set to lock in the upright position must be engaged as they are being raised to "kill" them. This gives the soldier a one-second time limit. At 15 meters (the maximum recommended range), an E-type silhouette engaged using pointed quick fire may be hit anywhere. Using aimed quick fire at the same target, hits should fall within a 10-inch circle located center of target.

> ✍ **NOTE**
> Repeated live-fire exercises are necessary to train the soldier. If 5.56-mm service ammunition is in short supply, the 5.56-mm practice ammunition and M2 bolt or the .22-caliber rim fire adapter device may be used.

Unit. Unit MOUT LFXs should include the use of quick-fire. Targets should be presented at 25 meters or less and soldiers must engage them within one second.

SECTION V. MOPP FIRING

All soldiers must effectively fire their weapons to accomplish combat missions in an NBC environment. With proper training and practice, soldiers can gain confidence in their ability to effectively hit targets in full MOPP equipment. MOPP firing proficiency must be a part of every unit's training program.

EFFECTS OF MOPP EQUIPMENT ON FIRING

Firing weapons is only part of overall NBC training. Soldiers must first be familiar with NBC equipment, its use, and proper wear before they progress to learning the techniques of MOPP firing. Trainers must consider the impact of MOPP equipment (hood/mask, gloves, overgarments) on the soldier's ability to properly apply the fundamentals of marksmanship and combat firing skills.

Immediate Action. Under normal conditions a soldier should be able to clear a stoppage in three to five seconds. Under full MOPP, however, this may take as long as ten seconds to successfully complete. Dry-fire practice under these conditions is necessary to reduce time and streamline actions. Hood/mask and gloves must be worn. Care must be taken not to snag or damage the gloves or dislodge the hood/mask during movements. Applying immediate action to a variety of stoppages during dry-fire must be practiced using dummy or blank ammunition until such actions can be performed by instinct.

Target Detection. Techniques and principles outlined in Chapter 3 remain valid for target detection while in MOPP, but considerations must be made for limiting factors imposed by MOPP equipment.

Vision is limited to what can be seen through the mask lenses/faceplate. Peripheral vision is severely restricted. The lenses/faceplate may be scratched or partly fogged, thus further restricting vision. Soldiers requiring corrective lenses must be issued insert lenses before training.

Scanning movement may be restricted by the hood/mask. Any of these factors could adversely affect the soldier's ability to quickly and accurately detect targets. Additional skill practice should be conducted.

Marksmanship Fundamentals. Although the four marksmanship fundamentals remain valid during MOPP firing, some modifications may be needed to accommodate the equipment.

Steady position. Due to the added bulk of the overgarments, firing positions may need adjustment for stability and comfort. Dry and live firing while standing, crouching, or squatting may be necessary to reduce body contact with contaminated ground or foliage. A consistent spot/stock weld is difficult to maintain due to the shape of the protective masks. This requires the firer to hold his head in an awkward position to place the eye behind the sight.

Aiming. The wearing of a protective mask may force firers to rotate (cant) the rifle a certain amount to see through the rear aperture. The weapon should be rotated the least amount to properly see through and line up the sights, as previously discussed in Chapter 3. The center tip of the front sight post should be placed on the ideal aiming point. This ideal aiming procedure (Figure 4-7, page 4–16) should be the initial procedure taught and practiced. If this cannot be achieved, a canted sight picture may be practiced.

Breath control. Breathing is restricted and more difficult while wearing the protective mask. Physical exertion can produce labored breathing and make settling down into a normal breath control routine much more difficult. More physical effort is needed to move around when encumbered by MOPP equipment, which can increase the breath rate. All of these factors make holding and controlling the breath to produce a well-aimed shot more energy- and time-consuming. Emphasis must be placed on rapid target engagement during the limited amount of time a firer can control his breath.

Trigger squeeze. Grasping the pistol grip and squeezing the trigger with the index finger are altered when the firer is wearing MOPP gloves. The action of the trigger finger is restricted, and the fit of the glove may require the release of the swing-down trigger guard. Because the trigger feels different, control differs from that used in bare-handed firing. This difference cannot be accurately predicted. Dry-fire training using dime (washer) exercises is necessary to ensure the firer knows the changes he will encounter during live-fire.

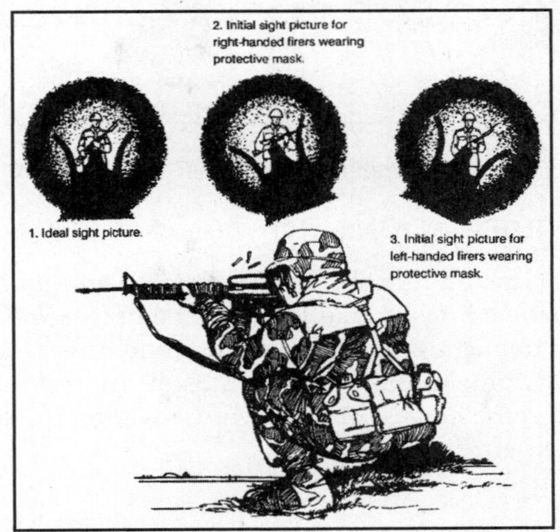

Figure 4-7: Sight picture when canting the rifle (75-meter target).

EFFECTS OF AIMING MODIFICATIONS

The normal amount of cant needed by most firers to properly see through the sights has a limited influence on rounds fired at ranges of 75 meters or less. At longer ranges, however, the change in bullet strike becomes more pronounced.

Rifle ballistics (Appendix F) causes the strike of the bullet to impact low in the direction of the cant (when a cant is used) at longer ranges. Due to this shift in bullet strike and the many individual differences in sight alignment when wearing a protective mask, it is important to conduct downrange feedback training (Appendix G) at ranges beyond 75 meters. This allows soldiers to determine what aiming adjustments are needed to achieve center target hits. Figure 4-8 shows what might be expected for a right-handed firer engaging a target at 175 meters with no cant, a certain amount of cant, and the adjustment in point of aim needed to move the bullet strike to the center of the target. Figure 4-9 shows what might be expected for a right-handed firer engaging a 300-meter target (the adjustments in point of aim for left-handed firers are the opposite of those shown in Figures 4-8 and 4-9).

Although bullet strike is displaced when using a cant, individual differences are such that center-of-mass aiming should be used until the individual knows what aiming adjustment is needed. When distant targets are missed, a right-handed firer should usually adjust his point of aim to the right and high; a left-handed firer should adjust to the left and high. Then, the aiming rules are clear. All targets should initially be engaged by aiming center mass, regardless of cant. When targets are missed while using a cant, firers should adjust the point of aim higher and opposite the direction of the cant. Actual displacement of the aiming point must be determined by using downrange feedback targets at ranges beyond 75 meters.

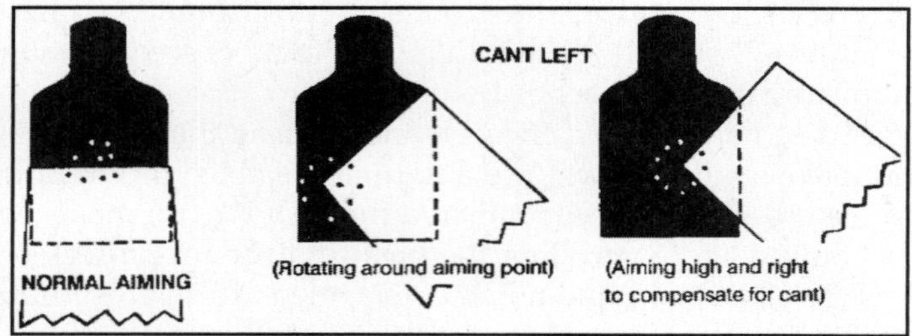

Figure 4-8: Engagement of 175-meter target.

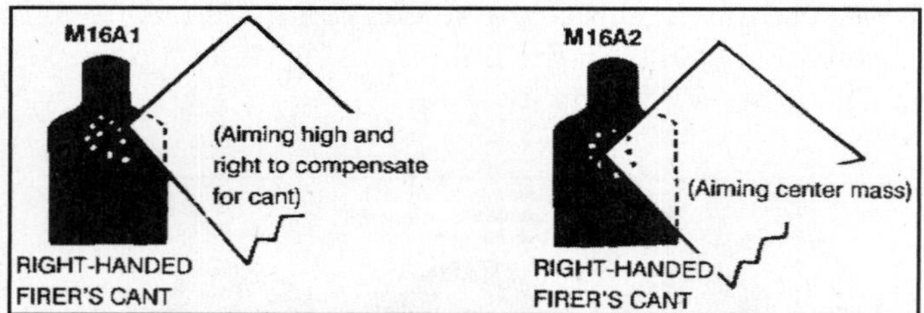

Figure 4-9: Engagement of 300-meter target.

OPERATION AND FUNCTION MODIFICATIONS

Handling the rifle, performing operation and function checks, loading and unloading, and cleaning are affected by MOPP equipment. Movements are slowed, tasks take longer to complete and often require more effort, vision is impaired, and care is needed to avoid damaging MOPP equipment and possible exposure to lethal agents. Because of the great differences between no MOPP and MOPP4, soldiers must be trained in all aspects of operation and maintenance of the weapon while practicing at the highest MOPP level. Only through repeated training and practice can the soldier be expected to perform all tasks efficiently.

MOPP FIRE EXERCISES

The many difficulties the soldier encounters while firing with MOPP gear must be experienced and overcome during training.

Dry-Fire MOPP Exercises. Repeated dry-fire exercises covering all aspects of MOPP firing are the most effective means available to ensure all soldiers can function during a live-fire MOPP situation. Multiple dry-fire exercises must be conducted before the first live round is fired. Otherwise, valuable ammunition and training time are wasted in trying to teach soldiers the basics. The soldier is trained in the fundamentals; repeated dry-fire or Weaponeer exercises are conducted; grouping, zeroing, qualifying, and evaluating are performed using standard non-MOPP firing; the differences and modifications are trained for MOPP firing; and repeated MOPP dry-fire exercises are conducted. The soldier is now ready to move on to MOPP live-fire.

Live-Fire MOPP Exercises. These exercises further develop the learned firing skills and allow the soldier to experience the effects of wearing MOPP equipment on downrange performance.

Individual. Application of immediate action, rapid magazine changes, grouping, and adjusted point of aim at 25 meters should all be tested and evaluated for further training. After soldiers exhibit proficiency at these tasks, further training and evaluation at extended ranges are indicated.

Unit. Parts of unit LFXs should be conducted in the highest MOPP level with a planned system of target hit evaluation. As in all aspects of marksmanship training, the emphasis is on soldier knowledge and skills displayed.

Basic 25-meter proficiency course. Initial live-fire exercises are conducted at 25 meters. This training provides all soldiers the basic techniques and introduces firing the rifle in MOPP equipment. This basic proficiency exercise must be fired while wearing gloves and protective mask with hood. The basic 25-meter proficiency exercise is fired to standard and is an annual/semiannual GO/NO-GO requirement for most soldiers. It is entered on the record fire scorecard when completed.

The course of fire can be conducted on any range equipped with mechanical target lifters. Soldiers are given initial instruction and a demonstration of the techniques of firing in MOPP equipment.

Each soldier is issued 20 rounds of 5.56-mm ball ammunition to engage 20 three-to-five-second exposures of F-type silhouette targets at 25 meters. Initial firing is performed with 10 rounds from the individual fighting position (supported), and 10 rounds from a prone unsupported position. Each soldier must obtain a minimum of 11 target hits out of 20 exposures to meet the basic requirement. This initial basic 25-meter exercise prepares soldiers for future individual and unit training in full MOPP gear.

Downrange feedback. Once the soldier has mastered basic marksmanship proficiency, he should be introduced to firing at range. This phase of firing should provide the maximum hit-and-miss performance feedback; it can be conducted on a KD or modified field fire range at 75, 175, and 300 meters.

Practice firing under full MOPP can also be conducted on the standard RETS ranges—for example, the standard record fire tables may be fired in MOPP. MOPP fire must also be part of unit tactical exercises, which are fired on MPRC as part of STXs.

> ✍ **NOTE**
> The .22-caliber rimfire adapter or plastic practice ammunition may be used during live-fire practice at scaled 25-meter targets when 5.56-mm ammunition is not available.

When the rimfire adapter, plastic ammunition, or live-fire range is not available, the Weaponeer device may be used. Scaled silhouette targets may also be used at this distance to introduce the many target sizes common at longer ranges.

Having mastered the 25-meter firing phase, the soldier is then introduced to firing at range, using the standard 75-, 175-, and 300-meter downrange feedback targets (Chapter 3). Adjusted point of aim, for individual differences of cant, is first used during this training. Live-fire training is conducted on a KD or modified field fire range, giving the soldier feedback on targets engaged at many ranges.

SECTION VI. MOVING TARGET ENGAGEMENT

The enemy normally moves by rushing from one covered or concealed position to another. While making the rush, the enemy soldier presents a rapidly moving target. However, for a brief time as he begins, movement is slow since many steps are needed to gain speed. Many steps are needed to slow down at the new position. A moving target is open to aimed fire both times.

MOVING TARGET TECHNIQUES

There are two primary techniques of engaging moving targets.

Tracking. Tracking is a more accurate technique of engaging targets by experienced firers. It involves the establishment and maintaining of the aiming point in relationship to the target and maintaining that sight picture (moving with the target) while squeezing the trigger. As the target moves, this technique puts the firer in position for a second shot if the first one misses.

Trapping. Trapping is the setting up of an aiming point forward of the target and along the target path. The trigger is squeezed as the target comes into the sights. This is a technique that works on targets with slow lateral movement. It does not require tracking skills. It does require that the firer know precisely when the rifle is going to fire. Some soldiers can squeeze the trigger without reacting to the rifle firing, and they may fire better using this technique.

Another technique is to use a modified 25-meter scaled timed-fire silhouette (see Figure 4-10). Trainers evaluate performance based on where shot groups are placed when the lead rule is applied. This target can be used for both the M16A1 and M16A2 rifles.

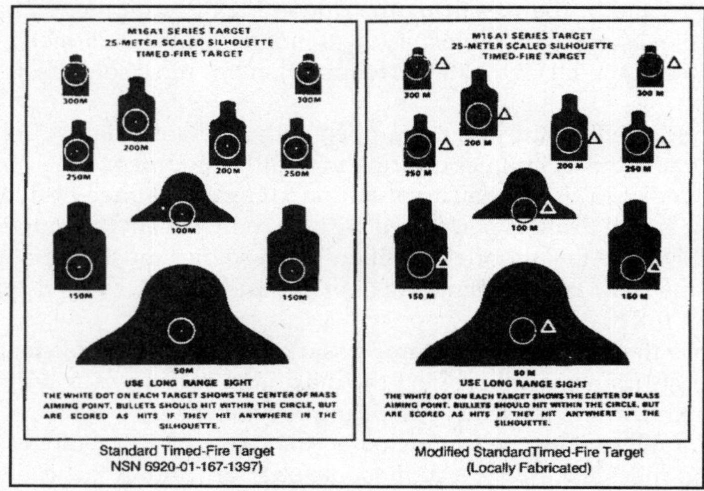

Standard Timed-Fire Target NSN 6920-01-167-1397)

Modified StandardTimed-Fire Target (Locally Fabricated)

Figure 4-10: Timed-fire targets.

MOVING TARGET FUNDAMENTALS

The fundamentals needed to hit moving targets are similar to those needed to hit stationary targets. The main skill is to engage moving targets with the least changes to procedures. Another consideration is that soldiers in a combat defensive position do not know if their next target will be stationary or moving—they must fire immediately at whatever targets occur.

The fundamentals for engaging stationary targets are steady position, aiming, breath control, and trigger squeeze. They are also used to engage moving targets. Considering the environment and the variables of the rifle and ammunition, the well-trained soldier should be able to hit 300-meter stationary silhouette targets with a .5 PH. When the target has lateral movement, hits at 150 meters may be seven out of ten times, which is a good performance. Therefore, twice as much variability, twice as much dispersion, and a few more erratic shots are expected when soldiers are trained to hit moving targets.

The procedures used to engage moving targets vary as the angle and speed of the target vary. For example, when a moving target is moving directly at the firer, the same procedures are used as would be used if the target were stationary. However, if it is a close, fast-moving target at a 90-degree angle, the rifle and entire upper body of the firer must be free from support so that the target can be tracked. To hit moving targets, the firer must move the rifle smoothly and steadily as the target moves. The front sight post is placed with the trailing edge at target center, breath is held, and the trigger is squeezed. Several factors complicate this process.

Steady position. When firing from a firing position, the firer is in the standard supported position and is flexible enough to track any target in his sector. When a moving target is moving directly at the firer, directly away, or at a slight angle, the target is engaged without changing the firing position. When targets have much lateral movement, only minor changes are needed to allow for effective target engagement. Most moving targets are missed in the horizontal plane (firing in front of or behind the target) and not in the vertical plane (firing too low or too high). Therefore, a smooth track is needed on the target, even if the support arm must be lifted. Other adjustments include the following:

- *Nonfiring hand.* The grip of the nonfiring hand may need to be increased and more pressure applied to the rear. This helps to maintain positive control of the rifle and steady it for rapid trigger action.

- *Nonfiring elbow.* The elbow is lifted from the support position only to maintain a smooth track.
- *Grip of the right hand.* Rearward pressure may be applied to the pistol grip to steady the rifle during trigger squeeze.
- *Firing elbow.* The firing elbow is lifted from support only to help maintain a smooth track.

> ✍ **NOTE**
> The rifle pocket on the shoulder and the stock weld are the same for stationary targets.

Aiming. The trailing edge of the front sight post is at target center.

Breath control. Breathing is locked at the moment of trigger squeeze.

Trigger squeeze. Rearward pressure on the handguard and pistol grip is applied to hold the rifle steady while pressure is applied to the trigger. The trigger is squeezed fast (almost a controlled jerk). Heavy pressure is applied on the trigger (at least half the pressure it takes to make the rifle fire) before squeezing the trigger.

SINGLE-LEAD RULE FOR MOVING TARGETS

A target moving directly toward the firer can be engaged the same way as a stationary target. However, to hit a target moving laterally, the firer places the trailing edge of the front sight post at target center. The sight-target relationship is shown in Figure 4-11 (page 4–22). The single-lead rule automatically increases the lead as the range to the target increases.

Figure 4-12 (page 4–22) shows how this works, with the front sight post covering about 1.6 inches at 15 meters and about 16 inches at 150 meters. Since the center of the front sight post is the actual aiming point, this technique of placing the trailing edge of the front sight post at target center provides for an .8-inch lead on a 15-meter target, and an 8-inch lead on a target at 150 meters.

This rule provides for a dead-center hit on a 15-meter target that is moving at 7 mph at a 25-degree angle because the target moves .8 inch between the time the rifle is fired and the bullet arrives at the target. A 150-meter target moving at 7 mph at a 25-degree angle moves 8 inches between the time the weapon is fired and the bullet arrives. This rule provides for hits on the majority of high-priority combat targets.

Figure 4-11: Single-lead rule.

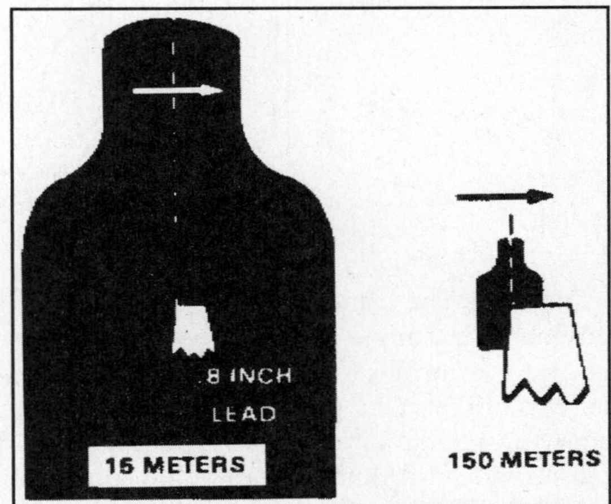

Figure 4-12: Lead increasing at greater ranges.

LEAD REQUIREMENTS

To effectively engage moving targets on the battlefield, soldiers must understand lead requirements. Figure 4-13 shows the amount of lead required to hit a 300-meter target when it is moving 8 mph at an angle of 90 degrees. Aiming directly at the target would result in missing it. When an enemy soldier is running 8 mph, 90 degrees to the firer, and at a range of 300 meters, he covers 4 1/2 feet while the bullet is traveling toward him. To get a hit, the firer must aim and fire at position D when the enemy is at position A. This indicates the need for target lead and for marksmanship trainers to know bullet speed and how it relates to the range, angle, and speed of the target. Soldiers must understand that targets moving fast and laterally are led by some distance if they are to be hit.

Target Speed. Figure 4-14 reflects the differences in lateral speed for various angles of target movement for a target that is traveling at 8 mph at a distance of 150 meters from the firer. The angle of target movement is the angle between the target-firer line and the target's direction of movement. An 8-mph target moves 24 inches during the bullet's flight time. If the target is moving on a 15-degree angle, it moves 6 inches (the equivalent of 2 mph). For the firer to apply precise lead rules, he must accurately estimate speed, angle, and range to the target during the enemy soldier's brief exposure. The single-lead rule (place the trailing edge of the front sight post at target center) places effective fire on most high-priority combat targets. At 100 meters, the rule begins to break down for targets moving at slight and large angles.

Since the target lead is half the perceived width of the front sight post, at 100 meters the standard sight provides for 5.4 inches of lead for the M16A1 and M16A2 front sights (Figure 4-15, page 4–24).

Figure 4-13: Lead requirement based on distance and approach angle.

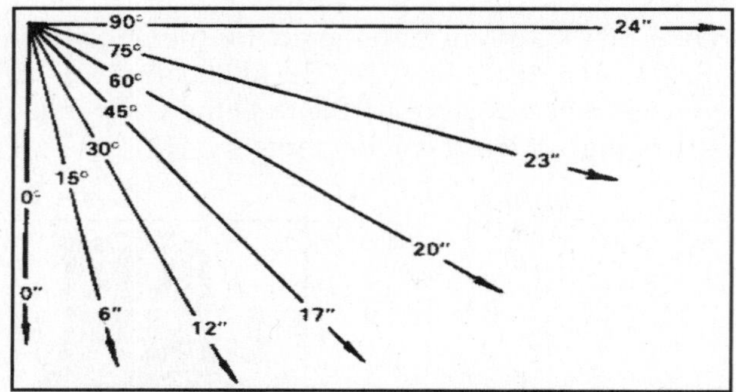

Figure 4-14: Target movement (distance) at various angles.

Target Distance. The front sight post covers only a small part of close-in targets, providing for target hits on close targets moving at any angle and any speed. However, if the lead rule is applied on more distant targets moving at a slight angle—for example, 5 degrees at 100 meters—the bullet strikes forward of target center, about 4 inches with standard sights and about 7 inches with LLLSS sights. Therefore, soldiers are taught to fire at targets as though they are stationary until lateral movement is observed (15 degrees).

The rule provides for many speed-angle combinations that place the bullet within 2 inches of target center (Figure 4-16, page 4–25). Since the soldier is expected to fire a 12-inch group on moving targets at 100 meters, the rule provides for hits on the majority of targets. Even the worst case (a 90-degree target moving at 8 mph) would result in the shot-group center being located 9.8 inches behind target center. If bullets were evenly distributed within a 12-inch group, this would result in hitting the target 40 percent of the time.

Soldiers should be taught to increase their lead when targets are missed. This increases their probability of hitting all targets. The amount of additional lead required should be developed through experience with only general guidance provided. For example, if there is much lateral movement of the target and the soldier feels by applying the lead rule and firing fundamentals he has missed the target, then he should increase his lead.

The training program must be simple and provide soldiers with only relevant information to improve their performance in combat. First, all soldiers should understand and apply the single-lead rule in the absence of more

ANGLE OF TARGET MOVEMENT	RANGE: 100 METERS (STANDARD SIGHT) TARGET SPEED		
	4 MPH	6 MPH	8 MPH
5°	+4.9"	+4.5"	+4.3"
10°	+4.1"	+3.5"	+2.7"
15°	+3.5"	+2.5"	+1.5"
20°	+2.8"	+1.5"	+.2"
25°	+2.2"	+.7"	-1.0"
30°	+1.7"	-.2"	-2.0"
35°	+1.1"	-1.1"	-3.2"
40°	+.6"	-1.9"	-4.3"
45°		-2.7"	-5.4"
50°	-.4"	-3.3"	-6.2"
55°	-.8"	-4.0"	-7.0"
60°	-1.2"	-4.5"	-7.7"
65°	-1.5"	-4.9"	-8.4"
70°	-1.7"	-5.3"	-8.8"
75°	-1.9"	-5.6"	-9.2"
80°	-2.0"	-5.9"	-9.6"
85°	-2.1"	-5.9"	-9.7"
90°	-2.1"	-6.0"	-9.8"

NOTE: Plus (+) indicates bullet strike in the direction of movement; minus (-) indicates bullet strike behind the target center.

Figure 4-15: Angle of target movement.

information. Second, soldiers should understand that moving targets coming toward them or on a slight angle (0 to 15 degrees) should be engaged as stationary targets. Third, information should be presented and practice allowed on applying additional lead to targets for soldiers who demonstrate an aptitude for this skill.

Target Angle. The rule does not apply to targets moving at small and large angles (Figure 4-16). For example, a walking enemy soldier at 250 meters is hit dead center when he is moving at 40 degrees. Hits can be obtained if he is moving on any angle between 15 and 75 degrees. When he is running (a center hit is obtained when the target is on an angle of 18 degrees), misses occur when he exceeds an angle of 30 to 35 degrees. The information provided in Figures 4-13, page 4–23, and 4–14, page 4–24, is designed to enhance instructor understanding so proper concepts are presented during instruction. For example, a target at 100 meters moving at 6 mph receives a center hit when moving at 29 degrees. When moving at an angle less than 29 degrees, the bullet strikes somewhat in front of target center. When moving at an angle of more than 29 degrees, the bullet strikes somewhat behind target center.

(STANDARD SIGHT)

RANGE	4 MPH	6 MPH	8 MPH
25M	48°	30°	22°
50M	47°	30°	22°
100M	45°	29°	21°
150M	44°	28°	20°
200M	41°	27°	19°
250M	40°	26°	18°
300M	33°	21°	16°
350M	38°	24°	18°
400M	35°	22°	17°
450M	33°	21°	16°

Figure 4-16: Target angle when dead center: hits accure using single lead rule.

MULTIPURPOSE RANGE COMPLEX TRAIN-UP

MPRCs require soldiers to hit moving targets. Ranges are used for collective training. Commanders should try to use the MPRCs for individual training and to teach the individual to engage moving targets. If no MPRCs are available for individual training, any range can be used that will support any type of moving target. Building a moving target range is limited only by the imagination of the trainer, but always within safety constraints. The following are examples that can be incorporated on many ranges.

Popsicle Sticks. This requires placing an E-type silhouette on a long stick and having an individual walk back and forth behind a high berm (high enough to protect the individual from fire) the length of the berm. Feedback should be made available for the firer such as for lowering the target when a hit is scored or reversing direction upon a hit.

Sled Targets. This requires constructing a simple sled that has one or more targets attached. The sled is pulled by a rope or cable across and off the range safely by a vehicle.

CHAPTER 5

Night Firing

All units must be able to fight during limited visibility. All soldiers should know the procedures for weapons employment during such time. Soldiers must experience the various conditions of night combat—from total darkness, to the many types of artificial illumination, to the use of surveillance aids. All units must include basic, unassisted night fire training annually in their unit marksmanship programs. Combat units should conduct tactical night fire training at least quarterly. This tactical training should include MILES during force-on-force training as well as live-fire. Night-fire training must include the use of applicable night vision devices when this equipment is part of a TOE. The many effects darkness has on night firing are discussed herein.

> ✍ **NOTE**
> Although this chapter addresses night firing, the appropriate modifications to the fundamentals of firing may be applied whenever visibility is limited.

CONSIDERATIONS

Trainers must consider the impact of limited visibility on the soldier's ability to properly apply the fundamentals of marksmanship and combat firing skills. These fundamentals / skills include:

Operation and Maintenance of the Weapon. Handling the weapon, performing operation and function checks, loading and unloading, and maintenance are affected by nighttime conditions. Movements are slowed, tasks take longer to complete, vision is impaired, and equipment is more easily misplaced or lost. Because combat conditions and enforcement of noise and light discipline restrict the use of illumination, soldiers must be trained to operate (load, unload, and clear), service, and clean their weapons using the lowest lighting conditions. Although initial practice of these tasks should occur during daylight (using simulated darkness) to facilitate control and error correction, repeated practice during actual nighttime conditions should be integrated with other training. Only through repeated practice and training can the soldier be expected to perform all tasks efficiently.

Immediate Action. Under normal conditions, a soldier should clear a stoppage in three to five seconds. After dark, this task usually takes longer. Identifying the problem may be frustrating and difficult for the soldier. A tactile (hands only) technique of identifying a stoppage must be taught and practiced. Clearing the stoppage using few or no visual indicators must also be included. The firer must apply immediate action with his eyes closed. Dry-fire practice using dummy or blank rounds under these conditions is necessary to reduce time and build confidence. Training should be practiced first during daylight for better control and error correction by the trainer. Practice during darkness can be simulated by closing the eyes or using a blindfold. Once the soldier is confident in applying immediate action in daylight or darkness, he can perform such actions rapidly on the firing line.

Target Detection. Light from a cigarette or flashlight, discharge of a rifle (muzzle flash), or reflected moonlight/ starlight are the main means of target location. Sounds may also be indicators of target areas. Because the other techniques of detection (movement, contrast) are less apparent at night, light and sound detection must be taught, trained, and reviewed repeatedly in practice exercises. Exercises should also emphasize shortened scanning ranges, night vision adaptation, and use of off-center vision. Target detection exercises should be integrated into all collective training tasks.

> ✍ **NOTE**
> Binoculars are often overlooked as night vision aids. Because they amplify the available light, binoculars or spotting/rifle scopes can provide the firer with another means to locate targets during limited visibility. Also, the use of MILES equipment is effective for use in engaging detected targets.

Marksmanship Fundamentals. The four marksmanship fundamentals apply to night firing. Some modifications are needed depending on the conditions. The firer must still place effective fire on the targets or target areas that have been detected.

Steady position. When the firer is firing unassisted, changes in his head position/stock weld will be necessary, especially when using weapon-target alignment techniques. When using rifle-mounted night vision devices, head position/stock weld must be changed to bring the firing eye in line with the device. Also, such mounted devices alter the rifle's weight and center of gravity, forcing a shift in placement of the support (nonfiring arm or sandbags). Repeated dry-fire practice, followed by live-fire training, is necessary to learn and refine these modifications and still achieve the most steady position.

Aiming. Modifications to the aiming process vary from very little (when using LLLSSs) to extensive (when using modified quick-fire techniques). When firing unassisted, the firer's off-center vision is used instead of pinpoint focus. When using a mounted night vision device, the firer's conventional iron sights are not used. The soldier uses the necessary aiming process to properly use the device.

Breathing. Weapon movement caused by breathing becomes more apparent when using night vision devices that magnify the field of view. This fundamental is not greatly affected by night fire conditions.

Trigger squeeze. This important fundamental does not change during night fire. The objective is to not disrupt alignment of the weapon with the target.

PRINCIPLES OF NIGHT VISION

For a soldier to effectively engage targets at night, he must apply the three principles of night vision:

Dark Adaptation. Moving from lighted to darkened areas (as in leaving a tent) can be temporarily blinding. After several minutes have passed, the soldier can slowly see his surroundings. If he remains in this completely darkened environment, he adapts to the dark in about 30 minutes. This does not mean he can see in the dark at the end of this time. After about 30 minutes, his visibility reaches its maximum level. If light is encountered, the eyes must adapt again. The fire on the end of a cigarette or a red-lensed flashlight can degrade night vision; larger light sources cause more severe losses.

Off-Center Vision. During the day, the soldier focuses his vision on the object he wants to see. Shifting this pinpoint focus slightly to one side causes the object to become blurry or lose detail. At night, the opposite is true. Focusing directly on an object after dark results in that object being visible for only a few seconds. After that, the object becomes almost invisible. To view an object at night, the soldier must shift his gaze slightly to one side. This allows the light-sensitive parts of the eye (parts not used during daylight) to be used. These can detect faint light sources or reflections and relay their image to the brain (Figures 5-1 and 5-2).

> ✍ **NOTE**
> Vision is shifted slightly to one side, but attention is still on the object. Because of the blind spot at the center of vision, directing attention to an off-centered objective is possible (with practice).

Scanning. Scanning is the short, abrupt, irregular movement of the soldier's eyes around an object or area every 4 to 10 seconds. Off-center vision is used. Scanning ranges vary according to visibility.

TARGET ENGAGEMENT TECHNIQUES

Night fire usually occurs under three general conditions.

Unassisted Firing Exercise. The firer must detect and engage targets without artificial illumination or night vision devices. Potential target areas are scanned. When a target is detected, the firer should engage it using a modified

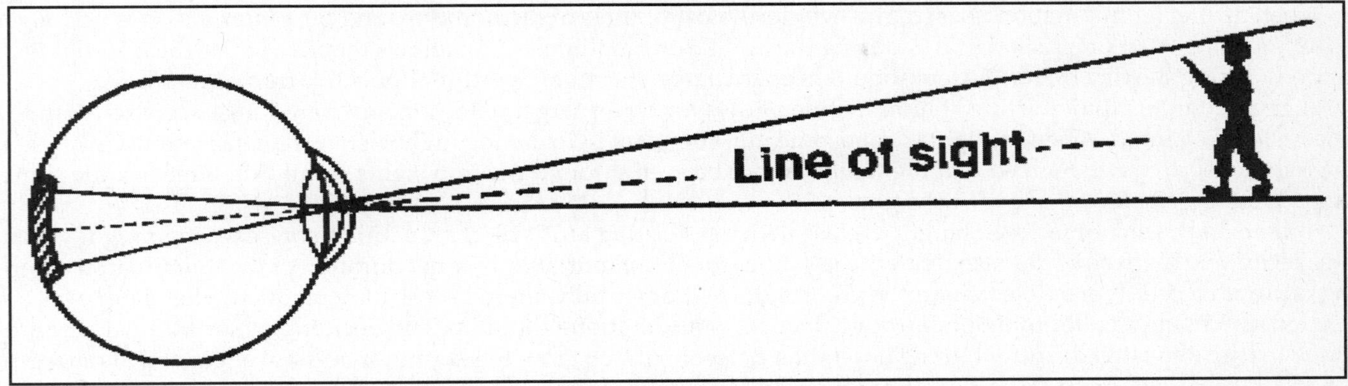

Figure 5-1: Daytime field of view using pinpoint focus.

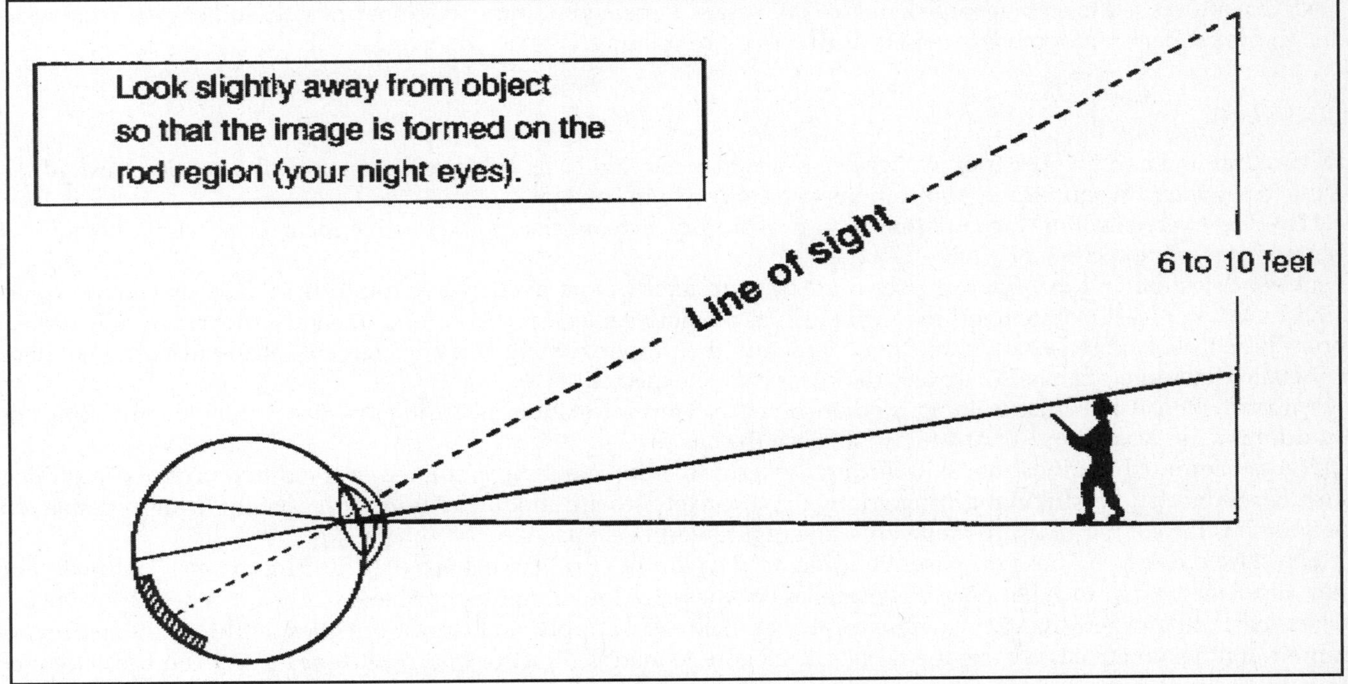

Figure 5-2: Nighttime field of view using off-center vision.

quick-fire position. His head is positioned high so that he is aligning the weapon on the target and looking just over the iron sights. His cheek should remain in contact with the stock.

The firer should take a few seconds to improve weapon/target alignment by pointing slightly low to compensate for the usual tendency to fire high. Both eyes are open to the maximum advantage of any available light, and the focus is downrange. Off-center vision is used to keep the target in sight. Tracer ammunition may provide feedback on the line of trajectory and facilitate any adjustments in weapon/target alignment.

Repeated dry-fire training, target detection, and proper aiming practice are the most efficient means to ensure the soldier can successfully engage short-range targets (50 meters or closer) unassisted during MILES exercises, and then live-fire training.

Artificial Illumination. Targets as distant as 175 meters can be engaged successfully with some type of artificial illumination. Illumination may be from hand flares, mortar or artillery fire, or bright incandescent lights such as searchlights.

When artificial illumination is used, the eyes lose most of their night adaption, and off-center vision is no longer useful. Aiming is accomplished as it is during the day. Artificial illumination allows the firer to use the iron sights as he does during the day (M16A2 users should keep the large rear sight aperture flipped up during darkness).

Engaging targets under artificial illumination allows for better target detection and long-range accuracy than the unassisted technique. When the light is gone, time must be spent in regaining night vision and adaptation. Only when the light level drops enough so that the target cannot be seen through the iron sights should the firer resume short-range scanning, looking just over the sights.

Soldiers have sometimes been taught to close their eyes during artificial illumination to preserve their night vision. This technique is effective but also renders the soldier (or entire unit) blind for the duration of the illumination. Keeping one eye closed to preserve its night vision results in a drastically altered sense of perception when both eyes are opened, following the illumination burnout. Tactical considerations should be the deciding factor as to which technique to use. Repeated dry-fire training and target detection practice are the keys to successful engagement of targets out to 150 meters or more during live-fire under artificial illumination.

Night Vision Devices. Rifle-mounted night vision devices are the most effective night fire aids. By using these devices, the firer can observe the area, detect and engage any suitable targets, and direct the fire of soldiers who are firing unassisted.

NVDs can be used to engage targets out to 300 meters. Repeated training, dry-fire practice, and correct zeroing are vital to the proper employment of NVDs during live-fire training.

TRAINING

Dry-fire training and live-fire training are necessary to mastering basic rifle marksmanship. The soldier must adhere to the following procedures and applications to be effective in combat.

Dry-Fire Exercises. Repeated training and dry-fire practice are the most effective means available to ensure all soldiers can function efficiently after dark.

Target detection and dry-fire exercises must be conducted before the first live round is fired. They can take place almost anywhere—elaborate live-fire range facilities are not needed. Modified fundamentals can be taught in a classroom/practical exercise situation. Further training in the proper zeroing and engagement techniques can take place anywhere that targets can be set up and darkness can be expected.

Without extensive dry-fire training, soldiers do not perform to standards during live-fire. Valuable range time and ammunition are wasted in a final attempt to teach the basics.

The soldier must demonstrate skill during daylight live-fire. Next, he is trained in the differences and modifications needed for successful night firing. Many dry-fire exercises are conducted until skill at night firing is displayed. Only then is the soldier ready to move on to the night live-fire exercises.

Live-Fire Exercises. These exercises continue to develop the firing skills acquired during dry-fire exercises, and they allow the soldier to experience the effects of darkness on downrange performance.

The basic unassisted live-fire exercise allows all soldiers to apply night-fire principles, and to gain confidence in their abilities to effectively engage targets at 25 and 50 meters. Practice and proficiency firing can be conducted on any range equipped with mechanical lifters and muzzle flash simulators. A small square of reflective material and a shielded low wattage flashing light (protected from bullet impact) may be used to facilitate target detection (Figures 5-3, page 5–6). The light should be placed to highlight the center of the target with a flashing, faint glow (intended to represent a muzzle flash). The light should not be on constantly, when the target is not exposed, or on when the target is exposed but not being used in actual engagement. The light should provide the firer with a momentary indication that a target is presenting itself for engagement. It should not be attached to the target or provide the firer with a distinct aiming point, regardless of how dim it may be. Practice can also be accomplished by the use of MILES equipment and target interface devices.

When an automated record fire range (RETS) is used for this exercise, the two 50-meter mechanisms are used. Before training, one E-type silhouette target is replaced with an F-type silhouette target. The F-type silhouette target is engaged at 25 meters from the prone unsupported position. The soldier is issued one magazine of 15 rounds (5 rounds ball; 10 rounds tracer) and presented 15 ten-second exposures. The firing line is moved, and the soldier engages the E-type silhouette target at 50 meters. He is issued a second 15-round magazine (5 rounds ball; 10 rounds tracer) to engage 15 ten-second exposures.

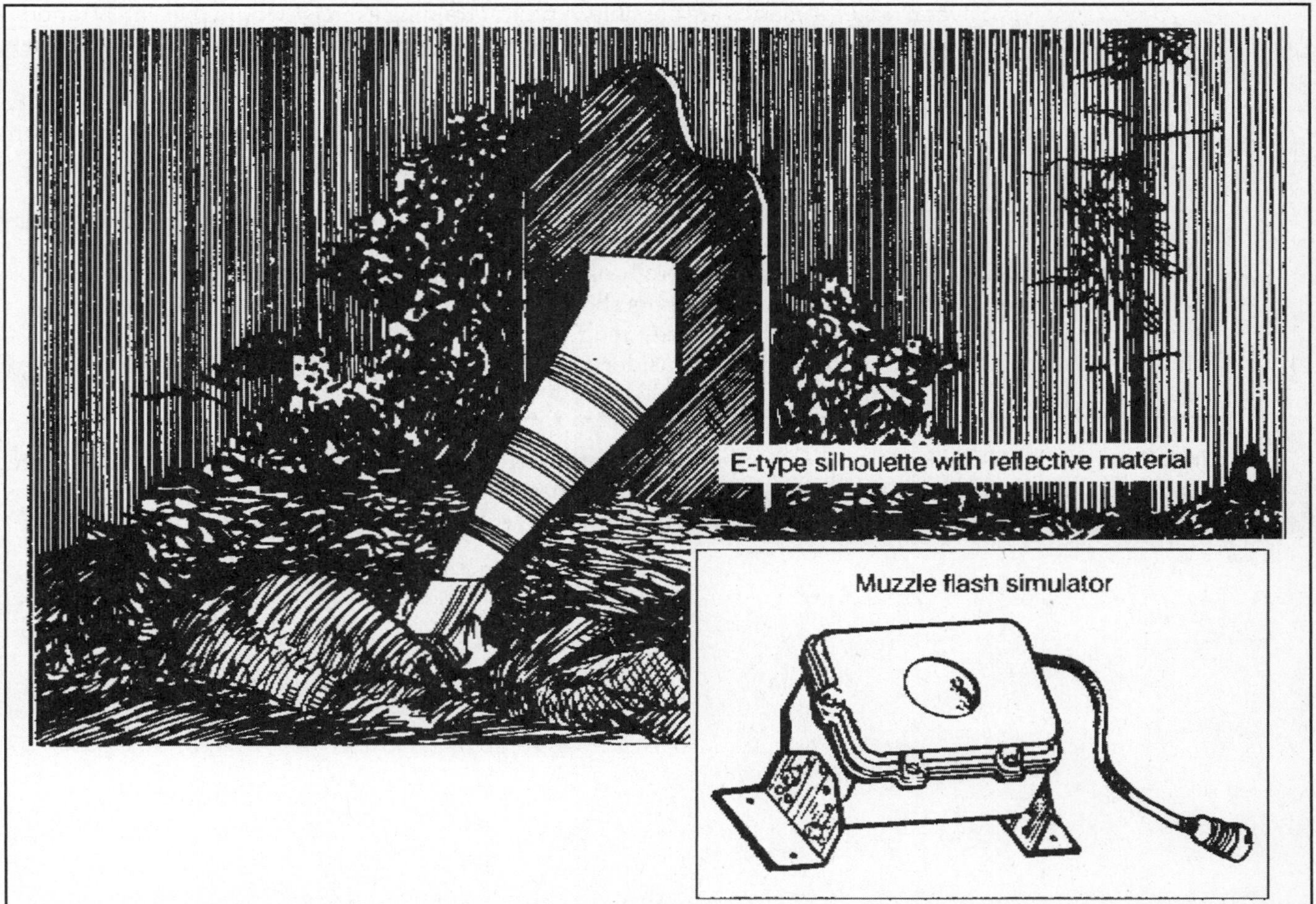

Figure 5-3: Night fire target.

When the automated range is used, the soldier's performance is recorded in the tower. If automatic scoring is not available, F-type and E-type silhouette paper facings are attached to the mechanical target, and bullet holes are counted. Facings may be repaired or replaced for each firer.

To meet the annual/semiannual minimum performance requirements, all soldiers must hit and kill seven separate targets out of 30 exposures. The results are annotated on the soldier's record fire scorecard.

- *Individual.* Application of immediate action, rapid magazine changes, and refinements of the modified quick-fire aiming point should be tested and evaluated for further training.
  - *Unassisted.* After soldiers exhibit proficiency of individual tasks, training and evaluation at ranges beyond those possible using only the rifle are indicated.
  - *Artificial illumination.* After mastering the unassisted night fire task and after repeated dry-fire training under artificial illumination, the soldier is ready to be tested and evaluated using live-fire under illumination. Pop-up or stationary targets at ranges out to 175 meters (depending on light conditions, terrain features, and vegetation) may be used. Illumination is provided by flares, mortar/artillery, or floodlights. Once these tasks are mastered, further training and evaluation using NVDs is indicated. Multipurpose range complexes can be used for night firing by using artificial illumination. Automated field fire or record fire ranges can also be used by adding lighting. During this training, soldiers engage targets at

75 to 175 meters. Several target scenarios are possible. A typical training exercise would present 30 random exposures of the 75-meter and 175-meter targets (or optional 100-meter and 200-meter targets). Soldiers should be expected to hit at least 10 targets. Tracer ammunition can be used to enhance training.

– *Night vision devices.* Repeated training and dry-fire practice on the proper use of NVDs are essential to the successful conduct of any live-fire training using these devices. Firers must understand the equipment and skillfully employ it. NVDs can provide engagement capabilities out to 300 meters.

> ✍ **NOTE**
>
> Spotlights or floodlights can be modified through use of a rheostat to simulate the flickering, bright/dim nature of artificial illumination. Lights should not be used to continuously spotlight targets. Unanticipated artificial illumination may render NVDs difficult to see through or may shut the device off. Live-fire training should consider any problems incurred by such unexpected illumination.

- *Unit.* Parts of unit STXs, FTXs, and LFXs should be conducted at night. This training should include target detection, unassisted MILES and live-fire, artificial illumination, and NVDs. Targets out to 300 meters may be used, depending on the existing conditions. Emphasis is on soldier knowledge and skills displayed.

Sniper Training

CHAPTER 1

Introduction to Sniper Training

The sniper has special abilities, training, and equipment. His job is to deliver discriminatory highly accurate rifle fire against enemy targets, which cannot be engaged successfully by the rifleman because of range, size, location, fleeting nature, or visibility. Sniping requires the development of basic infantry skills to a high degree of perfection. A sniper's training incorporates a wide variety of subjects designed to increase his value as a force multiplier and to ensure his survival on the battlefield. The art of sniping requires learning and repetitiously practicing these skills until mastered. A sniper must be highly trained in long-range rifle marksmanship and field craft skills to ensure maximum effective engagements with minimum risk.

1-1. MISSION

The primary mission of a sniper in combat is to support combat operations by delivering precise long-range fire on selected targets. By this, the sniper creates casualties among enemy troops, slows enemy movement, frightens enemy soldiers, lowers morale, and adds confusion to their operations. The secondary mission of the sniper is collecting and reporting battlefield information.

a. A well-trained sniper, combined with the inherent accuracy of his rifle and ammunition, is a versatile supporting arm available to an infantry commander. The importance of the sniper cannot be measured simply by the number of casualties he inflicts upon the enemy. Realization of the sniper's presence instills fear in enemy troop elements and influences their decisions and actions. A sniper enhances a unit's firepower and augments the varied means for destruction and harassment of the enemy. Whether a sniper is organic or attached, he will provide that unit with extra supporting fire. The sniper's role is unique in that it is the sole means by which a unit can engage point targets at distances beyond the effective range of the M16 rifle. This role becomes more significant when the target is entrenched or positioned among civilians, or during riot control missions. The fires of automatic weapons in such operations can result in the wounding or killing of noncombatants.

b. Snipers are employed in all levels of conflict. This includes conventional offensive and defensive combat in which precision fire is delivered at long ranges. It also includes combat patrols, ambushes, countersniper operations, forward observation elements, military operations in urbanized terrain, and retrograde operations in which snipers are part of forces left in contact or as stay-behind forces.

1-2. ORGANIZATION

In light infantry divisions, the sniper element is composed of six battalion personnel organized into three 2-man teams. The commander designates missions and priorities of targets for the team and may attach or place the team under the operational control of a company or platoon. They may perform dual missions, depending on the need. In the mechanized infantry battalions, the sniper element is composed of two riflemen (one team) located in a rifle squad. In some specialized units, snipers may be organized according to the needs of the tactical situation.

a. Sniper teams should be centrally controlled by the commander or the sniper employment officer. The SEO is responsible for the command and control of snipers assigned to the unit. In light infantry units, the SEO will be the reconnaissance platoon leader or the platoon sergeant. In heavy or mechanized units, the SEO may be the company commander or the executive officer. The duties and responsibilities of the SEO areas follows:

(1) To advise the unit commander on the employment of snipers.
(2) To issue orders to the team leader.
(3) To assign missions and types of employment.
(4) To coordinate between the sniper team and unit commander.

(5) To brief the unit commander and team leaders.
(6) To debrief the unit commander and team leaders.
(7) To train the teams.

b. Snipers work and train in 2-man teams. One sniper's primary duty is that of the sniper and team leader while the other sniper serves as the observer. The sniper team leader is responsible for the day-to-day activities of the sniper team. His responsibilities areas follows:
(1) To assume the responsibilities of the SEO that pertain to the team in the SEO's absence.
(2) To train the team.
(3) To issue necessary orders to the team.
(4) To prepare for missions.
(5) To control the team during missions.

c. The sniper's weapon is the sniper weapon system. The observer has the M16 rifle and an M203, which gives the team greater suppressive fire and protection. Night capability is enhanced by using night observation devices.

1-3. PERSONNEL SELECTION CRITERIA

Candidates for sniper training require careful screening. Commanders must screen the individual's records for potential aptitude as a sniper. The rigorous training program and the increased personal risk in combat require high motivation and the ability to learn a variety of skills. Aspiring snipers must have an excellent personal record.

a. The basic guidelines used to screen sniper candidates are as follows:
(1) ***Marksmanship.*** The sniper trainee must be an expert marksman. Repeated annual qualification as expert is necessary. Successful participation in the annual competition-in-arms program and an extensive hunting background also indicate good sniper potential.
(2) ***Physical condition.*** The sniper, often employed in extended operations with little sleep, food, or water, must be in outstanding physical condition. Good health means better reflexes, better muscular control, and greater stamina. The self-confidence and control that come from athletics, especially team sports, are definite assets to a sniper trainee.
(3) ***Vision.*** Eyesight is the sniper's prime tool. Therefore, a sniper must have 20/20 vision or vision correctable to 20/20. However, wearing glasses could become a liability if glasses are lost or damaged. Color blindness is also considered a liability to the sniper, due to his inability to detect concealed targets that blend in with the natural surroundings.
(4) ***Smoking.*** The sniper should not be a smoker or use smokeless tobacco. Smóke or an unsuppressed smoker's cough can betray the sniper's position. Even though a sniper may not smoke or use smokeless tobacco on a mission, his refrainment may cause nervousness and irritation, which lowers his efficiency.
(5) ***Mental condition.*** When commanders screen sniper candidates, they should look for traits that indicate the candidate has the right qualities to be a sniper. The commander must determine if the candidate will pull the trigger at the right time and place. Some traits to look for are reliability, initiative, loyalty, discipline, and emotional stability. A psychological evaluation of the candidate can aid the commander in the selection process.
(6) ***Intelligence.*** A sniper's duties require a wide variety of skills. He must learn the following:
- Ballistics.
- Ammunition types and capabilities.
- Adjustment of optical devices.
- Radio operation and procedures.
- Observation and adjustment of mortar and artillery fire.
- Land navigation skills.
- Military intelligence collecting and reporting.
- Identification of threat uniforms and equipment.

b. In sniper team operations involving prolonged independent employment, the sniper must be self-reliant, display good judgment and common sense. This requires two other important qualifications: emotional balance and field craft.

(1) ***Emotional balance.*** The sniper must be able to calmly and deliberately kill targets that may not pose an immediate threat to him. It is much easier to kill in self-defense or in the defense of others than it is to kill without apparent provocation. The sniper must not be susceptible to emotions such as anxiety or remorse. Candidates whose motivation toward sniper training rests mainly in the desire for prestige may not be capable of the cold rationality that the sniper's job requires.

(2) ***Field craft.*** The sniper must be familiar with and comfortable in a field environment. An extensive background in the outdoors and knowledge of natural occurrences in the outdoors will assist the sniper in many of his tasks. Individuals with such a background will often have great potential as a sniper.

c. Commander involvement in personnel selection is critical. To ensure his candidate's successful completion of sniper training and contribution of his talents to his unit's mission, the commander ensures that the sniper candidate meets the following prerequisites before attending the U.S. Army Sniper School:

- Male.
- PFC to SFC (waiverable for MSG and above).
- Active duty or ARNG and USAR.
- Good performance record.
- No history of alcohol or drug abuse.
- A volunteer (with commander recommendation).
- Vision of 20/20 or correctable to 20/20.
- No record of disciplinary action.
- Expert marksman with M16A1 or M16A2 rifle.
- Minimum of one-year retrainability.
- Career management field 11.
- Pass APFT (70 percent, each event).

1-4. SNIPER AND OBSERVER RESPONSIBILITIES

Each member of the sniper team has specific responsibilities. Only through repeated practice can the team begin to function properly. Responsibilities of team members areas follows:

a. The sniper—

- Builds a steady, comfortable position.
- Locates and identifies the designated target.
- Estimates the range to the target.
- Dials in the proper elevation and windage to engage the target.
- Notifies the observer of readiness to fire.
- Takes aim at the designated target.
- Controls breathing at natural respiratory pause.
- Executes proper trigger control.
- Follows through.
- Makes an accurate and timely shot call.
- Prepares to fire subsequent shots, if necessary.

b. The observer—

- Properly positions himself.
- Selects an appropriate target.
- Assists in range estimation.
- Calculates the effect of existing weather conditions on ballistics.
- Reports sight adjustment data to the sniper.
- Uses the M49 observation telescope for shot observation.
- Critiques performance.

1-5. TEAM FIRING TECHNIQUES

A sniper team must be able to move and survive in a combat environment. The sniper team's mission is to deliver precision fire. This calls for a coordinated team effort. Together, the sniper and observer—

- Determine the effects of weather on ballistics.
- Calculate the range to the target.
- Make necessary sight changes.
- Observe bullet impact.
- Critique performance before any subsequent shots.

CHAPTER 2

Equipment

This chapter describes the equipment necessary for the sniper to effectively peform his mission. The sniper carries only what is essential to successfully complete his mission. He requires a durable rifle with the capability of long-range precision fire. The current U.S. Army sniper weapon system is the M24. (See Appendix B for the M21 sniper weapon system.)

SECTION I. M24 SNIPER WEAPON SYSTEM

The M24 sniper weapon system is a 7.62-mm, bolt-action, six-shot repeating rifle (one round in the chamber and five rounds in the magazine). It is designed for use with either the M3A telescope (day optic sight) (usually called the M3A *scope*) or the metallic iron sights. The sniper must know the M24's components, and the procedures required to operate them (Figure 2-1). The deployment kit is a repair/maintenance kit with tools and repair parts for the operator to perform operator level maintenance (Figure 2-2).

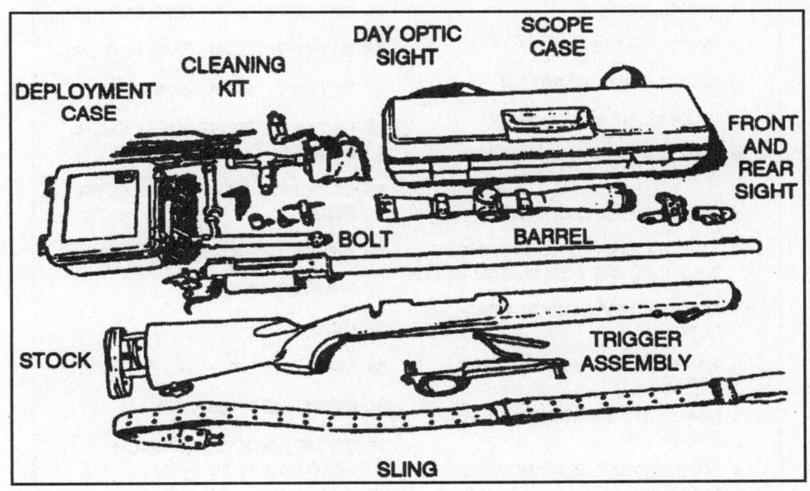

Figure 2-1: M24 sniper weapon system.

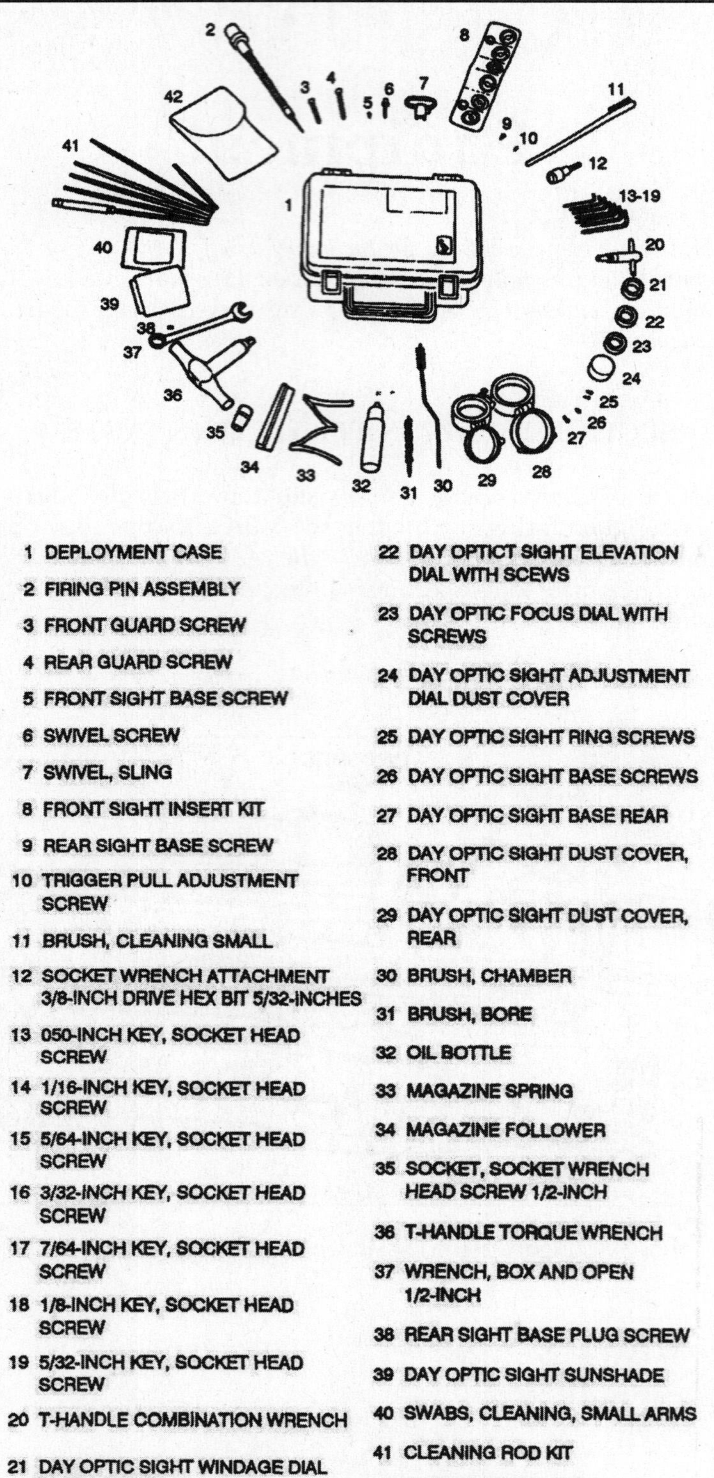

Figure 2-2: The deployment kit.

2-1. OPERATIONS AND FUNCTIONS

To operate the M24 sniper weapon system, the sniper must know the information and instructions pertaining to the safety, bolt assembly, trigger assembly, and stock adjustment.

a. **Safety.** The safety is located on the right rear side of the receiver. When properly engaged, the safety provides protection against accidental discharge in normal usage.
   (1) To engage the safety, place it in the "S" position (Figure 2-3).
   (2) Always place the safety in the "S" position before handling, loading, or unloading the weapon.
   (3) When the weapon is ready to be fired, place the safety in the "F" position (Figure 2-3).

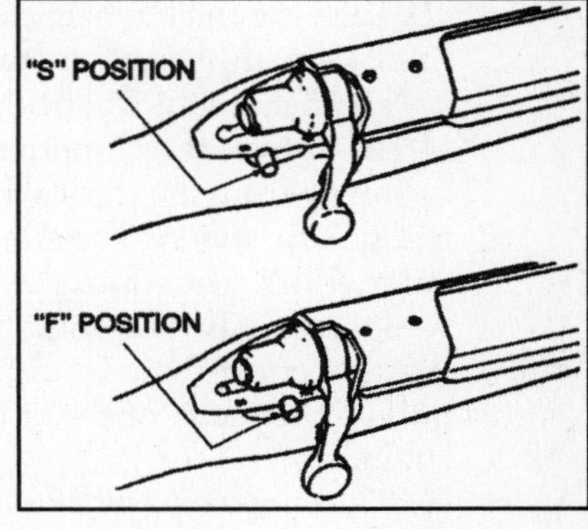

Figure 2-3: Safety.

b. **Bolt Assembly.** The bolt assembly locks the cartridge into the chamber and extracts the cartridge from the chamber.
   (1) To remove the bolt from the receiver, release the internal magazine, place the safety in the "S" position, raise the bolt handle, and pull it back until it stops. Then push the bolt stop release (Figure 2-4) and pull the bolt from the receiver.
   (2) To replace the bolt, ensure the safety is in the "S" position, align the lugs on the bolt assembly with the receiver (Figure 2-5), slide the bolt all the way into the receiver, and then push the bolt handle down.

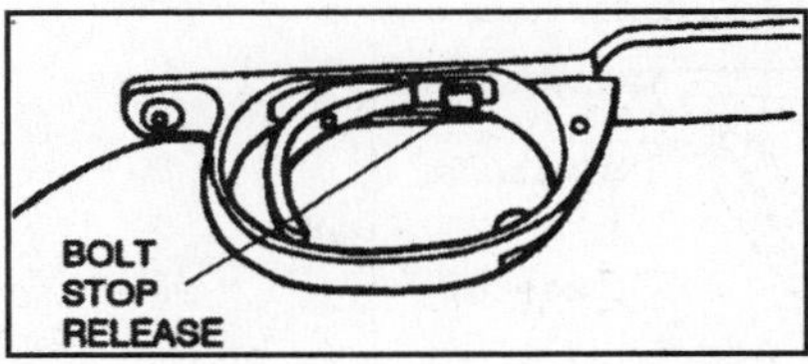

Figure 2-4: Bolt stop release.

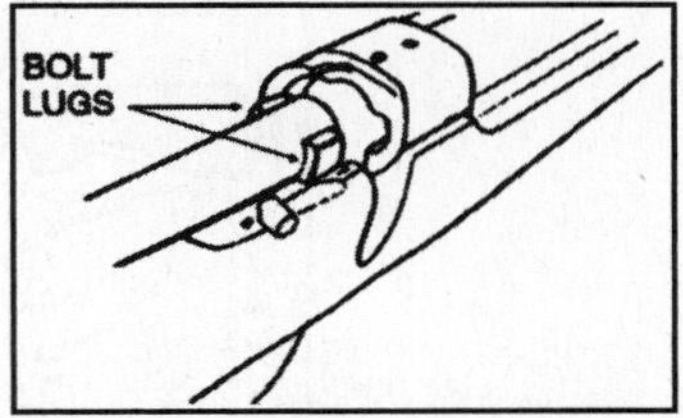

Figure 2-5: Bolt alignment.

WARNING

Never remove the trigger mechanism, or make adjustments to the trigger assembly, except for the trigger pull force adjustment.

c. **Trigger Assembly.** Pulling the trigger fires the rifle when the safety is in the "F" position. The operator may adjust the trigger pull force from a minimum of 2 pounds to a maximum or 8 pounds. This is done using the 1/16-inch socket head screw key provided in the deployment kit. Turning the trigger adjustment screw (Figure 2-6) clockwise increases the force needed to pull the trigger. Turning it counterclockwise decreases the force needed. This is the only trigger adjustment the sniper should make.

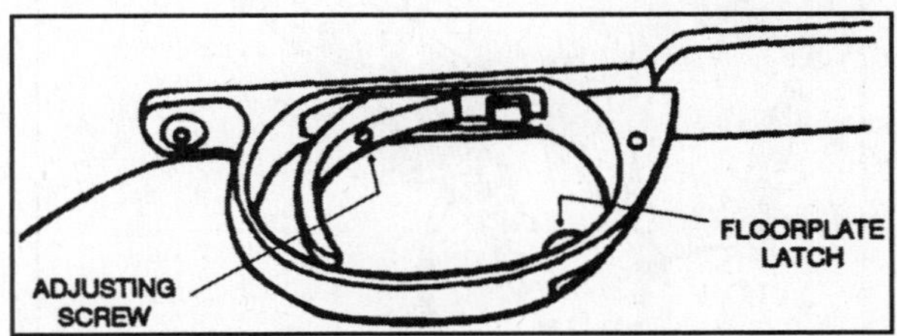

Figure 2-6: Trigger adjustment.

d. **Stock Adjustment.** The M24's stock has an adjustable butt plate to accommodate the length of pull. The stock adjustment (Figure 2-7) consists of a thin wheel and a thick wheel. The thick wheel adjusts the shoulder stock. The thin wheel locks the shoulder stock.
   (1) Turn the thick wheel clockwise to *lengthen* the stock.
   (2) Turn the thick wheel counterclockwise to *shorten* the stock.
   (3) To lock the shoulder stock into position, turn the thin wheel clockwise against the thick wheel.
   (4) To unlock the shoulder stock, turn the thin wheel counterclockwise away from the thick wheel.

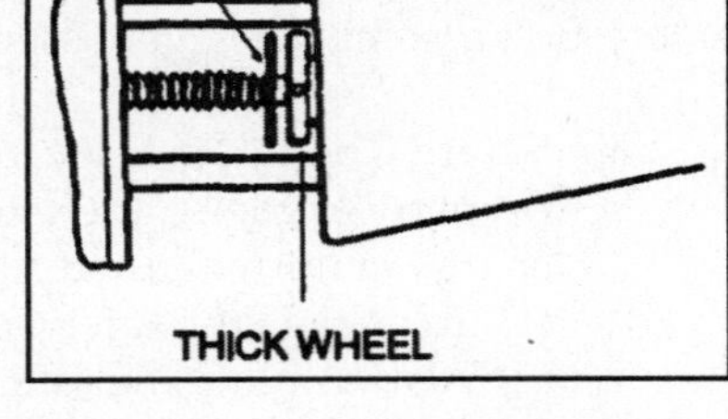

Figure 2-7: Stock adjustment.

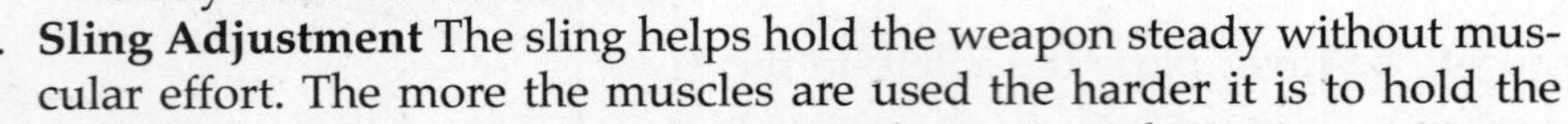

e. **Sling Adjustment** The sling helps hold the weapon steady without muscular effort. The more the muscles are used the harder it is to hold the weapon steady. The sling tends to bind the parts of the body used in aiming into a rigid bone brace, requiring less effort than would be necessary if no sling were used. When properly adjusted, the sling permits part of the recoil of the rifle to reabsorbed by the nonfiring arm and hand, removing recoil from the firing shoulder.
   (1) The sling consists of two different lengths of leather straps joined together by a metal D ring (Figure 2-8). The longer strap is connected to the sling swivel on the rear stud on the forearm of the rifle. The shorter strap is attached to the sling swivel on the buttstock of the rifle. There are two leather loops on the long strap known as keepers. The keepers are used to adjust the tension on the sling. The frogs are hooks that are used to adjust the length of the sling.

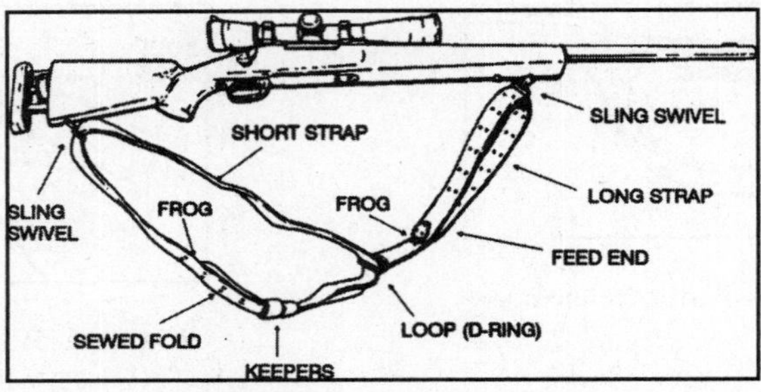

Figure 2-8: Leather sling.

   (2) To adjust the sling, the sniper disconnects the sling from the buttstock swivel. Then, he adjusts the length of the metal D ring that joins the two halves of the sling. He then makes sure it is even with the comb of the stock when attaching the sling to the front swivel (Figure 2-9).

Figure 2-9: Sling adjustment.

(3) The sniper adjusts the length of the sling by placing the frog on the long strap of the sling in the 4th to the 7th set of adjustment holes on the rounded end of the long strap that goes through the sling swivel on the forearm (Figure 2-10).

(4) After adjusting the length, the sniper places the weapon on his firing hip and supports the weapon with his firing arm. The sniper turns the sling away from him 90 degrees and inserts his nonfiring arm.

Figure 2-10: Adjusting the length of the sling.

(5) The sniper slides the loop in the large section of the sling up the nonfiring arm until it is just below the armpit (Figure 2-11). He then slides both leather keepers down the sling until they bind the loop snugly round the nonfiring arm.

Figure 2-11: Placing the sling around the nonfiring arm.

(6) The sniper moves his nonfiring hand from the outside of the sling to the inside of the sling between the rifle and the sling. The sniper then grasps the forearm of the weapon, just behind the sling swivel with his nonfiring hand. He forces it outward and away from his body with the nonfiring hand (Figure 2-12).

(7) The sniper pulls the butt of the weapon into the pocket of his shoulder with the firing hand. He then grasps the weapon at the small of the stock and begins the aiming process.

Figure 2-12: Proper placement of the sling.

2-2. INSPECTION

The sniper performs PMCS on the M24 SWS. Deficiencies that cannot be repaired by the sniper requires manufacturer repair. He must refer to TM 9-1005-306-10 that is furnished with each weapon system. The sniper must know this technical manual. He should cheek the following areas when inspecting the M24:

a. Check the appearance and completeness of all parts.
b. Check the bolt to ensure it locks, unlocks, and moves smoothly.
c. Check the safety to ensure it can be positively placed into the "S" and "F" positions easily without being too hard or moving too freely.
d. Check the trigger to ensure the weapon will not fire when the safety is in the "S" position, and that it has a smooth, crisp trigger pull when the safety is in the "F" position.
e. Check the trigger guard screws (rear of trigger guard and front of internal magazine) for proper torque (65 inch-pounds).
f. Check the scope mounting ring nuts for proper torque (65 inch-pounds).
g. Check the stock for any cracks, splits, or any contact it may have with the barrel.
h. Inspect the scope for obstructions such as dirt, dust, moisture, or loose or damaged lenses.

2-3. CARE AND MAINTENANCE

Maintenance is any measure taken to keep the M24 SWS in top operating condition. It includes inspection, repair, cleaning and lubrication-inspection reveals the need for repair, cleaning, or lubrication. It also reveals any damages or defects. When sheltered in garrison and infrequently used, the M24 SWS must be inspected often to detect dirt, moisture, and signs of corrosion, and it must be cleaned accordingly. The M24 SWS that is in use and subject to the elements, however, requires no inspection for cleanliness, since the fact of its use and exposure is evidence that it requires repeated cleaning and lubrication.

a. **M24 SWS Maintenance.** The following materials are required for cleaning and maintaining the M24 SWS:
   - One-piece plastic-coated .30 caliber cleaning rod with jag (36 inches).
   - Bronze bristle bore brushes (.30 and .45 calibers).
   - Cleaning patches (small and large sizes).
   - Carbon cleaner.
   - Copper cleaner.
   - Rust prevention.
   - Cleaner, lubricant, preservative.

- Rifle grease.
- Bore guide (long action).
- Swabs.
- Pipe cleaners.
- Medicine dropper.
- Shaving brush.
- Pistol cleaning rod.
- Rags.
- Camel's-hair brush.
- Lens tissue.
- Lens cleaning fluid (denatured or isopropyl alcohol).

b. **M24 SWS Disassembly.** The M24 SWS will be disassembled only when necessary, not for daily cleaning. For example, when removing an obstruction from the SWS that is stuck between the stock and the barrel. When disassembly is required, the recommended procedure is as follows:
   - Place the weapon so that is it pointing in a safe direction.
   - Ensure the safety is in the "S" position.
   - Remove the bolt assembly.
   - Loosen the mounting ring nuts on the telescope and remove the telescope.
   - Remove the action screws.
   - Lift the stock from the barrel assembly.

c. **M24 SWS Cleaning Procedures.** The M24 SWS must always be cleaned *before* and *after firing.*
   (1) The SWS must always be cleaned *before firing.* Firing a weapon with a dirty bore or chamber will multiply and speed up any corrosive action. Oil in the bore and chamber of a SWS will cause pressures to vary and first-round accuracy will suffer. Clean and dry the bore and chamber before departure on a mission and use extreme care to keep the SWS clean and dry en route to the objective area. Firing a SWS with oil or moisture in the bore will cause smoke that can disclose the firing position.
   (2) The SWS must be cleaned *after firing* since firing produces deposits of primer fouling, powder ashes, carbon, and metal fouling. Although ammunition has a noncorrosive primer that makes cleaning easier, the primer residue can still cause rust if not removed. Firing leaves two major types of fouling that require different solvents to remove *carbon* fouling and *copper* jacket fouling. The SWS must be cleaned within a reasonable time after firing. Use common sense when cleaning between rounds of firing. Repeated firing will not injure the weapon if it is properly cleaned before the first round is fired.
   (3) Lay the SWS on a table or other flat surface with the muzzle away from the body and the sling down. Make sure not to strike the muzzle or telescopic sight on the table. The cleaning cradle is ideal for holding the SWS.
   (4) Always clean the bore from the chamber toward the muzzle, attempting to keep the muzzle lower than the chamber to prevent the bore cleaner from running into the receiver or firing mechanism. Be careful not to get any type of fluid between the stock and receiver. If fluid does collect between the stock and receiver, the receiver will slide on the bedding every time the SWS recoils, thereby decreasing accuracy and increasing wear and tear on the receiver and bedding material.
   (5) Always use a bore guide to keep the cleaning rod centered in the bore during the cleaning process.
   (6) Push several patches saturated with carbon cleaner through the barrel to loosen the powder fouling and begin the solvent action on the copper jacket fouling.
   (7) Saturate the bronze bristle brush (NEVER USE STAINLESS STEEL BORE BRUSHES-THEY WILL SCRATCH THE BARREL) with carbon cleaner (shake the bottle regularly to keep the ingredients mixed) using the medicine dropper to prevent contamination of the carbon cleaner. Run the bore brush through at least 20 times. Make sure the bore brush passes completely through the barrel before reversing its direction; otherwise, the bristles will break off.
   (8) Use a pistol cleaning rod and a .45 caliber bronze bristle bore brush, clean the chamber by rotating the patch-wrapped brush 8 to 10 times. DO NOT scrub the brush in and out of the chamber.
   (9) Push several patches saturated with carbon cleaner through the bore to push out the loosened powder fouling.
   (10) Continue using the bore brush and patches with carbon cleaner until the patches have no traces of black/gray powder fouling and are green/blue. This indicates that the powder fouling has been removed and

only copper fouling remains. Remove the carbon cleaner from the barrel with several clean patches. This is important since solvents should never be mixed in the barrel.

(11) Push several patches saturated with copper cleaner through the bore, using a scrubbing motion to work the solvent into the copper. Let the solvent work for 10 to 15 minutes (NEVER LEAVE THE COPPER CLEANER IN THE BARREL FOR MORE THAN 30 MINUTES).

(12) While waiting, scrub the bolt with the toothbrush moistened with carbon cleaner and wipe down the remainder of the weapon with a cloth.

(13) Push several patches saturated with copper cleaner through the barrel. The patches will appear dark blue at first, indicating the amount of copper fouling removed. Continue this process until the saturated patches have no traces of blue/green. If the patches continue to come out dark blue after several treatments with copper cleaner, use the bronze brush saturated with copper cleaner to increase the scrubbing action. Be sure to clean the bronze brush thoroughly afterwards with hot running water (quick scrub cleaner/degreaser is preferred) as the copper cleaner acts upon its bristles as well.

(14) When the barrel is clean, dry it with several tight fitting patches. Also, dry the chamber using the .45 caliber bronze bristle bore brush with a patch wrapped around it.

(15) Run a patch saturated with rust prevention (*not* CLP) down the barrel and chamber if the weapon is to be stored for any length of time. Stainless steel barrels are not immune from corrosion. Be sure to remove the preservative by running dry patches through the bore and chamber before firing.

(16) Place a small amount of rifle grease on the rear surfaces of the bolt lugs. This will prevent galling of the metal surfaces.

(17) Wipe down the exterior of the weapon (if it is not covered with camouflage paint) with a CLP-saturated cloth to protect it during storage.

d. **Barrel Break-in Procedure.** To increase barrel life, accuracy, and reduce cleaning requirement the following barrel break-in procedure must be used. This procedure is best accomplished when the SWS is new or newly rebarreled. The break-in period is accomplished by polishing the barrel surface under heat and pressure. This procedure should only be done by qualified personnel. The barrel must be cleaned of all fouling, both powder and copper. The barrel is dried, and one round is fired. The barrel is then cleaned again using carbon cleaner and then copper cleaner. The barrel must be cleaned again, and another round is fired. The procedure must be repeated for a total of 10 rounds. After the 10th round the SWS is then tested for groups by firing three-round shot groups, with a complete barrel cleaning between shot groups for a total of five shot groups (15 rounds total). The barrel is now broken in, and will provide superior accuracy and a longer usable barrel life. Additionally, the barrel will be easier to clean because the surface is smoother. Again the barrel should be cleaned at least every 50 rounds to increase the barrel life.

e. **Storage.** The M24 SWS should be stored (Figure 2-13) using the following procedures:

- Clear the SWS, close the bolt, and squeeze the trigger.
- Open the lens caps to prevent gathering of moisture.
- Hang the weapon upside down by the rear sling swivel.
- Place all other items in the system case.
- Transport the weapon in the system case during nontactical situations.
- Protect the weapon at all times during tactical movement.

✍ **NOTE**

Rod clean swabs through the bore before firing. This procedure ensures first-round accuracy and reduces the signature.

f. **Cold Climates.** In temperatures below freezing, the SWS must be kept free of moisture and heavy oil, both of which will freeze, causing the working parts to freeze or operate sluggishly. The SWS should be stored in a room with the temperature equal to the outside temperature. When the SWS is taken into a warm area, condensation occurs, thus requiring a thorough cleaning and drying before taking it into the cold. Otherwise, the condensation causes icing on exposed metal parts and optics. The firing pin should be disassembled and cleaned thoroughly with a degreasing agent. It should then be lubricated with CLP. Rifle grease hardens and causes the firing pin to fall sluggishly.

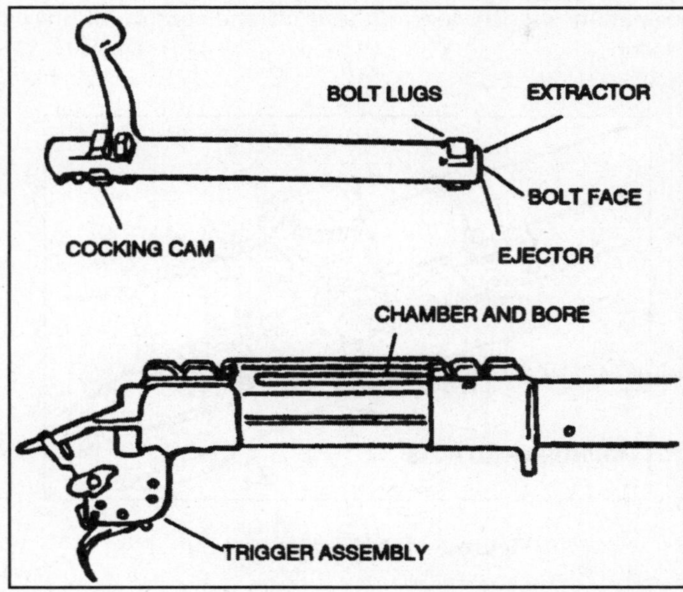

Figure 2-13: Maintenance for storing or using.

g. **Salt Water Exposure.** Saltwater and saltwater atmosphere have extreme and rapid corrosive effects on the metal parts of the SWS. During periods of exposure, the SWS must be checked and cleaned as often as possible, even if it means only lubricating the SWS. The SWS should always be well lubricated, including the bore, except when actually firing. Before firing, always run a dry patch through the bore, if possible.
h. **Jungle Operations** (High Humidity). In hot and humid temperatures, keep the SWS lubricated and cased when not in use. Protect the SWS from rain and moisture whenever possible. Keep ammunition clean and dry. Clean the SWS, the bore, and the chamber daily. Keep the caps on the telescope when not in use. If moisture or fungus develops on the inside of the telescope, replace it. Clean and dry the stock daily. Dry the carrying case and SWS in the sun whenever possible.
i. **Desert Operations.** Keep the SWS dry and free of CLP and grease except on the rear of the bolt lugs. Keep the SWS free of sand by using the carrying sleeve or carrying case when not in use. Protect the SWS by using a wrap. Slide the wrap between the stock and barrel, then cross over on top of the scope. Next, cross under the SWS (over the magazine) and secure it. The SWS can still be placed into immediate operation but all critical parts are covered. The sealed hard case is preferred in the desert if the situation permits. Keep the telescope protected from the direct rays of the sun. Keep ammunition clean and protected from the direct rays of the sun. Use a toothbrush to remove sand from the bolt and receiver. Clean the bore and chamber daily. Protect the muzzle and receiver from blowing sand by covering with a clean cloth. To protect the free-floating barrel of the SWS, take an 8- or 9-inch strip of cloth and tie a knot in each end. Before going on a mission, slide the cloth between the barrel and stock all the way to the receiver and leave it there. When in position, slide the cloth out, taking all restrictive debris and sand with it.

2-4. DISASSEMBLY

Occasionally, the weapon requires disassembly however, this should be done only when absolutely necessary, not for daily maintenance. An example of this would be to remove an obstruction that is stuck between the forestock and the barrel. When disassembly is required, the recommended procedure is as follows:

a. Point the rifle in a safe direction.
b. Put the safety in the "S" position.
c. Remove the bolt assembly.

d. Use the 1/2-inch combination wrench, loosen the front and rear mounting ring nuts (Figure 2-14) on the scope, and remove the scope.

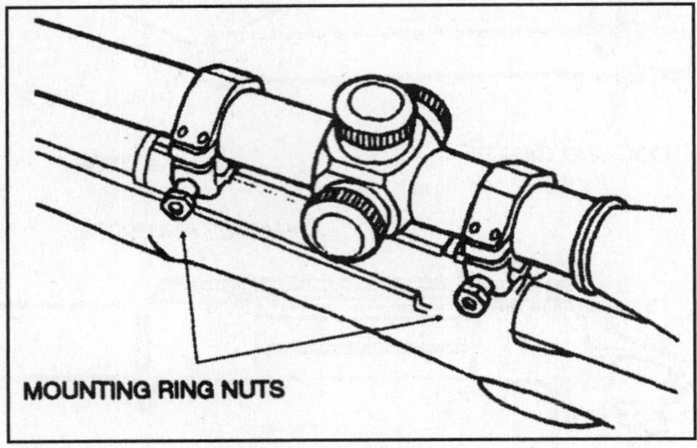

Figure 2-14: Mounting ring nuts.

e. Loosen the front and rear trigger guard screws (Figure 2-15).
f. Lift the stock assembly from the barrel assembly (Figure 2-16).
g. Reassemble in reverse order.

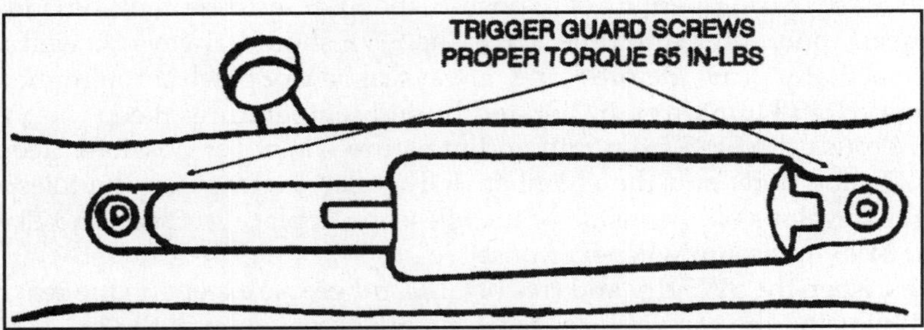

Figure 2-15: Trigger guard screws.

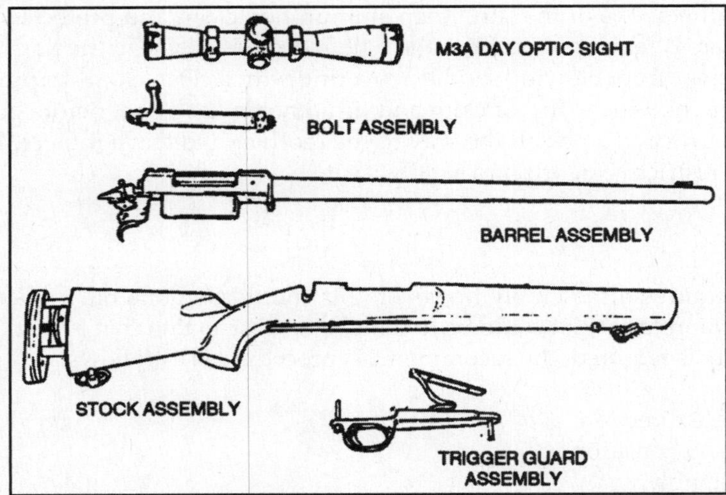

Figure 2-16: Disassembled weapon.

WARNING

Always keep fingers away from the trigger until ready to fire, make sure the rifle is not loaded by inspecting the magazine and chamber, use authorized ammunition and check the condition before loading the rifle.

2-5. LOADING AND UNLOADING

Before loading, the sniper should ensure that the M24 SWS is on SAFE, and the bolt is in a forward position. Before unloading, he should ensure the M24 SWS is on SAFE, and the bolt is toward the rear.

a. **Loading.** The M24 has an internal, five-round capacity magazine. To load the rifle—

(1) Point the weapon in a safe direction.
(2) Ensure the safety is in the "S" position.
(3) Raise the bolt handle. Then pull the bolt handle all the way back.
(4) Push five cartridges of 7.62-mm special ball ammunition one at a time through the ejection port into the magazine. Ensure the bullet end of the cartridges is aligned toward the chamber.
(5) To ensure proper functioning, cartridges should be set fully rearward in the magazine.
(6) Use a finger to push the cartridges into the magazine and all the way down. Slowly slide the bolt forward so that the bolt slides over the top of the cartridges in the magazine.
(7) Push the bolt handle down. The magazine is now loaded.
(8) To chamber a cartridge, raise the bolt and pull it back until it stops.
(9) Push the bolt forward. The bolt removes a cartridge from the magazine and pushes it into the chamber.
(10) Push the bolt handle down.
(11) To fire, place the safety in the "F" position and squeeze the trigger.

WARNING

Ensure the chamber and magazine are clear of cartridges.

b. **Unloading.** To unload the M24 SWS—

(1) Point the muzzle in a safe direction.
(2) Ensure the safety is in the "S" position.
(3) Raise the bolt handle.
(4) Put one hand over the top ejection port. Slowly pull the bolt handle back with the other hand to remove the cartridge from the chamber.
(5) Remove the cartridge from the rifle.
(6) Put a hand under the floor plate.
(7) Push the floor plate latch to release the floor plate (Figure 2-17). The magazine spring and follower will be released from the magazine.
(8) Remove the released cartridges.
(9) Push in the magazine follower, then close the floor plate.

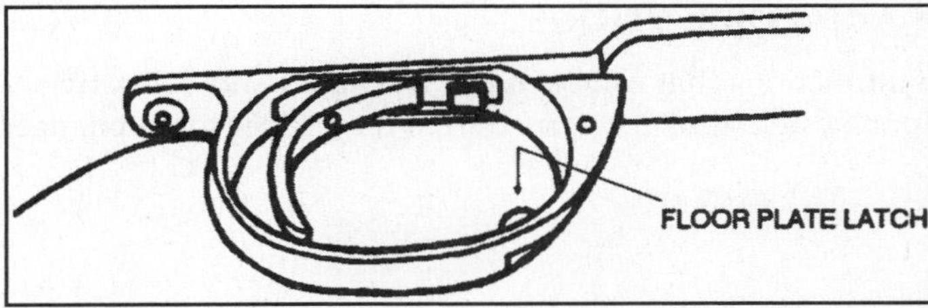

Figure 2-17: Floor plate latch.

2-6. STORAGE

The M24 SWS should be stored as follows:

a. Hang the weapon in an upside down position by the rear sling swivel.
b. Close the bolt and squeeze the trigger.
c. Open the lens caps to prevent gathering of moisture.
d. Place all other items in the system case.
e. Protect the weapon at all times during tactical movement. (See Chapter 4.)

SECTION II. AMMUNITION

The sniper uses the 7.62-mm special ball (M118) ammunition with the sniper weapon system. The sniper must rezero the weapon each time he fires a different type or lot of ammunition. This information should be maintained in the sniper data book.

2-7. TYPES AND CHARACTERISTICS

The types and characteristics of sniper ammunition are described in this paragraph.

a. **M118 Special Ball Bullet.** The 7.62-mm special ball (M118) bullet consists of a gilding metal jacket and a lead antimony slug. It is a boat-tailed bullet (rear of bullet is tapered) and weighs 173 grains. The tip of the bullet is not colored. The base of the cartridge is stamped with the year of manufacture and a circle that has vertical and horizontal lines, sectioning it into quarters. Its spread (accuracy standard) for a 10-shot group is no more than 12 inches at 550 meters (fired from an accuracy barrel in a test cradle).
b. **M82 Blank Ammunition.** The 7.62-mm M82 blank ammunition is used during sniper field training. It provides the muzzle blast and flash that can be detected by trainers during the exercises that evaluate the sniper's ability to conceal himself while firing his weapon.

✍ NOTE

Regular 7.62-mm ball ammunition should be used only in an emergency situation. No damage will occur to the barrel when firing regular 7.62-mm ball ammunition. The M3A scope's bullet drop compensator is designed for M118 special ball, and there will be a significant change in zero. Therefore the rifle will not be as accurate when firing regular 7.62-mm ball ammunition. The 7.62-mm ball ammunition should be test fired and the ballistic data recorded in the data book.

2-8. ROUND-COUNT BOOK

The sniper maintains a log of the number of cartridge fired through the M24 SWS. It is imperative to accurately maintain the round-count book as the barrel should be replaced after 5,000 rounds of firing. The round-count book is issued and maintained in the arms room.

2-9. M24 MALFUNCTIONS AND CORRECTIONS

Table 2-1 does not reflect all malfunctions that can occur, or all causes and corrective actions. If a malfunction is not correctable, the complete weapon system must be turned in to the proper maintenance/supply channel for return to the contractor.

Table 2-1: M24 malfunctions and corrections.

MALFUNCTION	CAUSE	CORRECTION
Fail to fire	Safety in "S" position	1. Move safety to "F" position
	Defective ammunition	2. Eject cartridge
	Firing pin damaged	3. Change firing pin assembly
	Firing pin binds	4. Change firing pin assembly
	Firing pin protrudes	5. Change firing pin assembly
	Firing control out of adjustment	6. Turn complete system in to the maintenance/supply channel for return to contractor
	Trigger out of adjustment	7. Turn in as above
	Trigger does not retract	8. Turn in as above
	Trigger binds on trigger guard	9. Turn in as above
	Firing pin does not remain in the cocked position with bolt closed	10. Turn in as above
Bolt binds	Action screw protudes into bolt track	11. Turn in as above
	Scope base protrudes into bolt track	12. Turn in as above
Fail to feed	Bolt override of cartridge	13. Seat cartridge fully rearward in magazine
	Cartridges stems chamber	14. Pull bolt fully rearward; remove stemmed cartridge from ejection port area; reposition cartridge fully in magazine
	Magazine in backward	15. Remove magazine spring, and reinstall with long leg follower
	Weak or broken magazine spring	16. Replace spring
Fail to eject	Broken ejector	17. Turn the complete weapon system in to the maintenance/supply channel for return to contractor
	Fouled ejector plunger	18. Inspect and clean bolt face; if malfunction continues, turn in as above
Fail to extract	Broken extractor	19. Turn in as above

SECTION III. SNIPER SIGHTING DEVICES

The sniper has two sighting devices: the M3A scope and iron sights. The M3A scope allows the sniper to see the cross hairs and the image of the target with identical sharpness. It can be easily removed and replaced with less than 1/2 minute of angle change in zero. However, the M3A scope should be left on the rifle. Iron sights are used only as a backup sighting system and can be quickly installed.

2-10. M3A SCOPE

The M3A scope is an optical instrument that the sniper uses to improve his ability to see his target clearly in most situations. Usually, the M3A scope presents the target at an increased size (as governed by scope magnification), relative to the same target at the same distance without a scope. The M3A scope helps the sniper to identify recognize the target. His increased sighting ability also helps him to successfully engage the target.

> ✍ **NOTE**
>
> The adjustment dials are under the adjustment dust cover.

a. **M3A Scope Adjustments.** The sniper must use the following adjustment procedures on the M3A scope:

(1) ***Focus adjustment dial.*** The focus adjustment dial (Figure 2-18) is on the left side of the scope barrel. This dial has limiting stops with the two extreme positions shown by the infinity mark and the largest dot. The focus adjustment dial keeps the target in focus. If the target is close, the dial is set at a position near the largest dot.

> ✍ **NOTE**
>
> Each minute of angle is an angular unit of measure.

(2) ***Elevation adjustment dial.*** The elevation adjustment dial (Figure 2-18) is on top of the scope barrel. This dial has calibrated index markings from 1 to 10. These markings represent the elevation setting adjustments needed at varying distances: 1 = 100 meters, 3 = 300 meters, 7 = 700 meters, and so on. Each click of the elevation dial equals 1 minute of angle.

(3) ***Windage adjustment dial.*** The windage adjustment dial (Figure 2-18) is on the right side of the scope barrel. This dial is used to make lateral adjustments to the scope. Turning the dial in the indicated direction moves the point of impact in that direction. Each click on the windage dial equals .5 minute of angle.

(4) ***Eyepiece adjustment.*** The eyepiece (Figure 2-19) is adjusted by turning it in or out of the barrel until the reticle appears crisp and clear. Focusing the eyepiece should be done after mounting the scope. The sniper grasps the eyepiece and backs it away from the lock ring. He does not attempt to loosen the lock ring first; it loosens automatically when he backs away from the eyepiece (no tools needed). The eyepiece is turned several turns to move it at least 1/8 inch. It takes this much change to achieve any measurable effect on the focus. The sniper looks through the scope at the sky or a blank wall and checks to see if the reticle appears sharp and crisp. He locks the lock ring after achieving reticle clarity.

WARNINGS

1. Securely fasten the mounting base to the rifle. Loose mounting may cause the M3A scope and base mount assembly to come off the rifle when firing, possibly injuring the firer.
2. During recoil prevent the M3A scope from striking the face by maintaining an average distance of 2 to 3 inches between the eye and the scope.

b. **M3A Scope Mount.** The M3A scope mount has a baseplate with four screws; a pair of scope rings with eight ring screws, each with an upper and lower ring half with eight ring screws and two ring mounting bolts with

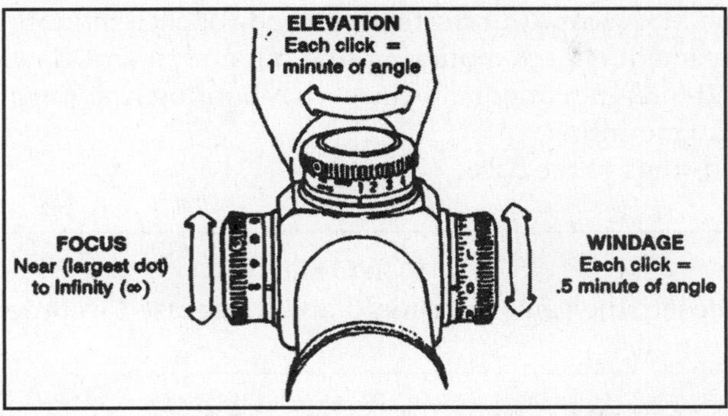

Figure 2-18. Focus, elevation, and windage adjustment dials.

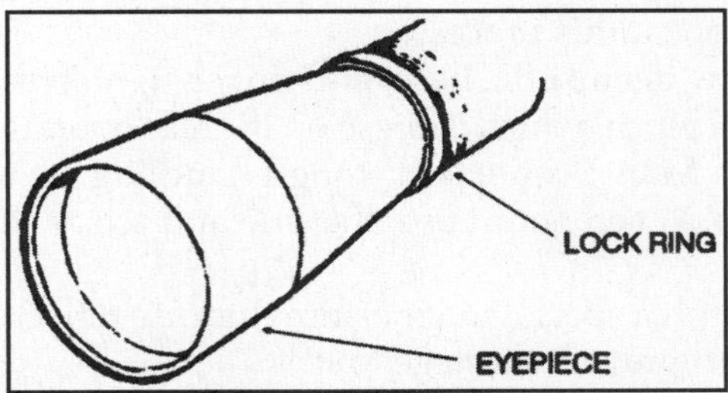

Figure 2-19: Eyepiece adjustment.

nuts (Figure 2-20). The baseplate is mounted to the rifle by screwing the four baseplate screws through the plate and into the top of the receiver. The screws must not protrude into the receiver and interrupt the functioning of the bolt. After the baseplate is mounted, the scope rings are mounted.

> ✍ **NOTE**
>
> The M3A scope has two sets of mounting slots. The sniper selects the set of slots that provides proper eye relief (the distance that the eye is positioned behind the telescopic sight). The average distance is 2 to 3 inches. The sniper adjusts eye relief to obtain a full field of view.

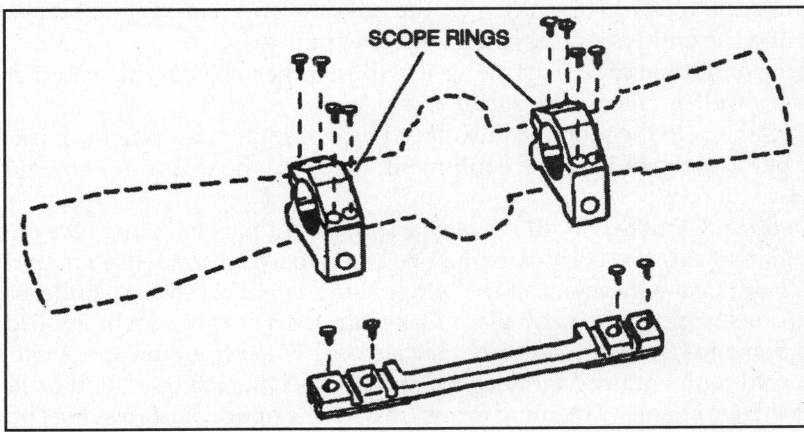

Figure 2-20: Scope mount.

(1) Before mounting the M3A scope, lubricate the threads of each mounting ring nut.
(2) Ensure smooth movement of each mounting ring nut and mount claw.
(3) Inspect for burrs and foreign matter between each mounting ring nut and mount claw. Remove burrs or foreign matter before mounting.
(4) Mount the sight and rings to the base.

> ✍ **NOTE**
> Once a set of slots is chosen, the same set should always be used in order for the SWS to retain zero.

(5) Ensure the mounting surface is free of dirt, oil, or grease.
(6) Set each ring bolt spline into the selected slot.
(7) Slide the rear mount claw against the base and finger-tighten the mounting ring nut.
(8) If the scope needs to be adjusted loosen the mounting ring nuts and align the ring bolts with the other set of slots on the base Repeat this process.
(9) Slide the front mount claw against the base, and finger-tighten the mounting ring nut.
(10) Use the T-handle torque wrench, which is preset to 65 inch-pounds, to tighten the rear mounting ring nut.

c. **Care and Maintenance of the M3A Scope.** Dirt, rough handling, or abuse of optical equipment will result in inaccuracy and malfunction. When not in use, the rifle and scope should be cased, and the lens should be capped.

(1) ***Lens.*** The lens are coated with a special magnesium fluoride reflection-reducing material. This coat is thin and great care is required to prevent damage to it.
(a) To remove dust, lint, or other foreign matter from the lens, lightly brush the lens with a clean camel's-hair brush.
(b) To remove oil or grease from the optical surfaces, apply a drop of lens cleaning fluid or robbing alcohol on a lens tissue. Carefully wipe off the surface of the lens in circular motions (from the center to the outside edge). Dry off the lens with a clean lens tissue. In the field, if the proper supplies are not available, breathe heavily on the glass and wipe with a soft, clean cloth.

(2) ***Scope.*** The scope is a delicate instrument and must be handled with care. The following precautions will prevent damage.
(a) Check and tighten all mounting screws periodically and always before an operation. Be careful not to change the coarse windage adjustment.
(b) Keep the lens free from oil and grease and never touch them with the fingers. Body grease and perspiration can injure them. Keep the cap on the lens.
(c) Do not force the elevation and windage screws or knobs.
(d) Do not allow the scope to remain in direct sunlight, and avoid letting the sun's rays shine through the lens. The lens magnify and concentrate sunlight into a pinpoint of intense heat, which is focused on the mil-scale reticle. This may melt the mil dots and damage the scope internally. Keep the lens covered and the entire scope covered when not in use.
(e) Avoid dropping the scope or striking it with another object. This could permanently damage the telescope as well as change the zero.
(f) To avoid damage to the scope or any other piece of sniper equipment, snipers or armorers should be the only personnel handling the equipment. Anyone who does not know how to use this equipment could cause damage.

(3) ***Climate conditions.*** Climate conditions play an important part in taking care of optical equipment.
(a) *Cold climates.* In extreme cold, care must be taken to avoid condensation and congealing of oil on the glass of the optical equipment. If the temperature is not excessive, condensation can be removed by placing the instrument in a warm place. Concentrated heat must not be applied because it causes expansion and damage can occur. Moisture may also be blotted from the optics with lens tissue or a soft, dry cloth. In cold temperatures, oil thickens and causes sluggish operation or failure. Focusing parts are sensitive to freezing oils. Breathing forms frost, so the optical surfaces must be cleaned with lens tissue, preferably dampened lightly with alcohol. DO NOT apply alcohol on the glass of the optics.

(b) *Jungle operations* (*high humidity*). In hot and humid temperatures, keep the caps on the scope when not in use. If moisture or fungus develops on the inside of the telescope, replace it.
(c) *Desert operations.* Keep the scope protected from the direct rays of the sun.
(d) *Hot climate and salt water exposure.* The scope is vulnerable to hot, humid climates and salt water atmosphere. It MUST NOT be exposed to direct sunlight. In humid and salt air conditions, the scope must be inspected, cleaned, and lightly oiled to avoid rust and corrosion. Perspiration can also cause the equipment to rust; therefore, the instruments must be thoroughly dried and lightly oiled.

d. **M3A Scope Operation.** When using the M3A scope, the sniper looks at the target and determines the distance to it by using the mil dots on the reticle. The mil-dot reticle (Figure 2-21) is a duplex-style reticle that has thick outer sections and thin inner sections. Superimposed on the thin center section of the reticle is a series of dots. There are 4 dots on each side of the center and 4 dots above and below the center. These 4 dots are spaced 1 mil apart, and 1 mil from both the center and the start of the thick section of the reticle. This spacing allows the sniper to make close estimates of target range, assuming there is an object of known size (estimate) in the field of view. For example, a human target appears to be 6 feet tall, which equals 1.83 meters tall, and at 500 meters, 3.65 dots high (nominally, about 3.5 dots high). Another example is a 1-meter target at a 1,000-meter range. This target is the height between 2 dots, or the width between 2 dots. If the sniper is given a good estimate of the object's size, then he may accurately determine target range using the mil-dot system.

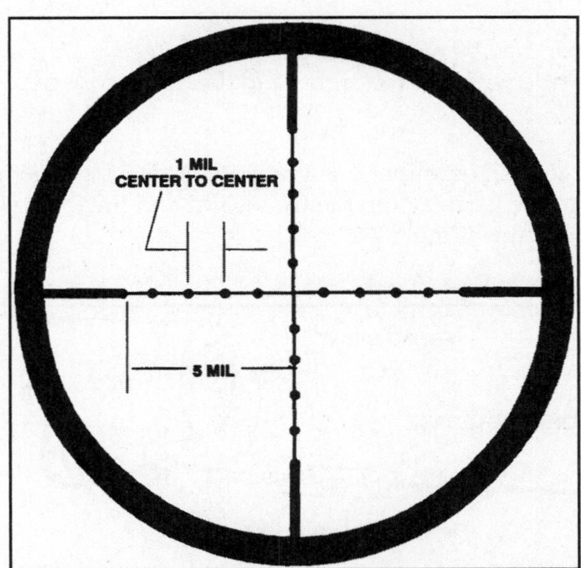

Figure 2-21: Mil-dot reticle.

e. **Zeroing.** Zeroing the M3A scope should be done on a known-distance range (preferably 900 meters long) with bull's-eye-type targets (200-yard targets). When zeroing the scope, the sniper—
(1) Assumes a good prone-supported position 100 meters from the target.
(2) Ensures the "1" on the elevation dial is lined up with the elevation index line, and the "0" on the windage dial is lined up with the windage index line.
(3) Fires three rounds at the center of the target, keeping the same aiming point each time and triangulate.
(4) After the strike of the rounds has been noted, turns the elevation and windage dials to make the needed adjustments to the scope.
- Each click on the elevation dial equals one minute of angle.
- One minute of angle at 100 meters equals 1.145 inches or about 1 inch.
- Each click on the windage dial equals .5 minute of angle.
- .5 minute of angle at 100 meters equals about .5 inch.

(5) Repeats steps 3 and 4 until a three-round shot group is centered on the target.

(6) Once the shot group is centered, loosens the hex head screws on the elevation and windage dials. He turns the elevation dial to the index line marked "1" (if needed). He turns the windage dial to the index line marked "0" (if needed) and tighten the hex head screws.

(7) After zeroing at 100 meters and calibrating the dial, confirms this zero by firing and recording sight settings (see Chapter 3) at 100-meter increments through 900 meters.

f. **Field-Expedient Confirmation/Zeroing.** The sniper may need to confirm zero in a field environment. Examples are shortly after receiving a mission, a weapon was dropped, or excessive climatic changes as may be experienced by deploying to another part of the world. Two techniques of achieving a crude zero are the 25-yard/900-inch method and the observation of impact method.

(1) ***25-yard/900-inch method.*** Dial the scope to 300 meters for elevation and to "0" for windage. Aim and fire at a target that is at a 25-yard distance. Adjust the scope until rounds are impacting 5/8 of an inch above the point of aim. To confirm, set the elevation to 500 meters. The rounds should impact 2 1/4 inches above the point of aim.

(2) ***Observation of impact method.*** When a known distance range is unavailable, locate a target so that the observer can see the impact of rounds clearly. Determine the exact range to the target, dial in the appropriate range, and fire. Watch the impact of the rounds; the observer gives the sight adjustments until a point of aim or point of impact is achieved.

2-11. IRON SIGHTS

Depending on the situation, a sniper may be required to deliver an effective shot at ranges up to 900 meters or more. This requires the sniper to zero his rifle with the iron sights and the M3A scope at most ranges that he can be expected to fire.

a. **Mounting.** To mount iron sights, the sniper must remove the M3A scope first.

(1) Attach the front sight to the barrel, align the front sight and the front sight base, and slide the sight over the base and tighten the screw (Figure 2-22).

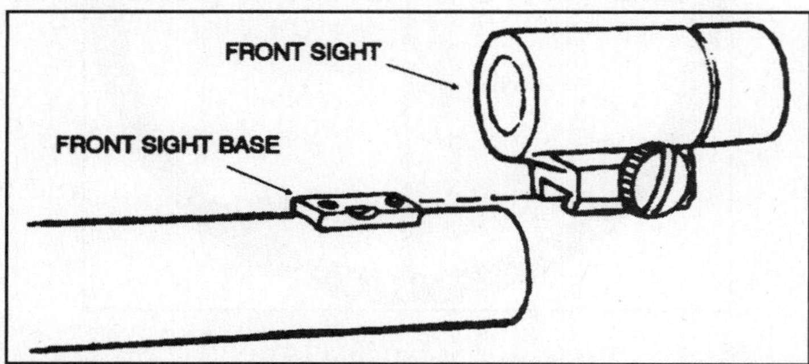

Figure 2-22: Front sight attachment.

(2) The aperture insert may be either skeleton or translucent plastic (Figure 2-23). The skeleton aperture is the most widely used. The translucent plastic aperture is preferred by some shooters and is available in clear plastic. Both apertures are available in various sizes. A common error is selecting an aperture that is too small. Select an aperture that appears to be at least twice the diameter of the bull's-eye. An aperture selected under one light condition may, under a different light, form a halo around the bull or make the bull appear indistinct or oblong. The aperture selected should reveal a wide line of white around the bull and allow the bull to standout in clear definition against this background.

(3) Remove one of the three sets of screws from the rear sight base located on the left rear of the receiver. Align the rear sight with the rear sight base taking care to use the hole that provides the operator the desired eye relief. Then tighten the screw to secure the rear sight to the base.

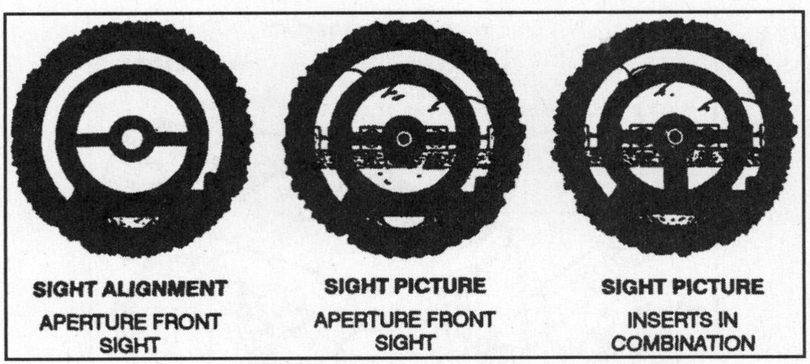

Figure 2-23: Aperture insert.

> ✍ NOTE
>
> Operator-desired eye relief determines the set screw that must be removed.

b. **Adjustment Scales.** Adjustment scales are of the vernier type. Each graduation on the scale inscribed on the sight base equals 3 minutes of angle. (See the minutes of angle chart in Chapter 3.) Each graduation of the adjustable scale plates equals 1 minute of angle. To use the vernier-type adjustment scales—
   (1) Note the point at which graduations on both the top and the bottom scales are aligned.
   (2) Count the numbers of full 3 minutes of angle graduations from "0" on the fixed scale to "0" on the adjustable scale. Add this figure to the number of 1 minute angle graduations from "0" on the adjustable scale to the point where the two graduations are aligned.

c. **Zeroing.** Zeroing iron sights should be done on the same type of range and targets as in paragraph 2-10a. To set a mechanical zero on the iron sights for windage, the sniper turns the windage dial all the way to the left or right, then he counts the number of clicks it takes to get from one side to the other. He divides this number by 2—for example, 120 divided by 2 equals 60. The sniper turns the windage dial 60 clicks back to the center. If the two zeros on the windage indicator plate do not align, he loosens the screw on the windage indicator plate and aligns the two zeros. The sniper uses the same procedure to set a mechanical zero for elevation. Once a mechanical zero has been set, he assumes a good prone-supported position, 100 meters from the target. He fires three rounds at the center of the target, observing the same aiming point each time. After noting the strike of the rounds, the sniper turns the *elevation* and *windage* dials to make needed adjustments to the iron sights as follows (Figure 2-24):
   (1) Each click of adjustment is 1/4 minute of angle (one minute of angle equals about 1 inch at 100 yards, 6 inches at 600 yards, and so forth). There are twelve 1/4 minutes of angle, equaling 3 minutes of angle adjustments in each dial revolution. The total elevation adjustment is 60 minutes of angle (600 inches at 1,000 yards) total windage adjustment is 36 minutes of angle (360 inches at 1,000 yards).
   (2) Turn the elevation dial in the direction marked *UP* to raise the point of impact: turn the elevation dial in the opposite direction to lower the point or impact. Turn the windage dial in the direction marked *R* to move the point of impact to the right; then turn the windage dial in the opposite direction to move the point of impact to the left.
   (3) Continue firing and adjusting shot groups until the point of aim or point of impact is achieved.

After zeroing the rifle sight to the preferred range, the sniper loosens the elevation and windage indicator plate screws with the socket head screw key provided. Now, he loosens the spring tension screw, aligns the "0" on the plate with the "0" on the sight body, and retightens the plate screws. Then the sniper loosens the spring tension screws and set screws in each dial, and aligns the "0" of the dial with the reference line on the sight. He presses the dial against the sight, tightens the set screws, and equally tightens the spring tension screws until a definite "click" can be felt when the dial is turned. This click can be sharpened or softened to preference by equally loosening or tightening the spring screws on each dial. The sniper makes windage and elevation corrections, and returns quickly to "zero" standard.

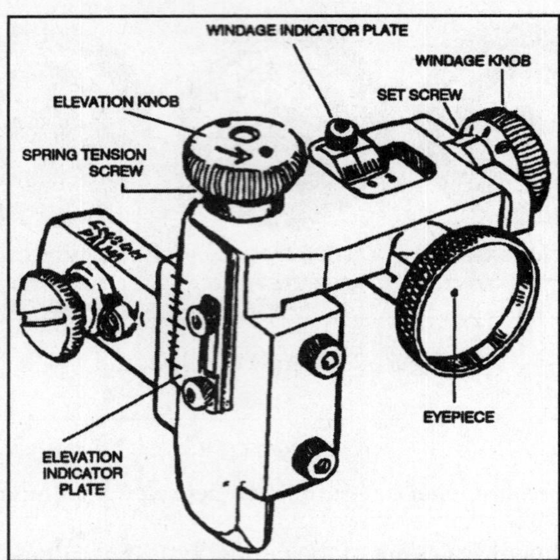

Figure 2-24: Zeroing adjustment dials.

SECTION IV. OTHER EQUIPMENT

The sniper must use special equipment to reduce the possibility of detection. The types and characteristics are discussed in this section.

2-12. M16A1/A2 RIFLE WITH M203 GRENADE LAUNCHER

The observer carries the M16A1/A2 rifle with the M203 grenade launcher. The sniper, carrying the M24 SWS, lacks the firepower required to break contact with enemy forces-that is, ambush or chance contact. The rapid-fire ability of the M16A1/A2 rifle, combined with the destructive abilities of the M203 40-mm grenade launcher (Figure 2-25), gives the sniper team a lightweight, easily operated way to deliver the firepower required to break contact.

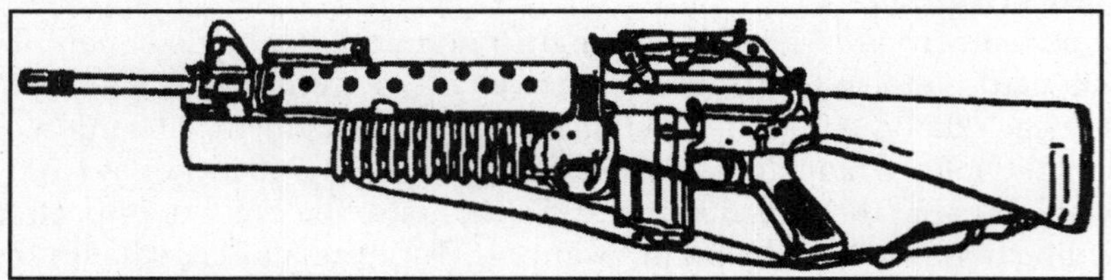

Figure 2-25: The M203 40-mm grenade launcher attached to M16A1 rifle.

2-13. IMAGE INTENSIFICATION AND INFRARED DEVICES

The sniper team employs night and limited visibility devices to conduct continuous operations.

a. **Night Vision Sight, AN/PVS-4.** The AN/PVS-4 is a portable, battery-operated, electro-optical instrument that can be hand-held for visual observation or weapon-mounted for precision fire at night (Figure 2-26). The observer can detect and resolve distant targets through the unique capability of the sight to amplify reflected ambient light (moon, stars, or sky glow). The sight is passive thus, it is free from enemy detection by visual or electronic means. This sight, with appropriate weapons adapter bracket, can be mounted on the M16 rifle.
   (1) ***Uses.*** The M16 rifle with the mounted AN/PVS-4 is effective in achieving a first-round hit out to and beyond 300 meters, depending on the light conditions. The AN/PVS-4 is mounted on the M16 since the

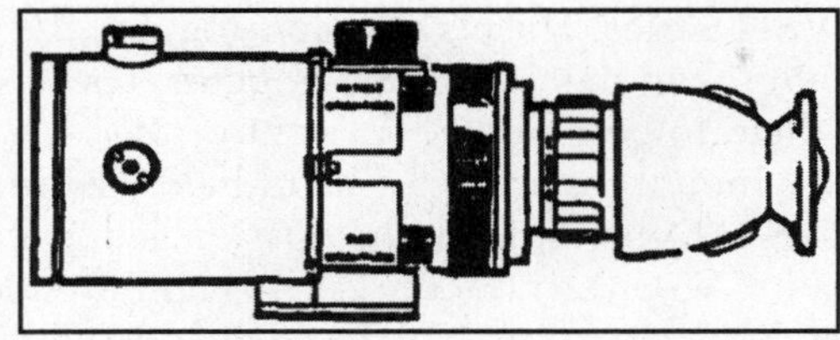

Figure 2-26: Night vision sight, AN/PVS-4.

nightsight's limited range does not make its use practical for the sniper weapon system. This avoids problems that may occur when removing and replacing the sniperscope. The nightsight provides an effective observation ability during night combat operations. The sight does not give the width, depth, or clarity of daylight vision; however, a well-trained operator can see enough to analyze the tactical situation, to detect enemy targets, and to place effective fire on them. The sniper team uses the AN/PVS-4 to accomplish the following:

(a) To enhance their night observation capability.
(b) To locate and suppress hostile fire at night.
(c) To deny enemy movement at night.
(d) To demoralize the enemy with effective first-round kills at night.

(2) ***Employment factors.*** Since the sight requires target illumination and does not project its own light source, it will not function in total darkness. The sight works best on a bright, moonlit night. When there is no light or the ambient light level is low (such as in heavy vegetation), the use of artificial or infrared light improves the sight's performance.

(a) Fog, smoke, dust, hail, or rain limit the range and decrease the resolution of the instrument.
(b) The sight does not allow seeing through objects in the field of view. For example, the operator will experience the same range restrictions when viewing dense wood lines as he would when using other optical sights.
(c) The observer may experience eye fatigue when viewing for prolonged periods. Viewing should be limited to 10 minutes, followed by a rest period of 10 minutes. After several periods of viewing, he can safely extend this time limit. To assist in maintaining a continuous viewing, capability and to reduce eye fatigue, the observer should use one eye then the other while viewing through the sight.

(3) ***Zeroing.*** The operator may zero the sight during daylight or darkness; however, he may have some difficulty in zeroing just before darkness. The light level at dusk is too low to permit the operator to resolve his zero target with the lens cap cover in place, but it is still intense enough to cause the sight to automatically turnoff unless the lens cap cover is in position over the objective lens. The sniper normally zeros the sight for the maximum practical range that he can be expected to observe and fire, depending on the level or light.

b. **Night Vision Goggles, AN/PVS-5.** The AN/PVS-5 is a lightweight, passive night vision system that gives the sniper team another means of observing an area during darkness (Figure 2-27). The sniper normally carries the goggles, because the observer has the M16 mounted with the nightsight. The goggles make it easier to see due to their design. However, the same limitations that apply to the nightsight also apply to the goggles.

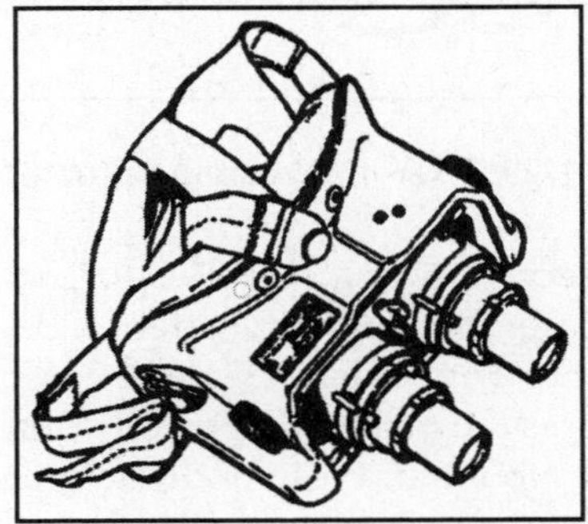

Figure 2-27: Night vision goggles, AN/PVS-5.

c. **Night Vision Goggles, AN/PVS-7 Series.** The night vision goggles, AN/PVS-7 series (Figure 2-28) has a better resolution and viewing ability than the AN/PVS-5 goggles. The AN/PVS-7 series goggles have a head-mount assembly that allows them to be mounted in front of the face so that both hands can be free. The goggles can be used without the mount assembly for hand-held viewing.

d. **Laser Observation Set AN/GVS-5.** Depending on the mission, snipers can use the AN/GVS-5 to determine the range to the target. The AN/GVS-5 (LR) (Figure 2-29) is an individually operated, hand-held, distance-measuring device designed for distances from 200 to 9,990 meters (with an error of plus or minus 10 meters). It measures distances by firing an infrared beam at a target and by measuring the time the reflected beam takes to return to the operator. It then displays the target distance, in meters, inside the viewer. The reticle pattern in the viewer is graduated in 10-mil increments and has display lights to indicate low battery and multiple target hits. If the beam hits more than one target, the display gives a reading of the closest target hit. The beam that is fired from the set poses a safety hazard; therefore, snipers planning to use this equipment should be thoroughly trained in its safe operation.

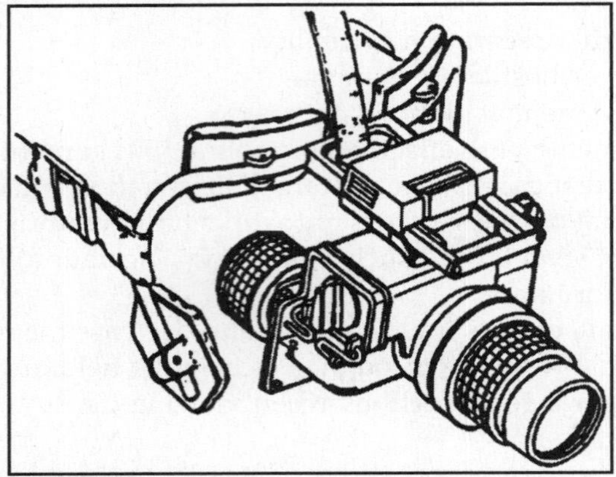

Figure 2-28: Night vision goggles, AN/PVS-7 series.

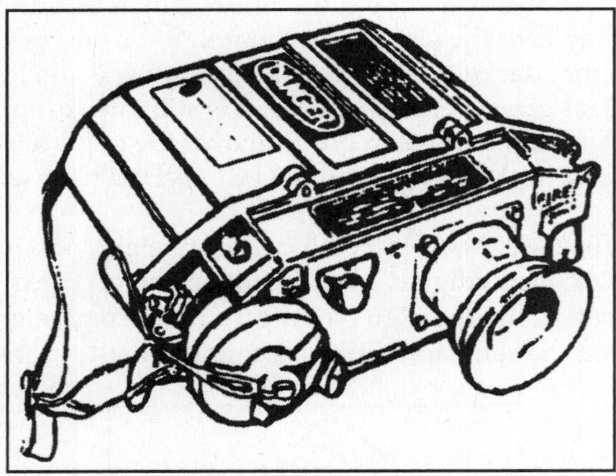

Figure 2-29: User observation set, AN/GVS-5.

e. **Mini-Eyesafe Laser Infrared Observation Set, AN/PVS-6.** The AN/PVS-6 (Figure 2-30) contains the following components: mini-eyesafe laser range finder; batteries, BA-6516/U, nonrechargeable, lithium thionyl chloride; carrying case; shipping case; tripod; lens cleaning compound and lens cleaning tissue; and operator's manual. The laser range finder is the major component of the AN/PVS-6. It is lightweight, individually operated, and hand-held or tripod mounted; it can accurately determine ranges from 50 to 9,995 meters in 5-meter increments and displays the range in the eyepiece. It can also be mounted with and bore-sighted to the night observation device, AN/TAS-6, long-range.

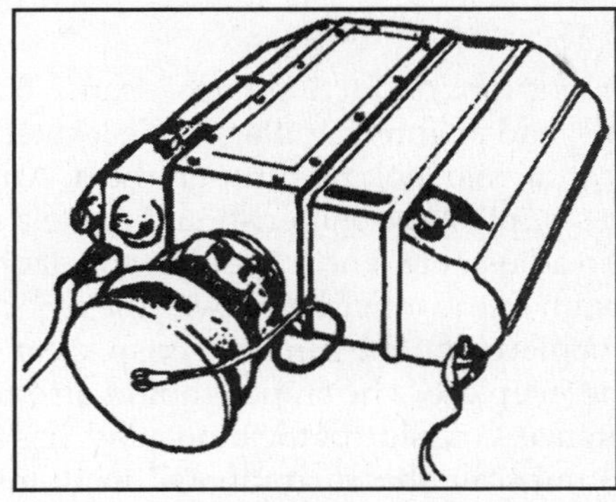

Figure 2-30: Mini-eyesafe laser infrared observation set AV/PVS-6.

2-14. M49 OBSERVATION TELESCOPE

The M49 observation telescope is a prismatic optical instrument of 20-power magnification (Figure 2-31). The telescope is focused by turning the eyepiece in or out until the image of the object being viewed is crisp and clear to the viewer. The sniper team carries the telescope on all missions. The observer uses the telescope to determine wind speed and direction by reading mirage, observing the bullet trace, and observing the bullet impact. The sniper uses this information to make quick and accurate adjustments for wind conditions. The lens are coated with a hard film of magnesium fluoride for maximum light transmission. Its high magnification makes observation, target detection, and target identification possible where conditions and range would otherwise preclude this ability. Camouflaged targets and those in deep shadows can be more readily distinguished. The team can observe troop movements at greater distances and identify selective targets with ease.

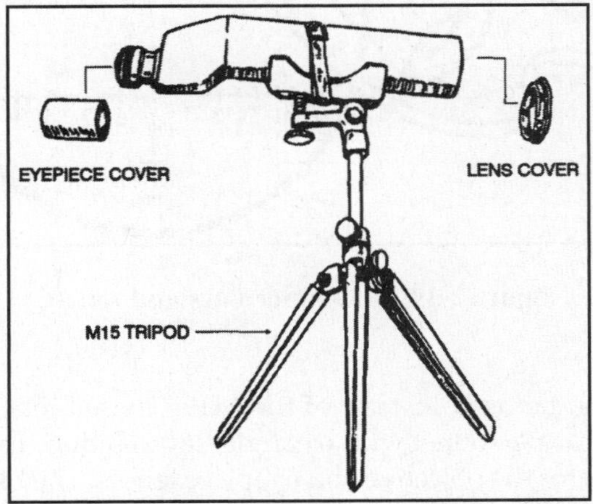

Figure 2-31: M49 observation telescope.

a. **Components.** Components of the telescope include a removable eyepiece and objective lens covers, an M15 tripod with canvas carrier, and a hard ease carrier for the telescope.

b. **Storage.** When storing the M49 observation telescope, the sniper must remove it from the hard case earner and remove the lens caps to prevent moisture from gathering on the inside of the scope. Maintenance consists of—

(1) Wiping dirt and foreign materials from the scope tube, hard case carrier, and M15 tripod with a damp rag.

(2) Cleaning the M49 lens with lens cleaning solution and lens tissue only.

(3) Brushing dirt and foreign agents from the M15 carrying case with a stiff-bristled brush; cleaning the threading of lens caps on the M49 and the tripod elevation adjustment screw on the M15 with a toothbrush, then applying a thin coat of grease and moving the lens caps and elevation adjustment screw back and forth to evenly coat threading.

2-15. M19 BINOCULARS

The M19 is the preferred optical instrument for conducting hasty scans. This binocular (Figure 2-32) has 7-power magnification with a 50-mm objective lens, and an interpupillary scale located on the hinge. The sniper should adjust the binocular until one sharp circle appears while looking through them. After adjusting the binoculars' interpupillary distance (distance between a person's pupils), the sniper should make a mental note of the reading on this scale for future reference. The eyepieces are also adjustable. The sniper can adjust one eyepiece at a time by turning the eyepiece with one hand while placing the palm of the other hand over the objective lens of the other monocular. While keeping both eyes open, he adjusts the eyepiece until he can see a crisp, clear view. After one eyepiece is adjusted, he repeats the procedure with the remaining eyepiece. The sniper should also make a mental note of the diopter scale reading on both eyepieces for future reference. One side of the binoculars has a laminated reticle pattern (Figure 2-32) that consists of a vertical and horizontal mil scale that is graduated in 10-mil increments. Using this reticle pattern aids the sniper in determining range and adjusting indirect-fires. The sniper uses the binoculars for—

- Calling for and adjusting indirect fires.
- Observing target areas.
- Observing enemy movement and positions.
- Identifying aircraft.
- Improving low-light level viewing.
- Estimating range.

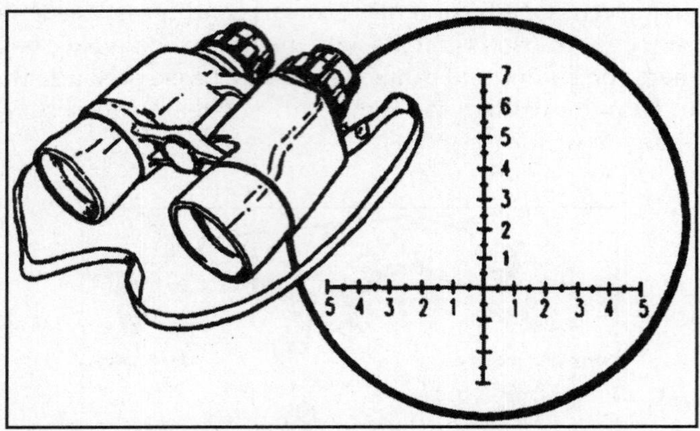

Figure 2-32: M19 binoculars and reticle.

2-16. M22 BINOCULARS

The M22 binoculars (Figure 2-33) can be used instead of the M19. These binoculars have the same features as the M19, plus fold-down eyepiece cups for personnel who wear glasses to reduce the distance between the eyes and the eyepiece. It also has protective covers for the objective and eyepiece lenses. The binoculars have laser protection filters on the inside of the objective lenses (direct sunlight can reflect off these lenses). The reticle pattern (Figure 2-33) is different than the M19 binocular reticle.

2-17. OTHER SNIPER EQUIPMENT

Other equipment the sniper needs to complete a successful mission follows:

a. **Sidearms.** Each member of the team should have a sidearm, such as an M9, 9-mm Beretta, or a caliber .45 pistol. A sidearm gives a sniper the needed protection from a nearby threat while on the ground moving or while in the confines of a sniper position.
b. **Compass.** Each member of the sniper team must have a lensatic compass for land navigation.
c. **Maps.** The team must have military maps of their area of operations.
d. **Calculator.** The sniper team needs a pocket-size calculator to figure distances when using the mil-relation formula. Solar-powered calculators usually work well, but under low-light conditions, battery power may

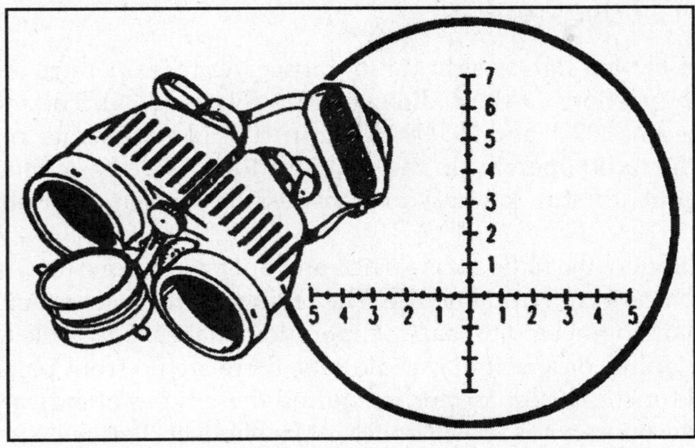

Figure 2-33: M22 binoculars and reticle.

be preferred. If a battery-powered calculator is to be used in low-light conditions, it should have a lighted display.

e. **Rucksack.** The sniper's rucksack should contain at least a two-quart canteen, an entrenching tool, a first-aid kit, pruning shears, a sewing kit with canvas needles and nylon thread, spare netting and garnish, rations, and personal items as needed. The sniper also carries his ghillie suit (Chapter 4, paragraph 4–4) in his rucksack until the mission requires its use.

f. **Measuring Tape.** A standard 10-foot to 25-foot metal carpenter's tape allows the sniper to measure items in his operational area. This information is recorded in the sniper data book. (See Chapter 4 for range estimation.)

SECTION V. COMMUNICATIONS EQUIPMENT

The sniper team must have a man-portable radio that gives the team secure communications with the units involved in their mission.

2-18. AN/PRC-77 RADIO

The basic radio for the sniper team is the AN/PRC-77 (Figure 2-34). This radio is a short-range, man-pack portable, frequency modulated receiver-transmitter that provides two-way voice communication. The set can net with all other infantry and artillery FM radio sets on common frequencies. The AN/KY-57 should be installed with the AN/PRC-77. This allows the sniper team to communicate securely with all units supporting or being supported by the sniper team.

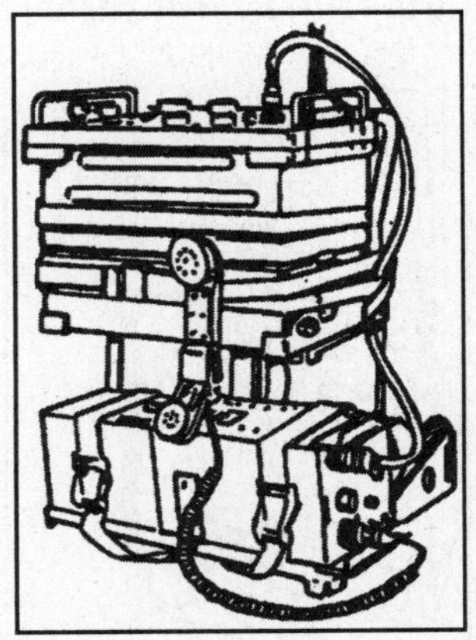

Figure 2-34: AN/PRC-77 radio.

2-19. AN/PRC-104A RADIO TRANSCEIVER

The AN/PRC-104A is a state-of-the-am lightweight radio transceiver that operates in the high frequency and in the upper part of the low frequency portions of the radio spectrum (Figure 2-35). The receiver/transmitter circuits can be tuned to any frequency between 2.0000 and 29.9999 MHz in 100 Hz increments, making it possible to tune up to 280,000 separate frequencies. The radio operates in the upper or lower side bank modes for voice communications, CW for Morse code, or FSK (frequency-shift keying) for transmission of teletype or other data.

a. In the man-pack configuration, the radio set is carried and operated by one man or, with the proper accessories, it can be configured for vehicle or fixed-station use. The radio set with antenna and handset weighs 15.7 pounds.
b. The control panel, human-engineered for ease of operation, makes it possible to adjust all controls even while wearing heavy gloves. Unlike older, similar radio sets, there are no front panel meters or indicator lights on the AN/PRC-104A. All functions that formerly required these types of indicators are monitored by the radio and communicated to the operator as special tones in the handset. This feature is highly useful during tactical blackout operations. The superior design and innovative features of the AN/PRC-104A radio set make it possible to maintain a reliable long-range communications link. The radio uses lightweight, portable equipment that can be operated by personnel who have minimum training.

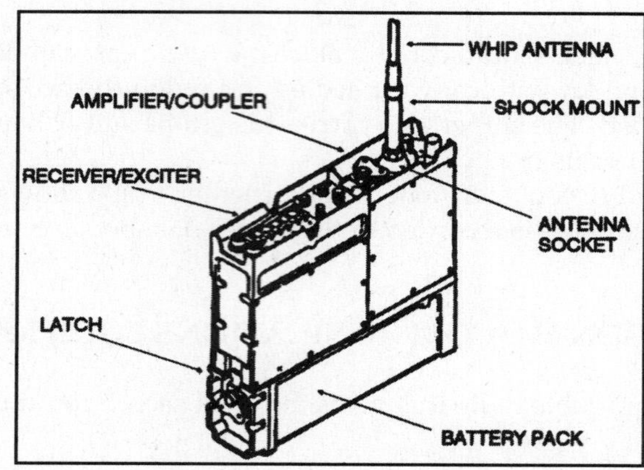

Figure 2-35: AN/PRC-104A radio transceiver.

2-20. AN/PRC-119 RADIO

The AN/PRC-119 (Figure 2-36) replaces the AN/PRC-77, although the AN/PRC-77 is still in use. The AN/PRC-119 is a man-pack portable, VHF/FM radio that is designed for simple, quick operation using a 16-element keypad for push-button tuning. It can also be used for short-range and long-range operation for voice, FSK, or digital data communications. It can also be used for single-channel operation or in a jam-resistant, frequency-hopping mode, which can be changed as needed This radio has a built-in self-test with visual and audio readbacks. It is compatible with the AN/KY-57 for secure communications.

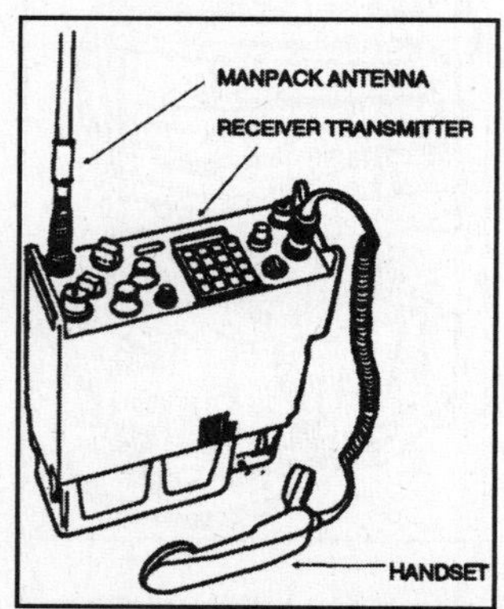

Figure 2-36: AN/PRC-119 radio.

CHAPTER 3

Marksmanship

Sniper marksmanship is an extension of basic rifle marksmanship and focuses on the techniques needed to engage targets at extended ranges. To successfully engage targets at increased distances, the sniper team must be proficient in marksmanship fundamentals and advanced marksmanship skills. Examples of these skills are determining the effects of weather conditions on ballistics, holding off for elevation and windage, engaging moving targets, using and adjusting scopes, and zeroing procedures. Markmanship skills should be practiced often.

SECTION I. FUNDAMENTALS

The sniper team must be thoroughly trained in the fundamentals of marksmanship. These include assuming a position, aiming, breath control, and trigger control. These fundamentals develop fixed and correct firing habits for instinctive application. Every sniper should periodically refamiliarize himself with these fundamentals regardless of his experience.

3-1. STEADY POSITION ELEMENTS

The sniper should assume a good firing position (Figure 3-1) in order to engage targets with any consistency. A good position enables the sniper to relax and concentrate when preparing to fire.

a. **Position Elements.** Establishing a mental checklist of steady position elements enhances the sniper's ability to achieve a first-round hit.

(1) ***Nonfiring hand.*** Use the nonfiring hand to support the butt of the weapon. Place the hand next to the cheat and rest the tip of the butt on it. Bail the hand into a fist to raise the weapon's butt or loosen the fist to lower the weapon's butt. An effective method is to hold a sock full of sand in the nonfiring hand and to place the weapon butt on the sock. This reduces body contact with the weapon. To raise the butt, squeeze the sock and to lower it, loosen the grip on the sock.

(2) ***Butt of the stock.*** Place the butt of the stock firmly in the pocket of the shoulder. Insert a pad on the ghillie suit (see Chapter 4) where contact with the butt is made to reduce the effects of pulse beat and breathing, which can be transmitted to the weapon.

(3) ***Firing hand.*** With the firing hand, grip the small of the stock. Using the middle through little fingers, exert a slight rearward pull to keep the butt of the weapon firmly in the pocket of the shoulder. Place the thumb over the top of the small of the stock. Place the index finger on the trigger, ensuring it does not touch the stock of the weapon. This avoids disturbing the lay of the rifle when the trigger is squeezed.

(4) ***Elbows.*** Find a comfortable position that provides the greatest support.

(5) ***Stock weld.*** Place the cheek in the same place on the stock with each shot. A change in stock weld tends to cause poor sight alignment, reducing accuracy.

(6) ***Bone support.*** Bone support is the foundation of the firing position; they provide steady support of the weapon.

(7) ***Muscle relaxation.*** When using bone support, the sniper can relax muscles, reducing any movement that could be caused by tense or trembling muscles. Aside from tension in the trigger finger and firing hand, any use of the muscle generates movement of the sniper's cross hairs.

(8) ***Natural point of aim.*** The point at which the rifle naturally rest in relation to the aiming point is called natural point of aim.

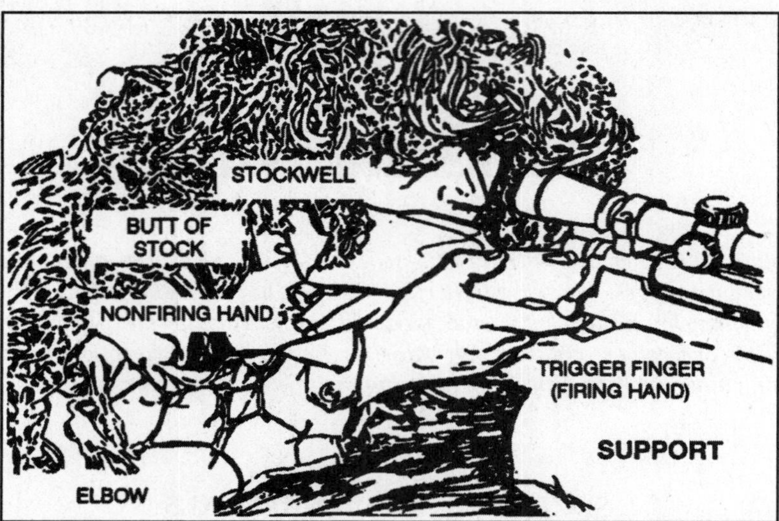

Figure 3-1: Firing position.

(a) Once the sniper is in position and aimed in on his target, the method for checking for natural point of aim is for the sniper to close his eyes, take a couple of breaths, and relax as much as possible. Upon opening his eyes, the scope's cross hairs should be positioned at the sniper's preferred aiming point. Since the rifle becomes an extension of the sniper's body, it is necessary to adjust the position of the body until the rifle points naturally at the preferred aiming point on the target.

(b) Once the natural point of aim has been determined, the sniper must maintain his position to the target. To maintain his natural point of aim in all shooting positions, the natural point of aim can be readjusted and checked periodically.

(c) The sniper can change the elevation of the natural point of aim by leaving his elbows in place and by sliding his body forward or rearward. This raises or lowers the muzzle of the weapon, respectively. To maintain the natural point of aim after the weapon has been fired, proper bolt operation becomes critical. The sniper must practice reloading while in the prone position without removing the butt of the weapon from the firing shoulder. This may be difficult for the left-hand firer. The two techniques for accomplishing this task are as follows:

- After firing, move the bolt slowly to the rear while canting the weapon to the right. Execution of this task causes the spent cartridge to fall next to the weapon.
- After firing, move the bolt to the rear with the thumb of the firing hand. Using the index and middle fingers, reach into the receiver and catch the spent cartridge as it is being ejected. This technique does not require canting the weapon.

> ✍ **NOTE**
> The sniper conducts bolt operation under a veil or equivalent camouflage to improve concealment.

b. **Steady Firing Position.** On the battlefield, the sniper must assume a steady firing position with maximum use of cover and concealment. Considering the variables of terrain, vegetation, and tactical situations, the sniper can use many variations of the basic positions. When assuming a firing position, he must adhere to the following basic rules:

(1) Use any support available.

(2) Avoid touching the support with the barrel of the weapon since it interferes with barrel harmonics and reduces accuracy.

(3) Use a cushion between the weapon and the support to prevent slippage of the weapon.

(4) Use the prone supported position whenever possible.

c. **Types of Firing Positions.** Due to the importance of delivering precision fire, the sniper makes maximum use of artificial support and eliminates any variable that may prevent adhering to the basic rules. He uses the prone supported; prone unsupported; kneeling unsupported; kneeling, sling supported; standing supported; and the Hawkins firing positions.

(1) ***Prone supported position.*** The prone supported position is the steadiest position; it should be used whenever possible (Figure 3-2). To assume the prone supported position, the sniper should—

(a) Lie down and place the weapon on a support that allows pointing in the direction of the target. Keep the position as low as possible. (For field-expedient weapon supports, see paragraph 3–1d.)

(b) Remove the nonfiring hand from underneath the fore-end of the weapon by folding the arm underneath the receiver and trigger, grasping the rear sling swivel. This removes any chance of subconsciously trying to exert control over the weapon's natural point of aim. Keep the elbows in a comfortable position that provides the greatest support.

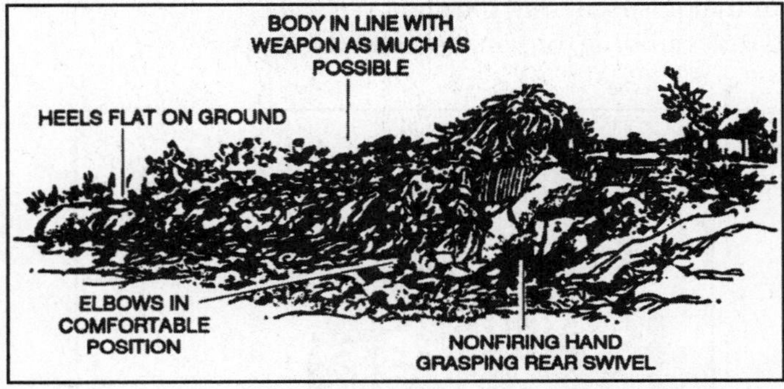

Figure 3-2: Prone supported position.

(c) Keep the body in line with the weapon as much as possible-not at an angle. This presents less of a target to the enemy and more body mass to absorb recoil.

(d) Spread legs a comfortable distance apart with the heels on the ground or as close as possible without causing strain.

(2) ***Prone unsupported position.*** The prone unsupported position (Figure 3-3) offers another stable firing platform for engaging targets. To assume this position, the sniper faces his target, spreads his feet a comfortable distance apart, and drops to his knees. Using the butt of the rifle as a pivot, the firer rolls onto his nonfiring side. He places the rifle butt in the pocket formed by the firing shoulder, grasps the pistol grip in his firing hand, and lowers the firing elbow to the ground. The rifle rests in the V formed by the thumb and fingers of the nonfiring hand. The sniper adjusts the position of his firing elbow until his shoulders are about level, and pulls back firmly on the rifle with both hands. To complete the position, he obtains a stock weld and relaxes, keeping his heels close to the ground.

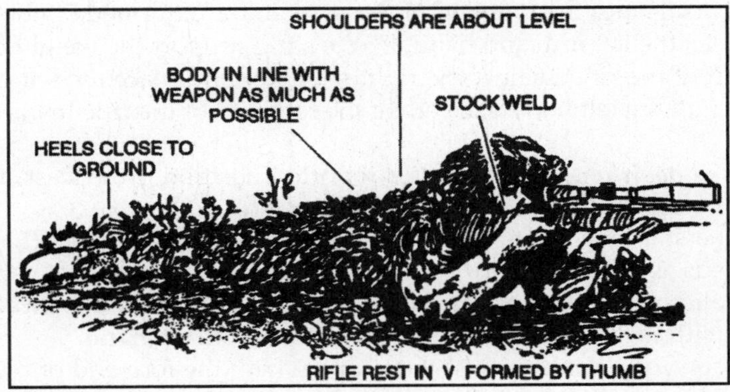

Figure 3-3: Prone unsupported position.

(3) ***Kneeling unsupported position.*** The kneeling unsupported position (Figure 3-4) is assumed quickly. It places the sniper high enough to see over small brush and provides for a stable position.

(a) Place the body at a 45-degree angle to the target.

(b) Kneel and place the right knee on the ground.

(c) Keep the left leg as perpendicular to the ground as possible; sit back on the right heel, placing it as directly under the spinal column as possible. A variation is to turn the toe inward and sit squarely on the right foot.

(d) Grasp the small of the stock of the weapon with the firing hand, and cradle the fore-end of the weapon in a crook formed with the left arm.

(e) Place the butt of the weapon in the pocket of the shoulder, then place the meaty underside of the left elbow on top of the left knee.

(f) Reach under the weapon with the left hand, and lightly grasp the firing arm.

(g) Relax forward and into the support position, using the left shoulder as a contact point. This reduces transmission of the pulsebeat into the sight picture.

(h) Lean against a tree, building, or vehicle for body support.

Figure 3-4: Kneeling unsupported position.

(4) ***Kneeling, sling supported position.*** If vegetation presents a problem, the sniper can raise his kneeling position by using the rifle sling. To assume the kneeling, sling supported position, he executes the first three steps for assuming a kneeling unsupported position. With the leather sling mounted to the weapon, the sniper turns the sling one-quarter turn to the left. The lower part of the sling will then form a loop.

(a) Place the left arm (nonfiring) through the loop; pull the sling up the arm and place it on the upper arm between the elbow and shoulder, but not directly over the biceps.

(b) Tighten the sling by sliding the sling keeper against the loop holding the arm.

(c) Rotate the left arm in a clockwise motion around the sling and under the rifle with the sling secured to the upper arm. Place the fore-end of the stock in the V formed by the thumb and forefinger of the left hand. Relax the left arm and hand, let the sling support the weight of the weapon.

(d) Place the butt of the rifle against the right shoulder and place the left elbow on top of the left knee (Figure 3-5). Pull the left hand back along the fore-end of the rifle toward the trigger guard to add to stability.

(5) ***Standing supported position.*** The standing supported position is the least steady of the supported positions and should be used only as a last resort (Figure 3-6).

(a) To assume the standing supported position with horizontal support, such as a wall or ledge, the sniper proceeds as follows:

- Locate a solid object for support. Avoid branches as they tend to sway when wind is present.
- Form a V with the thumb and forefinger of the nonfiring hand.
- Place the nonfiring hand against the support with the fore-end of the weapon resting in the V of the hand. This steadies the weapon and allows quick recovery from recoil.
- Then place the butt of the weapon in the pocket of the shoulder.

Figure 3-5: Kneeling, sling supported position.

Figure 3-6: Standing supported position (horizontal support).

(b) To use vertical support (Figure 3-7), such as a tree, telephone pole, comer of building, or vehicle, the sniper proceeds as follows:
- Locate stable support. Face the target, then turn 45 degrees to the right of the target, and place the palm of the nonfiring hand at arm's length against the support.
- Lock the left arm straight, let the left leg buckle, and place body weight against the nonfiring hand. Keep the trail leg straight.
- Place the fore-end of the weapon in the V formed by extending the thumb of the nonfiring hand.
- Exert more pressure to the rear with the firing hand.

(6) ***Hawkins position.*** The Hawkins position (Figure 3-8) is a variation of the prone unsupported position. The sniper uses it when firing from a low bank or a depression in the ground, over a roof, or so forth. It cannot be used on level ground since the muzzle cannot be raised high enough to aim at the target. It is

Figure 3-7: Standing supported position (vertical support).

a low-profile position with excellent stability and aids concealment. To assume this position, the sniper uses the weapon's sling and proceeds as follows:

⚠ CAUTION
Lock the nonfiring arm straight or the face will absorb the weapon's recoil.

(a) After assuming a prone position, grasp the upper sling swivel and sling with the nonfiring hand, forming a fist to support the front of the weapon.
(b) Ensure the nonfiring arm is locked straight since it will absorb the weapon's recoil. Wearing a glove is advisable.
(c) Rest the butt of the weapon on the ground and place it *under* the firing shoulder.

The sniper can make minor adjustments in muzzle elevation by tightening or relaxing the fist of the nonfiring hand. If more elevation is required, he can place a support under the nonfiring fist.

Figure 3-8: Hawkins position.

d. **Field-Expedient Weapon Support.** Support of the weapon is critical to the sniper's success in engaging targets. Unlike a well-equipped firing range with sandbags for weapon support, the sniper can encounter situations where weapon support relies on common sense and imagination. The sniper should practice using these supports at every opportunity and select the one that best suits his needs. He must train as if in combat to avoid confusion and self-doubt. The following items are commonly used as field-expedient weapon supports

(1) ***Sand sock.*** The sniper needs the sand sock when delivering precision fire at lone ranges. He uses a standard issue, olive-drab wool sock filled one-half to three-quarters full of sand and knotted off. He places it under the rear sling swivel when in the prone supported position for added stability (Figure 3-9). By limiting minor movement and reducing pulse beat, the sniper can concentrate on trigger control and aiming. He uses the nonfiring hand to grip the sand sock, rather than the rear sung swivel. The sniper makes minor changes in muzzle elevation by squeezing or relaxing his grip on the sock. He uses the sand sock as padding between the weapon and a rigid support also.

Figure 3-9: Sand sock.

(2) ***Rucksack.*** If the sniper is in terrain without any natural support, he may use his rucksack (Figure 3-10). He must consider the height and presence of rigid objects within the rucksack. The rucksack must conform to weapon contours to add stability.

(3) ***Sandbag.*** The sniper can fill an empty sandbag (Figure 3-11) on site.

Figure 3-10: Rucksack.

Figure 3-11: Sandbag.

(4) ***Tripod.*** The sniper can build a field-expedient tripod (Figure 3-12) by tying together three 12-inch long sticks (one thicker than the others) with 550 cord or the equivalent. When tying the sticks, he wraps the cord at the center point and leaves enough slack to fold the legs out into a triangular base. Then, he places the fore-end of the weapon between the three uprights.

(5) ***Bipod.*** The sniper can build a field-expedient bipod (Figure 3-12) by tying together two 12-inch sticks, thick enough to support the weight of the weapon. Using 550 cord or the equivalent, he ties the sticks at the center point, leaving enough slack to fold them out in a scissor-like manner. He then places the weapon between the two uprights. The bipod is not as stable as other field-expedient items, and it should be used only in the absence of other techniques.

(6) ***Forked stake.*** The tactical situation determines the use of the forked stake. Unless the sniper can drive a forked stake into the ground, this is the least desirable of the techniques; that is, he must use his nonfiring hand to hold the stake in an upright position (Figure 3-12). Delivering long-range precision fire is a near-impossibility due to the unsteadiness or the position.

Figure 3-12: Field-expedient tripod, bipod, and forked stake.

e. **Sniper and Observer Positioning.** The sniper should find a place on the ground that allows him to build a steady, comfortable position with the best cover, concealment, and visibility of the target area. Once established, the observer should position himself out of the sniper's field of view on his firing side.

(1) The closer the observer gets his spotting telescope to the sniper's line of bore, the easier it is to follow the trace (path) of the bullet and observe the point of impact. A position at 4 to 5 o'clock (7 to 8 o'clock for left-handed firers) from the firing shoulder and close to (but not touching) the sniper is best (Figure 3-13).

> ✍ **NOTE**
>
> Trace is the visible trail of a bullet and is created by the shock wave of a supersonic bullet. The Shockwave compresses the air along the leading edge of a bullet causing water vapor in the air to momentary condense and become visible. To the observer, located to the rear of the sniper, trace appears as a rapidly moving V-shaped vortex in the air following the trajectory of the bullet. Through close observation and practice, trace can be used to judge the bullet's trajectory relative to the aiming point, making corrections easier for a follow-up shot. Trace can best be seen if the observer's optics are directly in line with the axis of the sniper's rifle barrel. Watching the trace and the effects of the bullet's impact are the primary means by which the observer assists the sniper in calling the shot.

Figure 3-13: Sniper team positioning.

(2) If the sniper is without weapon support in his position, he uses the observer's body as a support (Figure 3-14). This support is not recommended since the sniper must contend with his own movement and the observer's body movement. The sniper should practice and prepare to use an observer supported position. A variety of positions can be used; however, the two most stable are when the observer is in a prone or sitting position.

(a) *Prone.* To assume the prone position, the observer lies at a 45-to 75-degree angle to the target and observes the area through his spotting telescope. The sniper assumes a a prone supported position, using the back of the observer's thigh for support. Due to the offset angle, the observer may only see the bullet impact.

Figure 3-14: Prone observer supported position.

(b) *Sitting.* If vegetation prevents the sniper from assuming a prone position, the sniper has the observer face the target area and assume a cross-legged sitting position. The observer places his elbows on his knees to stabilize his position. For observation, the observer uses binoculars held in his hands. The spotting telescope is not recommended due to its higher magnification and the unsteadiness of this position. The sniper is behind the observer in an open-legged, cross-legged, or kneeling position, depending on the target's elevation (Figure 3-15). The sniper places the fore-end of the weapon across the observer's left shoulder, stabilizing the weapon with the forefinger of the nonfiring hand. When using these positions, the sniper's effective engagement of targets at extended ranges is difficult and used only as a last resort. When practicing these positions, the sniper and observer must enter respiratory pause together to eliminate movement from breathing.

Figure 3-15: Sitting position.

3-2. AIMING

The sniper begins the aiming process by aligning the rifle with the target when assuming a firing position. He should point the rifle naturally at the desired point of aim. If his muscles are used to adjust the weapon onto the point of aim, they automatically relax as the rifle fires, and the rifle begins to move toward its natural point of aim. Because this movement begins just before the weapon discharge, the rifle is moving as the bullet leaves the muzzle. This causes inaccurate shots with no apparent cause (recoil disguises the movement). By adjusting the weapon and body as a single unit, rechecking, and readjusting as needed, the sniper achieves a true natural point of aim. Once the position is established, the sniper then aims the weapon at the exact point on the target. Aiming involves: eye relief, sight alignment, and sight picture.

a. **Eye Relief.** This is the distance from the sniper's firing eye to the rear sight or the rear of the scope tube. When using iron sights, the sniper ensures the distance remains consistent from shot to shot to preclude changing what he views through the rear sight. However, relief will vary from firing position to firing position and from sniper to sniper, according to the sniper's neck length, his angle of head approach to the stock, the depth of his shoulder pocket, and his firing position. This distance (Figure 3-16) is more rigidly controlled with telescopic sights than with iron sights. The sniper must take care to prevent eye injury caused by the scope tube striking his brow during recoil. Regardless of the sighting system he uses, he must place his head as upright as possible with his firing eye located directly behind the rear portion of the sighting system. This head placement also allows the muscles surrounding his eye to relax. Incorrect head placement causes the sniper to look out of the top or corner of his eye, resulting in muscular strain. Such strain leads to blurred vision and can also cause eye strain. The sniper can avoid eye strain by not staring through the telescopic or iron sights for extended periods. The best aid to consistent eye relief is maintaining the same stock weld from shot to shot.

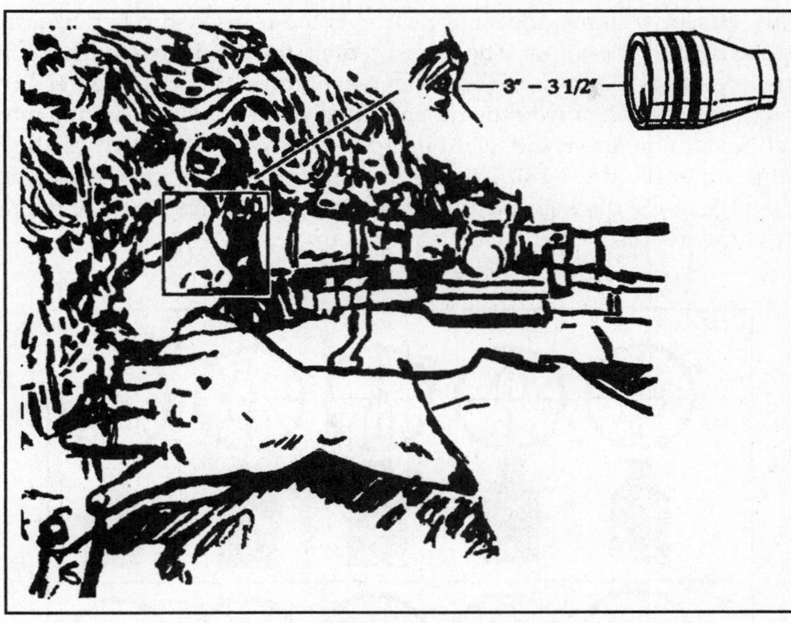

Figure 3-16: Eye relief.

b. **Sight Alignment.** With telescopic sights, sight alignment is the relationship between the cross hairs (reticle) and a full field of view as seen by the sniper. The sniper must place his head so that a full field of view fills the tube, with no dark shadows or crescents to cause inaccurate shots. He centers the reticle in a full field of view, ensuring the vertical cross hair is straight up and down so the rifle is not canted. Again, the center is easiest for the sniper to locate and allows for consistent reticle placement. With iron sights, sight alignment is the relationship between the front and rear sights as seen by the sniper (Figure 3-17). The sniper centers the top edge of the front sight blade horizontally and vertically within the rear aperture. (The center of aperture is easiest for the eye to locate and allows the sniper to be consistent in blade location.)

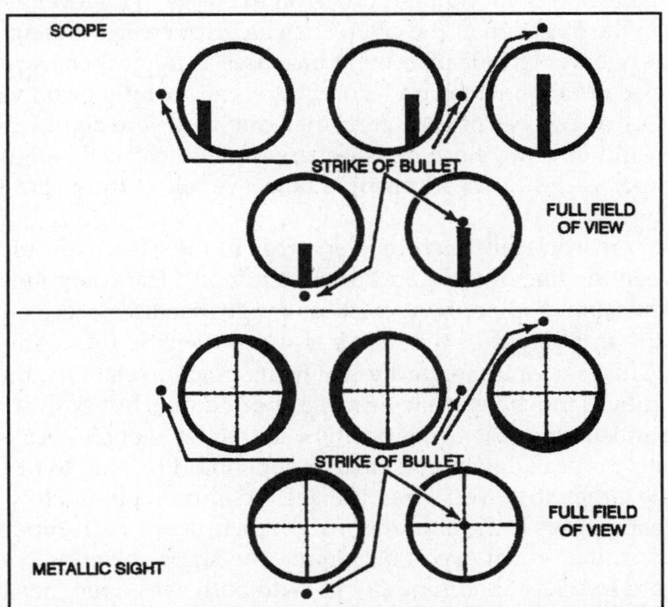

Figure 3-17: Sight alignment.

c. **Sight Picture.** With telescopic sights, the sight picture is the relationship between the reticle and full field of view and the target as seen by the sniper. The sniper centers the reticle in a full field of view. He then places the reticle center of the largest visible mass of the target (as in iron sights). The center of mass of the target is easiest for the sniper to locate, and it surrounds the intended point or impact with a maximum amount of target area. With iron sights, sight picture is the relationship between the rear aperture, the front sight blade, and the target as seen by the sniper (Figure 3-18). The sniper centers the top edge of the blade in the rear aperture. He then places the top edge of the blade in the center of the largest visible mass of the target (disregard the head and use the center of the torso).

Figure 3-18: Sight picture.

d. **Sight Alignment Error.** When sight alignment and picture are perfect (regardless of sighting system) and all else is done correctly, the shot will hit center of mass on the target. However, with an error insight alignment, the bullet is displaced in the direction of the error. Such an error creates an angular displacement between the line of sight and the line of bore. This displacement increases as range increases; the amount of bullet displacement depends on the size of alignment error. Close targets show little or no visible error. Distant targets can show great displacement or can be missed altogether due to severe sight misalignment. An inexperienced sniper is prone to this kind of error, since he is unsure of what correctly aligned sights look like (especially telescopic sights); a sniper varies his head position (and eye relief) from shot to shot, and he is apt to make mistakes while firing.

e. **Sight Picture Error.** An error in sight picture is an error in the placement of the aiming point. This causes no displacement between the line of sight and the line of bore. The weapon is simply pointed at the wrong spot on the target. Because no displacement exists as range increases, close and far targets are hit or missed depending on where the front sight or the reticle is when the rifle fires. All snipers face this kind of error every time they shoot. This is because, regardless of firing position stability, the weapon will always be moving. A supported rifle moves much less than an unsupported one, but both still move in what is known as a *wobble area.* The sniper must adjust his firing position so that his wobble area is as small as possible and centered on the target. With proper adjustments, the sniper should be able to fire the shot while the front sight blade or reticle is on the target at, or very near, the desired aiming point. How far the blade or reticle is from this point when the weapon fires is the amount of sight picture error all snipers face.

f. **Dominant Eye.** To determine which eye is dominant, the sniper extends one arm to the front and points the index finger skyward to select an aiming point. With both eyes open, he aligns the index finger with the aiming point, then closes one eye at a time while looking at the aiming point. One eye will make the finger appear to move off the aiming point; the other eye will stay on the aiming point. The dominant eye is the eye that does not move the finger from the aiming point. Some individuals may have difficulty aiming because of interference from their dominant eye, if this is not the eye used in the aiming process. This may require the sniper to fire from the other side of the weapon (right-handed firer will fire left-handed). Such individuals must close the dominant eye while shooting.

3-3. BREATH CONTROL

Breath control is important with respect to the aiming process. If the sniper breathes while trying to aim, the rise and fall of his chest causes the rifle to move. He must, therefore, accomplish sight alignment during breathing. To do this, he first inhales then exhales normally and stops at the moment of natural respiratory pause.

a. A respiratory cycle lasts 4 to 5 seconds. Inhalation and exhalation require only about 2 seconds. Thus, between each respiratory cycle there is a pause of 2 to 3 seconds. This pause can be extended to 10 seconds without any special effort or unpleasant sensations. The sniper should shoot during this pause when his breathing muscles relax. This avoids strain on his diaphragm.
b. A sniper should assume his firing position and breathe naturally until his hold begins to settle. Many snipers then take a slightly deeper breath, exhale, and pause, expecting to fire the shot during the pause. If the hold does not settle enough to allow the shot to be fired, the sniper resumes normal breathing and repeats the process.
c. The respiratory pause should never feel unnatural. If it is too long, the body suffers from oxygen deficiency and sends out signals to resume breathing. These signals produce involuntary movements in the diaphragm and interfere with the sniper's ability to concentrate. About 8 to 10 seconds is the maximum safe period for the respiratory pause. During multiple, rapid engagements, the breathing cycle should be forced through a rapid, shallow cycle between shots instead of trying to hold the breath or breathing. Firing should be accomplished at the forced respiratory pause.

3-4. TRIGGER CONTROL

Trigger control is the most important of the sniper marksmanship fundamentals. It is defined as causing the rifle to fire when the sight picture is at its best, without causing the rifle to move. Trigger squeeze is uniformly increasing pressure straight to the rear until the rifle fires.

a. Proper trigger control occurs when the sniper places his firing finger as low on the trigger as possible and still clears the trigger guard, thereby achieving maximum mechanical advantage and movement of the finger to the entire rifle.
b. The sniper maintains trigger control beat by assuming a stable position, adjusting on the target, and beginning a breathing cycle. As the sniper exhales the final breath toward a natural respiratory pause, he secures his finger on the trigger. As the front blade or reticle settles at the desired point of aim, and the natural respiratory pause is entered, the sniper applies initial pressure. He increases the tension on the trigger during the respiratory pause as long as the front blade or reticle remains in the area of the target that ensures a well-placed shot. If the front blade or reticle moves away from the desired point of aim on the target, and the pause is free of strain or tension, the sniper stops increasing the tension on the trigger, waits for the front blade or reticle to return to the desired point, and then continues to squeeze the trigger. If movement is too large for recovery or if the pause has become uncomfortable (extended too long), the sniper should carefully release the pressure on the trigger and begin the respiratory cycle again.
c. As the stability of a firing position decreases, the wobble area increases. The larger the wobble area, the harder it is to fire the shot without reacting to it. This reaction occurs when the sniper—
   (1) ***Anticipates recoil.*** The firing shoulder begins to move forward just before the round fires.
   (2) ***Jerks the trigger.*** The trigger finger moves the trigger in a quick, choppy, spasmodic attempt to fire the shot before the front blade or reticle can move away from the desired point of aim.
   (3) ***Flinches.*** The sniper's entire upper body (or parts thereof) overreacts to anticipated noise or recoil. This is usually due to unfamiliarity with the weapon.

(4) ***Avoids recoil.*** The sniper tries to avoid recoil or noise by moving away from the weapon or by closing the firing eye just before the round fires. This, again, is caused by a lack of knowledge of the weapon's actions upon firing.

3-5. FOLLOW-THROUGH

Applying the fundamentals increases the odds of a well-aimed shot being fired. When mastered, additional skills can make that first-round kill even more of a certainty. One of these skills is the follow-through.

a. Follow-through is the act of continuing to apply all the sniper marksmanship fundamentals as the weapon fires as well as immediately after it fires. It consists of—
   (1) Keeping the head infirm contact with the stock (stock weld).
   (2) Keeping the finger on the trigger all the way to the rear.
   (3) Continuing to look through the rear aperture or scope tube.
   (4) Keeping muscles relaxed.
   (5) Avoiding reaction to recoil and or noise.
   (6) Releasing the trigger only after the recoil has stopped.

b. A good follow-through ensures the weapon is allowed to fire and recoil naturally. The sniper/rifle combination reacts as a single unit to such actions.

3-6. CALLING THE SHOT

Calling the shot is being able to tell where the round should impact on the target. Because live targets invariably move when hit, the sniper will find it almost impossible to use his scope to locate the target after the round is fired. Using iron sights, the sniper will find that searching for a downrange hit is beyond his abilities. He must be able to accurately call his shots. Proper follow-through will aid in calling the shot. The dominant factor in shot calling is knowing where the reticle or blade is located when the weapon discharges. This location is called the *final focus point.*

a. With iron sights, the final focus point should be on the top edge of the front sight blade. The blade is the only part of the sight picture that is moving (in the wobble area). Focusing on it aids in calling the shot and detecting any errors insight alignment or sight picture. Of course, lining up the sights and the target initially requires the sniper to shift his focus from the target to the blade and back until he is satisfied that he is properly aligned with the target. This shifting exposes two more facts about eye focus. The eye can instantly shift focus from near objects (the blade) to far objects (the target).

b. The final focus is easily placed with telescopic sights because of the sight's optical qualities. Properly focused, a scope should present both the field of view and the reticle in sharp detail. Final focus should then be on the target. While focusing on the target, the sniper moves his head slightly from side to side. The reticle may seem to move across the target face, even though the rifle and scope are motionless. This movement is *parallax.* Parallax is present when the target image is not correctly focused on the reticle's focal plane. Therefore, the target image and the reticle appear to be in two separate positions inside the scope, causing the effect of reticle movement across the target. The M3A scope on the M24 has a focus adjustment that eliminates parallax in the scope. The sniper should adjust the focus knob until the target's image is on the same focal plane as the reticle. To determine if the target's image appears at the ideal location, the sniper should move his head slightly left and right to see if the reticle appears to move. If it does not move, the focus is properly adjusted and no parallax will be present.

3-7. INTEGRATED ACT OF FIRING

Once the sniper has been taught the fundamentals of marksmanship, his primary concern is his ability to apply it in the performance of his mission. An effective method of applying fundamentals is through the use of the integrated act of firing one round. The integrated act is a logical, step-by-step development of fundamentals whereby the sniper can develop habits that enable him to fire each shot the same way. The integrated act of firing can be divided into four distinct phases:

a. **Preparation Phase**. Before departing the preparation area, the sniper ensures that—
   (1) The team is mentally conditioned and knows what mission they are to accomplish.
   (2) A systematic check is made of equipment for completeness and serviceability including, but not limited to—
      (a) Properly cleaned and lubricated rifles.
      (b) Properly mounted and torqued scopes.
      (c) Zero-sighted systems and recorded data in the sniper data book.
      (d) Study of the weather conditions to determine their possible effects on the team's performance of the mission.

b. **Before-Firing Phase.** On arrival at the mission site, the team exercises care in selecting positions. The sniper ensures the selected positions support the mission. During this phase, the sniper—
   (1) Maintains strict adherence to the fundamentals of position. He ensures that the firing position is as relaxed as possible, making the most of available external support. He also makes sure the support is stable, conforms to the position, and allows a correct, natural point of aim for each designated area or target.
   (2) Once in position, removes the scope covers and checks the field(s) of fire, making any needed corrections to ensure clear, unobstructed firing lanes.
   (3) Makes dry firing and natural point of aim checks.
   (4) Double-checks ammunition for serviceability and completes final magazine loading.
   (5) Notifies the observer he is ready to engage targets. The observer must be constantly aware of weather conditions that may affect the accuracy of the shots. He must also stay ahead of the tactical situation.

c. **Firing Phase.** Upon detection, or if directed to a suitable target, the sniper makes appropriate sight changes, aims, and tells the observer he is ready to fire. The observer then gives the needed windage and observes the target. To fire the rifle, the sniper should remember the key word, "BRASS." Each letter is explained as follows:
   (1) ***Breathe.*** The sniper inhales and exhales to the natural respiratory pause. He checks for consistent head placement and stock weld. He ensures eye relief is correct (full field of view through the scope; no shadows present). At the same time, he begins aligning the cross hairs or front blade with the target at the desired point of aim.
   (2) ***Relax.*** As the sniper exhales, he relaxes as many muscles as possible, while maintaining control of the weapon and position.
   (3) ***Aim.*** If the sniper has a good, natural point of aim, the rifle points at the desired target during the respiratory pause. If the aim is off, the sniper should make a slight adjustment to acquire the desired point of aim. He avoids "muscling" the weapon toward the aiming point.
   (4) **Squeeze.** As long as the sight picture is satisfactory, the sniper squeezes the trigger. The pressure applied to the trigger must be straight to the rear without disturbing the lay of the rifle or the desired point of aim.

d.**After-Firing Phase.** The sniper must analyze his performance If the shot impacted at the desired spot (a target hit), it may be assumed the integrated act of firing one round was correctly followed. If however, the shot was off call, the sniper and observer must check for Possible errors.
   (1) Failure to follow the keyword, BRASS (partial field of view, breath held incorrectly, trigger jerked, rifle muscled into position, and so on).
   (2) Target improperly ranged with scope (causing high or low shots).
   (3) Incorrectly compensated for wind (causing right or left shots).
   (4) Possible weapon/ammunition malfunction (used only as a last resort when no other errors are detected).

Once the probable reasons for an off-call shot is determined the sniper must make note of the errors. He pays close attention to the problem areas to increase the accuracy of future shots.

SECTION II. BALLISTICS

As applied to sniper marksmanship, types of ballistics may be defined as the study of the firing, flight, and effect of ammunition. Proper execution of marksmanship fundamentals and a thorough knowledge of ballistics ensure the successful completion of the mission. Tables and formulas in this section should be used only as guidelines since every rifle performs differently. Maximum ballistics data eventually result in a well-kept sniper data book and knowledge gained through experience.

3-8. TYPES OF BALLISTICS

Ballistics are divided into three distinct types: internal external, and terminal.

a. Internal-the interior workings of a weapon and the functioning of its ammunition.
b. External-the flight of the bullet from the muzzle to the target.
c. Termninal-what happens to the bullet after it hits the target. (See paragraph 3-16.)

3-9. TERMINOLOGY

To fully understand ballistics, the sniper should be familiar with the following terms:

a. Muzzle Velocity-the speed of the bullet as it leaves the rifle barrel, measured in feet per second. It varies according to various factors, such as ammunition type and lot number, temperature, and humidity.
b. Line of Sight-straight line from the eye through the aiming device to the point of aim.
c. Line of Departure-the line defined by the bore of the rifle or the path the bullet would take without gravity.
d. Trajectory-the path of the bullet as it travels to the target.
e. Midrange Trajectory/Maximum Ordinate-the highest point the bullet reaches on its way to the target. This point must be known to engage a target that requires firing underneath an overhead obstacle, such as a bridge or a tree. In attention to midrange trajectory may cause the sniper to hit the obstacle instead of the target.
f. Bullet Drop—how far the bullet drops from the line of departure to the point of impact.
g. Time of Flight-the amount of time it takes for the bullet to reach the target from the time the round exits the rifle.
h. Retained Velocity-the speed of the bullet when it reaches the target. Due to drag, the velocity will be reduced.

3-10. EFFECTS ON TRAJECTORY

To be effective, the sniper must know marksmanship fundamentals and what effect gravity and drag will have on those fundamentals.

a. **Gravity.** As soon as the bullet exits the muzzle of the weapon, gravity begins to pull it down, requiring the sniper to use his elevation adjustment. At extended ranges, the sniper actually aims the muzzle of his rifle above his line of sight and lets gravity pull the bullet down into the target. Gravity is always present, and the sniper must compensate for this through elevation adjustments or hold-off techniques.
b. **Drag.** Drag is the slowing effect the atmosphere has on the bullet. This effect decreases the speed of the bullet according to the air—that is, the less dense the air, the leas drag and vice versa. Factors affecting drag/density are temperature, altitude/barometric pressure, humidity, efficiency of the bullet, and wind.
   (1) ***Temperature.*** The higher the temperature, the less dense the air. (See Section III.) If the sniper zeros at 60 degrees F and he fires at 80 degrees, the air is leas dense, thereby causing an increase in muzzle velocity and higher point of impact. A 20-degree change equals a one-minute elevation change in the strike of the bullet.
   (2) ***Altitude/barometric pressure.*** Since the air pressure is less at higher altitudes, the air is less dense. Thus, the bullet is more efficient and impacts higher due to less drag. (Table 3-1 shows the approximate effect of change of the point of impact from sea level to 10,000 feet if the rifle is zeroed at sea level.) Impact will be the point of aim at sea level. For example, a rifle zeroed at sea level and fired at a range of 700 meters at an altitude of 5,000 feet will hit 1.6 minutes high.
   (3) ***Humidity.*** Humidity varies along with the altitude and temperature. Figure 3-19 considers the changes in altitudes. Problems can occur if extreme humidity changes exist in the area of operations. That is,

Table 3-1: Point of Impact rises as altitude Increases (data are in MOA).

RANGE (METERS)	2,500 FEET *(ASL)	5,000 FEET (ASL)	10,000 FEET (ASL)
100	.05	.08	.13
200	.1	.2	.34
300	.2	.4	.6
400	.4	.5	.9
500	.5	.9	1.4
600	.8	1.0	1.8
700	1.0	1.6	2.4
800	1.3	1.9	3.3
900	1.6	2.8	4.8
1,000	1.8	3.7	6.0
*ABOVE SEA LEVEL			

when humidity goes up, impact goes down; when humidity goes down, impact goes up. Since impact is affected by humidity, a 20 percent change in humidity equals about one minute as a rule of thumb. Keeping a good sniper data book during training and acquiring experience are the best teachers.

(4) ***Efficiency of the bullet.*** This is called a *bullet's ballistic coefficient.* The imaginary perfect bullet is rated as being 1.00. Match bullets range from .500 to about .600. The 7.62-mm special ball (M118) is rated at .530 (Table 3-2).

(5) ***Wind.*** Wind is discussed in Section III.

Table 3-2: Muzzle velocity data for 7.62-mm special ball (M118).

RANGE (METERS)	(A)	(B)	(C)	(D)
100	2,407	.7	NA	.1
200	2,233	3.0	1.5	.2
300	2,066	7.3	3.0	.4
400	1,904	14.0	3.5	.5
500	1,750	24.0	4.0	.7
600	1,603	37.6	4.5	.9
700	1,466	56.2	5.0	1.0
800	1,339	80.6	5.0	1.3
900	1,222	112.5	6.0	1.5
1,000	1,118	153.5	7.0	1.8

(A) RETAINED VELOCITY (FEET PER SECOND).
(B) MIDRANGE TRAJECTORY (INCHES).
(C) BULLET DROP IN 100-METER INCREMENTS (MINUTES).
(D) TIME OF FLIGHT (SECONDS).

3-11. ANGLE FIRING

Most practice firing conducted by the sniper team involves the use of military range facilities, which are relatively flat. However, as a sniper being deployed to other regions of the world, the chance exists for operating in a mountainous or urban environment. This requires target engagements at higher and lower elevations. Unless the sniper takes corrective action, bullet impact will be above the point of aim. How high the bullet hits is determined by the range and angle to the target (Table 3-3). The amount of elevation change applied to the telescope of the rifle for angle firing is known as *slope dope*.

Table 3-3: Bullet rise at given angle and range in minutes.

RANGE (METERS)	SLANT DEGREES											
	5	10	15	20	25	30	35	40	45	50	55	60
100	.01	.04	.09	.16	.25	.36	.49	.63	.79	.97	1.2	1.4
200	.03	.09	.2	.34	.53	.76	1.	1.3	1.7	2.	2.4	2.9
300	.03	.1	.3	.5	.9	1.2	1.6	2.1	2.7	3.2	3.9	4.5
400	.05	.19	.43	.76	1.2	1.7	2.3	2.9	3.7	4.5	5.4	6.3
500	.06	.26	.57	1.	1.6	2.3	3.	3.9	4.9	6.	7.2	8.4
600	.08	.31	.73	1.3	2.	2.9	3.9	5.	6.3	7.7	9.2	10.7
700	.1	.4	.9	1.6	2.5	3.6	4.9	6.3	7.9	9.6	11.5	13.4
800	.13	.5	1.	2.	3.	4.4	5.9	7.7	9.6	11.7	14.	16.4
900	.15	.6	1.3	2.4	3.7	5.3	7.2	9.3	11.6	14.1	16.9	19.8
1,000	.2	.7	1.6	2.8	4.5	6.4	8.6	11.	13.9	16.9	20.2	23.7
*RANGE GIVEN IS SLANT RANGE (METERS), NOT MAP DISTANCE.												

SECTION III. EFFECTS OF WEATHER

For the highly trained sniper, the effects of weather are the main causes of error in the strike of the bullet. Wind, mirage, light, temperature, and humidity affect the bullet, the sniper, or both. Some effects are minor; however, sniping is often done in extremes of weather and all effects must be considered.

3-12. WIND CLASSIFICATION

Wind poses the biggest problem for the sniper. The effect that wind has on the bullet increases with range. This is due mainly to the slowing of the bullet's velocity combined with a longer flight time. This allows the wind to have a greater effect on the round as distances increase. The result is a loss of stability.

a. Wind also has a considerable effect on the sniper. The stronger the wind, the more difficult it is for him to hold the rifle steady. This can be partly offset by training, conditioning and the use of supported positions.
b. Since the sniper must know how much effect the wind will have on the bullet, he must be able to classify the wind. The best method is to use the clock system (Figure 3-19). With the sniper at the center of the clock and the target at 12 o'clock, the wind is assigned three values: full, half, and no value. Full value means that the force of the wind will have a full effect on the flight of the bullet. These winds come from 3 and 9 o'clock. Half

value means that a wind at the same speed, but from 1, 2, 4, 5, 7, 8, 10, and 11 o'clock, will move the bullet only half as much as a full-value wind. No value means that a wind from 6 or 12 o'clock will have little or no effect on the flight of the bullet.

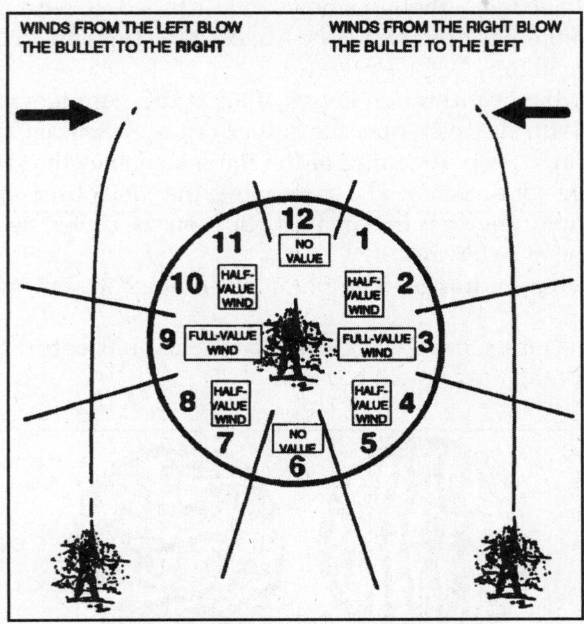

Figure 3-19: Clock system.

3-13. WIND VELOCITY

Before adjusting the sight to compensate for wind, the sniper must determine wind direction and velocity. He may use certain indicators to accomplish this. These are range flags, smoke, trees, grass, rain, and the sense of feel. However, the preferred method of determining wind direction and velocity is reading mirage (see paragraph d below). In most cases, wind direction can be determined simply by observing the indicators.

a. A common method of estimating the velocity of the wind during training is to watch the range flag (Figure 3-20). The sniper determines the angle between the flag and pole, in degrees, then divides by the constant number 4. The result gives the approximate velocity in miles per hour.

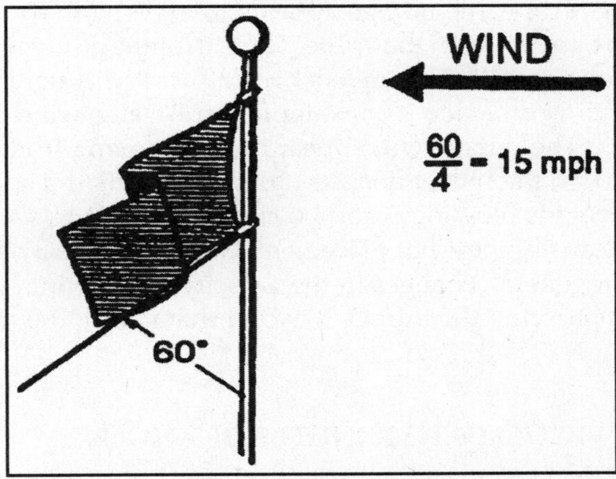

Figure 3-20: The Flag method.

b. If no flag is visible, the sniper holds a piece of paper, grass, cotton, or some other light material at shoulder level, then drops it. He then points directly at the spot where it lands and divides the angle between his body and arm by the constant number 4. This gives him the approximate wind velocity in miles per hour.

c. If these methods cannot be used, the following information is helpful in determining velocity. Winds under 3 miles per hour can barely be felt, although smoke will drift. A 3- to 5-mile-per-hour wind can barely be felt on the face. With a 5- to 8-mile-per-hour wind, the leaves in the trees are in constant motion, and with a 12- to 15-mile-per-hour wind, small trees begin to sway.

d. A mirage is a reflection of the heat through layers of air at different temperatures and density as seen on a warm day (Figure 3-21). With the telescope, the sniper can see a mirage as long as there is a difference in ground and air temperatures. Proper reading of the mirage enables the sniper to estimate wind speed and direction with a high degree of accuracy. The sniper uses the M49 observation telescope to read the mirage. Since the wind nearest to midrange has the greatest effect on the bullet, he tries to determine velocity at that point. He can do this in one of two ways:

(1) He focuses on an object at midrange, then places the scope back onto the target without readjusting the focus.

(2) He can also focus on the target, then back off the focus one-quarter turn counterclockwise. This makes the target appear fuzzy, but the mirage will be clear.

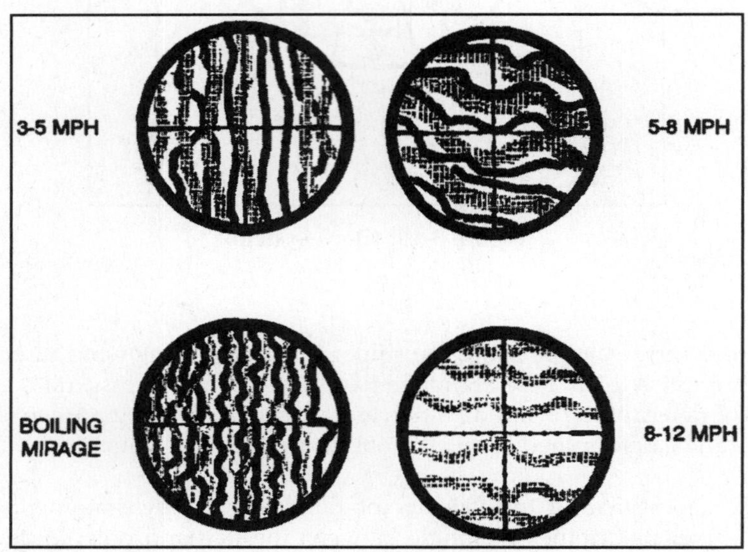

Figure 3-21: Types of mirages.

e. As observed through the telescope, the mirage appears to move with the same velocity as the wind, except when blowing straight into or away from the scope. Then, the mirage gives the appearance of moving straight upward with no lateral movement. This is called a *boiling mirage.* A boiling mirage may also be seen when the wind is constantly changing direction. For example, a full-value wind blowing from 9 o'clock to 3 o'clock suddenly changes direction. The mirage will appear to stop moving from left to right and present a boiling appearance. When this occurs, the inexperienced observer directs the sniper to fire with the "0" wind. As the sniper fires, the wind begins blowing from 3 o'clock to 9 o'clock, causing the bullet to miss the target therefore, firing in a "boil" can hamper shot placement. Unless there is a no-value wind, the sniper must wait until the boil disappears. In general, changes in the velocity of the wind, up to about 12 miles per hour, can be readily determined by observing the mirage. Beyond that speed, the movement of the mirage is too fast for detection of minor changes.

3-14. CONVERSION OF WIND VELOCITY TO MINUTES OF ANGLE

All telescopic sights have windage adjustments that are graduated in minutes or angle or fractions thereof. A minute of angle is 1/60th of a degree (Figure 3-22). This equals about 1 inch (1.145 inches) for every 100 meters.

EXAMPLE
1 MOA = 2 inches at 200 meters
1 MOA = 5 inches at 500 meters

a. Snipers use minutes of angle (Figure 3-22) to determine and adjust the elevation and windage needed on the weapon's scope. After finding the wind direction and velocity in miles per hour, the sniper must then convert it into minutes of angle, using the wind formula as a rule of thumb only. The wind formula is—

$$\frac{\text{RANGE (hundreds) divided by 100 VELOCITY (mph)}}{\text{CONSTANT}} = \text{Minutes full-value winc}$$

The constant depends on the target's range.

100 to 500 "C" = 15
600 "C" = 14
700 to 800 "C" = 13
900 "C" = 12
1,000 "C" = 11

If the target is 700 meters away and the wind velocity is 10 mph, the formula is—

$$\frac{7 \times 10}{13} = 5.38 \text{ minutes or } 5\ 1/2 \text{ minutes}$$

This determines the number of minutes for a full-value wind. For a half-value wind, the 5.38 would be divided in half.

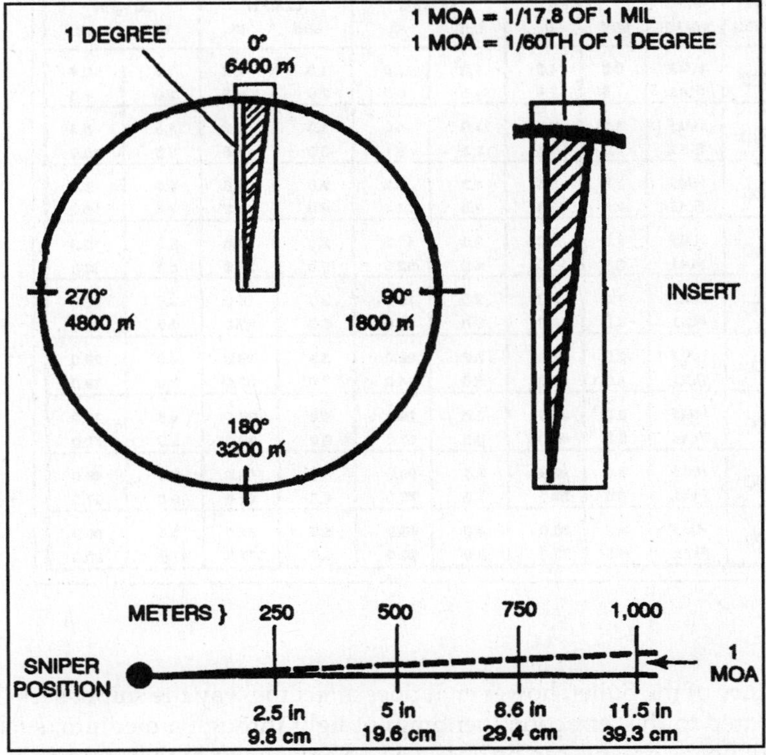

Figure 3-22: Minutes of angle.

b. The observer makes his own adjustment estimations, then compares them to the wind conversion table, which can be a valuable training tool. He must not rely on this table; if it is lost, his ability to perform the mission could be severely hampered. Until the observer gains skill in estimating wind speed and computing sight changes, he may refer to Table 3-4.

Table 3-4: Wind conversion table.

RANGE (METERS)	WIND VALUE	3 MPH MIN	3 MPH IN	5 MPH MIN	5 MPH IN	7 MPH MIN	7 MPH IN	10 MPH MIN	10 MPH IN
200	HALF	0.0	0.4	0.5	0.6	0.5	0.8	0.5	1.2
	FULL	0.5	0.8	0.5	1.2	1.0	1.7	1.0	2.4
300	HALF	0.5	0.9	0.5	1.3	0.5	1.9	1.0	2.7
	FULL	0.5	1.7	1.0	2.7	1.0	3.8	1.5	5.4
400	HALF	0.5	1.4	0.5	2.4	1.0	3.3	1.0	4.8
	FULL	0.5	2.9	1.0	4.8	1.5	6.7	2.0	9.6
500	HALF	0.5	2.3	0.5	3.8	1.0	5.3	1.5	7.5
	FULL	1.0	4.5	1.5	7.5	2.0	10.5	2.5	15.0
600	HALF	0.5	3.0	1.0	5.0	1.0	8.0	1.5	11.0
	FULL	1.0	7.0	1.5	11.0	2.5	15.0	3.5	21.0
700	HALF	0.5	4.0	'1.0	7.0	1.5	10.0	2.0	15.0
	FULL	1.0	9.0	2.0	15.0	2.5	21.0	4.0	29.0
800	HALF	0.5	6.0	1.0	10.0	1.5	13.0	2.0	19.0
	FULL	1.5	11.0	2.0	19.0	3.0	27.0	4.5	38.0
900	HALF	0.5	7.0	1.0	12.0	1.5	17.0	2.5	24.0
	FULL	3.5	15.0	2.5	24.0	3.5	34.0	5.0	49.0
1000	HALF	1.0	9.0	1.5	15.0	2.0	21.0	2.5	3.00
	FULL	1.5	18.0	2.5	30.0	4.0	42.0	5.5	60.0

RANGE (METERS)	WIND VALUE	12 MPH MIN	12 MPH IN	15 MPH MIN	15 MPH IN	18 MPH MIN	18 MPH IN	20 MPH MIN	20 MPH IN
200	HALF	0.5	1.3	1.0	1.8	1.0	2.2	1.0	2.4
	FULL	1.5	2.9	1.5	3.6	2.0	4.3	2.0	4.8
300	HALF	1.0	3.3	1.0	4.0	1.5	4.9	1.5	5.4
	FULL	2.0	6.5	2.5	8.1	3.0	9.8	3.5	10.9
400	HALF	1.5	5.8	1.5	7.2	2.0	8.6	2.0	9.6
	FULL	2.5	11.5	3.5	14.4	4.0	17.3	4.5	19.2
500	HALF	1.5	9.0	2.0	11.3	2.5	13.5	2.5	15.0
	FULL	3.5	18.0	4.0	22.6	5.0	27.0	5.5	30.0
600	HALF	1.5	13.0	2.5	16.0	3.0	19.0	3.5	22.0
	FULL	4.0	26.0	5.0	32.0	6.0	39.0	6.5	43.0
700	HALF	2.5	18.0	3.0	22.0	3.5	26.0	4.0	29.0
	FULL	4.5	36.0	6.0	44.0	7.0	53.0	7.5	59.0
800	HALF	2.5	23.0	3.5	29.0	4.0	35.0	4.5	38.0
	FULL	5.5	46.0	6.5	57.0	8.0	69.0	9.0	77.0
900	HALF	3.0	29.0	3.5	36.0	4.5	44.0	5.0	49.0
	FULL	6.0	58.0	7.5	73.0	9.0	97.0	10.0	97.0
1000	HALF	3.5	36.0	4.0	45.0	5.0	54.0	5.5	60.0
	FULL	6.5	72.0	8.0	90.0	10.0	103.0	11.5	120.0

3-15. EFFECTS OF LIGHT

Light does not affect the trajectory of the bullet; however, it does affect the way the sniper sees the target through the scope. This effect can be compared to the refraction (bending) of light through a medium, such as a prism or a fish bowl. The same effect, although not as drastic, can be observed on a day with high humidity and with sunlight from high angles. The only way the sniper can adjust for this effect is to refer to past firing recorded in the sniper data book.

He can then compare different light and humidity conditions and their effect on marksmanship. Light may also affect firing on unknown distance ranges since it affects range determination capabilities.

3-16. EFFECTS OF TEMPERATURE

Temperature affects the firer, ammunition, and density of the air. When ammunition sits in direct sunlight, the bum rate of powder is increased, resulting in greater muzzle velocity and higher impact. The greatest effect is on the density of the air. As the temperature rises, the air density is lowered. Since there is less resistance, velocity increases and once again the point of impact rises. This is in relation to the temperature at which the rifle was zeroed. If the sniper zeros at 50 degrees and he is now firing at 90 degrees, the point of impact rises considerably. How high it rises is best determined once again by past firing recorded in the sniper data book. The general role, however, is that when the rifle is zeroed, a 20-degree increase in temperature will raise the point of impact by one minute; conversely, a 20-degree decrease will drop the point of impact by one minute.

3-17. EFFECTS OF HUMIDITY

Humidity varies along with the altitude and temperature. The sniper can encounter problems if drastic humidity changes occur in his area of operation. Remember, if humidity goes up, impact goes down; if humidity goes down, impact goes up. As a rule of thumb, a 20-percent change will equal about one minute, affecting the point of impact. The sniper should keep a good sniper data book during training and refer to his own record.

SECTION IV. SNIPER DATA BOOK

The sniper data book contains a collection of data cards. The sniper uses the data cards to record firing results and all elements that had an effect on firing the weapon. This can vary from information about weather conditions to the attitude of the firer on that particular day. The sniper can refer to this information later to understand his weapon, the weather effects, and his shooting ability on a given day. One of the most important items of information he will record is the cold barrel zero of his weapon. A cold barrel zero refers to the first round fired from the weapon at a given range. It is critical that the sniper shoots the first round daily at different ranges. For example, Monday, 400 meters; Tuesday, 500 meters; Wednesday, 600 meters. When the barrel warms up, later shots begin to group one or two minutes higher or lower, depending on specific rifle characteristics. Information is recorded on DA Form 5785-R (Sniper's Data Card) (Figure 3-23). (A blank copy of this form is located in the back of this publication for local reproduction.)

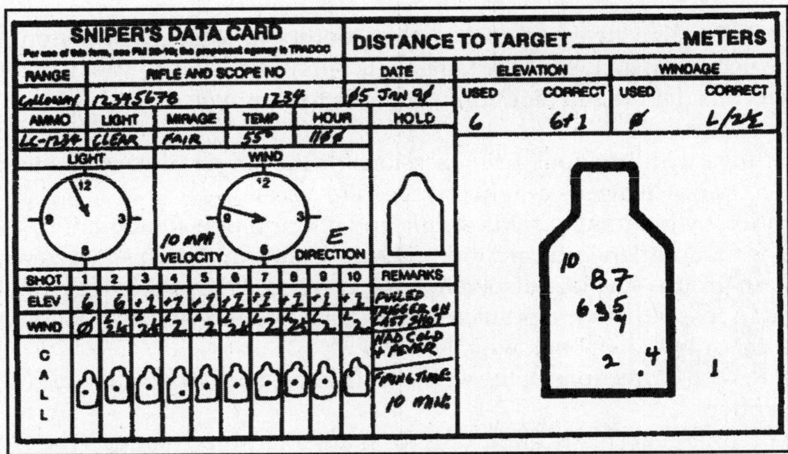
SNIPER'S DATA CARD
DISTANCE TO TARGET ______ METERS
RANGE: Galloway | RIFLE AND SCOPE NO: 12345678 1234 | DATE: 05 JAN 96
ELEVATION — USED: 6 | CORRECT: 6+1
WINDAGE — USED: Ø | CORRECT: L/2½
AMMO: LC-1234 | LIGHT: CLEAR | MIRAGE: FAIR | TEMP: 55° | HOUR: 1100 | HOLD
LIGHT
WIND: 10 mph VELOCITY | E DIRECTION
SHOT 1 2 3 4 5 6 7 8 9 10
ELEV
WIND
CALL
REMARKS: PULLED TRIGGER ON LAST SHOT; HAD COLD + FEVER; FIRING TIME: 10 MIN.

Figure 3-23: Example of completed DA Form 5785-R.

3-18. ENTRIES

Three phases in writing information on the data card (Figure 3-23) are *before firing, during firing*, and *after firing.*

a. **Before Firing.** Information that is written before firing is—
   (1) ***Range.*** The distance to the target.
   (2) ***Rifle and scope number.*** The serial numbers of the rifle and scope.
   (3) ***Date.*** Date of firing.
   (4) ***Ammunition.*** Type and lot number of ammunition.
   (5) ***Light.*** Amount of light (overcast, clear, and so forth).
   (6) ***Mirage.*** Whether a mirage can be seem or not (good, bad, fair, and so forth).
   (7) ***Temperature.*** Temperature on the range.
   (8) ***Hour.*** Time of firing.
   (9) ***Light (diagram).*** Draw an arrow in the direction the light is shining.
   (10) ***Wind.*** Draw an arrow in the direction the wind is blowing, and record its average velocity and cardinal direction (N, NE, S, SW, and so forth).

b. **During Firing.** Information that is written while firing is—
   (1) ***Elevation.*** Elevation setting used and any correction needed. For example: The target distance is 600 meters; the sniper sets the elevation dial to 6. The sniper fires and the round hits the target 6 inches low of center. He then adds one minute (one click) of elevation (+1).
   (2) ***Windage.*** Windage setting used and any correction needed. For example The sniper fires at a 600-meter target with windage setting on 0; the round impacts 15 inches right of center. He will then add 21/2 minutes left to the windage dial (L/21/2).
   (3) ***Shot.*** The column of information about a particular shot. For example: Column 1 is for the first round; column 10 is for the tenth round.
   (4) ***Elevation.*** Elevation used (6 +1, 6,6 -1, and so on).
   (5) ***Wind.*** Windage used (L/2 1/2, O, R/1/2, and so on).
   (6) ***Call.*** Where the aiming point was when the weapon fired.
   (7) ***Large silhouette.*** Used to record the exact impact of the round on the target. This is recorded by writing the shot's number on the large silhouette in the same place it hit the target.

c. **After Firing.** After firing, the sniper records any comments about firing in the remarks section. This can be comments about the weapon, firing conditions (time allowed for fire), or his condition (nervous, felt bad, felt good, and so forth).

3-19. ANALYSIS

When the sniper leaves the firing line, he compares weather conditions to the information needed to hit the point of aim/point of impact. Since he fires in all types of weather conditions, he must be aware of temperature, light, mirage, and wind. The sniper must consider other major points or tasks to complete

a. Compare sight settings with previous firing sessions. If the sniper always has to fine-tune for windage or elevation, there is a chance he needs a sight change (slip a scale).
b. Compare ammunition by lot number for best rifle and ammunition combination.
c. Compare all groups fired under each condition. Check the low and high shots as well as those to the left and the right of the main group—the less dispersion, the better. If groups are tight, they are easily moved to the center of the target; if loose, there is a problem. Check the scope focus and make sure the rifle is cleaned correctly. Remarks in the sniper data book will also help.
d. Make corrections. Record corrections in the sniper data book, such as position and sight adjustment information, to ensure retention.
e. Analyze a group on a target. This is important for marksmanship training. The firer may not notice errors during firing, but errors become apparent when analyzing a group. This can only be done if the sniper data book has been used correctly. A checklist that will aid in shot group/performance analysis follows:

(1) Group tends to be low and right.
- Left hand not positioned properly.
- Right elbow slipping.
- Improper trigger control.

(2) Group scattered about the target.
- Incorrect eye relief or sight picture.
- Concentration on the target (iron sights).
- Stock weld changed.
- Unstable firing position.

(3) Good group but with several erratic shots.
- *Flinching.* Shots may be anywhere.
- *Bucking.* Shots from 7 to 10 o'clock.
- *Jerking.* Shots may be anywhere.

(4) Group strung up and down through the target.
- Breathing while firing.
- Improper vertical alignment of cross hairs.
- Stock weld changed.

(5) Compact group out of the target.
- Incorrect zero.
- Failure to compensate for wind.
- Bad natural point of aim.
- Scope shadow.

(6) Group center of the target out the bottom.
- Scope shadow.
- Position of the rifle changed in the shoulder.

(7) Horizontal group across the target.
- Scope shadow.
- Canted weapon.
- Bad natural point of aim.

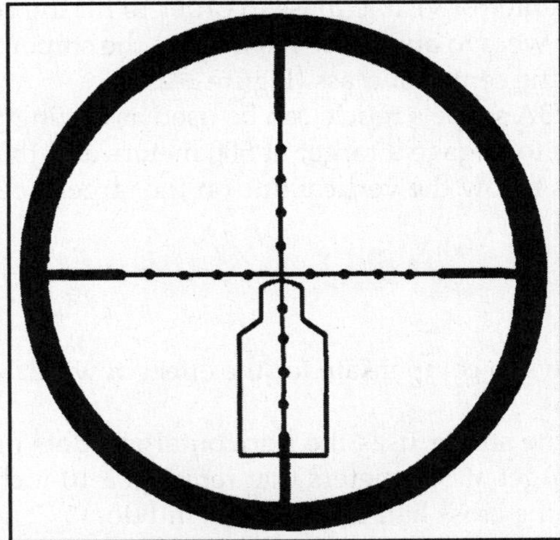

Figure 3-24: Elevation.

SECTION V. HOLDOFF

Holdoff is shifting the point of aim to achieve a desired point of impact. Certain situations, such as multiple targets at varying ranges and rapidly changing winds, do not allow proper windage and elevation adjustments. Therefore, familiarization and practice of elevation and windage holdoff techniques prepare the sniper to meet these situations.

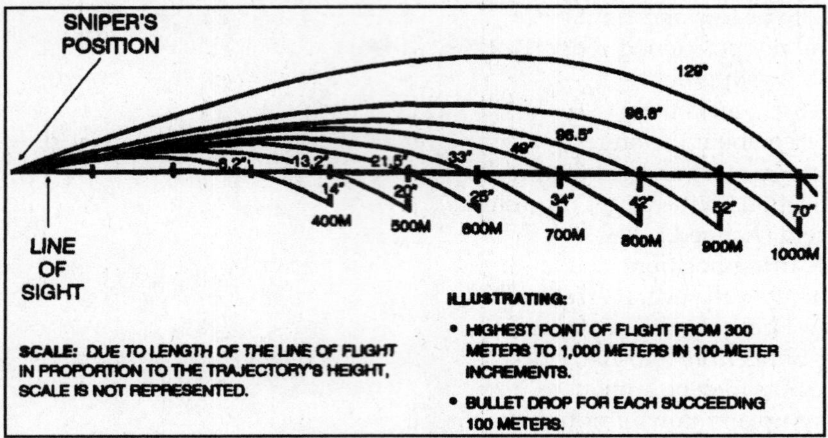

Figure 3-25: Trajectory chart.

3-20. ELEVATION

This technique is used only when the sniper does not have time to change his sight setting. The sniper rarely achieves pinpoint accuracy when holding off, since a minor error in range determination or a lack of a precise aiming point might cause the bullet to miss the desired point. He uses holdoff with the sniperscope only if several targets appear at various ranges, and time does not permit adjusting the scope for each target.

a. The sniper uses holdoff to hit a target at ranges other than the range for which the rifle is presently adjusted. When the sniper aims directly at a target at ranges greater than the set range, his bullet will hit below the point of aim. At lesser ranges, his bullet will hit higher than the point of aim. If the sniper understands this and knows about trajectory and bullet drop, he will be able to hit the target at ranges other than that for which the rifle was adjusted. For example, the sniper adjusts the rifle for a target located 500 meters downrange and another target appears at a range of 600 meters. The holdoff would be 25 inches, that is, the sniper should hold off 25 inches above the center of visible mass in order to hit the center of mass of that particular target (Figure 3-24). If another target were to appear at 400 meters, the sniper would aim 14 inches below the ureter of visible mass in order to hit the center of mass (Figure 3-25).

b. The vertical mil dots on the M3A scope's reticle can be used as aiming points when using elevation holdoffs. For example, if the sniper has to engage a target at 500 meters and the scope is set at 400 meters, he would place the first mil dot 5 inches below the vertical line on the target's center mass. This gives the sniper a 15-inch holdoff at 500 meters.

3-21. WINDAGE

The sniper can use holdoff in three ways to compensate for the effect of wind.

a. When using the M3A scope, the sniper uses the horizontal mil dots on the reticle to hold off for wind. For example, if the sniper has a target at 500 meters that requires a 10-inch holdoff, he would place the target's center mass halfway between the cross hair and the first mil dot (1/2 mil) (Figure 3-26).

b. When holding off, the sniper aims into the wind. If the wind is moving from the right to left, his point of aim is to the right. If the wind is moving from left to right, his point of aim is to the left.

c. Constant practice in wind estimation can bring about proficiency in making sight adjustments or learning to apply holdoff correctly. If the sniper misses the target and the point of impact of the round is observed, he notes the lateral distance of his error and refires, holding off that distance in the opposite direction.

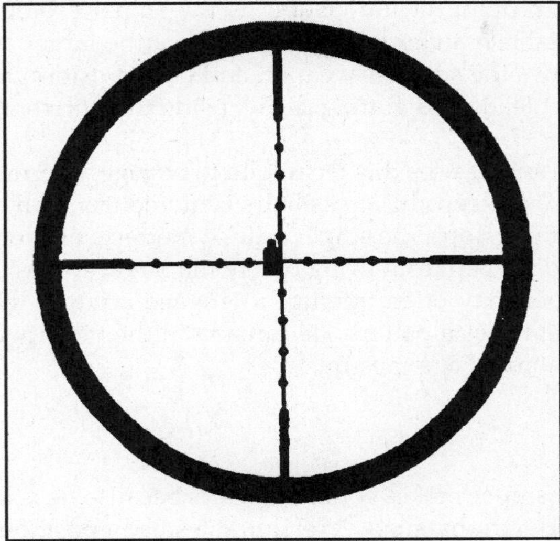

Figure 3-26: Holdoff for 7.62-mm special ball (M118).

SECTION VI. ENGAGEMENT OF MOVING TARGETS

Engaging moving targets not only requires the sniper to determine the target distance and wind effects on the round, but he must also consider the lateral and speed angle of the target, the round's time of flight, and the placement of a proper lead to compensate for both. These added variables increase the chance of a miss. Therefore, the sniper should engage moving targets when it is the only option.

3-22. TECHNIQUES

To engage moving targets, the sniper employs the following techniques:

- Leading.
- Tracking.
- Trapping or ambushing.
- Tracking and holding.
- Firing a snap shot.

a. **Leading.** Engaging moving targets requires the sniper to place the cross hairs ahead of the target's movement. The distance the cross hairs are placed in front of the target's movement is called a *lead.* There are four factors in determining leads:

(1) ***Speed of the target.*** As a target moves faster, it will move a greater distance during the bullet's flight. Therefore, the lead increases as the target's speed increases.

(2) ***Angle of movement.*** A target moving perpendicular to the bullet's flight path moves a greater lateral distance than a target moving at an angle away from or toward the bullet's path. Therefore, a target moving at a 45-degree angle covers less ground than a target moving at a 90-degree angle.

(3) ***Range to the target.*** The farther away a target is, the longer it takes for the bullet to reach it. Therefore, the lead must be increased as the distance to the target increases.

(4) ***Wind effects.*** The sniper must consider how the wind will affect the trajectory of the round. A wind blowing against the target's direction of movement requires less of a lead than a wind blowing in the same direction as the target's movement.

b. **Tracking.** Hacking requires the sniper to establish an aiming point ahead of the target's movement and to maintain it as the weapon is fired. This requires the weapon and body position to be moved while following the target and firing.

c. **Trapping or Ambushing.** Trapping or ambushing is the sniper's preferred method of engaging moving targets. The sniper must establish an aiming point ahead of the target and pull the trigger when the target reaches it. This method allows the sniper's weapon and body position to remain motionless. With practice, a sniper can determine exact leads and aiming points using the horizontal stadia lines in the mil dots in the M3A.

d. **Tracking and Holding.** The sniper uses this technique to engage an erratically moving target. That is, while the target is moving, the sniper keeps his cross hairs centered as much as possible and adjusts his position with the target. When the target stops, the sniper quickly perfects his hold and fires. This technique requires concentration and discipline to keep from firing before the target comes to a complete halt.

e. **Firing a Snap Shot.** A sniper may often attempt to engage a target that only presents itself briefly, then resumes cover. Once he establishes a pattern, he can aim in the vicinity of the target's expected appearance and fire a snap shot at the moment of exposure.

3-23. COMMON ERRORS

When engaging moving targets, the sniper makes common errors because he is under greater stress than with a stationary target. There are more considerations, such as retaining a steady position and the correct aiming point, how fast the target is moving, and how far away it is. The more practice a sniper has shooting moving targets, the better he will become. Some common mistakes are as follows:

a. The sniper has a tendency to watch his target instead of his aiming point. He must force himself to watch his lead point.

b. The sniper may jerk or flinch at the moment his weapon fires because he thinks he must fire NOW. This can be overcome through practice on a live-fire range.

c. The sniper may hurry and thus forget to apply wind as needed. Windage must be calculated for moving targets just as for stationary targets. Failure to do this when squiring a lead will result in a miss.

3-24. CALCULATION OF LEADS

Once the required lead has been determined, the sniper should use the mil scale in the scope for precise holdoff. The mil scale can be mentally sectioned into 1/4-mil increments for leads. The chosen point on the mil scale becomes the sniper's point of concentration just as the cross hairs are for stationary targets. The sniper concentrates on the lead point and fires the weapon when the target is at this point. The following formulas are used to determine moving target leads:

TIME OF FLIGHT X TARGET SPEED = LEAD.
Time of flight = flight time of the round in seconds.
Target speed = speed the target is moving in fps.
Lead = distance aiming point must be placed ahead of movement in feet.

Average speed of a man during—
Slow patrol = 1 fps/0.8 mph
Fast patrol = 2 fps/1.3 mph
Slow walk = 4 fps/2.5 mph
Fast walk = 6 fps/3.7 mph

To convert leads in feet to meters:
LEAD IN FEET X 0,3048 = METERS

To convert leads in meters to mils:

$$\frac{\text{LEAD IN METERS X 1,000}}{\text{RANGE TO TARGET}} = \text{MIL LEAD}$$

SECTION VII. NUCLEAR, BIOLOGICAL, CHEMICAL

Performance of long-range precision fire is difficult at best. Enemy NBC warfare creates new problems for the sniper. Not only must the sniper properly execute the fundamentals of marksmanship and contend with the forces of nature, he must overcome obstacles presented by protective equipment. Testing conducted by the U.S. Army Sniper School, Fort Benning, GA during 1989 to 1990 uncovered several problem areas. Evaluation of this testing discovered ways to help the sniper overcome these problems while firing in an NBC environment.

3-25. PROTECTIVE MASK

The greatest problem while firing the M24 with the M17-series protective mask was that of recoil breaking the seal of the mask. Also, due to filter elements and hard eye lenses, the sniper could not gain and maintain proper stock weld and eye relief. Additionally, the observer could not gain the required eye relief for observation through his M49 observation telescope. However, testing of the M25-series protective mask provided the following results:

a. Because of its separate filtering canister, the stock weld was gained and maintained with minimal effort.
b. Its flexible face shield allowed for excellent observation. This also allowed the sniper and observer to achieve proper eye relief, which was needed for observation with their respective telescopes.

3-26. MISSION-ORIENTED PROTECTION POSTURE

Firing while in MOPP has a significant effect on the ability to deliver precision fire. The following problems and solutions have been identified

a. **Eye Relief.** Special emphasis must be made in maintaining proper eye relief and the absence of scope shadow. Maintaining consistent stock weld is a must.
b. **Trigger Control.** Problems encountered with trigger control consist of the sense of touch and stock drag.
   (1) ***Sense of touch.*** When gloves are worn, the sniper cannot determine the amount of pressure he is applying to the trigger. This is of particular importance if the sniper has the trigger adjusted for a light pull. Training with a glove will be beneficial; however, the trigger should be adjusted to allow the sniper to feel the trigger without accidental discharge.
   (2) ***Stock drag.*** While training, the sniper should have his observer watch his trigger finger to ensure that the finger and glove are not touching any part of the rifle but the trigger. The glove or finger resting on the trigger guard moves the rifle as the trigger is pulled to the rear. The sniper must wear a well-fitted glove.
c. **Vertical Sight Picture.** The sniper naturally cants the rifle into the cheek of the face while firing with a protective mask.
d. **Sniper/Observer Communications.** The absence of a voice emitter on the M2S-series protective mask creates an obstacle in relaying information. The team either speaks louder or uses written messages. A system of foot taps, finger taps, or hand signals may be devised. Communication is a must; training should include the development and practice of communications at different MOPP levels.

CHAPTER 4

Field Techniques

The primary mission of the sniper team is to eliminate selected enemy targets with long-range precision fire. How well the sniper accomplishes his mission depends on knowledge, understanding and application of various field techniques that allow him to move, hide, observe, and detect targets. This chapter discusses the field techniques and skills that the sniper must learn before employment in support of combat operations. The sniper's application of these skills will affect his survival on the battlefield.

SECTION I. CAMOUFLAGE

Camouflage is one of the basic weapons of war. It can mean the difference between a successful or unsuccessful mission. To the sniper team, it can mean the difference between life and death. Camouflage measures are important since the team cannot afford to be detected at any time while moving alone, as part of another element, or while operating from a firing position. Marksmanship training teaches the sniper to hit a target, and a knowledge of camouflage teaches him how to avoid becoming a target. Paying attention to camouflage fundamentals is a mark of a well-trained sniper.

4-1. TARGET INDICATORS

To become proficient in camouflage, the sniper team must first understand target indicators. Target indicators are anything a soldier does or fails to do that could result in detection. A sniper team must know and understand target indication not only to move undetected, but also to detect enemy movement. Target indicators are sound, movement, improper camouflage, disturbance of wildlife, and odors.

a. Sound.
- Most noticeable during hours of darkness.
- Caused by movement, equipment rattling, or talking.
- Small noises may be dismissed as natural, but talking will not.

b. Movement.
- Most noticeable during hours of daylight.
- The human eye is attracted to movement.
- Quick or jerky movement will be detected faster than slow movement.

c. Improper camouflage.
- Shine.
- Outline.
- Contrast with the background.

d. Disturbance of wildlife.
- Birds suddenly flying away.
- Sudden stop of animal noises.
- Animals being frightened.

e. Odors.
- Cooking.
- Smoking.
- Soap and lotions.
- Insect repellents.

4-2. BASIC METHODS

The sniper team can use three basic methods of camouflage. It may use one of these methods or a combination of all three to accomplish its objective. The three basic methods a sniper team can use are hiding, blending, and deceiving.

a. **Hiding.** Hiding is used to conceal the body from observation by lying behind an objector thick vegetation.
b. **Blending.** Blending is used to match personal camouflage with the surrounding area to a point where the sniper cannot be seen.
c. **Deceiving.** Deceiving is used to fool the enemy into false conclusions about the location of the sniper team.

4-3. TYPES OF CAMOUFLAGE

The two types of camouflage that the sniper team can use are *natural* and *artificial.*

a. **Natural.** Natural camouflage is vegetation or materials that are native to the given area. The sniper augments his appearance by using natural camouflage.
b. **Artificial.** Artificial camouflage is any material or substance that is produced for the purpose of coloring or covering something in order to conceal it. Camouflage sticks or face paints are used to cover all exposed areas of skin such as face, hands, and the back of the neck. The parts of the face that form shadows should be lightened, and the parts that shine should be darkened. The three types of camouflage patterns the sniper team uses are striping, blotching, and combination.
   (1) ***Striping.*** Used when in heavily wooded areas and when leafy vegetation is scarce.
   (2) ***Blotching.*** Used when an area is thick with leafy vegetation.
   (3) ***Combination.*** Used when moving through changing terrain. It is normally the best all-round pattern.

4-4. GHILLIE SUIT

The ghillie suit is a specially made camouflage uniform that is covered with irregular patterns of garnish or netting (Figure 4-1).

a. Ghillie suits can be made from BDUs or one-piece aviator-type uniforms. Turning the uniform inside out places the pockets inside the suit. This protects items in the pockets from damage caused by crawling on the ground. The front of the ghillie suit should be covered with canvas or some type of heavy cloth to reinforce it. The knees and elbows should be covered with two layers of canvas, and the seam of the crotch should be reinforced with heavy nylon thread since these areas are prone to wear out quicker.
b. The garnish or netting should cover the shoulders and reach down to the elbows on the sleeves. The garnish applied to the back of the suit should be long enough to cover the sides of the sniper when he is in the prone position. A bush hat is also covered with garnish or netting. The garnish should belong enough to breakup the outline of the sniper's neck, but it should not be so long in front to obscure his vision or hinder movement.
c. A veil can be made from a net or piece of cloth covered with garnish or netting. It covers the weapon and sniper's head when in a firing position. The veil can be sewn into the ghillie suit or carried separately. A ghillie suit does not make one invisible and is only a camouflage base. Natural vegetation should be added to help blend with the surroundings.

4-5. FIELD-EXPEDIENT CAMOUFLAGE

The sniper team may have to use field-expedient camouflage if other means are not available. Instead of camouflage sticks or face paint, the team may use charcoal, walnut stain, mud, or whatever works. The team will not use oil or grease due to the strong odor. Natural vegetation can be attached to the body by boot bands or rubber bands or by cutting holes in the uniform.

a. The sniper team also camouflages its equipment. However, the camouflage must not interfere with or hinder the operation of the equipment.

Figure 4-1: Ghillie suit.

(1) ***Rifles.*** The sniper weapon system and the M16/M203 should also. be camouflaged to break up their outlines. The sniper weapon system can be carried in a "drag bag" (Figure 4-2), which is a rifle case made of canvas and covered with garnish similar to the ghillie suit.
(2) ***Optics.*** Optics used by the sniper team must also be camouflaged to breakup the outline and to reduce the possibility of light reflecting off the lenses. Lenses can be covered with mesh-type webbing or nylon hose material.
(3) ***ALICE pack.*** If the sniper uses the ALICE pack while wearing the ghillie suit, he must camouflage the pack the same as the suit.

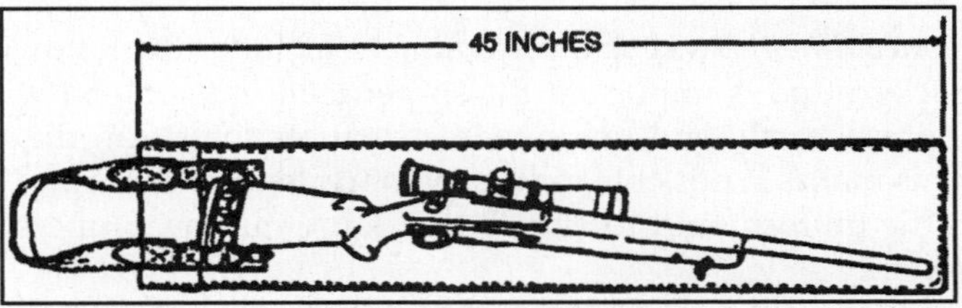

Figure 4-2: Drag bag.

b. The sniper team alters its camouflage to blend in with changes in vegetation and terrain in different geographic areas. Examples of such changes are as follows:
   (1) ***Snow areas.*** Blending of colors is more effective than texture camouflage in snowy areas. In areas with heavy snow or in wooded areas with trees covered with snow, a full white camouflage suit should be worn. In areas with snow on the ground but not on the trees, white trousers with green and brown tops should be worn.
   (2) ***Desert areas.*** In sandy desert areas that have little vegetation, the blending of tan and brown colors is important. In these areas, the sniper team must make full use of the terrain and the vegetation that is available to remain unnoticed.
   (3) ***Jungle areas.*** In jungle areas, textured camouflage, contrasting colors, and natural vegetation must be used.
   (4) ***Urban areas.*** In urban areas, the sniper team's camouflage should be a blended color (shades of gray usually work best). Texutred camouflage is not as important in these environments.
c. The sniper team must be camouflage conscious from the time it departs on a mission until it returns. It must constantly use the terrain, vegetation, and shadows to remain undetected. At no other time during the mission will the sniper team have a greater tendency to be careless than during its return to a friendly area. Fatigue and undue haste may override caution and planning. Therefore, the team needs to pay close attention to its camouflage discipline on return from missions.

4-6. COVER AND CONCEALMENT

The proper understanding and application of the principles of cover and concealment used with the proper application of camouflage protects the sniper team from enemy observation.

a. Cover is natural or artificial protection from the fire of enemy weapons. Natural cover (ravines, hollows, reverse slopes) and artificial cover (fighting positions, trenches, walls) protect the sniper team from flat trajectory fires and partly protect it from high-angle fires and the effects of nuclear explosions. Even the smallest depression or fold in the ground may provide some cover when the team needs it most. A 6-inch depression, properly used, may provide enough cover to save the sniper team under fire. Snipers must always look for and take advantage of all the cover that the terrain provides. By combining this habit with proper movement techniques, the team can protect itself from enemy fire. To get protection from enemy fire when moving, the team uses routes that put cover between itself and the enemy.

b. Concealment is natural or artificial protection from enemy observation. The surroundings may provide natural concealment that needs no change before use (bushes, grass, and shadows). The sniper team creates artificial concealment from materials such as burlap and camouflage nets, or it can move natural materials (bushes, leaves, and grass) from their original location. The sniper team must consider the effects of the change of seasons on the concealment provided by both natural and artificial materials. The principles of concealment include the following

(1) ***Avoid unnecessary movement.*** Remain still—movement attracts attention. The position of the sniper team is concealed when the team remains still, but the sniper's position is easily detected when the team moves. Movement against a stationary background makes the team stand out clearly. When the team must change positions, it moves carefully over a concealed route to a new position, preferably during limited visibility. Snipers move inches at a time, slowly and cautiously, always scanning ahead for the next position.

(2) ***Use all available concealment.*** Available concealment includes the following:

(a) *Background.* Background is important the sniper team must blend with it to prevent detection. The trees, bushes, grass, earth, and man-made structures that form the background vary in color and appearance. This makes it possible for the team to blend with them. The team selects trees or bushes to blend with the uniform and to absorb the figure outline. Snipers must always assume they are under observation.

(b) *Shadows.* The sniper team in the open stands out clearly, but the sniper team in the shadows is difficult to see. Shadows exist under most conditions, day and night. A sniper team should never fire from the edge of a wood line; it should fire from a position inside the wood line (in the shade or shadows provided by the tree tops).

(3) ***Stay low to observe.*** A low silhouette makes it difficult for the enemy to see a sniper team. Therefore, the team observes from a crouch, a squat, or a prone position.

(4) ***Avoid shiny reflections.*** Reflection of light on a shiny surface instantly attracts attention and can be seen from great distances. The sniper uncovers his rifle scope only when indexing and aiming at a target. He uses optics cautiously in bright sunshine because of the reflections they cause.

(5) ***Avoid skylining.*** Figures on the skyline can be seen from a great distance, even at night, because a dark outline stands out against the lighter sky. The silhouette formed by the body makes a good target.

(6) ***Alter familiar outlines.*** Military equipment and the human body are familiar outlines to the enemy. The sniper team alters or disguises these revealing shapes by using the ghillie suit or outer smock that is covered with irregular patterns of garnish. The team must alter its outline from the head to the soles of the boots.

(7) ***Observe noise discipline.*** Noise, such as talking, can be picked up by enemy patrols or observation posts. The sniper team silences gear before a mission so that it makes no sound when the team walks or runs.

SECTION II. MOVEMENT

A sniper team's mission and method of employment differ in many ways from those of the infantry squad. One of the most noticeable differences is the movement technique used by the sniper team. Movement by teams must not be detected or even suspected by the enemy. Because of this, a sniper team must master individual sniper movement techniques.

4-7. RULES OF MOVEMENT

When moving, the sniper team should always remember the following rules:

a. Always assume the area is under enemy observation.
b. Move slowly. A sniper counts his movement progress by feet and inches.
c. Do not cause overhead movement of trees, bushes, or tall grasses by rubbing against them.
d. Plan every movement and move in segments of the route at a time.
e. Stop, look, and listen often.
f. Move during disturbances such as gunfire, explosions, aircraft noise, wind, or anything that will distract the enemy's attention or conceal the team's movement.

4-8. INDIVIDUAL MOVEMENT TECHNIQUES

The individual movement techniques used by the sniper team are designed to allow movement without being detected. These movement techniques are sniper low crawl, medium crawl, high crawl, hand-and-knees crawl, and walking.

a. **Sniper Low Crawl.** The sniper low crawl (Figure 4-3) is used when concealment is extremely limited, when close to the enemy, or when occupying a firing position.

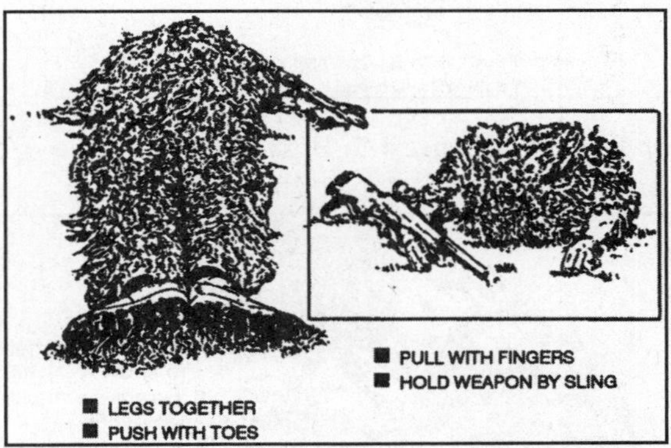

Figure 4-3: Sniper low crawl.

b. **Medium Crawl.** The medium crawl (Figure 4-4) is used when concealment is limited and the team needs to move faster-than the sniper low crawl allows. The medium crawl is similar to the infantryman's low crawl.
c. **High Crawl.** The high crawl (Figure 4-5) is used when concealment is limited but high enough to allow the sniper to raise his body off the ground. The high crawl is similar to the infantry high crawl.
d. **Hand-and-knees Crawl.** The hand-and-knees crawl (Figure 4-6) is used when some concealment is available and the sniper team needs to move faster than the medium crawl.
e. **Walking.** Walking (Figure 4-7) is used when there is good concealment, it is not likely the enemy is close, and speed is required.

4-9. SNIPER TEAM MOVEMENT AND NAVIGATION

Due to lack of personnel and firepower, the sniper team cannot afford detection by the enemy nor can it successfully fight the enemy in sustained engagements.

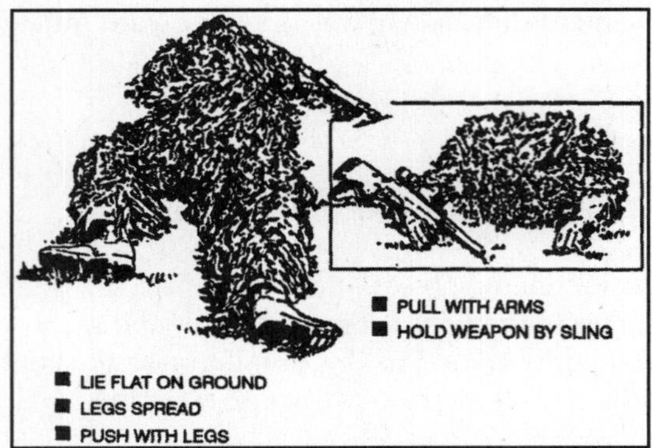

Figure 4-4: Medium crawl.

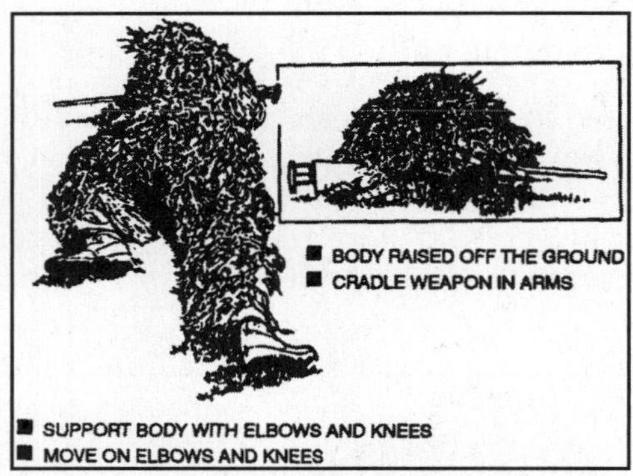

Figure 4-5: High crawl.

Figure 4-6: Hand-and-knees crawl.

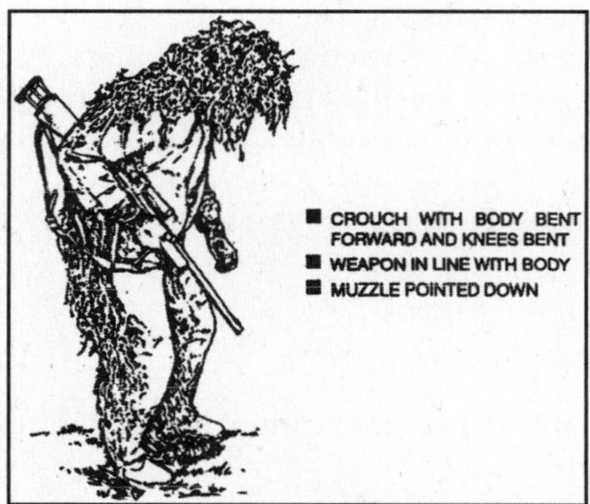

Figure 4-7: Walking.

a. When possible, the sniper team should be attached to a security element (squad/platoon). The security element allows the team to reach its area of operations quicker and safer than the team operating alone. Plus, the security element provides the team a reaction force should the team be detected. Snipers use the following guidelines when attached to a security element:
   (1) The security element leader is in charge of the team while it is attached to the element.
   (2) The sniper team always appears as an integral part of the element.
   (3) The sniper team wears the same uniform as the element members.
   (4) The sniper team maintains proper intends and positions in all formations.
   (5) The sniper weapon system is carried in line and close to the body, hiding its outline and barrel length.
   (6) All equipment that is unique to sniper teams is concealed from view (optics, ghillie suits, and so forth).
b. Once in the area of operation, the sniper team separates from the security element and operates alone. Two examples of a sniper team separating from security elements are as follows:
   (1) The security element provides security while the team prepares for operation.
      (a) The team dons the ghillie suits and camouflages itself and its equipment (if mission requires).
      (b) The team ensures all equipment is secure and caches any nonessential equipment (if mission requires).
      (c) Once the team is prepared, it assumes a concealed position, and the security element departs the area.
      (d) Once the security element has departed, the team waits in position long enough to ensure neither itself nor the security element has been compromised. Then, the team moves to its tentative position.
   (2) The security element conducts a short security halt at the separation point. The sniper team halts, ensuring they have good available concealment and know each other's location. The security element then proceeds, leaving the sniper team in place. The sniper team remains in position until the security element is clear of the area. The team then organizes itself as required by the mission and moves on to its tentative position. This type of separation also works well in MOUT situations.
c. When selecting routes, the sniper team must remember its strengths and weaknesses. The following guidelines should be used when selecting routes:
   (1) Avoid known enemy positions and obstacles.
   (2) Seek terrain that offers the best cover and concealment.
   (3) Take advantage of difficult terrain (swamps, dense woods, and so forth).
   (4) Do not use trails, roads, or footpaths.
   (5) Avoid built-up or populated areas.
   (6) Avoid areas of heavy enemy guerrilla activity.
d. When the sniper team moves, it must always assume its area is under enemy observation. Because of this and the size of the team with the small amount of firepower it has, the team uses only one type of formation-the sniper movement formation. Characteristics of the formation are as follows:
   (1) The observer is the point man; the sniper follows.
   (2) The observer's sector of security is 3 o'clock to 9 o'clock; the sniper's sector of security is 9 o'clock to 3 o'clock (overlapping).
   (3) Visual contact must be maintained even when lying on the ground.
   (4) An interval of no more than 20 meters is maintained.
   (5) The sniper reacts to the point man's actions.
   (6) The team leader designates the movement techniques and routes used.
   (7) The team leader designates rally points.
e. A sniper team must never become decisively engaged with the enemy. The team must rehearse immediate action drills to the extent that they become a natural and immediate reaction should it make unexpected contact with the enemy. Examples of such actions are as follows:
   (1) ***Visual contact.*** If the sniper team sees the enemy and the enemy does not see the team, it freezes. If the team has time, it will do the following:
      (a) Assume the best covered and concealed position.
      (b) Remain in position until the enemy has passed.

✍ NOTE

The team will not initiate contact.

(2) ***Ambush.*** In an ambush, the sniper team's objective is to break contact immediately. One example of this involves performing the following
(a) The observer delivers rapid fire on the enemy.
(b) The sniper throws smoke grenades between the observer and the enemy.
(c) The sniper delivers well-aimed shots at the most threatening targets until smoke covers the area.
(d) The observer then throws fragmentation grenades and withdraws toward the sniper, ensuring he does not mask the sniper's fire.
(e) The team moves to a location where the enemy cannot observe or place direct fire on it.
(f) If contact cannot be broken, the sniper calls for indirect fires or a security element (if attached).
(g) If team members get separated, they should return to the next-to-last designated en route rally point.

(3) ***Indirect fire.*** When reacting to indirect fires, the team must move out of the area as quickly as possible. This sudden movement can result in the team's exact location and direction being pinpointed. Therefore, the team must not only react to indirect fire but also take actions to conceal its movement once it is out of the impact area.
(a) The team leader moves the team out of the impact area using the quickest route by giving the direction and distance (clock method).
(b) Team members move out of the impact area the designated distance and direction.
(c) The team leader then moves the team farther away from the impact area by using the most direct concealed route. They continue the mission using an alternate route.
(d) If team members get separated, they should return to the next-to-last designated en route rally point.

(4) ***Air attack.***
(a) Team members assume the best available covered and concealed positions.
(b) Between passes of aircraft, team members move to positions that offer better cover and concealment.
(c) The team does not engage the aircraft.
(d) Team members remain in positions until attacking aircraft depart.
(e) If team members get separated, they return to the next-to-last designated en route rally point.

f. To aid the sniper team in navigation, the team should memorize the route by studying maps, aerial photos, or sketches. The team notes distinctive features (hills, streams, roads) and its location in relation to the route. It plans an alternate route in case the primary route cannot be used. It plans offsets to circumvent known obstacles to movement. The team uses terrain countdown, which involves memorizing terrain features from the start point to the objective, to maintain the route. During the mission, the sniper team mentally counts each terrain feature, thus ensuring it maintains the proper route.

g. The sniper team maintains orientation at all times. As it moves, it observes the terrain carefully and mentally checks off the distinctive features noted in the planning and study of the route. Many aids are available to ensure orientation. The following are examples:
(1) The location and direction of flow of principal streams.
(2) Hills, valleys, roads, and other peculiar terrain features.
(3) Railroad tracks, power lines, and other man-made objects.

SECTION III. SELECTION, OCCUPATION, AND CONSTRUCTION OF SNIPER POSITIONS

Selecting the location for a position is one of the most important tasks a sniper team accomplishes during the mission planning phase of an operation. After selecting the location, the team also determines how it will move into the area to locate and occupy the final position.

4-10. SELECTION

Upon receiving a mission, the sniper team locates the target area and then determines the best location for a tentative position by using one or more of the following sources of information: topographic maps, aerial photographs, visual reconnaissance before the mission, and information gained from units operating in the area.

a. The sniper team ensures the position provides an optimum balance between the following considerations:
   - Maximum fields of fire and observation of the target area.
   - Concealment from enemy observation.
   - Covered routes into and out of the position.
   - Located no closer than 300 meters from the target area.
   - A natural or man-made obstacle between the position and the target area.

b. A sniper team must remember that a position that appears to be in an ideal location may also appear that way to the enemy. Therefore, the team avoids choosing locations that are—
   - On a point or crest of prominent terrain features.
   - Close to isolated objects.
   - At bends or ends of roads, trails, or streams.
   - In populated areas, unless it is required.

c. The sniper team must use its imagination and ingenuity in choosing a good location for the given mission. The team chooses a location that not only allows the team to be effective but also must appear to the enemy to be the least likely place for a team position. The following are examples of such positions:
   - Under logs in a deadfall area.
   - Tunnels bored from one side of a knoll to the other.
   - Swamps.
   - Deep shadows.
   - Inside rubble piles.

4-11. OCCUPATION

During the mission planning phase, the sniper also selects an objective rally point. From this point, the sniper team reconnoiters the tentative position to determine the exact location of its final position. The location of the ORP should provide cover and concealment from enemy fire and observation, be located as close to the selected area as possible, and have good routes into and out of the selected area.

a. From the ORP, the team moves foward to a location that allows the team to view the tentative position area (Figure 4-8). One member remains in this location to cover the other member who reconnoiters the area to locate a final position. Once a suitable location has been found, the covering team member moves to the position. While conducting the reconnaissance or moving to the position, the team—
   - Moves slowly and deliberately, using the sniper low crawl.
   - Avoids unnecessary movement of trees, bushes, and grass.
   - Avoids making any noises.
   - Stays in the shadows, if there are any.
   - Stops, looks, and listens every few feet.

b. When the sniper team arrives at the firing position, it—
   - Conducts a detailed search of the target area.
   - Starts construction of the firing position, if required.
   - Organizes equipment so that it is easily accessible.
   - Establishes a system of observing eating resting, and latrine calls.

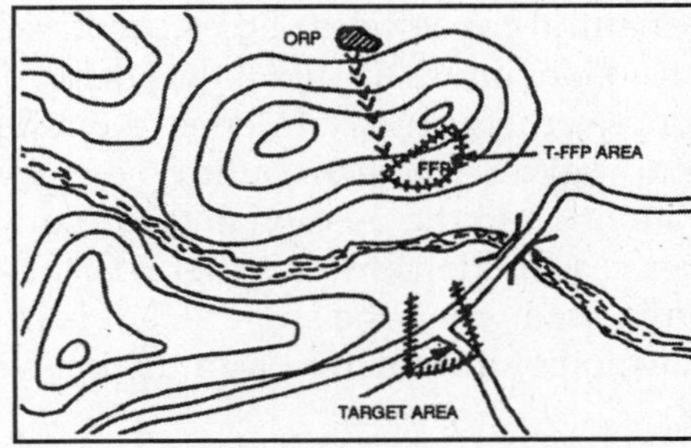

Figure 4-8: Tentative position areas.

4-12. CONSTRUCTION

A sniper mission always requires the team to occupy some type of position. These positions can range from a hasty position, which a team may use for a few hours, to a more permanent position, which the team could occupy for a few days. The team should always plan to build its position during limited visibility.

a. **Sniper Position Considerations.** Whether a sniper team is in a position for a few minutes or a few days, the basic considerations in choosing a type of position remain the same.
  (1) ***Location:***
    (a) *Type of terrain and soil.* Digging and boring of tunnels can be very difficult in hard soil or in fine, loose sand. The team takes advantage of what the terrain offers (gullies, holes, hollow tree stumps, and so forth).
    (b) *Enemy location and capabilities.* Enemy patrols in the area may be close enough to the position to hear any noises that may accidentally be made during any construction. The team also considers the enemy's night vision and detection capabilities.
  (2) ***Time:***
    (a) *Amount of time to be occupied.* If the sniper team's mission requires it to be in position for a long time, the team constructs a position that provides more survivability. This allows the team to operate more effectively for a longer time.
    (b) *Time required for construction.* The time required to build a position must be considered, especially during the mission planning phase.
  (3) ***Personnel and equipment:***
    (a) *Equipment needed for construction.* The team plans for the use of any extra equipment needed for construction (bow saws, picks, axes, and so forth).
    (b) *Personnel needed for construction.* Coordination is made if the position requires more personnel to build it or a security element to secure the area during construction.

b. **Construction Techniques.** Belly and semipermanent hide positions can be constructed of stone, brick, wood, or turf. Regardless of material, every effort is made to bulletproof the front of the hide position. The team can use the following techniques:
  - Pack protective jackets around the loophole areas.
  - Emplace an angled armor plate with a loophole cut into it behind the hide loophole.
  - Sandbag the loopholes from the inside.

  (1) ***Pit.*** Hide construction begins with the pit since it protects the sniper team. All excavated dirt is removed (placed in sandbags, taken away on a poncho, and so forth) and hidden (plowed fields, under a log, or away from the hide site).
  (2) ***Overhead cover.*** In a semipermanent hide position, logs should be used as the base of the roof. The sniper team places a dust cover over the base (such as a poncho, layers of empty sandbags, or canvas), a layer of dirt, and a layer of gravel, if available. The team spreads another layer of dirt, and then adds camouflage. Due to the various materials, the roof is difficult to conceal if not countersunk.
  (3) ***Entrance.*** To prevent detection, the sniper team should construct an entrance door sturdy enough to bear a man's weight.
  (4) ***Loopholes.*** The construction of loopholes (Figure 4-9) requires care and practice to ensure they afford adequate fields of fire. Loopholes must be camouflaged by foliage or other material that blends with or is natural to the surroundings.
  (5) ***Approaches.*** It is vital that the natural appearance of the ground remains unaltered and camouflage blends with the surroundings. Construction time is wasted if the enemy observes a team entering the hide; therefore, approached must be concealed. Teams try to enter the hide during darkness, keeping movement to a minimum and adhering to trail discipline. In built-up areas, a secure and quiet approach is needed. Teams must avoid drawing attention to the mission and carefully plan movement. A possible ploy is to use a house search with sniper gear hidden among other gear. Sewers may be used for movement also.

c. **Hasty Position.** A hasty position is used when the sniper team is in a position for a short time and cannot construct a position due to the location of the enemy, or immediately assumes a position. The hasty position is characterized by the following:
  (1) ***Advantages:***
    (a) *Requires no construction.* The sniper team uses what is available for cover and concealment.

Figure 4-9: Loopholes in hide position.

(b) *Can be occupied in a short time.* As soon as a suitable position is found, the team need only prepare loopholes by moving small amounts of vegetation or by simply backing a few feet away from the vegetation that is already thereto conceal the weapon's muzzle blast.

(2) ***Disadvantages:***

(a) *Affords no freedom of movement.* Any movement that is not slow and deliberate may result in the team being compromised.

(b) *Restricts observation of large areas.* This type of position is normally used to observe a specific target area (intersection, passage, or crossing).

(c) *Offers no protection from direct or indirect fires.*

(d) *Relies heavily on personal camouflage.* The team's only protection against detection is personal camouflage and the ability to use the available terrain.

(3) ***Occupation time.*** The team should not remain in this type of position longer than eight hours.

d. **Expedient Position.** When a sniper team is required to remain in position for a longer time than the hasty position can provide, an expedient position (Figure 4-10) should be constructed. The expedient position lowers the sniper's silhouette as low to the ground as possible, but it still allows him to fire and observe effectively. The expedient position is characterized by the following

(1) ***Advantages:***

(a) *Requires little construction.* This position is constructed by digging a hole in the ground just large enough for the team and its equipment. Soil dug from this position can be placed in sandbags and used for building firing platforms.

(b) *Conceals most of the body and equipment.* The optics, rifles, and heads of the sniper team are the only items that are above ground level in this position.

(c) Provides some protection from direct fires due to its lower silhouette.

Figure 4-10: Expedient position.

(2) ***Disadvantages:***

(a) *Affords little freedom of movement.* The team has more freedom of movement in this position than in the hasty position. Team members can lower their heads below ground level slowly to ensure a target indicator is not produced.

(b) *Allows little protection from indirect fires.* This position does not protect the team from shrapnel and debris falling into the position.

(c) *Exposes the head, weapons, and optics.* The team must rely heavily on the camouflaging of these exposed areas.

(3) ***Construction time:*** 1 to 3 hours (depending on the situation).

(4) ***Occupation time:*** 6 to 12 hours.

e. **Belly Hide.** The belly hide (Figure 4-11) is similar to the expedient position, but it has overhead cover that not only protects the team from the effects of indirect fires but also allows more freedom of movement. This position can be dugout under a tree, a rock, or any available object that provides overhead protection and a concealed entrance and exit. The belly hide is characterized by the following:

(1) ***Advantages:***

(a) *Allows some freedom of movement.* The darkened area inside this position allows the team to move freely. The team must remember to cover the entrance/exit door so outside light does not silhouette the team inside the position or give the position away.

(b) *Conceals all but the rifle barrel.* All equipment is inside the position except the rifle barrels. Depending on the room available to construct the position, the rifle barrels may also be inside.

(c) *Provides protection from direct and indirect fires.* The team should try to choose a position that has an object that will provide good overhead protection (rock tracked vehicle, rubble pile, and so forth), or prepare it in the same manner as overhead cover for other infantry positions.

(2) ***Disadvantages:***

(a) *Requires extra construction time.*

(b) *Requires extra materials and tools.* Construction of overhead cover requires saws or axes, waterproof material, and so forth.

(c) *Has limited space.* The sniper team will have to lay in the belly hide without a lot of variation in body position due to limited space and design of the position.

(3) ***Construction time:*** 4 to 6 hours.

(4) ***Occupation time:*** 12 to 48 hours.

Figure 4-11: Belly hide position.

f. **Semipermanent Hide.** The semipermanent hide (Figure 4-12) is used mostly in defensive situations. This position requires additional equipment and personnel to construct. However, it allows sniper teams to remain in place for extended periods or to be relieved in place by other sniper teams. Like the belly hide, this position can be constructed by tunneling through a knoll or under natural objects already in place. The semipermanent hide is characterized by the following:

(1) ***Advantages:***

(a) *Offers total freedom of movement inside the position.* The team members can move about freely. They can stand, sit, or even lie down.

(b) *Protects against direct and indirect fires.* The sniper team should look for the same items as mentioned in the belly hide.

(c) *Is completely concealed.* Loopholes are the only part of the position that can be detected. They allow for the smallest exposure possible; yet they still allow the sniper and observer to view the target area. These loopholes should have a large diameter (10 to 14 inches) in the interior of the position and taper down to a smaller diameter (4 to 8 inches) on the outside of the position. A position may have more than two sets of loopholes if needed to cover large areas. The entrance/exit to the position must be covered to prevent light from entering and highlighting the loopholes. Loopholes that are not in use should be covered from the inside with a piece of canvas or suitable material.

(d) *Is easily maintained for extended periods.* This position allows the team to operate effectively for a longer period.

(2) ***Disadvantages:***

(a) *Requires extra personnel and tools to construct.* This position requires extensive work and extra tools. It should not be constructed near the enemy. It should be constructed during darkness and be completed before dawn.

Figure 4-12: Semipermanent hide position.

(b) *Increases risk of detection.* Using a position for several days or having teams relieve each other in a position always increases the risk of detection.

(3) ***Construction time:*** 4 to 6 hours (4 personnel).

(4) ***Occupation time:*** 48 hours plus (relieved by other teams).

g. **Routines in Sniper Team positions.** Although the construction of positions may differ, the routines while in position are the same. The sniper and the observer should have a good firing platform. This gives the sniper a stable platform for the sniper weapon and the observer a platform for the optics. When rotating observation duties, the sniper weapon should remain in place, and the optics are handed from one member to the other. Sniper data book, observation logs, range cards, and the radio should be placed between the team where both members have easy access to them. A system of resting, eating, and latrine calls must be arranged between the team. All latrine calls should be done during darkness, if possible. A hole should be dug to conceal any traces of latrine calls.

4-13. POSITIONS IN URBAN TERRAIN

Positions in urban terrain are quite different than positions in the field. The sniper team normally has several places to choose. These can range from inside attics to street-level positions in basements. This type of terrain is ideal for a sniper, and a sniper team can stop an enemy's advance through its area of responsibility.

a. When constructing an urban position, the sniper team must be aware of the outside appearance of the structure. Shooting through loopholes in barricaded windows is preferred; the team must make sure all other windows are also barricaded. Building loopholes in other windows also provides more positions to engage targets. When building loopholes, the team should make them different shapes (not perfect squares or circles). Dummy loopholes also confuse the enemy. Positions in attics are also effective. The team removes the shingles and cuts out loopholes in the roof; however, they must make sure there are other shingles missing from the roof so the firing position loophole is not obvious.

(1) The sniper team should not locate the position against contrasting background or in prominent buildings that automatically draw attention. It must stay in the shadows while moving, observing, and engaging targets.

(2) The team must never fire close to a loophole. It should always back away from the hole as far as possible to hide the muzzle flash and to scatter the sound of the weapon when it fires. The snipers may be located in a different room than the loophole; however, they can make a hole through a wall to connect the rooms and fire from inside one room. The team must not fire continually from one position (more than one position should be constructed if time and situation permit). When constructing other positions, the team makes sure the target area can be observed. Sniper team positions should never be used by any personnel other than a sniper team.

b. Common sense and imagination are the sniper team's only limitation in the construction of urban hide positions. Urban hide positions that can be used are the room hide, crawl space hide, and rafter hide. The team constructs and occupies one of these positions or a variation thereof.

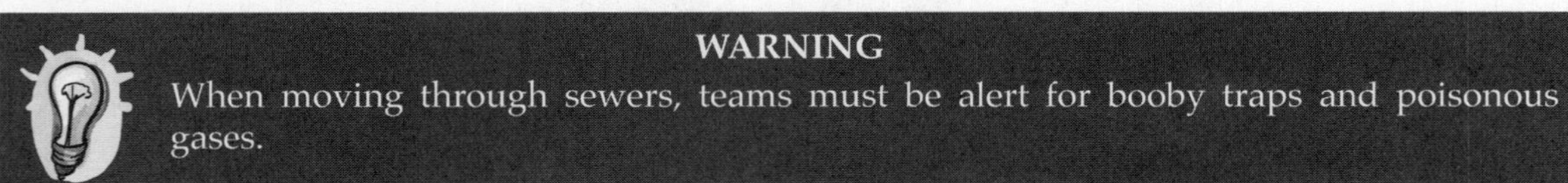

WARNING

When moving through sewers, teams must be alert for booby traps and poisonous gases.

(1) ***Room hide position.*** In a room hide position, the sniper team uses an existing room and fires through a window or loophole (Figure 4-13). Weapon support may be achieved through the use of existing furniture-that is, desks or tables. When selecting a position, teams must notice both front and back window positions. To avoid silhouetting, they may need to use a backdrop such as a dark-colored blanket, canvas, carpet, and a screen. Screens (common screening material) are important since they allow the sniper teams maximum observation and deny observation by the enemy. They must not remove curtains; however, they can open windows or remove panes of glass. Remember, teams can randomly remove panes in other windows so the position is not obvious.

Figure 4-13: Room hide position.

(2) ***Crawl space hide position.*** The sniper team builds a crawl space hide position in the space between floors in multistory buildings (Figure 4-14). Loopholes are difficult to construct, but a damaged building helps considerably. Escape routes can be holes knocked into the floor or ceiling. Carpet or furniture placed over escape holes or replaced ceiling tiles will conceal them until needed.

(3) ***Rafter hide position.*** The sniper team constructs a rafter hide position in the attic of an A-frame-type building. These buildings normally have shingled roofs (A and B, Figure 4-15). Firing from inside the attic around a chimney or other structure helps prevent enemy observation and fire.

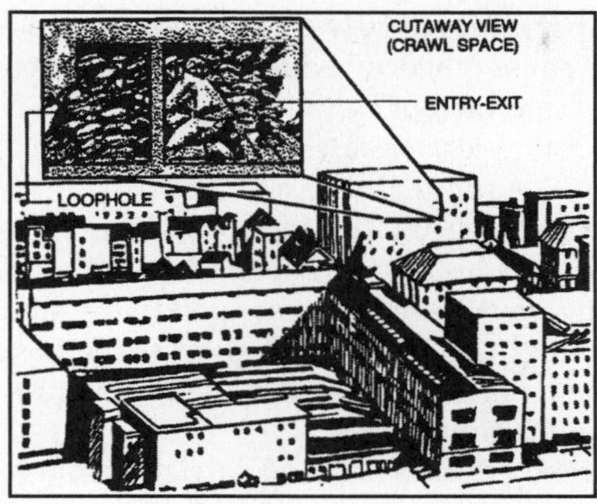

Figure 4-14: Crawl space hide position.

Figure 4-15: Rafter hide positions.

c. Sniper teams use the technique best suited for the urban hide position.
   (1) The second floor of a building is usually the best location for the position. It presents minimal dead space but provides the team more protection since passersby cannot easily spot it.
   (2) Normally, a window is the best viewing aperture/loophole.
      (a) If the window is dirty, do not clean it for better viewing.
      (b) If curtains are prevalent in the area, do not remove those in the position. Lace or net-type curtains can be seen through from the inside, but they are difficult to see through from the outside.
      (c) If strong winds blow the curtains open, staple, tack, or weight them.
      (d) Firing a round through a curtain has little effect on accuracy however, ensure the muzzle is far enough away to avoid muzzle blast.
      (e) When area routine indicates open curtains, follow suit. Set up well away from the loophole; however, ensure effective coverage of the assigned target area.
   (3) Firing through glass should be avoided since more than one shot may be required. The team considers the following options:
      (a) Break or open several windows throughout the position before occupation. This can be done during the reconnaissance phase of the operation; however, avoid drawing attention to the area.
      (b) Remove or replace panes of glass with plastic.
   (4) Other loopholes/viewing apertures are nearly unlimited.
      - Battle damage.
      - Drilled holes (hand drill).
      - Brick removal.
      - Loose boards/derelict houses.

(5) Positions can also be set up in attics or between the ceiling and roof. (See rafter hide positions.)
- Gable ends close to the eaves (shadow adding to concealment).
- Battle damage to gables and or roof.
- Loose or removed tiles, shingles, or slates.
- Skylights.

(6) The sniper makes sure the bullet clears the loophole. The muzzle must be far enough from the loophole to ensure the bullet's path is not in line with the bottom of the loophole.

(7) Front drops, usually netting, may have to be changed (if the situation permits) from dark to light colors at BMNT/EENT due to sunlight or lack of sunlight into the position.

(8) If the site is not multiroomed, partitions can be made by hanging blankets or nets to separate the operating area from the rest/administrative area.

(9) If sandbags are required, they can be filled and carried inside of rucksacks or can be filled in the basement, depending on the situation/location of the position site.

(10) Always plan an escape route that leads to the objective rally point. When forced to vacate the position, the team meets the security element at the ORP. Normally, the team will not be able to leave from the same point at which it gained access; therefore, a separate escape point may be required in emergency situations. The team must consider windows (other than the viewing apertures); anchored ropes to climb down buildings, or a small, preset explosive charge situated on a wall or floor for access into adjoining rooms, buildings, or the outside.

(11) The type of uniform or camouflage to be worn by the team will be dictated by the situation, how they are employed, and area of operation. The following applies:

(a) Most often, the BDU and required equipment are worn.

(b) Urban-camouflaged uniforms can be made or purchased. Urban areas vary in color (mostly gray [cinder block]; red [brick]; white [marble]; black [granite]; or stucco, clay, or wood). Regardless of area color, uniforms should include angular-line patterns.

(c) When necessary, most woodland-patterned BDUs can be worn inside out as they are a gray or green-gray color underneath.

(d) Soft-soled shoes or boots are the preferred footwear in the urban environment.

(e) Civilian clothing can be worn (native/host country populace).

(f) Tradesmen's or construction worker's uniforms and accessories can be used.

SECTION IV. OBSERVATION

Throughout history, battles have been won and nations conquered based on an accurate accounting and description of the opposing forces strength, equipment, and location. As the sniper team performs the secondary mission of collecting and reporting battlefield intelligence, the commander can act, rather than react. The purpose of observation is to gather facts and to provide information for a specific intent. Observation uses all of the sniper team's five senses but often depends on sight and hearing. For example, the sniper team is issued a PIR or OIR for a specific mission. Information gathered by the sniper team is reported, analyzed, and processed into intelligence reports. The sniper team's success depends upon its powers of observation. In addition to the sniperscope, the sniper team has an observation telescope, binoculars, night vision sight, and night vision goggles to enhance its ability to observe and engage targets. Team members must relieve each other when using this equipment since prolonged use can cause eye fatigue, greatly reducing the effectiveness of observation. Team members rotate periods of observation. During daylight, observation should be limited to 10 minutes followed by a 10-minute rest. When using night vision devices, the observer should limit his initial period of viewing to 10 minutes followed by a 10-minute rest. After several periods of viewing, he can extend the viewing period to 15 minutes and then a 15-minute rest.

4-14. HASTY AND DETAILED SEARCHES

While observing a target area, the sniper team alternately conducts two types of visual searches: hasty and detailed.

a. A hasty search is the first phase of observing a target area. The observer conducts a hasty search immediately after the team occupies the firing position. A hasty search consists of quick glances with binoculars at specific points, terrain features, or other areas that could conceal the enemy. The observer views the area closest to the team's position first since it could pose the most immediate threat. The observer then searches farther out until the entire target area has been searched. When the observer sees or suspects a target, he uses an M49 observation telescope for a detailed view of the target area. The telescope should not be used to search the area because its narrow field of view would take much longer to cover an area; plus, its stronger magnification can cause eye fatigue sooner than the binoculars.

b. After a hasty search has been completed, the observer then conducts a detailed search of the area. A detailed search is a closer, more thorough search of the target area, using 180-degree area or sweeps, 50 meters in depth, and overlapping each previous sweep at least 10 meters to ensure the entire area has been observed (Figure 4-16). Like the hasty search, the observer begins by searching the area closest to the sniper team position.

c. This cycle of a hasty search followed by a detailed search should be repeated three or four times. This allows the sniper team to become accustomed to the area; plus, the team will look closer at various points with each consecutive pass over the area. After the initial searches, the observer should view the area, using a combination of both hasty and detailed searches. While the observer conducts the initial searches of the area, the sniper should record prominent features, reference points, and distances on a range card. The team members should alternate the task of observing the area about every 30 minutes.

Figure 4-16: Detailed search.

4-15. ELEMENTS OF OBSERVATION

The four elements in the process of observation include awareness, understanding, recording, and response. Each of these elements may be accomplished as a separate processor accomplished at the same time.

a. **Awareness.** Awareness is being consciously attuned to a specific fact. A sniper team must always be aware of the surroundings and take nothing for granted. The team also considers certain elements that influence and distort awareness.
   (1) An object's size and shape can be misinterpreted if viewed incompletely or inaccurately.
   (2) Distractions degrade the quality of observations.
   (3) Active participation or degree of interest can diminish toward the event.
   (4) Physical abilities (five senses) have limitations.
   (5) Environmental changes affect accuracy.
   (6) Imagination may cause possible exaggerations or inaccuracy.

b. **Understanding.** Understanding is derived from education, training, practice, and experience. It enhances the sniper team's knowledge about what should be observed, broadens its ability to view and consider all aspects, and aids in its evaluation of information.

c. **Recording.** Recording is the ability to save and recall what was observed. Usually, the sniper team has mechanical aids, such as writing utensils, sniper data book, sketch kits, tape recorders, and cameras, to support the recording of events; however, the most accessible method is memory. The ability to record, retain, and recall depends on the team's mental capacity (and alertness) and ability to recognize what is essential to record. Added factors that affect recording include:

(1) The amount of training and practice in observation.
(2) Skill gained through experience.
(3) Similarity of previous incidents.
(4) Time interval between observing and recording.
(5) The ability to understand or convey messages through oral or other communications.

d. **Response.** Response is the sniper team's action toward information. It may be as simple as recording events in a sniper data book, making a communications call, or firing a well-aimed shot.

> ✍ **NOTE**
> See Chapter 9 for discussion on the keep-in-memory (KIM) game.

4-16. TWILIGHT TECHNIQUES

Twilight induces a false sense of security, and the sniper team must be extremely cautious. The enemy is also prone to carelessness and more likely to expose himself at twilight. During twilight, snipers should be alert to OP locations for future reference. The M3A telescope reticle is still visible and capable of accurate fire 30 minutes before BMNT and 30 minutes after EENT.

4-17. NIGHT TECHNIQUES

Without night vision devices, the sniper team must depend upon eyesight. Regardless of night brightness, the human eye cannot function at night with daylight precision. For maximum effectiveness, the sniper team must apply the following principles of night vision:

a. **Night Adaptation.** The sniper team should wear sunglasses or red-lensed goggles in lighted areas before departing on a mission. After departure, the team makes a darkness adaptation and listening halt for 30 minutes.

b. **Off-Center Vision.** In dim light, an object under direct focus blurs, appears to change, and sometimes fades out entirely. However, when the eyes are focused at different points, about 5 to 10 degrees away from an object, peripheral vision provides a true picture. This allows the light-sensitive portion of the eye, that's not used during the day, to be used.

c. **Factors Affecting Night Vision.** The sniper team has control over the following night vision factors:
(1) Lack of vitamin A impairs night vision. However, an overdose of vitamin A will not improve night vision capability.
(2) Colds, fatigue, narcotics, headaches, smoking, and alcohol reduce night vision.
(3) Exposure to bright light degrades night vision and requires a readaption to darkness.

4-18. ILLUMINATION AIDS

The sniper team may occasionally have artificial illumination for observing and firing. Examples are artillery illumination fire, campfires, or lighted buildings.

a. Artillery Illumination Fire. The M301A2 illuminating cartridge provides 50,000 candlepower.
b. Campfires. Poorly disciplined enemy soldiers may use campfires, or fires may be created by battlefield damage. These opportunities give the sniper enough illumination for aiming.
c. Lighted Buildings. The sniper can use lighted buildings to eliminate occupants of the building or personnel in the immediate area of the light source.

SECTION V. TARGET DETECTION AND SELECTION

Recording the type and location of targets in the area helps the sniper team to determine engageable targets. The sniper team must select key targets that will do the greatest harm to the enemy in a given situation. It must also consider the use of indirect fire on targets. Some targets, due to their size or location, may be better engaged with indirect fire.

4-19. TARGET INDEXING

To index targets, the sniper team uses the prepared range card for a reference since it can greatly reduce the engagement time. When indexing a target to the sniper, the observer locates a prominent terrain feature near the target. He indicates this feature and any other information to the sniper to assist in finding the target. Information between team members varies with the situation. The observer may sound like an FO giving a call for fire to an FDC depending on the condition of the battlefield and the total number of possible targets from which to choose.

a. **Purpose.** The sniper team indexes targets for the following reasons:
   (1) Sniper teams may occupy an FFP in advance of an attack to locate, index, and record target locations; and to decide on the priority of targets.
   (2) Indiscriminate firing may alert more valuable and closer enemy targets.
   (3) Engagement of a distant target may result in disclosure of the FFP to a closer enemy.
   (4) A system is needed to remember location if several targets are sighted at the same time.
b. **Considerations.** The sniper team must consider the following factors when indexing targets:
   (1) ***Exposure times.*** Moving targets may expose themselves for only a short time The sniper team must note the point of disappearance of each target, if possible, before engagement. By doing so, the team may be able to take several targets under fire in rapid succession.
   (2) ***Number of targets.*** If several targets appear and disappear at the same time, the point of disappearance of each is hard to determine; therefore, sniper teams concentrate on the most important targets.
   (3) ***Spacing/distance between targets.*** The greater the distance between targets, the harder it is to see their movement. In such cases, the team should locate and engage the nearest targets.
   (4) ***Evacuation of aiming points.*** Targets that disappear behind good aiming points are easily recorded and remembered, targets with poor aiming points are easily lost. Assuming that two such targets are of equal value and danger, the team should engage the more dangerous aiming point target first.
c. **Determination of Location of Hidden Fires.** When using the *crack-thump method*, the team listens for the crack of the round and the thump of the weapon being fired. By using this method, the sniper can obtain both a direction and a distance.
   (1) ***Distance to firer.*** The time difference between the crack and the thump can be converted into an approximate range. A one-second lapse between the two is about 600 yards with most calibers; a one-half-second lapse is about 300 yards.
   (2) ***Location of firer.*** By observing in the direction of the thump and near the predetermined range, the sniper team has a good chance of seeing the enemy's muzzle flash or blast from subsequent shots.
   (3) ***Limitations.*** The crack-thump method has the following limitations:
      (a) Isolating the crack and thump is difficult when many shots are being fired.
      (b) Mountainous areas, tall buildings, and so forth cause echoes and make this method ineffective.
d. **Shot-Hole Analysis.** Locating two or more shot holes in trees, walls, dummy heads, and so forth may make it possible to determine the direction of the shots. The team can use the dummy-head pencil method and triangulate on the enemy sniper's position. However, this method only works if all shots come from the same position.

4-20. TARGET SELECTION

Target selection may be forced upon the sniper team. A target moving rapidly may be lost while obtaining positive identification. The sniper team considers any enemy threatening its position as a high-value target. When selecting key targets, the team must consider the following factors:

a. **Threat to the Sniper Team.** The sniper team must consider the danger the target presents. This can be an immediate threat, such as an enemy element walking upon its position, or a future threat, such as enemy snipers or dog tracking teams.
b. **Probability of First-Round Hit.** The sniper team must determine the chances of hitting the target with the first shot by considering the following:
   - Distance to the target.
   - Direction and velocity of the wind.
   - Visibility of the target area.

- Amount of the target that is exposed.
- Amount of time the target is exposed.
- Speed and direction of target movement.

c. **Certainty of Target's Identity.** The sniper team must be reasonably certain that the target it is considering is the key target.

d. **Target Effect on the Enemy.** The sniper team must consider what effect the elimination of the target will have on the enemy's fighting ability. It must determine that the target is the one available target that will cause the greatest harm to the enemy.

e. **Enemy Reaction to Sniper Fire.** The sniper team must consider what the enemy will do once the shot has been fired. The team must be prepared for such actions as immediate suppression by indirect fires and enemy sweeps of the area.

f. **Effect on the Overall Mission.** The sniper team must consider how the engagement will affect the overall mission. The mission may be one of intelligence gathering for a certain period. Firing will not only alert the enemy to a team's presence, but it may also terminate the mission if the team has to move from its position as a result of the engagement.

4-21. KEY TARGETS

Key personnel targets can be identified by actions or mannerisms, by positions within formations, by rank or insignias, and/or by equipment being worn or carried. Key targets can also include weapon systems and equipment. Examples of key targets areas follows:

a. **Snipers.** Snipers are the number one target of a sniper team. The enemy sniper not only poses a threat to friendly forces, but he is also the natural enemy of the sniper. The fleeting nature of a sniper is reason enough to engage him because he may never be seen again.

b. **Dog Tracking Teams.** Dog tracking teams pose a great threat to sniper teams and other special teams that may be working in the area. It is hard to fool a trained dog. When engaging a dog tracking team, the sniper should engage the dog's handler first. This confuses the dog, and other team members may not be able to control it.

c. **Scouts.** Scouts are keen observers and provide valuable information about friendly units. This plus their ability to control indirect fires make them dangerous on the battlefield. Scouts must be eliminated.

d. **Officers.** Officers are another key target of the sniper team. Losing key officers in some forces is such a major disruption to the operation that forces may not be able to coordinate for hours.

e. **Noncommissioned Officers.** Losing NCOs not only affects the operation of a unit but also affects the morale of lower ranking personnel.

f. **Vehicle Commanders and Drivers.** Many vehicles are rendered useless without a commander or driver.

g. **Communications Personnel.** In some forces, only highly trained personnel know how to operate various types of radios. Eliminating these personnel can be a serious blow to the enemy's communication network.

h. **Weapon Crews.** Eliminating weapon crews reduces the amount of fire on friendly troops.

i. **Optics on Vehicles.** Personnel who are in closed vehicles are limited to viewing through optics. The sniper can blind a vehicle by damaging these optic systems.

j. **Communication and Radar Equipment.** The right shot in the right place can completely ruin a tactically valuable radar or communication system. Also, only highly trained personnel may attempt to repair these systems in place. Eliminating these personnel may impair the enemy's ability to perform field repair.

k. **Weapon Systems.** Many high-technology weapons, especially computer-guided systems, can be rendered useless by one well-placed round in the guidance controller of the system.

SECTION VI. RANGE ESTIMATION

A sniper team is required to accurately determine distance, to properly adjust elevation on the sniper weapon system, and to prepare topographical sketches or range cards. Because of this, the team has to be skilled in various range estimation techniques.

4-22. FACTORS AFFECTING RANGE ESTIMATION

Three factors affect range estimation: nature of the target, nature of the terrain, and light conditions.

a. **Nature of the Target.**
 (1) An object of regular outline, such as a house, appears closer than one of irregular outline, such as a clump of trees.
 (2) A target that contrasts with its background appears to be closer than it actually is.
 (3) A partly exposed target appears more distant than it actually is.

b. **Nature of the Terrain.**
 (1) As the observer's eye follows the contour of the terrain, he tends to overestimate distant targets.
 (2) Observing over smooth terrain, such as sand, water, or snow, causes the observer to underestimate distant targets.
 (3) Looking downhill, the target appears farther away.
 (4) Looking uphill, the target appears closer.

c. **Light Conditions.**
 (1) The more clearly a target can be seen, the closer it appears.
 (2) When the sun is behind the observer, the target appears to be closer.
 (3) When the sun is behind the target, the target is more difficult to see and appears to be farther away.

4-23. RANGE ESTIMATION METHODS

Sniper teams use range estimation methods to determine distance between their position and the target.

a. **Paper-Strip Method.** The paper-strip method (Figure 4-17) is useful when determining longer distances (1,000 meters plus). When using this method, the sniper places the edge of a strip of paper on the map and ensures it is long enough to reach between the two points. Then he pencils in a tick mark on the paper at the team position and another at the distant location. He places the paper on the map's bar scale, located at the bottom center of the map, and aligns the left tick mark with the 0 on the scale. Then he reads to the right to the second mark and notes the corresponding distance represented between the two marks.

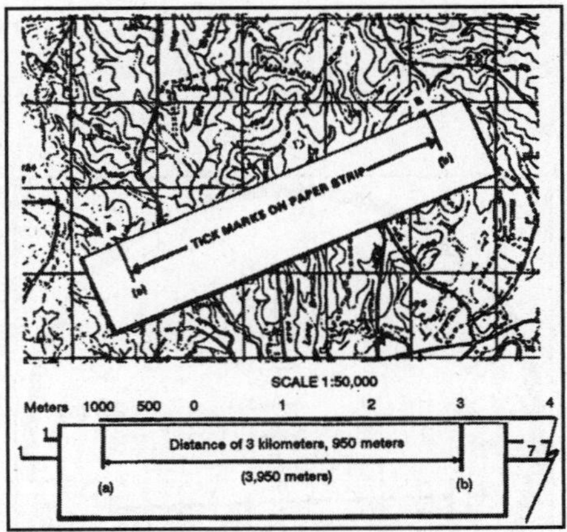

Figure 4-17: Paper-strip method.

b. **100-Meter-Unit-of-Measure Method.** To use this method (Figure 4-18), the sniper team must be able to visualize a distance of 100 meters on the ground. For ranges up to 500 meters, the team determines the number of 100-meter increments between the two objects it wishes to measure. Beyond 500 meters, it must select a point halfway to the object and determine the number of 100-meter increments to the halfway point, then double it to find the range to the object.

Figure 4-18: 100-meter-unit-of-measure method.

c. **Appearance-of-Object Method.** This method is a means of determining range by the size and other characteristic details of the object. To use the appearance-of-object method with any degree of accuracy, the sniper team must be familiar with the characteristic details of the objects as they appear at various ranges.
d. **Bracketing Method.** Using this method, the sniper team assumes that the target is no more than X meters but no less than Y meters away. An average of X and Y will be the estimate of the distance to the target.
e. **Range-Card Method.** The sniper team can also use a range card to quickly determine ranges throughout the target area. Once a target is seen, the team determines where it is located on the card and then reads the proper range to the target.
f. **Mil-Relation Formula.** The mil-relation formula is the preferred method of range estimation. This method uses a mil-scale reticle located in the M19 binoculars (Figure 4-19) or in the M3A sniperscope (Figure 4-20). The team must know the target size in inches or meters. Once the target size is known, the team then compares the target size to the mil-scale reticle and uses the following formula:

$$\frac{\text{Size of target in meters} \times 1{,}000}{\text{Size of object in mils}} = \text{Range to target in meters}$$

(To convert inches to meters, multiply the number of inches by .0254.)

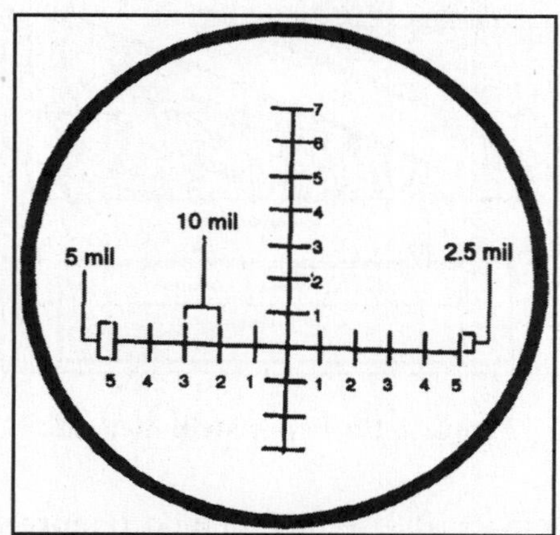

Figure 4-19: M19 mil-scale reticle.

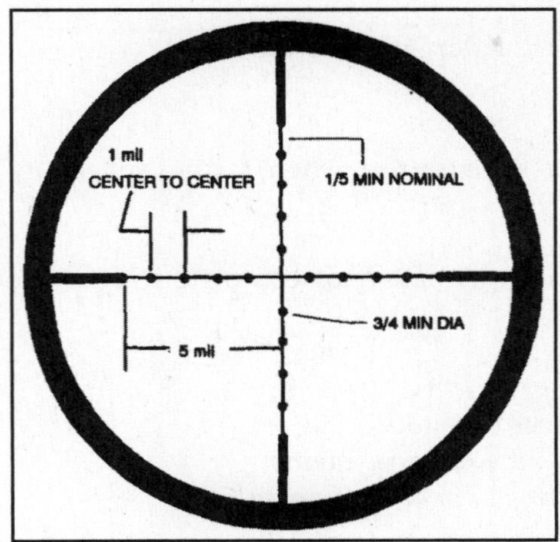

Figure 4-20: M3A mil-scale reticle.

g. **Combination Method.** In a combat environment, perfect conditions rarely exist. Therefore, only one method of range estimation may not be enough for the team's specific mission. Terrain with much dead space limits the accuracy of the 100-meter method. Poor visibility limits the use of the appearance-of-object method. However, by using a combination of two or more methods to determine an unknown range, an experienced sniper team should arrive at an estimated range close to the true range.

4-24. LASER RANGE FINDER

When the sniper team has access to a laser observation set, AN/GVS-5, the set should always be used. It can provide the sniper team range to a specific target with great accuracy. When aiming the laser at a specific target, the sniper should support it much the same as his weapon to ensure accuracy. If the target is too small, aiming the laser at a larger object near the target will suffice (that is, a building, vehicle, tree, or terrain feature).

4-25. ESTIMATION GUIDELINES

If mirage is too heavy to distinguish the bottom of a target, it should be halved.

> ☞ **EXAMPLE**
>
> When the target is estimated to be 70 inches high, divide the height into one-half. Use the following mil-relation formula:
>
> $$\frac{35 \text{ inches} \times .0254 \times 1{,}000}{\text{Size of target in mils}} = \text{Range to target in meters}$$

By using this technique, estimate range to targets that are only partly visible. Such as:

The normal distance from the breastbone to the top of the head is 19 inches.

$$\frac{19 \text{ inches} \times .0254 \times 1{,}000}{\text{Size of target in mils}} = \text{Range to target in meters}$$

OR

Normal height of the human head is 10 inches.

$$\frac{10 \text{ inches} \times .0254 \times 1{,}000}{\text{Size of target in mils}} = \text{Range to target in meters}$$

This example may prove to be of specific use when facing an enemy entrenched in bunkers or in dense vegetation.

a. The sniper team should keep a sniper data book complete with measurements.
   (1) ***Vehicles.***
   - Height of road wheels.
   - Vehicle dimensions.
   - Length of main gun tubes on tanks.
   - Lengths/sizes of different weapon systems.

   (2) ***Average height of human targets in area of operation.***
   (3) ***Urban environment.***
   - Average size of doorways.
   - Average size of windows.
   - Average width of streets and lanes (average width of a paved road in the United States is 10 feet).
   - Height of soda machines.

b. As the sniper team develops a sniper data book, all measurements are converted into constants and computed with different mil readings. An example of this is Table 4-1, which has already been computed for immediate use. This table should be incorporated into the sniper data book

Table 4-1: Range estimation table.

TABLE FOR 6-FOOT MAN		
HEIGHT IN MILS	STANDING	SITTING/ KNEELING
1	2000	1000
1.5	1333	666
2	1000	500
2.5	800	400
3	666	333
3.5	571	286
4	500	250
4.5	444	222
5	400	200
5.5	364	182
6	333	167
6.5	308	154
7	286	143
TABLE FOR 5-FOOT 6-INCH MAN		
HEIGHT IN MILS	STANDING	SITTING/ KNEELING
1	1800	900
1.5	1200	600
2	900	450
2.5	750	375
3	600	300
3.5	514	257
4	450	225
4.5	400	200
5	360	180
5.5	327	164
6	300	150
6.5	277	139

SECTION VII. INFORMATION RECORDS

The secondary mission of the sniper team is the collection and reporting of information. To accomplish this, the sniper team not only needs to be keen observers, but it also must accurately relay the information it has observed. To record this information, the team uses the sniper data book, which contains a range card, a military sketch, and an observation log.

4-26. RANGE CARD

The range card represents the target area drawn as seen from above with annotations indicating distances throughout the target area. Information is recorded on DA Form 5787-R (Sniper's Range Card) (Figure 4-21). (A blank copy of this form is located in the back of this publication for local reproduction.) The range card provides the sniper team with a quick-range reference and a means to record target locations, since it has preprinted range rings on it. These cards can be divided into sectors by using dashed lines. This provides the team members with a quick reference when locating targets-for example: "The intersection in sector A." A range card can be prepared on any paper the team has available. The sniper team position and distances to prominent objects and terrain features are drawn on the card. There is not a set maximum range on the range card, because the team may also label any indirect fire targets on its range card. Information contained on range cards includes:

a. Name, rank, SSN, and unit.
b. Method of obtaining range.

c. Left and right limits of engageable area.
d. Major terrain features, roads, and structures.
e. Ranges, elevation, and windage needed at various distances.
f. Distances throughout the area.
g. Temperature and wind. (Cross out previous entry whenever temperature, wind direction, or wind velocity changes.)
h. Target reference points (azimuth, distance, and description).

4-27. MILITARY SKETCH

DA Form 5788-R (Military Sketch) is used to record information about a general area, terrain features, or man-made structures that are not shown on a map. Military sketches provide intelligence sections a detailed, on-the-ground view of an area or object that is otherwise unobtainable. These sketches not only let the viewer see the area in different perspectives but also provide detail such as type of fences, number of telephone wires, present depth of streams, and so forth. There are two types of military sketches as stated in FM 21–26 panoramic sketches and topographic sketches. Information is recorded on DA Form 5788-R.

a. **Panoramic.** A panoramic sketch (Figure 4-22) is a representation of an area or object drawn to scale as seen from the sniper team's perspective. It shows details about a specific area or a man-made structure. Information considered in a panoramic sketch includes the following:

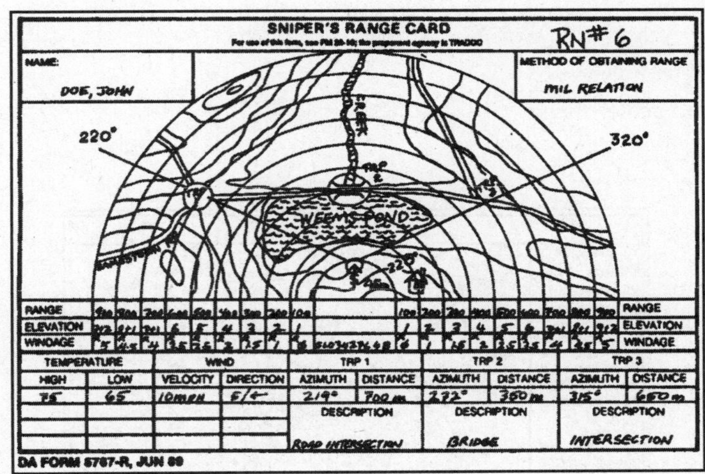
SNIPER'S RANGE CARD

RN# 6

NAME: DOE, JOHN

METHOD OF OBTAINING RANGE: MIL RELATION

220° 320°

RANGE	900	800	700	600	500	400	300	200	100		100	200	300	400	500	600	700	800	900	RANGE
ELEVATION	9+2	8+1	7+1	6	5	4	3	2	1		1	2	3	4	5	6	7+1	8+1	9+2	ELEVATION
WINDAGE	5	4.5	4	3.5	2.5	2	1.5	1	[illegible]	[illegible]	[illegible]	1	1.5	2	2.5	3.5	4	4.5	5	WINDAGE

TEMPERATURE		WIND		TRP 1		TRP 2		TRP 3	
HIGH	LOW	VELOCITY	DIRECTION	AZIMUTH	DISTANCE	AZIMUTH	DISTANCE	AZIMUTH	DISTANCE
75	65	10MPH	E/←	219°	700 m	272°	350 m	315°	650 m
				DESCRIPTION		DESCRIPTION		DESCRIPTION	
				ROAD INTERSECTION		BRIDGE		INTERSECTION	

DA FORM 5787-R, JUN 89

Figure 4-21: Example of completed DA Form 5787-R.

(1) Name, rank, SSN, and unit.
(2) Remarks section (two).
(3) Sketch name.
(4) Grid coordinates of sniper team's position.
(5) Weather.
(6) Magnetic azimuth through the center of sketch.
(7) Sketch number and scale of sketch.
(8) Date and time.

b. **Topographic Sketch.** A topographic sketch (Figure 4-23) is a topographic representation of an area drawn to scale as seen from above. It provides the sniper team with a method for describing large areas while showing reliable distance and azimuths between major features. This type of sketch is useful in describing road systems, flow of streams / rivers, or locations of natural and man-made obstacles. The field sketch can also be used as an overlay on the range card. Information contained in a field sketch includes the following:
(1) Grid coordinates of the sniper team's position.
(2) Name, rank, SSN, and unit.

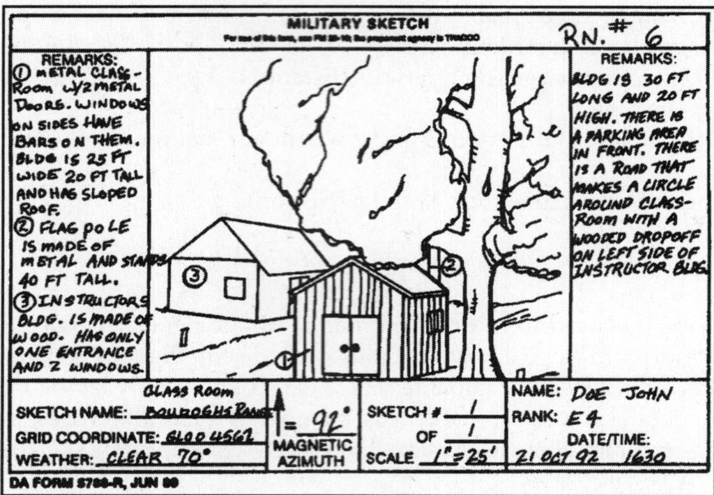

MILITARY SKETCH

RN. # 6

REMARKS:
① METAL CLASS-ROOM W/2 METAL DOORS. WINDOWS ON SIDES HAVE BARS ON THEM. BLDG IS 25 FT WIDE 20 FT TALL AND HAS SLOPED ROOF.
② FLAG POLE IS MADE OF METAL AND STANDS 40 FT TALL.
③ INSTRUCTORS BLDG. IS MADE OF WOOD. HAS ONLY ONE ENTRANCE AND 2 WINDOWS.

REMARKS:
BLDG IS 30 FT LONG AND 20 FT HIGH. THERE IS A PARKING AREA IN FRONT. THERE IS A ROAD THAT MAKES A CIRCLE AROUND CLASS-ROOM WITH A WOODED DROPOFF ON LEFT SIDE OF INSTRUCTOR BLDG.

SKETCH NAME: CLASS ROOM BOUDOGHS RANGE
GRID COORDINATE: GL00 4562
WEATHER: CLEAR 70°
= 92° MAGNETIC AZIMUTH
SKETCH # 1 OF 1
SCALE 1" = 25'
NAME: DOE JOHN
RANK: E4
DATE/TIME: 21 OCT 92 1630
DA FORM 5788-R, JUN 89

Figure 4-22: Example of completed DA Form 5788-R for panoramic sketch.

(3) Remarks.
(4) Sketch name.
(5) Grid coordinates.
(6) Weather.
(7) Magnetic azimuth.
(8) Sketch number and scale.
(9) Date and time.

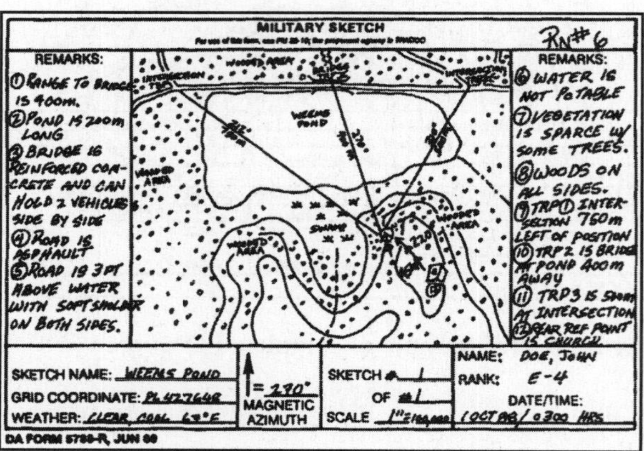

MILITARY SKETCH

RN # 6

REMARKS:
① RANGE TO BRIDGE IS 400m.
② POND IS 200m LONG
③ BRIDGE IS REINFORCED CONCRETE AND CAN HOLD 2 VEHICLES SIDE BY SIDE
④ ROAD IS ASPHAULT
⑤ ROAD IS 3 FT ABOVE WATER WITH SOFT SHOULDER ON BOTH SIDES.

REMARKS:
⑥ WATER IS NOT POTABLE
⑦ VEGETATION IS SPARCE W/ SOME TREES.
⑧ WOODS ON ALL SIDES.
⑨ TRP ① INTERSECTION 750m LEFT OF POSITION
⑩ TRP 2 IS BRIDGE AT POND 400m AWAY
⑪ TRP 3 IS SHOWN AT INTERSECTION
⑫ REAR REF POINT IS CHURCH

SKETCH NAME: WEEMS POND
GRID COORDINATE: PL 427648
WEATHER: CLEAR, COOL 65°F
= 270° MAGNETIC AZIMUTH
SKETCH # 1 OF # 1
SCALE 1" = 100,000
NAME: DOE, JOHN
RANK: E-4
DATE/TIME: 1 OCT 88 / 0300 HRS
DA FORM 5788-R, JUN 89

Figure 4-23: Example of completed DA Form 5788-R for topographic sketch.

c. **Guidelines for Drawing Sketches.** As with all drawings, artistic skill is an asset, but satisfactory sketches can be drawn by anyone with practice. The following are guidelines when drawing sketches:
(1) ***Work from the whole to the part.*** First determine the boundaries of the sketch. Then sketch the larger objects such as hills, mountains, or outlines of large buildings. After drawing the large objects in the sketch, start drawing the smaller details.
(2) ***Use common shapes to show common objects.*** Do not sketch each individual tree, hedgerow, or wood line exactly. Use common shapes to show these types of objects. Do not concentrate on the fine details unless they are of tactical importance.
(3) ***Draw in perspective; use vanishing points.*** Try to draw sketches in perspective. To do this, recognize the vanishing points of the area to be sketched. Parallel lines on the ground that are horizontal vanish at

a point on the horizon (Figure 4-24). Parallel lines on the ground that slope downward away from the observer vanish at a point below the horizon. Parallel lines on the ground that slope upward, away from the observer vanish at a point above the horizon. Parallel lines that recede to the right vanish on the right and those that recede to the left vanish on the left (Figure 4-24).

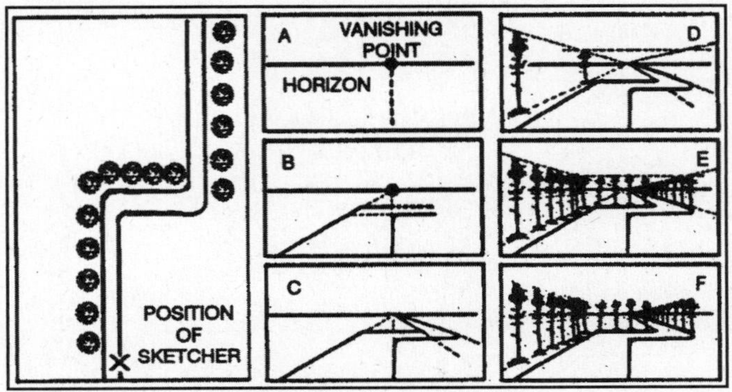

Figure 4-24: Vanishing points.

4-28. SNIPER DATA BOOK

The sniper data book is a written, chronological record of all activities and events that take place in a sniper team's area. It is used with military sketches and range cards; this combination not only gives commanders and intelligence personnel information about the appearance of the area, but it also provides an accurate record of the activity in the area. Information is recorded on DA Form 5786-R (Sniper's Observation Log) (Figure 4-25). (A blank copy of this form is in the back of this publication for local reproduction.) Information in the observation log includes: (Completion of this form is self-explanatory.)

a. Sheet number and number of total sheets.
b. Observer's name, rank, SSN, and unit.
c. Date and time of observation and visibility.
d. Grid coordinates of the sniper team's position.
e. Series number, time, and grid coordinates of each event.
f. The event that has taken place.
g. Action taken and remarks.

SNIPER'S OBSERVATION LOG — SHEET____OF____SHEETS

ORIGINATOR: DOE, JOHN R — DATE/TIME: 1 OCT 92 — LOCATION: GL03427648

SERIAL	TIME	GRID COORDINATE	EVENT	ACTIONS OR REMARKS
1	0300	GL03427648	OCCUPIED POSITION	OBSERVATION
2	0340	SAME	PFC JUDSON RESTED	NONE
3	0430	SAME	PFC JUDSON ASSUMED OBSERVATION	I RESTED
4	0530	SAME	BOTH OF US AWAKE	NONE
5	0630	SAME	PREPARED RANGE CARD AND TOPOGRAPHIC SKETCH	LIGHT ENOUGH TO SEE
6	0655	GL034276428	BRM CROSSED BRIDGE GOING SOUTH	OBSERVED
7	0700	GL034276428	PREPARED SKETCH OF BRIDGE GL03117631	COMPLETE
8	0900	GL034276428	MISSION COMPLETED - RETURN TO CP	END OF MISSION

DA FORM 5786-R, JUN 89

Figure 4-25: Example of completed DA Form 5786-R.

CHAPTER 5

Tracking/Countertracking

When a sniper follows a trail, he builds a picture of the enemy in his mind by asking himself questions: How many persons am I following? What is their state of training? How are they equipped? Are they healthy? What is their state of morale? Do they know they are being followed? To answer these questions, the sniper uses available indicators to track the enemy. The sniper looks for signs that reveal an action occurred at a specific time and place. For example, a footprint in soft sand is an excellent indicator, since a sniper can determine the specific time the person passed. By comparing indicators, the sniper obtains answers to his questions. For example, a footprint and a waist-high scuff on a tree may indicate that an armed individual passed this way.

SECTION I. TRACKING

Any indicator the sniper discovers can be defined by one of six tracking concepts: displacement, stains, weather, litter, camouflage, and immediate-use intelligence.

5-1. DISPLACEMENT

Displacement takes place when anything is moved from its original position. A well-defined footprint or shoe print in soft, moist ground is a good example of displacement. By studying the footprint or shoe print, the sniper determines several important facts. For example, a print left by worn footgear or by bare feet may indicate lack of proper equipment. Displacement can also result from clearing a trail by breaking or cutting through heavy vegetation with a machete. These trails are obvious to the most inexperienced sniper who is tracking. Individuals may unconsciously break more branches as they follow someone who is cutting the vegetation. Displacement indicators can also be made by persons carrying heavy loads who stop to rest; prints made by box edges can help to identify the load. When loads are set down at a rest halt or campsite, they usually crush grass and twigs. A reclining soldier also flattens the vegetation.

a. **Analyzing Footprints.** Footprints may indicate direction, rate of movement, number, sex, and whether the individual knows he is being tracked.
   (1) If footprints are deep and the pace is long, rapid movement is apparent. Long strides and deep prints with toe prints deeper than heel prints indicate running (A, Figure 5-1).
   (2) Prints that are deep, short, and widely spaced, with signs of scuffing or shuffling indicate the person is carrying a heavy load (B, Figure 5-1).
   (3) If the party members realize they are being followed, they may try to hide their tracks. Persons walking backward (C, Figure 5-1) have a short, irregular stride. The prints have an unnaturally deep toe, and soil is displaced in the direction of movement.
   (4) To determine the sex (D, Figure 5-1), the sniper should study the size and position of the footprints. Women tend to be pigeon-toed, while men walk with their feet straight ahead or pointed slightly to the outside. Prints left by women are usually smaller and the stride is usually shorter than prints left by men.

b. **Determining Key Prints.** The last individual in the file usually leaves the clearest footprints; these become the key prints. The sniper cuts a stick to match the length of the prints and notches it to indicate the width at the widest part of the sole. He can then study the angle of the key prints to the direction of march. The sniper looks for an identifying mark or feature, such as worn or frayed footwear, to help him identify the key prints. If the trail becomes vague, erased, or merges with another, the sniper can use his stick-measuring devices and, with close study, can identify the key prints. This method helps the sniper to stay on the trail.

A technique used to count the total number of individuals being tracked is the box method. There are two methods the sniper can use to employ the box method.

(1) The most accurate is to use the stride as a unit of measure (Figure 5-2) when key prints can be determined. The sniper uses the set of key prints and the edges of the road or trail to box in an area to analyze. This method is accurate under the right conditions for counting up to 18 persons.

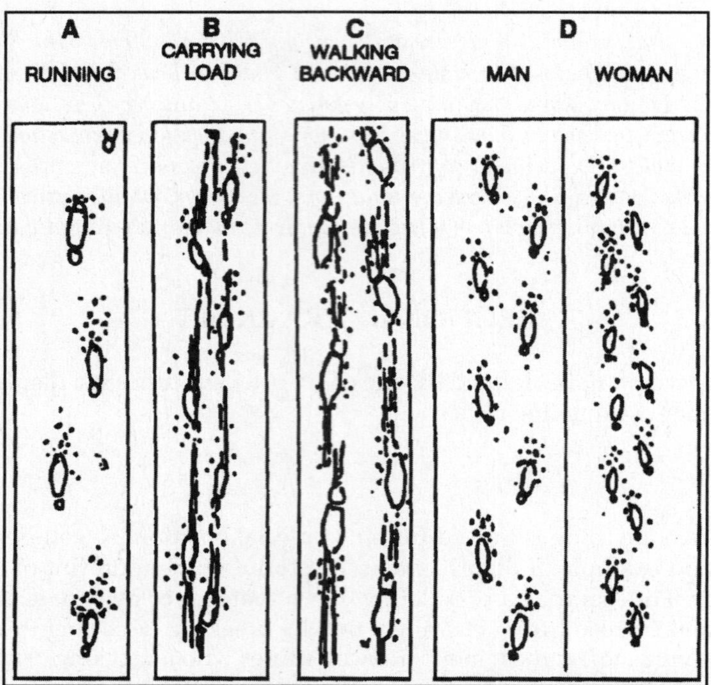

Figure 5-1: Different types of footprints.

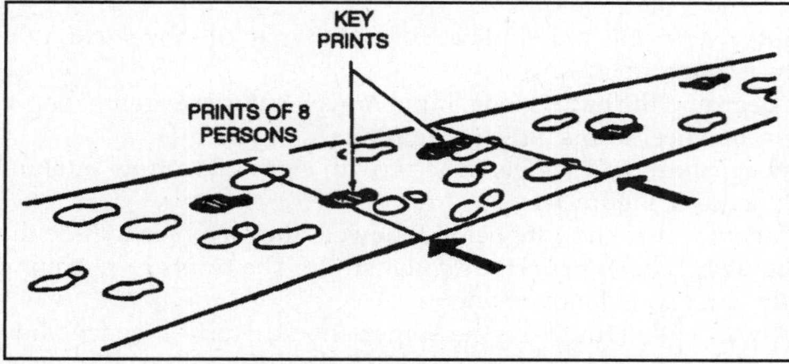

Figure 5-2: Stride measurement.

(2) The sniper may also use the the 36-inch box method (Figure 5-3) if key prints are not evident. To use the 36-inch box method, the sniper uses the edges of the road or trail as the sides of the box. He measures a cross section of the area 36 inches long, counting each indentation in the box and dividing by two. This method gives a close estimate of the number of individuals who made the prints; however, this system is not as accurate as the stride measurement.

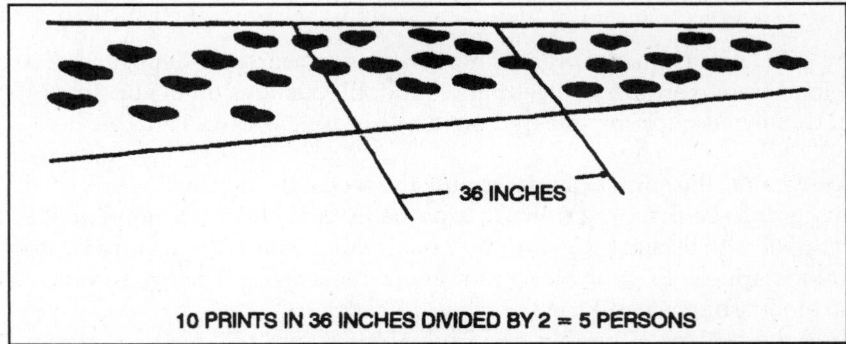

Figure 5-3: 36-inch box method.

c. **Recognizing Other Signs of Displacement.** Foliage, moss, vines, sticks, or rocks that are scuffed or snagged from their original position form valuable indicators. Vines may be dragged, dew droplets displaced, or stones and sticks overturned (A, Figure 5-4) to show a different color underneath. Grass or other vegetation may be bent or broken in the direction of movement (B, Figure 5-4).

(1) The sniper inspects all areas for bits of clothing, threads, or dirt from footgear that can be torn or can fall and be left on thorns, snags, or the ground.

(2) Flushed from their natural habitat, wild animals and birds are another example of displacement. Cries of birds excited by unnatural movement is an indicator; moving tops of tall grass or brush on a windless day indicates that someone is moving the vegetation.

(3) Changes in the normal life of insects and spiders may indicate that someone has recently passed. Valuable clues are disturbed bees, ant holes uncovered by someone moving over them, or torn spider webs. Spiders often spin webs across open areas, trails, or roads to trap flying insects. If the tracked person does not avoid these webs, he leaves an indicator to an observant sniper.

(4) If the person being followed tries to use a stream to cover his trail, the sniper can still follow successfully. Algae and other water plants can be displaced by lost footing or by careless walking. Rocks can be displaced from their original position or overturned to indicate a lighter or darker color on the opposite side. The person entering or exiting a stream creates slide marks or footprints, or scuffs the bark on roots or sticks (C, Figure 5-4). Normally, a person or animal seeks the path of least resistance; therefore, when searching the stream for an indication of departures, snipers will find signs in open areas along the banks.

Figure 5-4: Other displacements.

5-2. STAINS

A stain occurs when any substance from one organism or article is smeared or deposited on something else. The best example of staining is blood from a profusely bleeding wound. Bloodstains often appear as spatters or drops and are not always on the ground; they also appear smeared on leaves or twigs of trees and bushes.

a. By studying bloodstains, the sniper can determine the wound's location.
   (1) If the blood seems to be dripping steadily, it probably came from a wound on the trunk.
   (2) If the blood appears to be slung toward the front, rear, or sides, the wound is probably in the extremity.
   (3) Arterial wounds appear to pour blood at regular intervals as if poured from a pitcher. If the wound is veinous, the blood pours steadily.
   (4) A lung wound deposits pink, bubbly, and frothy bloodstains.
   (5) A bloodstain from a head wound appears heavy, wet, and slimy.
   (6) Abdominal wounds often mix blood with digestive juices so the deposit has an odor and is light in color.

The sniper can also determine the seriousness of the wound and how far the wounded person can move unassisted. These prompts may lead the sniper to enemy bodies or indicate where they have been carried.

b. Staining can also occur when muddy footgear is dragged over grass, stones, and shrubs. Thus, staining and displacement combine to indicate movement and direction. Crushed leaves may stain rocky ground that is too hard to show footprints. Roots, stones, and vines may be stained where leaves or berries are crushed by moving feet.
c. The sniper may have difficulty in determining the difference between staining and displacement since both terms can be applied to some indicators. For example, muddied water may indicate recent movement; displaced mud also stains the water. Muddy footgear can stain stones in streams, and algae can be displaced from stones in streams and can stain other stones or the bank. Muddy water collects in new footprints in swampy ground; however, the mud settles and the water clears with time. The sniper can use this information to indicate time; normally, the mud clears in about one hour, although time varies with the terrain.

5-3. WEATHER

Weather either aids or hinders the sniper. It also affects indicators in certain ways so that the sniper can determine their relative ages. However, wind, snow, rain, or sunlight can erase indicators entirely and hinder the sniper. The sniper should know how weather affects soil, vegetation, and other indicators in his area. He cannot determine the age of indicators until he understands the effects that weather has on trail signs.

a. By studying weather effects on indicators, the sniper can determine the age of the sign (for example, when bloodstains are fresh, they are bright red). Air and sunlight first change blood to a deep ruby-red color, then to a dark brown crust when the moisture evaporates. Scuff marks on trees or bushes darken with time; sap oozes, then hardens when it makes contact with the air.
b. Weather affects footprints (Figure 5-5). By carefully studying the weather process, the sniper can estimate the age of the print. If particles of soil are beginning to fall into the print, the sniper should become a stalker. If the edges of the print are dried and crusty, the prints are probably about one hour old. This varies with terrain and should be considered as a guide only.
c. A light rain may round the edges of the print. By remembering when the last rain occurred, the sniper can place the print into a time frame. A heavy rain may erase all signs.
d. Trails exiting streams may appear weathered by rain due to water running from clothing or equipment into the tracks. This is especially true if the party exits the stream single file. Then, each person deposits water into the tracks. The existence of a wet, weathered trail slowly fading into a dry trail indicates the trail is fresh.
e. Wind dries tracks and blows litter, sticks, or leaves into prints. By recalling wind activity, the sniper may estimate the age of the tracks. For example, the sniper may reason "the wind is calm at the present but blew hard about an hour ago. These tracks have litter in them, so they must be over an hour old." However, he must be sure that the litter was not crushed into them when the prints were made.

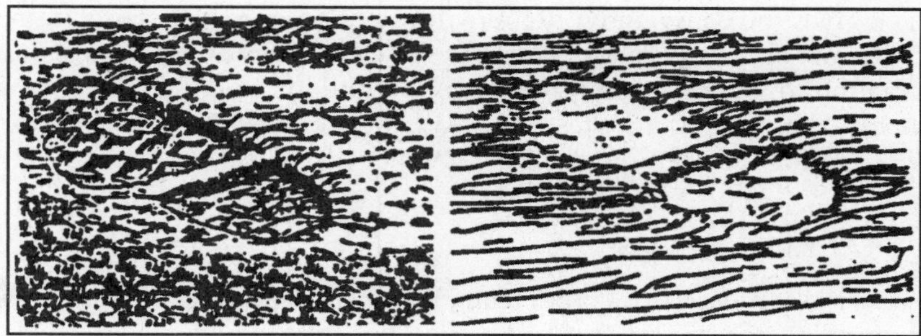

Figure 5-5: Weather effects on footprints.

(1) Wind affects sounds and odors. If the wind is blowing toward the sniper, sounds and odors may be carried to him; conversely, if the wind is blowing *away* from the sniper, he must be extremely cautious since wind also carries sounds toward the enemy. The sniper can determine wind direction by dropping a handful of dust or dried grass from shoulder height. By pointing in the same direction the wind is blowing, the sniper can localize sounds by cupping his hands behind his ears and turning slowly. When sounds are loudest, the sniper is facing the origin.

(2) In calm weather (no wind), air currents that may be too light to detect can carry sounds to the sniper. Air cools in the evening and moves downhill toward the valleys. If the sniper is moving uphill late in the day or at night, air currents will probably be moving toward him if no other wind is blowing. As the morning sun warms the air in the valleys, it moves uphill. The sniper considers these factors when plotting patrol routes or other operations. If he keeps the wind in his face, sounds and odors will be carried to him from his objective or from the party being tracked.

(3) The sun should also be considered by the sniper. It is difficult to fire directly into the sun, but if the sniper has the sun at his back and the wind in his face, he has a slight advantage.

5-4. LITTER

A poorly trained or poorly disciplined unit moving over terrain may leave a trail of litter. Unmistakable signs of recent movement are gum or candy wrappers, food cans, cigarette butts, remains of fires, or human feces. Rain flattens or washes litter away and turns paper into pulp. Exposure to weather can cause food cans to rust at the opened edge; then, the rust moves toward the center. The sniper must consider weather conditions when estimating the age of litter. He can use the last rain or strong wind as the basis for a time frame.

5-5. CAMOUFLAGE

Camouflage applies to tracking when the followed party employs techniques to baffle or slow the sniper. For example, walking backward to leave confusing prints, brushing out trails, and moving over rocky ground or through streams.

5-6. IMMEDIATE-USE INTELLIGENCE

The sniper combines all indicators and interprets what he has seen to form a composite picture for on-the-spot intelligence. For example, indicators may show contact is imminent and require extreme stealth.

a. The sniper avoids reporting his interpretations as facts. He reports what he has seen rather than stating these things exist. There are many ways a sniper can interpret the sex and size of the party, the load, and the type of equipment. Timeframes can be determined by weathering effects on indicators.

b. Immediate-use intelligence is information about the enemy that can be used to gain surprise, to keep him off balance, or to keep him from escaping the area entirely. The commander may have many sources of intelligence reports, documents, or prisoners of war. These sources can be combined to form indicators of the enemy's last location, future plans, and destination.

c. Tracking, however, gives the commander definite information on which to act immediately. For example, a unit may report there are no men of military age in a village. This information is of value only if it is combined with other information to make a composite enemy picture in the area. Therefore, a sniper who interprets trail signs and reports that he is 30 minutes behind a known enemy unit, moving north, and located at a specific location, gives the commander information on which he can act at once.

5-7. DOG/HANDLER TRACKING TEAMS

Dog/handler tracking teams are a threat to the sniper team. While small and lightly armed, they can increase the area that a rear area security unit can search. Due to the dog/handler tracking team's effectiveness and its lack of firepower, a sniper team may be tempted to destroy such an "easy" target. Whether a sniper should fight or run depends on the situation and the sniper. Eliminating or injuring the dog/handler tracking team only confirms that there is a hostile team operating in the area.

a. When looking for sniper teams, trackers use wood line sweeps and area searches. A wood line sweep consists of walking the dog upwind of a suspected wood line or brush line. If the wind is blowing through the woods and out of the wood line, trackers move 50 to 100 meters inside a wooded area to sweep the wood's edge. Since wood line sweeps tend to be less specific, trackers perform them faster. An area search is used when a team's location is specific such as a small wooded area or block of houses. The search area is cordoned off, if possible, and the dog/handler tracking teams are brought on line, about 25 to 150 meters apart, depending on terrain and visibility. The handler trackers then advance, each moving their dogs through a specific corridor. The handler tracker controls the dog entirely with voice commands and gestures. He remains undercover, directing the dog in a search pattern or to a likely target area. The search line moves forward with each dog dashing back and forth in assigned sectors.

b. While dog/handler tracking teams area potent threat, there are counters available to the sniper team. The beat defenses are basic infantry techniques: good camouflage and light, noise, and trash discipline. Dogs find a sniper team either by detecting a trail or by a point source such as human waste odors at the hide site. It is critical to try to obscure or limit trails around the hide, especially along the wood line or area closest to the team's target area. Surveillance targets are usually the major axis of advance. "Trolling the wood lines" along likely looking roads or intersections is a favorite tactic of dog/handler tracking teams. When moving into a target area, the sniper team should take the following countermeasures:
   (1) Remain as faraway from the target area as the situation allows.
   (2) Never establish a position at the edge of cover and concealment nearest the target area.
   (3) Reduce the track. Try to approach the position area on hard, dry ground or along a stream or river.
   (4) Urinate in a hole and cover it up. Never urinate in the same spot.
   (5) Bury fecal matter deep. If the duration of the mission permits, use MRE bags sealed with tape and take it with you.
   (6) Never smoke.
   (7) Carry all trash until it can be buried elsewhere.
   (8) Surround the hide site with a 3-cm to 5-cm band of motor oil to mask odor; although less effective but easier to carry, garlic may be used. A dead animal can also be used to mask smell, although it may attract unwanted canine attention.

c. If a dog/handler tracking team moves into the area, the sniper team can employ several actions but should first check wind direction and speed. If the sniper team is downwind of the estimated search area, the chances are minimal that the team's point smells will probably be detected. If upwind of the search area, the sniper team should attempt to move downwind. Terrain and visibility dictate whether the sniper team can move without being detected visually by the handlers of the tracking team. Remember, sweeps are not always conducted just outside of a wood line. Wind direction determines whether the sweep will be parallel to the outside or 50 to 100 meters inside the wood line.
   (1) The sniper team has options if caught inside the search area of a line search. The handlers rely on radio communications and often do not have visual contact with each other. If the sniper team has been generally localized through enemy radio detection-finding equipment, the search net will still be loose during

the initial sweep. A sniper team has a small chance of hiding and escaping detection in deep brush or in woodpiles. Larger groups will almost certainly be found. Yet, the sniper team may have the opportunity to eliminate the handler and to escape the search net.

(2) The handler hides behind cover with the dog. He searches for movement and then sends the dog out in a straight line toward the front. Usually, when the dog has moved about 50 to 75 meters, the handler calls the dog back. The handler then moves slowly forward and always from covered position to covered position. Commands are by voice and gesture with a backup whistle to signal the dog to return. If a handler is eliminated or badly injured after he has released the dog, but before he has recalled it, the dog continues to randomly search out and away from the handler. The dog usually returns to another handler or to his former handler's last position within several minutes. This creates a gap from 25 to 150 meters wide in the search pattern. Response times by the other searchers tend to be fast. Given the high degree of radio communication, the injured handler will probably be quickly missed from the radio net. Killing the dog before the handler will probably delay discovery only by moments. Dogs are so reliable that if the dog does not return immediately, the handler knows something is wrong.

(3) If the sniper does not have a firearm, one dog can be dealt with relatively easy if a knife or large club is available. The sniper must keep low and strike upward using the wrist, never overhand. Dogs are quick and will try to strike the groin or legs. Most attack dogs are trained to go for the groin or throat. If alone and faced with two or more dogs, the sniper should avoid the situation.

SECTION II. COUNTERTRACKING

If an enemy tracker finds the tracks of two men, this may indicate that a highly trained team may be operating in the area. However, a knowledge of countertracking enables the sniper team to survive by remaining undetected.

5-8. EVASION

Evasion of the tracker or pursuit team is a difficult task that requires the use of immediate-action drills to counter the threat. A sniper team skilled in tracking techniques can successfully employ deception drills to lessen signs that the enemy can use against them. However, it is very difficult for a person, especially a group, to move across any area without leaving signs noticeable to the trained eye.

5-9. CAMOUFLAGE

The sniper team may use the most used and the least used routes to cover its movement. It also loses travel time when trying to camouflage the trail.

a. **Most Used Routes.** Movement on lightly traveled sandy or soft trails is easily tracked. However, a sniper may try to confuse the tracker by moving on hard-surfaced, often-traveled roads or by merging with civilians. These routes should be carefully examined; if a well-defined approach leads to the enemy, it will probably be mined, ambushed, or covered by snipers.

b. **Least Used Routes.** Least used routes avoid all man-made trails or roads and confuse the tracker. These routes are normally magnetic azimuths between two points. However, the tracker can use the proper concepts to follow the sniper team if he is experienced and persistent.

c. **Reduction of Trail Signs.** A sniper who tries to hide his trail moves at reduced speed; therefore, the experienced tracker gains time. Common methods to reduce trail signs areas follows:

(1) Wrap footgear with rags or wear soft-soled sneakers, which make footprints rounded and leas distinctive.

(2) Brush out the trail. This is rarely done without leaving signs.

(3) Change into footgear with a different tread immediately following a deceptive maneuver.

(4) Walk on hard or rocky ground.

5-10. DECEPTION TECHNIQUES

Evading a skilled and persistent enemy tracker requires skillfully executed maneuvers to deceive the tracker and to cause him to lose the trail. An enemy tracker cannot be outrun by a sniper team that is carrying equipment, because he travels light and is escorted by enemy forces designed for pursuit. The size of the pursuing force dictates the sniper team's chances of success in employing ambush-type maneuvers. Sniper teams use some of the following techniques in immediate-action drills and deception drills.

a. **Backward Walking.** One of the basic techniques used is that of walking backward (Figure 5-6) in tracks already made, and then stepping off the trail onto terrain or objects that leave little sign. Skillful use of this maneuver causes the tracker to look in the wrong direction once he has lost the trail.

b. **Large Tree.** A good deception tactic is to change directions at large trees (Figure 5-7). To do this, the sniper moves in any given direction and walks past a large tree (12 inches wide or larger) from 5 to 10 paces. He carefully walks backward to the forward side of the tree and makes a 90-degree change in the direction of travel, passing the tree on its forward side. This technique uses the tree as a screen to hide the new trail from the pursuing tracker.

> ✍ **NOTE**
>
> By studying signs, a tracker may determine if an attempt is being made to confuse him. If the sniper team loses the tracker by walking backward, footprints will be deepened at the toe and soil will be scuffed or dragged in the direction of movement. By following carefully the tracker can normally find a turnaround point.

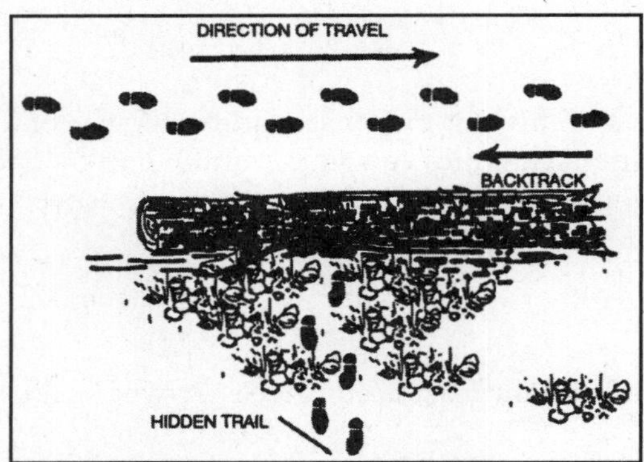

Figure 5-6: Walking backward.

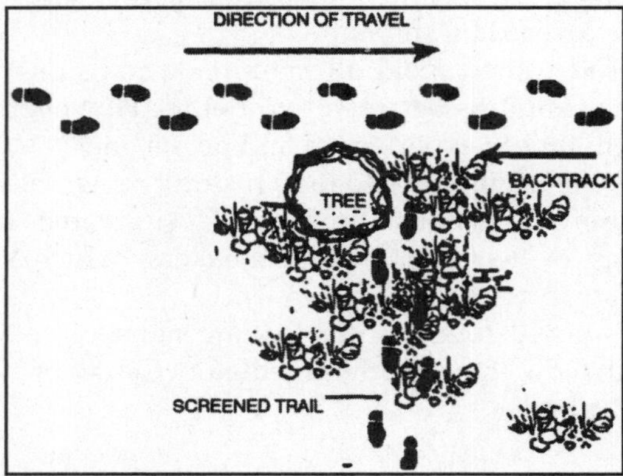

Figure 5-7: Large tree.

c. **Cut the Corner.** Cut-the-corner technique is used when approaching a known road or trail. About 100 meters from the road, the sniper team changes its direction of movement, either 45 degrees left or right. Once the road is reached, the sniper team leaves a visible trail in the same direction of the deception for a short distance on the road. The tracker should believe that the sniper team "cut the corner" to save time. The sniper team backtracks on the trail to the point where it entered the road, and then it carefully moves on the road without leaving a good trail. Once the desired distance is achieved, the sniper team changes direction and continues movement (Figure 5-8).

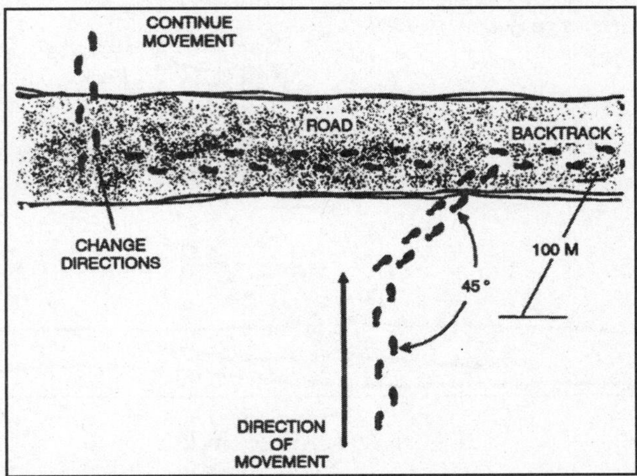

Figure 5-8: Cut the corner.

d. **Slip the Stream.** The sniper team uses slip-the-stream technique when approaching a known stream. The sniper team executes this method the same as the cut the comer technique. The sniper team establishes the 45-degree deception maneuver upstream, then enters the stream. The sniper team moves upstream to prevent floating debris and silt from compromising its direction of travel, and the sniper team establishes false trails upstream if time permits. Then, it moves downstream to escape since creeks and streams gain tributaries that offer more escape alternatives (Figure 5-9).

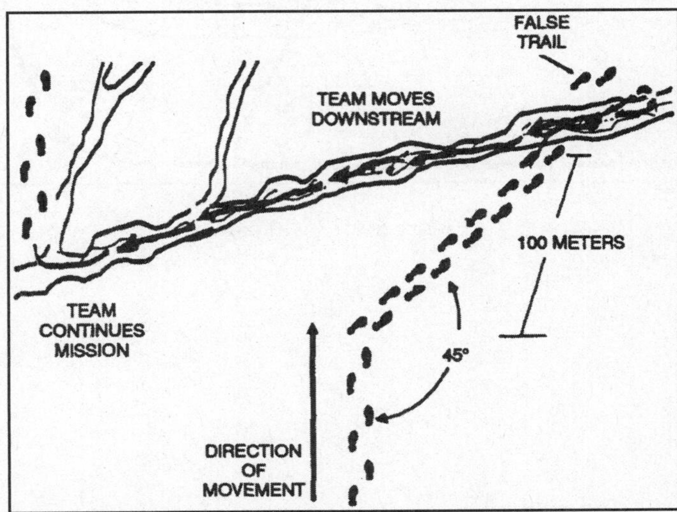

Figure 5-9: Slip the stream.

e. **Arctic Circle.** The sniper team uses the arctic circle technique in snow-covered terrain to escape pursuers or to hide a patrol base. It establishes a trail in a circle (Figure 5-10) as large as possible. The trail that starts on a road and returns to the same start point is effective. At some point along the circular trail, the sniper team removes snowshoes (if used) and carefully steps off the trail, leaving one set of tracks. The large tree maneuver can be used to screen the trail. From the hide position, the sniper team returns over the same steps and carefully fills them with snow one at a time. This technique is especially effective if it is snowing.

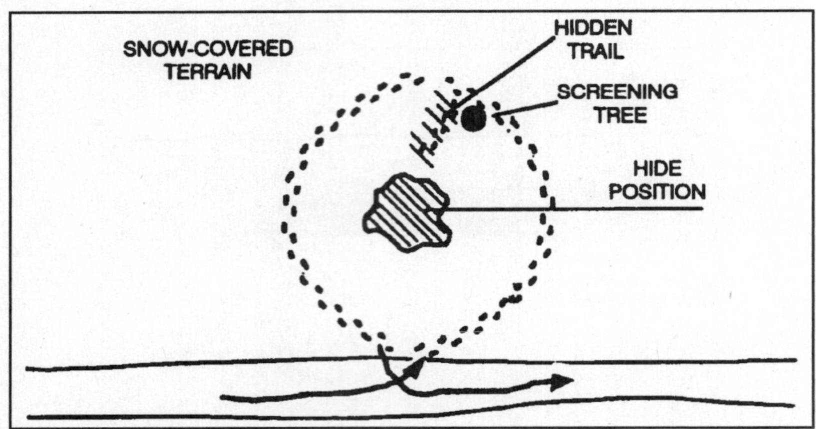

Figure 5-10: Arctic circle.

f. **Fishhook.** The sniper team uses the fishhook technique to double back (Figure 5-11) on its own trail in an overwatch position. The sniper team can observe the back trail for trackers or ambush pursuers. If the pursuing force is too large to be destroyed, the sniper team strives to eliminate the tracker. The sniper team uses the hit-and-run tactics, then moves to another ambush position. The terrain must be used to advantage.

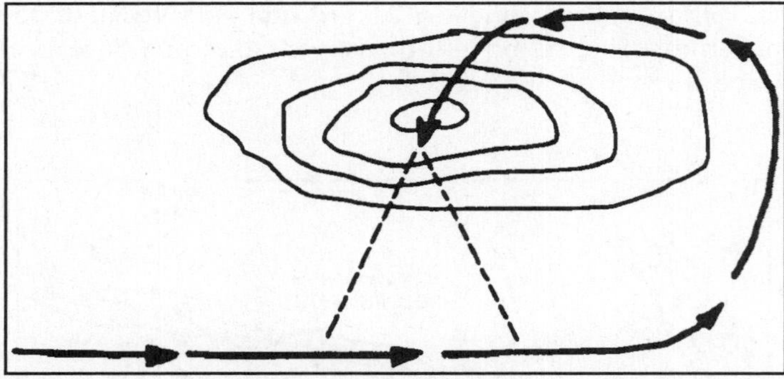

Figure 5-11: Fishhook.

The Army Combat Pistol

CHAPTER 1

Components and Functioning

This chapter describes the M9 and M11 semiautomatic pistols, their maintenance requirements, and their operation and functioning.

SECTION I. DESCRIPTION AND COMPONENTS

The M9 (Figure 1-1) and M11 (Figure 1-2) pistols are 9-mm, semiautomatic, magazine-fed, recoil-operation, double-action weapons chambered for the 9-mm cartridge.

Figure 1-1: 9-mm pistol, M9.

Figure 1-2: 9-mm pistol, M11.

1-1. DESCRIPTION

Table 1-1 summarizes equipment data for both pistols.

Table 1-1: Equipment Data, M9 and M11 pistols.

	M9 PISTOL	M11 PISTOL
Caliber	9-mm NATO	9-mm NATO
System of Operation	Short recoil, semiautomatic	Short recoil, semiautomatic
Locking System	Oscillating block	Oscillating block
Length	217 mm (8.54 inches)	180 mm (7.08 inches)
Width	38 mm (1.5 inches)	37 mm (1.46 inches)
Height	140 mm (5.51 inches)	136 mm (5.35 inches)
Magazine Capacity	**15 Rounds**	**13 Rounds**
Weight with Empty Magazine	960 grams (2.1 pounds)	745 grams (26.1 oz.)
Weight with 15-Round Magazine	1,145 grams (2.6 pounds)	830 grams (29.1 oz.)
Barrel Length	125 mm (4.92 inches)	98 mm (3.86 inches)
Rifling	Right-hand, six-groove (pitch 250 mm [about 10 inches])	Right-hand, six-groove (pitch 250 mm [9.84 inches])
Muzzle Velocity	375 meters per second (1,230.3 feet per second)	375 meters per second (1,230.3 feet per second)
Muzzle Energy	569.5 Newton meters (430 foot pounds)	569.5 Newton meters (430 foot pounds)
Maximum Range	1,800 meters (1,962.2 yards)	1,800 meters (1,962.2 yards)
Maximum Effective Range	50 meters (54.7 yards)	50 meters (54.7 yards)
Front Sight	Blade, integral with slide	Blade, integral with slide
Rear Sight	Notched bar, dovetailed to slide	Notched bar, dovetailed to slide
Sighting Radius	158 mm (6.22 inches)	158 mm (6.22 inches)
Safety Features	Decocking/safety lever, firing pin block.	Decocking/safety lever, firing pin block.
Hammer (half-cocked notch)	Prevents accidental discharge.	Prevents accidental discharge.
Basic Load	45 rounds	45 rounds
Trigger Pull	Single-action: 5.50 pounds Double-action: 12.33 pounds	Single-Action: 4.40 pounds Double-Action: 12.12 pounds

WARNING

The half-cocked position catches the hammer and prevents it from firing if the hammer is released while manually cocking the weapon. It is not to be used as a safety position. The pistol will fire from the half-cocked position if the trigger is pulled.

1-2. COMPONENTS

The major components of the M9 (Figure 1-3) and M11 (Figure 1-4) pistols are:

a. **Slide and Barrel Assembly**: Houses the firing pin, striker, and extractor. Cocks the hammer during recoil cycle.
b. **Recoil Spring and Recoil Spring Guide**: Absorbs recoil and returns the slide assembly to its forward position.
c. **Barrel and Locking Block Assembly**: Houses cartridge for firing, directs projectile, and locks barrel in position during firing.
d. **Receiver**: Serves as a support for all the major components. Houses action of the pistol through four major components. Controls functioning of the pistol.
e. **Magazine**: Holds cartridges in place for stripping and chambering.

Figure 1-3: Major components, M9.

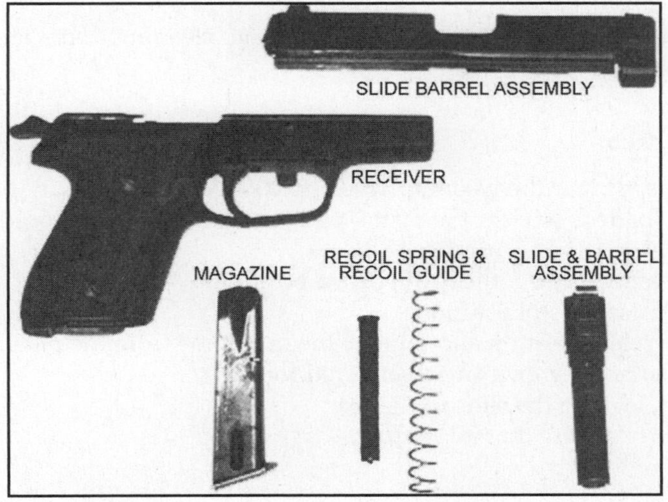

Figure 1-4: Major components, M11.

1-3. AMMUNITION

M9 and M11 pistols use several different types of 9-mm ammunition. Soldiers should use only authorized ammunition that is manufactured to U.S. and NATO specifications.

a. **Type and Characteristics.** The specific type ammunition (Figure 1-5) and its characteristics are as follows:
(1) Cartridge, 9-mm ball, M882 with/without cannelure.
(2) Cartridge, 9-mm dummy, M917.

WARNING

Do not fire heavily corroded or dented cartridges, cartridges with loose bullets, or any other rounds detected as defective through visual inspection.

b. **Care, Handling, and Preservation.**
   (1) Protect ammunition from mud, sand, and water. If the ammunition gets wet or dirty, wipe it off at once with a clean dry cloth. Wipe off light corrosion as soon as it is discovered. Turn in heavily corroded cartridges.
   (2) Do not expose ammunition to the direct rays of the sun. If the powder is hot, excessive pressure may develop when the pistol is fired.
   (3) Do not oil or grease ammunition. Dust and other abrasives that collect on greasy ammunition may cause damage to the operating parts of the pistol. Oiled cartridges produce excessive chamber pressure.

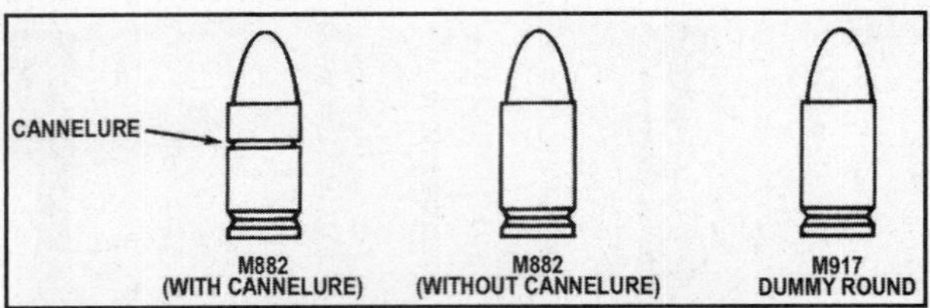

Figure 1-5: Ammunition.

SECTION II. MAINTENANCE

Maintenance procedures include clearing, dissembling, inspecting, cleaning, lubricating, assembling, and checking the functioning of the M9 or M11 pistol.

1-4. CLEARING PROCEDURES

The first step in maintenance is to clear the weapon. This applies in all situations, not just after firing. Soldiers must always assume the weapon is loaded. To clear the pistol, perform the following procedures:

a. Place the decocking/safety lever in the SAFE down position.
b. Hold the pistol in the raised pistol position.
c. Depress the magazine release button and remove the magazine from the pistol.
d. Pull the slide to the rear and remove any chambered round.
e. Push the slide stop up, locking the slide to the rear.
f. Look into the chamber to ensure that it is empty.

1-5. GENERAL DISASSEMBLE

To disassemble the pistol, perform the following procedures:

a. Depress the slide stop and let the slide go forward.
b. Hold the pistol in the right hand with the muzzle slightly raised.
c. Press the disassembly lever button with the forefinger.
d. Rotate the disassembly lever downward until it stops.
e. Pull the slide and barrel assembly forward and remove it from the receiver.
f. Carefully and lightly compress the recoil spring and spring guide. At the same time, lift up and remove them.
g. Separate the recoil spring from the spring guide.
h. Push in on the locking block plunger while pushing the barrel forward slightly.
i. Lift and remove the locking block and barrel assembly from the slide.

1-6. INSPECTION

Inspection begins with the pistol disassembled in its major components. Shiny surfaces do not mean the parts are unserviceable. Inspect all surfaces for visible damage, cracks, burns, and chips.

1-7. CLEANING, LUBRICATION, AND PREVENTIVE MAINTENANCE

The M9 or M11 pistol should be disassembled into its major components and cleaned immediately after firing. All metal components and surfaces that have been exposed to powder fouling should be cleaned using CLP on a bore-cleaning patch. The same procedure is used to clean the receiver. After it has been cleaned and wiped dry, a thin coat of CLP is applied by rubbing with a cloth. This lubricates and preserves the exposed metal parts during all normal temperature ranges. When not in use, the pistol should be inspected weekly and cleaned and lubricated when necessary.

> ⚠ **CAUTION**
> When using CLP, do not use any other type cleaner. Never mix CLP with RBC or LSA.

a. Clear and disassemble the weapon.
b. Wipe or brush dirt, dust, and carbon buildup from the disassembled pistol.
c. Use CLP to help remove carbon buildup and stubborn dirt and grime.
d. Pay particular attention to the bolt face, guide rails on the receiver, grooves on the slide, and other hard-to-reach areas.

> ✍ **NOTE**
> Do not use mineral spirits, paint thinner, or dry cleaning solvent to clean the pistol. Use only issued lubricants and cleaners, such as CLP or LSA.

e. Clean the bore and chamber using CLP and fresh swabs.
f. Lubricate the pistol by covering all surfaces including the bore and chamber with a light coat of CLP. In extremely hot or cold weather, refer to the technical manual for lubricating procedures and materials.

1-8. GENERAL ASSEMBLY

To assemble the M9 or M11 pistol, simply reverse the procedures used to disassemble the pistol.

a. Grasp the slide with the bottom facing up.
b. With the other hand, grasp the barrel assembly with the locking block facing up.
c. Insert the muzzle into the forward end of the slide and, at the same time, lower the rear of the barrel assembly by aligning the extractor cutout with the extractor.

> ✍ **NOTE**
> The locking block will fall into the locked position in the slide.

d. Insert the recoil spring onto the recoil spring guide.

> ⚠ **CAUTION**
> Maintain spring tension until the spring guide is fully seated in the cutaway on the locking block.

e. Insert the end of the recoil spring and the recoil spring guide into the recoil spring housing. At the same time, compress the recoil spring guide until it is fully seated on the locking block cutaway.

> ⚠ **CAUTION**
> Do not pull the trigger while placing the slide on the receiver.

f. Ensure that the hammer is unlocked, the firing pin block is in the DOWN position, and the decocking/safety lever is in the SAFE position.
g. Grasp the slide and barrel assembly with the sights UP, and align the slide on the receiver assembly guide rails.
h. Push until the rear of the slide is a short distance beyond the rear of the receiver assembly and hold. At the same time, rotate the disassembly latch lever upward. A click indicates a positive lock.

1-9. FUNCTION CHECK

Always perform a function check after the pistol is reassembled to ensure it is working properly. To perform a function check:

a. Clear the pistol in accordance with the unloading procedures.
b. Depress the slide stop, letting the slide go forward.
c. Insert an empty magazine into the pistol.
d. Retract the slide fully and release it. The slide should lock to the rear.
e. Depress the magazine release button and remove the magazine.
f. Ensure the decocking/safety lever is in the SAFE position.
g. Depress the slide stop. When the slide goes forward, the hammer should fall to the forward position.
h. Squeeze and release the trigger. The firing pin block should move up and down and the hammer should not move.
i. Place the decocking/safety lever in the fire POSITION.
j. Squeeze the trigger to check double action. The hammer should cock and fall.
k. Squeeze the trigger again. Hold it to the rear. Manually retract and release the slide. Release the trigger. A click should be heard and the hammer should not fall.
l. Squeeze the trigger to check the single action. The hammer should fall.

SECTION III. OPERATION AND FUNCTION

This section provides detailed information on the functioning of M9 and M11 pistols.

1-10. OPERATION

With the weapon loaded and the hammer cocked, the shot is discharged by pulling the trigger.

a. Trigger movement is transmitted by the trigger bar, which draws the sear out of register with the full-cock hammer notch via the safety lever. With a slight timing lag, the safety lever also cams the safety lock upward to free the firing pin immediately before the hammer drops. The hammer forces the firing pin forward to strike and detonate the cartridge primer.
b. Blowback reaction generated by the exploding charge thrusts the locked barrel/slide system rearward against the recoil spring. After recoiling about 3 mm (1/8″), the barrel and slide unlock, allowing the barrel to tilt down into the locked position. The slide continues rearward until it abuts against the receiver stop.
c. During slide recoil, the hammer is cocked; the spent case is extracted and ejected as it strikes the ejector. In the initial recoil phase, the safety lever and safety lock separate, automatically rendering the firing pin safety lock effective again. As recoil continues, the slide depresses the trigger bar, disconnecting it from the safety lever. Sear spring pressure returns the sear and safety lever to their initial positions.
d. After contacting the receiver stop, the slide is thrust forward by the compressed recoil spring, stripping a round from the magazine and chambering it on the way. Just before reaching the forward end position, the slide again locks up with the barrel. The complete system is then thrust fully into the forward battery position by recoil spring pressure. Releasing the trigger allows the trigger bar and safety lever to re-engage.
e. The weapon is now cocked and ready to fire. After firing the last shot, the slide is locked in the rearmost position by the slide catch lever. This catch is actuated positively by the magazine follower, which is raised by magazine spring pressure.

1-11. LOADING

To load the pistol—

- Hold the pistol in the raised pistol position.
- Insert the magazine into the pistol.
- Pull the slide to the rear and release the slide to chamber a round.
- Push the decocking/safety lever to the SAFE position.
    a. Always make sure the muzzle is pointing in a safe direction, with the finger off the trigger.
    b. Never attempt to load or unload any firearm inside a vehicle, building, or other confined space (except a properly constructed shooting range or bullet trap). Enclosed areas frequently offer no completely safe direction in which to point the firearm; if an accidental discharge occurs, there is great risk of injury or property damage.
    c. Before loading, always clean excess grease and oil from the bore and chamber, and ensure that no obstruction is in the barrel. Any foreign matter in the barrel could result in a bulged or burst barrel or other damage to the firearm and could cause serious injury to the shooter or to others.

1-12. UNLOADING AND CLEARING

To unload and clear the pistol—

- Hold the pistol in the raised pistol position.
- Depress the magazine release button and remove the magazine.
- Pull the slide to the rear and lock it in its rearward position by pushing up on the slide stop.
- Point the pistol skyward and look into the chamber to ensure it is clear.
- Let the slide go forward and pull the trigger to release the spring tension.
    a. Perform this task in an area designated for this process.
    b. Keep your finger off the trigger, and always make sure the muzzle is pointed in a safe direction.
    c. Remember to clear the chamber after removing the magazine.
    d. Never assume that a pistol is unloaded until you have personally checked it both visually and physically.
    e. After every shooting practice, make a final check to be certain the firearm is unloaded before leaving the range.

1-13. CYCLE OF OPERATION

Each time a cartridge is fired, the parts inside the weapon function in a given order. This is known as the functioning cycle or cycle of operation. The cycle of operation of the weapon is divided into eight steps: feeding, chambering, locking, firing, unlocking, extracting, ejecting, and cocking. The steps are listed in the order in which functioning occurs; however, more than one step may occur at the same time.

a. A magazine containing ammunition is placed in the receiver. The slide is pulled fully to the rear and released. As the slide moves forward, it strips the top round from the magazine and pushes it into the chamber. The hammer remains in the cocked position, and the weapon is ready to fire.

b. The weapon fires one round each time the trigger is pulled. Each time a cartridge is fired, the slide and barrel recoil or move a short distance locked together. This permits the bullet and expanding powder gases to escape from the muzzle before the unlocking is completed.

c. The barrel then unlocks from the slide and continues to the rear, extracting the cartridge case from the chamber and ejecting it from the weapon. During this rearward movement, the magazine feeds another cartridge, the recoil spring is compressed, and the hammer is cocked.

d. At the end of the rearward movement, the recoil spring expands, forcing the slide forward, locking the barrel and slide together. The weapon is ready to fire again. The same cycle of operation continues until the ammunition is expended.

e. As the last round is fired, the magazine spring exerts upward pressure on the magazine follower. The stop on the follower strikes the slide stop, forcing it into the recess on the bottom of the slide and locking the slide to the rear. This action indicates that the magazine is empty and aids in faster reloading.

SECTION IV. PERFORMANCE PROBLEMS

Possible performance problems of M9 and M11 pistols are sluggish operation and stoppages. This section discusses immediate and remedial action to correct such problems.

1-14. MALFUNTIONS

The following malfunctions may occur to the M9 and M11 pistols. Take these corrective actions to correct any problems that may occur.

a. **Sluggish Operation.** Sluggish operation is usually due to excessive friction caused by carbon build up, lack of lubrication, or burred parts. Corrective action includes cleaning, lubricating, inspecting, and replacing parts as necessary.
b. **Stoppages.** A stoppage is an interruption in the cycle of operation caused by faulty action of the pistol or faulty ammunition. Types of stoppages are:
   - Failure to feed.
   - Failure to chamber.
   - Failure to lock.
   - Failure to fire.
   - Failure to unlock.
   - Failure to extract.
   - Failure to eject.
   - Failure to cock.

1-15. IMMEDIATE ACTION

Immediate action is the action taken to reduce a stoppage without looking for the cause. Immediate action is taken within 15 seconds of a stoppage.

a. Ensure the decocking/safety lever is in the FIRE position.
b. Squeeze the trigger again.
c. If the pistol does not fire, ensure that the magazine is fully seated, retract the slide to the rear, and release.
d. Squeeze the trigger.
e. If the pistol again does not fire, remove the magazine and retract the slide to eject the chambered cartridge. Insert a new magazine, retract the slide, and release to chamber another cartridge.
f. Squeeze the trigger.
g. If the pistol still does not fire, perform remedial action.

1-16. REMEDIAL ACTION

Remedial action is the action taken to reduce a stoppage by looking for the cause.

a. Clear the pistol.
b. Inspect the pistol for the cause of the stoppage.
c. Correct the cause of the stoppage, load the pistol, and fire.
d. If the pistol again fails to fire, disassemble it for closer inspection, cleaning, and lubrication.

CHAPTER 2

Pistol Marksmanship Training

Marksmanship training is divided into two phases: preparatory marksmanship training and range firing. Each phase may be divided into separate instructional steps. All marksmanship training must be progressive. Combat marksmanship techniques should be practiced after the basics have been mastered.

SECTION I. BASIC MARKSMANSHIP

The main use of the pistol is to engage an enemy at close range with quick, accurate fire. Accurate shooting results from knowing and correctly applying the elements of marksmanship. The elements of combat pistol marksmanship are:

- Grip.
- Aiming.
- Breath control.
- Trigger squeeze.
- Target engagement.
- Positions.

2-1. GRIP

A proper grip is one of the most important fundamentals of quick fire. The weapon must become an extension of the hand and arm; it should replace the finger in pointing at an object. The firer must apply a firm, uniform grip to the weapon.

a. **One-Hand Grip.** Hold the weapon in the nonfiring hand; form a V with the thumb and forefinger of the strong hand (firing hand). Place the weapon in the V with the front and rear sights in line with the firing arm. Wrap the lower three fingers around the pistol grip, putting equal pressure with all three fingers to the rear. Allow the thumb of the firing hand to rest alongside the weapon without pressure (Figure 2-1). Grip the weapon tightly until the hand begins to tremble; relax until the trembling stops. At this point, the necessary pressure for a proper grip has been applied. Place the trigger finger on the trigger between the tip and second joint so that it can be squeezed to the rear. The trigger finger must work independently of the remaining fingers.

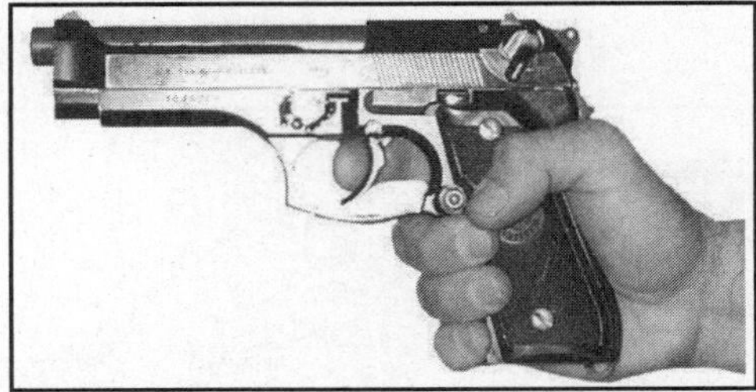

Figure 2-1: One-hand grip.

> ✍ **NOTE**
> If any of the three fingers on the grip are relaxed, the grip must be reapplied.

b. **Two-Hand Grip.** The two-hand grip allows the firer to steady the firing hand and provide maximum support during firing. The nonfiring hand becomes a support mechanism for the firing hand by wrapping the fingers of the nonfiring hand around the firing hand. Two-hand grips are recommended for all pistol firing.

WARNING

Do not place the nonfiring thumb in the rear of the weapon. The recoil upon firing could result in personal injury.

(1) ***Fist Grip.*** Grip the weapon as with the one-hand grip. Firmly close the fingers of the nonfiring hand over the fingers of the firing hand, ensuring that the index finger from the nonfiring hand is between the middle finger of the firing hand and the trigger guard. Place the nonfiring thumb alongside the firing thumb (Figure 2-2).

NOTE

Depending upon the individual firer, he may chose to place the index finger of his nonfiring hand on the front of the trigger guard since M9 and M11 pistols have a recurved trigger guard designed for this purpose.

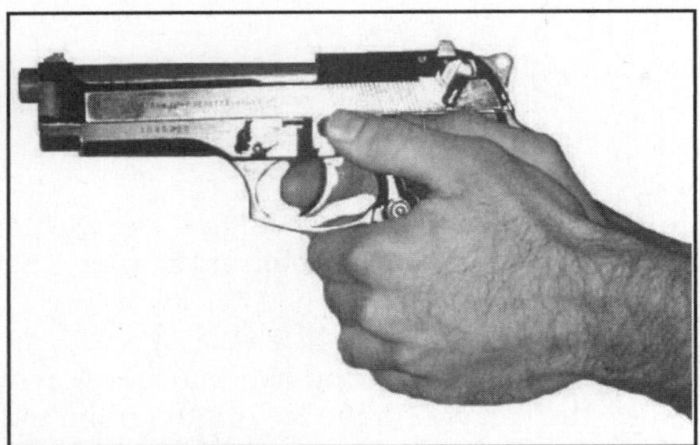

Figure 2-2: Fist grip.

(2) ***Palm-Supported Grip.*** This grip is commonly called the cup and saucer grip. Grip the firing hand as with the one-hand grip. Place the nonfiring hand under the firing hand, wrapping the nonfiring fingers around the back of the firing hand. Place the nonfiring thumb over the middle finger of the firing hand (Figure 2-3).

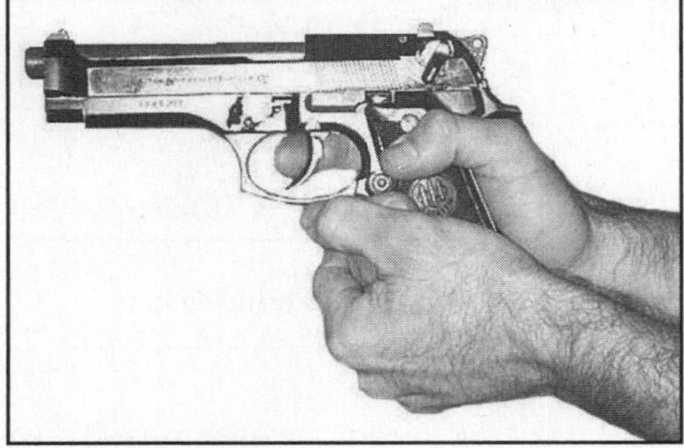

Figure 2-3: Palm-supported grip.

(3) ***Weaver grip.*** Apply this grip the same as the fist grip. The only exception is that the nonfiring thumb is wrapped over the firing thumb (Figure 2-4).

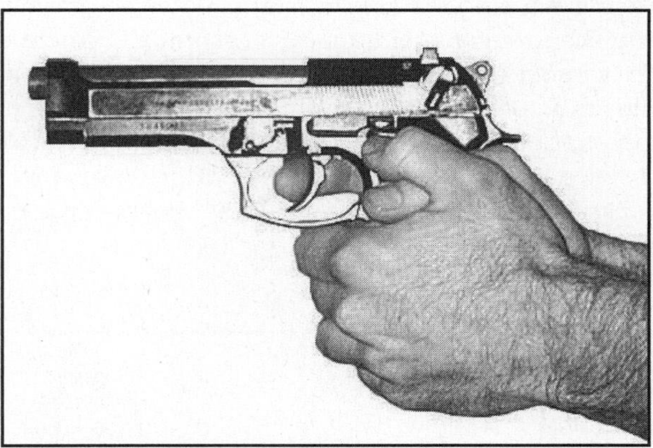

Figure 2-4: Weaver grip.

c. **Isometric Tension.** The firer raises his arms to a firing position and applies isometric tension. This is commonly known as the push-pull method for maintaining weapon stability. Isometric tension is when the firer applies forward pressure with the firing hand and pulls rearward with the nonfiring hand with equal pressure. This creates an isometric force but never so much to cause the firer to tremble. This steadies the weapon and reduces barrel rise from recoil. The supporting arm is bent with the elbow pulled downward. The firing arm is fully extended with the elbow and wrist locked. The firer must experiment to find the right amount of isometric tension to apply.

> ✍ **NOTE**
> The firing hand should exert the same pressure as the nonfiring hand. If it does not, a missed target could result.

d. **Natural Point of Aim.** The firer should check his grip for use of his natural point of aim. He grips the weapon and sights properly on a distant target. While maintaining his grip and stance, he closes his eyes for three to five seconds. He then opens his eyes and checks for proper sight picture. If the point of aim is disturbed, the firer adjusts his stance to compensate. If the sight alignment is disturbed, the firer adjusts his grip to compensate by removing the weapon from his hand and reapplying the grip. The firer repeats this process until the sight alignment and sight placement remain almost the same when he opens his eyes. With sufficient practice, this enables the firer to determine and use his natural point of aim, which is the most relaxed position for holding and firing the weapon.

2-2. AIMING

Aiming is sight alignment and sight placement (Figure 2-5).

a. Sight alignment is the centering of the front blade in the rear sight notch. The top of the front sight is level with the top of the rear sight and is in correct alignment with the eye. For correct sight alignment, the firer must center the front sight in the rear sight. He raises or lowers the top of the front sight so it is level with the top of the rear sight. Sight alignment is essential for accuracy because of the short sight radius of the pistol. For example, if a 1/10-inch error is made in aligning the front sight in the rear sight, the firer's bullet will miss the point of aim by about 15 inches at a range of 25 meters. The 1/10-inch error in sight alignment magnifies as the range increases—at 25 meters, it is magnified 150 times.

b. Sight placement is the positioning of the weapon's sights in relation to the target as seen by the firer when he aims the weapon (Figure 2-5). A correct sight picture consists of correct sight alignment with the front sight placed center mass of the target. The eye can focus on only one object at a time at different distances. Therefore, the last focus of the eye is always on the front sight. When the front sight is seen clearly, the rear sight and target will appear hazy. The firer can maintain correct sight alignment only through focusing on the front sight. His bullet will hit the target even if the sight picture is partly off center but still remains on the target. Therefore, sight alignment is more important than sight placement. Since it is impossible to hold the weapon completely still, the firer must apply trigger squeeze and maintain correct sight alignment while the weapon is moving in and around the center of the target. This natural movement of the weapon is referred to as wobble area. The firer must strive to control the limits of the wobble area through proper grip, breath control, trigger squeeze, and positioning.

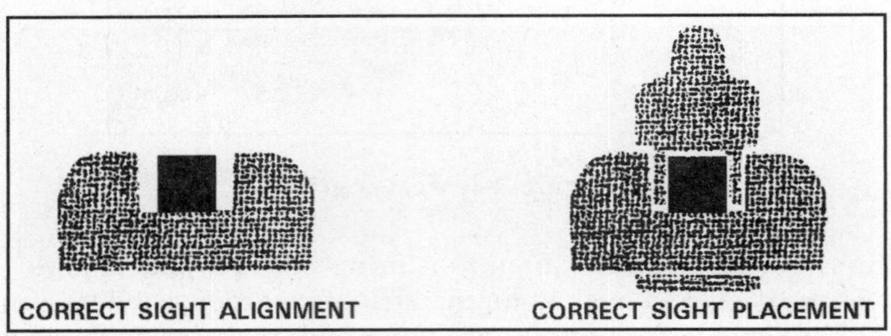

Figure 2-5: Correct sight alignment and sight placement.

c. Focusing on the front sight while applying proper trigger squeeze will help the firer resist the urge to jerk the trigger and anticipate the moment the weapon will fire. Mastery of trigger squeeze and sight alignment requires practice. Trainers should use concurrent training stations or have fire ranges to enhance proficiency of marksmanship skills.

2-3. BREATH CONTROL

To attain accuracy, the firer must learn to hold his breath properly at any time during the breathing cycle. This must be done while aiming and squeezing the trigger. While the procedure is simple, it requires explanation, demonstration, and supervised practice. To hold his breath properly, the firer takes a breath, lets it out, then inhales normally, lets a little out until comfortable, holds, and then fires. It is difficult to maintain a steady position keeping the front sight at a precise aiming point while breathing. Therefore, the firer should be taught to inhale, then exhale normally, and hold his breath at the moment of the natural respiratory pause (Figure 2-6). Breath control, firing at a single target. The shot must then be fired before he feels any discomfort from not breathing. When multiple targets are presented, the firer must learn to hold his breath at any part of the breathing cycle (Figure 2-7). Breath control must be practiced during dry-fire exercises until it becomes a natural part of the firing process.

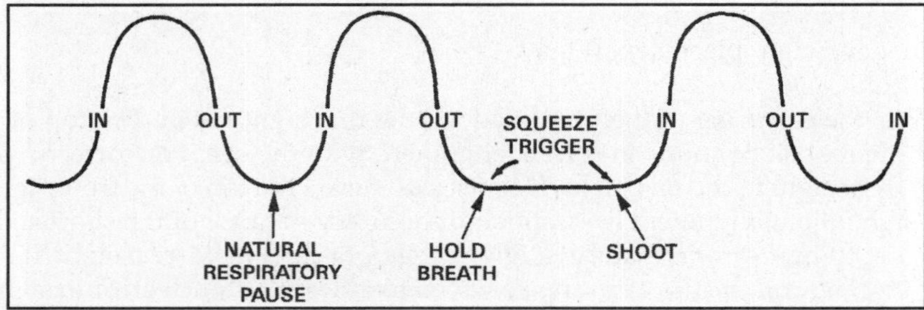

Figure 2-6: Breath control, firing at a single target.

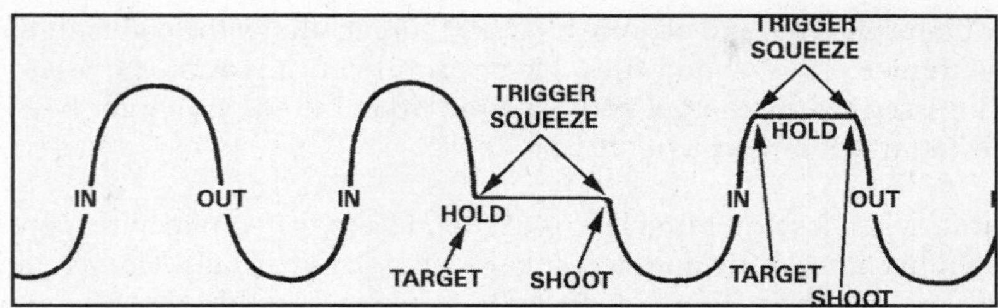

Figure 2-7: Breath control, firing at timed or multiple targets.

2-4. TRIGGER SQUEEZE

Improper trigger squeeze causes more misses than any other step of preparatory marksmanship. Poor shooting is caused by the aim being disturbed before the bullet leaves the barrel of the weapon. This is usually the result of the firer jerking the trigger or flinching. A slight off-center pressure of the trigger finger on the trigger can cause the weapon to move and disturb the firer's sight alignment. Flinching is an automatic human reflex caused by anticipating the recoil of the weapon. Jerking is an effort to fire the weapon at the precise time the sights align with the target. For more on problems in target engagement, see paragraph 2-5.

a. Trigger squeeze is the independent movement of the trigger finger in applying increasing pressure on the trigger straight to the rear, without disturbing the sight alignment until the weapon fires. The trigger slack, or free play, is taken up first, and the squeeze is continued steadily until the hammer falls. If the trigger is squeezed properly, the firer will not know exactly when the hammer will fall; thus, he will not tend to flinch or heel, resulting in a bad shot. Novice firers must be trained to overcome the urge to anticipate recoil. Proper application of the fundamentals will lower this tendency.

b. To apply correct trigger squeeze, the trigger finger should contact the trigger between the tip of the finger and the second joint (without touching the weapon anywhere else). Where contact is made depends on the length of the firer's trigger finger. If pressure from the trigger finger is applied to the right side of the trigger or weapon, the strike of the bullet will be to the left. This is due to the normal hinge action of the fingers. When the fingers on the right hand are closed, as in gripping, they hinge or pivot to the left, thereby applying pressure to the left (with left-handed firers, this action is to the right). The firer must not apply pressure left or right but should increase finger pressure straight to the rear. Only the trigger finger should perform this action. Dry-fire training improves a firer's ability to move the trigger finger straight to the rear without cramping or increasing pressure on the hand grip.

c. Follow-through is the continued effort of the firer to maintain sight alignment before, during, and after the round has fired. The firer must continue the rearward movement of the finger even after the round has been fired. Releasing the trigger too soon after the round has been fired results in an uncontrolled shot, causing a missed target.

(1) The firer who is a good shot holds the sights of the weapon as nearly on the target center as possible and continues to squeeze the trigger with increasing pressure until the weapon fires.

(2) The soldier who is a bad shot tries to "catch his target" as his sight alignment moves past the target and fires the weapon at that instant. This is called ambushing, which causes trigger jerk.

> ✍ **NOTE**
>
> The trigger squeeze of the pistol, when fired in the single-action mode, is 5.50 pounds; when fired in double-action mode, it is 12.33 pounds. The firer must be aware of the mode in which he is firing. He must also practice squeezing the trigger in each mode to develop expertise in both single-action and double-action target engagements.

2-5. TARGET ENGAGEMENT

To engage a single target, the firer applies the method discussed in paragraph 2-4. When engaging multiple targets in combat, he engages the closest and most dangerous multiple target first and fires at it with two rounds. This is called controlled pairs. The firer then traverses and acquires the next target, aligns the sights in the center of mass, focuses on the front sight, applies trigger squeeze, and fires. He ensures his firing arm elbow and wrist are locked during all engagements. If he has missed the first target and has fired upon the second target, he shifts back to the first and engages it. Some problems in target engagement are as follows:

a. **Recoil Anticipation.** When a soldier first learns to shoot, he may begin to anticipate recoil. This reaction may cause him to tighten his muscles during or just before the hammer falls. He may fight the recoil by pushing the weapon downward in anticipating or reacting to its firing. In either case, the rounds will not hit the point of aim. A good method to show the firer that he is anticipating the recoil is the ball-and-dummy method (see paragraph 2-14).
b. **Trigger Jerk.** Trigger jerk occurs when the soldier sees that he has acquired a good sight picture at center mass and "snaps" off a round before the good sight picture is lost. This may become a problem, especially when the soldier is learning to use a flash sight picture (see paragraph 2-7b).
c. **Heeling.** Heeling is caused by a firer tightening the large muscle in the heel of the hand to keep from jerking the trigger. A firer who has had problems with jerking the trigger tries to correct the fault by tightening the bottom of the hand, which results in a heeled shot. Heeling causes the strike of the bullet to hit high on the firing hand side of the target. The firer can correct shooting errors by knowing and applying correct trigger squeeze.

2-6. POSITIONS

The qualification course is fired from a standing, kneeling, or crouch position. During qualification and combat firing, soldiers must practice all of the firing positions described below so they become natural movements. Though these positions seem natural, practice sessions must be conducted to ensure the habitual attainment of correct firing positions. Practice in assuming correct firing positions ensures that soldiers can quickly assume these positions without a conscious effort. Pistol marksmanship requires a soldier to rapidly apply all the fundamentals at dangerously close targets while under stress. Assuming a proper position to allow for a steady aim is critical to survival.

> ✍ **NOTE**
> During combat, there may not be time for a soldier to assume a position that will allow him to establish his natural point of aim. Firing from a covered position may require the soldier to adapt his shooting stance to available cover.

a. **Pistol-Ready Position.** In the pistol-ready position, hold the weapon in the one-hand grip. Hold the upper arm close to the body and the forearm at about a 45-degree angle. Point the weapon toward target center as you move forward (Figure 2-8).

Figure 2-8: Pistol-ready position.

b. **Standing Position without Support.** Face the target (Figure 2-9). Place feet a comfortable distance apart, about shoulder width. Extend the firing arm and attain a two-hand grip. The wrist and elbow of the firing arm are locked and pointed toward target center. Keep the body straight with the shoulders slightly forward of the buttocks.

Figure 2-9: Standing position without support.

c. **Kneeling Position.** In the kneeling position, ground only your firing-side knee as the main support (Figure 2-10). Vertically place your firing-side foot, used as the main support, under your buttocks. Rest your body weight on the heel and toes. Rest your nonfiring arm just above the elbow on the knee not used as the main body support. Use the two-handed grip for firing. Extend the firing arm, and lock the firing-arm elbow and wrist to ensure solid arm control.

Figure 2-10: Kneeling position.

d. **Crouch Position.** Use the crouch position when surprise targets are engaged at close range (Figure 2-11). Place the body in a forward crouch (boxer's stance) with the knees bent slightly and trunk bent forward from the hips to give faster recovery from recoil. Place the feet naturally in a position that allows another step toward the target. Extend the weapon straight toward the target, and lock the wrist and elbow of the firing arm. It is important to consistently train with this position, since the body will automatically crouch under conditions of stress such as combat. It is also a faster position from which to change direction of fire.

Figure 2-11: Crouch position.

e. **Prone Position.** Lie flat on the ground, facing the target (Figure 2-12). Extend your arms in front with the firing arm locked. (Your arms may have to be slightly unlocked for firing at high targets.) Rest the butt of the weapon on the ground for single, well-aimed shots. Wrap the fingers of the nonfiring hand around the fingers of the firing hand. Face forward. Keep your head down between your arms and behind the weapon as much as possible.

Figure 2-12: Prone position.

f. **Standing Position with Support.** Use available cover for support—for example, a tree or wall to stand behind (Figure 2-13). Stand behind a barricade with the firing side on line with the edge of the barricade. Place the knuckles of the nonfiring fist at eye level against the edge of the barricade. Lock the elbow and wrist of the firing arm. Move the foot on the nonfiring side forward until the toe of the boot touches the bottom of the barricade.

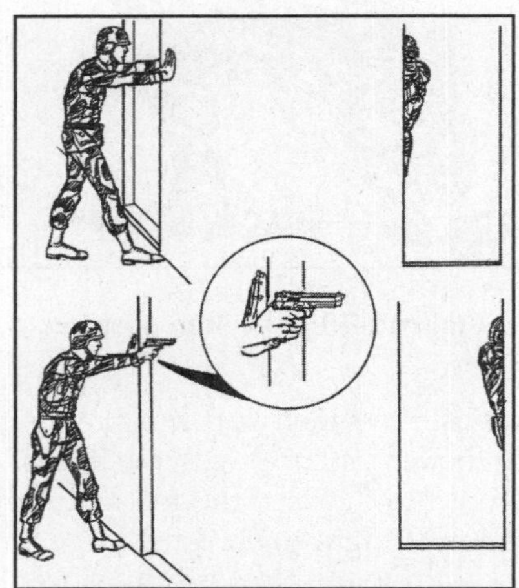

Figure 2-13: Standing position with support.

g. **Kneeling Supported Position.** Use available cover for support—for example, use a low wall, rocks, or vehicle (Figure 2-14). Place your firing-side knee on the ground. Bend the other knee and place the foot (nonfiring side) flat on the ground, pointing toward the target. Extend arms alongside and brace them against available cover. Lock the wrist and elbow of your firing arm. Place the nonfiring hand around the fist to support the firing arm. Rest the nonfiring arm just above the elbow on the nonfiring-side knee.

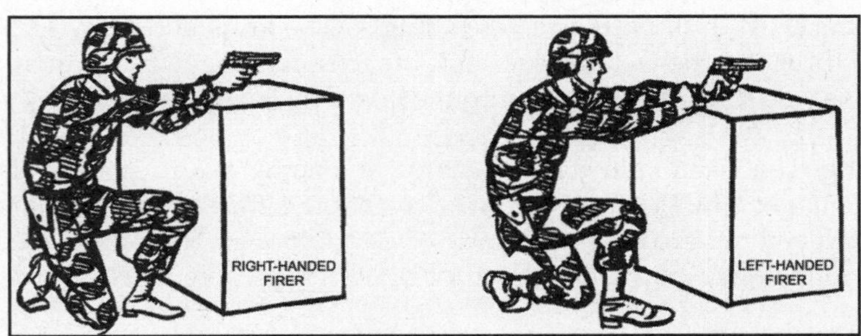

Figure 2-14: Kneeling supported.

SECTION II. COMBAT MARKSMANSHIP

After a soldier becomes proficient in the fundamentals of marksmanship, he progresses to advanced techniques of combat marksmanship. The main use of the pistol is to engage the enemy at close range with quick, accurate fire. In shooting encounters, it is not the first round fired that wins the engagement, but the first accurately fired round. The soldier should use his sights when engaging the enemy unless this would place the weapon within arm's reach of the enemy.

2-7. TECHNIQUES OF FIRING

Firing techniques include the use of hand-and-eye coordination, flash sight picture, quick-fire point shooting, and quick-fire sighting.

a. **Hand-and-Eye Coordination.** Hand-and-eye coordination is not a natural, instinctive ability for all soldiers. It is usually a learned skill obtained by practicing the use of a flash sight picture (see paragraph b below). The more a soldier practices raising the weapon to eye level and obtaining a flash sight picture, the more natural the relationship between soldier, sights, and target becomes. Eventually, proficiency elevates to a point so that the soldier can accurately engage targets in the dark. Each soldier must be aware of this trait and learn how to use it best. Poorly coordinated soldiers can achieve proficiency through close supervision from their trainers. Everyone has the ability to point at an object. Since pointing the forefinger at an object and extending the weapon toward a target are much the same, the combination of the two are natural. Making the soldier aware of this ability and teaching him how to apply it results in success when engaging enemy targets in combat.

(1) The eyes focus instinctively on the center of any object observed. After the object is sighted, the firer aligns his sights on the center of mass, focuses on the front sight, and applies proper trigger squeeze. Most crippling or killing hits result from maintaining the focus on the center of mass. The eyes must remain fixed on some part of the target throughout firing.

(2) When a soldier points, he instinctively points at the feature on the object on which his eyes are focused. An impulse from the brain causes the arm and hand to stop when the finger reaches the proper position. When the eyes are shifted to a new object or feature, the finger, hand, and arm also shift to this point. It is this inherent trait that can be used by the soldier to engage targets rapidly and accurately. This instinct is called hand-and-eye coordination.

b. **Flash Sight Picture.** Usually, when engaging an enemy at pistol range, the firer has little time to ensure a correct sight picture. The quick-kill (or natural point of aim) method does not always ensure a first-round hit. A compromise between a correct sight picture and the quick-kill method is known as a flash sight picture. As the soldier raises the weapon to eye level, his point of focus switches from the enemy to the front sight, ensuring that the front and rear sights are in proper alignment left and right, but not necessarily up and down. Pressure is applied to the trigger as the front sight is being acquired, and the hammer falls as the flash sight picture is confirmed. Initially, this method should be practiced slowly, with speed gained as proficiency increases.

c. **Quick-Fire Point Shooting.** This is for engaging an enemy at less than 5 yards and is also useful for night firing. Using a two-hand grip, the firer brings the weapon up close to the body until it reaches chin level. He then thrusts it forward until both arms are straight. The arms and body form a triangle, which can be aimed as a unit. In thrusting the weapon forward, the firer can imagine that there is a box between him and the enemy, and he is thrusting the weapon into the box. The trigger is smoothly squeezed to the rear as the elbows straighten.

d. **Quick-Fire Sighting.** This technique is for engaging an enemy at 5 to 10 yards away and only when there is no time available to get a full picture. The firing position is the same as for quick-fire point shooting. The sights are aligned left and right to save time, but not up and down. The firer must determine in practice what the sight picture will look like and where the front sight must be aimed to hit the enemy in the chest.

2-8. TARGET ENGAGEMENT

In close combat, there is seldom time to precisely apply all of the fundamentals of marksmanship. When a soldier fires a round at the enemy, he often does not know if he hits his target. Therefore, two rounds should be fired at the target. This is called controlled pairs. If the enemy continues to attack, two more shots should be placed in the pelvic area to break the body's support structure, causing the enemy to fall.

2-9. TRAVERSING

In close combat, the enemy may be attacking from all sides. The soldier may not have time to constantly change his position to adapt to new situations. The purpose of the crouching or kneeling 360-degree traverse is to fire in any direction without moving the feet.

a. **Crouching 360-Degree Traverse.** The following instructions are for a right-handed firer. The two-hand grip is used at all times except for over the right shoulder. The firer remains in the crouch position with feet almost parallel to each other. Turning will be natural on the balls of the feet.

(1) ***Over the Left Shoulder*** (Figure 2-15): The upper body is turned to the left, the weapon points to the left rear with the elbows of both arms bent. The left elbow is naturally bent more than the right elbow.

Figure 2-15: Traversing over the left shoulder.

(2) ***Traversing to the Left*** (Figure 2-16): The upper body turns to the right, and the right firing arm straightens out. The left arm is slightly bent.

(3) ***Traversing to the Front*** (Figure 2-17): The upper body turns to the front as the left arm straightens out. Both arms are straight forward.

Figure 2-16: Traversing to the left.

Figure 2-17: Traversing to the front.

(4) ***Traversing to the Right*** (Figure 2-18): The upper body turns to the right as both elbows bend. The right elbow is naturally bent more than the left.

Figure 2-18: Traversing to the right.

(5) ***Traversing to the Right Rear*** (Figure 2-19): The upper body continues to turn to the right until it reaches a point where it cannot go further comfortably. Eventually the left hand must be released from the fist grip, and the firer will be shooting to the right rear with the right hand.

Figure 2-19: Traversing to the right rear.

b. **Kneeling 360-Degree Traverse.** The following instructions are for right-handed firers. The hands are in a two-hand grip at all times. The unsupported kneeling position is used. The rear foot must be positioned to the left of the front foot.

(1) ***Traversing to the Left Side*** (Figure 2-20): The upper body turns to a comfortable position toward the left. The weapon is aimed to the left. Both elbows are bent with the left elbow naturally bent more than the right elbow.

(2) ***Traversing to the Front*** (Figure 2-21): The upper body turns to the front, and a standard unsupported kneeling position is assumed. The right firing arm is straight, and the left elbow is slightly bent.

(3) ***Traversing to the Right Side*** (Figure 2-22): The upper body turns to the right as both arms straighten out.

(4) ***Traversing to the Rear*** (Figure 2-23): The upper body continues to turn to the right as the left knee is turned to the right and placed on the ground. The right knee is lifted off the ground and becomes the forward knee. The right arm is straight, while the left arm is bent. The direction of the kneeling position has been reversed.

Figure 2-20: Traversing to the left, kneeling.

Figure 2-21: Traversing to the front, kneeling.

Figure 2-22: Traversing to the right, kneeling.

Figure 2-23: Traversing to the rear, kneeling.

(5) ***Traversing to the New Right Side*** (Figure 2-24): The upper body continues to the right. Both elbows are straight until the body reaches a point where it cannot go further comfortably. Eventually, the left hand must be released from the fist grip, and the firer is shooting to the right with the one-hand grip.

Figure 2-24: Traversing to the new right side, kneeling.

c. **Training Method.** This method can be trained and practiced anywhere and, with the firer simulating a two-hand grip, without a weapon. The firer should be familiar with firing in all five directions.

2-10. COMBAT RELOADING TECHNIQUES

Overlooked as a problem for many years, reloading has resulted in many casualties due to soldiers' hands shaking or errors such as dropped magazines, magazines placed in the pistol backwards, or empty magazines placed back into the weapon. The stress state induced by a life-threatening situation causes soldiers to do things they would not otherwise do. Consistent, repeated training is needed to avoid such mistakes.

> ✍ NOTE
> These procedures should be used only in combat, not on firing ranges.

a. Develop a consistent method for carrying magazines in the ammunition pouches. All magazines should face down with the bullets facing forward and to the center of the body.

b. Know when to reload. When possible, count the number of rounds fired. However, it is possible to lose count in close combat. If this happens, there is a distinct difference in recoil of the pistol when the last round has been fired. Change magazines when two rounds may be left—one in the magazine and one in the chamber. This prevents being caught with an empty weapon at a crucial time. Reloading is faster with a round in the chamber since time is not needed to release the slide.

c. Obtain a firm grip on the magazine. This precludes the magazine being dropped or difficulty in getting the magazine into the weapon. Ensure the knuckles of the hand are toward the body while gripping as much of the magazine as possible. Place the index finger high on the front of the magazine when withdrawing from the pouch. Use the index finger to guide the magazine into the magazine well.

d. Know which reloading procedure to use for the tactical situation. There are three systems of reloading: rapid, tactical, and one-handed. Rapid reloading is used when the soldier's life is in immediate danger and the reload must be accomplished quickly. Tactical reloading is used when there is more time and it is desirable to keep the replaced magazine because there are rounds still in it or it will be needed again. One-handed reloading is used when there is an arm injury.

(1) ***Rapid Reloading.***

(a) Place your hand on the next magazine in the ammunition pouch to ensure there is another magazine.

(b) Withdraw the magazine from the pouch while releasing the other magazine from the weapon. Let the replaced magazine drop to the ground.

(c) Insert the replacement magazine, guiding it into the magazine well with the index finger.

(d) Release the slide, if necessary.

(e) Pick up the dropped magazine if time allows. Place it in your pocket, not back into the ammunition pouch where it may become mixed with full magazines.

(2) ***Tactical Reloading.***

(a) Place your hand on the next magazine in the ammunition pouch to ensure there is a remaining magazine.

(b) Withdraw the magazine from the pouch.

(c) Drop the used magazine into the palm of the nonfiring hand, which is the same hand holding the replacement magazine.

(d) Insert the replacement magazine, guiding it into the magazine well with the index finger.

(e) Release the slide, if necessary.

(f) Place the used magazine into a pocket. Do not mix it with full magazines.

(3) ***One-Hand Reloading, Right Hand.***

(a) Push the magazine release button with the thumb.

(b) Place the safety ON with the thumb if the slide is forward.

(c) Place the weapon backwards into the holster.

✍ NOTE

If placing the weapon in the holster backwards is a problem, place the weapon between the calf and thigh to hold the weapon.

(d) Insert the replacement magazine.
(e) Withdraw the weapon from the holster.
(f) Remove the safety with the thumb if the slide is forward, or push the slide release if the slide is back.

(4) ***One-Hand Reloading, Left Hand.***
(a) Push the magazine release button with the middle finger.
(b) Place the weapon backwards into the holster.

✍ NOTE

If placing the weapon in the holster backwards is a problem, place the weapon between the calf and thigh to hold the weapon.

(c) Insert the replacement magazine.
(d) Remove the weapon from the holster.
(e) Remove the safety with the thumb if the slide is forward, or push the slide release lever with the middle finger if the slide is back.

2-11. POOR VISIBILITY FIRING

Poor visibility firing with any weapon is difficult since shadows can be misleading to the soldier. This is mainly true during EENT and EMNT (a half hour before dark and a half hour before dawn). Even though the pistol is a short-range weapon, the hours of darkness and poor visibility further decrease its effect. To compensate, the soldier must use the three principles of night vision.

a. **Dark Adaptation.** This process conditions the eyes to see during poor visibility conditions. The eyes usually need about 30 minutes to become 98-percent adapted in a totally darkened area.
b. **Off-Center Vision.** When looking at an object in daylight, a person looks directly at it. However, at night he would see the object only for a few seconds. To see an object in darkness, he must concentrate on it while looking 6 to 10 degrees away from it.
c. **Scanning.** This is the short, abrupt, irregular movement of the firer's eyes around an object or area every 4 to 10 seconds. When artificial illumination is used, the firer uses night fire techniques to engage targets, since targets seem to shift without moving.

2–12. NUCLEAR, BIOLOGICAL, CHEMICAL FIRING

When firing a pistol under NBC conditions, the firer should use optical inserts, if applicable. Firing in MOPP levels 1 through 3 should not be a problem for the firer. Unlike wearing a protective mask while firing a rifle, the firer's sight picture will be acquired the same as without a protective mask. MOPP4 is the only level that may present a problem for a firer since gloves are worn. Gloves may require the firer to adjust his grip to attain a proper grip and proper trigger squeeze. Firers should practice firing in MOPP4 to become proficient in NBC firing.

SECTION III. COACHING AND TRAINING AIDS

Throughout preparatory marksmanship training, the coach-and-pupil method of training should be used. The proficiency of a pupil depends on how well his coach performs his duties. This section provides detailed information on coaching techniques and training aids for pistol marksmanship.

2-13. COACHING

The coach assists the firer by correcting errors, ensuring he takes proper firing positions, and ensuring he observes all safety precautions. The criteria for selecting coaches are a command responsibility; coaches must have experience in pistol marksmanship above that of the student firer. Duties of the coach during instruction practice and record firing include:

a. Checking that the—
   - Weapon is cleared.
   - Ammunition is clean.
   - Magazines are clean and operational.

b. Observing the firer to see that he—
   - Takes the correct firing position.
   - Loads the weapon properly and only on command.
   - Takes up the trigger slack correctly.
   - Squeezes the trigger correctly (see paragraph 2-4).
   - Calls the shot each time he fires (except for quick fire and rapid fire).
   - Holds his breath correctly (see paragraph 2-3).
   - Lowers his weapon and rests his arm when he does not fire a round within 5 to 6 seconds.

c. Having the firer breathe deeply several times to relax if he is tense.

2-14. BALL-AND-DUMMY METHOD

In this method, the coach loads the weapon for the firer. He may hand the firer a loaded weapon or an empty one. When firing the empty weapon, the firer observes that in anticipating recoil he is forcing the weapon downward as the hammer falls. Repetition of the ball-and-dummy method helps to alleviate recoil anticipation.

2-15. CALLING THE SHOT

To call the shot is to state where the bullet should strike the target according to the sight picture at the instant the weapon fires—for example: "high," "a little low," "to the left," "to the right," or "bull's-eye." Another method of calling the shot is the clock system—for example, a three-ring hit at 8 o'clock, a four-ring hit at 3 o'clock. Another method is to provide the firer with a target center (placed beside him on the firing line). As soon as the shot is fired, the firer must place a finger on the target face or center where he expects the round to hit on the target. This method avoids guessing and computing for the firer. The immediate placing of the finger on the target face gives an accurate call. If the firer does not call his shot correctly in range firing, he is not concentrating on sight alignment and trigger squeeze. Thus, he does not know that his sight picture is as the weapon fires.

2-16. SLOW-FIRE EXERCISE

The slow-fire exercise is one of the most important exercises for both amateur and competitive marksmen. Coaches should ensure soldiers practice this exercise as much as possible. This is a dry-fire exercise.

a. To perform the slow-fire exercise, the firer assumes the standing position with the weapon pointed at the target. The firer should begin by using a two-hand grip, progressing to the one-hand grip as his skill increases. He takes in a normal breath and lets part of it out, locking the remainder in his lungs by closing his throat. He then relaxes, aims at the target, takes the correct sight alignment and sight picture, takes up the trigger slack, and squeezes the trigger straight to the rear with steady, increasing pressure until the hammer falls, simulating firing.

b. If the firer does not cause the hammer to fall in 5 or 6 seconds, he should come to the pistol ready position, and rest his arm and hand. He then starts the procedure again. The action sequence that makes up this process can be summed up by the key word BRASS. It is a word the firer should think of each time he fires his weapon:

Breathe	Take a normal breath, let part of it out, and lock the remainder in the lungs by closing the throat.
Relax	Relax the body muscles.
Aim	Take correct sight alignment and sight placement, and focus the eye at the top of the front sight.
Slack	Take up the trigger slack.
Squeeze	Squeeze the trigger straight to the rear with steadily increasing pressure without disturbing sight alignment until the hammer falls.

c. Coaches should observe the front sight for erratic movements during the application of trigger squeeze. Proper application of trigger squeeze allows the hammer to fall without the front sight moving. A small bouncing movement of the front sight is acceptable. Firers should call the shot by the direction of movement of the front sight (high, low, left, or right).

2-17. AIR-OPERATED PISTOL, .177 MM

The air-operated pistol is used as a training device to teach the soldier the method of quick fire, to increase confidence in his ability, and to afford him more practice firing. A range can be set up almost anywhere with a minimum of effort and coordination, which is ideal for USAR and NG. If conducted on a standard range, live firing of pistols can be conducted along with the firing of the .177-mm air-operated pistol. Due to light recoil and little noise of the pistol, the soldier can concentrate on fundamentals. This helps build confidence because the soldier can hit a target faster and more accurately. The air-operated pistol should receive the same respect as any firearm. A thorough explanation of the weapon and a safety briefing are given to each soldier.

2-18. QUICK-FIRE TARGET TRAINING DEVICE

The QTTD (Figures 2-25 and 2-26) is used with the .177-mm air-operated pistol.

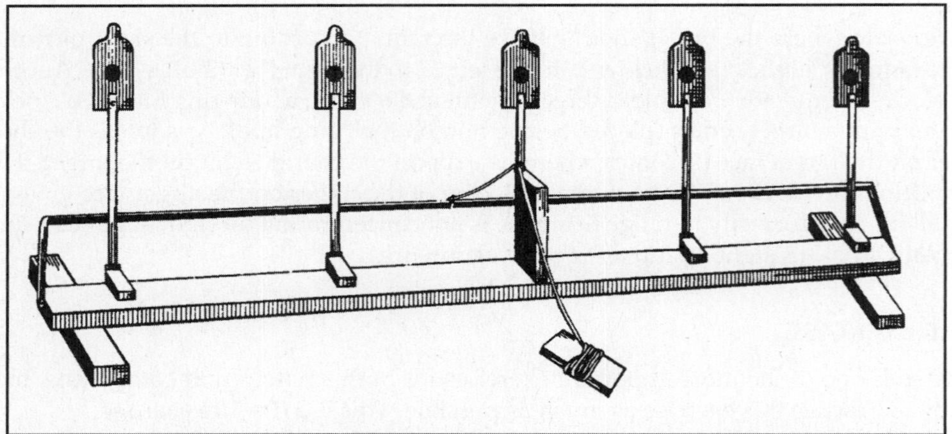

Figure 2-25: The quick-fire target training device.

a. **Phase I.** From 10 feet, five shots at a 20-foot miniature E-type silhouette. After firing each shot, the firer and coach discuss the results and make corrections.
b. **Phase II.** From 15 feet, five shots at a 20-foot miniature E-type silhouette. The same instructions apply to this exercise as for Phase I.
c. **Phase III.** From 20 feet, five shots at a 20-foot miniature E-type silhouette. The same instructions apply to this exercise as for Phases I and II.
d. **Phase IV.** From 15 feet, six shots at two 20-foot miniature E-type silhouettes. This exercise is conducted the same as the previous one, except that the firer is introduced to fire distribution. The targets on the QTTD are held in the up position so they cannot be knocked down when hit.

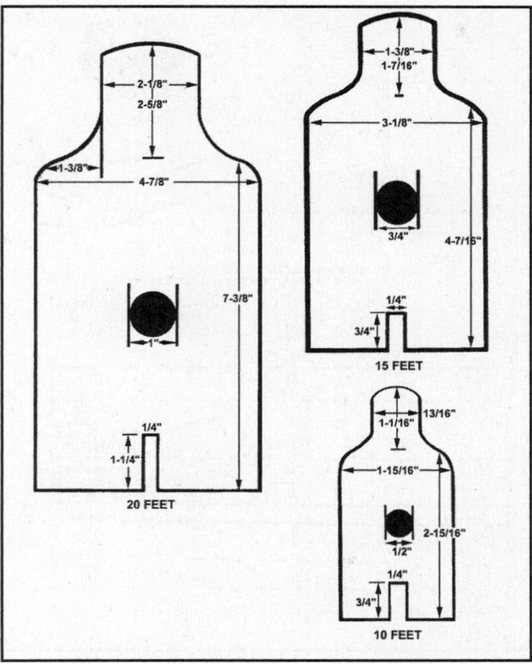

Figure 2-26: Dimensions for the QTTD.

(1) The firer first engages the 20-foot miniature E-type silhouette on the extreme right of the QTTD (see Figure 2-27). He then traverses between targets and engages the same type target on the extreme left of the QTTD. The firer again shifts back to reengage the first target. The procedure is used to teach the firer to instinctively return to the first target if he misses it with his first shot.

(2) The firer performs this exercise twice, firing three shots each time. Before firing the second time, the coach and firer should discuss the errors made during the first exercise.

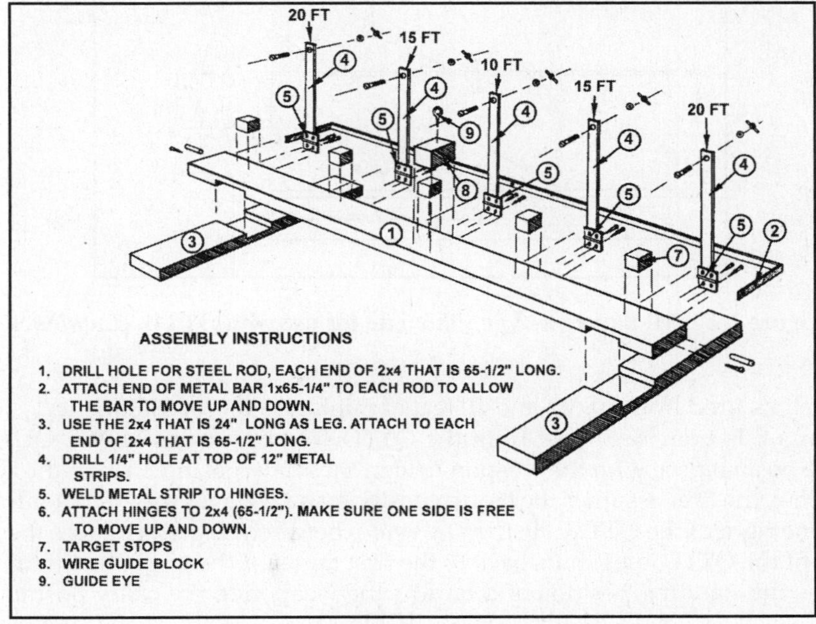

Figure 2-27: Miniature E-type silhouette for use with QTTD.

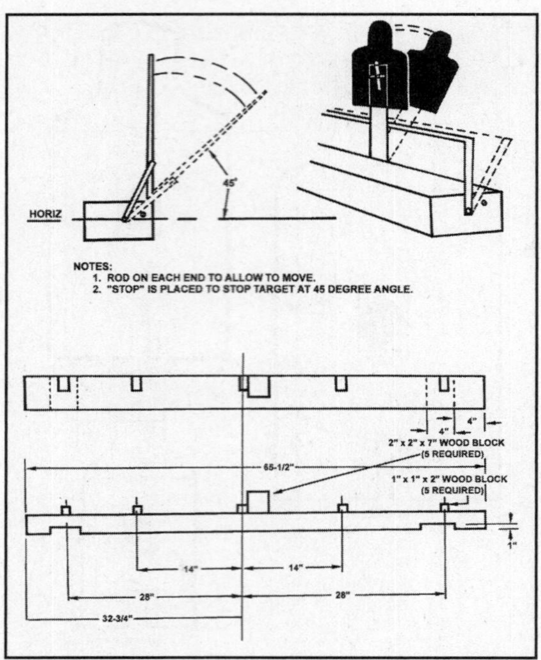

Figure 2-27: Miniature E-type silhouette for use with QTTD. ***(Continued)***

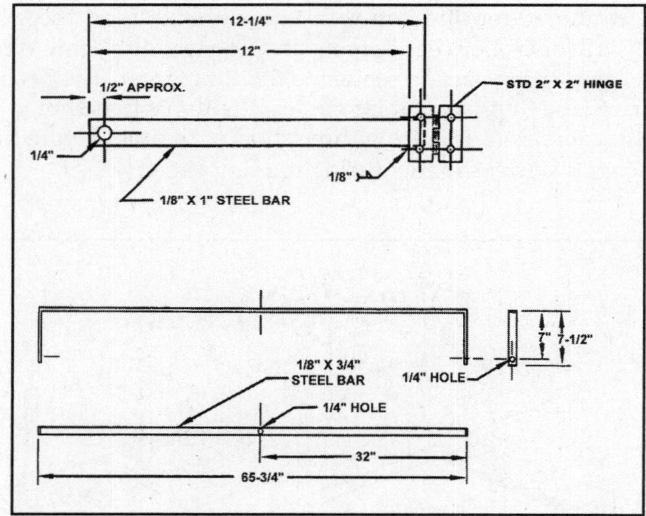

Figure 2-27: Miniature E-type silhouette for use with QTTD. ***(Continued)***

e. **Phase V.** Seven shots fired from 20, 15, and 10 feet at miniature E-type silhouettes.

(1) The firer starts this exercise 30 feet from the QTTD. The command MOVE OUT is given, and the firer steps out at a normal pace with the weapon held in the ready position. Upon the command FIRE (given at the 20-foot line), the firer assumes the crouch position and engages the 20-foot miniature E-type silhouette on the extreme right of the QTTD. He then traverses between targets, engages the same type target on the extreme left of the QTTD, and shifts back to the first target. If the target is still up, he engages it. The firer then assumes the standing position and returns the weapon to the ready position. (Upon completion of each exercise, the coach makes corrections as the firer returns to the standing position.)

(2) On the command MOVE OUT, the firer again steps off at a normal pace. Upon the command FIRE (given at the 15-foot line), he engages the 15-foot targets on the QTTD. The same sequence of fire distribution is followed as with the previous exercise.
(3) During this exercise, the firer moves forward on command until he reaches the 10-foot line. At the command FIRE, the firer engages the 10-foot miniature E-type silhouette in the center of the QTTD.

2-19. RANGE FIRING COURSES

Range firing is conducted after the firers have satisfactorily completed preparatory marksmanship training. The range firing courses are:

a. **Instructional.** Instructional firing is practice firing on a range, using the assistance of a coach.
   (1) All personnel authorized or required to fire the pistol receive 12 hours of preliminary instruction that includes the following:
   - Disassembly and assembly.
   - Loading, firing, unloading, and immediate action.
   - Preparatory marksmanship.
   - Care and cleaning.

   (2) The tables fired for instructional practice are prescribed in the combat pistol qualification course in Appendix A. During the instructional firing, the CPQC is fired with a coach or instructor.

b. **Combat Pistol Qualification.** The CPQC stresses the fundamentals of quick fire. It is the final test of a soldier's proficiency and the basis for his marksmanship classification. After the soldier completes the instructional practice firing, he shoots the CPQC for record. Appendix A provides a detailed description of the CPQC tables, standards, and conduct of fire. TC 25-8 provides a picture of the course.

> ✍ **NOTE**
> The alternate pistol qualification course (APQC) can be used for sustainment/qualification if the CPQC is not available.

c. **Military Police Firearms Qualification.** The military police firearms qualification course is a practical course of instruction for police firearms training (see FM 19-10).

SECTION IV. SAFETY

Safety must be observed during all marksmanship training. Listed below are the precautions for each phase of training. It is not intended to replace AR 385-63 or local range regulations. Range safety requirements vary according to the requirements of the course of fire. It is mandatory that the latest range safety directives and local range regulations be consulted to determine current safety requirements.

2-20. REQUIREMENTS

The following requirements apply to all marksmanship training.

a. Display a red flag prominently on the range during all firing.
b. Soldiers must handle weapons carefully and never point them at anyone except the enemy in actual combat.
c. Always assume a weapon is loaded until it has been thoroughly examined and found to contain no ammunition.
d. Indicate firing limits with red and white striped poles visible to all firers.
e. Never place obstructions in the muzzle of any weapon about to be fired.
f. Keep weapons in a prescribed area with proper safeguards.
g. Refrain from smoking on the range near ammunition, explosives, or flammables.

2-21. BEFORE FIRING

The following requirements must be met before conducting marksmanship training.

a. Close and post guards at all prescribed roadblocks and barriers.
b. Ensure all weapons are clear of ammunition and obstructions, and all slides are locked to the rear.
c. Brief all firers on the firing limits of the range and firing lanes. Firers must keep their fires within prescribed limits.
d. Ensure all firers receive instructions on how to load and unload the weapon and on safety features.
e. Brief all personnel on all safety aspects of fire and of the range pertaining to the conduct of the courses.
f. No one moves forward of the firing line without permission of the tower operator, safety officer, or OIC.
g. Weapons are loaded and unlocked only on command from the tower operator except during conduct of the courses requiring automatic magazine changes.
h. Weapons are not handled except on command from the tower operator.
i. Firers must keep their weapons pointed downrange when loading, preparing to fire, or firing.

2-22. DURING FIRING

The following requirements apply during marksmanship training.

a. A firer does not move from his position until his weapon has been cleared by safety personnel and placed in its proper safety position. An exception is the assault phase.
b. During Table 5 of the CPQC, firers remain on line with other firers on their right or left.
c. Firers must fire only in their own firing lane and must not point the weapon into an adjacent lane, mainly during the assault phase.
d. Firers treat the air-operated pistol as a loaded weapon, observing the same safety precautions as with other weapons.
e. All personnel wear helmets during live-fire exercises.
f. Firers hold the weapon in the raised position except when preparing to fire. They then hold weapons in the ready position, pointed downrange.

2-23. AFTER FIRING

Safety personnel inspect all weapons to ensure they are clear. A check is conducted to determine if any brass or live ammunition is in the possession of the soldiers. Once cleared, pistols are secured with the slides locked to the rear.

2-24. INSTRUCTIONAL PRACTICE AND RECORD QUALIFICATION FIRING

During these phases of firing, safety personnel ensure that—

a. The firer understands the conduct of the exercise.
b. The firer has the required ammunition and understands the commands for loading and unloading.
c. The firer complies with all commands from the tower operator.
d. Firers maintain proper alignment with other firers while moving downrange.
e. Weapons are always pointed downrange.
f. Firers fire within the prescribed range limits.
g. Weapons are cleared after each phase of firing, and the tower-operator is aware of the clearance.
h. Malfunctions or failures to fire that are due to no fault of the firer are reported immediately. On command of the tower operator, the weapon is cleared and action is taken to allow the firer to continue with the exercise.

Army Combat Machine Gun Fundamentals

CHAPTER 1

Machine Gun Marksmanship Training

This chapter aids trainers in preparing and conducting machine gun marksmanship training for the machine gun. Machine gun marksmanship training is conducted in three phases: preliminary gunnery, basic gunnery, and advanced gunnery in Chapter 2.

SECTION I. INTRODUCTION

Marksmanship begins with non-firing individual skill proficiency and concludes with collective proficiency firing under demanding conditions.

1-1. OBJECTIVES

The objectives of machine gun marksmanship training are to produce gunners that are thoroughly capable of the following:

a. **Accurate Initial Burst.** Obtaining an accurate initial burst of fire on the target is essential to good marksmanship. This requires the gunner to estimate range to the target, set the sights, and apply the fundamentals of marksmanship while engaging targets.
b. **Adjustment of Fire.** The gunner must observe the strike of the rounds when the initial burst is fired. If not on target, he manipulates the T&E mechanism until the rounds do strike the target. The assistant gunner must be proficient in observing the strike of rounds and in observing and using tracers so the gunner can rapidly relay the machine gun on the target for engagement.
c. **Speed.** Speed is also essential to good marksmanship; it is attained by practice in both dry-fire and live-fire exercises. It is an acquired skill gained through extensive training that combines other skills when delivering fire. Speed should not be stressed to the detriment of accuracy.

1-2. TRAINING PHASES

Marksmanship training for the machine gun is progressive in nature. It begins with nonfiring individual skill proficiency and concludes with collective proficiency firing under demanding conditions. Gunners and leaders must master the fundamentals before attempting individual and collective firings. More effective and efficient marksmanship occurs if live firing is preceded with good preliminary marksmanship training. Likewise, proficient individual firing will achieve more proficient collective firing.

a. **Preliminary Gunnery.** In this phase, the gunner learns and demonstrates proficiency on individual skills that prepare him to fire live ammunition. This includes mastering mechanical training, the four fundamentals of marksmanship, T&E manipulation, sight adjustments, crew drill, and fire commands.
b. **Basic Gunnery.** In this phase, the gunner applies the fundamentals in live-fire exercises during day and night conditions. This includes zeroing, 10-meter firing with crew drill, field zeroing, and transition firing with crew drill.
c. **Advanced Gunnery.** In this phase, gunners are trained on combat techniques of fire, techniques of employment, and live-fire exercise during NBC conditions.

1-3. TRAINING STRATEGY

Training strategy involves the overall concept for integrating resources into a program that trains individual and collective skills needed to perform a wartime mission. The goal of a marksmanship program is to produce well-trained gunners who can win and survive on the battlefield.

a. Leaders implement training strategies for machine gun marksmanship in TRADOC institutions (IET, NCOES, IOBC, and IOAC) and in units. The overall training strategy is multifaceted and is inclusive of the specific strategies used in institution and unit programs. Also included are the supporting strategies that use resources such as publications, ranges, ammunition, training aids, devices, simulators, and simulations. These strategies focus on developing critical soldier skills and leader skills that are required for the intended outcome.

b. The training strategies contain two components: initial training and sustainment training. Both may include individual and collective skills. Initial training is critical because a task that is taught correctly and learned well is retained longer. When an interim of nonuse occurs, well-trained skills are more quickly regained and sustained. The more difficult and complex the task, the harder it is to sustain the skill. Personnel turnover plays a major factor in the decay of collective skills, since the loss of critical team members requires retraining to regain proficiency. Retraining becomes necessary when a long period elapses between initial and sustainment training sessions or when the training doctrine is altered.

c. The training strategy for machine gun marksmanship begins in the institutions and continues in the unit. Figure 1-1, illustrates an example of this overall process, which provides a concept of the flow of unit sustainment training. Combat arms IET provides field units with soldiers who are familiar with standards in basic marksmanship tasks. The soldiers graduating from these courses have been trained to maintain their machine guns and to hit a variety of targets. They have learned range determination, target detection, application of marksmanship fundamentals, and other skills needed to engage a target.

d. Additional skills trained in the institution include techniques for employment, classes of fire, and fire commands. These skills must then be reinforced in the unit. Related soldier skills of camouflage, cover and concealment, maneuver, and preparation and selection of a fighting position are addressed in STP 21–24-SMCT, which must be integrated into tactical training.

e. Training continues in units on the basic skills taught in combat arms IET. Additional skills, such as suppressive fire and supporting fire, are trained and then integrated into collective training exercises, which include squad and platoon live-fire exercises. The strategy for sustaining the basic marksmanship skills that is taught in combat arms IET involves periodic preliminary gunnery, followed by 10-meter, transition firing, and qualification range firing. However, a unit must establish a year-round program to sustain skills. Key elements include training the trainers and refresher training of non-firing skills.

f. In the unit, individual proficiency and leader proficiency of marksmanship tasks are integrated into collective training that includes squad, section, and platoon drills and STXs. Collective tasks are evaluated to standard and discussed during leader and trainer after-action reviews. Objective evaluations of both individual and unit proficiency provide readiness indicators and future training requirements.

g. A critical step in the Army's overall marksmanship training strategy is to train the trainers and leaders first. Leader courses include limited machine gun training, but unit publications will help develop officer and NCO proficiency necessary to plan and conduct gunnery training and to evaluate the effectiveness of their programs. Proponent schools provide training support materials to include field manuals, training aids, devices, simulators, and programs that are doctrinal foundations and guidance for training the force.

h. Once the soldier understands the weapon, knows how to zero, and has demonstrated proficiency at 10-meter and transition ranges, he should be exposed to more difficult ranges and scenarios.

i. IET culminates in the soldier's proficiency assessment, which is conducted on the 10-meter and transition and record fire ranges. Unit training culminates in a collective, live-fire, tactical exercise that provides an overview of unit proficiency and training effectiveness.

1-4. TRAINING FOR COMBAT CONDITIONS

The trainer must realize that qualification is not an end but a step towards reaching combat requirements. To reach this goal, the gunner not only considers his position and the use of his weapon, but also some of the following combat conditions as well.

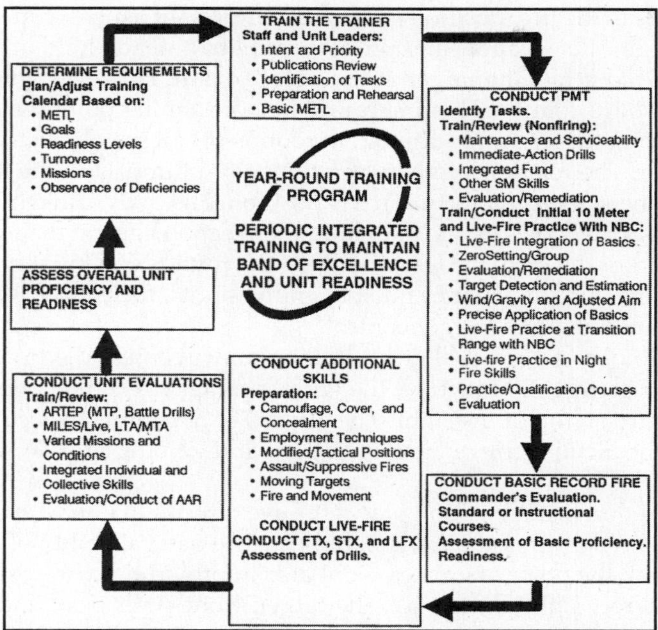

Figure 1-1: Unit marksmanship sustainment strategy.

a. Most engagements will be within 300 meters; however, the gunner must still engage targets out to the maximum range of the machine gun.
b. Enemy personnel are seldom visible except when assaulting.
c. Most combat fire must be directed at an area where the enemy has been detected or where he is suspected of being but cannot be seen. Area targets consist of objects or outlines of men irregularly spaced along covered and concealed areas (ground folds, hedges, borders of woods).
d. Most combat targets can be detected by smoke, flash, dust, noise, or movement, but the targets are only visible for a moment.
e. Some combat targets can be engaged by using reference points, predetermined fire, or range card data.
f. The nature of the target and irregularities of terrain and vegetation may require a gunner to move from one position to another to place effective fire on the target. The most stable position for the gunner is the prone tripod-supported position.
g. Most combat targets have a low contrast outline and are obscured. Therefore, choosing an aiming point in elevation is difficult.
h. Time-stressed fire in combat can be divided into three types: a single, fleeting target that must be engaged quickly; distributed targets that must be engaged within the time they remain available; and a surprise target that must be engaged at once with instinctive, accurate fire.

SECTION II. PRELIMINARY GUNNERY

Once a soldier is proficient in the characteristics and mechanical training of the machine gun, he is ready to be trained on the four fundamentals of marksmanship. As the gunner learns the fundamentals, he should be required to manipulate the sights, use his body to shift and lay the sights on the target, use the T&E mechanism to lay on the target, conduct crew drill, and respond to fire commands. Dry-fire exercises are an excellent method for training to proficiency.

1-5. MARKSMANSHIP FUNDAMENTALS

The four fundamentals for firing are the same for all machine guns, they are *steady position, aim, breath control, and trigger control.*

a. **Steady Position.** In automatic fire, position is the most important aspect of marksmanship. If the gunner has a good zero, correctly aims his weapon, and properly applies a steady hold in firing a burst of automatic fire, the first round of that burst hits the target at the point of aim. However, this procedure is not necessarily true of the second and third rounds. The first round hits the aiming point the same as when a round is fired singularly. The recoil from the first and subsequent rounds progressively disturbs the lay of the weapon with each round of the burst. The relationship between the point of impact of the first and subsequent rounds of the burst depends on the stability of the gunner's position. His body, directly behind the weapon, serves as the foundation, and his grip serves as a lock to hold the weapon against the foundation. The better the body alignment and the steadier the grip, the less dispersed the rounds of a burst of automatic fire will be.

b. **Aim.** To aim the machine gun, the gunner must align the sights, focus his eye, obtain a correct sight picture, control his breathing, and maintain trigger control.

(1) ***Sight Alignment.*** To obtain correct alignment, the gunner centers the front sight post in the aperture of the rear sight. For a correct sight picture, the gunner centers the target over the front sight post so that it appears to rest lightly on top of the sight. The aspects of obtaining an accurate initial burst through sight alignment and sight picture, trigger manipulation, and zeroing are the same for tripod training as for bipod training.

(2) ***Focus of the Eye.*** A good firing position places the eye directly in line with the center of the rear sight. The gunner must focus on the tip of the front sight post. The natural ability of the eye to center objects in the rear sight and to seek the point of greatest light aids in providing correct sight alignment.

(3) ***Sight Picture.*** A correct sight picture has the target, front sight post, and rear sight aligned. The sight picture consists of sight alignment and placement of the aiming point on the target. The gunner aligns the front sight post in the center of the rear sight and then aligns the sights with the target. The top of the front sight post is aligned on the center base of the target (Figure 1-2).

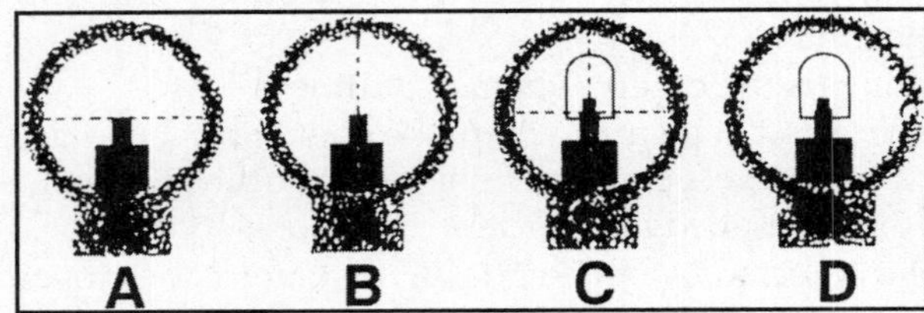

Figure 1-2: Sight picture.

c. **Breath Control.** When firing in bipod-mounted mode, two types of breath control are used. When firing single shots, as in zeroing, the gunner stops breathing after most of the air has been exhaled during the normal breathing cycle. He fires before he feels any discomfort. During automatic fire, ideally, the gunner exhales and stops his breath when pressing the trigger. He does not have time to take deep breaths between bursts. He must hold his breath before each burst or adapt his breathing by taking quick shallow breaths or taking deeper breaths between several bursts.

d. **Trigger Control.** Pressing the trigger straight to the rear and releasing it helps control the number of rounds in each burst and prevents disturbing the lay of the weapon. For this the gunner must learn how to manipulate the trigger so that he may get the desired burst he wishes to obtain.

1-6. FIRING POSITIONS

The bipod-supported prone and fighting positions and the tripod-supported prone and fighting positions are covered in preliminary gunnery.

a. **Prone Position, Bipod-Supported.**

(1) Assume a prone position to the rear of the weapon (place the shoulder rest on your firing shoulder for the M249 and M60 only). An imaginary line drawn through the weapon should bisect the firing shoulder and buttock, and continue through the heel of your foot.

(2) Spread your legs a comfortable distance apart with your heels as close to the ground as possible, yet comfortable.

(3) Grasp the pistol grip with your firing hand. Place the fleshy end of the index finger so that it rest lightly on the trigger. Place your non-firing hand on the small of the stock with your thumb curled underneath. Then slide your non-firing hand forward until your little finger touches the receiver, so your aiming point will always be the same.
(4) Place your cheek against the forefinger of your non-firing hand to form a stock weld. Try to position your non-firing hand and cheek at the same spot on the stock each time you fire the weapon. The stock weld should provide for a natural line of sight through the center of the rear sight aperture to the front sight post and to the target. Relax your neck so that your cheek rests on your forefinger naturally.
(5) Apply a firm, steady pressure rearward and down, holding the weapon tightly into the hollow of your shoulder while aiming and firing.
(6) Keep your shoulders level and elbows about an equal distance from the receiver of the weapon (Figure 1-3).

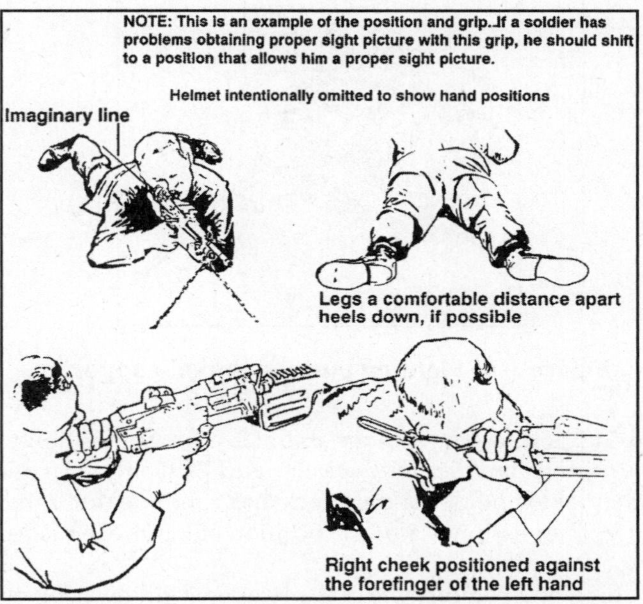

Figure 1-3: Prone position, bipod-supported.

✍ **NOTES**

1. The assistant gunner assumes a prone position along the left side of the gunner to load ammunition and observe.
2. Left-handed firing with the M249 and M60 is discouraged because the ejection pattern of some weapons is almost directly to the rear. When firing any machine gun using the tripod, the gunner must use his left hand to manipulate the T&E mechanism, therefore precluding the gunner from firing the machine gun left handed.
3. If a gunner has problems obtaining a proper sight picture, he should shift to a position that allows him to do so.

b. **Fighting Position, Bipod-Supported.** This is an excellent position that provides a stable firing platform. The depth of the fighting position and the support should be adjusted for the height and arm length of the gunner. This allows for a steadier position.
(1) Extend the bipod legs and place the machine gun in front of the position.
(2) Place your right (firing side foot) foot sideways against the rear of the fighting position and lean forward until your chest is squarely against the forward wall.
(3) Raise the folding shoulder rest and place it on your firing shoulder (M249 and M60 only). Keep your shoulders level or parallel to the ground.

(4) Grasp the pistol grip with your firing hand, place the fleshy end of the index finger so that it rests lightly on the trigger. Place your non-firing hand on the small of the stock and ensure that your thumb is curled underneath.
(5) Place your cheek against the forefinger of your non-firing hand to form a stock weld. Try to position your non-firing hand and cheek at the same spot on the stock each time you fire the weapon. The stock weld should provide for a natural line of sight through the center of the rear sight aperture to the front sight post and to the target. Relax your neck so that your cheek rests on your forefinger naturally.
(6) Apply a firm, steady pressure rearward and down, holding the weapon tight into the hollow of your shoulder while aiming and firing.
(7) Keep your shoulders level and elbows about an equal distance from the receiver of the weapon (Figure 1-4).

Figure 1-4: Fighting position, bipod-supported.

c. **Prone Position, Tripod-Supported.** The gunner assumes a prone position to the rear of the weapon (place the shoulder rest on your firing shoulder for the M249 and M60 only). An imaginary line drawn through the weapon should bisect the right shoulder and buttock and continue through the heel of his foot. When using the tripod, the assistant gunner assumes a prone position along the left side of the gunner to load ammunition and observe.
(1) The gunner spreads his legs a comfortable distance apart with his heels as close to the ground as possible and still be comfortable.
(2) Grasps the pistol grip with his right hand with the fleshy end of his index finger resting lightly on the trigger. (The machine gun is not fired left-handed with the tripod because turning the traverse handwheel with the right hand is difficult.)
(3) Grasps the elevating handwheel with his left hand, palm down. Exerts a firm downward pressure with both hands while aiming and firing.
(4) Places both elbows on the ground between the tripod legs and his body. The position of his elbows raises or lowers his body in relation to the machine gun.
(5) Places his shoulder lightly against the stock without applying any pressure.
(6) Rests his cheek lightly (if at all) against the stock (Figure 1-5).

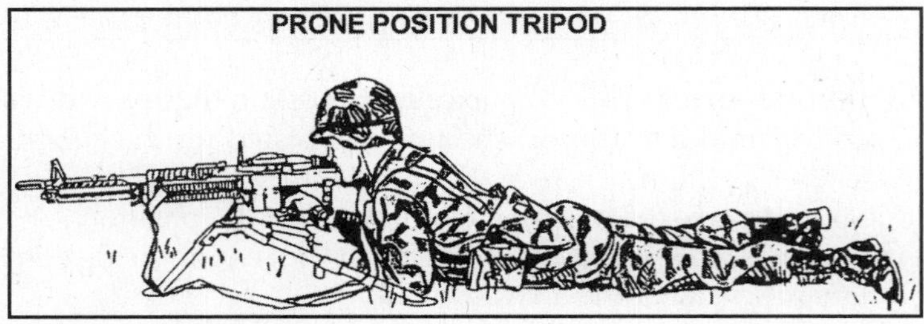

Figure 1-5: Prone position, tripod-supported.

d. **Fighting Position, Tripod-Supported.** (Figure 1-6.) The gunner places his right (firing side) foot sideways against the rear of the fighting position and leans forward until his chest is squarely against the wall.
   (1) The gunner grasps the pistol grip with his firing hand with the fleshy end of his index finger resting lightly on the trigger.
   (2) Places his left hand on the elevating handwheel, palm down, exerting a firm downward pressure to make either minor or major adjustments in deflection or elevation. (The weapon is stabilized by the support of the tripod.)
   (3) Places his elbows on the inside and does not touch the tripod.
   (4) Places little or no pressure against the stock of the gun.
   (5) Rests his cheek lightly, if at all, against the stock.

Figure 1-6: Fighting position, tripod-supported.

1-7. NIGHT FIRE

Although the same four fundamentals of marksmanship are used for night firing, adjustments must be made to accommodate the night vision devices.

a. **Bipod.**
   (1) ***Steady Position.*** When firing unassisted, changes in head position and stock weld are necessary especially when using weapon-target alignment techniques. Normally, the gunner positions his head so that he can align the weapon on the target and look over the sights. In some cases, the lower part of his jaw makes firm contact with his nonfiring hand on the stock, with his eyes an inch or so above the sights. The key is to use the natural pointing ability to align the machine gun on the target. When using NVDs, the head position and stock weld must be altered to be able to use the device. Sometimes height of the NVD may make this impossible. NVDs alter the machine gun's weight and center of gravity. The gunner must compensate by exerting greater pressure and control with his firing hand on the pistol grip and his nonfiring hand on the stock.
   (2) ***Aim.*** Various modifications are necessary when aiming the machine gun at night. When firing unassisted, the gunner uses off-center vision instead of pinpoint focus. Both eyes are open and focused downrange on the target and not on the sights. Rather than aim using the sights, the gunner looks over the sights and points the machine gun where he is looking. The normal tendency is to fire high so the gunner must improve weapon-target alignment by pointing slightly low to compensate. When using NVDs, the gunner uses the necessary aiming process to use the device.
   (3) ***Breath Control.*** This fundamental is not affected by night firing conditions; however, wobble is more pronounced when using NVDs, because they magnify the field of view.
   (4) ***Trigger Control.*** There is no change to this fundamental during night firing. The objective is to not disrupt alignment of the weapon with the target.

b. **Tripod.**
   (1) ***Steady Position.*** When firing at predetermined targets with the weapon laid on each target, there are no differences in steady position at night as compared to day. However, firing at night at targets of opportunity

requires modifications. The gunner is required to use weapon-target alignment techniques. He must align the weapon on the target and look over the sights. His head is higher and his lower jaw is lightly on the stock if at all. With night vision devices, the gunner must position his head so that his firing eye is in line with the device.

(2) ***Aim.*** For targets of opportunity, the gunner uses the same techniques as with a bipod during night firing except weapon-target alignment is achieved with the T&E mechanism.

(3) ***Breath Control.*** There are no changes in this fundamental.

(4) ***Trigger Control.*** There are no changes in this fundamental.

1-8. NUCLEAR, BIOLOGICAL, CHEMICAL FIRE

The four fundamentals remain valid in an NBC environment, although some modifications may be needed to accommodate the equipment.

a. **Bipod.**

(1) ***Steady Position.*** The bulk of overgarments may require adjustments to the position for stability and comfort. A consistent stock weld is difficult to maintain because of the shape of the protective masks. The gunner has to hold his head in an awkward position to see through the sight. If necessary, he may cant the weapon to overcome this situation. This procedure relieves the neck muscles and places the eye in line with the center of the rear sight.

(2) ***Aim.*** The gunner may have to rotate (cant) the machine gun to see through the rear sight aperture. He should rotate only enough to align the sights, and only if necessary. Ballistics cause rounds to impact low in the direction of the cant at long ranges. If canting at targets beyond 175 meters, the gunner must adjust his point of aim. The best technique is to aim at center base of the target initially and then make adjustments based on the strike of the rounds. Right-handed firers adjust point of aim to the right and high; left-handed firers to the left and high.

(3) ***Breath Control.*** Although breathing is somewhat restricted and more difficult while wearing the protective mask, the impact is negligible. Care must be taken to avoid hyperventilating during burst fire. The amount of oxygen inhaled by taking quick shallow breaths or deeper breaths between bursts is significantly reduced.

(4) ***Trigger Control.*** Trigger control is affected when the gunner wears gloves. The effect cannot be accurately predicted for each soldier; therefore, practice and training under these conditions is required.

b. **Tripod.**

(1) ***Steady Position.*** Modifications are similar to those in bipod firing. There are two other points of importance. Manipulating the T&E with gloves on is more difficult because the feel of the hand wheel differs. The gunner may not sense the same control as without gloves. Second, hearing is impaired. Together, reduced sense of touch and hearing impairment make T&E manipulations especially difficult. For these reasons, adjustments may be considerably slower.

(2) ***Aim.*** Unlike the bipod, the tripod does not allow the machine gun to be canted. This requires the gunner to position his head behind the stock to use the sight. Skilled gunners who make adjustments to the T&E quickly can confirm their sight picture and then look over the sights to observe the strike of the round while firing. This not only provides relief for the neck muscles but aids in making adjustments.

(3) ***Breath Control.*** Some considerations apply in the same way as with of the bipod; however, the stable platform of the tripod negates movement associated with breathing.

(4) ***Trigger Control.*** Like the bipod, control is different because the trigger feels different. Training familiarizes the gunner with the changes he must make while wearing gloves.

1-9. ENGAGEMENT OF MOVING TARGETS

The fundamentals used to hit moving targets are the same as those needed to hit stationary targets. However, the procedures to engage moving targets vary as the angle, speed, and range of the target varies. Targets moving directly at the gunner are engaged the same as a stationary target; there is no change in the application of the fundamentals. But fast-moving targets at varying ranges and angles do require changes in the application of steady position and aiming.

a. **Leads.** To hit a moving target, the machine gun must be aimed ahead of the target far enough to cause the bullet and target to arrive at the same time at the same point. This distance is measured in target lengths. One target length as seen by the gunner is one lead. Leads are measured from the center of mass. Table 1-1 gives the amount of lead needed to hit a target moving at right angles, to the gunner, and at speeds and ranges indicated. The gunner makes adjustments as conditions change. If target speed is 7½ mph, the amount of lead is half that shown on the table; at 30 mph, double that shown. The angle at which the target moves also changes the lead. If the target is moving on an oblique angle, only half the lead is required. For a target moving directly at the gunner, the aiming point is below the center base of the target depending on range and slope of the ground. For a target moving directly away from a gunner, the aiming point is above the center base of the target (Figure 1-7). Too much lead is better than too little because the target moves into the beaten zone, and observation of the strike of the rounds is easier in relation to the target.

Table 1-1: Vehicle lead table.

SPEED	RANGE OF TARGET		
	300 meters	500 meters	900 meters
15 mph	1/2 X Target length	1 X Target length	2 X Target lengths

NOTE

A soldier carrying a full combat load can run as fast as 8 mph for short distances on the battlefield.

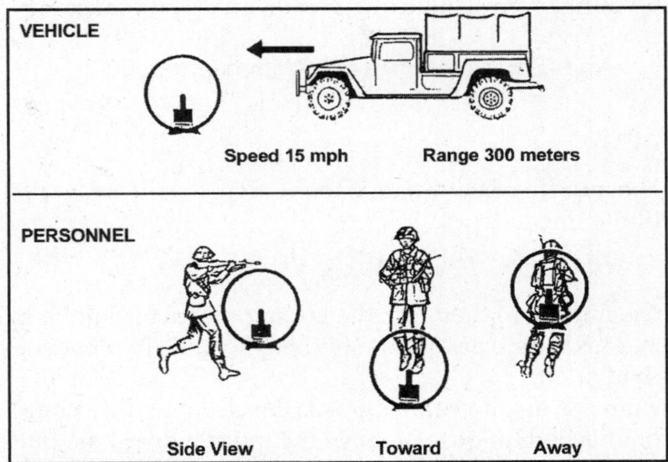

Figure 1-7: Moving-target aiming points.

b. **Tracking Techniques.** The gunner aims at a point ahead of the target equal to the estimated number of leads, maintains this lead by tracking the target (manipulates the weapon at the same angular speed as that of the target), and then fires. Tracking allows the gunner in position for a second burst if the first one misses.

c. **Trapping Techniques.** The gunner establishes an aiming point forward of the target and along the target path. He pulls the trigger as the target reaches the appropriate point in regard to lead.

d. **Position and Aim.**

(1) ***Steady Position.*** The gunner makes no change in position for targets moving directly toward or away from him. He manipulates the T&E mechanism to obtain the proper lead and sight picture. Some targets at varying speeds, angles, and ranges may require the gunner to reposition when in the prone position. The gunner redistributes his weight to his elbows and toes, raising his body directly behind the weapon. He uses the T&E mechanism to traverse on to the target.

(2) ***Aim.*** The gunner uses the T&E mechanism to acquire the appropriate sight picture in relation to leading the target. He must quickly determine speed, angle, and range to the target, decide whether to track or trap, acquire lead, and engage the target. He uses the traversing handwheel to maintain lead.

(3) ***Breath Control.*** The gunner makes no change, but he must be quick to hold his breath because of the fleeting nature of moving targets.

(4) ***Trigger Control.*** The gunner makes no change in applying this fundamental.

e. **Bipod Techniques.** For targets moving to or from a gunner using a bipod, the same procedures are used. From a prone position, the gunner may be required to adjust his position quickly depending on range, angle, and speed of the target.

(1) ***Steady Position.*** If appropriate lead cannot be achieved by shifting his shoulders right or left (traverse) or by moving his elbows closer or farther apart (search), the gunner redistributes his weight to his elbows and toes and raises his body off the ground. Using his toes, the gunner shifts his body right or left in the opposite direction of the target and pivots on his elbows until the aiming point is well ahead of the target. The gunner rapidly assumes a steady position, obtains the sight picture, and leads and engages the target. Trapping is the preferred technique. In order to apply this method, the bipod legs must move freely. When firing from a fighting position, the gunner must be flexible enough to track any target in his sector. If lead cannot be achieved, he slides the bipod legs in the appropriate direction (left or right) ahead of the target and continues as in the prone position. Trapping is still the preferred technique. If the terrain does not permit sliding the weapon left or right, the gunner lifts the bipod legs off the ground and places them where he can aim ahead of the target, reestablishes a steady position, and continues as before.

(2) ***Aim.*** The gunner determines angle, speed, and range quickly; acquires the appropriate lead; and engages the target. He aligns the front sight post in the proper position to lead the target. For targets moving directly away, he places the front sight post above center of mass. For targets moving directly at him, he aligns the front sight post below center of mass. For all other targets, he aligns the front sight with center base of the target applying the appropriate lead.

(3) ***Breath Control.*** The gunner must hold his breath quickly because of the fleeting nature of moving targets.

(4) ***Trigger Control.*** This is the same as for engaging stationary targets.

1-10. TRAVERSE AND SEARCH

The traverse technique moves the muzzle of the weapon to the left or right to distribute fire laterally. Search moves the muzzle up or down to distribute fire in depth.

a. **Tripod.**

(1) ***Traverse.*** To move the muzzle to the right, the gunner places his left hand on the traversing handwheel, thumb up, and pushes his thumb away from his body (right). To move the muzzle to the left, he pulls his thumb towards his body (left).

(2) ***Search.*** To move the muzzle up, the gunner grasps the elevating handwheel with his left hand and pushes his thumb away from his body (add). To move the muzzle down, he pulls his thumb towards his body (drop).

b. **Bipod.**

(1) ***Traverse.*** To make minor changes in direction, the gunner shifts his shoulders to the right or left to select successive aiming points in the target area. Major changes require him to redistribute his weight to his elbows and toes and raise his body off the ground. Using his toes, he shifts his body to the right or left to be in the opposite direction of the target, and pivots on his elbows until he is aligned with the target. The gunner rapidly assumes a steady position, obtains the proper sight picture, and engages the target.

(2) ***Search.*** To make changes in elevation, the gunner moves his elbows closer together to lower the muzzle or farther apart to raise the muzzle. He corrects gross errors in range by adjusting the range setting.

1-11. DIRECT LAY

The simplest, quickest, and most effective technique of delivering fire with the machine gun is to align the sights on the target and properly apply fire. This technique of fire is called *direct lay.*

1-12. APPLICATION OF FIRE

The gunner must aim, fire, and adjust on a certain point of the target. He always keeps the center of his beaten zone at the center base of the target for maximum effect from each burst of fire. When this procedure is done, bullets in the upper half of the cone of fire run through the target if it has height, and the bullets in the lower half of the beaten zone ricochet into the target.

1-13. FIRE ADJUSTMENT

The gunner initially sets his sights with the range to the target, lays on the target (sight alignment and sight picture on the center base of the target), fires a burst, and observes the strike of the rounds or flight of the tracers. When the initial burst is correct, he continues to fire until the target is covered. He must regain a good sight picture before each burst when using the bipod. When using the tripod, the gunner makes a rapid check of the sight picture after each traverse and search adjustment.

a. **Sight Corrections Method.** A gunner must observe and adjust fire rapidly to be effective. He observes bursts of fire by noting the strike of the rounds in the target area and the tracers in flight. The technique to adjust fire depends on time, range, and amount of adjustment. These factors assist the gunner in determining whether or not to make sight corrections or adjust position and point of aim. When the initial burst is not correctly placed, the gunner may change the elevation and windage on the sights and fire another burst on the target. This method is time-consuming, even for the well-trained soldier.

b. **Adjusted Aiming Point Method.** In this method of fire adjustment, the gunner uses his sight but does not make sight corrections. This method is quick. If the gunner misses the target with his initial burst, he must rapidly select a new aiming point the same distance from the target as the center of impact of the initial burst, but in the opposite direction. For example, if the initial burst is 20 meters beyond and 10 meters to the right of the target, the gunner rapidly selects an aiming point about 20 meters short and 10 meters to the left of the target, lays on that aiming point, and fires (Figure 1-8).

(1) When selecting a new aiming point from bipod mode, he may have to shift his shoulders slightly to the left or right for windage corrections. For elevation changes, he moves his elbows closer together (lowers the impact) or farther apart (raises the impact). For large corrections, he must move his elbows and realign his body to remain directly behind the weapon. He does this by redistributing weight to his elbows and toes and raises his body off the ground. He shifts his body using his toes, to the right or left, pivoting on his elbows until he is on line with the target. Then he assumes a steady position, obtains the sight picture, and engages the target.

(2) When selecting a new aiming point from tripod mode, the gunner may have to manipulate the T&E mechanism.

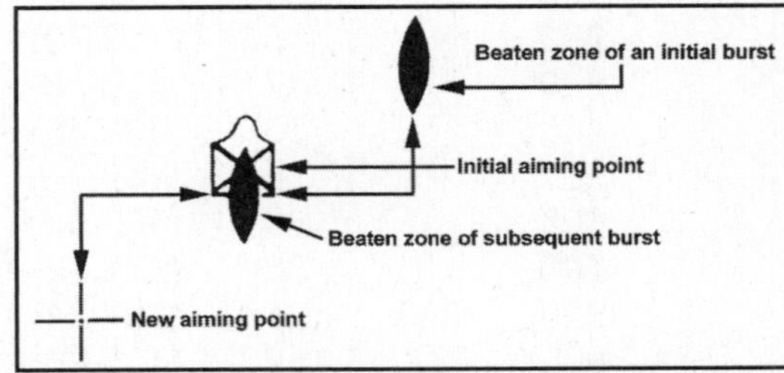

Figure 1-8: Adjusting aiming point method.

1-14. EFFECTS OF WIND

The effects of wind vary depending on changes in speed and direction. Wind is classified by the direction it is blowing in relationship to the firer and target line. The *clock system* is used to indicate wind direction and value (Figure 1-9).

a. **Clock System.** Winds that blow from the left (9 o'clock) or right (3 o'clock) are called *full-value winds,* because they have the most effect on the round. Winds that blow at an angle from the front or rear area are called *half-value winds,* because they have about one-half the effect on the round as full-value winds. Winds that blow straight into the gunner's face or winds that blow straight into the target are termed *no-value winds,* because their effect on the round is too small to be a concern. Effects of the wind increase as the range increases. Figure 1-10 shows the effects of a 10-mph wind at varying ranges. A 20-mph wind doubles the effect. Winds at other than right angles have less effect. As indicated in Figure 1-10, wind has almost no effect up to 300 meters.

> ✍ **NOTE**
> When in doubt, the gunner aims the initial burst directly at the center base of the target and, using the techniques of observation and adjustment of fire, adjusts the fire onto the target.

b. **Wind Measurement.** Wind is highly variable and sometimes quite different at the firing position than at the target position. Even though the wind is blowing hard at the firing position, trees, brush, or terrain could protect the path of the round. The wind can vary by several miles per hour between the time a measurement is taken and when the round is fired. Therefore, training time should not be wasted trying to teach gunners an exact way to measure wind speed. They should know that even though wind can affect trajectory, it can be overcome by adjusting fire. A wind gauge can be used for precise measurement of wind velocity. When a gauge is not available, velocity is estimated by one of the following methods.

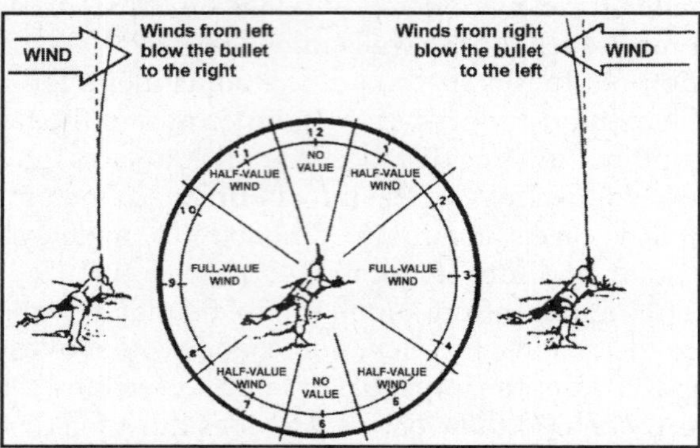

Figure 1-9: Clock method.

10-MILES PER HOUR WIND DRIFT	
RANGE IN METERS	**INCHES (CM)**
100	1 (2.54)
200	5 (12.70)
300	12 (30.48)
400	23 (53.42)
500	39 (49.06)
600	60 (152.04)
700	88 (223.52)
800	121 (307.34)
900	159 (403.86)
1,000 +	202 (513.08)

Figure 1-10: Effects of winds.

(1) ***Observation Method.*** The following information can assist in determining wind velocities.
   (a) Winds under 3 mph can barely be felt, but the presence of slight wind can be determined by drifting smoke.
   (b) Winds of 5 to 8 mph constantly move the leaves of trees.
   (c) Winds of 8 to 12 mph raise dust and loose paper.
   (d) Winds of 12 to 15 mph cause small trees to sway.

(2) ***Pointing Method.*** A piece of paper or other light material can be dropped from shoulder height. By pointing directly at the spot where it lands, the angle can be estimated. As shown in Figure 1-11, the angle is also divided by the constant number 4 to determine the wind speed in mph. However, this only indicates the conditions at the firing position; the conditions may be different at the target.

1-15. FIRE COMMANDS

The standard fire commands are used as means of control during preliminary, basic, and advanced gunnery. The fire command must be explained to the gunner. The elements are given (as appropriate) before each dry-fire or live-fire exercise. The gunner takes action as directed and repeats each element as it is announced. (For a detailed explanation of fire commands, see Chapter 2.) When using the basic 10-meter range target, the fire command elements are as follows:

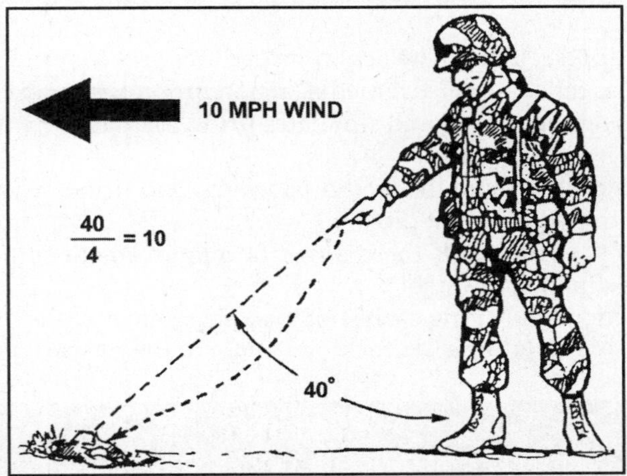

Figure 1-11: Pointing method.

a. **Alert.** The alert is given as "Fire mission." Upon hearing the alert, the gunner loads his weapon and places the safety on "F".
b. **Direction.** Direction is given as FRONT since the targets appear to the gunner's front on the basic range.
c. **Description.** Description is given as PASTER NUMBER (pasters 1 through 8 as appropriate), at which time the gunner lays his weapon on the announced paster.
d. **Range.** The elevation on the rear sight assembly is always used on the basic range. This is announced as FIVE HUNDRED or SEVEN HUNDRED, at which time the gunner must ensure that his rear sight assembly has the correct elevation setting.
e. **Method of Fire.** Firing on the basic range is at a point target, so the method of fire is announced as FIXED. The gunner fires either single rounds or bursts at a rate slower than the sustained rate; therefore, the rate-of-fire element is omitted.
f. **Command to Open Fire.** This is announced as AT MY COMMAND. When the gunner is ready, he announces "Up." When all gunners are ready to fire, the command FIRE is given.

1-16. DRY-FIRE EXERCISES

Dry-fire exercises train the techniques of loading, unloading, immediate action, remedial action, fundamentals of marksmanship, sight settings, and T&E manipulation.

a. **Ammunition.** These exercises may be conducted using blank or dummy ammunition and should be conducted using fire commands when appropriate. If the blank firing attachment is used, safety restrictions for its use must be enforced. While the gunner performs the tasks, the assistant gunner—
   - Checks the sight setting and initial lay.
   - Checks the gunner's position.

- Ensures the gunner simulates firing before adjusting his position.
- Checks for proper body adjustment or manipulation of T&E.
- Critiques the gunner at the end of the exercise.

b. **Loading and Unloading Exercises.** The procedures for loading and unloading are prescribed in Chapters 1, 2 and 3. They should be reinforced using dummy ammunition. This training instills confidence and proficiency in the operation of the weapon. It also provides training in clearing the weapon.

c. **Immediate Action and Remedial Action Exercise.** This exercise is conducted using linked dummy rounds and the basic machine gun target. The instructor should use salvage links to link the dummy rounds together. The gunner—

(1) Loads the weapon with dummy ammunition and aims at one of the aiming pasters on the basic machine gun target.

(2) Being conscious of the sight picture, pulls the trigger and the bolt goes forward (simulate firing the weapon). If the sight picture is disturbed, checks his position and grip, and maintains better control of the weapon.

(3) If he has a stoppage, applies immediate action procedures and continues to fire.

(4) If immediate action has failed, applies remedial action procedures and continue to fire.

d. **Operational Exercise.** The gunner aims and simulates firing each dummy round at the aiming paster on the basic machine gun target.

(1) Observes the sight picture through the feeding, locking, and firing cycle. (This provides feedback on his ability to maintain and hold the sight picture.)

(2) If at the completion of the firing cycle there is significant movement of the sight picture, his position is not steady enough or the tripod is not stable.

(3) Applies immediate action after firing each shot to extract and eject the dummy cartridge, and returns the bolt to the cocked position. Returns the cocking handle to the forward position.

WARNING

The M240B is carried loaded with the bolt locked to the *rear* in *tactical situations* where noise discipline is critical to the success of the mission. Trained gun crews are the only personnel authorized to load the M240B and only when command directs the crew to do so. During *normal training exercises*, the M240B is loaded and carried with the bolt in the *forward position.*

e. **Sight Setting and Sight Change Exercises.** These exercises are designed to train the gunner in the operation and adjustment of the rear sight, and making corrections in elevation and windage on the machine gun.

(1) For large adjustments in elevation (range), the gunner manipulates the rear sight to achieve different range settings. For fine adjustments in elevation, the gunner rotates the elevation knob for the machine gun.

(2) To make adjustments for windage, the gunner traverses the rear sight across the windage scale for the machine gun.

f. **Practice.** Before the dry-fire proficiency examination, soldiers should practice the tasks until they become proficient.

g. **Traversing and Searching Exercise.** After the gunner knows the principles of sighting and aiming and can assume a satisfactory firing position, he learns how to make minor and major body position changes to obtain an accurate initial lay. He practices shifting the direction of the weapon to successive points by moving his body. The basic machine gun target is placed 10 meters from the weapon for this exercise.

(1) Makes adjustments for large shifts in direction by using his elbows-and-toes technique described earlier. Makes small changes in direction by adjusting his shoulders.

(2) Makes major elevation changes by adjusting the range setting on the rear sight. Makes minor elevation changes by adjusting his elbows.

(3) Traverses and searches the target by sighting on the initial aiming paster (number 5 or 6) and then shifting to each of the other pasters in order (5 through 6 or its reverse).

(4) Upon receiving a fire command, the gunner repeats the instructions, sets the sights, lays the weapon on the designated paster, assumes the correct position, and reports *up.*

(5) At the command FIRE, the gunner simulates firing two single shots, then shifts to the next paster and simulates firing until the exercise is complete.

h. **T&E Manipulation Exercise.** After the gunner understands the principles of sighting and aiming and can assume a satisfactory firing position, he is instructed in manipulating the tripod-mounted machine gun to obtain an accurate initial lay. He is taught to shift the direction of the weapon to successive points with proficiency. The basic machine gun target is placed 10 meters from the weapon for this exercise.

(1) Makes large shifts in direction by releasing the traversing slide lock lever and moving the slide to the right or left. Makes minor changes in direction by using the traversing handwheel. (One click on the handwheel moves the strike of the round 1 cm on the target.)

(2) Adjusts for elevation by rotating the elevating handwheel with his left hand.

(3) Traverses and searches the target by laying on the initial aiming paster (number 5 or 6) and then shifts to each of the other pasters in order (5 through 6 or its reverse). (All major shifts in traverse are accomplished by loosening the traversing slide lockding lever.) When shifting from pasters number 7 through 8 or 8 through 7, uses the traversing handwheel.

(4) Upon receiving the command, the gunner repeats the instructions, sets the sights, lays the weapon on the designated paster, assumes the firing position, and reports UP.

(5) At the command FIRE, the gunner repeats the command, simulates firing two single shots, then shifts to the next paster and simulates firing until the exercise is completed.

i. **Dry-Fire Proficiency (Performance) Examination.** A gunner must demonstrate skill in all the tasks of the dry-fire proficiency examination before he is allowed to progress to 10-meter live firing. This examination emphasizes learning by doing. Proficiency is tested on a pass or fail basis.

j. **Remedial Training.** Remedial training must be given to soldiers who fail the performance objectives. Gunners who have passed the proficiency test may be used to assist in the training of soldiers having difficulty. Following retraining, the soldiers are retested in those tasks.

1-17. MULTIPURPOSE MACHINE GUN RANGE LAYOUT

The multipurpose machine gun range is used for conducting the 10-meter course as well as transition day, night, and integrated NBC firing. The firing area has 10 lanes. (Detailed setup and target configurations are described in TC 25-8. The layout is shown in Figure 1-12.) Personnel required for conducting the 10-meter range, as well as the transition firing, are the same, and they should perform the same duties for each training period. Local policy may dictate personnel requirements. The following are the minimum required personnel: OIC, NCOIC, safety officer or NCO, ammunition NCO, tower operator, lane NCOs, trainer and assistant gunners, or IAW TC 25-8.

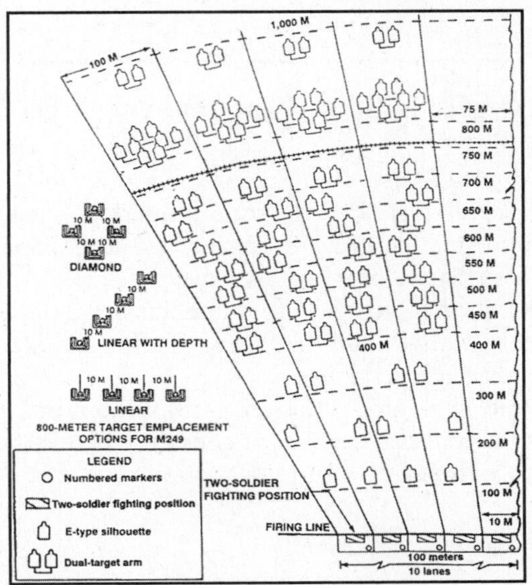

Figure 1-12: Multipurpose machine gun range layout.

NOTE

Targets beyond 800 meters are to be used with a machine gun optic and are not to be used during qualification without a machine gun optic.

1-18. BASIC MACHINE GUN TARGET

The basic machine gun target (FSN 6920-078-5128 and NSN 6920-00-078-5123) is used for the 10-meter firing exercise (Figure 1-13). The following explanation of the target, including the size of the aiming pasters and scoring spaces, aids in zeroing the machine guns and facilitates control during the 10-meter firing exercises. The target consists of four sections lettered A, B, C, and D. Each section has four point targets numbered 1, 2, 3, and 4; and two sets of area targets numbered 5 through 6 and 7 through 8. Each space is 4 cm wide and 5 cm high. The black aiming paster within the numbered scoring spaces is 1 cm square. The target is used to score one gunner—with one refire. Each gunner uses sections A, B and C. Sections C for qualification and section D for refire.

a. **Point Targets.** Point targets on the basic machine gun target are pasters 1 through 4 of sections A, B, C, and D. Firing at point targets exposes the gunner to zeroing techniques and controlled-burst fire techniques. Targets 1 through 4 can also be used for qualification.

b. **Area Targets.** Area targets on the basic machine gun target consist of pasters 5 through 6, and 7 through 8 of sections A, B, C, and D. Target group 5 through 6 provides the gunner with targets in depth and allows him to use a series of aiming points to disburse fire across the target by using the T&E mechanism. Target group 7 through 8 provides the gunner with linear targets with depth. This series of targets uses a series of aiming points to disburse fire across the target and in depth by using the T&E mechanism.

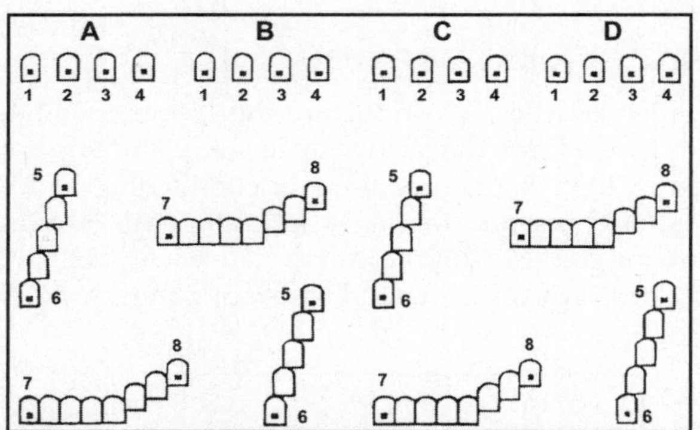

Figure 1-13: Basic machine gun target.

c. **Grid Square Overlay.** This device assists the gunner in zeroing his weapon at 10 meters, while using the basic machine gun target (Figure 1-14). The grid square overlay is used the same as an M16 25-meter zero target, except the material can be made of plastic or view graph transparency. Each square is equal to 1 cm.
1 CLICK = 1 CM. Turn the traversing handwheel to move the strike of the round left or right.
1 CLICK = 1 CM. Turn the elevation handwheel to move the strike of the round up or down.

(1) Sets the sights for 10-meter zeroing, then fires three single rounds to form a three-round shot group. Relays on the target using the T&E mechanism.

(2) After firing the three-round shot group (Figure 1-15), places the grid square overlay over the pasters (1 and 2) (Figure 1-16) and counts the number of clicks it will take for rounds to impact on the black aiming paster. (Corrections for Figure 1-16 would be turn the traverse handwheel to the right one click.)

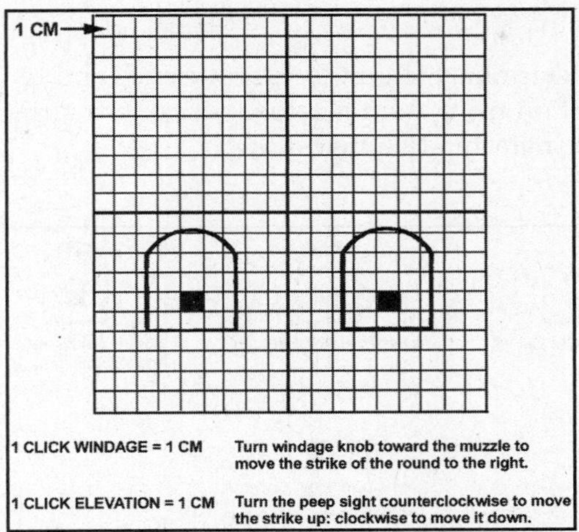

Figure 1-14: Grid square overlay.

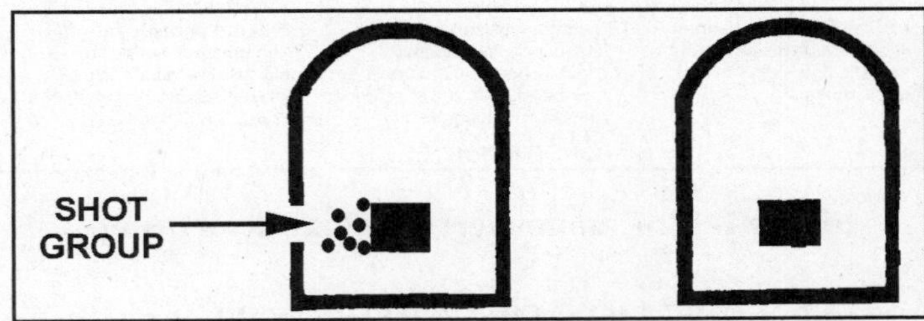

Figure 1-15: Shot group on basic machine gun target.

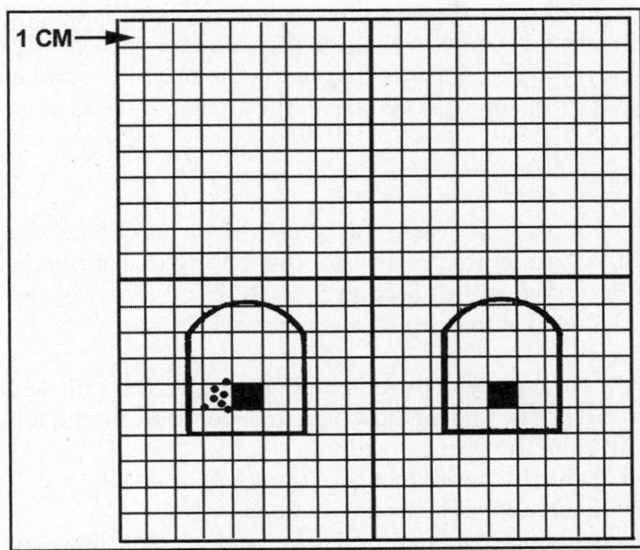

Figure 1-16: Overlay placed over pasters.

1-19. TARGET ANALYSIS

Targets are analyzed and scored to determine the gunner's proficiency and to reinforce the fundamentals of marksmanship. In a prone or fighting position firing with a zeroed weapon, a target is best analyzed by considering the common errors of machine gun marksmanship (Figure 1-17).

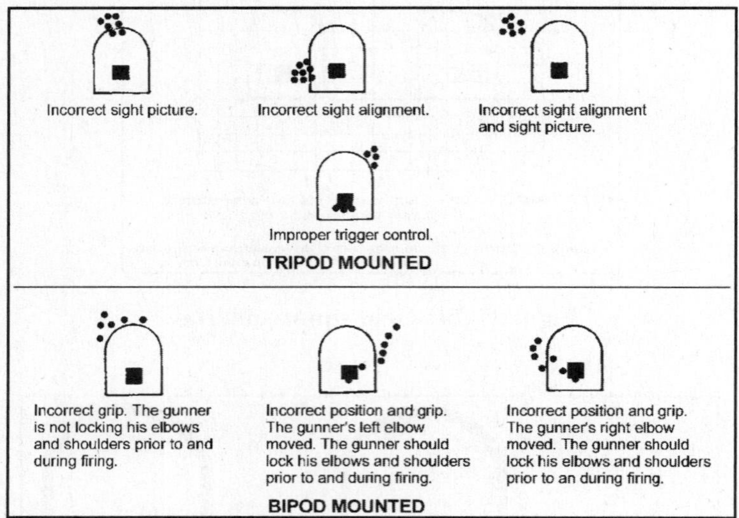

Figure 1-17: Common errors of marksmanship.

SECTION III. CREW DRILL

This section applies to all three machine guns and will be incorporated in *preliminary gunnery* and *basic gunnery.* The machine gun crew drill gives squad and platoon members training in the fundamentals of machine gun operation and confidence in their ability to put the machine gun into action with precision and speed. Rotation of duties during training ensures that every member becomes trained in the duties of each crew position. Precision is attained by learning and practicing correct procedures to include inspecting the machine gun before firing and observing safety procedures. Speed is acquired after precision has been developed. *Precision is never sacrificed for speed.*

1-20. PREPARATION

The crew drill will be conducted with preliminary gunnery and will be part of the 10-meter and transition firing practice and qualification, concurrently during other courses of fire, or anytime at the discretion of the unit commander. The organization for crew drill described in this section is for training crews in the fundamentals of machine gun operation; it is not the organization to be employed in every tactical situation.

a. To instill realism and relate the crew drill to actual situations, the unit leader should vary his method of instruction. Possible approaches to this method of instruction include the following:
   - Conduct the crew drill from the prone position.
   - Initiate the crew drill from all types of tactical formations.
   - Perform the crew drill in simulated tactical situations.

b. The crew drill, as discussed here, involves the leader and one machine gun crew. The machine gun crew consists of three members (a gunner, assistant gunner, and an ammunition bearer). There are two complete machine gun crews in the light headquarters section of infantry, air assault infantry platoons, and airborne infantry platoons.

c. All commands are given by a leader. This leader may be a team leader, squad leader, or someone placed in charge of the crew. The gunner and assistant gunner repeat all commands. After the machine gun is mounted, the assistant gunner transmits all signals from the leader to the gunner and from the gunner to the leader.

1-21. CREW EQUIPMENT

In addition to individual weapons and equipment, crew members carry equipment for both bipod and tripod training. The following is a suggested assignment of the equipment to the machine gun crew members:

a. **Day Time Equipment.**
   (1) Leader (designated)—binoculars, compass.
   (2) Gunner—machine gun, compass, MGO or AN/PAS-13, two bandoleers (with dummy ammunition).
   (3) Assistant Gunner—binoculars, spare barrel case (spare barrel and accessories), traversing and elevating mechanism, pintle assembly, and three bandoleers (with dummy ammunition).
   (4) Ammunition bearer—compass, tripod and four bandoleers (with dummy ammunition).

b. **Night Time Equipment.**
   (1) Leader (designated)—AN/PVS-7B with 3XMAG, compass.
   (2) Gunner—machine gun, compass, AN/PVS-4 or AN/PAS-13, two bandoleers (with dummy ammunition).
   (3) Assistant Gunner—AN/PVS-14 with 3XMAG, spare barrel case (spare barrel and accessories), traversing and elevating mechanism, pintle assembly, and three bandoleers (with dummy ammunition).
   (4) Ammunition bearer—AN/PVS-7B with 3XMAG, compass, tripod and four bandoleers (with dummy ammunition).

1-22. FORMATION (BIPOD OR TRIPOD)

The leader commands FORM FOR CREW DRILL. The crew forms in a file with five steps between each crew member in this order: gunner, assistant gunner, and ammunition bearer. The gunner is five steps from and facing the leader. When the crew members reach their positions, each assumes the prone position and is ready for the crew drill. (Figure 1-18, page 1-26.)

Figure 1-18: Crew in ready position.

1-23. CROSS-TRAINING PROCEDURES

Duties are rotated during the crew drill to train each soldier in the duties of all crew members. The command to rotate duties is FALL OUT, GUNNER. At this command, the gunner becomes the ammunition bearer, the assistant gunner becomes the gunner, and the ammunition bearer becomes the assistant gunner. When crew members have assumed their new positions, they call out their new duties in order: AMMUNITION BEARER, ASSISTANT GUNNER, GUNNER.

1-24. INSPECTION FOR BIPOD FIRE

An inspection of equipment is made at the beginning of each exercise.

a. **Command.** After the crew is formed for crew drill, the leader commands INSPECT EQUIPMENT BEFORE FIRING, BIPOD. At the command, each crew member inspects his equipment as explained below.

(1) ***Inspection by Gunner.*** The gunner inspects the ammunition first. He ensures that the ammunition is properly linked and free of dirt and corrosion, and that the double link is up (ready for loading). After he inspects the ammunition, he places the cloth slings over his shoulder (except for one bandoleer, which he prepares for loading). He then inspects the machine gun and takes his position parallel to the machine gun (his head on line with the feed tray). The night personnel also check the AN/PVS-4 or AN/PAS-13.
   (a) Holding the machine gun with his left hand, using his right hand he lowers the bipod legs and then rest the machine gun on the bipod.
   (b) Attaches the bandoleer to the machine gun.
   (c) Places the safety on "F", pulls the cocking handle to the rear, places the safety on "S", returns the cocking handle to the forward position, and raises the cover assembly.
   (d) Calls for the cleaning rod and receives it from the assistant gunner.
   (e) Crawls forward, then runs the cleaning rod through the barrel to ensure it is clear.
   (f) Checks the flash suppressor for cracks.
   (g) Checks the front sight for tightness and for damage to the blade.
   (h) Checks the carrying handle to ensure that it can be positioned so it will not be in the way during aiming and firing.
   (i) Ensures that the barrel is securely locked to the receiver.
   (j) Returns the cleaning rod to the assistant gunner.
   (k) Moves to the rear of the machine gun and checks the moving parts in the feed cover.
   - Ensures that the feed cam is clean and properly lubricated.
   - Pushes back and forth on the feed cam to check for freedom of movement.
   - Pushes on the belt feed pawl to ensure that it has spring tension.
   - Pushes on the cartridge guides to ensure that they a have spring tension.
   (l) Pushes the belt holding pawl to ensure that it has spring tension.
   (m) Lowers and latches the cover (without inserting the belt).
   (n) Pulls the trigger to check the functioning of the safety.
   (o) Places the safety on "F", pulls the cocking handle to the rear, pulls the trigger, eases the bolt forward manually with the cocking handle.
   (p) Checks the rear sight.

(2) ***Inspection by Assistant Gunner.*** Remaining in a prone position, the assistant gunner begins by inspecting his ammunition. He takes the cleaning rod from the carrying case and assembles the cleaning rod. He then takes the traversing and elevating mechanism from the case and prepares it as follows. Night personnel will also check AN/PVS-14 with 3X MAG.
   (a) Rotates the elevating handwheel, exposing 1½ inches or the width of two fingers of threads above the elevating handwheel.
   (b) Rotates the traversing slide sleeve, exposing 1½ inches or the width of two fingers of threads below the elevating handwheel.
   (c) Centers the traversing mechanism.
   (d) Checks the to ensure that the locking mechanism that attach to the machine gun are present and in working order.
   (e) Replaces the traversing and elevating mechanism in on the case and removes the spare barrel from the spare barrel case.
   (f) Checks the barrel.
   (g) Checks the flash suppressor for cracks.
   (h) Checks the front sight for tightness and for damage to the blade.
   (i) Checks the pintle assembly for proper functioning.
   (j) Places the spare barrel its case; disassembles the cleaning rod and returns it accessory pocket; and checks the ruptured cartridge extractor, bore brush, chamber brush, receiver brush, and heat protective mitten for serviceability.

(3) ***Inspection by Ammunition Bearer.*** Remaining in a prone position, the ammunition bearer inspects his ammunition as described above for gunner and assistant gunner. He then inspects the tripod, pintle assembly and T&E mechanism. Night personnel also check the AN/PVS-7 with the 3XMAG.
   (a) Ensures that the front leg will unfold properly and the rear legs unfold and lock securely in place with the sleeve latch.

(b) Checks the sleeve latch to ensure that it has spring tension and will function.
(c) Checks the pintle assembly to ensure that it is locked into the pintle bushing and that the pintle rotates freely within the bushing.
(d) Checks to ensure that the T&E mechanism will lock on the traversing bar and move freely when unlocked for major changes in direction.
(e) Unlocks the pintle and T&E mechanism from the tripod and return to the assistant gunner.
(f) Folds the rear legs by unlocking the sleeve latch and folds the front leg so that the tripod is in the carrying position.

b. **Report.** When crew members have completed their inspection of the equipment, they call out their report, without command, starting from the rear.
   (1) AMMUNITION BEARER CORRECT (or reports deficiencies).
   (2) AMMUNITION BEARER AND ASSISTANT GUNNER CORRECT (or reports the ammunition deficiencies.
   (3) GUNNER ALL CORRECT (or deficiencies found during the inspections).

1-25. PLACEMENT INTO ACTION (BIPOD)

To place the machine gun into action, the leader commands and signals MACHINE GUN TO BE MOUNTED HERE (pointing to the position where the machine gun is to be mounted), FRONT (pointing in the direction of fire), ACTION (raising fist to shoulder level and thrusting it several times in the direction of the selected position).

a. At the command ACTION, the gunner stands, grasps the carrying handle with his left hand, grasps the top of the stock with his right hand, raises the machine gun to a carrying position (muzzle to the front) and moves to the selected position.
b. Upon arrival at the position, the gunner places the machine gun on the ground. He then assumes a prone position to the rear of the machine gun, positions the carrying handle so that it will not interfere during aiming and firing, aligns the machine gun in the direction of fire, and set the rear sight. He places the safety on "F", pulls the bolt to the rear, places the safety on "S", and returns the cocking handle to the forward position. He then raises the feed cover, places the first round of ammunition in the cartridge feed tray groove, and closes the feed cover ensuring that the round does not slip out of the cartridge feed tray groove. He then places the machine gun to his shoulder and puts the safety on "F".

WARNING

The M240B is carried loaded with the bolt locked to the *rear* in *tactical situations* where noise discipline is critical to the success of the mission. Trained gun crews are the only personnel authorized to load the M240B and only when command directs the crew to do so. During *normal training exercises*, the M240B is loaded and carried with the bolt in the *forward position.*

c. The assistant gunner times his movements so that he arrives at the position as the gunner is assuming the prone position. He lies prone on his left hip, feet to the rear, and on the left side of the gunner. He places the spare barrel case parallel to the gun with the zippered side towards the machine gun. He opens the case and removes the spare barrel. He places the spare barrel on the case, muzzle to the front and even with the muzzle of the machine gun. (Figure 1-19.)
d. The ammunition bearer times his movements so that he arrives at the position as the assistant gunner is assuming the prone position. He places the folded tripod one step to the left of the muzzle of the machine gun and on line with the machine gun. He unslings his bandoleers and places them next to the folded tripod legs. He then lies prone 10 meters to the left and on line with the position, provides security, and prepares to fire into the target area with his rifle.
e. When ready to fire, the gunner puts the safety lever on "F" and reports UP. The assistant gunner signals READY to the leader.

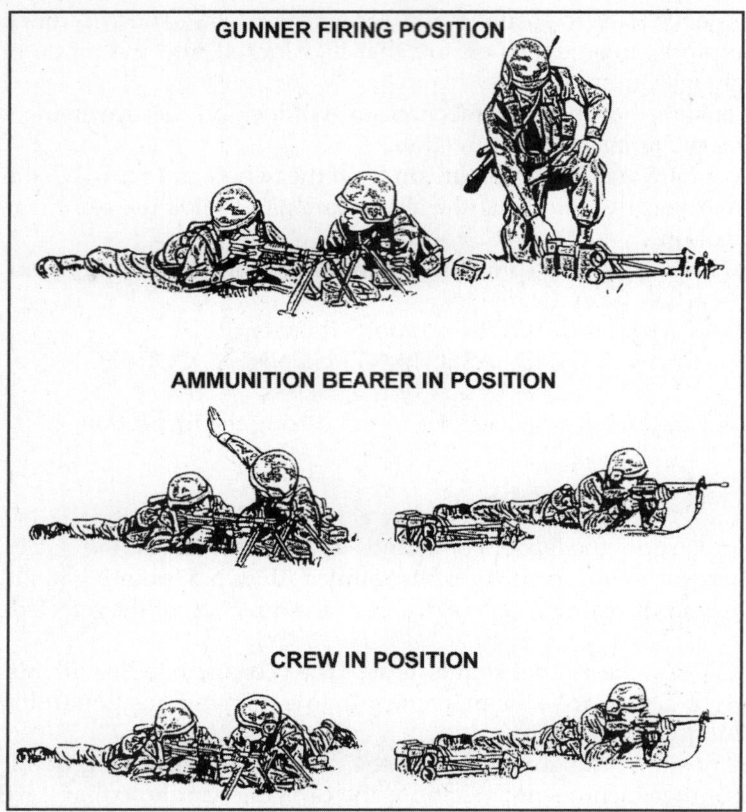

Figure 1-19: Crew members in firing position.

1-26. PROCEDURES FOR CHANGING THE BARREL (BIPOD)

To ensure proficiency and speed in changing barrels, the barrel changing process is included in crew drill. When the gunner has reported UP and the assistant gunner has signaled READY, the leader commands CHANGE BARRELS.

a. The gunner ensures that the bolt is to the rear, puts the safety on "S", and puts the stock on the ground. Next, he moves his left hand to the top of the stock to ensure the weapon stays parallel to the ground. He puts his right hand under the handguard / forearm assembly help support the machine gun when the assistant gunner removes the barrel.
b. The assistant gunner (wearing the heat protective mitten) unlocks the barrel locking lever, removes the barrel, and places the barrel on the spare barrel case. He holds the spare barrel and inserts it into the machine gun.
c. The gunner ensures that the barrel is locked and secured in the receive of the machine gun, moves the safety lever to "F", assumes the correct firing position, and reports UP. The assistant gunner signals READY to the squad leader.

1-27. REMOVAL FROM ACTION (BIPOD)

To take the machine gun out of action, the leader commands and signals OUT OF ACTION. The gunner and assistant gunner repeat the command.

a. At the command OUT OF ACTION, the ammunition bearer moves to the position, slinging his rifle. He picks up and slings the bandoleers that he previously left there. He gets the tripod and moves 15 steps to the rear of the machine gun. He lies prone, facing the position with the tripod in front of him.
b. The assistant gunner places the spare barrel and the heat protective mitten in the spare barrel case. Before standing, he closes the spare barrel case enough to retain the spare barrel and the traversing and elevating

mechanism. He moves 10 steps to the rear of the position and lies prone, facing the position. At this time, he fully closes the spare barrel case.

c. The gunner places the stock on the ground, ensures that the bolt is to the rear, places the safety on "S", and raises the feed cover. He removes the ammunition from the tray, puts it into the bandoleer, and closes the bandoleer. The gunner examines the chamber to ensure that it is clear; closes the feed cover; pulls the cocking handle to the rear; puts the safety on "F"; and pulls the trigger, easing the bolt forward. Standing, he pivots on his right foot; without turning the machine gun, he raises it to his left hip and moves five steps to the rear. He visually checks to ensure that the ammunition bearer and the assistant gunner are in their positions. He lies prone, facing the position with the machine gun on his right. He folds the bipod legs alongside the barrel and reports UP to the squad leader.

1-28. INSPECTION FOR TRIPOD FIRE

The inspection of equipment for tripod training is the same as for bipod training except that the leader's command to start the inspection of equipment is INSPECT EQUIPMENT BEFORE FIRING TRIPOD. Also, the gunner inspects the bipod legs and folds them to their position alongside the barrel.

1-29. PLACEMENT INTO ACTION (TRIPOD)

The leader commands and signals MACHINE GUN TO BE MOUNTED HERE, FRONT, ACTION. (Figure 1-20.)

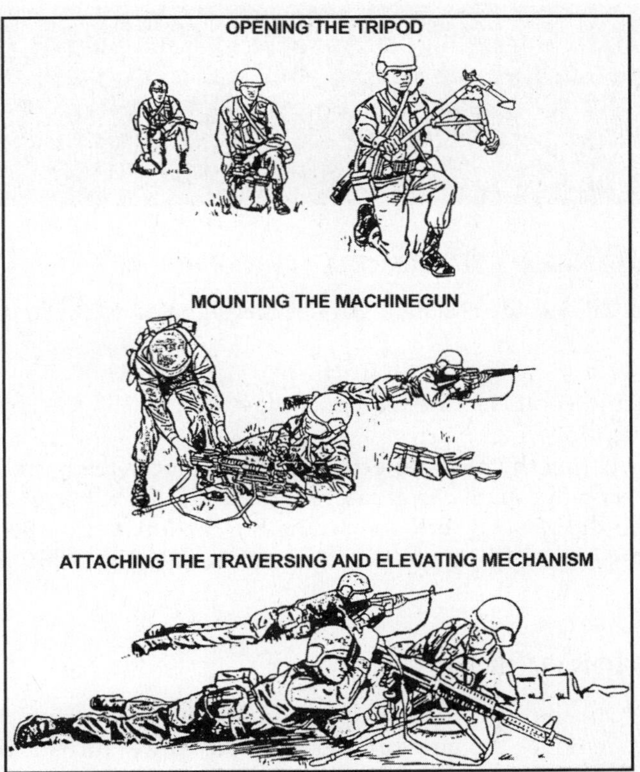

Figure 1-20: Placing the machine gun into action.

a. Upon the command ACTION, the ammunition bearer stands, holds the tripod with his right hand, and moves forward to the position. He kneels on his right knee and rests the shoes of the rear tripod legs on the ground, with the mount in a vertical position. Steadying the mount with his right hand near the tripod head, he raises the front leg with his left hand. He grasps the right shoe with his right hand and the left shoe with is left hand, and raises the tripod chest high. He separates the tripod legs with a quick jerk. Ensuring that the sleeve latch engages the sleeve, he places the tripod on the ground with the front leg pointing in the direction of fire. He rises to his feet and stamps the rear shoes into the ground. He then unslings his bandoleers and places them on line with the front leg of the tripod, one step to the left. He moves 10 meters to the left of the position, unslings his rifle, lies prone, provides security, and prepares to fire into the target area.

b. The assistant gunner times his movements and arrives at the position as the ammunition bearer leaves. He places the spare barrel case (zippered side towards the tripod) parallel to and in line with the spot where the muzzle of the machine gun will be when it is mounted. He lies on his left side, with his hip near the left tripod shoe. He unzips the spare barrel case and removes the spare barrel, mounting equipment necessary to mount the machine gun. He places the spare barrel on the spare barrel case with the muzzle forward.

c. The gunner times his movements and arrives at the position as the assistant gunner assumes the prone position. He stands, holds the carrying handle in his left hand and the stock in his right hand, and raises the gun to the carrying position (muzzle to the front). He mounts the machine gun on the tripod. He then positions the carrying handle to the right so it will not interfere with aiming and firing, raises the rear sight assembly, and lies prone.

d. The assistant gunner assists the gunner in mounting the machine gun to the tripod. They ensure that both the pintle and traversing and elevating mechanism are securely locked in place and working properly.

e. The gunner places the safety on "F", pulls the bolt to the rear, places the safety on "S", and returns the cocking handle to the forward position. The assistant gunner places the first round of ammunition in the tray groove and supports the belt, while the gunner closes the cover. The gunner takes the correct position and grip, places the safety on "F", and reports UP. The assistant gunner signals READY to the squad leader.

WARNING

The M240B is carried loaded with the bolt locked to the *rear* in *tactical situations* where noise discipline is critical to the success of the mission. Trained gun crews are the only personnel authorized to load the M240B and only when command directs the crew to do so. During *normal training exercises,* the M240B is loaded and carried with the bolt in the *forward position.*

1-30. PROCEDURES FOR CHANGING THE BARREL (TRIPOD)

When the gunner has reported UP and the assistant gunner has signaled READY, the leader commands CHANGE BARRELS.

a. The gunner ensures that the bolt is to the rear, puts the safety on "S". He also assists the assistant gunner in changing the barrel, if needed.

b. The assistant gunner (wearing the heat protective mitten) unlocks the barrel locking lever, removes the barrel, and places the barrel on the spare barrel case. He holds the spare barrel inserts it into the machine gun.

c. The gunner ensures that the barrel is lock and secured in the receiver of the machine gun, moves the safety lever to "F", assumes the correct firing position, and reports UP. The assistant gunner signals READY to the squad leader.

1-31. REMOVAL FROM ACTION (TRIPOD)

At the command OUT OF ACTION, the gunner ensures that the bolt is to the rear, places the safety on "S", and raises the cover. The assistant gunner removes the ammunition from the tray, returns it to the bandoleer, and closes the bandoleer. The gunner inspects the chamber to ensure that it is clear; closes the cover; pulls the cocking handle to the rear; puts the safety on "F"; pulls the trigger, easing the bolt forward. The gunner unlocks the rear of the machine gun from the tripod.

a. The assistant gunner will assist the gunner in dismounting the rear of the machine gun. He puts the spare barrel and heat protective mitten into the case and closes it enough to hold the contents. He stands, moves ten steps to the rear of the position, and lies prone, facing to the front. After receiving all mounting equipment from the ammunition bearer, he puts it in the spare barrel case and fully closes the spare barrel case.

b. After the assistant gunner leaves, the gunner stands, lowers the rear sight, and holds the carrying handle with his left hand. With his right hand, he dismounts the front of the machine gun from the tripod. Holding the stock with his right hand, he pivots to his right as he raises the machine gun to the carrying position. He then moves five steps to the rear of the position and lies prone, facing the front.
c. The ammunition bearer rises, slings his rifle, moves to the machine gun, and secures his bandoleers, timing his arrival so that the gunner and assistant gunner will be clear of the tripod. He grasps the tripod with his left hand and moves five steps to the rear of the position. He turns, facing the front, and kneels on his right knee. He places the tripod in a vertical position with the rear shoes on the ground and supports it with his right hand near the head of the tripod. At this time, he hands the assistant gunner all mounting equipment. He reaches up with his right hand down the right leg, and releases the sleeve latch. He then grasps the shoes and closes the tripod legs. He lowers the tripod to the ground, head to the left, lies prone behind it, and reports UP.

1-32. PRONE POSITION

Machine gun crew drill, as it is described in the preceding paragraphs, is an excellent training vehicle for the machine gun crew. A continuation or second phase of the crew drill is outlined in this paragraph. It should be used only as a technique for adding realism to training.

a. **Inspecting Equipment Before Firing.** The inspection of equipment for crew drill from the prone position is the same as that for bipod training and tripod training.
b. **Placing the Machine Gun Into Action.** The leader commands and signals MACHINE GUN TO BE MOUNTED HERE, FRONT, ACTION in the same manner as for bipod training. The procedures for bipod training are the same with one exception—crew members do not get to their feet and movements are executed in the low crawl. Once in position, all actions are performed from the prone position.
c. **Training With the Tripod.** Upon the command ACTION, the ammunition bearer crawls forward to the designated position and extends the front leg of the tripod. Grasping the rear legs firmly, he emplaces the front leg. Applying downward pressure, he emplaces the rear legs. He then crawls to a position about 10-meters to the left of the machine gun and gets into a good firing position with his rifle.
   (1) The assistant gunner crawls forward, timing his movement to arrive as the ammunition bearer leaves. Positioning himself on the left side and facing the tripod, he places the spare barrel case alongside the tripod, unzips the case, and removes the spare barrel and mounting equipment.
   (2) The procedures for mounting the machine gun on the tripod remain the same except all are performed in a prone position and all movements are in the low crawl.
d. **Taking the Machine Gun Out of Action.** The procedures for taking the machine gun out of action remain the same except all are performed in a prone position and all movements are in the low crawl.

SECTION IV. BASIC GUNNERY

In basic marksmanship, the gunner applies the fundamentals in live-fire exercises during day and night. This includes 10-meter zeroing, 10-meter firing, field zeroing, transition firing, and record firing.

1-33. ZERO

Zeroing aligns the sights with the barrel so that the point of aim equals the point of impact. Ten-meter zeroing is for conducting 10-meter fire only and has no further application. (Zeroing at range or field zeroing is the gunner's battlesight zero and must be recorded.) Remember to zero both barrels of the machine gun.

a. **10-Meter Zero, Set the Sights (Mechanical Zero).** The gunner indexes or places the range scale on a range of 500 meters. He assumes a prone position and sights on the target.
b. **Three-Round Group.** The gunner fires three single rounds loaded individually at the center base of the aiming points on the basic machine gun marksmanship target. He fires the three rounds without making any

adjustments to the sights. The shot group must be about a 4-cm circle or smaller to establish the center of the group in relation to the center base of the aiming paster.

c. **Grid Square Overlay.** For a more accurate adjustment, the gunner moves downrange and places the grid square overlay over pasters 1 and 2. He ensures that he aligns the overlay with the pasters and squares.
   (1) Counts the number of squares it will take to move the shot group to the aiming paster.
   (2) Upon completion, returns to the firing line to make corrections to the weapon. (Figure 1-21 illustrates a zero group size on which adjustments can be made and a group that is too loose for adjustments [bipod mode].) If a group is too loose, the gunner checks his position and group.

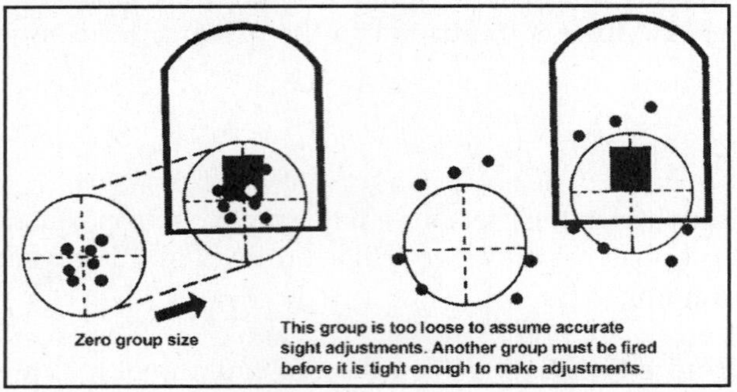

Figure 1-21: Zero group size.

d. **Windage Correction.** If the center of the group is to the left or right of the black aiming paster, the gunner must correct for windage.
e. **Elevation Correction.** If the center of the shot group is above or below of the black aiming paster, the gunner must correct for elevation.
f. **Confirmation.** The gunner fires another three-shot group (loaded singly) after making his corrections for windage and elevation. If the center of the group is still off the aiming point, he adjusts further until the group is centered on the point of aim.
g. **Recording of Zero.** There is no reason to record the 10-meter zero, because it applies only to firing at the 10-meter basic machine gun target.

✍ NOTE

Remember to zero both barrels.

WARNING

The M240B is carried loaded with the bolt locked to the *rear* in *tactical situations* where noise discipline is critical to the success of the mission. Trained gun crews are the only personnel authorized to load the M240B and only when command directs the crew to do so. During *normal training exercises*, the M240B is loaded and carried with the bolt in the *forward position.*

1-34. FIELD ZERO

A gunner must know how to zero the machine gun at distance. He should select a known distance target between 300 and 700 meters. As the range increases, it becomes more difficult to determine where the center of the beaten zone is in relation to the target. Therefore, the 500-meter target on the transition range is recommended because of the ease of determining adjustments.

a. **Setting of the Sights.** The gunner uses the same procedures as for 10-meter zeroing except that he places the rear sight on the range to the target. The recommended range is 500 meters.

b. **Burst.** Fire a burst of 5 to 7 rounds for the M249 or 7 to 9 for the M60/M240B. The gunner assumes a good stable position and fires bursts of 5 to 7 rounds for the M249 or 7 to 9 for the M60/M240B at the center base of the target and notes where the burst strikes.
c. **Correction for Windage.** If the center of the beaten zone is to the left or right of the target, he corrects for windage. He adjusts the windage accordingly.
d. **Correction for Elevation.** If the center of the beaten zone is high or low in relation to the target, he corrects for elevation. Because determining that relationship is difficult, the gunner relies on trial and error to gain sufficient experience in making reliable estimates. He makes corrections in the same manner as 10-meter zeroing.
e. **Confirmation.** After making corrections for windage and elevation, the gunner fires confirming bursts of 5 to 7 rounds for the M249 or 7 to 9 rounds for the M60/M240B. If the target is not hit, he repeats the procedures.
f. **Recording of Zero.** Upon confirming the zero, the gunner records it by counting the number of clicks he moved the sight for windage and elevation from the initial setting.

1-35. 10-METER FIRING

The 10-meter firing trains the gunner to apply the fundamentals of machine gun marksmanship in live-fire exercises. It familiarizes the soldier with the weapon's characteristics, noise, and recoil. It instills in the soldier confidence in his weapon. Each gunner learns to zero his machine gun, conducts crew drill, controlled-burst fire at point targets, and uses traverse and search techniques of fire at area targets. The 10-meter firing is conducted on a 10-meter range or a multipurpose range using the basic machine gun target. These exercises are fired with the machine gun on the bipod from both the prone position and the fighting position and with the tripod from prone and fighting positions. The 10-meter firing exercises are for practice as well as part of record qualification. All 10-meter firing exercises are recorded and scored to provide the gunner an assessment of his performance. The 10-meter firing is conducted IAW Firing Table I (Table 1-2). There are ten tasks.

a. **Task 1—Zero Bipod.** The gunner fires single shots to determine his weapon's zero for 10 meters. This task reinforces the dry-fire experience and allows the gunner to practice loading, while providing the most accurate and tight shot group obtainable. (A1 and A2)
b. **Task 2—Controlled-Burst Fire Bipod Fixed.** Using point targets, the gunner fires bursts of 5 to 7 rounds for the M249 or 7 to 9 rounds for the M60/M240B. This task exposes the gunner to automatic fire and the action of the weapon and at the same time introduces trigger control. (A3 and A4)
c. **Task 3—Controlled-Burst Fire Bipod Fixed.** This task requires the gunner to make body position to engage area targets in depth, to use controlled-burst firing, and to use a series of aiming points to disburse fire across the target. (A5 and A6)
d. **Task 4—Controlled-Burst Fire Bipod Fixed.** This task requires the gunner to make position changes to engage linear targets with depth, to use controlled-burst firing, and to use a series of aiming points to disburse fire across the target. (A7 and A8)
e. **Task 5—Zero Tripod.** The gunner fires single shots to determine his weapon's zero for 10 meters. This task reinforces the dry-fire experience and allows the gunner to practice loading, while providing the most accurate and tight shot group obtainable. (B1 and B2)
f. **Task 6—Controlled-Burst Fire Tripod.** Using point targets, the gunner fires bursts of 5 to 7 rounds for the M249 or 7 to 9 rounds for the M60/M240B. This task exposes the gunner to automatic fire and the action of the weapon and at the same time introduces trigger control. (B1 through B4)
g. **Task 7—Traverse and Search Fire.** This task requires the gunner to make position changes or manipulate the T&E mechanism to engage linear targets with depth, to use controlled-burst firing, and to use a series of aiming points to disburse fire across the target. (B7 through B8)
h. **Task 8—Traverse and Search Fire.** This task requires the gunner to make body position changes or manipulate the T&E mechanism to engage area targets in depth, to use controlled-burst firing, and to use a series of aiming points to disburse fire across the target, while wearing a protective mask and gloves. (B5 through B6)
i. **Task 9—Search and Traverse Fire Qualification.** This task requires the gunner to make position changes or manipulate the T&E mechanism to engage area targets in depth during timed conditions. (C5 through C6)

j. **Task 10—Traverse and Search Fire Qualification.** This task requires the gunner to engage area targets with width and depth, while making position changes or manipulating the T&E mechanism during timed conditions. (C7 through C8)

1-36. 10-METER CONDUCT OF FIRE

The gunners are instructed on the objectives and fundamentals of firing from the bipod and tripod-supported prone or fighting positions, on fire commands used on the basic range, on the basic machine gun marksmanship target, and on analyzing and scoring the target. The unit is organized in firing orders based on range constraints. Each firing order should consist of a gunner and an assistant gunner. The assistant gunner assists the gunner during prefire checks and zeroing. The assistant gunner also relays signals to the tower operator, checks the gunner's position, and assists him. During qualification, an assistant gunner is not used. The ten tasks are fired in the following manner:

a. **Task 1—Bipod, Zero.**

(1) The tower operator gives the command MACHINE GUN TO BE MOUNTED HERE (weapon squad leader's pointing to the firing points on the 10-meter line), FRONT (weapon squad leader's pointing to the 10-meter targets), ACTION.

(2) At the command ACTION the machine gun crew conducts, placing the machine gun into action (bipod mode).

(3) The gunner prepares the rear sight for zeroing and checks the front sight.

(4) The gunner assumes a good position.

(5) The tower operator instructs the gunner to prepare a single round.

(6) The following fire command is given. The gunner and assistant gunner repeat each element of the fire command as it is given.
FIRE MISSION (The gunner loads and moves the safety to "F".)
FRONT (The gunner focuses on the target or target area.)
PASTER A ONE (The gunner locates target.)
FIVE HUNDRED (The gunner adjusts sights and acquires the sight picture.)
FIXED, ONE ROUND (The gunner is given the method of fire.)
COMMENCE FIRING (The gunner fires on command from tower operator, but when ready.)

✍ NOTE

Throughout all firing exercises, the gunner performs the appropriate tasks during each element of the fire command. The number of rounds fired is used instead of the rate for METHOD OF FIRE. This is for control. (Omitting the rate specifies RAPID fire, which is not desirable for the tasks.)

WARNING

The M240B is carried loaded with the bolt locked to the *rear* in *tactical situations* where noise discipline is critical to the success of the mission. Trained gun crews are the only personnel authorized to load the M240B and only when command directs the crew to do so. During *normal training exercises*, the M240B is loaded and carried with the bolt in the *forward position.*

(7) The gunner loads one round, obtains the proper sight picture, and gives an UP to the assistant gunner.

(8) The assistant gunner relays the READY signal to the tower operator.

(9) The tower operator gives the command COMMENCE FIRING.

(10) The gunner engages paster A1 with three-single shots when he is ready.

(11) The gunner moves downrange to observe, mark, and triangulate the shot group. He makes adjustments as needed.

(12) Steps 3 through 10 are repeated, but the gunner fires at paster A2 firing a single round, then he adjusts.

> ✍ **NOTE**
> If the gunner should zero his weapon using 9 rounds, he uses the remaining 3 rounds to confirm his zero. If he is unable to zero with 12 rounds, he is removed from the firing line for remedial training.

> **WARNING**
> The M240B is carried loaded with the bolt locked to the *rear* in *tactical situations* where noise discipline is critical to the success of the mission. Trained gun crews are the only personnel authorized to load the M240B and only when command directs the crew to do so. During *normal training exercises,* the M240B is loaded and carried with the bolt in the *forward position.*

b. **Task 2—Bipod, Controlled-Burst Fire, Fixed.**

(1) The tower operator instructs the gunner to prepare two 7-round belts (M249) or two 9-round belts (M60/M240B).

(2) When the fire command is given, the gunner and assistant gunner repeat each element as it is given.

FIRE MISSION
FRONT
PASTER A THREE
FIVE HUNDRED
FIXED, FIVE- TO SEVEN-ROUND BURSTS (M249) or SEVEN- TO NINE-ROUND BURSTS (M60/M240B).
AT MY COMMAND

(3) The gunner acquires the proper sight picture and gives an UP to the assistant gunner.

(4) The assistant gunner relays the READY signal to the tower operator.

(5) The tower operator gives the command to FIRE.

(6) The gunner fires the first burst of 5 to 7 rounds (M249) or 7 to 9 rounds (M60/M240B) at paster A3.

(7) Steps 2 through 6 are repeated, but the gunner fires at paster A4.

c. **Task 3—Bipod, Controlled-Burst Fire, Fixed.**

(1) The tower operator instructs the gunner to prepare a 14-round belt (M249) or 18-round belt (M60/M240B).

(2) When the fire command is given, the gunner and assistant gunner repeat each element as it is given.

FIRE MISSION
FRONT
PASTER A FIVE
FIVE HUNDRED
TRAVERSE AND SEARCH, FIVE- TO SEVEN-ROUND BURSTS (M249) OR SEVEN- TO NINE-ROUND BURSTS (M60/M240B)
AT MY COMMAND

(3) The gunner acquires the proper sight picture and gives an UP to the assistant gunner.

(4) The assistant gunner relays the READY signal to the tower operator.

(5) The tower operator gives the command to FIRE.

(6) The gunner fires the first burst of 5 to 7 (M249) OR 7 TO 9 (M60/M240B) rounds at paster A5.

(7) Steps 2 through 6 are repeated, but the gunner fires at paster A6.

d. **Task 4—Bipod, Controlled-Burst Fire, Fixed.**

(1) The tower operator instructs the gunner to prepare 14-round belt (M249) or 18-round belt (M60/M240B).

(2) When the fire command is given, the gunner and assistant gunner repeat each element as it is given.

FIRE MISSION
FRONT
PASTER A SEVEN
FIVE HUNDRED

TRAVERSE AND SEARCH, FIVE- TO SEVEN-ROUND BURSTS (M249) or SEVEN- TO NINE-ROUND BURSTS (M60/M240B)
AT MY COMMAND

(3) The gunner acquires the proper sight picture and gives an UP to the assistant gunner.
(4) The assistant gunner relays the READY signal to the tower operator.
(5) The tower operator gives the command to FIRE.
(6) The gunner fires the first burst of 5 to 7 rounds (M249) or 7 to 9 rounds (M60/M240B) at paster A7.
(7) Steps 2 through 6 are repeated, but the gunner fires at paster A8.
(8) The gunner and assistant gunner moves downrange to observe and analyze his target and shot groups.
(9) The tower operator gives the following command when the gunner and assistant gunner return from downrange. OUT OF ACTION.
(10) At the command OUT OF ACTION the machine gun crew conducts, taking the machine gun out of action (bipod mode).

e. **Task 5—Tripod, Zero.** If the gunner should zero his weapon in 9 rounds, he uses the remaining 3 rounds to confirm his zero. If he is unable to zero in 12 rounds, he is removed from the firing line for remedial training.

(1) The tower operator gives the command MACHINE GUN TO BE MOUNTED HERE (weapon squad leaders point to the firing points on the 10-meter line), FRONT (weapon squad leader points to the 10-meter targets), ACTION.
(2) At the command ACTION the machine gun crew conducts, placing the machine gun into action (tripod mode)
(3) The gunner prepares the rear sight for zeroing and checks the front sight.
(4) The gunner assumes a good tripod position.
(5) The tower operator instructs the gunner to prepare a single round.
(6) The following fire command is given. The gunner and assistant gunner repeat each element of the fire command as it is given.
FIRE MISSION (The gunner loads and moves the safety to "F".)
FRONT (The gunner focuses on the target or target area.)
PASTER B ONE (The gunner locates target.)
FIVE HUNDRED (The gunner adjusts sights and acquires the sight picture.)
FIXED, ONE ROUND (The gunner is given the method of fire.)
COMMENCE FIRING (The gunner fires on command from tower operator, but when ready.)
(7) The gunner loads one round, obtains the proper sight picture, and gives an UP to the assistant gunner.
(8) The assistant gunner relays the READY signal to the tower operator.
(9) The tower operator gives the command COMMENCE FIRING.
(10) The gunner engages paster B1 with three single shots when he is ready.
(11) The gunner moves downrange to observe, mark, and triangulate the shot group. He makes adjustments as needed.
(12) Steps 3 through 10 are repeated, but the gunner fires at paster B2 firing a single round, then he adjusts.

f. **Task 6—Tripod, Controlled-Burst Fire, Traverse.**

(1) The tower operator instructs the gunner to prepare a 28-round belt (M249) or 36-round belt (M60/M240B).
(2) When the fire command is given, the gunner and assistant gunner repeat each element as it is given.
FIRE MISSION
FRONT
PASTERS B ONE THROUGH B FOUR
FIVE HUNDRED
FIXED, FIVE TO SEVEN-ROUND BURSTS (M249) or SEVEN- TO NINE-ROUND BURSTS (M60/M240B)
AT MY COMMAND
(3) The gunner acquires the proper sight picture and gives an UP to the assistant gunner.
(4) The assistant gunner relays the READY signal to the tower operator.
(5) The tower operator gives the command to FIRE.

(6) The gunner engages pasters B1 through B4, firing 5- to 7-round bursts (M249) or 7 to 9 round bursts (M60/M240B) at each paster, using traverse technique.

g. **Task 7—Tripod, Controlled-Burst Fire, Traverse and Search.**

(1) The tower operator instructs the gunner to prepare a 56-round belt (M249) or 63-round belt (M60/M240B).

(2) When the fire command is given, the gunner and assistant gunner repeat each element as it is given.
FIRE MISSION
FRONT
PASTERS B SEVEN THROUGH B EIGHT
FIVE HUNDRED
TRAVERSE AND SEARCH, FIVE- TO SEVEN-ROUND BURSTS (M249) or SEVEN- TO NINE-ROUND BURSTS (M60/M240B)
AT MY COMMAND

(3) The gunner acquires the proper sight picture and gives an UP to the assistant gunner.

(4) The assistant gunner relays the READY signal to the tower operator.

(5) The tower operator gives the command to FIRE.

(6) The gunner engages pasters B7 through B8, firing a 5- to 7-round bursts or 7- to 9-round bursts at each paster, using traverse and search technique.

h. **Task 8—Tripod, Controlled-Burst Fire, Search and Traverse.**

(1) The tower operator instructs the assistant gunner to prepare a 35-round belt (M249) or 45-round belt (M60/M240B).

(2) When the fire command is given, the gunner and assistant gunner repeat each element as it is given
FIRE MISSION
FRONT
PASTERS B FIVE THROUGH B SIX
FIVE HUNDRED
TRAVERSE AND SEARCH, FIVE- TO SEVEN-ROUND BURSTS (M249) or SEVEN- TO NINE-ROUND BURSTS (M60/M240B)
AT MY COMMAND

(3) The gunner acquires the proper sight picture and gives an UP to the assistant gunner.

(4) The assistant gunner relays the READY signal to the tower operator.

(5) The tower operator gives the command to FIRE.

(6) The gunner engages pasters B5 through B6, firing a three round burst at each paster, using search and traverse technique.

(7) The gunner and assistant gunner moves downrange to observe and analyze his targets.

i. **Task 9—Tripod, Qualification, Search and Traverse Fire.** On completion of all firing, the firing line is cleared and the instructors or safeties move downrange and score the targets. The firer will not score his own target.

(1) The tower operator instructs the assistant gunner to prepare a 35-round belt (M249) or 45-round belt (M60/M240B).

(2) When the fire command is given, the gunner and assistant gunner repeat each element as it is given
FIRE MISSION
FRONT
PASTERS C FIVE THROUGH C SIX
FIVE HUNDRED
TRAVERSE AND SEARCH, FIVE- TO SEVEN-ROUND BURSTS (M249) or SEVEN- TO NINE-ROUND BURSTS (M60/M240B)
AT MY COMMAND

(3) The gunner acquires the proper sight picture and gives an UP to the assistant gunner.

(4) The assistant gunner relays the READY signal to the tower operator.

(5) The tower operator gives the command to FIRE.

(6) The gunner engages pasters B5 through B6, firing a 5- to 7-round bursts (M249) or 7- to 9-round bursts (M60/M240B) at each paster, using search and traverse technique. The gunner has 30 seconds to engage as many pasters as he can during the time allowed.

j. **Task 10—Tripod, Qualification, Traverse and Search.** On completion of all firing, the firing line is cleared and the instructors or safeties move downrange and score the targets. The firer will not score his own target.
   (1) The tower operator instructs the gunner to prepare a 56-round belt (M249) or 72-round belt (M60/M240B).
   (2) When the fire command is given, the gunner and assistant gunner repeat each element as it is given.
   FIRE MISSION
   FRONT
   PASTERS C SEVEN THROUGH C EIGHT
   HUNDRED
   TRAVERSE AND SEARCH, FIVE- TO SEVEN-ROUND BURSTS (M249) or SEVEN- TO NINE-ROUND BURSTS (M60/M240B)
   AT MY COMMAND
   (3) The gunner acquires the proper sight picture and gives an UP to the assistant gunner.
   (4) The assistant gunner relays the READY signal to the tower operator.
   (5) The tower operator gives the command to FIRE.
   (6) The gunner engages pasters C7 through C8, firing 5- to 7-round bursts (M249) or 7- to 9-round bursts (M60/M240B) at each paster, using traverse and search technique. The gunner has 45 seconds to engage as many pasters as he can during the time allowed.
   (7) The tower operator gives the following command when the gunner and assistant gunner return from downrange. OUT OF ACTION.
   (8) At the command OUT OF ACTION the machine gun crew conducts, taking the machine gun out of action (tripod mode).

WARNING

The M240B is carried loaded with the bolt locked to the *rear* in *tactical situations* where noise discipline is critical to the success of the mission. Trained gun crews are the only personnel authorized to load the M240B and only when command directs the crew to do so. During *normal training exercises*, the M240B is loaded and carried with the bolt in the *forward position*.

1-37. 10-METER FIRING, QUALIFICATION

The first phase of qualification consists of firing tasks 2 through 8 of Firing Table I for practice, and tasks 9 and 10 of Firing Table I for record. Before firing, all soldiers must be familiar with the tasks, the time allowed, the ammunition allowances, the procedures to follow in the event of a stoppage, and the penalties imposed.

a. **Time and Ammunition.** Each gunner completes zeroing before record firing. Individual fire commands are given for each task. Task 9 is fired in 30 seconds, and task 10 is fired in 45 seconds.
b. **Stoppages.** If a stoppage occurs, the gunner must apply immediate action. If the stoppage is reduced, he continues to fire the course.
   (1) If a stoppage occurs that cannot be reduced by immediate action, the gunner raises his hand and awaits assistance.
   (2) Once the stoppage is reduced, the gunner completes firing beginning with the next task.
   (3) If a stoppage is caused by an error on the part of the gunner, additional time is not permitted. The gunner receives the score he earned before the stoppage occurred.
   (4) If it is necessary to replace the machine gun, the gunner must zero the new weapon. The gunner can fire the exercise again.
   (5) Gunners who cannot fire a task or cannot complete firing in the time allowed (because of malfunctions) can finish the exercise in an *alibi run* after all other gunners complete firing. They fire only those tasks they failed to engage because of the malfunction.
c. **Penalties.** Five points are deducted from the score of any gunner who fails to stop firing at the command or signal to cease fire. If a gunner fires at the wrong target or exercise, he loses the points for those rounds. A gunner whose target was fired upon by another gunner is permitted to refire the exercise.

Table 1-2: Firing Table I—Basic (10-meter) fire.

BASIC (10-METER) FIRE PRONE OR FIGHTING POSITION, BIPOD OR TRIPOD, PRACTICE AND QUALIFICATION						
TASK	TIME	RDS M249	RDS M60/ M240B	TYPE	TARGET	TYPE FIRE
1	No limit	12	12	Ball	Pasters A1 and A2	12 single rd (zero).
2	No limit	14	18	Ball	Pasters A3 and A4	5- to 7-rd bursts (M249) or 7- to 9-rd bursts (M60/ M240B) for each paster.
3	No limit	14	18	Ball	Pasters A5 and A6	5- to 7-rd bursts (M249) or 7- to 9-rd bursts (M60/ M240B) for each paster.
4	No limit	14	18	Ball	Pasters A7 and A8	5- to 7-rd bursts (M249) or 7- to 9-rd bursts (M60/ M240B) for each paster.
5	No limit	12	12	Ball	Pasters B1 and B2	12 single rd (zero).
6	No limit	28	36	Ball	Pasters B1 thru B4	5- to 7-rd bursts (M249) or 7- to 9-rd bursts (M60/ M240B) for each paster.
7	No limit	56	72	Ball	Pasters B7 thru B8	5- to 7-rd bursts (M249) or 7- to 9-rd bursts (M60/ M240B) for each paster traverse and search.
8	No limit	35	45	Ball	Pasters B5 thru B6	5- to 7-rd bursts (M249) or 7- to 9-rd bursts (M60/ M240B) for each paster.
*9	30 seconds	35	45	Ball	Pasters C5 thru C6	5- to 7-rd bursts (M249) or 7- to 9-rd bursts (M60/ M240B) for each paster.
*10	45 seconds	56	72	Ball	Pasters C7 thru C8	5- to 7-rd bursts (M249) or 7- to 9-rd bursts (M60/ M240B) for each paster.
NOTE: The unit commander determines the position to be used. A summary of the ammunition requirements is on page 4-54. *Indicates qualification tasks.						

d. **Scoring.** When scoring the 10-meter target, the trainer scores all scoring pasters (C5 through C6 and C7 through C8). One point is given for each round impacting within the scoring space. The maximum point value is 7 points (M249) or 9 points (M60/M240B) for each paster. Rounds touching the line on the paster are considered a HIT. When firing C5 though C6, the gunner engages 5 scoring pasters with 35 rounds. (M249) or 45 rounds (M60/M240B) The maximum possible is 35 points (M249) or 45 points (M60/M240B). When firing pasters C7 through C8, the gunner engages 8 scoring pasters with 56 rounds (M249) or 72 rounds (M60/M240B). The maximum possible is 56 points (M249) or 72 points (M60/M240B). Gunners do not score their own targets when firing for qualification. During qualification firing, at least 63 points (M249) or 81 points (M60/M240B) must he achieved on Firing Table I. DA Form 85-R is used to record scores (Figure 1-23).

e. **Position.** Based on his METL, the commander selects either the bipod-supported prone or fighting position for table A only. For qualification the position will be either tripod-supported prone or tripod-supported fighting position table B for practice and table C for qualification.

1-38. TRANSITION FIRE

Transition firing provides the gunner the experience necessary to progress from 10-meter firing to field firing at various types of targets at longer ranges. The gunner experiences and learns the characteristics of fire, field zeroing, and range determination, and engaging targets in a timed scenario. He uses the adjusted aiming-point method of fire adjustment. Transition firing is conducted on a machine gun transition range or the MPRC. These exercises are fired with the bipod prone or fighting position. Transition firing is fired and scored for practice and qualification to provide feedback to the gunner. Firing Table II consists of eight tasks (Table 1-3).

a. **Range Facilities.** The transition range should consist of several firing lanes. Each lane should be 10 meters wide at the firing line and 100 meters wide at a range of 800 meters. Ideally, each lane has a fighting position with an adjacent prone firing position.

b. **Targets** (Card board: NSN 6920-00-795-1806 and plastic: 6920-00-071-4780). The E-type silhouette targets are used—single and double are needed for qualification. The double represents an enemy automatic weapon, which for the gunner is a priority target (Figure 1-22). The targets are at various ranges that a gunner might engage. All targets should be plainly seen from the firing positions. Electrical targets are desirable.

c. **Stoppage.** The same procedures used in Firing Table I qualification firing are used.

d. **Penalties.** The same procedures used in Firing Table I qualification firing are used.

e. **Scoring.** Ten points are given for each target hit, whether hit on the first or second burst. The total possible points are 110. The gunner must hit at least 7 (70 points) targets out of 11 exposures to qualify. DA Form 85-R is used to record scores Figure 1-23.

f. **Position.** Based on his METL, the commander selects either the bipod-supported prone or bipod-supported fighting position for qualification.

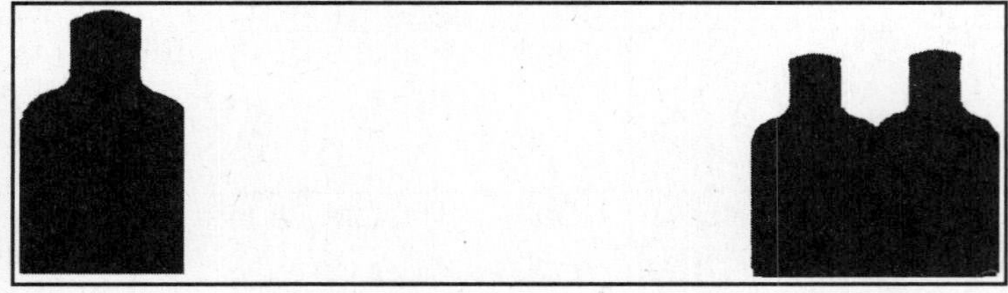

Figure 1-22: Single and double E-type silhouette targets.

1-39. TRANSITION CONDUCT OF FIRE, BIPOD

The unit is organized in firing orders based on range constraints. Each firing order should consist of a gunner and an assistant gunner. The assistant gunner assists the gunner during prefire checks and zeroing. He also relays signals to the tower operator, checks the gunner's position, and assists him during qualification in target detection and adjustments. The bipod-supported prone or fighting positions are used. The eight tasks are fired in the following manner.

a. **Task 1—Field Zero, 500-Meter, Double E-Type Silhouette.**

(1) The tower operator gives the command MACHINE GUN TO BE MOUNTED HERE (weapon squad leader's pointing to the firing points on the transition line), FRONT (weapon squad leader's pointing to the targets), ACTION.

(2) At the command ACTION the machine gun crew conducts, placing the machine gun into action (bipod mode).

(3) The gunner prepares the rear sight for field zeroing and checks the front sight blade. He sets the range to the zero target on the range scale. The preferred range is 500 meters.

(4) The gunner assumes a good position.
(5) The tower operator instructs the assistant gunner to prepare a 28-round belt (M249) or 36-round belt (M60/M240B).
(6) When the fire command is given, the gunner and assistant gunner repeat each element as it is given.
FIRE MISSION
FRONT
TARGETS: TROOPS IN THE OPEN
THREE HUNDRED
FIXED, FIVE- TO SEVEN-ROUND BURST (M249) or SEVEN- to NINE-ROUND BURST (M60/M240B)
AT MY COMMAND
(7) The gunner loads one 28-round belt of ammunition (M249) or 36-round belt of ammunition (M60/M240B), obtains the proper sight picture, and gives an UP to the assistant gunner.
(8) The assistant gunner relays the READY signal to the tower operator.
(9) The tower operator gives the command FIRE.
(10) The gunner fires a 5- to 7-round burst (M249) or 7- to 9-round burst (M60/M240B) at the target when ready.
(11) The gunner observes the beaten zone. If the rounds miss the target, he makes adjustments for windage and elevation.
(12) After adjustments have been made, the gunner repeats steps 8 through 9 with the remaining rounds until rounds are impacting on the target. He records his zero.

b. **Task 2—400-Meter, Double E-Type Silhouette.**
(1) The tower operator instructs the gunner to load one 154-round belt.
(2) When the fire command is given, the gunner and assistant gunner repeat each element as it is given. It is only given once for tasks 2 through 8.
FIRE MISSION
FRONT
TARGET: TROOPS IN THE OPEN
ONE HUNDRED TO EIGHT HUNDRED METERS
FIXED, FIVE- TO SEVEN-ROUND BURST (M249) or SEVEN- TO NINE-ROUND BURST (M60/M240B)
AT MY COMMAND
(3) The gunner gives an UP to the assistant gunner.
(4) The assistant gunner gives the READY signal to the tower operator.
(5) The tower operator gives the command FIRE.
(6) The gunner scans the sector.
(7) A 400-meter, double E-type target is exposed for 10 seconds.
(8) The gunner determines the range, places the proper setting on the rear sight, assumes the proper position, obtains the correct sight alignment and sight picture, and fires a 5- to 7-round burst (M249) or 7- to 9-round burst (M60/M240B).
(9) If the gunner fails to hit the target, he fires another 5- to 7-round burst (M249) or 7- to 9-round burst (M60/M240B) using the adjusted aiming point method of fire adjustment.

c. **Task 3—500-Meter, Double E-Type Silhouette.**
(1) The gunner and assistant gunner continues to scan the sector.
(2) A 500-meter, double E-type target is exposed for 10 seconds.
(3) The gunner determines the range, places the proper setting on the rear sight, assumes the proper position, obtains the correct sight alignment and sight picture, and fires a 5- to 7-round burst (M249) or 7- to 9-round burst (M60/M240B).
(4) If the gunner fails to hit the target, he fires another 5- to 7-round burst (M249) or 7- to 9-round burst (M60/M240B) using the adjusted aiming point method of fire adjustment.

d. **Task 4—600-Meter, Single E-Type Silhouette.**
(1) The gunner and assistant gunner continues to scan the sector.
(2) A 600-meter, single E-type target is exposed for 20 seconds.

(3) The gunner determines the range, places the proper setting on the rear sight, assumes the proper position, obtains the correct sight alignment and sight picture, and fires a 5- to 7-round burst (M249) or 7- to 9-round burst (M60/M240B).

(4) If the gunner fails to hit the target, he fires another 5- to 7-round burst (M249) or 7- to 9-round burst (M60/M240B) using the adjusted aiming point method of fire adjustment.

e. **Task 5—800-Meter, Single E-Type Silhouette.**

(1) The gunner and assistant gunner continues to scan the sector.

(2) A 800-meter, single E-type target is exposed for 30 seconds (total of six targets).

(3) The gunner determines the range, places the proper setting on the rear sight, assumes the proper position, obtains the correct sight alignment and sight picture, and fires a 5- to 7-round burst (M249) or 7- to 9-round burst (M60/M240B).

(4) If the gunner fails to hit the target, he fires another 5- to 7-round burst (M249) or 7- to 9-round burst (M60/M240B) using the adjusted aiming point method of fire adjustment.

f. **Task 6—400-Meter, Single E-Type Silhouette; and 600-Meter, Double E-Type Silhouettes.**

(1) The gunner and assistant gunner continue to scan the sector.

(2) A 400-meter single E-type target and a 600-meter double E-type target are exposed for 30 seconds.

(3) The gunner determines the range, places the proper setting on the rear sight, assumes the proper position, obtains the correct sight alignment and sight picture, and fires a 5- to 7-round burst (M249) or 7- to 9-round burst (M60/M240B) at each target.

Table 1-3: Firing Table II—Bipod transition fire.

BIPOD TRANSITION FIRE PRONE OR FIGHTING POSITION PRACTICE AND QUALIFICATION							
TASK	TIME	RDS M249	RDS M60/ M240B	TYPE	TARGET	RANGE	TYPE FIRE
1	No limit	28	36	X 4:1	Double E	500	Fixed, 5- to 7-rd burst (M249) or 7- to 9-rd burst (M60/M240B) (field zero)
*2	5 seconds	14	18	X 4:1	Double E	400	Fixed, 5- to 7-rd burst (M249) or 7- to 9-rd burst (M60/M240B)
*3	10 seconds	14	18	X 4:1	Double E	500	Fixed, 5- to 7-rd burst (M249) or 7- to 9-rd burst (M60/M240B)
*4	5 seconds	14	18	X 4:1	Double E	600	Fixed, 5- to 7-rd burst (M249) or 7- to 9-rd burst (M60/M240B)
*5	10 seconds	14	18	X 4:1	Double E	800	Fixed, 5- to 7-rd burst (M249) or 7- to 9-rd burst (M60/M240B)
*6	20 seconds	28	36	X 4:1	Single E Double E	400 600	Fixed, 5- to 7-rd burst (M249) or 7- to 9-rd burst (M60/M240B)
*7	20 seconds	28	36	X 4:1	Double E Double E	700 800	Fixed, 5- to 7-rd burst (M249) or 7- to 9-rd burst (M60/M240B)
*8	25 seconds	42	54	X 4:1	Single E Double E Double E	400 500 600	Fixed, 5- to 7-rd burst (M249) or 7- to 9-rd burst (M60/M240B)
NOTE: The unit commander determines the firing position.							
*Indicates qualification tasks.					**X** Indicates ball and tracer 4:1 mix.		

(4) If the gunner fails to hit the target, he fires another 5- to 7-round burst (M249) or 7- to 9-round burst (M60/M240B) using the adjusted aiming point method of fire adjustment at each target.

g. **Task 7—700-Meter and 800-Meter, Double E-Type Silhouettes.**

(1) The gunner and assistant gunner continue to scan the sector.

(2) A 700-meter and a 800-meter double E-type targets are exposed for 45 seconds (total of four targets at 700 meters and six targets at 800 meters).

(3) The gunner determines the range, places the proper setting on the rear sight, assumes the proper position, obtains correct sight alignment and sight picture, and fires a 5- to 7-round burst (M249) or 7- to 9-round burst (M60/M240B) at each target.

(4) If the gunner fails to hit the target, he fires another 7-round burst using the adjusted aiming point method of fire adjustment at each target.

h. **Task 8—400-Meter, Single E-Type Silhouette, and 500-Meter, 600-Meter, Double E-Type Silhouettes.**

(1) The gunner and assistant gunner continue to scan the sector.

(2) The 400-meter single E-type silhouettes, and 500- and 600-meter double E-type silhouettes are exposed for 45 seconds (total of two targets at 400 meters, four targets at 500 meters, and six targets at 600 meters).

(3) The gunner determines the range, places the proper setting on the rear sight, assumes the proper position, obtains correct sight alignment and sight picture, and fires a 5- to 7-round burst (M249) or 7- to 9-round burst (M60/M240B) at each target.

(4) If the gunner fails to hit the target, he fires another 5- to 7-round burst (M249) or 7- to 9-round burst (M60/M240B) using the adjusted aiming point method of fire adjustment at each target.

1-40. TRANSITION FIRE, LIMITED VISIBILITY

Night or limited visibility firing requires the soldier to apply the fundamentals of gunner marksmanship while using nightsights. This training instills confidence in the machine gunner. Each soldier learns how to engage targets using nightsight. He learns to mount the sight, boresight the weapon at 10-meters, and zero the aided vision devices at 10-meters using a 10-meter (M16A2) zero target. Finally, he learns to detect and engage a series of undetermined targets at various ranges with the aided vision device. Night firing exercises can be conducted during daylight with the AN/PVS-4 when the daylight cover is used. These exercises are for instructional, practice and qualification purposes. The commander can use this training to assess his unit's METL. Night firing is conducted on the same 10-meter range and transition range or a multipurpose machine gun range used for Firing Tables I and II. The tasks and conduct of fire in Firing Table III are the same as in Firing Table II. Therefore, a conduct of fire is not necessary.

a. **Time and Ammunition.** Table 4-4, Firing Table III outlines ammunition requirements.
b. **Stoppage.** The same procedures that are used in Firing Table II.
c. **Penalties.** No penalties are used.
d. **Scoring.** No points are given when the target is hit on the first or second hit, only a hit or miss. The gunner must hit 6 out of 11 targets in order to be a qualified gunner. The gunner must have qualified on both the 10-meter and transition in order to advance to this step.
e. **Conditions.** Table 1-3, Firing Table III is used for engaging targets out to 400 meters under ideal moonlight or during daylight conditions. If visibility is limited because of a lack of ambient light, commanders may use field-expedient means to identify targets.

> ✍ **NOTE**
> The commander may lower the ranges by 100 meters when the ambient conditions do not allow the gunners to engage targets at extended ranges.

f. **Targets.** Single E-type silhouette targets and double E-type silhouette targets are used.
g. **Position.** Based on his METL, the commander selects either the bipod-supported prone position or bipod-supported fighting position.
h. **Conduct of Fire.** Limited visibility is the same as Firing Table II. The only difference is time and distance of the targets to be engaged and firing the scanning, walking and IR discipline exercise.

1-41. AN/PVS-4 ZERO

⚠ CAUTION

When mounting the AN/PVS-4 to the mounting bracket, make sure the hole for the screw in the AN/PVS-4 is aligned and flush against the bracket screw. If not, it will strip the threads on the screw, and the AN/PVS-4 cannot be used with the M249 machine gun.

Table 1-4: Firing Table III—Transition fire, limited visibility.

TRANSITION FIRE, LIMITED VISIBILITY						
TASK	TIME	RDS M249	RDS M60/ M240B	TYPE	TARGET	TYPE FIRE
1	No limit	6	6	X 4:1	25-meter zero at 10 meters	6-single rounds
2	No limit	18	18	X 4:1	25-meter zero at 10 meters	18-single rounds
3	No limit	28	36	X 4:1	500	Fixed, 5- to 7- rd bursts (M249) or 7- to 9-rd bursts (M60/M240B)
*4	10 seconds	14	18	X 4:1	200	Fixed, 5- to 7- rd bursts (M249) or 7- to 9-rd bursts (M60/M240B)
*5	15 seconds	14	18	X 4:1	400	Fixed, 5- to 7- rd bursts (M249) or 7- to 9-rd bursts (M60/M240B)
*6	10 seconds	14	18	X 4:1	100	Fixed, 5- to 7- rd bursts (M249) or 7- to 9-rd bursts (M60/M240B)
*7	15 seconds	14	18	X 4:1	300	Fixed, 5- to 7- rd bursts (M249) or 7- to 9-rd bursts (M60/M240B)
*8	25 seconds	28	36		200 400	Fixed, 5- to 7- rd bursts (M249) or 7- to 9-rd bursts (M60/M240B)
*9	25 seconds	28	36		100 300	Fixed, 5- to 7- rd bursts (M249) or 7- to 9-rd bursts (M60/M240B)
*10	30 seconds	42	56	X 4:1	100, 200 400	Fixed, 5- to 7- rd bursts (M249) or 7- to 9-rd bursts (M60/M240B)
NOTE: The unit commander determines the position to be used.						
* Indicates qualification tasks.						**X** Indicates ball and tracer 4:1 mix

1-42. QUALIFICATION STANDARDS

Qualification with the M249, M60/M240B machine gun consists of achieving the minimum standards for 10-meter day and transition day firing tables. One point is allowed for each round impacting within the scoring space (maximum of 7 points [M249] or 9 points [M60/M240B] for each space) for Firing Table I. For Firing Table II, 7 points (M249) or 9 points (M60/M240B) are allowed for each target hit whether the target is hit on the first or second burst. For Firing Table III, place an X in the hit column and place an O in the miss column. The maximum possible score for Firing Table I is 91 points (M249), 117 points (M60/M240B). A minimum of 63 points (M249), 81 points (M60/M240B) is required. The maximum score for Firing Table II is 110 points; at least 70 points must be scored on this table to qualify. The maximum possible score for Firing Table III is 11 hits. A minimum of 7 hits is required. The combined minimum total score is 133 (M249), 151 (M240B); the combined maximum total score is 201 points (M249), 227 points (M240B). The overall ratings are as follows:

	M249	**M60/M240B**
EXPERT	182 to 201	206 to 227
GUNNER 1st CLASS	158 to 181	180 to 205
GUNNER 2nd CLASS	133 to 157	151 to 179
UNQUALIFIED	0 to 132	0 to 150

Use the following procedures to fill out the M249, M60/M240B scorecard:

1.	NAME:	Enter the gunner's last name, first name, middle initial, and rank.
2.	SSN:	Enter the gunner's social security number.
3.	UNIT:	Enter the gunner's unit designation.
4.	DATE:	Enter the date of firing.
5.	LANE:	Enter the lane number for the gunner's firing point.
6.	RECORD:	Tasks used for record and qualification are Firing Table I, tasks 9 through 10; Firing Table II, tasks 2 through 8; and Firing Table III, tasks 4 through 10.
7.	HIT/MISS:	For Table I, tasks 9 through 10, enter the number of rounds impacting within target spaces (maximum of 7 [M249] or 9 [M60/M240B] per space). For Table II, tasks 2 through 8, and Table III, tasks 4 through 10, enter an X for a hit and an O for a miss (regardless of whether the target is hit on the first or second burst).
8.	TOTAL HITS/ POINTS:	For Table I, tasks 9 through 10, give 1 point for each round impacting within a scoring space. For Table II, tasks 2 through 8, give 10 points for each target hit. For Table III, tasks 4 through 10, enter the number of targets hit (no points awarded).
9.	TOTAL SCORE:	Add points from Tables IV and V. Use the following qualification levels*:

	M249	M60/M240B
EXPERT GUNNER	182-201	206-227
GUNNER 1ST CLASS	158-181	180-205
GUNNER 2D CLASS	133-157	151-179
UNQUALIFIED	0-132	0-150

* The gunner must score 63 points (M249), 81 points (M60/M240B) on Table I, 70 points on Table II, and 6 hits on Table III to meet the minimum score for each.

The trainer uses DA Form 85-R (Scorecard for M249, M60/M240B Machine Gun) for recording the gunner's performance on the machine gun qualification range. The instructions for completing the scorecard are on its reverse side. For an example of a completed form, see Figure 1-23. A blank locally reproducible form is in the back of this manual. The instructions are on the back of the form explaining how to fill out the form.

The following is a summary of ammunition required:

	M249	M60/M240B	TYPE
Table I, Practice	185	231	Ball
Table I, Record	91	117	X4:1
Table II, Practice	182	236	X4:1
Table II, Record	154	200	X4:1
Table III, Practice	360	460	X4:1
Table III, Record	154	200	X4:1

✍ NOTE

See DA Pam 350-38 for STRAC ammunition requirements.

SCORECARD FOR M249, M60/M240B MACHINE GUNS

For use of this form, see FM 3-22.68; the proponent agency is TRADOC.
See back of this form for instructions.

PRIVACY ACT STATEMENT

AUTHORITY: 10 USC 30129(g) Executive Order 9397.

PRINCIPAL PURPOSE: Records individual's performance on record fire range.

ROUTINE USES: Evaluate individual's proficiency and basis for determination of award of proficiency badge; SSN is used for positive identification purposes only.

DISCLOSURE: Voluntary, individuals not providing information cannot be rated/scored on a mass basis.

NAME	SSN	UNIT	DATE (YYYYMMDD)	LANE
PVT DAVID JONES	123-45-6789	C Co. 2/45TH IN	12 DEC 02	3

TABLE I (10-METERS)

TASK	RANGE (meters)	TIME	HITS
1*	10	N/A	N/A
2*	10	N/A	N/A
3*	10	N/A	N/A
4*	10	N/A	N/A
5*	10	N/A	N/A
6*	10	N/A	N/A
7*	10	N/A	N/A
8*	10	N/A	N/A
9	10	40 SEC	30
10	10	50 SEC	52

TOTAL HITS (POINTS) 82

TABLE II (DAY TRANSITION)

TASK	RANGE (meters)	TIME	*PRACTICE		**QUALIFY	
			HIT	MISS	HIT	MISS
1*	500	N/A	N/A	N/A	N/A	N/A
2**	400	10 SEC	X		X	
3**	500	15 SEC	X		X	
4**	600	20 SEC		O	X	
5**	800	30 SEC	X			O
6**	400 600	30 SEC	X X		X X	
7**	700 800	45 SEC	X	O	X X	
8**	400 500 600	45 SEC	X X X		X X X	

**TOTAL POINTS 100

TABLE III (LIMITED VISIBILITY)

TASK	RANGE (meters)	TIME	*PRACTICE		**QUALIFY	
			HIT	MISS	HIT	MISS
1*	10	N/A	N/A	N/A	N/A	N/A
2*	10	N/A	N/A	N/A	N/A	N/A
3*	500	N/A	N/A	N/A	N/A	N/A
4	200	10 SEC	X		X	
5	400	15 SEC	X			O
6	100	10 SEC		O	X	
7	300	15 SEC	X		X	
8	200 400	25 SEC	X	O	X X	
9	100 300	25 SEC	X X		X X	
10	100 200 400	30 SEC	X X	O	X X X	

TOTAL HITS 9

TOTAL SCORE ____________

* NONSCORED TASKS
**10 POINTS PER HIT

CHECK APPROPRIATE WEAPON

EXPERT		FIRST CLASS		SECOND CLASS	
☑ M249 182-201	☐ M60/M240B 206-227	☐ M249 158-181	☐ M60/M240B 180-205	☐ M249 158-181	☐ M60/M240B 180-205

OIC SIGNATURE	GRADER	RATING
John Smith	Paul Davis	EXPERT

DA FORM 85-R, OCT 2002 DA FORM 85, SEP 62, IS OBSOLETE. Page 1 of 2
USAPA V1.00ES

Figure 1-23: Example of a completed DA Form 85-R

CHAPTER 2

Combat Techniques of Fire

Technique of fire is the method of delivering and controlling effective fire. The machine gunners must be trained in the standard methods of applying fire. This chapter discusses combat techniques of fire, application of fire on the battlefield, and advanced gunnery. Before the machine gun can be employed to its full potential, the soldier must know and be trained on characteristics of fire, classes of fire, types of targets, and application of fire.

SECTION I. CHARACTERISTICS OF FIRE

Each gunner must know the effects of rounds when fired. Factors influencing the path and strike of rounds are not limited to applying the fundamentals. They include the velocity of the round, gravity, terrain, atmospheric conditions, and the innate differences between each round.

2-1. TRAJECTORY

The trajectory is the path of the round in flight (Figure 2-l). The gunner must know the machine gun trajectory to effectively fire the weapon throughout its full range. The path of the round is almost flat at ranges up to 300 meters; then it begins to curve, and the curve becomes greater as the range increases.

2-2. MAXIMUM ORDINATE

Maximum ordinate is the highest point the trajectory reaches between the muzzle of the weapon and the base of the target. It always occurs about two-thirds of the distance from the weapon to the target. The maximum ordinate increases as the range increases (Figure 2-l).

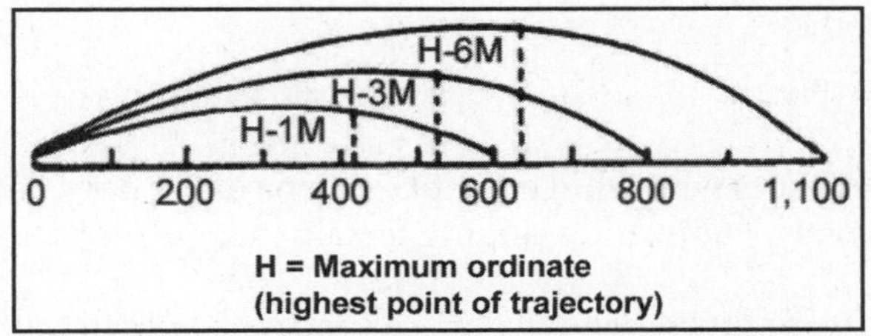

Figure 2-1: Trajectory and maximum ordinate.

2-3. CONE OF FIRE

When several rounds are fired in a burst from any machine gun, each round takes a slightly different trajectory. The pattern these rounds form on the way to the target is called a cone of fire (Figure 2-2). This pattern is caused primarily by vibration of the machine gun and variations in ammunition and atmospheric conditions.

2-4. BEATEN ZONE

The beaten zone (Figure 2-2) is the elliptical pattern formed by the rounds striking the ground or the target. The size and shape of the beaten zone changes when the range to the target changes or when the machine gun is fired on

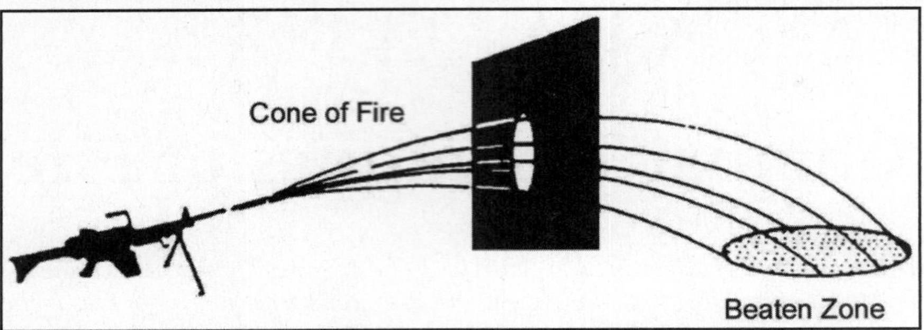

Figure 2-2: Cone of fire and beaten zone.

different types of terrain. On uniformly sloping or level terrain, the beaten zone is long and narrow. As the range to the target increases, the beaten zone becomes shorter and wider. When fire is delivered on terrain sloping down and away from the machine gun, the beaten zone becomes longer. When fire is delivered on rising terrain, the beaten zone becomes shorter. The terrain has little effect on the width of the beaten zone.

2-5. DANGER SPACE

The danger space is the space between the machine gun and the target where the trajectory does not rise above 1.8 meters (the average height of a standing soldier). This space includes the area of the beaten zone. When the machine gun is fired on level or uniformly sloping terrain at a target less than 700 meters away, the trajectory does not rise above the average height of a standing soldier. When targets are engaged on level or uniformly sloping terrain at ranges greater than 700 meters, the trajectory rises above the average height of a standing soldier, therefore, not all the distance between the machine gun and the target is danger space.

SECTION II. CLASSES OF FIRE

Machine gun fire is classified with respect to the ground, the target, and the weapon.

2-6. RESPECT TO THE GROUND

Fire with respect to the GROUND (Figure 2-3) includes grazing and plunging fires.

a. **Grazing Fire.** Grazing fire occurs when the center of the cone of fire does not rise more than 1 meter above the ground. When firing on level or uniformly sloping terrain, the gunner can obtain a maximum of 600 meters of grazing fire.
b. **Plunging Fire.** Plunging fire occurs when the danger space is confined to the beaten zone. Plunging fire also occurs when firing at long ranges, from high ground to low ground, into abruptly rising ground, or across uneven terrain, resulting in a loss of grazing fire at any point along the trajectory.

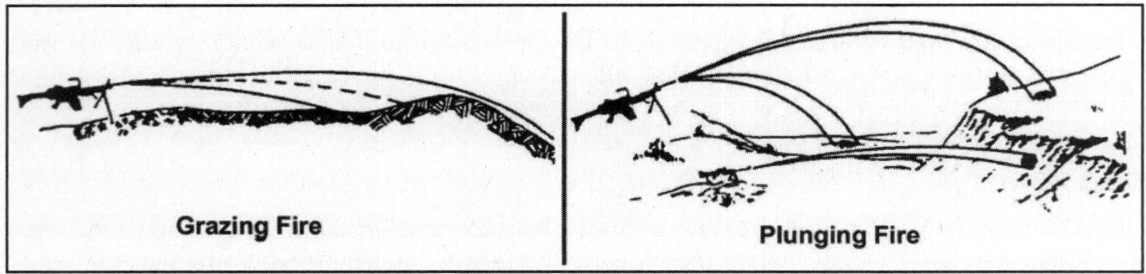

Figure 2-3: Classes of fire with respect to the ground.

2-7. RESPECT TO TARGET

Fire with respect to the TARGET includes frontal, flanking, oblique, and enfilade fires.

a. **Frontal Fire.** Frontal fire is when the long axis of the beaten zone is at a right angle to the front of the target. An example is when firing at the front of a target (Figure 2-4).
b. **Flanking Fire.** Flanking fire is firing at the side of a target (Figure 2-4).

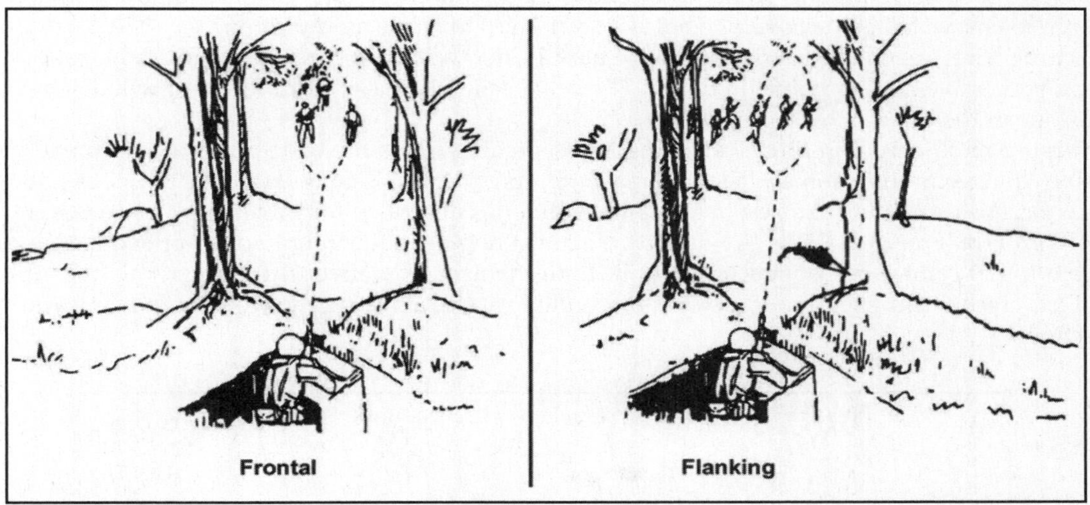

Figure 2-4: Frontal fire and flanking fire.

c. **Oblique Fire.** Oblique fire is when the long axis of the beaten zone is at an angle other than a right angle to the front of the target (Figure 2-5).
d. **Enfilade Fire.** Enfilade fire is when the long axis of the beaten zone coincides or nearly coincides with the long axis of the target. This type of fire is either frontal or flanking. It is the most desirable type of fire with respect to a target, because it makes maximum use of the beaten zone (Figure 2-5).

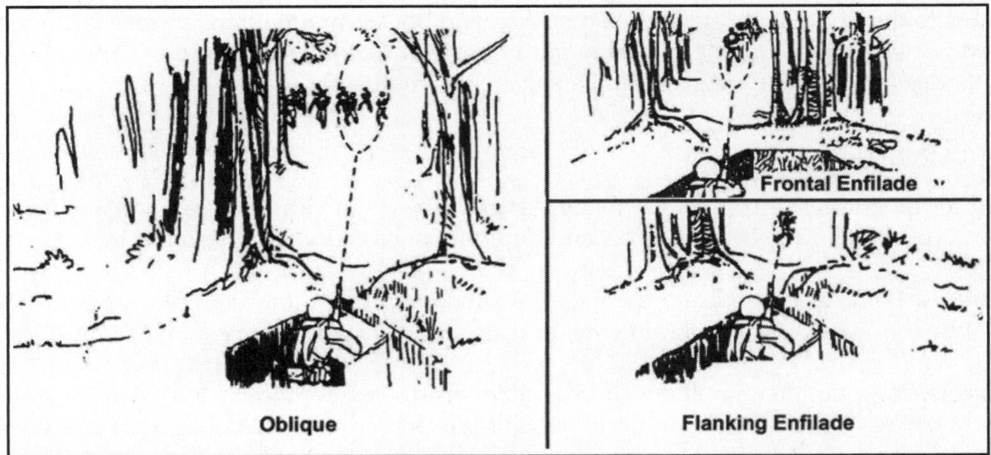

Figure 2-5: Oblique fire and enfilade fire.

2-8. RESPECT TO MACHINE GUN

Fire with respect to the machine gun (Figure 2-6) includes fixed, traversing, searching, and traversing and searching, and free-gun fires.

a. **Fixed Fire.** Fixed fire is fire delivered against a point target when the depth and width of the beaten zone covers the target. Fixed fire also means only one aiming point is necessary to provide coverage of the target.
b. **Traversing Fire.** Traversing fire is fire distributed in width by successive changes in direction. The gunner selects successive aiming points throughout the width of the target. These aiming points must be close enough to ensure adequate coverage but not so close as to waste ammunition.
c. **Searching Fire.** Searching fire is fire distributed in depth by successive changes in elevation. The gunner selects successive aiming points in depth. The changes made in each aiming point will depend on the range and slope of the ground.
d. **Traversing and Searching Fire.** Traversing and searching fire is fire distributed in width and depth by successive changes in direction and elevation. Combining traversing and searching provides good coverage of the target. Adjustments are made in the same manner as described for traversing and searching fire.
e. **Free-Gun Fire.** Free-gun fire is fire delivered against targets requiring rapid major changes in direction and elevation that cannot be applied with the T&E mechanism. To deliver this type of fire, the gunner removes the T&E mechanism from the traversing bar on the tripod, allowing the weapon to be moved freely in any direction.

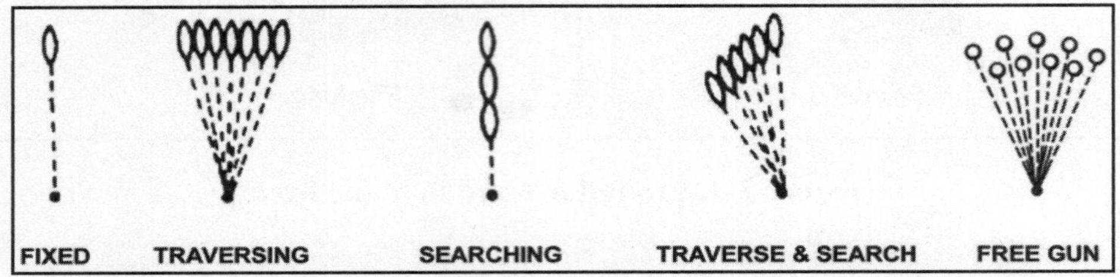

Figure 2-6: Classes of fire with respect to the machine gun.

SECTION III. APPLICATION OF FIRE

Application of fire consists of the methods the gunner uses to cover a target area. Training these methods of applying fire can be accomplished only after the soldiers have learned how to recognize the different types of targets they may find in combat, how to distribute and concentrate their fire, and how to maintain the proper rate of fire. Normally, the gunner is exposed to two types of targets in the squad or platoon sector: enemy soldiers and supporting automatic weapons. These targets have priority and should be engaged immediately.

2-9. TYPES OF TARGETS

Targets presented to the gunner in combat are usually enemy troops in various formations, which require distribution and concentration of fire. Targets with width and depth must be thoroughly covered by fire.

a. **Point Targets.** Point targets require the use of a single aiming point. Examples of point targets are enemy soldiers, bunkers, weapons emplacements, and lightly armored vehicles. Fixed fire is delivered at point targets.
b. **Area Targets.** Area targets may have considerable width and depth and may require extensive traversing and searching fire. These include targets in which the exact location of the enemy is unknown. The following are varieties of area targets likely to be engaged.
   (1) ***Linear Targets.*** Linear targets have sufficient width to require successive aiming points (traversing fire). The beaten zone effectively covers the depth of the target area (Figure 2-7). Traversing fire is delivered at linear targets.

(2) ***Deep Targets.*** Deep targets require successive aiming points (searching fire) (Figure 2-8). Searching fire is delivered at deep targets.

(3) ***Linear Targets with Depth.*** Linear targets with depth have sufficient width requiring successive aiming points in which the beaten zone does not cover the depth of the target area. A combined change in direction and elevation (traversing and searching) is necessary to effectively cover the target with fire (Figure 2-9). Traversing and searching fire are delivered at linear targets with depth.

Figure 2-7: Linear target.

Figure 2-8: Deep target.

Figure 2-9: Linear targets with depth.

2-10. DISTRIBUTION, CONCENTRATION, AND RATE OF FIRE

The size and nature of the target determine how the gunner applies his fire. He must manipulate the machine gun to move the beaten zone throughout the target area. The rate of fire must be controlled to adequately cover the target but not waste ammunition or destroy the barrel.

a. Distributed fire is delivered in width and depth such as at an enemy formation.
b. Concentrated fire is delivered at a point target such as an automatic weapon or an enemy fighting position.
c. The rates of fire that can be used with the machine gun are sustained, rapid, and cyclic. These rates enable leaders to control and sustain fire and prevent the destruction of barrels. More than anything else, the size of the target and ammunition supply dictate the selection of the rate of fire.
   (1) ***Sustained Fire.*** Sustained fire for the M249 is 85 rounds per minute in bursts of 3 to 5 rounds. The M60 and M240B are 100 rounds per minute in bursts of 6 to 9 rounds. The gunner pauses 4 to 5 seconds between bursts. The barrel should be changed after firing at sustained rate for 10 minutes. This is the normal rate of fire for the gunner.
   (2) ***Rapid Fire.*** Rapid fire for the M249, M60, and M240B gunner is 200 rounds per minute in bursts of (6 to 8 M249) 10 to 12 rounds. The gunner pauses 2 to 3 seconds between bursts. The barrel should be changed after firing at a rapid rate for 2 minutes. This procedure provides for an exceptionally high volume of fire, but for only a short period.
   (3) ***Cyclic Fire.*** Cyclic fire uses the most ammunition that can be used in 1 minute. The cyclic rate of fire with the machine gun is achieved when the trigger is held to the rear and ammunition is fed into the weapon uninterrupted for one minute. Normal cyclic rate of fire for the M249 is 850 rounds, M60 is 550 rounds, and for the M240B it is 650 to 950 rounds. Always change the barrel after firing at cyclic rate for 1 minute. This procedure provides the highest volume of fire that the machine gun can fire, but this adversely affects the machine gun, and should only be fired in combat under emergency purposes only.

2-11. TARGET ENGAGEMENT

The gunner engages targets throughout his sector. He must know how to effectively engage all types of targets either by himself or in conjunction with another gunner.

a. **Single Gunner.**
   (1) ***Point Target.*** When engaging a point target, the gunner uses fixed fire (Figure 2-10). If the target moves after the initial burst, the gunner adjusts fire onto the target by following its movement.

Figure 2-10: Engagement of point target.

   (2) ***Area Target.*** When engaging an area target, the gunner fires in the center of mass, then traverses and searches to either flank (Figure 2-11). Upon reaching the flank, he reverses direction and traverses and searches in the opposite direction. A leader may indicate the width and depth of the target.
   (3) ***Linear Target.*** When engaging a linear target, the gunner traverses the machine gun to distribute fire evenly onto the target. He must cover the entire width of a linear target. The initial point of aim is on the

midpoint. The gunner then manipulates to cover the rest of the target. If a linear target is hard to identify, a leader may designate the target by using a reference point (Figure 2-12). When this method is used, the leader determines the center of mass of the target and announces the number of meters from the reference point that will cause the gunner to aim on the center of mass. The reference point may be within or adjacent to the target (Figure 2-13). However, the reference point should be on line with the target for the best effect. After the command to fire has been given, the leader maintains and controls the fire by subsequent fire commands.

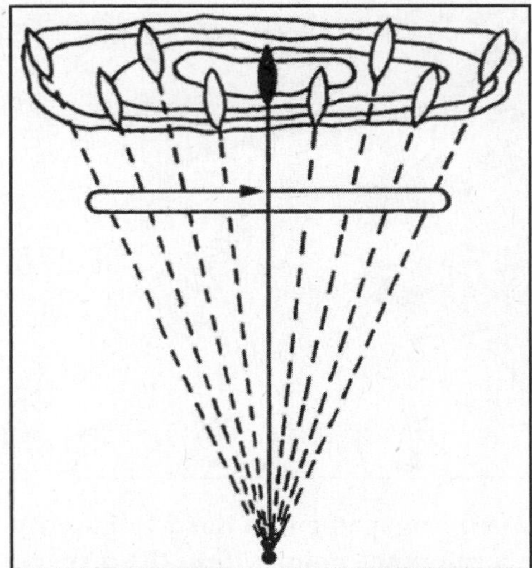

Figure 2-11: Engagement of area target.

Figure 2-12: Engagement of hard-to-identify linear targets with a reference point outside the target area.

(4) ***Deep Target.*** When engaging a deep target, the gunner must use searching fire. If the range is announced, he initially aims on the midpoint of a deep target unless another portion of the target is more critical or presents a greater threat. The gunner then searches down to one aiming point in front of the near end and back up to one aiming point beyond the far end. If a deep target is hard to identify, use the reference points to designate the center of mass. The extent (depth) of the target is always given in meters.

(5) ***Linear Target With Depth.*** When engaging a linear target with depth, the gunner uses traversing and searching fire. He begins engagement at the midpoint of the target unless another portion of the target is

more critical or presents a greater threat. He traverses and searches to the near flank, then back to the far flank. When engaging hard-to-identify linear targets with depth, he designates the flanks and midpoint with rifle fire. The reference-point method is not used because at least two reference points are required to show the angle of the target.

Figure 2-13: Engagement of hard-to-identify targets with a reference point within the target area.

b. **Pair of Gunners.**

(1) ***Area Targets.*** When using a pair of machine guns to engage area targets, the gunner on the right fires on the right half, and the gunner on the left fires on the left half. The point of initial aim and adjustment for both gunners is on the midpoint. After adjusting fire on the center of mass, both gunners distribute fire by applying direction and elevation changes that give the most effective coverage of the target area. The right gunner traverses to the right, applies the necessary amount of search, and fires a burst. He traverses and searches up and down until the right flank of the area target has been reached. The left gunner traverses and searches to the left flank in the same way. Both gunners then reverse the direction of manipulation and return to the center of mass, firing a burst after each combined direction and elevation change (Figure 2-14).

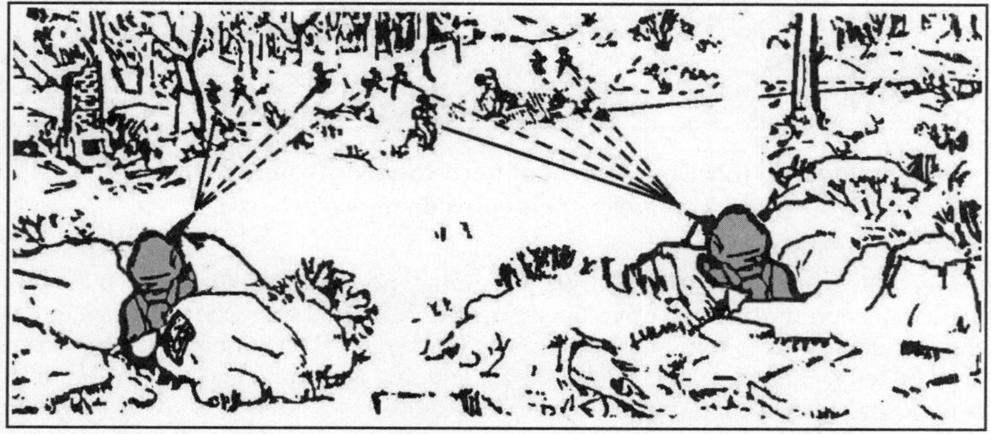

Figure 2-14: Engagement of area targets with a pair of gunners.

(2) ***Linear Targets.*** When using a pair of machine guns to engage a linear target, the target is divided at midpoint with the gunner on the right of the target firing on the right half, and the gunner on the left of the target firing on the left half (Figure 2-15).

Figure 2-15: Engagement of linear targets with a pair of gunners.

(a) Both gunners aim on the midpoint initially. After adjusting on the midpoint, the gunner on the right traverses right, firing a burst after each change in direction until the rounds reach one aiming point beyond the right flank (this ensures complete target coverage). The gunner on the left traverses to the left flank in the same way the gunner on the right did. Both gunners then reverse their directions and return to the midpoint. The gunner must select aiming points for each burst rather than "spray" the target area.

(b) If one part of the target is a greater threat, fire can be concentrated on the greater threat by dividing the target unevenly. This special division of the target is done with fire commands. To preclude confusion, the gunners initially aim on the midpoint regardless of the special division to be made.

(3) ***Deep Targets.*** When using a pair of machine guns to engage a deep target, the initial point of aim is also on the midpoint for both gunners. Normally, the gunner on the right has the near half and the gunner on the left has the far half. Since enfilade fire is being used, they do not adjust on the midpoint of the target, because the long beaten zone compensates for any range errors. After the initial burst, the gunner on the right searches down to one aiming point in front of the near end of the target, and the gunner on the left searches up to one aiming point beyond the far end. Both gunners then reverse their direction of search and return to the midpoint (Figure 2-16).

Figure 2-16: Engagement of deep targets with a pair of gunners.

(4) ***Linear Target With Depth.*** When using a pair of machine guns to engage a linear target with depth, the initial point of aim and the extent of manipulation for both gunners is the same as those prescribed for linear targets (Figure 2-17).

Figure 2-17: Engagement of linear target with depth with a pair of gunners.

2-12. TARGET ENGAGEMENT DURING LIMITED VISIBILITY

Gunners have problems detecting and identifying targets during limited visibility. The leader's ability to control the fires of his weapons is also reduced, therefore, he may instruct the gunners to fire without command when targets present themselves.

a. Gunners should engage targets only when they can identify the targets, unless ordered to do otherwise. For example, if one gunner detects a target and engages it, the other gunner observes the area fired upon and adds his fire only if he can identify the target or if ordered to fire.

b. Tracer ammunition helps a gunner engage targets during limited visibility and should be used, if possible. If firing unaided, gunners must be trained to fire low at first and adjust upward. This overcomes the tendency to fire high.

c. When two or more gunners are engaging linear targets, linear targets with depth, or deep targets, they do not engage these targets as they would when visibility is good. With limited visibility, the center and flanks of these targets may not be clearly defined; therefore, each gunner observes his tracers and covers what he believes to be the entire target.

2-13. OVERHEAD FIRE

Fire delivered over the heads of friendly soldiers is called overhead fire. It is used during training ONLY AFTER SOLDIER SAFETY IS CHECKED AND VERIFIED. The terrain and visibility dictate when overhead fire can be delivered safely. Overhead fire is delivered with any machine gun mounted on a tripod because the machine guns provide greater stability and accuracy, and because vertical mil angles can be measured by using the elevating mechanism.

☠ DANGER

Overhead fire cannot be safely delivered on a target at greater than 850 meters from the machine gun, and it is not delivered over level or uniformly sloping terrain. It can cause death or injury.

a. Ideally, overhead fire is delivered when there is a depression in the terrain between the machine gun position and the target. The depression should place the gunner's line of aim well above the heads of friendly soldiers.

b. The squad leader normally controls overhead fire. He lifts or shifts the fire when the friendly soldiers reach an imaginary line, parallel to the target, where further fire would cause casualties to friendly soldiers. This imaginary line is called the "safety limit." The leader of the friendly soldiers may direct lifting of fire by prearranged signals transmitted by radio, wire, or visual means. The safety limit can be determined by observing the fire or by using the gunner's rule (Figure 2-18).

(1) To determine the safety limit by observation, the leader uses binoculars to see how close the fire is to advancing friendly soldiers.

(2) A safety limit can be selected by using the gunner's rule before the weapon is fired. The accuracy and safety of this method depends on the machine gun being zeroed and the range to the target being known.

Figure 2-18: Overhead fire safety limit.

The gunner's rule is used only when the target is between 350 and 850 meters from the machine gun. The gunner's rule consists of the following procedure.

(a) Determine the range to the target and set the range on the rear sight.
(b) Aim the machine gun to hit the target.
(c) Set the rear sight to 1,000 meters.
(d) Depress the muzzle 10 mils by using the elevating handwheel (one click equals 1 mil).
(e) Look through the rear sight and note the point where the new line of aim strikes the ground. (An imaginary line drawn through this point and parallel to the target is the safety limit.)
(f) Reset the range to the target on the rear sight, aim on the target, and prepare to fire.
(g) Cease or shift fire when soldiers reach the safety limit.

c. The following safety measures MUST be applied when delivering overhead fire.

(1) Firmly emplace the tripod mount.
(2) Use field-expedient depression stops to prevent the muzzle from accidentally being lowered below the safety limit.
(3) Do not deliver overhead fire through trees.
(4) Inform commanders of friendly soldiers when fire is to be delivered over their heads.
(5) Ensure that all members of the crew are aware of the safety limit.
(6) Do not deliver overhead fire if the range from the machine gun to the target is less than 350 meters or more than 850 meters.
(7) Do not use a barrel that is badly worn.
(8) During training exercises, do not aim any machine gun where their trajectories will cross at a point directly over the heads of friendly soldiers.

2-14. DEFILADE POSITIONS

A machine gun is in defilade when the weapon and its crew are completely behind terrain that masks them from the enemy (usually on the reverse slope of a hill). Fire, from a defilade position, is controlled by an observer (the leader or a member of the crew who can see the target) that is in a position near the machine gun. (Figure 2-19.)

a. The machine gun must fire up and over the hill. Its fire must be observed and adjusted by a crewmember that can observe the target from a position on a flank or to the rear of the weapon (on higher ground). A defilade position allows little opportunity to engage new targets. The tripod mount is used when firing from defilade, because the gunner can measure vertical angles with it. This makes changes in elevation for adjusting fire easier, and if data is determined during daylight, the crew can fire from the same position after dark. A machine gun is in partial defilade when it is positioned just back of the crest of a hill, so that the crest provides some protection from enemy direct-fire and the machine guns are still able to engage its target by direct-lay techniques.

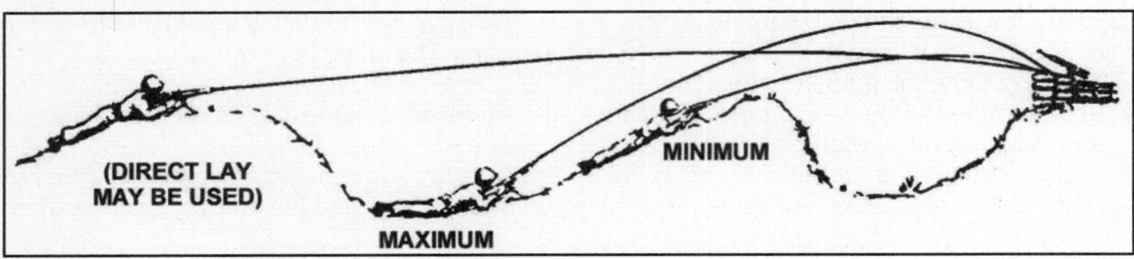

Figure 2-19: Defilade positions.

(1) ***Advantages.***
- The crew has cover and concealment from enemy direct-fire weapons.
- The crew has some freedom of movement near the position.
- Control and supply are easier.
- The smoke and flash of the machine gun are hidden from the enemy.

(2) ***Disadvantages.***
- Rapidly moving ground targets are hard to engage, because adjustment of fire must be made by using an observer.
- Targets close to the mask usually cannot be engaged.
- Final protective line is hard to understand.

b. The essential elements in the engagement of a target from a defilade position are mask clearance, direction, and adjustment of fire. If possible, a minimum mask clearance (minimum elevation) is determined for the entire sector of fire, however, a mask clearance for each target may be necessary (due to the slope of the mask). The elevation readings obtained using the methods below give the minimum elevation for the sector or target(s). The minimum elevation should be recorded on a range card.
(1) If the mask is 300 meters or less from the machine gun position, the gunner places a 300-meter range setting on the rear sight, aims on the top of the mask and adds 3 mils (clicks) of elevation with the elevating handwheel.
(2) If the mask is over 300 meters from the machine gun position, the gunner places the range setting to the mask on the rear sight, aims on the top of the mask, and adds 3 mils (clicks) of elevation.

c. The observer places himself to the rear of the machine gun on the gun-to-target line and in a position where he can see the machine gun and the target. He aligns the machine gun for general direction by directing the gunner to shift the machine gun until it is aligned on the target. A prominent terrain feature or landmark visible to the gunner through his sights is selected as an aiming point. This aiming point should be at a greater range than the target and at a higher elevation. When laying the machine gun on the aiming point, the range setting on the rear sight must correspond to the range to the target. (Figure 2-20.)

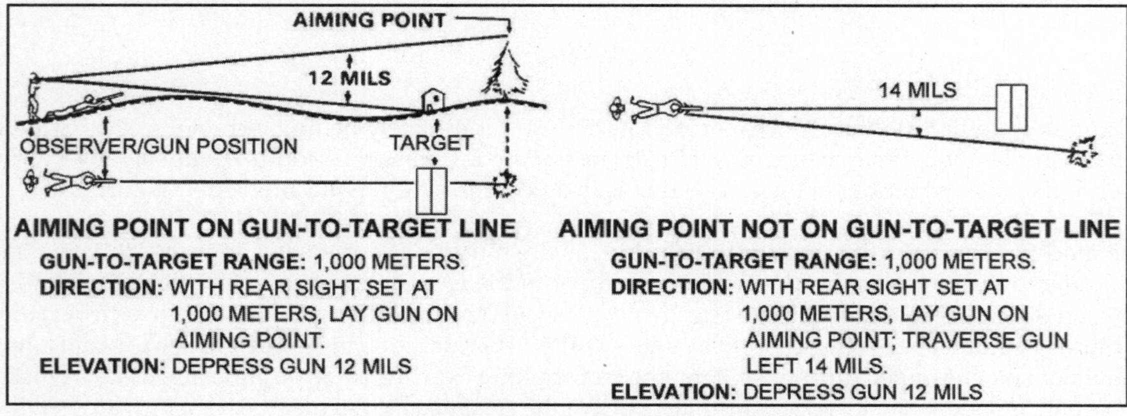

Figure 2-20: Observer adjusting fire.

(1) If the aiming point is on the gun-to-target line, the gun is laid on the aiming point and is thereby aligned for direction.
(2) If the aiming point is not on the gun-to-target line, the horizontal distance in mils is determined using the best means available (usually binoculars) and announced to the gunner. This measured distance is then set with the traversing handwheel.

d. The observer measures the vertical distance from the aiming point to the base of the target using the best means available and directs the gunner to depress the muzzle of the machine gun the number of mils measured. The machine gun should now be laid to hit the target.

SECTION IV. PREDETERMINED FIRES

Predetermined fires organize the battlefield for the gunners. They allow the leader and gunner to select potential targets or target areas that will most likely be engaged or that have tactical significance. This includes dismounted enemy avenues of approach, likely positions for automatic weapons, and probable enemy assault positions. The gunners do this by using sectors of fire, final protective lines, or a principal direction of fire and selected target areas. This preparation maximizes the effectiveness of the machine gun during good as well as limited visibility. It enhances fire control by reducing the time required to identify targets, determine range, and manipulate the weapon onto the target. Abbreviated fire commands and previously recorded data enable the gunner to aim or adjust fire on the target quickly and accurately. Selected targets should be fired on in daylight whenever practical to confirm data. The range card identifies the targets and provides a record of firing data.

2-15. TERMINOLOGY

Several terms are associated with predetermined fire that every gunner needs to know.

a. **Sector of Fire.** A sector of fire is an area to be covered by fire that is assigned to an individual, a weapon, or a unit. Gunners are normally assigned a primary and a secondary sector of fire.

b. **Final Protective Fire.** An FPF is an immediately available prearranged barrier of fire to stop enemy movement across defensive lines or areas.

c. **Final Protective Line.** An FPL is a predetermined line along which grazing fire is placed to stop an enemy assault. If an FPL is assigned, the machine gun is sighted along it except when other targets are being engaged. An FPL becomes the machine gun's part of the unit's final protective fires. An FPL is fixed in direction and elevation; however, a small shift for search must be employed to prevent the enemy from crawling under the FPL and to compensate for irregularities in the terrain or the sinking of the tripod legs into soft soil during firing. Fire must be delivered during all conditions of visibility.

d. **Principal Direction of Fire.** A PDF is a direction of fire assigned priority to cover an area that has good fields of fire or has a likely dismounted avenue of approach. It also provides mutual support to an adjacent unit. Machine guns are sighted using the PDF if an FPL has not been assigned. If a PDF is assigned and other targets are not being engaged, machine guns remain on the PDF. A PDF has the following characteristics.
(1) It is used only if an FPL is not assigned; it then becomes the machine gun's part of the unit's final protective fires.
(2) When the target has width, direction is determined by aiming on one edge of the target area and noting the amount of traverse necessary to cover the entire target.
(3) The gunner is responsible for the entire wedge-shaped area from the muzzle of the weapon to the target, but elevation may be fixed for a priority portion of the target.

e. **Grazing Fire.** A good FPL covers the maximum area with grazing fire. Grazing fire can be obtained over various types of terrain out to a maximum of 600 meters. To obtain the maximum extent of grazing fire over level or uniformly sloping terrain, the gunner sets the rear sight at 600 meters. He then selects a point on the ground that he estimates to be 600 meters from the machine gun, and he aims, fires, and adjusts on that point. To prevent enemy soldiers from crawling under grazing fire, he searches (downward) by lowering the muzzle of the weapon. To do this, the gunner separates his elbows.

f. **Dead Space.** The extent of grazing fire and the extent of dead space may be determined in two ways. In the preferred method, the machine gun is adjusted for elevation and direction. A member of the squad then walks along the FPL while the gunner aims through the sights. In places where the soldier's waist (midsection) falls below the gunner's point of aim, dead space exists. Arm-and-hand signals must be used to control the soldier who is walking and to obtain an accurate account of the dead space and its location. Another method is to observe the flight of tracer ammunition from a position behind and to the flank of the weapon.

g. **Fire Control.** Predetermined targets, including the FPL or PDF, are engaged on order or by SOP. The signal for calling for these fires is normally stated in the defense order. Control these predetermined targets by using arm-and-hand signals, voice commands, or pyrotechnic devices. Gunners fire the FPL or PDF at the sustained rate of fire unless the situation calls for a higher rate. When engaging other predetermined targets, the sustained rate of fire is also used unless a different rate is ordered.
h. **Primary Sector of Fire.** The primary sector of fire is the area to be covered by an individual or unit.
i. **Secondary Sector of Fire.** The secondary sector of fire is the same area covered by the same individual or unit after it has moved to a different location.

2-16. RANGE CARD

The standard range card (DA Form 5517-R) provides a record of firing data and aids defensive fire planning. (See FM 7-8 for a reproducible copy of this form.) Its use enhances fire control and rapid engagement of predetermined targets. It is also used in estimating ranges to other targets within the sector of fire. Each gunner makes two copies—one for his position and one for the squad leader. The squad leader uses his copy to prepare his sector sketch. The range card is prepared immediately upon occupation and is constantly revised. Each range card contains the following:

- Weapon symbol (Figure 2-21).
- Sector of fire.
- PDF or FPL.
- Range, azimuth, and number label to predetermined targets.
- Dead space.
- Distance and azimuth from a known point or eight-digit grid coordinate (reference point).
- Magnetic north arrow.
- Data section.

Figure 2-21: M249/M60 and M240B machine gun symbol.

a. **Procedures.** The machine gun is placed in the tripod-supported mode in the position it will be fired. The machine gun symbol is sketched on the range card pointing toward the most dangerous target in the sector.
   (1) If using the FPL, the gunner aims the machine gun along the FPL. This procedure will also be either the left or right limit of the sector of fire. To set the limit, he slides the T&E mechanism all the way to the left or right end of the traversing bar. Then, he moves the tripod until the barrel lines up on the FPL. The sector of fire with the FPL along one limit is now prepared. The FPL is always labeled target number 1.
   (2) To determine the range for all targets in the sector, the gunner ensures each circle, except the first one, represents 100 meters. Since the lowest setting on the M249 and M60 is 300 meters and the M240B is 200 meters, the first circle represents 200 or 300 meters. He indicates this on the range card in the data section just below the circles. On the top half of the range card, the gunner draws the left or right limits from the weapon position to the maximum effective range of the machine gun.
   (3) If the FPL is assigned, the machine gun symbol is drawn along that line (left or right limit) (Figure 2-22). The extent of grazing fire is determined. A shaded blade is sketched on the inside of the FPL to represent the extent of the grazing fire. If there is dead space along the FPL, it is shown by breaks in the shaded

area. The ranges to the *near* and *far* edges of the dead space are recorded above the FPL, and the *extent* of the grazing fire is recorded along the FPL. The magnetic azimuth of the FPL is determined and recorded below the shaded blade representing the FPL. The elevation reading and other data are recorded in the data section.

(4) If an FPL is not assigned, the gunner locks the T&E mechanism on 0 on the traversing bar scale and shifts the tripod until the muzzle points to the PDF. The machine gun symbol is sketched in the center of the left and right limits pointing in the direction of the PDF (Figure 2-23).

(5) The opposite primary sector limit is drawn. If a target is along this line, the target information is added to the data section. If the opposite side of the traversing bar cannot be used to mark the opposite side of the primary sector, a direction reading must be recorded in the sketch section.

(6) Next, the left and right limits of the secondary sector are drawn using a broken line. The area between the primary and secondary sector is labeled dead space.

(7) An arrow is drawn in the magnetic north block (upper right-hand corner) pointing in the direction of magnetic north.

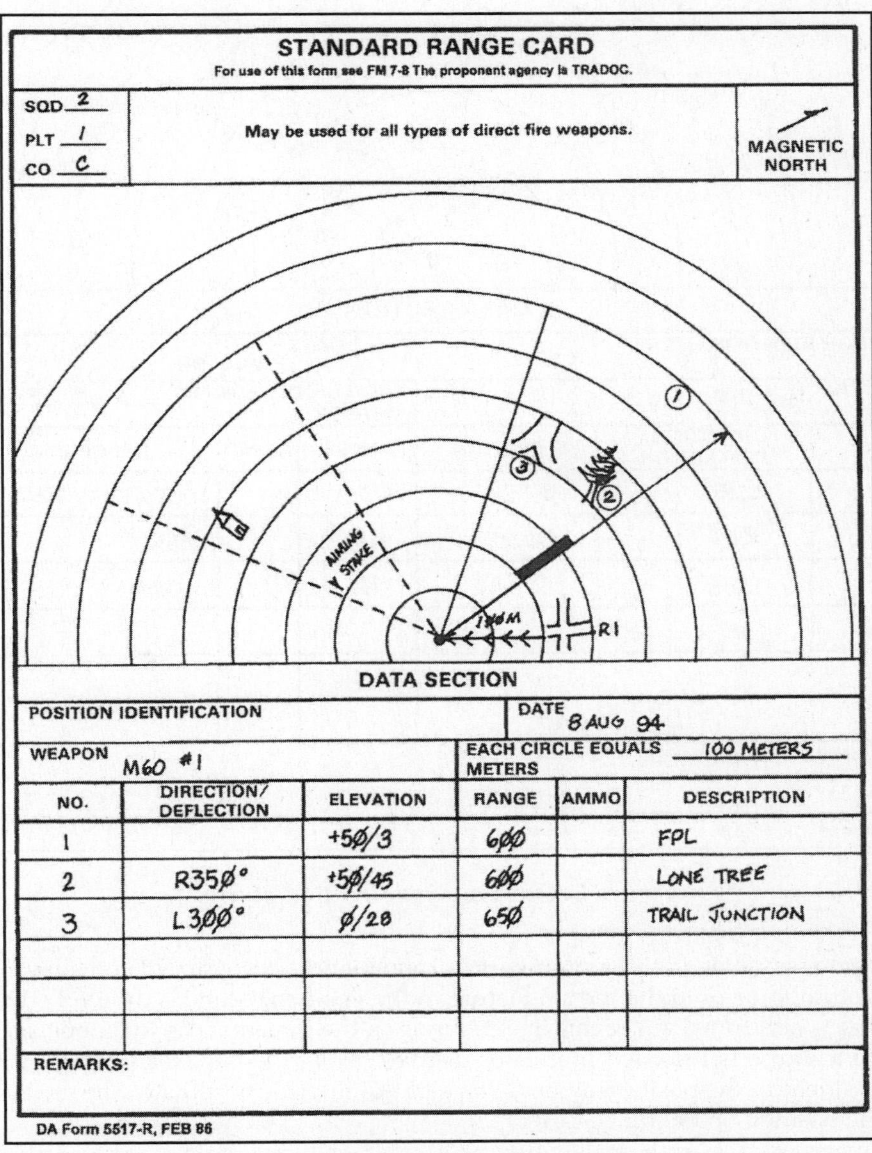

STANDARD RANGE CARD

For use of this form see FM 7-8 The proponent agency is TRADOC.

SQD 2
PLT 1
CO C

May be used for all types of direct fire weapons.

MAGNETIC NORTH

DATA SECTION

POSITION IDENTIFICATION

DATE 8 AUG 94

WEAPON M60 #1

EACH CIRCLE EQUALS 100 METERS METERS

NO.	DIRECTION/ DEFLECTION	ELEVATION	RANGE	AMMO	DESCRIPTION
1		+5∅/3	6∅∅		FPL
2	R35∅°	+5∅/45	6∅∅		LONE TREE
3	L3∅∅°	∅/28	65∅		TRAIL JUNCTION

REMARKS:

DA Form 5517-R, FEB 86

Figure 2-22: Final protective line.

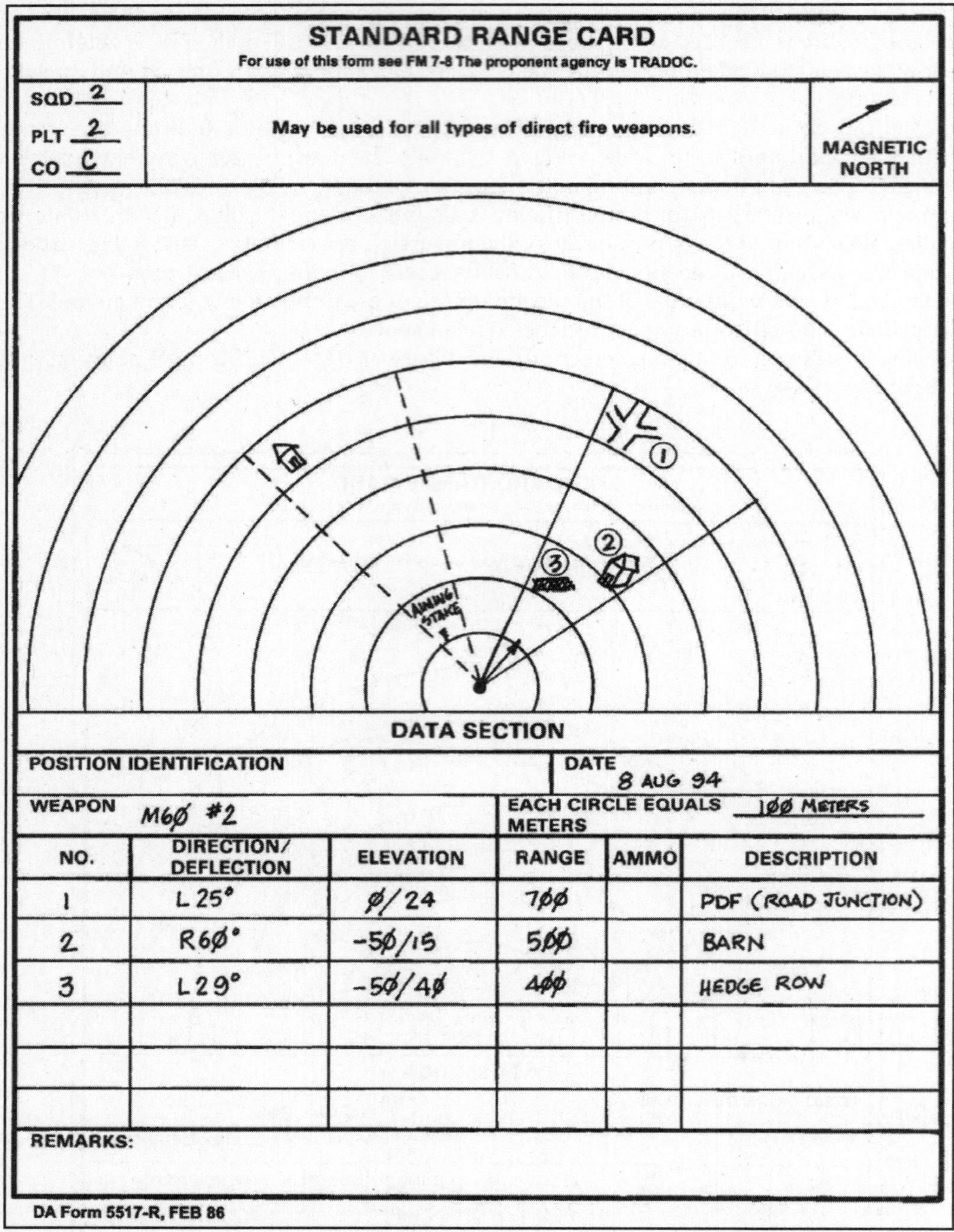

STANDARD RANGE CARD

For use of this form see FM 7-8 The proponent agency is TRADOC.

SQD 2
PLT 2
CO C

May be used for all types of direct fire weapons.

MAGNETIC NORTH

DATA SECTION

POSITION IDENTIFICATION

DATE 8 AUG 94

WEAPON M6Ø #2

EACH CIRCLE EQUALS 1ØØ METERS METERS

NO.	DIRECTION/ DEFLECTION	ELEVATION	RANGE	AMMO	DESCRIPTION
1	L 25°	Ø/24	7ØØ		PDF (ROAD JUNCTION)
2	R6Ø°	-5Ø/15	5ØØ		BARN
3	L29°	-5Ø/4Ø	4ØØ		HEDGE ROW

REMARKS:

DA Form 5517-R, FEB 86

Figure 2-23: Principal direction of fire.

(8) The position is oriented with a prominent terrain feature (recognizable on a map) by obtaining a magnetic azimuth to or from the terrain feature to the position. A line is drawn between these two points. Arrow barbs are drawn along this line pointing in the direction the magnetic azimuth was taken. The magnetic azimuth is recorded in mils or degrees below the line. If a prominent terrain feature is not available, identify the position by using an eight-digit grid coordinate. The grid coordinate is recorded below the position on the range card.

(9) The gunner's number, unit designation (SQD, PLT, CO), and date are recorded in the upper left-hand corner. For security, do not use a unit designation higher than a company.

(10) Targets within the sector are identified. A symbol is drawn to represent the target in the appropriate place within the sector of fire. Targets in the primary sector are shown by numbers and enclosed in circles. An FPL, when assigned, is always labeled target Number 1. Other targets are assigned subsequent numbers in order of tactical importance.

(a) Wide targets in the primary sector are usually engaged in the center; however, the initial burst can be positioned anywhere the leader designates. The gunner measures the target width and records it in the data section; for example, TW-20 (target width is 20 mils). The gunner lays on the point on the target where the initial burst will be placed, and traverses to one edge of the target, while counting the clicks. He records the number of clicks he traverses and the direction he moves the muzzle; for example, TW-20/R7 (target width, 20 mils; right 7 clicks). After the initial burst, the gunner traverses 7 clicks to the right edge of the target and back to the left 20 clicks to cover the target area. To lay on the left edge of the target, the gunner records TW-20/R20.

(b) When field expedients are used with the machine gun to engage targets, they are sketched above the drawing of the target. Predetermined targets in the secondary sector are sketched on the range card and ranges to these targets are recorded below the targets but not in the data section. Field expedients should be used for targets in the secondary sector.

b. **Field Expedients.** When laying the machine gun for predetermined targets, the gunner can use field expedients as a means of engaging targets when other sources are not available. These methods are not as effective as the traversing bar and T&E mechanism method.

(1) ***Base Stake Technique.*** A base stake is used to define sector limits and may provide the lay for the FPL or predetermined targets along a primary or secondary sector limit. This technique is effective in all visibility conditions. The gunner uses the following steps:

(a) Defines the sector limits by laying the gun for direction along one sector limit and by emplacing a stake along the outer edge of the folded bipod legs. Rotates the legs slightly on the receiver, so that the gunner takes up the "play". Uses the same procedure for placing a stake along the opposite sector limit.

(b) Lays the machine gun along the FPL by moving the muzzle of the machine gun to a sector limit. Adjusts for elevation by driving a stake into the ground, so that the top of the stake is under the gas cylinder extension, allowing a few mils of depression to cover irregularities in the terrain.

(c) Lays the machine gun to engage other targets within a sector limit, in a primary sector by using the procedure described previously, except keeps the elevation fixed.

(2) ***Notched-Stake or Tree-Crotch Technique.*** The gunner uses the notched-stake or tree-crotch technique (Figure 2-24) with the bipod mount to engage predetermined targets within a sector or to define sector limits. This technique is effective during all conditions of visibility, and it requires little additional material. The gunner uses the following steps:

(a) Drives either a notched stake or tree crotch into the ground where selected targets are anticipated. Places the stock of the machine gun in the nest of the stake or crotch and adjusts the weapon to hit the selected targets and to define his sector limits.

> ✍ **NOTE**
>
> If notched stakes and crotches are not available, tent poles can be used. It requires four poles for the left and right limits and additional poles for target areas. The gunner drives two poles in the ground in the shape of an X and then places the stock within that X as described with stakes and crotches.

(b) Digs shallow, curved trenches or grooves for the bipod feet. (These trenches allow for rotation of the bipod feet as the gunner moves the stock from one crotch or stake to another.)

(3) ***Horizontal Log or Board Technique.*** This technique is used with the bipod or tripod mount to mark sector limits and engage wide targets. This technique is good for all visibility conditions. It is best suited for flat, level terrain. The gunner uses the following steps:

(a) Using a bipod-mounted machine gun, places a log or board beneath the stock of the weapon, so that the stock can slide across it freely. Digs shallow, curved trenches or grooves for the bipod feet to allow rotation of the feet as he moves the stock along the log or board. (The gunner may mark the

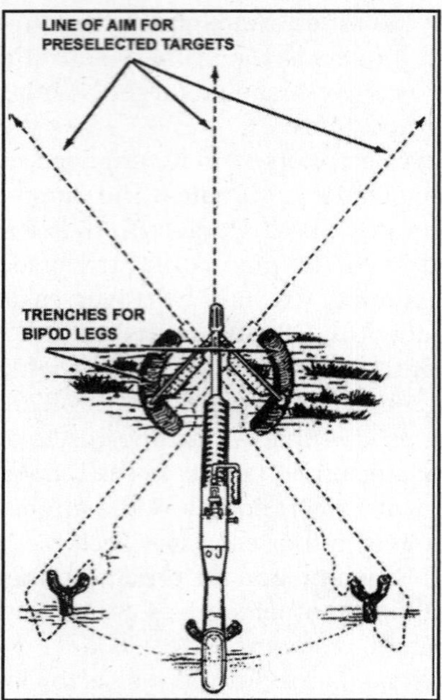

Figure 2-24: Notched-stake or tree-crotch technique.

sector limits by notching or placing stops on the log or board. The gunner uses the bipod firing position and grip.)

(b) Using a tripod-mounted machine gun, places a log or board beneath the barrel, positioning it so that the barrel, when resting on the log or board is at the proper elevation to obtain grazing fire. Marks the sector limits, when appropriate, as described for the bipod in the preceding paragraph. (This technique is used only if a T&E mechanism is not available.)

SECTION V. FIRE CONTROL

Fire control includes all actions of the leader and soldiers in planning, preparing, and applying fire on a target. The leader selects and designates targets. He also designates the midpoint and flanks or ends of a target, unless they are obvious to the gunner. The gunner fires at the instant desired. He then adjusts fire, regulates the rate of fire, shifts from one target to another, and ceases fire. When firing, the gunner should continue to fire until the target is neutralized or until signaled to do otherwise by the leader.

2-17. METHODS OF FIRE CONTROL

The noise and confusion of battle may limit the use of some of these methods; therefore, the leader must select a method or combination of methods that will accomplish the mission.

a. **Oral.** This can be an effective method of control, but sometimes the leader may be too far away from the gunner, or the noise of the battle may make it impossible for him to hear. The primary means of the oral fire control method is the issuance of a fire command.
b. **Arm-and-Hand Signals.** This is an effective method when the gunner can see the leader. All gunners must know the standard arm-and-hand signals. The leader gets the gunner's attention and then points to the target. When the gunner returns the READY signal, the leader commands FIRE.
c. **Prearranged Signals.** These are either visual or sound signals such as casualty-producing devices, pyrotechnics, whistle blasts, or tracers. These signals should be included in SOPs. If the leader wants to shift fire at a certain time, he gives a prearranged signal such as smoke or pyrotechnics. Upon seeing the signal, the gunner shifts his fire to a prearranged point.

d. **Personal Contact.** In many situations, the leader must issue orders directly to individual soldiers and is used more than any other method by small-unit leaders. The leader must use maximum cover and concealment to keep from disclosing the position or himself.

e. **Range Cards.** When using this method of fire control, the leader must ensure all range cards are current and accurate. Once this is accomplished, the leader may designate certain targets for certain weapons with the use of limiting stakes or with fire commands. He should also designate no-fire zones or restricted fire areas to others. The key factor, in this method of fire control, is that gunners must be well-disciplined and pay attention to detail.

f. **Standing Operating Procedures.** SOPs are actions to be executed without command that are developed during the training of the squads. Their use eliminates many commands and simplifies the leader's fire control. SOPs for certain actions and commands can be developed to make gunners more effective. Some examples follow:

(1) ***Observation.*** The gunners continuously observe their sectors.

(2) ***Fire.*** Gunners open fire without command on appropriate targets that appear within their sectors.

(3) ***Check.*** While firing, the gunners periodically check with the leader for instructions.

(4) ***Return Fire.*** The gunners return enemy fire without order, concentrating on enemy automatic weapons.

(5) ***Shift Fire.*** Gunners shift their fires without command when more dangerous targets appear.

(6) ***Rate of Fire.*** When gunners engage a target, they initially fire at the rate necessary to gain and maintain fire superiority.

(7) ***Mutual Support.*** When two or more gunners are engaging the same target and one stops firing, the other increases the rate of fire and covers the entire target. When only one gunner is required to engage a target and the leader has alerted two or more, the gunner not firing aims on the target and follows the movements of the target. This is so that he can fire instantly should the other machine gun malfunction or cease fire before the target has been eliminated.

2-18. FIRE COMMANDS

A fire command is given to deliver effective fire on a target quickly and without confusion. When the leader decides to engage a target that is not obvious to the squad, he must provide them with the information they need to effectively engage the target. He must alert the soldiers; give a target direction, description, and range; name the method of fire; and give the command to fire. There are initial fire commands and subsequent fire commands.

a. **Initial Fire Commands.** Initial fire commands are given to adjust onto the target, change the rate of fire after a fire mission is in progress, interrupt fire, or terminate the alert.

b. **Elements.** Fire commands for all direct-fire weapons follow a pattern that includes similar elements. There are six elements in the fire command for the machine gun: alert, direction, description, range, method of fire, and command to open fire. The gunners repeat each element of fire command as it is given.

(1) ***Alert.*** This element prepares the gunners for further instructions. The leader may alert both gunners in the squad and may have only one fire, depending upon the situation. To alert and have both gunners fire, the leader announces, "fire mission." If he desires to alert both gunners but have only one fire, he announces, "gun number one, fire mission." In all cases, upon receiving the alert, the gunners load their machine guns and place them on FIRE.

(2) ***Direction.*** This element indicates the general direction to the target and may be given in one or a combination of the following methods.

(a) *Orally.* The leader orally gives the direction to the target in relation to the position of the gunner (for example, FRONT, LEFT FRONT, RIGHT FRONT).

(b) *Pointing.* The leader designates a small or obscure target by pointing with his finger or aiming with a weapon. When he points with his finger, a soldier standing behind him should be able to look over his shoulder and sight along his arm and index finger to locate the target. When aiming his weapon at a target, a soldier looking through the sights should be able to see the target.

(c) *Tracer Ammunition.* Tracer ammunition is a quick and sure method of designating a target that is not clearly visible. When using this method, the leader should first give the general direction to direct the gunner's attention to the target area. To prevent the loss of surprise when using tracer ammunition, the leader does not fire until he has given all elements of the fire command except the command to fire. The leader may fire his individual weapon. The firing of the tracer(s) then becomes the last element of the fire command, and it is the signal to open fire.

> ✍ **NOTE**
>
> Soldiers must be aware that with the night vision device, temporary blindness "white out" may occur when firing tracer ammunition at night or when exposed to other external light sources. Lens covers may reduce this effect.

> ☞ **EXAMPLE**
>
> FIRE MISSION
>
> FRONT
>
> FIVE HUNDRED
>
> WATCH MY TRACER(S)

(d) *Reference Points.* Another way to designate obscure targets is to use easy-to-recognize reference points. All leaders and gunners must know terrain features and the terminology used to describe them (FM 21-26). When using a reference point, the word "reference" precedes its description. This is done to avoid confusion. The general direction to the reference point should be given.

> ☞ **EXAMPLE**
>
> FIRE MISSION
>
> FRONT
>
> REFERENCE: BUNKER, CENTER MASS
>
> TARGET: TROOPS EXTENDING SHORT ONE HUNDRED, OVER ONE HUNDRED
>
> FOUR HUNDRED
>
> FIRE

(Sometimes the reference point may be outside the target area.)

> ☞ **EXAMPLE**
>
> FIRE MISSION
>
> FRONT
>
> REFERENCE: BUNKER, RIGHT FOUR FINGERS, CENTER MASS
>
> TARGET: TROOPS EXTENDING SHORT ONE HUNDRED, OVER ONE HUNDRED
>
> THREE HUNDRED
>
> SEARCH
>
> AT MY COMMAND
>
> FIRE

(Sometimes a target must be designated by using successive reference points.)

☞ **EXAMPLE**

GUN NUMBER ONE, FIRE MISSION

RIGHT FRONT

REFERENCE: RED-ROOFED HOUSE, LEFT TO HAYSTACK, LEFT TO BARN

(Finger measurements can be used to direct the gunner's attention to the right or left of reference points.)

☞ **EXAMPLE**

FIRE MISSION

LEFT FRONT

REFERENCE: CROSSROADS, RIGHT FOUR FINGERS

(3) ***Description.*** The target description creates a picture of the target in the minds of the gunners. To properly apply their fire, the soldiers must know the type of target they are to engage. The leader should describe it briefly. If the target is obvious, no description is necessary.

(4) ***Range.*** The leader always announces the estimated range to the target. The range is given, so the gunner knows how far to look for the target and what range setting to put on the rear sight. Range is announced in meters; however, since the meter is the standard unit of range measurement, the word "meters" is not used. With machine gun's, the range is determined and announced to the nearest hundred or thousand (in other words, THREE HUNDRED, or ONE THOUSAND).

☞ **EXAMPLE**

FIRE MISSION

FRONT

REFERENCE: KNOCKED-OUT TANK, LEFT TWO FINGERS

TARGET: TROOPS

THREE HUNDRED

(5) ***Method of Fire.*** This element includes manipulation and rate of fire. Manipulation prescribes the class of fire with respect to the weapon. It is announced as FIXED, TRAVERSE, SEARCH, or TRAVERSE AND SEARCH. Rate controls the volume of fire (sustained, rapid, and cyclic). Normally, the gunner uses the sustained rate of fire. The rate of fire is omitted from the fire command. The method of fire for the machine gun is usually 3- to 5-round bursts (M249) and 6- to 9-round bursts (M60/M240B).

☞ **EXAMPLE**

FIRE MISSION

FRONT

REFERENCE: KNOCKED-OUT TANK, LEFT TWO FINGERS

TARGET: TROOPS

THREE HUNDRED

TRAVERSE

(6) ***Command to Open Fire.*** When fire is to be withheld so that surprise fire can be delivered on a target or to ensure that both gunners open fire at the same time, the leader may preface the command to commence firing with AT MY COMMAND or AT MY SIGNAL. When the gunners are ready to engage the target, they report READY to the leader. The leader then gives the command FIRE at the specific time desired.

☞ EXAMPLE

FIRE MISSION

FRONT

TROOPS

FOUR HUNDRED

AT MY COMMAND or AT MY SIGNAL (The leader pauses until the gunners are ready and fire is desired.)

FIRE (The gunners fire on prearranged signal.)

If immediate fire is required, the command FIRE is given without pause and the gunners fire as soon as they are ready.

c. **Subsequent Fire Commands.** These fire commands are used to make adjustments in direction and elevation, to change rates of fire after a fire mission is in progress, to interrupt fires, or to terminate the alert. If the gunner fails to properly engage a target, the leader must promptly correct him by announcing or signaling the desired changes. When these changes are given, the gunner makes the corrections and resumes firing without further command.

(1) Adjustments in direction and elevation with the machine gun are always given in meters; one finger is used to indicate 1 meter and so on. Adjustment for direction is given first. For example: RIGHT ONE ZERO METERS or LEFT FIVE METERS. Adjustment for elevation is given next. For example: ADD FIVE METERS or DROP ONE FIVE METERS. These changes may be given orally or with arm-and-hand signals.

(2) Changes in the rate of fire are given orally or by arm-and-hand signals.

(3) To interrupt firing, the leader announces "cease fire," or he signals to cease fire. The gunners remain on the alert. They resume firing when given the command FIRE.

(4) To terminate the alert, the leader announces "cease fire, end of mission."

d. **Doubtful Elements and Corrections.** When the gunner is in doubt about any element of the fire command, he replies "say again range, target." The leader then announces "the command was," repeats the element in question, and continues with the fire command.

(1) When the leader makes an error in the initial fire command, he corrects it by announcing "correction," and then gives the corrected element.

☞ EXAMPLE

FIRE MISSION

FRONT

TROOPS

SIX HUNDRED

CORRECTION

THREE HUNDRED

TRAVERSE

AT MY COMMAND

(2) When the leader makes an error in the subsequent fire command, he may correct it by announcing "correction," and then repeating the entire subsequent fire command.

> ☞ **EXAMPLE**
> LEFT FIVE METERS, DROP ONE METER
> CORRECTION
> LEFT FIVE METERS, DROP ONE HUNDRED METERS

e. **Abbreviated Fire Commands.** Fire commands need not be complete to be effective. In combat, the leader gives only the elements necessary to place fire on a target quickly and without confusion. During training, however, he should use all of the elements to get gunners in the habit of thinking and reacting properly when a target is to be engaged. After the gunner's initial training in fire commands, he should be taught to react to abbreviated fire commands, using one of the following methods.

(1) ***Oral.*** The leader may want to place the fire of one machine gun on an enemy machine gun.

> ☞ **EXAMPLE**
> GUN NUMBER ONE, FIRE MISSION
> MACHINE GUN
> FOUR HUNDRED
> FIRE

(2) ***Arm-and-Hand Signals.*** Battlefield noise and the distance between the gunner and the leader often make it necessary to use arm-and-hand signals to control fire (Figure 2-25). When an action or movement is to be executed by only one of the gunners, a preliminary signal is given to that gunner only. The following are commonly used signals for fire control.

Figure 2-25: Arm-and-hand signals.

(a) *Ready.* The gunner indicates that he is ready to fire by yelling "up" or having the assistant gunner raise his hand above his head toward the leader.

(b) *Commence Firing or Change Rate of Firing.* The leader brings his hand (palm down) to the front of his body about waist level, and moves it horizontally in front of his body. To signal an increase in the rate of fire, he increases the speed of the hand movement to signal slower fire, and he decreases the speed of the hand movement.

(c) *Change Direction or Elevation.* The leader extends his arm and hand in the new direction and indicates the amount of change necessary by the number of fingers extended. The fingers must be spread, so the gunner can easily see the number of fingers extended. Each finger indicates 1 meter of change for the weapon. If the desired change is more than 5 meters, the leader extends his hand the number of times necessary to indicate the total amount of change. For example, *right nine* would be indicated by extending the hand once with five fingers showing and a second time with four fingers showing for a total of nine fingers.

(d) *Interrupt or Cease Firing.* The leader raises his arm and hand (palm outward) in front of his forehead and brings it downward sharply.

(e) *Other Signals.* The leader can devise other signals to control his weapons.

SECTION VI. RANGE DETERMINATION

During combat, ranges are seldom known. Poor visibility and damp ground often make adjustment of fire by observation difficult if not impossible. Therefore, correct range determination is critical for accurate effective fire. Range estimation and lateral distance measurements are two methods used to determine the range to the target.

2-19. RANGE ESTIMATION

Range estimation is determining the distance between two points. In most situations, one of these points is the gunner's own position; the other point may be a target or prominent terrain feature. The gunner must accurately determine the range to set the sights and effectively fire on a target with the first burst.

a. Not only does the accurate estimation of range affect marksmanship, but it is also required in the reporting of information and the adjustment of artillery and mortar fire (Table 2-1).

b. There are several methods of estimating range. They include measuring distance on a map, pacing the distance between two points, and using an optical range finder. The gunner does not usually have a map and rarely has access to an optical range finder. He can pace the distance between two points if the enemy is not within range. Firing rounds to determine the range is not desirable, since it may reveal your position to the enemy. Most of the time, the gunner must use techniques that do not require equipment and can be used without exposing himself or revealing his position. There are two methods that meet these requirements: the appearance-of-objects and the 100-meter-unit-of-measure.

(1) ***Appearance-of-Objects Method.*** This method is a means of estimating range by the size and other characteristic details of the object.

(a) This is a common method of determining distances and is used most often. For example, a motorist trying to pass another car must judge the distance of oncoming vehicles based on his knowledge of how vehicles appear at various distances. In this example, the motorist is not interested in precise distances but only in having enough road space to safely pass the car. Suppose, however, the motorist knew that at a distance of 1 kilometer, an oncoming vehicle appeared to be 1 centimeter between headlights. Then, anytime he saw other oncoming vehicles that fit these dimensions, he would know they were about 1 kilometer away. This technique can be used by a gunner to estimate ranges on the battlefield. If the gunner knows the characteristic size and detail of men and equipment at known ranges, he can compare these characteristics to similar objects at unknown ranges. When characteristics match, so does the range.

(b) To use the appearance-of-objects method with any degree of accuracy, the gunner must know the characteristic details of objects as they appear at various ranges. For example, the gunner should study the appearance of a man standing at a range of 100 meters. He fixes the man's appearance firmly in his mind, carefully noting details of size and the characteristics of uniform and equipment. Next, he studies the same man in a kneeling position and then in a prone position. By comparing the appearance of the man at known ranges from 100 to 500 meters, the gunner can establish a series of mental images that will help determine range on unfamiliar terrain. Training should also be conducted in the appearance of other familiar objects such as weapons or vehicles. Because the

Table 2-1: Factors of range estimation.

FACTORS AFFECTING RANGE ESTIMATION	FACTORS CAUSING UNDERESTIMATION	FACTORS CAUSING OVERESTIMATION
The clearness of outline and details of the target.	When most of the target is visible and offers	When only a small portion of the target is small in relation to its surroundings.
Nature of terrain or position of the gunner.	When looking across a depression that is mostly hidden from view. When looking downward form high ground. When looking down a straight, open road or along a railroad. When looking over uniform surfaces like water, snow, desert, or grain fields.	When looking across a depression that is totally visible. When looking from low ground toward high ground. When vision is narrowly confined as in streets, draws, or forest trails.
Light and atmosphere.	In bright light or when the sun is shining from behind the gunner. When the target is in sharp contrast with the silhouette because of its size, shape, or color. When seen in the clear air of high altitudes.	In poor light such as dawn and dusk; in rain, snow, fog; or when the sun is in the gunner's eyes. When the target blends into the background or terrain.

successful use of this method depends upon visibility, anything that limits visibility (such as weather, smoke, or darkness) will also limit the effectiveness of this method.

(2) ***100-Meter-Unit-of-Measure Method.*** To use this method, the gunner visualizes a distance of 100-meters on the ground. For ranges up to 500-meters (Figure 2-26), he determines the number of 100-meter increments between the two points he wishes to measure. Beyond 500-meters (Figure 2-27), he selects a point halfway to the target, determines the number of 100-meter increments to the halfway point, and then doubles it to find the range to the target.

(a) During training, the gunner must become familiar with the effect that sloping terrain has on the appearance of a 100-meter increment. Terrain that slopes upward gives the illusion of longer distance, and observers have a tendency to overestimate the 100-meter increment. Terrain that slopes downward gives the illusion of shorter distance. In this case, the gunner's tendency is to underestimate the 100-meter increment and thus underestimate the range.

(b) Proficiency in the 100-meter-unit-of-measure method requires constant practice. When training in this technique, the gunner should make frequent comparisons between the range as determined by the himself and by pacing or other accurate means of measurement. The best training technique is to pace the range after he has visually determined it. In this way, he discovers the actual range for himself, which makes a much greater impression than if he is told the correct range.

(c) A limitation of the 100-meter-unit-of-measure method is that its accuracy is directly related to the amount of terrain visible to the gunner. This is particularly true at greater ranges. If a target appears at a range of 500 meters or more and the gunner can only see a portion of the ground between himself and the target, it becomes difficult to use the 100-meter-unit-of-measure method of range estimation with any degree of accuracy.

(3) ***Combination of Methods.*** Under ideal conditions, either the appearance-of-objects method or 100-meter-unit-of-measure method is an effective method of estimating range. However, ideal conditions rarely exist on the battlefield, so the gunner must use a combination of methods. The terrain might limit the use of the appearance-of-objects method. For example, a gunner may not be able to see all the terrain out to the target; however, he may see enough to get a general idea of the distance. A slight haze may obscure many of the target details, but the gunner should still be able to judge its size. By carefully considering

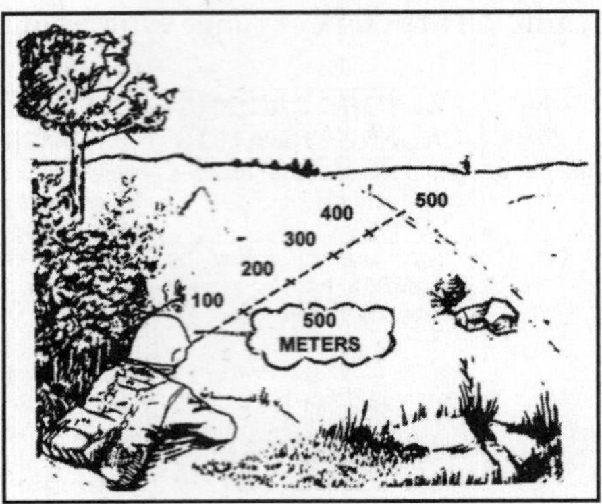

Figure 2-26: Applying the 100-meter-unit-of-measure method for ranges up to 500 meters.

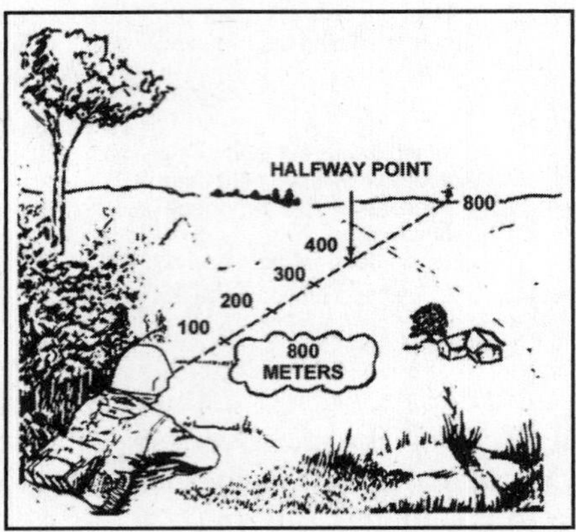

Figure 2-27: Applying the 100-meter-unit-of-measure method for ranges up to 800 meters

the ranges estimated by both methods, an experienced gunner should arrive at a figure close to the true range. The best way to reduce errors using these two methods is to train often.

2-20. LATERAL DISTANCE MEASUREMENT

In addition to estimating range accurately, the gunner needs a quick method of measuring lateral distance (right or left) from a reference point to a target. When the machine gun is tripod-mounted, width can be measured by aiming on a point, manipulating the traversing handwheel, and counting the clicks from one point of aim to another point of aim. Each click equals 1 mil and is equivalent to 1 meter at 1,000 meters, or half a meter at 500 meters. When the machine gun is bipod-mounted, the gunner can use his fingers to measure the lateral distance between a reference point and a target. He extends his arm with his palm outward, lowers his fingers, and locks his elbow. Then, he closes one eye, raises his index finger, and sights along its edge, placing the edge of his finger so that it appears to be along the flank of the target or reference point. The gunner fills the space remaining between the points by raising his fingers until the space is covered. He states the measurement from the reference point to the target as being one or more fingers, depending upon how many fingers are raised to cover this distance.

SECTION VII. ADVANCED GUNNERY

Once the gunner masters the four fundamentals of marksmanship in the prone position and fighting position, he needs practice in engaging targets that will most likely replicate the battlefield. The advanced gunnery field firing exercise for the gunner exposes him to different types of targets at various ranges to simulate combat conditions.

2-21. OBJECTIVES

The objectives of this training are to reinforce the fundamentals and increase the effectiveness of the gunner by building his confidence (*not for qualification*). He must acquire targets quickly and deliver an accurate volume of fire.

2-22. ORGANIZATION

The unit is assembled in the bleachers, given the training objectives, a range briefing, and a safety briefing. Gunners are then organized into firing orders with a gunner and an assistant gunner. (Concurrent training stations must be set up for those soldiers not on the firing line.)

2-23. AMMUNITION

This exercise requires 392 rounds of 7.62-mm linked ammunition (zero is included). The gunner is allotted two 7-round bursts for each target and fires twice.

2-24. FIRING SEQUENCE

The sequence of firing is to be conducted IAW Firing Table IV (Table 2-2). Commanders may score their soldiers to determine their most proficient gunners, to assess the marksmanship program, and to encourage competition.

a. **Task 1, Field Zeroing the 500-Meter, Single E-Type Silhouette.** The gunner is allocated 28 rounds of ammunition.
b. **Task 2, Engage Single E-Type Silhouettes From the Prone and Fighting Position, Bipod Supported (Point Targets) at Various Ranges.** The gunner will use his NBC equipment (Mask and Gloves). Targets are at 100, 200, 250, 300, and 400 meters. The gunner is allocated 70 rounds of ammunition.
c. **Task 3, Engage Double E-Type Silhouettes (Automatic Weapon Positions) at Various Ranges.** Targets are at 250, 300, 400, 500, and 600 meters. The gunner is allocated 70 rounds of ammunition.
d. **Task 4, Engage Linear E-Type Silhouettes (Troops on Line) at Various Ranges.** The gunner uses his NBC equipment (Mask and Gloves). Targets are at 300 and 600 meters. The gunner is allocated 28 rounds of ammunition.

WARNING

The M240B is carried loaded with the bolt locked to the ***rear*** in ***tactical situations*** where noise discipline is critical to the success of the mission. Trained gun crews are the only personnel authorized to load the M240B and only when command directs the crew to do so. During ***normal training exercises***, the M240B is loaded and carried with the bolt in the ***forward position.***

2-25. ALTERNATE FIRING POSITIONS

All gunners must master the bipod-supported prone firing fighting position, and tripod-supported prone firing position to be effective. But it is also equally important that they know other positions. Each gunner must be trained to assume different positions quickly during various combat conditions. The situation determines the appropriate position. The gunner must establish his position so that he can effectively observe and engage the target yet minimize his exposure to enemy fire.

a. **Positions.** The underarm firing position and the hip firing position are used.
   (1) ***Underarm Firing Position.*** This position is used almost exclusively when moving in and around the objective during the assault (Figure 2-28). To assume this position, the gunner—
      (a) Puts the bipod legs and rear sight down for instant use in the prone position if necessary.
      (b) Faces the target with his feet spread about shoulder width apart.
      (c) Places his left foot in front of the right with most of his weight on his left foot.

Table 2-2: Firing Table II.

TASK	RANGE (M)	TIME	TOTAL ROUNDS PER INDIVIDUAL	TARGET	AMMO	TYPE FIRE
1	500	No limit	28	E-type silhouette	4:1	Zeroing 7-round bursts
2*	100 200 250 300 400	60 seconds	70	Single E-type silhouette	4:1	7-round bursts
3	250 300 400 500 600	120 seconds	70	Single E-type silhouette	4:1	7-round bursts
4*	300 600	120 seconds	28	Linear target Single E-type 1 meter apart	4:1	7-round bursts
* Indicates tasks fired with protective mask and gloves as a minimum.						

(d) Bends both legs at the knees and leans forward at the waist.

(e) With his right hand, firmly grasps the pistol grip, and with his right forearm holds the stock firmly against the side of his body at a point between his armpit and waist.

(f) With his left hand, grasps the handguard firmly.

(g) Points his left foot in the direction of the target while his right foot provides stability.

(h) Depresses the muzzle of the machine gun slightly so the strike of rounds can be observed. (This reduces shooting high and takes advantage of ricochets.)

(i) Leans toward the target before and during firing.

(2) ***Hip Firing Position.*** This position is used when closing with the enemy, when a heavy volume of fire in the target area is required, and when rapid movement is not necessary (Figure 2-29). The only differences between this position and the underarm position are that the gunner—

(a) Holds the rear of the stock firmly against the forward position of his right thigh.

(b) Extends his arms fully downward.

b. **Alternate Firing Position Exercises.** The assault fire exercise challenges the gunner. It consists of point and area targets during a variety of conditions replicating the battlefield. These exercises, which involve fire and maneuver, must be carefully controlled for safety purposes.

(1) ***Objectives.*** This exercise gives the gunner practice on engaging targets as quickly as possible, using any of the alternate firing positions.

(2) ***Organization.*** The unit is assembled in the bleachers, given instructions, and briefed on training that will be conducted while they are on the range. After the briefing, they are organized into firing orders and moved to firing lanes. Lanes are conducted and used IAW local range policies.

(3) ***Ammunition.*** This exercise requires a total of 168 rounds of 7.62-mm linked ammunition. The gunner is allowed two bursts per exposure, and he is also required to conduct at least one rapid reload during the exercise and the gunner will fire this twice. The commander has the option of when the rapid reload may take place. Ammunition is configured into two belts of any size that requires the gunner to reload.

Figure 2-28: Underarm firing position

Figure 2-29: Hip firing position

(4) ***Firing Sequence.*** The sequence of firing is conducted IAW Firing Table V (Table 2-3). The suggested sequence of firing is as follows.

(a) ***Task 1, Dry Fire Walk-Through.*** Upon his arrival at the firing position, the gunner walks through his respective lane to become familiar with the targets. No ammunition is fired at this time. When he returns, he draws his ammunition.

> ✍ NOTE
> Commanders ensure that ammunition is used in such a manner that the gunner is required to rapidly reload sometime during his movement phases.

(b) ***Task 2, Engage Single E-Type Silhouette from the Hip-Firing Position.*** After being issued the ammunition, the gunner begins his movement. When targets are exposed, he uses the hip-firing technique. He is given a single exposed target at a distance of 25 meters, with an exposure time of 5 seconds.

(c) ***Task 3, Engage Single E-Type Silhouettes from the Underarm-Firing Position.*** As the gunner continues to move through the course, he is given two single exposed E-type silhouettes at distances of 50 and 25 meters, where he engages each silhouette using the underarm-firing position. The exposure time for each target is 5 seconds.

(d) ***Task 4, Engage Single E-Type Silhouettes from the Underarm or Hip-Firing Position.*** Once the gunner reaches this point, he is be given three single exposed E-type silhouettes at distances of 25, 50, and 75 meters. The exposure time for each target is 5 seconds.

Table 2-3: Firing Table VIII.

TASK	RANGE (M)	TIME	TOTAL ROUNDS PER INDIVIDUAL	TARGET	AMMO	TYPE FIRE
1	NA	No limit	NA	NA	NA	NA
2	25	5 seconds	14	Single E-type silhouette	4:1	7-round bursts
3	50	10 seconds	28	Single E-type silhouette	4:1	7-round bursts
4	25 50 75	15 seconds	42	Single E-type silhouette	4:1	7-round bursts

> ✍ NOTE
> The commander may integrate firing under NBC conditions for selected tasks while negotiating the course, or he may conduct the course during limited visibility unaided.

2-26. MOVEMENT, SPEED, AND ALIGNMENT

The gunner must keep up with the other soldiers of the assaulting element through individual movement techniques. To do this, he moves as rapidly as possible, consistent with his ability to fire accurately and maintain alignment.

2-27. RELOADING

The gunner must reload rapidly to avoid lulls in the firing. This can be achieved by practicing and by applying the following techniques.

a. Before the assault, the gunner conducts prefire checks on the machine gun. He inspects ammunition to ensure that it is clean and serviceable, and he checks the box for serviceability.
b. During the assault, the gunner must continue moving forward and reload as rapidly as possible. The sling allows the gunner to reload using both hands.

Army Combat Guide to Use & Identification of Hand Grenades

CHAPTER 1

Types of Hand Grenades

1-1. DESCRIPTION

The hand grenade is a handheld, hand-armed, and hand-thrown weapon. U.S. forces use colored smoke, white smoke, riot-control, special purpose, offensive, and practice hand grenades. Each grenade has a different capability that provides the soldier with a variety of options to successfully complete any given mission. Hand grenades give the soldier the ability to kill enemy soldiers and destroy enemy equipment. Historically, the most important hand grenade has been the fragmentation grenade, which is the soldier's personal indirect weapon system. Offensive grenades are much less lethal than fragmentation grenades on an enemy in the open, but they are very effective against an enemy within a confined space. Smoke and special purpose grenades can be used to signal, screen, control crowds or riots, start fires, or destroy equipment. The hand grenade is thrown by hand; therefore, the range is short and the casualty radius is small. The 4- to 5-second delay on the fuze allows the soldier to safely employ the grenade.

1-2. COMPONENTS

The hand grenade is made up of the following components:

a. **Body.** The body contains filler and, in certain grenades, fragmentation.
b. **Filler.** The filler is composed of a chemical or explosive substance, which determines the type of hand grenade for employment factors.
c. **Fuze Assembly.** The fuze causes the grenade to ignite or explode by detonating the filler.

1-3. MECHANICAL FUNCTION

The following is the sequence for the M67 fragmentation hand grenade safety clip insertion and arming.

a. **Insert the Safety Clip.** All hand grenades do not have safety clips (NSN 1330-00-183-5996). However, safety clips are available through Class V ammunition supply channels for some types of grenades. The safety clip is adaptable to the M26 and M67 series, the MK2, and the M69 practice grenade. The safety clip prevents the safety lever from springing loose even if the safety pin assembly is accidentally removed. The adjustment instructions are illustrated in Figure 1-1. The safety clip installation instructions are as follows:
   (1) Hold the fuzed grenade in the palm of the hand with the pull ring up.
   (2) Insert the small loop at the open end of the safety clip in the slot of the fuze body beneath the safety lever.
   (3) Press the clip across the safety lever until the closed end of the clip touches the safety lever and snaps securely into place around the safety lever.
b. **Arming Sequence.** First remove the safety clip, then the safety pin, from the fuze by pulling the pull ring. Be sure to maintain pressure on the safety lever: it springs free once the safety clip and the safety pin assembly are removed.
c. **Release Pressure on Lever.** Once the grenade is thrown, the pressure on the safety lever is released, and the striker is forced to rotate on its axis by the striker spring, throwing the safety lever off. The striker then detonates the primer, and the primer explodes and ignites the delay element. The delay element burns for the prescribed amount of time then activates either the detonator or the igniter. The detonator or igniter acts to either explode or burn the filler substance (Figure 1-2).

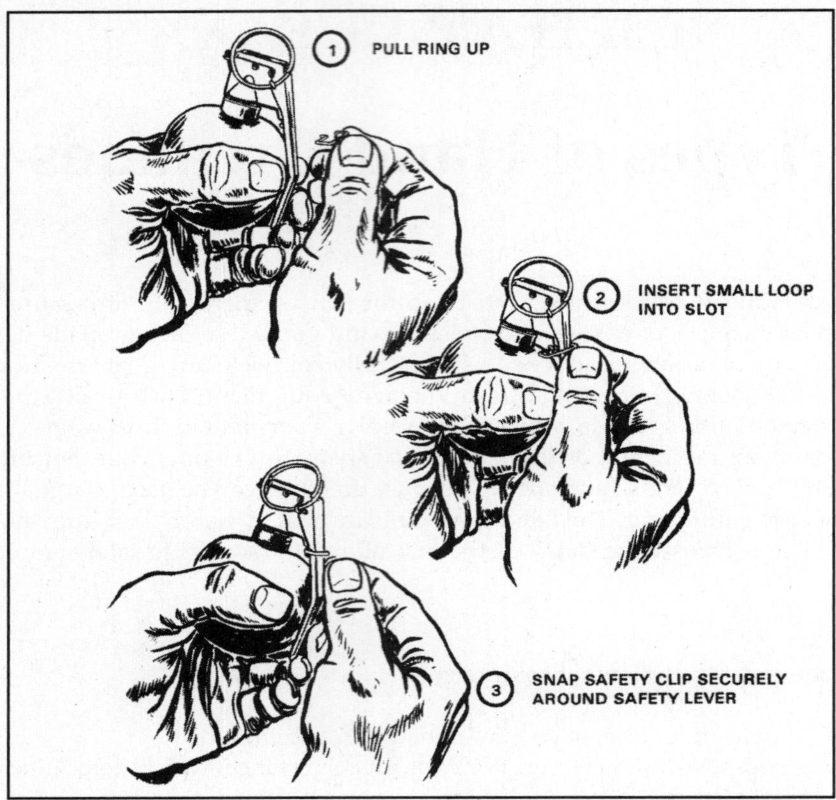

Figure 1-1: Safety clip insertion.

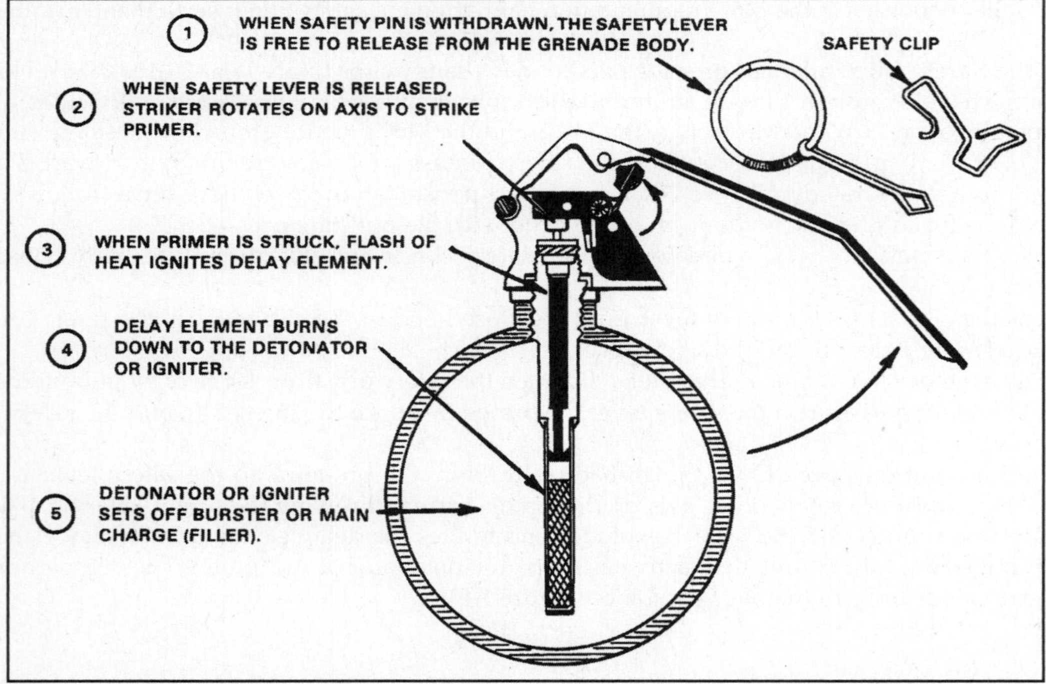

Figure 1-2: Fuze functioning.

1-4. FUZES

The two types of fuzes used in current U.S. hand grenades are detonating and ignition. Both function in the same manner; the difference is how they activate the filler substance.

a. **Detonating Fuze.** Detonating fuzes explode within the grenade body to initiate the main explosion of the filler substance. Detonating fuzes include the M213 and M228.

(1) ***M213 fuze.*** The M213 fuze (Figure 1-3) is designed for use with the M67 fragmentation grenade. It has a safety clip. The standard delay element is a powder train requiring 4 to 5 seconds to burn to the detonator. In some cases, the delay element may vary from less than 4 seconds to more than 5 seconds due to defective fuzes.

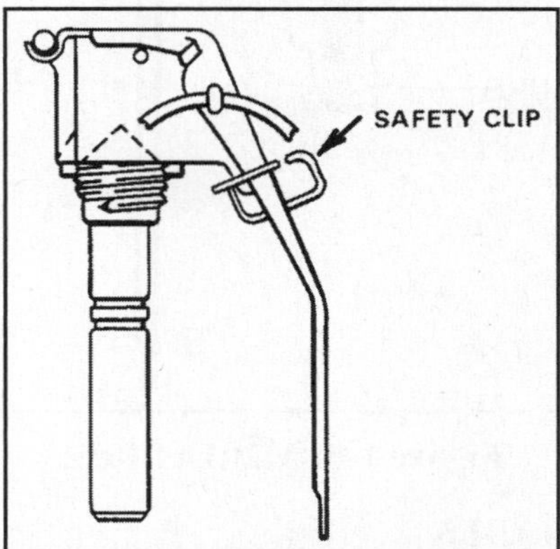

Figure 1-3: M213 fuze.

WARNING

If pressure on the safety lever is relaxed after the safety clip and safety pin have been removed, it is possible that the striker can rotate and strike the primer while the thrower is still holding the grenade. This is called "milking" the grenade. Throwers must be instructed to maintain enough pressure on the safety lever so the striker cannot rotate.

(2) ***M228 fuze.*** The M228 fuze (Figure 1-4) is used with the M69 practice grenade to replicate the fuze delay of the M67 fragmentation hand grenade. The time delay element is a powder train with a 4- to 5-second delay burn. In some cases, however, the delay element may vary from less than 4 seconds to more than 5 seconds due to defective fuzes.

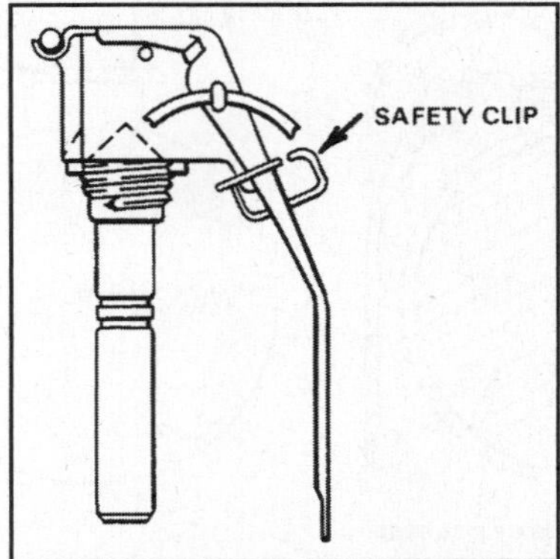

Figure 1-4: M228 fuze.

b. **Igniting Fuze.** Igniting fuzes are designed for use with chemical hand grenades. They burn at high temperatures and ignite the chemical filler. The M201A1 (Figure 1-5) is designed for use with the AN-M83HC white smoke grenade, the AN-M14 TH3 incendiary grenade, and the M18 colored smoke grenade. This fuze is interchangeable with any standard firing device. The time delay element is a powder train requiring 1.2 to 2 seconds to burn to the igniter. The igniter ignites the filler or a pyrotechnic starter with a violent burning action and expels the filler from the grenade body.

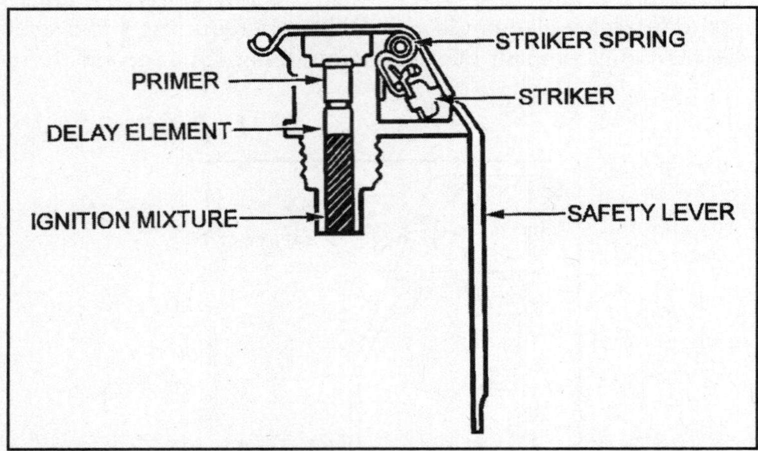

Figure 1-5: M201A1 fuze.

1-5. FRAGMENTATION HAND GRENADES

The following is a description of the M67 fragmentation hand grenade (Figure 1-6):

a. **Body.** The body is a steel sphere.
b. **Filler.** The filler has 6.5 ounces of Composition B.
c. **Fuze.** The fuze is an M213.
d. **Weight.** The grenade weighs 14 ounces.
e. **Safety Clip.** The grenade has a safety clip. (See paragraph 1-3.)
f. **Capabilities.** The average soldier can throw the M67 grenade 35 meters effectively. The effective casualty-producing radius is 15 meters and the killing radius is 5 meters.
g. **Color and Markings.** The grenade has an olive drab body with a single-yellow band at the top. Markings are in yellow.

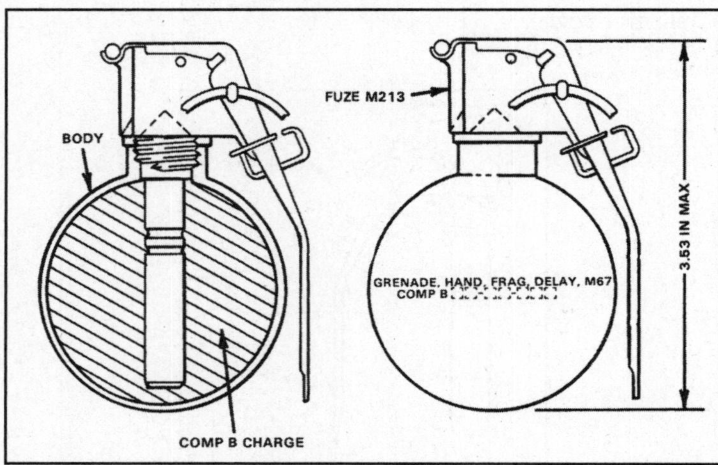

Figure 1-6: M67 fragmentation hand grenade.

WARNING

Although the killing radius of this grenade is 5 meters and the casualty-producing radius is 15 meters, fragmentation can disperse as far away as 230 meters.

1-6. SMOKE HAND GRENADES

Smoke hand grenades are used as ground-to-ground or ground-to-air signaling devices, target or landing zone marking devices, or screening devices for unit movements.

a. **M18 Colored Smoke Hand Grenade.** The following is a description of the M18 colored smoke hand grenade and its components (Figure 1-7).

(1) ***Body.*** The body has a sheet steel cylinder with four emission holes at the top and one at the bottom. The holes allow smoke to escape when the grenade is ignited.

(2) ***Filler.*** The filler has 11.5 ounces of colored smoke mixture (red, yellow, green and violet).

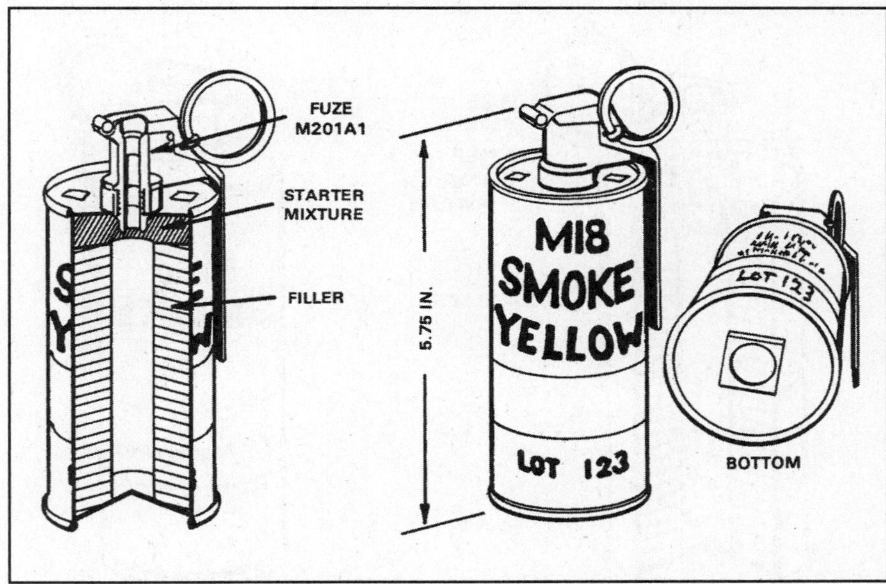

Figure 1-7: M18 colored smoke hand grenade.

(3) ***Fuze.*** The fuze is an M201A1.

(4) ***Weight.*** The grenade weighs 19 ounces.

(5) ***Safety clip.*** This grenade does not have a safety clip.

(6) ***Capabilities.*** The average soldier can throw this grenade 35 meters. It produces a cloud of colored smoke for 50 to 90 seconds.

(7) ***Color and markings.*** The grenade has an olive drab body with the top indicating the smoke color.

(8) ***Field expedient.*** In combat, you may need to use the M18 hand grenade without the fuze. Use the following procedures *in combat only*:

- Remove the tape from the grenade bottom to expose the filler.
- Remove the fuze by unscrewing it from the grenade.
- Ignite the starter mixture with an open flame.
- Throw the grenade immediately to avoid burn injury.

WARNING

Do not use a smoke grenade in an enclosed area. If you must remain in the area with the smoke, always wear a protective mask.

b. **AN-M83 HC White Smoke Hand Grenade.** The AN-M83 HC white smoke hand grenade (Figure 1-8) is used for screening the activities of small units and for ground-to-air signaling.
   (1) ***Body.*** The body is a cylinder of thin sheet metal, 2.5 inches in diameter.
   (2) ***Filler.*** The filler has 11 ounces of terephthalic acid.
   (3) ***Fuze.*** The fuze is an M201A1.
   (4) ***Weight.*** The grenade weighs 16 ounces and is 2.5 inches in diameter and 5.7 inches in length.
   (5) ***Safety clip.*** This grenade does not have a safety clip.
   (6) ***Capabilities.*** The AN-M83 produces a cloud of white smoke for 25 to 70 seconds.
   (7) ***Color and markings.*** The grenade has a forest green body with light green markings, a blue band, and a white top.

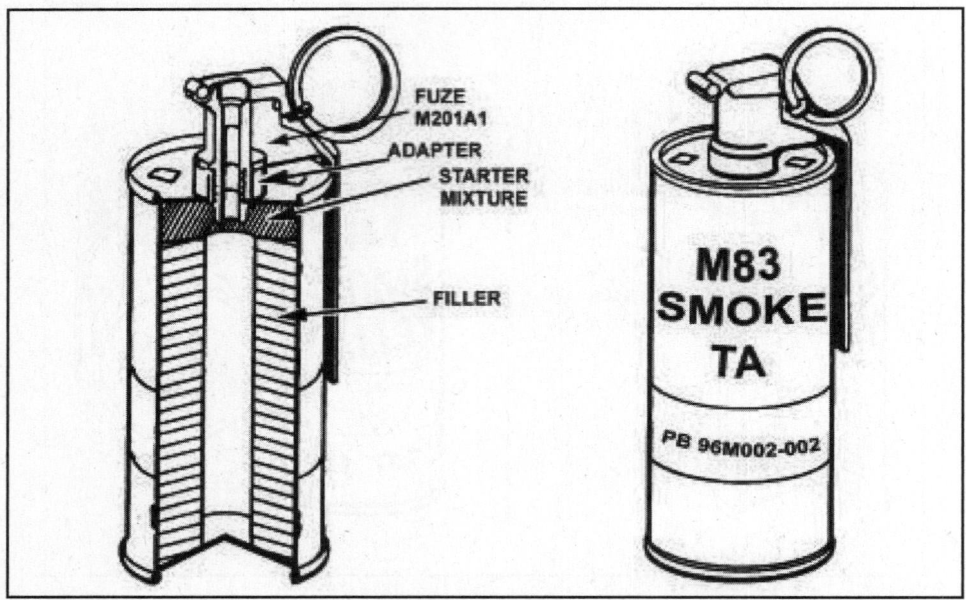

Figure 1-8: AN-M83 white smoke hand grenade.

1-7. RIOT-CONTROL HAND GRENADES

The ABC-M7A2 and ABC-M7A3 riot-control hand grenades (Figure 1-9) contain only CS as a filler. They differ only in the amount of filler and the form of the CS they contain. Description and components are as follows:

a. **Body.** The bodies of both grenades are sheet metal with four emission holes at the top and one at the bottom.
b. **Filler.** The ABC-7A2 grenade has 5.5 ounces of burning mixture and 3.5 ounces of CS in gelatin capsules. The ABC-M7A3 has 7.5 ounces of burning mixture and 4.5 ounces of pelletized CS agent.
c. **Fuze.** The fuze for either grenade is an M201A1.
d. **Weight.** Each grenade weighs about 15.5 ounces.
e. **Safety.** These grenades do not have safety clips.
f. **Capabilities.** The average soldier can throw these grenades 40 meters. Both grenades produce a cloud of irritant agent for 15 to 35 seconds.
g. **Color and Markings.** Both grenades have gray bodies with red bands and markings.

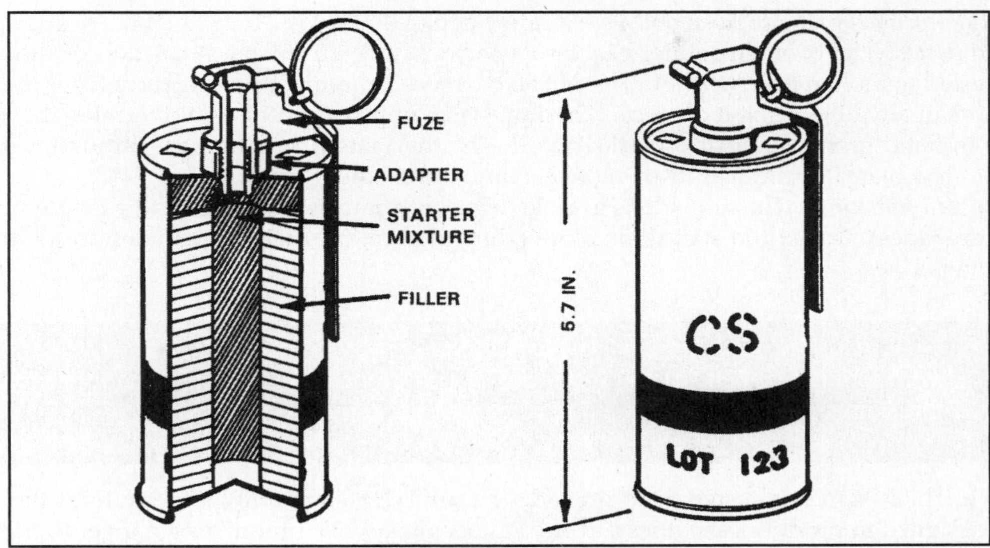

Figure 1-9: ABC-M7A2 and M7A3 riot-control hand grenades.

WARNING
Do not use a riot control grenade in an enclosed area. If you must remain in the area, always wear a protective mask.

1-8. SPECIAL-PURPOSE HAND GRENADES

a. **Incendiary.** The AN-M14 TH3 incendiary hand grenade (Figure 1-10) is used to destroy equipment or start fires. It can also damage, immobilize, or destroy vehicles, weapons systems, shelters, or munitions. The description and components are as follows:

(1) ***Body.*** The body is sheet metal.
(2) ***Filler.*** The filler has 26.5 ounces of thermate (TH3) mixture.
(3) ***Fuze.*** The fuze is an M201A1.
(4) ***Weight.*** The grenade weighs 32 ounces.

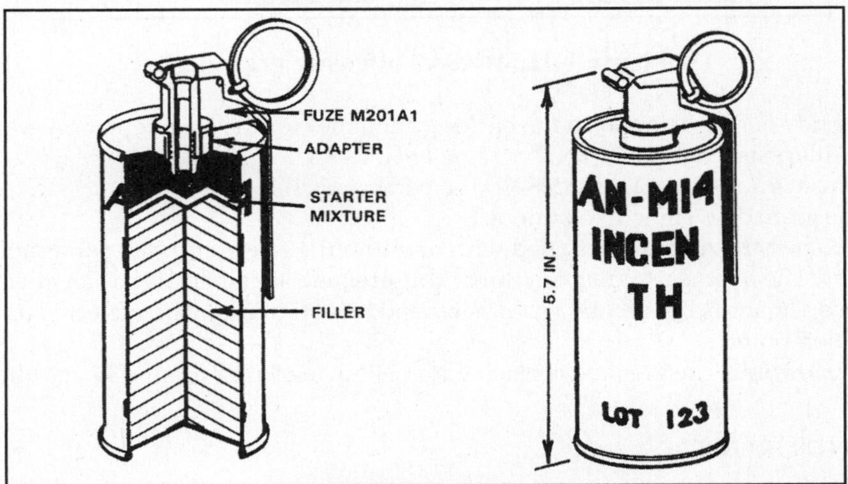

Figure 1-10: AN-M14 TH3 incendiary hand grenade.

(5) ***Safety clip.*** This grenade does not have a safety clip.

(6) ***Capabilities.*** The average soldier can throw this grenade 25 meters. A portion of thermate mixture is converted to molten iron, which burns at 4,000 degrees Fahrenheit. The mixture fuzes together the metallic parts of any object that it contacts. Thermate is an improved version of thermite, the incendiary agent used in hand grenades during World War II. The thermate filler can burn through a 1/2-inch homogenous steel plate. It produces its own oxygen and burns under water.

(7) ***Color and markings.*** The grenade is gray in color with purple markings and a single purple band (current grenades). Under the standard color-coding system, incendiary grenades are light red with black markings.

WARNING

Avoid looking directly at the incendiary hand grenade as it burns. The intensity of the light is hazardous to the retina and can cause permanent eye damage.

b. **Offensive.** The MK3A2 offensive hand grenade (Figure 1-11), commonly referred to as the concussion grenade, is designed to produce casualties during close combat while minimizing danger to friendly personnel. The grenade is also used for concussion effects in enclosed areas, for blasting, and for demolition tasks. The shock waves (overpressure) produced by this grenade when used in enclosed areas are greater than those produced by the fragmentation grenade. It is, therefore, very effective against enemy soldiers located in bunkers, buildings, and fortified areas.

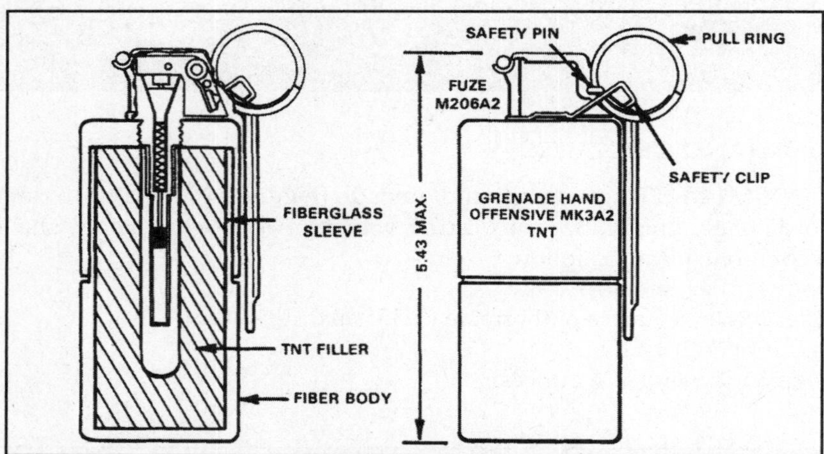

Figure 1-11: MK3A2 offensive grenade.

(1) ***Body.*** The body is fiber (similar to the packing container for the fragmentation grenade.)

(2) ***Filler.*** The filler has 8 ounces of TNT.

(3) ***Fuze.*** The fuze is an M206A1 or M206A2 (see paragraph 1-4).

(4) ***Weight.*** The grenade weighs 15.6 ounces.

(5) ***Safety clip.*** The MK3A2 may be issued with or without a safety clip (see paragraph 1-3).

(6) ***Capabilities.*** The average soldier can throw this grenade 40 meters. It has an effective casualty radius of 2 meters in open areas, but secondary missiles and bits of fuze may be projected as far as 200 meters from the detonation point.

(7) ***Color and markings.*** The grenade is black with yellow markings around its middle.

1-9. PRACTICE HAND GRENADES

The M69 practice hand grenade (Figure 1-12) simulates the M67 series of fragmentation hand grenades for training purposes. The grenade provides realistic training and familiarizes the soldier with the functioning and characteristics of the fragmentation hand grenade. The following is a description of the M69 practice hand grenade and its components:

a. **Body.** The body is a steel sphere.
b. **Fuze.** The fuze is an M228, which is inserted into the grenade body.
c. **Weight.** The grenade weighs 14 ounces.
d. **Safety Clip.** The M69 grenade has a safety clip.
e. **Capabilities.** The average soldier can throw the M69 hand grenade 40 meters. After a delay of 4 to 5 seconds, the M69 emits a small puff of white smoke and makes a loud popping noise. The grenade body can be used repeatedly by replacing the fuze assembly.
f. **Color and Markings.** The grenade is light blue with white markings. The safety lever of the fuze is light blue with black markings and a brown tip.

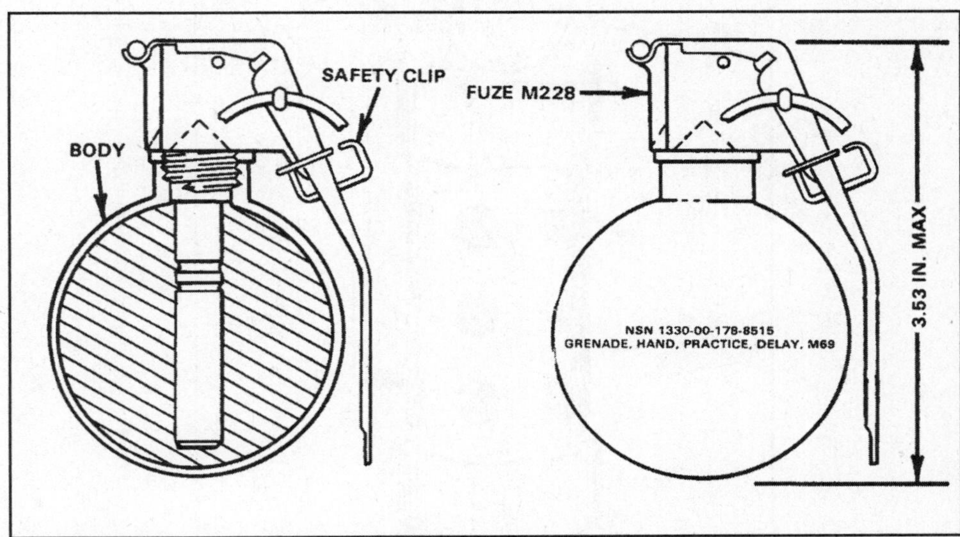

Figure 1-12: M69 practice hand grenade.

WARNING
Fuze fragments may exit the hole in the base of the grenade body and cause injuries.

1-10. STUN HAND GRENADES

Stun hand grenades are used as diversionary or distraction devices during building and room clearing operations when the presence of noncombatants is likely or expected and the assaulting element is attempting to achieve surprise. The following is a description of the M84 diversionary/flash-bang stun hand grenade and its components (Figure 1-13).

a. **Body.** The body is a steel hexagon tube with holes along the sides to allow for the emission of intense light and sound when the grenade is ignited.
b. **Fuze and safety pin.** The fuze is the M201A1. The M84 also has a secondary safety pin with a triangular pull ring.
c. **Weight.** The grenade weighs 8.33 ounces.

d. **Capabilities.** The handheld device is designed to be thrown into a room (through an open door, a standard glass window, or other opening) where it delivers a loud bang and bright flash sufficient to temporarily disorient personnel in the room.

e. **Field-expedient early warning device.** In combat, you may need to use the M84 stun hand grenade as an early warning device. Use the following procedures in combat only:
   (1) Attach the grenade to a secure object such as a tree, post, or picket.
   (2) Attach a tripwire to a secure object, extend it across a path, and attach it to the pull ring of the grenade.
   (3) Bend the end of the pull pin flat to allow for easy pulling.
   (4) Remove the secondary safety pin.

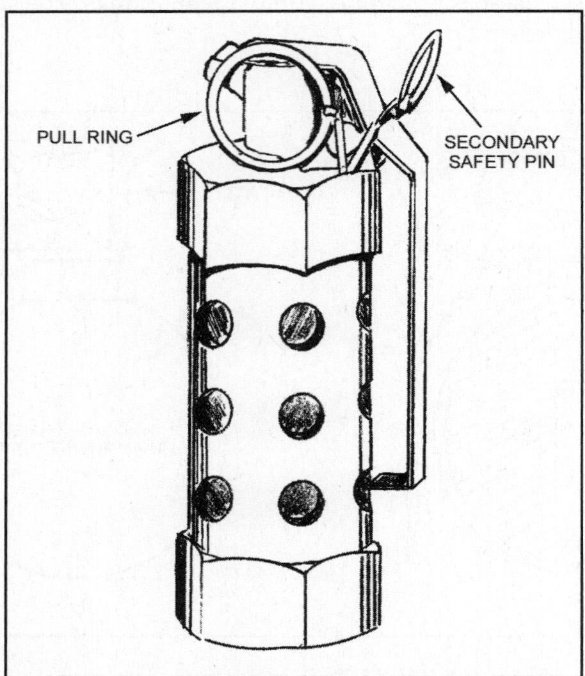

Figure 1-13: M84 stun hand grenade.

⚠ **CAUTION**

Use stun grenades as field-expedient early warning devices only when in a combat environment.

CHAPTER 2

Maintenance

2-1. GENERAL ASSEMBLY

Hand grenades within the U.S. inventory are composed of a body and a fuze. Most hand grenades come assembled with the exception of the M69 practice hand grenade and the fuzes for the M69, which come in flats of 45 fuzes.

2-2. INSPECTION PROCEDURES

Hand grenades within the U.S. inventory are specifically designed and manufactured to overcome any situation during combat or training missions. Grenades can be used to save or take lives. Hand grenades are simple yet powerful weapons used in combat or any training mission. As simple as they may seem, however, hand grenades—like any other weapon—must be inspected before use in order to avoid serious injury or death. The following inspection procedures apply to all hand grenades within the U.S. inventory.

a. **Newly Issued Hand Grenades.**
   (1) Remove the tape and the top cover from the shipping canister.
   (2) Look down into the canister; if the hand grenade is upside down, return the canister to the issuing person (NCOIC or OIC).
   (3) Ensure all required safeties are properly attached to the hand grenade. If a safety pin is missing, return it.
   (4) Check the hand grenade for rust on the body or the fuze. If it has rusted, return it.
   (5) Check for holes on the body and the fuze. If any holes are visible, return the hand grenade.
   (6) If the hand grenade seems to be in order, remove the grenade carefully from the canister and make a visual check for proper fitting of the safety pins. Then, properly secure the grenade to the ammunition pouch.

b. **Grenades That Are Unpacked or Stored on Ammunition Pouches.**
   (1) Inspect unpacked grenades daily to ensure safety pins are present. Under hostile conditions, the safety clip must be removed from the fragmentation hand grenade since soldiers under stressful situations sometimes forget to remove the clip when throwing the grenade.
   (2) Check the body for rust or dirt.
   (3) Make sure the lever is not broken or bent.

2-3. CLEANING, LUBRICATION, AND PREVENTIVE MAINTENANCE

Hand grenades are like any other weapon; they must be inspected and cleaned weekly when exposed to the environment. The body of the hand grenade is made of metal, which rusts when it is exposed to moisture or submerged in water. If not removed, dirt or rust can cause the hand grenade to malfunction.

a. **Cleaning.** Wipe the dirt off the body of the hand grenade using a slightly damp cloth or a light brush. For the fuze head, a light brush is recommended since it can reach into the crevices.

b. **Lubrication.** Depending on weather conditions, a light coat of CLP may be needed.

c. **Preventive Maintenance.** For most hand grenades, keeping them clean and lubricated is sufficient maintenance. With the M69 practice grenade, however, maintenance is more difficult since the bodies are used repeatedly. The M69 practice grenade must be cleaned with a wire brush and painted at least quarterly. The threads must be cleaned with a wire brush on a monthly basis, and fuze residue must be removed from the body immediately after each use. Cleaning the threads and removing the residue from the hand grenade body make replacement of the fuzes easier. The grenade body lasts longer if these preventive maintenance procedures are performed.

CHAPTER 3

Employment of Hand Grenades

SECTION I. INTRODUCTION TO HAND GRENADE TRAINING

The rifle, the bayonet, and the hand grenade are the soldier's basic lethal weapons. Historically, hand grenade training has received less emphasis than marksmanship and bayonet training. The hand grenade must receive greater emphasis in training programs and field training exercises. The proper use of hand grenades could determine the fate of the soldier or the success of the mission.

Leaders at all levels should study the employment of grenades in conjunction with the unit mission and implement a training program that supports that mission. Once soldiers can safely arm and throw live fragmentation grenades, units should integrate the use of grenades into collective tasks, rather than training these skills as a separate event. Hand grenades must be integrated with other available weapons systems to enhance the unit's combat power on the modern battlefield. We must conduct hand grenade training in the same manner in which we plan to fight.

We cannot let the danger associated with hand grenades deter our training efforts. Proper control and safety procedures allow us to conduct hand grenade training in a safe manner. Train soldiers to standard, and safety is inherent.

Hand grenades include more than casualty-producing instruments of war. They are used to signal, screen, and control crowds. The current inventory provides a specific hand grenade for most circumstances. Soldiers must be familiar with current grenades, their descriptions, and how best to employ each.

3-1. HAND GRENADE STORING

The storing of hand grenades on ammunition pouches is one of the most neglected aspects of hand grenade training. Experiences of American infantry, both in combat and in training, point out the need for specific training in storing hand grenades on ammunition pouches and integration of this type of training into tactical training exercises. Commanders should make every effort to issue training hand grenades for wear and use during all training activities. The soldier must be as confident in carrying and using hand grenades as he is with his rifle and bayonet. Before storing a hand grenade, take the following safety precautions:

a. Check the grenade fuze assembly for tightness. It must be tightly fitted in the grenade fuze well to prevent the grenade from working loose and separating from the grenade body. Never remove the fuze from a grenade.

b. If the grenade safety lever is broken, do not use the grenade. A broken safety lever denies the thrower the most critical safety mechanism of the grenade.

c. Do not bend the ends of the safety pin back flush against the fuze body. This practice, intended to preclude the accidental pulling of the pin, makes the removal of the safety pin difficult. Repeated working of the safety pin in this manner causes the pin to break, creating a hazardous condition.

d. Carry hand grenades either on the ammunition pouch, using the carrying safety straps that are designed specifically for this purpose (Figure 3-1), or in the grenade pockets of the enhanced tactical load-bearing vest (Figure 3-2).

   (1) ***Standard ammunition pouch.*** Open the web carrying sleeve on the side of the ammunition pouch and slide the grenade into the sleeve with the safety lever against the side of the ammunition pouch. Be sure the pull ring is in the downward position. Wrap the carrying strap around the neck of the fuze and snap the carrying strap to the carrying sleeve.

   (2) ***Enhanced tactical load-bearing vest.*** The enhanced tactical load-bearing vest (ETLBV) has slanted pockets for carrying hand grenades. The grenades are not exposed and are safer to carry than in the standard ammunition pouch. The ETLBV is intended to provide the combat soldier with a comfortable and efficient method of transporting the individual fighting load.

Figure 3-1: Standard ammunition pouch.

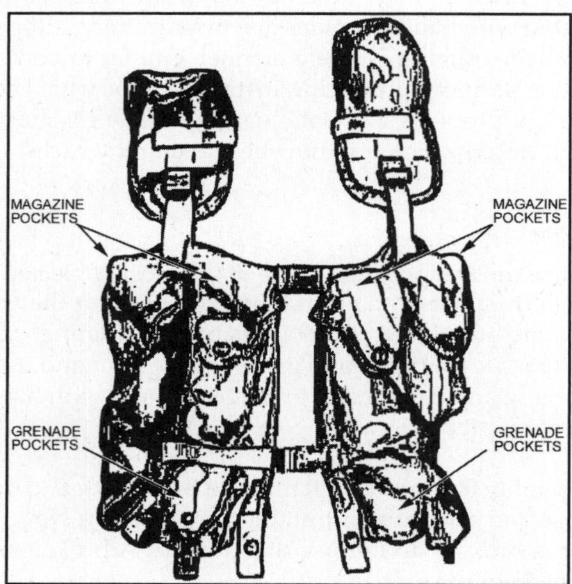

Figure 3-2: Enhanced tactical load-bearing vest.

- **Description.** The ETLBV has permanently attached ammunition and grenade pockets. The vest is compatible with the standard equipment belt. It incorporates adjustments to allow for proper fitting.
- **Components materials.** The ETLBV has 7 yards and 5 ounces of nylon fabric and nylon webbing.
- **Color.** The coloring of the ETLBV is woodland camouflage.
- **Weight.** The ETLBV weighs 1.9 pounds.
- **Size.** The ETLBV comes in one size that fits all.
- **Basis of issue.** Each infantry soldier should receive one ETLBV.

3-2. HAND GRENADE GRIPPING PROCEDURES

The importance of properly gripping the hand grenade cannot be overemphasized. Soldiers must understand that a grenade not held properly is difficult to arm. Sustainment training is the key to maintaining grip efficiency. Gripping procedures differ slightly for right- and left-handed soldiers:

a. Holding the grenade in the throwing hand with the safety lever placed between the first and second joints of the thumb provides safety and throwing efficiency.
b. Right-handed soldiers hold the grenade upright with the pull ring away from the palm of the throwing hand so that the pull ring can be easily removed by the index or middle finger of the free hand (Figure 3-3).
c. Left-handed soldiers invert the grenade with the fingers and thumb of the throwing hand positioned in the same manner as by right-handed personnel (Figure 3-4).

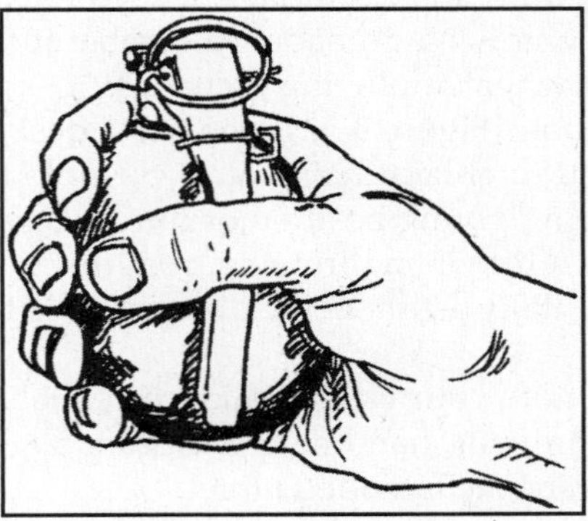

Figure 3-3: Right-handed grip.

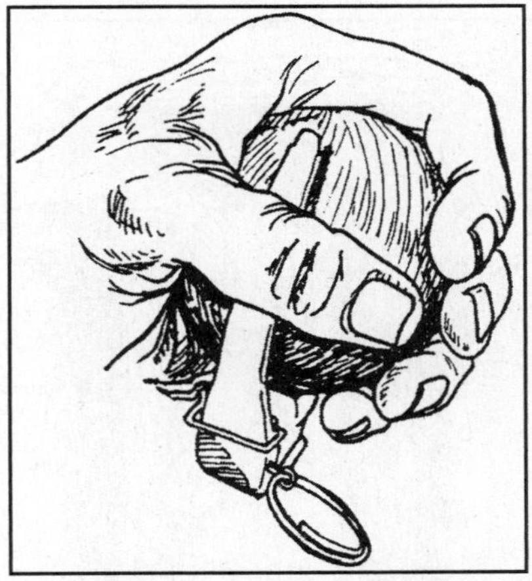

Figure 3-4: Left-handed grip.

3-3. HAND GRENADE THROWING

Since few soldiers throw in the same manner, it is difficult to establish firm rules or techniques for throwing hand grenades. How accurately they are thrown is more important than how they are thrown. If a soldier can achieve more distance and accuracy using his own personal style, he should be allowed to do so as long as his body is facing sideways, towards the enemy's position, and he throws basically overhand. There is, however, a recommended method of throwing hand grenades.

a. **Employ Grenades.** Use the following procedures:
   (1) Observe the target to mentally establish the distance between your throwing position and the target area. In observing the target, minimize your exposure time to the enemy (no more than 3 seconds).
   (2) Grip the hand grenade in your throwing hand.
   (3) Grasp the pull ring with the index or middle finger of your nonthrowing hand. Remove the safety pin with a pulling and twisting motion. If the tactical situation permits, observe the safety pin's removal.

(4) Look at the target and throw the grenade using the overhand method so that the grenade arcs, landing on or near the target.

(5) Allow the motion of your throwing arm to continue naturally once you release the grenade. This follow-through improves distance and accuracy and lessens the strain on your throwing arm.

(6) Practice the necessary throws that are used in combat, such as the underhand and sidearm throws. Soldiers can practice these throws with practice grenades, but they must throw live fragmentation grenades overhand in a training environment.

b. **Throwing Positions.** In training, throwing positions are used for uniformity, control, and to familiarize soldiers with the proper manner of throwing grenades in combat if the situation gives you a choice. Consider the following throwing positions when employing grenades:

(1) ***Standing.*** The standing position (Figure 3-5) is the most desirable and natural position from which to throw grenades. It allows you to obtain the greatest possible throwing distance. Soldiers normally use this position when occupying a fighting position or during operations in fortified positions or urban terrain. Use the following procedures when throwing from this position:

(a) Observe the target to mentally estimate the distance. Use the proper handgrip and arm the grenade while behind cover.

(b) Assume a natural stance with your weight balanced equally on both feet. Hold the grenade shoulder high and hold the nonthrowing hand at a 45-degree angle with the fingers and thumb extended, joined, and pointing toward the intended target.

(c) Throw the grenade with a natural motion, using the procedures described in paragraph 3-3.

(d) Seek cover to avoid being hit by fragments or direct enemy fire. If no cover is available, drop to the prone position with your Kevlar facing the direction of the grenade's detonation.

Figure 3-5: Standing throwing position.

(2) ***Kneeling.*** The kneeling position (Figure 3-6) reduces the distance a soldier can throw a grenade. It is used primarily when a soldier has only a low wall, a shallow ditch, or similar cover to protect him. Use the following procedures when throwing from this position:

(a) Observe the target to mentally estimate the throwing distance. Using the proper grip, arm the grenade while behind cover.

(b) Hold the grenade shoulder high and bend your nonthrowing knee at a 90-degree angle, placing that knee on the ground. Keep your throwing leg straight and locked, with the side of your boot firmly on the ground. Move your body to face sideways toward the target position. Keep your nonthrowing hand at a 45-degree angle with your fingers and thumb extended, joined, and pointing toward the enemy position.

(c) Throw the grenade with a natural throwing motion. Push off with your throwing foot to give added force to your throw. Follow through with your throwing arm as described in paragraph 3-3.

Figure 3-6: Kneeling throwing position.

(d) Drop to the prone position or behind available cover to reduce exposure to fragmentation and direct enemy fire.

(3) ***Alternate prone.*** The alternate prone position (Figure 3-7) reduces both distance and accuracy. It is used only when an individual is pinned down by hostile fire and is unable to rise to engage his target. Use the following procedures when throwing from this position:

(a) Lie down on your back with your body parallel to the grenade's intended line of flight. Hold the grenade at chin-chest level and remove the safety pins.

(b) Cock your throwing leg at a 45-degree angle, maintaining knee-to-knee contact and bracing the side of your boot firmly on the ground. Hold the grenade 4 to 6 inches behind your ear with your arm cocked for throwing.

(c) With your free hand, grasp any object that is capable of giving added leverage to increase your throwing distance. In throwing the grenade, push off with your rearward foot to give added force to

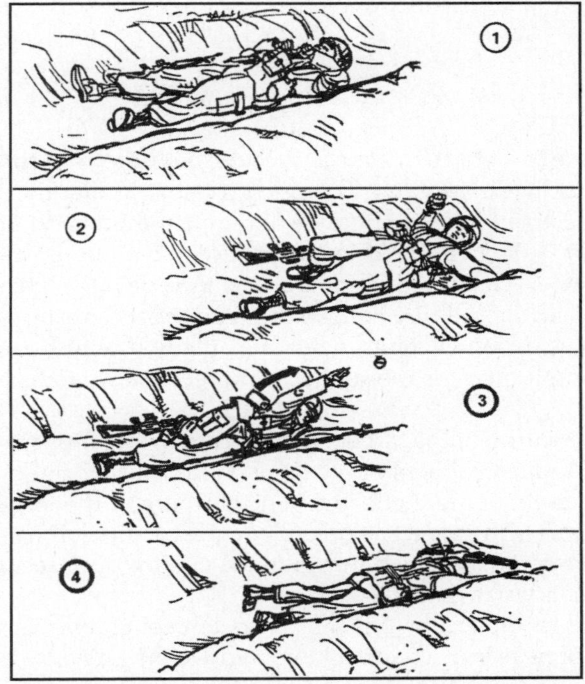

Figure 3-7: Alternate prone throwing position.

your throw. Do not lift your head or body when attempting to throw a grenade as this exposes you to direct enemy fire.

(d) After throwing the grenade, roll over onto your stomach and press flat against the ground.

SECTION II. TACTICAL EMPLOYMENT

Hand grenades provide the individual soldier with a number of highly versatile and effective weapons systems. Soldiers employ hand grenades throughout the spectrum of warfare, from low to high intensity conflict, to prevent giving away positions, to save ammunition, and to inflict greater casualties.

3-4. APPLICATION

Soldiers use hand grenades in defensive missions, offensive missions, and retrograde operations. All soldiers use hand grenades during close, deep, and rear operations, during all conditions of combat, and in all types of terrain. Hand grenades have the following specific applications:

- Fragmentation hand grenades are mainly used to kill or wound enemy soldiers but can also be used to destroy or disable equipment.
- Incendiary hand grenades are mainly used to destroy equipment and start fires but can also be used to destroy or disable vehicles and weapons.
- Colored smoke is mainly used to identify or mark positions but can also be used to mark areas for ground-to-ground operations or ground-to-air operations.
- White smoke is mainly used to conceal or create a smoke screen for offensive or retrograde operations.
- Riot-control hand grenades are used to control crowds or riots.
- Stun grenades are used to temporarily stun or disorient the occupants of an enclosed area such as a building or room.

While all hand grenades have application in modern combat, the fragmentation hand grenade remains the most important because it is not only the primary killing hand grenade but also the most dangerous to employ. Fragmentation hand grenades are equally lethal to friendly and enemy soldiers; therefore, we must employ them properly to protect our own soldiers.

3-5. CLOSE COMBAT

On the modern battlefield, the close-in fight can occur anywhere, anytime. The rifle, bayonet, and hand grenade are basic weapons of warfare for the individual soldier. The rifle gives the soldier the ability to kill enemy soldiers with direct fire out to the maximum effective line-of-sight range. Fragmentation hand grenades, on the other hand, allow the soldier to effectively engage and kill enemy soldiers located within a radius of 40 meters where line-of-sight systems, including the rifle, are no longer effective. Since there is no muzzle flash, grenades also help conceal a soldier's position as he engages the enemy. While the rifle is the safest and most discriminating weapon at close ranges, the fragmentation hand grenade is the weapon of choice when the enemy is within range but the terrain masks engagement areas. The fragmentation hand grenade is the soldier's indirect-fire weapon system.

a. Many times in combat, the nature of the targets confronting the infantryman make normal methods of target engagement inadequate. Against soldiers or weapons in trenches or fighting positions, for example, having a grenade burst over the target is more effective. Furthermore, if the targets are on sloping ground, then a grenade needs to detonate as near impact as possible to prevent its rolling away from the target before detonating. Such aboveground detonation also prevents the enemy from securing the grenade and throwing it back within the 4- to 5-second fuze delay.

b. Aboveground detonation is especially critical when engaging bunker-type emplacements. To achieve aboveground detonation or near-impact detonation, remove the grenade's safety pin, release the safety lever, count ONE THOUSAND ONE, ONE THOUSAND TWO, and throw the grenade. This is called *cooking-off.* Cooking-off expends a sufficient period (about 2 seconds) of the grenade's 4- to 5-second delay. This causes the grenade to detonate above ground or shortly after impact with the target. Do not cook-off fragmentation or white phosphorous hand grenades when in training.

> ⚠ **CAUTION**
> Use cook-off procedure only when in a combat environment.

3-6. PLANS AND PREPARATIONS FOR COMBAT

The theater commander normally establishes basic and combat loads of hand grenades. The combat load is not a fixed quantity; it can be altered as the situation dictates. Units vary their combat load depending upon the commander's analysis of METT-T. The most important factor in determining the combat load for hand grenades is unit mission. It influences the type and quantity of hand grenades needed. Other factors used in determining the hand grenade combat load are as follows:

a. **Weight.** Each hand grenade weighs close to one pound. Consequently, each grenade that the soldier carries adds another pound to his total load.
b. **Weapons Tradeoff.** Soldiers cannot carry everything commanders would like to take into battle. Commanders must consider the value of various weapons and munitions with a view toward determining which contribute the most to the mission accomplishment. For example, tradeoff may be required between hand grenades and mines, between hand grenades and mortar ammunition, or between different types of grenades.
c. **Balance.** Different types of hand grenades are required on all missions. Generally, fragmentation and colored smoke grenades are required for all missions. Distribute hand grenades selected for a mission among several soldiers, if not among all of them.
d. **Individual Duties.** Distribute to each soldier the hand grenades that are required for his job and assigned tasks.

3-7. EMPLOYMENT RULES

The rules to remember before employing hand grenades, or when in areas where they are in use, are as follows:

- Know where all friendly forces are located.
- Know your sector of fire.
- Use the buddy or team system.
- Ensure the projected arc of the fragmentation hand grenade is clear of obstacles.
- Evacuate positions into which you plan to throw a fragmentation hand grenade, if possible. If not, then use the grenade sump.

3-8. OFFENSIVE EMPLOYMENT

The fragmentation hand grenade is the primary type of grenade used during offensive operations. These grenades provide the violent, destructive, close-in firepower essential for the individual soldier to overcome and kill the enemy. The fragmentation hand grenade makes the individual soldier's movement easier by suppressing the enemy and disrupting the continuity of the enemy's defensive fires. Fragmentation hand grenades contribute greatly in destroying the enemy's will to continue the fight. The noise, flash, and concussion generated by fragmentation hand grenades have severe psychological effects on enemy soldiers. Offensive grenades are much less lethal than fragmentation grenades on an enemy in the open, but they are very effective against an enemy within a confined space. The concussion they produce is capable of killing or severely injuring enemy personnel, not just stunning them. Consider the following factors when employing hand grenades:

a. The critical phase of the attack is the final assault, that moment when a soldier closes with the enemy to kill him. The individual soldier uses the rifle, the hand grenade, and the bayonet during the assault. The soldier first uses the rifle, firing controlled, well-aimed shots at known or suspected enemy positions. The soldier does this as part of a buddy team, fire team, and squad. He is controlled and disciplined in his movement and application of fires by using the established unit SOPs and battle drills. These battle drills are rehearsed extensively during preparation for combat. As the soldier closes to hand grenade range, he engages the enemy with a combination of rifle fire and hand grenades. He uses fragmentation grenades to kill and suppress enemy soldiers in the open, in defilades, or in trenches. Movement toward the enemy is rapid and violent.

b. Soldiers must throw hand grenades accurately into enemy positions to reduce the chances of hand grenades hitting friendly forces. Movement forward is done as part of a buddy team. One soldier within the buddy team provides overwatching, direct suppressive fire while the other soldier moves forward. Both soldiers must take advantage of the grenade explosion to immediately continue their movement forward. If the enemy is located in an enclosed area, such as a bunker or room within a building, the offensive grenade may be more appropriate than the fragmentation hand grenade. Choosing between them depends upon availability and mission analysis beforehand. Offensive grenades are less lethal to the enemy, but because of this, they are also safer to employ in confined spaces. Soldiers should follow offensive grenade employment immediately with violent rifle fire unless capturing enemy personnel is a mission requirement. Remember, an enemy who is only temporarily stunned can still kill you. The shock waves from an offensive grenade also provide better overall interior effect in an enclosed space. Another advantage of the offensive grenade is that it covers more of an enclosed space than the fragmentation grenade.

c. In an assault against a dug-in, well-prepared enemy, the soldier uses hand grenades to clear crew-served weapons first. Once the first defensive belt has been penetrated, he uses hand grenades in a priority effort to attack command bunkers and communications equipment and to kill or capture enemy leaders within those bunkers.

d. In the assault, the soldier participates as a squad member in clearing trenches, destroying bunkers, and clearing rooms. The soldier employs unit procedures, which have been rehearsed during preparation for combat. In clearing a trench within a fortified position (Figure 3-8), the buddy team forms the basis for all fragmentation grenade employment in the following manner:

Figure 3-8: Enemy trench assault.

(1) Before entering the trench, the first clearing team throws or drops hand grenades into the trench, attempting to keep the individual grenades separated by at least five meters.

(2) After the grenades explode, the first clearing team rolls into the trench, landing on their feet and firing their weapons down both directions of the trench.

(3) The first clearing team holds the entry point.
(4) The teams following the first clearing team enter at the same position and begin clearing in one direction only.
(5) As the lead buddy team moves to the right (or left), one soldier is the designated grenadier. He moves along the wall closest to the next bend in the trench. His movement is covered by his buddy, who is ready to fire at any enemy soldiers advancing toward them. The grenadier holds a grenade at the ready as he moves rapidly down the trench.
(6) At the bend in the trench, the designated grenadier throws a grenade around the bend. After the explosion, the rifleman moves rapidly around the bend and fires rapid bursts horizontally and alternately along the long axis of the trench.
(7) Movement down the trench continues by alternating the designated rifleman and grenadier roles or maintaining the same roles throughout. Fire teams and squads are bounded forward to continue clearing the trench line.

> ✍ **NOTE**
> The unit SOP specifies many of these tasks. If a three-man clearing team is used, the third member guards the back of the other team members and stands by to provide fire on point targets.

e. Clearing an enemy bunker and killing the enemy soldiers inside requires violence and speed of execution, plus synchronization of effort at the buddy and squad level, in order to succeed. The following are procedures for clearing a bunker (Figure 3-9):

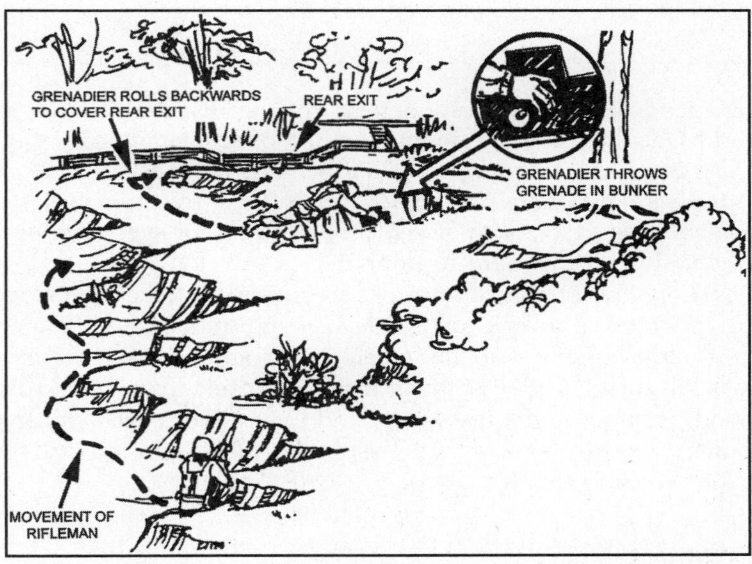

Figure 3-9: Enemy bunker assault.

(1) A two-man team assaults a single bunker using a combination of grenades and rifle fire. One member of the buddy team provides overwatching suppressive fire while the other member moves rapidly toward the bunker, using a combination of individual movement techniques. He uses the best available covered route to move toward the bunker.
(2) As he approaches to within 75 meters of the bunker, the grenadier can use white smoke to help conceal his movement for the remaining distance. The white smoke grenade should be thrown on line with the bunker and as close to the enemy's firing port as possible.
(3) Once the grenadier member of the buddy team is at the side of the bunker, he holds the grenade at a 90-degree angle from his body, releases the safety lever, mentally counts two seconds (ONE THOUSAND ONE, ONE THOUSAND TWO), and throws or pushes the grenade into the firing port of the bunker.

Once he releases the grenade, he rolls away from the bunker and faces to the rear of the bunker, prepared to engage escaping enemy soldiers with his rifle.

(4) After the grenade detonates, he enters the position from the rear to kill or capture remaining enemy soldiers.

f. When clearing a room or moving through an urban area, the following considerations apply:
- What types of grenades do the ROE permit and restrict?
- What effect do I want to achieve—kill, stun, obscure, destroy equipment, mark a location, and so forth?
- Does the structural integrity of the room and building permit the types of grenades selected for use?
- Will the scheme of maneuver permit the use of fragmentation grenades and not cause fratricide?
- Will the type of grenade used cause an urban fire in an undesired location?

If employing grenades during room clearing, the following procedure should be used in conjunction with Battle Drill 6, or Battle Drill 5:

(1) The Number 2 man throws a grenade into the room and yells FRAG OUT, STUN OUT, or CONCUSSION OUT, if stealth is not a factor, to alert friendly personnel that a grenade has been thrown toward the threat. After the grenade explodes, the Number 1 man enters the room, eliminates any threat, and moves to his point of domination IAW Battle Drill 6.

(2) Numbers 3 and 4 men enter the room, move to their points of domination, and eliminate any threat.

(3) The team clears and marks the room IAW unit SOP.

> ✍ **NOTE**
>
> Grenades tend to roll back down stairs and either nullify the desired effect(s) or cause friendly casualties.

g. The use of hand grenades during raids always depends on the mission. The raid, as a type of offensive operation, is characterized by heavy use of fragmentation and offensive grenades, but it may also require other types of grenades. Use grenades according to the following guidelines:

(1) If the mission is to secure prisoners, the employment of offensive grenades is appropriate.

(2) If the mission calls for the destruction of vehicles, weapons, or special equipment, then incendiary grenades and fragmentation grenades are appropriate.

(3) Smoke grenades are often used to create a smoke screen covering the advance of friendly forces or to mark the location of friendly forces and pickup points. Colored smoke is used mainly for signaling purposes.

h. Reaction to an enemy ambush requires an immediate, rapid, and violent response. The longer friendly forces remain in the ambush kill zone, the greater the probability of friendly force destruction. Using a combination of fragmentation hand grenades to kill the enemy and white smoke grenades to obscure the enemy's sight and rifle fire, the soldiers within a squad assault the enemy force. Train and drill soldiers to throw fragmentation grenades first, then smoke grenades.

3-9. DEFENSIVE EMPLOYMENT

Hand grenades are used in defensive operations during the final phase of the close-in battle. The primary hand grenade in all defensive operations is the fragmentation grenade. It is used in conjunction with other weapons and man-made or natural obstacles to destroy remnants of the attacking enemy force that have succeeded in penetrating the more distant barriers and final protective fires. The fragmentation hand grenade further disrupts the continuity of the enemy attack, demoralizes the enemy soldier, and forces the enemy into areas covered by direct-fire weapons, such as rifle and machine gun fire and Claymore mines. Using fragmentation hand grenades on dismounted enemy forces at a critical moment in the assault can be the final blow in taking the initiative away from the enemy.

a. **Defense From Individual Fighting Positions** (Figure 3-10). From individual fighting positions, fragmentation hand grenades are used primarily to cover close-in dead space approaches on the friendly side of the protective wire and in front of a squad's position. Soldiers should use these grenades in conjunction with ground flares positioned along the protective wire. Enemy soldiers who are stopped at the protective wire are engaged first with Claymore mines. If time permits during the preparation of the defensive position, soldiers should identify dead space in their sectors, especially dead space that may intersect the protective wire and move toward the friendly fighting positions. These potential avenues of approach through the protective wire should be marked with a reference to identify them as primary hand grenade targets. The following rules apply when employing fragmentation hand grenades from fighting positions:

(1) Clear overhead obstructions that may interfere with the path of the thrown grenade. Do this at the same time direct-fire fields of fire are cleared.
(2) Rehearse grenade employment; know where your primary target is located.
(3) Keep 50 percent of your fragmentation grenades at the ready in your fighting position, leaving the remaining fragmentation grenades on your load-carrying equipment (LCE).
(4) Rehearse actions needed if an enemy grenade lands in your fighting position.
(5) Employ fragmentation hand grenades against enemy soldiers located in defilade positions as first priority. This lessens the danger to friendly soldiers and helps cover terrain not covered by direct-fire weapons. Use the rifle to kill enemy soldiers not in defilade positions.
(6) Reconnoiter the alternate and supplementary positions and determine the priority for the fragmentation hand grenade target.
(7) Redistribute hand grenades after each enemy engagement.

WARNING

Former Soviet Union grenades use fuzes with only a 3- to 4-second delay, which means you have very little time to react. The preferred course of action if an enemy grenade lands in your position or near you is to immediately roll out of your fighting position or throw yourself flat on the ground.

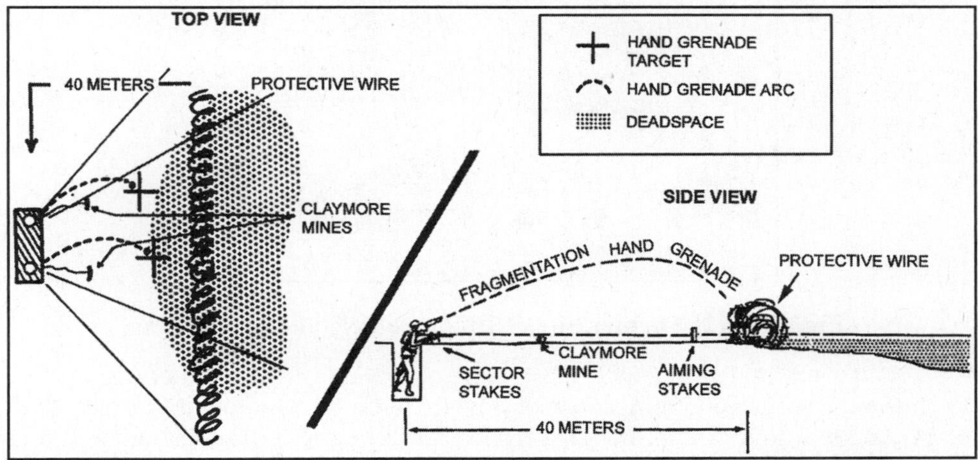

Figure 3-10: Defense from an individual fighting position.

b. **Defense Against Enemy Armored and Tracked Vehicles** (Figure 3-11). On occasion, friendly dismounted soldiers may come in close contact with enemy armored formations. Dismounted infantry should first use antitank weapons to defeat enemy armor and motorized infantry. Soldiers can also use satchel charges, as described in FM 5-250, to defeat enemy armor. If these are not available, it is still possible to destroy, immobilize, or render inoperative the vehicle or system, or to kill the crew inside the vehicle. In either case, the soldier must approach the armored vehicle to kill it or the crew with hand grenades. An understanding of some characteristics and vulnerabilities of former Soviet Union armor can help kill or disable the enemy armored vehicle or its crew. Vulnerabilities common to most threat vehicles are the fuel cells, ammunition storage areas, and power trains. Figure 3-12 highlights vulnerable areas on selected threat vehicles.

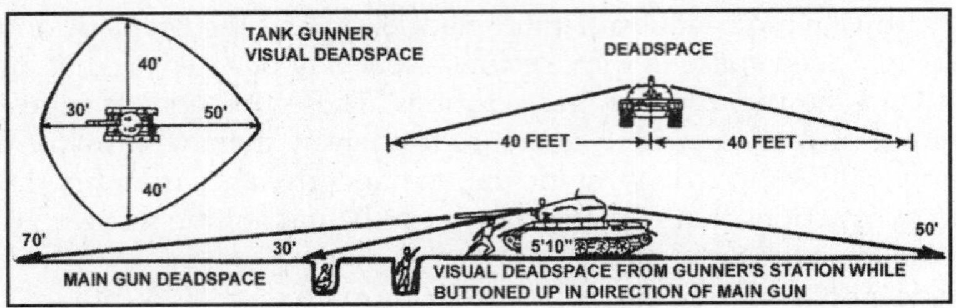

Figure 3-11: Attack of a former Soviet Union tank.

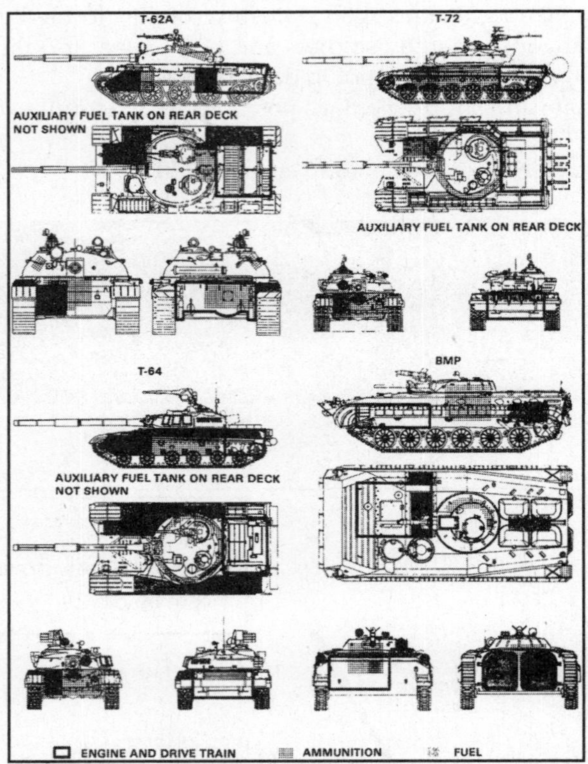

Figure 3-12: Former Soviet Union vehicle vulnerabilities.

(1) ***Turret rotation.*** The turrets of older former Soviet Union tanks rotate much slower than those on U.S. and NATO tanks. It takes more than 21 seconds for T60- and T70-series tanks to rotate through a full 360 degrees. The T80- and T90-series (Figure 3-13) tanks rotate a full 360 degrees in just 6 seconds, which is as fast as the US's Ml Abrams and M2 BFV. With the older former Soviet Union tanks, a soldier can actually run around the tank before the turret traverses from the front deck to the rear. The newer tanks have been fitted with explosive reactive armor, which makes them more difficult to engage with antitank weapons. Therefore, engagement with hand grenades should be considered only as a last resort.

(2) ***Visual dead space.*** From the gunner's station of a former Soviet Union tank, nothing at ground level within 30 feet can be seen through the frontal 180 degrees of turret rotation. If the turret is oriented over the rear 180 degrees (the rear deck), the dead space increases to 50 feet. This means gunners on former Soviet Union tanks cannot see soldiers in fighting positions within these distances of the tank.

(3) ***Fire extinguisher system.*** A fire extinguisher system can be triggered manually or automatically by one of eight heat sensors. The fire extinguisher's ethylene bromide gas creates a poisonous vapor when exposed to flames. If the extinguisher discharges, the crew may have to bail out. Any weapon that can trigger a fire and the fire extinguisher system might possibly knock out a former Soviet Union tank.

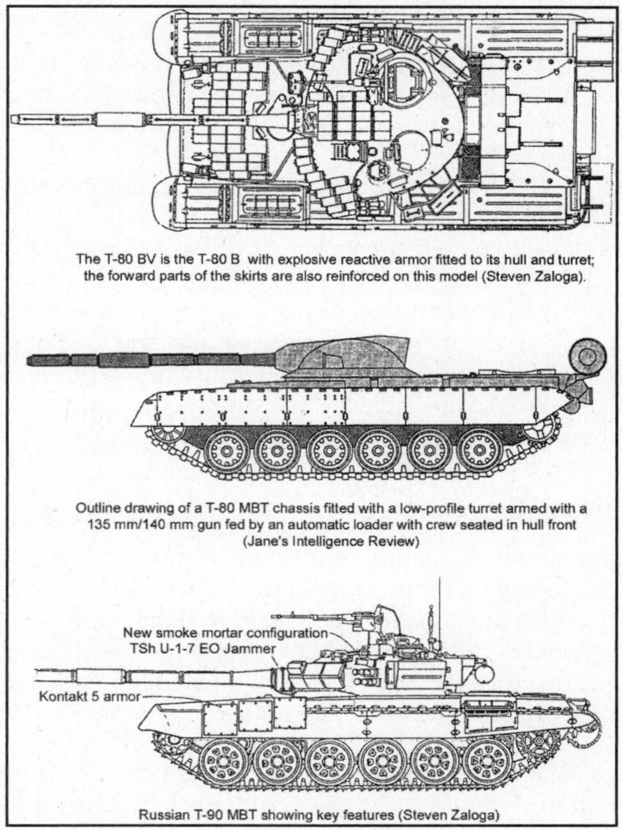

Figure 3-13: T80- and T90-series former Soviet Union tanks.

(4) ***BMP visual dead space.*** The BMP has nine vision blocks for the eight infantrymen in the rear of the vehicle. Eight of these vision blocks, four on each side, correspond to the firing ports for the squad's weapons. These vision blocks are oriented at a 45-degree angle toward the vehicle's direction of movement. The soldier at the left rear of the vehicle mans either the left rear vision block or the last vision block and firing port on the left side. If the flank firing port is being manned, the vehicle is vulnerable to an approach from the rear. Dismounted soldiers should attempt to destroy or disable enemy armor only as a last resort. When employing hand grenades for this purpose, follow these procedures:

- Remain in a covered fighting position until the vehicle closes to within its visual dead space. Approach the vehicle from the rear, moving aggressively.
- Place an incendiary grenade over the engine compartment.
- Attempt to drop a fragmentation grenade into an open hatch if incendiary grenades are not available.
- Engage any crewmen who exit the vehicle.

c. **Defensive Employment on Urban Terrain.** The considerations for the defensive employment of grenades on urban terrain are generally the same as offensive considerations with respect to ROE, structural integrity of the building, fratricide avoidance, and desired effects of the type of grenade to be used. Additionally, the following also apply:

(1) Fragmentation grenades can be very effective in producing casualties when thrown at assaulting enemy troops between buildings or on streets from windows, doors, mouseholes, or other building apertures.

(2) Stun grenades can cause confusion and hesitation when thrown at assaulting enemy soldiers, allowing time for withdrawal from rooms. This is especially useful if the structural integrity of the building does not permit the use of fragmentation or concussion grenades.

(3) Use of smoke grenades inside buildings may displace oxygen in poorly ventilated rooms and make breathing difficult while also rendering protective masks ineffective.

3-10. RETROGRADE OPERATIONS EMPLOYMENT

Most of the employment considerations applicable to the use of hand grenades in the defense are equally applicable to retrograde operations. Special applications or considerations for hand grenade use during retrograde operations relate to creating obstacles, marking friendly force locations, and breaking contact.

a. **Create Obstacles.** When terrain conditions permit, soldiers can use incendiary grenades to impede and disrupt enemy movement by initiating fires in specific areas.
b. **Mark Locations.** Soldiers can use colored smoke hand grenades to mark friendly force positions and identify friendly forces.
c. **Break Contact.** During retrograde operations, some elements of the friendly force most often become decisively engaged. Soldiers can use fragmentation, white smoke, and CS grenades to break contact and regain flexibility of maneuver. Use of hand grenades in volley fire following the employment of white smoke is especially effective. The smoke obscures enemy observation of friendly force movement from covered positions, and the fragmentation grenades force the enemy to cover.

3-11. REAR AREA OPERATIONS EMPLOYMENT

Army operations doctrine recognizes that the nature of a future war poses a significant threat to rear areas. These threats range from large operational maneuver groups to highly trained, special operating forces and even terrorists. All U.S. soldiers in combat, CS, and CSS units must be prepared to fight using small arms, antitank weapons, Claymore mines, and fragmentation grenades. At every element level throughout the corps battle area, individual U.S. soldiers must react to every action by aggressive, violent employment of grenades, and individual weapons. There is no safe zone on the battlefield; therefore, leaders must plan for the following:

a. **Special Considerations.** Two features of rear area operations provide for unique considerations concerning hand grenade employment. In certain areas of the world, the U.S. Army and its allies must anticipate a large number of civilian refugees moving into and through the rear area. This situation can be confusing with the large numbers of CS and CSS units operating throughout the rear area. These factors dictate the following guidelines for hand grenade employment in the rear areas:
   (1) ***Offensive grenades.*** Individual soldiers throw offensive grenades at enemy soldiers in situations where noncombatants and support troops may be intermingled with threat forces.
   (2) ***Riot-control grenades.*** It is reasonable to expect enemy special forces, special agent provocateurs, and fifth columnists to attempt to incite riots in our rear areas, especially if the conflict begins to stalemate and does not result in the rapid victory for either side. Forces in the rear area must quell these riots as rapidly as possible while reducing damage to the lives and property of noncombatants. Riot-control grenades, which are usually associated with peacetime law and order functions, also have relevancy in maintaining control of the rear area.
b. **Base Cluster Defense.** Base cluster commanders must organize the defense of their positions in much the same manner as tactical commanders in the MBA. Accordingly, the employment of hand grenades from defense positions surrounding the base cluster should follow the same considerations as hand grenade employment by combat units in the MBA.

3-12. USE UNDER ADVERSE CONDITIONS

While hand grenade procedures do not change when employed under adverse conditions, special cautions must be considered.

a. **MOPP4.** Exercise additional caution when employing hand grenades in MOPP gear. The thrower should execute arming and throwing procedures carefully and deliberately and should concentrate on using the proper grip. Observing each arming action (removal of safety clip and safety pin) is also recommended in MOPP. Note that wearing gloves inhibits the thrower's feel and could decrease his throwing ability and range.
b. **Night.** Throwers must have clear fields of fire with no overhead obstructions. Depth perception is generally impaired under limited visibility conditions.

CHAPTER 4

Threat Hand Grenades

This chapter provides general information on common threat hand grenade identification, functions, and capabilities. North Korea, China, and many former Soviet Union nations have an extensive inventory of hand grenades. As with most equipment in use by these nations, older hand grenades remain in circulation and use long after being classified obsolete.

SECTION I. FORMER SOVIET UNION NATIONS

4-1. RGN OFFENSIVE HAND GRENADE

- Type: Offensive. (Figure 4-1)
- Weight: 310 grams.
- Body Material: Aluminum.
- Filler Material: 114 grams A-1X-1 (RDX 96 percent, wax 4 percent) explosive.
- Fuze Type: Striker release, impact, or self-destruct.
- Fuze Delay: Impact, 1 to 2 seconds; time, 3.5 to 4 seconds (self-destruct).
- Range Thrown: 30 meters.
- Lethal Radius: 4 meters.

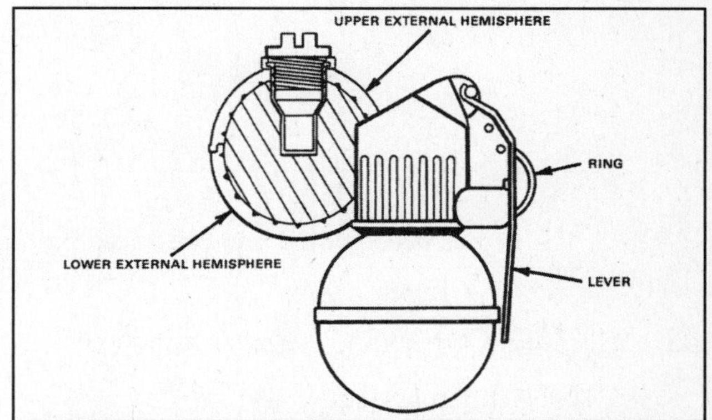

Figure 4-1: RGN hand grenade.

4-2. RGO DEFENSIVE HAND GRENADE

- Type: Defensive. (Figure 4-2)
- Weight: 530 grams.
- Body Material: Aluminum.
- Filler Material: 92 grams A-1X-1 (RDX 96 percent, wax 4 percent) explosive.
- Fuze Type: Striker release, impact, or self-destruct.
- Fuze Delay: Impact, 1 to 2 seconds; time, 3.5 to 4 seconds.
- Range Thrown: 30 to 40 meters.
- Lethal Radius: 6 meters.

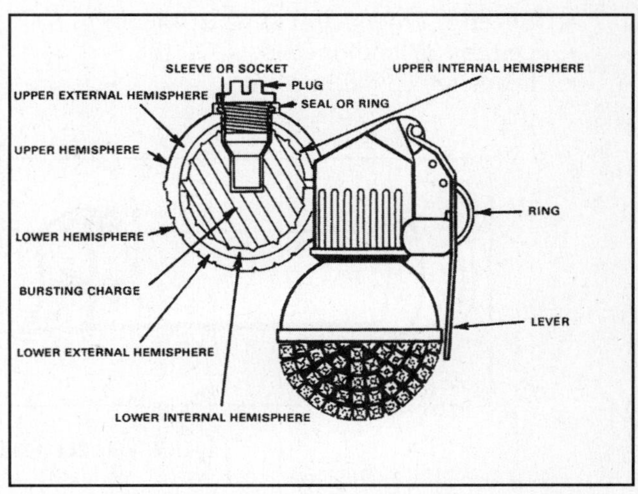

Figure 4-2: RGO hand grenade.

4-3. F1 FRAGMENTATION HAND GRENADE

- Type: Fragmentation. (Figure 4-3)
- Weight: 700 grams.
- Body Material: Cast iron.
- Filler Material: 60 grams TNT.
- Fuze Type: Striker release.
- Fuze Delay: 3 to 4 seconds; for booby traps, 0 to 13 seconds.
- Range Thrown: 30 meters.
- Lethal Radius: 20 to 30 meters.

Figure 4-3: F1 hand grenade.

> ✍ **NOTE**
> The F1 has been copied and produced by numerous other countries throughout the world.

4-4. RKG-3M ANTITANK HAND GRENADE

- Type: Antitank. (Figure 4-4)
- Weight: With fuze, 1.07 kilograms.
- Weight of HE Filling: TNT/RDX, 540 grams.
- Penetration: 125 millimeters.
- Fuze Type: Instantaneous impact, base detonating.
- Effective Fragment Radius: 20 meters.
- Length: 350 millimeters.
- Diameter: 65 millimeters.

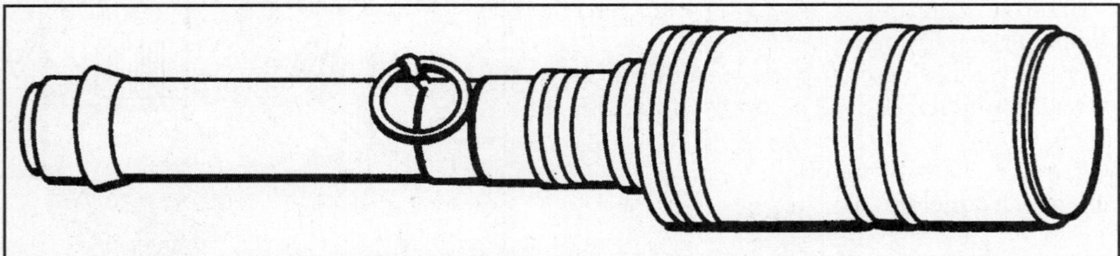

Figure 4-4: RKG-3M antitank hand grenade.

> ✍ **NOTE**
> The RKG-3 family of grenades has been copied and produced by numerous other countries throughout the world.

4-5. RGD-5 FRAGMENTATION HAND GRENADE

- Type: Fragmentation. (Figure 4-5)
- Weight: 310 grams.
- Filler Material: 110 grams of TNT.
- Fuze Delay: 3 to 4 seconds.
- Range Thrown: 40 meters.
- Effective Fragment Radius: 15 to 20 meters, maximum fragment range about 30 meters.

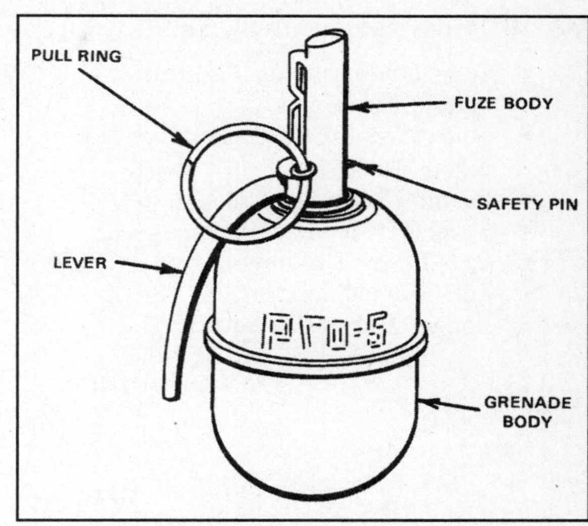

Figure 4-5: RGD-5 hand grenade.

> ✍ NOTE
> The RGD-5 has been copied and produced by numerous other countries throughout the world.

4-6. RG-42 FRAGMENTATION HAND GRENADE

- Type: Fragmentation. (Figure 4-6)
- Weight: 435 grams.
- Body Material: Steel.
- Filler Material: 110 to 120 grams TNT.
- Fuze Type: Striker release.
- Fuze Delay: 3.2 to 4.2 seconds.
- Range Thrown: 30 meters.
- Effective Fragment Radius: 20 meters.

Figure 4-6: RG-42 hand grenade.

> ✍ NOTE
> The RG-42 has been copied and produced by numerous other countries throughout the world.

4-7. RDG-1

- Type: Hand, smoke. (Figure 4-7)
- Weight: 500 grams.
- Body Material: Cardboard, handle wood / cardboard.
- Burning Time: 60 to 90 seconds.
- Fuze: Friction fuze.
- Fuze Delay: Unknown.
- Filler: Smoke mixture.
- Range Thrown: 35 meters.

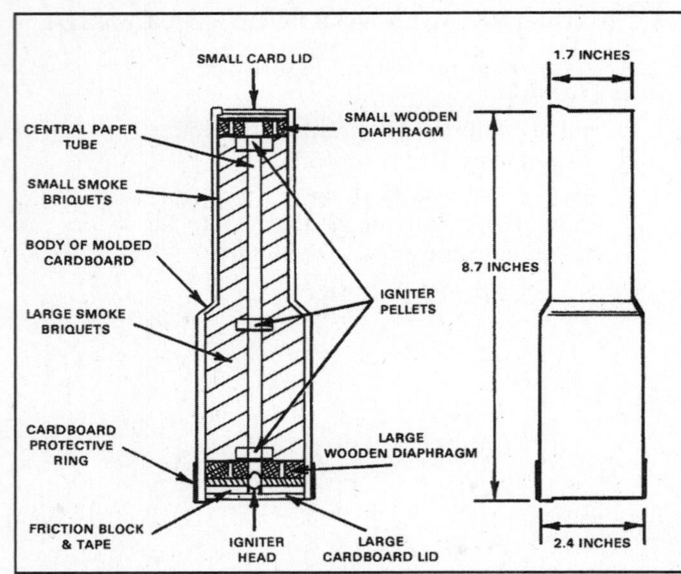

Figure 4-7: RDG-1 smoke grenade.

> ✍ **NOTE**
> This grenade is used to screen river crossings because it floats.

4-8. RDG-2 AND RDG-3

- Type: Smoke. (Figure 4-8)
- Weight: 500 grams.
- Body Material: Cardboard coated with wax, handle wood / cardboard.
- Burning Time: 50 to 90 seconds.
- Fuze: Friction fuze.
- Fuze Delay: Unknown.
- Filler: Smoke mixture.
- Range Thrown: 35 meters.

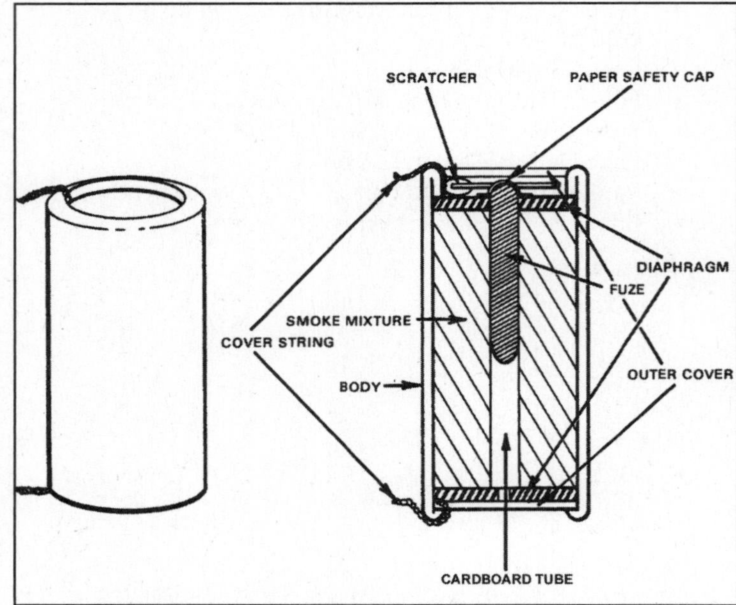

Figure 4-8: RDG-2 and RDG-3 smoke grenade.

> ✍ **NOTE**
> This grenade does not float and is unsuitable for water use.

SECTION II. NORTH KOREA

4-9. ROUND FRAGMENTATION GRENADE

- Type: Fragmentation. (Figure 4-9)
- Weight: 600 grams.
- Body Material: Cast aluminum body with 140 to 150 cast iron balls embedded in it.
- Fuze: Striker release.
- Fuze Delay: 3.2 to 4.2 seconds.
- Filler: TNT, 60 grams.
- Effective Casualty Radius: 20 meters.

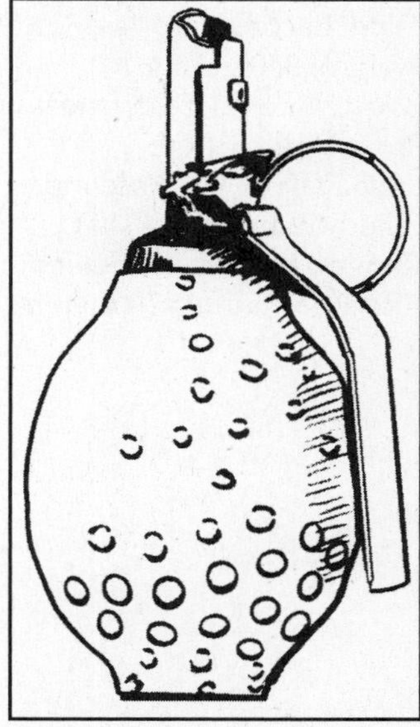

Figure 4-9: North Korean fragmentation grenade (round).

> ✍ **NOTE**
> A variation of this grenade has a plastic body.

4-10. RECTANGULAR FRAGMENTATION GRENADE

- Type: Fragmentation. (Figure 4-10)
- Weight: 370 grams.
- Body Material: Sheet steel with about 1,300 steel balls in a cavity between the outer wall and the explosive filler.
- Fuze: Striker release.
- Fuze Delay: 3.2 to 4.2 seconds.
- Filler: Composition B, 55 grams.
- Effective Casualty Radius: 20 meters.

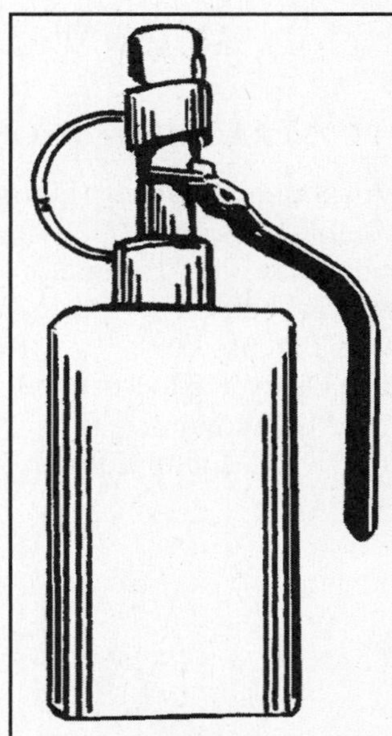

Figure 4-10: North Korean fragmentation grenade (rectangular).

4-11. LACHRYMATORY GRENADE

- Type: Lachrymatory. (Figure 4-11)
- Weight: 350 grams.
- Body Material: Sheet steel with a wooden handle.
- Fuze: Pull friction.
- Fuze Delay: 3 to 4 seconds.
- Filler: CS mixture/TNT.
- Range Thrown: 20 meters.
- Effective Radius: 10 meters.

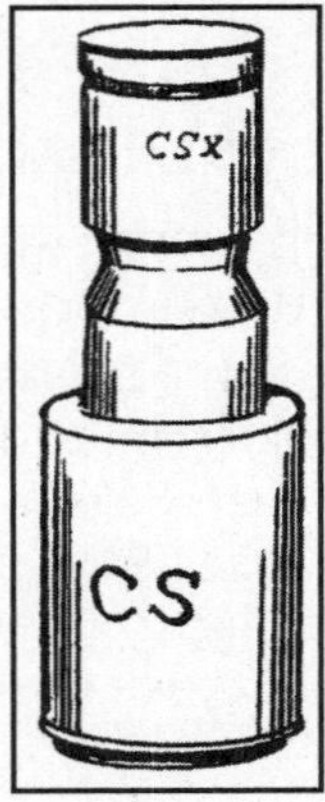

Figure 4-11: North Korean lachrymatory grenade.

SECTION III. CHINA

4-12. TYPE 1 FRAGMENTATION GRENADE

- Type: Fragmentation. (Figure 4-12)
- Weight: 600 grams.
- Body Material: Cast iron.
- Fuze: Striker release.
- Fuze Delay: 3 to 4 seconds.
- Filler: TNT, 50 grams.
- Lethal Range: 20 meters.

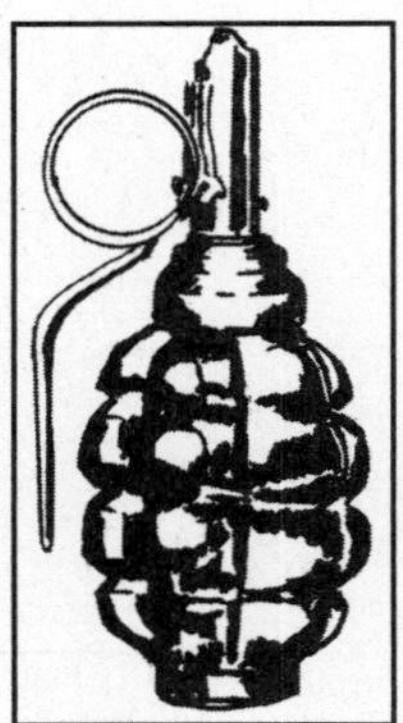

Figure 4-12: Type 1 fragmentation grenade.

4-13. TYPE 73 FRAGMENTATION GRENADE

- Type: Fragmentation. (Figure 4-13)
- Weight: 190 grams.
- Body Material: Two-piece sheet metal body enclosing a layer of 580 steel balls.
- Fuze: Percussion.
- Fuze Delay: 0.5 to 1 second.
- Filler: Unknown.
- Effective Casualty Radius: 7 meters.

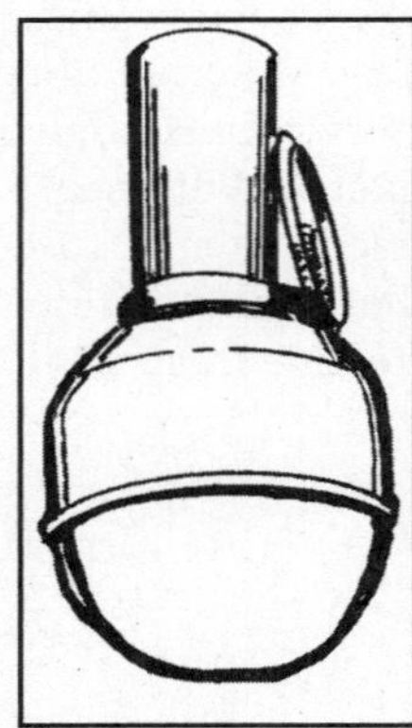

Figure 4-13: Type 73 fragmentation grenade.

> ✍ **NOTE**
> A variation of this grenade may be in use as a rifle grenade with a tail fin assembly.

4-14. TYPE 77-1 FRAGMENTATION STICK

- Type: Fragmentation. (Figure 4-14)
- Weight: 380 grams.
- Body Material: Cast iron with a plastic handle and sheet metal or plastic fuze cover cap.
- Fuze: Pull friction.
- Fuze Delay: 2.8 to 4 seconds.
- Filler: TNT, 70 grams.
- Lethal Radius: 7 meters.

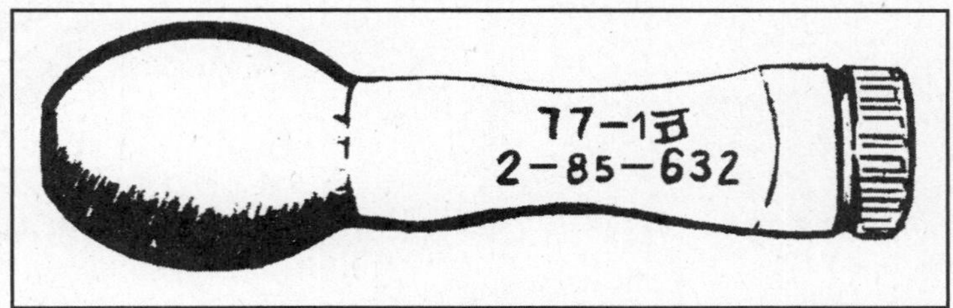

Figure 4-14: Type 77-1 fragmentation stick.

4-15. SC-2 LACHRYMATORY GRENADE

- Type: Lachrymatory (explosively dispersed). (Figure 4-15)
- Weight: 110 grams.
- Body Material: Plastic.
- Fuze: Striker release or friction.
- Fuze Delay: 2.8 to 3.6 seconds.
- Filler: Tear agent, 25 grams.
- Coverage: 300 cubic meters.

Figure 4-15: SC-2 lachrymatory grenade.

4-16. SC-2 LACHRYMATORY/SMOKE GRENADE

- Type: Lachrymatory / smoke. (Figure 4-16)
- Weight: 110 grams.
- Body Material: Plastic.
- Fuze: Striker release or friction.
- Fuze Delay: 1.8 to 2.8 seconds.
- Filler: Tear agent / smoke mixture, 70 grams.
- Coverage: 300 cubic meters.

Figure 4-16: SC-2 lachrymatory/smoke grenade.

4-17. JYD-1

- Type: Rubber ball. (Figure 4-17)
- Weight: 150 grams.
- Body Material: Plastic.
- Fuze: Striker release or friction.
- Fuze Delay: 2.8 to 3.4 seconds.
- Filler: 840 rubber balls; bursting charge, 4 grams.
- Effective radius: 0.3 to 3 meters.

Figure 4-17: JYD-1 rubber ball grenade.

4-18. JYB-1

- Type: Stun. (Figure 4-18)
- Weight: 150 grams.
- Body Material: Plastic.
- Fuze: Striker release or friction.
- Fuze Delay: 3 to 4 seconds.
- Filler: Pyrotechnic mixture, 45 grams.
- Coverage: Sound level over 150 decibels within 10 meters.

Figure 4-18: JYB-1 stun grenade.

4-19. JYS-1

- Type: Flash/bang. (Figure 4-19)
- Weight: 45 grams.
- Body Material: Plastic.
- Fuze: Striker release or friction.
- Fuze Delay: Unknown.
- Filler: Pyrotechnic mixture, 25 grams.
- Effective Range: 10 meters.
- Flash Intensity: 40,000,000 candella.

Figure 4-19: JYS-1 flash/bang grenade.

CHAPTER 5

Obsolete Hand Grenades

This chapter provides data for identifying and understanding the description and capabilities of obsolete U.S. hand grenades. Although these grenades are no longer common to the U.S. inventory, the majority of them are still in use by other services or nations.

5-1. M30 PRACTICE HAND GRENADE

The M30 practice grenade (Figure 5-1) simulates the M26 series of fragmentation hand grenades for training purposes. The M30 adds realism to training and familiarizes the soldier with the functioning and description of the fragmentation hand grenade.

a. **Body.** The grenade body is cast iron and is reusable.
b. **Fuze.** The fuze is an M205A1 or M205A2.
c. **Weight.** The grenade weighs 16 ounces.
d. **Safety Clip.** See paragraph 1–3.
e. **Capabilities.** The average soldier can throw the grenade 40 meters. The M30 emits a small puff of white smoke after a delay of 4 to 5 seconds and makes a loud popping sound.
f. **Color and Markings.** The grenade is light blue with white markings.

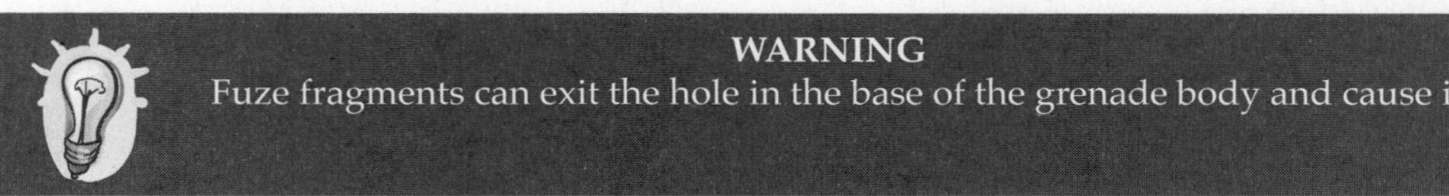

WARNING
Fuze fragments can exit the hole in the base of the grenade body and cause injury.

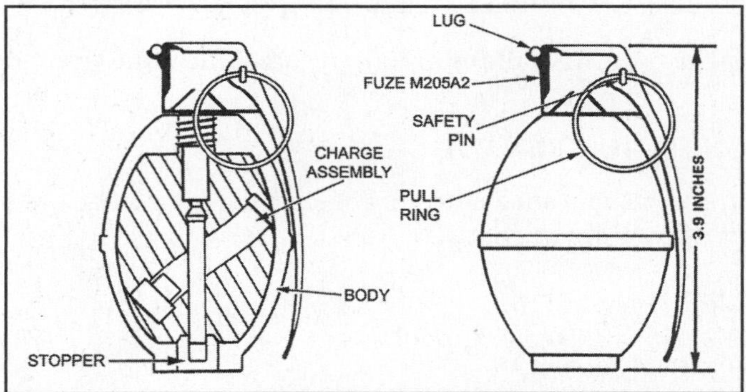

Figure 5-1: M30 practice grenade.

5-2. MK1 ILLUMINATION HAND GRENADE

The MK1 illumination hand grenade (Figurg 5-2) is a ground signaling and ground pyrotechnic signal, except that the grenade burns only at ground level whereas pyrotechnic signals burn in flight or while suspended from a parachute. The MK1 should not be used in deep mud or swampy ground, which would result in little or no illumination. The grenade burns with a very hot flame and may be used as an incendiary agent. Because it is incendiary, soldiers should use caution to prevent fires that would be detrimental to tactical operations.

a. **Body.** The body of the MK1 illumination grenade is sheet metal.
b. **Filler.** The filler has 3.5 ounces of illuminating pyrotechnic composition.
c. **Fuze.** The fuze is a special igniter, which differs from other igniting type fuzes in that it contains a quick match rather than a powder delay train. The quick match has a burning time of 7 seconds, after which it sets off an igniter charge. The igniter charge initiates the burning process of the grenade's filler.
d. **Weight.** The grenade weighs 10 ounces.
e. **Capabilities.** The average soldier can throw the MK1 40 meters. The filler burns for 25 seconds, producing 55,000 candlepower and illuminating an area 200 meters in diameter.
f. **Color and Markings.** Older MK1 grenades are white with black markings; newer models are unpainted with black markings.

WARNING
Avoid looking directly at the illumination grenade as it burns, since the intensity of the light may damage the retina.

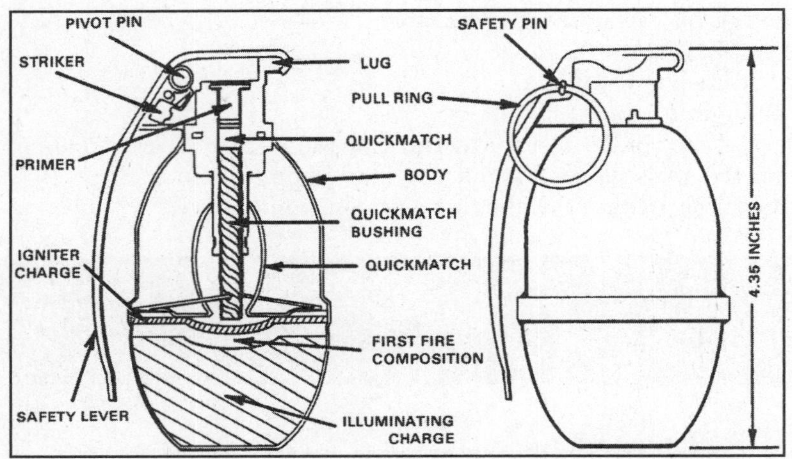

Figure 5-2: MK1 illumination pyrotechnic hand grenade.

5-3. MK2 FRAGMENTATION HAND GRENADE

The MK2 (Figure 5-3) is used to supplement small arms fire against the enemy in close combat. The grenade produces casualties by high-velocity projection of fragments.

a. **Body.** The MK2 grenade body is cast iron.
b. **Filler.** The filler has TNT, either flaked or granular.
c. **Fuze.** The fuze is an M204A1 or M204A2.
d. **Weight.** The grenade weighs 21 ounces.
e. **Capabilities.** The average soldier can throw the grenade 30 meters. The MK2 grenade has a bursting radius of 10 meters.
f. **Color and Markings.** The grenade has an olive drab body with a single yellow band, which indicates a high-explosive filler.

WARNING
If the fuze is loose, do not try to tighten it. This could set off the granular TNT in the grenade.

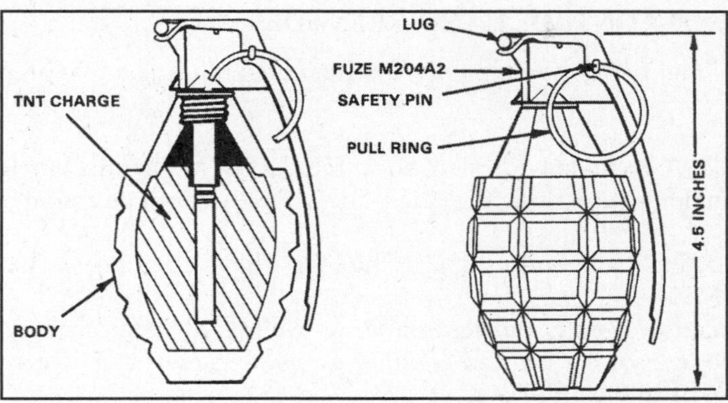

Figure 5-3: MK2 fragmentation hand grenades.

5-4. M26 AND M26A1 FRAGMENTATION HAND GRENADES

These grenades (Figure 5-4) are used to supplement small arms fire against an enemy in close combat. They produce casualties through the high-velocity projection of fragments.

a. **Body.** The M26 and M26A1 grenade bodies are cast iron.
b. **Filler.** The fillers have TNT, either flaked or granular.
c. **Fuze.** The fuze is an M204A1 or M204A2.
d. **Weight.** Each grenade weighs 21 ounces.
e. **Capabilities.** The average soldier can throw these grenades 40 meters. They have an effective casualty radius of 15 meters.
f. **Color and Markings.** These grenades have an olive drab body with a single yellow band at the top and yellow markings, which indicate a high-explosive filler.

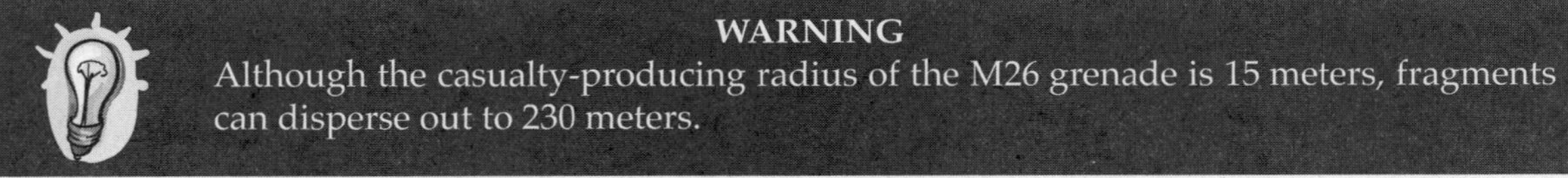

WARNING
Although the casualty-producing radius of the M26 grenade is 15 meters, fragments can disperse out to 230 meters.

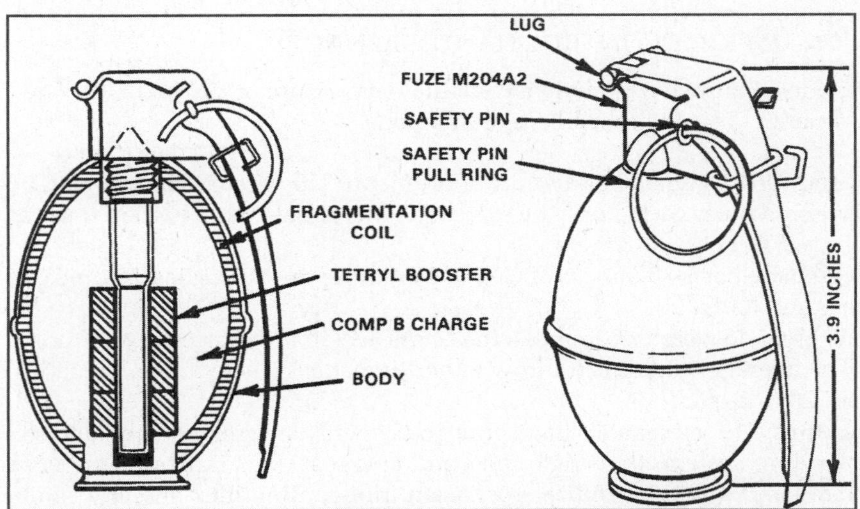

Figure 5-4: M26 and M26A1 fragmentation hand grenade.

5-5. M7 AND M7A1 CN RIOT-CONTROL HAND GRENADES

The M7 and M7A1 grenades (Figure 5-5) contain only CN (tear gas) filler. The two grenades differ in the amount of filler they contain.

a. **Body.** The M7 and M7A1 grenade bodies are sheet metal. The M7 has six emission holes at the top and two rows of nine emission holes each along the sides. The M7A1 has four emission holes at the top and one at the bottom.
b. **Filler.** The M7 grenade has 10.25 ounces of CN; the M7A1 has 12.5 ounces of CN.
c. **Fuze.** The fuze is an M201A1.
d. **Weight.** The M7 grenade weighs 17 ounces; the M7A1 weighs 18.5 ounces.
e. **Capabilities.** The average soldier can throw either grenade 35 meters. The grenades produce a dense cloud of irritant agent for 20 to 60 seconds.
f. **Color and Markings.** Each grenade has a gray body with a single red band and red markings.

WARNING
Friendly forces should don protective masks before using these grenades.

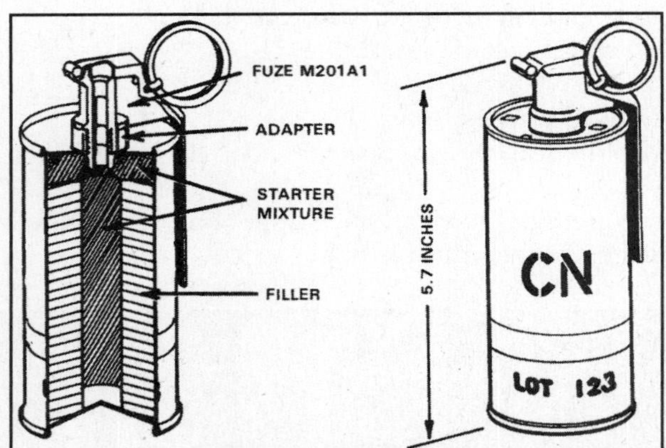

Figure 5-5: M7 and M7A1 tear gas hand grenade.

5-6. M6 AND M6A1 CN-DM RIOT-CONTROL HAND GRENADES

The M6 and M6A1 grenades (Figure 5-6) contain a combination mixture of CN and DM. They differ chiefly in external appearance and the manner in which the filler is combined.

a. **Body.** The M6 and M6A1 grenade bodies are sheet metal. The M6 has six emission holes at the top and two rows of nine emission holes each along the sides. The M6A1 has four emission holes at the top and one at the bottom.
b. **Filler.** The M6 grenade has 10.5 ounces of CN-DM mixture; the M6A1 has 9.5 ounces of CN-DM mixture.
c. **Fuze.** The fuze is an M201A1.
d. **Weight.** The M6 grenade weighs 17 ounces; the M6A1 weighs 20 ounces.
e. **Capabilities.** The average soldier can throw either grenade 35 meters. The grenades emit a dense cloud of irritant agent for 20 to 60 seconds.
f. **Color and Markings.** These grenades have gray bodies with a single red band and red markings. (Under the standard color-coding system, the single red band and markings indicate nonpersistent riot-control filler. A double red band and markings indicate persistent riot-control filler, and any combination of green bands and markings indicates casualty-producing filler. Currently, there are no casualty-producing agents in hand grenade form.)

WARNING
Friendly forces should don protective masks before using these grenades.

Figure 5-6: M6 and M6A1 riot-control hand grenade.

5-7. ABC-M25A1 AND ABC-M25A2 RIOT-CONTROL HAND GRENADES

The ABC riot-control hand grenade is a bursting munition with an integral fuze (Figure 5-7). The M25A2 grenade is an improved version of the M25A1 grenade. The two types of grenades differ primarily in body construction. They are used to deliver all three types of riot-control agents presently used in hand grenades.

a. **Body.** The body of this grenade is compressed fiber or plastic sphere.
b. **Filler.** The fillers of the M25 series of riot-control hand grenades vary in weight and composition according to the type of agent contained in the grenade. All fillers are mixed with silica aerosol for increased dissemination efficiency.
c. **Fuze.** The fuze type is integral.
d. **Weight.** Each grenade weighs 7.5 to 8 ounces, depending on the type of filler.
e. **Capabilities.** The average soldier can throw the grenade 50 meters. The M25 series of riot-control hand grenades have a radius burst (visible cloud grenade) of about 5 meters, but fragments of the grenade are occasionally projected up to 25 meters.
f. **Color and Markings.** The color and markings are the same as the M6 and M6A1 grenades (paragraph 5–6f). Most grenades of the M25 series currently in use are not painted according to any color-coding system. They are either totally unpainted or have only a red band and red markings.

WARNING
When the ABC-M25A1 grenade is employed, do not drop it because it may go off immediately. Do not attempt to replace a pulled safety pin and do not relax thumb pressure arming sleeve after the safety pin is pulled. Friendly forces should don protective masks before using these grenades.

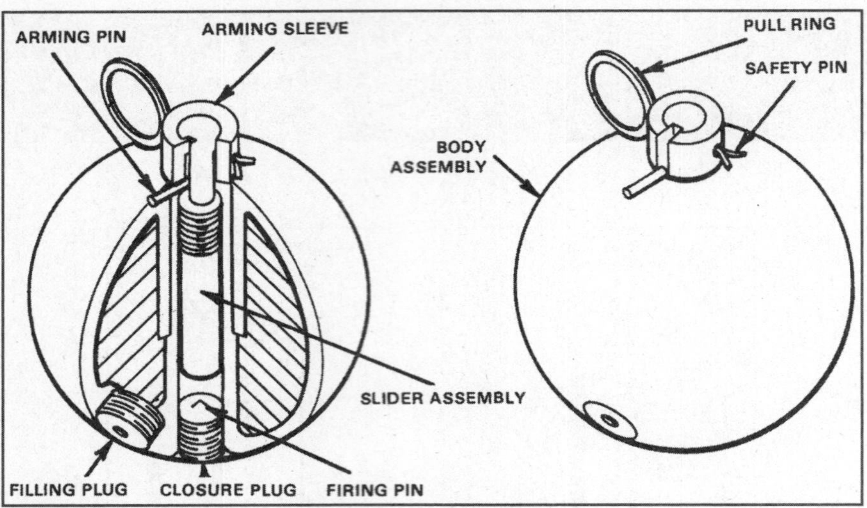

Figure 5-7: The ABC-M25A1 riot-control hand grenade.

5-8. M34 WHITE PHOSPHORUS HAND GRENADE

The M34 chemical smoke grenade is the most versatile of all hand grenades (Figure 5-8). The grenade can be used for signaling, screening, or incendiary missions, or for producing casualties. The use of this grenade also has a psychological impact on the enemy.

a. **Body.** The M34 WP grenade body is compressed fiber or plastic sphere.
b. **Filler.** The filler has 15 ounces of white phosphorous.
c. **Fuze.** The fuze is an M206A2.
d. **Weight.** The grenade weighs 27 ounces.
e. **Capabilities.** The average soldier can throw the grenade 30 meters. The grenade has a bursting radius of 35 meters. All friendly personnel within this 35-meter area should be in a covered position to avoid being struck by burning particles. The WP filler burns for about 60 seconds at a temperature of 5,000 degrees Fahrenheit. This intense heat causes the smoke produced by the grenade to rise rapidly, especially in cool climates, making the M34 grenade less desirable for use as a screening agent. (The M15WP smoke hand grenade is similar to the M34. For more information, refer to TM 9-1330-200-12.)
f. **Color and Markings.** Under the old ammunition color-coding system, the white phosphorous grenade is light gray with a single yellow band and yellow markings. Under the new standard color-coding system, the M34 grenade is light green with a single yellow band and light red markings.

> ✍ NOTE
> Most M34WP smoke hand grenades presently in use were manufactured before the standard color-coding system agreement and are painted according to the old color code.

> WARNING
> The M34 has a bursting radius of 35 meters, which is farther than the average soldier can throw it; therefore, the thrower must be in a covered or protected position.

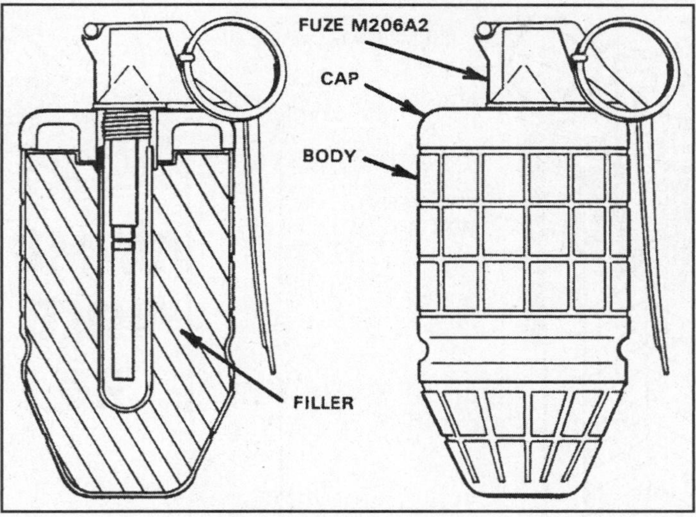

Figure 5-8: M34WP smoke hand grenade.

5-9. AN-M8 HC WHITE SMOKE

This grenade is used to produce dense clouds of white smoke for signaling and screening (Figure 5-9).

a. **Body.** The grenade body is a sheet steel cylinder.
b. **Filler.** The filler has 19 ounces of Type C, HC smoke mixture.
c. **Fuze.** The fuze is an M201A1.
d. **Weight.** The grenade weighs 24 ounces.
e. **Capabilities.** The average soldier can throw the AN-M8 30 meters. The grenade emits a dense cloud of white smoke for 105 to 150 seconds.
f. **Color and Markings.** The grenade has a light green body with black markings and a white top.

WARNING

The AN-M8 hand grenade produces harmful hydrochloric fumes that irritate the eyes, throat, and lungs. It should not be used in closed-in areas unless soldiers are wearing protective masks.

WARNING

Any damaged AN-M8 HC grenades that expose the filler are hazardous. Exposure of the filler to moisture and air could result in a chemical reaction that will ignite the grenade.

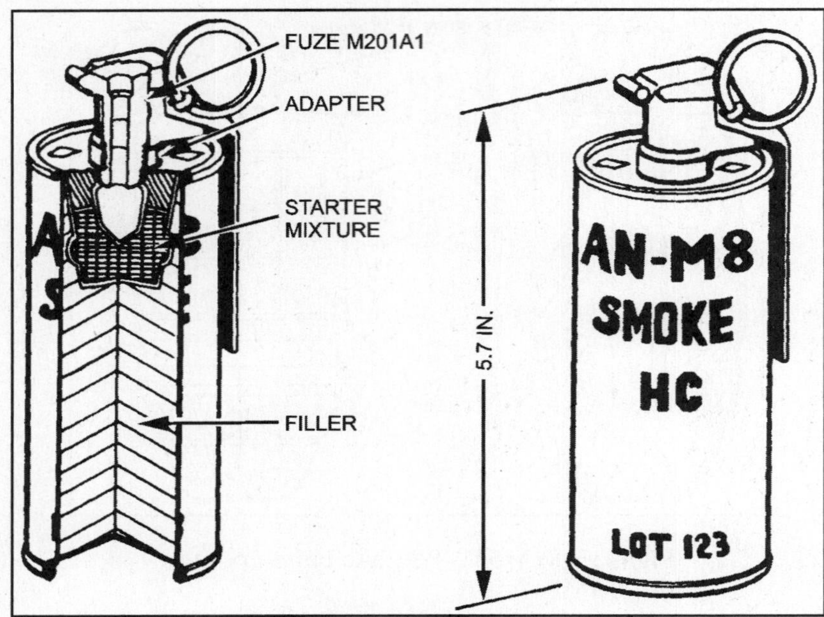

Figure 5-9: AN-M8 HC white smoke grenade.

5-10. SAFETY CLIPS

Improvements have been made in safety clips. There are four types of safety clips that might be encountered on the obsolete grenades (Figure 5-10).

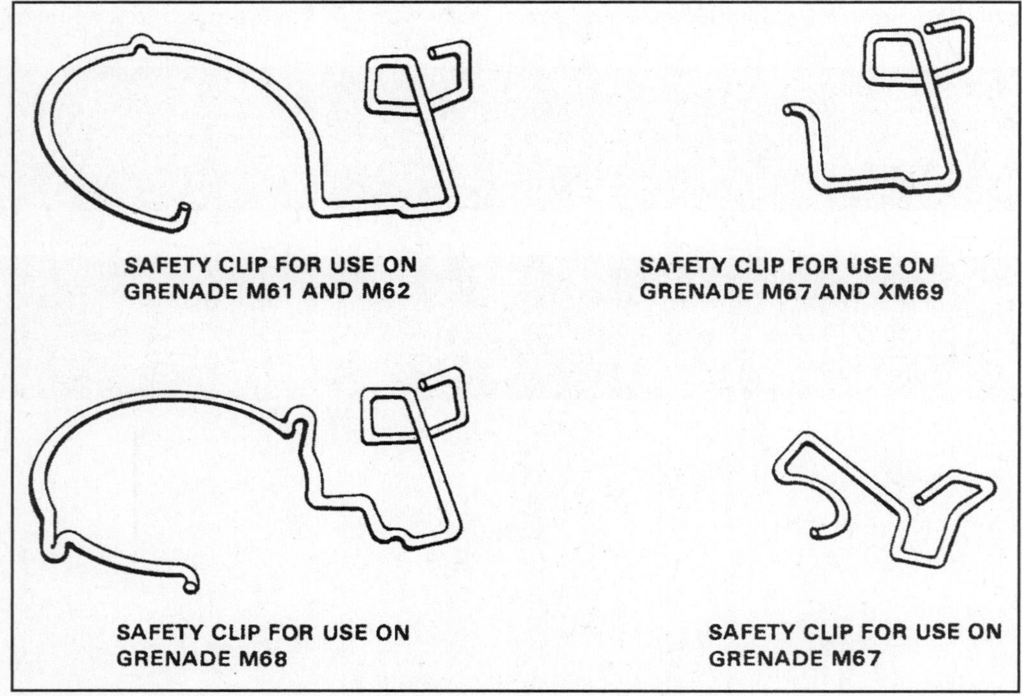

Figure 5-10: Safety clips on obsolete grenades.

CHAPTER 6

NATO Hand Grenades

This chapter provides general information on the identification, functions, and capabilities of NATO hand grenades. The North Atlantic Treaty Organization nations have an extensive inventory of grenades. This chapter describes only the more common grenades that the U.S. soldier might encounter during joint operations.

SECTION I. NETHERLANDS

6-1. NR17

- Type: Offensive. (Figure 6-1)
- Weight: 475 grams.
- Length: 125 millimeters.
- Diameter: 56 millimeters.
- Body Material: Plastic.
- Fuze Type: Striker release.
- Filler Material: TNT.
- Filler Weight: 205 grams.
- Fuze Delay: 3–4 seconds.
- Effective Radius: 5 meters.
- Range Thrown: 30 to 40 meters.

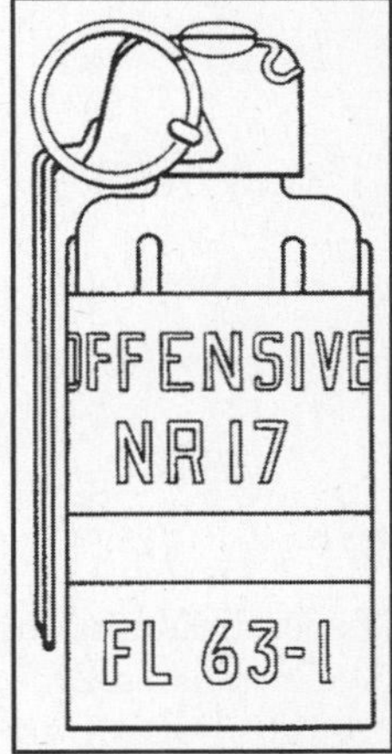

Figure 6-1: NR17 hand grenade.

6-2. NR13C1

- Type: Fragmentation, offensive. (Figure 6-2)
- Weight: 475 grams.
- Length: 143 millimeters.
- Diameter: 54 millimeters.
- Body Material: Steel.
- Filler Weight: 225 grams.
- Filler Material: High explosive.
- Fuze Type: Pyrotechnic delay.
- Fuze Delay: 5 seconds.
- Range Thrown: 30 meters.

Figure 6-2: NR13C1 fragmentation hand grenade.

6-3. MARK 2

- Type: Fragmentation. (Figure 6-3)
- Length: 114 millimeters.
- Diameter: 57 millimeters:
- Body Material: Cast iron.
- Filler Weight: 55 grams.
- Filler Material: TNT powdered.
- Fuze Type: Pyrotechnic delay.
- Fuze Delay: 3 seconds.

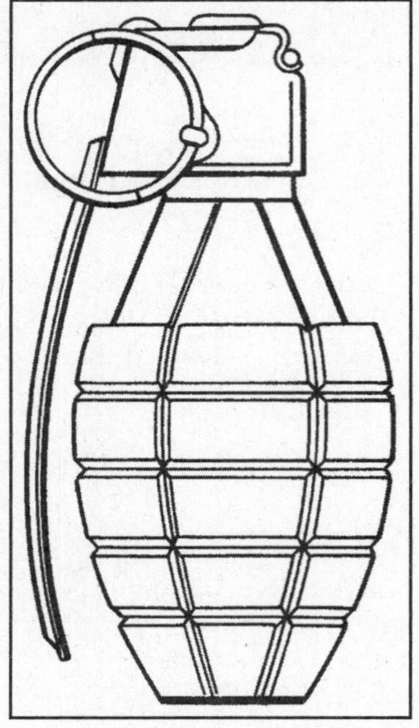

Figure 6-3: Mark 2 fragmentation hand grenade.

6-4. NR1C1

- Type: Fragmentation. (Figure 6-4)
- Weight: 670 grams.
- Length: 122 millimeters.
- Body Material: Cast iron.
- Filler Weight: 55 grams.
- Filler Material: TNT powdered.
- Fuze Type: Pyrotechnic delay.
- Fuze Delay: 3 seconds.

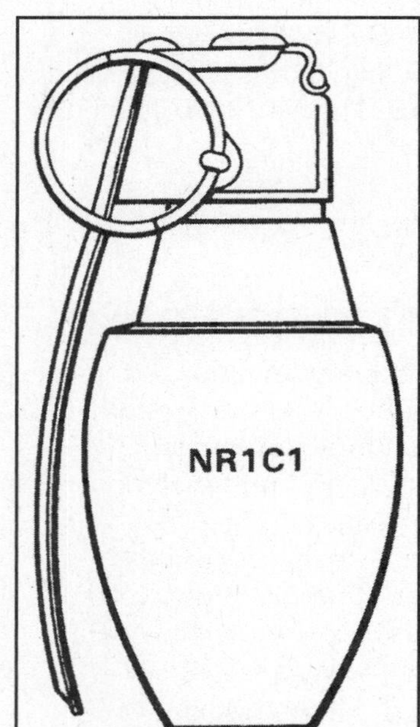

Figure 6-4: NR1C1 fragmentation hand grenade.

6-5. JNS 62–65

- Type: Smoke. (Figure 6-5)
- Weight: 660 grams.
- Length: 151 millimeters.
- Diameter: 63 millimeters.
- Body Material: Tinned steel.
- Filler Material: Colored smoke.
- Fuze Delay: 2 to 3 seconds.
- Burn Time: 1 to 2 minutes.

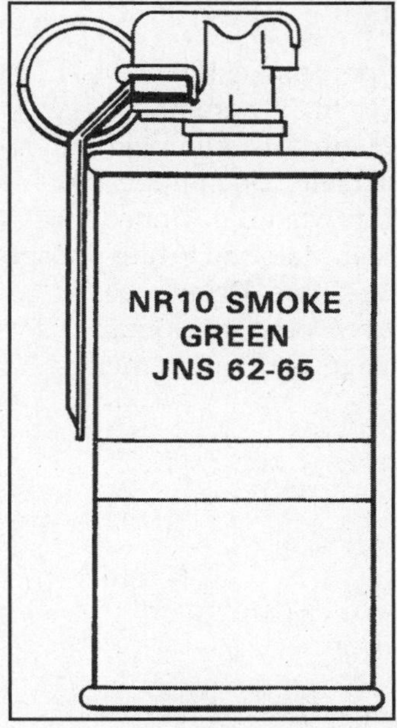

Figure 6-5: JNS 62-65 smoke hand grenade.

6-6. NR12

- Type: Incendiary. (Figure 6-6)
- Weight: 820 grams.
- Length: 153 millimeters.
- Diameter: 63 millimeters.
- Body Material: Tinned steel.
- Filler Material: Thermite.
- Fuze Type: Striker release.
- Fuze Delay: 1 to 3 seconds.
- Range Thrown: 40 meters.
- Burn Time: 40 seconds.
- Peak Intensity: 2200°C

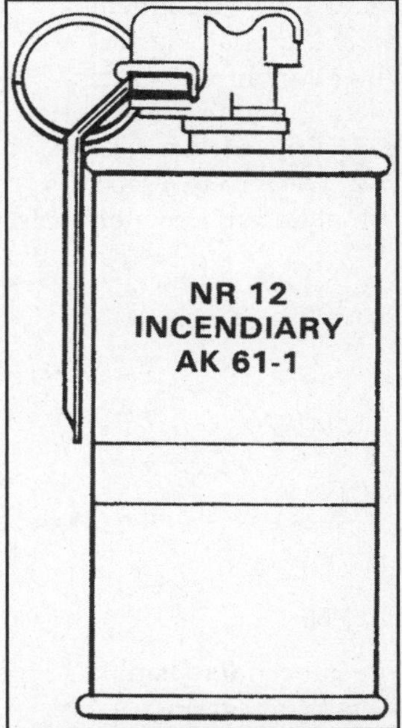

Figure 6-6: NR12 incendiary hand grenade.

6-7. NR16

- Type: Smoke. (Figure 6-7)
- Weight: 284 grams.
- Length: 101 millimeters.
- Diameter: 50 millimeters.
- Body Material: Tinned Steel.
- Filler Material: White phosphorus.
- Fuze Type: Delay.
- Fuze Delay: 4 seconds.
- Range Thrown: 37 meters.

Figure 6-7: NR16 smoke hand grenade.

6-8. NR20C1

- Type: Fragmentation. (Figure 6-8)
- Weight: 390 grams.
- Length: 103 millimeters.
- Diameter: 60 millimeters.
- Body Material: Plastic.
- Filler Weight: 150 grams.
- Filler Material: Composition B.
- Fuze Type: Striker release.
- Fuze Delay: 3 to 4 seconds.
- Lethal Radius: 5 meters, safety range 15 to 20 meters.

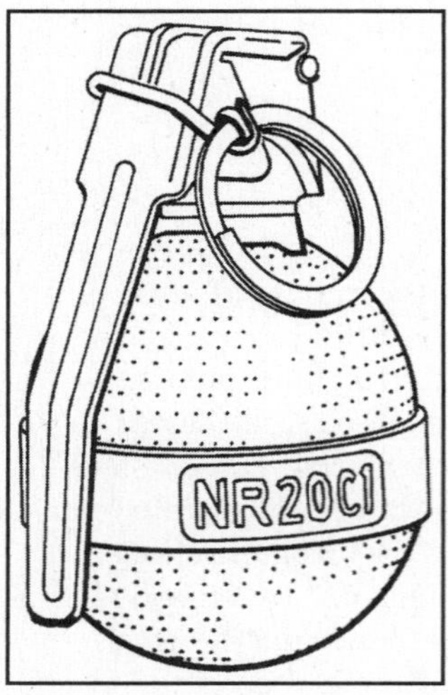

Figure 6-8: NR20C1 fragmentation hand grenade.

SECTION II. GERMANY

6-9. DM 24/68

- Type: Incendiary smoke. (Figure 6-9)
- Weight: 340 grams.
- Length: 133 millimeters.
- Diameter: 67 millimeters.
- Body Material: Plastic.
- Filler Weight: 255 grams.
- Filler Material. Red phosphorus.
- Fuze Type: Mechanical ignition.
- Fuze Delay: 2.5 seconds after ignition.
- Burn Time: 5 minutes.

Figure 6-9: DM 24/68 incendiary hand grenade.

6-10. HC DM 15

- Type: Smoke. (Figure 6-10)
- Weight: 1,200 grams.
- Length: 175 millimeters.
- Diameter: 76 millimeters.
- Body Material: Hexachlorethane.
- Fuze Type: Mechanical ignition.
- Fuze Delay: 2.5 seconds after ignition.
- Burn Time: 2.5 minutes.

Figure 6-10: HC DM 15 smoke hand grenade.

6-11. M-DN 11

- Type: Fragmentation, defensive. (Figure 6-11)
- Weight: 467 grams.
- Length: 97 millimeters.
- Diameter: 60 millimeters.
- Body Material: Plastic.
- Filler Weight: 43 grams, plasticized PETN.
- Fuze Type: Striker release.
- Fuze Delay: 3.5 to 4.5 seconds.

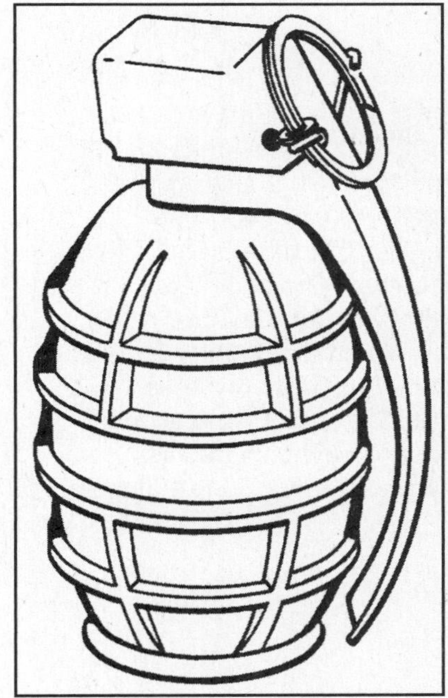

Figure 6-11: M-DN 11 fragmentation hand grenade.

SECTION III. BELGIUM

6-12. 35×65 MECAR

- Type: Fragmentation, defensive. (Figure 6-12)
- Weight: 230 grams.
- Length: 88 millimeters.
- Diameter: 35 millimeters.
- Body Material. Metal.
- Filler Material: Composition B.
- Fuze Type: Delay.
- Fuze Delay: 4 seconds.
- Range Thrown: 40 meters.
- Effective Radius: 10 meters.

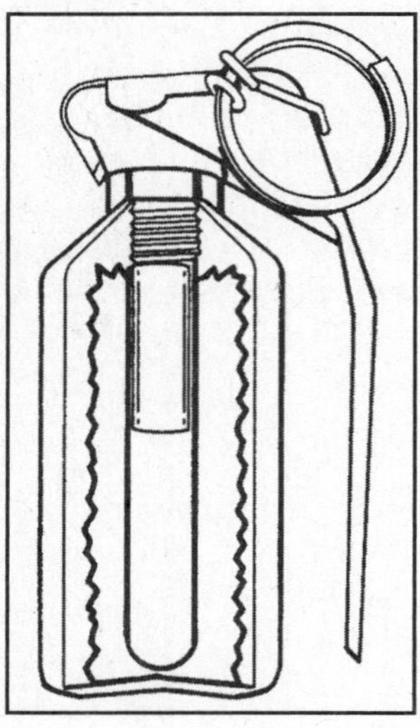

Figure 6-12: 35×65 MECAR fragmentation hand grenade.

SECTION IV. UNITED KINGDOM

6-13. NO. 36M

- Type: Defensive. (Figure 6-13)
- Weight: 600 grams.
- Length: 102 millimeters.
- Diameter: 60 millimeters.
- Body Material: Cast iron.
- Filler Weight: TNT, 60 grams.
- Fuze Type: Striker release.
- Fuze Delay: 3.5 to 4.5 seconds.
- Range Thrown: 25 meters.
- Effective Radius: 30 to 100 meters (40 fragments).

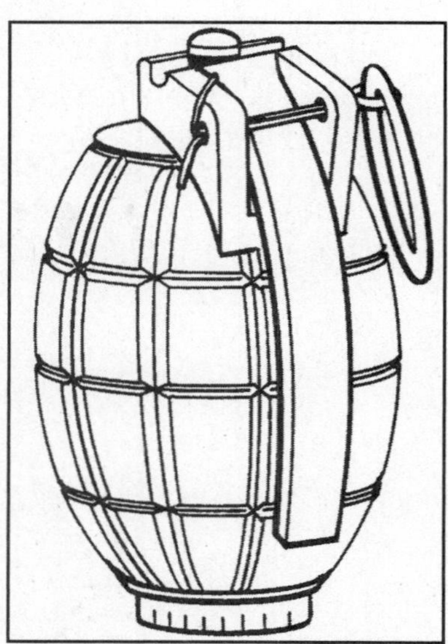

Figure 6-13: No. 36M hand grenade.

6-14. PC1

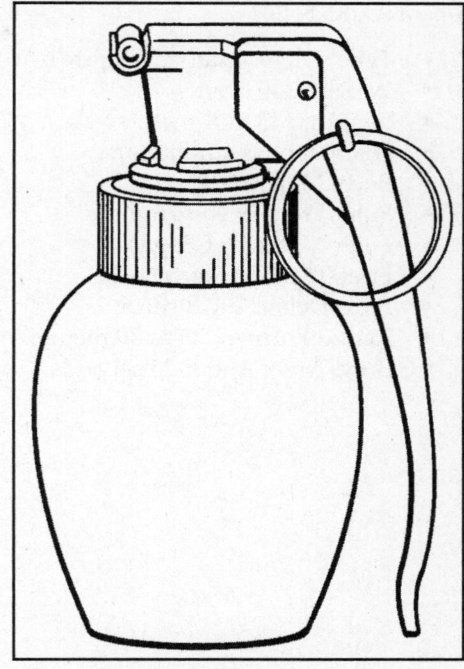

- Type: Practice. (Figure 6-14)
- Weight: 265 grams.
- Length: 95 millimeters.
- Diameter: 56 millimeters.
- Body Material: Soft plastic.
- Filler Weight: 80 grams.
- Filler Material: White powder.
- Fuze Type: Delay.
- Fuze Delay: 4.4 seconds + 0.5 seconds.
- Range Thrown: 40 meters.

Figure 6-14: PC1 practice hand grenade.

6-15. L2A2

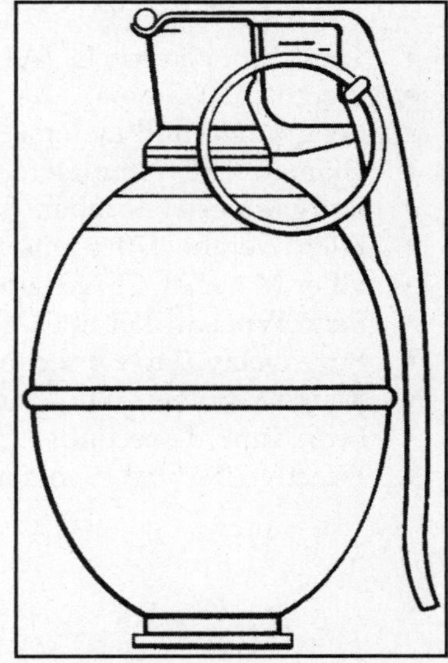

- Type: Fragmentation. (Figure 6-15)
- Weight: 395 grams.
- Length: 106 millimeters.
- Diameter: 60 millimeters.
- Body Material: Two-piece sheet-steel body with spiral wrapped fragmentation sleeve inside.
- Filler Material: RDX/TNT, 170 grams.
- Fuze Type: Striker release.
- Fuze Delay: 4 to 5 seconds.
- Range Thrown: 40 meters.
- Lethal Radius: 10 meters.

Figure 6-15: L2A2 hand grenade.

> ✍ **NOTE**
> Copy of U.S. M26, being replaced by RO 01A1, a product improved model.

6-16. NO. 83 N 201

- Type: Lachrymatory. (Figure 6-16)
- Weight: 340 grams.
- Length: 135 millimeters.
- Diameter: 63 millimeters.
- Body Material: Tin.
- Filler Weight: 205 grams.
- Filler Material: CS, gas.
- Fuze Type: Striker release.
- Fuze Delay: 2 to 3 seconds.
- Range Thrown: 25 to 30 meters.
- Burn Time: About 25 seconds.

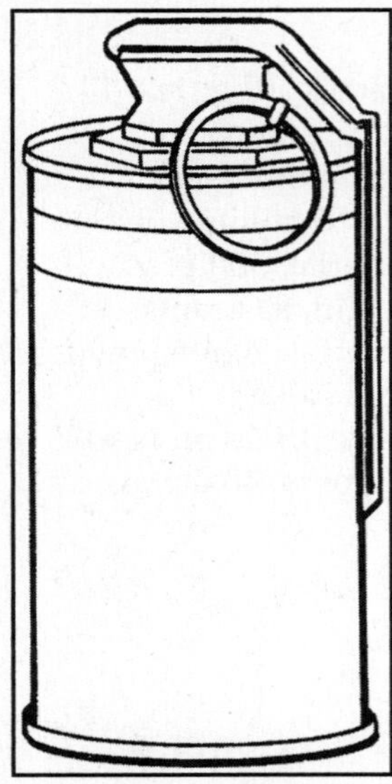

Figure 6-16: No. 83 N 201 riot-control hand grenade.

6-17. RUBBER BURSTING CS

- Type: Riot control, L13A1 (N225 is similar). (Figure 6-17)
- Weight: 550 Grams.
- Length: 175 millimeters.
- Diameter: 66 millimeters.
- Body Material: Rubber.
- Filler Weight: 470 grams.
- Filler Material: CS, 23 separate CS pellets.
- Fuze Type: Striker release.
- Fuze Delay: 2 to 2.4 seconds.
- Range Thrown: 25 to 35 meters.
- Burn Time: 12 seconds.
- Effective Radius: 15 meters.

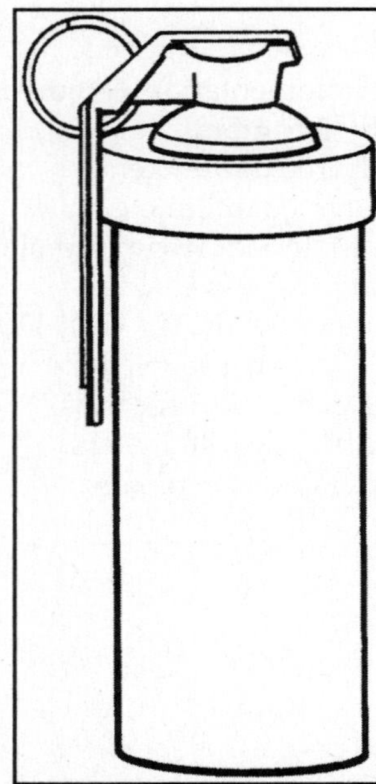

Figure 6-17: Rubber bursting CS hand grenade.

SECTION V. AUSTRIA

6-18. SPL HGR 77

- Type: Defensive. (Figure 6-18)
- Weight: 470 grams.
- Length: 96 millimeters.
- Diameter: 63 millimeters.
- Body Material: Rigid plastic.
- Filler Material: Plasticized PETN, 70 g.
- Fuze Type: Striker release.
- Fuze Delay: 3.5 to 4.5 seconds.
- Range Thrown: 45 meters.
- Effective Radius: 10 to 12 meters.

Figure 6-18: Spl HGr 77 hand grenade.

6-19. HDGR 78

- Type: Defensive. (Figure 6-19)
- Weight: 520 grams.
- Length: 115 millimeters.
- Diameter: 60 millimeters.
- Body Material: Plastic with steel pellets.
- Filler Weight: 70 grams.
- Filler Material: Plasticized PETN.
- Fuze Type: Striker release.
- Fuze Delay: 3 to 5 seconds.
- Range Thrown: 35 to 40 meters.
- Effective Radius: 10 meters.

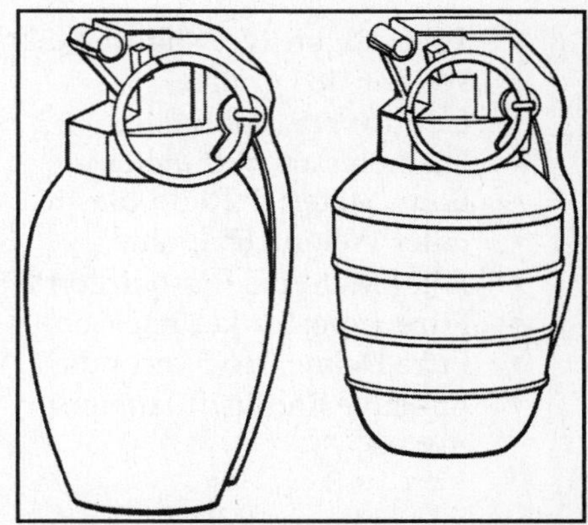

Figure 6-19: HdGr 78 hand grenade.

6-20. HGR 79

- Type: Defensive. (Figure 6-20)
- Weight: 370 grams.
- Length: 96 millimeters.
- Diameter: 58 millimeters.
- Body Material: Plastic.
- Filler Weight: 45 grams.
- Filler Material: Plasticized PETN.
- Fuze Type: Striker release.
- Fuze Delay: 3.5 to 4.5 seconds.
- Range Thrown: 45 meters.
- Effective Radius: 10 meters.

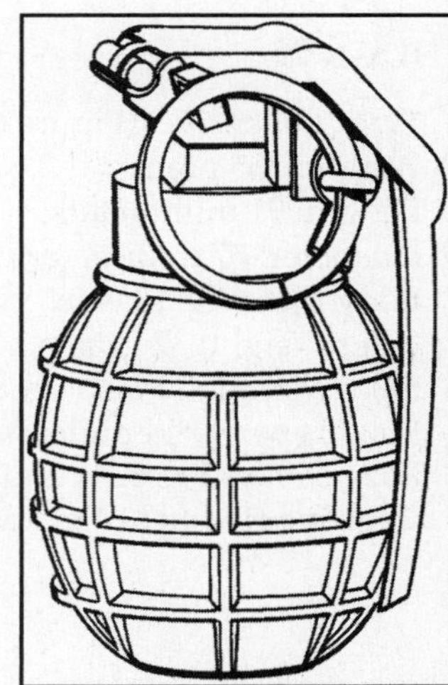

Figure 6-20: HGr 79 hand grenade.

6-21. SPL HGR 84

- Type: Defensive. (Figure 6-21)
- Weight: 490 grams.
- Length: 115 millimeters.
- Diameter: 61 millimeters.
- Body Material: Plastic.
- Filler Weight: 96 grams.
- Fuze Type: Striker release.
- Fuze Delay: 3.5 to 4.5 seconds nominal.
- Range Thrown: 35 to 40 meters.
- Effective Radius: 10 meters.

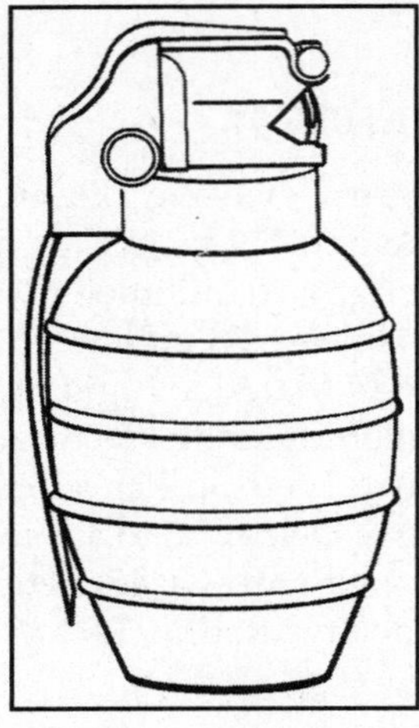

Figure 6-21: Spl HGr 84 hand grenade.

6-22. HDGR 72

- Type: Defensive. (Figure 6-22)
- Weight: 485 grams.
- Length: 115 millimeters.
- Diameter: 60 millimeter.
- Body Material: Rigid plastic.
- Filler Weight: 65 grams.
- Filler Material: Plasticized PETN.
- Fuze Type: Striker release.
- Fuze Delay: 3 to 5 seconds.
- Effective Radius: 10 meters.

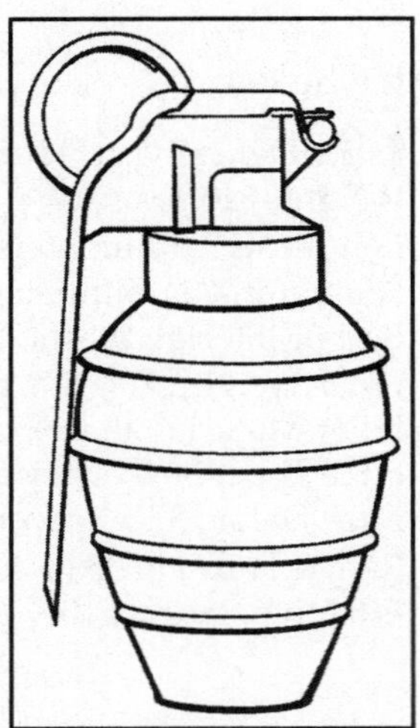

Figure 6-22: HdGr 72 hand grenade.

6-23. HDGR 73

- Type: Defensive. (Figure 6-23)
- Weight: 355 grams.
- Length: 91 millimeters.
- Diameter: 57 millimeters.
- Body Material: Plastic.
- Filler Weight: 37 grams.
- Filler Material: Plasticized PETN.
- Fuze Type: Striker release.
- Fuze Delay: 3 to 5 seconds.
- Effective Radius: 10 meters.

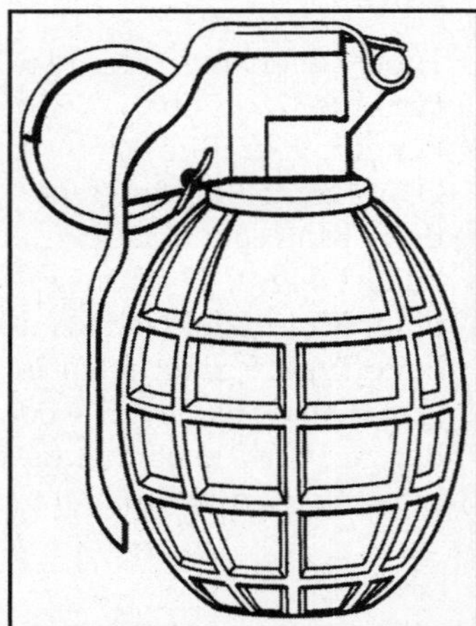

Figure 6-23: HdGr 73 hand grenade.

The Claymore Antipersonnel Mine

CHAPTER 1

Introduction

SECTION I. GENERAL

1. PURPOSE AND SCOPE

a. This manual provides guidance for commanders and instructors presenting instruction and training on the functioning, installation, and employment of the antipersonnel mine, CLAYMORE.

b. This manual describes the M18A1 antipersonnel mine, CLAYMORE, its functioning, and installation. It provides a basis for conducting training utilizing the electric firing system issued with the mine. It also gives guidance for tactical employment and safety requirements. An earlier model of the CLAYMORE antipersonnel mine, the M18, is covered in appendix II.

c. The material contained herein is applicable without modification to both nuclear and nonnuclear warfare.

d. Users of this manual are encouraged to submit recommended changes or comments to improve the publication. Comments should be keyed to the specific page, paragraph, and line of the text in which the change is recommended. Reasons should be provided for each comment to insure understanding and complete evaluation. Comments should be forwarded direct to the Commandant, United States Army Infantry School, Fort Benning, Ga. 31905.

2. ROLES OF THE ANTIPERSONNEL MINE, CLAYMORE

The number of ways in which the CLAYMORE may be employed is limited only by the imagination of the user. The CLAYMORE is used primarily as a defensive weapon, but has its application in the offensive role. It must be emphasized that when the CLAYMORE is referred to as a weapon, this implies that it is employed in the controlled role. In the uncontrolled role, the CLAYMORE is considered a mine or boobytrap (FM 20–32).

SECTION II. DESCRIPTION

3. GENERAL

The M18A1 antipersonnel mine was standardized in 1960, and replaced the M18 antipersonnel mine (app. II). Both mines are similar in appearance and functioning. The M18A1 (fig. 1) is a directional, fixed-fragmentation mine. When employed in the controlled role, it is treated as a one-shot weapon. It is primarily designed for use against massed infantry attacks; however, its fragments are also effective against light vehicles. The M18A1 mine is equipped with a fixer plastic slit-type sight (knife-edge sight on later model), adjustable legs, and two detonator wells. An instruction sheet for the M18A1 mine is attached to the inside cover of the bandoleer. The instruction sheet which accompanies the M18A1 mine having the knife-edge sight is shown in figure 3.

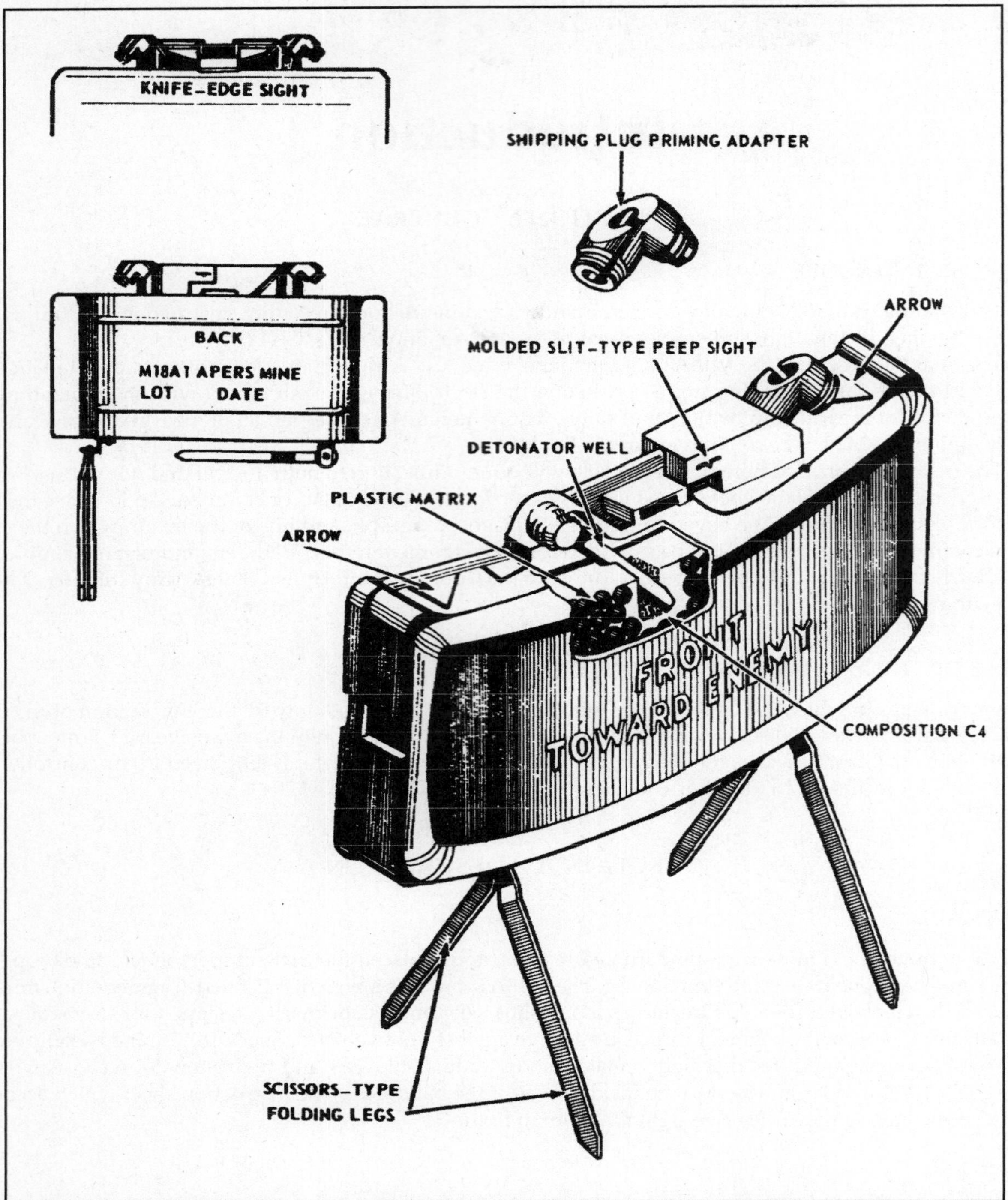

Figure 1: The M18A1 antipersonnel mine (CLAYMORE).

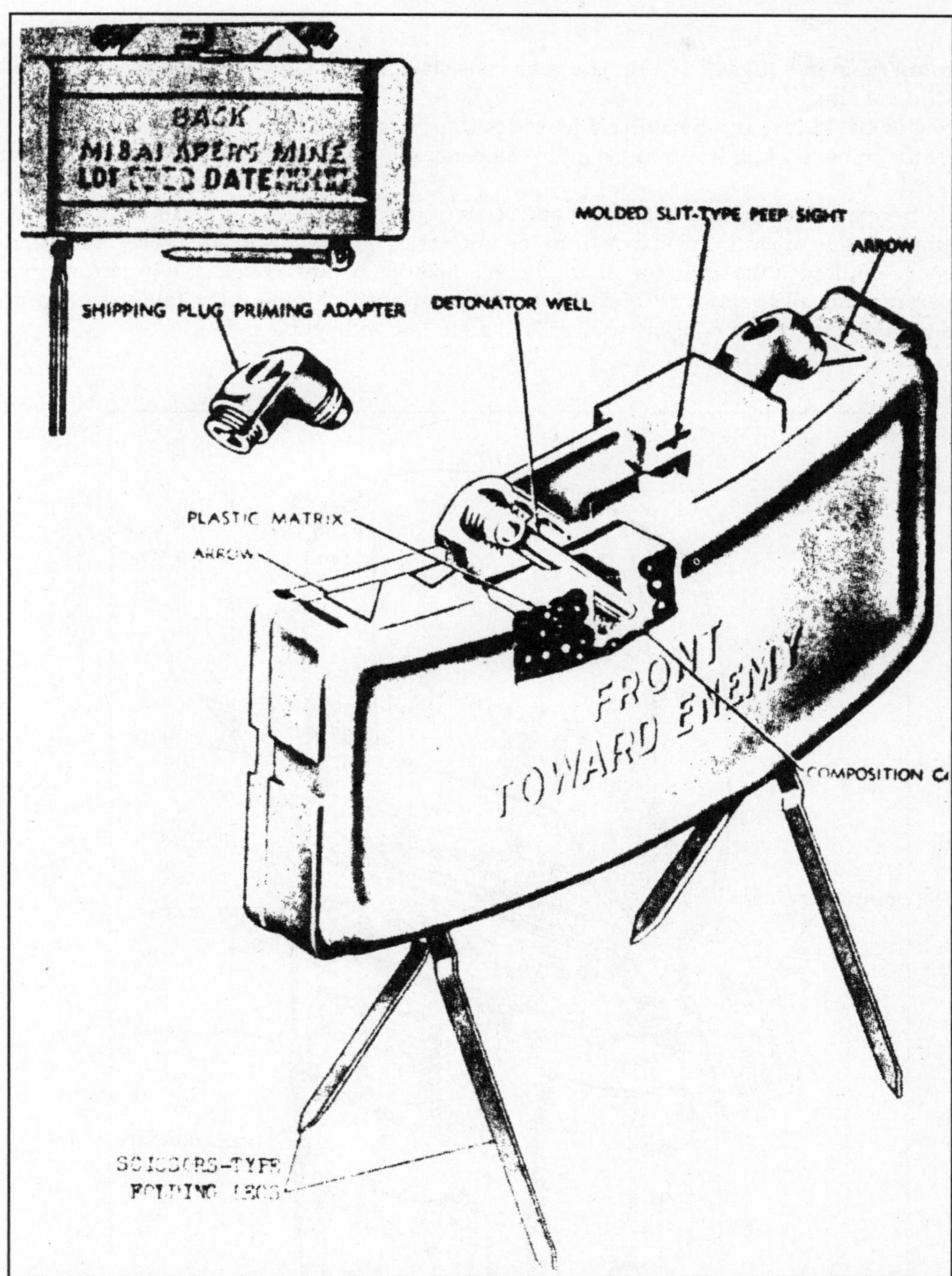

4. CASUALTY EFFECTS

When detonated, the M18A1 mine will deliver spherical steel fragments over a 60° fan-shaped pattern that is 2 meters high and 50 meters wide at a range of 50 meters (fig. 4). These fragments are moderately effective up to a range of 100 meters and can travel up to 250 meters forward of the mine. The optimum effective range (the range at which the most desirable balance is achieved between lethality and area coverage) is 50 meters.

5. DANGER AREA

a. **Danger From Fragments** (fig. 4). The danger area consists of a 180° fan with a radius of 250 meters centered in the direction of aim.

b. **Danger Area of Backblast and Secondary Missiles** (figs. 4 and 24). Within an area of 16 meters to the rear and sides of the mine, backblast can cause injury by concussion (ruptured eardrums) and create a secondary missile hazard.

(1) Friendly troops are prohibited to the rear and sides of the mine within a radius of 16 meters.

(2) The minimum safe operating distance from the mine is 16 meters. At this distance, and regardless of how the mine is employed, the operator should be in a foxhole, behind cover, or lying prone in a depression. The operator and all friendly troops within 100 meters of the mine must take cover to prevent being injured by flying secondary objects such as sticks, stones, and pebbles.

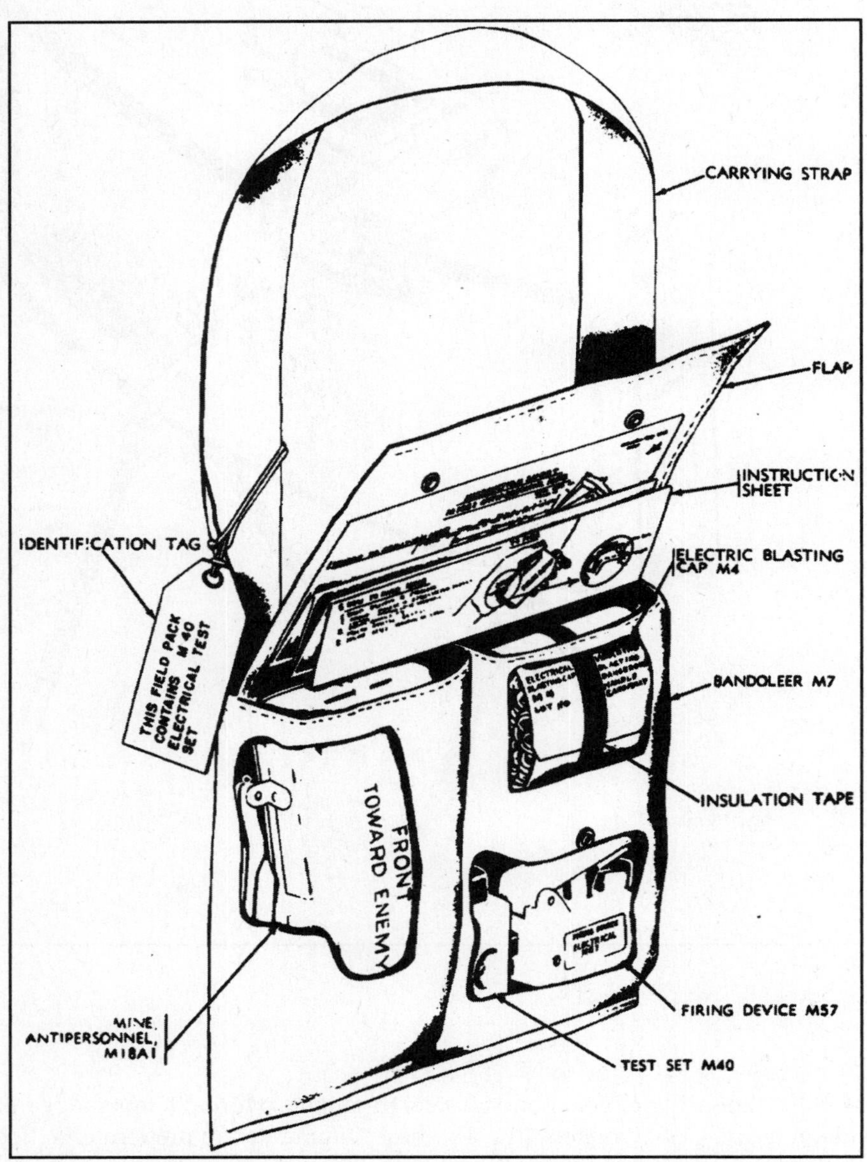

Figure 2: The M18A1 antipersonnel mine and accessories packed in the M7 bandoleer.

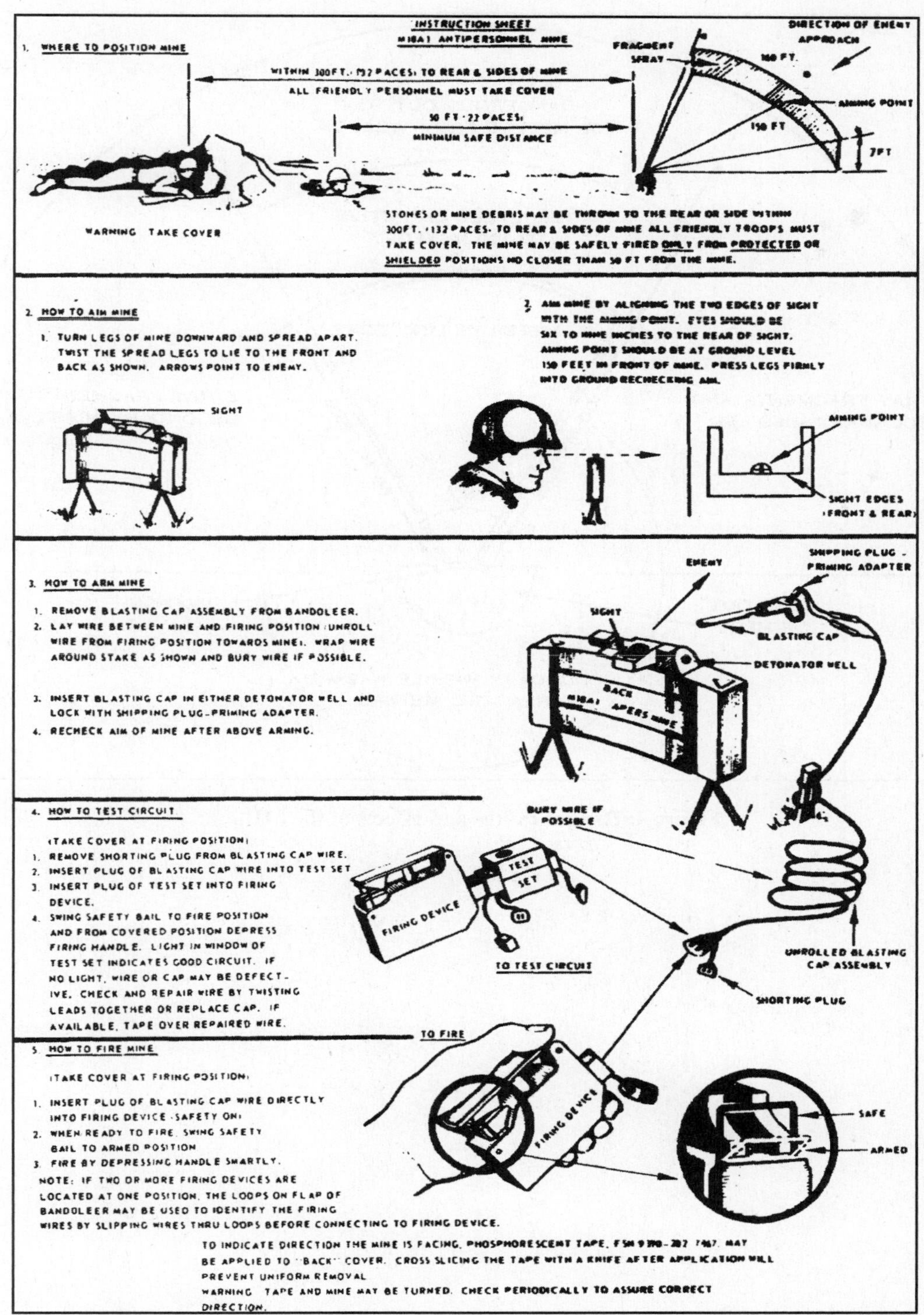

INSTRUCTION SHEET
M18A1 ANTIPERSONNEL MINE

1. WHERE TO POSITION MINE

WITHIN 300 FT. (132 PACES) TO REAR & SIDES OF MINE
ALL FRIENDLY PERSONNEL MUST TAKE COVER

50 FT (22 PACES)
MINIMUM SAFE DISTANCE

FRAGMENT SPRAY
DIRECTION OF ENEMY APPROACH
160 FT.
AIMING POINT
150 FT
7 FT

WARNING TAKE COVER

STONES OR MINE DEBRIS MAY BE THROWN TO THE REAR OR SIDE WITHIN 300 FT. (132 PACES). TO REAR & SIDES OF MINE ALL FRIENDLY TROOPS MUST TAKE COVER. THE MINE MAY BE SAFELY FIRED ONLY FROM PROTECTED OR SHIELDED POSITIONS NO CLOSER THAN 50 FT FROM THE MINE.

2. HOW TO AIM MINE

1. TURN LEGS OF MINE DOWNWARD AND SPREAD APART. TWIST THE SPREAD LEGS TO LIE TO THE FRONT AND BACK AS SHOWN. ARROWS POINT TO ENEMY.

2. AIM MINE BY ALIGNING THE TWO EDGES OF SIGHT WITH THE AIMING POINT. EYES SHOULD BE SIX TO NINE INCHES TO THE REAR OF SIGHT. AIMING POINT SHOULD BE AT GROUND LEVEL 150 FEET IN FRONT OF MINE. PRESS LEGS FIRMLY INTO GROUND RECHECKING AIM.

SIGHT
AIMING POINT
SIGHT EDGES (FRONT & REAR)

3. HOW TO ARM MINE

1. REMOVE BLASTING CAP ASSEMBLY FROM BANDOLEER.
2. LAY WIRE BETWEEN MINE AND FIRING POSITION (UNROLL WIRE FROM FIRING POSITION TOWARDS MINE). WRAP WIRE AROUND STAKE AS SHOWN AND BURY WIRE IF POSSIBLE.
3. INSERT BLASTING CAP IN EITHER DETONATOR WELL AND LOCK WITH SHIPPING PLUG-PRIMING ADAPTER.
4. RECHECK AIM OF MINE AFTER ABOVE ARMING.

ENEMY
SHIPPING PLUG - PRIMING ADAPTER
SIGHT
BLASTING CAP
DETONATOR WELL
BACK
M18A1 APERS MINE

4. HOW TO TEST CIRCUIT

(TAKE COVER AT FIRING POSITION)
1. REMOVE SHORTING PLUG FROM BLASTING CAP WIRE.
2. INSERT PLUG OF BLASTING CAP WIRE INTO TEST SET
3. INSERT PLUG OF TEST SET INTO FIRING DEVICE.
4. SWING SAFETY BAIL TO FIRE POSITION AND FROM COVERED POSITION DEPRESS FIRING HANDLE. LIGHT IN WINDOW OF TEST SET INDICATES GOOD CIRCUIT. IF NO LIGHT, WIRE OR CAP MAY BE DEFECTIVE. CHECK AND REPAIR WIRE BY TWISTING LEADS TOGETHER OR REPLACE CAP. IF AVAILABLE, TAPE OVER REPAIRED WIRE.

BURY WIRE IF POSSIBLE
TEST SET
FIRING DEVICE
TO TEST CIRCUIT
UNROLLED BLASTING CAP ASSEMBLY
SHORTING PLUG

5. HOW TO FIRE MINE

(TAKE COVER AT FIRING POSITION)
1. INSERT PLUG OF BLASTING CAP WIRE DIRECTLY INTO FIRING DEVICE (SAFETY ON)
2. WHEN READY TO FIRE, SWING SAFETY BAIL TO ARMED POSITION
3. FIRE BY DEPRESSING HANDLE SMARTLY.

NOTE: IF TWO OR MORE FIRING DEVICES ARE LOCATED AT ONE POSITION, THE LOOPS ON FLAP OF BANDOLEER MAY BE USED TO IDENTIFY THE FIRING WIRES BY SLIPPING WIRES THRU LOOPS BEFORE CONNECTING TO FIRING DEVICE.

TO FIRE
FIRING DEVICE
SAFE
ARMED

TO INDICATE DIRECTION THE MINE IS FACING, PHOSPHORESCENT TAPE, FSN 9390-202-7467, MAY BE APPLIED TO "BACK" COVER. CROSS SLICING THE TAPE WITH A KNIFE AFTER APPLICATION WILL PREVENT UNIFORM REMOVAL.
WARNING: TAPE AND MINE MAY BE TURNED. CHECK PERIODICALLY TO ASSURE CORRECT DIRECTION.

Figure 3: The instruction sheet attached to the M7 bandoleer.

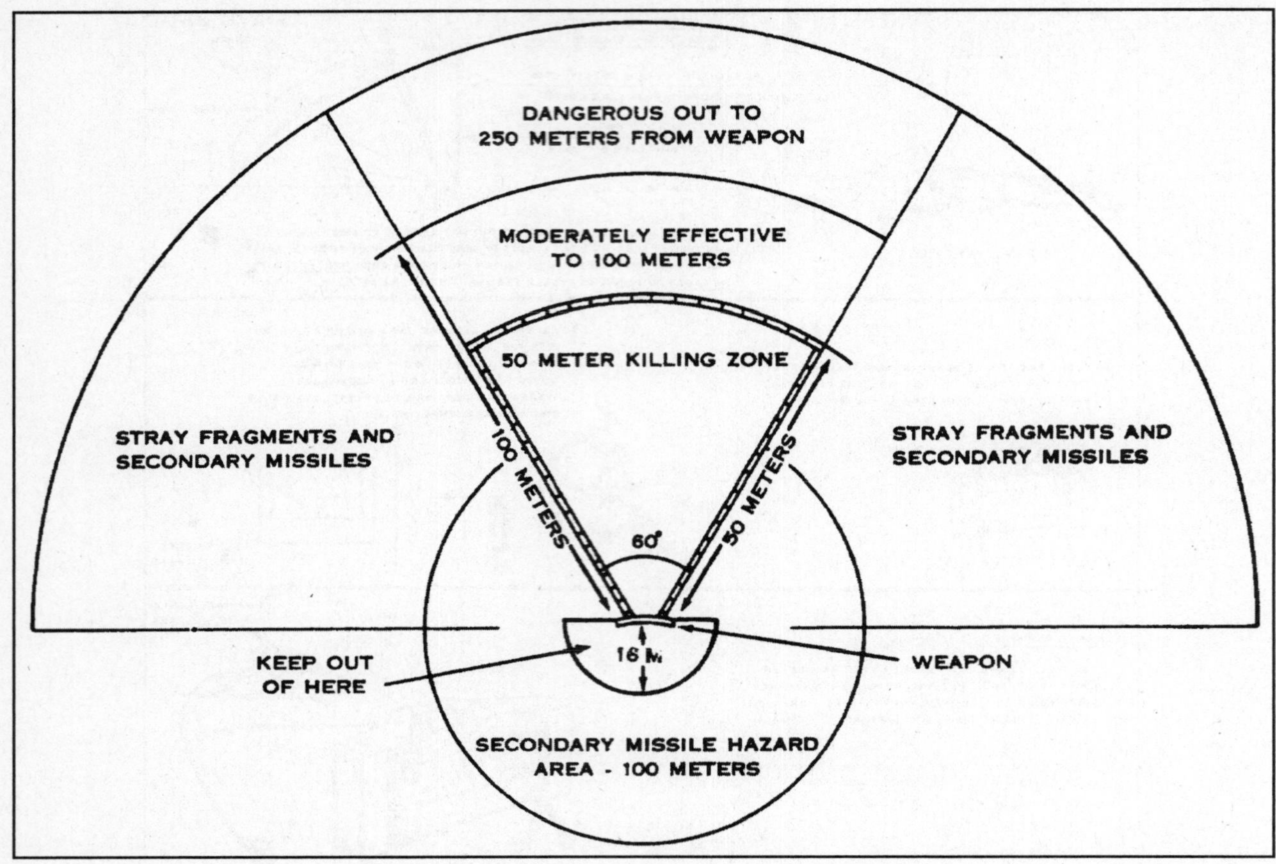

Figure 4: Danger radius and effects of the M18A1.

CHAPTER 2

Mechanical Training

SECTION I. INTRODUCTION

6. GENERAL

This section describes and illustrates the M18A1 antipersonnel mine and the electric and nonelectric firing systems that can be used to detonate the mine.

7. DETAILED DESCRIPTION

a. **Mine.**

(1) ***Nomenclature*** Mine, antipersonnel, M18A1.

(2) ***Common name*** CLAYMORE.

(3) ***Type*** Antipersonnel.

(4) ***Weight*** 3½ pounds.

(5) ***Dimensions*** 8½ inches long; 1⅜ inches wide; 3¼ inches high (legs folded); 6¾ inches high (legs unfolded).

(6) ***Firing unit construction*** The outer surface of the mine is a curved, rectangular, olive-drab, molded case of fiberglass-filled polystyrene (plastic). In the front portion of the case is a fragmentation face containing steel spheres embbedded in a plastic matrix. The back portion of the case behind the matrix contains a layer of explosive.

(7) ***Explosive*** 1½ pounds of composition C4.

(8) ***Detonator wells.*** Two detonator wells are located on the top of the mine which allows for single or dual priming. These wells are sealed by the plug ends of the shipping plug priming-adapters which prevent entry of foreign materials into the detonator wells. The slotted end of the shipping plug priming-adapter is used to hold an electric blasting cap in place when the mine is armed. The shipping plug priming-adapter is merely reversed when the mine is to be armed.

(9) ***Sight and arrows.*** The molded slit-type peepsight (or knife-edge sight) and arrows (fig. 10) located on top of the mine are used to aim the mine.

(10) ***Legs.*** Two pairs of scissors-type folding legs located on the bottom of the mine enable it to be emplaced on the ground. The mine can also be tied to posts, trees, etc.

b. **Accessories.**

(1) ***M57 firing device.***

(a) One M57 electrical firing device is issued with each M18A1. This device is a hand-held pulse generator. A squeeze of the handle produces a double (one positive, one negative) 3-volt electric pulse of sufficient energy to fire the electric blasting cap through the 100 feet of firing wire which is issued with the mine. The M57 device is 4 inches long, approximately 1½ inches wide, 3¼ inches high, and weighs three-fourths of a pound. On one end of the firing device is a rubber connecting plug with a dust cover. The M57 firing device is shown in figure 5.

(b) The safety bail on the M57 electrical firing device (fig. 6) has two positions. In the upper SAFE position, it acts as a block between the firing handle and the pulse generator. In the lower FIRE position, it is clear of the firing handle and allows the pulse generator to be activated. The M18 A1 antipersonnel mine with the M57 firing device connected is shown in figure 7.

(c) The M57 electrical firing device and firing wire should not be discarded after initial use. Another electric blasting cap can be attached to the firing wire and the M57 device can be used to fire other

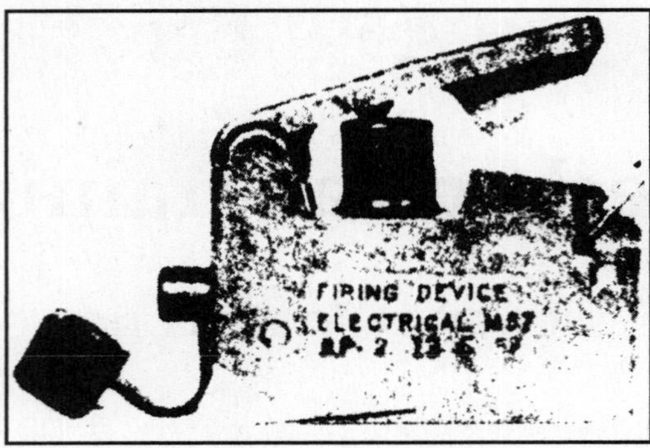

Figure 5: The M57 firing device.

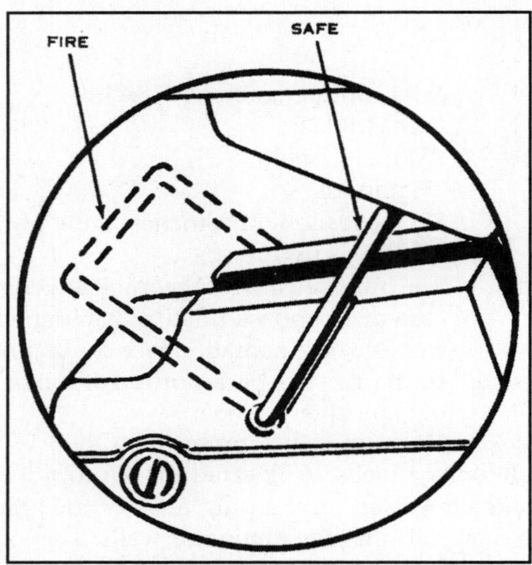

Figure 6: The M57 firing device safety bail.

devices, such as fougasse bombs and demolition charges, provided no more than 100 feet of firing wire and one M6 blasting cap are used.

(2) ***M4 electric blasting cap.*** The M4 electric blasting cap assembly (fig. 7) consists of an M6 electric blasting cap attached to 100 feet of firing wire. Attached to the firing wire connection is a combination shorting plug and dust cover. The shorting plug prevents accidental functioning of the blasting cap by static electricity; the dust cover prevents dirt and moisture from entering the connector. The firing wire is wrapped around a flat paper and then rolled to form a package 6 inches long, 4 inches wide, and 2 inches high. A piece of insulating tape is used to hold the package together.

> ✍ **NOTE**
> With minus of later manufacture, the M4 electrical blasting cap assembly is Willed on a spool.

(3) ***M40 test set.*** The M40 test set (figs. 17 and 18) is an instrument used for checking the continuity of the initiating circuit of the mine. (For further details on the M40 test set, see para 15.)

✍ NOTE
Only one of the six bandoleers in each packing box contains a test set. The bandoleer containing the test set is marked by an identification tag on the carrying strap (fig. 2).

c. **M7 Bandoleer.** The M7 bandoleer (fig. 2) is constructed of water resistant canvas (olive-drab color) and has snap fasteners which secure the flap. The bandoleer has two pockets; one pocket contains the mine and the other contains a firing device, a test set, and an electric blasting cap assembly. A 2-inch wide web strap, which is used as a shoulder carrying strap, is sewn to the bag. An instruction sheet is sewn to the inside flap (fig. 3).

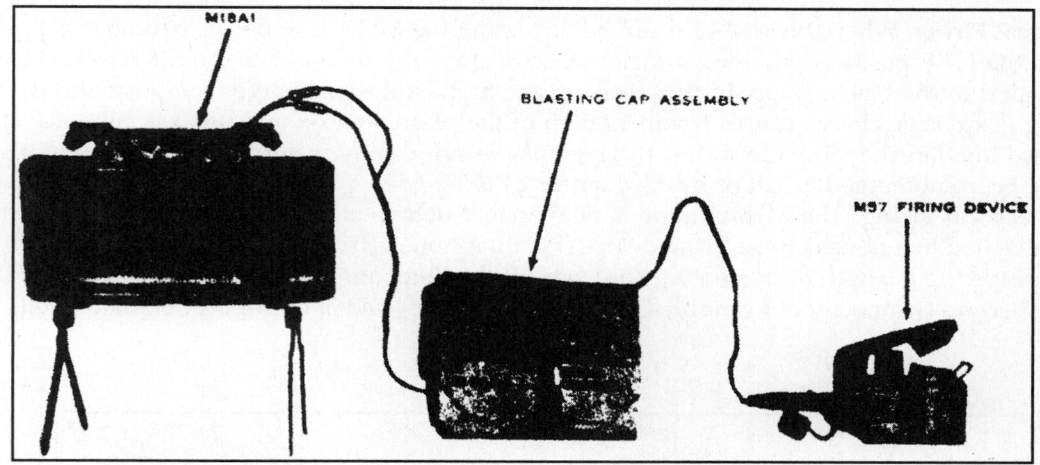

Figure 7: The M18A1 antipersonnel mine with the M57 firing device connected.

SECTION II. COVERAGE AND METHODS OF FIRE

8. FIRE DISCIPLINE

Since the M18A1 mine can be fired only once, fire discipline is of paramount importance. The mine should not be used against single personnel targets; rather, it should be used for its intended purpose—massed personnel. When lead elements of an enemy formation approach within 20 to 30 meters of the mine, it should be detonated. If practicable, and to insure fire discipline, actual authority and responsibility for target selection and timely detonation should rest with squad leaders or their superiors.

9. CONTROLLED FRONTAL COVERAGE

a. For effective coverage of the entire front of a position, mines can be placed in a line no closer than 5 meters and no farther apart than 45 meters. Preferred lateral and rearward separation distance is 25 meters (fig. 8).
b. If mines are placed in depth (from front to rear), the minimum rearward separation distance is 5 meters, provided secondary missiles are removed. This distance is sufficient to prevent possible disturbance or damage to the rearward mines.

10. METHODS OF FIRE

The M18A1 mine can be employed in either the controlled or uncontrolled role.

a. **Controlled Role.** The mine is detonated by the operator as the forward edge of the enemy approaches a point within the killing zone (20 to 30 meters) where maximum casualties can be inflicted. Controlled detonation may be accomplished by use of either an electrical or nonelectrical firing system (fig. 9). When mines are employed in the controlled role, they are treated the same as individual weapons and are reported for inclusion in the unit fire plan. They are not reported as mines; however, the emplacing unit must insure that the mines are either removed, detonated, or turned over to a relieving unit.

b. **Uncontrolled Role.** Uncontrolled firing is accomplished when the mine is installed in such a manner as to cause an unsuspecting enemy to detonate the mine. Mines employed in this manner must be reported and recorded as land mines.

SECTION III. FUNCTIONING AND INSTALLATION

11. FUNCTIONING

a. **Electrical Firing.** When the M18A1 is armed, actuating the M57 firing device handle (fig. 5) with the safety bail in the FIRE position provides sufficient electrical energy to detonate the M6 electric blasting cap. The detonation of the blasting cap, in turn, sets off the high explosive charge (composition C4). Detonation of the high explosive charge causes fragmentation of the plastic matrix and projects spherical steel fragments outward in a fan-shaped pattern (fig. 4). This mine is sufficiently waterproof to function satisfactorily after having been submerged in salt or fresh water for 2 hours.

b. **Nonelectrical Firing.** The M18A1 mine is deliberately detonated by the operator pulling or cutting a trip wire attached to a nonelectrical firing device (fig. 9). A nonelectric blasting cap attached to the firing device and crimped to a length of detonating cord sets off the detonating cord. At the other end of the detonating cord, a second crimped nonelectric blasting cap, which is inserted in one of the detonator wells, detonates the mine.

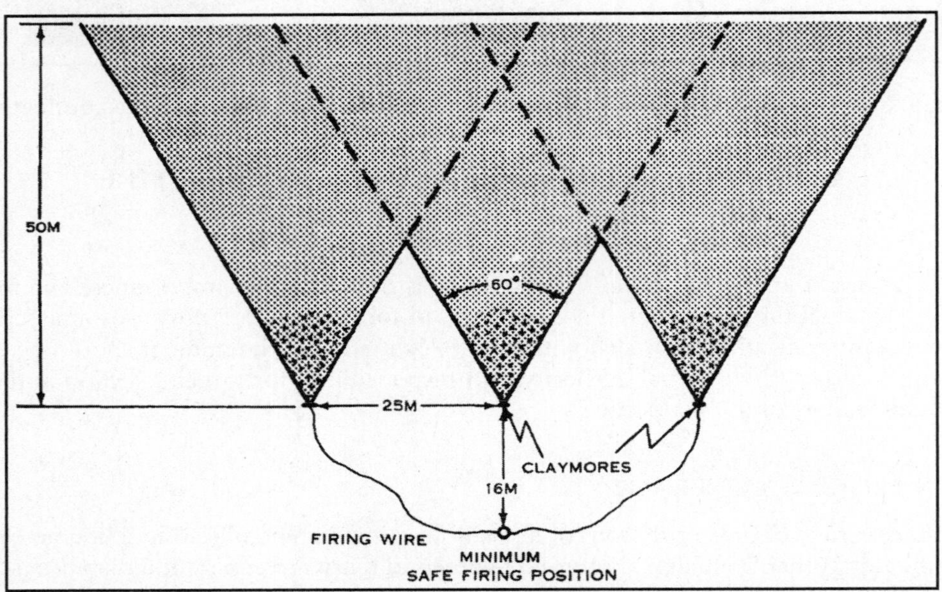

Figure 8: Diagram of lateral separation pattern of (CLAYMORES).

12. INSTALLATION FOR ELECTRICAL FIRING

a. **Laying and Aiming.**

(1) ***Laying.***

(a) Check to see that the mine and all accessories (fig. 2) are in the bandoleer. Read the instruction sheet (fig. 3) attached inside the bandoleer cover before installing the mine.

(b) Remove the electrical firing wire leaving the mine and other accessories in the bandoleer.

WARNING

During installation the M57 firing device must be kept in the possession of the man installing the mine to prevent accidental firing by a second man.

(c) Secure the shorting plug end of the firing wire at the firing position. Place the bandoleer on your shoulder and unroll the firing wire to the position selected for emplacing the mine.

NOTE

The instructor sheet which accompanies the M18A1 mine with slit-type peepsight indicates that the firing wire can be unrolled from the mine or from the firing position; however, the firing wire should always be laid from the firing psition to the mine emplacement.

(d) Remove the mine from the bandoleer; turn the legs rearward and then downward. Spread each pair of legs about 45 degrees. One leg should protrude to the front and one to the rear of the mine. Position the mine with the surface marked "FRONT TOWARD ENEMY" and the arrows on top of the mine pointing in the direction of the enemy or the desired area of fire. On snow or extremely soft ground the bandoleer may be spread beneath the mine for support.

(e) To prevent tipping in windy areas or when the legs cannot be pressed into the ground, spread the legs to the maximum (about 180° so that the legs are to the front and rear of the mine). A top view of the M18A1 antipersonnel mine is shown in figure 10.

(2) ***Aiming.***

(a) *Mines with slit-type peepsight.*

1. Select an aiming point which is about 50 meters (150 feet) to the front of the mine and about 2½ meters (8 feet) above the ground (fig. 11).
2. Position the eye about 15 centimeters (6 inches) to the rear of the sight. Aim the mine by sighting through the peepsight. The groove of the sight should be in line with the aiming point. The aiming point should be in the center of the desired area of coverage, and the bottom edge of the peepsight should be parallel to the ground that is to be covered with the fragment spray.

(b) *Mines with knife-edge sight.*

1. Select an aiming point at ground level that is about 50 meters (150 feet) in front of the mine.
2. Position the eye about 15 centimeters (6 inches) to the rear of the sight. Aim the mine by alining the two edges of the sight with the aiming point (fig. 11.1).

b. **Arming and Electrical Firing.**

(1) Secure the firing wire about 1 meter behind the mine so it will not become misalined should the firing wire be disturbed.

(2) Test the firing device, test set, and blasting cap assembly as described in paragraph 15.

WARNING

Make certain that the combination shorting plug and dust cover are assembled to the connector of the firing wire before proceeding with installation of the mine.

(3) Unscrew one of the shipping plug priming adapters from the mine. Slide the slotted end of the shipping plug priming adapter (fig. 12) onto the firing wires of the blasting cap between the crimped connections and the blasting cap. Pull the excess wire through the slotted end of the adapter until the top of the blasting cap is firmly seated in the bottom portion of the shipping plug priming adapter. Screw the adapter with blasting cap into the detonator.

WARNING

Make certain that the face of the mine marked "Front Toward Enemy" and the arrows on top of the mine point in the direction of the enemy.

(4) Recheck the aim of the mine. Camouflage the mine and, if possible, bury the firing wire to protect it from fire and enemy detection. Make certain you have the bandoleer and other accessories and then move back to the firing position.

WARNING

The mine firing position should be in a foxhole or covered position at least 16 meters to the rear or the side of the emplaced mine.

(5) Before connecting the M57 firing device (fig. 5) to the firing wire, make certain that the safety bail is in the SAFE position and that all friendly troops within 250 meters of the front and sides and 100 meters of the rear of the mine are under cover. Do not connect the firing device to the firing wire until the actual time of firing.

(6) To fire the mine, remove the dust cover on the firing device, remove the combination shorting plug and dust cover from the end of the firing wire, and connect the firing device to the firing wire. Fire the mine by positioning the firing device safety bail in the FIRE position and actuating the firing device handle with a firm, quick squeeze.

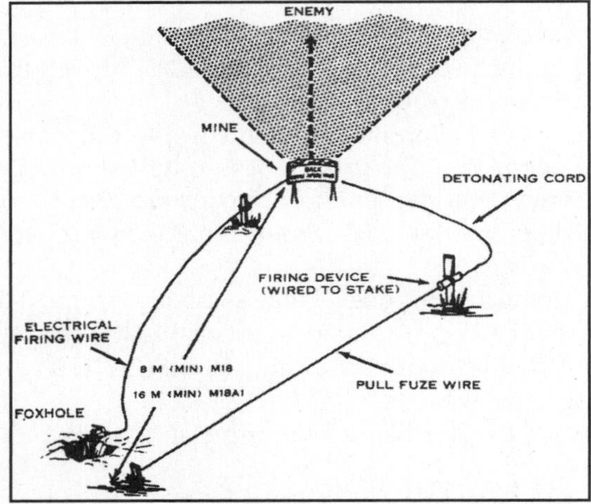

Figure 9: Diagram of the M18A1 antipersonnel mine installed for controlled nonelectrical and electrical detonation.

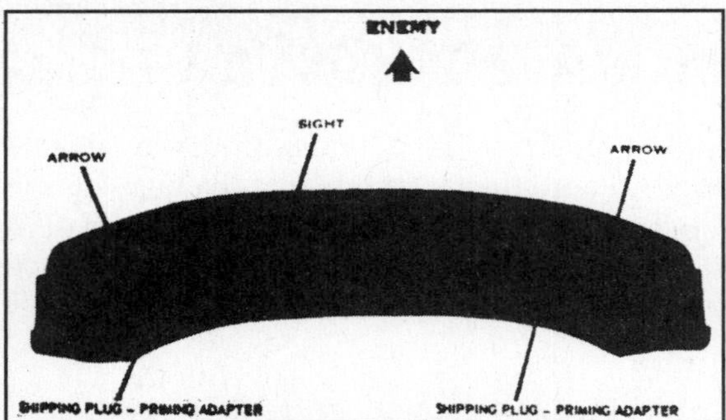

Figure 10: Top view of the M18A1 antipersonnel mine.

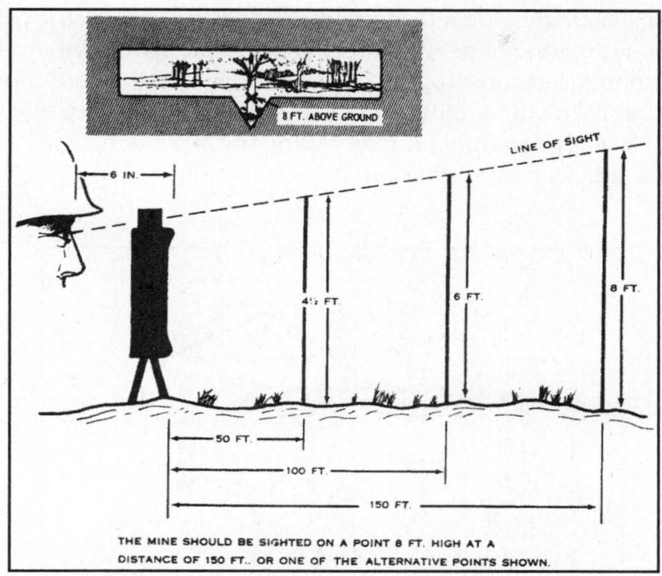

Figure 11: Aiming the M18A1 antipersonnel mine.

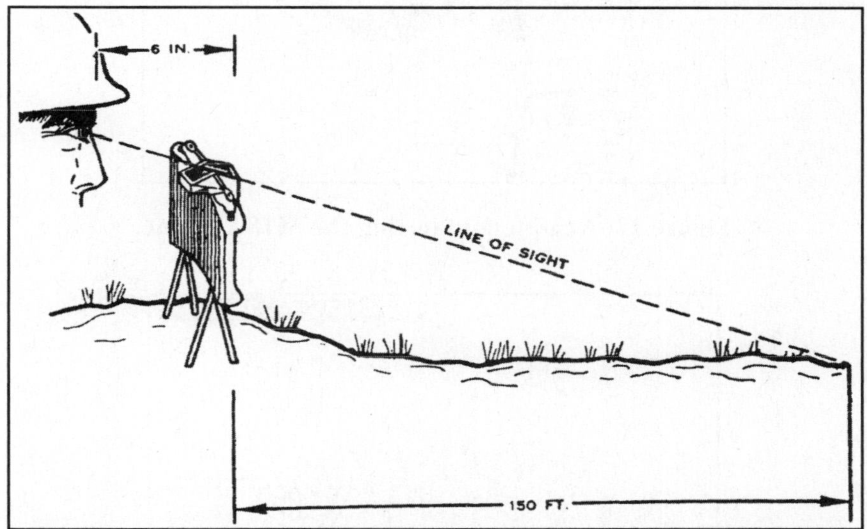

Figure 11.1: Aiming the M18A1 antipersonnel mine equipped with the knife-edge sight.

13. INSTALLATION FOR NONELECTRICAL FIRING

A nonelectric firing system utilizing a ring main is shown in figure 13. Instructions for laying, aiming, and arming the mine using two nonelectric M7 blasting caps, a piece of detonating cord approximately 25 feet long, a pull wire, and a pull-type or pull release-type firing device, such as the M1 or the M3 is discussed in *a* and *b* below. Instructions for laying, aiming, and arming the mine using a dual firing system and a ring main is discussed in *c* below. To arm the mine by the methods described below, a thorough knowledge of explosives and demolition materials and the use and installation of land mines and boobytraps is required.

a. **Pull Wire Initiation of the Mine (controlled).**

(1) Laying and aiming the mine are performed in the same manner as for electrical firing. For details on laying and aiming, see paragraph 12*a*.

(2) Crimp a nonelectric blasting cap to a firing device. With the nonelectric blasting cap attached, fasten the firing device to the detonating cord with tape. Using tape, wire, twine or cord, fasten the firing device securely to a firmly emplaced stake (fig. 13). Insert the detonating cord into a second nonelectric blasting cap and crimp the cap to the detonating cord. Carefully insert the cap into the detonator well. Secure the cap in the detonator well by carefully taping or tying the detonating cord to the mine. A method of taping detonating cord to a nonelectric blasting cap is shown in figure 14.

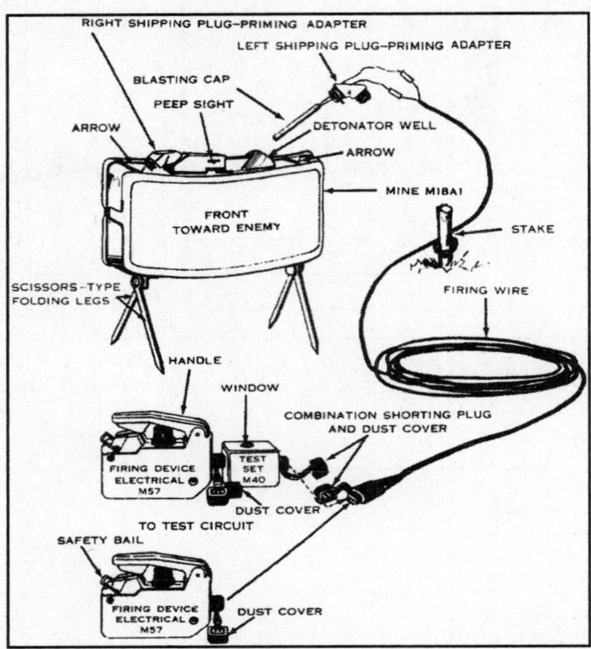

Figure 12: Arming and testing the M18A1 mine.

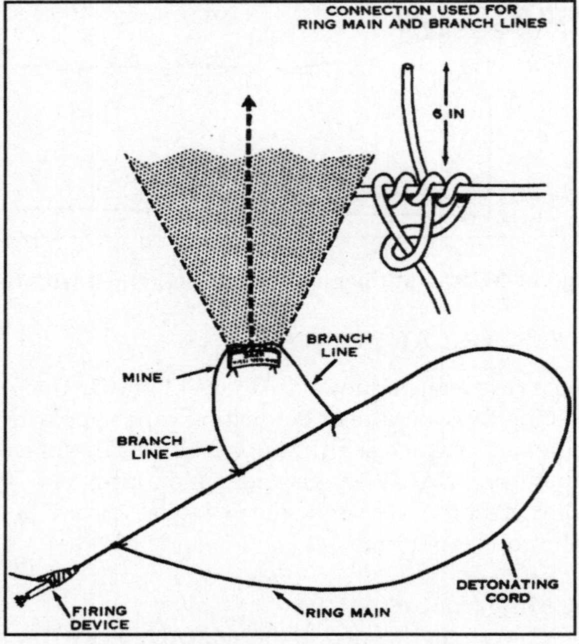

Figure 13: Nonelectric firing system.

(3) Attach a pull wire securely to the pull ring of the firing device. The pull wire should be sufficiently long to allow actuation of the firing device from a protected position at least 16 meters to the rear of the mine. Care must be taken during emplacement to secure the firing device so that the mine will not be dislodged by a pull of the detonating cord of the tripwire.

b. **Tripwire Initiation of the Mine (uncontrolled).**

(1) Laying and aiming the mine are performed in the same manner as for electrical firing. For details on laying and aiming, see paragraph 12*a*.

(2) The preliminary steps used to arm the mine are the same as those described in *a* (1) through (3) above.

(3) The tripwire and the firing device, which are stretched across a trail or other avenues of approach, must be securely attached to two stakes firmly emplaced in the ground at a distance of 20 to 30 meters forward of the mine (fig. 15).

c. **Nonelectric Method Using Dual Firing or Ring Main.**

(1) ***Dual firing.***

(a) Obtain two 10-meter lengths of detonating cord, four M7 nonelectric blasting caps, and two pull-type firing devices.

(b) Remove both shipping plug priming-adapters from the mine.

(c) Crimp an M7 nonelectric blasting cap to the end of each piece of detonating cord. Insert the caps into the detonator wells, and carefully tape or tie the detonating cord to the mine. While moving back to a safe firing position, unwind the detonating cord.

(d) Emplace the mine and the detonating cord as described in a (1) through (3) above.

(e) Attach a pull-type firing device and a tripwire (or pull wire) to the free end of each piece of detonating cord (fig. 13). Use the procedures described in *a* or *b* above.

(2) ***Ring Main.***

(a) Follow the instructions in (1) *(a)* through *(d)* above.

(b) Make a ring main.

(c) When mines are emplaced one behind the other, the one nearest the enemy is generally fired first. Mines emplaced laterally may be fired in any order or simultaneously.

(d) The mine and the danger area around the mine must be visible from the firing position so that friendly personnel in the vicinity of the mine may be seen.

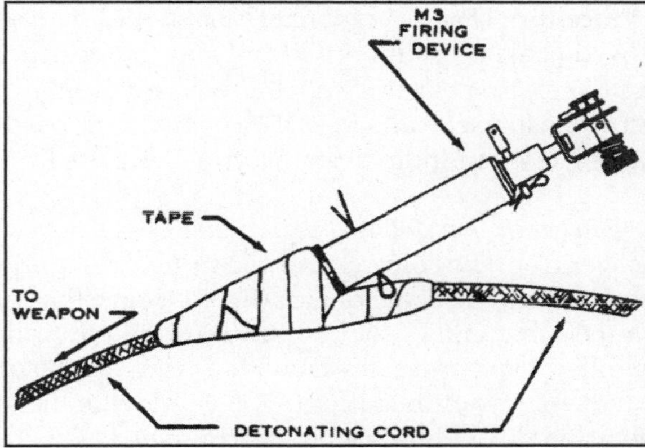

Figure 14: Method of taping MS firing device to detonating cord.

14. CAMOUFLAGE

a. Although the M18A1 is painted olive-drab to facilitate camouflaging, it is necessary to blend the mine into its surroundings to prevent its detection.

b. Only lightweight foliage, such as leaves and grass should be used to avoid increasing the secondary missile hazard to the rear of the mine.

c. Both the front and rear of the mine should be camouflaged with foliage. The firing wire should also be camouflaged or buried underground. If used, detonating cord should not be buried; however, it may be covered with light foliage.

15. TESTING

a. **M40 Test Set.** One M40 test set is provided with each case of six M18A1's. The test set is an instrument used for checking the continuity of the electrical firing circuit. A shipping tag on the carrying strap marks the bandoleer which contains the test set. The test set is 2 inches long, 1½ inches high, and weighs 8 ounces. A small window is located on top of the test set and is used for observing the flashes of the indicating lamp (figs. 17 and 18). The M18 A1 antipersonnel mine set up for circuit testing is shown in figure 16.

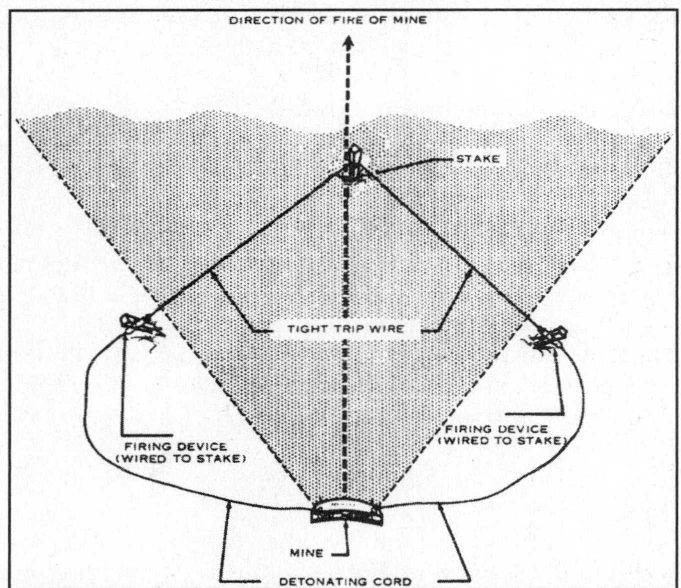

Figure 15: Diagram of the M18A1 antipersonnel mine installed for uncontrolled firing.

b. **Detailed Circuit Testing Procedure.** The firing circuit test should be conducted before the blasting cap is placed into the detonator well. This precaution will prevent the destruction of the mine if the testing set malfunctions and detonates the electric blasting cap. If the blasting cap is detonated during testing, it can be replaced by a standard electric blasting cap attached to the remaining firing wire. Before and after completion of the firing device and blasting cap continuity tests, ascertain that the firing device safety bail is in the SAFE position.

(1) ***Testing the M57 firing device and the M40 test set.***

(a) Remove the dust cover from the connector of the firing device and from the female connector of the test set. Plug the test set into the firing device (fig. 5). Leave the combination shorting plug and dust cover assembly on the other end of the test set. Position the firing device bail to the FIRE position and actuate the handle of the firing device with a firm, quick squeeze and observe the flashing of the lamp through the window of the test set. The window of the test set should be held near the eye when checking the firing device and blasting cap circuitry. This minimizes the risk of enemy observation in the dark and enables the operator to see the lamp flashing, even in bright sunlight.

(b) Flashing of the lamp indicates that the firing device is functioning properly. If the lamp does not flash (on and off), it could be caused by corrosion on the electric connectors of the test set. The firer can overcome this by connecting and disconnecting the shorting plug dust cover on the M40 test set. If the test set indicates that several firing devices are faulty, retest with another set since the first one may be defective. Side and top views of the M40 test set are shown in figures 17 and 18.

(2) ***Testing the blasting cap.***

(a) After determining that the firing device and test set are operative, remove the shorting plug dust cover from the connector of the firing wire and from the end of the test set. Plug the connector of the firing wire into the test set. Position the M57 firing device bail to the FIRE position. Insure that no friendly personnel are near the blasting cap, as it may detonate.

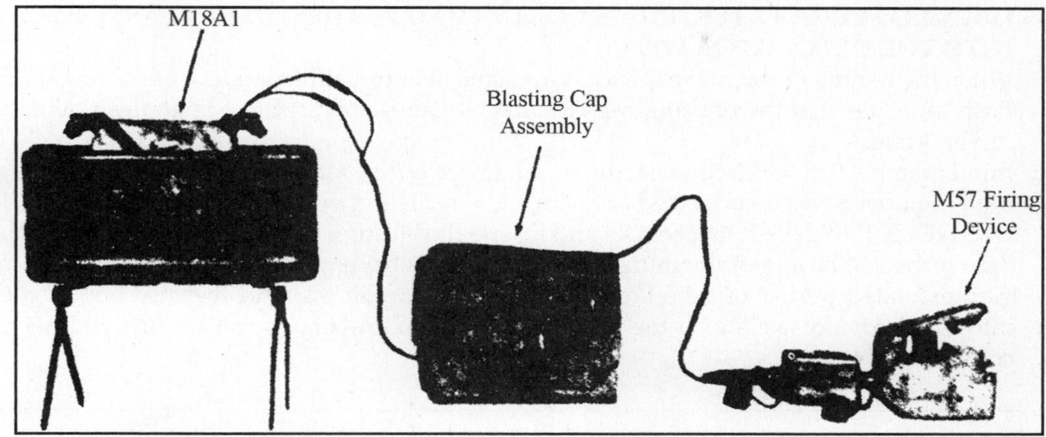

Figure 16: The M18A1 antipersonnel mine set up for circuit testing.

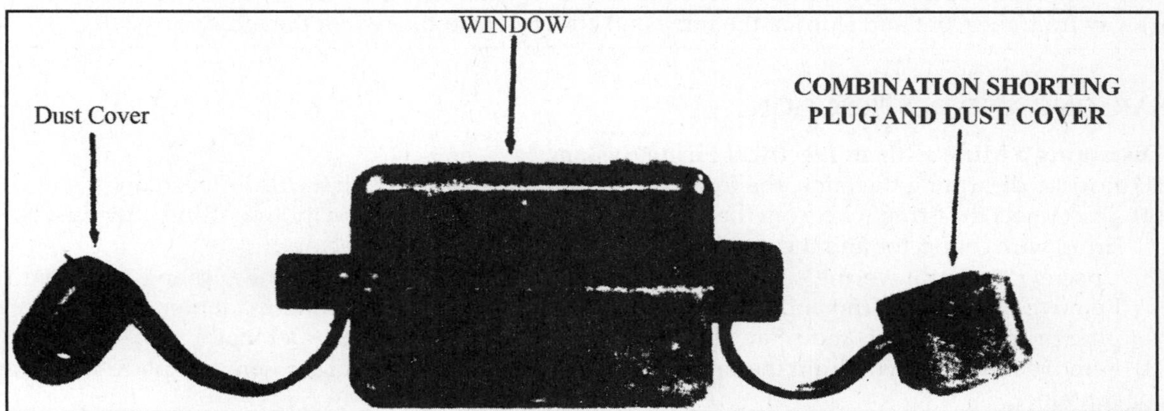

Figure 17: Side view of the M40 test set.

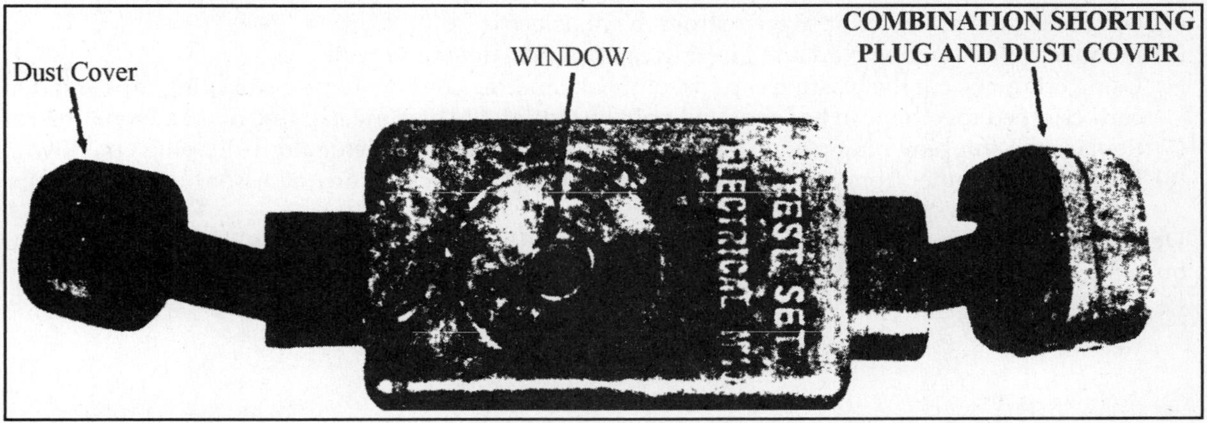

Figure 18: Top view of the M40 test set.

DETAILED CIRCUIT TESTING IS CONDUCTED WITHOUT THE BLASTING CAP INSERTED INTO THE DETONATOR WELL.

(b) When the handle of the firing device is actuated, a lamp in the window of the test set will flash. This flash indicates that the blasting cap circuitry is satisfactory. If there is no flash, replace the blasting cap and retest.

(c) Immediately after the circuit test, the firing device is disconnected from the firing wire and the shorting plug dust cover is connected to the firing wire. The operator returns to the mine WITH THE FIRING DEVICE IN HIS POSSESSION and inserts the blasting cap into the detonator well. The operator then rechecks the aim of the mine and returns to his firing position.

(d) If an extended period of time lapses between the circuit test and the insertion of the blasting cap into the detonator well, or if the area is subjected to artillery or mortar fire, another test should be conducted.

> ✍ **NOTE**
>
> If time available precludes the conduct of a circuit test with the blasting cap removed from the mine, then an abbreviated test may be conducted with the blasting cap inserted into the detonator well. If an abbreviated test is conducted, all personnel must be under cover at least 250 meters away from the front and sides of the mine and 100 meters to the rear of the mine.

16. DISARMING AND DESTRUCTION

a. **Disarming a Mine with an Electrical Firing System.**

(1) Prior to disarming the mine, the firing device safety bail must be in the SAFE position.

(2) Disconnect the firing wire from the firing device. Replace the combination shorting plug dust cover on the firing wire connector and the dust cover on the firing device connector.

(3) Unscrew and remove the shipping plug priming-adapter containing the blasting cap from the mine. Remove the blasting cap and firing wire from the shipping plug priming-adapter. Reverse the shipping plug priming-adapter, and screw the plug end of the adapter into the detonator well.

(4) Remove the firing wire from the stake. Reroll the blasting cap and firing wire and place it in its cardboard container.

(5) Remove the mine from its emplacement. Repack the mine and its accessories into their respective pockets in the bandoleer.

b. **Disarming a Mine with a Nonelectrical Firing System.**

(1) Prior to performing (2) through (6) below, render the firing device safe by replacing all safety pins.

(2) Disconnect the pull wire or tripwire from the nonelectric firing device.

(3) Remove the detonating cord and blasting cap from the detonator well.

(4) Using crimpers, cut the blasting cap free of the detonating cord. Nonelectric blasting caps and detonating cord crimped together can be separated only by cutting the blasting cap free of the detonating cord.

(5) Replace the shipping plug priming-adapter and screw it into the detonator well, plug end down.

(6) Remove the mine from its emplaced position and repack. Store accessory items in appropriate containers.

c. **Destruction of Mine to Prevent Enemy Use.** CLAYMORES can be most quickly destroyed by detonation or burning.

CHAPTER 3

Tactical Employment

17. GENERAL

The M18A1 mine is primarily a defensive weapon. It may be employed to a limited extent in certain phases of offensive operations. The M18A1 has the same basic capabilities as antipersonnel mines and can be used in most situations where other types of antipersonnel mines are employed. In addition, the M18A1 has the capability of being sighted directionally to provide fragmentation over a specific area and does not necessarily rely upon chance detonation by the enemy. The M18A1 is adaptable for covering the ranges between maximum hand grenade throwing distance and the minimum safe distance of mortar and artillery supporting fires.

18. DEFENSE

a. **General.** The M18A1 normally is employed in the controlled role as an antipersonnel mine. When used in conjunction with other types of antipersonnel and antitank mines, the employment of the M18A1 will be governed by the procedures described in FM 20-32.

b. **Minefields.**

(1) Ease of transportation, installation, and removal facilitates the use of the M18A1 in protective, defensive, and nuisance minefield.

(2) The M18A1, with its controlled dispersion pattern, is designed to cover areas where enemy personnel attacks in force are anticipated. They may be located singly, or in multiples (fig. 8).

(3) CLAYMORES may be mixed with antipersonnel and antitank mines in conjunction with nuisance minefield and arranged for detonation by tripwire.

(4) The M18A1 can supplement other mines within a protective minefield, and can be installed and employed in either the controlled or uncontrolled roles. The configuration and composition of the minefield pattern varies with the terrain and tactical situation.

(5) The M18A1 can be used to cover portions of defensive minefield by emplacing it on the minefield perimeter, or within the field to cover lanes between mines. The controlled method of employment is desirable. Care should be taken to insure that the mine is properly aimed to provide fragmentation effect over and not into the minefield. This can be accomplished by securing the mine to trees or other elevated objects which are at least 2 meters above ground level.

c. **Find Protective Fires.** The M18A1 can be employed to fill the dead space of the final protective fires of automatic weapons in defensive positions. Depending on the importance of the area being protected, CLAYMORE mines may be emplaced behind each other in relatively close proximity. To avoid the risk of sympathetic detonation, mines should be placed no closer than 5 meters apart. Normally, mines closest to the enemy will be detonated first. If the enemy continues to approach a defender's position, he will successively detonate rearward mines as he comes within their range. In determining positions for emplacing CLAYMORE mines, consideration must be given to the effects of back blast on friendly positions.

d. **Security of Outposts.** CLAYMORE mines are easily transported and rapidly emplaced for security of outposts. The mines can be installed for complete perimeter coverage of a position. Time permitting, several rows can be employed. The mine can also be emplaced to assist in covering withdrawals from outposts.

e. **Defense of Command, Combat Support, Combat Service Support Installations, and Reserve Forces.**

(1) CLAYMORE mines can be utilized to assist in the local security of command posts and support installations; and they can be carried in vehicles located within these areas. In addition to providing local protection for these installations, the mines also provide protection for the vehicles.

(2) CLAYMORE mines so emplaced should be employed in the electrically controlled role as a protective measure against inflicting casualties on friendly personnel.

(3) It is necessary to mark, record, and report all such positions as described in FM 20-32. The shorting plug dust cover must be attached to the firing wire and the firing device should not be attached until actual firing, particularly in rear areas where friendly personnel move about extensively.

(4) Reserve forces in blocking positions or assembly areas can use CLAYMORES to augment their local security forces.

f. **Local Security of Halted Columns.** CLAYMORES may be carried on tanks and other types of vehicles and emplaced for perimeter defense of such vehicles when they are halted. As soon as they are halted, personnel will emplace the CLAYMORES for close-in protection of the vehicles. Controlled electrical firing should be employed for simplicity, speed, and safety.

g. **Roadblocks and Obstacles.**

(1) In conjunction with roadblocks, CLAYMORES should have a clear field of fire to cover the avenue of approach. Additional CLAYMORES should be placed on the friendly side of a roadblock. When used to cover obstacles, the CLAYMORE should be placed 20 to 30 meters on the friendly side of the obstacle. This distance also applies to barbed wire obstacles.

(2) Controlled detonation is most desirable, since the firer can best judge the exact moment of detonation. However, uncontrolled detonation may be employed allowing the enemy to activate the mine when he attempts to breach the obstacle (para 10).

h. **Boobytraps.** Using standard firing devices, CLAYMORE mines can be employed as boobytraps (para 13). Concealment of the mine and a positive detonation system is essential. The mine must be emplaced and sighted to cover the desired area. In order to allow for the full effects of the dispersion pattern of the mine, it is best to locate it away from the boobytrap actuation device. The mine is adaptable to many varied situations of boobytrapping, limited only by the ingenuity of the individual emplacing the mine. Authority to emplace boobytraps requires approval by the field army commander.

i. **Retrograde Operations.**

(1) During a *delay* while on position, CLAYMORES will be employed in the same manner as they are when employed in the defense. During movement between positions, CLAYMORES will be employed in the same manner as a withdrawal.

(2) During a *night-type withdrawal*, which is conducted without enemy pressure, CLAYMORES may be emplaced for use by the detachments left in contact, using both controlled and uncontrolled methods of employment. CLAYMORES may be used to assist in covering the gaps left by the main force. They may be used singly or in conjunction with other mines to mine routes of withdrawal.

(3) If used, the rear guard can also employ M18Al's using the uncontrolled means of firing to assist in covering its withdrawal to the rear. Utilization of the M18A1 in this manner provides added security for the detachments left in contact, or the rear guard, and can delay the enemy's advance. However, since the M18A1 is employed in the uncontrolled role, it must be reported and recorded as a mine.

(4) If a covering force is used during a *daylight-type withdrawal*, CLAYMORES can be employed by the covering force in a manner similar to that used in any blocking position and also employed using the same techniques as used during a night-type withdrawal.

19. OFFENSE

a. **General.** The M18A1 can be employed in certain phases of offensive combat, and provisions for its use should be considered in planning offensive operations. The mine easily can be transported by attacking troops for defense of assembly areas, to provide security during the conduct of the attack, and for protection during the reorganization and consolidation of the objective. The M18A1 also provides an economical means for establishing effective ambushes.

b. **Offensive Combat.**

(1) ***Preparation for the attack.*** When a unit is approaching the enemy and occupies an assembly area prior to an attack, it is particularly vulnerable to surprise enemy attacks. CLAYMORE mines can be quickly emplaced around the perimeter of the assembly area to cover the unit during its preparation for the attack.

(2) ***Conduct of the attack.*** During the conduct of the attack, CLAYMORES can be employed by the flank security forces. The ease of employment and disarmament of the M18A1 facilitates its use in this manner.

(3) ***Reorganization and consolidation.*** During the conduct of the attack, assaulting troops may carry CLAYMORES for employment during reorganization and consolidation. After a unit has overrun an enemy position and pursued him by fire, it must immediately begin consolidation of the objective. The prompt emplacement of CLAYMORES will provide the base for an immediate defense against possible counterattack, while leaders reorganize their units and prepare to continue the attack. When the final objective is captured, mines should be immediately emplaced. The emplaced CLAYMORES can be integrated into the defensive plans as they are developed.

(4) ***Defense of supporting elements during the attack.***

(a) CLAYMORE mines can be utilized in command posts or in the defense of supporting units, such as mortar and artillery batteries. Immediately after displacement, and as the first echelon of these supporting units moves into new positions, adequate defense measures will be established. CLAYMORES should be emplaced initially to cover likely avenues of enemy approach; eventually, they should be integrated with the fully developed defensive position. When displacements occur, the mines will be disarmed, collected, and moved to the next position. If the area is to be occupied by other units, the mines may be left in position by mutual arrangement with the relieving unit.

(b) When CLAYMORE mines are employed in the defense of command posts, supporting unit installations, or reserve forces in the rear of the battle positions, they must be well-marked and personnel should be familiarized with their location.

c. **Ambush.** CLAYMORE mines provide an excellent, economical means for establishing effective ambushes deep in enemy territory with a minimum use of friendly personnel. Small groups can easily transport a large number of CLAYMORES; for example, one man can carry six CLAYMORES, enough to cover a frontage up to 300 meters. CLAYMORES may be employed in any or all of the following ways:

(1) ***Laterally along the killing zone of the ambush, between the ambush element and the killing zone.*** This method inflicts maximum damage on dismounted troops and is particularly useful in countering enemy immediate action drills that include assault into the ambush element.

(2) ***At the front and rear of the killing zone*** (fig. 19). This method provides enfilade fire into the killing zones, greater economy of employment, and is particularly useful when the route through the killing zone is restricted in width. It also provides a good counter in enemy immediate action drills that include withdrawal or forward movement out of the killing zone along the original route.

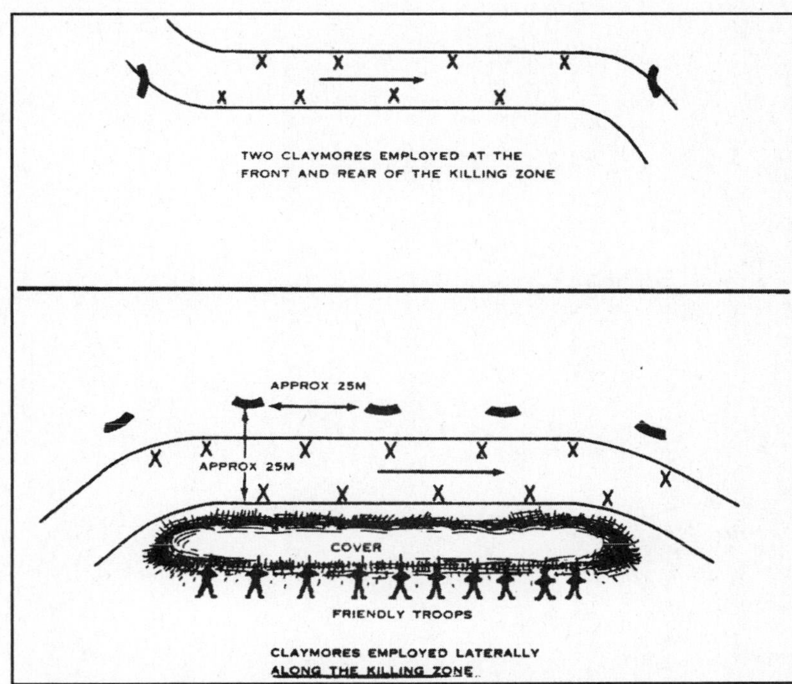

Figure 19: CLAYMORES employed in ambush.

(3) ***Laterally or at the front and rear of the killing zone, on the far side of the killing zone from the ambush element*** (fig. 19). This method of employment is particularly effective in countering enemy immediate action drills that include maneuver or withdrawal out of the killing zone by moving away from the ambush element. Care must be taken to insure the ambush element is protected from the fragmentation of the M18A1.

(4) ***Defiles.*** CLAYMORES are particularly effective in covering areas that might afford the enemy cover from small-arms fire, such as defiles. CLAYMORES used in ambushes may be emplaced on the ground, in trees, or on other upright objects which insure a clear, unobstructed, sighted field of fire. Controlled detonation is desirable, since this permits the firing to be delayed until that portion of the enemy which the commander desires to catch in the ambush is in the killing zone. Mines should be carefully camouflaged to prevent their detection.

CHAPTER 4

Safety

20. GENERAL

This chapter covers the safety precautions to be observed when firing the M18A1 antipersonnel mines for training purposes. These safety precautions will assist the instructor in conducting CLAYMORE training. They are intended as a guide only and must be used in conjunction with appropriate safety measures prescribed in Army and/or local installation regulations.

21. SAFETY PRECAUTIONS

a. Before firing, the *officer in charge* (OIC) will check all mines to insure that—
   (1) Mines are installed correctly.
   (2) The fragmentation face of the mine is pointed into the impact area and away from friendly troops.
b. CLAYMORES will be installed only on command of the OIC.
c. All mines will be kept under guard until the OIC directs their issue.
d. Once a mine has been emplaced for firing it will not be disarmed, except by order of the OIC.
e. The firing wire will not be connected to the firing device until ordered by the OIC.
f. When more than one mine is to be fired, the OIC will insure that a previous firing has not dislodged other mines in the impact area.
g. No one will enter the impact area without the approval of the OIC.
h. After firing, the impact area will be inspected to insure that all mines have detonated.

22. OPERATIONAL SAFETY FACTORS

a. An individual installing a mine will carry the firing device on his person.
b. Mines must be installed in a manner that will prevent them from becoming disoriented.
c. Blasting caps will not be inserted into the detonator wells until the mine has been emplaced in its firing position and aimed.
d. The safety bail on the firing device must be in the SAFE position after the completion of the firing circuit test.
e. The shunt will not be removed from the firing wire of the Ml8 until the operator is ready to connect it to the firing device. Before installing batteries and firing, leads can be shunted by attaching both leads to the clip on the battery holder.
f. Firing wire leads of the M18 mines that are tactically employed must be twisted together and taped at two or more equidistant places.

23. MISFIRES

a. **Electrical Firing System.** A misfire of an electrically employed M18A1 must be investigated immediately. If the mine is dual-primed with both electric and nonelectric caps, it will then be necessary to wait 30 minutes before investigating the cause of the misfire. When handling electrical misfires, the following steps will be taken:
   (1) Shout MISFIRE (nontactical).
   (2) Check the firing device connection to the firing wire connector; make two attempts to fire the mine.
   (3) Using the M40 test set, check the continuity of the electric firing circuit.

> ✍ **NOTE**
> Only one man at a time will investigate the cause of an electric misfire.

b. **Nonelectrical Firing System.** If the non electric blasting cap initiator attached to the detonating cord fails to function, delay investigation for at least 30 minutes. Then cut the detonating cord between the firing device and the mine and fasten a new firing device to the detonating cord. If the detonating cord leading to the mine detonates, but the mine fails to detonate, delay investigation until it is certain that the mine is not burning. If the mine is not damaged, insert a new blasting cap with detonating cord. In training, if the mine appears to be damaged, it should be treated as a dud and destroyed.

24. SURFACE DANGER AREA FOR THE CLAYMORE ANTIPERSONNEL MINE

a. When employing the antipersonnel mines, careful consideration must be given to the safety of friendly troops. Emphasis must be placed on the danger areas to the rear and sides of the mine, as well as the killing zone to the front. Care must be exercised when installing mines to prevent the creation of secondary missile hazards.

b. No personnel will be allowed within 16 meters of the rear of the mine. Personnel from 16 to 100 meters in a 180° arc to the rear of the mine will be in a covered position, lying prone in a depression, or behind some form of protection.

c. When a mine is installed on a tree or some other object, the secondary missile hazard cannot be eliminated. When mines are used in this manner, friendly troops in a 16- to 100-meter radius in a 180° arc must be in a covered position.

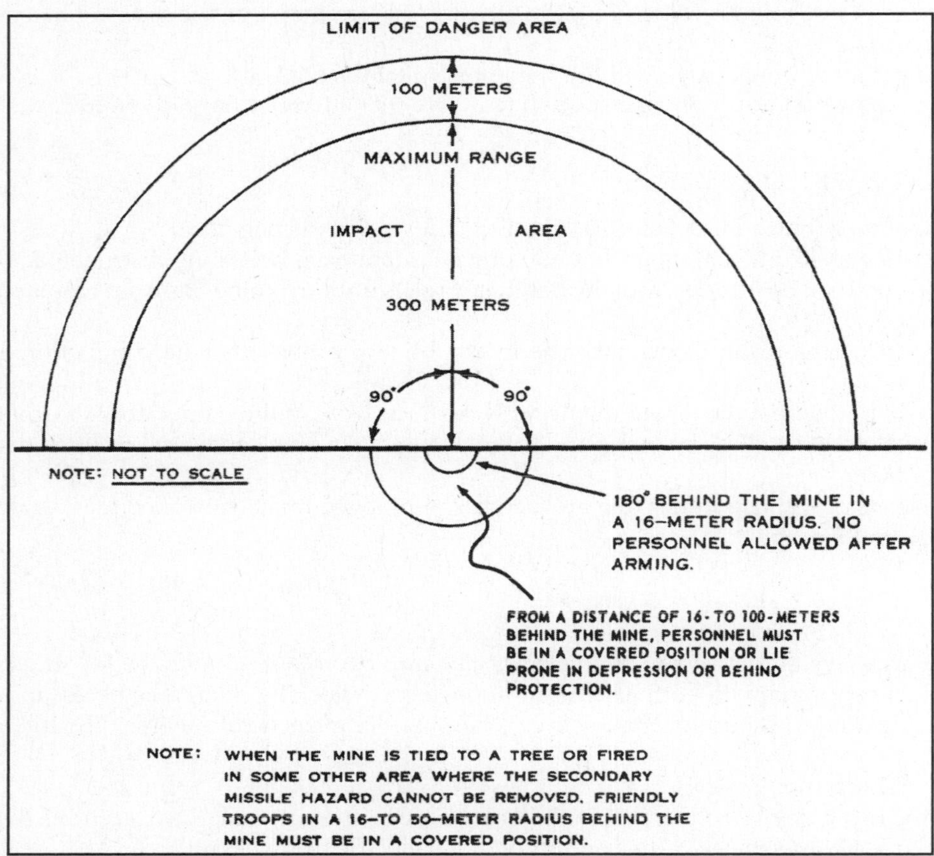

Figure 20: Surface danger area for CLAYMORE.

Boobytraps

CHAPTER 1

Characteristics of Boobytraps

SECTION I. INTRODUCTION

1. PURPOSE AND SCOPE

a. This manual contains procedures, techniques, and expedients for the instruction of the soldier in the assembly, use, detection, and removal of boobytraps in combat.
b. Included are descriptions and discussions of the design and functioning characteristics of standard demolition items—firing devices, explosives, and accessories—and missiles, such as hand grenades, mortar ammunition, artillery ammunition, and bombs.
c. This manual also contains information on a variety of items and indigenous materials useful for improvising firing devices, explosives, and pyrotechnic mixtures for guerrilla warfare applications.
d. Factory-produced boobytraps (dirty trick devices) are described. Most of these have been developed and used in the field by foreign armies.
e. Safety measures pertinent to boobytrapping operations are provided for the protection of troops from casualty.
f. The contents of this manual are applicable to nuclear and nonnuclear warfare.

2. COMMENTS

Users of this manual are encouraged to forward comments or recommendations for changes for improvement. Comments should be referenced to the page, paragraph, and line of text. The reason for each comment should be given to insure proper interpretation and evaluation. Forward all comments directly to the Commandant, U.S. Army Engineer School, Fort Belvoir, Virginia 22060.

SECTION II. PRINCIPLES OF OPERATION

3. TYPES OF BOOBYTRAPS

A boobytrap is an explosive charge cunningly contrived to be fired by an unsuspecting person who disturbs an apparently harmless object or performs a presumably safe act. Two types are in use—improvised and manufactured. Improvised boobytraps are assembled from specially provided material or constructed from materials generally used for other purposes. Manfactured boobytraps are dirty trick devices made at a factory for issue to troops. They usually imitate some object or article that has souvenir appeal or that may be used by the target to advantage.

4. ASSEMBLING BOOBYTRAPS

A boobytrap consists of a main charge, firing device, standard base (not always used), and detonator. Another item, the universal destructor, is an adapter for installing a firing device assembly in a loaded projectile or bomb to make an improvised boobytrap. Also, firing device assemblies are often attached to the main charge by means of a length of detonating cord.

5. BOOBYTRAP FIRING CHAIN

The firing chain is a series of initiations beginning with a small quantity of highly sensitive explosive and ending with a comparatively large quantity of insensitive explosive.

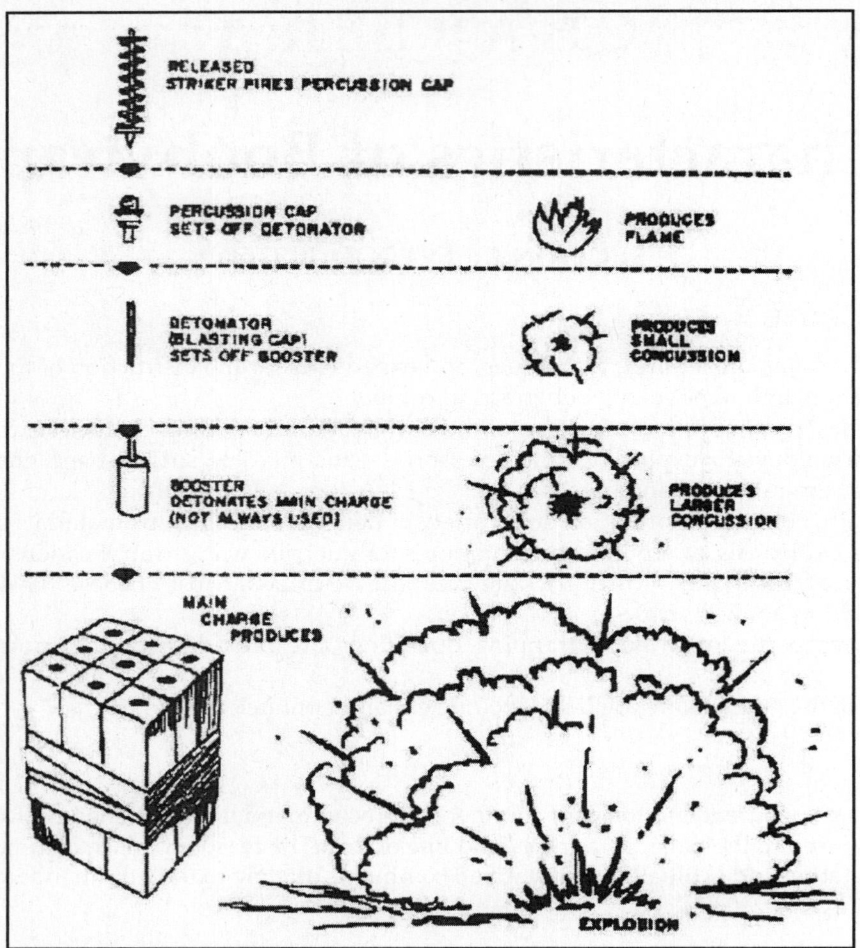

6. INITIATING ACTIONS

The initiating action starts the series of explosions in the boobytrap firing chain.

a. Pressure: Weight of foot starts explosive action.

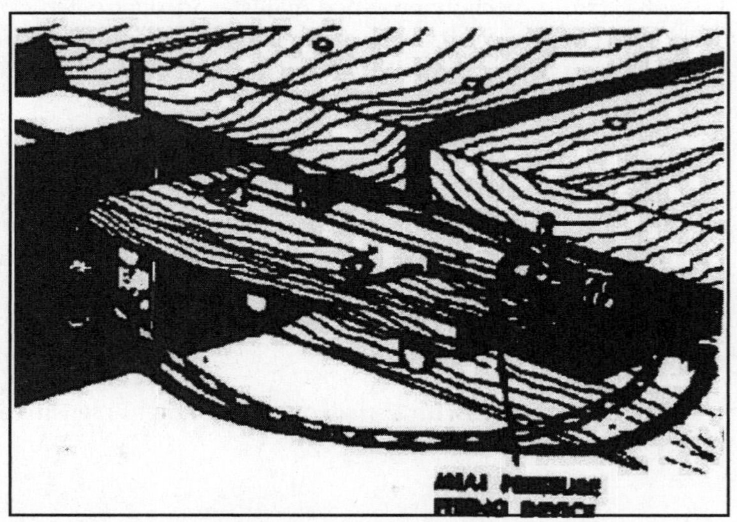

b. Pull: Lifting the souvenir starts explosive action.
c. Pressure-release: Moving the stone starts explosive action.

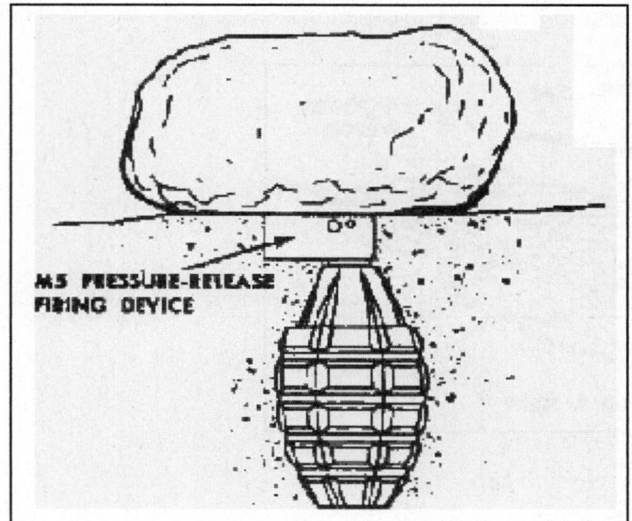

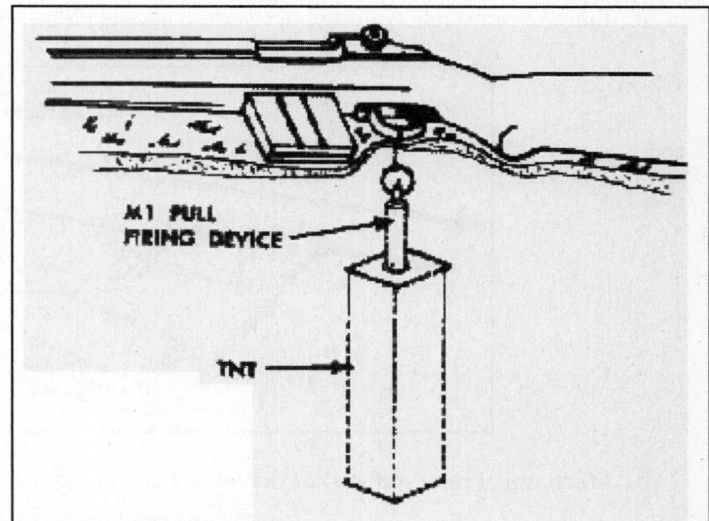

d. Tension-release: Raising lower sash starts explosive action.

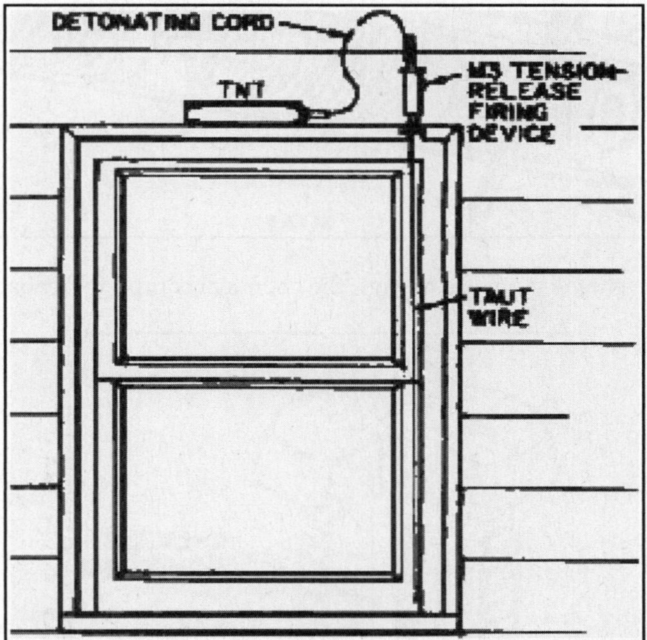

7. FIRING DEVICE INTERNAL ACTIONS

A firing device when actuated may function internally in many ways to initiate the firing chain.

a. Electric removal of wedge between contacts closes circuit and fires electric cap.

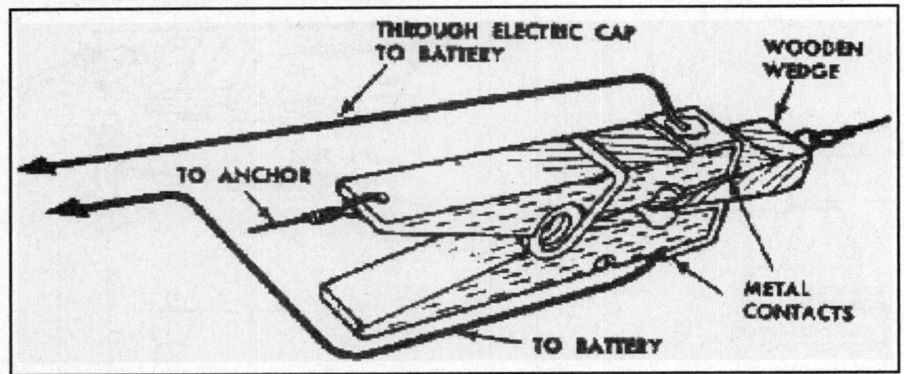

b. Mechanical released striker driven by its spring, fires percussion cap.

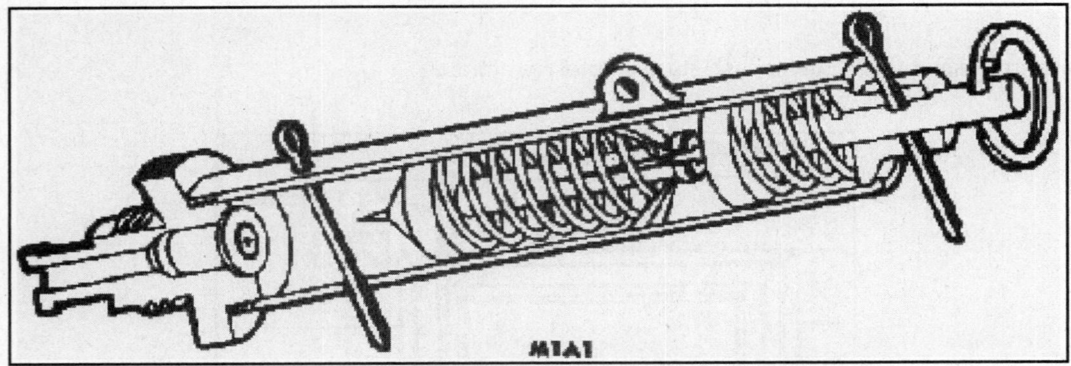

c. Pull-friction pulling the chemical pellet through the chemical compound causes flash that fires the detonator.

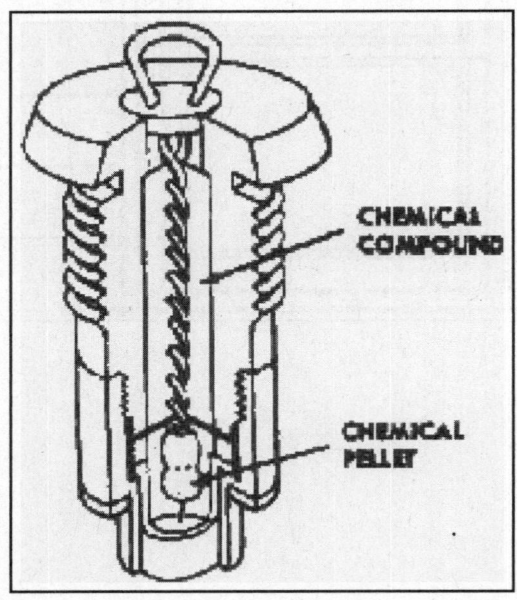

d. Pressure-friction pressure on top of the striker forces its cone-shaped end into the phosphorus and glass mixture in the mating sleeve, causing a flash that fires the detonator.

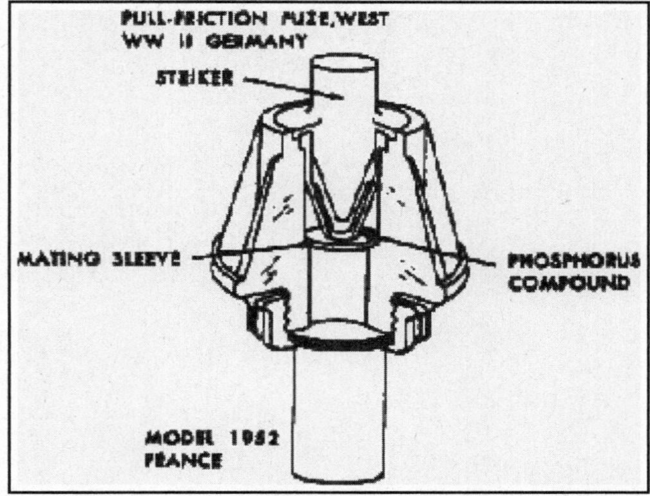

e. Chemical
   (1) Pressure pressure on the top breaks the vial, the sulphuric acid to mix with the flash powder, producing a flams that fires the detonator.
   (2) Delay causing the ampule releases the chemical to corrode the retaining wire, freeing the striker to fire the detonator, the delay is determined by the time needed for the chemical to corrode the retaining wire.

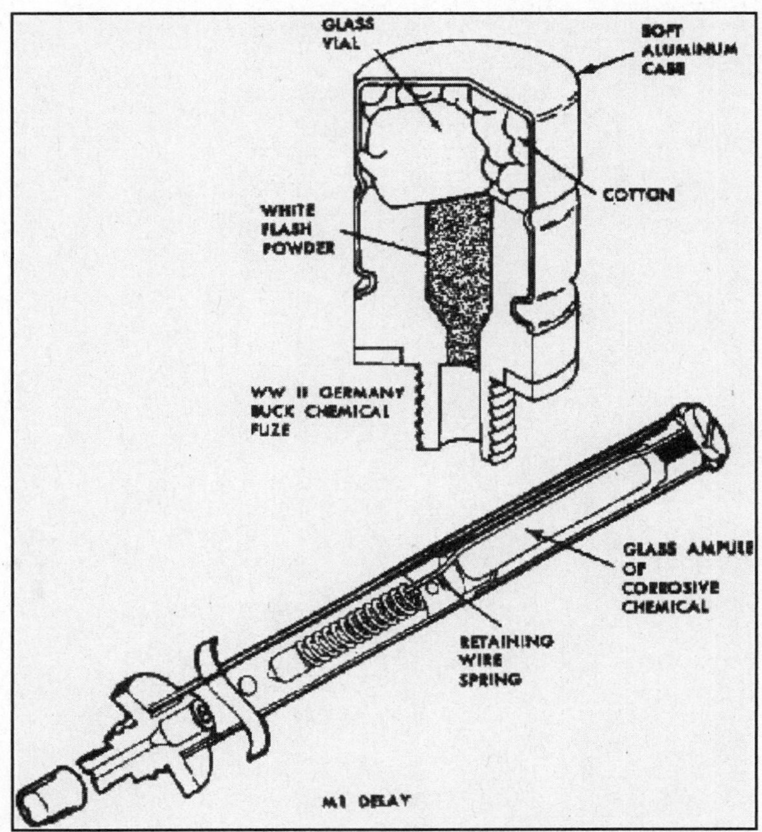

CHAPTER 2

Use of Boobytraps

SECTION I. BASIC DOCTRINE

8. TACTICAL PRINCIPLES

Boobytraps supplement minefields by increasing their obstacle value. They add to the confusion of the enemy, inflict casualties, destroy material, and lower morale. Boobytraps are usually laid by specialists. All military personnel, however, are trained in handling explosives and other boobytrapping material, so that they may, if necessary, boobytrap a mine or install a simple boobytrap.

9. AUTHORITY

a. Army commanders issue special instructions for the use of boobytraps within their command. Supplies are authorized and provided as required to meet boobytrapping needs.
b. Army and higher commanders may delegate authority to lay boobytraps to as low as division commanders. All higher commanders, however, may revoke this authority for a definite or indefinite period, as the tactical situation may require.
c. Records of all boobytraps laid are prepared and forwarded to higher headquarters.
d. Enemy boobytraped areas, as soon as discovered, are reported to higher headquarters to keep all interested troops advised of enemy activities. If possible, all boobytraps are neutralized; otherwise they are properly marked by warning signs.

SECTION II. PLANNING

10. TACTICAL EFFECTS

a. The ingenious use of local resources and standard items is important in making effective boobytraps. They must be simple in construction, readily disguised, and deadly. They may produce unexpected results if conceived in sly cunning and built in various forms. Boobytraps cause uncertainty and suspicion in the mind of the enemy. They may surprise him, frustrate his plans, and inspire in his soldiers a fear of the unknown.
b. In withdrawal, boobytraps may be used in much the same way as nuisance mines. Buildings and other forms of shelter, roads, paths, diversions around obstacles, road blocks, bridges, fords, and similar areas are suitable locations for concealing boobytraps.
c. In defense, boobytraps, placed in the path of the enemy at strategic locations in sufficient numbers, may impede his programs, prevent detailed reconnaissance, and delay disarming and removal of minefields.

11. BASIC PRINCIPLES

Certain basic principles, as old as warfare itself, must be followed to get the optimum benefit from boobytraps. Knowledge of these principles will aid the soldier, not only in placing boobytraps expertly, but in detecting and avoiding those of the enemy.

a. Appearances: Concealment is mandatory to success. All litter and other evidences of boobytraping must be removed.
b. Firing: An obvious firing assembly may distract attention from a cunningly hidden one.
c. Likely Areas: Defiles or other constructed areas are excellent locations.

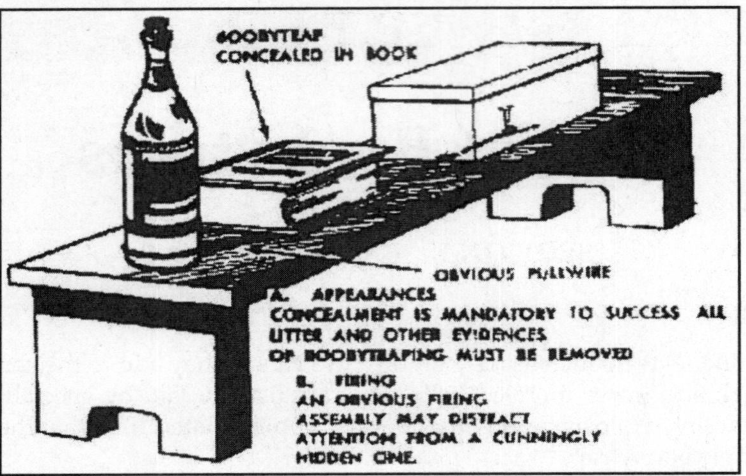

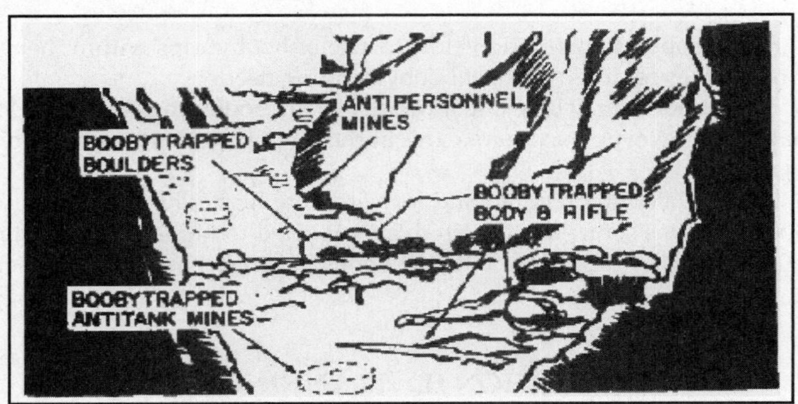

d. Obstacles: Road blocks, fallen trees, litter, etc, are ideal locations.

e. Gathering Places: In buildings, at building entrances, and in similar places where soldiers may move or gather, delay charges pay off.

f. Appeal to Curiosity: Boobytraps laid in bold positions to dare the curious get results.
g. Bluff: Dummy boobytraps, consistency repeated, may encourage carelessness an obvious boobytrap may mask another and perhaps a more deadly one.

h. Lures: Boobytraps may be raited. The unexpected detonation of a delay action incendiary or explosive boobytrap may scatter troops or detour them into a more heavily laid area.

12. LOCATION OF CHARGES

a. **Preparation.** Small compact boobytraps are the most desirable for use in raids in enemy-held territory. Each member of a team must carry his own supplies and be able to operate independently. Boobytraps should be assembled, except for the attachment of the firing device, before entering enemy territory. This will reduce the work at the site to the minimum.

b. **Location.** Charges should be placed when they will do the most damage. A charge detonated against a stone wall will expend its force in magnified intensity away from the wall. The force of an explosion on the ground will affect the surrounding air more if the charge is placed on a hard surface. This deflects the explosive wave upward. A charge detonating 6 to 10 feet above the ground will damage a larger area than one laid on or below the surface.

c. **Characteristics.** Many inexpensive boobytraps, simple to make and easy to lay, will delay and confuse the enemy more than a small number of the expensive and complex kind. Complex mechanisms cost more, require more care in laying, and offer little more advantage than the simple type.

13. RECONNAISSANCE

Complete reconnaissance of an area is essential to good planning. Without this and the preparation of a program, boobytraps may not be used effectively. Boobytrap teams are best suited to survey a combat area to determine its boobytrapping possibilities.

14. PLAN OF OPERATION

a. The commander with authority to use boobytraps coordinates his plans with other tactical plans. Timing of boobytrap operations with movement plans is extremely essential. Boobytraps should not be laid in areas where friendly troops will remain for any appreciable length of time. Plans will indicate what is to be done, where and when it will be done, and the troops to be used. Generally, trained troops are assigned such tasks.

b. The plan authorizes the use of boobytraps and the types and densities required in specified areas, depending on the terrain, time, personnel, and material available. The completion of the detailed plan is delegated to the commander responsible for installation. Materials are obtained from unit supply stocks on the basis of the proposed action.

c. Complete coordination between the troop commandar and the officer supervising boobytrap activities is essential. The area should be evacuated immediately following the completion of the job.

d. The commander installing boobytraps prepares a detailed plan indicating the site and the location, number, type, and setting. He assigns boobytrap teams to specific areas and the laying of specified types. The plan covers arrangements for supplies and transportation and designates the location where all preliminary work on boobytraps will be done. Time tables are established to insure completion of the work to comply with withdrawal phases of tactical plane.

e. In hasty withdrawal, when there is no time for planning, each team will be given a supply of material with instructions for making the best possible use of it in the time allowed.

f. Boobytrap planning must give proper consideration to all known characteristics of the enemy. Members of teams should study the personal habits of enemy soldiers, constantly devising new methods to surprise them. Repetitions may soon become a pattern easily detected by an alert enemy.

g. Withdrawal operations are the most desirable of all for laying boobytraps. When an enemy meets a boobytrap at the first obstacle, his progress throughout the area will be delayed even though no others have been laid. A few deadly boobytraps and many dummies, laid indiscriminately, can inspire great caution. Dummies, however, should be unserviceable or useless items. Never throw away material that may return to plague friendly forces!

SECTION III. INSTALLATION

15. RESPONSIBILITIES

a. A commander authorized to use boobytraps is responsible for all within his zone of command. He will keep adequate records showing their type, number, and location, and prepare information on those laid and on practices followed by the enemy.
b. Management of boobytrap services may be delegated to the engineer staff officer.
c. Unit commanders must know the location of all boobytraps is their areas and keep all subordinates so advised. Subordinates are also responsible for reporting to higher headquarters all new information obtained on enemy boobytraps.
d. Officers responsible for laying boobytraps prepare plans, supervise preliminary preparations, and direct their installation. They forward to proper authority a detailed report of their progress, advise all concerned when changes are made, and report to engineer intelligence units the discovery of any new enemy devices or low-cunning practices.
e. Engineer and infantry units, with special training, have the responsibility of installing and neutralizing boobytraps. Since adequate numbers of trainees may not always be available, all troops are given familiarity instruction in boobytrapping.

16. PROCEDURES

Like all activities involving explosives, boobytrapping is dangerous only because of mistakes men make. Prescribed methods must be followed explicitly in the interest of personal safety and overall effectiveness.

a. Before assembling a boobytrap, all components should be inspected for serviceability. They must be complete and in working order. All safeties and triggering devices must be checked to insure proper action, and for rust or dents that might interfere with mechanical action.
b. If a boobytrapping plan is not available, one must be prepared on arrival at the site, so that the material obtained will be required items only. A central control point should be established in each boobytrap area where supplies may be unloaded and from which directions may be given. In areas where many boobytraps are concentrated, safe passage routes from the control point to each location most be marked clearly. Lines of tape may be useful where vegetation is heavy. The control man is the key man.
c. Several teams may operate from one control point. Each team (rarely more than two men) is assigned to a specific area and supplies are issued only as needed. Each detail commander must make certain that every man knows his job and is competent to do it. Teams will remain separated so that one may not suffer from the mistake of another. When a job is completed, all teams must report to the control man before going elsewhere.
d. One person in each team is designated leader to direct all work. If possible, members of a team will avoid working close together when a boobytrap is assembled. One member should do all technical work and the other be a helper to carry supplies, provide assistance needed, and learn the skills needed.
e. Boobytraps laid during raids into enemy held territory should be small, simple, and easily installed. Each member of a party must carry the supplies he needs. The use of boobytraps under these conditions, when accurate records are impossible, may be a hazard to friendly troops if raids into the same area should become necessary.
f. Procedure for installing boobytraps is as fallows:
   (1) Select the site that will produce the optimum effect when the boobytrap is actuated.
   (2) Lay the charge, then protect and conceal it.
   (3) Anchor the boobytrap securely, with nails, wire, rope, or wedges, if necessary.
   (4) Camouflage or conceal, if necessary.
   (5) Teams arm boobytraps systematically, working toward a safe area.
   (6) Leave the boobytrapped area clean. Carry away all items that might betray the work that has been done, such as loose dirt, empty boxes, tape, and broken vegetation. Obliterate footprints.

17. REPORTING, RECORDING, AND MARKING

Boobytraps are reported and recorded for the information of tactical commanders and the protection of friendly troops from casualty. Boobytrap installations are reported and recorded as nuisance minefields, whether the area contains both boobytraps and mines or boobytraps alone.

a. **Reports**

(1) ***Intent.*** This is transmitted by the fastest means available consistent with signal security. It includes the location of the boobytrapped area selected, the number and type of mines to be laid (if antitank mine are boobytrapped), bootstraps to be laid, the estimated starting and completing time, and the tactical purpose. The report is initiated by the commander authorized to lay the field and forwarded to higher headquarters.

(2) ***Initiation of Laying.*** This report is transmitted by the fastest means available consistent with signal security. It contains the location and extent of the field, total number of mines and boobytraps to be laid, and estimated time of completion. The commander of the unit installing the field sends the report to the commander that directed him to lay it.

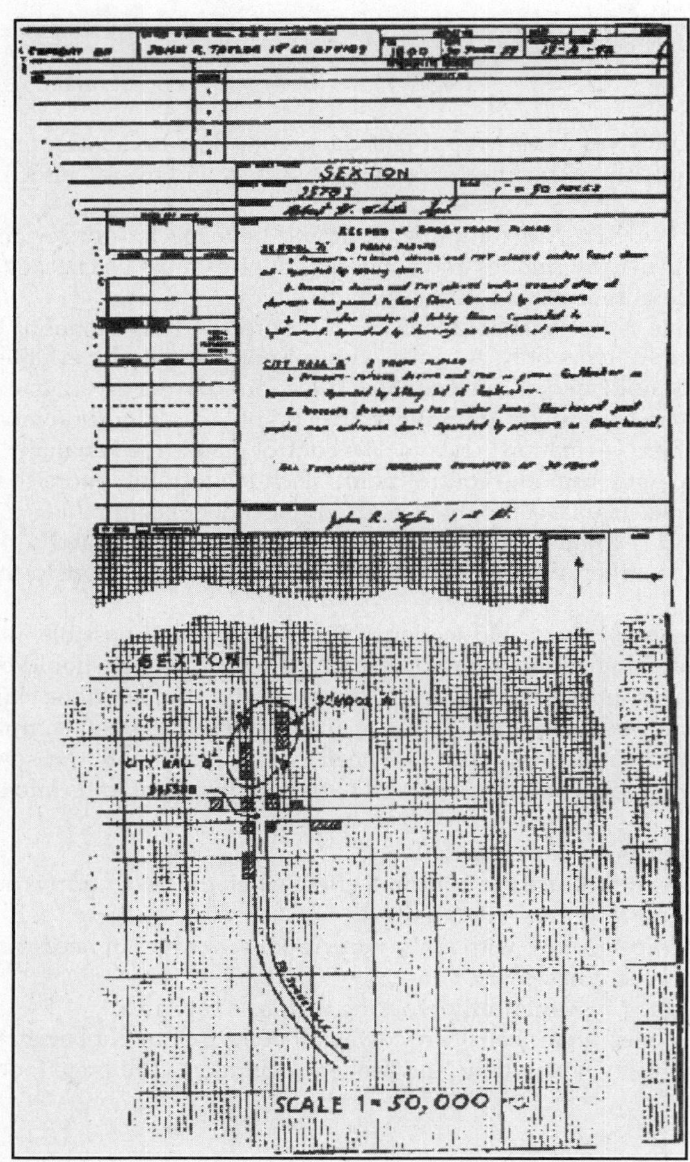

(3) ***Completion.*** The report of completion is transmitted by the fastest possible means. It contains the number and type of boobytraps laid, location and extent of the field or area and the time of completion. The report is forwarded to army level. When boobytraps are laid, either alone or with mines, the report of intent and the report of initiation of laying will include the estimated number of boobytraps to be placed and the report of completion, the number placed.

b. **Records.** Boobytraps are recorded as nuisance mine fields on the standard mine field record form. It is filled in as follows:

(1) The general locations are shown on the sketch, using the appropriate symbol. Boobytrapped areas or buildings are lettered serially, "A" being the nearest to the enemy.

(2) The number, types, locations, and method of operation of boobytraps are entered in the NOTES section of the form. If space in lacking, additional sheets may be attached. If the boobytrap cannot be adequately described in a few short sentences, a sketch of minimum details will be included.

(3) The record is prepared simultaneously with the laying of the boobytrap and forwarded through channels to army level without delay. If a standard form is not available, the data required must be entered and submitted on an expedient form.

(4) Nuisance mine fields containing both mines and boobytraps are recorded as prescribed in FM 20–32. When the specific locations of boobytraps and manufactured devices cannot be accurately recorded (scattered laying in open areas) their number and type are entered in the notes section of the form and identified by grid coordinates.

c. **Marking.** Boobytraps are marked by special triangular signs painted red on both sides. On the side facing away from the danger area, a 3-inch diameter white disc, is centered in the triangle and the word BOOBYTRAPS is painted in white across top in 1-inch letters. The STANAG or new sign is similar except for the 1-inch white stripe below the inscription. Signs may be made of metal, wood, plastic, or similar material. They are placed above ground, right-angled apex downwards, on wire fences, trees, or doors, windows, or other objects or by pushing the apex in the ground. These working signs are used by all troops to identify friendly boobytraps during the period preceding withdrawal from an area, or to warn friendly forces of the presence of active enemy boobytraps.

d. **Abandonment.** When abandoning a boobytrapped area to the enemy, all markers, wire, etc., are removed.

e. **Signs.** Signs are also used to mark enemy boobytraps or boobytrapped areas.

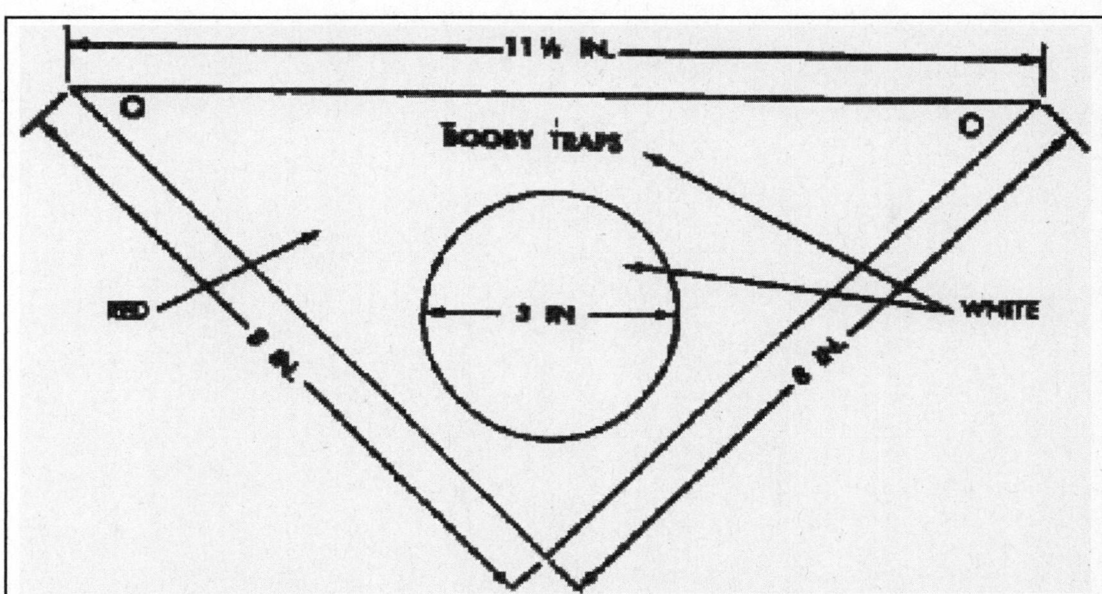

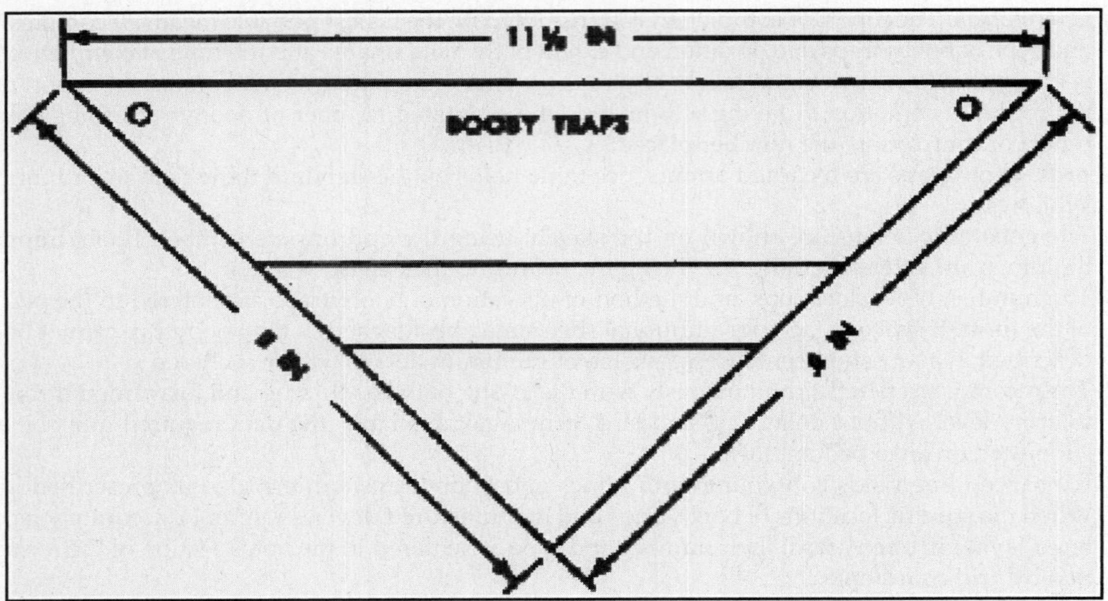
BOOBY TRAPS

CHAPTER 3

Boobytrapping Equipment

SECTION I. FIRING DEVICES

18. INTRODUCTION

Many triggering devices are available for use in boobytraps. They include fuzes, igniters, and firing devices. All U.S. standard firing devices have the following advantages over improvisations: established supply, speed of installation, dependability of functioning, resistance to weather, and safety. All have a standard base coupling by which they may readily be attached to a variety of charges. For more detailed information see TM9-1375-200.

19. M1A1 PRESSURE FIRING DEVICE

a. **Characteristics.**

	Dimensions				
Case	Color	Depth	Length	Internal Action	Initiating Action
Metal	OD	7/8	2 3/8 in	Spring-driven striker with keyhole slot release	20 lbs of pressure or more

Safeties	Accessories	Packaging
Safety clip and positive safety pin	3-pronged pressure head and extension rod	Five units with standard bases packed in cardboard carton. Thirty cartons shipped in wooden box.

b. **Functioning.** A pressure of 20 pounds or more on the pressure cap moves the trigger pin downward until the striker spindle passes through the keyhole slot. This releases the striker to fire the percussion cap.

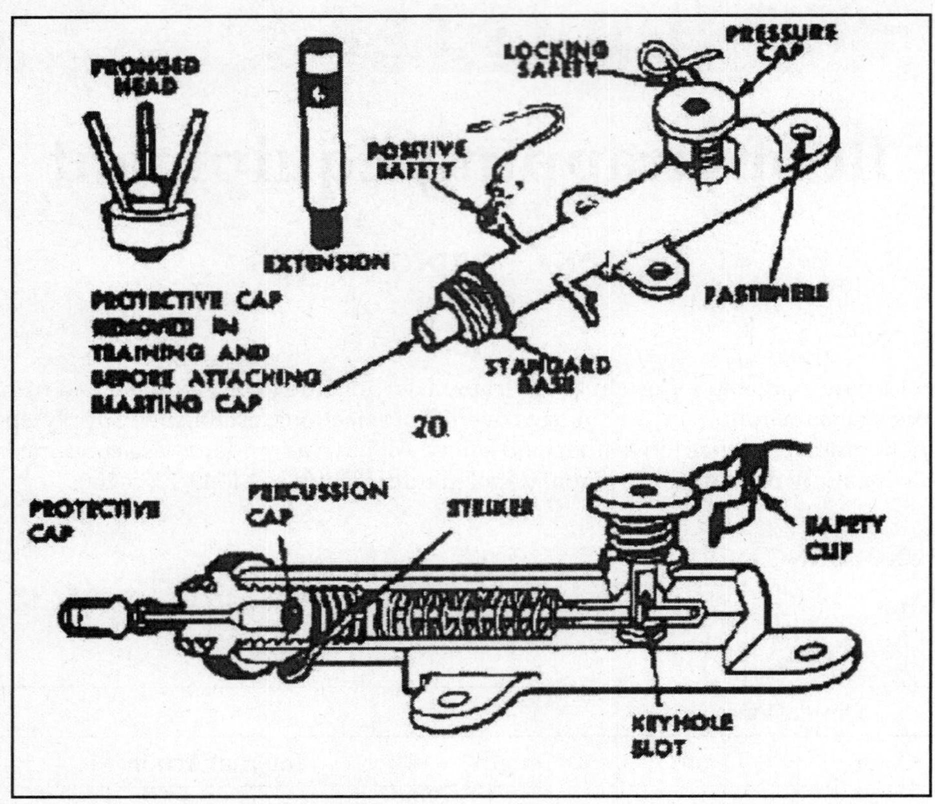

c. **Installing.**

(1) Remove protective cap from base and crimp on a non-electric blasting cap, *Crimper jaws should be placed no further than 1/4 inch from open and of blasting cap.*
(2) Assemble 3-pronged pressure head and extension rod and screw in top of pressure cap, if needed.
(3) Attach firing device assembly to standard base.
(4) Attach firing device assembly to charge.

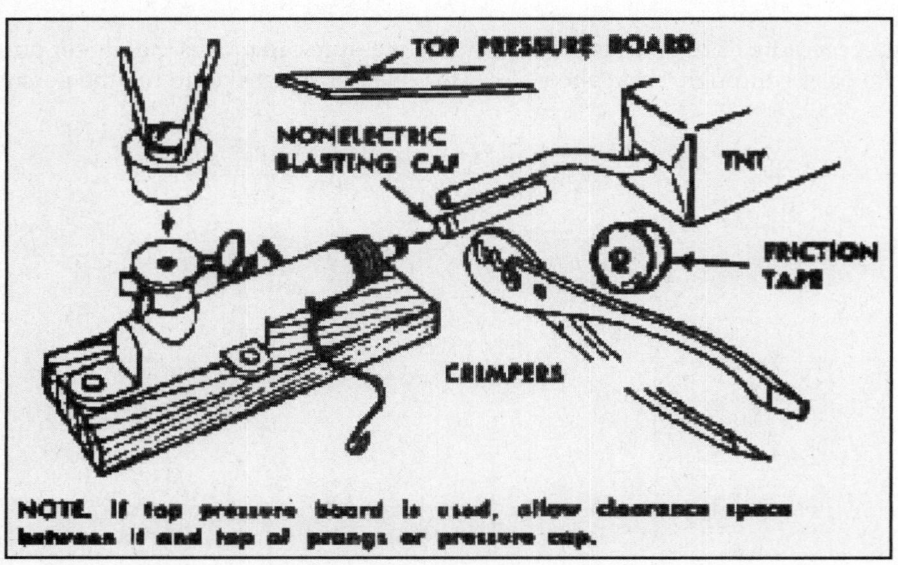

d. **Arming.** Remove safety clip first and *positive pin last*.

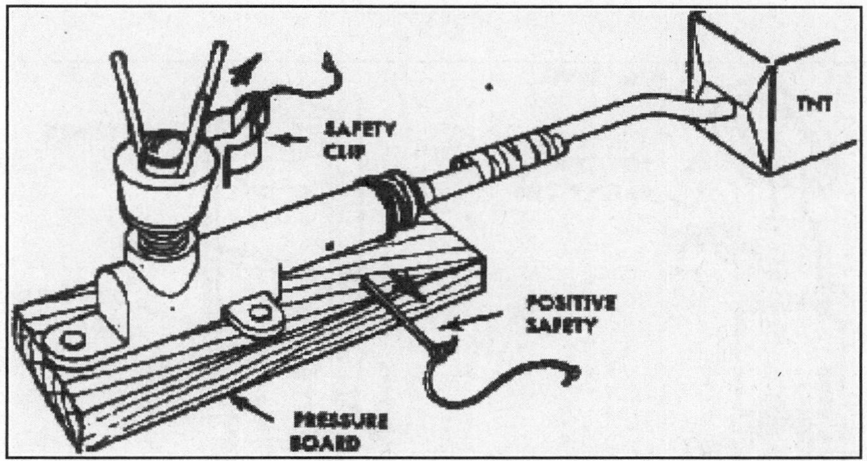

e. **Disarming.**
(1) Insert length of wire, nail, or original pin in positive safety pin hole.
(2) Replace safety clip, if available.
(3) Separate firing device and explosive block.
(4) Unscrew standard bass assembly from firing device.

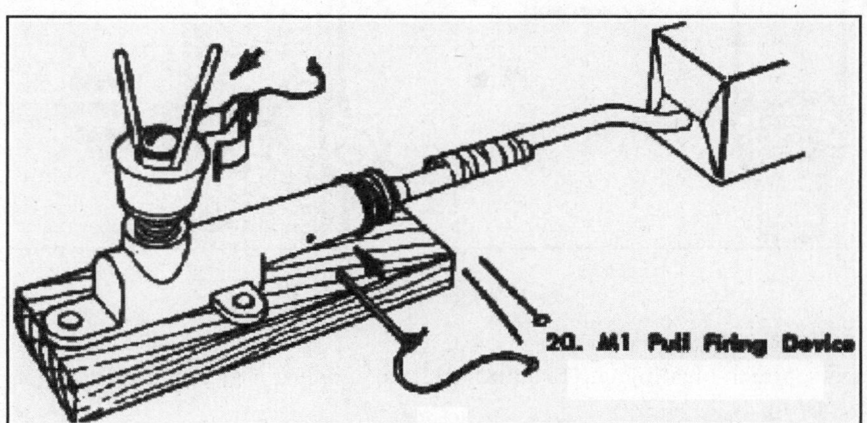

20. M1 PULL FIRING DEVICE

a. **Characteristics.**

	Dimensions				
Case	Color	Depth	Length	Internal Action	Initiating Action
Metal	OD	9/16 in	3 5/16 in	Mechanical with split-head striker release	3–5 lbs of pull on trip wire

Safeties	Packaging
Locking and positive safety pin.	Five units complete with standard bases and two 80-ft spools of trip wire, chipboard container. Thirty packed in wooden box.

b. **Functioning.** A pull of 3 to 5 lb. on trip wire withdraws tapered end of release pin from split head of striker. This frees striker to fire the percussion cap.

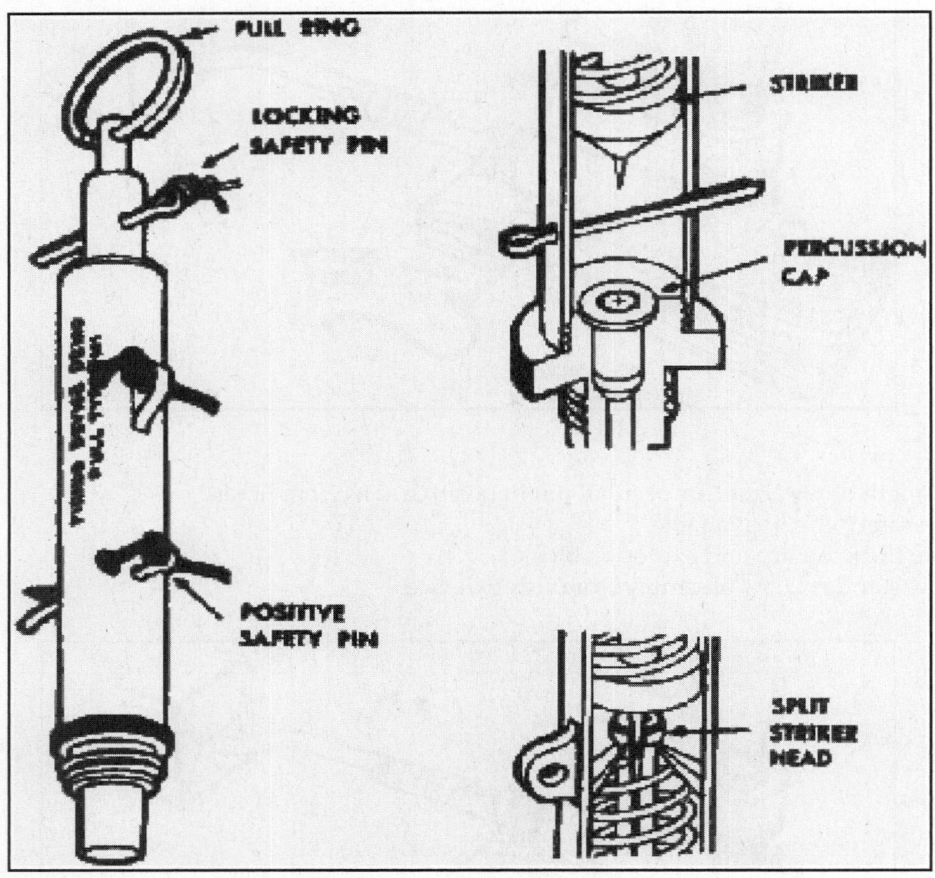

c. **Installing.**
   (1) Remove protective cap.
   (2) With crimpers, attach blasting cap to standard base. *Crimper jaws should be placed no farther than ¼ in. from open end of blasting cap.*
   (3) Attach firing device assembly to charge.

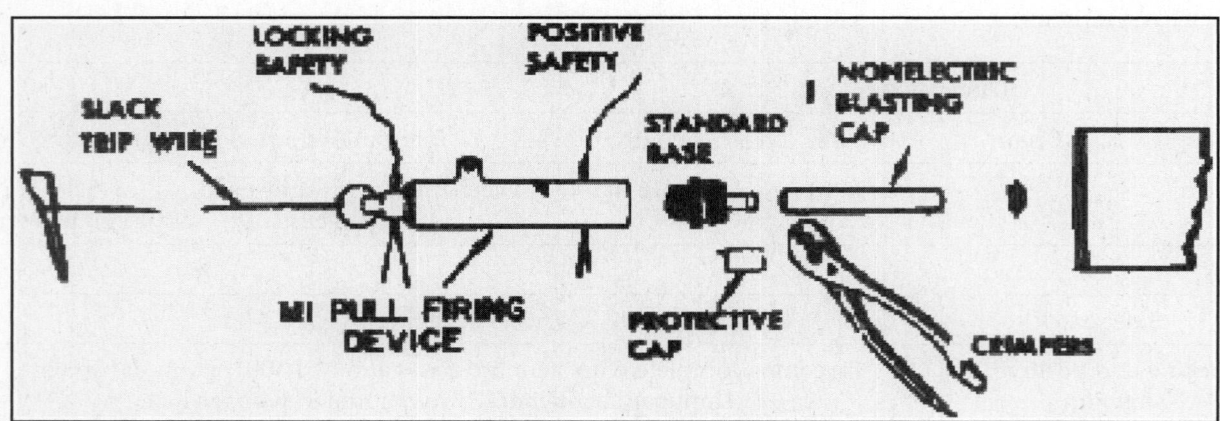

d. **Arming.**
   (1) Anchor trip wire and fasten other and to pull ring.
   (2) Remove locking safety pin first and *positive safety pin last.*

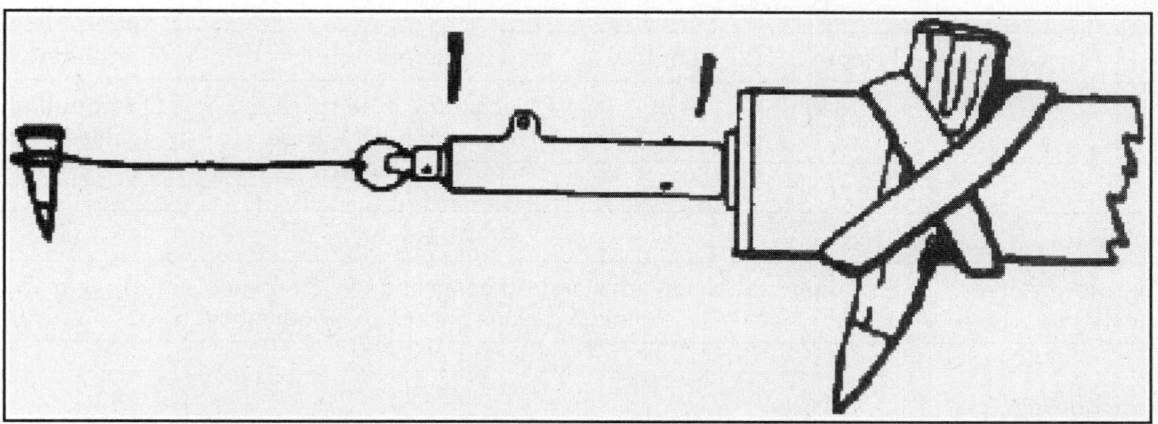

e. **Disarming**
   (1) Insert nail, length of wire, or original safety pin in positive safety pin hole *first.*
   (2) Insert a similar pin in locking safety pin hole.
   (3) Cut trip wire.
   (4) Separate firing device and charge.

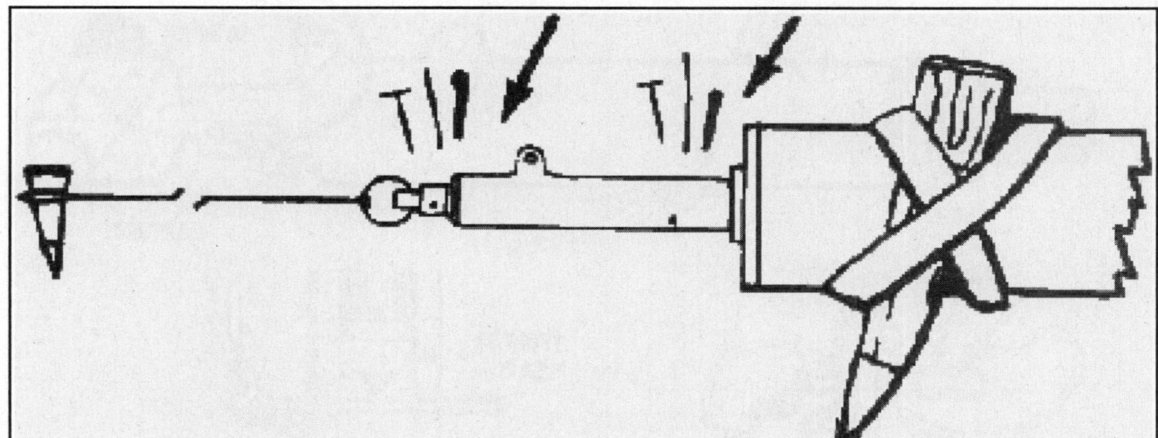

21. M3 PULL-RELEASE FIRING DEVICE

a. **Characteristics.**

		Dimensions			
Case	Color	Depth	Length	Internal Action	Initiating Action
Metal	OD	9/16 in	4 in	Mechanical with spreading striker head release	Direct pull of 6–10 lbs or release of tension

Safeties	Packaging
Locking and positive safety pin.	Five units complete with standard bases and two 80-ft spools of trip wire in carton, and 5 cartons packed in wooden box.

b. **Functioning.**

(1) Pull. A pull of 6 to 10 1b. on taut trip wire raises release pin until shoulder passes constriction in barrel. The striker jaws then spring open, releasing striker to fire percussion cap.

(2) Tension-release. Release of tension (cutting of taut trip wire) permits spring-driven striker to move forward, separate from release and fire percussion cap.

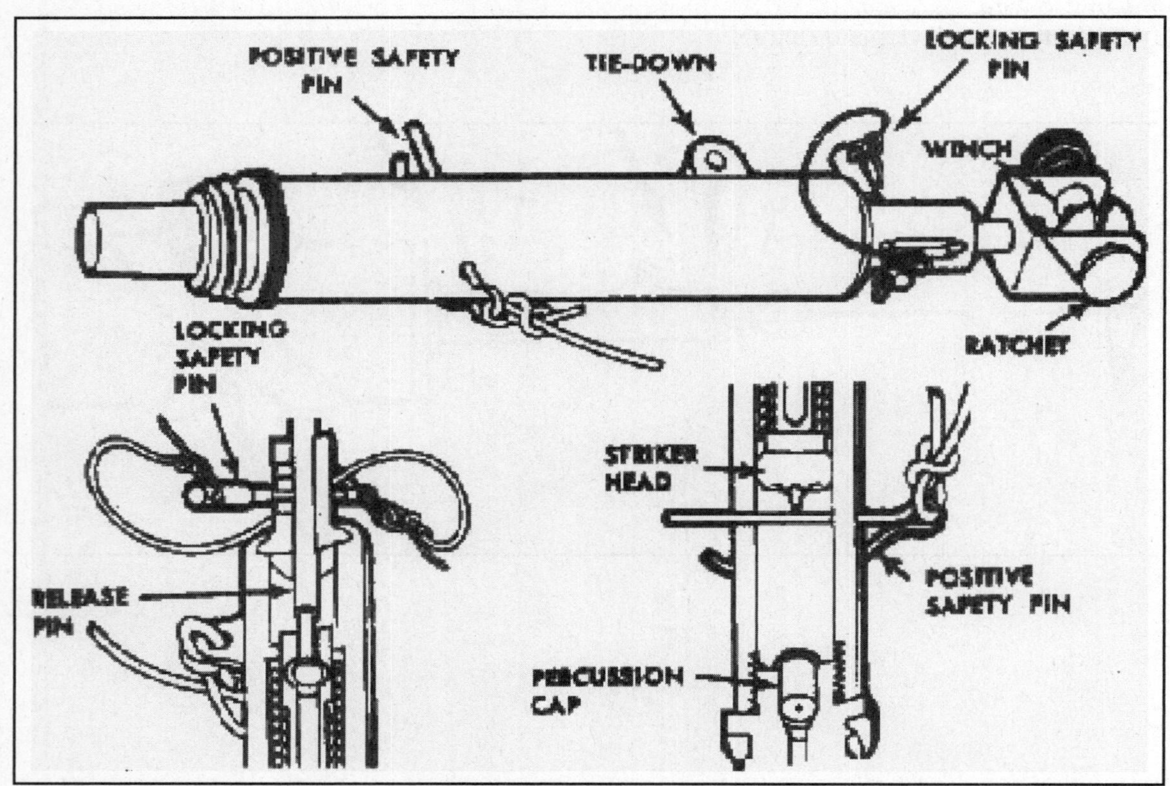

c. **Installing.**
   (1) Remove protective cap.
   (2) With crimpers, attach blasting cap to standard base. *Crimper jaws should be placed no farther than ¼ in. from open end of blasting cap.*
   (3) Attach firing device assembly to anchored charge (must be firm enough to withstand pull of at least 20 lb.).
   (4) Secure one end of trip wire to anchor and place other end in hole in winch.
   (5) With knurled knob draw up trip wire until locking safety pin is pulled into wide portion of safety pin hole.

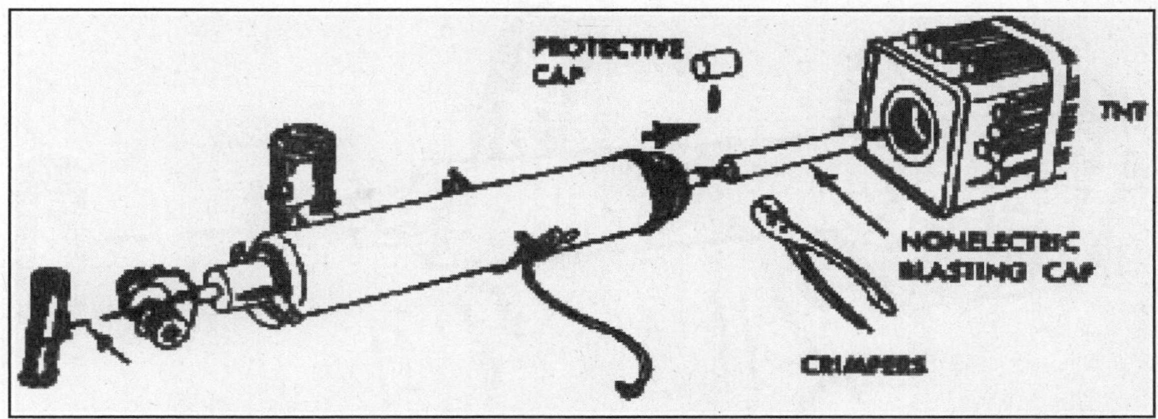

d. **Arming.**
   (1) With cord, remove small cotter pin from locking safety pin and withdraw locking safety pin. If it does not pull out easily, adjust winch winding.
   (2) With cord, pull out positive safety pin. This should pull out easily. If not, disassemble and inspect.

e. **Disarming.**

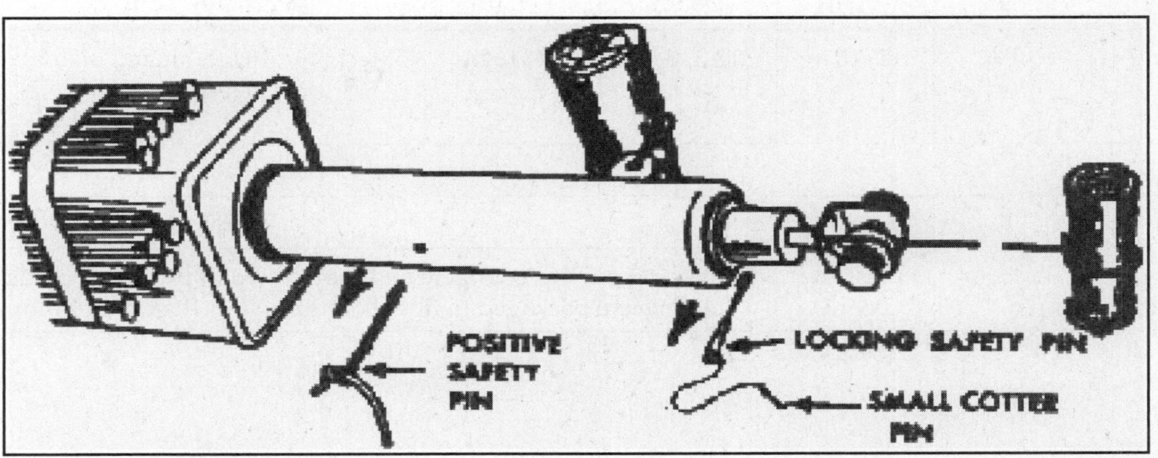

(1) Insert length of wire, nail, or cotter pin in positive safety pin hole.
(2) Insert length of wire, nail, of safety pin in locking safety pin hole.
(3) Check both ends and cut trip wire.
(4) Separate firing device from charge.

> ✍ **NOTE**
> Insert positive safety pin first. Cut trip wire last.

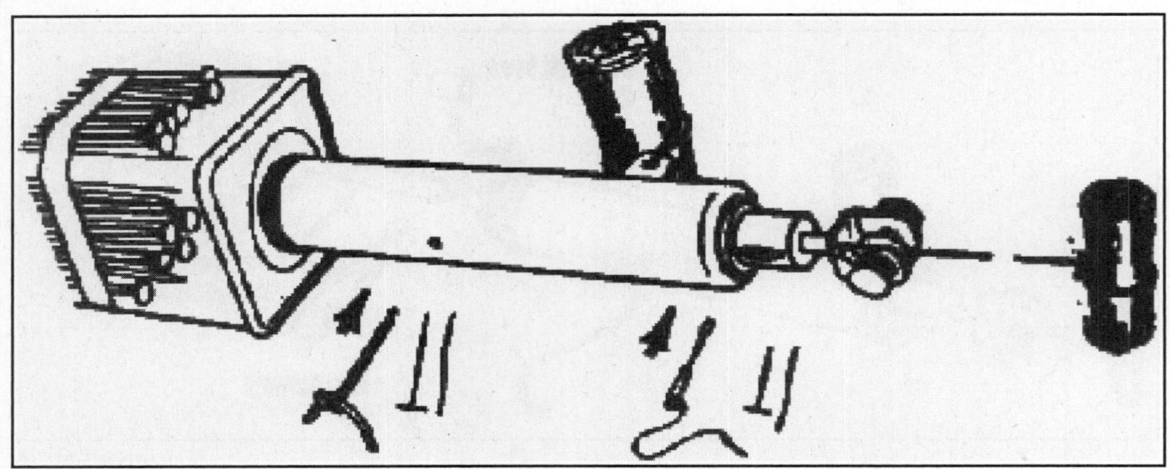

22. M5 PRESSURE-RELEASE FIRING DEVICE

a. **Characteristics.**

		Dimensions				
Case	Color	Width	Depth	Length	Internal Action	Initiating Actio
Metal	OD	15/16 in	12 3/8 in	11/16 in	Mechanical with hinged plate release	Removal of restrai ing weight, 5 lbs more

Safeties	Accessories	Packaging
Safety pin and hole for interceptor pin	Pressure board	Four firing devices complete and four plywood pressure boards in paper carton. Fi cartons are packaged in fiber board box and 10 of these shipped in wooden box.

b. **Functioning.** Lifting or removing retaining weight releases striker to fire the percussion cap.

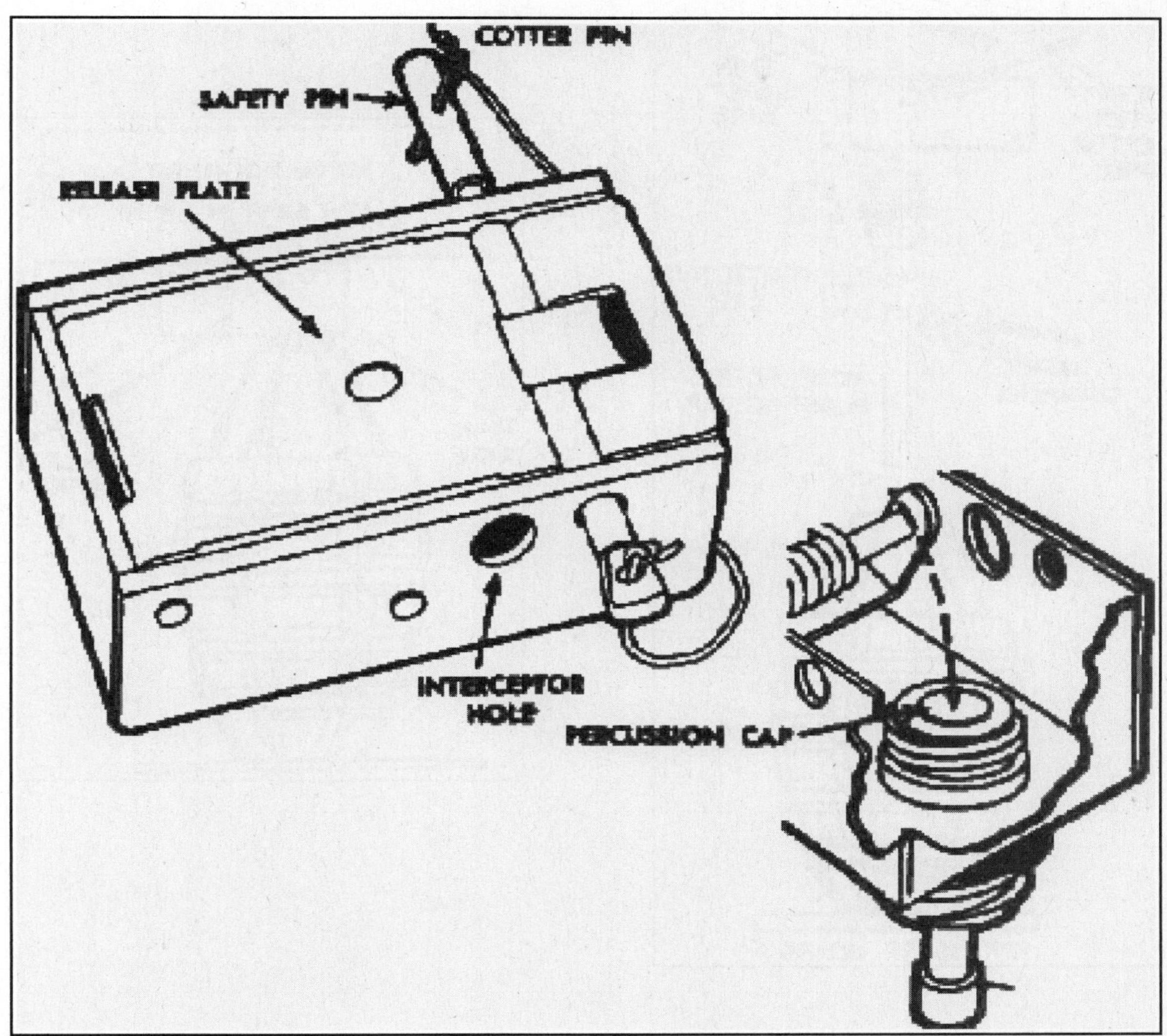

c. **Installing.**
   (1) Insert a length of 10-gage wire in interceptor hole. Bend slightly to prevent dropping out.
   (2) Remove small cotter pin from safety pin.
   (3) Holding release plate down, replace safety pin with length of No. 18 wire. Bend wire slightly to prevent dropping out.
   (4) Remove protective cap from base and with crimpers, attach blasting cap. *Crimper jaws should be placed no farther than ¼ inch from open end of blasting cap.*
   (5) Secure firing device assembly in charge.

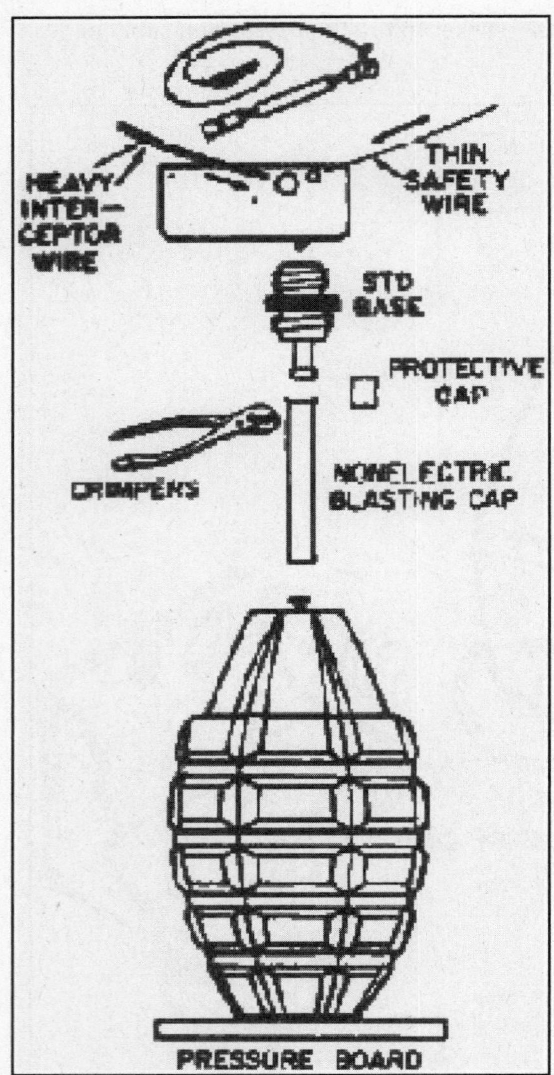

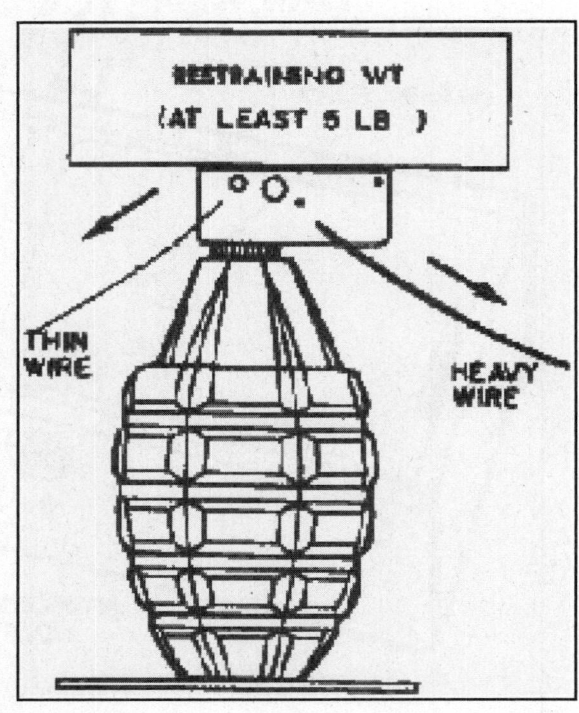

d. **Arming.**
   (1) Place restraining weight on top of firing device.
   (2) Remove thin wire from safety pin hole. If wire does not come out easily, restraining weight is either insufficient or improperly placed.
   (3) Remove heavy wire from interceptor hole. It should move freely. *Note. Withdraw thin wire first and heavy wire last. Follow arming procedure carefully.*

e. **Disarming.**
   (1) Insert length of heavy gage wire in interceptor hole. Bend wire to prevent dropping out. *Proceed carefully, as the slightest disturbance of the restraining weight might initiate the firing device.*
   (2) Separate firing device from charge.

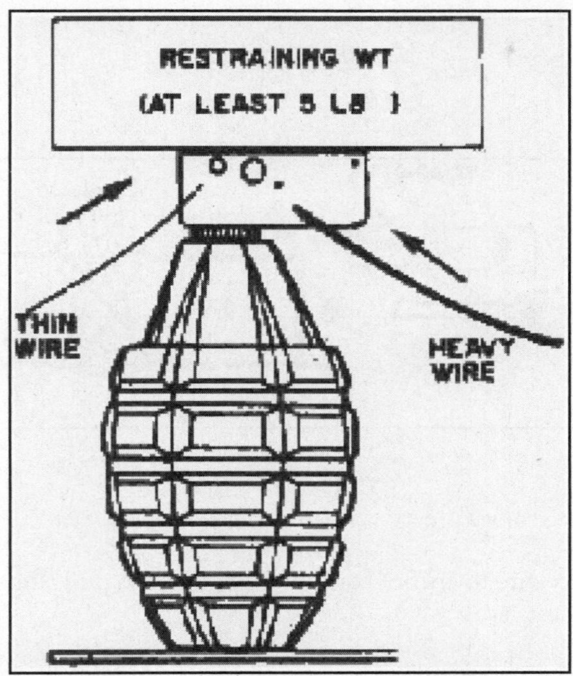

23. 15-SECOND DELAY DETONATOR

a. **Characteristics.** This device consists of a pull-friction fuse igniter, 15-second length of fuse, and blasting cap. The blasting cap is protected by a transit cap screwed on the base.

b. **Functioning.** A strong pull on the pull ring draws the friction igniter through the flash compound, causing a flame which ignites the time fuse.

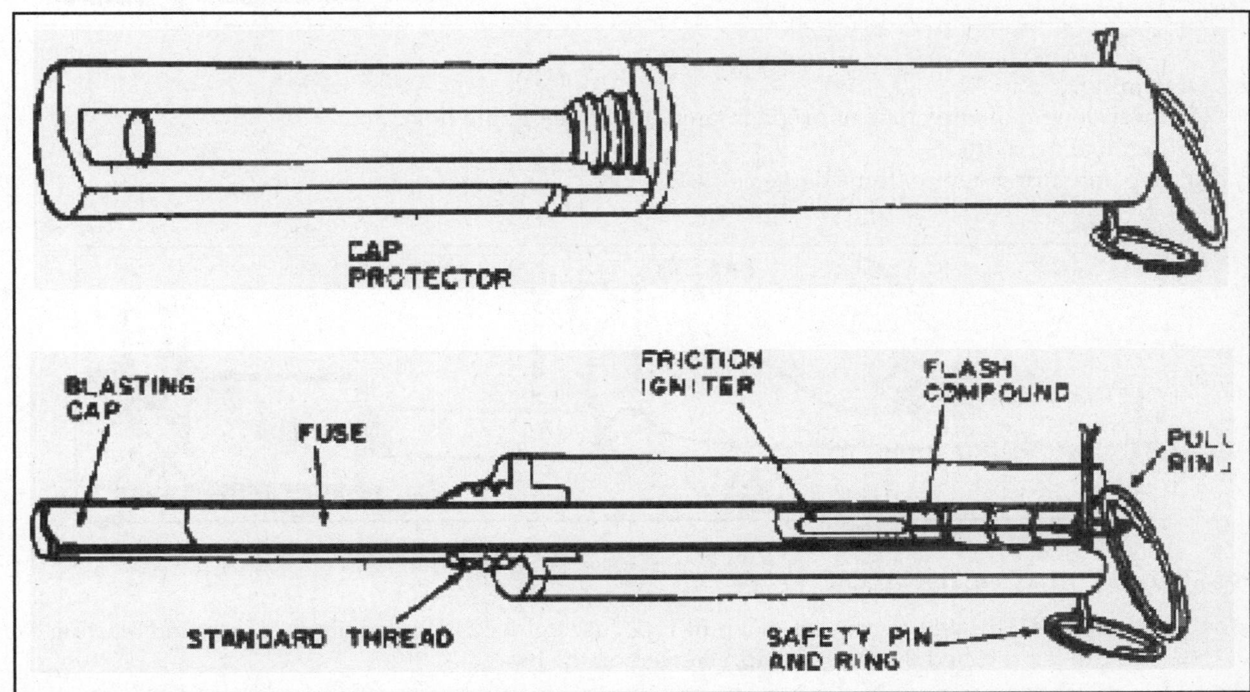

c. **Installing.**
   (1) Unscrew transit cap from base.
   (2) Secure device in charge.

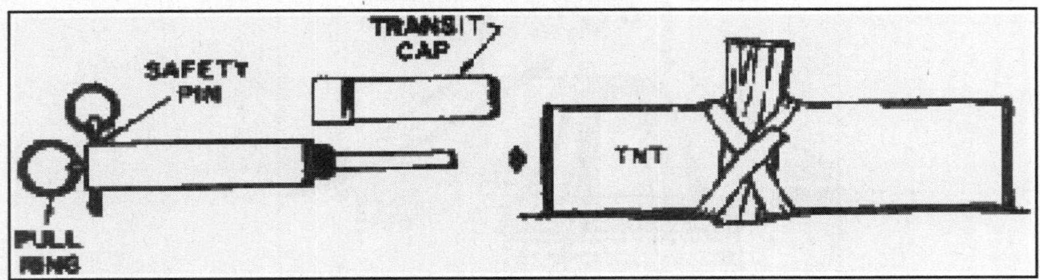

d. **Arming.**
   (1) ***Manual initiation.*** Remove safety pin.
   (2) ***Trip wire initiation.***
      (a) Attach one end of trip wire to anchor stake and the other to pull ring.
      (b) Remove safety pin.

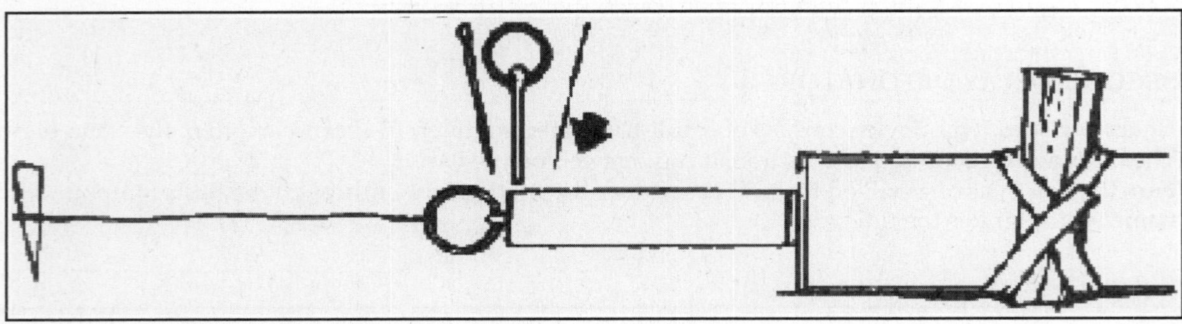

e. **Disarming.**
   (1) Insert length of wire, nail, or original safety pin in safety pin hole.
   (2) Remove trip wire.
   (3) Separate firing device from charge.

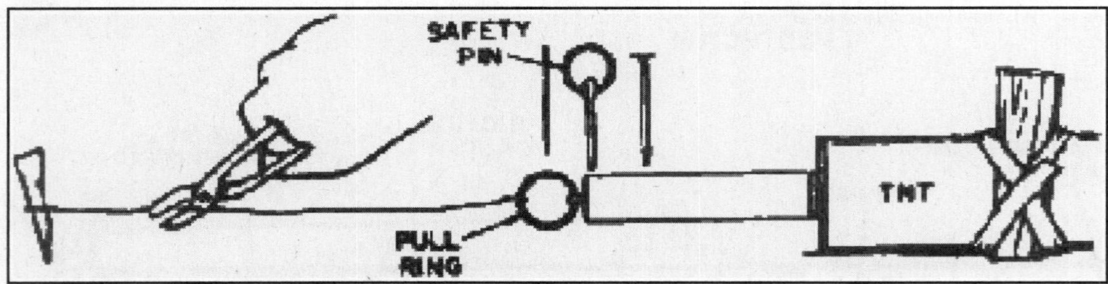

24. 8-SECOND DELAY DETONATOR

a. **Characteristics.** This device consists of a pull-type fuse lighter, 8-second length of fuse, and blasting cap. The blasting cap is protected by a transit cap, screwed on the base.

b. **Functioning.** A strong pull on the T-shaped handle draws the friction igniter through the flash compound, causing a flame that ignites the time fuse.

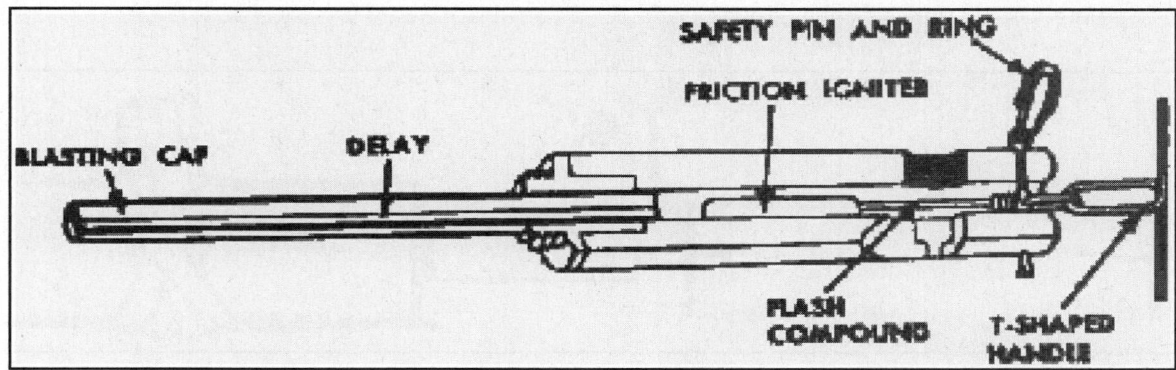

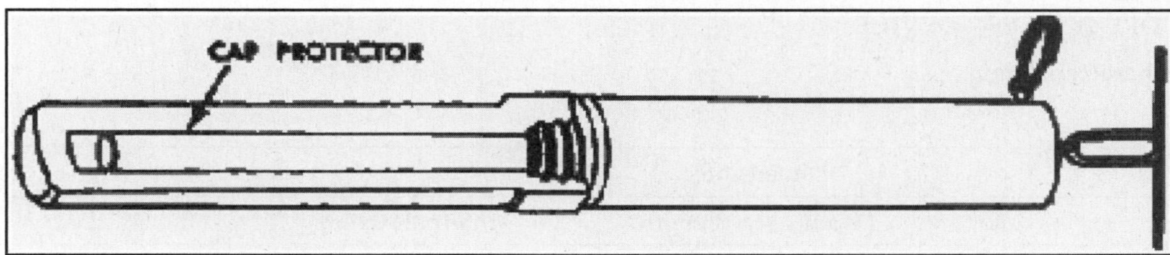

c. **Installing.**
(1) Unscrew transit cap from base.
(2) Secure device in charge.

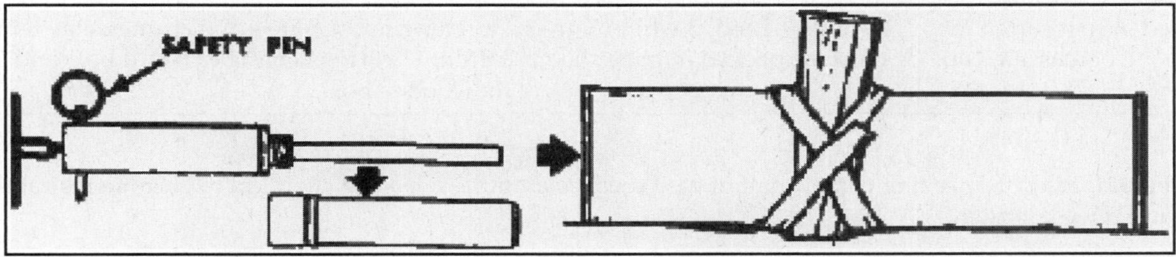

d. **Arming.**
(1) Manual initiation. Remove safety pin.
(2) Trip wire initiation.
(a) Attach one end of trip wire to anchor stake and the other to pull ring.
(b) Remove safety pin.

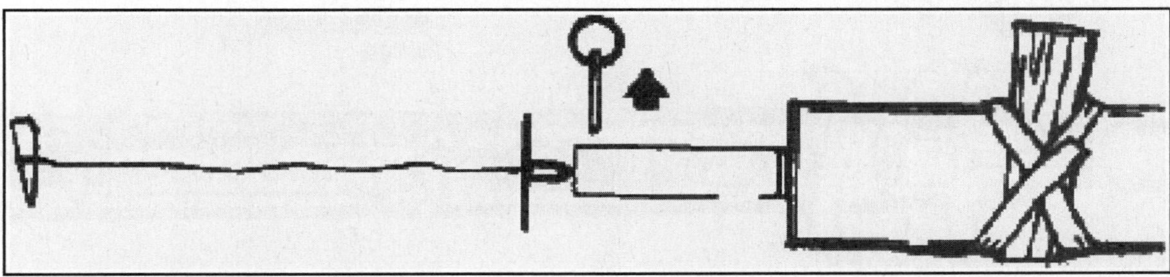

e. **Disarming.**
   (1) Insert length of wire, nail, or safety pin in safety pin hole.
   (2) Remove trip wire.
   (3) Separate firing device from charge.

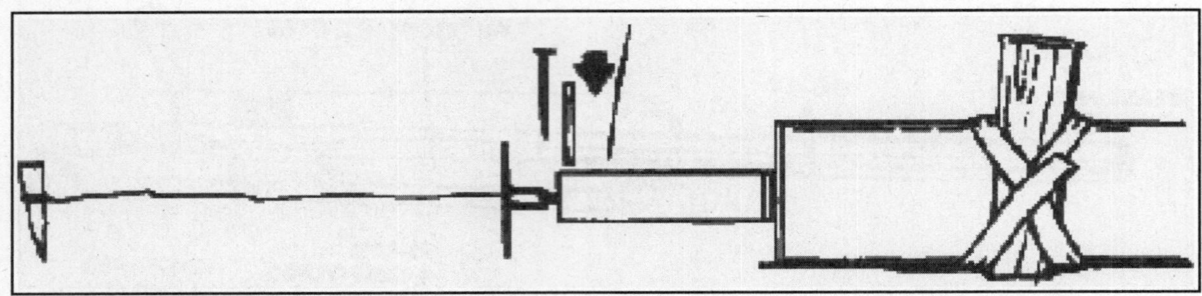

25. M1 DELAY FIRING DEVICE

a. **Characteristics.**

		Dimensions			
Case	Color	Depth	Length	Internal Action	Delay
Copper and brass	Natural Metal	7/16 in	6 1/2 in	Mechanical with corrosive chemical release	4 min to 9 hrs, identified by color of safety strip

Safeties	Packaging
Colored strip inserted in hole above percussion cap.	10 units—2 red, 3 white, 3 green, 1 yellow, and 1 blue—and a time delay temperature chart packed in paper board carton, 10 cartons in a fiber board box, and 5 boxes in wooden box.

b. **Functioning.** Squeezing copper half of case crushes ampule, releasing chemical to corrode restraining wire and release striker.

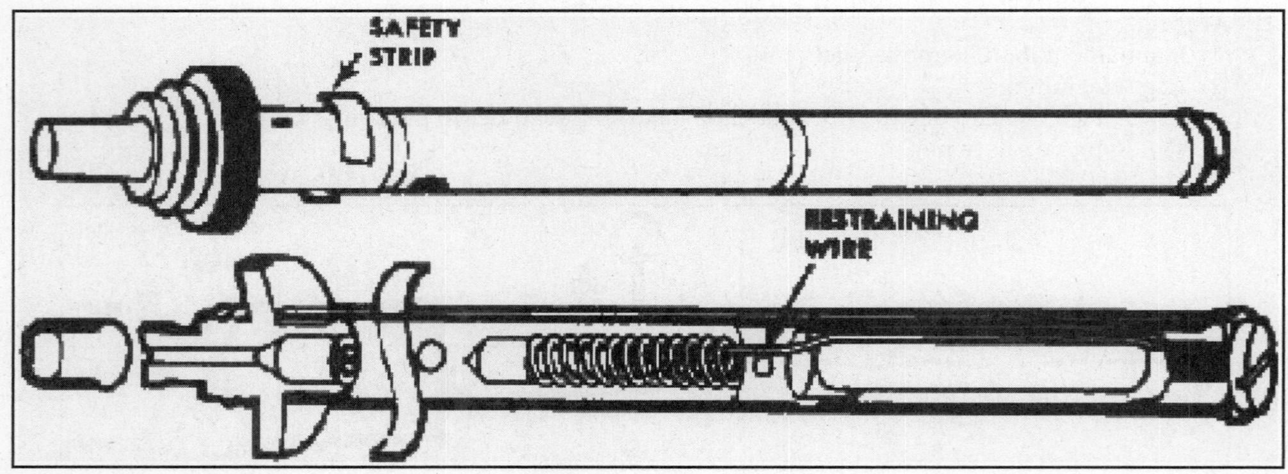

c. **Installing.**
   (1) Select device of proper delay.
   (2) Insert nail in inspection hole to make sure that firing pin has not been released.
   (3) Remove protective cap from base.
   (4) With crimpers, attach blasting cap to base. *Crimper jaws should be placed no further than ¼ in. from open end of blasting cap.*
   (5) Secure firing device assembly in destructor and then in charge.

d. **Arming.**
   (1) Crush ampule by squeezing the copper portion of case.
   (2) Remove safety strip.

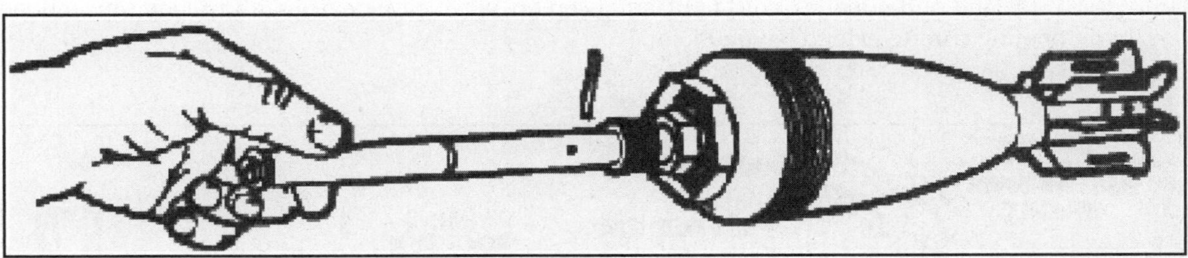

e. **Disarming.** *There is no safe way of disarming this firing device.* If disarming is necessary, insert an improvised safety pin through inspection holes.

26. M1 PRESSURE-RELEASE FIRING DEVICE

a. **Characteristics.**

	Dimensions					
Case	Color	Depth	Width	Height	Internal Action	Delay
Metal	OD	3 in	2 in	2 in	Mechanical with springed latch release	3 lbs or more

Safeties	Packaging
Safety pin and hole for interceptor pin.	Obsolete, but many are still available.

b. **Functioning.** Lifting or removing restraining weight unlatches lever, releasing striker to fire percussion cap.

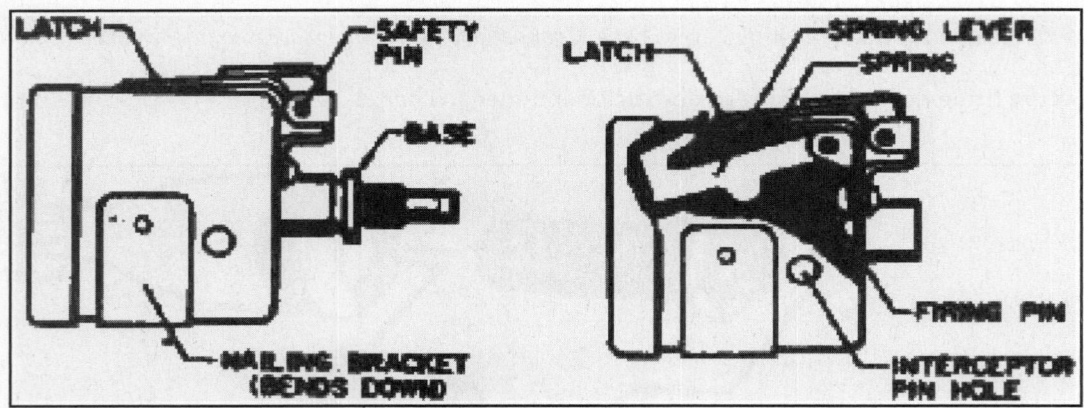

c. **Installing.**
   (1) Insert a length of heavy gage wire in interceptor hole. Bend slightly to prevent dropping out.
   (2) Holding down latch, remove safety pin and replace with length of thin wire.
   (3) Remove protective cap from base and with crimpers attach nonelectric blasting cap. *Crimper jaws should be placed no farther than ¼ in. from open end of blasting cap.*
   (4) Assemble length of detonating cord, priming adapter, nonelectirc blasting cap, and explosive block.
   (5) Attach free and of detonating cord to blasting cap on M1 release device with friction tape, allowing 6 in. of detonating cord to extend beyond joint.

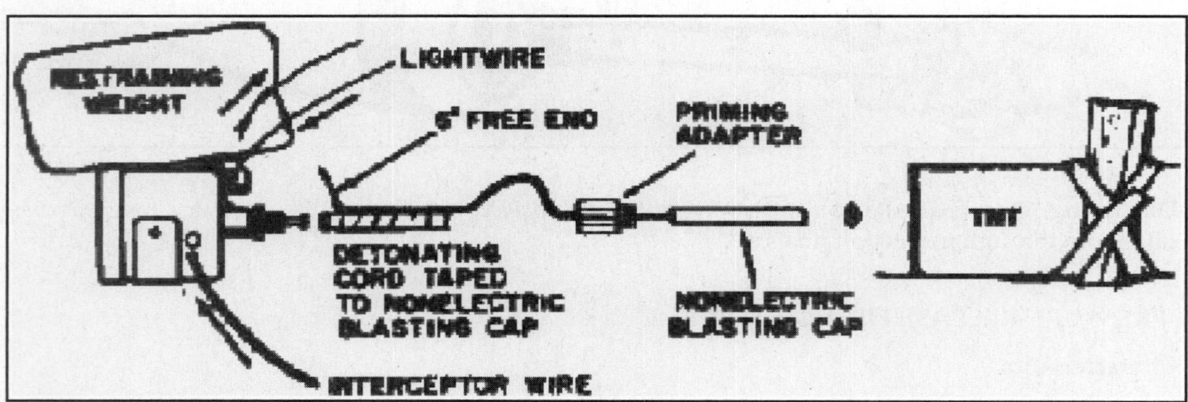

d. **Arming.**
   (1) Place restraining weight on top of firing device.
   (2) Remove thin wire from safety pin hole. If it does not come out easily, restraining weight in either insufficient or improperly placed.
   (3) Remove heavy wire from interceptor hole.

> ✍ **NOTE**
> Proceed carefully.

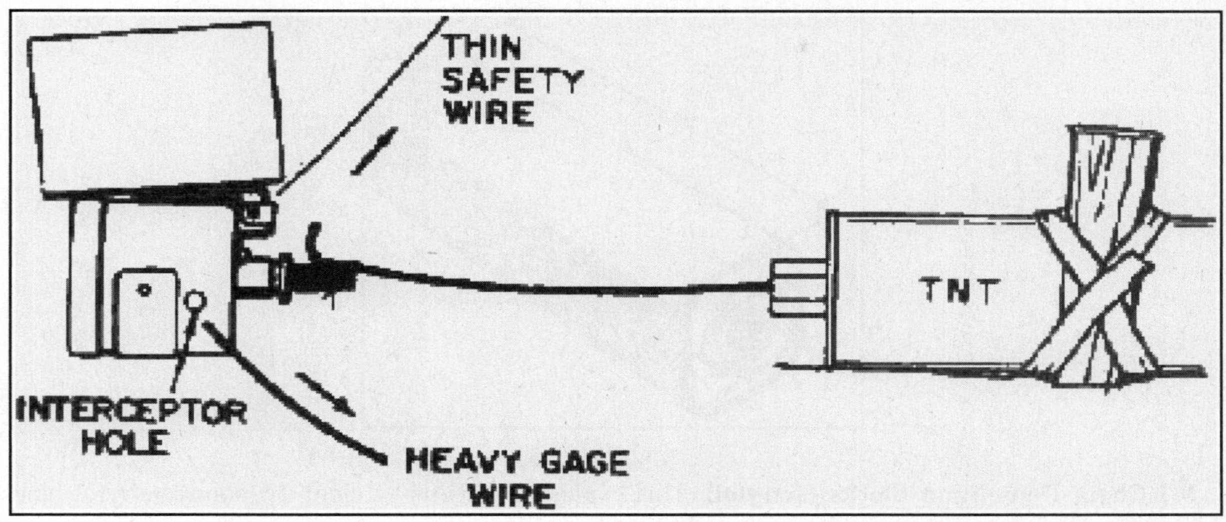

e. **Disarming.**
   (1) *Proceed carefully as the slightest disturbance of restraining weight might unlatch lever and detonate the mine.* Insert length of heavy gage wire in interceptor hole. Bend wire to prevent dropping out.
   (2) Insert length of thin wire in safety pin hole, if possible.
   (3) Separate firing device assembly and explosive charge.

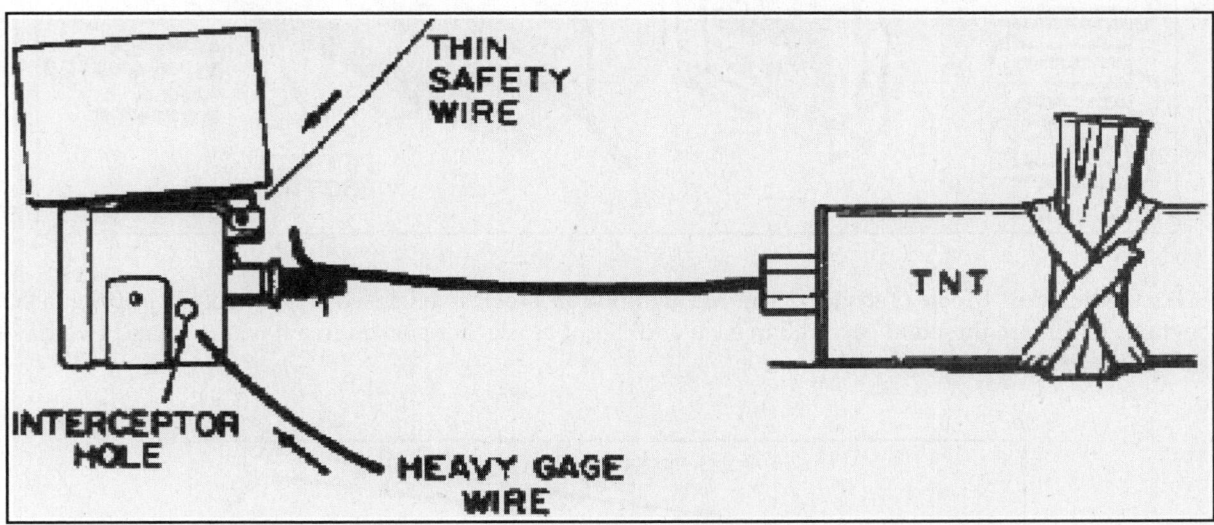

SECTION II. DEMOLITION MATERIALS

27. EXPLOSIVES AND ACCESSORIES (FOR MORE DETAILED INFORMATION SEE FM5–25 AND TM 9-1375-200.)

a. **TNT.** This is issued in ¼, ½ and 1-pound blocks in a cardboard container with lacquered metal ends. One end has a threaded cap well. Half-pound blocks are obtained by cutting a 1-pound package in the center.

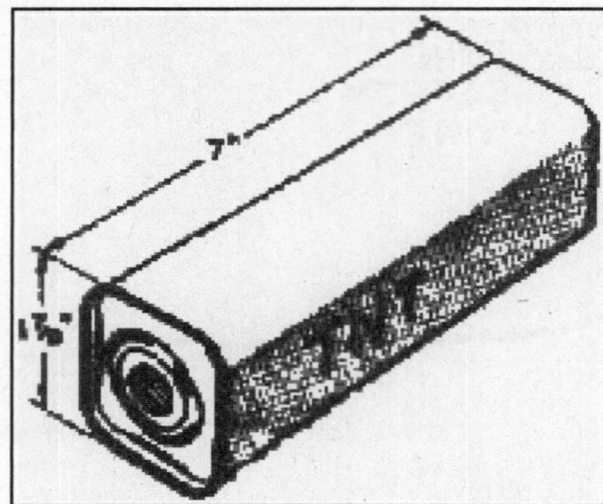

b. **M1 Chain Demolition Blocks (Tetrytol).** This explosive consists of eight 2½-pound tetrytol blocks cast 8 inches apart onto a single line of detonating cord, which extends 2 feet beyond the end blocks. All blocks have a tetryl booster in each end. Each chain is packed in a have sack, and two haversacks in a wooden box.

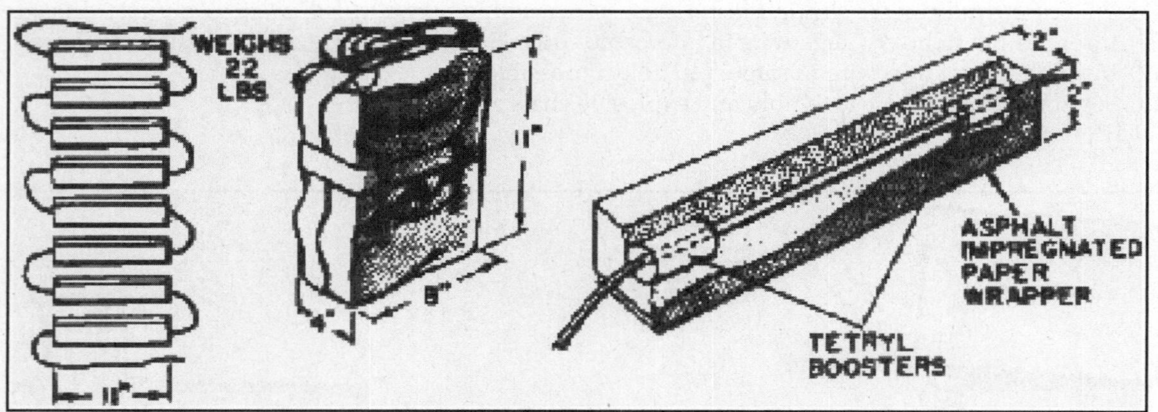

c. **M2 Demolition Block (Tetrytol).** The M2 demolition block is enclosed in an asphalt impregnated paper wrapper. It has a threaded cap well in each end. Eight blocks are packed in a haversack, and two haversacks in a wooden box.

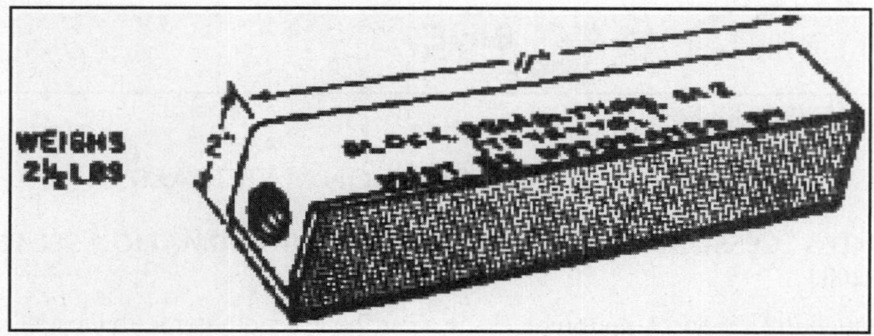

d. **M3 and M5 Demolition Blocks (Composition C3).** These consist of a yellow, odorous, plastic explosive more powerful than TNT. The M3 block has a cardboard wrapper perforated around the middle for easy opening. The M5 Block has a plastic container with a threaded cap well. Eight M3 or M5 blocks are packed in a haversack; and two haversack, in a wooden box.

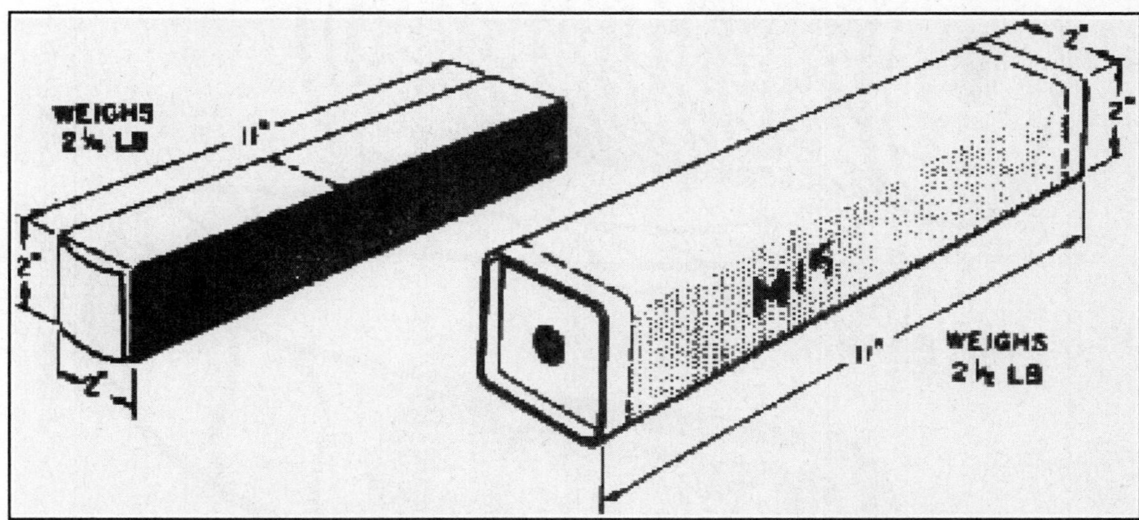

e. **M5A1 Demolition Block (Composition C4).** This is a white plastic explosive more powerful than TNT, but without the odor of C3. Each block is wrapped in plastic covering with a threaded cap well in each end. Twenty-four blocks are packed in a wooden box.

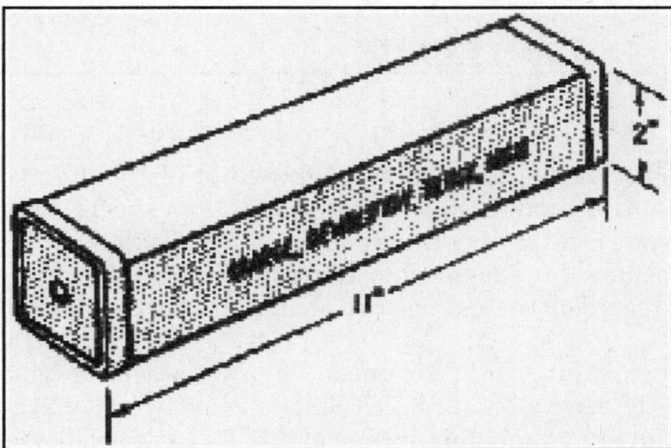

f. **M112 Demolition Charge (Composition C4).** This is composition C4 in a new package measuring 1 in. x 2 in x 12 in. Each block has an adhesive compound on one face. Further information is not available.

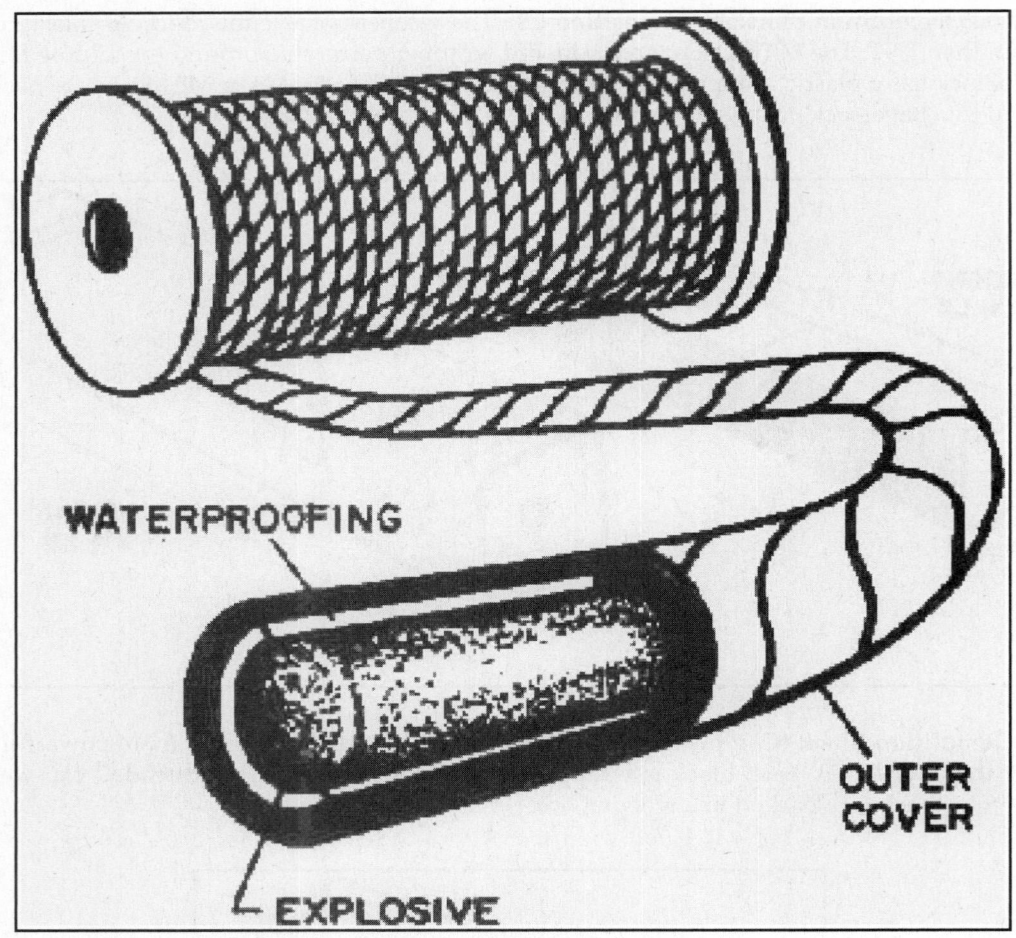

g. **M118 Demolition Charge.** The M118 charge is composed of PETN and plasticizers. The detonating rate is approximately 23,000 ft. per second. Each package contains four sheets ¼ in. x 3 in. x 12 in. Each sheet has an adhesive compound on one face. Further information is unavailable.
h. **Composition B.** Composition B is a high explosive with a relative effectiveness higher than TNT, and more sensitive. Because of its high dentonation rate and shattering power, it is used in certain bangalore torpedoes and in shaped charges.
i. **PETN.** This is used in detonating cord. It is one of the most powerful military explosives, almost equal to nitroglycerine and RDX. In detonating cord, PETN has a velocity rate of 21,000 feet per second.
j. **Amatol.** Amatol, a mixture of ammonium nitrate and TNT, has a relative effectiveness higher than that of TNT, Amatol (80/20) is used in the bangalore torpedo.
k. **RDX.** This is the base charge in the M6 and M7 electric and nonelectric blasting caps. It is highly sensitive, and has a shattering effect second only to nitroglycerine.
l. **Detonating Cord.**
   (1) ***Types I and II.*** These consist of a flexible braided seamless cotton tube filled with PETN. On the outside is a layer of asphalt covered by a layer of rayon with a wax gum composition finish. Type II has the larger diameter and greater tensile strength.
   (2) ***Type IV.*** This is similar to types I and II, except for the special smooth plastic covering designed for vigorous use and rough weather.

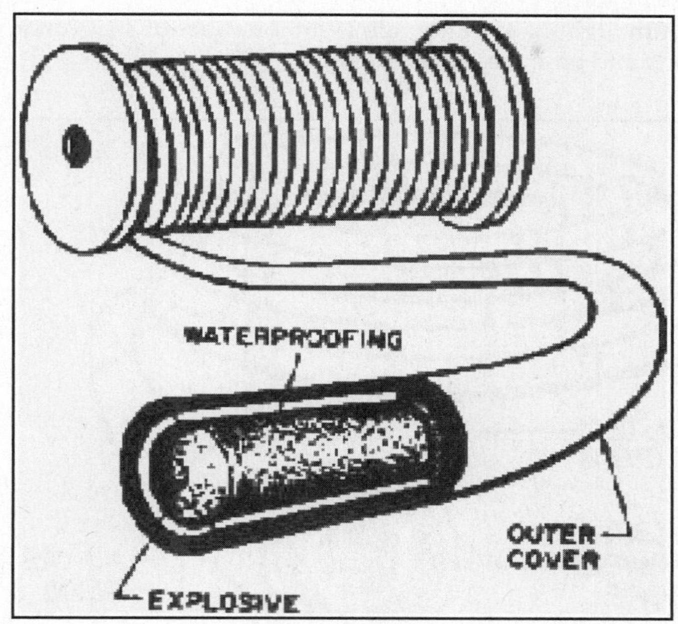

m. **Blasting Time Fuse.** This consists of black powder tightly wrapped in layers of fabric and waterproofing materials. It may be any color, orange being the most common. As burning rate varies from about 30 to 45 seconds per foot, each roll must be tested before using by burning and timing a 1-foot length.

n. **Safety Fuse M700.** *This* fuse is a dark green cord with a plastic cover, either smooth or with single pointed abrasive bands around the outside at 1-foot or 18-inch intervals and double pointed abrasive bands at 5-foot

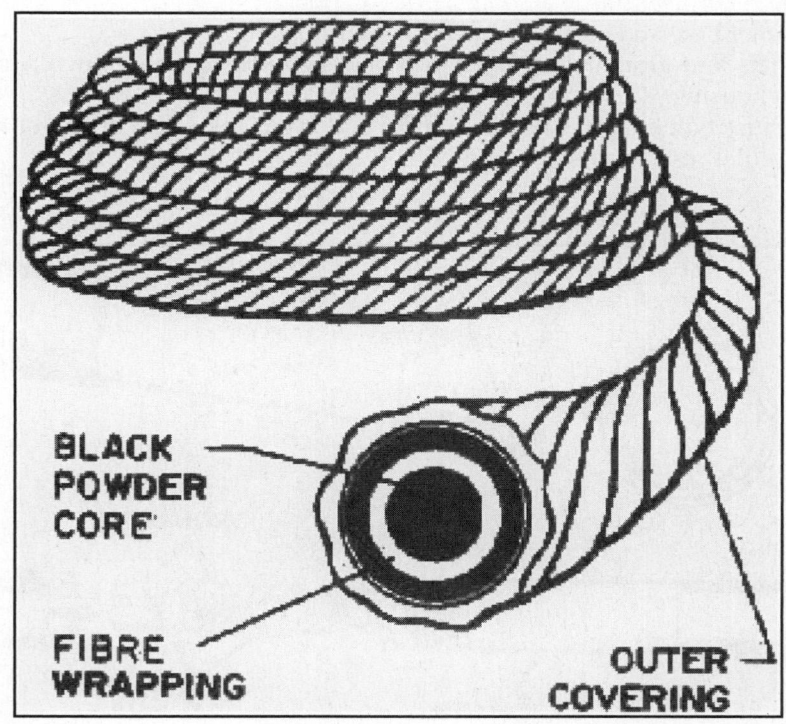

or 90-inch intervals. Although the burning rate is uniform (about 40 seconds per foot), it should be tested before using by burning and timing a 1-foot length.

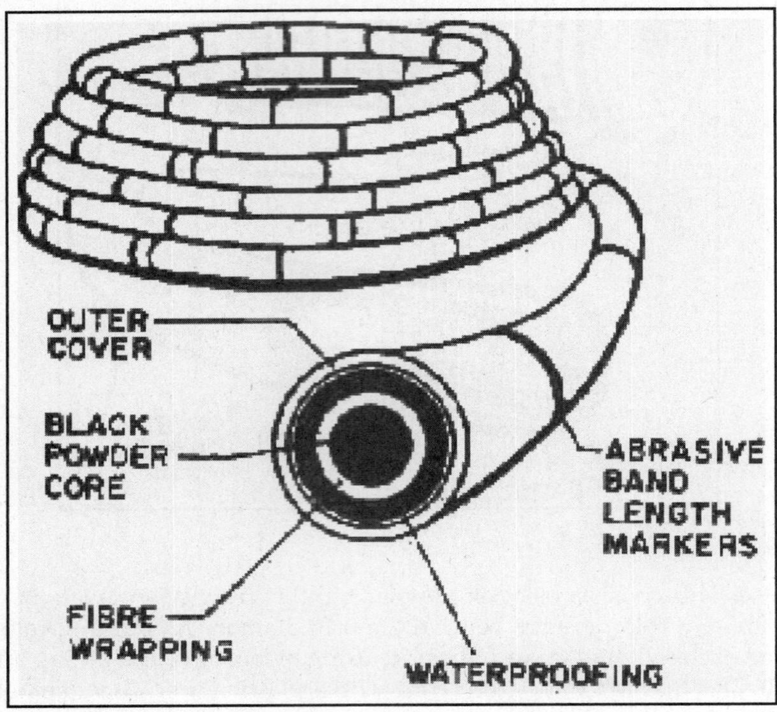

o. **M60 Fuse Lighter.**
   (1) ***To install:*** *Unscrew the fuse holder cap, remove shipping* plug, insert time fuse, and tighten cap.
   (2) ***To reload;***
      (a) Insert primer base and primer in end of lighter housing.
      (b) Put washers and grommets in open end of fuse holder cap as shown, and screw fuse holder cap firmly on housing.
      (c) Unscrew fuse holder cap about three turns and insert a freshly cut end of time fuse into the hole in the cap until it rests against the primer.
      (d) Tighten cap.

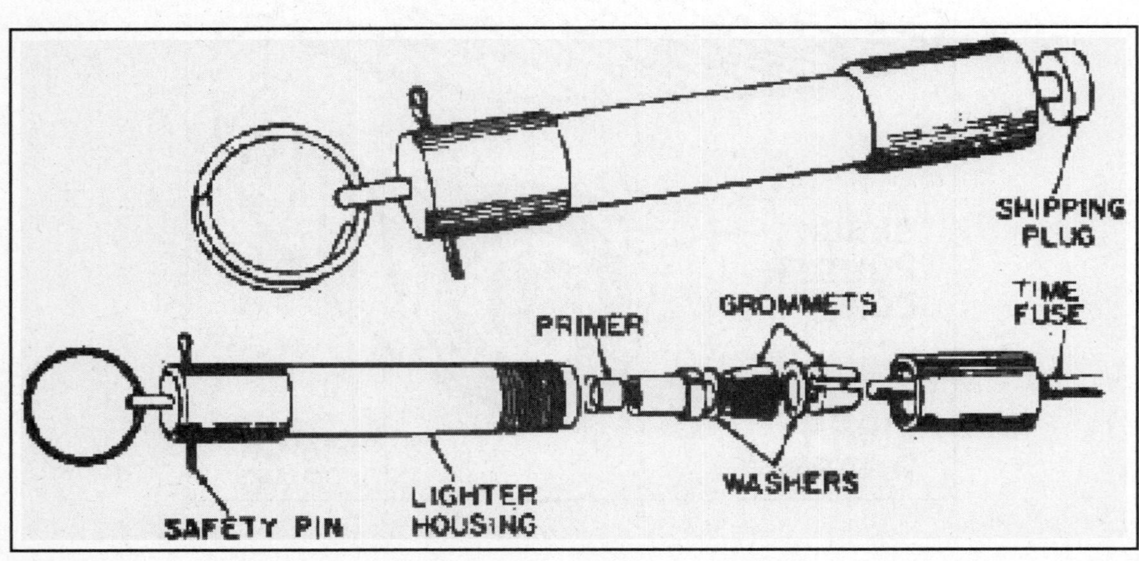

(3) *To fire:*
   (a) Remove safety pin
   (b) Pull on pull ring.

> ✍ **NOTE**
> Lighter is reusable after the insertion of a new primer and the reassembly of parts.

p. **Electric Blasting Caps.** Electric blasting caps have three lengths of leads—short (4 to 10 ft.), medium (12 to 14 ft), and long (50 to 100 ft). The short-circuit tab or shunt prevents accidental firing. It must be removed before the cap is connected in the firing circuit. Military blasting caps are required to insure detonation of military explosives.

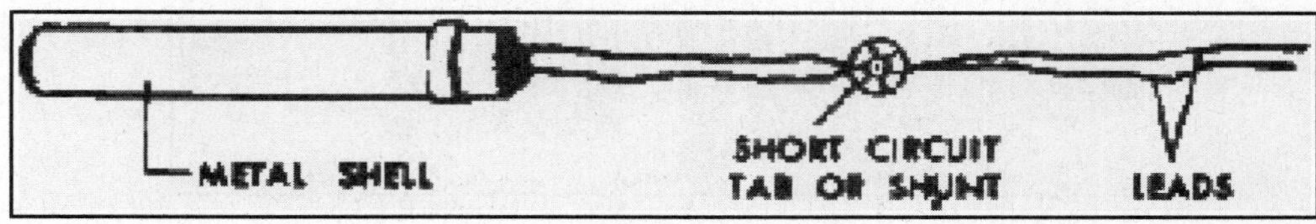

q. **Nonelectric Blasting Cape.** Two types are available, the No. 8 and the special M7, which resembles the No. 8 in appearance except for the expanded open end.

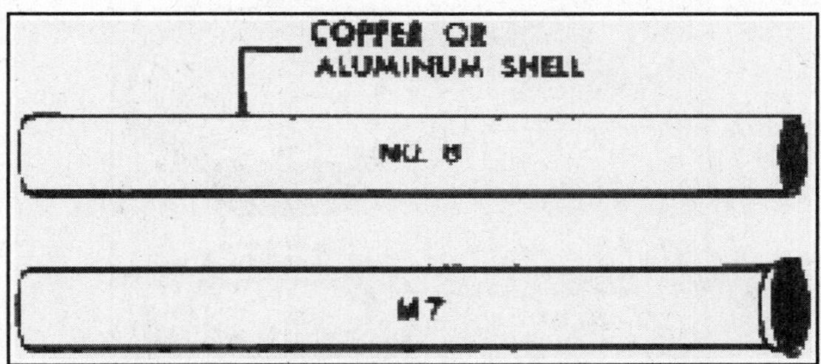

r. **Priming Adapter.** This is a plastic device with a threaded end for securing electric and nonelectric primers in the threaded cap wells of military explosives. A groove for easy insertion of the electric lead wires extends the full length of the adapter.

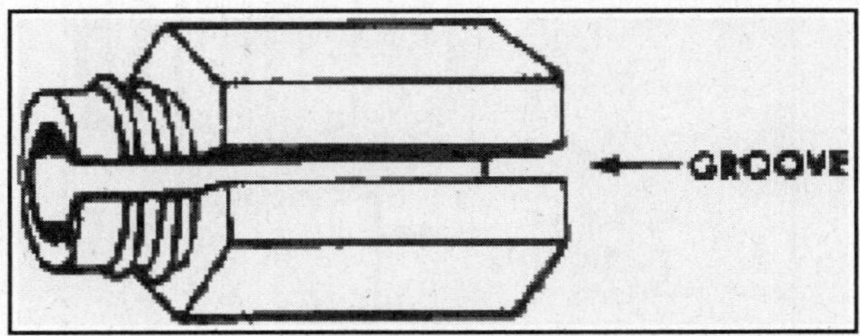

s. **M10 Universal Destructor.** The destructor is used to convert loaded projectiles, missiles, and bombs into improvised charges. The destructor has booster caps containing tetryl pellets. All standard firing devices with the standard base coupler screw into the top.

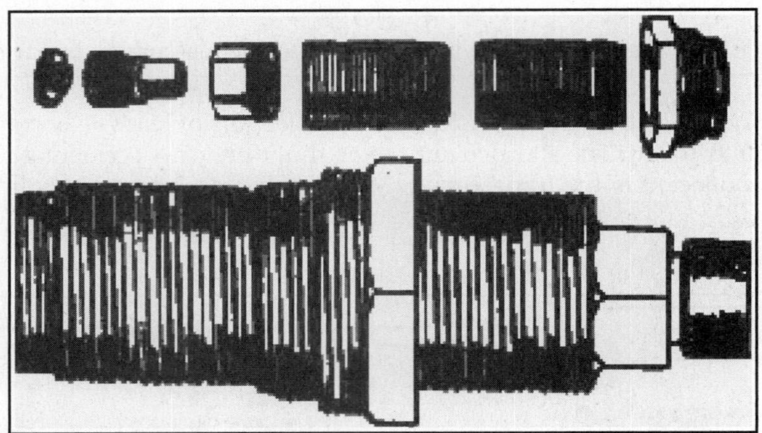

t. **Antitank Mine Activator.** This is a detonator designed for boobytrapping antitank mines. The top is threaded to receive all standard firing devices, and the base to screw in antitank mine activator wells.

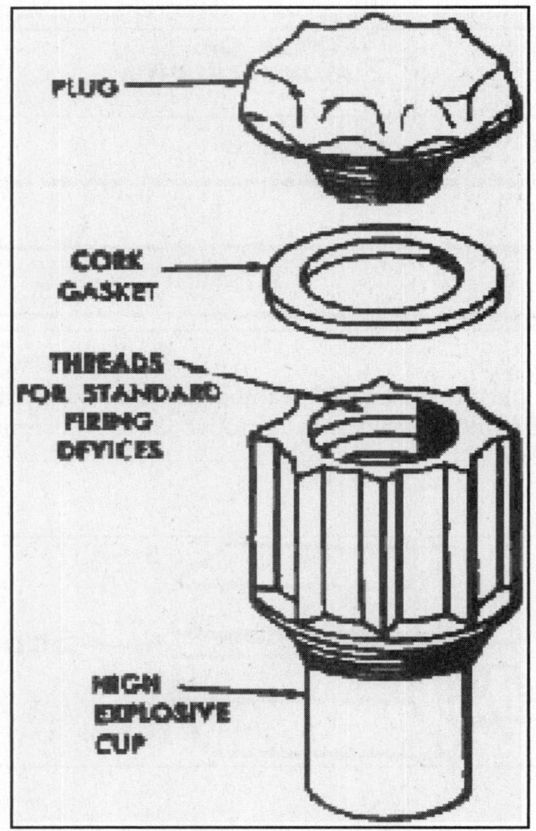

28. BANGALORE TORPEDO

The bangalore torpedo is a group of 10 loading assemblies (steel tubes filled with high explosive) with nose sleeve and connecting sleeves. The loading assemblies may be used singly, in series, or in bundles. They are primed in four ways: by a standard firing device; a standard firing device, nonelectric blasting cap, length of detonating cord, priming adaptor, and nonelectric blasting cap (para 29); a standard firing device, and length of detonating cord attached by the clove hitch and two extra turns around the cap well at either end of the loading assembly; and electrical methods (para 29).

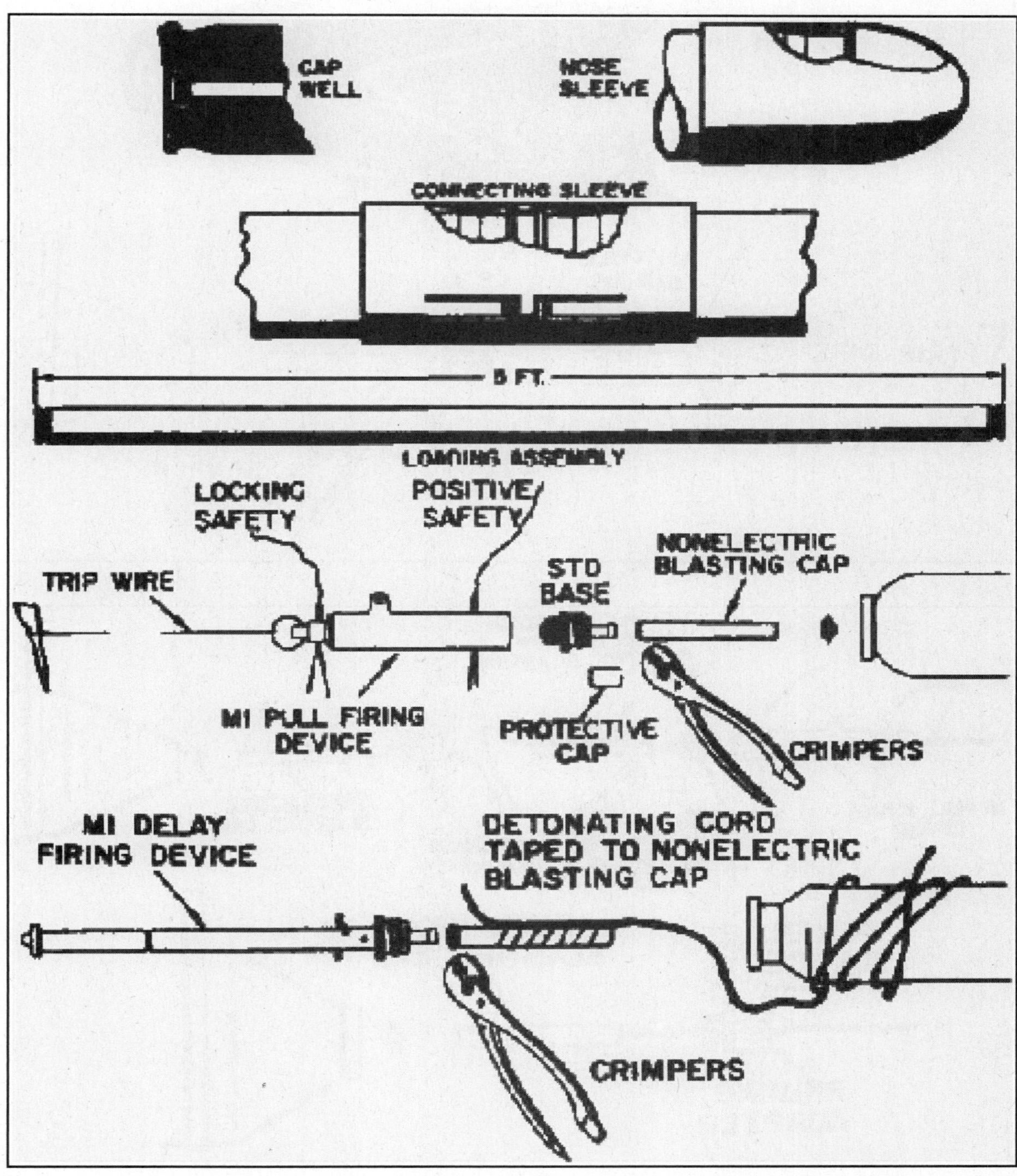

29. M2A3 SHAPED CHARGE

This charge consists of a conical top, conical liner integral standoff, threaded cap well, and 11½ pounds of explosive. It may be primed in three ways; by a standard firing device; a standard firing device, nonelectric blasting cap, length of detonating cord, priming adapter, and nonelectric blasting cap; and a priming adapter and electric blasting cap connected to power source.

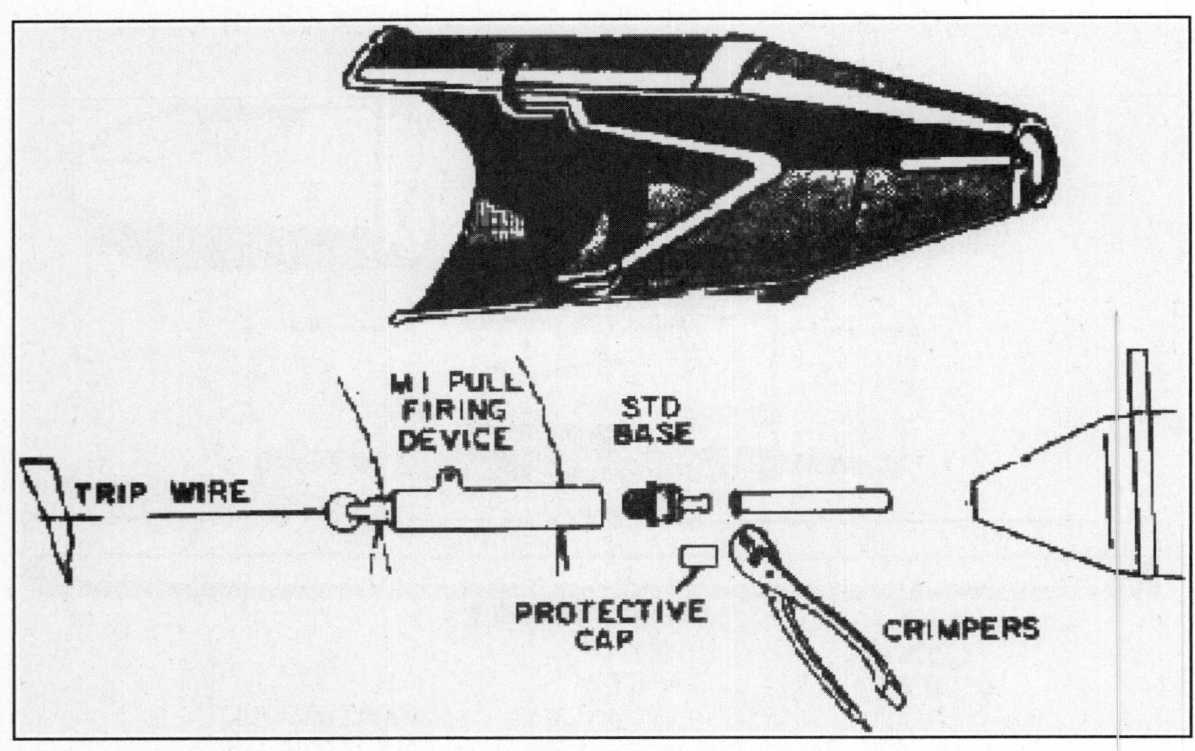

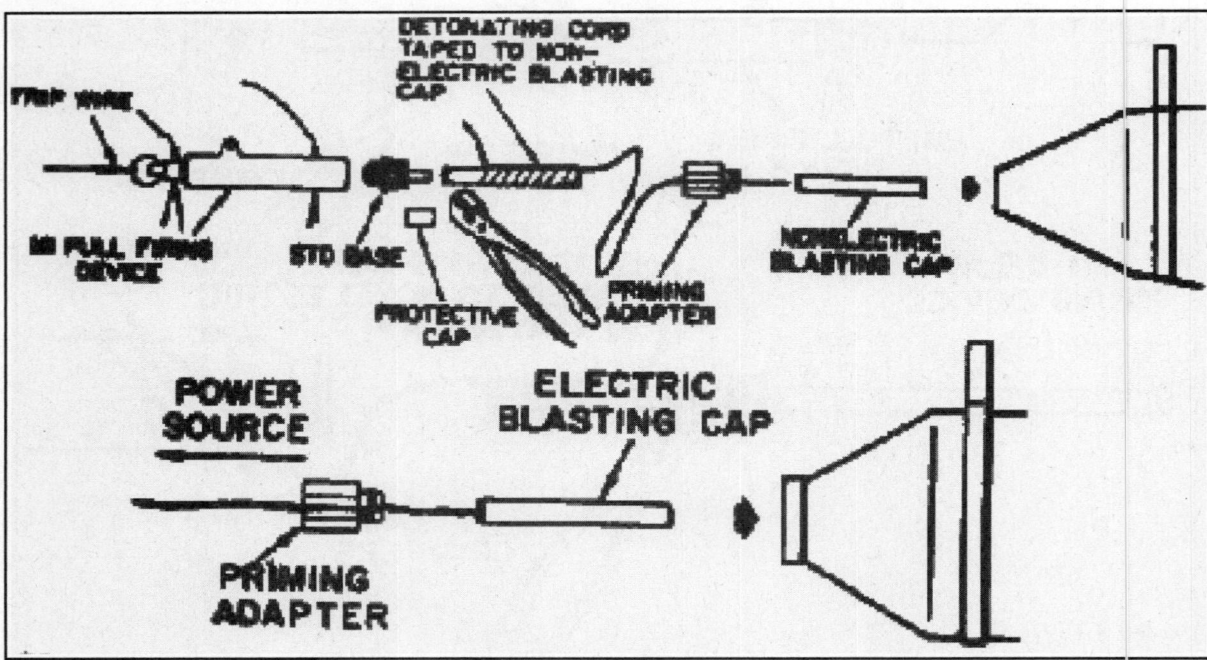

30. M3 SHAPED CHARGE

Tin M3 shaped charge is a metal container with a conical top, conical liner, threaded cap well, 30 pounds of explosive, and a metal tripod standoff. It may be primed in the same manner as the M2A3 shaped charge above.

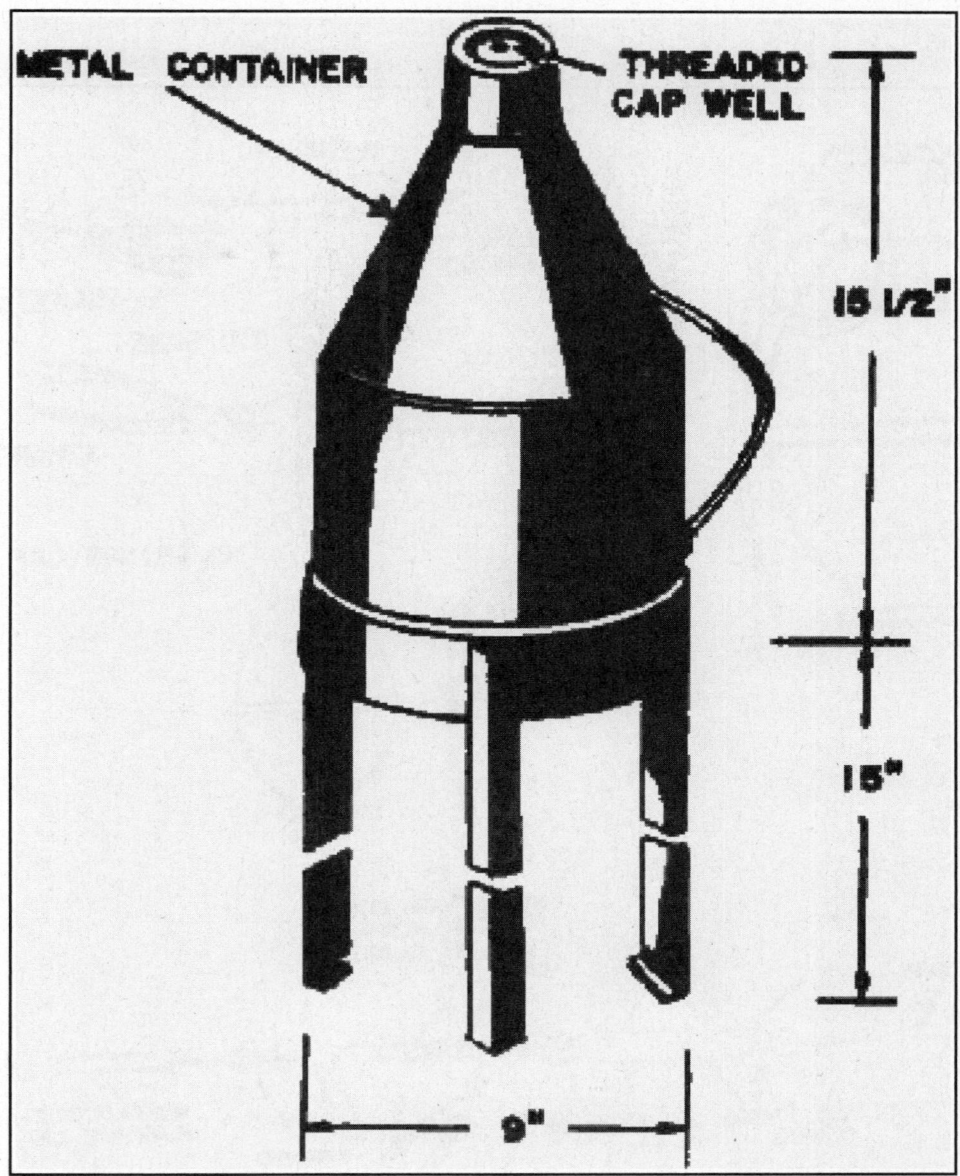

SECTION III. MISSILES

31. INTRODUCTION

Hand grenades, bombs, and mortar and artillery ammunition have wide application as improvised explosives charges. The only portion of these useful in boobytrapping, however, are the container and its explosive filler. The fuse is replaced by a standard firing devices and an M10 universal destructor—an adapter designed especially for this purpose. The number and types of missiles useful in boobytrapping, however, are not limited to the examples given below.

32. HAND GRENADES

The M26 hand grenades, an improved model, consists of a thin metal body lined with a wire-wound fragmentation coil, fuse, and composition B explosive charge. It has a variety of applications to boobytrapping. The fuse is removed and a standard firing device is screwed directly into the fuse well or remotely connected by a length of detonating cord, priming adapter, and a nonelectric blasting cap.

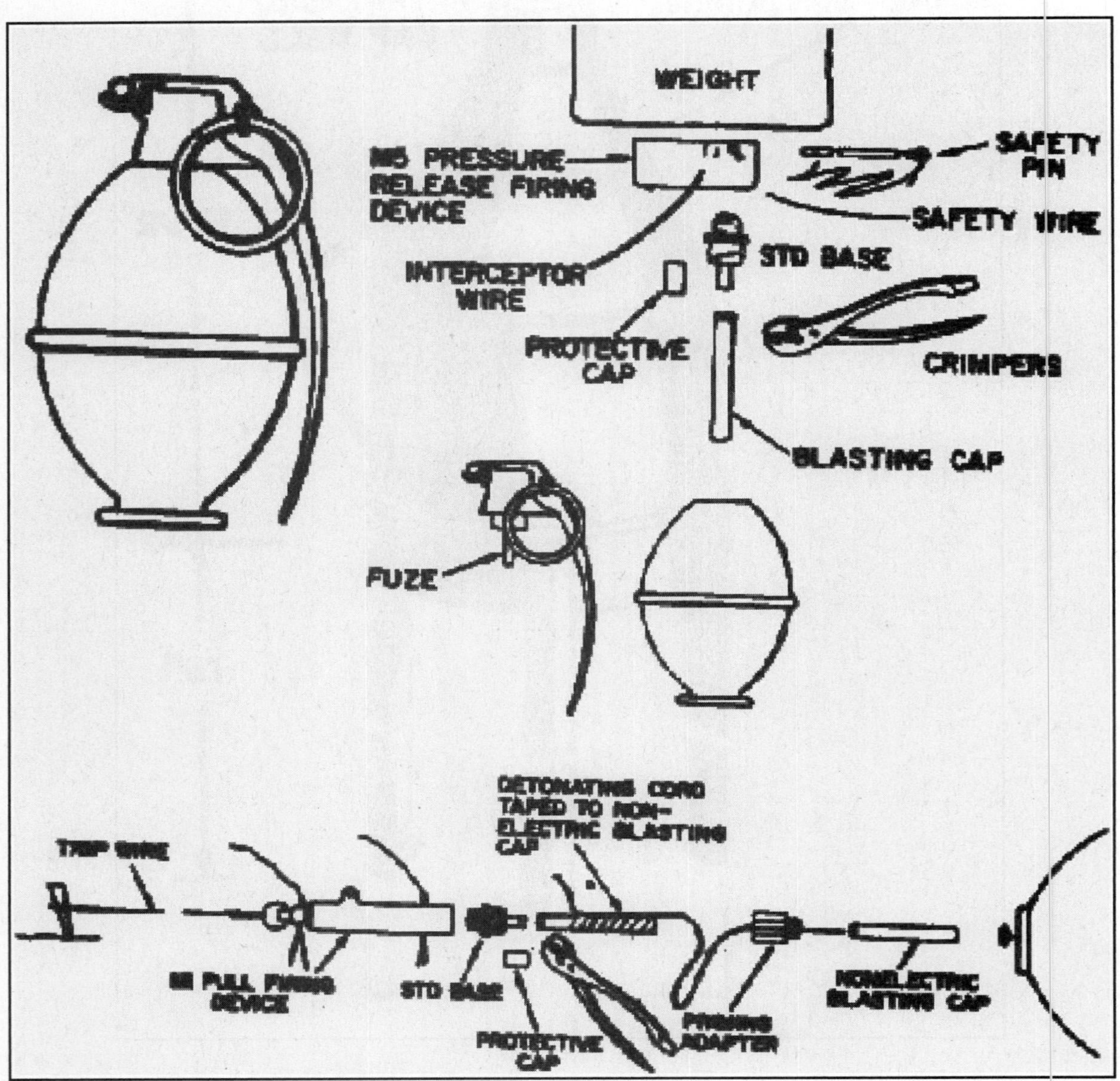

33. SIMM MORTAR SHELL

This is converted by replacing the fuse with a standard firing device and a properly assembled destructor or by a firing device, length of detonating cord, priming adapter, nonelectric blasting cap, and a properly assembled destructor. If a destructor is not available the detonating cord and nonelectric blasting cap are packed firmly in the fuse well with C4 explosive.

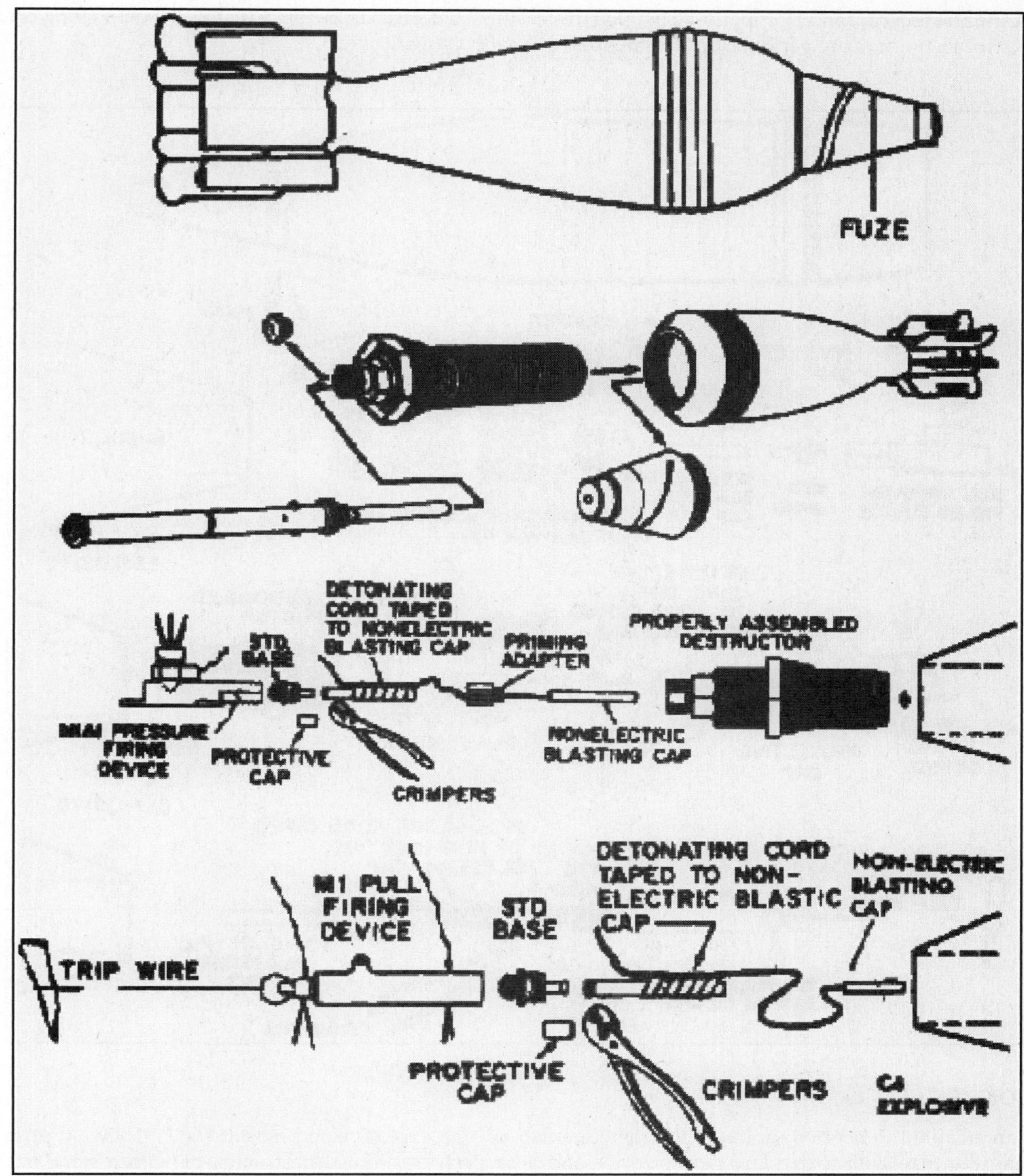

34. HIGH EXPLOSIVE SHELL

The high explosive shell is readily adapted to boobytrapping. The fuze is removed and replaced by a standard firing device and a properly-assembled destructor or a standard firing device, length or detonating cord, priming adapter, nonelectric blasting cap, and a properly-assembled destructor. If a destructor is not available, the detonating cord and nonelectric blasting cap are packed firmly in the fuze well with C4 explosive.

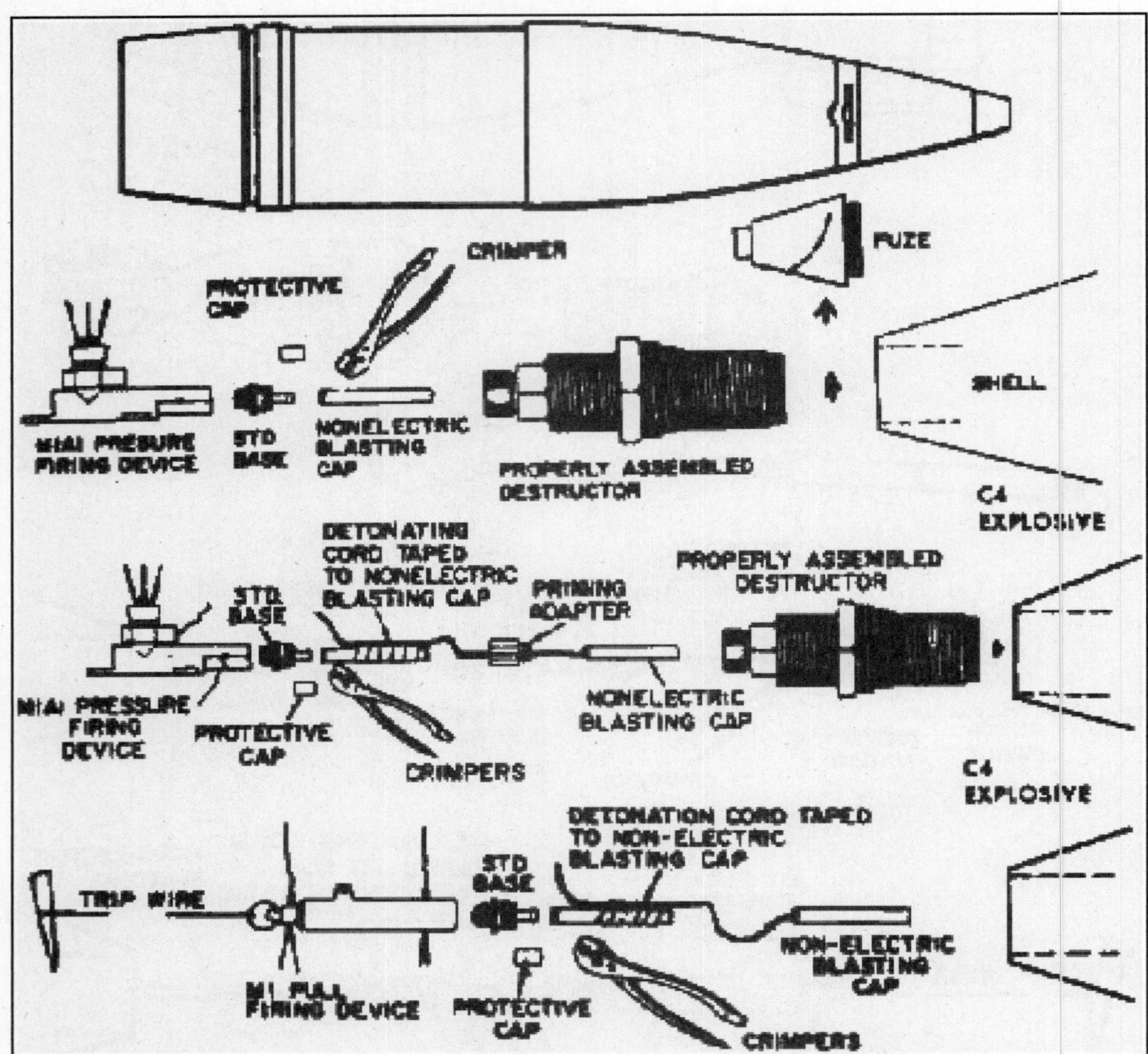

35. BOMBS

These are adapted to boobytrapping in the same manner as high explosive and mortar shells. They are primed by replacing the fuze with a standard firing device and a properly-assembled destructor, or with a standard firing device, length of detonating cord, priming adapter, nonelectric blasting cap, and a properly-assembled destructor. If a destructor is not available, the detonating cord and blasting cap are packed firmly in the fuze well with C4 explosive.

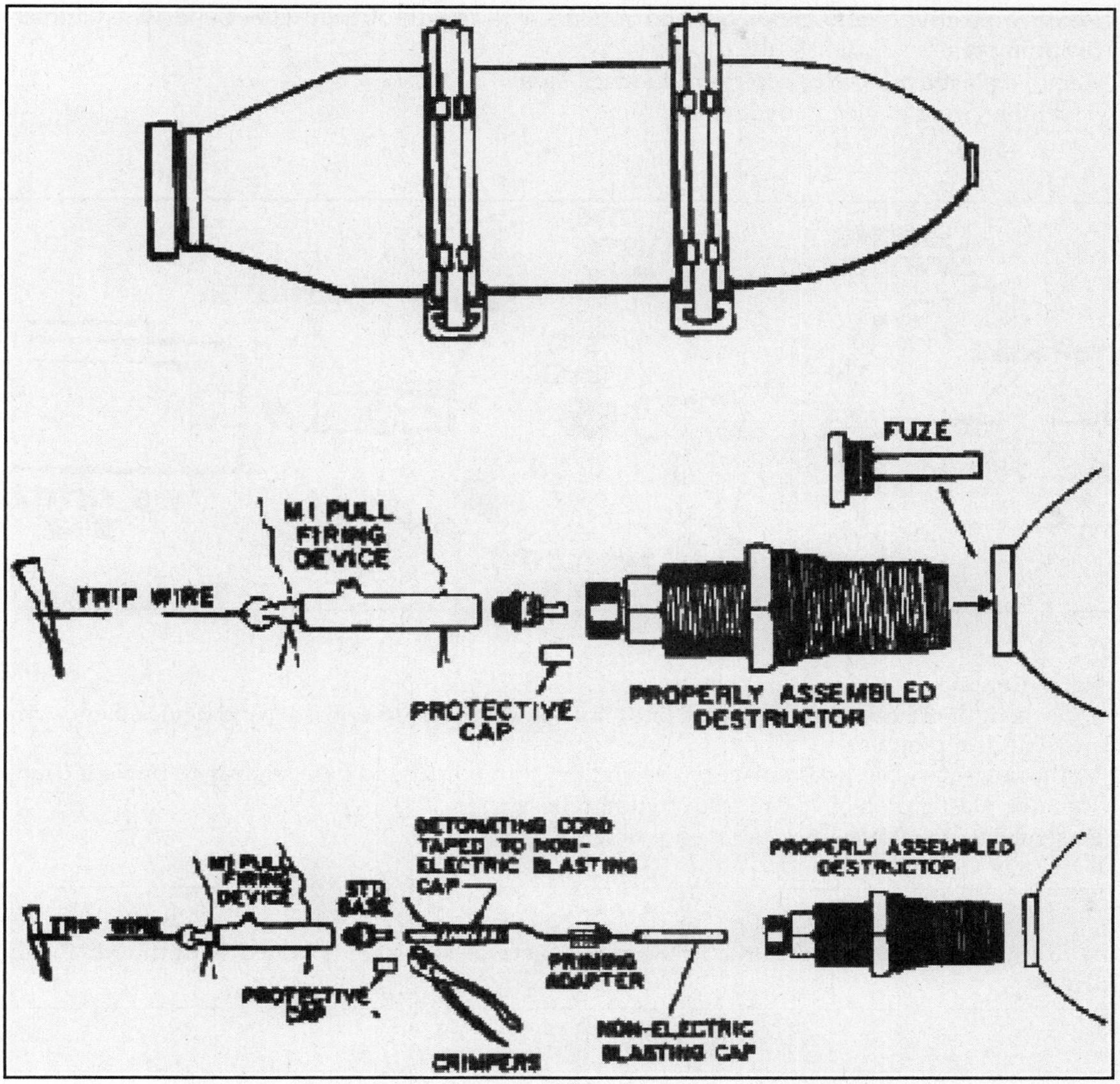

FUZE
M1 PULL FIRING DEVICE
TRIP WIRE
PROTECTIVE CAP
PROPERLY ASSEMBLED DESTRUCTOR
DETONATING CORD TAPED TO NON-ELECTRIC BLASTING CAP
PROPERLY ASSEMBLED DESTRUCTOR
M1 PULL FIRING DEVICE
STD BASE
TRIP WIRE
PRIMING ADAPTER
PROTECTIVE CAP
NON-ELECTRIC BLASTING CAP
CRIMPERS

DETONATION CORD TAPED TO NON-ELECTRIC BLASTING CAP
STD BASE
TRIP WIRE
NON-ELECTRIC BLASTING CAP
M1 PULL FIRING DEVICE
PROTECTIVE CAP
CRIMPERS
C4 EXPLOSIVE

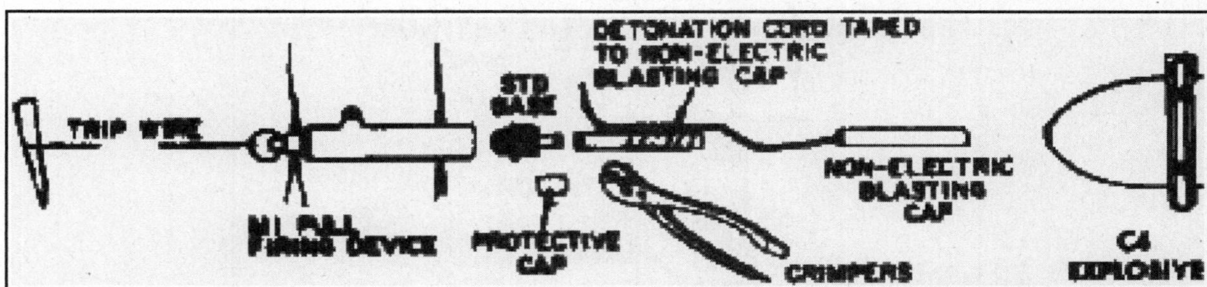

36. ANTITANK MINES

A land mine may be used as the main charge in a boobytrap by removing the fuze and attaching a standard pull or pressure-release firing device in an auxiliary fuze well.

a. **Pull.**
   (1) Remove locking safety cotter pin in M1 pull firing device and replace with length of thin wire. Bend wire slightly to prevent dropping out.

(2) Remove positive safety cotter pin and replace with length of thin wire. Bend wire slightly to prevent dropping out.
(3) Remove plastic protective cap from standard base.
(4) Assemble firing device, activator, and mine.

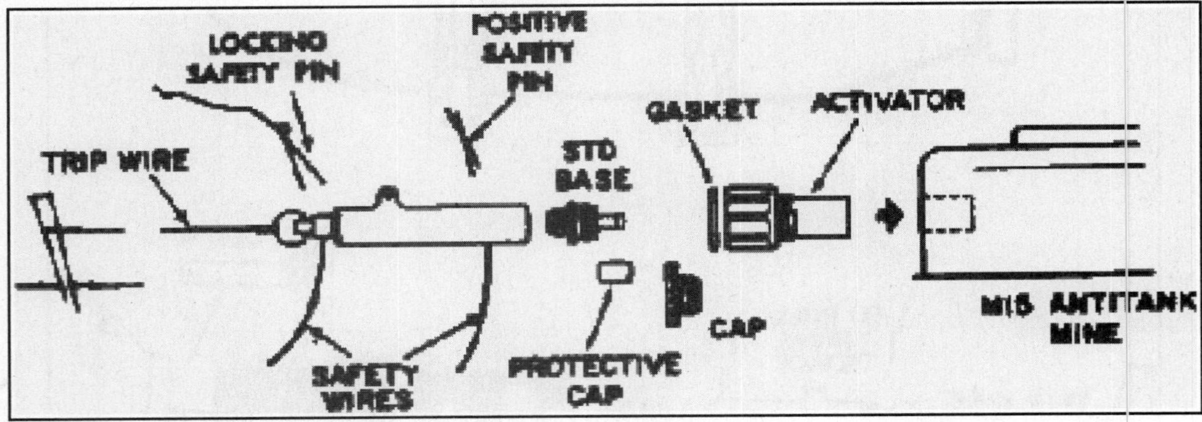

b. **Pressure-Release.**
(1) Insert length of heavy wire in interceptor hole in M5 pressure-release firing device. Bend wire slightly to prevent dropping out.
(2) Withdraw safety pin and replace with length of thin wire. Bend wire slightly to prevent dropping out.
(3) Remove plastic protective cap from standard base.
(4) Assemble firing device, activator, and mine.

> ✍ NOTE
> The firing device must be set on a firm base. A piece of masonite is issued with the M5 for this purpose.

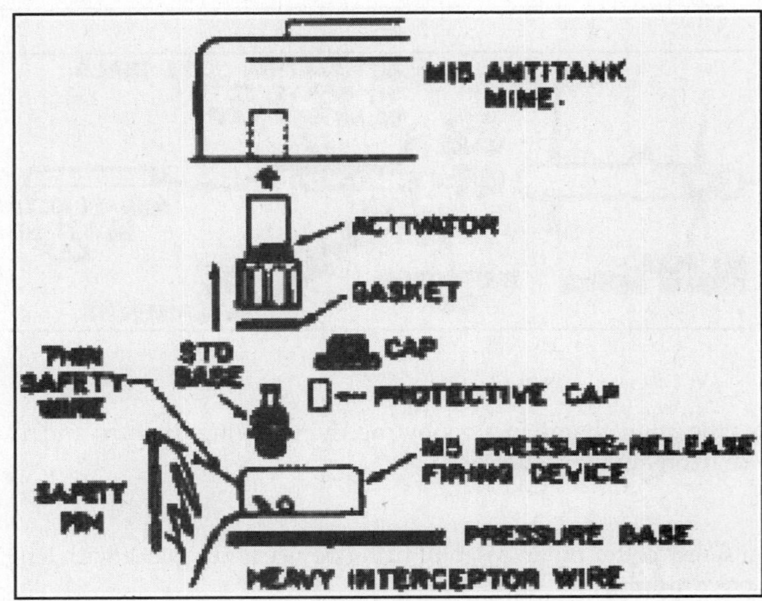

CHAPTER 4

Construction Techniques

SECTION I. BOOBYTRAPPING MINES IN MINEFIELDS

37. TACTICAL PURPOSE

Antitank mines laid in mine fields are boobytrapped (or activated) primarily to make breaching and clearing as dangerous, difficult, and time consuming as possible in order to confuse, demoralize, and delay the enemy. Most standard U.S. antitank mines and many foreign antitank mine have auxiliary fuze wells for this purpose. See FM20–32 for more detailed information.

38. METHODS

U.S. standard antitank mines are generally boobytrapped by means of a pull or a pressure-release firing device, or both, if desirable.

a. **Pull.** Dig hole to proper depth to bury mine on firm foundation with top of pressure plate even with or slightly above ground level. Arm mine before boobytrapping.

(1) ***Installing.***

(a) Remove locking safety cotter pin and replace with length of thin wire. Bend wire slightly to prevent dropping out.

(b) Remove positive safety cotter pin and replace with length of thin wire. Bend wire slightly to prevent dropping out.

(c) Remove protective cap from standard base and assemble firing device, activator, and mine.

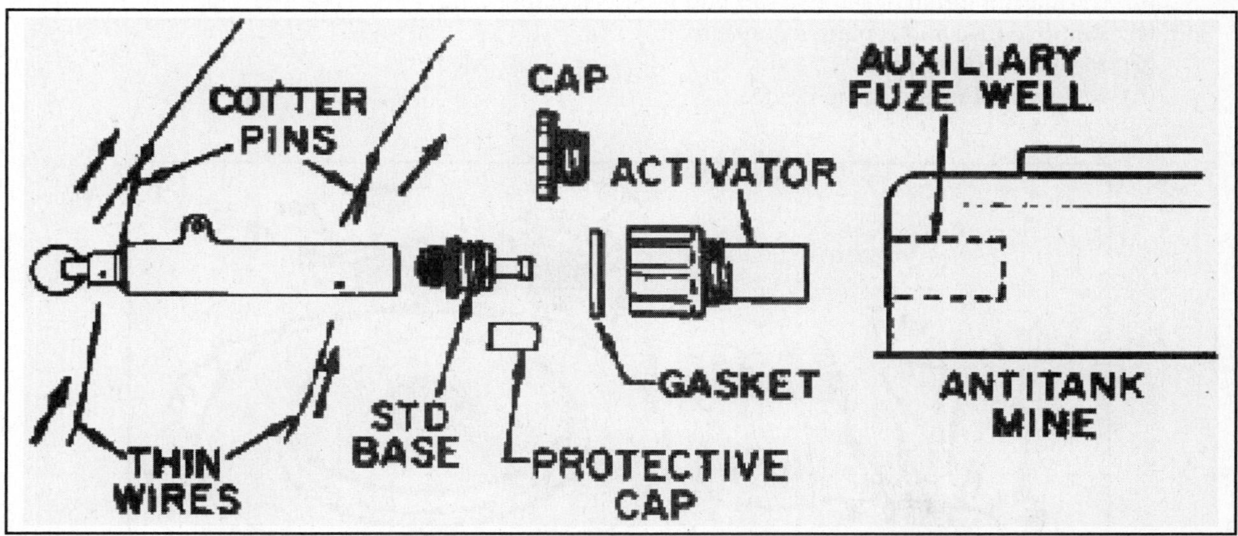

(2) ***Arming.***

(a) Anchor one end of trip wire to stake and fasten the other to pull ring.
(b) *Remove locking safety wire first.*
(c) Remove positive safety *last.*
(d) Camouflage.

(3) ***Disarming.***

(a) Uncover mine carefully.
(b) Locate boobytrap assembly.
(c) Replace positive safety *first,* then locking safety.
(d) Cut trip wire.
(e) Turn arming dial of mine to *safe* and remove arming plug.
(f) Remove fuse and replace safety clip.
(g) Replace arming plug.
(h) Recover mine and firing device.

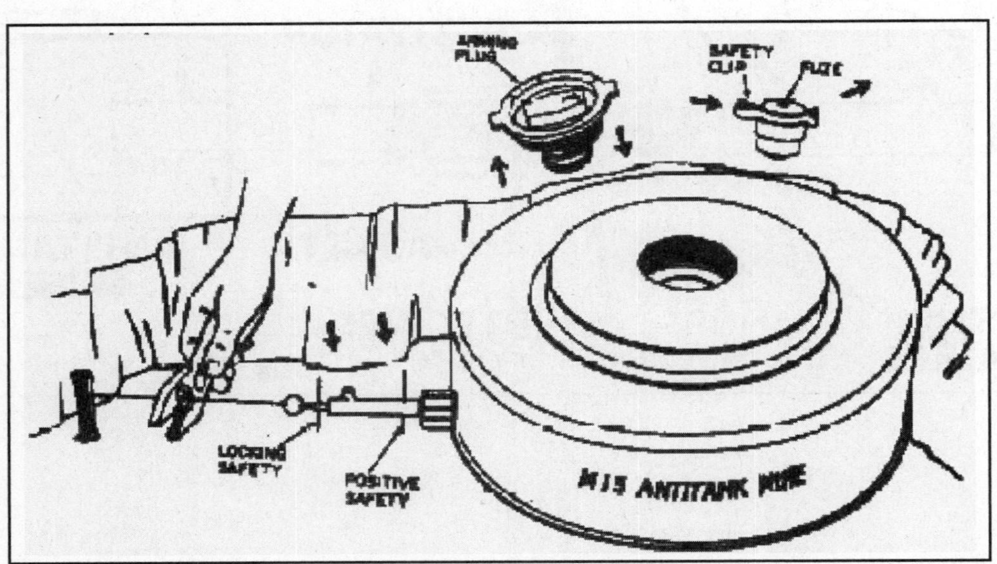

b. **Pressure-Release.** Dig hole to proper depth to bury mine on firm foundation, with top of pressure plate even with or slightly above ground level.

(1) ***Installing.***

(a) Insert length of heavy wire in interceptor hole. Bend wire slightly to prevent dropping out.

(b) Remove safety pin. Apply pressure on release plate until pin comes out easily.

(c) Insert length of light wire in safety pin hole and bend slightly to prevent dropping out.

(d) Remove protective cap from standard base and assemble firing device, activator, and mine.

(e) Place mine and firing assembly in hole, using pressure board to insure a solid foundation for firing device.

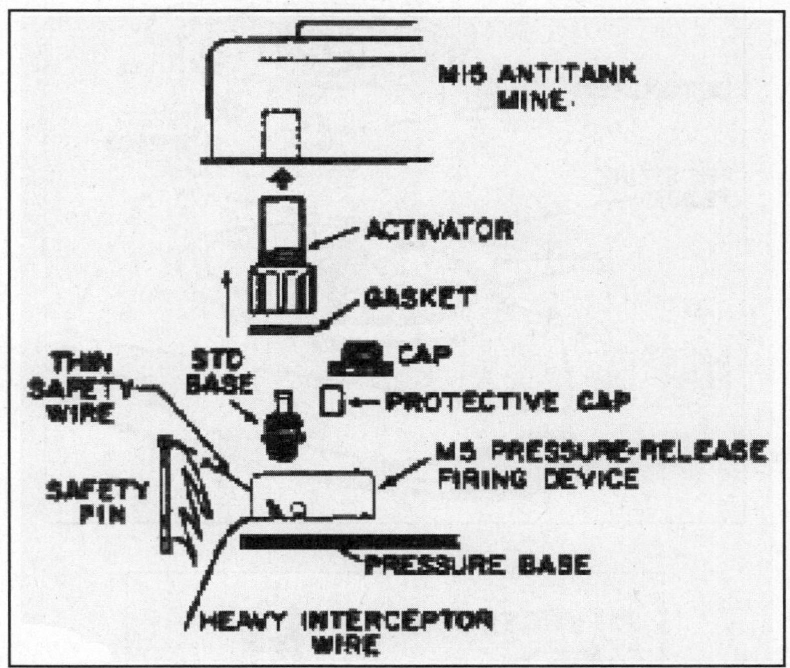

(2) ***Arming.***

(a) Camouflage mine, leaving hole at side to remove safeties.

(b) Carefully remove thin safety wire *first*, then the interceptor wire.

(c) Complete camouflage.

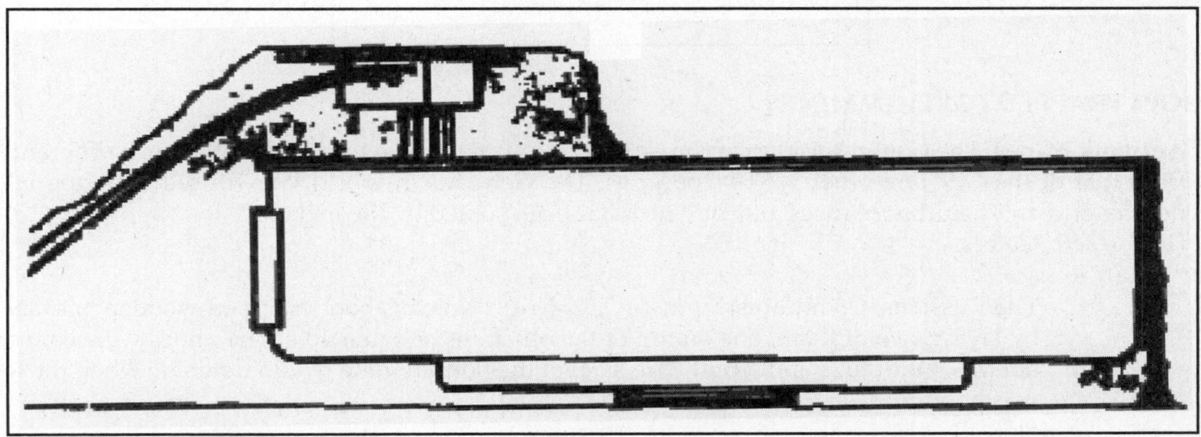

(3) ***Disarming.***
- (a) Uncover mine carefully.
- (b) Locate boobytrap assembly.
- (c) Insert length of heavy wire in interceptor hole.
- (d) Turn dial on pressure plate to "S" (safe) and replace safety fork.
- (e) Recover mine and firing device assembly.
- (f) Remove pressure plate, unscrew detonator, and replace shipping plug.
- (g) Reassemble mine.

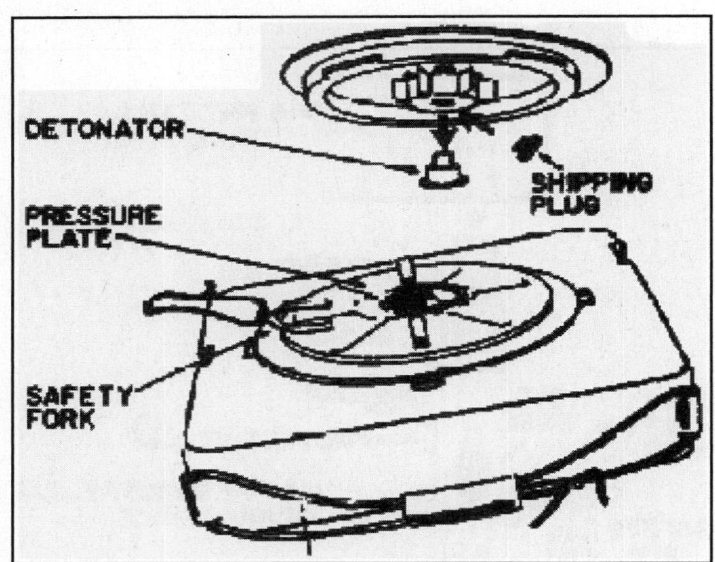

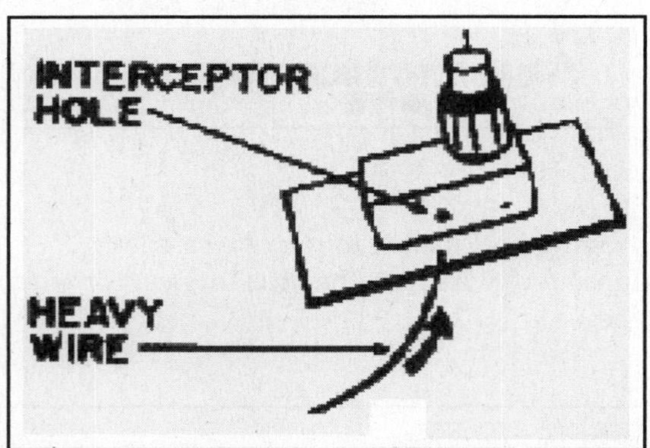

39. BOOBYTRAPPED FOREIGN MINES

a. **Antitank Mines.** The Communist European and Asiatic armies boobytrap mines in a much different fashion from that of the U.S. and other NATO countries. The Germans in World War II used both special antilift devices and antidisturbance fuzes, one of which has been copied by the French.

(1) ***Antilift devices.***

(a) *Russia*

1. The Russians, Communist Chinese, and North Koreans boobytrapped wooden antitank mines by laying two of them, one on top of the other, in the same hole. The mines were connected by am MUV pull fuze and a pull wire, so that the bottom mine would detonate when the top mine was lifted.

2. The Russians in World War II also had a more sophisticated method — a special wooden antilift device, placed under the mine. This, however was readily located by probing. It consisted of an outer case, a charge, an MUV pull fuze, a pressure release lid supported on two coil springs, and a fuze access hole. Lifting the mine initiated the antilift. *This device is too dangerous to disarm.* Even though the pressure-release might be secured by a rope or length of wire, the chances of additional pull wires and boobytrap charges are too great to risk. Also deterioration of the wooden case from prolonged burial adds to the difficulty. *The best procedure is to blow all wooden antitank mines and antilifts in place.*

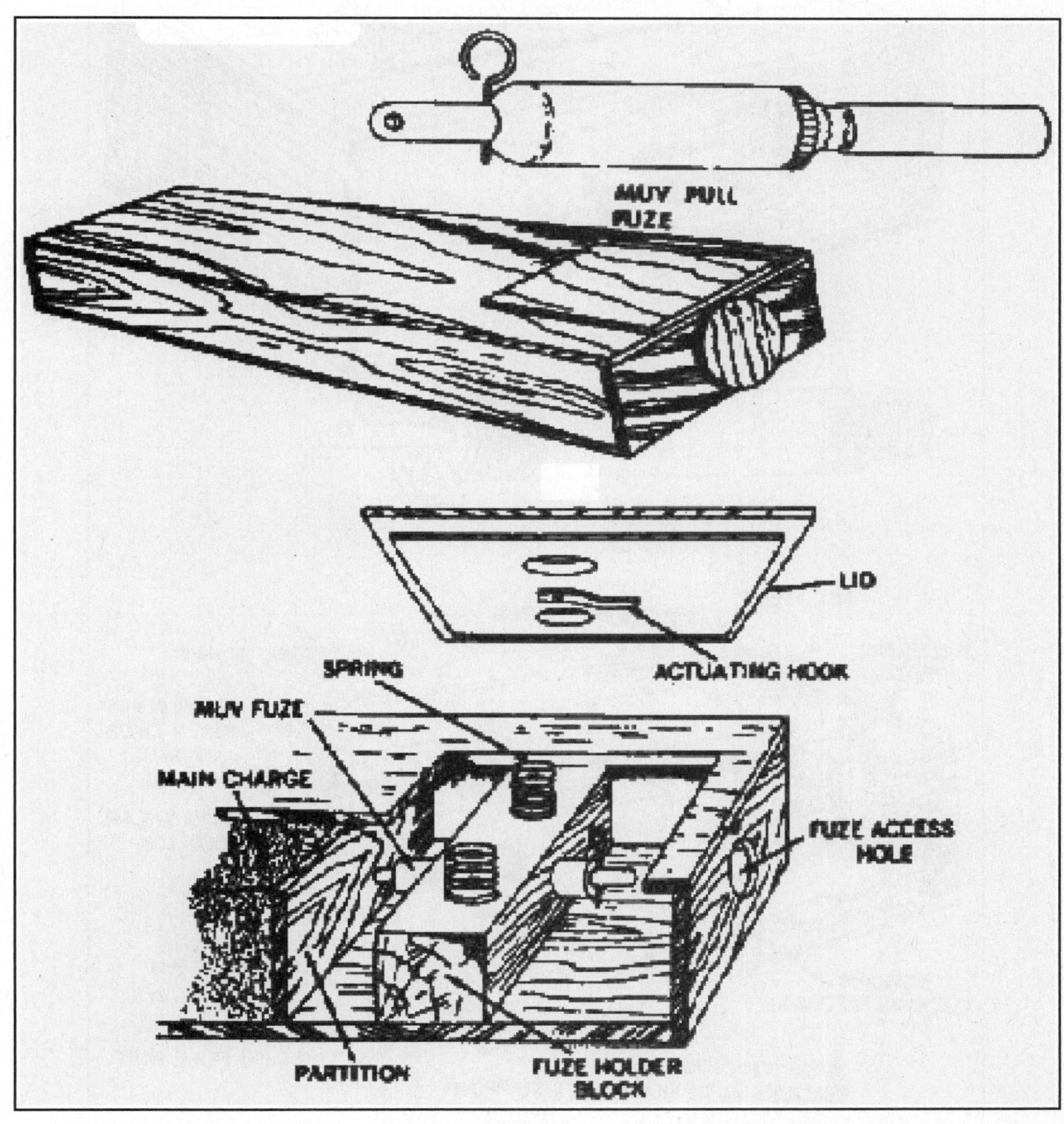

(b) *Czechoslovakia.* This satellite country has a wooden antitank mine (PT-M1-D) that may prove extremely hazardous to breaching and clearing parties. Having an RO-1, pull fuze in each end, it is easily boobytrapped by means of wire anchored to a stake underneath the mine and extended through a hole in the bottom of the case to the fuze pull pin.

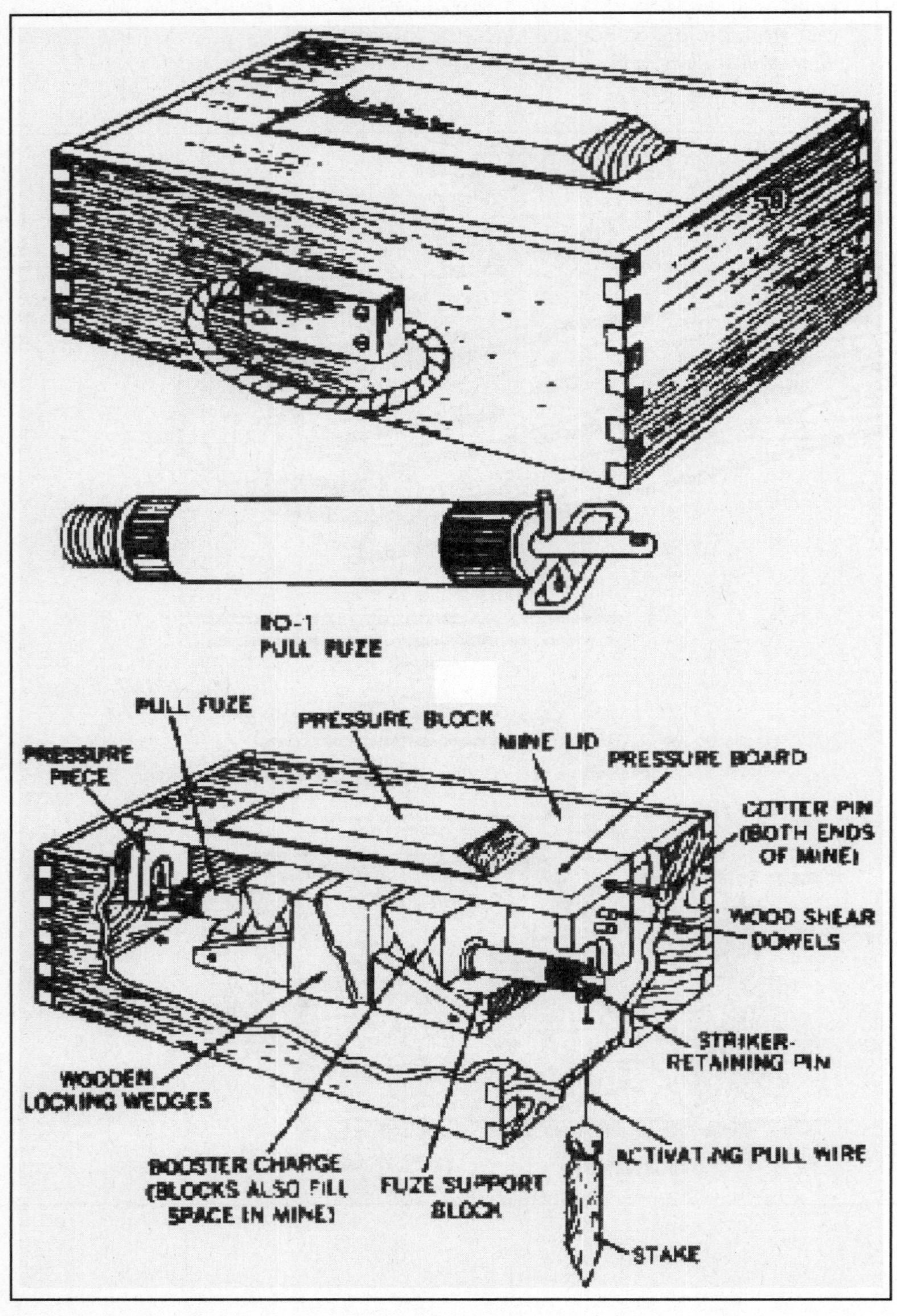

(c) *World War II Germany.* The German armies had several pressure-release devices for boobytrapping antitank mines. In a future war in Europe, these or facsimiles may appear on any battlefield.

1. *Nipolite all explosive antilift.* This consisted of two oblong blocks of moulded explosives joined together with brass bolts and recessed to contain the metal striker assembly. It may be disarmed by inserting a safety in the lower safety pin hole.

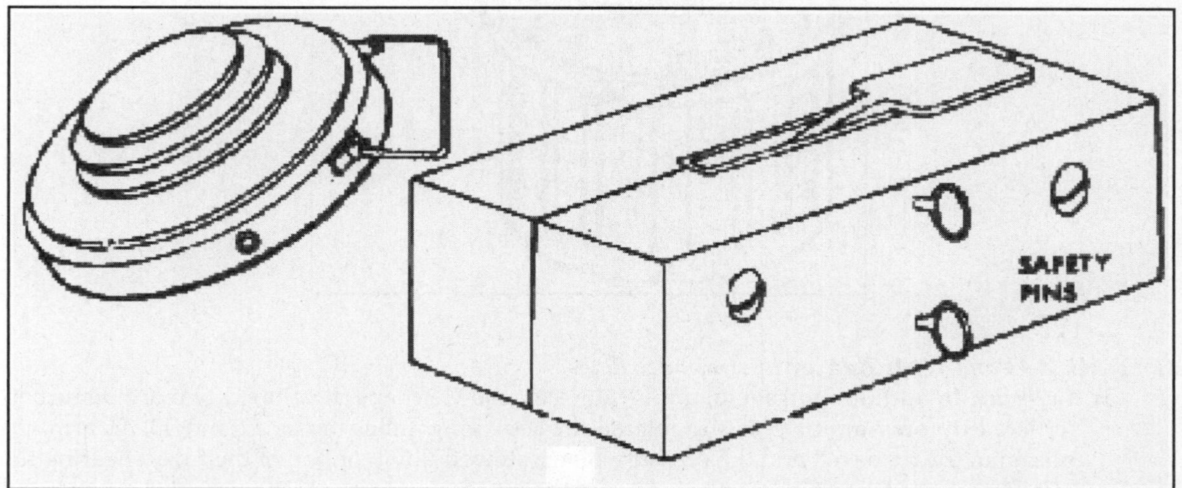

2. *EZ. SM2 (EZ 44).* This device consists of an explosive charge, a pressure-release firing mechanism, a safety bar and a metal case. When the safety bar is removed, the device arms itself by means of clockwork inside the case. *This device cannot be disarmed.*

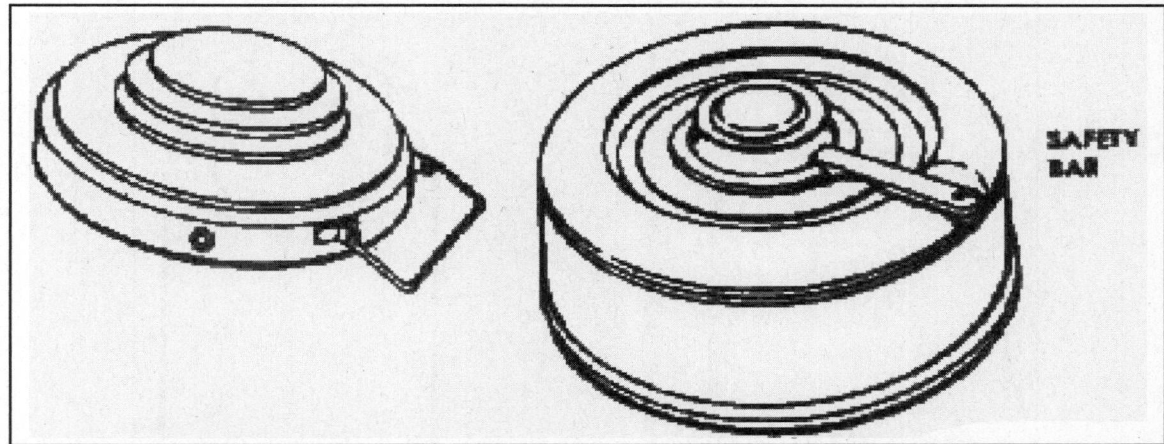

3. *SF3.* This antilift consists of an explosive charge, pressure-release striker assembly, safety bar, and chemical arming equipment. A turn of the safety bar crushes the glass vial, releasing the chemical to dissolve the safety pellet. *This device cannot be disarmed.*

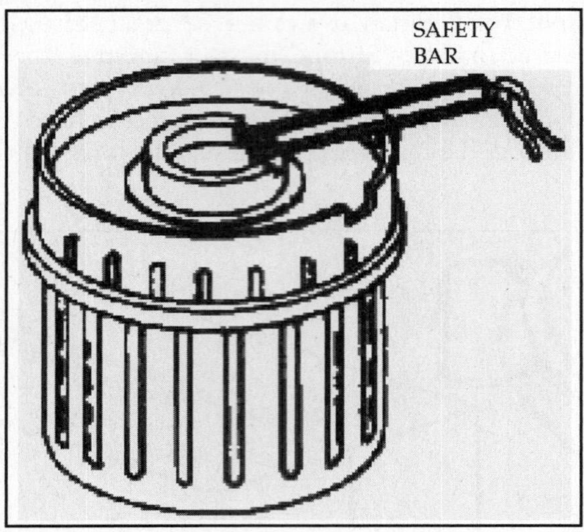

(2) ***T. Mi. Z 43 and T. Mi Z 44 antidisturbance fuzes.***

(a) *Germany.* In addition to several antilift devices, the Germans developed two antidisturbance fuzes initiated by pressure or pressure-release for activating Teller mines 42 and 43. To arm, the fuze is placed in the fuze well and the pressure plate screwed down on top of the fuze, shearing the arming pin. Removal of the pressure plate initiates the pressure-release mechanism and detonates the mine. Although the T. Mi. Z 44 was an experimental model that never reached the field, copies of both fuzes are now in use in several European armies. *Mines armed with these fuzes can neither be identified by size, shape, marking, or color of the case, nor be disarmed.*

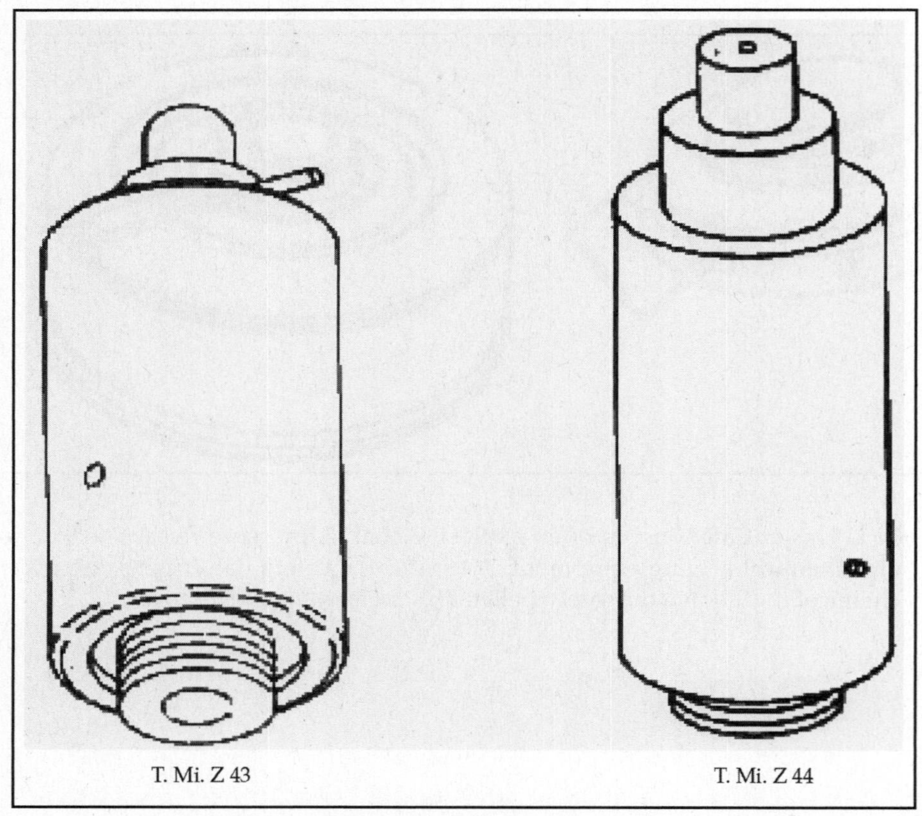

(b) *France.* The French have a copy of the T. Mi. Z 43 antidisturbance (pressure and pressure-release) fuze, and Teller mine 43, named models 1952 and 1948 respectively. The fuze is placed in the fuze well and the pressure plate screwed down on top, shearing the arming pin. Removing the pressure plate actuates the pressure-release element, detonating the mine.

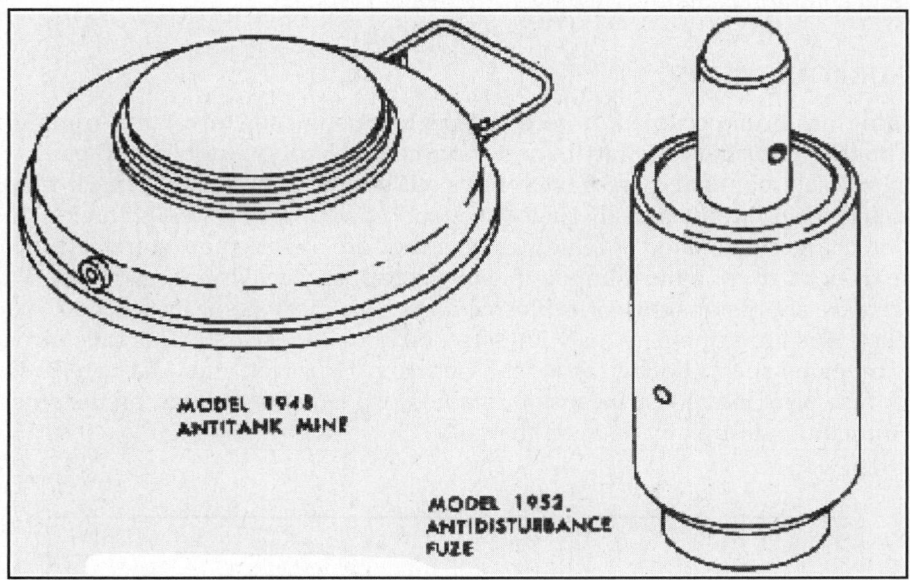

b. **Antipersonnel Mines.** Antipersonnel mines are laid in antitank minefields to halt and delay enemy troops and make breaching and clearing as difficult, dangerous, and time consuming as possible. Enemy mine layers may increase this harrassment substantially by laying small blast type antipersonnel mines near the anchors and along the trip wires, which, according to procedure, must be traced from pull ring to anchor before cutting. These are extremely hazardous to breaching and clearing specialists who may detonate them unawares by the pressure of a hand, knee, or elbow on the pressure plate.

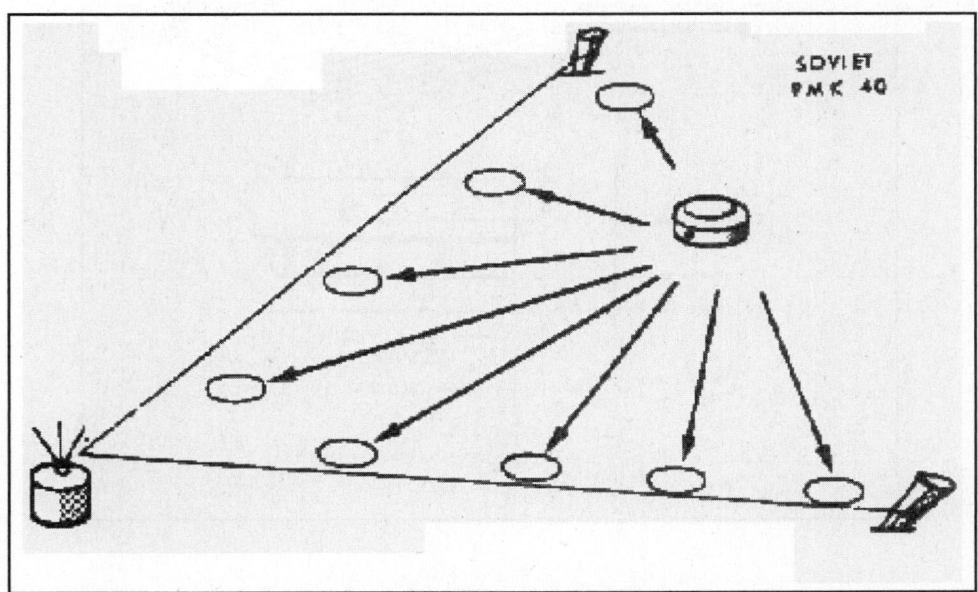

SECTION II. BOOBYTRAPPING BUILDINGS

40. ADVANTAGES

Boobytraps laid in buildings and their surroundings can be very effective. Buildings are very attractive to fighting men for they provide a degree of comfort and shelter from the elements. They are also useful for headquarters where plans may be made and communications carried on with greater dispatch.

41. IMMEDIATE SURROUNDINGS

a. Once a building has been occupied, it becomes the focal point for travel and communication from many directions. Thus the immediate vicinity becomes a potential location for boobytraps.
b. Dwellings in sparsely populated areas often have out buildings, wood piles, fruit trees, wells, fences with gates, walks, and other locations easily rigged to wound or destroy careless soldiers.
c. Delayed action charges detonated in buildings after they are occupied are extremely effective. Such charges, however, are difficult if not almost impossible to conceal, especially in large masonry and steel buildings, which may require a large quantity of explosive for serious damage or destruction. None but a most ingenious specialist, given time, help, and a wide selection of material can do this satisfactorily. In World War II, the Russians prepared such a boobytrap for the Germans. However, after lone careful search the charge and its clockwork fuze were located by means of a stethoscope. Small buildings, on the other hand, may be only moderately difficult to destroy by delayed charges.

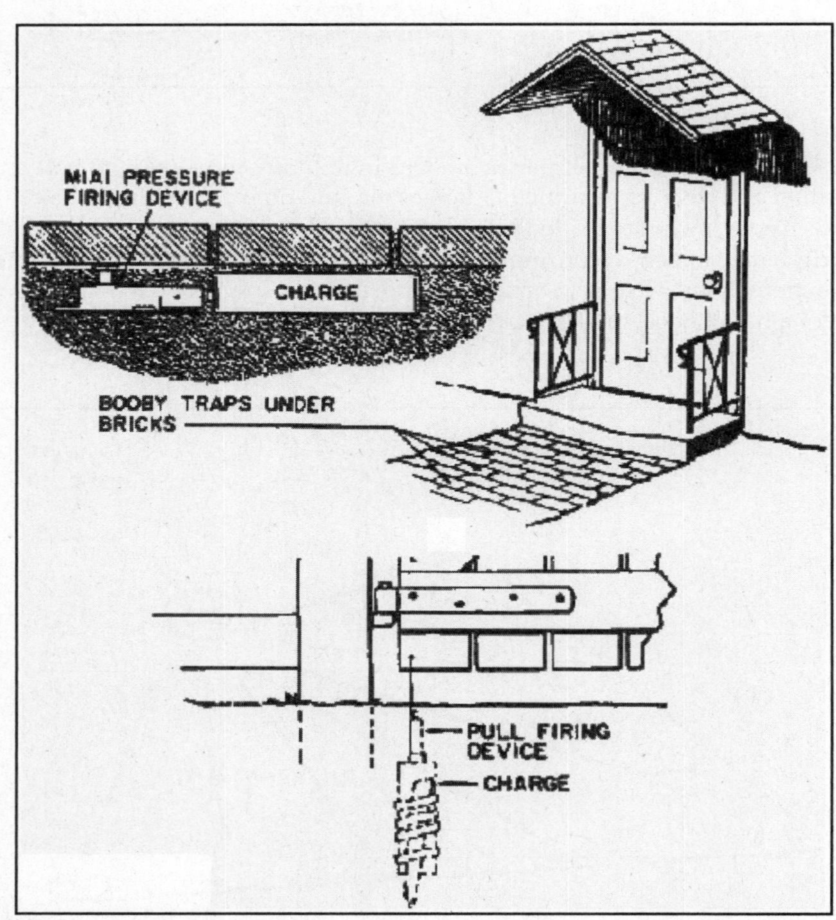

42. ENTRANCES

Curiosity prompts a soldier to investigate hurriedly an interesting building in his path. Women, loot, or mere inquisitiveness may be the motive. His rush to be the first inside makes all entrances excellent spots for boobytraps. For the foolish, a rigging connected to the front door, side door, or back doors may be sufficient. But for the experienced soldier, who may carefully seek entry to the basement first and then try to clear the building story by story, careful and ingenious effort may be required.

a. **Basement Windows.** Here boobytraps must be concealed to prevent detection by the enemy's breaking the pane or kicking out a door panel. Basement windows should be boobytrapped at the top or in the floor underneath.

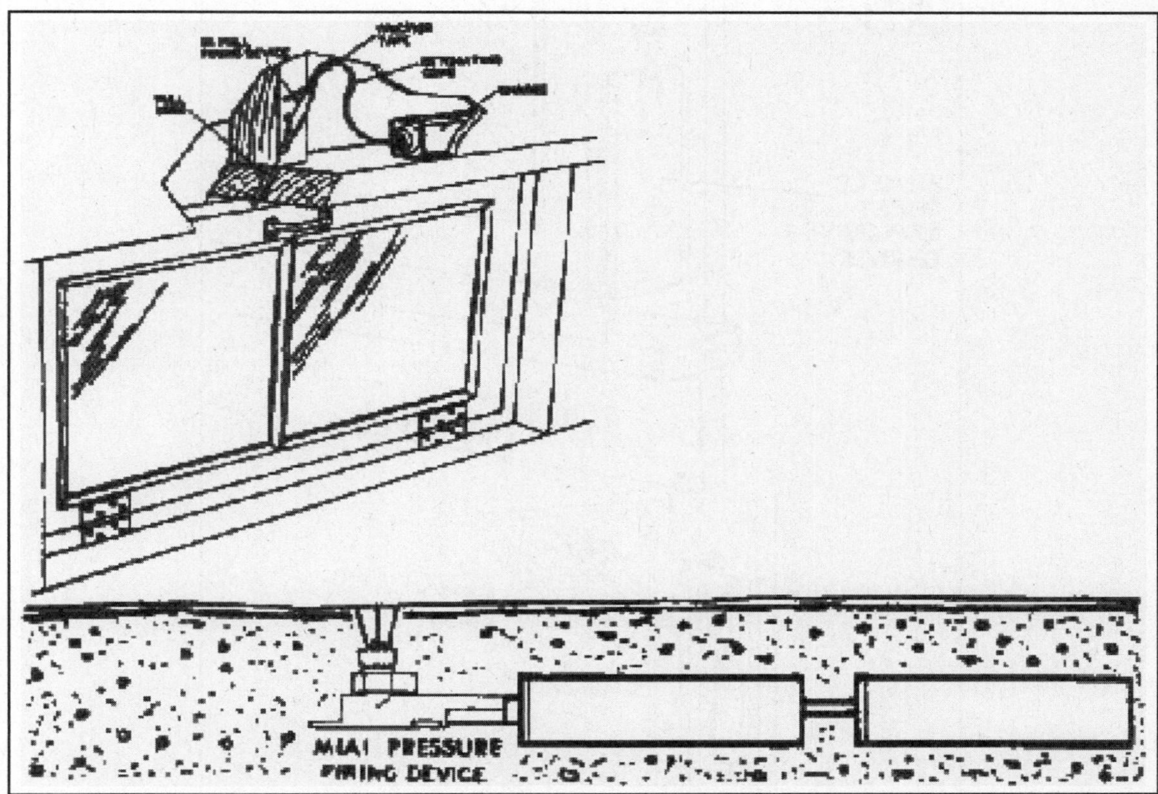

b. **Upper Floor Windows.** Window charges are easier concealed in the weight box behind the jamb than in the wall or under the floor. Experienced hands can remove and replace window trim without obvious damage.
   (1) ***Nonelectric firing.***
      (a) Assemble M3 pull-release firms device, standard base, and blasting cap.
      (b) Place sheet explosive in weight box.
      (c) Bore hole in side jamb for pull wire.
      (d) Anchor one end of pull wire to window, and thread through hole in side jamb.
      (e) Attach free end of pull wire to ratchet on firing device.
      (f) Arm firing device.
      (g) Conceal boobytrap.

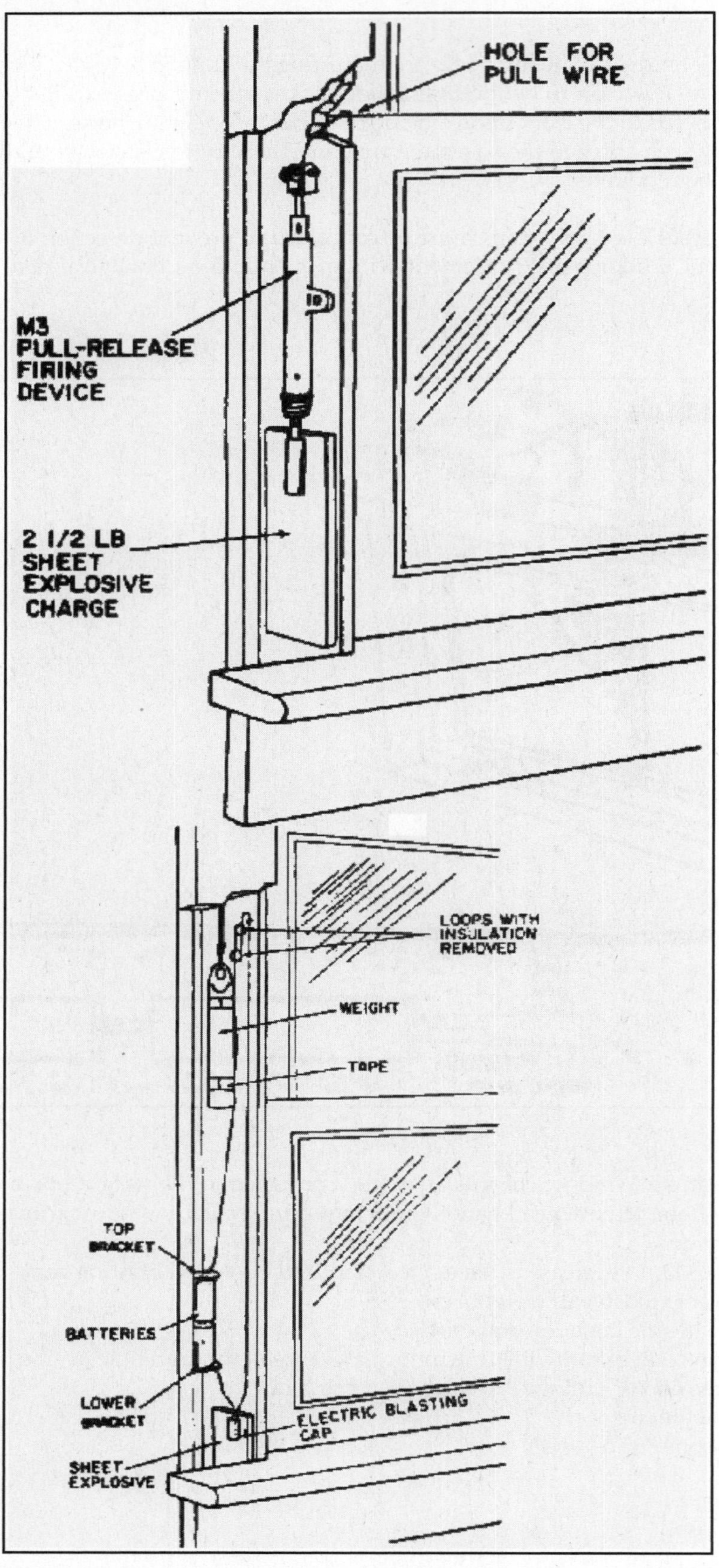
HOLE FOR
PULL WIRE
M3
PULL-RELEASE
FIRING
DEVICE
2 1/2 LB
SHEET
EXPLOSIVE
CHARGE
LOOPS WITH
INSULATION
REMOVED
WEIGHT
TAPE
TOP
BRACKET
BATTERIES
LOWER
BRACKET
ELECTRIC BLASTING
CAP
SHEET
EXPLOSIVE

(2) ***Electric firing.***

(a) Fasten two metal brackets to side of weight box close enough to wedge two flashlight batteries between.
(b) Place sheet explosive charge in weight box.
(c) Insert electric blasting cap in charge.
(d) Cut one leg wire and attach to lower bracket.
(e) Cut other leg wire to proper length to twist an uninsulated loop on end and fasten to hang in place just above top of window weight.
(f) On a length of leg wire twist on uninsulated loop around the leg wire hanging above the weight. Thread other end through other uninsulated loop and fasten to top clamp. Tape wire to window weight.
(g) Test circuit with galovonmeter first, then insert batteries between brackets.
(h) Conceal boobytrap.

c. **Doors.** Improved detection methods have made the use of boobytraps on doors, with charges, firing devices, and wires exposed, a waste of time and material, except for purposes of deception. The best location is the head or side jamb, not the sill, which is often recommended. The sill is exposed, so that one experienced clearing unit may easily locate the rigging while in the jamb, it is concealed by the doorstop.

(1) ***Head jamb rigging.***

(a) Assemble M1 pull firing device, standard base, and nonelectric blasting cap.
(b) Assemble length of detonating cord, priming adapter, nonelectric blasting cap and explosive block.
(c) Attach firing device firmly to stud and tape free end of length of detonating cord to nonelectric blasting cap.
(d) Drill hole at proper place in header and head jamb.
(e) Anchor one end of pull wire at proper place on door and thread free end through holes.
(f) Close door and attach pull wire to pull ring.
(g) Arm and conceal boobytrap.

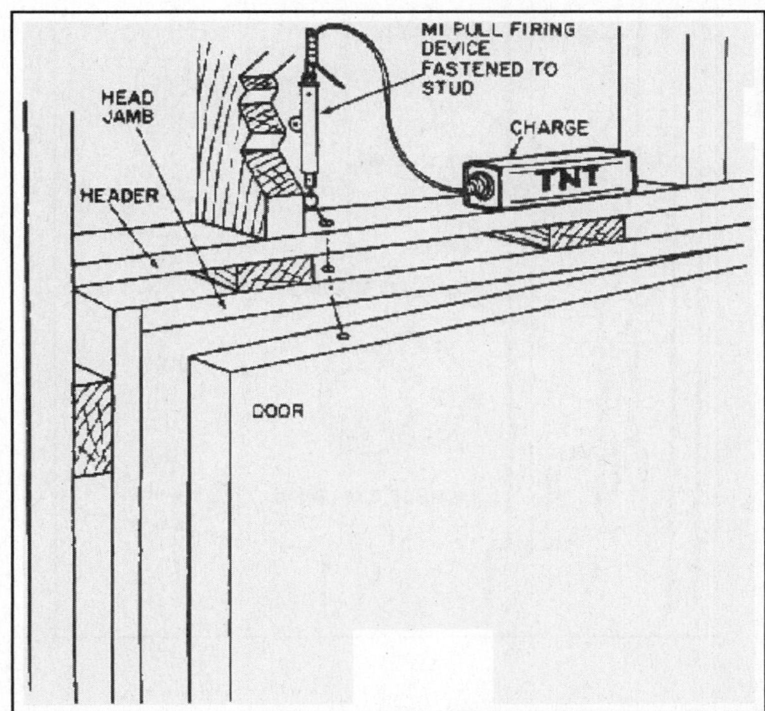

(2) ***Side jamb rigging.***

(a) Attach metal brackets to side jamb close enough to wedge two flashlight batteries between.
(b) Insert sheet explosive charge snugly between stud and jamb.
(c) Place electric blasting cap in charge, and fasten one leg wire to top bracket.
(d) Bore pull wire hole at proper spot inside jamb.
(e) Cut other leg wire long enough to twist on an insulated loop on one end and fit over pull wire hole. Loop should be about ½ inch in diameter.
(f) Twist on uninsulated loop on one end of leg wire and secure to lower bracket so that loop fits over pull wire hole. Fasten wire to jamb.
(g) Anchor one end of insulated pull wire at proper spot on door, and thread free end through pull wire hole and loop fastened to jamb.
(h) Close door. Fasten free end of pull wire to other loop to hold it snugly against stud.
(i) Check circuit with galvonometer first, then
(j) Install batteries between brackets.
(k) Conceal boobytrap.

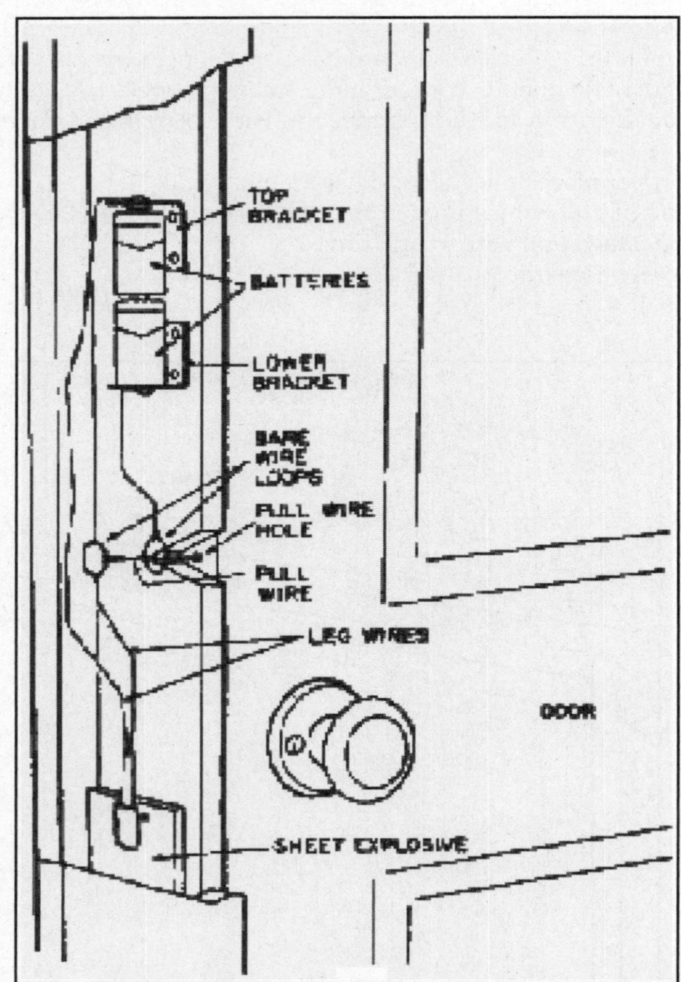

43. STRUCTURAL FRAMEWORK

a. In a building charges should be placed where detonation will seriously impair its structural strength, such as walls, chimneys, beams, and columns. Charges and firing devices must be carefully concealed to avoid detection.

b. In boobytrapping load-bearing walls, several charges should be laid to detonate simultaneously near the base. Chimneys and fireplaces are difficult to boobytrap for charges placed there are readily detected. These should detonate from intense heat.

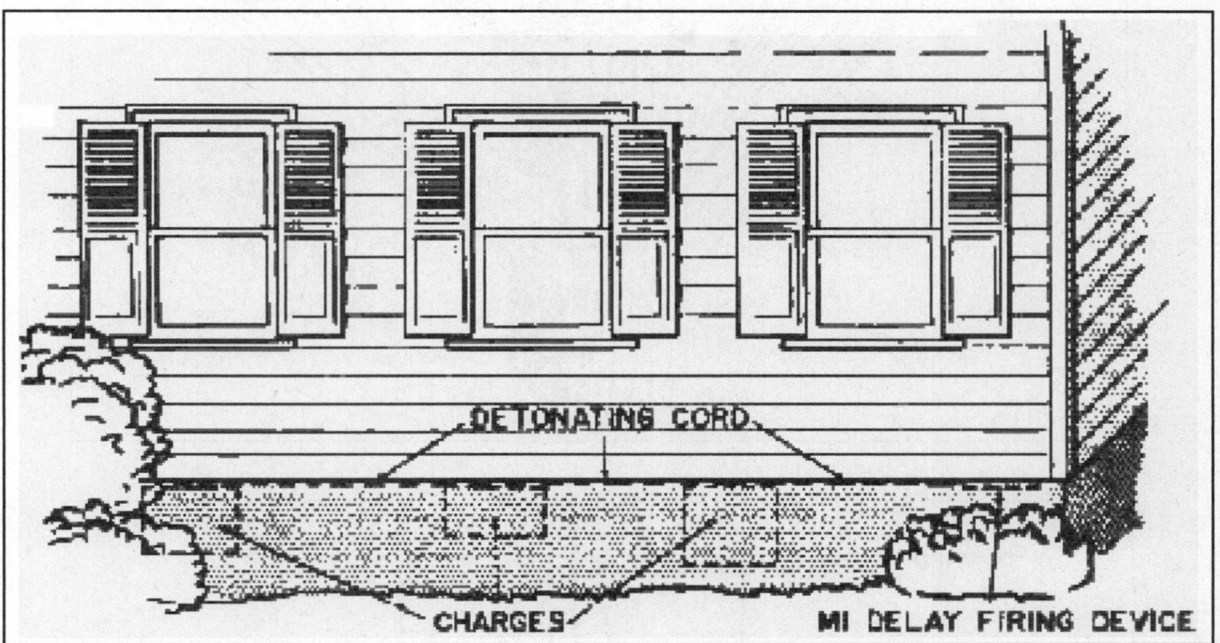

c. Beams and columns when they collapse cause much more damage than walls because they bear much mere weight.

(1) In wooden beams, holes for concealed explosives should be bored close enough together for sympathetic detonation. An M1 delay firing device and detonator placed in a hole within the bulk explosive charge should suffice. Buildings of masonry and steel construction may also be boobytrapped with delay charges. The difficulty of the job depends often on the interior finish, type of decoration, heating ducts, air conditioning, and type of floors.

(2) A column may be destroyed by a charge buried below ground level at its base. Although heavy delay charges like these are often considered mines, they are shown here because they may be found in boobytrap locations.

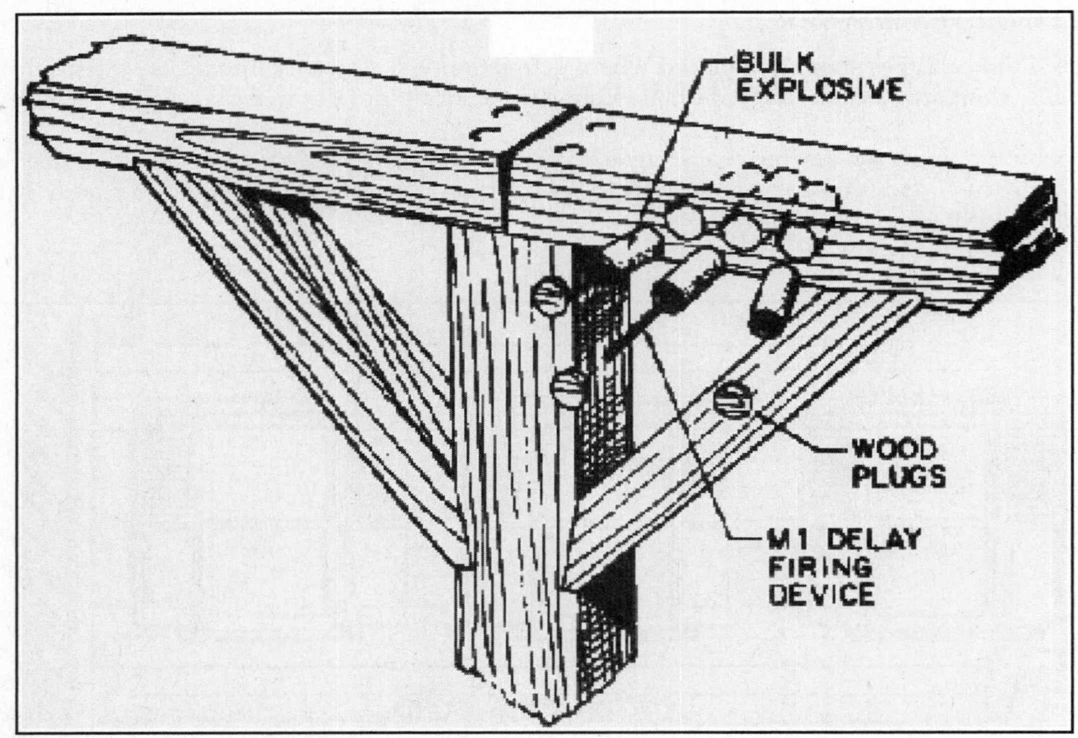
BULK EXPLOSIVE
WOOD PLUGS
M1 DELAY FIRING DEVICE

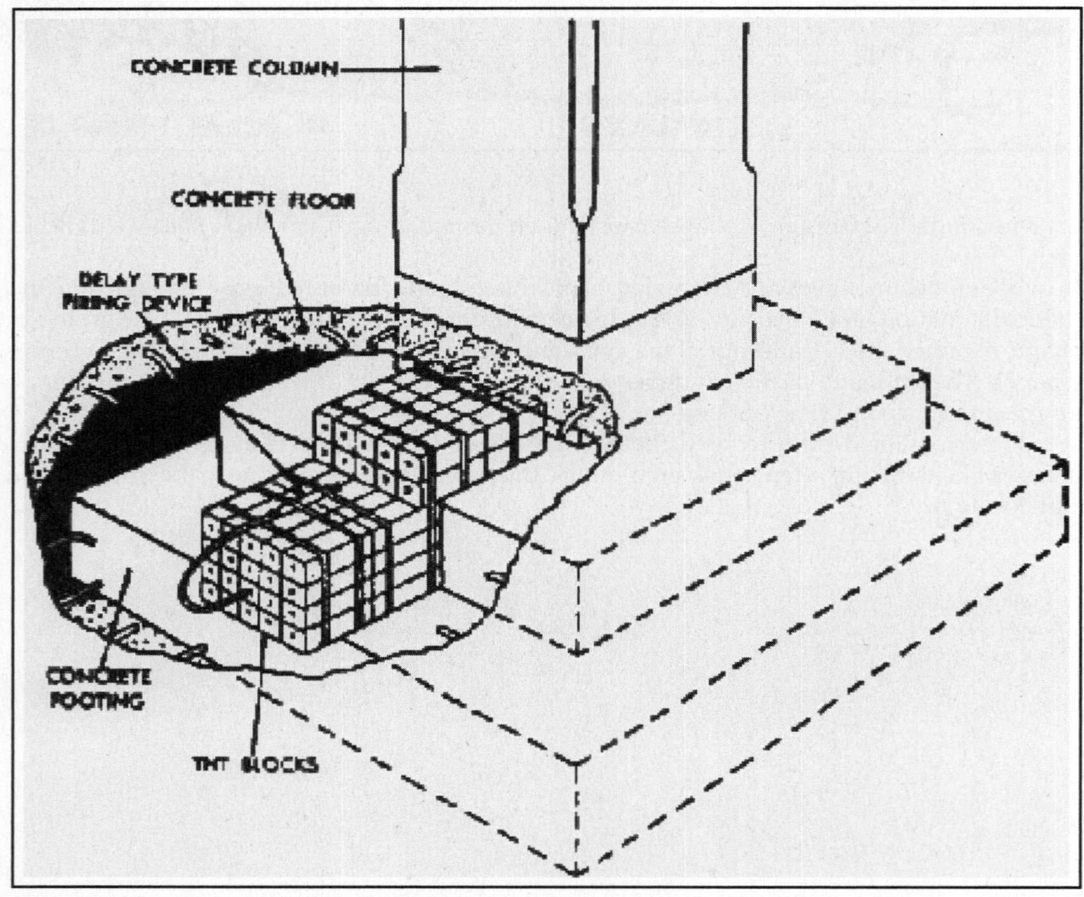
CONCRETE COLUMN
CONCRETE FLOOR
DELAY TYPE FIRING DEVICE
CONCRETE FOOTING
TNT BLOCKS

d. Loose floor boards sometimes are excellent objects for boobytrapping. The rigging must escape detection, however; otherwise, it will be ineffective. This rigging might be harder to detect if the support underneath is chiseled out to let the floorboard sink about ¼ inch when tramped on.

e. A double delay chain detonating boobytrap should be very effective if timed right and skillfully laid. *First*, is the explosive of a minor charge laid in an upper story damaging the building only slightly. *Then*, after a curious crowd has gathered, a second heavy charge or series of charges go off, seriously damaging or destroying the building and killing or wounding many onlookers.

44. INTERIOR FURNISHINGS

Vacated buildings provide much opportunity for boobytrapping. Hurriedly departing occupants usually leave behind such odds and ends as desks, filing cases, cooking utensils, table items, rugs, lamps, and furniture. Electric light and power fixtures are also exploitable.

a. **Desk.** Because of its construction a desk is easily boobytrapped. If carefully placed the rigging may be non-detectable and if properly constructed, cannot be neutralized. Electric firing systems are the most suitable for this purpose. Sheet explosive is much better than other types, because its adhesive surface holds it firmly in place. Check the circuit with a galvonometer *before* installing the batteries.

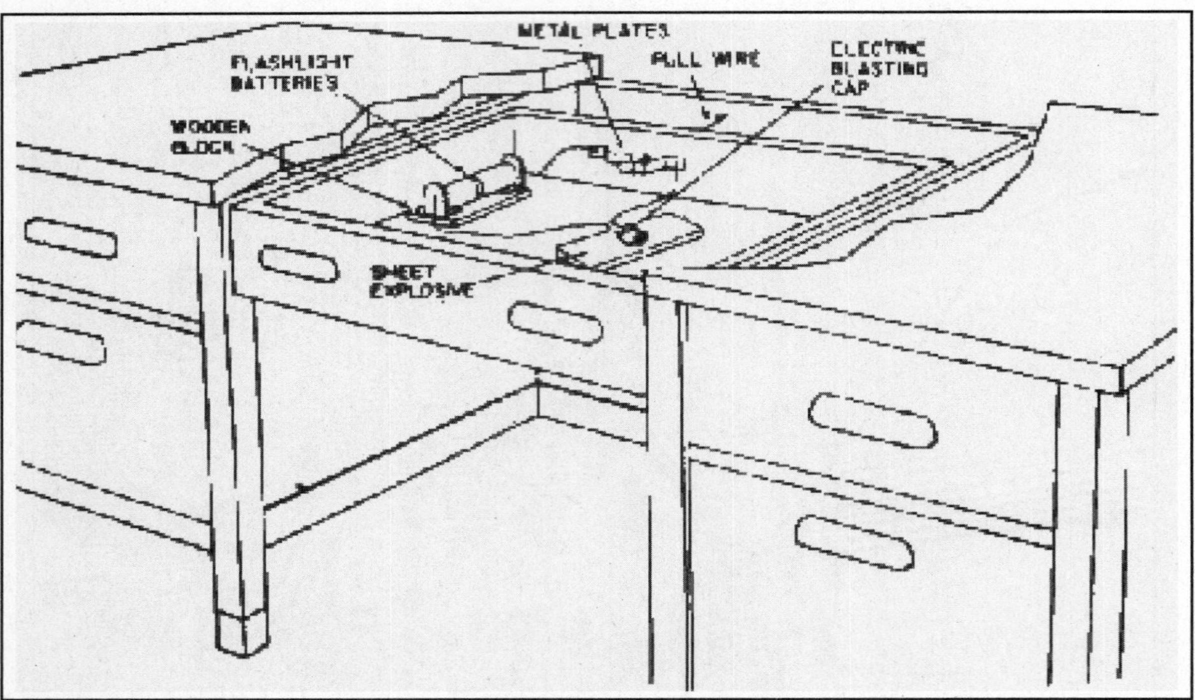

b. **Office Equipment.** Many items used in offices have boobytrap potential.
  (1) ***Telephone list finder.***
    (a) Remove contents from finder.
    (b) Assemble sheet explosive, shrapnel, and blasting cap.
    (c) Remove insulation from ends of wire and twist to form loop switch.
    (d) Place boobytrap in finder so that the raising of the lid draws the loops together.
    (e) Insulate inside of case from contact with loops with friction tape.
    (f) Check circuit with galvanometer *first*, then install batteries.

> ✍ **NOTE**
> Batteries may be connected to legwires by wrapping them tightly in place with friction tape.

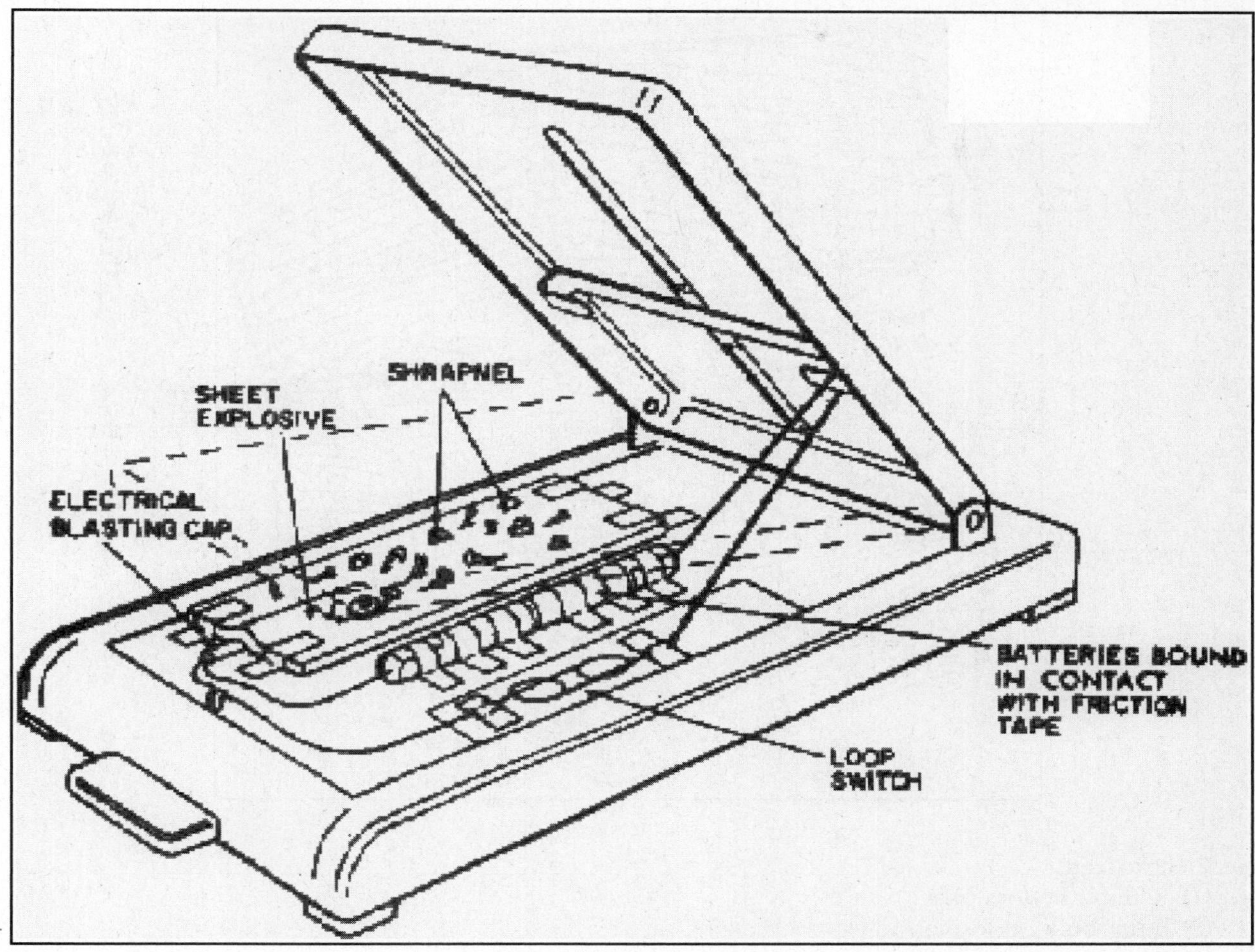

(2) ***Card File.*** A wooden card file can be boobytrapped effectively by the use of a mousetrap rigged as a trigger, a standard base with blasting cap attached, a support block fastened inside to hold the firing assembly at the proper level for operation, and a trigger block to hold the trigger in armed position.

- (a) Rig wire trigger of mousetrap with screw and metal strip.
- (b) Locate support block on strips at proper level to fix trigger in trigger block.
- (c) Bore hole in support block at proper place to admit standard base and blasting cap so that sheet metal screw will strike percussion cap.
- (d) Insert explosive, then support block with mousetrap, standard base, and blasting cap in position.
- (e) Raise trigger and close lid so that trigger is fixed in firing position.

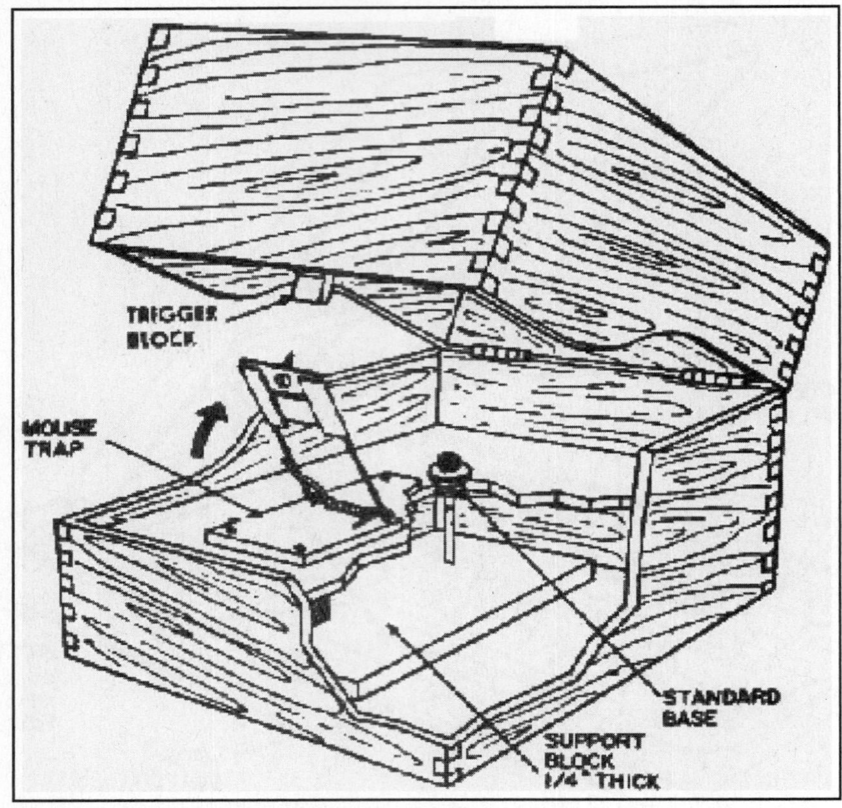

c. **Electric Iron.**
   (1) Remove bottom plate.
   (2) Insert bulk explosive and electric blasting cap.
   (3) Attach shortened leg wires to power inlet.

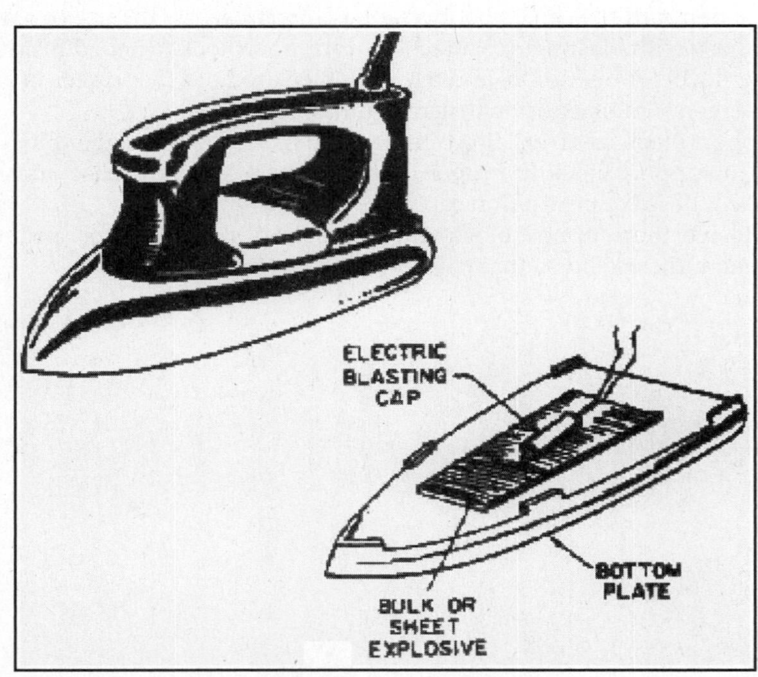

d. **Teakettle.**
   (1) Assemble sheet explosive, electric blasting cap and mercury element in teakettle.
   (2) Cheek circuit with galvanometer first, then install batteries.

> ✍ NOTE
> Batteries may be bound tightly in circuit with friction tape. For safety and ease of assembly, use a wrist watch delay in circuit (para 60*d*).

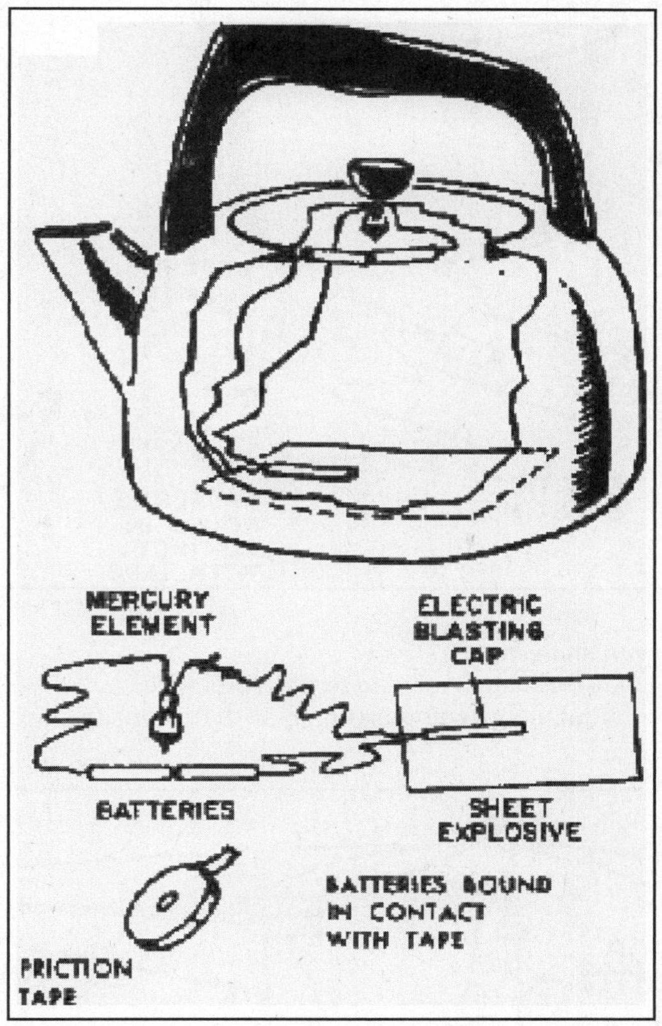

e. **Pressure Cooker.**
   (1) ***Antidisturbance circuit.***
      (a) Assemble sheet explosive, mercury element, and electric blasting cap in cooker.
      (b) Check circuit with galvanometer *first,* then install batteries.

> ✍ NOTE
> Batteries may be bound tightly in circuit with friction tape. For safety and ease of assembly, use a wrist watch delay in circuit (para 60*d*).

(2) ***Loop switch.***

(a) Assemble sheet explosive and electric blasting cap.

(b) Cut leg wires to proper length. Remove insulation from ends and twist to form loop switch.

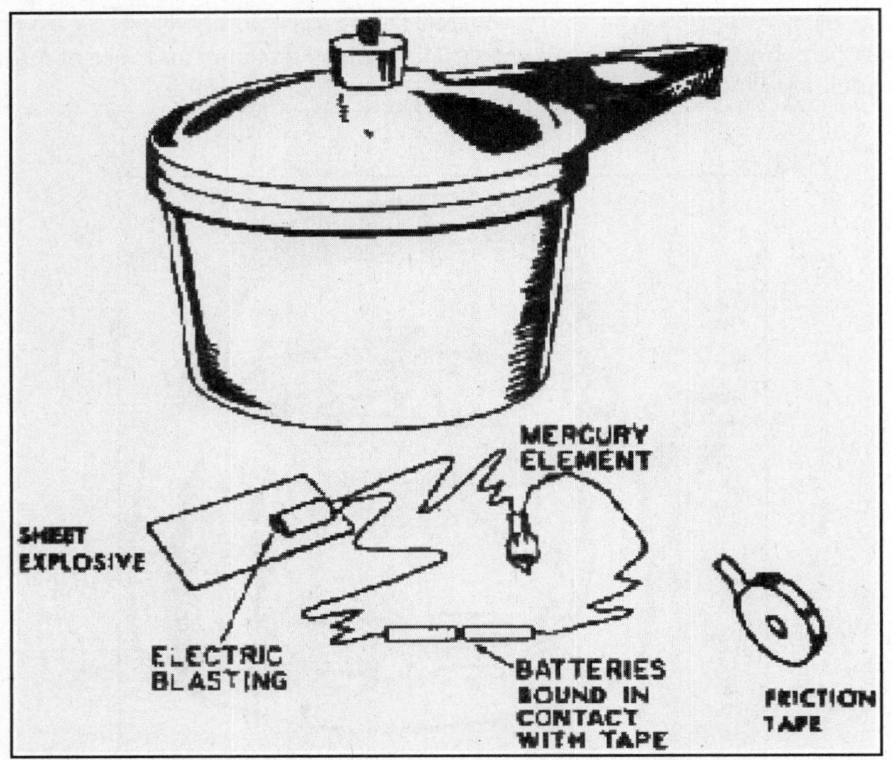

(3) ***Check circuit with galvanometer.***

(a) Fasten one leg wire (insulated) to lid to serve as pull wire.

(b) Secure batteries in circuit by wrapping tightly with friction tape.

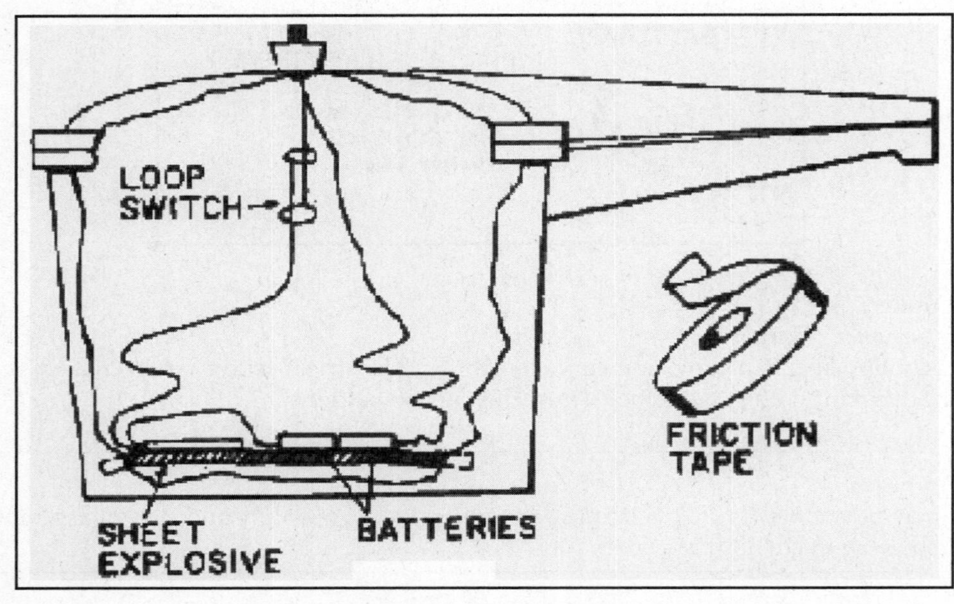

f. **Radio and Television Sets.** Both sets may be boobytrapped by assembling a charge and an electric blasting cap inside the case.

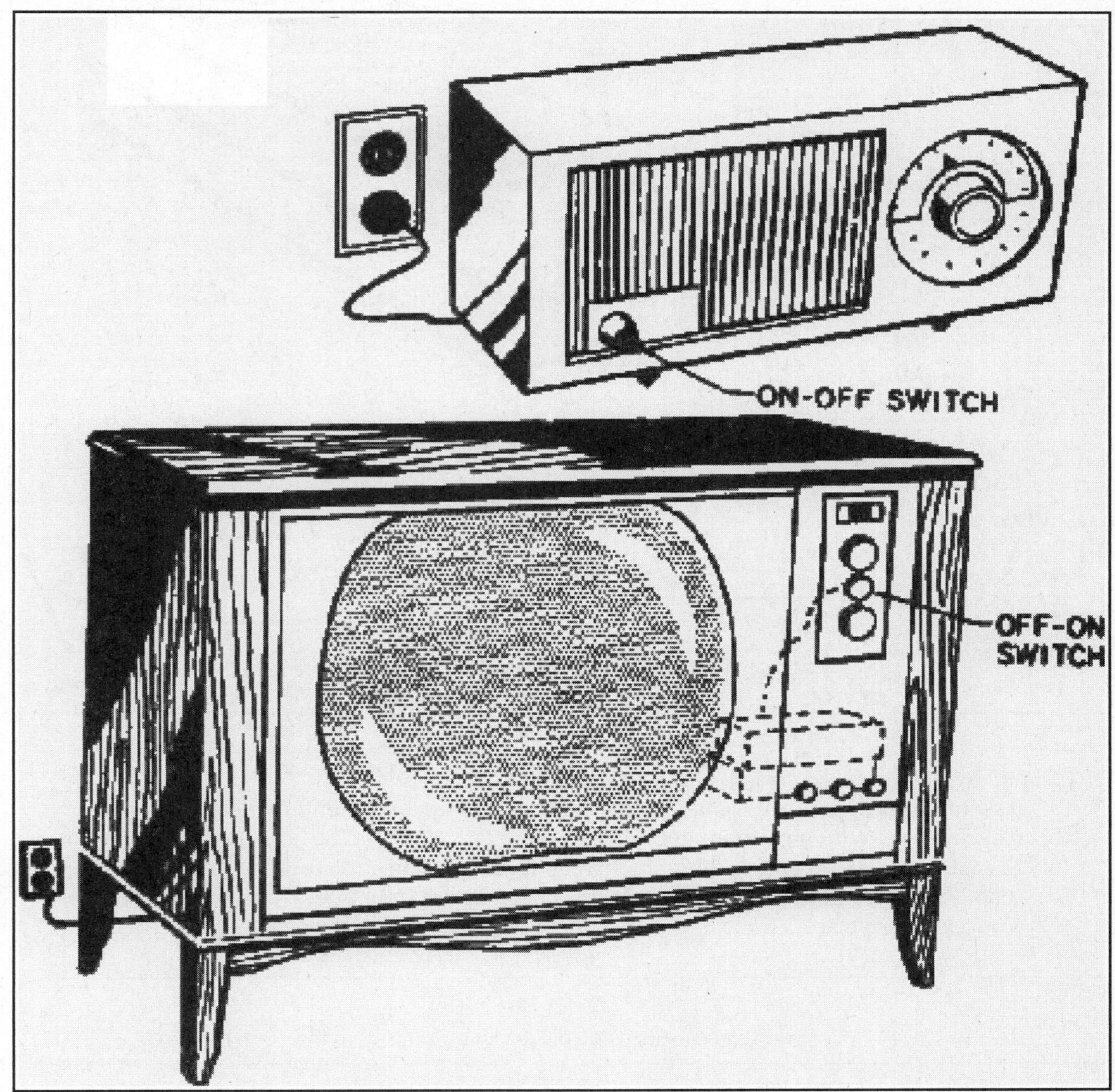

The leg wires are connected in the circuit for detonation at turning of off-on switch.
Extreme care is required in connecting leg wires to prevent premature explosion.

g. **Bed.** Two methods may be used — a charge, nonelectric blasting cap, and pull firing device or a charge, batteries, electric blasting cap, and a mercury switch element.

(1) ***Nonelectric rigging.***

(a) Assemble pull wire, M1 will firing device, blasting cap, and sheet explosive charge.

(b) Anchor pull wire so that a person sitting or lying on bed will initiate firing device.

(c) Conceal boobytrap.

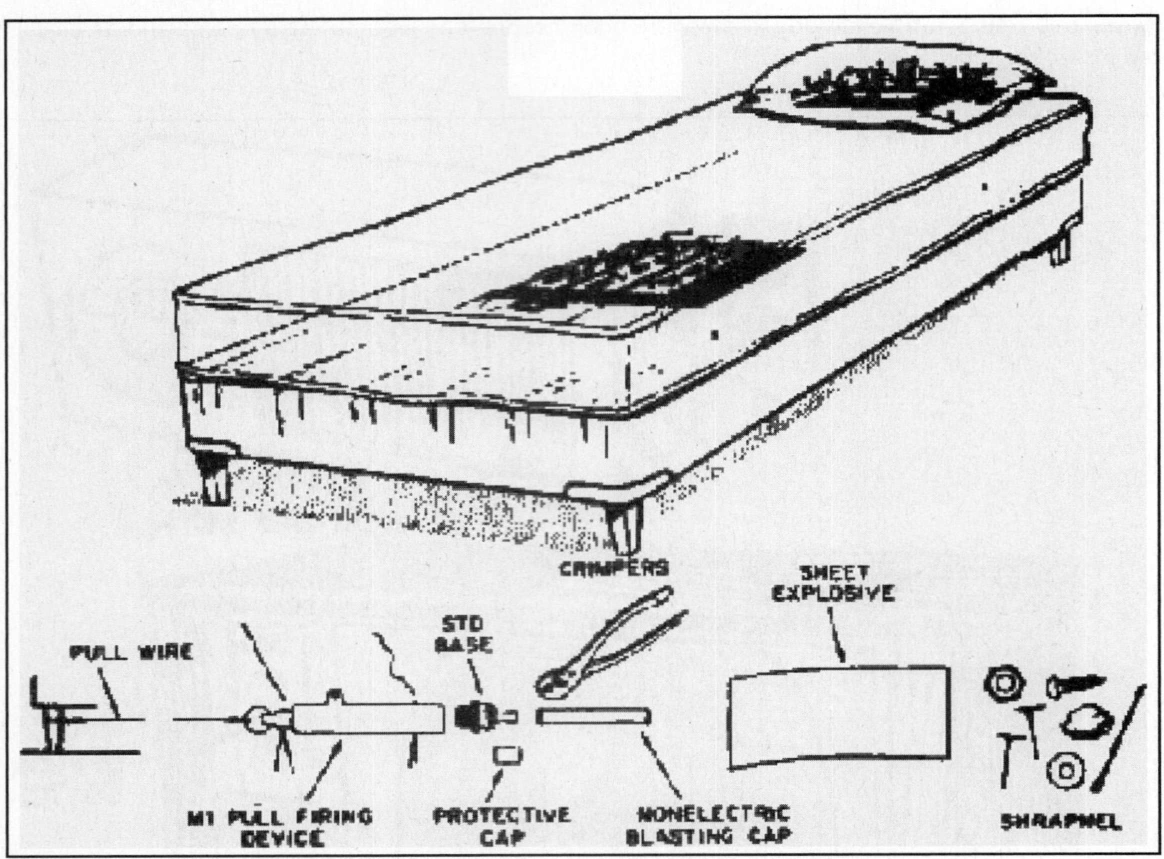

(2) *Electric rigging.*

(a) Assemble sheet explosive charge, electric blasting cap, and mercury element.
(b) Check circuit with galvanometer.
(c) Place boobytrap on bed to initiate when its level position is disturbed.
(d) Install batteries in circuit by wrapping tightly with friction tape.
(e) Conceal boobytrap.

> ✍ **NOTE**
> For safety and ease of assembly, use a wrist watch delay in circuit (para 60*d*).

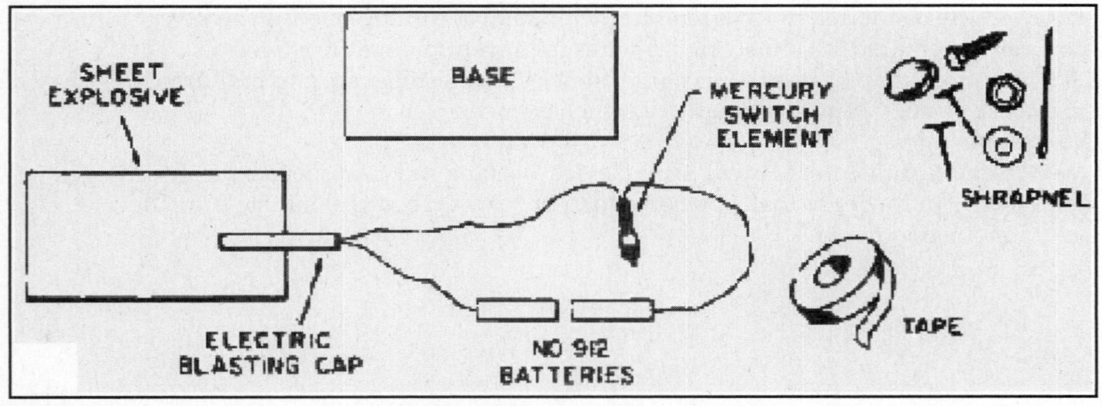

h. **Chairs and Sofas.** These may be boobytrapped nonelectrically and electrically as in *f* above. For nonelectric rigging the M1A1 pressure firing device, nonelectric blasting cap and sheet explosive charge are probably the most suitable. The sofa because of its size should have more than one rigging. If the electrical method is used *the circuit should be tested with the galvanometer before the batteries are installed.*

i. **Book.** A book with an attractive cover is sure to invite examination.
(1) Cut hole in book large enough to accommodate the rigging.

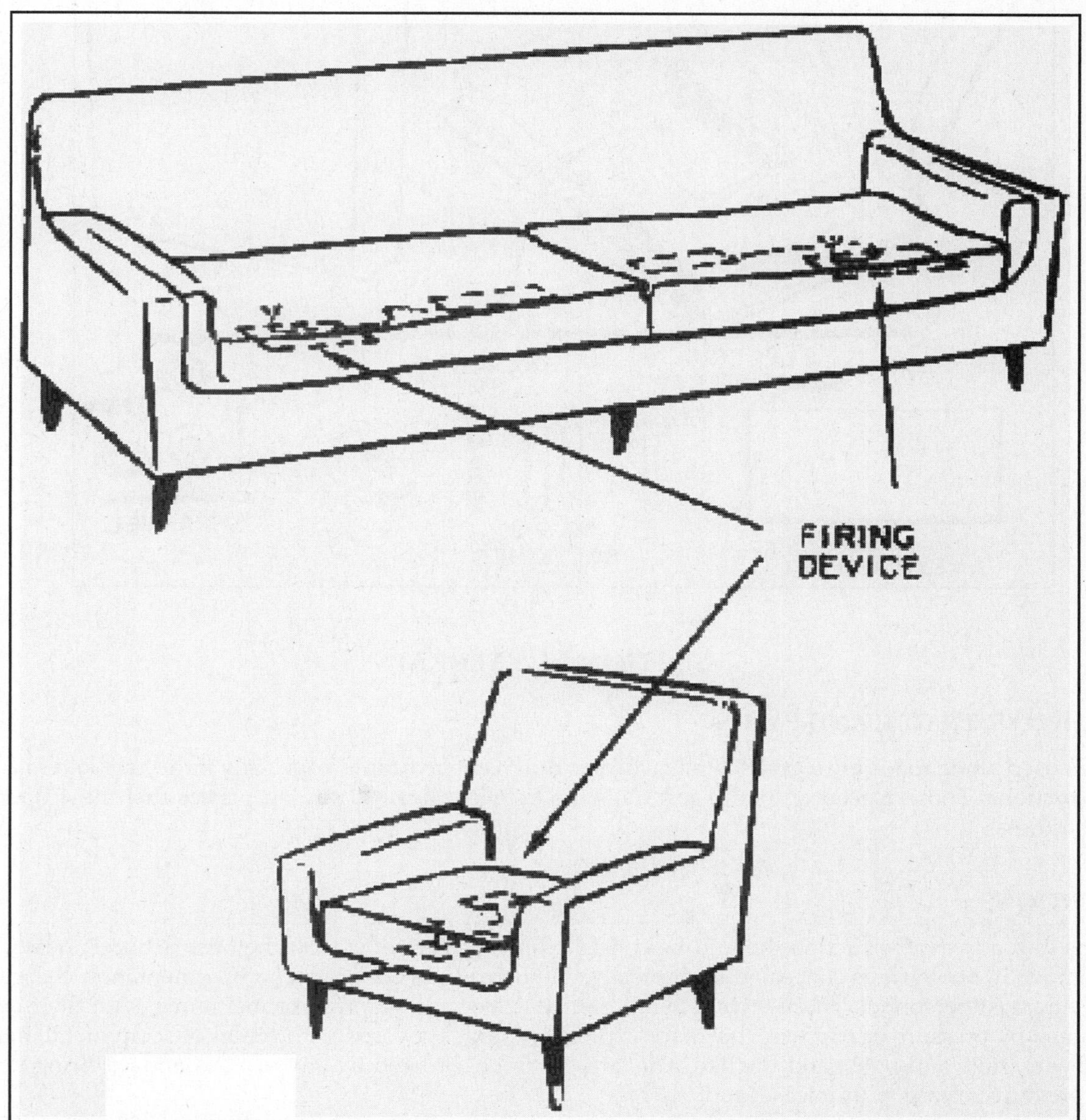

(2) Assemble sheet explosive, electric blasting cap, mercury element, and shrapnel.
(3) *Test circuit with galvanometer first,* then
(4) Secure batteries in circuit by wrapping tightly with friction tape.

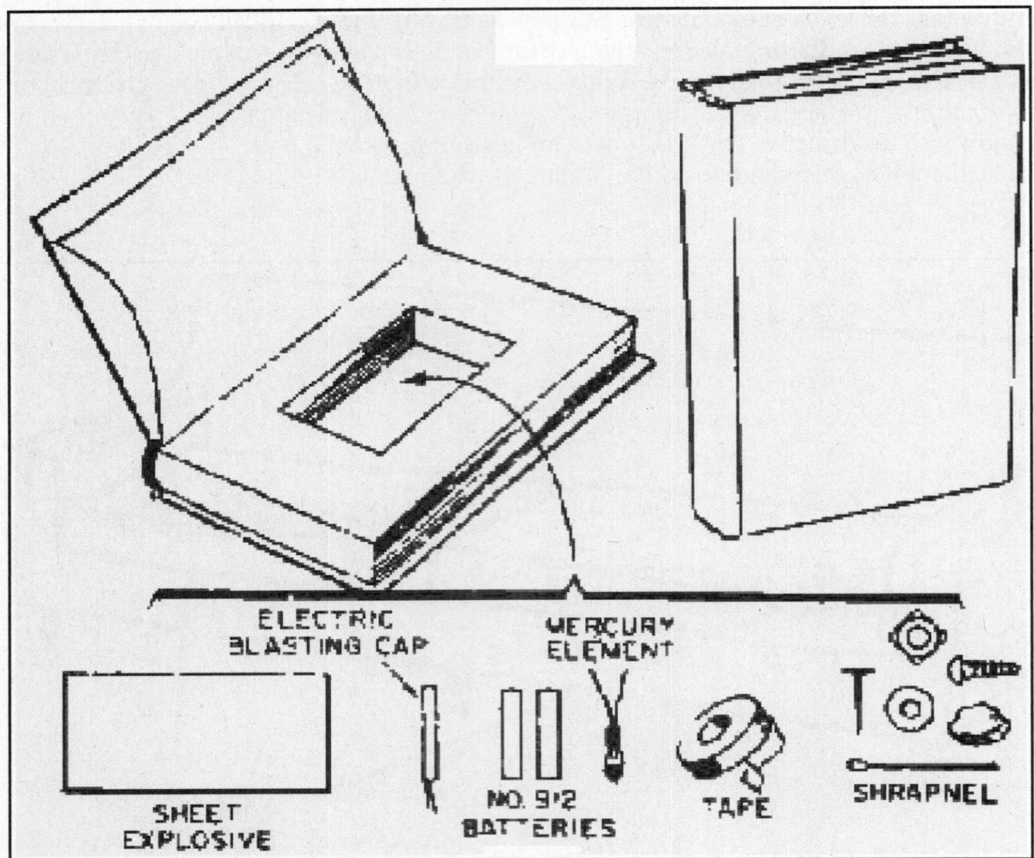

SECTION III. TERRAIN

45. HIGHWAYS, TRAILS, AND PATHS

Boobytraps used along roads are a great help in slowing down enemy traffic, especially if they are laid in and around other obstructions. Those placed on paths and trails are excellent against raiding parties that must operate under cover of darkness.

46. LOCATIONS

Boobytraps in roadway obstructions should be concealed on the enemy side. If the obstruction is heavy, requiring force to remove it, boobytraps concealed underneath will increase its effectiveness. Fragmentation charges are very destructive against personnel. These include hand grenades; bounding antipersonnel mines with their own special fuzes actuated by pressure or trip wire; ordinary explosive charges covered with pieces of scrap metal, nails, gravel, lengths of wire, nuts and bolts; and the like. The latter may be actuated by any of the standard firing devices—by pressure, pressure-release, pull-release, and pull.

a. The jet of the M2A3 shaped charge from the roadside directed into a moving vehicle is very destructive.
   (1) Assemble an M3 pull-release firing device and detonator, length of detonating cord, priming adapter, and nonelectric blasting cap.
   (2) Drive anchor stake in berm at side of road and attach pull wire. Drive stake or lay log, stone, or other object on other side to support pull wire at proper height off ground.
   (3) Attach firing device assembly to stake at proper position.
   (4) Fix shaped charge in position to direct explosive jet into vehicle when front wheels hit trip wire.
   (5) Attach free end of pull wire in hole in winch and draw taut.
   (6) Screw priming adapter and nonelectric blasting cap in threaded cap well.
   (7) Conceal boobytrap.
   (8) Arm firing device.

✍ **NOTE**
Cone may be filled wish fragments.

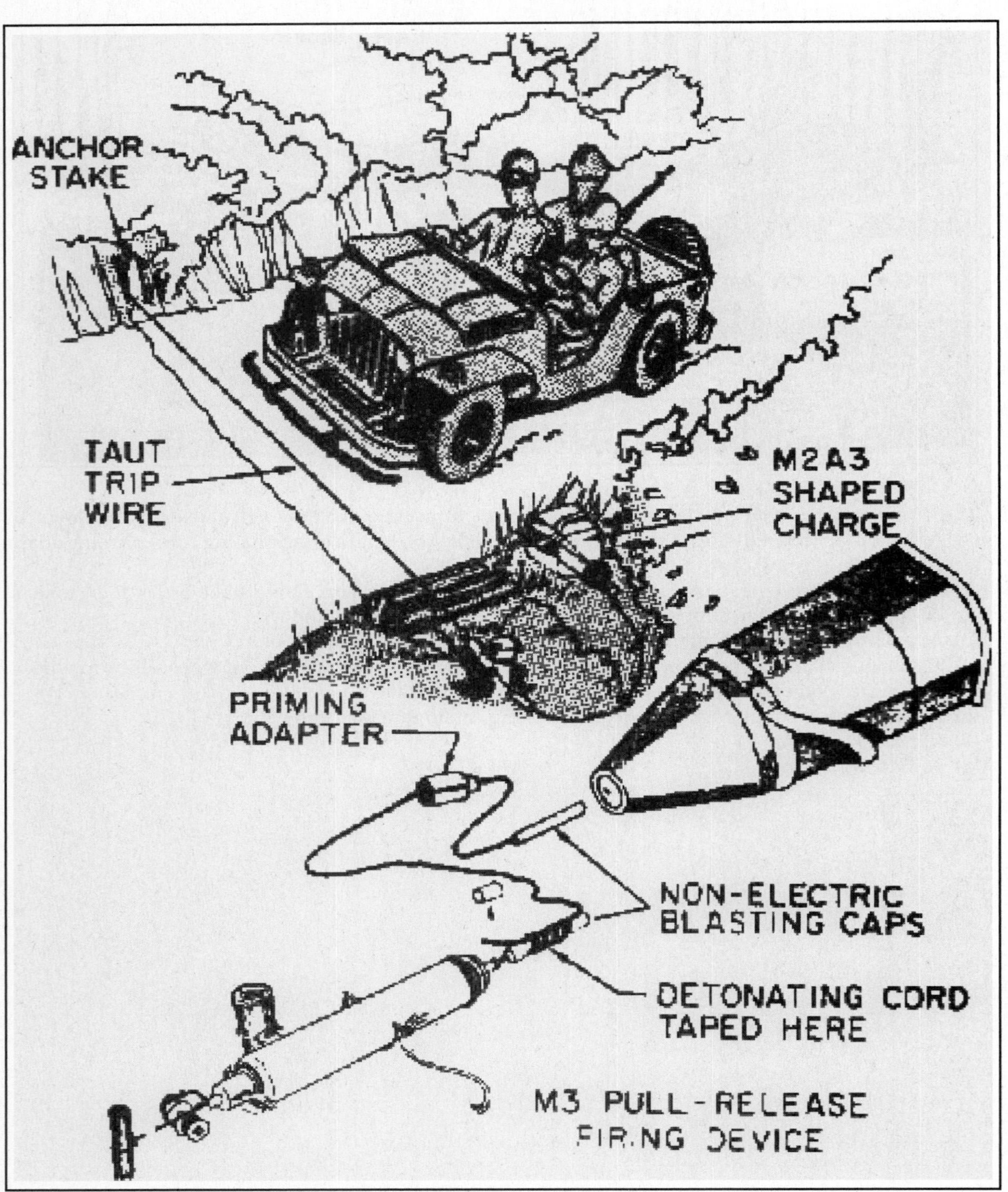

b. An M3 shaped charge boobytrap placed overhead in a tree in a wooded area will destroy both tank and crew if located properly. Trip wire, being very thin and camoufloage-colored, is not easily detected by a driver.
   (1) Assemble two firing devices (only one may be necessary) with detonators and lengths of detonating cord and a detonating cord primer.
   (2) Attach firing assemblies and MS shaped charge in position in tree, so that when the vehicle contacts the trip wires, the explosive jet will penetrate the crew compartment.
   (3) Arm boobytrap.

c. Boobytraps laid in and along a narrow path may prove delaying or frustrating obstacles to foot troops. These may be improvised shrapnel charge with a pressure-release firing device concealed under a stone, piece of wood, or other object, or with a pull or pull-release firing device and a trip wire. The latter would be very effective against patrols.

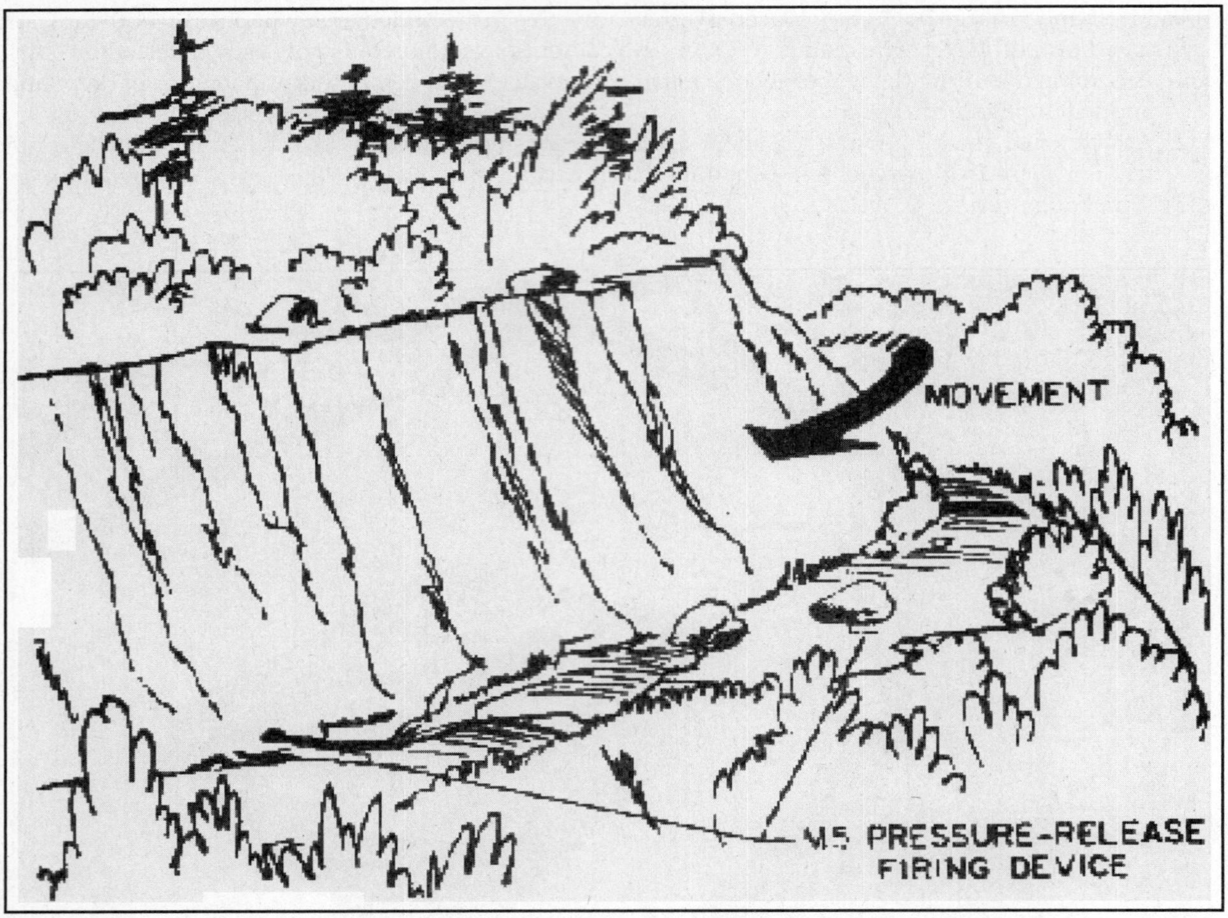

MOVEMENT

M5 PRESSURE-RELEASE FIRING DEVICE

47. SPECIAL LOCATIONS

a. Abandoned serviceable or repairable items are frequently boobytrapped if time and equipment are available. Even unserviceable items may be rigged against scavengers who may search through the wreckage for useful things.

b. Abandoned ammunition should be exploited to the maximum. Chain detonations of connected mines or sections of bangalore torpedo are particularly effective.

c. Boobytraps are applicable to storage areas where materials cannot be removed or destroyed. Several charges strategically laid will prove very rewarding. A lumber pile provides excellent concealment for an explosive rigging. Sheet explosive may be used in many places where TNT is impractical, because of its size and shape. Here again chain detonations of explosive blocks and bangalore torpedos will do extensive damage, if the firing mechanism is properly located and cunningly concealed.

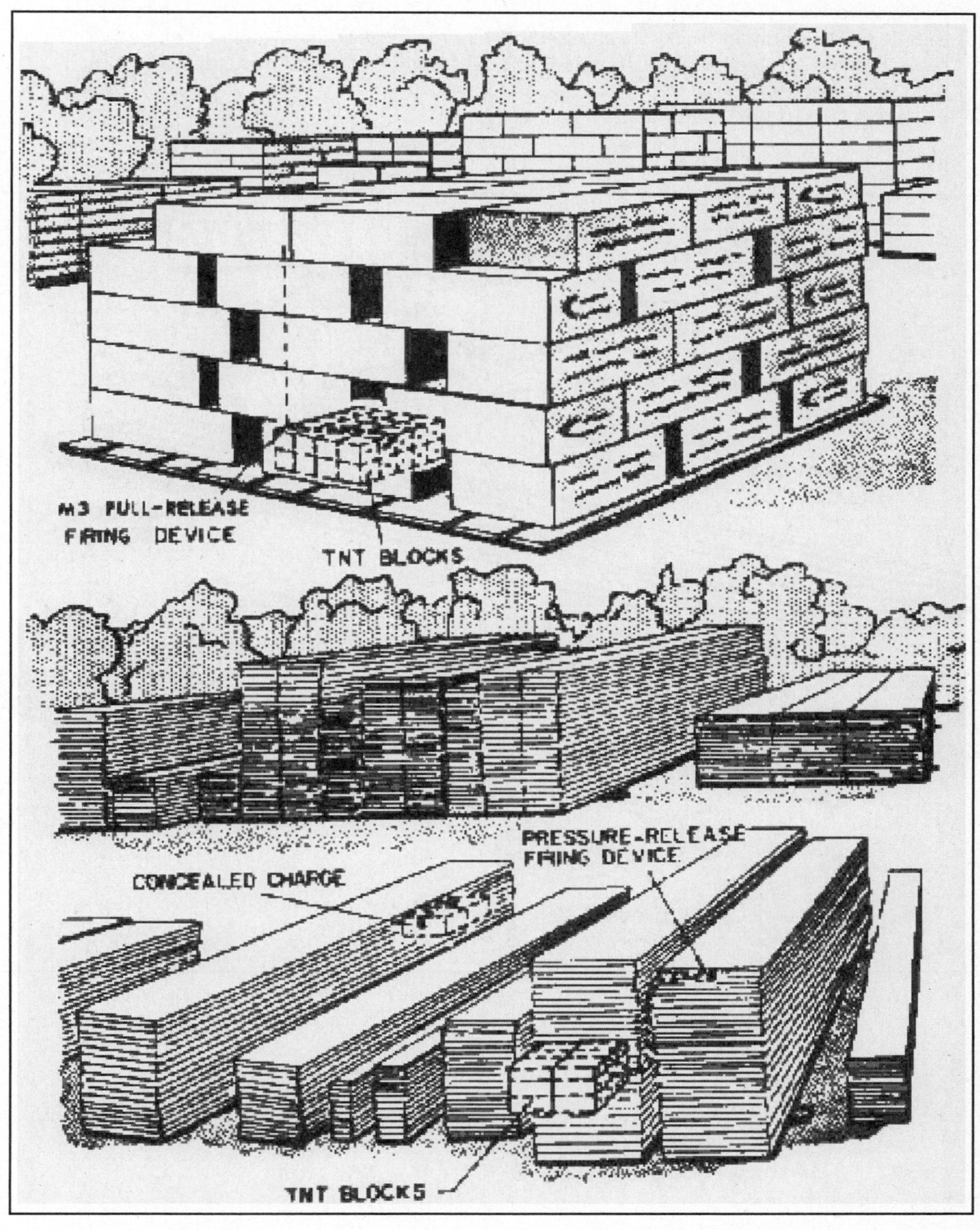

48. ABANDONED VEHICLES

a. **Truck Wheel.**

(1) Insert length of heavy wire in interceptor hole in firing device.

(2) Remove safety pin and replace with length of thin wire. Bend both wires slightly to prevent falling out.

(3) Assemble standard base, nonelectric blasting cap, and firing device.

(4) Assemble two 2-block explosive charges, nonelectric blasting caps, priming adapters, and length of detonating cord.

(5) In hole prepared under truck wheel, assemble bearing blocks (take weight off explosive charge), charges, bearing board, protective blocks (take weight off firing device), and firing device.

(6) Arm firing device.

(7) Cover boobytrap, and camouflage.

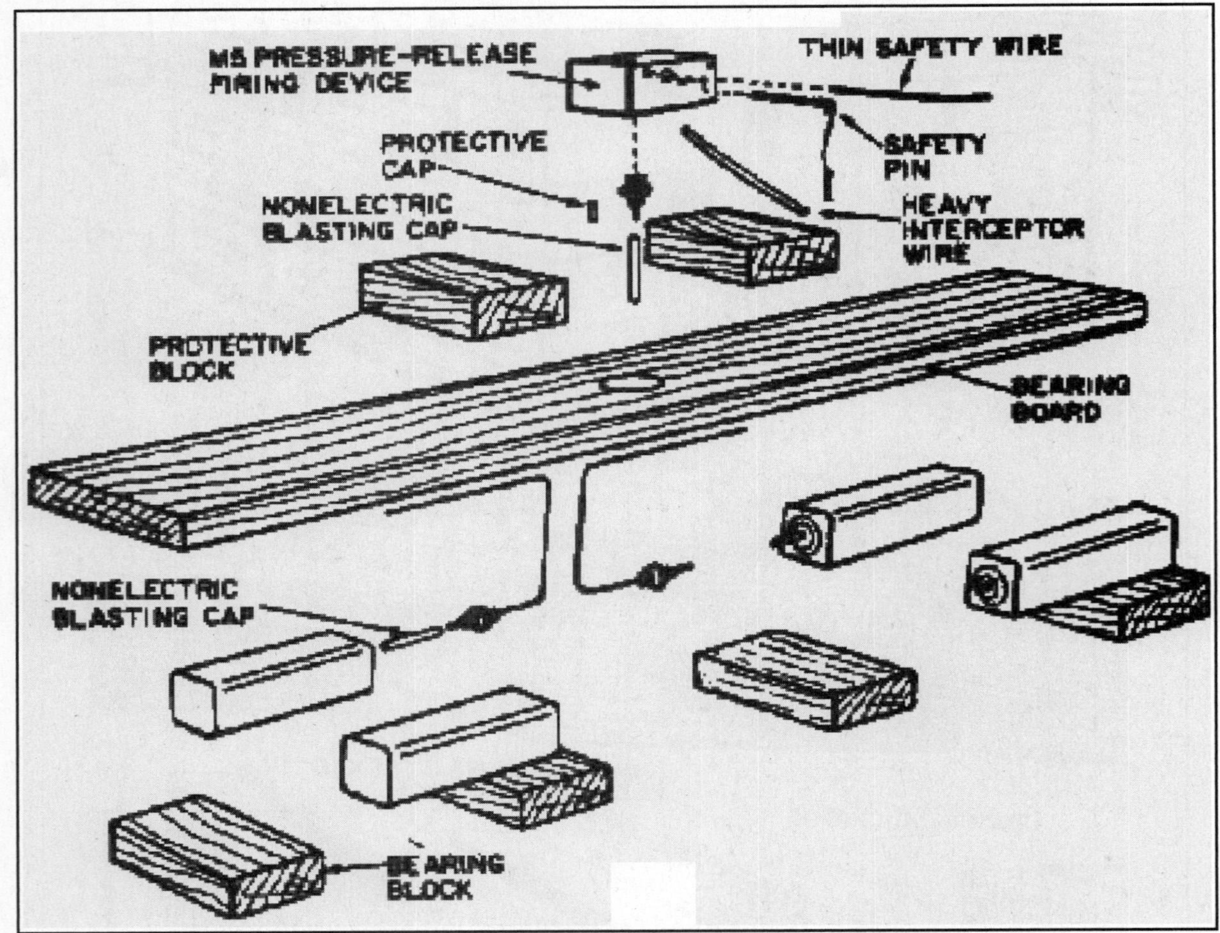

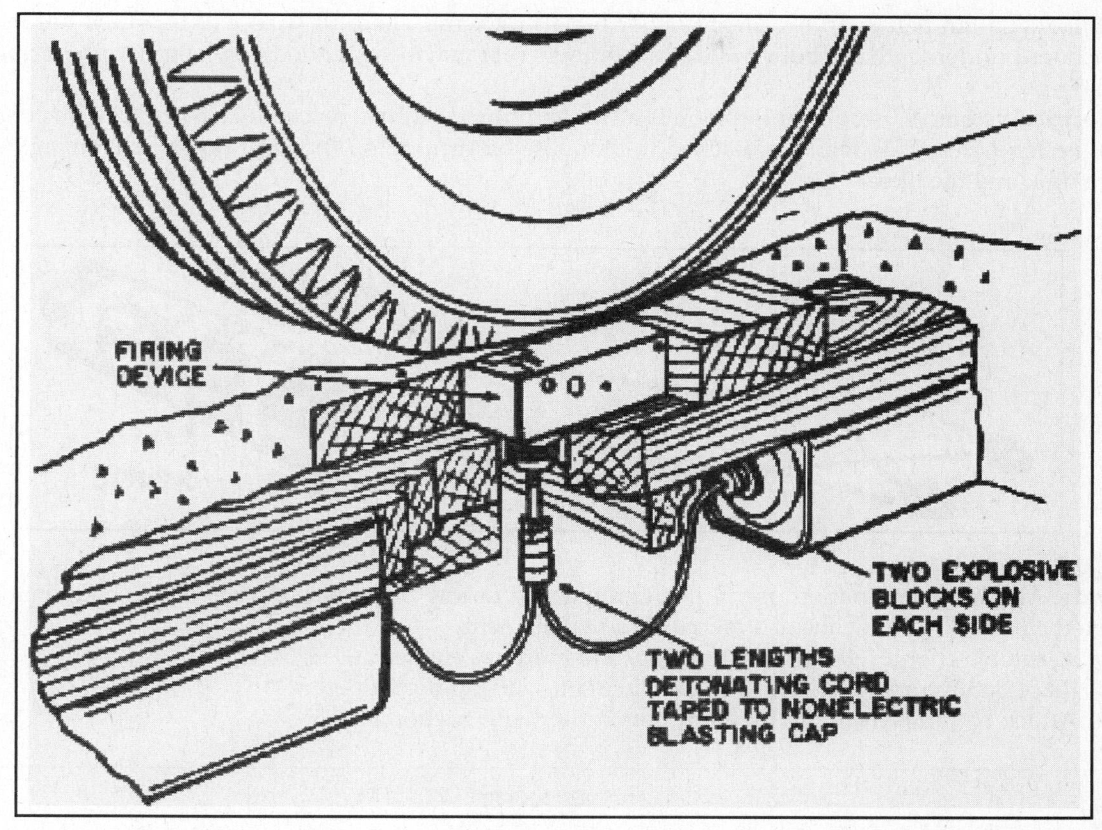
FIRING
DEVICE
TWO EXPLOSIVE
BLOCKS ON
EACH SIDE
TWO LENGTHS
DETONATING CORD
TAPED TO NONELECTRIC
BLASTING CAP

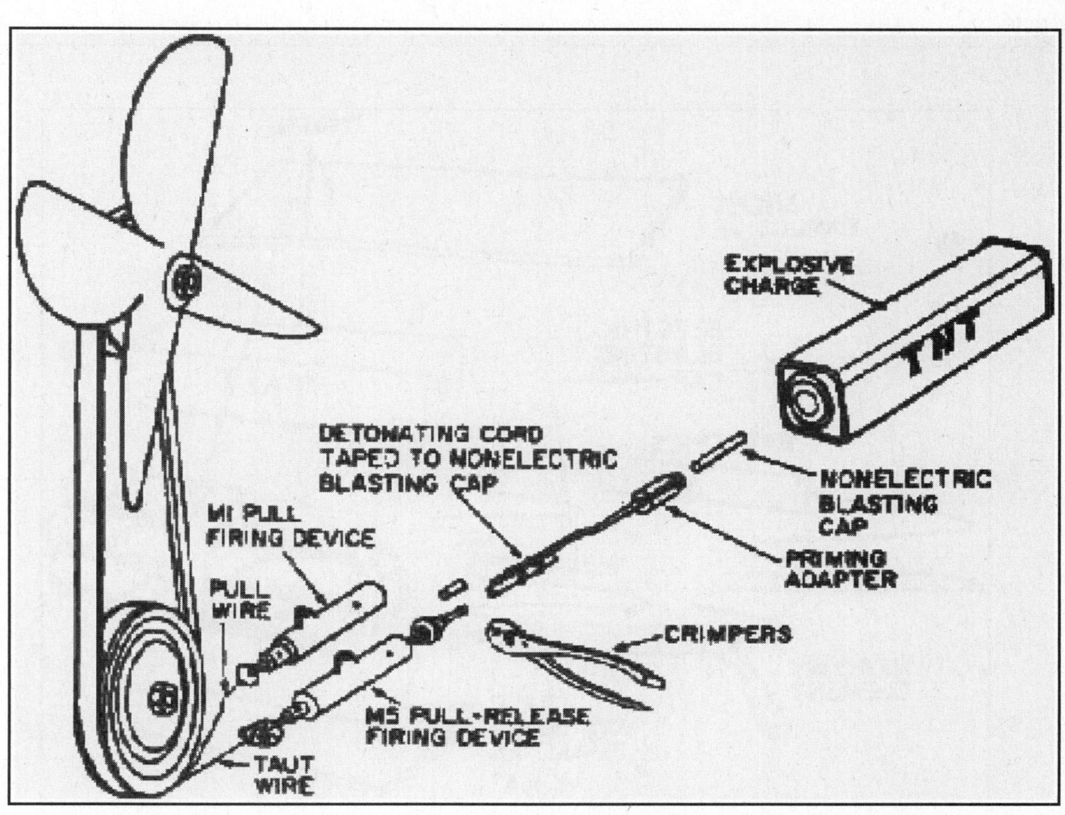
EXPLOSIVE
CHARGE
TNT
DETONATING CORD
TAPED TO NONELECTRIC
BLASTING CAP
NONELECTRIC
BLASTING
CAP
M1 PULL
FIRING DEVICE
PRIMING
ADAPTER
PULL
WIRE
CRIMPERS
M5 PULL-RELEASE
FIRING DEVICE
TAUT
WIRE

b. **Motor.** The fan belt is an excellent anchor for a pull wire. The pull wire will be much harder to detect if anchored underneath the bottom pulley, from where it may be extended any length to the firing device and charge.

c. **Electric System.** A useful combination is a charge primed with an electric blasting cap with clamps attached to the leg wires. This may be attached to detonate by turning on the ignition switch, engaging the starter, braking, and the like.

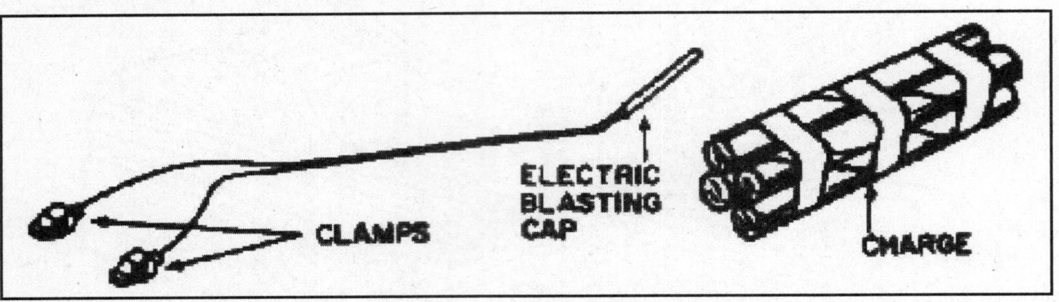

d. **Body.** Another combination useful in rigging a seat or any other part of the vehicle body is a charge detonated electrically by means of a mercury switch element.
   (1) Assemble charge, electric blasting cap, and mercury element.
   (2) Place boobytrap in position and check circuit with a galvanometer.
   (3) Attach batteries in circuit by wrapping tightly with friction tape.

> ✍ **NOTE**
>
> Always check circuit before attaching batteries. This rigging may be assembled in a small package for use in a seat cushion or separated for convenience for another location in the body of the vehicle.

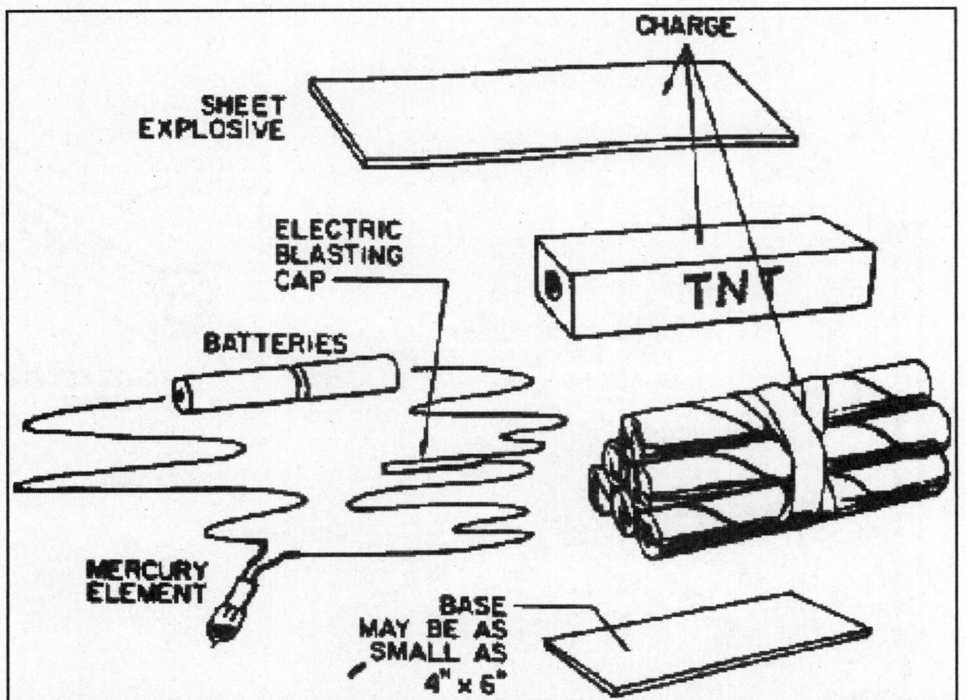

CHAPTER 5

Miscellaneous Boobytraps

SECTION I. STANDARD BOOBYTRAPS

49. TACTICAL USE

In World War II, every major power manufactured boobytraps to use against the enemy. Most of them were charged imitations of useful objects, which maimed or killed helpless soldiers that handled them. The defect common to all standard boobytraps however, is that after the first or second explosion, all others of the same type become ineffective. A "one-shot" job hardly justifies production costs.

50. FOREIGN TYPES

a. The Soviets used more standard boobytraps in World War II than any other combatant. A weird assortment of charged imitations of items issued to German soldiers were dropped from Soviet planes. Some of these were:
   (1) Cartridge boxes, apparently filled with ammunition, containing high explosives and detonators.
   (2) Bandage packets containing detonators and shrapnel.
   (3) Bandage cases with Red Cross insignia rigged as mines.
   (4) Rubber balls, about twice the size of a fist that detonated upon impact.
   (5) Silver-grey light metal boxes or flasks that exploded when the lid was raised.
   (6) Cognac bottles filled with incendiary liquid.
   (7) Small red flags marked with an M and attached to mines that detonated when the flag was removed.
   (8) Imitation earth-grey colored frogs that detonated when pressed on.
   (9) Flashlights containing high explosive which detonated when the switch was moved.
   (10) Mechanical pencils, watches, cigarette cases, cigarette lighters, salt cellars, and similar items that detonated when handled.

b. Knowing the German interest in books, the Soviets prepared a book boobytrap. The charge inside detonated when the cover was raised.

c. The British also had a book boobytrap; but it was slightly more complicated than the Soviet version above.

d. All sorts of dirty-trick devices were used by the enemy.
   (1) A flashlight was rigged with a charge and an electric detonator powered and actuated by the original dry cell battery switch, and circuit.

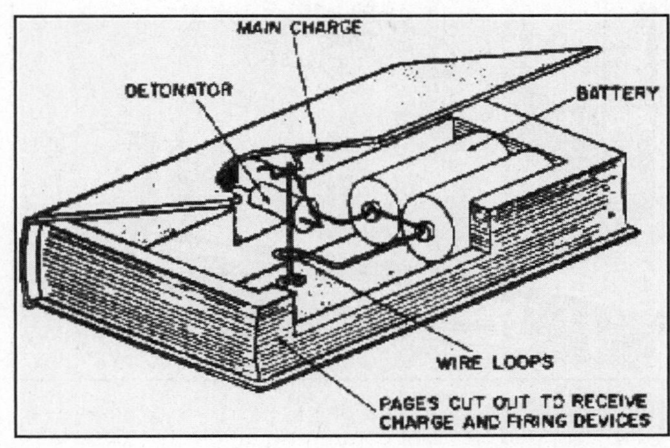

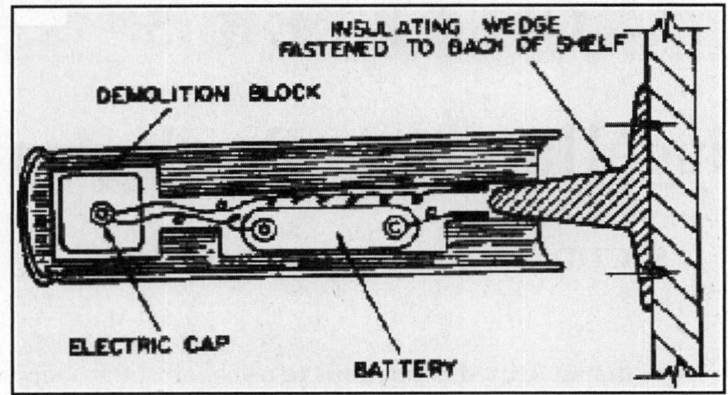

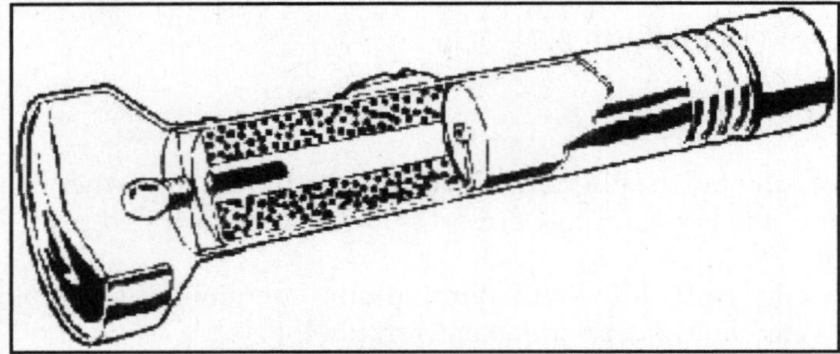

(2) Bottles designed to look like liquor bottles were filled with a liquid explosive detonated by a pull-friction fuze attached to the cork.
(3) A fountain pen, though very small was rigged with an explosive charge, a spring driven striker to fire a percussion cap, and a detonator.
(4) The Japanese manufactured a pipe boobytrap with a charge, detonator, and spring-loaded striker.

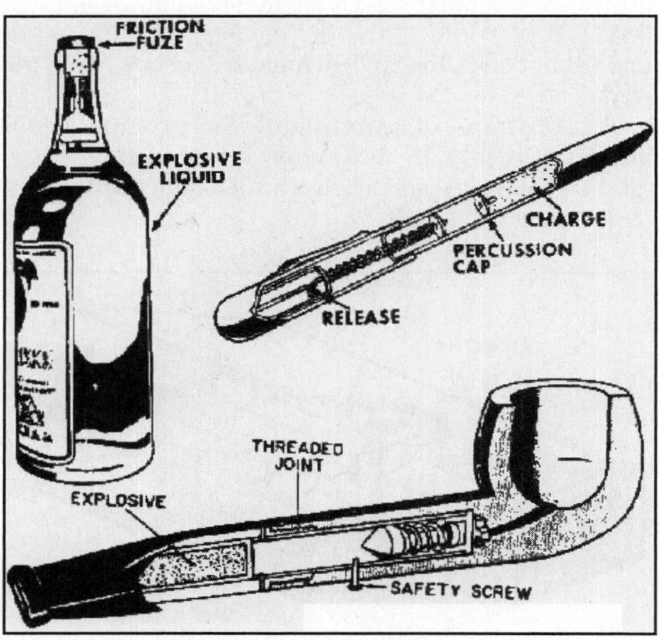

(5) The Italians had a boobytrapped headset containing an electric detonator connected to the terminals on the back. The connection of the headset into the live communication line initiated detonation.

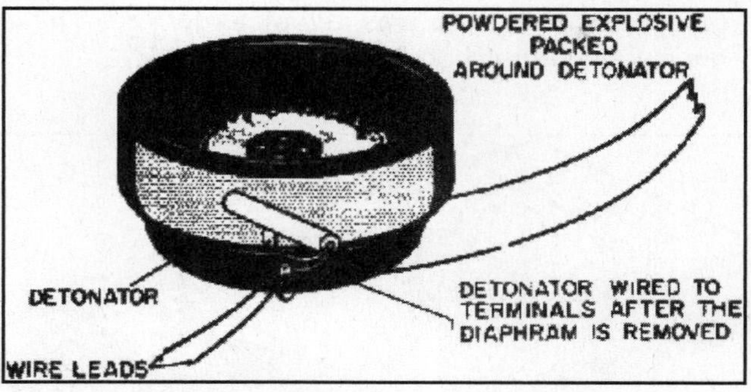

(6) The Germans converted their own and enemy standard canteens into boobytraps. The explosive charge was detonated by a pull fuze and a pull wire connected to the cap. When partially filled with water and placed in its canvas case, it was very deceptive. The canteen boobytrap had an effective radius of 3 to 5 yards.

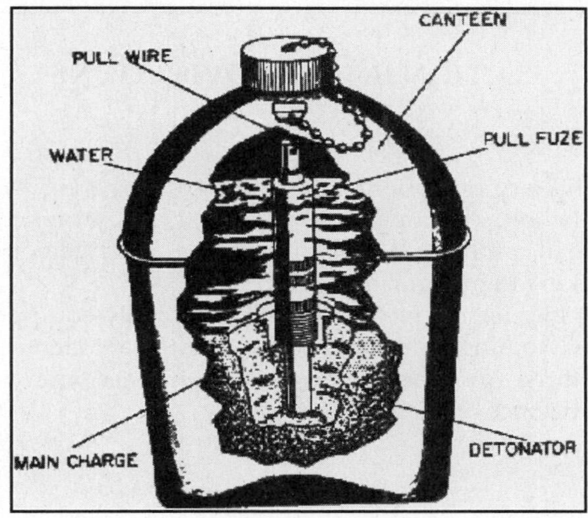

(7) Another German device was the boobytrap whistle. This consisted of a policeman's or referee's whistle with a charge and a metal ball covered with a layer of friction compound. Blowing the whistle moved the ball, igniting the friction compound and detonating the charge.

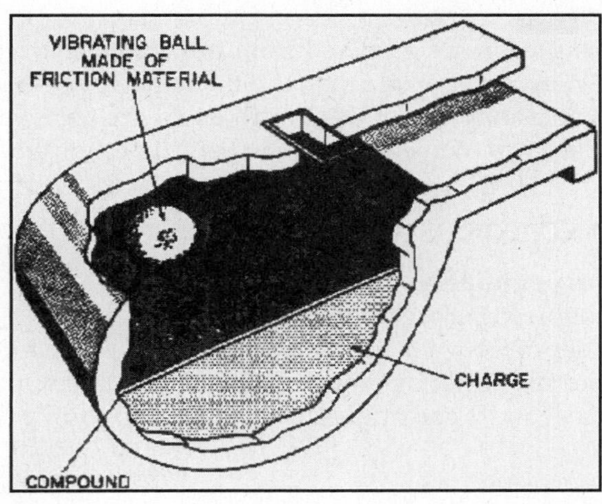

(8) The German Peters candy bar boobytrap was ingenious indeed. The explosive charge, fuze, and thin canvas pull device were covered with chocolate.

SECTION II. IMPROVISATIONS

51. INGENUITY

a. Through information on military operations in World War II, the U.S. soldier has been well-prepared for the dangerous mission of laying, detecting, and disarming boobytraps in conventional warfare. However, he now is virtually a novice in comparison with the cunning and ingenious present day guerrilla, who at the start was almost totally lacking in material and equipment.

b. Experience has shown that in guerrilla warfare, carried on by illy-equipped native populations, boobytrapping success depends largely on ingenuity. Explosive, a necessary element, is either improvised from commercial ingredients or captured from the enemy. Captured mines, ammunition, and other similar material are disassembled and every ounce of explosive saved.

52. TRAINING

Every soldier should have some training in the lessons learned from the guerrillas, for many items they have improvised and the way they have used them are also applicable to conventional warfare. With little effort, a soldier may be trained so that with no military equipment what so ever, but with ample funds, he may prepare himself to fight effectively with materials available from merchants, junk piles, and salvage.

53. APPLICATION

The improvisations included in this section are gathered from numerous sources. Some may have wider application to boobytrapping than others. How the guerrilla may use them, however, is unpredictable. All are presented to stimulate initiative and arouse enthusiasm to out-do backward enemy peoples in devising and placing boobytraps and to develop a higher level of proficiency than ever before in their detection and removal.

54. IMPROVISED TIME FUSE AND EXPLOSIVE CAPS

a. **Fast burning fuse (40 inches per minute).**

(1) Braid three lengths of cotton string together.

(2) Moisten fine black powder to form a paste. Rub paste into twisted string with fingers and allow to dry. If a powder is not available, mix 25 parts potassium nitrate (salt-peter) in an equal amount of water and add 3 parts pulverized charcoal and 2 parts pulverized sulphur to form a paste. Rub paste into twisted string and allow to dry.

(3) Check burning rate before using.

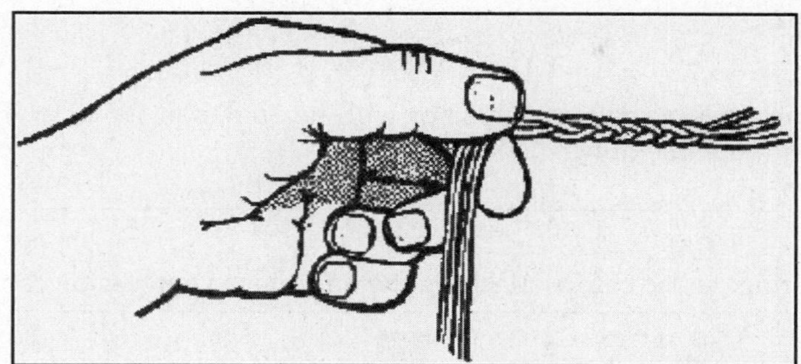

b. **Slow burning fuse (2 inches per minute).**
   (1) Wash three lengths of string or three shoelaces in hot soapy water and rinse.
   (2) Dissolve 1 part potassium nitrate or potassium chlorate and 1 part granulated sugar in 2 parts hot water.
   (3) Soak string or shoelaces in solution and braid three strands together. Allow to dry.
   (4) Check burning rate.
   (5) Before using, coat several inches of the end to be inserted into cap or material to be ignited with black powder paste (*a* (2) above).

c. **Electric Blasting Cap.**
   (1) With files other instrument make hole in end of light bulb.
   (2) If jacket is not available, solder or securely fasten two wires to bulb—one on metal threads at side and other at metal contact on bottom.
   (3) Fill bulb and empty portion of blasting cap with black powder. Tape blasting cap on top of bulb.

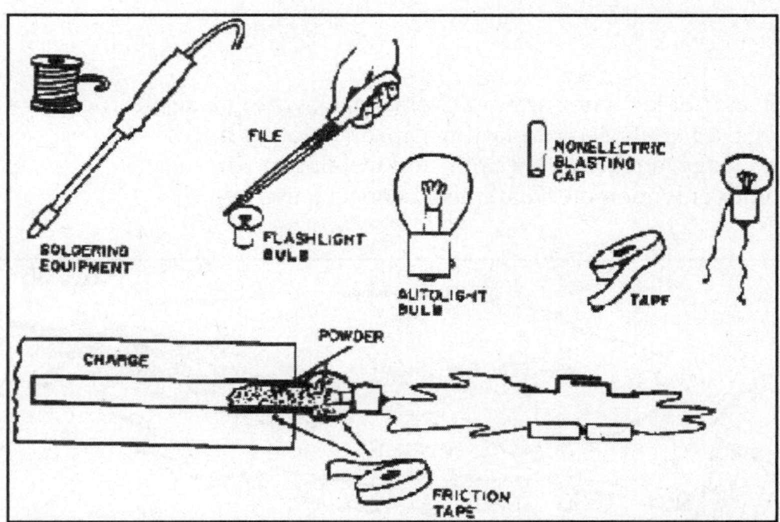

d. **Percussion Cap Assembly.**
   (1) Remove projectile, but not powder from small arms cartridge.
   (2) Tape nonelectric blasting cap securely in cartridge.

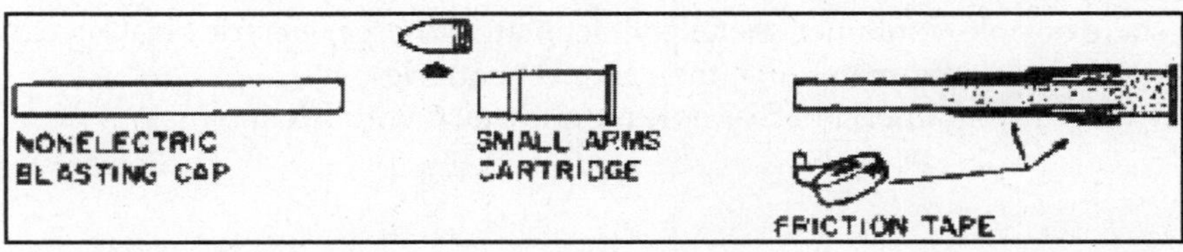

55. PULL FIRING DEVICES

a. **Tube and Striker.**
Assemble tube, spring, striker shaft with hole or with hex nut, soft wood or metal top plug, pull pin, and improvised percussion cap assembly.

> ✍ **NOTE**
> Always assemble firing device before attaching the improvised percussion cap assembly.

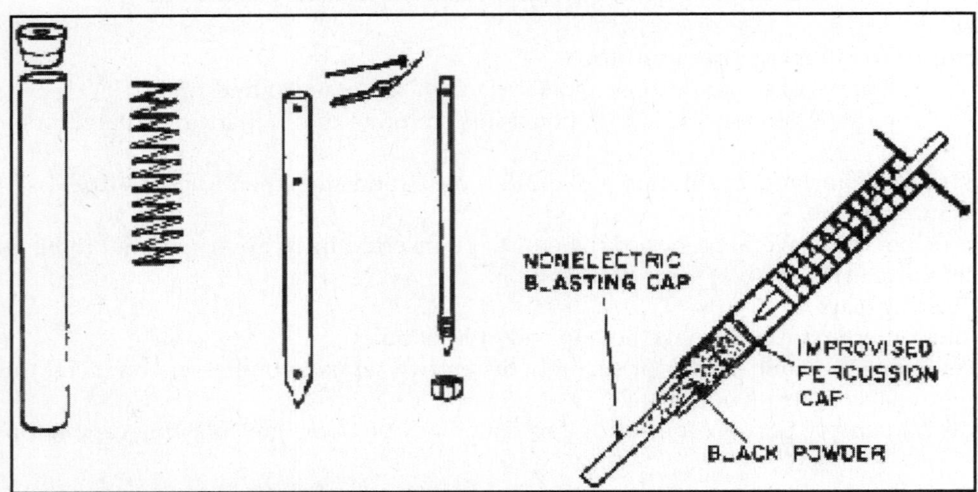

b. **Clothes Pin.**
(1) Wrap stripped ends of leg wires around clothes pin jaws to make electrical contact.
(2) Assemble charge, adapter, electric blasting cap, and clothes pin.
(3) Insert wooden wedge, anchor clothes pin, and install trip wire.
(4) Check circuit with galvonometer *first*, then, connect batteries.

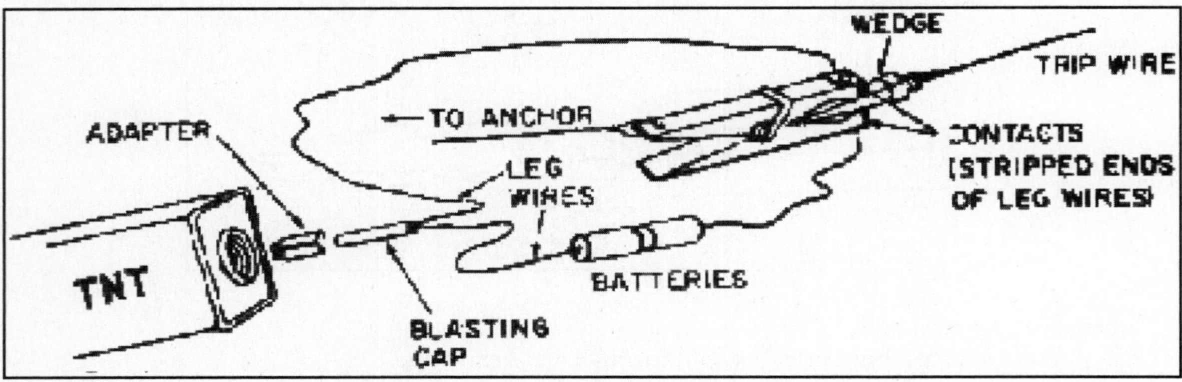

c. **Stake or Pole Initiator.**
(1) Assemble stake or pole, container, metal contact plates, charge, electric blasting cap, and pull cord.
(2) Check circuit with galvonometer *first*, then connect batteries.
(3) Fasten down top of container and seal hole around stake with friction tape.

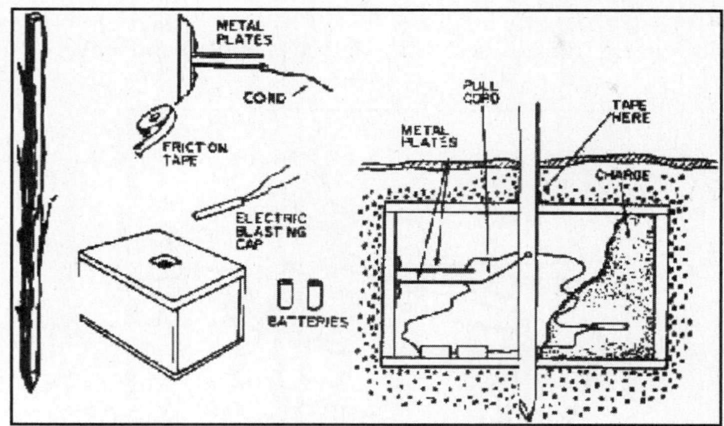

d. **Rope and Cylinder.**
   (1) Cut leg wires to proper length.
   (2) Prepare wooden end plugs and bore hole in one to receive leg wires.
   (3) Thread leg wires through hole in block.
   (4) Strip end of one leg wire and twist into loop, and secure other leg wire in position.
   (5) Test circuit with galvonometer.
   (6) Assemble metal cylinder, contact bolt, pull cord, charge, blasting cap, end blocks, and batteries.

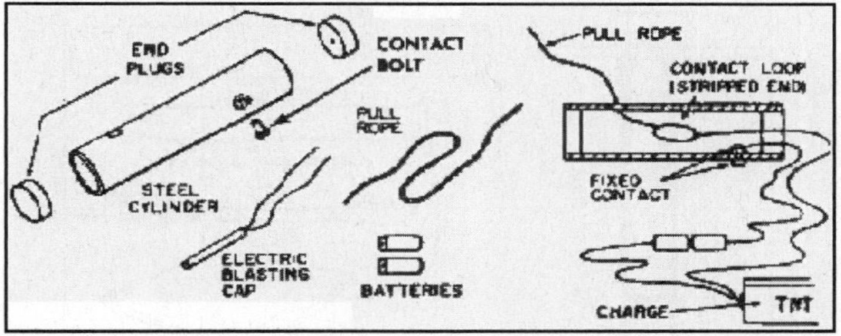

e. **Trip Lever and Pull Pin.**
   (1) ***Flat placement.***
   Assemble container, charge, improvised pull firing device (*a* above) and trip lever.

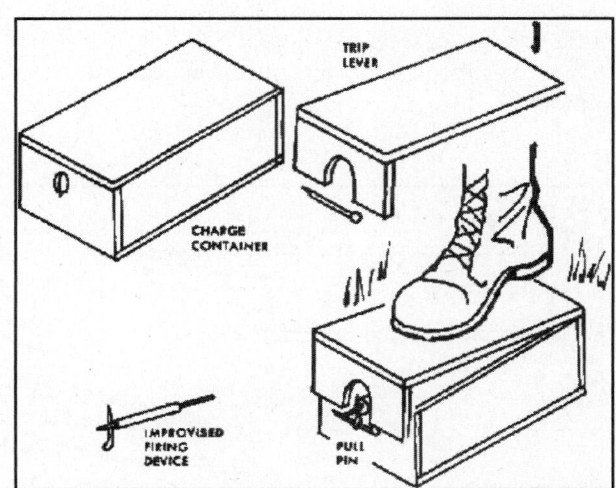

(2) ***Sloping placement.***
Assemble container, charge, improvised firing device (*a* above) and stake.

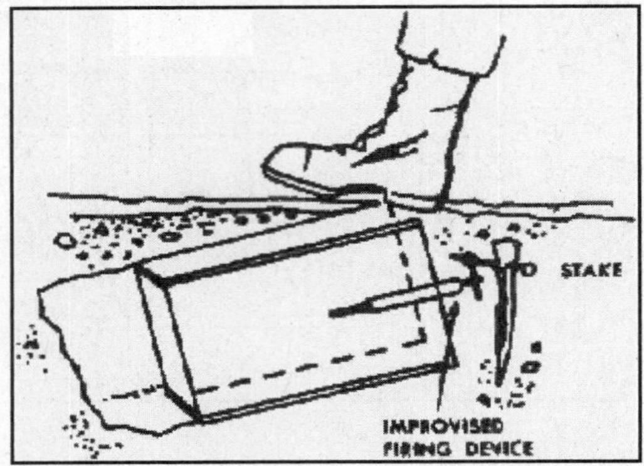

56. PRESSURE FIRING DEVICES

a. **Mechanical Concussion.**
(1) Force striker into hole in pressure board.
(2) Insert wood or soft metal shear pin in shear pin hole.
(3) Assemble striker, metal tube, and improvised blasting cap (para 54).

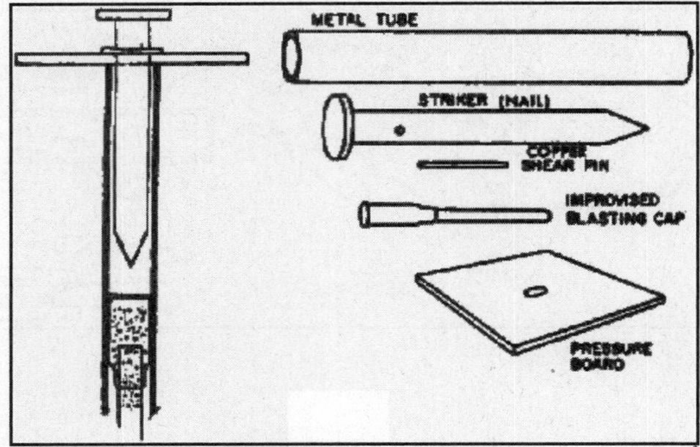

b. **Electrical.**
(1) ***Lever arm.***
(a) Attach contact blocks to ends of wooden levers.
(b) Assemble wooden levers, rubber strip, and plastic sponge.
(c) Attach leg wire contacts.

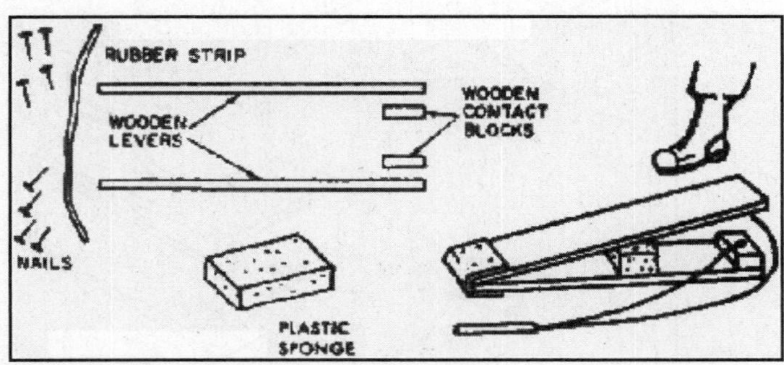

(2) ***Flexible side.***

(a) Attach metal contact plates to bearing boards.
(b) Thread leg wires through holes in lower bearing board and attach to contact plates.
(c) Attach flexible sides.

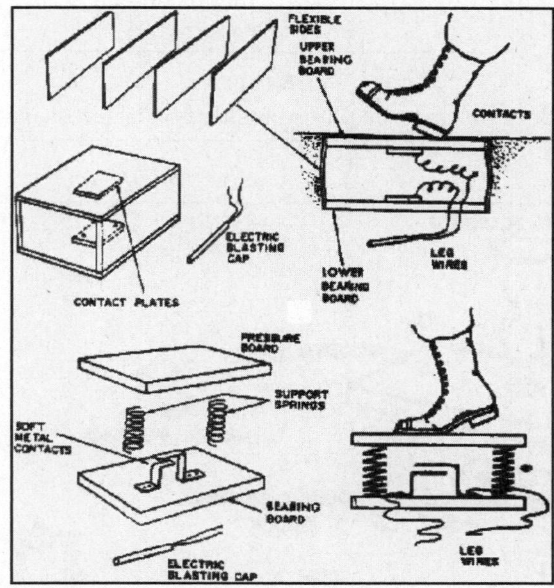

(3) ***Springed pressure board.***

(a) Assemble metal contacts, springs, bearing board, and pressure board.
(b) Attach leg wires to metal contacts.

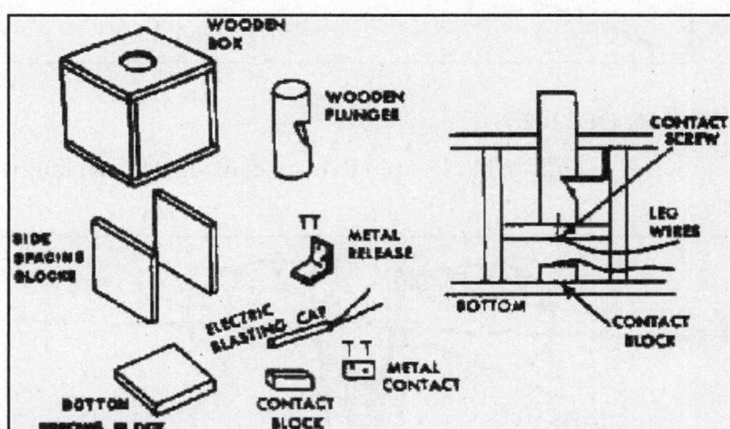

(4) ***Wooden plunger.***

(a) Assemble box, leaving one side open.
(b) Assemble contact plate and three spacing blocks inside box.
(e) Drill holes in spacing block for leg wires.
(d) Assemble plunger, metal release, contact block, metal contact, and contact screw.
(e) Thread leg wires through holes in spacing block and attach to contacts.

(5) ***Metal box.***
- (a) Attach metal contact to wooden contact block.
- (b) Assemble contact block and metal contact, brackets, metal release, plunger, and wooden box lid.
- (c) Bore hole in side of box for leg wires.
- (d) Thread leg wires through hole in box.
- (e) Attach one leg wire to plunger, the other to metal contact.

> ✍ NOTE
> Batteries may be placed inside box if necessary.

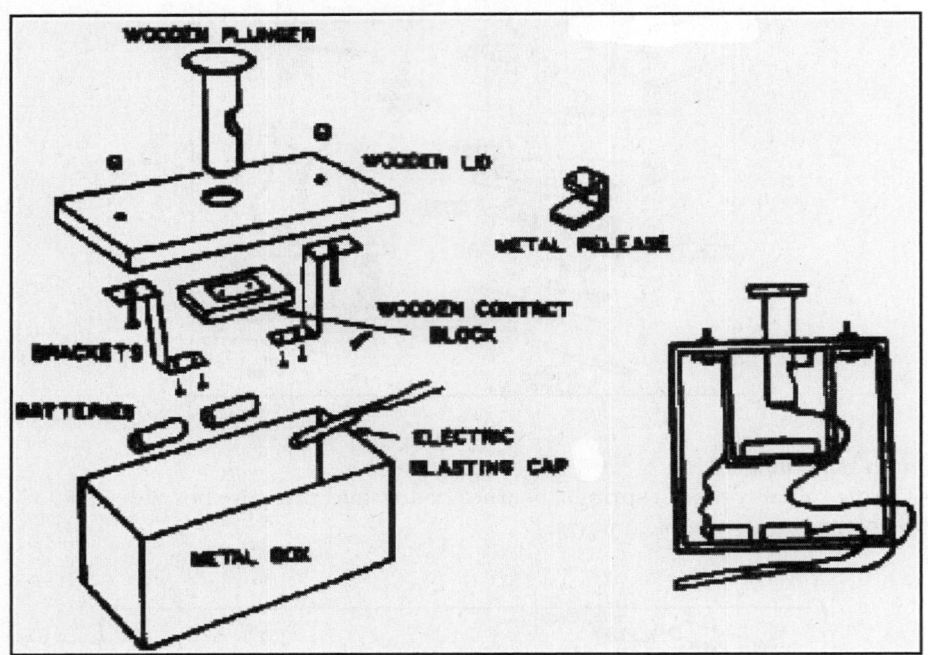

57. TENSION-RELEASE FIRING DEVICE

Attach stripped ends of circuit wires to ends of clothes pin to farm contacts. Attach taut trip wires below contacts.

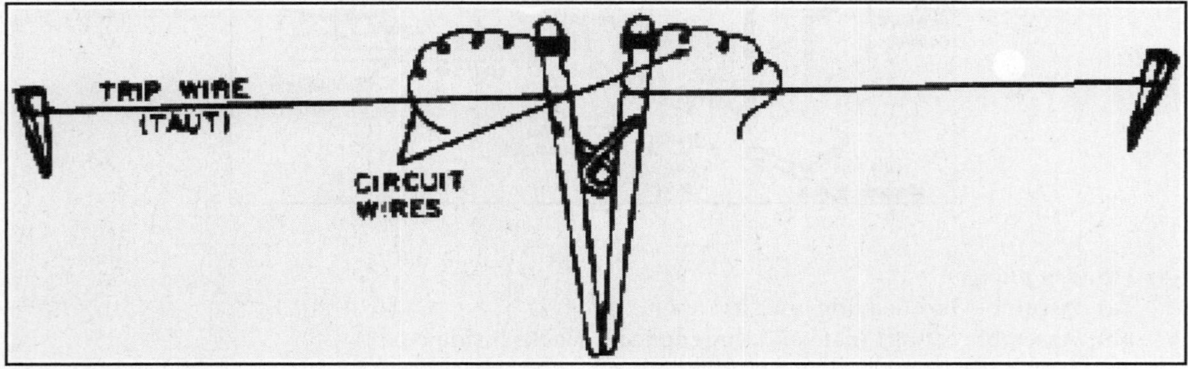

58. PRESSURE-RELEASE

a. **Double Contact.**
   (1) Bore holes in top of mine body to accommodate long contacts.
   (2) Assemble pressure board, coil springs, wooden contact board and metal contacts.
   (3) Attach circuit wires.

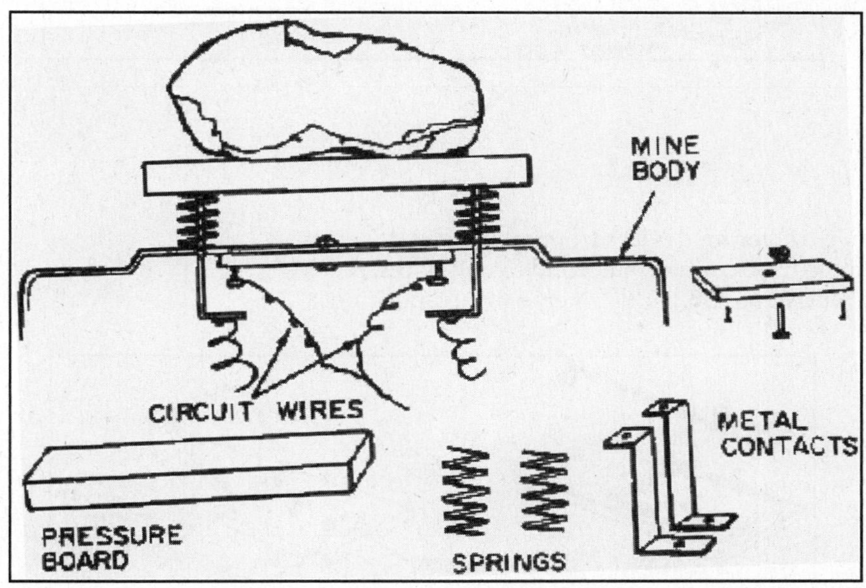

b. **Clothes Pin.**
   (1) Attach stripped ends of circuit wires to clothes pin to make contacts.
   (2) Place mine on top, keeping contacts apart.

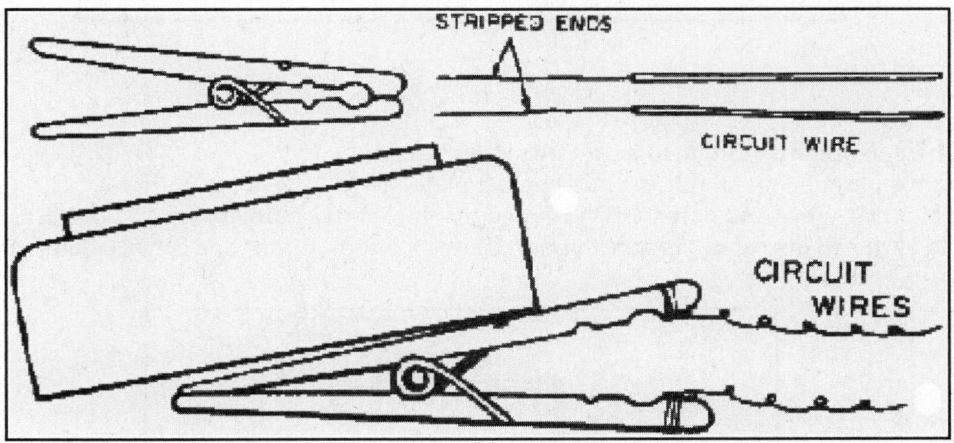

c. **Bottom Plunger.**
   (1) Bore hole in bottom of mine case to admit plunger.
   (2) Attach lower metal contact over hole.
   (3) Assemble mine, pressure block, upper metal contact, and nonmetallic plunger.
   (4) Attach circuit wires.

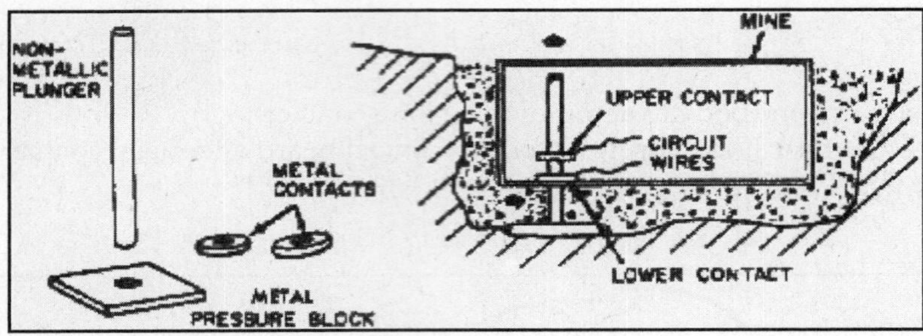

d. **Mousetrap.**
   (1) ***Mechanical***
   See para 44 *b* (2)
   (2) ***Electrical***
      (a) Remove triggering devices from mousetrap.
      (b) Assemble trap, contact plate, and circuit wires.
      (c) Place weight on top with striker in armed position.

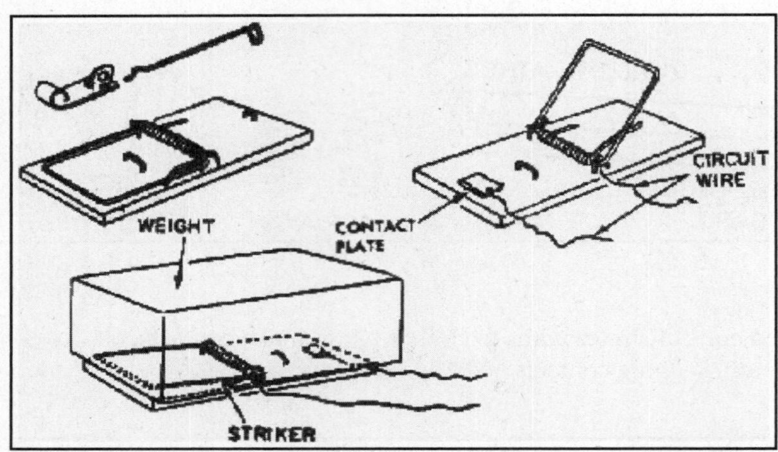

59. ANTI-LIFE DEVICES

a. **Loop Contact.**
   (1) Drill hole in bottom of mine to admit insulated pull wire.
   (2) Assemble plunger, metal release, and contact plate.
   (3) Attach circuit wires and bare loop to plunger contact and contact plate.
   (4) Thread anchored insulated trip wire through holes in bottom of mine and contact plate and attach to bare loop.

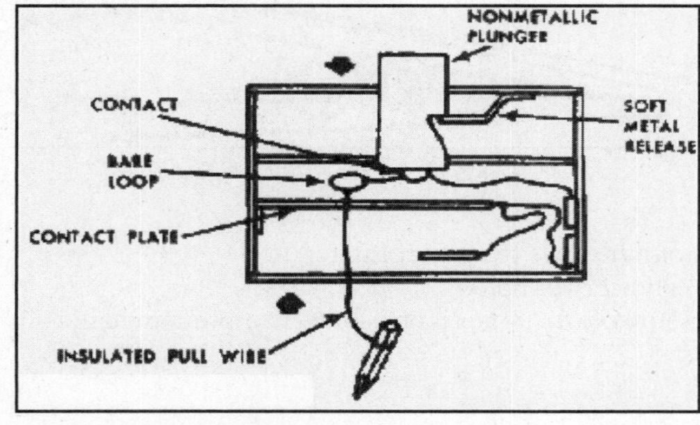

b. **Double Detonator.**

(1) Drill three holes—one in bottom, one in partition, and one in side—to admit nonmetallic plunger and two electric blasting caps.
(2) Assemble blasting cap, leg wires, contact plates, plunger, and pressure block.
(3) *Check circuit with galvanometer first.* Then connect batteries with friction tape.
(4) Install blasting cap connected to pressure firing device in side of mine.

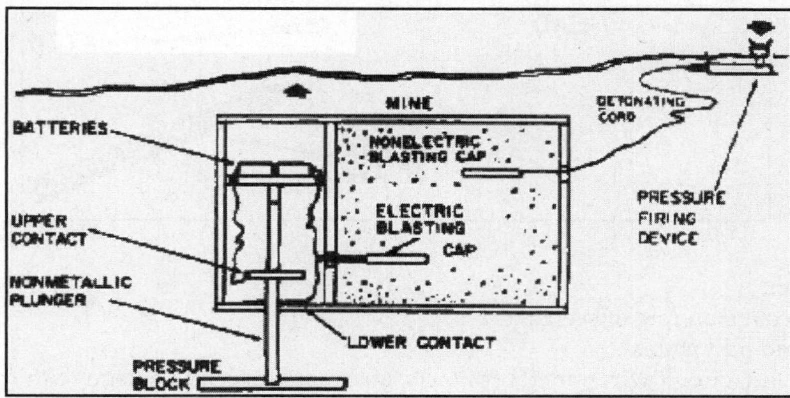

c. **Sliding Contact.**

(1) Assemble metal cap, nonmetallic tube or carton, sliding contact, wooden plug, and leg wires at contacts.
(2) *Check circuit with a galvonometer first,* then connect batteries with friction tape.
(3) Install assembly in tube.

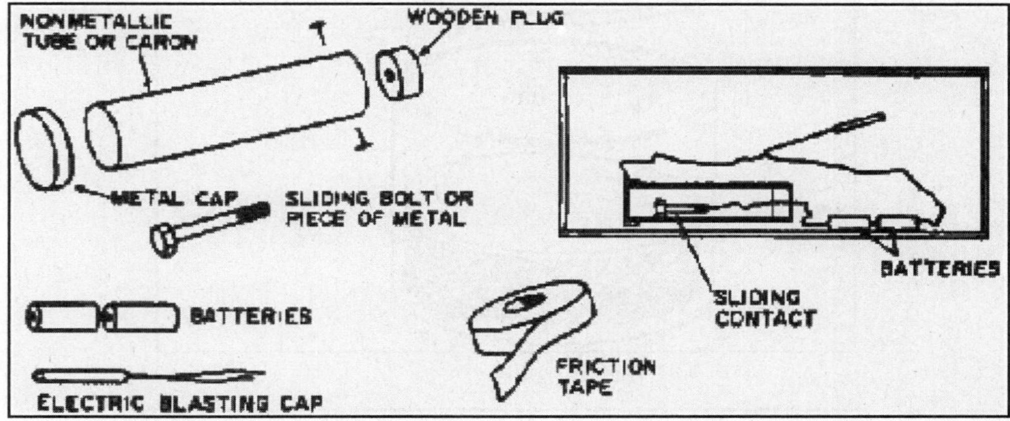

60. DELAY FIRING DEVICES

a. **Cigarette Timer.**

(1) Test burning rate of time fuze and cigarette. (A cigarette usually burns at the rate of 1 inch in 7 to 8 minutes.)
(2) Cut sloping end on length of time fuze.
(3) Assemble slopped end of time fuze, match head, and cigarette.

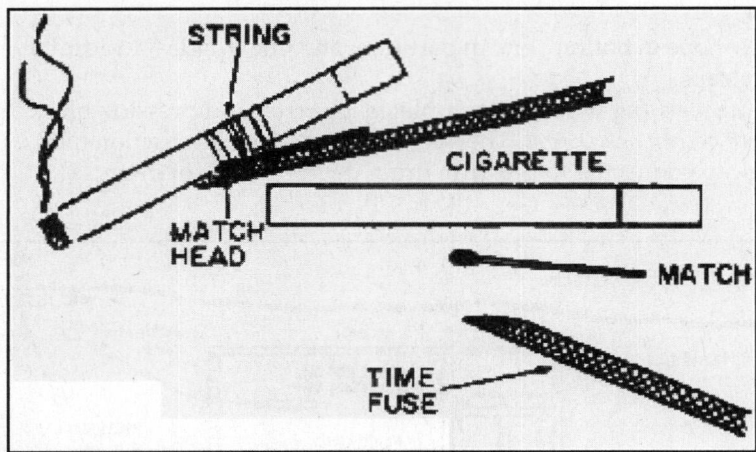

b. **Dried Seed Timer.**
   (1) Determine expansion rate of seeds.
   (2) Place in jar and add water.
   (3) Assemble jar, lid, circuit wires, metal contacts, and metal disk and secure with friction tape.

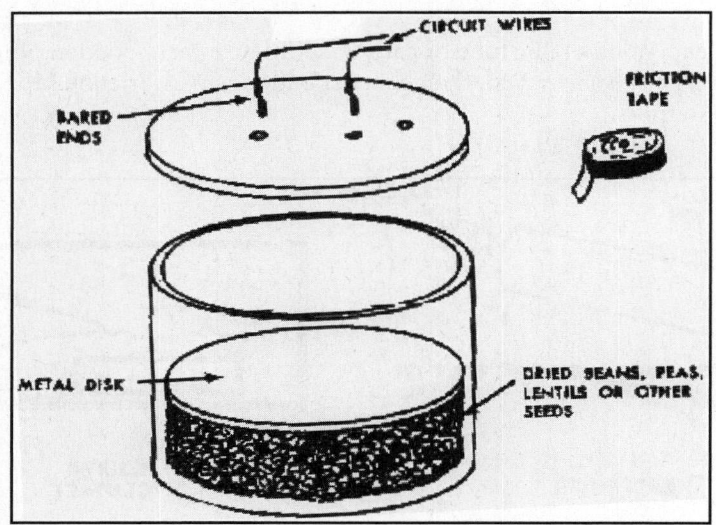

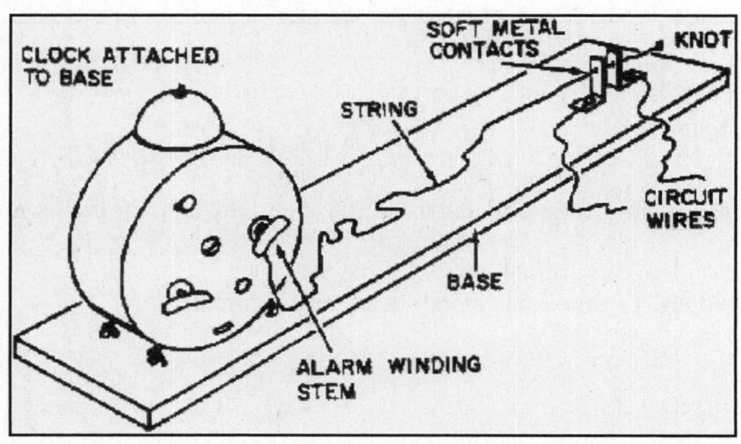

c. **Alarm Clock Timers.**

(1) ***Electric.***

(a) Assemble base, metal contacts, and alarm clock.

(b) Tie knot in one end of string. Thread other end through metal contacts and attach to alarm winding stem, which winches string and closes circuit.

> ✍ **NOTE**
> An alarm clock, being a very versatile delay, may be connected in many other ways.

(2) ***Nonelectric.***

(a) Drill hole in board of proper size to hold standard base tightly.

(b) Remove standard safety pin from firing device and replace with easily removed pin.

(c) Remove protective cap from standard base and crimp on nonelectric blasting cap.

(d) Screw standard base with blasting cap into firing device.

(e) Assemble alarm dock and firing device on board.

(f) Attach one end of length of string to eye in safety pin and the other to alarm winding stem, which winches string and removes safety pin.

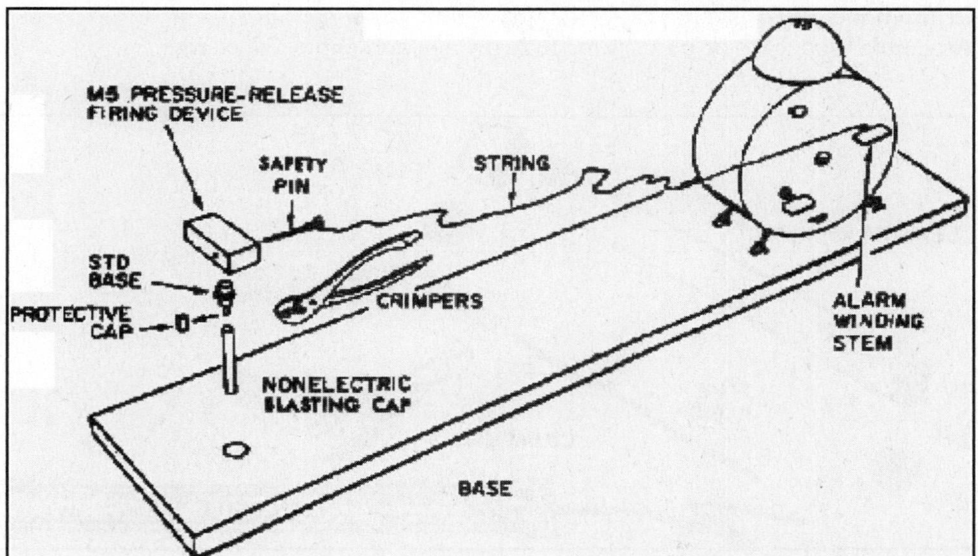

d. **Wrist Watch Timer.**

(1) ***One-hour delay or less.***

(a) Drill small hole in plastic crystal and attach circuit wire with screw of proper length to contact minute hand.

(b) Attach other circuit wire to case.

(2) ***Twelve-hour delay or less.***

(a) Remove minute hand.

(b) Drill small hole in plastic crystal and attach circuit wire with screw of proper length to contact hour hand.

(c) Attach other circuit wire to case.

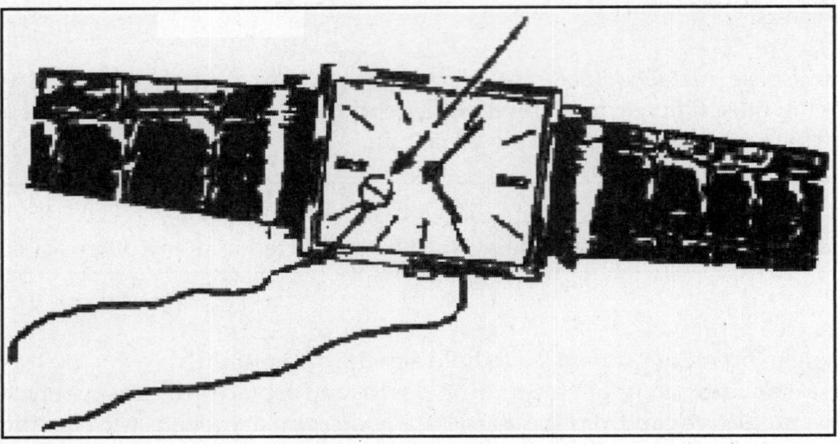

61. BOMBS

a. **Pipe Bombs.**

(1) ***Grenade.***

(a) Drill hole in cap or plug to admit length of time fuze.

(b) Crimp nonelectric blasting cap to length of time fuze.

(c) Assemble pipe, caps or plugs, time fuze primer, and explosive charge.

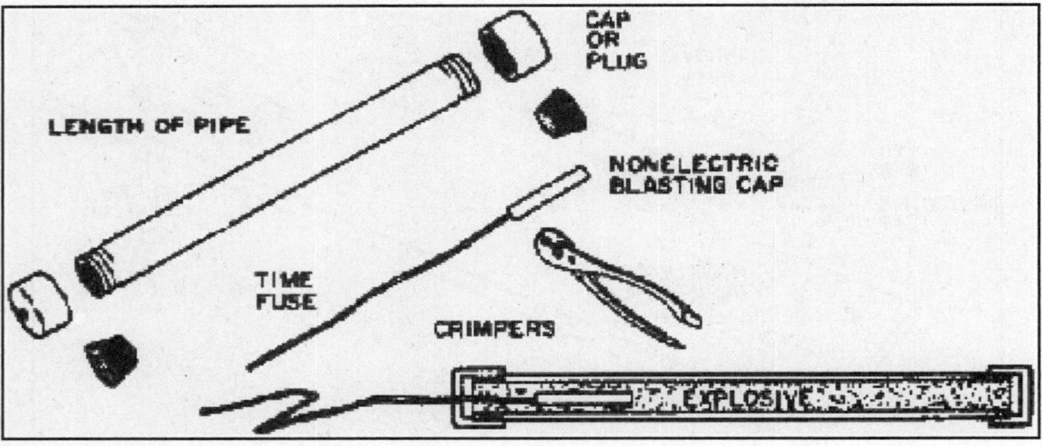

(2) ***Antidisturbance bomb.***

(a) Drill hole in end cap to admit length of burnt time fuze to make a bomb look like a "dud."

(b) Attach electric cap and mercury element on base.

(c) Test circuit with galvonometer *first*, then connect batteries with friction tape.

(d) Assemble bomb.

> ⚠ CAUTION
>
> If possible, assemble bomb *in place*, as the mercury element, when disturbed, may cause premature explosion. To assemble more safely and easily, attach wrist watch timer in circuit.

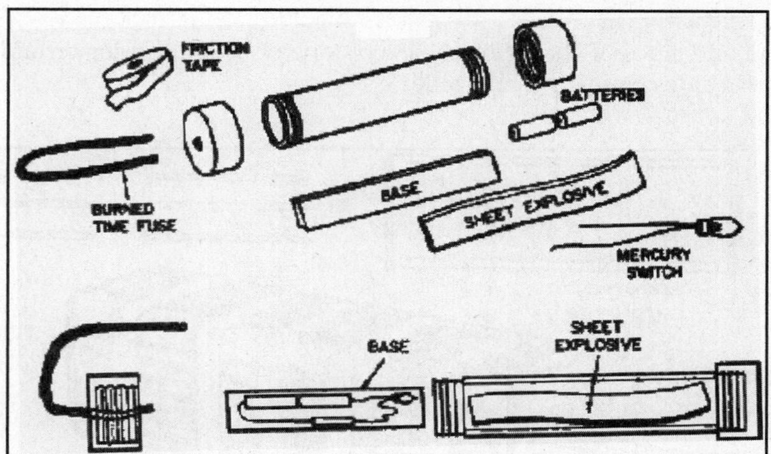

(3) ***Shotgun bomb.***

(a) Close one end of pipe with hammer, allowing opening for detonating cord primer or electric blasting cap.

(b) Remove protective cap from M1A1 pressure or M1 pull firing device and crimp on nonelectric blasting cap.

(c) Screw standard base with blasting cap into firing device.

(d) Assemble pipe, shrapnel, wadding, explosive, nonelectric primer or electric blasting cap (for controlled firing), and proper firing device.

> ✍ **NOTE**
> The force of the explosive and the strength of the pipe are important in calculating the size of the charge.

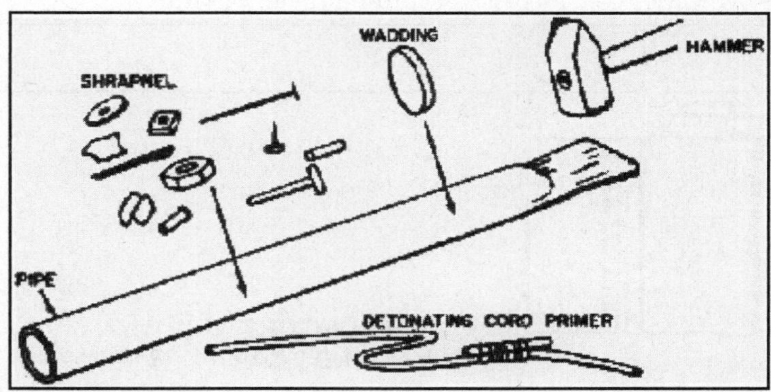

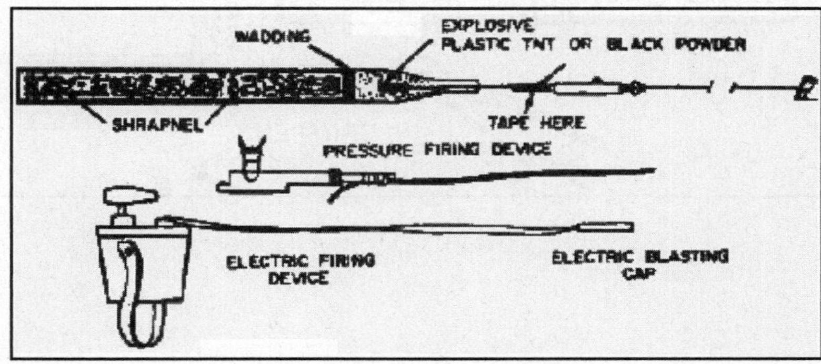

b. **Nail Grenade.**
Attach nails to top and sides of charge by means of tape or string. Under certain conditions, nails may be required on only two sides, or even on one side.

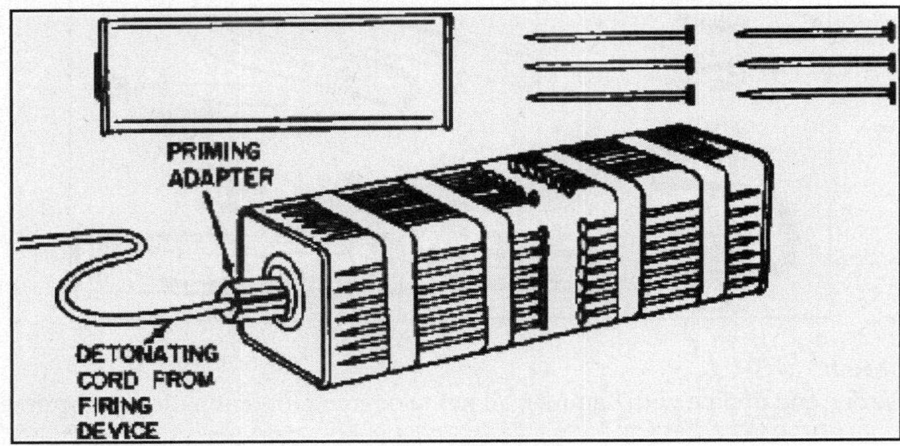

c. **Delay Bomb.**
(1) ***Chemical delay.***
(a) Crimp nonelectric blasting cap on base of appropriate M1 delay firing device.
(b) Assemble firing device and charge in package.
(c) Crush copper end of firing device with fingers.
(d) Place package in suitcase or container.

> ✍ **NOTE**
> Use this bomb only when delay is necessary but accuracy is secondary, as the delay time of any chemical firing device varies considerably according to temperature.

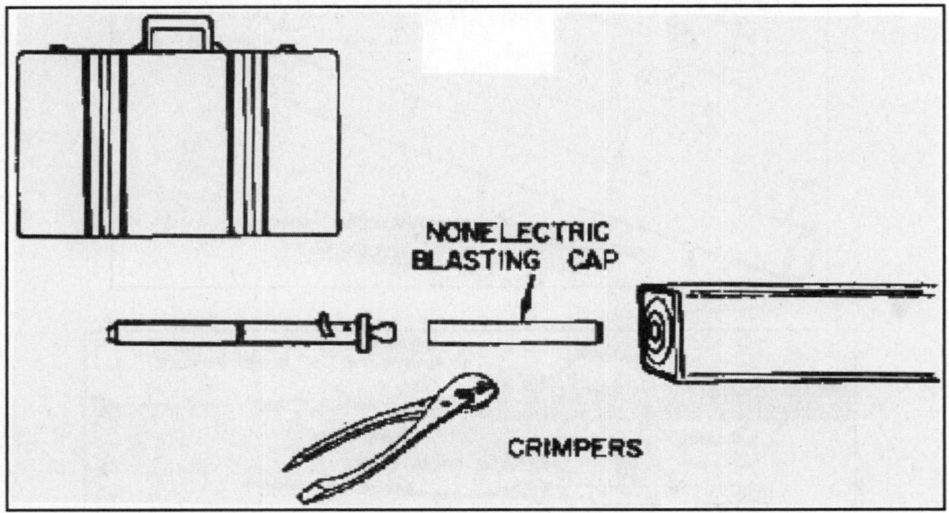

(2) ***Alarm clock delay.***

(a) Drill hole in wooden base of proper size to hold standard base firmly.
(b) Remove standard safety pin from M5 pressure-release firing device and replace with easily-removed pin.
(c) Crimp nonelectric blasting cap on standard base and attach to firing device.
(d) Assemble alarm clock and firing device on wooden base.
(e) Attach one end of string in eye in pull pin and the other to the alarm winding stem so that its turning will winch the string and withdraw the pin.
(f) Place assembly in suitcase or container.

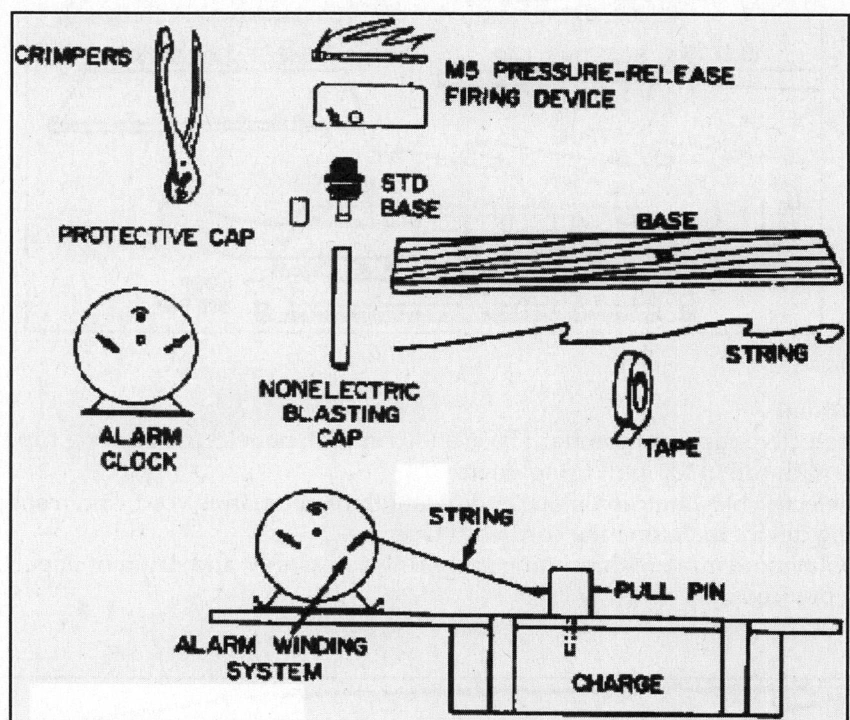

d. **Envelope Bomb.**

(1) Cut leg wires of electric blasting cap of proper length to make circuit.
(2) Strip insulation off ends of circuit wires and twist into ¼-inch loops to make loop switch.
(3) Test circuit with galvanometer *first,* then attach batteries.
(4) Assemble cardboard base, batteries, electric blasting cap, and explosive as package.
(5) Attach one end of string to loop switch so that it will pull the bared loops together to close circuit.
(6) Cut hole inside of envelope under flap.
(7) Fix package in envelope firmly and thread string through hole.
(8) Attach string firmly but concealed to underside of flap.
(9) Close envelope with elastic band.

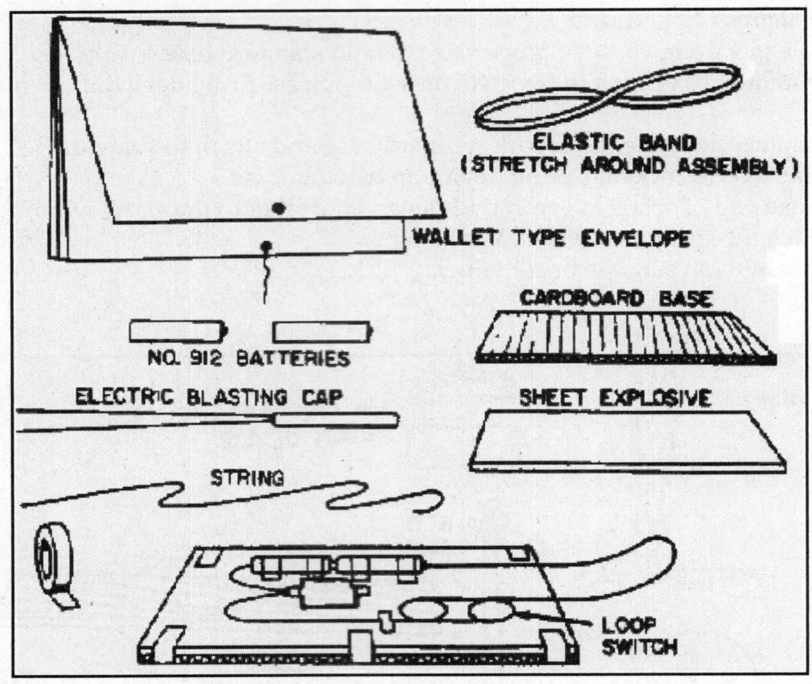

e. **Hot Shrapnel Bomb.**
   (1) Remove protective cap from standard base and crimp on nonelectric blasting cap.
   (2) Screw base with cap in M1 pull firing device.
   (3) Crimp nonelectric blasting cap on one end of length of detonating cord, and install in Claymore mine.
   (4) Attach firing device to detonating cord with tape.
   (5) Assemble Claymore mine with priming and firing accessories and drum of napalm.
   (6) Arm firing device.

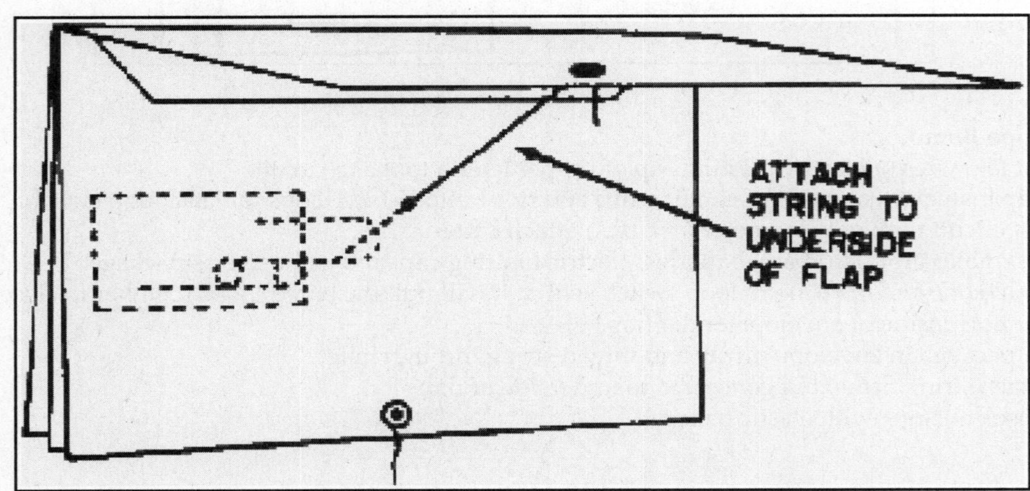

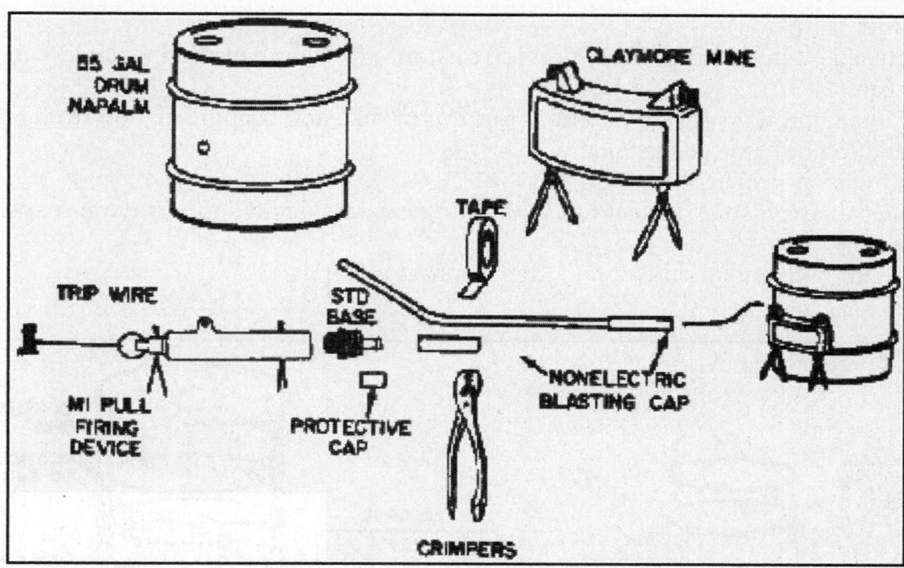

f. **Rise Paddy Bomb.**
   (1) Remove protective cap from standard base and crimp on nonelectric blasting cap.
   (2) Screw standard base with cap in M1 pull firing device.
   (3) Assemble firing device, detonating cord, priming adapter, nonelectric blasting cap, and explosive charge.
   (4) Attach charge to drum of napalm.
   (5) Arm firing device.

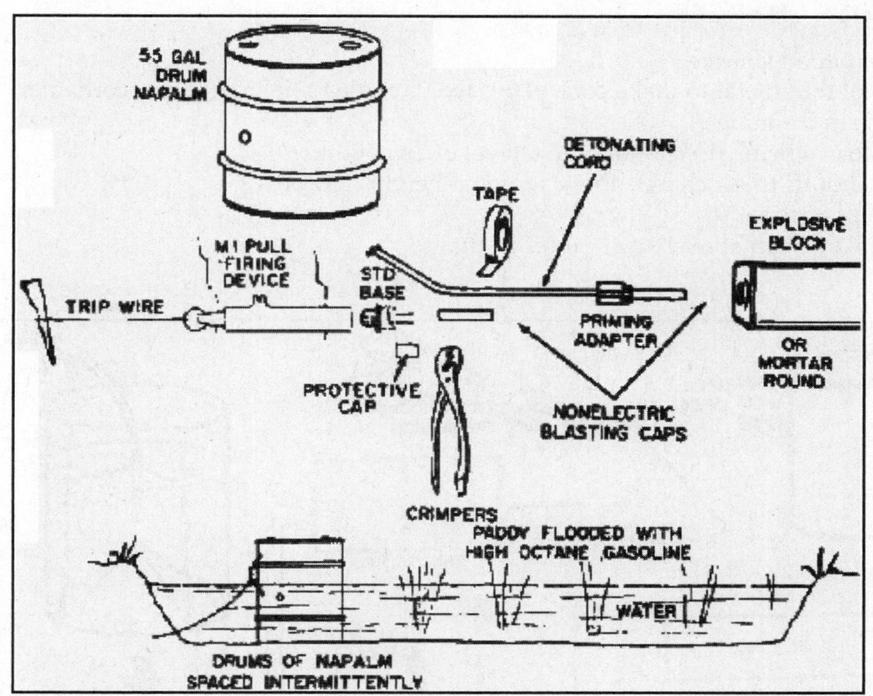

g. **Tin Can Bomb.**

(1) Cut a notched metal contact disk to provide clearance for length of stiff insulated wire and ⅛ to ¼ in. from walls of can.

(2) Cut stiff insulated wire of proper length to support disk and strip insulation from both ends. Bend hook on one end to hold bars suspension wire.

(3) Bend stiff wire to proper shape.

(4) Assemble can, explosive, contact to can, blasting cap, insulated support wire, suspension wire and contact disk.

(5) Check circuit with galvanometer *first*, then connect batteries.

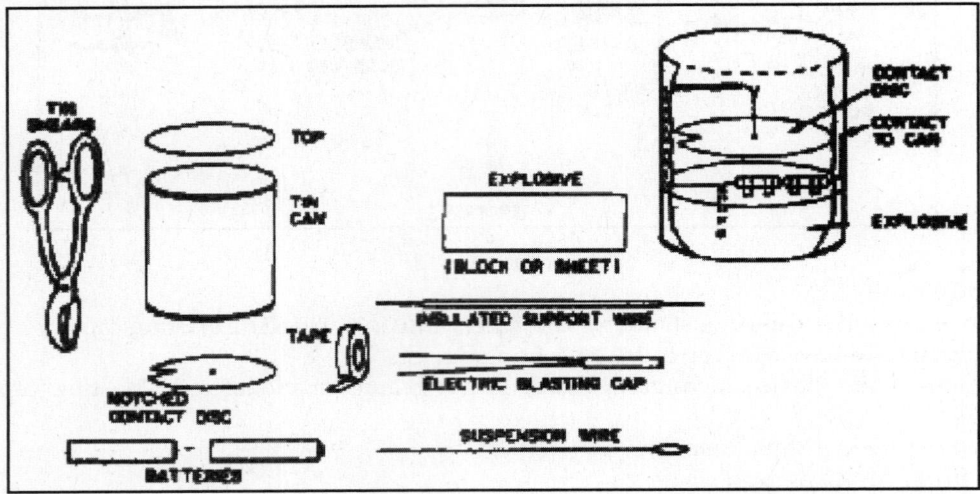

62. MISCELLANEOUS CHARGES

a. **Improvised Shaped Charge.**

(1) Cut strip of thin metal to make cone of 30° to 60° angle to fit snugly into container.

(2) Place cone in container.

(3) Pack explosive firmly in container to a level of 2x height.

(4) Attach standoffs to set charge above target at height of cone.
2x diameter of cone.

(5) Attach blasting cap at rear dead center of charge.

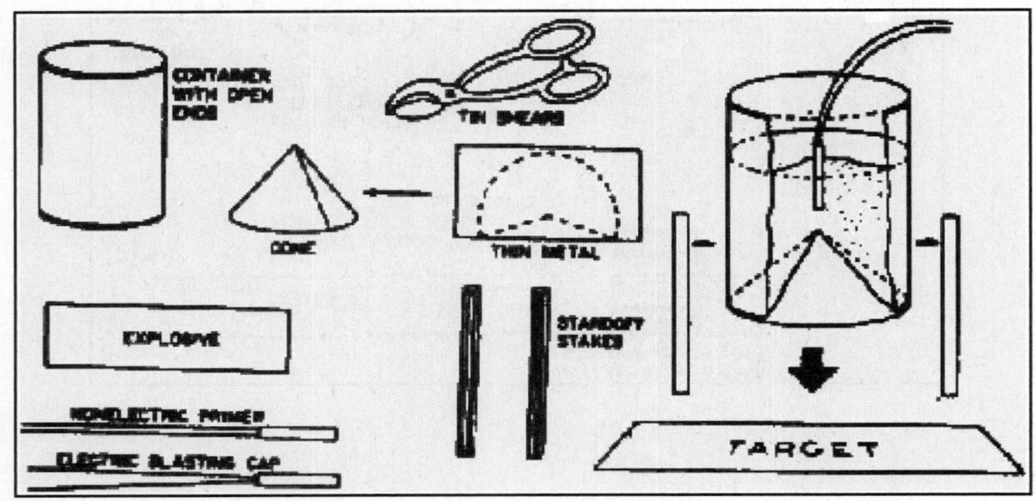

b. **Improvised Antipersonnel Mine.**

(1) Assemble container, explosive, separator, and shrapnel. *Explosive must be packed to uniform density and thickness* (should be ¼ weight of shrapnel).
(2) Remove protective cap from standard base and crimp on nonelectric blasting cap.
(3) Screw standard base with blasting cap into proper firing device.
(4) Secure firing device in place.
(5) Fix primer in rear center of explosive and tape to firing device.
(6) Arm firing device.

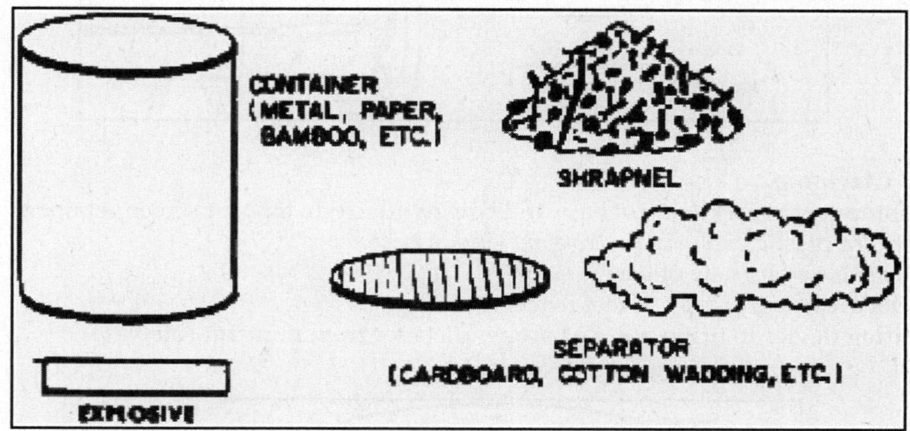

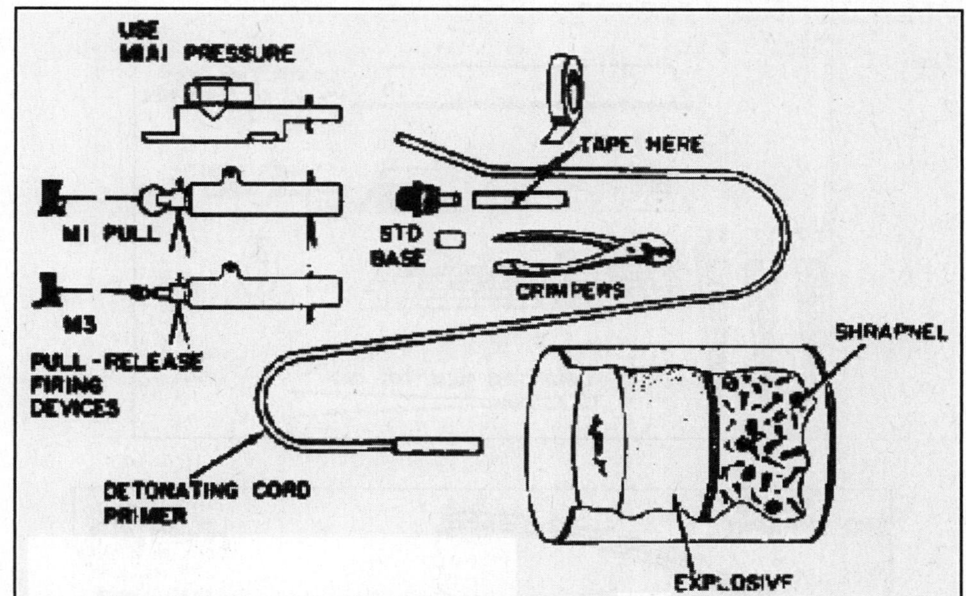

c. **Platter Charge.**

(1) Assemble container, charge, and platter. Charge should weigh same as platter.
(2) Place primer in rear center of charge.
(3) Align center of platter with center of target mass.
(4) Attach and arm firing device.

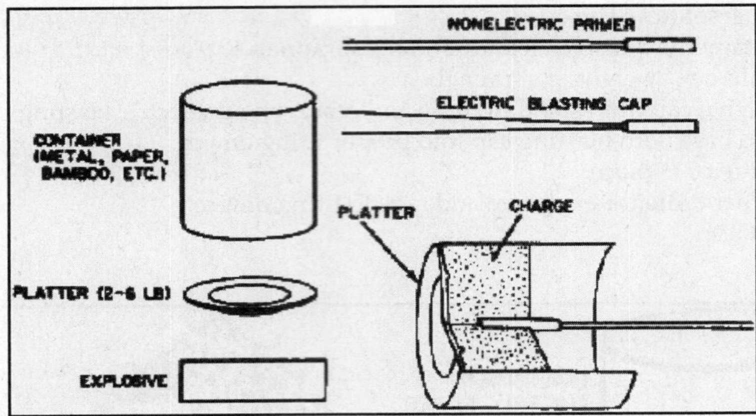

d. **Improvised Claymore.**
   (1) Attach shrapnel to *convex* side of base and cover with cloth, tape, or screen retainer.
   (2) Place layer of plastic explosive on *concave* side of base.
   (3) Attach legs to *concave* side of base.
   (4) Attach electric blasting cap at exact rear center.
   (5) Attach firing device to firing wires at proper distance from mine for safety.

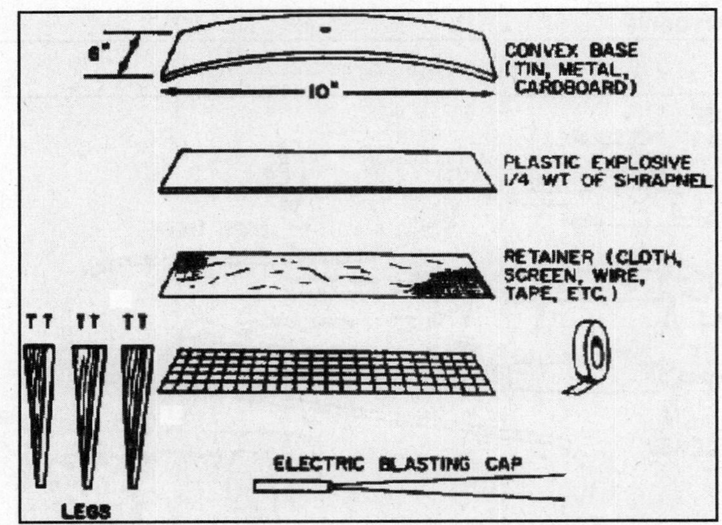

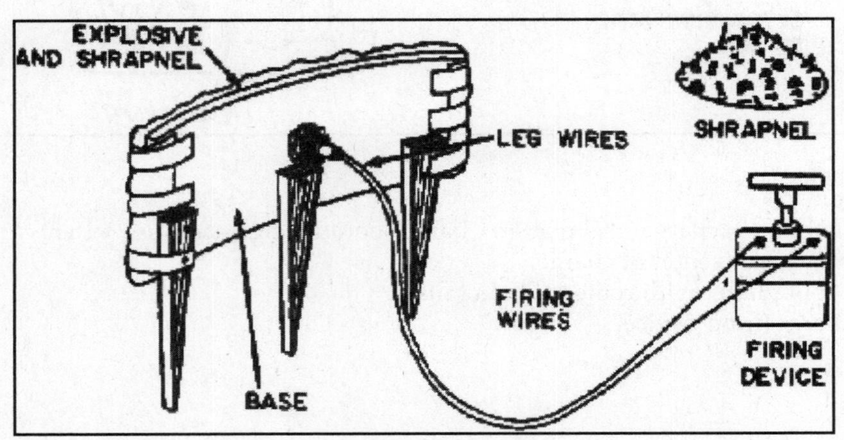

CHAPTER 6

Boobytrap Detection and Removal

SECTION I. CLEARING METHODS

63. TECHNICIANS

a. Although engineer and infantry specialists are responsible far boobytrap detection and removal, all military organizations assigned to combat zone missions must provide trained men to assist them.
b. If possible, trained engineer, infantry, or explosive ordnance disposal units will search out and neutralize all boobytraps in front of friendly troops or prepare safe passage lanes. When discovered, boobytraps will either be disarmed immediately or marked by warning signs. Only the simple ones will be disarmed during attack. Those more complicated will be marked and reported for removal.
c. To avoid casualty, boobytrapped areas, especially villages and other inhabited places, should be bypassed, to be cleared by specialists later. Tactical units will neutralize boobytraps only when necessary for continued movement or operation.

64. CLEARANCE TEAMS

Men who clear boobytraps are organized into disposal teams and assigned to specific areas according to their training and experience.

a. Direction and control is the responsibility of the person in charge of clearance activities, who will—
   (1) Maintain a control point near at hand and remain in close contact with his clearance parties.
   (2) Give assistance to disposal teams when required.
   (3) Preserve new types of enemy equipment found for more careful examination by engineer intelligence teams.
b. Searching parties will be sufficient in number to cover an area promptly, without interfering with each other.
c. In clearing a building, one person will direct all searching parties assigned.
d. Open area clearance will be preceded by reconnaissance if the presence of boobytraps is suspected. Once boobytraps are found, search must be thorough.
e. Searching parties must be rested frequently. A tired man, or one whose attention is attracted elsewhere, is a danger to himself and others working with him.

65. TOOLS AND EQUIPMENT

a. ***Body Armor.*** Armor of various kinds is available. Special boots and shoe pacs, also issued, will give greater protection against blast than boots generally worn.
b. ***Mine Detectors.***
   (1) Three mine detectors useful in the removal of boobytraps are issued: AN/PRS-3 (Polly Smith) and the transistorized, aural indication model, designed for metal detection, and AN/PRS-4 for nonmetallic detection. Of the metal detectors, the transistorized model is the lighter and more powerful. All three models have the same deficiences. They may signal a small piece of scrap as well as a metal-cased explosive or signal an air pocket in the soil, a root, or disturbed soil generally.
   (2) Operating time should not exceed 20 minutes to avoid operator fatigue. *Tired operators often become careless operators.*
c. ***Grapnels.*** These are hooks attached to a length of stout cord or wire, long enough for the operator to pull a mine or boobytrap from place from a safe distance or from at least 50 meters behind cover.

d. ***Probes.*** Lengths of metal rod or stiff wire, or bayonets, are good probes for locating buried charges. Searching parties sometimes work with rolled-up sleeves better to feel trip wires and hidden objects.
e. ***Markers.*** Standard markers are carried by disposal teams to designate the location of known boobytraps, pending their removal.
f. ***Tape.*** Marking tape is useful for tracing safe routes and identifying dangerous areas.
g. ***Hand Tools.*** Small items, such as nails, cotter pins, pieces of wire, friction tape, safety pins, pliers, pocket knife, hand mirror, scissors, flashlight, and screw driver are very useful in boobytrap clearance.

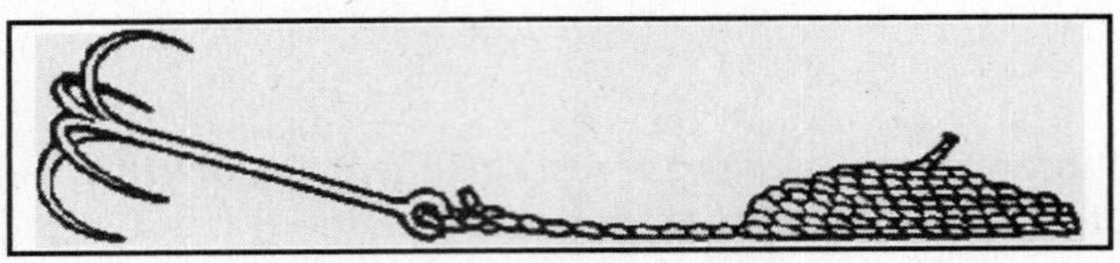

66. DETECTION

a. The most careful observation is required for the detection of boobytraps. Soldiers must be trained and disciplined to be on guard, especially when moving over an area previously held by the enemy. Although a soldier may not be assigned the responsibility for their detection and clearance, he must be alert for any sign that may indicate their presence. He must also discipline himself to look carefully for concealed boobytraps before performing many acts of normal life.
b. Often prisoners of war through interrogation give information on new or unknown boobytrap devices that may aid in their identification and handling later on. Local inhabitants also often provide information on boobytraps laid in the neighborhood.
c. Searching for boobytraps and delayed charges is difficult and tedious, particularly when intelligence is lacking or inadequate. The extent of search required, the ease of placing and camouflaging, and the great number of devices available to the enemy make the clearance of all charges almost impossible. Searching parties, before being sent out, will be briefed on all that is known about enemy activities in the area.

67. OUTDOOR SEARCHING TECHNIQUES

As boobytraps are so deadly and as a rule cunningly conceived and hidden, outdoor searching parties should be suspicious of—

a. All movable and apparently valuable and useful property.
b. All disturbed ground and litter from explosive containers.
c. Marks intentionally left behind to attract or divert attention.
d. Evidence of former camouflage.
e. Abrupt changes or breaks in the continuity of any object, such as unnatural appearances of fences, paint, vegetation, and dust.
f. Unnecessary things like nails, wire, or cord that may be part of a boobytrap.
g. Unusual marks that may be an enemy warning of danger.
h. All obstructions, for they are ideal spots for boobytraps. Search carefully before lifting a stone, moving a low hanging limb, or pushing aside a broken-down wheelbarrow.
i. Queer imprints or marks on a road, which may lead a curious person to danger.
j. Abandoned vehicles, dugouts, wells, machinery, bridges, gullies, defiles, or abandoned stores. Also walk carefully in or around these as pressure-release devices are easily concealed under relatively small objects.
k. Areas in which boobytraps are not found immediately. Never assume without further investigation that entire areas are clear.
l. Obvious trip wires. The presence of one trip wire attached to an object does not mean that there are no others. Searching must be complete.

68. INDOOR SEARCHING TECHNIQUES

Those in charge of disposal teams should:

a. Assign no more than one man to a room in a building.
b. Indicate the finding of a large charge by a prearranged signal. All teams except those responsible for neutralizing large charges must then vacate the building immediately by the original route of entry.
c. Examine both sides of a door before touching a knob. Observe through a window or break open a panel. If doors and windows must be opened and both sides cannot be examined, use a long rope.
d. Move carefully in all buildings, for boobytraps may be rigged to loose boards, moveable bricks, carpets, raised boards or stair treads, window kicks, or door knobs.
e. Never move furniture, pictures, or similar objects before checking them carefully for release devices or pull wires.
f. Never open any box, cupboard door, or drawer without careful checking. Sticky doors, drawers, or lids should be pulled with a long rope.
g. Not sit on any chair, sofa, or bed before careful examination.
h. Never connect broken wires or operate switches before checking the entire circuit. Such action may connect power to a charge.
i. Remove all switch plates and trace all wires that appear foreign to a circuit. Examine all appliances.
j. Investigate all repaired areas. Look for arming holes. Enlarge all wall and floor punctures. Cavities may be examined by reflecting a flashlight beam off a hand mirror (this is also applicable for searching under antitank mines).
k. Empty all fire boxes, remove the ashes, check fire wood, and move the coal pile.
l. Always work from the basement upward. Check, move, and mark everything movable including valves, taps, levers, controls, screens, and the like. A clockwork delay may not be heard if it is well hidden.
m. Double check basements and first floors—especially chimney flues, elevator and ventilator shafts, and insulated dead-air spaces. Check straight flues and shafts by observing from one end against a light held at the other. Dog-leg flues may be checked by lowering a brick from a safe distance.
n. Guard all buildings until they are occupied.
o. When possible and only after a thorough check, turn on all utilities from *outside* the building.

> ✍ **NOTE**
> A soldier by training can develop his sense of danger. Also by experience and careful continuous observation of his surroundings while in a combat area, he can develop an acute instinct that warns him of danger—a most valuable asset toward self-protection.

SECTION II. DISARMING METHODS

69. NEUTRALIZATION

a. This is the making of a dangerous boobytrap safe to handle. If this is not possible, however, it must be destroyed. Neutralization involves two steps—*disarming* or replacing safeties in the firing assembly and *defuzing* or separating the firing assembly from the main charge and the detonator from the firing assembly.

b. Although types of boobytraps found in conventional warfare in a combat zone vary greatly, equipment used by most armies is basically similar except in construction details. Accordingly, a knowledge of the mechanical details and techniques in the use of standard U.S. boobytrapping equipment in conventional warfare prepares a soldier to some extent for dealing with that of the enemy. This, however is not true in guerrilla warfare. Most enemy boobytraps found recently in guerrilla infested areas, were cunningly and ingeniously improvised and laid. Such boobytraps can rarely be neutralized even by the most experienced specialists. These are discussed and illustrated in chapter 5.

c. Boobytraps may be neutralized by two methods. (1) Whenever the location permits, they may be destroyed by actuating the mechanism from a safe distance or detonating a charge near the main charge. These should be used at all times unless tactical conditions are unfavorable. (2) When necessary, boobytraps may be disassembled by hand. As this is extremely dangerous, it should be undertaken only by experienced and extremely skillful specialists.

> ✍ **NOTE**
> Complete knowledge of the design of the boobytrap should be obtained before any neutralization is attempted.

d. In forward movements, all complicated mechanisms found are bypassed. These are marked and reported for neutralization later, when more deliberate action may be taken without hartassment by enemy fire.

e. All boobytraps exposed to blast from artillery fire or aerial bombing should be destroyed in place.

f. Boobytraps with unrecognizable or complicated firing arrangements should be marked and left for specialists to disarm.

   (1) Electrically fired boobytraps are among the most dangerous of all. Though rare in the past, they now turn up frequently in guerrilla warfare. Some may be identified by the presence of electric lead wires, dry cells, or other batteries. Some are small containers with all elements placed inside which actuate at the slightest disturbance. These can hardly be disarmed even by experts.

   (2) Another difficult type has delay fuzing—a spring-wound or electric clockwork for long delay periods or chemical action firing devices. As the line of detonation is uncertain, such boobytraps should be destroyed in place, if possible or tactically feasible.

70. RULES OF CONDUCT

a. Keep in constant practice by inspecting and studying all known boobytrap methods and mechanisms.
b. Develop patience. A careless act may destroy you and others as well.
c. Remember that knowledge inspires confidence.
d. Let only one man deal with boobytrap. Keep all others out of danger.
e. If in doubt, get help from an expert.
f. Never group together when there is danger.
g. Be suspicious of every unusual object.

PART III

Region - Specific Combat

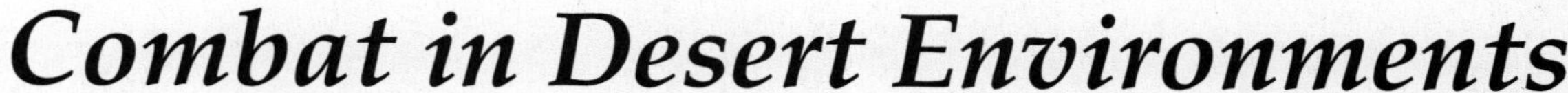

Combat in Desert Environments

Introduction

Arid regions make up about one-third of the earth's land surface, a higher percentage than that of any other type of climate. As we have seen in the recent past, some of these regions – because of diverse and conflicting cultures, strategic importance, and natural resources – have become centers of conflict.

Military leaders have long recognized the potential for U.S. involvement in conflict in these regions. Exercises at the Army's National Training Center, Fort Irwin and the Marine Corps' Marine Air Ground Combat Center, Twentynine Palms, California, have provided an opportunity for virtually all our ground forces to experience desert conditions. The success of Operation Desert Storm can be directly attributed to this realistic training.

Desert operations demand adaptation to the environment and to the limitations imposed by terrain and climate. Success depends on an appreciation of the effects of arid conditions on soldiers (both physically and psychologically), on equipment and facilities, and on combat and support operations. Leaders and soldiers must continually evaluate the situation and be ready to react to changing conditions. Equipment and tactics must be modified and adapted to a dusty, rugged landscape where temperatures vary from extreme highs to freezing lows and where visibility can change from 30 miles to 30 feet in a matter of minutes.

The key to success in desert operations is mobility. This was clearly evident in the ground operations of Desert Storm. The tactics employed to achieve victory over Iraq were wide, rapid flanking movements similar to those executed by Montgomery and Rommel during World War II. During Desert Storm, however, new technologies increased higher-echelon headquarters' ability to target, attack, and fight deep operations simultaneously. Modern weapon systems like the M1A1 Abrams tank, Bradley fighting vehicle, light armored vehicle, and assault amphibious vehicle, coupled with newly developed navigation and targeting devices, contributed immeasurably. Tactical units were able to fight battles with minimal direction; leaders were able to exercise initiative based on a clear understanding of their commanders' intent. Current doctrine—focused on improving mobility and implemented through the planning, preparation, and execution processes, battle drills, and tactical SOPs, paved the way for the overwhelming triumph.

Arid regions create both opportunities and restraints for soldiers and marines at all levels. The U.S. military's performance in Desert Storm shows it understands these factors and has successfully addressed the effects of desert warfare on troops, equipment, and operations. As they prepare for the future, leaders, soldiers, and marines must study past campaigns and use the lessons they learn to reduce casualties, use the environment to their advantage, and ensure victory on the desert battlefield.

CHAPTER 1

The Environment and Its Effects on Personnel and Equipment

SECTION I. THE ENVIRONMENT

Successful desert operations require adaptation to the environment and to the limitations its terrain and climate impose. Equipment and tactics must be modified and adapted to a dusty and rugged landscape where temperatures vary from extreme highs down to freezing and where visibility may change from 30 miles to 30 feet in a matter of minutes. Deserts are arid, barren regions of the earth incapable of supporting normal life due to lack of water. See Figure 1-1 for arid regions of the world. Temperatures vary according to latitude and season, from over 136 degrees Fahrenheit in the deserts of Mexico and Libya to the bitter cold of winter in the Gobi (East Asia). In some deserts, day-to-night temperature fluctuation exceeds 70 degrees Fahrenheit. Some species of animal and plant life have adapted successfully to desert conditions where annual rainfall may vary from 0 to 10 inches.

Desert terrain also varies considerably from place to place, the sole common denominator being lack of water with its consequent environmental effects, such as sparse, if any, vegetation. The basic land forms are similar to those in other parts of the world, but the topsoil has been eroded due to a combination of lack of water, heat, and wind to give deserts their characteristic barren appearance. The bedrock may be covered by a flat layer of sand, or gravel, or may have been exposed by erosion. Other common features are sand dunes, escarpments, wadis, and depressions. This environment can profoundly affect military operations. See Figure 1-2 for locations of major deserts of the world.

It is important to realize that deserts are affected by seasons. Those in the Southern Hemisphere have summer between 21 December and 21 March. This 6-month difference from the United States is important when considering equipping and training nonacclimatized soldiers/marines for desert operations south of the equator.

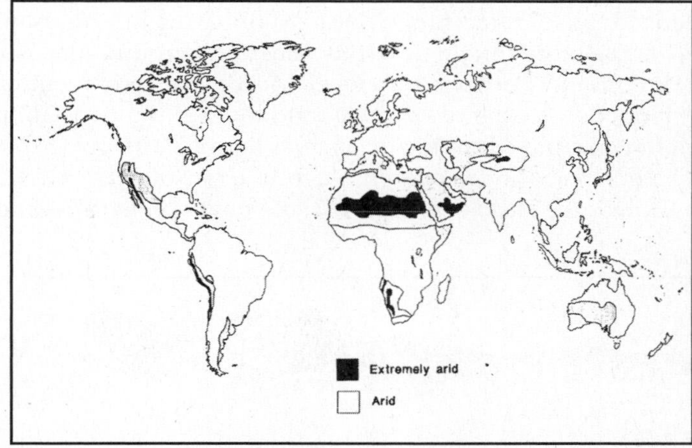

Figure 1-1: Deserts of the world.

TERRAIN

Key terrain in the desert is largely dependent on the restrictions to movement that are present. If the desert floor will not support wheeled vehicle traffic, the few roads and desert tracks become key terrain. Crossroads are vital as they control military operations in a large area. Desert warfare is often a battle for control of the lines of communication

(LOC). The side that can protect its own LOC while interdicting those of the enemy will prevail. Water sources are vital, especially if a force is incapable of long distance resupply of its water requirements. Defiles play an important role, where they exist. In the Western Desert of Libya, an escarpment that paralleled the coast was a barrier to movement except through a few passes. Control of these passes was vital. Similar escarpments are found in Saudi Arabia and Kuwait.

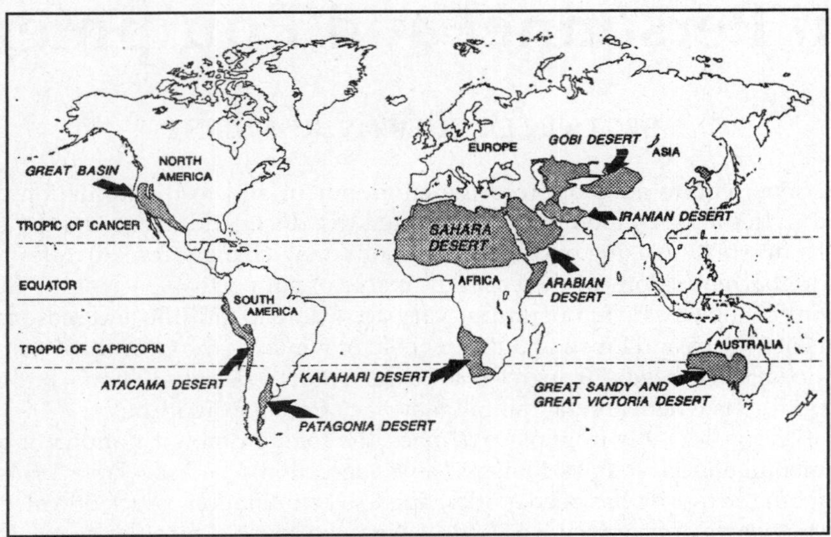

Figure 1-2: Desert locations of the world.

Types of Desert Terrain

There are three types of desert terrain: mountain, rocky plateau, and sandy or dune terrain. The following paragraphs discuss these types of terrain.

Mountain Deserts

Mountain deserts are characterized by scattered ranges or areas of barren hills or mountains, separated by dry, flat basins. See Figure 1-3 for an example of mountain desert terrain. High ground may rise gradually or abruptly from flat areas, to a height of several thousand feet above sea level. Most of the infrequent rainfall occurs on high ground and runs off in the form of flash floods, eroding deep gullies and ravines and depositing sand and gravel around the edges of the basins. Water evaporates rapidly, leaving the land as barren as before, although there may be short-lived vegetation. If sufficient water enters the basin to compensate for the rate of evaporation, shallow lakes may develop, such as the Great Salt Lake in Utah or the Dead Sea; most of these have a high salt content.

Figure 1-3: Example of mountain desert terrain.

Rocky Plateau Deserts

Rocky plateau deserts are extensive flat areas with quantities of solid or broken rock at or near the surface. See Figure 1-4 for an example of a rocky plateau desert. They may be wet or dry, steep-walled eroded valleys, known as wadis, gulches, or canyons. Narrow valleys can be extremely dangerous to men and materiel due to flash flooding after rains; although their flat bottoms may be superficially attractive as assembly areas. The National Training Center and the Golan Heights are examples of rocky plateau deserts.

Figure 1-4: Example of rocky plateau desert terrain.

Sandy or Dune Deserts

Sandy or dune deserts are extensive flat areas covered with sand or gravel, the product of ancient deposits or modern wind erosion. "Flat" is relative in this case, as some areas may contain sand dunes that are over 1,000 feet high and 10–15 miles long; trafficability on this type of terrain will depend on windward/leeward gradients of the dunes and the texture of the sand. See Figure 1-5 for an example of a sandy desert. Other areas, however, may be totally flat for distances of 3,000 meters and beyond. Plant life may vary from none to scrub, reaching over 6 feet high. Examples of this type of desert include the ergs of the Sahara, the Empty Quarter of the Arabian desert, areas of California and New Mexico, and the Kalahari in South Africa. See Figure 1-6 for an example of a dune desert.

Figure 1-5: Example of sandy desert terrain.

Figure 1-6: Example of dune desert terrain.

Trafficability

Roads and trails are rare in the open desert. Complex road systems beyond simple commercial links are not needed. Road systems have been used for centuries to connect centers of commerce, or important religious shrines such as Mecca and Medina in Saudi Arabia. These road systems are supplemented by routes joining oil or other mineral deposits to collection outlet points. Some surfaces, such as lava beds or salt marshes, preclude any form of routine vehicular movement, but generally ground movement is possible in all directions. Speed of movement varies depending on surface texture. Rudimentary trails are used by minor caravans and nomadic tribesmen, with wells or oasis approximately every 20 to 40 miles; although there are some waterless stretches which extend over 100 miles. Trails vary in width from a few meters to over 800 meters.

Vehicle travel in mountainous desert country may be severely restricted. Available mutes can be easily blinked by the enemy or by climatic conditions. Hairpin turns are common on the edges of precipitous mountain gorges, and the higher passes may be blocked by snow in the winter.

Natural Factors

The following terrain features require special considerations regarding trafficability.

Wadis or dried water courses, vary from wide, but barely perceptible depressions of soft sand, dotted with bushes, to deep, steep-sided ravines. There frequently is a passable route through the bottom of a dried wadi. Wadis can provide cover from ground observation and camouflage from visual air reconnaissance. The threat of flash floods after heavy rains poses a significant danger to troops and equipment downstream. Flooding may occur in these areas even if it is not raining in the immediate area. See Figure 1-7 for an example of a wadi.

Figure 1-7: Example of a wadi.

Salt marsh (sebkha) terrain is impassable to tracks and wheels when wet. When dry it has a brittle, crusty surface, negotiable by light wheel vehicles only. Salt marshes develop at points where the water in the subsoil of the desert rose to the surface. Because of the constant evaporation in the desert, the salts carried by the water are deposited, and results in a hard, brittle crust.

Salt marshes are normally impassable, the worst type being those with a dry crust of silt on top. Marsh mud used on desert sand will, however, produce an excellent temporary road. Many desert areas have salt marshes either in the center of a drainage basin or near the sea coast. Old trails or paths may cross the marsh, which are visible during the dry season but not in the wet season. In the wet season trails are indicated by standing water due to the crust being too hard or too thick for it to penetrate. However, such routes should not be tried by load-carrying vehicles without prior reconnaissance and marking. Vehicles may become mired so severely as to render equipment and units combat ineffective. Heavier track-laying vehicles, like tanks, are especially susceptible to these areas, therefore reconnaissance is critical.

Man-made Factors

The ruins of earlier civilizations, scattered across the deserts of the world, often are sited along important avenues of approach and frequently dominate the only available passes in difficult terrain. Control of these positions maybe imperative for any force intending to dominate the immediate area. Currently occupied dwellings have little impact on trafficability except that they are normally located near roads and trails. Apart from nomadic tribesmen who live in tents (see Figure 1-8 for an example of desert nomads), the population lives in thick-walled structures with small windows, usually built of masonry or a mud and straw (adobe) mixture. Figure 1-9 shows common man-made desert structures.

Figure 1-8: Example of desert nomads.

Figure 1-9: Common man-made desert structures.

Because of exploration for and production of oil and other resources, wells, pipelines, refineries, quarries, and crushing plants may be of strategic importance in the desert. Pipelines are often raised 1 meter off the ground—where this is the case, pipelines will inhibit movement. Subsurface pipelines can also be an obstacle. In Southwest Asia, the subsurface pipelines were indicated on maps. Often they were buried at such a shallow depth that they could be damaged by heavy vehicles traversing them. Furthermore, if a pipeline is ruptured, not only is the spill of oil a consideration, but the fumes may be hazardous as well.

Agriculture in desert areas has little effect on trafficability except that canals limit surface mobility. Destruction of an irrigation system, which may be a result of military operations, could have a devastating effect on the local population and should be an important consideration in operational estimates. Figure 1-10 shows an irrigation ditch.

TEMPERATURE

The highest known ambient temperature recorded in a desert was 136 degrees Fahrenheit (58 degrees Celsius). Lower temperatures than this produced internal tank temperatures approaching 160 degrees Fahrenheit (71 degrees Celsius) in the Sahara Desert during the Second World War. Winter temperatures in Siberian deserts and in the Gobi reach minus 50 degrees Fahrenheit (minus 45 degrees Celsius). Low temperatures are aggravated by very strong winds producing high windchill factors. The cloudless sky of the desert permits the earth to heat during sunlit hours, yet cool to near freezing at night. In the inland Sinai, for example, day-to-night temperature fluctuations are as much as 72 degrees Fahrenheit.

Figure 1-10: Irrigation ditch.

WINDS

Desert winds can achieve velocities of near hurricane force; dust and sand suspended within them make life intolerable, maintenance very difficult, and restrict visibility to a few meters. The Sahara "Khamseen", for example, lasts for days at a time; although it normally only occurs in the spring and summer. The deserts of Iran are equally well known for the "wind of 120 days," with sand blowing almost constantly from the north at wind velocities of up to 75 miles per hour.

Although there is no danger of a man being buried alive by a sandstorm, individuals can become separated from their units. In all deserts, rapid temperature changes invariably follow strong winds. Even without wind, the telltale clouds raised by wheels, tracks, and marching troops give away movement. Wind aggravates the problem. As the day gets wanner the wind increases and the dust signatures of vehicles may drift downwind for several hundred meters.

In the evening the wind normally settles down. In many deserts a prevailing wind blows steadily from one cardinal direction for most of the year, and eventually switches to another direction for the remaining months. The equinoctial gales raise huge sandstorms that rise to several thousand feet and may last for several days. Gales and sandstorms in the winter months can be bitterly cold. See Figure 1-11 for an example of wind erosion.

Figure 1-11: Example of wind erosion.

Sandstorms are likely to form suddenly and stop just as suddenly. In a severe sandstorm, sand permeates everything making movement nearly impossible, not only because of limited visibility, but also because blowing sand damages moving parts of machinery.

WATER

The lack of water is the most important single characteristic of the desert. The population, if any, varies directly with local water supply. A Sahara oasis may, for its size, be one of the most densely occupied places on earth (see Figure 1-12 for a typical oasis).

Desert rainfall varies from one day in the year to intermittent showers throughout the winter. Severe thunderstorms bring heavy rain, and usually far too much rain falls far too quickly to organize collection on a systematic basis. The water soon soaks into the ground and may result in flash floods. In some cases the rain binds the sand much like a beach after the tide ebbs allowing easy maneuver however, it also turns loam into an impassable quagmire obstacle. Rainstorms tend to be localized, affecting only a few square kilometers at a time. Whenever possible, as storms approach, vehicles should move to rocky areas or high ground to avoid flash floods and becoming mired.

Permanent rivers such as the Nile, the Colorado, or the Kuiseb in the Namib Desert of Southwest Africa are fed by heavy precipitation outside the desert so the river survives despite a high evaporation rate.

Subsurface water may be so far below the surface, or so limited, that wells are normally inadequate to support any great number of people. Because potable water is absolutely vital, a large natural supply may be both tactically and strategically important. Destruction of a water supply system may become a political rather than military decision, because of its lasting effects on the resident civilian population.

SECTION II. ENVIRONMENTAL EFFECTS ON EQUIPMENT

Conditions in an arid environment can damage military equipment and facilities. Temperatures and dryness are major causes of equipment failure, and wind action lifts and spreads sand and dust, clogging and jamming anything that has moving parts. Vehicles, aircraft, sensors, and weapons are all affected. Rubber components such as gaskets and seals become brittle, and oil leaks are more frequent. Ten characteristics of the desert environment may adversely affect equipment used in the desert:

- Terrain.
- Heat.
- Winds.
- Dust and sand.
- Humidity.
- Temperature variations.
- Thermal bending.
- Optical path bending.

- Static electricity.
- Radiant light.

The relative importance of each characteristic varies from desert to desert. Humidity, for example, can be discounted in most deserts but is important in the Persian Gulf.

TERRAIN

Terrain varies from nearly flat, with high trafficability, to lava beds and salt marshes with little or no trafficability. Drivers must be well trained in judging terrain over which they are driving so they can select the best method of overcoming the varying conditions they will encounter.

Track vehicles are well suited for desert operations. Wheel vehicles may be acceptable as they can go many places that track vehicles can go; however, their lower speed average in poor terrain maybe unacceptable during some operations. Vehicles should be equipped with extra fan belts, tires, (and other items apt to malfunction), tow ropes (if not equipped with a winch), extra water cans, and desert camouflage nets. Air-recognition panels, signal mirrors, and a tarpaulin for crew sun protection are very useful. Wheel vehicles should also carry mats, or channels as appropriate, to assist in freeing mired vehicles.

The harsh environment requires a very high standard of maintenance, which may have to be performed well away from specialized support personnel. Operators must be fully trained in operating and maintaining their equipment. Some types of terrain can have a severe effect on suspension and transmission systems, especially those of wheel vehicles. Tanks are prone to throw tracks when traveling over rocks.

Track components require special care in the desert. Grit, heat, and bad track tension accelerate track failure. Sprockets wear out quickly in sandy conditions. Track pins break more easily in high temperatures and high temperatures also increase rubber / metal separation on road wheels. Proper track tension is critical, as loose track is easily thrown and excessive tension causes undue stress on track components.

Increase the unit PLL of tires and tracks as sand temperatures of 165 degrees Fahrenheit are extremely detrimental to rubber, and weaken resistance to sharp rocks and plant spines, Items affected by mileage such as wheels, steering, track wedge bolts and sprocket nuts, and transmission shafts, must be checked for undue wear when conducting before-, during-, and after-operations maintenance.

HEAT

Vehicle coding and lubrication systems are interdependent. A malfunction by one will rapidly place the other system under severe strain. In temperature extremes, all types of engines are apt to operate above optimum temperatures, leading to excessive wear, or leaking oil seals in the power packs, and ultimately, engine failure. Commanders should be aware which types of vehicles are prone to excessive overheating, and ensure extra care is applied to their maintenance. The following are considerations for ensuring engines do not overheat:

- Check oil levels frequently to ensure proper levels are maintained (too high may be as bad as too low), that seals are not leaking, and oil consumption is not higher than normal.
- Keep radiators and air flow areas around engines clean and free of debris and other obstructions.
- Fit water-cooled engines with condensers to avoid steam escaping through the overflow pipe.
- Cooling hoses must be kept tight (a drip a second loses 7 gallons of fluid in 24 hours).
- Operators should not remove hood side panels from engine compartments while the engine is running as this causes air turbulence and leads to ineffective cooling.

Batteries do not hold their charge efficiently in intense heat. Check them twice daily. The following are additional considerations for maintaining batteries in intense heat:

- Change battery specific gravity to adjust to the desert environment (see vehicle TMs for details).
- Keep batteries full, but not overfilled, and carry a reserve of distilled water.
- Keep air vents clean, or vapors may build up pressure and cause the battery to explode.

- Set voltage regulators as low as practical.
- Increase dry battery supplies to offset high attrition rate caused by heat exposure.

Severe heat increases pressure in closed pressurized systems such as the M2 fire burner unit, and increases the volume of liquids. Ensure that the working pressure of all equipment is within safety limits and be careful when removing items such as filler caps.

Treat Halon fire extinguishers with care. High temperatures may cause them to discharge spontaneously. Put wet rags on them during the hottest part of the day to keep them coder.

Some items of equipment are fitted with thermal cutouts that open circuit breakers whenever equipment begins to overheat. Overheating is often caused by high ambient temperatures, and can be partly avoided by keeping the item in the shade or wrapping it in a wet cloth to maintain a lower temperature by evaporation.

Flying time and performance of helicopters are degraded as the altitude and heat increases. Helicopter performance is also affected by humidity. Aircraft canopies have been known to bubble under direct heat and should be covered when not in use.

Ammunition must be out of direct heat and sunlight. Use camouflage nets and tarpaulins to provide cover. Ammunition cool enough to be held by bare hands is safe to fire.

Wood shrinks in a high-temperature, low-humidity environment. Equipment, such as axes carried on track vehicles, can become safety hazards as heads are likely to fly off shrunken handles.

Radiators require special attention. Proper cooling-system operation is critical in high-temperature environments. Check cooling systems for serviceability prior to deployment. Local water may be high in mineral content which will calcify in cooling systems. Distilled water is better since tap water contains chemicals that will form a crusty coating inside the radiator and will ultimately clog it. A mixture of 40 percent antifreeze and 60 percent water is usually acceptable—check your appropriate technical manual to be certain.

During movement, and at operation sites where extremely hot temperatures exist, continuous protection from the heat is necessary for medical items and supplies, which deteriorate rapidly.

Air and all fluids expand and contract according to temperature. If tires are inflated to correct pressure during the cool of night, they may burst during the heat of day. If fuel tanks are filled to the brim at night, they will overflow at midday. Servicing these items during the heat of day can result in low tire pressure, overheating of tires, and a lack of endurance if the fuel tanks were not filled to their correct levels. Air pressure in tires must be checked when the equipment is operating at efficient working temperatures, and fuel tanks must be filled to their correct capacity as defined in the appropriate technical manual. These items should be checked several times a day and again at night.

The major problem with radios in a desert environment is overheating. The following steps can help prevent overheating of radios:

- Keep radios out of direct sunlight.
- Place a piece of wood on top of the radio. Leaving space between the wood and the top of the radio will help cool the equipment. Operating on low power whenever possible will also help.
- Place wet rags on top of radios to help keep them cool and operational. Do not cover the vents.

Any oil or fuel blown onto a cooler (heat exchanger) will gather and quickly degrade cooling. Fix even slight leaks promptly. Do not remove cooling ducts or shrouds. Check them for complete coverage—use tape to seal cracks. Do not remove serviceable thermostats if overheating occurs.

WINDS

Desert winds, by their velocity alone, can be very destructive to large and relatively light materiel such as aircraft, tentage, and antenna systems. To minimize the possibility of wind damage, materiel should be sited to benefit from wind protection and should be firmly picketed to the ground.

DUST AND SAND

Dust and sand are probably the greatest danger to the efficient functioning of equipment in the desert. It is almost impossible to avoid particles settling on moving parts and acting as an abrasive. Sand mixed with oil forms an abrasive paste.

Lubricants must be of the correct viscosity for the temperature and kept to the recommended absolute minimum in the case of exposed or semiexposed moving parts. Lubrication fittings are critical items and should be checked frequently. If they are missing, sand will enter the housing causing bearing failure. Teflon bearings require constant inspection to ensure that the coating is not being eroded.

Proper lubrication is crucial for success. Wipe off all grease fittings before you attach the grease gun and after use. Keep cans of grease covered to prevent sand contamination. Preserve opened grease containers by covering and sealing with plastic bags. Use of grease cartridges in lieu of bulk grease is preferred. All POL dispensing tools must be stored in protected areas to prevent contamination. Place a tarpaulin, or other material, under equipment being repaired to prevent tools and components from being lost in the sand. The automotive-artillery grease possesses a significantly high-temperature capability. If not available, an alternative is general purpose wide-temperature range (WTR) aircraft grease.

Oil should be changed about twice as often under desert conditions as under U.S. or European conditions, not only because grit accumulates in the oil pan, but also because noncombusted low-octane fuel seeps down the cylinder walls and dilutes the reservoir. Diluted lubricants cool less effectively, and evaporate at the higher temperatures generated during engine operation. Oil changes and lubrication of undercarriage points at more frequent intervals will prolong engine and vehicle life under desert conditions. Units employed in desert environments should reevaluate their engine oil requirements and plan accordingly.

Keeping sand out of maintenance areas is critical due to the strong possibility of sand or dust entering the cylinders or other moving parts when the equipment is stripped. Baggies, cloth, or plastic can be used to protect open or disassembled components from blowing sand and dust. The same applies for disconnected water, oil, or other fluid lines. Be sure to cover both ends of the connection if stored. It is essential to have screens against blowing sand (which also provides shade for mechanics). The surrounding ground may be soaked in used oil or covered with rocks to bind it down. Mechanics must keep their tools clean.

Dust and sand can easily cause failure of such items as radio and signal distribution panels, and circuit breakers, and cause small electrical motors to burn out. Wheel and flight control bearings may require daily cleaning and repacking, and engines should be flushed of contaminants daily.

Rotor heads have reduced life, requiring more frequent inspections than in temperate climates. Pay particular attention to sand-caused wear on rotor heads, leading edges of rotor blades, and exposed flight controls. Over 200 pounds of dirt has been known to accumulate in the fuselage area of helicopters operating in desert conditions. These areas must be routinely checked and cleaned to prevent a pound-for-pound reduction in aircraft-lift capability.

Filters must be used when refueling any type of vehicle, and the gap between the nozzle and the fuel tank filler pipe must be kept covered. It takes comparatively little dirt to block a fuel line. Fuel filters will require more frequent cleaning and will need to be checked and replaced often. Engine oil should be changed more often and oil filters replaced more frequently than in temperate climates.

Compression-ignition engines depend on clean air; therefore, examine and clean air cleaners of every type of equipment at frequent intervals. The exact interval depends on the operating conditions, but as a minimum, should be checked at least daily.

Air compressors are valuable pieces of equipment in the desert. They are essential for cleaning air filters and removing dust and sand from components. Intake filters require cleaning daily.

Windblown sand and grit, in addition to heat, will damage electrical wire insulation over a period of time. All cables that are likely to be damaged should be protected with tape before insulation becomes worn. Sand will also find its way into parts of items such as "spaghetti cord" plugs, either preventing electrical contact or making it impossible to join the plugs together. Use a brush, such as an old toothbrush, to brush out such items before they are joined. Electrical tape placed over the ends of spaghetti cords also works.

Radio is the primary means of communications in the desert. It can be employed effectively in desert climates and terrain to provide the reliable communications demanded by widely dispersed forces. However, desert terrain provides poor electrical ground, and a counterpoise (an artificial ground) is needed to improve the range of certain antennas.

Some receiver-transmitters have ventilating ports and channels that can get clogged with dust. These must be checked regularly and kept clean to prevent overheating. Mobile subscriber equipment may require the deployment of additional radio access units (RAU) AN/VRC-191. These assemblages are the primary link for the mobile subscriber radio telephone terminal (MSRT) AN/VRC-97s which are located down to battalion level. The normal operating range of the receiver-transmitter used with these radios may only be 10 kilometers in the desert.

Dust and sand adversely affect the performance of weapons. Weapons may jam or missiles lock on launching rails due to sand and dust accumulation. Sand- or dust-clogged barrels lead to in-bore detonations. Daily supervised cleaning of weapons is essential. Particular attention should be given to magazines which are often clogged, interrupting the feeding of weapons. Cover missiles on launchers until required for use. To avoid jamming due to the accumulation of sand, the working parts of weapons must have the absolute minimum amount of lubrication. It may even be preferable to have them totally dry, as any damage caused during firing will be less than that produced by the sand / oil abrasive paste. Paintbrushes are among the most useful tools to bring to the desert; they are extremely effective in cleaning weapons and optics.

Take precautions to prevent exposure of floppy disks and computers to dust or sand. Covering them in plastic bags is a technique that has worked for several different units. A number of units have successfully operated PLL computers in inflatable medical NBC shelters (MIS 1). This technique has obvious drawbacks since the shelter was not designed for this; however, until a materiel fix is developed, this sort of innovation may be necessary. Compressed air cans, locally purchased from computer vendors, will facilitate the cleaning of keyboards and other components of computer systems.

All optics are affected by blown sand, which gradually degrade their performance due to small pitting and scratching. It is necessary to guard against buildup of dust on optics, which may not be apparent until the low light optical performance has severely deteriorated. It may be advisable to keep optics covered with some form of cellophane film until operations are about to start, especially if the unit is in a sandstorm. A cover that has no sand on the underside should also be used and must be secured so it cannot vibrate against the wind screen. Both of these measures are equally important to tactical security as sun reflected from these optics will reveal positions.

Sand and dirt can easily accumulate in hull bottoms of armored vehicles. This accumulation, combined with condensation or oil, can cause jamming of control linkages. Sand accumulation at the air-bleeder valve can inhibit heat from escaping from the transmission and result in damage to the transmission. Park tactical wheeled vehicles with the rear facing the wind to keep sand out of the radiator. Tracked vehicles should park to protect the engine compartment (grille doors away from wind) from the same sort of damage. The operator's checks and services increase in importance in this environment.

HUMIDITY

Some deserts are humid. Where this is the case, humidity plus heat encourages rust on bare metal and mold in enclosed spaces such as optics. Bare metal surfaces on equipment not required for immediate use must be kept clean and very lightly lubricated.

Items such as optics must be stored in dry conditions; those in use should be kept where air can circulate around them, and should be purged at frequent intervals. Aircraft must be washed daily, particularly if there is salt in the air, using low-pressure sprays.

TEMPERATURE VARIATIONS

In deserts with relatively high-dew levels and high humidity, overnight condensation can occur wherever surfaces (such as metal exposed to air) are cooler than the air temperature. Condensation can affect such items as optics, fuel lines, and air tanks. Drain fuel lines both at night and in the morning (whenever necessary). Clean optics and weapons frequently. Weapons, even if not lubricated, accumulate sand and dirt due to condensation.

THERMAL BENDING

Weapon systems such as the tank cannon are affected in several ways by the desert. One is thermal bending, which is the uneven heating and cooling of a gun lube due to ambient temperature changes. Modem tanks, like the MI, have been designed to compensate for these factors. The muzzle reference system (MRS) allows the crew to monitor any loss of gun sight relationship and to comet for any error using the MRS update at regular intervals. MI-series tanks are equipped with a thermal shroud, allowing for more even heating and cooling o the gun tube. Both factors can greatly reduce the accuracy of a tank weapon system. By boresighting at regular intervals and constant monitoring of the fire control system, the tank crew can maximize its readiness. "Gun tube droop" can be countered using the MRS update at least four times in a 24-hour period: at dawn as part of stand-to; at noon to compensate for gun tube temperature change: before EENT, for TIS reticle confirmation; and at 0100 hours to compensate for gun tube temperature changes.

OPTICAL PATH BENDING

The apparent illusion of target displacement is commonly called refraction. Under certain light and environmental conditions, the path of light (line of sight) may not appear to travel in a straight line. Refraction may cause problems for tank crews attempting engagements at ranges beyond 1,500 meters. Figure 1-17 shows an example of optical path bending in the desert. Refraction may occur in the following conditions:

- Day-Clear sky, flat terrain, winds less than 10 miles per hour.
- Night-Clear sky, flat terrain, winds under 4 miles per hour.

The effect of refraction is to make the target appear lower during the day; the sight picture, though it appears center of visible mass to the gunner, is actually below the target. This may result in a short round. At night, the effects are the opposite and may result in an over round. Crews must not be fooled by what appears to be a good range from their laser range finder (LRF); the laser beam will refract with other light rays and still hit the desired target.

> ✍ **NOTE**
> Any time heat shimmer is present, refraction may also exist.

The most effective measure available to the crew to minimize refraction is an elevated firing position. A position at least 10 meters above intervening terrain will generally negate any effects. If this type of position is not available, a crew operating under conditions favorable to refraction, and having missed with their first round, should apply the following:

> ✍ **NOTE**
> Crews do not need to make a correction for refraction at ranges of less than 1,500 meters.

- Day—Adjust sight picture up 1/2 target form. See Figures 1-18 and 1-19 for examples of day and night refraction, respectively.
- Night—Adjust sight picture down 1/2 target form.

Boresight does not correct refraction, but crews must ensure that all prepare-to-fire checks and boresighting procedures are performed correctly. When a crew is missing targets under these conditions, the cause is refraction and not crew error or loss of boresight due to improper procedures.

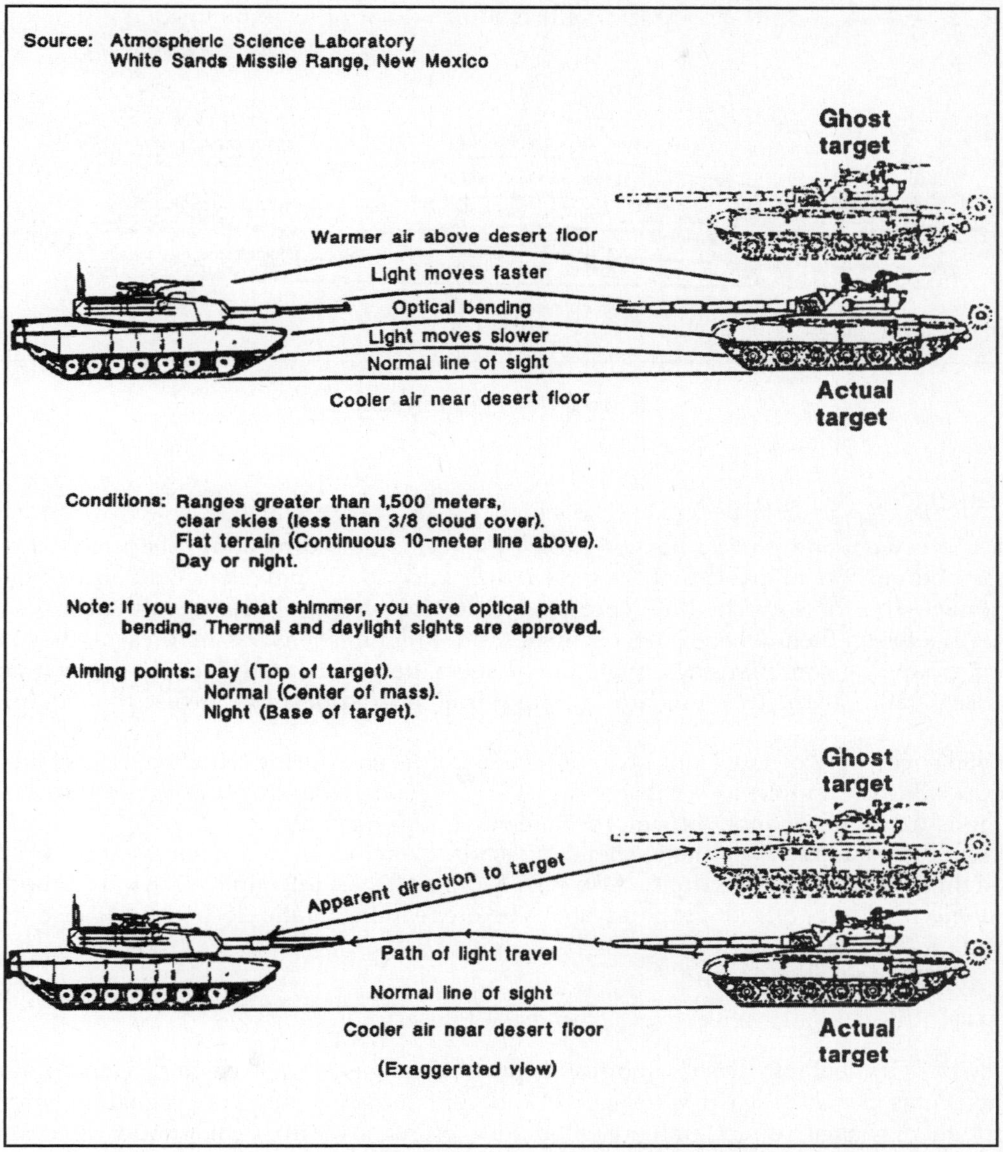

Source: Atmospheric Science Laboratory
White Sands Missile Range, New Mexico
Ghost target
Warmer air above desert floor
Light moves faster
Optical bending
Light moves slower
Normal line of sight
Cooler air near desert floor
Actual target
Conditions: Ranges greater than 1,500 meters, clear skies (less than 3/8 cloud cover). Flat terrain (Continuous 10-meter line above). Day or night.
Note: If you have heat shimmer, you have optical path bending. Thermal and daylight sights are approved.
Aiming points: Day (Top of target). Normal (Center of mass). Night (Base of target).
Ghost target
Apparent direction to target
Path of light travel
Normal line of sight
Cooler air near desert floor
(Exaggerated view)
Actual target

Figure 1-12: Optical path bending in the desert.

Cooler air above desert floor
Actual target
Light moves slower
Optical bending
Light moves faster
Normal line of sight
Warmer air near desert floor
Conditions: Ranges greater than 1,500 meters, clear skies (less than 3/8 cloud cover), Flat terrain.
Ghost target

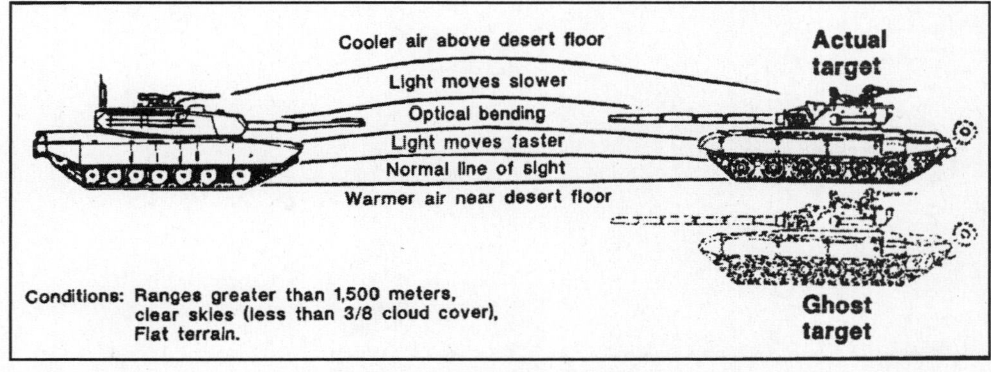

Figure 1-13: Day refraction.

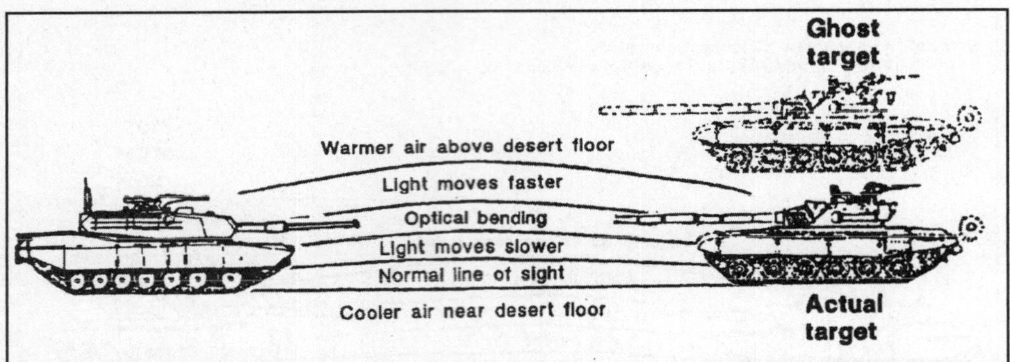

Figure 1-14: Night refraction.

STATIC ELECTRICITY

Static electricity is prevalent and poses a danger in the desert. It is caused by atmospheric conditions coupled with an inability to ground out due to dryness of the terrain. It is particularly prevalent with aircraft or vehicles having no conductor contact with the soil. The difference of electrical potential between separate materials may cause an electrical discharge between them when contact is made, and if flammable gases are present, they may explode and cause a fire. Poor grounding conditions aggravate the problem. Be sure to tape all sharp edges (tips) of antennas to reduce wind-caused static electricity. If you are operating from a fixed position, ensure that equipment is properly grounded.

Establish a metal circuit between fuel tankers and vehicles before and during refueling. Ensure the fuel tankers and vehicles are grounded (for example, by a cable and picket or by a crowbar). Grounding of vehicles and equipment should be accomplished in accordance with appropriate operations manuals.

Static electricity is also a hazard with helicopter sling loads. Exercise care when handling and transporting unlike materials that might generate static electricity. Also turn off all switches, uncouple electrical connectors, and ground vehicle or aircraft electrically-operated weapon systems before reaming. Static electricity will also ruin circuit boards and other electronic equipment.

RADIANT LIGHT

Radiant light may be detrimental to plastics, lubricants, pressurized gases, some chemicals, and infrared tracking and guidance systems. Items like C02 fire extinguishers, M13 decontamination and reimpregnating kits, and Stinger missiles must be kept out of constant direct sunlight. Optics nave been known to discolor under direct sunlight (although this is unusual), so it is wise to minimize their exposure to the sun's rays.

CHAPTER 2

Desert Concealment and Camouflage

In the desert, camouflage problems are encountered that require imagination, ingenuity, and intelligence. The lack of natural overhead cover, the increased range of vision, and the bright tones of the desert terrain place emphasis upon siting, dispersion discipline, and the skillful employment of decoys to achieve deception and surprise. Total concealment is rarely achieved, yet proper camouflage measures can reduce the effectiveness of enemy observation, and consequently enemy operations.

Cover from enemy direct fire may be afforded by dunes, hills, and other irregularities in the desert terrain. Camouflage is an essential part of all operations in the desert and the importance of the concept must be impressed upon fresh units and individual replacements upon their arrival in theater. Poor camouflage may also compromise a high-level plan and lead to an operational failure. One poorly concealed vehicle can compromise an entire task force. Improvisation of available assets is just as important as being able to properly use camouflage systems. As previously described, deserts generally do not offer much natural concealment or means for camouflage; therefore, make maximum use of any artificial means available.

VEHICLES AND AIRCRAFT

Movement of vehicles produces dust, diesel plumes, and distinctive track marks. The slower the speed, the less dust that is produced; however, the need for speed must be balanced against the amount of dust that may be produced. Drivers must avoid harsh use of accelerators, the main cause of diesel plumes.

Shine from optical instruments (which should be kept shaded), and matte paint that has been polished by continual wear, or from tracks, particularly if rubber blocks have been removed, are difficult to camouflage during the desert day. See Figure 2-1 for shading optics. Running gear on tracks that has been polished by wear should be covered with burlap when stationary. Windscreens and windows should be removed or lowered to prevent reflection of the sun and heat. Vehicle silhouettes can be reduced in the forward areas by removing cabs and tops.

Disruptive pattern painting for vehicles and aircraft is described in FM 20–3. Local materials can also be used. The color and texture of the local terrain is best represented by placing dirt on vehicles and using a little water to make it stick.

The effects are increased by covering a vehicle with a wide-mesh net and using foliage brackets to attach local vegetation. Twine or wire may be used as an alternative to the mesh net, provided vegetation is available.

Some or all of the equipment listed in the following paragraphs should be available for every vehicle and aircraft, although aircraft will not necessarily be able to carry all of it.

The preferred net is the lightweight camouflage screen system (LCSS), desert version, which provides concealment against visual, near IR, and radar target acquisition/surveillance sensor devices. Additionaly, the transparent version of the LCSS allows U.S. units to camouflage radars (less CW type radars) without degrading operations. A desert camouflage net should be a complete cover, as it depends on its Imitation of the ground surface, and both color and texture, for its effect. The alternatives to the LCSS in order of priority include the following:

- The specially produced desert-pattern net of the lightweight screen system.
- An open-weave cloth (colored as appropriate to the soil or "patched") stitched to an ordinary wide-mesh net and used with the string uppermost. This provides both color and texture and can be suitably garnished with radar-scattering plastic, such as that used in the lightweight screening system, and with any local vegetation.
- A cover of close-weave cloth, colored as appropriate.
- A standard net garnished solid, threaded in long straight strips that have been colored to harmonize with the terrain. The garnishing must be maintained.

Figure 2-l: Shade optics to prevent shine.

The number of nets issued depends on the size of the equipment to be covered, but should be sufficient to allow a gradual slope of not more than 15 degrees from the top of the equipment to the earth. Each company-size unit should be equipped with a spray gun and various tints of paint to provide for temporary variations in net color to match the terrain.

When using nets for stationary equipment—

- Do not allow nets to touch sensitive items such as helicopter rotor heads and radio antennas which may cause a net to catch fire.
- Do not pull nets so tight that each supporting pole stands out.
- Ensure the net does not prevent the equipment from fulfilling its primary task. In some equipment, such as helicopters, a net must be easily removable to reduce reaction time.
- Avoid straight-edged patterns on the ground, which indicate something is there.
- Use burlap spray-painted in a nondescript desert color to cover all reflecting surfaces (excluding fire control optics) and shadow-producing areas under vehicle bodies, including tank suspensions. Aircraft equipped with windscreen covers will not require it.
- Cut desert scrub in the immediate area.
- Use poles, natural or man-made, to raise the nets from the equipment, thereby hiding its shape. They must be brought into the area of operations by the force and are extremely difficult to replace in the desert if lost or damaged.
- Make a "mushroom" out of thin iron tubing locally, It resembles an open umbrella without its cloth cover and with the end of the spokes joined together. Slotted into a socket that has been welded onto the top of a tank, self-propelled gun, or personnel carrier, it lifts the net above the vehicle, concealing its shape, increasing air circulation, and permitting the crew or team to use the top hatches.
- Hook and hold a camouflage net to the ground away from the vehicle by using wooden pegs or long steel pins, depending on soil consistency.
- Use mallets to drive pegs and pins into the ground.

After dismounting local security, camouflage is the first priority when a vehicle halts. Actions to be taken are—

- Site in vegetation or shadow, if available.
- Cover shiny surfaces and shadow areas with burlap screens.

- Drape the net.
- Add any available vegetation to the net.
- Blot out vehicle tracks for 50 meters behind vehicles.

Stationary aircraft take a relatively long time to conceal as they are fragile in comparison with other equipment, have a considerable heat signature, and must also be readily accessible for maintenance. The more they are concealed, the greater their response time is likely to be. Tactical flying is discussed in Appendix B, but take the following actions in sequence when approaching a landing site where aircraft will stay for some time:

- Ensure aircraft approach the site terrain-masked from enemy surveillance.
- Close down aircraft as soon as possible.
- Cover all reflective surfaces.
- Move aircraft into shadow if it can be towed or pushed.
- Shift the main rotor (depending on the type) until it is at a 45-degree angle with the fuselage and drape a net over the rotor and fuselage. The rotor must be picketed to the ground.
- Conceal the remainder of the aircraft.

POSITION SELECTION

Position selection is critical at all levels. One of the fundamentals of camouflage in any environment, but particularly the desert, is to fit into the existing ground pattern with a minimum of change to the terrain. A wadi bottom with vegetation or a pile of boulders that can be improved with grey burlap and chickenwire are good examples. Sites chosen must not be so obvious that they are virtually automatic targets for enemy suppressive frees, and antennas must be screened against the enemy, if possible.

Shadows, particularly in the morning and evening, identify objects; so equipment must be placed in total shadow (rarely found), or with its maximum vertical area facing the sun so that minimum shadow falls on the ground ("maximum vertical area" is the rear of a 5-ton truck with canopy, but the front of an M88, for example). See Figure 2-2 for the effects of shadows. The shadow can be broken up, which is normally achieved by siting equipment next to scrub or broken surfaces, such as rocks. Equipment should not be sited broadside to the sun, and it is usually necessary to move as the sun moves. Digging in reduces the length of any shadow that is cast (on the principle that the lower the object, the shorter the shadow).

Vehicles passing over pebbles or heavy ground surfaces press the pebbles or gravel into the soil, causing track marks to be prominent when viewed from the air. Avoid such areas if possible. Use existing trails and blend new trails into old ones whenever possible.

Soil texture suitable for digging must be a consideration when reconnoitering for battle positions. Holes must be covered to avoid shadows being cast. If vehicles will be in position for more than a day, trenches should be dug for them.

Figure 2-2: Camouflage: the effects of shadows.

In forward areas, tactical operations centers are probably the most difficult positions to hide although their need for concealment is great. They require strict camouflage discipline. Vehicles and aircraft should not be allowed to approach closer than 300–400 meters. They must be dispersed and concealed so nets may have to be readily available for aircraft. Pay special attention to lights and noise at night.

Generators will have to be dug-in and allowed adequate air space for cooling. Radios and antenna systems must be remoted as far out as possible, and in different directions. Whenever possible, dig in the entire command post. Use engineer assets to build a berm around the perimeter and to help break up the silhouette and to enhance security. Other equipment should not be placed too close to minimize the possibility of the enemy's attention being attracted to the site.

Engineer activity often precedes operations, which makes it important that such work be concealed from enemy surveillance. The following guidelines should be used to conceal engineer activity:

- Employ the minimum number of equipment and personnel.
- Keep equipment well away from the site, and dispersed and concealed if not in use.
- Complete all possible preparations well away from the site.
- Follow the ground pattern, if possible.

Combat service and support assets must rely on concealment for most of their protection. The following guidelines will assist unit commanders in concealing trains while stationary or on the move:

- All vehicles of a given type should look alike. This will make it difficult for an enemy to pick out critical vehicles, such as water and fuel trucks, in a column. Canopies over fuel trucks disguise them and prevent radiant heat from striking the fuel containers.
- Vehicles should follow the tracks of the preceding vehicle if it is possible to do so without breaking through the crust, as this reduces the possibility of an enemy intelligence analyst to calculate how many vehicles have passed.
- Screen exhaust systems to reduce heat signature.
- Vehicles must never form a pattern, either when stationary or on the move.

SUPPLY POINTS

A supply point is likely to be in a location where its main threat of detection will be either by the eye or by photograph. Normally, greater emphasis can be placed on selecting supply positions from the point of view of concealment rather than for tactical efficiency, particularly in situations where air defense cover may be limited. The following guidelines should be used when setting up supply points:

- The location should be selected where trails already exist. Vehicles must use existing trails to the extent possible.
- Stocks should be irregularly spaced, both in length and depth, to the maximum extent possible so that there is no definite pattern.
- Stocks should be piled as low as possible and preferably dug-in. For example, a stack of gasoline cans should be only one can high.
- The shape of the area should not be square or rectangular, but should follow the local ground pattern.
- Stocks should be covered with sand, gravel, burlap, netting, or anything else that harmonizes with the local terrain, and the sides should be gradually sloped with soil filled to the top of the dump.
- The contents of each supply point should be mixed so that the destruction of one supply point will not cause an immediate shortage of a particular commodity.

CHAPTER 3

Operations in Desert Conditions

SECTION I. HOW THE DESERT ENVIRONMENT AFFECTS TACTICAL OPERATIONS

The key to success in desert operations is mobility, and this was clearly evident in ground operations in Desert Storm. The tactics employed to achieve victory over Iraq were wide and rapid flanking movements similar to those Rommel and Montgomery executed in North Africa.

Trafficability and cross-country movement become critical to desert operations when using these tactics. Trafficability is generally good in the desert and cross-country movement is a lesser problem, but not always. Salt marshes can create NO-GO conditions during the rainy season. Sand can also bog down traffic and make foot movement slow and exhausting. The steep slopes of dunes and rocky mountains can make vehicular movement a NO-GO. The wadis create cross-compartmented terrain. The banks of these stream beds can be steep and unconsolidated. Then, when it rains, it becomes a torrent of dangerously rushing water, leading to flat lake beds that can create NO-GO mud conditions. Rock quarries and mining areas can also adversely affect mobility and trafficability. Often these areas are not reflected on maps. Satellite imagery can be helpful in identifying these areas, as was the case in Kuwait during Operation Desert Storm. In rocky terrain, tires can easily be punctured by sharp angular debris; however, overall movement is mostly uninhibited. Given ample fuel, water, and other resources, units can go around natural and man-made obstacles.

Movement can easily be detected because of sand and dust signatures left due to the loose surface material. In an actual engagement, this may not be all that bad because a unit is obscured from direct fire while advancing, but the element of surprise may be lost. Moving at night becomes the logical choice. The dust is still there, and vehicles (which should be widely spaced) can get separated. But at night, reflection of the sun's rays from glass, mirrors, or metal, which can give away movement and positions up to 20 kilometers away, is not a concern.

Using the ability to make fast and wide flanking movements, a unit can encircle and cut off enemy forces. The Israeli forces under General Ariel Sharon did just that to the Egyptian Third Army in the 1973 War, and the British did the same to the Italians in North Africa in January 1941. In Desert Storm, the night-fighting AH-64 helicopters, combined with field artillery fires, made for an unbeatable team in this regard.

Land navigation is a challenge during movement in the wide expanses of many arid regions. There are few landmarks to key on, and maps and even photos can become dated quickly, especially in the sandy deserts where dunes migrate. The global positioning system (GPS) with the small lightweight GPS receivers (SLGRs) is a major aid for desert operations.

Refuel and resupply operations require periods in which forces assume the defense, but only temporarily. The flat sandy desert topography that is characteristic of Saudi Arabia is not conducive to defense, compared to rocky plateau topography. In mountains and canyons, a defensive posture can be favorable. Controlling the passes, as mentioned earlier, can essentially close off vast areas to an attacker and make it extremely costly for him.

While a unit is in the defense, it needs both ground and air reconnaissance to detect enemy movement at long range. Obstacles must be placed in all types of topography, primarily to slow advances and channel columns. Neglecting these security measures in the flat, sandy regions can lead to disaster.

MILITARY ASPECTS OF THE TERRAIN

The following paragraphs describe how terrain affects tactical operations in the desert. This discussion follows the outline of the terrain analysis process summarized by the factors of OCOKA.

Observation and Fields of Fire

Observation and fields of fire are generally excellent in most desert areas. The atmosphere is stable and dry, allowing unrestricted view over vast distances, but this can also be a problem. Range estimation by "gut feeling" is subject to error. The effective ranges of weapons can easily be reached, and a correct estimation of maximum ranges is critical for all weapons, especially for wire-guided munitions.

Flat desert terrain permits direct-fire weapons to be used to their maximum range. Open terrain and a predominantly clear atmosphere generally offer excellent long-range visibility; but at certain times of the day visibility may be limited or distorted by heat.

Two primary considerations in the desert environment are longer range observation, and fields of fire at the maximum effective ranges for weapons. However, rapid heating and cooling of the atmosphere hinder these factors and cause distortion of ranges to the aided and unaided eye. Mechanical and electronic means must be used to verify estimated ranges such as GSR and laser range finders. Boresight and zero more frequently at standard ranges.

The desert is not absolutely flat, so weapons are sited to provide mutual support. Dead space is a problem. Even though the landscape appears flat, upon closer inspection it can be undulating with relatively deep wadis and depressions. These areas must be covered by indirect fire.

When on the offense, attacks should be initiated with the sun at or near one's back whenever possible. This eliminates most shadows that degrade optical weapon guidance and makes visual target acquisition difficult.

When there is no usable dominant terrain available, the only means of observation may be from an aeroscout, or limited to short-range observation by the vehicle commander. Other visibility problems are caused by heat distortion. Heat waves at the desert surface cause images to shimmer making positive identification difficult and degrade depth perception. Ranges to targets may be distorted from heat rising from the desert surface. Use range finders to verify correct distances. Be prepared to use bracketing techniques with large adjustments to hit an enemy target with artillery.

Radars are unlikely to be affected by heat haze so they could be valuable on flat terrain during midday heat if optical vision is hopelessly distorted; however, they are almost useless in sandstorms. Image intensification is of limited value in sandstorms, and depends on the phase of the moon at night. If there is no moon, use artificial illumination outside the field of view of the system.

Since thermal imagery devices depend on the difference between ambient temperature and equipment temperature, they are more useful at night than in the day. Because of the distinct advantages of thermal sights, they should be used as the primary sighting systems for vehicles so equipped.

Correction of field artillery fires, especially those of larger pieces, may be complicated by dust hanging in the air following the impact of ranging rounds. Forward observers should consider placing initial rounds beyond a target rather than short of the target. Observation of fires, especially direct fires by tanks, may be difficult due to dust clouds, so wingmen may have to observe direct fires.

Cover and Concealment

Cover and concealment are generally scarce in the desert. The flat, sandy deserts provide little if any natural cover or concealment, especially from aerial attack or reconnaissance. Ground concealment and protection from fire can be found behind dunes or in wadis. Troops must be aware of the potential for flash floods when using wadis for ground concealment.

Some arid regions have vegetation that can provide limited concealment from ground observation. In rocky, mountainous deserts, cover and concealment are best found behind boulders and in crevices. Daytime vehicular movement eliminates nearly any possibility of surprise, as dust trails created by the traffic can be spotted for miles. At night noise and light discipline is critical, as both sound and light travel great distances because of the unobstructed flatness of the terrain and atmospheric stability. Camouflage can be effectively employed to improve on natural cover and concealment. See chapter 2 for additional information on concealment and camouflage.

Obstacles

Natural obstacles do exist in the desert, and arid regions are well suited for man-made obstacles. The wadis and steep slopes of escarpments, mountains, hills, and dunes hinder cross-country movement. Sand dunes may stretch for miles and prevent direct movement across their length. These sand dunes are often more than 100 feet in elevation and consist of loose sand with high, steep downwind faces that make vehicular traversing next to impossible. Aerial reconnaissance immediately before any large movement is advisable because sand dunes migrate with shifting winds, and they may not be where maps or even photographs show them.

In the Desert Storm area, the salt marshes have a crust on the top that can deceive a vehicle driver. These dry lake beds can become obstacles, especially in the wetter seasons when the water table is higher. A top crust forms on the surface, but below the crust the soil is moist, similar to marsh conditions. The surface may look like it has good trafficability, but the crust will collapse with the weight of a vehicle, and the vehicle becomes mired. The high premium on fuel and time makes it costly to go around these natural obstacles.

Sandy deserts are ideal for employing minefield. Although windstorms can reveal previously buried mines, these mines can still channel movement and deny access to certain areas. The battles of the Bi'R Hacheim Line and El Alamein were influenced by minefield. Other obstacles include ditches, revetments, and barriers, such as the Bar Lev Line along the Suez Canal, made by bulldozing sand mounds or by blasting in rocky mountainous areas to close passes.

Key Terrain

Key terrain in the desert can be any man-made feature, mountain pass, or source of water, and of course, high ground. Because there are few man-made features in the desert, those that do exist can become important, perhaps even key.

Passes through steep topography are also likely to be key, again because they are so few. The North African campaigns of World War II focused on the control of passes, specifically the Sollum and Halfaya. In the Sinai Wars between Egypt and Israel, the Mitla, Giddi, and Sudar passes were key. In Afghanistan, control of the mountain passes provided the Mujahideen safe haven from the Soviets. Oases, where wells exist, become important for water resupply. The high ground in desert terrain is usually key terrain. The relative flatness and great distances of some deserts, such as in Iraq, make even large sand dunes dominant features.

Avenues of Approach

Avenues of approach are not clearly defined in arid regions. The vast, relatively flat areas permit maneuver from virtually any direction. This point became obvious to units establishing defensive positions in Desert Storm. Wide envelopments are possible, as demonstrated in the Desert Storm ground campaign. Modem sensor technology, limited natural concealment, and improved observation make the element of surprise a challenge. Yet, surprise was achieved during Desert Storm—Iraqi commanders were shocked when they discovered U.S. tanks in their perimeters.

The major limitation with respect to avenues of approach may be fuel. The great distances a unit must travel to outflank enemy positions require significant amounts of fuel and complicate resupply. In mountainous and canyon topography avenues are much more limited, and the wadis and valleys are likely to be the only possible access routes. Any roads that do exist are probably in the valleys. Nevertheless, none of the considerations outlined above are reasons to disregard flanking movements.

MANEUVER

Army operations are ideally suited to desert environments. Its thrust of securing and retaining the initiative can be optimized in the open terrain associated with the desert environments of the world. In that environment, the terrain aspect of METT-T offers the potential to capitalize on the four basic tenets of the doctrine initiative, agility, depth, and synchronization.

Initiative

Israeli efforts in 1967 and initial Egyptian assaults in 1973 clearly illustrate the effects of initiative in the desert environment.

Agility

The Egyptian success in 1973 was negated by their failure to ensure agility. Conversely, the Israeli actions on the flanks of the Egyptian force demonstrated the effects of a force capable of rapid and bold maneuver.

Depth

Depth does not necessarily relate to distance. In the nonlinear battlefield offered by the desert, depth often equates to an agile reserve force of sufficient size to counter enemy efforts into flanks and rear areas. Depth is also a concept of all-around defense for forces—the ability to fight in any direction.

Synchronization

To a large measure, the German successes against the British in the Western Desert were due to their ability to synchronize their operating systems. More recent events illustrate this tenet between and internal to, operating systems. Heavy / light operations have demonstrated that light forces can be key to achieving tactical and operational momentum. The Israeli airmobile assault against supporting artillery in the 1967 battle of Abu Ageila is a good example of the effective use of light forces in this type of environment.

Maneuver must be at the maximum tactical speed permitted by the terrain, dust conditions, and rate of march of the slowest vehicle, using whatever cover is available. Even a 10-foot sand dune will cover and conceal a combat vehicle. Air defense coverage is always necessary as aircraft can spot movement very easily due to accompanying dust clouds. In some situations movement may be slowed to reduce dust signatures. Rapid movement causes dramatic dust signatures and can reveal tactical movements.

Another consideration during maneuver is dust from NOE flight, which can be seen as far as 30 kilometers. This is especially true when the enemy is stationary. Aeroscouts must use caution to avoid blundering into enemy air defense weapons.

To achieve surprise, maneuver in conditions that preclude observation, such as at night, behind smoke, or during sandstorms. In certain circumstances, there may be no alternative to maneuvering in terrain where the enemy has long-range observation. Then it is necessary to move at the best speed possible while indirect fires are placed on suspected enemy positions. Speed, suppressive fires, close air support, and every other available combat multiplier must be brought to bear on the enemy.

Tactical mobility is the key to successful desert operations. Most deserts permit good to excellent movement by ground troops similar to that of a naval task force at sea. Use of natural obstacles may permit a force to establish a defensive position that theoretically cannot be turned from either flank; however, these are rare. Desert terrain facilitates bypassing enemy positions and obstacles, but detailed reconnaissance must be performed first to determine if bypassing is feasible and will provide an advantage to friendly forces.

Dismounted infantry may be used to clear passes and defiles to eliminate enemy ATGM positions prior to the mounted elements moving through.

Avenues of approach of large forces may be constrained due to limited cross-country capability of supply vehicles coupled with longer lines of communications. The limited hard-surface routes that do exist are necessary for resupply.

RECONNAISSANCE

Reconnaissance is especially important in desert environments. Reconnaissance is a mission undertaken to obtain information by visual observation, or other detection methods, about the activities and resources of an enemy, or about the meteorologic, hydrographic, or geographic characteristics of a particular area. The desert environment may influence any or all of these techniques. The environmental effects on troops and their equipment may also influence observation techniques, or the frequency of vehicle and equipment maintenance that is required. Reconnaissance produces combat information. Combat information is a by-product of all operations, acquired as they are in progress. Reconnaissance, however, is a focused collection effort. It is performed prior to or in advance of other combat operations, as well as during that operation, to provide information used by the commander to confirm or modify his concept. Cavalry is the Army corps or division commander's principal reconnaissance organization.

Surveillance is a primary task of Army cavalry during reconnaissance operations. Surveillance is the systematic observation of airspace or surface areas by visual, aural, electronic, photographic, or other means. Scouts, ground and air, are the principal collectors of information. Scouts and their associated equipment are particularly affected by the environmental aspects of deserts. They require equipment that enhances their senses allowing them to conduct mounted and dismounted surveillance with stealth, at long-range, and in limited visibility, all of which can be adversely influenced by the desert environment.

SECURITY

Security operations obtain information about the enemy and provide reaction time, maneuver space, and protection to the main body. Security operations are characterized by aggressive reconnaissance to reduce terrain and enemy unknowns, gaining and maintaining contact with the enemy to ensure continuous information, and providing early and accurate reporting of information to the protected force. Security operations may be affected by various aspects of the desert environment including the sun, wind, sand, vegetation, sandstorms, terrain, and heat. Security operations include:

- Screen
- Guard
- Cover

Counterreconnaissance is an inherent task in all security operations. Counterreconnaissance is the sum of actions taken at all echelons to counter enemy reconnaissance and surveillance efforts through the depth of the area of operation. It is active and passive and includes combat action to destroy or repel enemy reconnaissance elements. It also denies the enemy information about friendly units.

COMMAND, CONTROL, AND COMMUNICATIONS

The following paragraphs describe command, control, and communications considerations when operating in a desert environment.

Command

The effort to synchronize battlefield operating systems during the planning process can be negated by the failure to continue the synchronization effort during the preparation phase of a mission. This is especially true in the construction of engagement areas for defensive operations. Direct fire, indirect fire, and obstacles are linked, and the adjustment of one requires the adjustment of all. The commander must know and have a feel for what his unit can do, how long his unit takes to accomplish a mission, and what he really wants his unit to accomplish.

Adjustment of the elements of the battlefield operating systems can unravel the focus of a commander's intent. This is especially true in open terrain. Tactical commanders should personally direct the synchronization of engagement areas. Obstacles should be positioned, indirect fires adjusted, and direct fires rehearsed under the personal supervision of the commander. The commander controls operations using a highly mobile command group located well forward. He personally directs the battle, but must not be drawn into personally commanding an isolated segment of the force to the detriment of the remainder of the command. As previously mentioned, dry desert conditions can sometimes reduce radio signal strength and create unforeseen blind spots, even in aircraft operating nap of the earth.

Units may employ either a jump TOC or retransmission stations to facilitate communications with rear areas, as maneuver units are unlikely to be in one place very long. (If wire is used it should be buried to a minimum depth of 12 inches to avoid damage from track vehicles or shell fire.) There must be plenty of slack in the line to allow for sand shift, and accurate map plots of buried wire should be kept. If overhead wire must be used, it should be mounted on posts erected in the form of tripods to avoid falling during severe weather.

Air or vehicle mounted liaison officers can be used if units are stationary or under listening silence. They should be proficient in navigation and sufficiently equipped to facilitate parallel planning. Liaison officers are highly effective and should be employed at every opportunity.

Continuous Operations

Continuous operations are affected by a number of factors in a desert environment. Fatigue is probably the foremost degrader of performance. Performance and efficiency begin to deteriorate after 14 to 18 hours of continuous work and reach a low point after 22 to 24 hours. Most tasks involving perceptual skills begin to show a performance degradation after 36 to 48 hours without sleep. Soldiers/marines cease to be effective after 72 hours without sleep. Performance decreases dramatically in an NBC environment and sleep becomes more difficult in MOPP gear. Sleep deprivation coupled with the environmental factors of the desert and the stresses of combat can significantly affect mission accomplishment.

The two categories of personnel who can be expected to show signs of fatigue first are young immature soldiers/marines who are not sure of themselves and seasoned old soldiers/marines upon whom others have relied and who have sustained them at a cost to themselves. Commanders and leaders often regard themselves as being the least vulnerable to fatigue. Tasks requiring quick reaction, complex reasoning, and detailed planning make leaders the most vulnerable to sleep deprivation. Leaders denying themselves sleep as an example of self-control is extremely counterproductive. These factors are complicated by the environmental aspects of desert operations and should be considerations for operational planning.

Control

Clear identification of engagement areas is necessary to facilitate the massing and distribution of fires. In the absence of identifiable terrain, target reference points (TRPs) can be created with damaged/destroyed vehicles that are moved into required locations at the direction of commanders invested with the responsibility for specific engagement areas. Other types of TRPs could be used. For example, marker panels, visible and infrared chemical lights, flags, and white phosphorus/illumination rounds could be used. The construction or fabrication of TRPs must be resourced and well planned in order to be effective. For example, how will TRPs be replaced for subsequent defensive operations? Another common problem is TRP proliferation, which makes TRPs difficult to identify when each echelon of command has allocated too many TRPs.

Pyrotechnics are usually more effective in desert climates than in temperate climates; however, heat mirages and duststorms may impair or restrict their use. Even heliographs (signal mirrors) may be useful as they are directional and therefore can aid security. Sound communications are usually impractical due to distance, vehicular noise, and storms, but can be used for local alarm systems.

Colored flags with prearranged meanings can be used as a means of communication in the flat open terrain of the desert. Colored flags tied to antennas may also assist in vehicle/unit recognition during limited visibility operations and offensive operations.

As previously described, the desert offers excellent fields of fire. Tanks and heavy antitank weapons should be sited to take advantage of their long range and accuracy. Firing first and accurately are the most important considerations in desert operations.

Target identification is the recognition of a potential military target as being a particular object (such as a specific vehicle, by type). At a minimum, this identification must determine the potential target as friendly or threat (identify friend, foe, or neutral [IFFN]). Because it is easy to become disoriented, it is often necessary to mark sectors of fire on the ground with poles or rocks, if available.

Communications

Communications support is also adversely affected by high temperatures. The heat causes anomalies in radio and other electrical transmissions, and radio battery life is reduced. Radio range is shorter during the day than at night. At night, range improves but static electricity may cause interference. FM communications range can be reduced by as much as 50 percent because of high temperatures. HF ground wave propagation over the dry sandy soil is reduced.

Night communications make communications security a concern, as it always should be. Experience in Desert Shield and Desert Storm indicates vastly expanded ranges of FM radios. Communications between units 40 to 50 kilometers apart was not unusual. Communications obviously affect command and control as well as intelligence collection and dissemination, and their importance must not be underestimated.

COMBAT SUPPORT

A force operating in the desert must be a balanced force with combat support and combat service support—it must be a combined arms team. While principles of combat support operations are found in doctrinal manuals dealing with a specific arm of service, there are some techniques that must be modified or emphasized in the desert.

INTELLIGENCE

The relative importance of intelligence sources may vary from that expected in more conventional areas. Enemy prisoners of war require immediate interrogation as the flexibility of operations will rapidly make their information outdated. Information given by civilians encountered in desert operations should be treated with caution unless corroborated. Military intelligence teams located in the area of operations can determine if these EPWs and civilians are in fact what they say they are, or infiltrators sent to harass the rear area and commit acts of sabotage. Electronic support measures are a major source of intelligence in desert warfare. Enemy activity, or the lack of it, is a good source of information; so punctual, accurate reports by all sources, both positive and negative, are necessary.

FIRE SUPPORT

The Allies in North Africa in 1942 found that placing small field artillery units in support of small maneuver units gave the units a sense of security, but produced limited results. Field artillery was effective only when massed (battalion or higher) and only when continued for some time because of the protective posture and mobility of the target. Typically, the control of massed fires was the responsibility of the division artillery.

The Allies in North Africa in 1942 experienced heavy casualties from Axis units overrunning the artillery positions after penetrating the armor and infantry positions. Often, the Axis units would attack from the east at one time, from the west later, and from several directions simultaneously. At first, the Allies simply emphasized direct fire. Later, the Allies attached antitank gun units to the artillery battalions to increase the artillery's antitank ability.

When armor and infantry units move, the artillery must move with them. The most useful technique is for the artillery to move in a formation with a lead vehicle so that, immediately upon stopping, the artillery is in a position or formation to deliver fire in any direction and simultaneously defend the position from any direction. The Allies in North Africa in 1942 and units in Desert Shield/Storm found that the armor and infantry units would outdistance the artillery unless the artillery moved with them. The artillery moved within 2–3 kilometers of the leading troops to provide responsive fires. The armor and infantry provided protection for the artillery. The whole group moved in one cohesive formation, sometimes in a large box or diamond formation.

Due to the fluid nature of desert operations and the possibilities for excellent enemy observation, close and continuous field-artillery support for all levels of the force is necessary. Field-artillery pieces should be at least as mobile as the force they are supporting. Crews must be proficient in direct fire and prepared to defend against a ground attack.

Due to the threat of immediate counterbattery fire, field artillery units must be prepared to move into position, fire, and rapidly displace to another position. A battery should be prepared to displace several times a day.

Field artillery units employed in desert operations should be equipped with the most sophisticated survey devices available. Manual systems are slower and not necessarily as accurate, thus affecting tactical employment and reducing response time.

Aerial observation may often be extremely difficult due to enemy air defense, so most adjustment is by ground observers. How the environment affects observation of fires was described previously in this chapter in the paragraph, "Observation and Fields of Fire." Recompute weather conditions frequently as weather conditions can change rapidly from the morning to the evening, and thus affect the accuracy of fires.

Fires are planned as in temperate climates. When there are no significant terrain features along a route of advance, targets are planned using coordinates.

A moving force in a desert is at a disadvantage in comparison with a stationary unit due to lack of concealment and the presence of dust clouds. The defender may engage with missiles from an unexpected direction or from terrain features of no apparent significance. The attacker must be prepared to rapidly shift fires to suppress unforeseen targets. Tactical aircraft may be used to suppress or destroy targets. Targets for aircraft can be marked with indirect- or direct-fire smoke. White phosphorus or illuminating rounds set for low-air burst are also effective.

Indirect fires are used to slow the enemy advance, to suppress enemy weapons and observers, and to conceal movement between positions using smoke. Defensive operations in deserts are characterized by long-range engagement with tanks and ATGMs.

AIR DEFENSE

Identification of friend or foe is difficult. Throughout the entire theater of operations there will be numerous weapon systems that are common to both sides of the conflict. The individual soldier/marine is going to be faced with the monumental task of separating friend from foe by more than just from the recognition of the manufacturer or silhouette of a piece of equipment. This will be true of both air and ground systems. This identification problem will be compounded by the nonlinear battlefield where the focus of operations will not be separated by a line.

The desert is an outstanding environment for employing aircraft. Every unit must be extremely proficient at passive and active air defense. The Allies in North Africa and the Israelis in the Middle East found that dispersion limited the effects of air attacks, and small arms air-defense techniques were effective. Almost every weapon in North Africa had a secondary antiaircraft or antitank mission.

Emphasize to each unit that, when in position, units must disperse very widely making a less lucrative target. When moving in column and under air attack, units must move at least 40 to 50 meters off the road because aircraft normally have nose guns trained on both sides of the road. A vehicle on the road or on both sides of the road will die.

Because of the wide open spaces characteristic of many deserts and the relatively large areas associated with desert operations, forces fighting in the desert should be reinforced with additional air-defense weapons. Still, there may not be sufficient dedicated air-defense systems to fully cover the force. When this is the case, commanders must be especially careful when establishing air-defense priorities in view of relatively long lines of communication and the tendency to maneuver over relatively large areas. In any event, all units must include a scheme for countering air attacks in their battle plans using both active and passive measures.

Although Army armored and mechanized infantry division air-defense weapons are tracked, this does not necessarily apply to corps medium-altitude air defense units. However, Army corps surface-to-air missile (SAM) units have considerably greater ranges and are equipped with more sophisticated early warning and control systems. Some corps units should be employed well forward. These weapons will have to displace by section to ensure continuous coverage.

Air-defense units should be located close to elements of supported units to provide for ground defense. When the supported unit moves, the air defense unit must also move, which requires careful coordination to ensure that movement of the supported unit is not delayed. Airspace management difficulties are compounded in the multinational environment. SOPS should be exchanged among multinational forces to lessen the confusion of airspace management.

ENGINEERS

Engineer operations in the desert are similar to those in temperate climates although there are fewer natural terrain obstacles to be crossed. Depending on the terrain anticipated in the operations area, a dry-gap crossing capability may have to be obtained from corps support units. Important tasks for engineers in desert operations include:

- Mobility/countermobility/survivability support, including construction of obstacles, logistics facilities and routes, field fortifications, airfields, and helicopter landing pads.
- Water supply.
- Topographic support (map-making).

Mobility

The vastness of the desert makes mobility a prime concern. Roads are usually scarce and primitive. Cross-country mobility is possible in some areas, but trafficability is poor in soft sand, rocky areas, and salt flats. Engineers assist maneuver by reducing slopes, smoothing rock steps, and bridging dry gaps.

Expanded engineer reconnaissance capability will be needed to identify routes, existing obstacles, and minefield locations. Flat, open areas provide good sites for aircraft landing strips; however, in most cases the soil must be stabilized. Normally, desert soil produces extensive dust and has limited weight-bearing capacity.

Engineers use various agents to alleviate severe dust conditions (diesel, JP4, or oil mixtures for example). This is particularly critical in reducing engine wear in areas supporting rotary wing aircraft. It is also important along heavily traveled roads and in cantonment areas. Engineers also use soil-stabilization techniques to increase soil-bearing capacity for airstrips and MSRs.

The application of the fundamentals of breaching—suppress, obscure, secure, and reduce—and the organization of the force in terms of supporting, breaching, and assaulting elements, are even more important in the desert due to the enhanced observation and fields of fire. However, the desert does offer greater opportunities to bypass enemy obstacles because of the greater range of mobility afforded by desert terrain. Caution must be exercised when choosing to bypass enemy obstacles since the bypass may lead the force to the enemy's kill sack.

The increased mobility in the desert makes it easier for the enemy to counterattack exposed flanks of attacking forces. Plan obstacles to protect flanks during offensive operations. Beyond conventionally emplaced minefield, FASCAM, which includes artillery-delivered mines, GEMSS, and air-delivered Gator munitions, are all systems that lend themselves to situational development. FASCAM and conventional minefield maybe appropriate, but consider the time required to employ FASCAM when selecting this option. Artillery-delivered FASCAM does not deploy well in soft sand and removes a majority of your indirect-fire assets from the fight.

Countermobility

Due to the mobility inherent in desert operations, obstacles must be extensive and used in conjunction with each other and with any natural obstacles, and covered by direct and indirect fires. Isolated obstacles are easily bypassed.

Mines are easily emplaced in a sand desert, and blowing sand will effectively conceal evidence of emplacement. However, the following potential problem areas must be considered when emplacing mines:

- Large quantities of mines are required for effectiveness.
- Sand can cause malfunctioning.
- Shifting sand can cause mine drift.
- An excessive accumulation of sand over the mines can degrade performance.
- Sand may be blown away and expose the mines.

In suitable terrain, antitank ditches that exceed the vertical step of enemy main battle tanks may be used. Because antitank ditches cannot be conceded, they must be dug so they do not outline a defensive front or flank. They have the advantage of not requiring as much logistic support as minefields. They must be covered by observation and fire to prohibit enemy infantry using them as ready-made trenches.

Because of limited off-road mobility of most combat service support vehicles, considerable engineer efforts may be necessary to construct and maintain routes forward to maneuver units. Local resources, such as salt-marsh mud laid on sand, can be used. Track vehicles should not use these routes since they could easily ruin them.

Most desert regions have a natural terrain structure that restricts maneuver such as sandy dunes, rocky plateaus, mountains, and wadis. These structures must be interpreted rapidly and correctly, and then reinforced with obstacles to fix, turn, or disrupt enemy movement, according to the commander's plan.

Minefield and antitank ditches are the primary means of creating obstacles in the desert. Antitank ditches require extensive preparations, but they are effective when adequate preparation time is available. Many desert villages have irrigation ditches that can be used tactically. Other countermobility methods are generally not effective. Road craters, for example, are usually easy to bypass. In sandy areas, ditches can easily be filled in, so they are not good obstacles. Opportunities for bridge destruction are rare, and local materials for expedient obstacles are scarce.

Engineers and combat forces should coordinate the siting of planned obstacles to support the defensive concept. In defensive operations the effectiveness of obstacles requires synchronization.

Survivability

Desert terrain varies from region to region. Generally, however, observation is excellent and concealment is difficult. Deserts provide little cover and concealment from ground-based observers and even less from aircraft. These conditions make modern weapon systems more lethal in deserts than in any other environment.

In the desert, hull and turret defilades for tactical vehicles are essential. This allows the defending force to take advantage of their long-range weapon systems in the face of enemy fires. Dispersion and frequent moves are other survivability techniques that can be used.

The preparation of fortifications in the desert is difficult. Fortifications in sandy soil often require revetments. In rocky plains or plateaus it may be impossible to dig. To counter this problem, build up emplacements with rocks and use depressions.

Camouflage is very effective when properly employed; however, patterns and techniques must be carefully selected to match the local desert environment. Camouflage nets should be provided for all equipment. See Appendix E for additional comments on desert concealment and camouflage.

DESERT SURVIVABILITY POSITIONS

Defensive positions are very vulnerable to offensive fire due to long-range observation and fields of fire in the desert. This, coupled with a lack of natural obstacles, may lead the commander to invest the bulk of his engineer effort into survivability positions. Survivability positions enhance the ability of all direct-fire elements to survive indirect-fire and to return fire on the enemy. Survivability positions are normally more important than antitank ditches, especially in open terrain. See Figures 3-1 through 3-6 for examples of survivability positions. The following are some things you should or should not do when preparing survivability positions:

DO –

- Ensure adequate material is available.
- Dig down as much as possible.
- Maintain, repair, and improve positions continuously.
- Inspect and test position safety daily, after heavy rain, and after receiving direct and indirect fires.
- Revet excavations in sandy soil.
- Interlock sandbags for double-walled constructions and corners.
- Check stabilization of wall bases.
- Fill sandbags approximately 75 percent.
- Construct to standard.
- Use common sense.

DO NOT –

- Fail to supervise.
- Use sand for structural support.
- Forget to camouflage.
- Drive vehicles within 6 feet of a position.
- Overfill sandbags.
- Put troops in marginally safe bunkers.
- Take shortcuts.
- Build above ground unless absolutely necessary.
- Forget lateral bracing on stringers.

The commander's responsibilities during construction of survivability positions are to:

- Protect troops.
- Continuously improve and maintain unit survivability.
- Provide materials.
- Periodically inspect.
- Plan and select fighting position sites.
- Get technical advice from engineers, as required.

In a combat situation, it may be necessary to improvise construction of a survivability position by using materials not normally associated with the construction. Some examples of field-expedient materiel are:

Wall Revetment

- Sheet metal.
- Corrugated sheet metal.
- Plastic sheeting.
- Plywood.
- Air mat panels.
- Air Force air-load pallets.

Wall Construction (Building up)

- Sand-grid material.
- 55-gallon drums filled with sand.
- Expended artillery shells filled with sand.
- Shipping boxes/packing material.
- Prefabricated concrete panels.
- Prefabricated concrete traffic barriers.

Overhead Cover Stringers

- Single pickets.
- Double pickets.
- Railroad rails.
- "T" beams.
- Two-inch diameter pipe or larger.
- Timbers 2″ × 4″, 4″ × 4″, and larger.
- Reinforced concrete beams.
- 55-gallon drums cut in half longitudinally
- Large diameter pipe/culvert, cut in half.
- Precast concrete panels, 6–8 inches thick.
- Airfield panels.
- Air Force air-load pallets.
- Shipping pallets.

Stand-Alone Positions

- Prefab concrete catch basins, valve pits, and utility boxes.
- Military vans.
- Connexes or shipping containers.
- Large diameter pipe/culvert.
- Steel water tanks.
- Other storage tanks (cleaned and ventilated).
- Vehicle hulks.

The following is a suggested inspection checklist to follow when preparing survivability positions:

- Location is sited tactically sound.
- Low profile is maintained.
- Materials are of structural quality (standard construction material).
- Excavation-walls are sloped.
- The setback for overhead is a minimum of 1 foot or ¼ the depth of cut.
- Stringers—
  - Are firmly on a structural support.
  - Have lateral bracing emplaced along supports.
- 2″ × 4″ or 2″ × 6″ stringers are used on the edge; the strength is on the depth of the lumber.
- Supports—

  - Stringers are firmly on supports.
  - Supports extend past the excavation by ½ the depth of cut.
- Revetments—
  - Quality of construction is checked.
  - Sheeting is supported by pickets.
  - Pickets are tied back.
- Overhead cover—
  - Quality of structural layer is inspected.
  - Quality of dust layer—plywood or panels—is inspected.
  - Layer is cushioned at least 18 inches deep.

The one-man fighting position is the individual's basic defensive position. The one-man fighting position with overhead cover (see Figure 3-1) provides protection from airburst weapon fragments. A good position has overhead cover that allows the soldier / marine to fire from beneath it. Stringers extend at least 1 foot on each side of the position to provide a good load-bearing surface for overhead cover.

Figure 3-1: One-man fighting position with overhead cover.

Generally, the two-man fighting position is preferred over a one-man position since one soldier / marine can provide security while the other is digging or resting. The position can be effectively manned for longer periods of time; if one soldier / marine becomes a casualty, the position is still occupied. Further, the psychological effect of two men working together permits occupation of the position for longer periods. Overhead cover also improves the position's effectiveness; it is made as described for the one-man position (see Figure 3-2).

Figure 3-2: Two-man fighting position with overhead cover.

Fighting positions for machine guns are constructed so the fires are to the front or oblique; the primary sector of fire is usually oblique so the gun can fire across the unit's front. The position is shaped so the gunner and assistant gunner can get to the gun and fire it to either side of the frontal direction. Overhead cover is built over the middle of the position (see Figure 3-3). It is constructed as described for the one-man position.

Protective shelters and fighting bunkers are usually constructed using a combination of the components of positions mentioned thus far. Protective shelters are primarily used as command posts, observation posts, medical aid

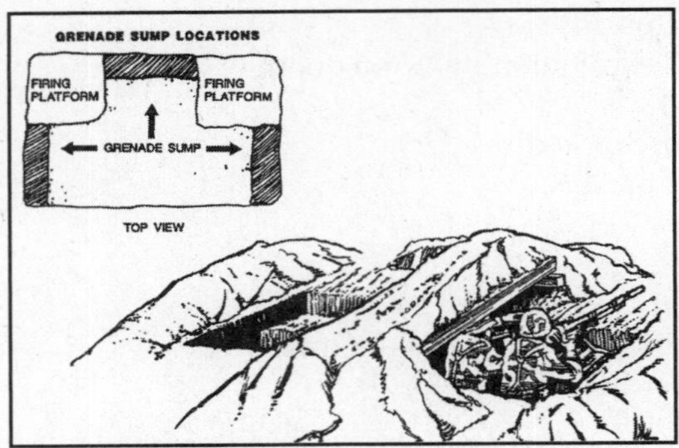

Figure 3-3: Machine-gun position with overhead cover.

stations, supply and ammunition shelters, and sleeping or resting shelters. Figure 3-4 shows an example of a command bunker.

The Dragon position requires some unique considerations. The soldier/marine must consider the Dragon's extensive backblast and muzzle blast, as well as cleared fields of fire. When a Dragon is fired, the muzzle extends 6 inches

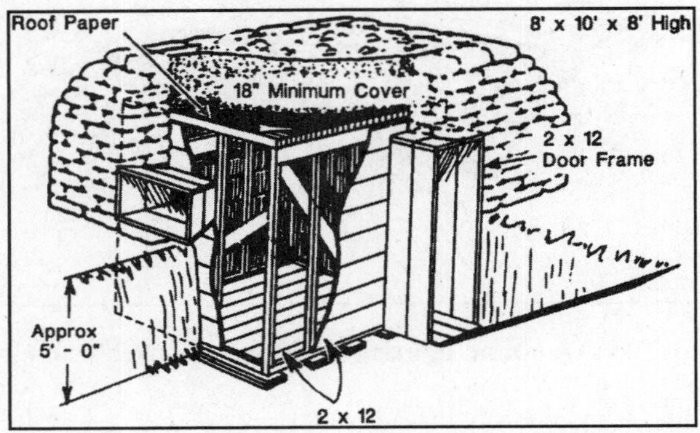

Figure 3-4: Command bunker.

beyond the front of the position, and the rear of the launcher extends out over the rear of the position. As the missile leaves the launcher, stabilizing fins unfold. Therefore, the soldier keeps the weapon at least 6 inches above the ground when firing to leave room for the fins. A waist-deep position will allow the gunner to move while tracking a target. Because of the Dragon's above ground height, soldiers/marines should construct frontal cover high enough to hide the soldier's/marine's head and, if possible, the Dragon's backblast. The soldier/marine must dig a hole in the front of the position for the biped legs. If cover is built on the flanks of a Dragon position, it must cover the tracker, missiles, and the gunner. Overhead cover that would allow firing from beneath it is usually built if the backblast area is clear (see Figure 3-5).

Figure 3-5: Dragon position.

A fighting position for the dismounted TOW must not interfere with the launch or tracking operations of the weapon. As with Dragon and LAW positions allowances for backblast effects are necessary. Backblast and deflection requirements restrict the size of overhead cover for the weapon. See Figure 3-6.

Figure 3-6: Dismounted TOW position.

Designers of fighting positions and protective positions in desert areas must consider the lack of available cover and concealment. Fighting positions should have the lowest profile possible, but mountain and plateau deserts have rocky soil or "surface chalk" soil which makes digging difficult. In these areas, rocks and boulders are used for cover. Because target acquisition and observation are relatively easy in desert terrain, camouflage and concealment, as well as light and noise discipline, are important considerations during position construction.

Indigenous materials are usually used in desert position construction. However, prefabricated structures and revetments, if available, are ideal for excavations. Metal culvert revetments can be quickly emplaced in easily excavated sand. Sandbags and sand-filled ammunition boxes are also used to prevent side walk of positions from collapsing.

FM 5-103 discusses vehicle fighting positions in detail and should be consulted for more information. Figure 3-7 provides specifications for vehicle survivability defilade positions that can be dug by the D-7 dozer.

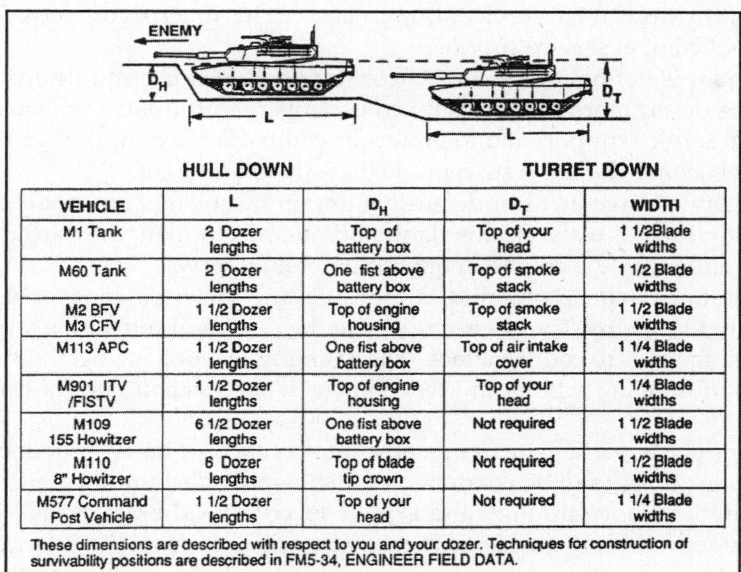

VEHICLE	L	D_H	D_T	WIDTH
M1 Tank	2 Dozer lengths	Top of battery box	Top of your head	1 1/2Blade widths
M60 Tank	2 Dozer lengths	One fist above battery box	Top of smoke stack	1 1/2 Blade widths
M2 BFV M3 CFV	1 1/2 Dozer lengths	Top of engine housing	Top of smoke stack	1 1/2 Blade widths
M113 APC	1 1/2 Dozer lengths	One fist above battery box	Top of air intake cover	1 1/4 Blade widths
M901 ITV /FISTV	1 1/2 Dozer lengths	Top of engine housing	Top of your head	1 1/4 Blade widths
M109 155 Howitzer	6 1/2 Dozer lengths	One fist above battery box	Not required	1 1/2 Blade widths
M110 8" Howitzer	6 Dozer lengths	Top of blade tip crown	Not required	1 1/2 Blade widths
M577 Command Post Vehicle	1 1/2 Dozer lengths	Top of your head	Not required	1 1/4 Blade widths

These dimensions are described with respect to you and your dozer. Techniques for construction of survivability positions are described in FM5-34, ENGINEER FIELD DATA.

Figure 3-7: Survivability defilade positions.

Logistics areas (BSA/DSA) require additional survivability support. Desert operations require that logistics concentrations such as BSAs and DSAs be given additional considerations for survivability support. These sites are large, datively static, and difficult to camouflage. As a result, these support areas are vulnerable to enemy interdiction. Military vans or connexes should be covered with sandbags to improve protection. Additionally, if they are covered with heavy plastic, with plastic drapes over the entrances, protection against NBC effects can be improved.

Engineer digging assets, such as bulldozers, should be tasked to provide survivability support to these sites with particular emphasis placed on hardening ammunition and fuel storage locations. Caution should be used when digging foxholes and tank hide positions since some areas have a tendency to cave in.

Water Supply

Water supply is the most important mission of engineers in the desert. The search for water sources requires continuous, intensive reconnaissance. Water may be obtained by drilling beds of dry water courses, or by deepening dry wells. Once found, water must be made potable and stored or transported. Since water purification trucks may be high-priority targets and barely sufficient for the task, any force operating in the desert must be augmented with water supply units (including well drilling), water purification and water distillation teams, and transportation teams. Another possible water source is the reverse osmosis water purification unit (ROWPU). This unit is an ISO frame-mounted, portable water purification system capable of purifying water from almost any shallow well, deep well, and surface water or raw water source. The ROWPU is capable of removing NBC contaminants, minerals, and biological impurities. The single greatest benefit of the reverse osmosis process is the ability to desalinate sea water. The ROWPU is capable of producing potable water at a rate of 600 gph. The ROWPU is powered by a 30-kilowatt generator set.

SECTION II. OFFENSIVE OPERATIONS

This section discusses offensive operations as they are modified by desert terrain.

GENERAL

The main purpose of offensive operations in desert terrain is to destroy the enemy. Operations may be undertaken to secure key or decisive terrain, to deprive the enemy of resources or decisive terrain, to deceive and divert the enemy, to develop intelligence, and to hold the enemy in position. Destruction of the enemy can be accomplished by concentrating friendly forces at a weak point in the enemy's defense and destroying enemy combat units, or by driving deep into the enemy's rear to destroy his combat service support and cut his lines of communication. No force can survive in the desert for long without combat service support.

An imaginative commander is not bound by terrain constraints in seeking and destroying the enemy. Due to the scarcity of key terrain in the desert, normally the only constraints placed upon a maneuvering force is its ability to maintain responsive combat service support and to protect its combat service support from enemy attack. The longer the lines of communication become, the more susceptible they are to being cut.

In most deserts, the scarcity of large areas of defensible terrain means that an enemy force has at least one flank open to attack. The attacking force must seek this flank and attempt to maneuver around it into the enemy's rear before the enemy can react and block the envelopment with mobile reserves.

Successful offensive operations depend on rapid, responsive, and violent maneuver, seeking a vulnerable enemy flank while exposing none to the enemy. The enemy, realizing the danger of remaining stationary in this terrain, may choose to conduct spoiling attacks or to counterattack. The resulting meeting engagement between the two attacking forces will often be a series of flanking actions and reactions with success going to the one who can find the other's unguarded flank first.

Attacking forces may conduct or participate in movement to contacts or hasty or deliberate attacks. Within a division, lead elements of forward units may be conducting a deliberate attack on the enemy's weak point or flank to open a gap for following units to move through and exploit success. Lead units of the exploiting force will be conducting a movement to contact and hasty attacks to overcome pockets of enemy resistance.

FUNDAMENTALS OF THE OFFENSE

The attacker must conduct active and aggressive reconnaissance to the front, flanks, and rear, not only to locate and identify enemy obstacles, units, weak points, and flanks, but also to give early warning of threats to his flanks and combat service support elements. A moving force is at a disadvantage in the desert due to a lack of concealment.

Therefore, it is necessary to push reconnaissance units as far out from the main body as possible to allow early warning and to deny the enemy close-in observation.

Information gathered by this reconnaissance must be passed promptly to all units. In the desert, a negative report may be as important as an enemy sighting. Commanders and staffs must avoid the two extremes of either passing too little information or overwhelming their subordinates with useless trivia. Similarly, reconnaissance units must also avoid extremes. There is a very real possibility that extensive reconnaissance in one area will alert the enemy of intended operations in that area. Therefore, the need for reconnaissance must be tempered with the need for deception. In fact, reconnaissance may even serve as a deceptive measure to draw the enemy's attention away from the real objective or area of operations.

Concentrate on overwhelming combat power. Mass is achieved in both time and space. Units must be able to rapidly concentrate at a given time and place, and then disperse just as rapidly to avoid offering a lucrative target to the enemy. Concentration does not necessarily mean that vehicles and men are massed in a small area, but that units have the ability to place an overwhelming concentration of fires on the enemy.

Mutual support is as important in the desert as in temperate climates. Due to the large distances covered by maneuver in the desert, mutual support does not mean that any one unit is always in position to fire against an enemy threatening another unit. However, units must be capable of maneuvering in support of one another without disrupting the scheme of maneuver.

Concentration requires movement, and possibly weakening of forces facing the enemy in another part of the zone. Due to the enemy's observation capabilities, movement should take place at night or in conditions of limited visibility whenever possible. Deception measures play an important part in concentration, either to mislead the enemy as to the strength or true intentions of the opposing forces, or their avenues of approach. In this environment of negligible concealment, deception cannot be overemphasized.

The enemy's objective is to stop and destroy the attacking force by direct and indirect fires, obstacles, and counterattacks. The attacker must in turn suppress enemy weapon and surveillance systems to degrade their effects and their intelligence-gathering capability.

Attack helicopters and high-performance aircraft are extremely useful due to their ability to maneuver and apply firepower over a large battlefield in a short time. So, suppression of enemy air defense has a high priority during offensive operations. The destruction of enemy antitank capabilities must also have a high priority due to the shock potential of armor in the desert. No target that has a long-range antitank capability should be disregarded. Good gunnery and well-planned fire distribution are preeminent.

In featureless desert terrain, the requirement to shock, overwhelm, and destroy the enemy demands accurate reconnaissance to identify actual positions from false positions, and excellent navigation so that a commander may be certain of the deployment of his forces. Reconnoiter to find a gap or assailable flank (without alerting the enemy that the area is being reconnoitered) and concentrate the main body to go through or around it with suppressive fires on the flank(s). A gap must be wide enough to allow one unit to bypass another unit that could be stalled. Obstacles are likely to be placed so that attempts to go around them will often lead the attacker into a tire sack. Equipment capable of breaching obstacles must be located well forward.

ENVIRONMENTAL CONSIDERATIONS

As a general rule, a force attacking in daylight should try to wait until the sun is comparatively low and position behind it. This enables enemy targets to be plainly seen without their shadows, while the defenders are handicapped by glare, mirages, and haze. It is not always possible (nor essential) for the sun to be directly behind the attackers. To rely on this leads to a stereotyped method of attack which could become evident to the defenders. The commander of a maneuver force should attempt to keep the sun somewhere on a 3,200-mil arc to his flanks or rear, giving a wide choice of angle of attack.

Dust is an observational hazard to a maneuvering force, especially where there is little or no wind. Teams should move in echelon with overmatching elements on the upwind side, and observers and attack helicopters should operate well to the flank. Since it is impossible to disguise movement during daylight, the assault should be as rapid as possible to minimize enemy reaction time.

The decision to move through a sandstorm will depend on the unit's distance from the enemy, trafficability, the presence of minefield, and the direction and density of the storm. If the advancing unit is caught in a storm blowing from the enemy's direction, the safest alternative is to halt until it abates, although this may not always be possible. In some situations it may be possible for platoons to form close column, using taillights only, and continue movement.

When the storm is blowing toward the enemy it is possible (and extremely effective) to conduct an attack immediately behind the storm.

In certain circumstances equipment or positions that are camouflaged and are less than 1 meter from the ground are invisible to an observer at the same height out to approximately 2,000 meters. At the same time, mirages allow observation of objects below the horizon, although these may be distorted, enlarged, or fuzzy to the point of being unrecognizable. These effects often depend entirely on the angle of the sun to the observer and are best combated by—

- Maintaining observers as high above the desert floor as possible, even if only in hull-down positions behind sand dunes.
- Allowing a vehicle's crew on one side of a position to warn a crew on the other side of a possible threat to his front by crews observing over wide areas.

Many offensive operations take place at night. Observation in these conditions varies according to the amount of ambient light. During nights when the moon is full or almost full, the clear desert sky and ample ambient light allow good observation, both with the naked eye and with night observation devices. Maneuvering units using night-vision devices must continually scan the surrounding terrain to pick up enemy activity that normally would be acquired by peripheral vision in the daylight.

The desert night is extremely dark when there is little or no moon. Under these conditions passive-vision devices, with the exception of thermal imagery, are of little value unless artificial light is used. Active light sources will have to be relied upon. Employment of artificial light must be strictly controlled by the headquarters directing the operation to maintain surprise. As a general rule, direct-fire weapons should not illuminate their target themselves, as their vision will be obscured by debris kicked up due to muzzle blast. Following contact, when some targets should be on fire, passive devices can be used.

MANEUVER

If the terrain permits masking of maneuvering units, and trafficability is good, normal fundamentals of fire and maneuver are used. Trafficability may be restricted by rocky terrain as in the Golan Heights, or the ground may be so flat that the defender has total observation of the area. Movement in these circumstances requires speed of maneuver, deception, and considerable suppression to degrade enemy observation and fires. Frontal attacks should be avoided, especially in conditions of restricted trafficability. It is preferable to maintain pressure on enemy units in unfavorable terrain, while other forces find enemy weaknesses in terrain that is more favorable for an attack.

Lack of clearly defined terrain features complicates navigation and phased operations. Units conducting an enveloping maneuver are apt to lose direction unless routes have been carefully reconnoitered by the maximum number of leaders.

SECTION III. DEFENSIVE OPERATIONS

This section discusses defensive operations as they are modified by desert terrain.

GENERAL

It is unlikely that a U.S. force will be fully deployed in a desert country before an enemy attack. The more probable situation, assuming a secure lodgement area, will be that part of the force will be in position supporting an allied force, while the remainder is moving in by air and sea. Tactically, the allied force will be outnumbered, so the initial mission will be to gain time until the entire force is present in the operational area. This will require a defensive posture initially, but a defense undertaken so aggressively as to convince the enemy that his offensive action will be too costly in personnel and equipment to be worth maintaining. The enemy will be well aware that U.S. forces are arriving in the area, and will make every effort to conclude his operation successfully before the force is fully prepared for combat operations.

The force may conduct defensive operations during subsequent stages of the operation for several reasons. Portions of the force may be required to defend the important types of terrain described below:

- Man-made features such as ports, key logistic installations, roads, railroads, water pumping stations, airfields, and wells.
- Natural features, such as mountain passes, or dominating ground, such as Mount Hermon on the border of Syria and Israel, or the Sollum escarpment near the sea between Libya and Egypt.
- Key or decisive terrain that need not necessarily be a major feature, but one whose loss will inhibit the force in some manner. For example, the loss of terrain relatively close to a lodgement area may hinder the planned rate of buildup.

With the exception of the above cases, the retention of desert terrain normally makes little difference to the final outcome of battle. This does not mean that a commander has complete discretion to move his force wherever and whenever he wishes, as this movement will affect the dispositions of other U.S. forces or allies. It means that possession of terrain is less important than the destruction of enemy forces. Although it will be necessary to dominate certain terrain or retain freedom to maneuver in large areas of the desert, there is no more sense in permanently occupying such areas than occupying a patch of sea. Assuming equal equipment capabilities for both opposing forces, the critical factor in defense will be the force ratios involved and the state of morale and training of the opposing forces.

A defense using aggressive maneuver at all levels is the best way to destroy large numbers of enemy without being destroyed in the process. If the defending force fails to remain mobile and active, the enemy will easily outflank it and strike directly at vital targets, such as the lodgement area. It is almost certain that one flank or the other will be open as were the south flanks of the British and German forces in Egypt and Libya in 1940–43. Since it will not be possible to maintain an unbroken line between strategic obstacles, air and ground security forces must be positioned in width and depth to guard against an enemy trying to outflank the defender.

Obstacles, both natural and artificial, are used to slow, contain, or isolate enemy units in order to defeat and destroy his units one at a time. Forward units block the enemy and canalize him into one or two avenues where he can be engaged from the flank. A reserve can then counterattack to destroy any remaining enemy.

Mutual support is normally a factor of time rather than weapon range due to the large areas to be covered. Gaps in initial positions may have to be accepted between and within task forces; although the ideal is to site units in such a manner that forces in at least two positions can engage an enemy maneuvering on any one of them. This greatly reduces any possibility of defeat in detail. When gaps exist they must be kept under surveillance. The defensive plan must include provisions for maneuvering to fire on any part of a gap before the enemy can move through it. A unit's area of responsibility must be defined by higher headquarters and should be clearly identifiable on the ground, which, due to the absence of significant terrain features, may require marking by artificial means.

FUNDAMENTALS OF THE DEFENSE

The following paragraphs discuss some points to remember in desert operations as they apply to the fundamentals of defense.

Reconnaissance and security units and force surveillance systems must focus on:

- What is the enemy's short-term objective?
- What are the enemy's avenues of approach, and what force is employed on each of them?
- Are the apparent movements real or feints?

As soon as these questions have been answered the commander will be able to maneuver to destroy the enemy. Until they are confirmed he can do nothing more than react to enemy initiatives. This is dangerous in any circumstance and doubly so in the desert as the side with the greatest potential for maneuver is more likely to win.

Direct-fire weapons must be used to their maximum effective range both by day and night. Limitations in night-vision equipment cannot be allowed to reduce depth or frontages; so plans for field artillery or mortar illumination are made for defense during limited visibility.

It is essential that all elements of a force retain their tactical mobility and efficient communications so that they can immediately react to changes in the commander's plans. Each individual weapon must be sited in a number of firing positions, even though vehicular movement may be exposed to air attack. Infantry fighting vehicles must remain in positions where they are concealed, capable of giving fire support to the dismounted squad, and available for immediate remounting.

Combined arms teams are essential to give the commander the capability he requires to fight the defensive battle. Defending forces orient on primary enemy approaches but units must also be prepared for attack from any other direction. It is neither possible nor necessary to have maximum firepower in all directions, provided weapons can be moved to threatened areas before the enemy reaches them. Air cover or an air defense umbrella is necessary for a successful defense.

It is rare to find positions where any substantial part of the unit area of operations can be protected by natural obstacles. This require extensive use of artificial obstacles, depending on time, personnel, and combat service support available. Obstacles are used to divide the enemy force to improve local force ratios, and to slow the enemy's advance, thus permitting a flank attack. Conventional minefield must be clearly marked on the friendly side and recorded to avoid unnecessary losses if friendly forces later maneuver over the area.

STRONG POINTS

Strongpoints are rare in desert warfare; however, they may be necessary to defend an oasis, mountain pass, or other key terrain essential to the defender's scheme of maneuver. When it is necessary to deny terrain to an enemy force, it is far better to initiate the defense well forward of the terrain feature, conduct the defense in depth, and destroy the enemy or force him to break off his attack before he reaches the critical feature.

In some cases the level of fortification and the deployment of the enemy maybe a function of time, or the enemy's intention and his understanding of what our forces are intending to do, The effectiveness of these strongpoints depends on the range of fires, the level of fortifications, and the decision of the opponent to attack them.

Deeply dug and well-prepared strongpoints surrounded by a minefield and having underground accommodations are usually used in the desert. Although these strongpoints may be neutralized by air or artillery fire and bypassed, eventually they will have to be assaulted. If they have been carefully sited and are well defended they can be quite effective. Variations of the strongpoint defense are used in rear operations. Combat service support units will use this method in perimeter defenses or base-cluster defenses. See Figure 3-8 for an example of a strongpoint and Figure 3-9 for an example of a strongpoint holding key terrain.

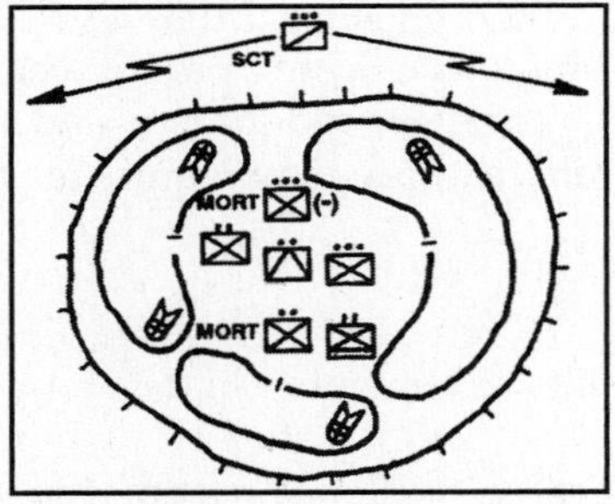

Figure 3-8: Strongpoint.

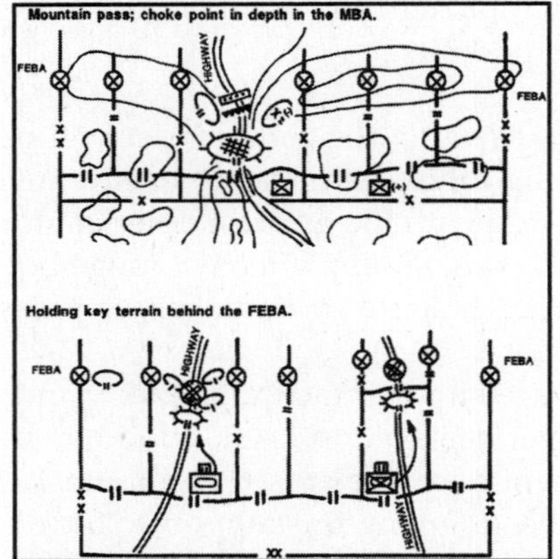

Figure 3-9: Strongpoint holding key terrain.

REVERSE SLOPE DEFENSE

The use of the reverse slope defense takes on added importance in the desert. Concealment is hard to achieve in the open desert. Detection of a unit's location invites both direct and indirect fires in abundance. The use of reverse slope positions will deny the enemy direct observation of positions until he is within the range of direct-fire weapons. Reverse slopes can even be found on seemingly flat desert floors; an intervisibility line will provide the reference for the establishment of engagement areas to support a reverse slope defense. A common misconception is that the desert is flat, when in fact, deserts are normally very uneven, with large breaks in the terrain.

Desert environments give special significance to the terrain aspect of METT-T. Commanders at all levels should place emphasis on the impact of desert terrain as it relates to the other factors of METT-T. The reverse slope defense in desert terrain warrants special considerations.

Direct-fire positions should be placed at the maximum effective ranges from the intervisibility line. This is where the enemy cannot see or engage a force with direct fire until he is within its engagement area. He can only deploy limited forces at a time. This allows the defender to mass fires on one portion of the enemy force at a time. The attacking force will have difficulty in observing and adjusting indirect fires. Obstacles may not be seen by the enemy until he is upon them and force him to breach under massed frees. Observation posts (OPs) positioned forward to see the advance of the enemy can influence the fight through indirect fires. The OPs can direct indirect fires on enemy forces that are slowed or stopped outside direct-fire ranges.

This defensive technique may be used in all defensive missions. Light infantry units use the reverse slope for protection against enemy long-range fires and to reduce the effects of massive indirect fires (artillery and close air support). The reverse slope defense brings the battle into the defender's weapons' ranges. Use of the reverse slope provides an opportunity to gain surprise.

The goal is to cause the enemy to commit his forces against the forward slope of the defense, resulting in his force attacking in an uncoordinated fashion across the crest. A reverse slope defense is organized on the portion of a terrain feature or slope that is masked from enemy direct fires and observation by the topographical crest, and extends rearward from the crest to maximize the range of the defender's weapon systems. See Figure 3-10 for an example of a reverse slope defense and Figure 3-11 for the organization of the reverse slope defense.

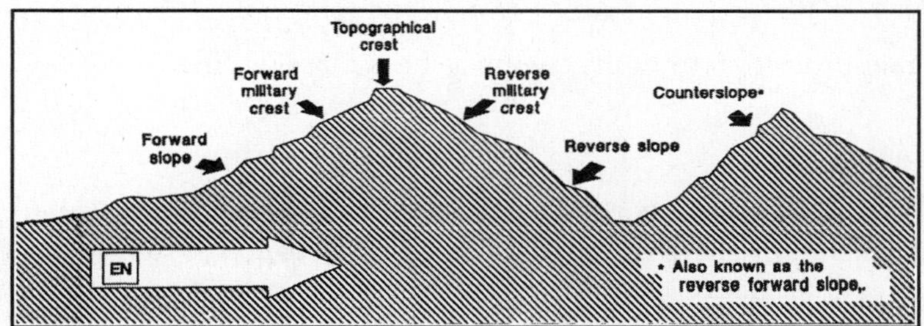

Figure 3-10: Reverse slope defense.

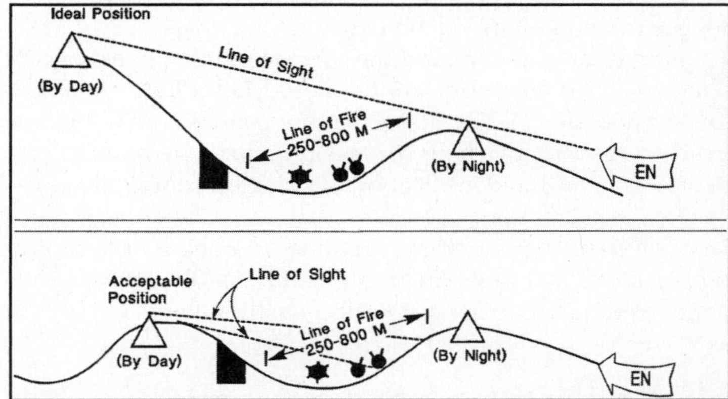

Figure 3-11: Organization of the reverse slope defense.

A disadvantage maybe that the maximum ranges of weapon systems may not be employed due to the terrain available. The desert may be the best environment for the reverse slope defense. It may allow the use of weapons at maximum ranges as well as facilitating advantages. The following are advantages of a reverse slope defense:

- It hinders or prevents enemy observation of the defensive position.
- Attacking forces will not be able to receive direct-fire support from following forces.
- Enemy long-range antitank fires will be degraded.
- Attacking enemy forces will be silhouetted on the crest of the hill.
- Engineer work can be conducted away from direct-fire and observation from the enemy.

Reverse slope defense is not one concept, but a series of concepts that produce the potential for success. The concepts are:

- Pursue offensive opportunities through surprise and deceptive actions, with the intent of stealing the initiative, imposing the commander's will on the enemy, and breaking the enemy's morale.
- Afford the defender a variety of options in positioning his troops, with each option designed to draw the enemy into unfamiliar terrain.
- Enhance light infantry effectiveness and survivability.

A hasty or deliberate reverse slope defense may be considered when any of the following conditions exist:

- When the forward slope lacks cover and concealment, and effective enemy fire makes that position untenable.
- When the terrain on the reverse slope affords appreciably better fields of fire than those available on the forward slope.
- When it is desirable to avoid creating a distortion or dangerous salient in friendly lines by relying on forward slope positions.
- When it is essential to surprise and deceive the enemy as to the unit's true defensive positions or main effort.
- When seeking to gain protection from the enemy as he is massing fires.

DELAY OR WITHDRAWAL

When it is necessary to delay or withdraw, a desert offers many advantages to the defender. Long-range fields of fire allow engagements at maximum effective range of direct-fire weapon systems, and disengagement before the defender's position. However, dust clouds created by a moving force make it necessary to disengage under cover of smoke or darkness. Even a sandstorm can be used to the advantage. Field artillery, U.S. Air Force fighter bombers, and attack helicopters can also be used to allow a ground maneuver unit to disengage and move rapidly to the next position.

When it is necessary to trade space for time, often a counterattack to destroy enemy advance units will do more good than trying to defend longer from an intermediate position.

Commanders at all levels should clearly understand the scheme of maneuver concept of the operation, and what it is they are expected to do, especially if communications should fail. Plans must include provisions for alternate means of communication. Routes should be clearly marked and reconnoitered to the maximum extent practical.

Due to the distances involved and constantly changing task organization, passage of lines is more difficult to coordinate and control. Pay extra attention to the identification of vehicles, routes of passage, signals, and coordination of movements.

Deception should be a part of all desert retrograde operations. The object of deception is to conceal the fact that a retrograde operation is taking place and that units are thinning out. Smoke and dummy positions can be used, false radio messages transmitted, and even dust clouds used to deceive the enemy.

ENVIRONMENTAL CONSIDERATIONS

In the desert it is necessary to modify the techniques of defense as described in doctrinal manuals applicable to each level of command and according to the mission, the fundamentals described in the preceding paragraph, and to the environmental considerations that are described in the following paragraphs.

Observation

The enemy will try to attack when the sun is low and behind him so as to dazzle the defender. The defender's observers must be as high as possible above the desert floor to see the advancing enemy as soon as possible.

Active light sources can be detected from great distances, especially during nights with low ambient light. Positive control of active light sources must be maintained until the battle is joined. Even then, the force equipped with passive devices will have the advantage over the force that is not equipped with these devices.

Heat from combat vehicles can give an enemy using thermal imagery devices a complete picture of the defensive scheme. So, combat vehicles should not prematurely occupy battle positions at night.

Sandstorms

Sandstorms may be used by the enemy to hide an offensive operation especially if the storm is blowing from the enemy's direction. When this is the case, units should immediately occupy their battle positions before the storm arrives. The unit should remain there until it ends, ready to fire and maneuver against the attacker after the storm abates. If vehicle patrolling is possible, a scout platoon or similar unit should cover all gaps, preferably moving in pairs, and on straight lines in view of navigational difficulties.

Terrain

From the point of view of a defending brigade or battalion task force commander, avenues of approach will often seem unlimited. Long-range observation must be maximized and scouts employed well forward to offset this problem. Radars should also be used extensively to provide early warning. It is necessary to identify the enemy's main effort early in order to move to concentrate.

Lack of concealment, especially from the aerial detection, prohibits units from occupying firing positions until just before engaging the enemy. Combat vehicles must displace immediately after engagement or risk destruction. Because of frequent displacement, mutes between battle positions should be reconnoitered and marked when possible, without revealing the scheme of defense. Smoke must be used frequently to conceal movement.

TACTICAL DECEPTION OPERATIONS

Analysis of desert operations from World War II to the present day indicates that tactical deception and surprise are clearly linked to the ability to move and mass forces during periods of limited visibility.

Operational planning should emphasize night movement of units. To minimize the problems of dust and to enhance deception, movement should be accomplished using multiple routes. Place priority on training to support this requirement. Associated with night movement is the requirement for night passage through lanes in minefield and forward passage through friendly forces.

In every modern desert war, deception has played a major role. The lack of concealment leads commanders to believe that with a reasonable reconnaissance effort they can gain an accurate picture of the enemy's dispositions. Reconnaissance by German, British, Israeli, Egyptian, and Syrian forces in modern desert warfare has been sufficient to detect the presence of combat forces in the desert. Deception has been successfully used in each of the modem desert conflicts to mislead commanders.

Since the desert environment makes it difficult to hide forces, the alternative is to make them look like something else—trucks and plywood made to look like tanks, and tanks made to look like trucks.

The movement of personnel and equipment and the placement of logistic support installations are normally indicators of a force's intent. The movement of empty boxes or pallets of ammunition and the establishment of fuel storage areas with real or dummy assets can deceive the enemy as to planned offensive actions. Use minimal actual transportation assets and make numerous, visible trips to simulate a large effort.

There are many examples of successful deception efforts by U.S. forces from World War II. In September 1944, the 43rd Cavalry Reconnaissance Squadron (Reinforced) occupied a 23-mile fronton the left flank of XX (U.S.) Corps on the Metz Front. This squadron portrayed an armored division for several weeks and was so successful that the German Order of Battle Maps showed the 14th (U.S.) Armored Division (AD) to be in the area. The 14th AD was not even in Europe at the time. Expertise in deception operations is critical to success.

Deception plays a key part in offensive operations and has two objectives: the first objective is to weaken the local defense by drawing reserves to another part of the battlefield. This may be done by making a small force seem larger than it is. The second objective is to conceal the avenue of approach and timing of the main attack. Some deception methods that can be used in offensive operations are:

- Using dummy units and installations.
- Using phony radio traffic.
- Using movement and suppressive fires in other areas timed to coincide with the real attack.
- Using small convoys to generate dust clouds.
- Filling ration boxes with sand and stacking them at landfills.
- Moving trucks into and out of the area giving it the appearance of being a storage facility or logistic base.
- Emulating damage to induce the enemy to leave important targets alone. For example, ragged patterns can be painted on the walls and roof of a building with tar and coal dust, and covers placed over them.
- Stacking debris nearby and wiring any unused portions for demolition. During an attack, covers are removed under cover of smoke generators, debris scattered, and demolitions blown. Subsequent enemy air photography will disclose a building that is too badly damaged to be used. Troops using the building after an attack must guard against heat emissions after dark and care must be taken to control electromagnetic emissions.
- Using phony minefield to simulate live minefields. For example, disturb the ground so that it appears that mines have been emplaced and mark boundaries with appropriate warnings.
- Making a real minefield to appear as phony or camouflaging it. For example, once a real minefield is settled, a wheel or a specially made circular wooden tank track marker can be run through the field, leaving track or tire marks to lure the enemy onto live mines. Antipersonnel mines should not be sown in such a field until the track marks have been laid. Another method is to leave gaps in the mechanically laid field, run vehicles through the gaps, and then close them with hand-laid mines without disturbing the track marks.
- Using decoys to confuse the enemy as to the strength of friendly forces and the unit's identity, or to conceal unit movement by being sited in a position after the real unit has moved.

LONG-RANGE SURVEILLANCE OPERATIONS

Desert characteristics affecting LRS operations are: lack of water (a major problem), scarcity of vegetation, extensive sand areas, extreme temperature ranges, brilliant sunlight, and usually excellent observation. Movement using animals, vehicles, or by foot may be considered and is generally restricted to darkness. More training in land or air navigation and terrain orientation procedures may be necessary.

CHAPTER 4

Operations in Mountains

This chapter describes special conditions associated with operating in mountains such as those in the southern Sinai and on the shores of the Red Sea. It does not address tactics and techniques for mountain operations that are equally applicable to all mountains, except for the purpose of clarity.

TERRAIN

Mountains are high and rugged, with very steep slopes. Valleys running into a range become more and more narrow with the sides becoming gradually steeper. Valleys are usually the only routes that allow ground movement of men and equipment at any speed or in any quantity. Water is nonexistent on hilltops and unusual in valleys except during flash floods after rains. Lateral ground communications are limited unless the force is moving across the spines of mountain ranges. Navigation may be difficult, as maps are likely to be inaccurate.

PERSONNEL

Troops operating in mountainous country must be in peak physical condition. Regardless of their normal physical condition, personnel operating in mountainous areas require additional stamina and energy. They must also possess the ability to conduct sustained physical exertion and recover from it quickly.

Acclimatization to height, which varies much more among individuals than that for heat, must also be considered for operations in mountains. Lack of oxygen at high altitudes can cause unacclimatized troops to lose up to 50 percent of their normal physical efficiency when operating in altitudes over 6,000 feet. Mountain sickness may occur at altitudes over 7,800 feet and is usually characterized by severe headache, loss of appetite, nausea and dizziness, and may last from 5 to 7 days. Troops can acclimatize by appropriate staging techniques. It may take several weeks to become completely acclimatized, depending on altitude and the individual's personal physical reactions.

The risk of sunburn, particularly to the uncovered face, is greater in mountains than on the desert floor due to thinner atmosphere. Use antisunburn ointment and keep the face in shade around midday, using face nets or sweat rags. An individual camouflage net or scarf is particularly useful for this purpose. Recognition of heat illnesses in higher altitudes may not be as apparent as at lower altitudes because sweat evaporates very quickly. Measures to avoid dehydration and salt loss are extremely important. Daily temperature variations may be considerable making it necessary to ensure troops do not become chilled at night. Layering of clothing is essential. Troops who have been sweating heavily before the temperature starts to drop should take their wet shirts off and place them over relatively dry shirts and sweaters. Soldiers/marines should add layers of clothing as it gets colder and remove them as needed. This may have to be leader supervised and disciplined in the same manner as water consumption.

Requirements for hygiene areas important in mountainous areas as in the desert itself. Normal rocky ground will make it extremely difficult to dig any form of latrine so cover excrement with rocks in a specially marked area.

GENERAL CONSIDERATIONS

Infantry is the basic maneuver force in mountains. Mechanized infantry is confined to valleys and foothills (if these exist), but their ability to dismount and move on foot enables them to reach almost anywhere in the area. Airmobile infantry can also be extensively used. Consideration should be given to modifying the TOE of infantry units operating in barren mountains. A strong antitank platoon may not be necessary. However, the infantry requires extra radars and radios for the number of observation posts and separate positions that they may expect to occupy.

Mountains are not a good environment for tank and armored cavalry operations, because tanks and armored cavalry are unable to maximize their mobility, flexibility, and firepower.

Avenues of approach at ground level are few. Roads or trails are limited and require extensive engineer effort to maintain. Off-road trafficability varies from relatively easy to very difficult. Most movement and maneuver in this type of terrain is either by air or on foot. Unnecessary vertical foot or vehicle movement should be avoided. Rock slides and avalanches, although not as common as in high cold mountains, do exist and can restrict movement.

Air cavalry is the major reconnaissance means but they must guard against being ambushed by ground troops located at their own altitude or even higher. Security of units must include observation, especially at night, of all avenues of approach including those within the capabilities of skilled mountaineers.

It is relatively easier to conceal troops in barren mountains than on the desert floor due to rugged ground, deep shadows (especially at dawn and dusk), and the difficulties an observer encounters when establishing perspective. Carefully placed rocks can be used to hide equipment; however, rocks can chip and splinter under small arms fire. The normal-type camouflage net, which breaks up outline by shadow, may be used rather than the overall cover normally used in the desert.

Helicopter units of all types can be used, although they may be slightly inhibited by altitude and rugged terrain. Payloads and endurance are degraded due to density and attitude. Winds are turbulent with considerable fluctuations in air flow strength and direction, particularly on the lee side of mountains. These winds, combined with the terrain, produce extra strain on crews as they have little margin for error. Flight crews should receive training in these conditions before flying in operations under these conditions.

When using men on foot for navigation, use all available maps, the lensatic compass, and a pocket altimeter. The pocket altimeter is essentially a barometer, measuring height by means of varying air pressure. If a navigator can only establish his location in the horizontal plane by resection on one point, the altimeter tells him his height, and thus his exact position. The instrument must be reset at every known altitude as it is affected by fluctuations of air pressure. Air photographs can also be helpful if they are scaled and contoured.

Supply of water and ammunition and the evacuation of wounded, especially if helicopters cannot land, can complicate operations. Water and ammunition may have to be transported by unit or civilian porters using A-frames or other suitable devices, or even by animal transport such as camel or mule.

OFFENSIVE OPERATIONS

The objective in mountainous areas of operations is normally to dominate terrain from which the enemy can be pinned down and destroyed. Avenues of approach are normally few, with very limited lateral movement except by helicopter. Reconnaissance must be continuous using all available means, as enemy defensive positions will be difficult to find. Observation posts are emplaced on high ground, normally by helicopter.

When contact is made, airmobile infantry can be used to outflank and envelop the enemy while suppressive fires and close air support are placed on all suspected positions, especially on dominating ground. Engineers should be well forward to assist in clearing obstacles. If airmobile infantry is unable to outflank the enemy, it will be necessary to launch a deliberate attack.

Frontal attacks in daylight, even with considerable supporting frees, have a limited chance of success against a well-emplaced enemy. Flank attacks on foot take a lot of time. The best opportunity is at night or in very poor visibility, but progress of men on foot will be slow and objectives should be limited.

The force should make every effort to secure ground higher than enemy positions to allow the attack to be downhill. Mobile forces should select objectives to the enemy's rear to kill the enemy as they reposition or counterattack. Foot mobile forces must seek adequate terrain (restrictive) to equalize the enemy's mounted mobility advantage.

Air superiority is required to allow a continuous flow of supplies and combat support by helicopter. Friendly mobile units must concentrate to destroy enemy command and control, artillery, service support, and air defense assets. It may be possible to infiltrate to a position behind the enemy, preferably using the most difficult, and hence, unlikely route. Although this is very slow, it normally has the advantage of surprise.

The importance of dominating terrain, together with the enemy's knowledge that troops on the objective will be physically tired and dehydrated, makes an immediate counterattack likely. Supporting weapons must be brought forward at once, preferably by helicopter, and casualties removed by the same method.

Airmobile and attack helicopter units are well suited for pursuit operations. They can be used to outflank retreating enemy, and set up positions overlooking likely withdrawal routes. Small engineer parties can be emplaced to block defiles and interdict trails. Close air support and field artillery are used to reinforce airmobile and attack helicopter units and to counter efforts by enemy engineers to create obstacles.

DEFENSIVE OPERATIONS

A defense from a series of strongpoints is normal in hot mountains due to the need to hold dominating terrain and restrictions on ground mobility. Due to the amount of rock in the soil, it takes more time to prepare positions and normally requires engineer support.

It is necessary to hold terrain dominating avenues of approach. Any terrain that dominates a friendly position must either be held, or denied to the enemy by fire. It may be necessary to stock several days' supplies, especially water, ammunition, and medical equipment in a position in case helicopters or supply vehicles are unable to reach it.

When a covering force is used, it is organized around cavalry reinforced with attack helicopters, supported by field and air defense artillery. Airmobile infantry operates on ridge lines. If the enemy closes on a battle position it is difficult to extract airmobile infantry, so sheltered landing sites nearby should be available. In any event, extractions must be covered by air or ground suppressive fires. Stay-behind observers should be used to call down field artillery fires on targets of opportunity or to report enemy activity. When tanks are a threat and terrain is suitable, the covering force is reinforced with tank-heavy units and antitank weapon systems.

Combat in the main battle area is usually a series of isolated actions fought from strongpoints on ridge lines and in valleys. Patrols are used extensively to harass the enemy and prevent infiltration; all possible routes must be covered. If the enemy attempts to outflank the friendly force, he must be blocked by attack helicopters, if available, or airmobile infantry.

Reserves should be kept centrally located and deployed by air to block or counterattack. If this is not possible, reserves may have to be split up and placed behind key terrain where they are available for immediate counterattack.

If retrograde operations are necessary, mountainous terrain is as good a place to conduct them as anywhere. More time is required to reconnoiter and prepare rearward positions, and they should be prestocked as much as possible. Unlike the desert floor where movement between positions is likely to cover relatively great distances, movement in these conditions is usually from ridge to ridge. Routes must be covered by flank guards, especially at defiles or other critical points, as the enemy will attempt to block them or cut off rear guards.

COMBAT SUPPORT

It may be difficult to find good gun positions at lower altitudes due to crest clearance problems—so high-angle fire is often used. The best weapons are light field artillery and mortars that are airmobile and can be manhandled so they can be positioned as high as possible.

Field artillery observation posts are emplaced on the highest ground available, although in low-cloud conditions it will be necessary to ensure that they are staggered in height. Predicted fire may be inaccurate due to rapidly changing weather conditions making observed fire a more sure method for achieving the desired results.

Like field artillery, there is limited use for self-propelled weapons in this environment, although some may be used in valleys. Airmobile towed weapons allow employment throughout the mountainous area of operations.

Major tasks for engineer, even in an airmobile force, are: construction, improvement, and route repair, and their denial to the enemy. Mining is important due to the limited number of routes. Lines of communication require constant drainage and possibly bridging to overcome the problem of flash flooding.

Because of the frequent interdictions of mountainous roadways, military police will experience multiple defile operations. Use temporary traffic signs to expedite traffic movement to the front. The number of stragglers may be expected to increase in this environment. Because of difficulty in resupply, the supply points for water, POL, food, and ammunition will become especially lucrative targets for enemy attack. Military police rear area security elements must develop plans for relief and for augmenting base defense forces.

Combat in Jungle Environments

CHAPTER 1

The Jungle

SECTION I. GENERAL

This chapter introduces jungle environments—where they are found and what they are like. Later chapters build on this information, providing guidance on fighting and living in the jungle.

Field Marshal Slim's words reflect the image of the jungle most armies carry into jungle warfare. At first, the jungle seems to be very hostile, but the hostility wanes as troops learn more about the jungle environment.

Jungles, in their various forms, are common in tropical areas of the world—mainly Southeast Asia, Africa, and Latin America.

> *"To our men...the jungle was a strange, fearsome place; moving and fighting in it were a nightmare. We were too ready to classify jungle as 'impenetratable'...To us it appeared only as an obstacle to movement; to the Japanese it was a welcome means of concealed maneuver and suprise...The Japanese reaped the deserved reward...we paid the penalty."*
>
> —Field Marshall Slim, Victor in Burma, World War II
> (Concerning the dark, early days of the Burma Campaign)

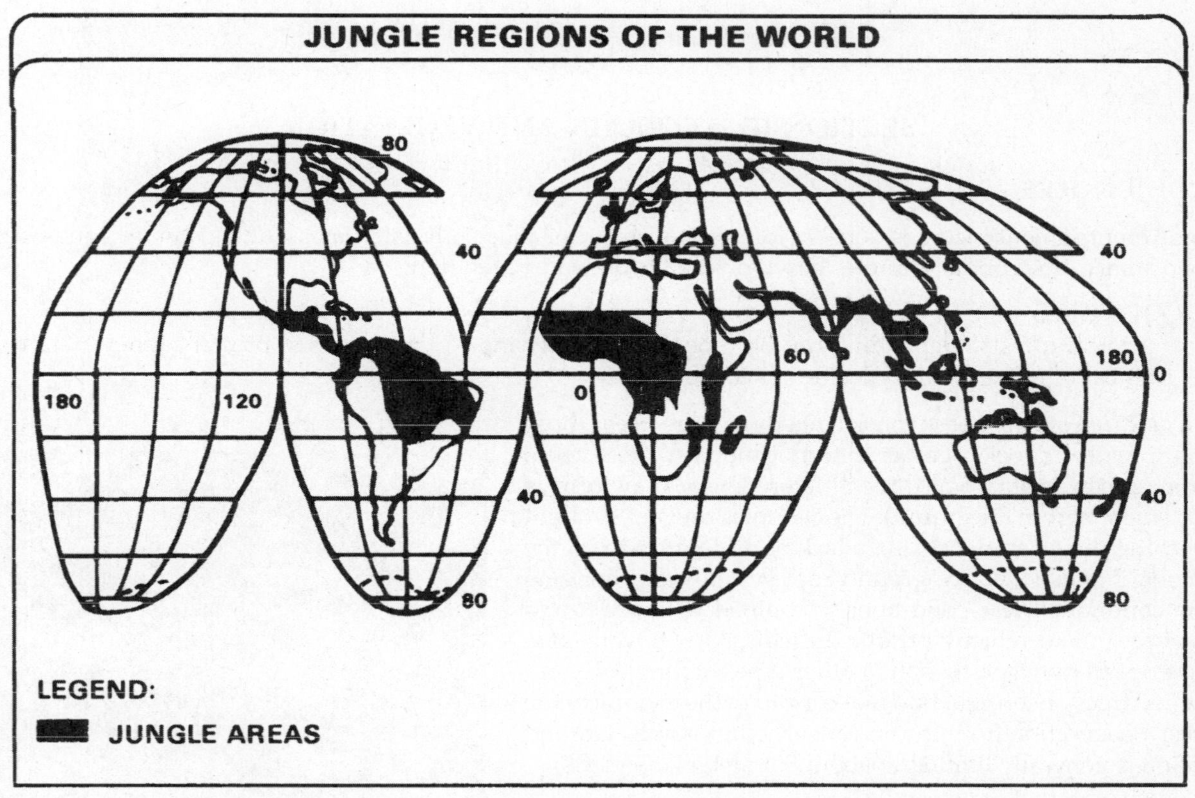

SECTION II. CLIMATE AND WEATHER

The climate in jungles varies with location. Close to the equator, all seasons are nearly alike, with rains throughout the year; farther from the equator, especially in India and Southeast Asia, jungles have distinct wet (monsoon) and dry seasons. Both zones have high temperatures (averaging 78 to 95+ degrees Fahrenheit), heavy rainfall (as much as 1,000 centimeters [400+ inches] annually), and high humidity (90 percent) throughout the year.

Severe weather also has an impact on tactical operations in the jungle. The specific effects of weather on operations are discussed throughout this manual.

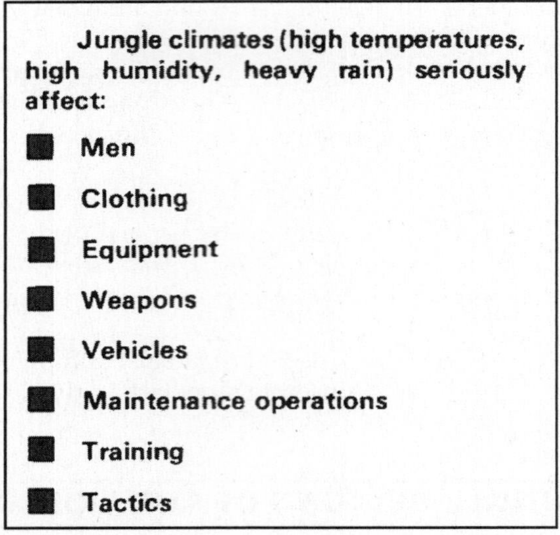

Jungle climates (high temperatures, high humidity, heavy rain) seriously affect:

- **Men**
- **Clothing**
- **Equipment**
- **Weapons**
- **Vehicles**
- **Maintenance operations**
- **Training**
- **Tactics**

SECTION III. TERRAIN AND VEGETATION

TYPES OF JUNGLES

The jungle environment includes densely forested areas, grasslands, cultivated areas, and swamps. Jungles are classified as primary or secondary jungles based on the terrain and vegetation.

PRIMARY JUNGLES

These are tropical forests. Depending on the type of trees growing in these forests, primary jungles are classified either as tropical rain forests or as deciduous forests.

Tropical Rain Forests. These consist mostly of large trees whose branches spread and lock together to form canopies. These canopies, which can exist at two or three different levels, may form as low as 10 meters from the ground. The canopies prevent sunlight from reaching the ground, causing a lack of undergrowth on the jungle floor. Extensive above-ground root systems and hanging vines are common. These conditions, combined with a wet and soggy surface, make vehicular traffic difficult. Foot movement is easier in tropical rain forests than in other types of jungle. Except where felled trees or construction make a gap in the canopy of the rain forest, observation from the air is nearly impossible. Ground observation is generally limited to about 50 meters (55 yards).

Deciduous Forests. These are found in semitropical zones where there are both wet and dry seasons. In the wet season, trees are fully leaved; in the dry season, much of the foliage dies. Trees are generally less dense in deciduous forests than in rain forests. This allows more rain and sunlight to filter to the ground, producing thick undergrowth. In the wet season, with the trees in full leaf, observation both from the air and on the ground is limited. Movement is more difficult than in the rain forest. In the dry season, however, both observation and trafficability improve.

SECONDARY JUNGLES

These are found at the edge of the rain forest and the deciduous forest, and in areas where jungles have been cleared and abandoned. Secondary jungles appear when the ground has been repeatedly exposed to sunlight. These areas are typically overgrown with weeds, grasses, thorns, ferns, canes, and shrubs. Foot movement is extremely slow and difficult. Vegetation may reach to a height of 2 meters. This will limit observation to the front to only a few meters.

COMMON JUNGLE FEATURES

SWAMPS

These are common to all low jungle areas where there is water and poor drainage. There are two basic types of swamps—mangrove and palm.

Mangrove Swamps. These are found in coastal areas wherever tides influence water flow. The mangrove is a shrub-like tree which grows 1 to 5 meters high. These trees have tangled root systems, both above and below the water level, which restrict movement to foot or small boats. Observation in mangrove swamps, both on the ground and from the air, is poor. Concealment is excellent.

Palm Swamps. These exist in both salt and fresh water areas. Like movement in the mangrove swamps, movement through palm swamps is mostly restricted to foot (sometimes small boats). Vehicular traffic is nearly impossible except after extensive road construction by engineers. Observation and fields-of-fire are very limited. Concealment from both air and ground observation is excellent.

SAVANNA

This is a broad, open jungle grassland in which trees are scarce. The thick grass is broad-bladed and grows 1 to 5 meters high. Movement in the savanna is generally easier than in other types of jungle areas, especially for vehicles. The sharp-edged, dense grass and extreme heat make foot movement a slow and tiring process. Depending on the height of the grass, ground observation may vary from poor to good. Concealment from air observation is poor for both troops and vehicles.

BAMBOO

This grows in clumps of varying size in jungles throughout the tropics. Large stands of bamboo are excellent obstacles for wheeled or tracked vehicles. Troop movement through bamboo is slow, exhausting, and noisy. Troops should bypass bamboo stands if possible.

CULTIVATED AREAS

These exist in jungles throughout the tropics and range from large, well-planned, and well-managed farms and plantations to small tracts cultivated by individual farmers. There are three general types of cultivated areas—rice paddies, plantations, and small farms.

Rice Paddies. These are flat, flooded fields in which rice is grown. Flooding of the fields is controlled by a network of dikes and irrigation ditches which make movement by vehicles difficult even when the fields are dry. Concealment is poor in rice paddies. Cover is limited to the dikes, and then only from ground fire. Observation and fields of fire are excellent. Foot movement is poor when the fields are wet because soldiers must wade through water about ½ meter (2 feet) deep and soft mud. When the fields are dry, foot movement becomes easier. The dikes, about 2 to 3 meters tall, are the only obstacles.

Plantations. These are large farms or estates where tree crops, such as rubber and coconut, are grown. They are usually carefully planned and free of undergrowth (like a well-tended park). Movement through plantations is generally easy. Observation along the rows of trees is generally good. Concealment and cover can be found behind the trees, but soldiers moving down the cultivated rows are exposed.

Small Farms. These exist throughout the tropics. These small cultivated areas are usually hastily planned. After 1 or 2 years' use, they usually are abandoned, leaving behind a small open area which turns into secondary jungle. Movement through these areas may be difficult due to fallen trees and scrub brush.

Generally, observation and fields-of-fire are less restricted in cultivated areas than in uncultivated jungles. However, much of the natural cover and concealment are removed by cultivation, and troops will be more exposed in these areas.

CHAPTER 2

Life in the Jungle

SECTION I. GENERAL

Soldiers must understand that the environment affects everyone. The degree to which soldiers are trained to live and fight in harsh environments will determine their unit's success or failure.

> *"Jungle fighting is not new to U.S. soldiers, nor does the enemy have a monopoly on jungle know-how. U.S. units adapted well to jungle fighting, and when we operated against the North Vietnamese Army along the Cambodian border we found that they had as much difficulty operating in the area as we did. The prisoners we captured were, as a rule, undernourished, emaciated, and sick with malaria. They stated that almost everyone in their unit had malaria, and many had died from it."*
>
> Report, 25th Infantry Division, Republic of Vietnam

There is very little to fear from the jungle environment. Fear itself can be an enemy. Soldiers must be taught to control their fear of the jungle. A man overcome with fear is of little value in any situation. Soldiers in a jungle must learn that the most important thing is to keep their heads and calmly think out any situation.

Many of the stories written about out-of-the-way jungle places were written by writers who went there in search of adventure rather than facts. Practically without exception, these authors exaggerated or invented many of the thrilling experiences they relate. These thrillers are often a product of the author's imagination and are not facts.

Most Americans, especially those raised in cities, are far removed from their pioneer ancestors, and have lost the knack of taking care of themselves under all conditions. It would be foolish to say that, without proper training, they would be in no danger if lost in the jungles of Southeast Asia, South America, or some Pacific island. On the other hand, they would be in just as much danger if lost in the mountains of western Pennsylvania or in other undeveloped regions of our own country. The only difference would be that a man is less likely to panic when he is lost in his homeland than when he is lost abroad.

SECTION II. JUNGLE HAZARDS

EFFECT OF CLIMATE

The discomforts of tropical climates are often exaggerated, but it is true that the heat is more persistent. In regions where the air contains a lot of moisture, the effect of the heat may seem worse than the same temperature in a dry climate. Many people experienced in jungle operations feel that the heat and discomfort in some U.S. cities in the summertime are worse than the climate in the jungle.

Strange as it may seem, there may be more suffering from cold in the tropics than from the heat. Of course, very low temperatures do not occur, but chilly days and nights are common. In some jungles, in winter months, the nights are cold enough to require a wool blanket or poncho liner for sleeping.

Rainfall in many parts of the tropics is much greater than that in most areas of the temperate zones. Tropical downpours usually are followed by clear skies, and in most places the rains are predictable at certain times of the day. Except in those areas where rainfall may be continuous during the rainy season, there are not many days when the sun does not shine part of the time.

People who live in the tropics usually plan their activities so that they are able to stay under shelter during the rainy and hotter portions of the day. After becoming used to it, most tropical dwellers prefer the constant climate of the torrid zones to the frequent weather changes in colder climates.

INSECTS

Malaria-carrying mosquitoes are probably the most harmful of the tropical insects. Soldiers can contract malaria if proper precautions are not taken.

Precautions against malaria include:

- **Taking Dapsone and chloroquine-primaquine**
- **Using insect repellent**
- **Wearing clothing that covers as much of the body as possible**
- **Using nets or screens at every opportunity**
- **Avoiding the worst-infested areas when possible**

PROTECTION AGAINST MALARIA

Mosquitoes are most prevalent early at night and just before dawn. Soldiers must be especially cautious at these times. Malaria is more common in populated areas than in uninhabited jungle, so soldiers must also be especially cautious when operating around villages. Mud packs applied to mosquito bites offer some relief from itching.

Wasps and bees may be common in some places, but they will rarely attack unless their nests are disturbed. When a nest is disturbed, the troops must leave the area and reassemble at the last rally point. In case of stings, mud packs are helpful. In some areas, there are tiny bees, called sweatbees, which may collect on exposed parts of the body during dry weather, especially if the body is sweating freely. They are annoying but stingless and will leave when sweating has completely stopped, or they may be scraped off with the hand.

The larger centipedes and scorpions can inflict stings which are painful but not fatal. They like dark places, so it is always advisable to shake out blankets before sleeping at night, and to make sure before dressing that they are not hidden in clothing or shoes. Spiders are commonly found in the jungle. Their bites may be painful, but are rarely serious. Ants can be dangerous to injured men lying on the ground and unable to move. Wounded soldiers should be placed in an area free of ants.

In Southeast Asian jungles, the rice-borer moth of the lowlands collects around lights in great numbers during certain seasons. It is a small, plain-colored moth with a pair of tiny black spots on the wings. It should never be brushed off roughly, as the small barbed hairs of its body may be ground into the skin. This causes a sore, much like a burn, that often takes weeks to heal.

LEECHES

Leeches are common in many jungle areas, particularly throughout most of the Southwest Pacific, Southeast Asia, and the Malay Peninsula. They are found in swampy areas, streams, and moist jungle country. They are not poisonous, but their bites may become infected if not cared for properly. The small wound that they cause may provide a point of entry for the germs which cause tropical ulcers or "jungle sores." Soldiers operating in the jungle should watch for leeches on the body and brush them off before they have had time to bite. When they have taken hold, they should not be pulled off forcibly because part of the leech may remain in the skin. Leeches will release themselves if touched with insect repellent, a moist piece of tobacco, the burning end of a cigarette, a coal from a fire, or a few drops of alcohol.

Straps wrapped around the lower part of the legs ("leech straps") will prevent leeches from crawling up the legs and into the crotch area. Trousers should be securely tucked into the boots.

SNAKES

A soldier in the jungle probably will see very few snakes. When he does see one, the snake most likely will be making every effort to escape.

If a soldier should accidently step on a snake or otherwise disturb a snake, it will probably attempt to bite. The chances of this happening to soldiers traveling along trails or waterways are remote if soldiers are alert and careful. Most jungle areas pose less of a snakebite danger than do the uninhabited areas of New Mexico, Florida, or Texas. This does not mean that soldiers should be careless about the possibility of snakebites, but ordinary precautions against them are enough. Soldiers should be particularly watchful when clearing ground.

Treat all snakebites as poisonous.

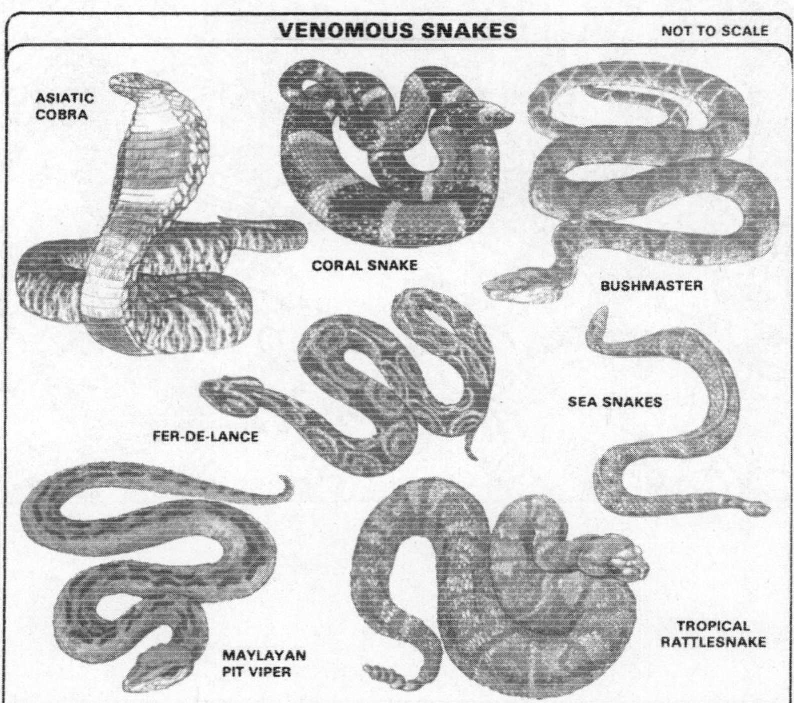

SNAKEBITE TREATMENT

Follow these steps if bitten:

- **Remain calm, but act swiftly, and chances of survival are good. (Less than one percent of properly treated snakebites are fatal. Without treatment, the fatality rate is 10 to 15 percent.)**
- **Immobilize the affected part in a position below the level of the heart.**
- **Place a lightly constricting band 5 to 10 centimeters (2 to 4 inches) closer to the heart than the site of the bite. Reapply the constricting band ahead of the swelling if it moves up the arm or leg. The constricting band should be placed tightly enough to halt the flow of blood in surface vessels, but not so tight as to stop the pulse.**
- **Do not attempt to cut open the bite or suck out venom.**
- **Seek medical help. If possible, the snake's head with 5 to 10 centimeters (2 to 4 inches) of its body attached should be taken to the medics for identification. Identification insures use of the proper antivenom.**

CROCODILES AND CAYMANS

Crocodiles and caymans are meat-eating reptiles which live in tropical areas. "Crocodile-infested rivers and swamps" is a catch-phrase often found in stories about the tropics. Asian jungles certainly have their share of crocodiles, but there are few authenticated cases of crocodiles actually attacking humans. Caymans, found in South and Central America, are not likely to attack unless provoked.

WILD ANIMAL

In Africa, where lions, leopards, and other flesh-eating animals abound, they are protected from hunters by local laws and live on large preserves. In areas where the beasts are not protected, they are shy and seldom seen. When encountered, they will attempt to escape. All large animals can be dangerous if cornered or suddenly startled at close quarters. This is especially true of females with young. In the jungles of Sumatra, Bali, Borneo, Southeast Asia, and Burma there are tigers, leopards, elephants, and buffalo. Latin America's jungles have the jaguar. Ordinarily, these will not attack a man unless they are cornered or wounded.

Certain jungle animals, such as water buffalo and elephants, have been domesticated by the local people. Soldiers should also avoid these animals. They may appear tame, but this tameness extends only to people the animals are familar with.

POISONOUS VEGETATION

Another area of danger is that of poisonous plants and trees. For example, nettles, particularly tree nettles, are one of the dangerous items of vegetation. These nettles have a severe stinging that will quickly educate the victim to recognize the plant. There are ringas trees in Malaysia which affect some people in much the same way as poison oak. The poison ivy and poison sumac of the continental U.S. can cause many of the same type troubles that may be experienced in the jungle. The danger from poisonous plants in the woods of the U.S. eastern seaboard is similar to that of the tropics. Thorny thickets, such as rattan, should be avoided as one would avoid a blackberry patch.

Some of the dangers associated with poisonous vegetation can be avoided by keeping sleeves down and wearing gloves when practical.

HEALTH AND HYGIENE

The climate in tropical areas and the absence of sanitation facilities increase the chance that soldiers may contract a disease. Disease is fought with good sanitation practices and preventive medicine. In past wars, diseases accounted for a significantly high percentage of casualties.

Before going into a jungle area, leaders must:

- **Make sure immunizations are current.**
- **Get soldiers in top physical shape.**
- **Instruct soldiers in personal hygiene.**

Upon arrival in the jungle area, leaders must:

- **Allow time to adjust (acclimate) to the new environment.**
- **Never limit the amount of water soldiers drink. (It is very important to replace the fluids lost through sweating.)**
- **Instruct soldiers on the sources of disease. Insects cause malaria, yellow fever, and scrub typhus. Typhoid, dysentery, cholera, and hepatitis are caused by dirty food and contaminated water.**

WATERBORNE DISEASES

Water is vital in the jungle and is usually easy to find. However, water from natural sources should be considered contaminated. Water purification procedures must be taught to all soldiers. Germs of serious diseases, like dysentery, are found in impure water. Other waterborne diseases, such as blood fluke, are caused by exposure of an open sore to impure water.

Soldiers can prevent waterborne diseases by:

- **Obtaining drinking water from approved engineer water points.**
- **Using rainwater; however, rainwater should be collected after it has been raining at least 15 to 30 minutes. This lessens the chances of impurity being washed from the jungle canopy into the water container. Even then the water should be purified.**
- **Insuring that all drinking water is purified.**
- **Not swimming or bathing in untreated water.**
- **Keeping the body fully clothed when crossing water obstacles.**

FUNGUS DISEASES

These diseases are caused by poor personal health practices. The jungle environment promotes fungus and bacterial diseases of the skin and warm water immersion skin diseases. Bacteria and fungi are tiny plants which multiply fast under the hot, moist conditions of the jungle. Sweat-soaked skin invites fungus attack. The following are common skin diseases that are caused by long periods of wetness of the skin:

Warm Water Immersion Foot. This disease occurs usually where there are many creeks, streams, and canals to cross, with dry ground in between. The bottoms of the feet become white, wrinkled, and tender. Walking becomes painful.

Chafing. This disease occurs when soldiers must often wade through water up to their waists, and the trousers stay wet for hours. The crotch area becomes red and painful to even the lightest touch.

Most skin diseases are treated by letting the skin dry.

To prevent these diseases, soldiers should:

- **Bathe often, and air- or sun-dry the body as often as possible.**
- **Wear clean, dry, loose-fitting clothing whenever possible.**
- **Not sleep in wet, dirty clothing. Soldiers should carry one dry set of clothes just for sleeping. Dirty clothing, even if wet, is put on again in the morning. This practice not only fights fungus, bacterial, and warm-water immersion diseases but also prevents chills and allows soldiers to rest better.**
- **Not wear underwear during wet weather. Underwear dries slower than jungle fatigues, and causes severe chafing.**
- **Take off boots and massage feet as often as possible.**
- **Dust feet, socks, and boots with foot powder at every chance.**
- **Always carry several pairs of socks and change them frequently.**
- **Keep hair cut short.**

HEAT INJURIES

These result from high temperatures, high humidity, lack of air circulation, and physical exertion. All soldiers must be trained to prevent heat disorders.

HEAT INJURIES

TYPE	CAUSE	SYMPTOMS	TREATMENT
Dehydration	Dehydration is caused by the loss of too much water. About two-thirds of the human body is water. When water is not replaced as it is lost, the body becomes dried out—dehydrated.	The symptoms are sluggishness and listlessness.	The treatment is to give the victim plenty of water.
Heat Exhaustion	Heat exhaustion is caused by the loss of too much water and salt.	The symptoms are: Dizziness. Nausea. Headache. Cramps. Rapid, weak pulse. Cool, wet skin.	The treatment consists of: Moving the victim to a cool, shaded place for rest. Loosening the clothing. Elevating the feet to improve circulation. Giving the victim cool salt water (two salt tablets dissolved in a canteen of water). Natural sea water should not be used.
Heat Cramps	Heat cramps are caused by the loss of too much salt.	The symptom is painful muscle cramps which are relieved as soon as salt is replaced.	The treatment is the same as for heat exhaustion.
Heatstrokes	Heatstroke (sunstroke) is caused by a breakdown in the body's heat control mechanism. The most likely victims are those who are not acclimated to the jungle, or those who have recently had bad cases of diarrhea. Heatstroke can kill if not treated quickly.	The symptoms are: Hot, red, dry skin (most important sign). No sweating (when sweating would be expected). Very high temperature (105 to 110 degrees). Rapid pulse. Spots before eyes. Headache, nausea, dizziness, mental confusion. Sudden collapse.	Treatment consists of: Cooling the victim immediately. This is achieved by putting him in a creek or stream; pouring canteens of water over him; fanning him; and using ice, if available. Giving him cool salt water (prepared as stated earlier) if he is conscious. Rubbing his arms and legs rapidly. Evacuating him to medical aid as soon as possible.

Heat injuries are prevented by:

- **Drinking plenty of water.**
- **Using extra salt with food and water.**
- **Slowing down movement.**

NATIVES

Like all other regions of the world, the jungle also has its native inhabitants. Soldiers should be aware that some of these native tribes can be hostile if not treated properly.

There may be occasions, however, when hostile tribes attack without provacation. If they attack, a small force should be able to disperse them.

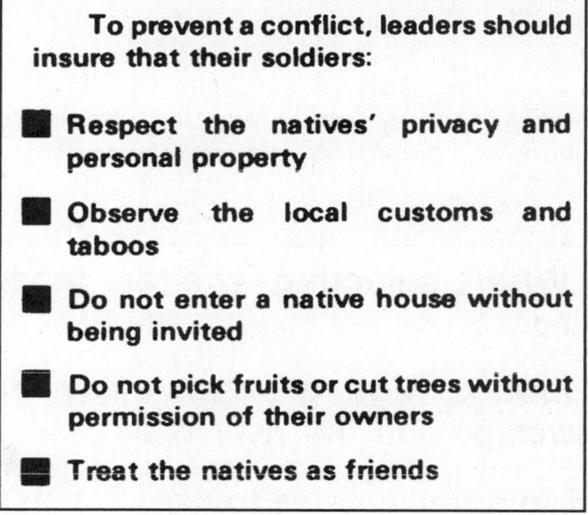

To prevent a conflict, leaders should insure that their soldiers:

- **Respect the natives' privacy and personal property**
- **Observe the local customs and taboos**
- **Do not enter a native house without being invited**
- **Do not pick fruits or cut trees without permission of their owners**
- **Treat the natives as friends**

SECTION III. JUNGLE SURVIVAL

FOOD

Food of some type is always available in the jungle—in fact, there is hardly a place in the world where food cannot be secured from plants and animals. All animals, birds, reptiles, and many kinds of insects of the jungle are edible. Some animals, such as toads and salamanders, have glands on the skin which should be removed before their meat is eaten. Fruits, flowers, buds, leaves, bark, and often tubers (fleshy plant roots) may be eaten. Fruits eaten by birds and monkeys usually may be eaten by man.

Meats that can be found in most jungles include:	The following types of fruits and nuts are common in jungle areas:		Vegetables found in most jungles include:
Wild fowl	Bananas	Wild raspberries	Taro *
Wild cattle	Coconuts	Nakarika	Yam *
Wild pig	Oranges and lemons	Papaya	Yucca *
Freshwater fish *	Navele nuts	Mangoes	Hearts of palm trees
Saltwater fish	Breadfruit		
Fresh-water crawfish			

*These items must be cooked before eating.

There are various means of preparing and preserving food found in the jungle. Fish, for example, can be cleaned and wrapped in wild banana leaves. This bundle is then tied with string made from bark, placed on a hastily constructed wood griddle, and roasted thoroughly until done. Another method is to roast the bundle of fish underneath a pile of red-hot stones.

Other meats can be roasted in a hollow section of bamboo, about 60 centimeters (2 feet) long. Meat cooked in this manner will not spoil for three or four days if left inside the bamboo stick and sealed.

Yams, taros, yuccas, and wild bananas can be cooked in coals. They taste somewhat like potatoes. Palm hearts can make a refreshing salad, and papaya a delicious dessert.

SHELTER

Jungle shelters are used to protect personnel and equipment from the harsh elements of the jungle. Shelters are necessary while sleeping, planning operations, and protecting sensitive equipment.

When selecting shelter, leaders should:

- **Choose high ground, away from swamps and dry river beds**
- **Avoid trails, game tracks, or villages**

NAVIGATION

Navigation in thick jungle areas is difficult even for the most experienced navigators. Soldiers navigating in the jungle must use various aids. The compass is an obvious aid, but a soldier would never be able to move very fast in the jungle if he had to constantly move along a magnetic azimuth. Movement along a terrain feature, such as a ridgeline, is easier but can be extremely dangerous when establishing a pattern of consistency. A soldier must trust the compass, map, and pace count. A soldier should not keep his eyes riveted on the compass; however, it should be used as a check.

The shadows caused by the sun are an easily observed and accurate aid to direction. Allowances must be made for the gradual displacement of the shadows as the sun moves across the sky.

Other aids to maintaining direction include prominent objects, the course of rivers, prevailing winds, the stars, and the moon.

OBSERVATION

All movements of animals and men are marked by tracks and signs. Soldiers must learn to read signs left in soft ground, in streambeds, on roads and trails, and near watering places and salt licks. Animals seldom move without a reason; a few fresh tracks supply information about their maker, his direction, and probable intentions.

Animals avoid man. The animals, their tracks, and their behavior can reveal whether or not men are in the area. Jungle fighters can listen to the cries of animals and learn to recognize their alarm calls.

The ability to track and to recognize signs in the jungle are valuable skills. Throughout the soldier's time in the jungle, he should practice these skills.

CLOTHING AND EQUIPMENT

Before deploying for jungle operations, troops are issued special uniforms and equipment. Some of these items are:

JUNGLE FATIGUES

These fatigues are lighter and faster drying than standard fatigues. To provide the best ventilation, the uniform should fit loosely. It should never be starched.

JUNGLE BOOTS

These boots are lighter and faster drying than all-leather boots. Their cleated soles will maintain footing on steep, slippery slopes. The ventilating insoles should be washed in warm, soapy water when the situation allows.

INSECT (MOSQUITO) BAR

The insect (mosquito) bar or net should be used any time soldiers sleep in the jungle. Even if conditions do not allow a shelter, the bar can be hung inside the fighting position or from trees or brush. No part of the body should touch the insect net when it is hung, because mosquitoes can bite through the netting. The bar should be tucked or laid loosely, not staked down. Although this piece of equipment is very light, it can be bulky if not folded properly. It should be folded inside the poncho as tightly as possible.

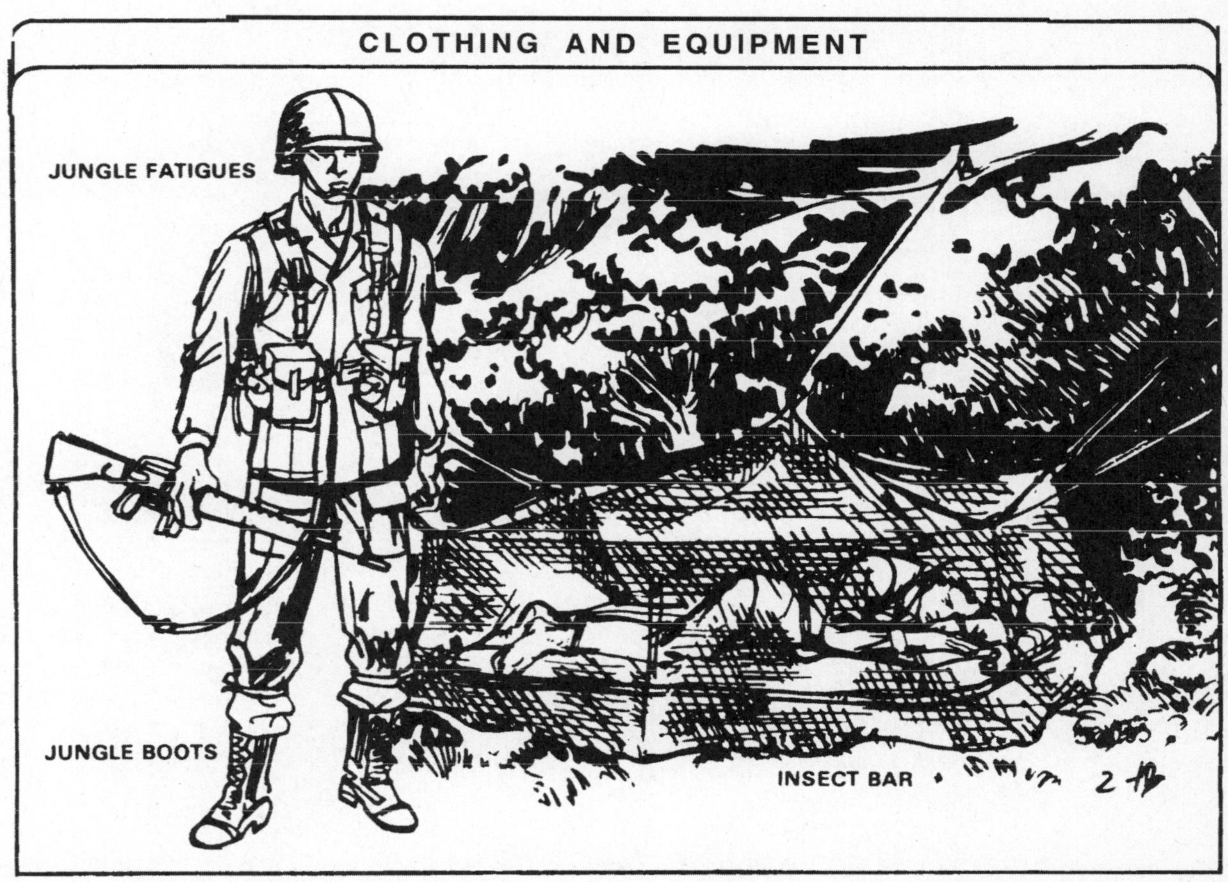

CHAPTER 3

Preparation and Training to Deploy to Jungle Areas

SECTION I. GENERAL

Chapters 1 and 2 describe the jungle environment. Since many soldiers are unaccustomed to such an environment, they must make preparations before conducting jungle operations.

This chapter lists the factors to be considered when preparing for jungle operations and presents training tips for conducting jungle training.

SECTION II. FACTORS TO BE CONSIDERED WHEN PREPARING FOR JUNGLE OPERATIONS

When a unit is alerted for training or actual combat operations in a jungle environment, the commander must first consider the following:

- Where will the unit be training or operating?
- What are the climatic and terrain conditions of the objective area?
- How much time does the unit have to prepare?
- What available training areas have climate and terrain resembling the objective area?
- What type operations are to be conducted—conventional or counter-guerrilla?
- Will the unit be taking its own equipment?
- Does any of the unit's equipment require modification (including camouflage painting)?
- What special equipment does the unit require?
- Does the unit have any jungle warfare instructors, soldiers with jungle experience, or linguists?
- What training assistance is available? Outside instructors? Training aids?
- Does higher headquarters have special standing operating procedures (SOP) for jungle war?
- Are all soldiers physically fit?
- What information is available about the enemy?
- What information is available about local civilians and allied forces in the objective area?

Once these questions have been answered, the commander can develop a program to prepare his unit to operate in the jungle.

The idea that a unit is technically and tactically proficient is only a small part of a unit's preparation. Emphasis should be placed on the mental, physical, and psychological aspects of operating in a jungle environment. The key to overcoming these problems lies with the unit chain of command in their efforts to develop a "will to win" as well as "will to train to win."

SECTION III. TRAINING TIPS

Units committed to jungle operations may have to fight as soon as they arrive in the operational area. Commanders must make the best use of the preparation time available. Measures which commanders should consider include:

Making use of time in garrison. Certain jungle subjects can be taught using classroom instruction. This training should begin as soon as possible, so that time in jungle training areas can be devoted to more advanced techniques.

Making use of local training areas. Although these training areas may not resemble jungle terrain, some jungle techniques can be introduced in them. This will provide a training base which can be expanded when the unit deploys to its jungle training or operational areas. In addition, physical training should begin in the local training area as early as possible before deployment.

Integrating individual training into unit training exercises. Rather than devote field training time to the individual skills required to live in the jungle, these skills should be introduced early in classes, and then practiced during unit training exercises.

The following lists can be used as a guide to subjects that should be covered:

INDIVIDUAL TRAINING

Common Subjects:

- Jungle environment and acclimation
- Living in the jungle
- Survival, evasion, and escape
- Camouflage and concealment
- Tracking
- Operational area orientation
- Jungle navigation
- Equipment recognition
- Enemy orientation
- Physical conditioning

Staff and Leader Subjects:

- Jungle maintenance and supply techniques
- Jungle terrain appreciation
- Enemy order of battle and tactics
- Airmobile techniques

Specialist Subjects:

- Language
- Demolitions
- Field expedient antennas
- Medevac techniques

UNIT TRAINING

- Movement
- Obstacles and Barriers
- Scouting, Surveillance, Patrolling, and Tracking
- Air Defense
- Adjustment and Conduct of Fires
- Immediate Action Drill
- Communications
- Jungle Operations:
  - Ambush/counterambush
  - Raid
  - Attack
  - Defense
  - Infiltration
  - Airmobile operations
  - Waterborne operations
  - River crossing
  - Road clearing

FIRE TEAM AND CREWMEMBERS

- Identification and Marking of Mines and Booby-traps
- Working with Helicopters
- Weapons Training

ACCLIMATION

The first priority in preparation for jungle warfare is acclimation (getting accustomed to jungle climate). Troops who are not conditioned properly will not perform jungle warfare tasks reliably. Different people become acclimated to hot weather at different rates, but the following methods can be used in most units.

Exercise is the best method for acclimation, because troops in good physical condition will adapt easily to new climates. A 7- to 14-day conditioning period should be sufficient for most soldiers. Exercises should be moderately strenuous at the beginning, and become more demanding each day. Troops from warm climates will adapt faster than troops deploying from colder climates. Physical training in heated gymnasiums prior to deployment will also ease the acclimation process.

Leaders must be alert for symptoms of heat disorders during the acclimation period.

SURVIVAL, EVASION, AND ESCAPE

Convincing a soldier that he will survive alone in the jungle will go a long way in building his self-confidence. *The Ultimate Guide to U.S. Army Survival Skills, Tactics, and Techniques* contains details on survival, evasion, and escape training.

SWIMMING

Swimming is also a vital skill for the jungle fighter. Falling into a jungle pool or river can be a terrible experience, especially for a nonswimmer. All troops should be "drown proofed." Units should identify their strong swimmers for lifeguard training and other more difficult swimming tasks.

CAMOUFLAGE AND CONCEALMENT

Training to conceal soldiers and equipment from ground and air observation is equally important to combat, combat support, and combat service support units. Proper use of camouflage will help to make up for an enemy's superior knowledge of the jungle area.

JUNGLE LIVING

Following a short period of classroom instruction, soldiers should experience jungle living conditions in the field. This training can be incorporated into other unit training.

Subjects which should be stressed include:

- **Heat disorders**
- **Survival**
- **First aid**
- **Health, hygiene, and field sanitation**
- **Proper wearing of clothing**
- **Use of equipment in a jungle environment**
- **Prevention and treatment of snakebites and insect bites**

During this period of training, use of garrison facilities should be kept to a minimum. Supplies should be brought to the field rather than the unit returning to the rear for them. Soldiers should learn to live without unnecessary personal comforts.

Land navigation should be practiced using jungle movement techniques. (*See* chapter 6).

TARGET AREA ORIENTATION

Classes on the host country should stress those facts which apply to operations.

Subjects could include:

- **Terrain appreciation**
- **Climate**
- **Population and culture**
- **Language (phrase books may be issued)**
- **Road, railroad, and canal system**
- **Standards of conduct for US Army personnel**
- **Allied armed forces**
- **Reasons for US involvement**

JUNGLE TACTICS

Chapter 5 describes tactics common to jungle fighting. These tactics should be taught first to leaders down to squad level. The leaders then train their own units. Stress should be placed on small unit tactics and operations with Army aviation. Since night operations, especially ambushes, are common in jungle fighting, units should emphasize night training.

MOVEMENT

Units should train in tactical marches.

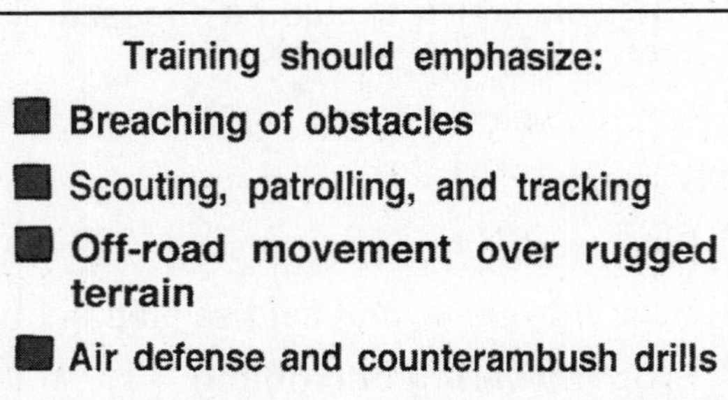

Training should emphasize:

- **Breaching of obstacles**
- **Scouting, patrolling, and tracking**
- **Off-road movement over rugged terrain**
- **Air defense and counterambush drills**

WEAPONS TRAINING

Most jungle fighting takes place at close range. Soldiers should be trained in "quick fire," as outlined in *chapter 8, FM 23-9* Advanced training should be conducted on a "jungle range." On this range, soldiers move down a trail and engage pop-up and moving targets which appear suddenly at close range. Targets are operated by an assistant on signals from a lane grader. Targets should be exposed for 3 to 6 seconds. Only 2 or 3 rounds should be fired at each target. At a later stage, boobytraps and obstacles can be emplaced on the trail.

INTELLIGENCE

Soldiers should be trained in specific intelligence subjects.

These include:

- Enemy organization and tactics
- Equipment recognition
- National markings
- Sound or signature recognition

This last subject is particularly important in jungle operations, because soldiers will more often hear weapons firing than see them. If captured enemy weapons and equipment are available, they should be used as aids in this training.

MAINTENANCE AND LOGISTICS

Operators need to learn techniques to keep their equipment operational in the jungle environment.

Subjects to be covered include:

- Effects of climate on equipment
- Jungle operational techniques
- Preventive maintenance
- Recovery and repair techniques

Staff members and leaders should receive familiarization training on these techniques in order to supervise the operators. In addition, staff and leaders should learn those special supply requirements and procedures in the operational area. They should also be familiar with the capabilities of those logistical units supporting the force.

CHAPTER 4

The Threat in Jungle Areas

SECTION I. GENERAL

The jungle is an environment which stretches in a broad belt around the tropical areas of the world. Each of these areas has its own military, political, and economic conditions. As a result, it is impossible to describe one threat which applies to all jungle areas. Potential enemies which U.S. forces might face in the jungle run the spectrum from lightly armed guerrillas all the way to conventional forces.

This chapter describes the main features of guerrilla and conventional forces as they are found in the jungle, and briefly outlines the types of potential threat forces in various jungle regions.

SECTION II. GUERRILLA FORCES

WHAT GUERRILLAS ARE

Guerrillas are irregular forces. They normally constitute the military faction of a political resistance or a subversive movement. These forces engage in unconventional operations in order to undermine the power of an established government or to take political control away from other factions. Their goal is normally to establish a new government, often according to a radical political philosophy.

The basic guerrilla organization is a three- to five-man cell. These cells are capable of independent action. They also can be brought together for larger operations and dispersed later. Guerrillas are organized into cells for two reasons. One is for security. The fewer the people who can identify members of a guerrilla force, the better the chances are that it will survive. The second reason is for support. Guerrillas must live off the land to a large degree, and small cells are easier to support in this manner.

HOW GUERRILLAS FIGHT

Guerrillas are usually weaker than conventional forces in terms of total resources. For that reason, guerrillas will not attempt to overwhelm large units of their opponents in combat. They will instead try to inflict as much damage as possible in lightning actions, withdrawing before the opposing forces can react. Guerrillas are most effective when they strike widely separated targets over a long period of time. This type of action will confuse, demoralize, and frustrate their opponents.

Typical missions which guerrillas conduct to accomplish their goals include:

- **Destroying or damaging vital installations, equipment, or supplies**
- **Capturing supplies, equipment, or key governmental or military personnel**
- **Diverting government forces from other operations**
- **Creating confusion and weakening government morale**

These missions are not normally accomplished by the use of conventional attacks and defenses. Instead, guerrillas rely on speed, surprise, and security. Guerrilla operations include raids, ambushes, mining and boobytrapping, and sniping.

Targets are selected by the guerrilla based on an analysis of how much the elimination of the target will disrupt the government, what the effect on the populace will be, the risk of being killed or captured, and the amount of weapons or supplies which can be seized. This analysis calls for timely intelligence, which is gained by active patrolling.

The retention of the initiative is the key to success in guerrilla operations. Guerrillas rely on their ability to strike where they are least expected, at points where the government forces are least prepared. If the guerrillas lose the initiative, and are forced to react to the operations of conventional forces, their effectiveness is greatly reduced.

Guerrillas are not normally organized or equipped for stand-and-fight type defensive operations. They prefer to defend themselves by moving, by dispersing into small groups, or by diverting the opponent's attention while they withdraw. Whenever possible, these operations are accomplished by offensive operations against the opponent's flank or rear. If the government forces persist in their attack, the guerrillas are prepared to disengage to keep their freedom of action. If forced to disperse into small groups, the guerrilla forces become less effective until they regroup to resume offensive operations.

One of the most important needs of guerrilla forces is support. This support can come from a number of sources. Food, for example, can be stolen or supplied by political sympathizers. Weapons can be gathered from raids on government installations. A foreign power may provide secret training, and shipments of food, weapons, ammunition, and equipment. If the guerrillas can be cut off from these sources of support, they will be much less effective.

To protect their operations, jungle guerrillas will normally establish bases from which they can operate. These bases will be in remote areas. The bases will be secured by a combination of guerrilla outposts and by a grapevine intelligence network established by political sympathizers. Although they may be difficult to find, there will normally be concealed routes into the bases, from which the guerrillas have access to their targets and sources of support.

GUERRILLA STRENGTHS AND WEAKNESSES

Guerrillas operate most effectively in countries where the people are discontented with government policies. If the people are apathetic or passively hostile to their government, the guerrillas will seek to develop this feeling into a popular base of support. If no such feeling exists among the people, it will be much harder for guerrillas to set up operations.

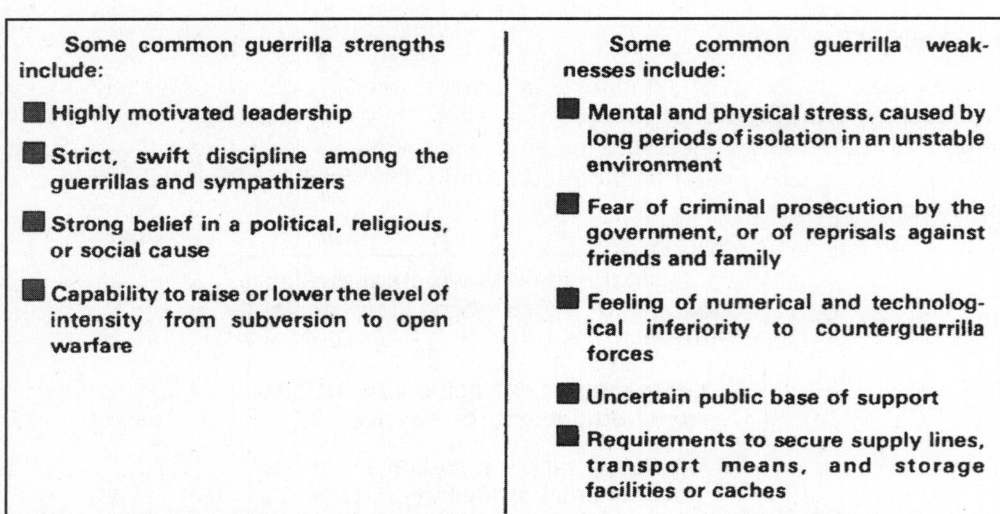

Some common guerrilla strengths include:

- Highly motivated leadership
- Strict, swift discipline among the guerrillas and sympathizers
- Strong belief in a political, religious, or social cause
- Capability to raise or lower the level of intensity from subversion to open warfare

Some common guerrilla weaknesses include:

- Mental and physical stress, caused by long periods of isolation in an unstable environment
- Fear of criminal prosecution by the government, or of reprisals against friends and family
- Feeling of numerical and technological inferiority to counterguerrilla forces
- Uncertain public base of support
- Requirements to secure supply lines, transport means, and storage facilities or caches

SECTION III. CONVENTIONAL FORCES

TYPES OF CONVENTIONAL FORCES IN THE JUNGLE

Conventional forces committed to jungle operations can perform any one of a number of missions. The lowest level of involvement is the use of conventional forces to advise and assist native guerrilla or paramilitary forces, teaching them either how to fight or how to operate sophisticated equipment. A higher level of involvement is the use of conventional forces as a military cadre in units which are composed of native forces. Finally, the highest level of involvement is the operation of conventional forces in a conventional role, fighting major battles in the jungle.

Conventional jungle enemies may come from a number of places. It is possible that U.S. forces committed to jungle operations will fight native conventional forces. It is also possible that U.S. forces will fight conventional forces brought in from a sponsoring hostile power. In either case, most potential jungle enemies are infantry forces, supported with artillery, mortars, and armored vehicles, organized along the lines of Soviet forces. These forces may also have a capability to conduct tactical air (TACAIR) operations and nuclear, biological, chemical (NBC) warfare. They may be equipped with weapons and equipment that are a generation or two older than those found in more modern armies.

HOW CONVENTIONAL FORCES FIGHT IN THE JUNGLE

The way in which a potential conventional threat army fights in the jungle depends on the terrain, the combat experience of that army, and the degree to which it models itself after the forces of a sponsoring power.

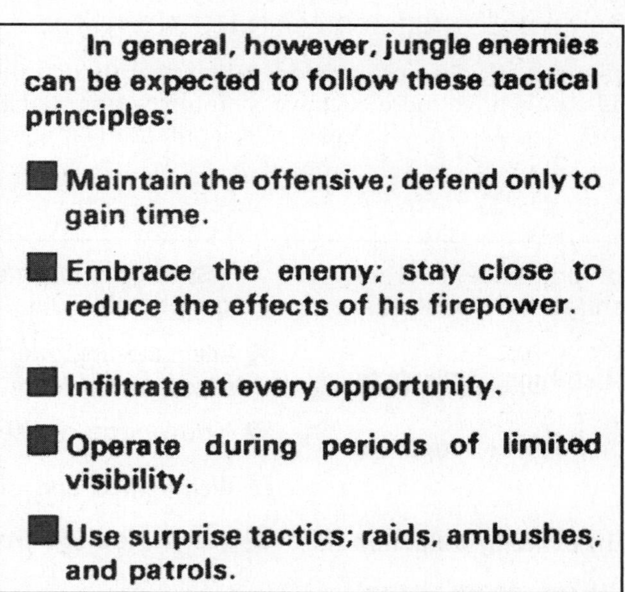

In general, however, jungle enemies can be expected to follow these tactical principles:

- **Maintain the offensive; defend only to gain time.**
- **Embrace the enemy; stay close to reduce the effects of his firepower.**
- **Infiltrate at every opportunity.**
- **Operate during periods of limited visibility.**
- **Use surprise tactics; raids, ambushes, and patrols.**

A jungle enemy can be expected to be skilled in the art of camouflage, the chief means he has to evade his opponent's firepower. Camouflage will be for him a way of life. He will probably use bunkers and tunnels as protective survival measures. To slow opposing forces, he may use obstacles, mines, and boobytraps. He will move on covered and concealed routes, using darkness to conceal most of his operations. He will probably depend heavily on streams and rivers to provide concealed routes of movement and drinking water.

He can be expected to remove all intelligence indicators from the battlefield. He will go to great lengths to remove his dead, wounded, weapons, and even expended cartridges from the battlefield. He will try to leave no information relating to order of battle, strength, dispositions, or intentions.

> *"We captured numerous enemy documents which either condemned or commended certain units for the police of the battle field."*
>
> —Report, 25th Infantry Division, Kontum Province, Republic of Vietnam

Jungle enemies have also used deception means, such as explosive bullets and firecrackers, to mislead U.S. units as to the size and disposition of the forces opposing them. Communications deception and jamming have also been used by jungle enemies against opponents.

Since the U.S. Army is noted for employing an abundance of firepower, jungle enemies in the past have preferred to engage U.S. units at extremely close range. At times, it is impossible for U.S. commanders to use their supporting indirect fires without taking friendly casualties. The specific effects that this technique has on offensive and defensive operations will be discussed later. In general, however, the U.S. ground commander must operate in such a manner that all his fire support can always be used effectively.

Jungle enemies can be expected to train hard to use the jungle to their advantage. In the offense, for example, they use the thick foliage to infiltrate positions and eliminate command posts (CP), key weapons, and vital facilities. These operations are conducted to take away their opponent's advantages in command and control, fire support, and logistical means. The intent is to put their forces on a more equal footing with their opponents. This situation can be exploited by a force with superior knowledge of the terrain.

When forced to defend, these forces will quite often prepare elaborate defensive positions, well camouflaged and concealed. In addition, defenders may use snipers, boobytraps, and ambushes to delay, create a sense of confusion and insecurity, and cause the attacker to surrender the initiative.

It is also possible that U.S. forces committed to jungle operations will fight Warsaw Pact forces, probably members of airborne divisions. Although these troops will have newer and more sophisticated weapons than some of the troops native to jungle areas, *they probably will not be familiar with the local terrain and may not be well trained in jungle operations.*

STRENGTHS AND WEAKNESSES OF CONVENTIONAL JUNGLE ENEMIES

Much of a conventional jungle enemy's effectiveness depends on familiarity with the terrain. In general, this means that armies native to a battlefield area will be more effective than forces from outside. Even if these outside forces have a greater amount of firepower than the native forces, the lack of terrain familiarity may limit their ability to use that firepower.

Weaknesses of potential conventional jungle enemies will probably include:

- Larger units, much more difficult to
- Bigger targets for close-air support or artillery
- More difficulty in evading detection
- Less information from local sympathizers

Strengths of potential conventional jungle enemies will probably include:

- Adequate firepower for conventional attacks and defense
- Knowledge of the terrain and area
- Well-trained and disciplined soldiers
- Independence from local support

HOW THE THREAT DEFENDS

The threat defense is a temporary measure, adopted only when necessary. This does not imply, however, that the threat defense consists of half measures or that he is unskilled in defense techniques. Jungle enemies will use every trick possible to survive against massive amounts of firepower. His defense will be cleverly and carefully prepared.

A typical jungle enemy defensive position consists of a complex series of earth and timber bunkers, spider holes, and tunnels. These are positioned to achieve mutual support. Bunkers are built low to make them more difficult to see and engage by fire. They are well camouflaged—even the fields-of-fire may be cut from the waist down, so that they will be unnoticeable to a standing man. Weapons positions are planned to provide interlocking fires—lethal even during limited visibility. Boobytraps and obstacles are integrated into the defense to slow, demoralize, and confuse the attacker.

The jungle threat's concept of the defense is to trap the attacker by allowing him to move into prepared fields-of-fire. Fire is opened at extremely close range, sometimes at 50 meters or less. This is done for two reasons—first, to bring fires to bear from all sides, and, second, to force the attacker to remove himself before he can call for supporting fires.

While the key part of the jungle threat's defense is automatic weapons positions in bunkers, the enemy will also put snipers in the trees. In this way, the attacker cannot devote his full attention to the bunkers, because he must also deal with the snipers.

If the attacker is too strong, the jungle threat will attempt to withdraw over routes that have been planned and scouted to make the withdrawal as rapid as possible. Stay-behind ambushes, snipers, mines, and obstacles are used to slow the attacker.

HOW THE CONVENTIONAL ENEMY ATTACKS

Attack is the preferred form of combat for potential jungle enemies. Because most of these forces expect to have a disadvantage in firepower and technology when fighting U.S. forces, most of them have developed special techniques to help make up the difference through surprise. They may, for example, probe a defensive position until the defender reveals the location of his key weapons. These weapons are then eliminated by infiltrators before the main attack. They may use firecrackers to create a diversion, drawing the defender's fire and deceiving him as to the size of the attacking force. They may infiltrate the defense to eliminate command posts, mortars, or artillery units.

> *"Decoy the Americans from one direction by smoke, firing, or shouting. Then attack him from an unexpected direction."*
>
> —Captured Japanese Document, World War II

Threat units will avoid attacking prepared defenses when possible. They prefer to attack a weak point, using the jungle, weather, and their own special training as much as possible. Sapper squads are specially trained to infiltrate minefields and obstacles in order to neutralize key positions or create a gap in the defense. The enemy may also isolate a position, so that their opponents will be tied down in trying to relieve it, or they may conduct raids to disrupt operations and lower the defender's morale. Darkness, poor weather, and rough terrain will be used to conceal these operations.

A commander should never assume that any jungle area is impassable to a well-trained jungle enemy. Experience has shown that such enemies are very adept at using extremely difficult terrain effectively as avenues of approach.

> *"Use fog and rain to catch the Americans off guard. Make an assault suddenly, from positions which the Americans believe unapproachable, such as cliffs, rivers, and jungles."*
>
> —Captured Japanese Document, World War II

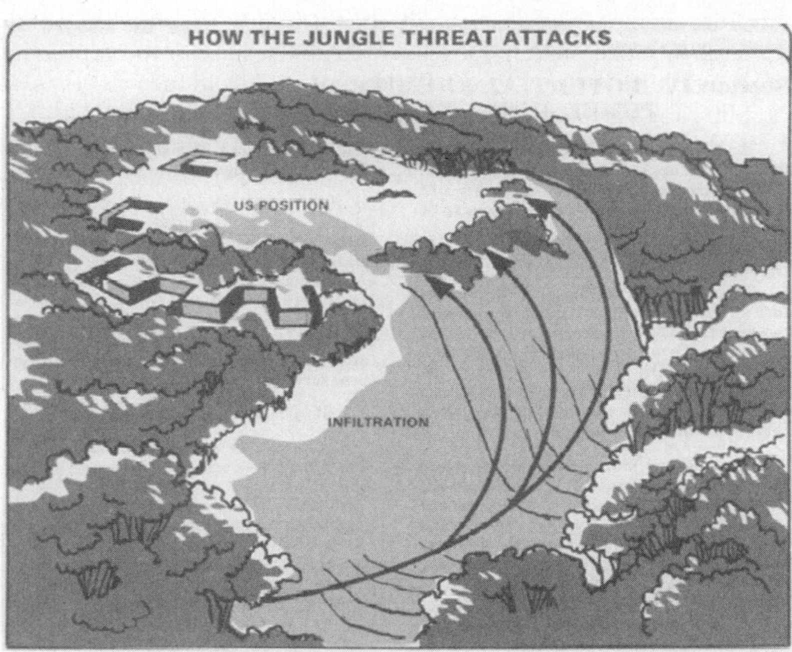

Although the jungle enemy attacks swiftly, his attacks are planned in minute detail. If he is allowed to attack according to plan, the jungle enemy is an effective force. If the defender can interrupt even a minor part of the plan, the enemy will have difficulty in adjusting, and the attack will probably fail. This aspect of enemy operations places a high premium on the struggle for the initiative at all levels.

If the defending force can be pushed out of its positions and forced to retreat, the jungle enemy will probably make every effort to maintain contact through pursuit. He will harass the rear guard, at the same time sending forces to outrun and cut off the retreating force. He will then try to destroy the retreating force by ambush or encirclement.

SECTION IV. POTENTIAL ENEMIES IN THREE JUNGLE REGIONS

It is impossible to describe one jungle threat which applies to all areas of the world. There are, however, certain characteristics of potential threat forces that are peculiar to specific jungle regions.

LATIN AMERICA

The most likely threat the U.S. forces may face in Latin American jungles are insurgent movements. These movements aim at the overthrow of a wealthy ruling class to install a new regime. The U.S. is often viewed by the insurgents as an ally of the government, and U.S. facilities and institutions are often targets for these movements.

The military faction of these insurgent movements consists of guerrilla forces similar to those described earlier. They are organized into small cells, are lightly armed, and are capable of concentrating for acts against major facilities and then dispersing after the operation. Although their ultimate objective will often be the establishment of control over the urban areas, they may use the jungle to provide a concealed and secure base of operations. The support of the local people is very important to their survival.

At the time U.S. forces are committed to fight in Latin American areas, guerrilla forces are likely to be augmented with military aid and personnel from other sponsoring countries in the region. These forces may perform any one of a number of roles: advisors, guerrilla cadre, or limited conventional combat. Logistical and intelligence support may also come from these forces.

SUBSAHARAN AFRICA

The conflicts in this region since World War II have been waged by insurgent groups against perceived vestiges of colonialism or imperialism. Most of these colonialist and imperialist institutions are connected in the minds of the insurgents with the Western European powers. As a result, the instability in some areas of this region has provided a tempting target for provocation. To make matters more complicated, many of the conflicting factions are also struggling among themselves, due to political or ancient tribal differences. This in turn creates even more regional turmoil, and an even greater vulnerability for exploitation.

Conflicting factions in Subsaharan Africa consist primarily of guerrilla groups. These guerrillas, however, are often more heavily armed than Latin American guerrillas for two reasons. First, these groups have mortars, artillery, and recoilless weapons from national army formations which have been defeated or disbanded. Second, external powers have backed their favorite factions by supplying arms, ammunition, and equipment. For the most part, these guerrillas subsist by acquiring food and supplies from the countryside.

Foreign involvement in these guerrilla movements has consisted of advisors and cadre from sponsoring nations. Should U.S. forces ever fight in this region, it is likely that they will encounter troops foreign to the nation. In addition, there is also a possibility that Warsaw Pact troops, primarily airborne or tactical aviation units, would be committed to such a region to fight U.S. troops.

SOUTHEAST ASIA

In many respects, the potential threat array in Southeast Asia is the most complicated of any jungle region. There are active guerrilla movements in most Southeast Asian countries as well as tribal and cultural conflicts. There is a good possibility of foreign support or intervention.

The unique development in this region has been the rise of a regional power. Since the end of U.S. involvement in Southeast Asia, this power has developed a potent conventional force, using equipment captured from the U.S. and its allies or supplied by communist countries. More than any other potential threat native in a jungle region, it possesses the ability for sustained conventional operations against any U.S. forces which might be deployed in the area. Its capabilities span the range from clandestine guerrilla operations to large-scale conventional attacks, supported by tanks, motorized units, artillery, and aviation.

Because there are already strong forces in this region, the probability of involvement of large numbers of world power forces is not great. There is a good possibility, however, that U.S. troops committed in these areas might encounter weapons and equipment supplied by a world power. They might also encounter advisors from world powers that instruct and aid the native forces in the use of sophisticated equipment.

Finally, of all the regions discussed thus far, the chemical warfare threat will probably be greatest for U.S. forces conducting operations in Southeast Asia.

SECTION V. WEAPONS USED BY POTENTIAL JUNGLE ENEMIES

Although potential jungle enemy forces vary widely from region to region, there are certain types of weapons which are commonly found in jungle countries. U.S. forces should become familiar with these basic types of weapons in order to be able to recognize them on the jungle battlefield. They should also have a basic knowledge of the weapons' characteristics and know where the weapons are found in typical communist forces organizations.

Although guerrilla forces do not have the same type of organizational structure as conventional forces, they too will probably carry many of these weapons.

RIFLE PLATOON

The threat rifle platoon normally has three rifle squads of 6 to 10 men each. Weapons found in the platoon will include small arms, one to three light machineguns, and one to three grenade launchers. Typical weapons include:

AKM ASSAULT RIFLE

Recognition features are the pistol grip, the curved-box magazine, and the "underslung" barrel without a bipod. The AKM fires the M-1943 7.62-mm cartridge, also used in the SKS, RPD, and RPK. The AKM also comes with a metal folding stock.

CHARACTERISTICS OF AKM

Caliber and ammo	7.62 mm, M-1943
Cyclic rate of fire	600 rpm
Practical rate of fire:	
auto	100 rpm
semi	40 rpm
Magazine capacity	30 rounds
Effective range	400 m

AK-74 ASSAULT RIFLE

A new, small caliber version of the tried-and-proven AKM which takes advantage of modern ammunition technology. Two models are being produced: the standard stock AK-74 and the folding stock AKS-74.

CHARACTERISTICS OF AK-74

Caliber	5.45 mm
Ammunition	high-velocity ball (somewhat similar to US M16 rd)
Mode of fire	automatic and semiautomatic
Cyclic rate of fire	650 rpm
Maximum effective range	350 m

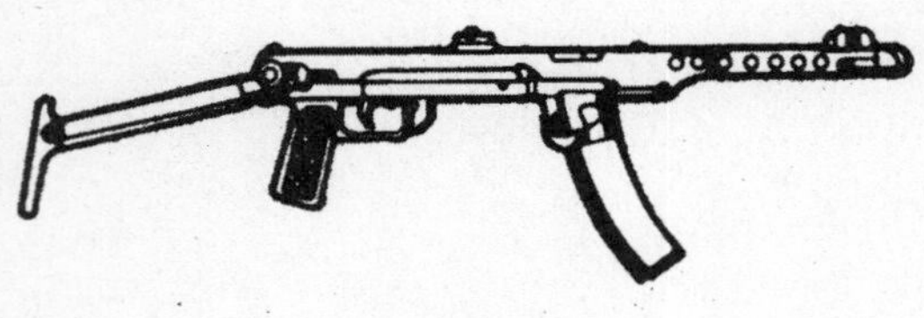

PPS SUBMACHINEGUN

The PPS is a fully automatic weapon. It has a hinged stock which folds up and forward. It also has a compensator welded on front of the barrel jacket. It fires the 7.62-mm M-1930 "P" ammunition from a curved-box magazine.

CHARACTERISTICS OF PPS

Cyclic rate of fire	650 rpm
Practical rate of fire	100 rpm
Magazine capacity	35 rounds
Effective range	200 m

RIFLE PLATOON CONTINUED

SKS CARBINE

This light, shoulder-fired weapon is recognized by a characteristic folding bayonet, a sporting rifle appearance, and triangular portion of the magazine which extends through the lower side of the stock, just forward of the trigger guard.

CHARACTERISTICS OF SKS

Caliber and ammo	7.62 mm, M-1943
Operation	gas, semiautomatic
Magazine capacity	10 rounds
Effective range	400 m

M-1890/1930 SNIPER RIFLE

The M-1890/1930 sniper rifle is a Soviet model fielded during World War II. It is still a standard weapon in many satellite armies. The M-1890/1930 mounts a telescopic sight. This sight is similar to the sight used on US hunting rifles.

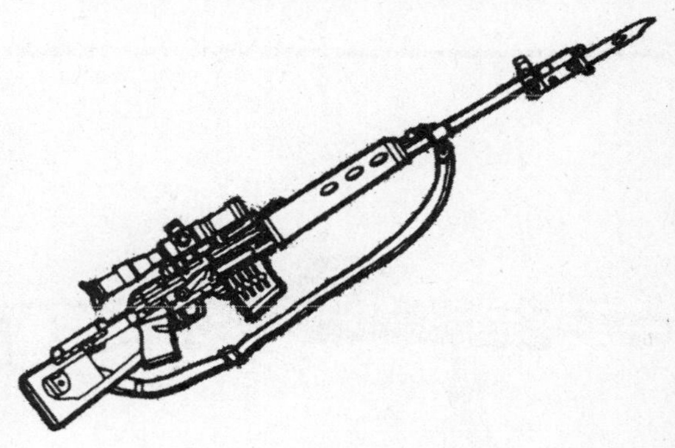

CHARACTERISTICS OF M-1890/1930

Caliber and ammo	7.62 mm, M-1908
Operation	turning bolt
Magazine capacity	5 rounds
Effective range	800 m
Maximum range	1,300 m

RPG-2 GRENADE LAUNCHER

The RPG-2 recoilless antitank rocket is fired from the shoulder. Recognition features are the warhead of the projectile which is larger than the launching tube, and the launcher itself, which is long, slender, and has a pistol grip handle and two sights.

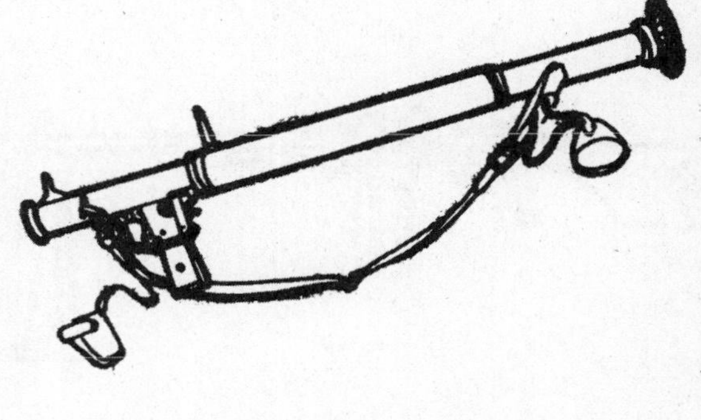

CHARACTERISTICS OF RPG-2

Caliber of tube	40 mm (1.58 in)
Caliber of projectile	82 mm (3.2 in)
Effective range	100 m
Rate of fire	4 to 6 rpm

RIFLE PLATOON CONTINUED

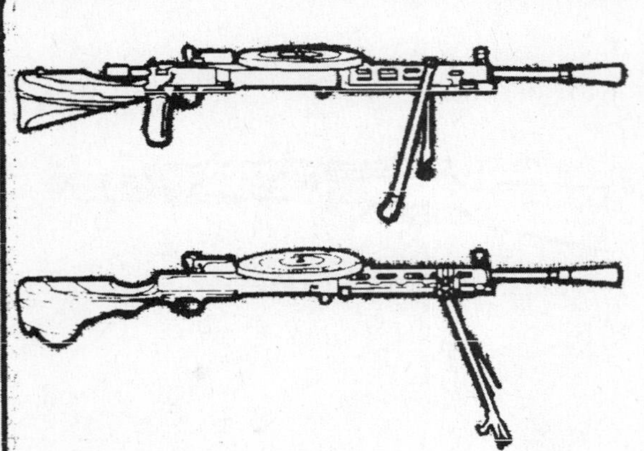

DPM AND DP LIGHT MACHINEGUNS

These machineguns can be recognized by the pan-type drum magazine on top of the receiver, slotted barrel casing, wooden stock with cheek rest, the fixed bipod, and flash suppressor. The DPM has a pistol grip and an operating-rod-spring housing projecting to the rear of the receiver. The DP has no pistol grip, and the operating-rod-spring housing does not project to the rear of the receiver.

CHARACTERISTICS OF DPM/DP LMG

Caliber and ammo	7.62 mm, M-1908
Cyclic rate of fire	550 rpm
Practical rate of fire	80 rpm
Magazine capacity	47 rounds
Effective range	800 m

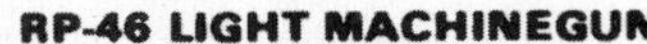

RP-46 LIGHT MACHINEGUN

The RP-46 was developed from the DP series. It has a detachable belt-feed mechanism that can be replaced by a DP type drum-feed mechanism. It is distinguishable from the DP and DPM by its carrying handle and heavier, thicker barrel.

CHARACTERISTICS OF RP-46

Caliber and ammo	7.62 mm, M-1980
Cyclic rate of fire	600 rpm
Practical rate of fire	230 to 250 rpm
Magazine capacity	200- or 250-round belt
Effective range	800 m

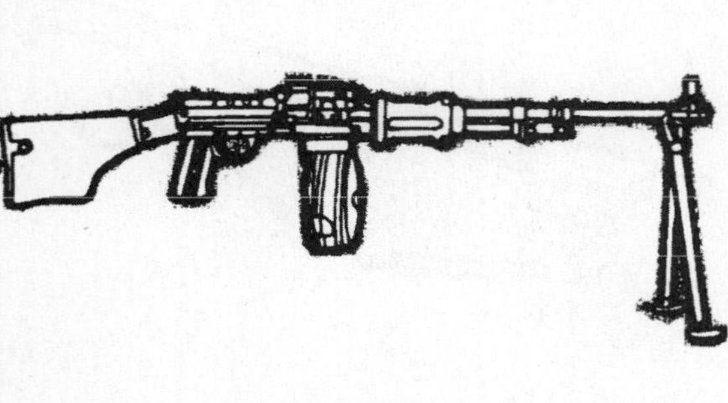

RPD LIGHT MACHINEGUN

The RPD uses the same ammunition as the AK-47 rifle. It has a drum (which houses a metallic link belt), a pistol grip, a permanently attached bipod, and an upper hand-guard which is flared at the ends. The RPD can fire full automatic only and has a chrome-plated barrel.

CHARACTERISTICS OF RPD

Caliber and ammo	7.62 mm, M-1943
Cyclic rate of fire	650 rpm
Practical rate of fire	150 rpm
Magazine capacity	100-round belt in drum
Effective range	800 m

RIFLE COMPANY

The rifle company usually has three rifle platoons and a mortar platoon with two or three 60-mm mortars.

60-MM MORTAR

CHARACTERISTICS OF 60-mm MORTAR

Length of tube	.724 m (28.5 in)
Weight	20.4 kg (45.0 lbs)
Elevation	40 to 85 degrees
Traverse	14 degrees
Maximum range	1,530 m

RIFLE BATTALION

The rifle battalion normally has three rifle companies. It may also have a heavy machinegun company, with 6 to 9 heavy machineguns, and a mortar company with 6 to 12 82-mm mortars.

DshK HEAVY MACHINEGUN

The DshK is used in a ground role, and on tanks and assault guns as an antiaircraft weapon. It has radial cooling fins on the barrel. In the ground role it has a wheeled mount and a shield.

CHARACTERISTICS OF DshK

Caliber	12.7 mm
Cyclic rate of fire	540 to 600 rpm
Practical rate of fire	125 rpm
Feed	50-round belt
Effective range; ground targets	1,500 m
Effective range; air targets	1,000 m

RIFLE BATTALION CONTINUED

82-MM MORTAR

There are three versions of the 82-mm mortar, but the M-1937 is by far the most common. All fire the same ammunition and can also use US 81-mm mortar rounds. (The US 81-mm mortar cannot fire the 82-mm ammunition.) The mortar is disassembled into three-pack loads for transport.

CHARACTERISTICS OF 82-MM MORTAR

Weight, travel position	56 kg (123 lbs)
Barrel length	1.22m (48.03 in)
Elevation	45 to 85 degrees
Traverse	6 degrees
Maximum range	3,040 m
Rate of fire	15 to 25 rpm
Projectile types	HE and smoke
Projectile weight:	
HE	3.3 kg (7.3 lbs)
Smoke	3.67 kg (8.0 lbs)

82-MM RECOILLESS RIFLE/TYPE 65

CHARACTERISTICS OF 82-MM RCLR

Weight	28.2 kg (62 lbs)
Caliber	82 mm
Effective range	450 m
Rate of fire	6 rpm
Ammunition	HEAT

75-MM RCLR

The 75-mm RCLR type 52 is a copy of the old US M20. The type 56 is a further development with the same performance as the type 52, but with a different mounting.

CHARACTERISTICS OF 75-MM RCLR

Length of tube:	
type 52	2.250 m (56.92 in)
type 56	2.280 m (58.16 in)
Weight, firing position:	
type 52	85 kg (187 lbs)
type 56	87 kg (190 lbs)
Rate of fire	10 rpm
Maximum range	6,675 m
Effective range	640 m

DIVISION AND HIGHER

Support from division and higher may include fire from 120-mm mortars, 76-mm guns, 122-mm howitzers, or 122-mm rockets.

120-MM MORTAR M-1938/1943

The 120-mm mortar in firing position looks like the 82-mm mortar but is much larger. It can be trigger-fired or drop-fired. An easily attached transport limber is provided for towing the mortar with a truck or armored personnel carrier. In addition to high explosive rounds, this mortar also fires smoke and incendiary rounds.

CHARACTERISTICS OF 120-MM MORTAR

Length of tube	1.854 m (51.66 in)
Weight in firing position	275 kg (605 lbs)
Elevation	65 to 80 degrees
Traverse	8 degrees
Maximum rate of fire	15 rpm
Maximum range	5,700 m
Weight of projectile: HE	15.4 kg (33.9lbs)

122-MM HOWITZER M-1938 (M-30)

This is a standard divisional artillery piece. The recoil mechanism is in a cradle below the tube, and the recuperator is above the tube.

CHARACTERISTICS OF 122-MM HOWITZER

Length of tube	2.8 m (9.2 ft)
Weight, firing position	2,500 kg (5,500 lbs)
Elevation	-3 to 63.5 degrees
Traverse	49 degrees
Rate of fire	5 to 6 rpm
Maximum range	11,800 m
Weight of projectile: HE	21.8 kg (48.0 lbs)

DIVISION AND HIGHER CONTINUED

122-MM SINGLE TUBE ROCKET LAUNCHER

The Soviet 122-mm rocket can be fired from a single tube launcher, consisting of a shortened BM-21 tube, mounted on a light tripod. The single-fired rocket has less range, but has the same warhead as the version fired from the multiple rocket launcher. The single-fired 122-mm rocket was used extensively in Vietnam; however, currently the BM-21 multiple rocket launcher is the most prevalent.

CHARACTERISTICS OF 122-MM ROCKET LAUNCHER

Length of tube	2.50 m (98 in)
Weight, tube/tripod	21.8/27.7 kg (48.0/60.9 lb)
Height, firing position	1.00 m (39.5 in)
Elevation	-4.5 to 42 degrees
Traverse	14 degrees
Maximum range	11,000 m

THREAT VEHICLES

TYPE 59

The type 59 tank is a Chinese version of the Soviet T-54. The major differences between the type 59 and the T-54 appear to be the type 59's lack of a gun stabilizer and infrared equipment, and the omission of power traverse. Both the gunner and loader have hand-traverse mechanisms. This results in a slow rate of engagement and difficulty in target identification on anything but a flat fire position.

PT-76

The PT-76 is the standard Soviet reconnaissance tank. The suspension of the PT-76 consists of six large, evenly spaced road wheels with no track return rollers. The drive sprocket is at the rear. The turret is circular and has flat sloping sides. The gun tube has a multibaffle or double-baffle muzzle brake. The PT-76 is amphibious. In the water, it is propelled by hydrojets which shoot water through ports in the rear of the tank. The gun fires the same ammunition as the 76-mm divisional gun M-1942 (ZIS-3).

CHAPTER 5

Tactical Operations

SECTION I. GENERAL

There are special techniques which help to insure success in the jungle. These techniques result from the restricted maneuver, slow tempo, close combat, and limited visibility commonly found in the jungle.

Combat in the jungle is characterized by long periods of developing the situation and looking for the enemy, and by short periods of violent, and sometimes unexpected, combat.

To meet these conditions, units must have:

- **Aggressive intelligence-gathering procedures**
- **Disciplined soldiers**
- **Solid SOPS proven in training and updated on a continuous basis**
- **Aggressive and tough-minded leadership**

These four points must be emphasized when a unit is engaged in jungle operations. The need for discipline is evident when one considers the extended periods of looking, often fruitlessly, for the enemy. When contact is made, maximum advantage can only be achieved through aggressive and violent action predicated upon solid SOPs. Aggressive leadership at the small-unit (squad and platoon) level is the one element that ties together the discipline and the training.

CHARACTERISTICS OF THE JUNGLE BATTLEFIELD

The thick foliage and rugged terrain of most jungles limit fields of fire and speed of movement.

The following limitations may restrict fire and movement:

- **Lack of line-of-sight and clearance may prevent visual contact between units, interlocking fires, and the use of tube-launched, optically-tracked, wire-guided missile (TOW) or Dragon missiles.**
- **Tree limbs may block mortars, flame weapons, 40-mm grenades, and hand grenades.**
- **Machineguns may not be able to attain grazing fire.**
- **Adjustment of indirect fire support is difficult due to limited visibility and may have to be accomplished by sound.**
- **Noise conditions differ in the jungle. There are large numbers of animals in jungle areas, and their noise (or lack of it) can give an indication of something out of the norm.**
- **Sounds in the jungle do not carry as far as on the conventional battlefield due to the amount of jungle foliage. The result is that noises are closer than first believed.**
- **Movement through jungle areas is also very difficult because:**

  Heat, thick vegetation, and rugged terrain will tire troops rapidly, especially those carrying heavy weapons or radios.

  A lack of roads will hinder resupply and evacuation.

These terrain characteristics make jungle fighting different from fighting on more open terrain. To be effective jungle fighters, soldiers must learn to use these characteristics to their advantage. Potential jungle enemies train to exploit the jungle; so must the U.S. Army.

CHARACTERISTICS OF JUNGLE OPERATIONS

The aspects of terrain and enemy discussed above result in fewer set-piece battles. Rather than conventional attacks conducted against conventional defenses, jungle battles are more often ambushes, raids, and meeting engagements. Battles are not fought for high ground as frequently as conventional battles. *Orientation is on the enemy rather than on the terrain.* Hills in the jungle are often too thickly vegetated to permit observation and fire, and therefore do not always qualify as key terrain. In the jungle, roads, rivers and streams, fording sites, and landing zones are more likely to be key terrain features.

The frequency of ambushes, raids, and meeting engagements makes it very important that units in the jungle practice immediate action drills. In the jungle firefight, the side which initiates contact and gains fire superiority in the first few seconds will normally have a decisive advantage.

Control

Command and control are difficult in the jungle. The thick foliage allows leaders to see and control only a portion of their units.

To cope with this problem, commanders and leaders must:

- **Plan their operations carefully**
- **Issue mission type orders**
- **Ensure that each soldier understands his part of the mission**

In addition, the thick jungle foliage and heavy monsoon rains often weaken radio signals, making communications difficult. To reduce the effects of the problem, use of the helicopter as a command and control vehicle is recommended. In that the heavy monsoon rains may not allow helicopters to always fly, an alternate means of command and control must be planned for.

Flexibility

While an appreciation of battlefield characteristics, jungle enemies, and characteristics of jungle operations is useful, flexibility is important to any leader involved in jungle operations. Successful operations require an extraordinary command adaptability—sometimes, a departure from orthodox thinking in favor of new and often untried procedures. Soldiers must learn to live *with* the jungle and adapt to its initially apparent disadvantages. Having done this, the unit can concentrate on the use of concealment, covered movement, and surprise.

Security and intelligence

Commanders must stress effective security measures and aggressive intelligence-gathering techniques to prevent being surprised. The key is to give the front-line soldier an appreciation of the things to look for. Food remnants and feces can indicate how long ago an enemy unit occupied an area. Captured documents, equipment, and weapons may provide order of battle information and an idea of the enemy's logistical situation. Even an ammunition crate may yield a lot number and packing date. From this an intelligence specialist may be able to trace the enemy unit's place in the order of battle.

In the past, U.S. forces operating in jungle warfare have generally been augmented by native scouts, attached down to platoon level. These scouts were auxiliaries, paid by the unit they supported from a fund established by higher headquarters for that purpose. Scouts familiar with the terrain and the enemy can be an extremely valuable asset. Local security regulations should provide guidance as to what friendly information can be given to scouts.

Surveillance, target acquisition, and night observation (STANO) devices, especially infrared, starlight scopes, and unattended ground sensors, are quite effective in gathering information about troop movements in the jungle. Radars and photography are not as effective because of the concealment of the foliage.

The local populace is one of the most valuable intelligence sources. Whether hostile, friendly, or indifferent, the people can provide information which, when processed, will help complete the intelligence picture.

Security prevents the enemy from gaining intelligence on U.S. units. Active security measures, such as patrolling and the use of observation posts (OP), helps prevent U.S. units from being ambushed or attacked by surprise. These measures do not lessen the need for passive security. Camouflage and noise and light discipline conceal U.S. forces from enemy observation. To prevent being tracked by the enemy, bivouacs and trails must be policed. Odor discipline is also a security measure. The enemy can follow such odors as heat tabs, cigarette smoke, deodorant, and C rations.

TROOP-LEADING PROCEDURES FOR JUNGLE OPERATIONS

Standing Operating Procedures

A unit's jungle operations SOP should include actions which the unit does on a routine basis or actions that are earned out essentially the same way each time they are done. Examples of such actions include organizing for combat, resupply, bivouac and shelter preparation, movement techniques, and battle drill. Use of SOPs will save planning time.

Planning use of time

A unit planning for jungle combat follows the same planning sequence as in any other type of combat operation. In planning the use of available time, leaders must consider that many tasks in the jungle take more time than the same tasks in other environments. More time must be allowed for movement and security. This means that units may have to begin movements earlier in order to accomplish their missions within a specified time. This may leave less time for planning and preparation.

Inspection

Prior to beginning a misssion, unit leaders should inspect their troops to insure that:

- **They have all their needed equipment**
- **They have no unnecessary equipment**
- **Weapons are cleaned, lubricated, and zeroed**
- **Equipment and weapons are in working order**
- **Everyone understands his job and the unit's SOP**

Control of equipment

Those troops who carry extra equipment should not be allowed to discard it. Captured U.S. equipment has been used by jungle enemies in the past. In Southeast Asia and in the Pacific, recovered equipment was a major source of enemy supply.

Supervision

Supervision must continue throughout the conduct of the operation. As the troops become tired after long periods of marching or digging in, they will tend to get lax and ignore good security habits. This is an especially common trend if they have not been in contact for a few days. Tight supervision is a must to ensure that security patrols and OPs are dispatched and doing their jobs; that troops remain alert; and that fire, noise, and light discipline are not relaxed.

JUNGLE MOVEMENT

Planning and route selection

Before conducting a move in the jungle, leaders should make a map and aerial photograph reconnaissance. This reconnaissance will indicate possible danger areas, obstacles, and roads or clearings suitable for resupply.

In planning the route, leaders should consider the following:

- **Lines of drift, such as ridgelines, are easy to guide on because they avoid streams and gullies and because they are usually less vegetated.**
- **Danger areas, such as streambeds and draws, are usually more thickly vegetated. They offer excellent concealment, but travel along them is slow and difficult.**
- **Roads and trails should be avoided. Although they are easy to move on, they offer little concealment. These are the areas most likely to be under enemy observation. They are easy to ambush and are very likely to be mined or boobytrapped.**

Movement techniques

Units moving in the jungle should normally use the jungle movement technique, but may use traveling overwatch and bounding overwatch when necessary. The file formation should be avoided in all but the most thickly vegetated areas.

To effectively use the jungle movement technique, certain key factors must be understood. They include the following:

- **Only the platoon should employ this movement technique.**
- **The lead fire team of the lead squad is always in a wedge (modified).**
- **The support elements may move with the headquarters element or be attached to a squad(s) depending upon likely threats.**
- **Each squad maintains an azimuth and pace.**
- **Immediate action drill (SOP) is essential.**
- **This technique is most effective during daylight movement.**

This movement technique is basically characterized as a formation of multiple columns which are mutually supporting.

Advantages of the jungle movement technique:	
■ Centralized control. ■ Rapid deployment to maneuver or reinforce. ■ Ease of movement (three routes). ■ 360-degree security during movement and at halts. ■ Multiple navigational aids (three azimuths and pace counts).	■ Flexibility of adjustment during movement (danger areas, choke points). **Disadvantages of the jungle movement technique:** ■ Possibility of loss of contact at major obstacles due to multiple routes. ■ Vulnerability to effectiveness of indirect fire weapons.

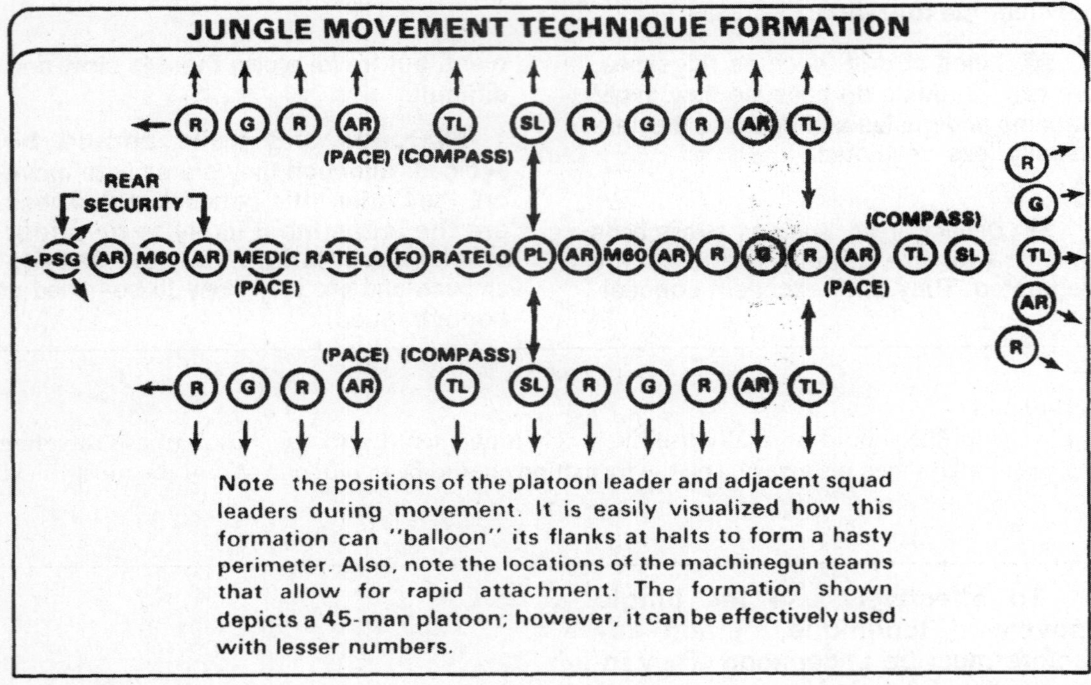

In traveling overwatch, the lead element performs the mission of point security, with troops from the rest of the unit performing rear and flank security. When contact is imminent, the unit moves into bounding overwatch. Bounds, as terrain allows, are normally 50 meters or less.

Security

The thick foliage makes ambush a constant danger. Point, flank, and rear security teams will help keep a force from being ambushed. These teams must be far enough away from the main body that if they make contact the whole force will not be engaged. They should not be so far away, however, that they cannot be supported. These security elements must be alert to signs of the enemy, and should carry as light a load as possible so they are able to maneuver. Security duties should be rotated often to avoid fatigue. Scout dogs may also be used with the security element. These dogs often detect the enemy before he is detected by humans. The jungle heat is hard on them, however, and they must be rested frequently.

If contact is broken between elements or individuals, the rear element should remain in position. Those in front should return to establish contact.

Halts

Units should plan halts on terrain which lends itself to all-round defense. During short halts, soldiers drop to one knee and face outward, their weapons at the ready. If the halt occurs at a trail crossing, security elements are sent out along the trail. The security element remains in place until the unit clears the crossing. During longer halts, units establish a perimeter defense. They run security patrols around their positions, and employ Claymore mines and early warning devices. Before an overnight halt, units should stop while there is still enough daylight to establish a secure perimeter defense, prepare ambushes, and dispatch patrols as necessary. If halted units are separated, connecting patrols should be run periodically to detect enemy infiltration.

SECTION II. RECONNAISSANCE, SURVEILLANCE, AND SECURITY OPERATIONS

RECONNAISSANCE

Reconnaissance operations are always important in jungle warfare. Many offensive operations in the jungle take on the aspects of a reconnaissance operation during their early stages. This is because the success of offense in the jungle depends on ability to find the enemy. The excellent concealment found in the jungle enables the enemy to operate unobserved both by day and night. Extensive patrolling is necessary to obtain information on his locations, strength, and disposition.

Reconnaissance is a responsibility of all leaders during jungle operations. Units with the capability to conduct reconnaissance should conduct frequent short patrols during the conduct of normal missions. These patrols should be coordinated with higher and adjacent units. In some situations, reconnaissance may become the primary objective of a major jungle operation.

Planning for a jungle reconnaissance should be thorough and well coordinated. Coordination with higher and adjacent headquarters will help insure maximum results from each patrol and eliminate duplication of effort. Radio is the primary means used to control reconnaissance operations. Each reconnaissance patrol must be prepared to make contact, develop the situation, and report to its controlling headquarters.

Ground reconnaissance

In the jungle, these operations are accomplished by means of OPs and long- or short-range reconnaissance patrols. The value of OPs is somewhat reduced in the jungle because of the limited visibility. OPs are most effective when used along trails, roads, and streams to detect enemy movement. (Although OPs in other areas may not provide much useful information on the enemy, they still are effective in providing early warning.) Reconnaissance patrols in the jungle are normally squad-size. These patrols move in a manner to take advantage of natural concealment, and avoid becoming engaged with the enemy. The use of helicopters increases the depth behind enemy lines that such patrols can be employed. For further details on reconnaissance patrols, *see section VI.*

Visual reconnaissance

From the air, key terrain features can often be identified and the enemy detected in areas where there are gaps in the jungle canopy. Aerial photographs are important sources of information because photograph interpretation can disclose hidden enemy camps not visible to the air observer. Photographs can also be used to locate helicopter landing zones. Decoy reconnaissance flights can be used to confuse or deceive the enemy about upcoming operations.

Reconnaissance-in-force

This method may be used to gather intelligence which cannot be gained by any other reconnaissance means. Examples of such intelligence include the enemy commander's plan for committing his reserves, or the trails used by a guerrilla force.

The commander conducting the reconnaissance-in-force will normally organize his unit into a number of reconnoitering forces. These reconnoitering forces conduct movements to contact, hasty or deliberate attacks, raids, reconnaissance, or patrols. Once the unit makes contact with the enemy, the commander must react on the intelligence gained. He must be prepared to exploit success or, if necessary, extricate the forces.

The size of the unit that conducts a reconnaissance-in-force depends on the nature of the intelligence to be gained and the chance that the reconnoitering force will have to fight on unfavorable terms. For example, if a battalion commander wants to find out how an enemy commander will commit his reserve, he may conduct a reconnaissance-in-force with his companies conducting limited objective attacks. If, on the other hand, a commander wants to find the routes used by a number of small guerrilla groups, the reconnaissance-in-force mission may be assigned to a company, which in turn will have its platoons conduct movements to contact.

Reconnaissance-by-fire

When using this method, the force fires on suspected enemy positions to cause the enemy to disclose his position by moving or returning fire. Reconnaissance-by-fire risks the loss of surprise. Its most effective use in the jungle is to find the flanks or gaps in enemy lines. Reconnaissance-by-fire from attack helicopters will often reveal the location of well-concealed enemy troops. Likewise, a reconnaissance-by-fire from armored vehicles firing into a wood line, either while moving crosscountry or along a road, can neutralize an enemy ambush. When using reconnaissance-by-fire, commanders must consider the difficulties of ammunition resupply in the jungle.

SURVEILLANCE

Surveillance operations in the jungle include using all techniques for establishing a continuous, thorough watch of the battlefield. This watch must be established both over large jungle areas and at selected key points such as trails, streams, and clearings. Surveillance operations are usually planned to support other missions.

Ground surveillance radars

These radars are best employed in those jungle areas where vegetation and terrain do not restrict line of sight. Night observation devices are also useful in such areas during periods of darkness. Unattended ground sensors, which are not affected by poor line of sight, are very useful in watching specific key areas. These electronic devices are affected by poor weather and are difficult to move in thickly forested areas. As a result, the use of manned OPs in jungle areas should always be planned.

Air surveillance

Surveillance of jungle areas from the air is most effective when pilots are familiar with ground operations and can recognize changes from normal patterns. Repeated flights by the same crews will attain this level of familiarity. In addition to visual surveillance, photographic coverage of an area can assist the surveillance effort. Side-looking airborne radar (SLAR) is not very effective in thick foliage, but can be used for surveillance along roads, trails, or streams. Likewise, infrared detection devices are limited by fog, clouds, rain, and vegetation. Airborne personnel detector devices (sniffers) were developed during the Vietnam war to detect human odors. These devices are extremely effective in detecting base camps of nonmechanized forces, but are limited by fog, rain, and windy conditions.

SECURITY OPERATIONS

Security must be a primary part of all jungle operations; therefore, specific security measures are covered as they apply to other operations throughout this chapter. Compared with operations in other types of terrain, security measures in the jungle must be intensified because of the poor observation and difficulties of control and movement. Operations must be slower than normal, and security forces must be closer to the units secured in order to provide adequate security in the jungle. Because it provides all-round security, the perimeter defense will be the defensive technique used most often by units operating independently in the jungle.

The "stand-to" is an important security technique in jungle fighting. When a unit stands-to, all of its soldiers don their fighting loads and occupy their fighting positions. The unit is 100 percent alert and ready to fight an attacking enemy. Stand-to procedures differ from unit to unit, but common stand-to times are before first light, before last light, before helicopter resupply, and before movement.

SECTION III. OFFENSIVE OPERATIONS

SPECIAL FACTORS

The purpose and fundamentals of the offense as outlined in field manuals for other environments generally apply as well to offensive operations in the jungle.

There are, however, factors which require the use of special offensive techniques:

- **Thick foliage makes it difficult for leaders to control their soldiers or to detect the enemy**
- **Fire support is difficult to observe and adjust**
- **Momentum and speed are difficult to maintain**

FUNDAMENTALS OF THE JUNGLE OFFENSE

When considering the use of special offensive techniques, commanders must remember that some offensive fundamentals acquire a new significance in the jungle.

Probably the most important and most difficult of these fundamentals is the requirement to *see the battlefield.* Above all else, the attacker must know the battlefield. As a result, he relies heavily on security patrols, information provided by air and ground reconnaissance, and proper movement techniques.

Key to effective operations in jungle warfare is the fundamental of using weapon systems to their best advantage. In addition to organic weapons, the ground commander must closely coordinate the employment of the supporting weapons available to him. The dense foliage found in some jungles may prevent heavy weapons from moving directly with the infantry. In those cases, TACAIR support and helicopter weapons must make up the difference. TOWs and Dragons, on the other hand, are of limited use in most jungle environments. The soldiers that man these weapons may be more effective as security forces or as reinforcements for maneuver elements. The primary jungle weapons are individual infantry small arms, supported by machineguns and mortars.

To *concentrate overwhelming combat power* against enemy weakness in jungle operations, the attacker must be able to bring up other elements quickly to support an element that is engaged. In determining how far he can separate his subordinate units, the commander must consider the factors of mission, enemy, terrain and weather, and troops and time available (METT). The separation may be expressed in time or in distance. The ability to provide mutual support must not be overlooked. Gaps between units should be covered by scouts and connecting patrols. Targets should be planned along the unit's route so that supporting fires can be responsive. The use of helicopters will permit even more rapid concentration of forces and provide additional firepower.

The jungle also increases the difficulty of efforts to *provide continuous support.* The key is constant planning, coordination, and maximum use of helicopters. Fires must be planned along the attack route so that they can be delivered in the shortest amount of time. Procedures for calling attack helicopters must be standardized and rehearsed. Likewise, combat service support must be timely and responsive. Ammunition and water must be loaded on pallets in the trains so that they can be brought forward as soon as needed.

CONDUCT OF THE JUNGLE OFFENSE

Because it is so hard to gather intelligence, jungle offensive tactics must be characterized by continuous reconnaissance. A unit attacking without timely information on the location of the enemy may subject its elements to enemy ambush without being able to support them. In such a situation, they may be defeated in detail.

> *"It is a situation that too frequently occurs in the Vietnam fighting. The forward element, losing men and becoming pinned down, compromises the position of all others. What has started out as an attack loses all form and deteriorates into a costly rescue act."*
>
> —S.L.A. Marshall, BIRD

Successful jungle attacks usually combine dispersion and concentration. For example, a rifle company may move out in a dispersed formation so that it can find the enemy. Once contact is made, its platoons close on the enemy from all directions. In this way, they move to support each other and destroy the enemy.

Operations are enemy-oriented, not terrain-oriented. Wherever the enemy is found, that is where he should be destroyed. If he is allowed to escape, he will only have to be found again, with all the risks involved.

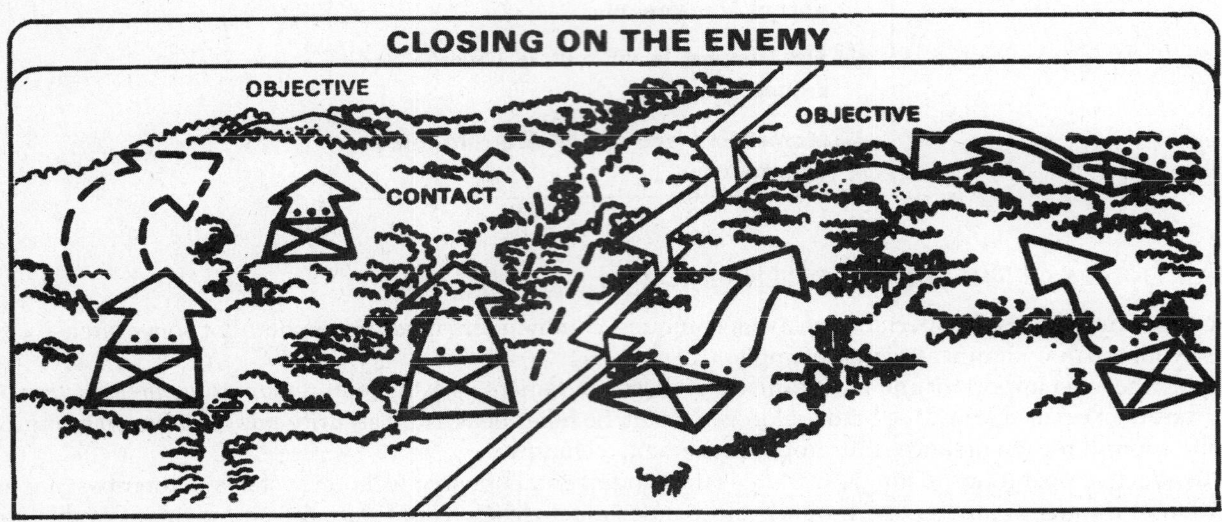

MOVEMENT TO CONTACT AND HASTY ATTACK

These two forms of combat are discussed together since they account for the majority of combat actions in the jungle. The successful follow-on action to movement to contact is a violently executed hasty attack. This action capitalizes on the advantage of surprise and the confusion prevalent in the jungle. The decision to employ single or multiple columns may depend solely on terrain and foliage considerations.

For companies and battalions, multiple columns are a sound movement practice because this formation provides more firepower to the front and because it is easier to deploy troops from two or three columns than from one file. In order to speed up deployment, units should develop and rehearse SOPs and immediate action drills. Troops should try to maintain a distance of five to seven paces between men, but must maintain visual contact. All-round defense and security measures must be maintained throughout movement.

Once contact with the enemy is made, the unit's first action is to build up a large volume of fire. The commander then assesses the situation and deploys his unit to overrun the enemy's positions while they are still suppressed. In this way, he seizes the initiative. There should be no delay in the troops' movement from the march formation into assault formation. Security elements protect the rear and prevent the enemy's counterattack. These forces may be used later to exploit a success, but should not be committed until the commander understands the situation.

The slowness of jungle maneuver makes a rapid call for supporting indirect fire important. Upon making contact, fires on the enemy should be immediately requested and adjusted from planned targets. To receive effective and timely fire support, accurate and continuous land navigation is necessary. Means for controlling attack helicopters are also important; this includes both radio and visual means. Adjustment techniques should be established by SOP.

Supporting fires and TACAIR or attack helicopters can place fires on suspected withdrawal routes, placing further pressure on the enemy. The success of the hasty attack depends to a large degree on the unit's vigorous execution of unit SOPs and the leadership of the squad and platoon leaders.

As the situation is developed and an enemy position is located, a violent assault should be made over the enemy's position. Soldiers stay on the alert for hidden enemy positions, snipers in the trees, and tunnels through which the enemy might move to attack the attacker's rear. This thorough technique will also provide enough information of the enemy and security to permit the commander to use his reserve force for exploitation, if needed.

The assault should be made using fire and maneuver. Soldiers should cover each other, moving by crawls and short rushes. Fire should be well-aimed shots and short bursts of automatic fire.

In such a fast-moving situation, it might be possible, for example, for a platoon to receive a fragmentary order (FRAGO), move to a pickup zone (PZ), and conduct an air assault to an objective. In this case, the planning might take place on the PZ or even in the vicinity of the objective rally point (ORP).

After the objective is seized, it must be secured immediately with a hasty perimeter, OPs, and early warning devices. This is to detect and repel an enemy counterattack or to allow the attacker to prepare to continue the attack.

THE DELIBERATE ATTACK

Based on information gained from reconnaissance and other sources, the commander may formulate a plan to attack a larger objective using a deliberate attack. Jungle terrain favors reduced distances and intervals between troops and units, and the deployment from movement to attack formation as far forward as possible. *In thickly vegetated terrain, the use of some of the same control techniques used in a night attack may be required.*

Fire support is as essential in the jungle as in other types of terrain. Unsupported troops are likely to incur heavy casualties when attacking jungle positions, especially considering the difficulties of employing organic weapons. Targets must be pinpointed by reconnaissance, and fires must be adjusted within very close range of attacking troops. During the assault, these supporting fires must continue until shifted by the assaulting commander. They are then adjusted onto targets which will assist the progress of attacking forces by blocking enemy counterattacks or withdrawal. Due to poor observation, indirect fire may have to be adjusted by sound.

Assaulting troops move over the objective using aggressive fire and movement to overcome enemy resistance. Assaulting troops again must be alert to snipers, mines and boobytraps, hidden positions, and tunnels which would permit the enemy to maneuver into the rear of attacking forces. Assaulting platoons and squads move in a single direction, with fires concentrated on enemy positions as they are located. Attacking elements must adjust their progress using base elements and phase lines. Smoke may be used to screen the flanks of the penetration from enemy observation and reduce his ability to deliver effective fires. Once an initial penetration is secured, it is exploited until the objective is taken.

After the objective is overrun, it must be secured immediately with a hasty perimeter, OPs, and early warning devices to detect and repel an enemy counterattack or to allow the attacker to prepare to continue the attack (*see IV*).

INFILTRATION

Jungle areas are ideal for infiltration. Dense vegetation and rugged terrain limit the enemy's ability to detect movement. As a technique to move through the enemy's positions, infiltration can be used with other offensive maneuvers to gain an advantage in the jungle. Although jungle infiltrations are normally conducted on foot, under certain circumstances helicopters or watercraft may be used.

Infiltrations are normally difficult to control. Chances for success are better if troops are well trained, well briefed, and well rehearsed. Roads, trails, and streams should be avoided because they will normally be under enemy surveillance. Movement by stealth is normally slow and exhausting. Phase lines (PL), infiltration routes, and adequate communications must be used to control the operation and to coordinate fires with movement.

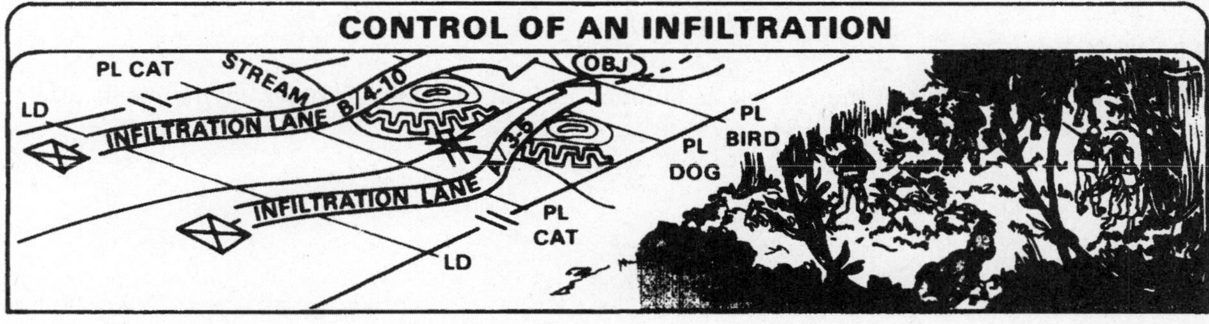

EXPLOITATION AND PURSUIT

Local successes should be exploited as soon as possible to cut off the retreat of isolated enemy forces. Airmobile troops are most effective to block enemy retreat in the jungle. They can also disrupt and harass enemy reserve, logistical, and command operations. Artillery, TACAIR support, and attack helicopters may also be used to block escape routes. Tanks may be used along trails or roads or in less dense areas if properly secured with infantry. During exploitations, rear areas must be secured against the actions of bypassed or infiltrating enemy.

Pursuit operations in the jungle should be conducted to maintain contact with the enemy. The precautions required to secure against ambush can slow pursuit operations considerably. Because attacking troops become more fatigued than defending troops, pursuit operations should be conducted using troops from the reserve. As is the case with most jungle offensive operations, airmobile forces, air cavalry, and attack helicopters can be used very effectively in pursuit operations.

ATTACK AGAINST A FORTIFIED POSITION

As mentioned earlier, jungle enemies have often used strongly fortified defensive positions to protect themselves from the effects of U.S. firepower. If it is necessary to attack such a position, troops will probably encounter bunkers, barbed wire, mines, and boobytraps. The enemy will often have to be burned or blasted out of such positions. These operations will require attacks on a narrow front, great amounts of firepower, and limited objective attacks.

Fortified enemy positions in dense jungle are often so well concealed that troops are not aware of their presence until they have physically encountered them. In these cases, the best course of action is usually to adjust forward dispositions enough to allow use of supporting indirect fires, to deploy additional forces to block possible withdrawal routes, and then to maneuver under the cover of supporting fires to defeat the fortifications in detail.

Maximum use of combat intelligence is required when attacking fortified areas. Aerial photographs, electronic intelligence, interrogation of prisoners of war (PW), and aggressive patrolling are all means of gaining the required information. Patrols also keep the enemy off balance and limit the enemy's ability to patrol.

In addition, combat engineer, and special weapons (such as flame) and equipment should be attached to the maneuver forces to assist in destroying the fortifications.

Destruction of the enemy in those types of positions takes a lot of time and effort. Other means should be used as much as possible. Here is a technique that proved successful in the past:

> *"The use of CS riot control gas could not be overlooked... On one occasion, a battalion made a night attack with gas masks following an aerial CS attack. A helicopter made several low passes on the windward side of the area and dispersed about 250 CS grenades. This was followed by 20 minutes of artillery fire, about half of which was VT fuze fired into the enemy positions. Behind a walking barrage of artillery fire, one company assaulted, and, once inside the objective, flareships lit up the area. Eighteen enemy were killed, while no casualties were suffered by the friendly troops."*
>
> —Report, 25th Infantry Division, Duang Nhgai Province, Republic of Vietnam

SECTION IV. DEFENSIVE OPERATIONS

SPECIAL FACTORS

The purpose and fundamentals of the defense as outlined in field manuals for other environments also apply to defensive operations in the jungle.

There are, however, certain factors which require the use of special techniques:

- **Thick foliage makes it difficult to detect the approach of an attacking enemy**
- **Slowness of jungle movement makes it difficult to react to an enemy threat**
- **Limited visibility between defensive positions**
- **Limited fields of fire**
- **Psychological impact of fighting in a strange environment**

FUNDAMENTALS OF THE JUNGLE DEFENSE

As in the offense, jungle defensive operations are based on the same fundamentals used in other area operations. Some of these fundamentals acquire a special significance in the jungle.

To succeed in the jungle defense, a commander must *understand the enemy and see the battlefield.* The enemy will probably be expert in using the environment to his advantage, and the defender must understand enemy techniques. To counter the threat of infiltration, the defender must employ all-round defense and all surveillance means available. No amount of electronic means can eliminate the need for frequent patrolling.

The defender must *exploit every advantage* that he has, particularly the abundant concealment provided by the foliage and the weather. A force which remains concealed may disrupt an enemy's attack by using surprise fire from hidden locations. Though not as common as in other types of terrain, features which lend themselves to the defense, such as rivers, gorges, and ridges, should be used if they dominate likely avenues of approach. The defender must appreciate the defensive characteristics of the terrain and environment.

The defender must *maximize the effectiveness of key weapons,* which in the jungle are infantry small arms, mortars, and artillery. The poor trafficability also increases the importance of attack helicopters and TACAIR.

In planning to *concentrate combat power at critical times and places,* the defender must first plan the massing of small-arms fire. Since fields-of-fire will be limited, positions must be placed close together for mutual support. To move troops and weapons rapidly to supplementary or alternate positions, it maybe necessary to cut paths through the bush. Units should rehearse these maneuvers.

As in the offense, the problem of *providing continuous support* is to a large degree solved by effective communications and the use of helicopters.

PLAN OF THE JUNGLE DEFENSE

Planning for the jungle defense should provide for a covering force area, a main battle area, and a rear area. Forces in each area must be provided fire support. Obstacles are planned to improve the natural defensive strength of the terrain. Plans are also formulated for counterattacks. The following factors should be considered when planning for the jungle defense:

Day and night in jungle regions are each roughly 12 hours long. Nights, especially under jungle canopies, are extremely dark. Defensive preparations should begin at least 2 hours before nightfall.

The heat and humidity will fatigue troops rapidly.

Tropical rain will flood positions unless they are adequately drained. During the rainy season, defensive positions should be dug on high ground, if possible.

Because jungle terrain favors infiltration, the use of starlight scopes, OPs, and early warning devices is very important.

After the commander organizes the ground and secures the area to be defended, he then positions his Dragons, if they can be used effectively, and machineguns and clears fields of fire. Leaders must insure that troops do not cut too much vegetation. In order to be mutually supporting, positions will be closer together than on other types of terrain. In addition to attaining mutual support, this helps prevent enemy infiltration. Mines and obstacles should be emplaced where they are covered by friendly fires. These should be located beyond hand grenade throwing range of the defensive positions.

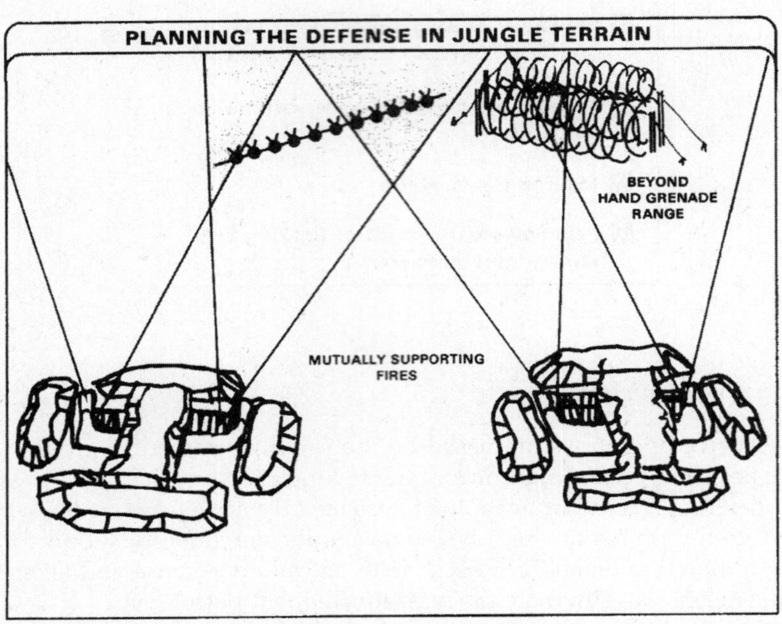

Security

Since enemy tactics, jungle terrain, and bad weather favor attacks conducted by stealth, security should be the leader's first concern. OPs, early warning devices, ambushes, and patrols are all measures which will prevent a unit from being surprised. Patrols must be planned according to an irregular schedule. A system of recognition signals must be used to prevent the engagement of friendly units.

> **NOTE**
>
> If mechanical ambushes are used, units should stop patrolling in that area, and should provide some means, such as communications wire, to guide OP personnel and prevent them from straying into the mechanical ambush.

Defensive formations

The basic defensive technique in the jungle is the perimeter defense. Two other very effective defensive techniques for jungle operations are the triangle and "Y" formations (*see app J*). Whether a unit is operating independently or as part of a larger defensive position, it must be prepared to defend itself against an attack from any direction. Initially, these formations will be formed by platoons or by companies. Larger units should position their companies in depth to provide all-round defense. Alert and aggressive patrols and OPs will defeat enemy attempts to infiltrate between positions. Later, if time permits, platoon and company formations can be connected with fighting positions and trenches. Even then, however, companies and platoons must be prepared for all-round defense.

Priority of work

Units in the defense must pay particular attention to their priority of work. Since more security measures must be taken than normal, fewer troops will be available to prepare defensive positions at any one time. Positions should be prepared and camouflaged as in any other situation. Overhead cover should be prepared using strong wood and sandbags. Claymore mines and trip flares should be emplaced in front of the defensive positions. Fields of fire should be cut low, leaving enough foliage so as not to reveal the location of the defensive position.

To counter enemy reconnaissance efforts, units should shift the positions of machineguns after dark. After a few days, the entire unit's position should be changed. If a unit remains in position for a longer period of time, it is more likely to be reconnoitered by the enemy and subject to attack.

Command and control

Command and control are extremely difficult in the jungle defense. Commanders must place great emphasis on planning, coordination, and small-unit leadership. Decentralized control is important to ensure that subordinate units can react to multiple threats. Aggressive leadership at the small-unit level is necessary in fighting off isolated assaults at close range. Alternate communications means must be established wherever possible. An example might be a communications system using wire as the primary means, radio as the secondary means, and pyrotechnics for certain prearranged signals.

Defensive targets for artillery and mortars should be planned on stream and trail junctions, and any other likely enemy avenues of approach. Artillery and mortar fire should also be used to cover the many areas of dead space found in jungle terrain. It is also a good idea to confirm the location of the defense on the ground by using artillery marking missions integrated into registration missions. Signals for the employment of TACAIR and attack helicopters, both day and night, and for medevac and resupply helicopters must also be planned.

CONDUCT OF THE JUNGLE DEFENSE

There are occasions when a unit will have to establish a defense with minimum planning time. This normally occurs when an attack is stalled, at dusk when the unit is still in contact with the enemy and no night attack is planned, or when an intermediate objective must be secured before continuing the attack. These situations are more dangerous in the jungle than in other areas because of the dense foliage and the closeness of the enemy.

The normal course of action in these cases is to establish a perimeter defense. Dragons, if they can be used effectively, and machineguns are positioned immediately where they have the best fields of fire. As soon as possible, OPs and other local security measures are established. Frontages are smaller than in other types of terrain, especially at night, to guard against enemy infiltration. Indirect fires are registered and fighting positions are dug as soon as possible.

Once these actions have been completed, steps are taken to improve the defense. A primary consideration in improving a defense is to expand the perimeter to gain "working room." This may require limited attacks, massed artillery and mortar fire, or close-in machinegun fire to force the enemy to withdraw. If the position will be occupied for a long time, it should be made as strong as possible.

This may be done as follows:

- **A small reserve is formed as soon as possible to react to enemy threats**
- **Local security is pushed forward**
- **Counterattack plans are developed**
- **Wire communications are established and pyrotechnic signals planned**
- **Machineguns are employed singly in order to cover as many enemy approaches as possible**

If troops remain in a defensive position for a long time, they must not become complacent. Leaders must inspect weapons, positions, and the cleanliness of troops. They must also develop plans for alerts, feeding, maintenance, and bathing. These activities must be scheduled according to a random pattern so that the enemy cannot take advantage of a set routine.

An alert system must be established, so that a portion of the defensive force is always awake. Although the poor observation in jungles favors the enemy's attack at any time, the early hours of the morning afford him the greatest chance of surprise unless positive alert measures are taken. All troops should stand-to before dawn.

The jungle enemy will try to probe a position to locate the flanks of positions and key weapons. Soldiers must not give away their positions by premature firing. Claymores and hand grenades should be used to engage these probes. When probed, riflemen near machineguns should fire, not the machinegunners. Machinegunners must use their pistols for self-defense instead of their machineguns. When the enemy attacks, he will try to isolate friendly positions and destroy them one at a time. Well-planned, mutually supporting fires will prevent this.

Counterattack

If enemy forces penetrate a position, a counterattack is the best way to expel them. Troops in the area of the penetration must stay in their positions and continue to fire to support the counterattack. If they leave their positions while the enemy is being expelled, they increase the chance that they will be hit with friendly fires.

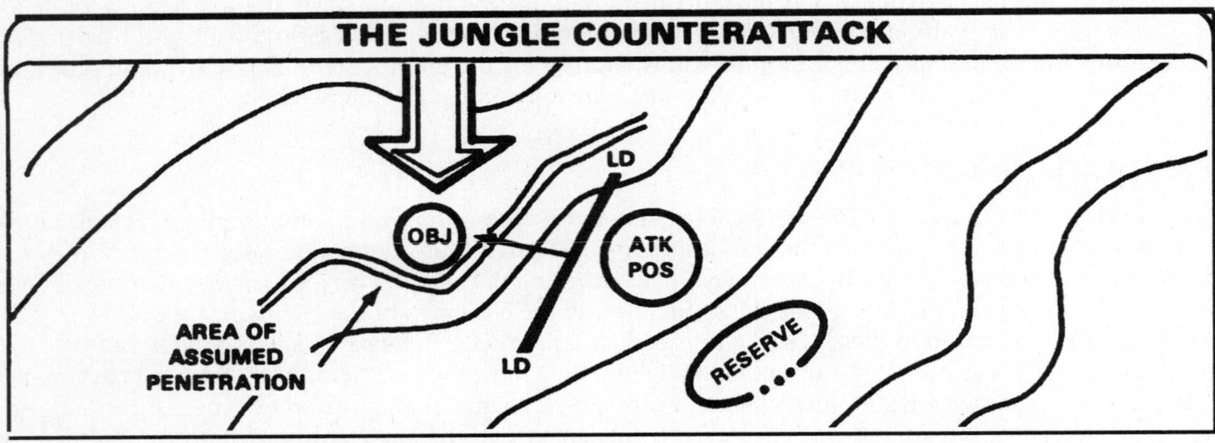

THE BATTALION COMBAT BASE

When engaged in tactical operations in the jungle, elements of the battalion will often establish a base for command and control and fire support resources, protected by a perimeter defense. These resources are called the battalion combat base.

The location of the perimeter defense to defend the battalion combat base will depend upon the:

- **Forces available to defend the combat base**
- **Ability to support subordinate units with indirect fire**
- **Defensibility of terrain**
- **Ability to communicate with subordinate units**

Prior to establishing the battalion combat base, the commander should conduct a reconnaissance to determine the defensibility of the terrain. He also plans forces required for the defense. While the defense must be capable of defeating the largest attack which the enemy is likely to conduct, it must use the minimum forces necessary. The combat support company, reinforced as necessary with an attached infantry platoon, is the largest force that is realistically available for preparing and defending the perimeter. To use a larger force would probably leave insufficient forces to fight the more important combat. Since some elements, such as the antitank platoon of the combat support company, may not be employed effectively in the jungle, they will often be available for use in the perimeter defense. The battalion commander will normally designate the combat support company or headquarters and headquarters company commander to be the battalion combat base commander and will have him take charge of the construction and execution of the perimeter defense.

Forces normally under control of the battalion combat base commander include:

- **The antitank platoon**
- **A Redeye section, if attached (both to man the perimeter and to provide anti-aircraft fire)**
- **The heavy mortar platoon (both to man the perimeter and provide fire support)**
- **A rifle platoon, if provided for the perimeter defense**

The scout platoon is normally used for patrolling or screening missions, rather than being used in manning the combat base perimeter.

During construction of the perimeter defense, it is vulnerable to enemy attack. Consequently, it is imperative to complete the perimeter defense as quickly as possible and to provide maximum security during construction.

The threat of infiltration attacks must be emphasized. The enemy may not be able to conduct large scale attacks on fortified positions, but he may be capable of disrupting operations by infiltrating one- or two-man teams through the perimeter to place explosive devices on command and control facilities, artillery pieces or mortars, or ammunition storage areas. This infiltration is often preceded by a deceptive attack or probe by ground forces. Troops in the perimeter must maintain constant security, using early warning systems and continuous patrolling. Starlight scopes, OPs, unattended ground sensors, and tripflares are also used. Wire obstacles should be used to keep infiltrators out of critical facilities.

A battalion combat base may have to remain in place for a long time. Continuous firing of mortars and landing of helicopters makes concealing its location very difficult. These two factors make it necessary to harden the perimeter defense. Overhead cover and sandbagged bunkers must be provided for all fighting positions. The tactical operations center (TOC) and CP should have similar protection and may also be dug underground. Mortars and artillery pieces should be dug in or fortified with sandbags.

ORGANIZATION OF THE DEFENSE

A reserve for the defense may be constituted from attachments, such as engineers (if available), or from off-shift personnel from TOC and CP elements. This reserve will react to enemy attacks, and will reinforce the defense or counterattack. They must be rehearsed on signals and actions until they become proficient. Mortars are employed to provide close-in fire support. Artillery pieces can provide direct fire but probably will not be able to provide indirect fire support of the perimeter. Hence, the perimeter should be located within range of other artillery and mortar units for additional protection.

The battalion combat base commander assigns sectors to subordinate platoons, insuring that likely avenues of approach are dominated by Dragons, machineguns, and artillery in direct fire role, if possible. He then plans indirect fires. The commander specifies points at which adjoining platoons must coordinate. The platoon leader selects each position and designates the personnel to man it.

The platoon leader must insure that he has complete coverage throughout his sector to deal with not only a mass attack but also infiltration of small elements.

Once the positions are selected, the platoon leader insures that a priority of work is adhered to.

EXAMPLE OF PRIORITIES OF WORK

Work should be accomplished in the following steps, consistent with the tactical situation and the availability of resources.

Step I :	**Air assault/ground assault seizes the site.**
	Immediate security established to include OPs.
	Area swept for boobytraps.
	Mortars laid.
Step II :	**Communications established.**
	CP set up.
	Position of TOC dug in.
	Selected TOC personnel displaced to perimeter defense.
Step III:	**Perimeter positions established.**
	Fields of fire cleared.
	Reserve force established.
	Wire to all positions.
Step IV:	**Barriers and obstacles placed around perimeter defense.**
	Early warning devices emplaced.
	Security/ambush patrol plans established.
	Final protective fire (FPF) fired in.
Step V:	**Positions sustained.**
	Positions are hardened with overhead cover.
	All other positions improved.
	More fields of fire cleared.
	Landing zone enlarged.
	Latrine, generators, and ammunition supply point (ASP) established.

NOTE: Throughout work, camouflage must be applied.

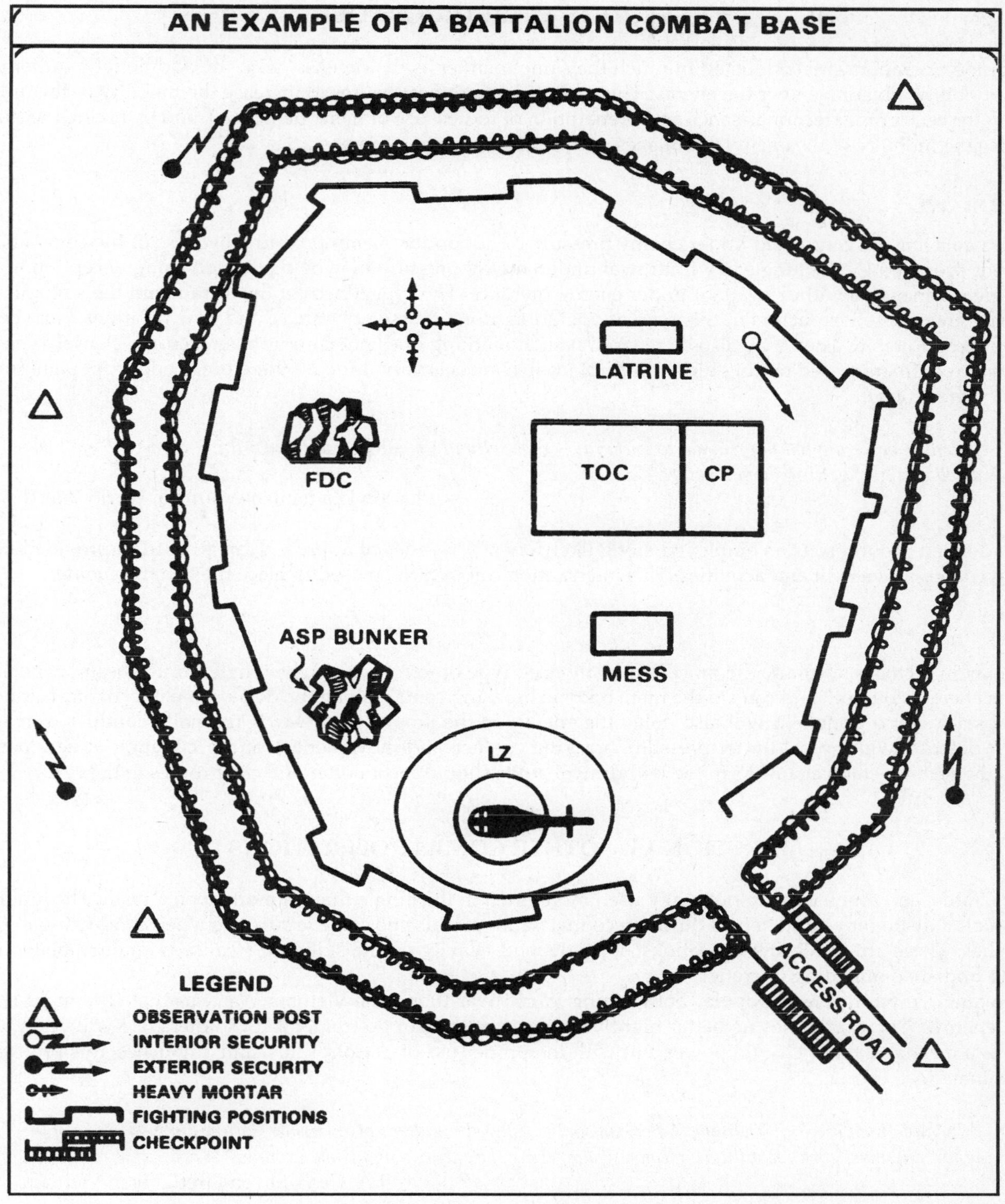
AN EXAMPLE OF A BATTALION COMBAT BASE
LATRINE
FDC
TOC
CP
ASP BUNKER
MESS
LZ
ACCESS ROAD
LEGEND
OBSERVATION POST
INTERIOR SECURITY
EXTERIOR SECURITY
HEAVY MORTAR
FIGHTING POSITIONS
CHECKPOINT

SECTION V. RETROGRADE

Retrograde operations are conducted in much the same manner as the defense, with the additional requirement to gain a mobility advantage over the enemy. This is done by taking measures to increase the mobility of the unit conducting the retrograde (reconnaissance and preparation of routes, use of helicopters, etc.), and by taking measures to decrease the mobility of the enemy (ambushes, artillery fires, mines, wire obstacles, etc.).

WITHDRAWL

Withdrawals may be conducted under enemy pressure or not under enemy pressure. Because of the cover and concealment provided by the jungle, a withdrawal under enemy pressure may be conducted using deception in much the same manner as a withdrawal not under enemy pressure. The ruggedness of the terrain and the strength of the attacking enemy are key factors in this type of operation. Routes, assembly areas, and new positions must be thoroughly reconnoitered. They may also be marked if such marking does not compromise security. Densely vegetated areas will require increased use of guides. Control in such areas is very difficult; therefore, leadership, planning, and rehearsal are crucial.

> *"I will never again tell my platoon to withdraw - especially in the jungle - without telling it where to go. I had a hell of a time getting them together."*
>
> —Platoon Leader, New Guinea, World War II

Unattended ground sensors employed along likely enemy avenues of approach can be used to provide information on enemy movement and activities. This information can in turn be used to place fires on the enemy.

DELAY

The delay in sector is normally the most frequently used type of retrograde in the jungle. Ambushes may be used to halt the enemy's pursuit, and can aid the main body in breaking contact along the delay route. Mechanical ambushes, wire obstacles, and minefield will also delay the enemy. In the jungle, the delay is normally conducted in several phases: defense, withdrawal under pressure, breaking contact, and movement to and occupation of new positions where the defense starts again. As in the withdrawal, units should reconnoiter and clear routes to the rear.

SECTION VI. OTHER COMBAT OPERATIONS

Patrols, raids, and ambushes are not really used more often in the jungle than in more open terrain. The jungle permits small units to move undetected during reconnaissance patrols and achieve surprise when conducting raids and ambushes. These are small-unit operations. They depend heavily on the skill and stealth of infantry platoons and squads, and are demanding operations.

One jungle myth that was popular both during World War II and the Vietnam War was that "the night belongs to the enemy." The enemy has no better night vision or stealth than do trained U.S. soldiers. He will often use the night as a means to avoid U.S. firepower, but with the proper use of patrols, raids, and ambushes, this problem can be eliminated.

> *"On any given night in Vietnam, American soldiers staged hundreds of ambushes, for the ambush is one of the oldest and most effective military means of hampering the enemy's nighttime exploits."*
>
> —J.A. Cash, Seven Firefights in Vietnam

Successful jungle patrols, raids, and ambushes result from detailed planning, intensive training, and constant rehearsal. Troops must be alert. A unit which has moved cross-country through the jungle until late in the afternoon will not be in a condition to succeed if it has to go out on ambush that night. Commanders must realize that such operations require time to prepare, train, and rest.

Specific techniques which are effective in jungle operations are described below.

PATROLS

A patrol is a detachment sent out by a larger unit to conduct a combat or reconnaissance operation. The operation itself is also called a patrol. The mission to conduct a patrol may be given to a fire team, squad, platoon, or company. The leader of the detachment conducting a patrol is referred to as the patrol leader.

Categories of patrols

The planned action at the objective determines the patrol's category. There are two categories of patrols:

Combat (ambush, raid, or security) Patrol. This patrol provides security and harasses, destroys, or captures enemy troops, equipment, and installations. A combat patrol also collects and reports information, whether related to its mission or not.

Reconnaissance (area or zone) Patrol. This patrol collects information or confirms or disproves the accuracy of information previously gained.

Regardless of the category of the patrol, there are four key principles to successful patrolling. These are:

- **Detailed planning.**
- **Thorough reconnaissance.**
- **Positive control.**
- **All-round security.**

Organization for a patrol

The patrol leader decides what elements and teams are needed for his patrol, selects men or units for these elements and teams, and decides what weapons and equipment are needed. He should, however, use his unit's normal organization (squads and platoons) and chain of command (squad and platoon leaders) as much as possible to meet these needs. For example, a combat patrol may be organized like this: the company headquarters is the patrol headquarters; the 1st platoon is the assault element; the 2nd platoon is the security element; and the 3rd platoon and weapons platoon make up the support element.

General organization

A patrol generally consists of a patrol headquarters and the elements needed for the mission.

Patrol Headquarters. The headquarters (HQ) of a company-size patrol normally consists of the same number of men as a regular company headquarters. However, regardless of a patrol's size, its leader tailors the headquarters to meet mission needs. The patrol headquarters has the same responsibilities as any other command element.

Reconnaissance Patrol. In an area reconnaissance (recon), a patrol has a reconnaissance element and a security element. In a zone reconnaissance, a patrol has several reconnaissance elements. Each one provides its own security.

Combat Patrol. A combat patrol normally has an assault element, a security element, and a support element. At times, the support element may be omitted by combining it with the assault element.

In general, jungle terrain affords excellent concealment, provides some cover, and hinders enemy observation and movement. During rainy periods, the sound of movement is less obvious. Wet ground and wet vegetation also muffle noise. All of these factors favor the patrolling unit.

On the other hand, the difficulties of movement and control and the ease with which the enemy can infiltrate friendly units are disadvantages to units patrolling in the jungle. These factors can best be overcome by training and discipline.

Silence, in both voice and movement, is essential at all times during a jungle patrol. With practice, it is possible to move steadily, deliberately, and carefully through the jungle, parting the undergrowth instead of crashing through it or cutting through it with machetes. Troops should avoid walking on dry leaves, sticks, rotten wood, or anything that would make noise. Machetes should be used to cut trails only as a last resort. Talking should be done in a whisper, and arm-and-hand signals should be used whenever possible.

Trails should be avoided. Patrols should make every effort to hide signs of movement, especially when moving through untraveled territory or near enemy positions.

Some techniques which may be used include:

- **Requiring all troops to wear boots that have the same pattern on their soles.**
- **Requiring troops to carry only the mission essentials, and do not let them litter.**
- **Cautioning troops to avoid small saplings, when going up hill. The shaking of overhead branches can be seen and heard at a distance.**
- **Requiring troops to keep off trails. If necessary to monitor or guide on a trail, patrols should move parallel to the trail and not on it.**

Native scouts are valuable in patrolling because they are often very familiar with the terrain. Patrol leaders must realize, however, that a scout's function is only to show direction and provide information. He should never lead the patrol. The correct position of a scout is with the patrol leader, so that the leader can make decisions based on the scout's advice.

RAID

Raids in the jungle environment must be keyed to reliable intelligence. The actions of the raiding unit must be decisive and rapid in order to catch an elusive jungle enemy. A raid's success depends on good intelligence and a sound plan.

Jungles favor raid operations. The excellent concealment enables skilled raiding patrols to operate deep in enemy territory. Platoon-sized units are best suited to jungle raids. Supporting artillery fires should be planned, but due to difficulties of control, timing, and communications, jungle raids may be executed without artillery support. Surprise is a key ingredient of a successful raid.

Raids that require deep penetration into enemy-held areas are best executed by establishing a patrol base in the general area of the final objective. From there, reconnaissance patrols can be sent to scout enemy positions while the remainder of the force completes its preparations for the raid. Helicopters and watercraft are effective means of transporting a raiding force rapidly to the vicinity of its objective without depleting their physical strength in a difficult march.

AMBUSHES

The ambush is more important, more effective, and more frequently used in jungle fighting than in any other type of combat. Jungle terrain provides many opportunities for a well-concealed force to gain surprise. Surprise is essential for a successful ambush.

Destruction of enemy forces is the primary purpose of most ambushes, but other benefits result from a well-executed ambush program.

More than in any other type of terrain, jungle ambushes require high standards of discipline. Soldiers on an ambush must be prepared to remain in the same position for hours at a time, without being able to sleep, talk, or smoke. They must endure insects and resist the desire to make any quick moves to swat or brush the insects away. All these require extensive training to develop the patience and self-discipline required.

These benefits include:

- **Disruption of enemy operations, since troops become reluctant to move and fight in areas where ambushes are frequent.**
- **Capture of prisoners and equipment which may yield intelligence data.**
- **Capture of supplies, thus increasing combat effectiveness at the expense of the enemy. In some instances, this is the primary source of supplies for guerrilla forces.**

The location for an ambush should be chosen after a careful analysis of the terrain, using maps, aerial photographs, and personal reconnaissance. The site chosen must contribute to the surprise of the ambush. Many times the selection of a site for surprise alone will be more effective than attempting to ambush from a site which is in other respects tactically sound but at which the enemy is sure to be suspicious. Covered routes of approach and withdrawal, good fields of fire, and canalization of the enemy are characteristics of a good site. The site should always be reconnoitered and approached from the rear.

In no other operation is camouflage more important than in the ambush. Weapons should fire through screens of undisturbed, living foliage. Spoilage resulting from the preparation of positions must be removed from sight. There can be no unnecessary noise or movement. If reliefs are used, they should be scheduled so that only a few men move at any one time. One or two men moving are harder to detect than an entire relief moving at once.

DEFENSE AGAINST AMBUSH

Since ambushes are more frequent and effective in the jungle than in any other type of terrain, a unit moving through the jungle must take all possible measures to reduce its vulnerability to ambush. The most effective means of countering an ambush is to detect it before entering the kill zone. This, however, is not always possible.

Dismounted troops have an advantage over mounted troops in avoiding ambushes because they do not have to move on roads or trails. Commanders of dismounted units should make a map and aerial photograph reconnaissance to detect likely ambush sites and plan routes which avoid them. During movement, security to the front, rear, and flanks should be maintained at all times. Alert troops, good noise discipline, and well-rehearsed signals are other means which will reduce the chances of ambush. Accurate land navigation, continuous fire support planning, and counterambush drills are also important antiambush techniques.

Mounted troops are very vulnerable to jungle ambushes, especially where the foliage grows up to the edge of a road. Ambush of vehicular columns traditionally has been a primary tactic of jungle enemies. As a result, traffic in jungle areas must be tightly controlled and kept to a minimum. All vehicles should have armed riders. Armored vehicles should escort convoys, and traffic information should be carefully guarded. Fire planning and route selection and reconnaissance are important for mounted troops as well as for dismounted troops.

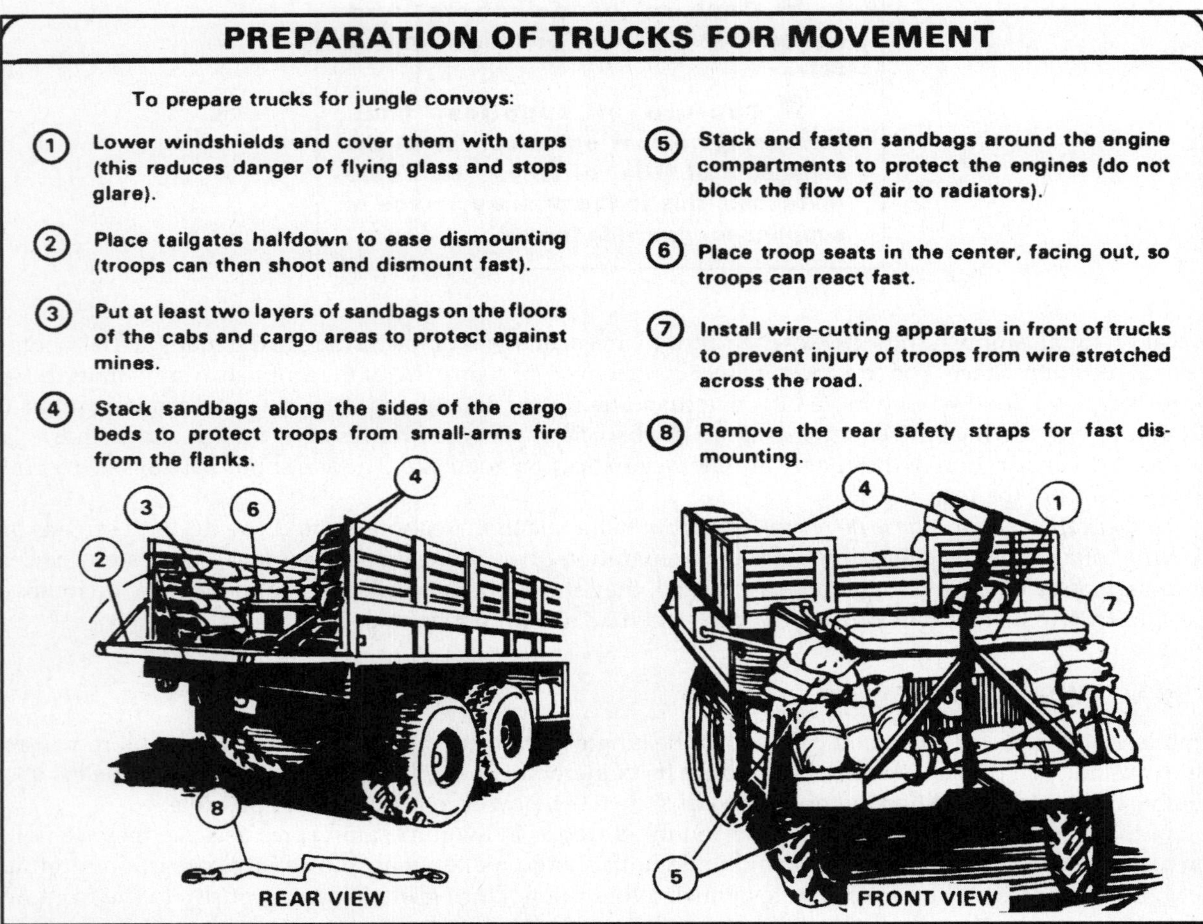

COUNTERAMBUSH MEASURES

Troops must also be trained in counter-ambush measures. The key is early detection followed by reflex-type counteraction, a high volume of return fire, and relentless pursuit. The most effective counterambush measures are well-rehearsed immediate action drills. Every soldier must know exactly what he is supposed to do.

Dismounted troops should react to an ambush immediately, firing into the ambushers without orders. Building and retaining fire superiority is the best initial defense against an ambush. If a patrol finds itself in an enemy ambush, it must get out of the kill zone immediately. It must take the following immediate actions:

Troops in the kill zone, without order or signal, immediately return fire, and quickly move out of the kill zone by the safest way. (There is no set way to do this; it must be each soldier's decision for his situation.) Smoke grenades can help conceal the troops in the kill zone.

Troops not in the kill zone fire to support the withdrawal of the troops in the kill zone.

If a dismounted patrol is ambushed, it should attempt to break contact and reorganize in the last designated rally point.

Mounted troops who are ambushed should attempt to drive rapidly out of the kill zone. Vehicles approaching the kill zone should stop so they do not enter it. Troops should then dismount and maneuver to destroy the ambush.

In any case, the rapid call for supporting artillery and mortar fire will help the ambushed force to gain fire superiority and will assist the maneuver to destroy the ambush.

REACTING TO AMBUSH

CHAPTER 6

Navigation and Tracking

SECTION I. JUNGLE NAVIGATION

Navigating in the jungle can be difficult for those troops not accustomed to it. This chapter outlines techniques which have been used successfully in jungle navigation. With training and practice, troops should be able to use these techniques to navigate in even the thickest jungle.

NAVIGATION TOOLS MAPS

Because of the isolation of many jungles, the rugged ground, and the presence of the canopy, topographic survey is difficult and is done mainly from the air. Therefore, although maps of jungle areas generally depict the larger features (hill, ridges, larger streams, etc.) fairly accurately, some smaller terrain features (gullies, small or intermittent streams, small swamps, etc.), which are actually on the ground, may not appear on the map. Also, many older maps are inaccurate. So, before going into the jungle, commanders and staff should bring their maps up to date.

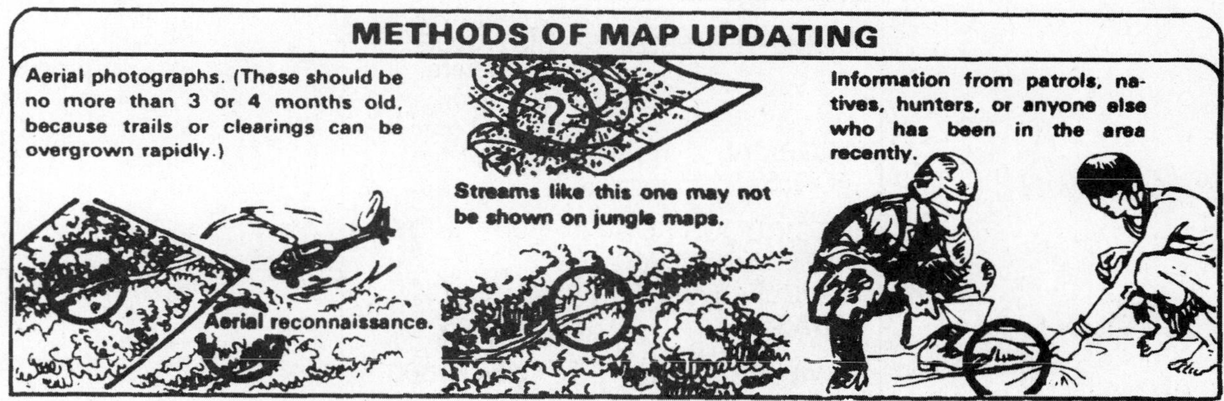

COMPASS

No one should move in the jungle without a compass. It should be tied to the clothing by a string or bootlace. The three most common methods used to follow the readings of a compass are:

Sighting along the desired azimuth. The compass man notes an object to the front (usually a tree or bush) that is on line with the proper azimuth and moves to that object. *This is not a good method in the jungle as trees and bushes tend to look very much alike.*

Holding the compass at waist level and walking in the direction of a set azimuth. *This is a good method for the jungle. The* compass man sets the compass for night use with the long, luminous line placed over the luminous north arrow and the desired azimuth under the black index line. There is a natural tendency to drift either left or right using this method. Jungle navigators must learn their own tendencies and allow for this drift.

Sighting along the desired azimuth and guiding a man forward until he is on line with the azimuth. The unit then moves to the man and repeats the process. This is the most accurate method to use in the jungle during daylight hours, but it is slow. In this method, the compass man cannot mistake the aiming point and is free to release the compass on its string and use both hands during movement to the next aiming point.

The keys to navigation are maintaining the right direction and knowing the distance traveled. Skill with the compass (acquired through practice) takes care of the first requirement. Ways of knowing the distance traveled include checking natural features with the map, knowing the rate of movement, and pacing.

CHECKING FEATURES

Major recognizable features (hills, rivers, changes in the type of vegetation) should be noted as they are reached and then identified on the map. Jungle navigators must BE CAUTIOUS ABOUT TRAILS—the trail on the ground may not be the one on the map.

RATE OF MOVEMENT

Speed will vary with the physical condition of the troops, the load they carry, the danger of enemy contact, and the type of jungle growth. *The normal error is to overestimate the distance traveled.* The following can be used as a rough guide to the maximum distance covered in 1 hour during daylight.

DAYLIGHT MOVEMENT	
TYPE TERRAIN	MAXIMUM DISTANCE (in meters per hour)
TROPICAL RAIN FOREST	1,000
DECIDUOUS FOREST, SECONDARY JUNGLE, TALL GRASS	500
SWAMPS	100 TO 300
RICE PADDIES (WET)	800
RICE PADDIES (DRY)	2,000
PLANTATIONS	2,000
TRAILS	1,500

PACING

In thick jungle, this is the best way of measuring distance. It is the only method which lets the soldier know how far he has traveled. With this information, he can estimate where he is at any given time-something that must be known to call for indirect fire support in a hurry. To be accurate, soldiers must practice pacing over different types of terrain. Each soldier should make a PERSONAL PACE TABLE like this one—

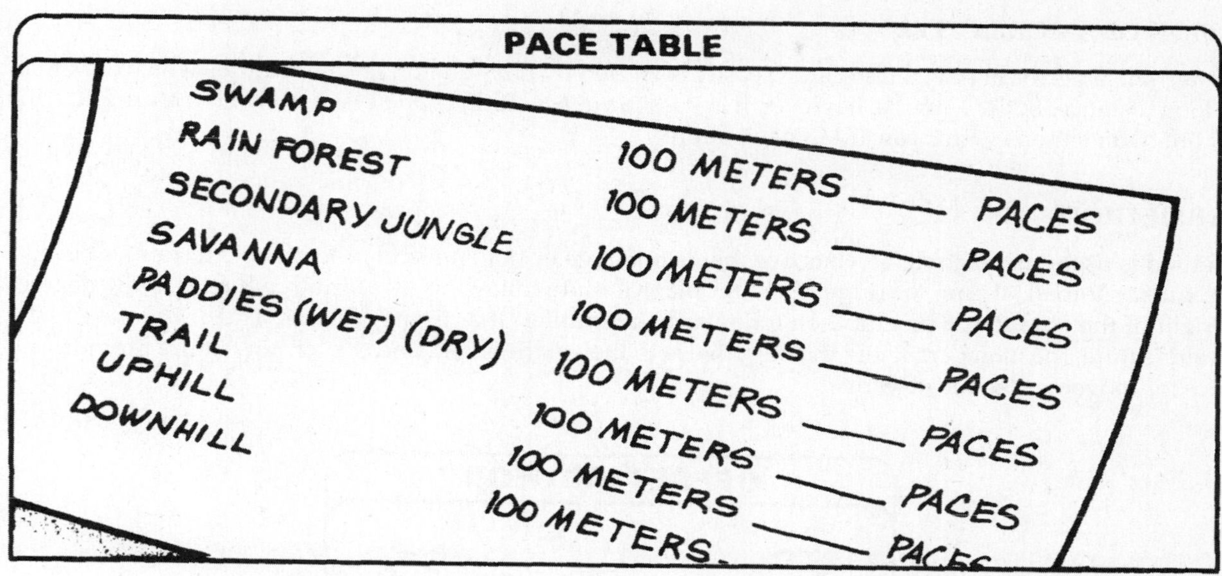

At least two men in each independent group should be compass men, and three or four should be keeping a pace count. The artillery fire support team (FIST) chief should keep an accurate fix on his location, as should the platoon forward observers (FO). He can be a great help to the rifle company commander in matters of navigation. When in doubt, the commander should do a resection, using artillery marking rounds.

> ✍ **NOTE**
> Jungle foliage will often require that artillery marking rounds be sensed by sound.

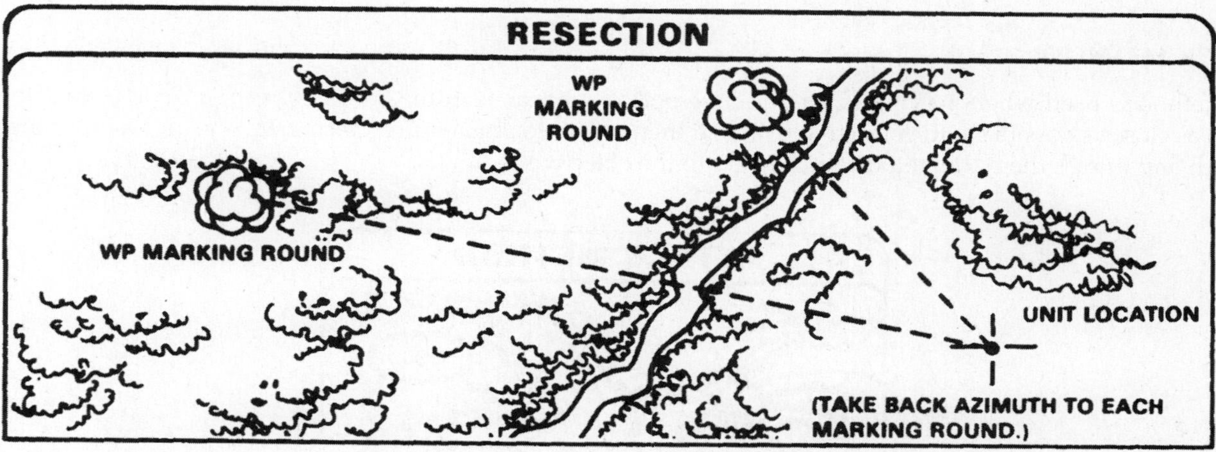

To locate a position by resection, the general location must be known. White phosphorus rounds (airbursts) are then called on two widely separated grids which are not on terrain features like the one the unit is occupying and which are a safe distance from the estimated location. A back azimuth to each of these rounds is taken and plotted on the map. The point where they intersect is the observer's approximate location.

LOCATION OF AN OBJECTIVE

In open terrain, an error in navigation can be easily corrected by orienting on terrain features which are often visible from a long distance. In thick jungle, however, it is possible to be within 50 meters of a terrain feature and still not see it. Here are two methods which can aid in navigation.

OFFSET METHOD

This method is useful in reaching an objective that is not large or not on readily identifiable terrain but is on a linear feature, such as a road, stream, or ridge. The unit plans a route following an azimuth which is a few degrees to the left or right of the objective. The unit then follows the azimuth to that terrain feature. Thus, when the unit reaches the terrain feature, the members know the objective is to their right or left, and the terrain feature provides a point of reference for movement to the objective.

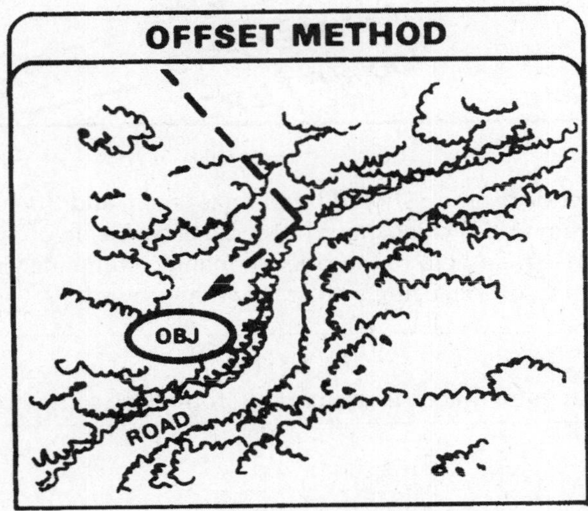

ATTACK METHOD

This method is used when moving to an objective not on a linear feature. An easily recognizable terrain feature is chosen as close as possible to the objective. The unit then moves to that feature. Once there, the unit follows the proper azimuth and moves the estimated distance to get to the objective.

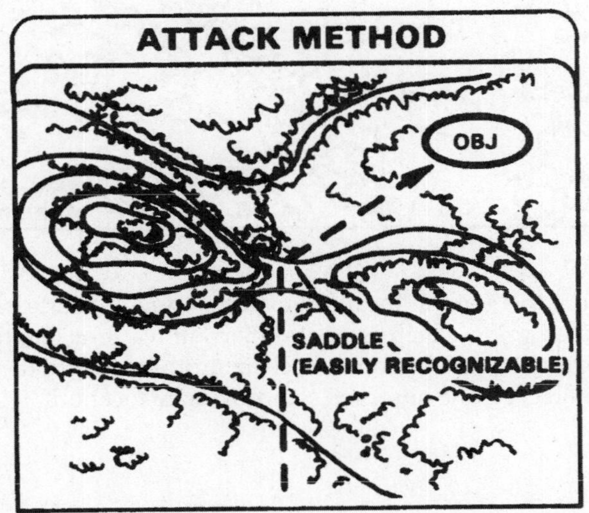

WHAT TO DO IF LOST

Do not panic. Few soldiers have ever been permanently lost in the jungle, although many have taken longer to reach their destination than they should.

Disoriented navigators should try to answer these questions. (If there are other navigators in the group, they all should talk it over.)

What was the last known location?

Did the unit go too far and pass the objective? (They should compare estimates of time and distance traveled.)

Does the terrain look the way it should? (They should compare the surroundings with the map.)

What features in the area will help to fix the unit's location? (They should try to find these features.)

If the unit is unable to locate itself using these techniques, the leader can call for an air or artillery orienting round. However, this may cause a loss of security, particularly if the unit is moving by stealth.

An airspot can usually be obtained from Army or Air Force aircraft. The pilot can be contacted and guided to the general location by radio. A mirror, smoke, panels, or some other signal can be shown to the pilot. He will be able to determine the unit's location and report it to them.

This, also, is a loss of security and should only be a last resort.

NIGHT MOVEMENT

The principles for navigation at night are the same as those for day movement. The problem in night movement is one of control, not navigation. In clear weather, through sparse vegetation and under a bright moon, a unit can move almost as fast by night as by day. If the sky is overcast, vegetation is thick, or there is little or no moon, movement will be slow and hard to control. The following points can assist a unit during night movement.

Attach *luminous tape* to the back of each soldier's headgear. Two strips, side by side, each about the size of a lieutenant's bar, are recommended. *The two strips aid depth perception and reduce the hypnotic effect that one strip can cause.*

When there is no light at all, distance between soldiers should be reduced. When necessary to prevent breaks in contact, each soldier should hold on to the belt or the pack of the man in front of him.

The leading man should carry a long stick to probe for sudden dropoffs or obstacles.

In limited visibility conditions, listening may become more important to security than observing. A unit which hears a strange noise should halt and listen for at least 1 minute. If the noise is repeated or cannot be identified, patrols should be sent out to investigate. Smell, likewise, can be an indication of enemy presence in an area.

All available night vision devices should be used.

NAVIGATIONAL TIPS

- Trust the map and compass, but understand the map's possible shortcomings. Use the compass bezel ring, especially during night navigation.
- Break brush. Do not move on trails or roads.
- Plan the move, and use the plan.
- Do not get frustrated. If in doubt, stop and think back over the route.
- Practice leads to confidence.

SECTION II. TRACKING

Visual tracking is following the paths of men or animals by the signs they leave, primarily on the ground or vegetation. Scent tracking is following men or animals by the odors they leave.

Practice in tracking is required to achieve and maintain a high standard of skill. Because of the excellent natural concealment the jungle offers, all soldiers should be familiar with the general techniques of visual tracking to enable them to detect the presence of a concealed enemy, to follow the enemy, to locate and avoid mines or boobytraps, and to give early warning of ambush.

Tracking is important in counterguerrills operations where it is often difficult to locate the enemy. Guerrillas who conduct raids and ambushes will normally return to their bases as quickly as possible. Well-developed tracking skills will help units to maintain contact with the enemy.

SIGNS

Men or animals moving through jungle areas leave signs of their passage. Some examples of these signs are listed below.

TRACKING POINTS	
SAVANNA	**ROCKY GROUND**
NOTE:If the grass is high, above 3 feet, trails are easy to follow because the grass is knocked down and normally stays down for several days. If the grass is short, it springs back in a shorter length of time. ■ **Grass that is tramped down will point in the direction that the person or animal is traveling.** ■ **Grass will show a contrast in color with the surrounding undergrowth when pressed down.** ■ **If the grass is wet with dew, the missing dew will show a trail where a person or an animal has traveled.** ■ **Mud or soil from boots may appear on some of the grass.** ■ **If new vegetation is showing through a track, the track is old.** ■ **In very short grass (12 inches or less) a boot will damage the grass near the ground and a footprint can be found.**	■ **Small stones and rocks are moved aside or rolled over when walked on. The soil is also disturbed, leaving a distinct variation in color and an impression. If the soil is wet, the underside of the stones will be much darker in color than the top when moved.** ■ **If the stone is brittle, it will chip and crumble when walked on. A light patch will appear where the stone is broken and the chips normally remain near the broken stone.** ■ **Stones on a loose or soft surface are pressed into the ground when walked upon. This leaves either a ridge around the edge of the stone where it has forced the dirt out, ora hole where the stone has been pushed below the surface of the ground.** ■ **Where moss is growing on rocks or stones, a boot or hand will scrape off some of the moss.**

TRACKING POINTS CONTINUED

PRIMARY JUNGLES

NOTE: Within rain forests and deciduous forests, there are many ways to track. This terrain includes undergrowth, live and dead leaves and trees, streams with muddy or sandy banks, and moss on the forest floor and on rocks, which makes tracking easier.

■ Disturbed leaves on the forest floor, when wet, show up a darker color when disturbed.

■ Dead leaves are brittle and will crack or break under pressure of a person walking on them. The same is true of dry twigs.

■ Where the undergrowth is thick, especially on the edges of the forest, green leaves of the bushes that have been pushed aside and twisted will show the underside of the leaf—this side is lighter in color than the upper surface. To find this sort of trail, the tracker must look through the jungle instead of directly at it.

■ Boot impressions may be left on fallen and rotting trees.

■ Marks may be left on the sides of logs lying across the path.

■ Roots running across a path may show signs that something has moved through the area.

■ Broken spiderwebs across a path indicate that something has moved through the area.

SECONDARY JUNGLE

■ Broken branches and twigs.

■ Leaves knocked off bushes and trees.

■ Branches bent in the direction of travel.

■ Footprints.

■ Tunnels made through vegetation.

■ Broken spiderwebs.

■ Pieces of clothing caught on the sharp edges of bushes.

RIVERS, STREAMS, MARSHES, AND SWAMPS

■ Footprints on the banks and in shallow water.

■ Mud stirred up and discoloring the water.

■ Rocks splashed with water in a quietly running stream.

■ Water on the ground at a point of exit.

■ Mud on grass or other vegetation near the edge of the water.

DECEPTION

The enemy may use any of the following methods to deceive or discourage trackers. They may, at times, mislead an experienced tracker.

These deceptions include:

- **Walking backwards. The heel mark tends to be deeper than that of the ball of the foot. The pace is shorter.**
- **More than one person stepping in the same tracks.**
- **Walking in streams.**
- **Splitting up into small groups.**
- **Walking along fallen trees or stepping from rock to rock.**
- **Covering tracks with leaves.**

WARNING

A tracker should always be alert to the possibility that the enemy is leaving false to lead the unit into an ambush.

CHAPTER 7

Jungle Obstacles

SECTION I. GENERAL

Units operating in the jungle will have to cross many obstacles. The most difficult obstacles will be streams and cliffs. In addition, units operating in the jungle will frequently have to insert or extract soldiers and units in places where helicopters cannot land. This chapter covers the skills required to perform these tasks.

Before learning these skills, however, soldiers must be familiar with ropes and knots.

SECTION II. CHARACTERISTICS AND USE OF EQUIPMENT

ROPES AND KNOTS TYPES OF ROPE

Nylon. Nylon rope is most commonly used in climbing and rappelling. The rope is seven-sixteenths of an inch in diameter and is issued in 120-foot lengths. Its dry breaking strength averages 3,840 pounds (plus or minus 5 percent). Strength is reduced by about 20 percent when the rope is wet. It will also stretch about one-third of its length when wet. Nylon sling (utility) ropes are commonly prepared by a unit in 12-foot lengths from older ropes that are no longer used for climbing or rappelling.

Vegetable Fiber. This is readily available in jungle areas as it is made primarily from the fibers of tropical plants.

Manila rope is made from the fibers of the leaves of a banana tree. The lighter the color of the rope, the better the quality. This rope is superior to nylon rope for suspension traverses and rope bridges because it does not stretch as much as nylon, and it is not weakened when wet.

> **The breaking strength and safe load capacity (respectively) for the sizes of manila rope most often used by jungle troops are:**
>
> **1-inch-diameter rope-9,000 pounds/ 2,250 pounds**
>
> **1/2-inch-diameter rope-3,650 pounds/ 660 pounds**

Hemp rope is made from the fibers of the hemp plant. This is the strongest of the fiber ropes. It is usually soaked in tar to preserve the rope from damage caused by dampness, but this tar tends to reduce the rope's strength. Also, because of its greater weight, tarred hemp is not practical for use by infantry troops.

> ✍ **NOTE**
> The breaking strength of a rope is always greater than its safe working capacity. The difference is a "safety factor." Individual ropes can vary greatly in minimum breaking strength. Even though a rope may not break under this load, the fibers are stretched beyond their elastic limit. Thereafter the strength of the rope is permanently reduced. Exposure, wear, use, and bending decrease a rope's strength over a period of time. This should be allowed for in estimating the strength of a used rope. The strength of a rope that is slung over a hook or contains a knot is reduced by about 30 percent; sharp bends over corners will cut strength by 50 percent; sand or grit between the fibers will quickly cut the fibers, and sharply drop the overall strength of the rope.

CARE OF A ROPE

Clean a muddy rope by washing it in water, but not in salt water.

Do not pull a rope over sharp edges. Place layers of heavy cloth or grass between the rope and any sharp edge to prevent the cutting of fibers.

Do not drag a rope through sand and dirt, or step on it, or drive over it.

Keep a rope dry. If it gets wet, dry it as soon as possible to prevent rotting. (A mildewed rope will have a musty odor and inner fibers will have a dark, stained look.)

Do not leave a rope knotted or tightly stretched any longer than needed.

Never splice a climbing or rappelling rope.

Inspect a rope often, both the outside and the inside. Untwist a few strands at different points to open the rope to check the inside.

Melted nylon and dark streaks indicate burns. Nylon rope burns when it rubs against other nylon ropes. Nylon ropes should never be tied in such a way that there is rope-to-rope friction.

Dirt and sawdust-like material inside the rope indicates damage.

A rope should be checked at a number of different places—any weak point in it weakens the entire rope.

Whenever any unsafe conditions are found in a rope, it should be destroyed or cut up in short pieces. This will prevent use of the rope for hoisting. The short pieces can be used for toggle ropes and for other purposes which do not involve load bearing operations.

KNOT-TYING TERMS

Knots to tie the end of a rope to an object (anchor knots).

The bowline will not slip under strain, yet it is easily untied.

Clove hitch used as an intermediate anchor with tension applied at all times to prevent slipping.

Round turn with two half-hitches.

Knots to tie the ends of two ropes together.

A square knot is used to tie ropes of equal diameter together.

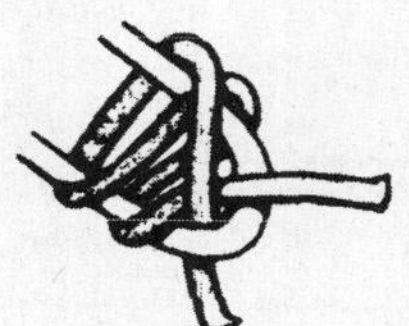

The double sheet bend knot is used to tie ropes of unequal diameter together.

Middle-of-rope knots.

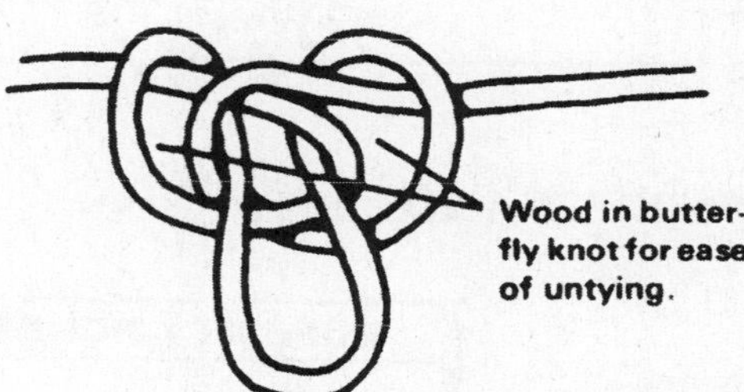

Wood in butterfly knot for ease of untying.

The butterfly knot is used to pull a line tight.

NOTE: After a butterfly knot is tied for a rope bridge, or for any other purpose where a great amount of strain or tension is applied to the knot, it becomes almost impossible to untie. Pieces of wood or pipe inserted through the two loops or wings of the knot will make it easier to untie.

Special knots.

The Prusik knot is used to tie one rope around another. One rope will slide along the other if there is no tension, and it will hold if tension is applied. This knot should be tied off with a bowline.

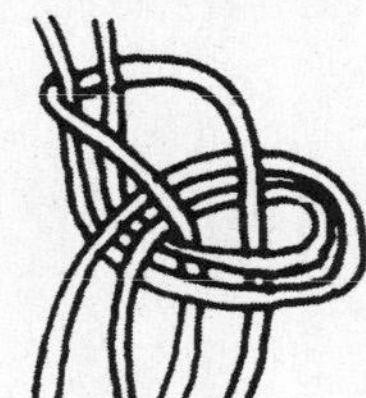

Bowline on a bight forms a double loop.

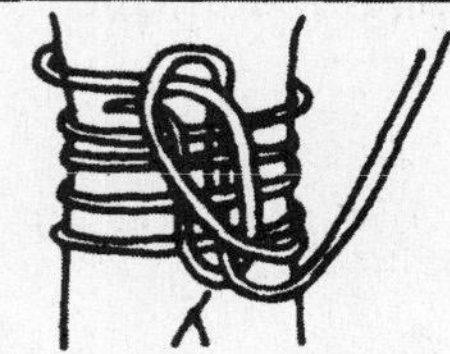

Bowline on a coil can be used by the first and last man on a climbing rope to take up unnecessary slack. A half-hitch must be employed behind the knot.

SEAT-HIP RAPPEL

The seat-hip rappel is a fast method. In this rappel, friction is taken up by getting down from a steep hill or cliff, and the snaplink inserted in a rappel seat is fastened. It is also used to rappel from helicopters.

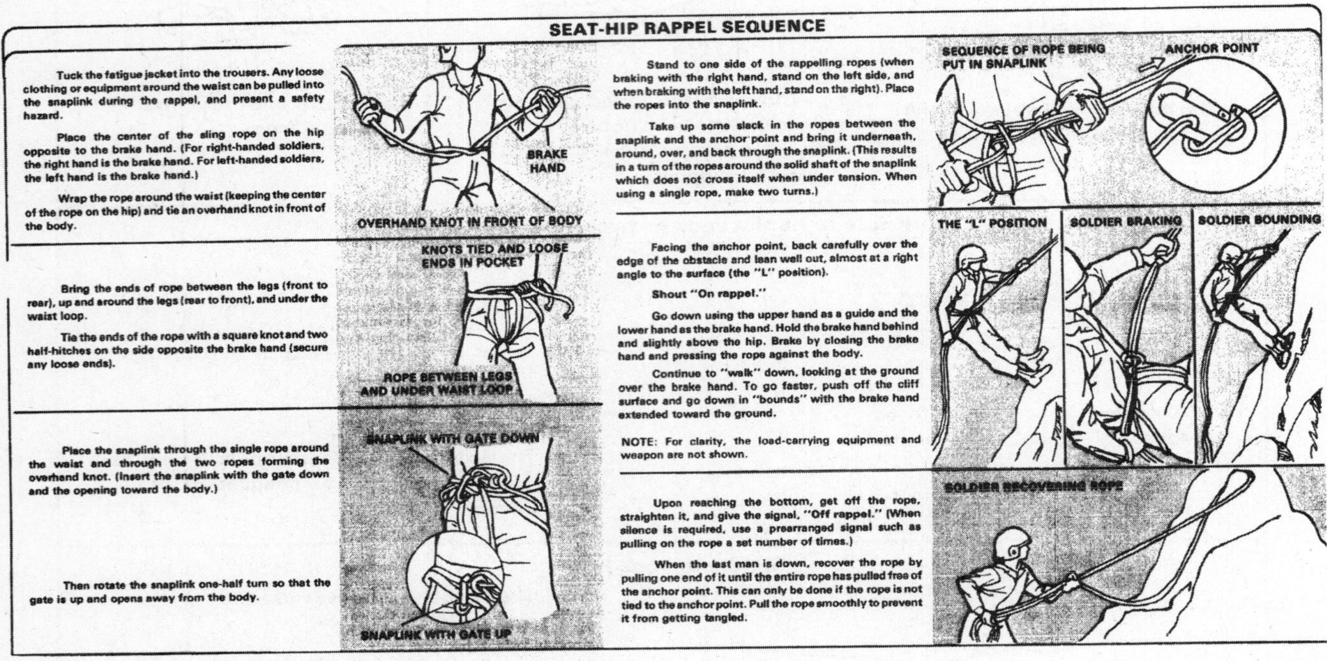

SECTION III. MOVING DOWN HILLS AND CLIFFS

RAPPELLING

Rappelling is a means to move quickly down very steep hills and cliffs. Rappelling involves sliding down a rope which has been anchored around a firm object (anchor point) such as a tree, projecting rock, or piton.

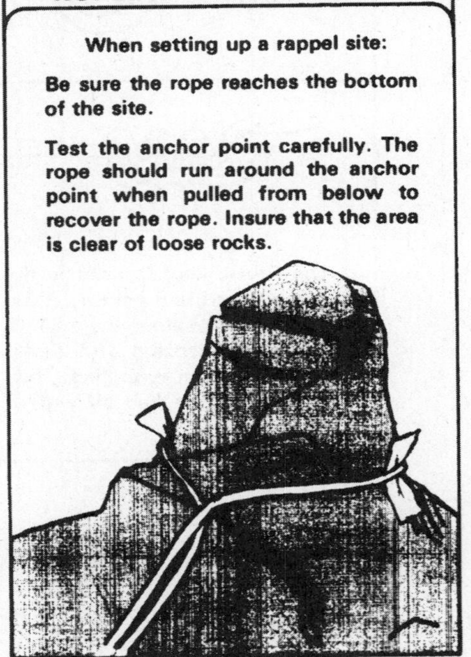

HASTY RAPPEL

The hasty rappel is a fast, easy way to get down a moderately steep slope or cliff. A soldier must wear a shirt to do a hasty rappel.

HASTY RAPPEL

To conduct a hasty rappel:

Face slightly sideways to the anchor point and place the ropes across the back. The hand nearest the anchor is the guide hand, and the lower hand is the brake hand.

Walk sideways down the hill or cliff, letting the rope move through the hands and across the back.

To stop, bring the brake hand across in front of the body, locking the rope. At the same time, turn and face up toward the anchor point.

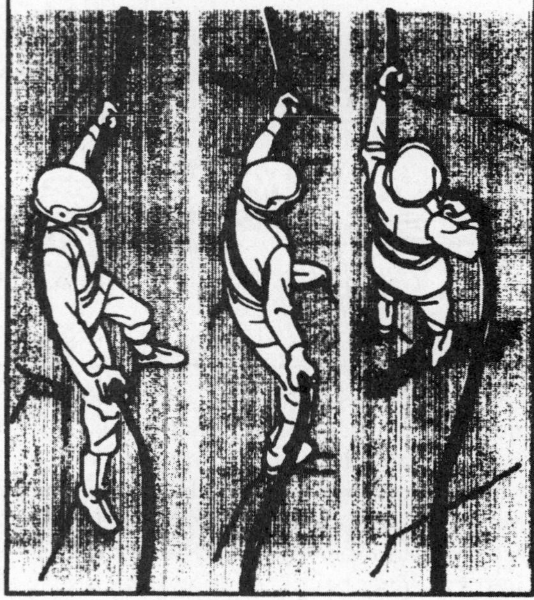

> ⚠ CAUTION
>
> Gloves must be worn during all rappelling to protect the hands from severe rope burns.

SECTION IV. MOVING BY HELICOPTER

RAPPELLING FROM HELICOPTERS

In the jungle, there are many places where the vegetation or the ruggedness of the terrain will not permit a helicopter to land. Therefore, it maybe necessary to rappel from a helicopter to get on the ground. Special equipment is required to rappel from helicopters. There are no safe field expedients. The following paragraphs describe the equipment and procedure used in rappelling from helicopters and furnish information on other extraction means.

EQUIPMENT

The *donut ring* is the primary anchoring device (anchor point) inside a helicopter. The floating safety ring is the secondary anchor point. The donut ring consists of a 12-inch solid ring of ½-inch cold-rolled steel cable; seven parachute static line snap hooks; four ½-inch U-bolts; and 12 inches of chain or ½-inch cable.

The *log coil* helps the double rappelling rope fall clear of the aircraft. To prepare it, start with the running end of the rope and coil the rope evenly and tightly around the log. Use a log approximately 2 to 3 inches in diameter and 16 to 24 inches long.

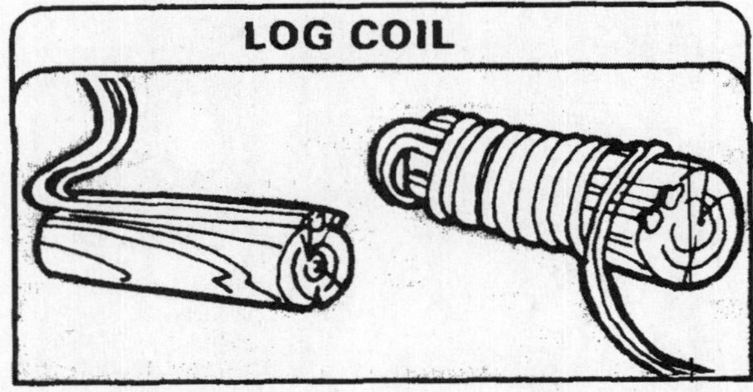

A system that has proven to be almost ideal for rope deployment in helicopter rappel operations is that of the rope deployment bag. The rope deployment bag is issue as a component of the Stabo extraction system The ropes are prepared in the normal rappel configuration and stretched to full length The D-bag is placed at the loose ends of rope opposite the snaplinks. After insur that all rubber bands are present all stowing lines of the D-bag, a bight is formed in the two runnings ends of the rappel ropes and then placed in the center retainer band just above the stow pocket. The rope is then folded and stowed in the retainer bands working from side to side of the D-bag, while making sure that folds do not extend past either side of the D-bag. Six to eight folds of rope are placed in each retainer band, working towards the top of the D-bag. Once the top of the bag is reached, a bight is formed in the climbing ropes 24 inches below the first snaplink and stowed in the top center retainer band. After the D-bag is inspected, the bag is rolled, going from bottom to top, leaving the snaplinks exposed. Tape is used to secure the top flap of the bag.

PROCEDURES

The rappelling rope is connected to the donut ring and the floating safety ring, in the following order, and in the manner described.

CONNECTION OF A RAPPELLING ROPE

The No. 1 snaplink is attached to the donut ring in the following manner:

Take a bight (loop of rope) approximately 5 feet from the end of the working end of the rope.

Insert the rope into the snaplink.

Make one turn through the snaplink, forming a round turn.

Secure the round turn to the snaplink with two half-hitches.

NOTE: Again, for clarity, a single rope is shown. But a double rope would be actually used.

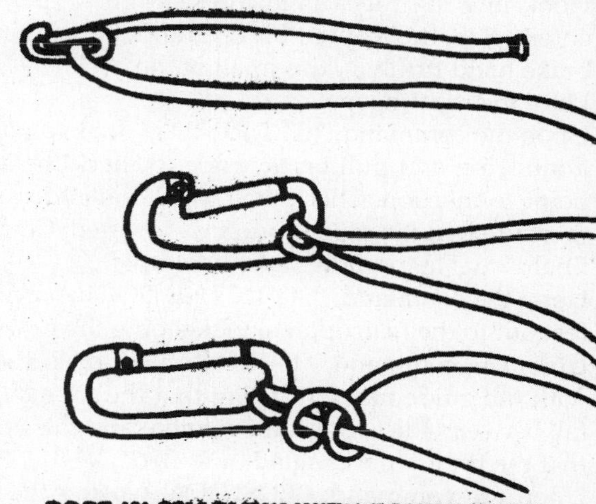

ROPE IN SNAPLINK WITH ROUND TURN AND TWO HALF-HITCHES

Snap the snaplink (gate upward and facing away from the knot) to the donut ring cable.

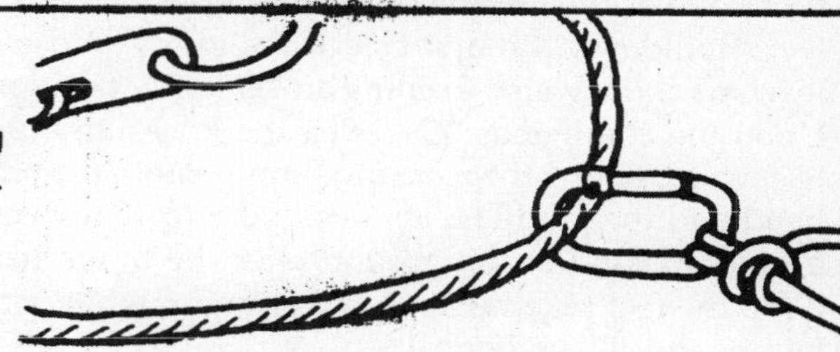

SNAPLINK SNAPPED TO CABLE

The No. 2. snaplink is attached to the floating safety ring in the same manner as the No. 1 snaplink, with the following exceptions:

Take a bight approximately 2 feet from the end of the working end of the rope.

Connect the snaplink to the rope in the same manner as the first connection. Tape the end of the working end of the rope and the knots with masking tape to secure them in place.

Snap the snaplink (gate upward and facing away from the knot) to the floating safety ring.

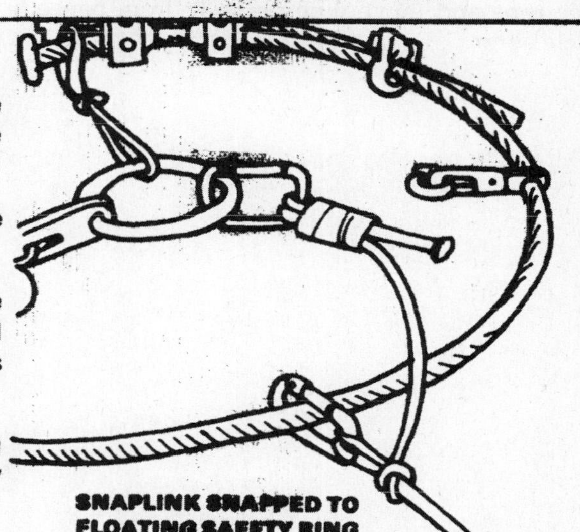

SNAPLINK SNAPPED TO FLOATING SAFETY RING

To rappel from a helicopter:

- Hook into the rope, as in the seat-hip rappel, upon entering the helicopter. Sit on the floor, keeping the brake hand firmly in the small of the back.
- Place the rope in lap.
- Upon the command, "GET READY," look toward the donut ring and pull on the rope to check the anchor point connection. Check the rappel seat and snaplink to insure that the rope is properly inserted. Conduct a final visual inspection of the hookup.
- Upon the command, "SIT IN THE DOOR," swing the feet out to the helicopter skid, keeping the brake on.
- Upon the command, "DROP ROPE," drop the rope with the guide hand, insuring that the rope does not fall between the cargo compartment and the skid and that the rope is not tangled or fouled.
- Upon the command, "POSITION," using the guide hand to assist, pivot 180 degrees on the helicopter and skid bar. Face the inside of the helicopter. Spread the feet shoulder-width apart; lock the knees; and bend forward at the waist, forming an "L" body position.
- Upon the command, "*Go,*" flex the knees and jump backward, letting the rope run through both the brake hand and the guide hand. Descend 5 to 10 meters at a time, looking at the ground over the brake hand. Keep the feet together and legs straight, while maintaining the "L" body position.
- Upon reaching the ground, back all the way out of the rope and move quickly away from beneath the helicopter.

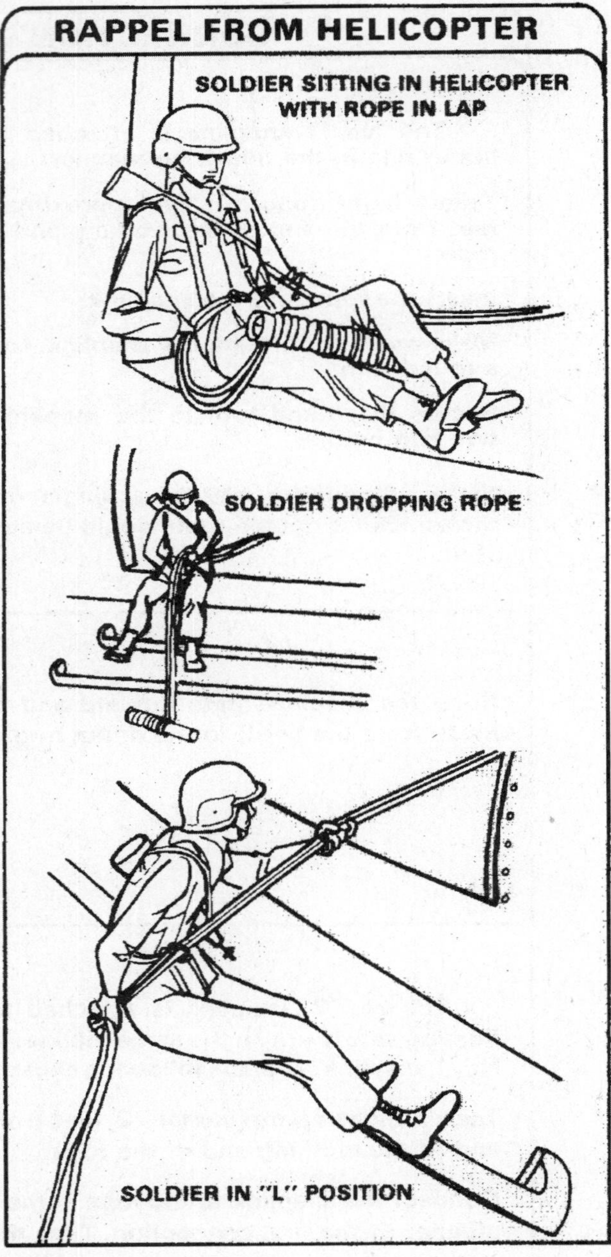

OTHER MEANS OF ENTERING AND LEAVING HELICOPTERS

The *troop ladder* is a good method for larger groups to enter or leave an area where the helicopter cannot land. Installation of the ladder is an aviation responsibility. The crew chief will control the number of troops on the ladder. Only five or six troops will be allowed on the ladder at a time.

Use the legs for climbing and descending; the arms for stability and holding the ladder close to the body.

If possible, each soldier, and especially those carrying heavy loads, should tie a rappel seat with a snaplink attached before ascending. Then, if he becomes tired, he can "snap in," avoiding the chance of a fall.

When going down a ladder, the first soldier on the ground steadies the ladder for the remaining troops. When climbing up a ladder, the soldier designated to hold the ladder steady is the last one up the ladder. If the helicopter starts going up before everyone is loaded, the soldier holding the ladder on the ground should release it at once.

When on the ladder, remain calm at all times. If the helicopter should start settling to the ground, stay calm, watch the ground, and stay on the ladder until reaching the ground.

Once on the ground, move from underneath the helicopter.

TROOP LADDER

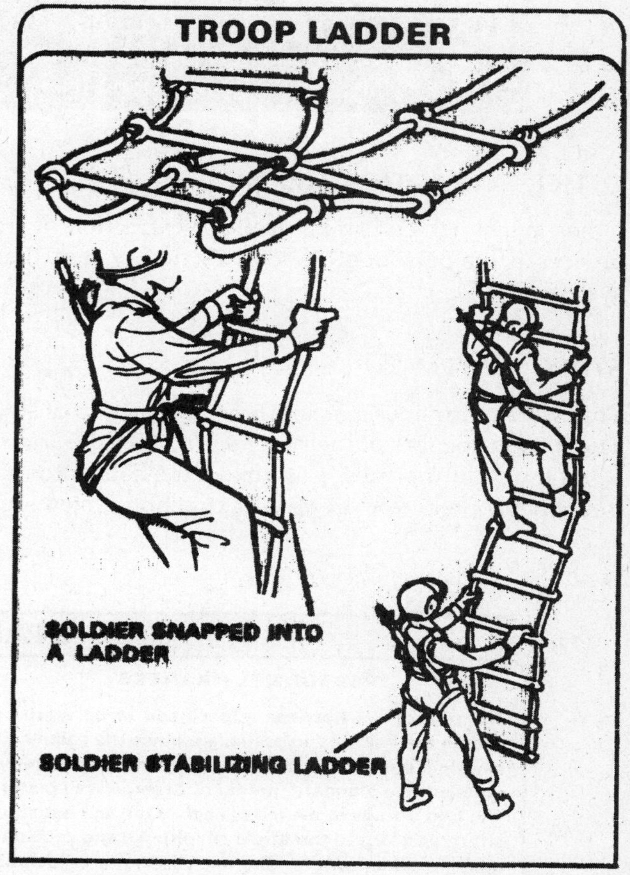

The *jungle penetrator* is a metal seat rescue assembly attached to a winch on a helicopter. The seats remain folded when the device is being lowered. The seats are unfolded when the device is on the ground. A conical nose allows it to penetrate the jungle foliage. One to three soldiers (two is a standard load) can be placed on it. Nylon straps are placed under the arms of the soldier(s) to be hoisted. The device lifts the soldier(s) into the helicopter.

JUNGLE PENETRATOR

WARNING

While the penetrator is being lowered. Static electricity can build up on the metal surface. The penetrator should touch the ground before anyone touches it. To allow the static electricity to ground itself.

OTHER EXTRACTION MEANS

Other means which can be used for extraction of troops where landing zones (LZ) are not available include such devices as the personnel Stabo extraction system, the Maguire rig, the Palmer rig, or the jungle operations extraction system (JOES).

STABO SYSTEM

This system provides a means for rapid pickup of soldiers by helicopter from areas where the helicopter cannot land. The system consists of the *personnel harness*, the *bridle, the suspension rope*, the *safety rope*, and the *deployment bag*.

As the pickup process is initiated, the helicopter hovers over the pickup zone at altitudes up to 150 feet. A member of the helicopter crew drops the extraction system deployment bag from the left door of the helicopter. (A maximum

STABO SYSTEM

PERSONNEL HARNESS

The **personnel harness** is designed to be worn by the user in the field and to partially replace the soldier's load-carrying equipment. It is made of nylon webbing and stitched to a standard, medium, or large web pistol belt. The two V-rings at the top of each of the harness shoulder straps connect to the bridle snaphooks and provide a lift point for the harness. The leg straps are adjustable for comfort. When the user is in the field, leg straps may be disconnected, folded, and secured to a suitable point on the harness.

BRIDLE

The **bridle** is also made of nylon webbing. During use, the D-ring is connected to a suspension rope snaphook while the two bridle snaphooks are attached to the two personnel harness lift V-rings.

SUSPENSION ROPE

The **suspension rope** is the same nylon rope that is used for rappelling. It has snaphooks attached to both ends: one to connect to the bridle and one to connect to the anchor point in the helicopter.

SAFETY ROPE

The **safety rope** is 3 meters long and made of nylon. Each end is looped and spliced, with a snaphook attached to each loop. It is used when two or three soldiers are extracted together, and it provides a means for them to hold together to minimize wind buffeting and oscilation during pickup and flight.

DEPLOYMENT BAG

The **deployment bag** is made of cotton duck and contains the bridle, suspension rope, and safety rope.

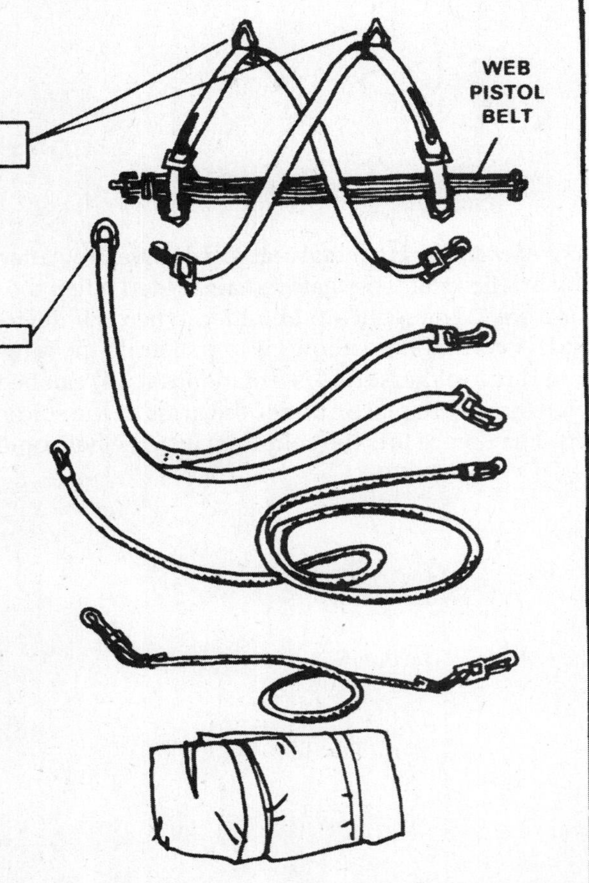

of three units may be connected and dropped simultaneously.) As the deployment bag descends, the suspension rope deploys until the bag reaches the ground. The soldier to be extracted then attaches the bridle snaphooks to the lift V-rings on his harness. After insuring that the leg straps are connected and tight the soldier notifies the helicopter by radio or hand signals that liftoff may begin. The helicopter then lifts the soldier from the area and, carrying him suspended beneath the helicopter, moves to an area where a safe landing can be made. The helicopter then lowers the suspended soldier to the ground, lands nearby, and allows him to board the helicopter.

SOLDIER IN HARNESS BEING LIFTED OFF

PALMER RIG

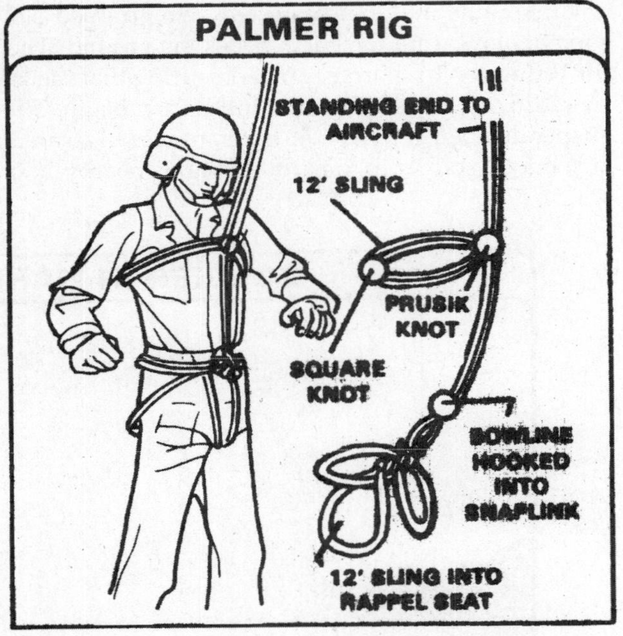

This rig is constructed with the 120-foot nylon rope and two 12-foot nylon sling ropes. One end of the 120-foot rope is secured to the donut ring. The running end of the 120-foot rope is tied with an end of the rope bowline knot at the end of the rope. One of the 12-foot sling ropes is tied 3 feet above the bowline with a Prusik knot, and the loose ends are tied off with a square knot to form a loop. The rider uses the remaining sling rope to form a rappel seat. He then fastens a snaplink to the rappel seat and the bowline knot, places his arms up and through the upper loop, and is extracted. The Palmer rig is relatively safe and may be used when evacuating wounded personnel.

MAGUIRE RIG

This rig is also simple and easy to construct. It is made with an 8-foot by 2-inch piece of nylon webbing sewn together at the ends to form a loop containing a D-ring. A smaller slip loop (wrist loop) is sewn 12 inches down from the top of the larger loop. During extraction, the rider simply sits in the seat of the large loop. He then places his wrist in the slip loop and tightens the loop, insuring that he does not fall from the larger loop during extraction.

JUNGLE OPERATIONS EXTRACTION SYSTEM

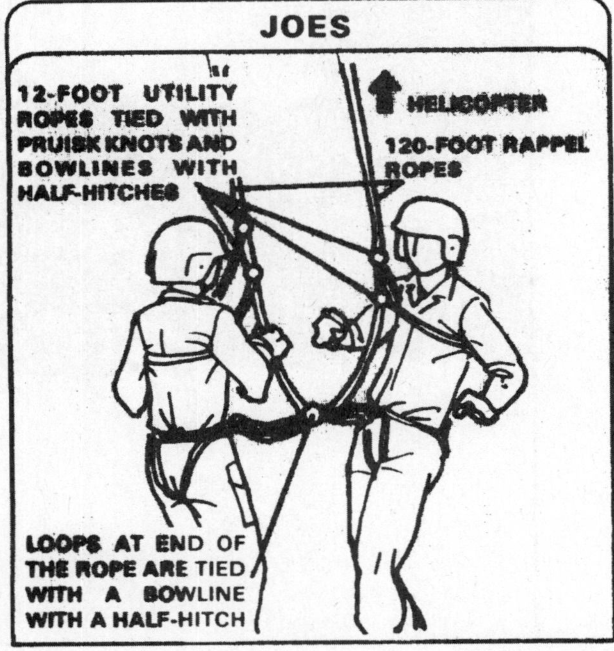

This system was developed after careful evaluation of the three previously mentioned systems, while considering those items of equipment available to the individual soldier. The JOES can be quickly constructed from components readily available from the supply system. The individual soldier requires very little (10 to 15 minutes) training in what he will be required to do if he needs to be extracted, and only a maximum of 5 minutes is required for him to actually prepare for extraction.

CONSTRUCTION OF A JOES FOR TWO INDIVIDUALS

Material needed:

- **Anchor system for helicopter (donut ring).**
- **Two 120-foot rappel ropes.**
- **Three military snaplinks.**
- **Two 12-foot utility ropes.**
- **One deployment system.**

Once all equipment has been thoroughly inspected, the JOES is prepared in the following manner.

- **Lay out both 120-foot rappel ropes side by side.**
- **Move to one end and, taking both ropes as one, tie a round turn and two half-hitches around a snaplink approximately 5 feet from the end.**
- **From the first knot, move 18 inches toward the short end of the rope and tie another round turn and two half-hitches around another snaplink. Tape any excess rope. This now becomes the fixed end of the rope and will be attached to the anchor system in the helicopter.**
- **Move to the working end of the rope and, taking both ropes as one, tie a bowline with a half-hitch. The loops formed by this bowline should be approximately 12 inches in diameter, Any excess over 6 inches should be taped to help eliminate confusion during hook up.**
- **Approximately 18 inches from the top of the bowline knot toward the fixed end of the rope, take one end of a 12-foot utility rope and tie a Prusik knot and a bowline with a half-hitch around one 1 20-foot rappel rope.**
- **On the same rope, using the other end of the 12-foot utility rope, tie the same knot directly below the first.**
- **Repeat steps 5 and 6 with another sling rope on the other 120-foot rappel rope.**
- **Pack JOES in D-bag.**

Each individual who is to be extracted must have a 12-foot utility rope and a snaplink. If the individual does not have these items, they can be dropped to him with the JOES. The individual to be extracted makes a rappel seat out of the 12-foot utility rope and installs the snaplink as if he were going to make a rappel.

When JOES is dropped, he and his buddy move to the bag. Each individual hooks his snaplink into one loop at the end of the rope bowline, and places the loop formed by one of the 12-foot utility ropes over his shoulders and under his armpits. He and his buddy stay as far back from the helicopter as practical until it starts to lift up, and as tension is put on the rope, they move forward until they are directly underneath it and linked up with other personnel. All soldiers should link up by holding onto the adjacent person's equipment.

SECTION V. MOVING ACROSS WATER OBSTACLES

CROSSING RIVERS AND STREAMS

There are several expedient ways to cross rivers and streams. The ways used in any situation depends on the width and depth of the water, the speed of the current, the time and equipment available, and the friendly and enemy situation.

There is always a possibility of equipment failure. For this reason, every soldier should be able to swim. In all water crossings several strong swimmers should be stationed either at the water's edge or, if possible, in midstream to help anyone who gets into trouble.

If a soldier accidentally falls into the water, he should swim with the current to the nearer bank. Swimming against the current is dangerous because the swimmer is quickly exhausted by the force of the current.

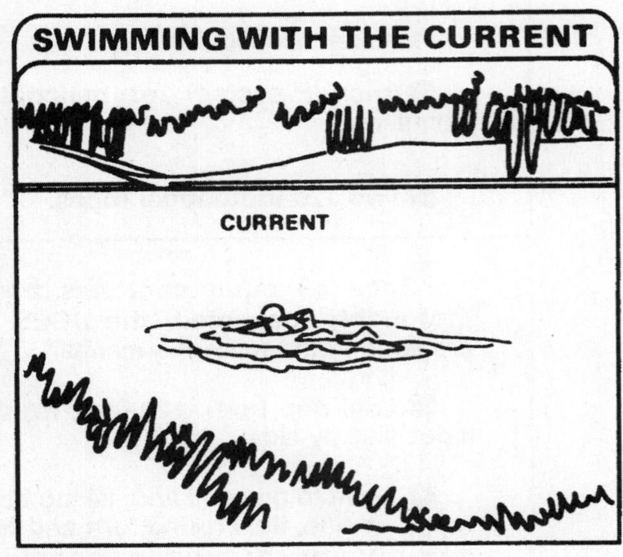

FORDING

A good site to ford a stream has these characteristics:

- Good concealment on both banks.
- Few large rocks in the river bed. (Submerged large rocks are usually slippery and make it difficult to maintain footing.)
- Shallow water or a sandbar in the middle of the stream. Troops may rest or regain their footing on these sandbars.
- Low banks to make entry and exit easier. High banks normally mean deep water. Deep water near the far shore is especially dangerous as the soldiers may be tired and less able to get out.

A unit should cross at an angle against the current. Each soldier should keep his feet wide apart and drag his legs through the water, not lift them, so that the current will not throw him off balance. Poles can be used to probe in front of the troops to help find deep holes and maintain footing.

FLOATING AIDS

For deeper streams which have little current, soldiers can use a number of floating aids such as the following:

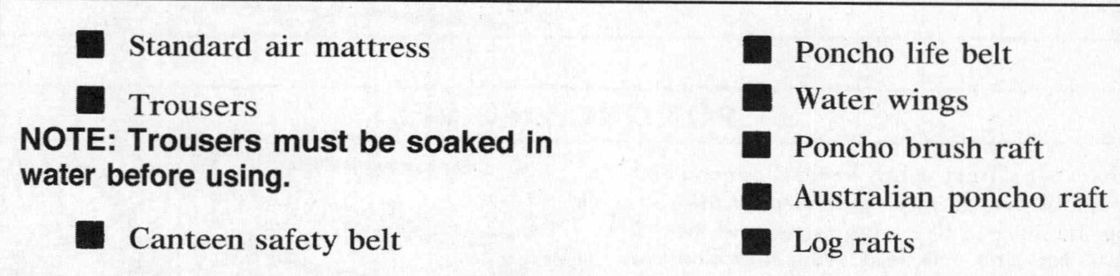

- Standard air mattress
- Trousers

NOTE: Trousers must be soaked in water before using.

- Canteen safety belt
- Poncho life belt
- Water wings
- Poncho brush raft
- Australian poncho raft
- Log rafts

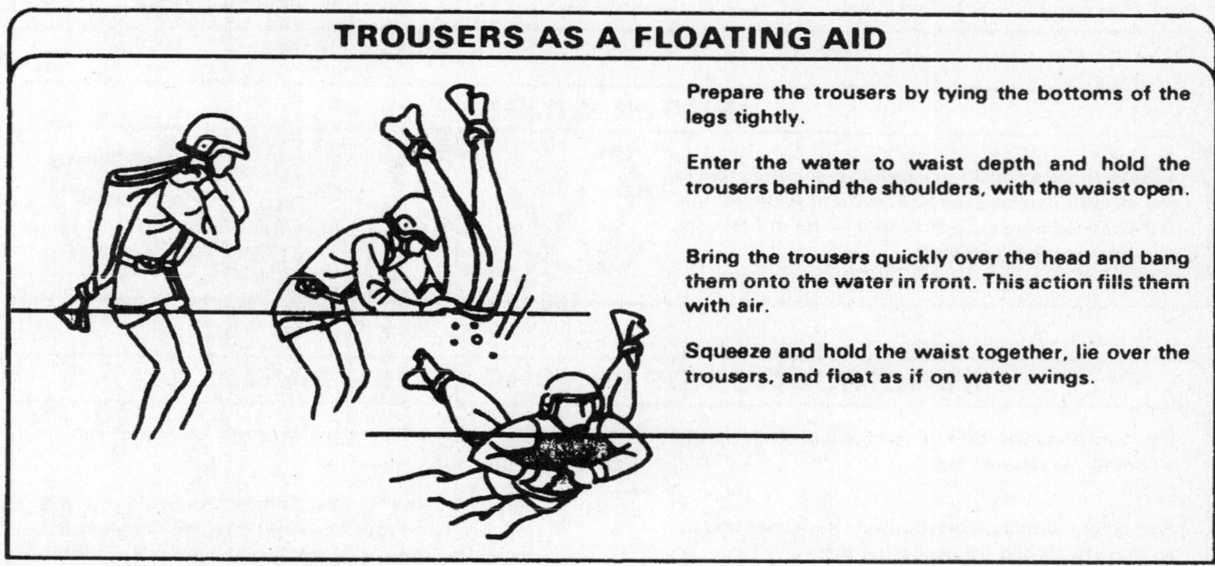

CANTEEN SAFETY BELT

Attach at least eight empty plastic canteens to a pistol belt (or tie them to a rope which can then be used as a belt). Insure that the caps are screwed on tightly.

PONCHO LIFE BELT

Roll green vegetation tightly inside a poncho and fold the ends over to make a watertight life belt. Roll up the life belt like a big sausage at least 8 inches in diameter and tie it. Wear it around the waist or across one shoulder and under the opposite arm like a bandoleer.

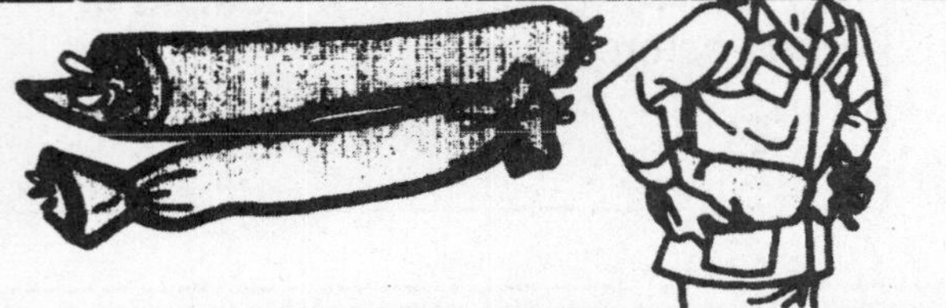

WATER WINGS

Two or more air-filled plastic bags, securely tied at the mouth, can be used as expedient water wings. Other expedients include empty water or fuel cans and ammunition canisters.

CONSTRUCTION OF PONCHO BRUSH RAFT

Use two ponchos, and tie the neck of each tightly by using the drawstring.

Spread one poncho on the ground with the hood up so that it will end up inside the raft.

Cut fresh, green brush (avoid thick branches or wood stakes) and pile it on the poncho to a height of 18 inches.

Place an X-frame made of small saplings (1 to 1 1/2 inches in diameter and 3 to 4 feet long) on the brush. Anchor this frame by tying the drawstring of the poncho to the center of the X-frame.

Pile another 18 inches of brush on top of the X-frame.

Compress the brush slightly and fold up the poncho, tying ropes or vines diagonally across the corner grommets and straight across from side grommets. The sides of the poncho should not touch.

Spread the second poncho on the ground, with hood up, next to the bundle made of the first poncho and brush. Roll the bundle over onto the center of the second poncho and tie the second poncho across the sides and diagonally across the corners. This raft will safely float 250 pounds and is very stable.

CONSTRUCTION OF AUSTRALIAN PONCHO RAFT

When there is not enough time to gather a lot of brush, this raft is made by using a soldier's combat equipment for bulk. Normally, two soldiers make this poncho together. It is more waterproof than the poncho brush raft but will float only about 80 pounds of weight. Two soldiers make this raft as follows.

Place one poncho on the ground with the hood facing up. Close the neck opening by tying it off with the drawstring.

Place two poles (or branches), about 1 to 1 1/2 inches in diameter and 4 feet long, in the center of the poncho about 18 inches apart.

Next, place the rucksack, and any other equipment desired, between the poles.

Snap the poncho together. Hold the snapped portion of the poncho in the air and roll it tightly down toward the equipment. Roll from the center out to both ends. At the ends, twist the poncho to form "pigtails." Fold the pigtails inward toward each other and tie them tightly together with boot laces, vines, communication wire, or other available tying material.

Spread the second poncho on the ground, neck closed and facing up.

Place the equipment bundle formed with the first poncho, with the seam (tied pigtails) facing down, on the second poncho.

Roll and tie the second poncho in the same way as the first.

An empty canteen tied to one end of a rope with the other end tied to the raft helps in towing. One soldier pulls on the rope while the other pushes the raft. Place weapons on top of the raft and secure them with ropes. The weapons should be secured to the raft by the use of quick releases. The raft is now ready for the water.

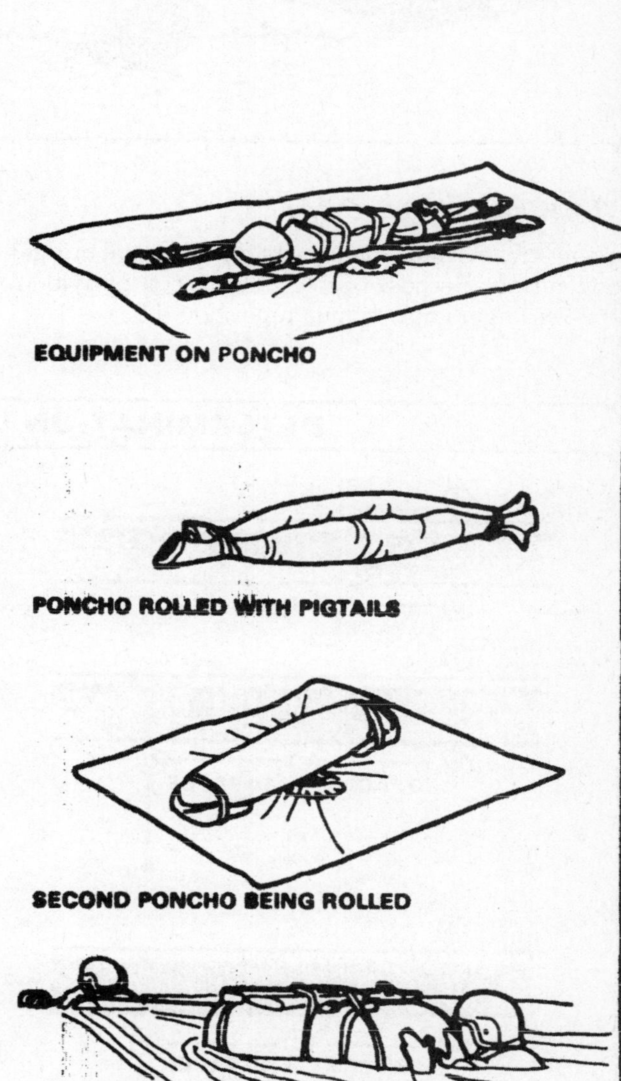

When launching any poncho raft or leaving the water with it, take care not to drag it on the ground as this will cause punctures or tears.

CONSTRUCTION OF LOG RAFT

Logs, either singly or lashed together, can be used to float soldiers and equipment. Be careful when selecting logs for rafts. Some jungle trees will not float. To see whether certain wood is suitable, put a wood chip from a tree in the water. If the chip sinks, so will a raft made of that wood.

ROPE BRIDGES

For crossing streams and small rivers quickly, rope bridges offer a suitable temporary system, especially when there is a strong current. Because of the stretch factor of nylon ropes, they should not be used to cross gaps of more than 20 meters. For larger gaps, manila rope should be used.

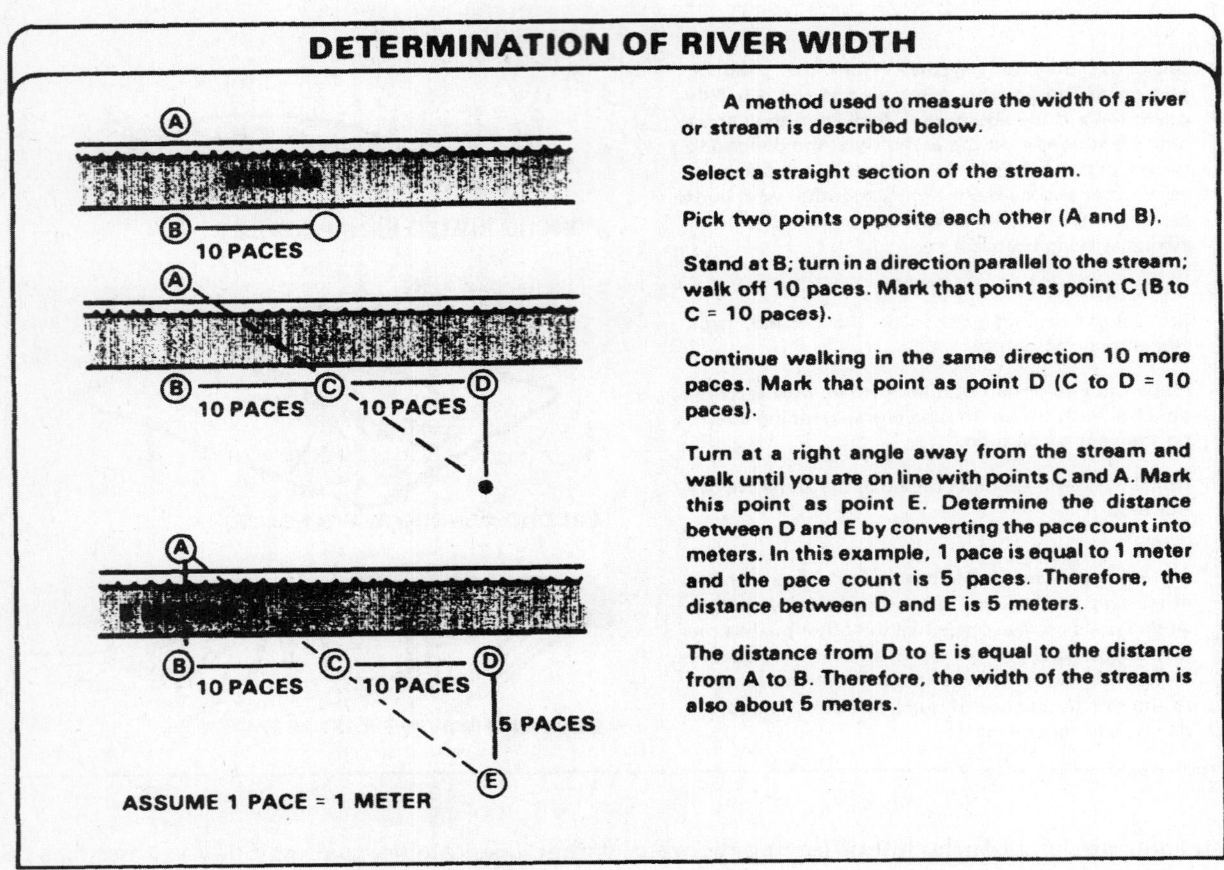

In order to erect a rope bridge, the first thing to be done is to get one end of the rope across the stream. This task can be frustrating when there is a strong current. To get the rope across, anchor one end of a rope that is at least double the width of the stream at point A. Take the other end of the line upstream as far as it will go. Then, tie a sling rope around the waist of a strong swimmer and, using a snaplink, attach the line to him. He should swim diagonally downstream to the far bank, pulling the rope across.

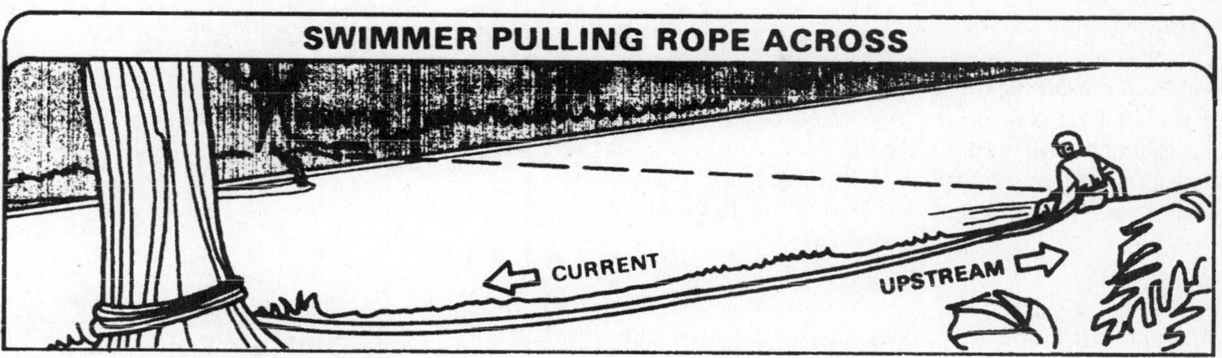

SWIMMER PULLING ROPE ACROSS

One-Rope Bridge. A one-rope bridge can be constructed either above water level or at water level. The leader must decide which to construct. The bridge is constructed the same regardless of the level.

CONSTRUCTION OF ONE-ROPE BRIDGE

To construct this bridge:

The bridge rope is pulled around the upstream side of the far side anchor point and temporarily secured without tying a knot. On the near side, a transport-tightening system is placed in the bridge rope by tying a double butterfly knot and placing two snaplinks in the butterfly. The running end of the bridge rope is then passed around the downstream side of the near side anchor point and through the two snaplinks.

When this transport-tightening system is prepared, the soldier on the far side pulls the butterfly knot approximately a third of the distance across the river. He then secures the bridge rope to the far side anchor point using a round turn and two half-hitches. Soldiers on the near side then pull the slack out of the bridge rope until the butterfly knot is back on the near side. (The bridge rope must be as tight as possible so that it will not sag when used.) The bridge rope is then tied off against itself using two half-hitches with a quick release in the last half-hitch.

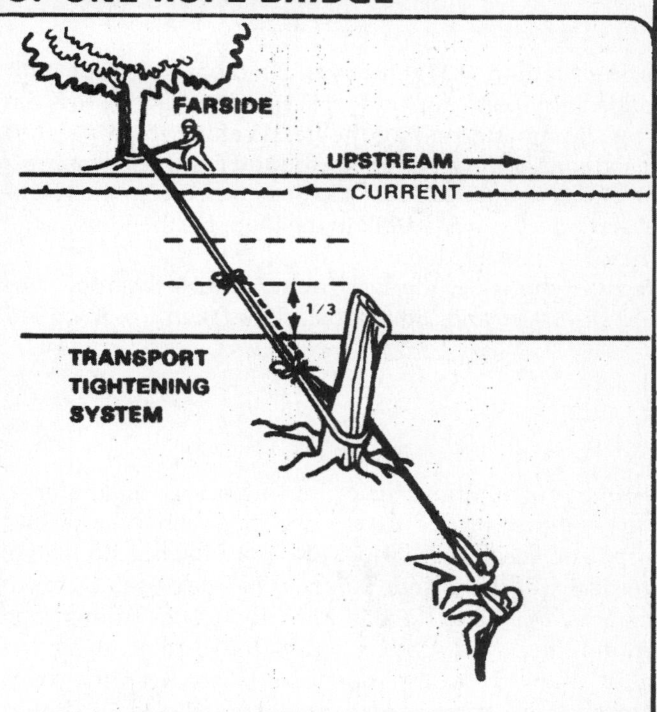

Crossing Method above Water Level. Use one of the following methods.

Commando crawl. Lie on the top of the rope with the instep of the right foot hooked on the rope. Let the left leg hang to maintain balance. Pull across with the hands and arms, at the same time pushing on the rope with the right foot. (For safety, each soldier ties a rappel seat and hooks the snaplink to the rope bridge.)

Monkey crawl. Hang suspended below the rope, holding the rope with the hands and crossing the knees over the top of the rope. Pull with the hands and push with the legs. (For safety, each soldier ties a rappel seat and hooks the snaplink to the rope bridge.) This is the safest and the best way to cross the one-rope bridge.

Crossing Method at Water Level. Hold onto the rope with both hands, face upstream, and walk into the water. Cross the bridge by sliding and pulling the hands along the rope. (For safety, each soldier ties a sling rope around his waist, leaving a working end of about 3 to 4 feet. He ties a bowline in the working end and attaches a snaplink to the loop. He then hooks the snaplink to the rope bridge.)

To recover the rope, the last soldier unties the rope, ties it around his waist and, after all slack is taken up, is pulled across.

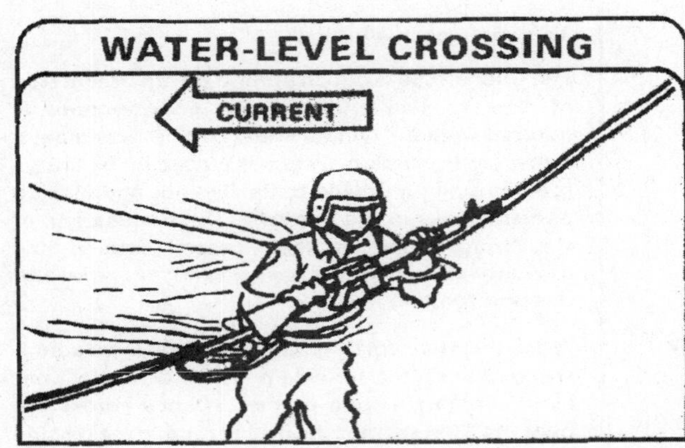

Two-rope bridge. Construction of this bridge is similar to that of the one-rope bridge, except two ropes, a hand rope and a foot rope, are used. These ropes are spaced about 1.5 meters apart vertically at the anchor points. (For added safety, make snaplink attachments to the hand and foot ropes from a rope tied around the waist. Move across the bridge using the snaplink to allow the safety rope to slide.) To keep the ropes a uniform distance apart as men cross, spreader ropes should be tied between the two ropes every 15 feet. A sling rope is used and tied to each bridge rope with a round turn and two half-hitches.

OTHER CROSSING MEANS

Suspension traverses, bridges, and cableways can be used to move large numbers of soldiers or heavy equipment over wide rivers and ravines, or up and down cliffs in a short period of time. Because heavy or bulky material or equipment is needed to construct these expedients, their use is practical only if the needed items can be transported to the site by air or surface means (watercraft, pack animals, etc.).

CHAPTER 8

Waterborne Operations

SECTION I. GENERAL

The inland waterways and jungle coastal or delta regions are land environments dominated by water routes. There may be one or more major waterways and an extensive network of smaller waterways. Usable roads are scarce, and cross-country movement is extremely difficult. The following describes jungle waterways.

UPPER SECTOR (HEADWATERS)

The headwaters of a waterway are usually formed in a mountainous region. The headwaters consist of numerous tributaries which merge to form a river system as the water flows down to the valley. Headwaters are characterized by waterfalls, rapids, and variations in water depth, all of which restrict the use of watercraft.

MIDDLE SECTOR (CENTRAL VALLEY)

When the waterway reaches the central valley, it has formed a broad river which is usually navigable for great distances inland. This river is usually fed by numerous tributaries. In those jungles where there are definite dry and rainy seasons, many of the tributaries found during the rainy season may not exist during the dry season. The river in the valley is wide, slow, and often meanders. During periods of heavy rainfall, the course of the river may change. The jungle vegetation grows up along the riverbanks to form an almost solid wall. The banks of the river are often steep and slippery. Many of the navigable tributaries feeding the major river will often be completely overgrown with vegetation and contain obstacles such as fallen trees.

LOW SECTOR (DELTA)

When the river reaches the low coastal area, it spreads over a flat, alluvial plain and becomes a number of river tributaries (small streams or channels spreading fanlike from the main channel) disbursing a great amount of sediment into a gulf, bay, or ocean. Usually, there are many large and small tidal streams and channels, whose current may change speed or reverse with the tide in a predictable manner. Bottoms of the tributaries normally slope up to a crest or bar at the river's mouth. In some instances, only watercraft with a draft (that part of the craft under water) of 1 to 2 meters will be able to cross the crest or bar at high tide.

SECTION II. PREPARING FOR OPERATIONS

WATERBORNE COMBAT OPERATIONS

The fundamentals and tactics applicable in conventional ground operations apply in waterborne operations. However, special organization, equipment, and techniques are required when ground forces are supported by Navy ships and craft. The waterborne force should be employed with all available modes of transportation to seek out and destroy the enemy and his installations. One portion of the force may enter the area by watercraft; another may enter by helicopters; still another may enter the area by moving overland. All units then maneuver to attack the enemy. All available fire support should be used in the operation: close air support, attack helicopters, waterborne and land-based artillery, and naval gunfire. Special considerations in the conduct of jungle waterborne operations include the following:

- The heavy vegetation along the banks of inland waterways offers excellent concealment and enhances the effectiveness of ambushes against watercraft. Therefore, counterambush measures must be planned in conjunction with all water movements. Steep, slippery river banks coupled with dense vegetation often make committing the waterborne force in a coordinated assault landing extremely difficult.
- Security measures during the movement phase along a jungle waterway include proper watercraft formations, constant water patrolling, and air observation, when possible. Fire support to include mortar, artillery, close air support, and available naval gunfire must be preplanned for all water movements.
- Intelligence is critical along jungle waterways. While aerial reconnaissance yields a considerable amount of information, it will have to be supplemented by reconnaissance by boat, especially in areas where tributaries are overgrown by vegetation.

SECTION III. USING JUNGLE WATERWAYS

SMALL BOAT HANDLING

The use of inland and coastal waterways can add flexibility, surprise, and speed to tactical operations in jungle areas. Use of these waterways will also increase the load-carrying capacity of units which normally operate dismounted. Thus, every combat leader should be familiar with the tactical and technical aspects of small boat handling.

Boats may be powered by outboard motors, paddles, or oars. The mission, availability, and the river itself dictate the method of propulsion to be used.

Motors are noisy. On the other hand, they provide speed, reduce fatigue, and free personnel for security missions. The noise form motors can be heard for distances of 500 to 1,000 meters by day and up to 5,000 meters at night

EQUIPMENT

There are several types of small craft available.

RB-3

Reconnaissance Boat, Inflatable: RB-3

Length: 3 meters

Width: 1.3 meters

Weight: 24 pounds, 33 pounds w/paddles and pump

Load: A two-man crew and 500 pounds or a three-man crew and 300 pounds.

Powered by: Paddles

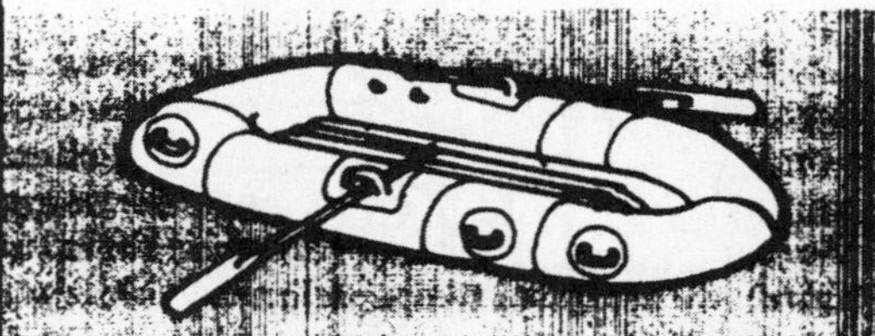

RB-15

Assault Boat, Pneumatic: RB-15

Length: 5.2 meters

Width: 1.8 meters

Weight: 260 pounds

Crew: 1 coxswain, 10 paddlers

Load: A maximum of 15 men (11-man crew and 4 passengers) with equipment or 3,300 pounds.

Powered by: Paddles or a 25-horsepower outboard motor

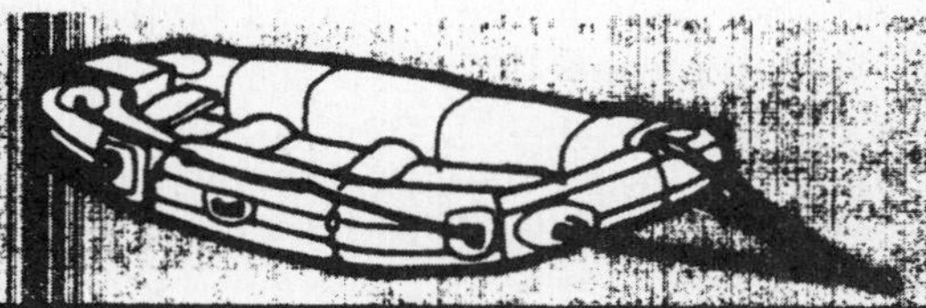

RB-7

Landing Boat Pneumatic: RB-7

Length: 4 meters

Width: 2 meters

Weight: 150 pounds

Crew: 1 coxswain, 6 paddlers

Load: 10 men (7-man crew and 3 passengers) with equipment.

Powered by: Paddles

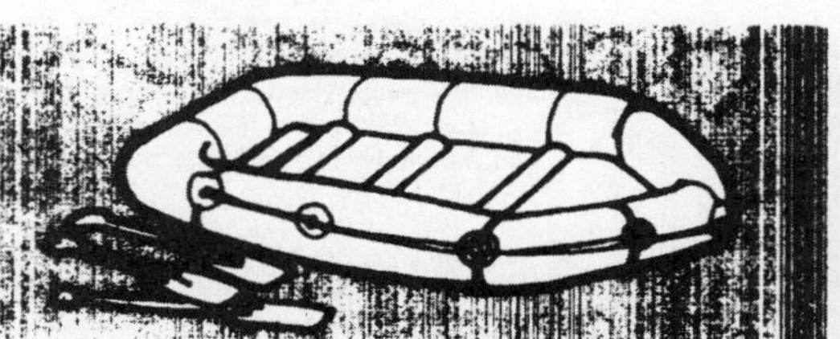

PAB

Plastic Assault Boat, M3: PAB

Length: 4.9 meters

Width: 1.7 meters

Weight: 300 pounds

Crew: 1 coxswain, 10 paddlers

Load: A maximum of 15 men (11-man crew and 4 passengers) with equipment or 3,200 pounds.

Powered by: Paddles or a 25-horsepower outboard motor

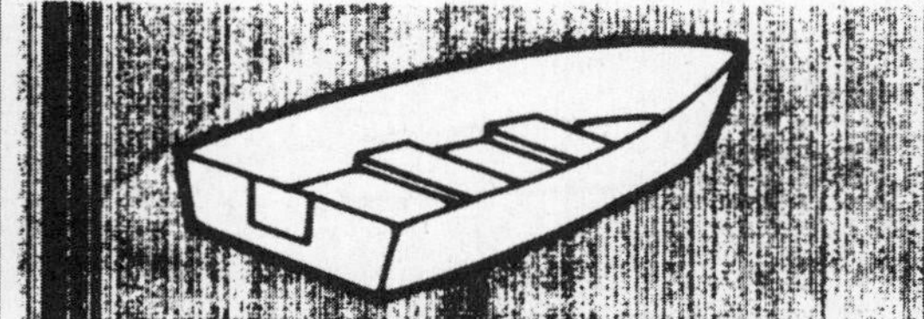

(sound carries better in the quieter, cooler night air). Provided the craft is not seen and the motor does not change pitch, however, it is difficult to estimate the direction of the sound and exactly how far away it is. Bearing these factors in mind, troops may be able to disguise a movement by deceptive tactics such as having other craft work the area. Stopping the motor when traveling downstream will also aid the security of movement.

Paddling is a slow and tiring process, but it is quieter than using motors. (With plastic, wooden, or metal craft, paddles may need to be wrapped with cloth to reduce noise when the paddles strike the craft.)

PADDLES WRAPPED TO REDUCE NOISE

ORGANIZATION

Before a waterborne operation, each person in a boat is assigned a specific boat position and a corresponding number. (This is the long count method of organization.)

> ✍ **NOTE**
> The unit, normally a squad, that uses the RB-15 for transportation actually comprises the crew that operates it. All others that do not operate the boat are passengers.

First, the crewmembers are assigned their positions. Next, the passengers are assigned their positions. When using an RB-15, for example, the crewmembers are assigned positions 1 through 11, and the passengers are assigned positions 12 through 15. One person is designated as the boat commander (normally the coxswain). Two persons are designated as a navigator-observer team.

For operational purposes, the crew is organized into pairs. Passengers are not numbered in this method. (This is the short count method of organization.) When using the RB-15, for example, the crewmembers (in pairs) are assigned to operational positions 1 through 5.

RB-15 WITH POSITIONS NUMBERED—LONG COUNT

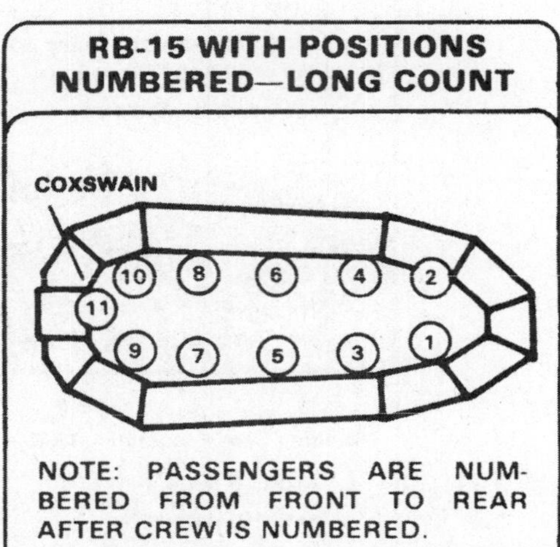

RB-15 WITH POSITIONS NUMBERED—SHORT COUNT

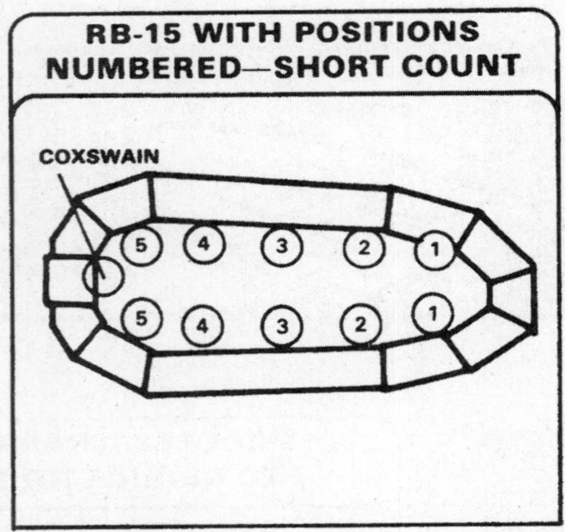

Crew duties:

- The coxswain is responsible for the control of the boat and action of the crew. He supervises the loading, lashing, and distribution of equipment, He also maintains the course and speed of the boat.
- The number 1 paddler (long count method) is the observer and is responsible for the storage and use of the bowline.
- The number 2 paddler (long count method) is responsible for setting the stroke.
- All paddlers are responsible for loading and lashing the equipment in their respective compartment.

PREPARATION OF PERSONNEL AND EQUIPMENT

Each crewmember and passenger must wear a life preserver.

The load-carrying equipment harness is worn unbuckled at the waist.

The rifle is slung outside of thelife preserver, opposite the outboard side, with the muzzle down.

Crew-served weapons, radios, ammunition, and other bulk equipment are lashed securely to the boat to prevent loss if the boat should overturn.

Radios, batteries, and unboxed ammunition are waterproofed.

Hot weapons are cooled prior to being placed in the boat to prevent damage to the boat or injury to personnel.

Pointed objects are padded to prevent puncture of the boat.

The most effective equipment-lashing system that has been developed is the RB-15 lashing system. This system is quick and easy to install, requires no special equipment, and prevents loss of equipment in the event the craft is capsized. It also allows the craft to be easily righted.

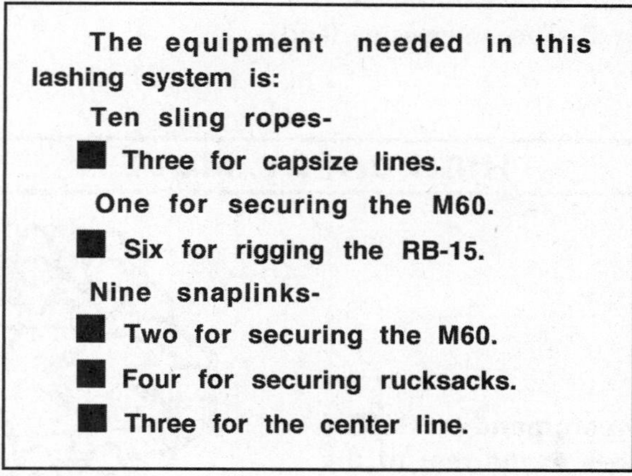

The equipment needed in this lashing system is:

Ten sling ropes-

- **Three for capsize lines.**

One for securing the M60.

- **Six for rigging the RB-15.**

Nine snaplinks-

- **Two for securing the M60.**
- **Four for securing rucksacks.**
- **Three for the center line.**

The average squad can fully rig and lash an RB- 15, using this system, in approximately 15 minutes.

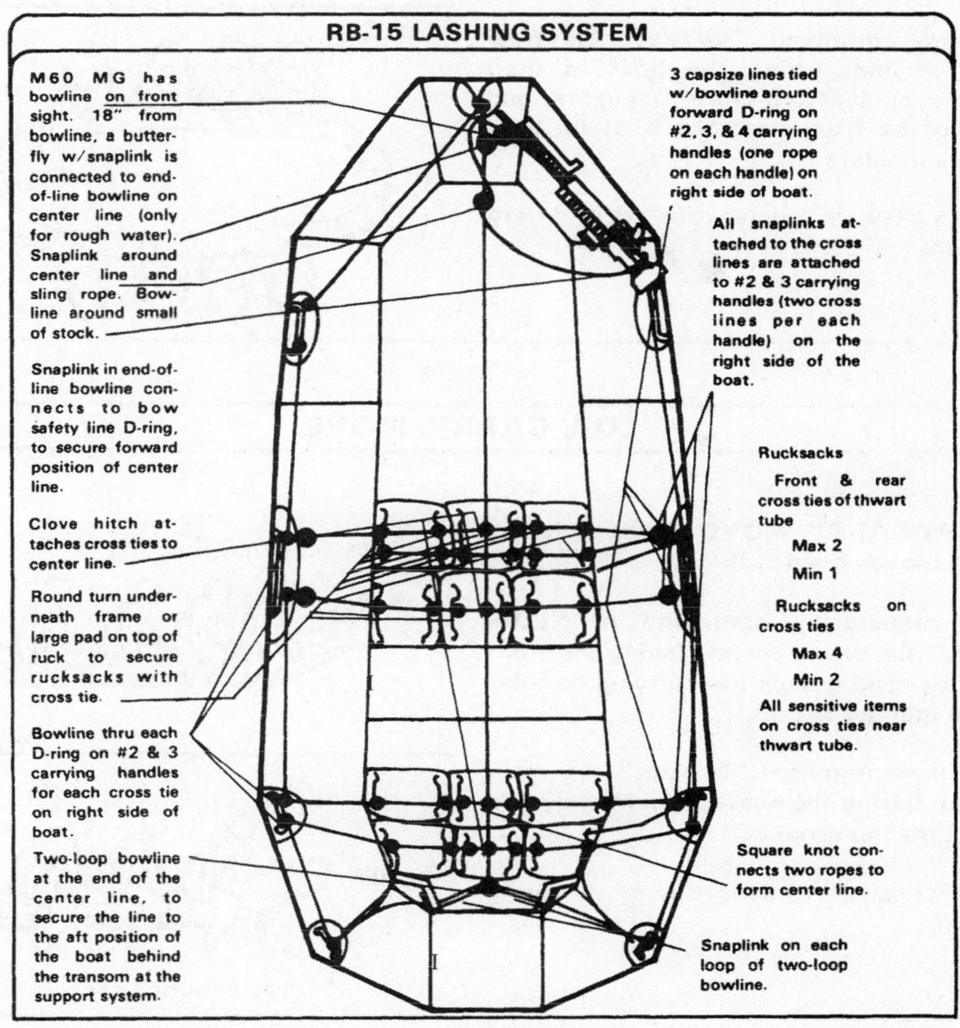

COMMANDS

"Short Count, count off." Crew counts *off* their positions by pairs, for example, 1, 2, 3, 4, 5, coxswain (RB-15).

"Long count, count off." Crew counts off their positions by individuals, for example, 1, 2, 3, 4, 5, 6, 7, 8, 9, 10, coxswain (RB-15).

"Boat stations." Crew takes position along side of boat.

"High carry, move" (used for long distance moves overland).

HIGH CARRY, MOVE

On the preparatory command of **"HIGH CARRY,"** the crew faces to the rear of the boat and squats down grasping carrying handles with the inboard hand.

On the command, **"MOVE,"** the crew swivels around, lifting the boat to their shoulders, so that the crew is standing and facing to the front with the boat on their inboard shoulders.

The coxswain guides the crew during movement.

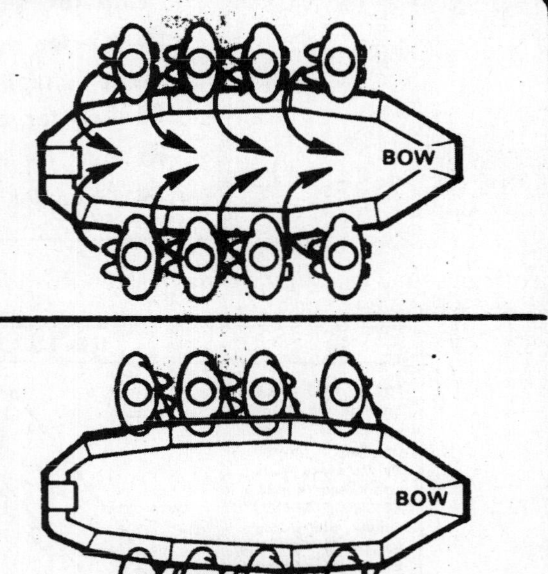

LOW CARRY, MOVE

"LOW CARRY, MOVE" (used for short distance moves overland).

On preparatory command of **"LOW CARRY,"** the crew remains facing the front of the boat and grasps the carrying handles with the inboard hand.

On the command, **"MOVE,"** the crew stands up raising the boat approximately 6 to 8 inches off the ground.

The coxswain guides the crew during movement.

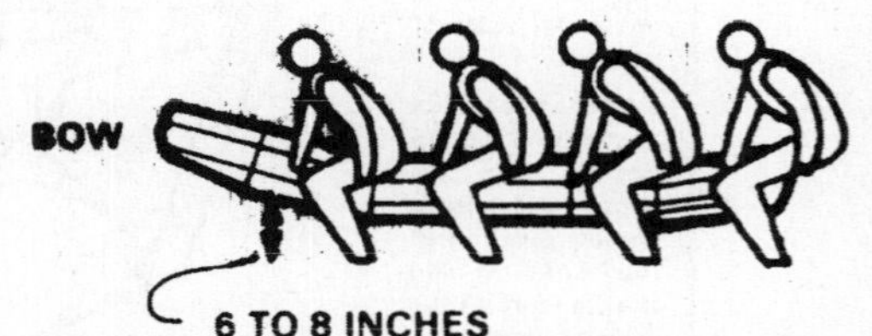

"Lower the boat, move." Crew lowers the boat gently to the ground using carrying handles.

"Give way together." Crew paddles to the front, with Number 2 setting the stroke for the rest of the crew.

"Hold." Entire crew keeps paddles motionless in the water, thereby stopping the boat.

"Hold left (right)." Left crewmembers hold, right crewmembers continue with previous command.

"Back paddle." Entire crew paddles backward. This action propels the boat to the rear.

"Back paddle left (right)." Left crewmembers back paddle causing the boat to turn left, right crewmembers continue with previous command.

"Rest paddles." Crewmembers place paddles on their laps with blades outboard. This command may be given to pairs, i.e., *"Number 1's rest paddles."*

LAUNCHING AND LANDING

When launching, the crew maintains a firm grip on the boat until they are inside the boat; similarly, when landing, they hold onto the boat until it is completely out of the water.

The crew stays as low as possible when entering and leaving the boat to avoid capsizing it.

Crewmembers can load or unload a boat either by individuals or in pairs. They load and unload a boat by individuals at steep river banks and along shoreline where the water is deep near the shore. They also load or unload from or into a larger vessel such as a landing craft, mechanized (LCM), by individuals.

The crewmembers load or unload individually according to their number in the long count method. The coxswain directs them by saying, *"One in (out), two in (out),"* etc.

The crewmembers load and unload a boat in pairs when at shallow water riverbanks. They load or unload in pairs according to their number in the short count method. The coxswain directs them by saying, *"Ones in (out), twos in (out),"* etc.

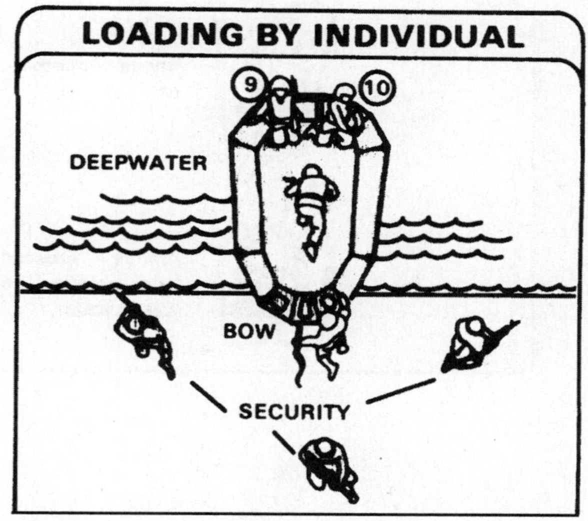

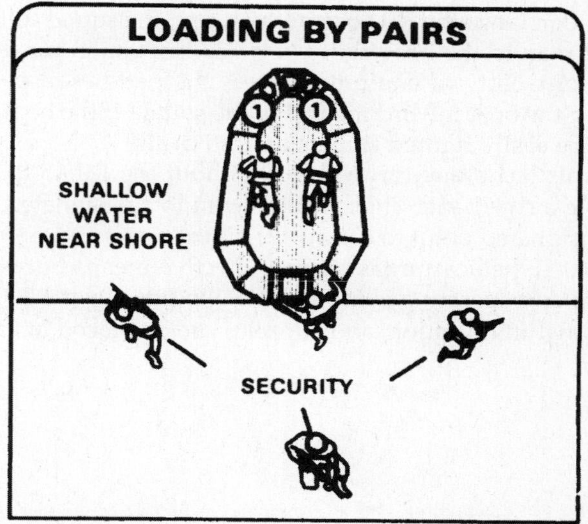

HELOCASTING

Helocasting is an excellent method for deploying troops and equipment in any terrain in which water courses exist. This technique involves a CH-47 helicopter, a 15-man rubber boat (RB-15), and a squad. The RB-15 is loaded with the squad's rucksacks, crew-served weapons, radios, and other heavy mission-essential items. All this equipment is kept in the RB-15 by a lashing system. At the desired time, the RB-15 is pushed off the ramp and into the water. The squad follows it, exiting the CH-47 in two columns off the tailgate. Drop speed is 20–25 knots and drop altitude is 10–20 feet. The water should have little or no current and should be free of all obstacles, including seaweed and stumps, and be at least 15 feet deep.

The only preparation necessary for the CH-47 is that two lengths of rollers must be installed in the center of the tailgate. The two rearward set of seats on each side of the CH-47 must be raised to fit the RB-15 inside. Personnel wear fatigues (boots unbloused, shirts out, sleeves rolled down, top button fastened), load-carrying equipment, and an individual life preserver. The individual weapon is tied to the individual in such a manner that it can be raised overhead when the individual exits the CH-47.

The RB-15 lashing system is used in rigging and lashing the rubber boat with the respective equipment. The boat is placed on the roller system and moved into the CH-47, bow first. On signal, it is pushed out by the castmaster and coxswain or RB-15 commander. Once the RB-15 is in the water, the squad follows it. The first man to the boat makes a quick inspection for damage and accountability of equipment, frees the paddles, and starts paddling the boat toward the rest of the squad. If the boat capsizes, it can be easily righted using standard drills.

This technique can be used without the RB-15 to cast scouts along a riverbank. They would swim to a designated shore or to a designated point to conduct their mission.

RB-15 helocasting is also an effective means of resupplying a company operating along a water obstacle. Over 1,000 pounds of rations, ammunition, and supplies can be placed in each boat.

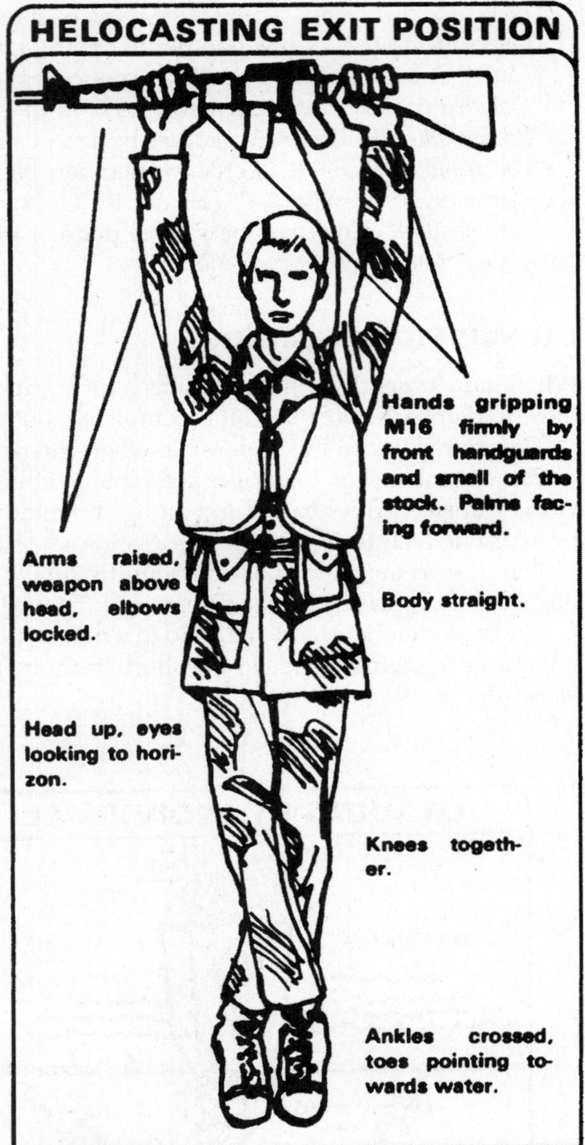

RIVER MOVEMENT

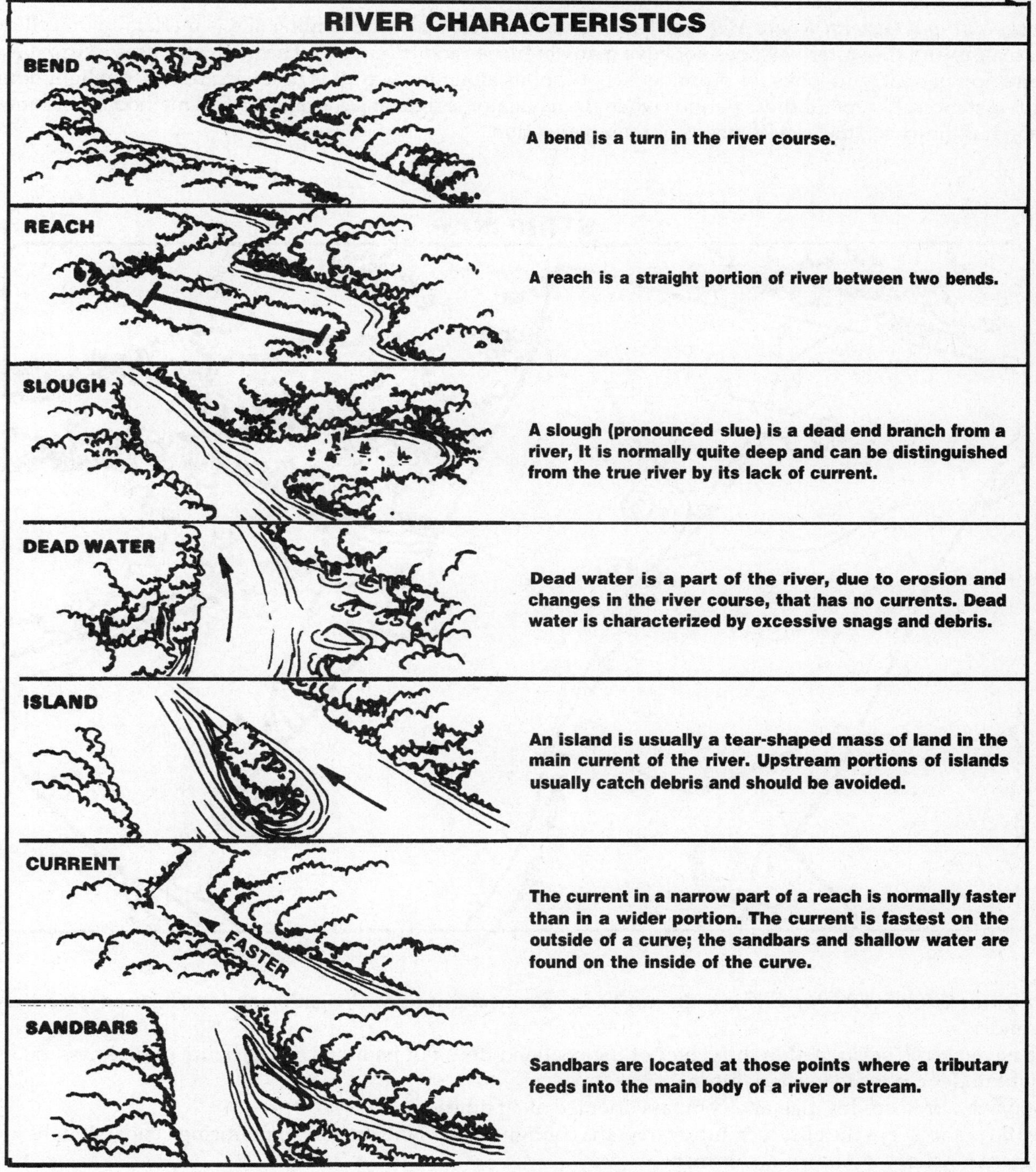

NAVIGATION

There are two acceptable methods of river navigation.

Checkpoint and General Route Method. This method is used when the landing site is marked by a well-defined terrain feature and the waterway does not have many branches and tributaries. The navigator uses a strip map, with the route drawn on it, and looks for prominent checkpoints along the way. It is best used during daylight hours and for short distances. Except for those periods when the navigator is right at a checkpoint, this method is not completely accurate. It is, however, the easiest means of river navigation.

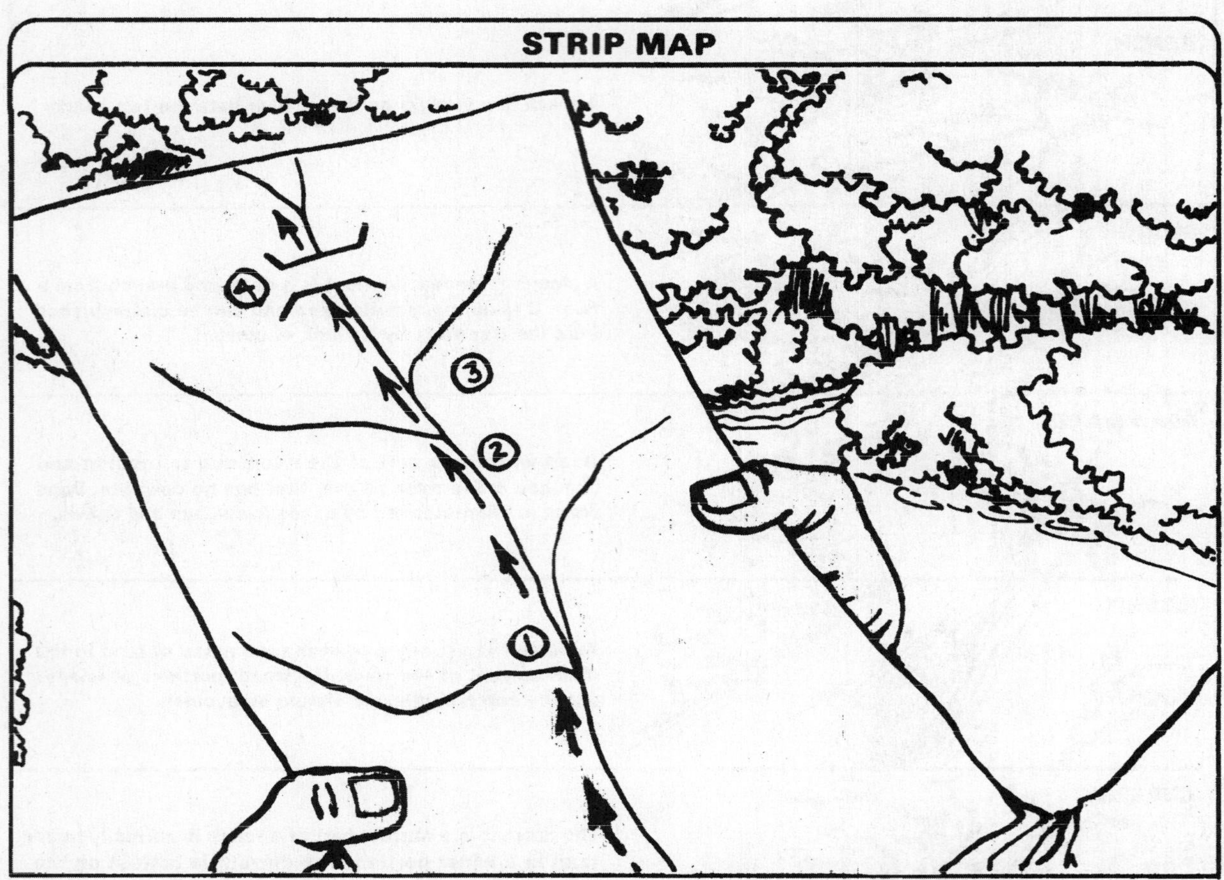

Navigator-Observer Method. This is the most accurate means of river navigation and can be used effectively in all light conditions.

The navigator is positioned in the center of the boat and does not paddle. During hours of darkness, he uses his flashlight under a poncho to check his map.

The navigator keeps his map and compass oriented at all times.

The navigator keeps the observer informed of the configuration of the river by announcing bends, sloughs, reaches, and stream junctions as shown on his map.

The observer compares this information with the bends, sloughs, reaches, and stream junctions he actually sees. When these are confirmed the navigator notes the boat's location on his map.

The navigator also keeps the observer informed of the general azimuths of reaches as shown on his map. The observer confirms these with actual compass readings.

The navigator announces only one configuration at a time to the observer and does not announce another until the first is confirmed and noted.

At night, a strip map drawn on clear acetate backed with luminous tape may be used instead of a map. It should be to scale or a schematic. It should show all curves and the azimuth and distance of all reaches. It should also show terrain features, streams, junctions, and sloughs.

TACTICAL MOVEMENT

The techniques of tactical river movement are very similar to those employed on land. As on land, movement techniques depend primarily on the likelihood of enemy contact and must be based on the concepts of traveling, traveling overwatch, and bounding overwatch.

Distances between elements will vary depending upon observation, range of weapons, and means of communication used. Each boat must maintain visual contact with the boat to its front.

Boats move close to the shoreline, taking advantage of the natural concealment.

When bends in the river deny observation, a unit sends a reconnaissance team ashore to reconnoiter the river beyond the bend. When the reconnaissance team determines that the area is clear, it signals the boats to move forward.

Troops in the boats are assigned specific sectors in which to observe and fire.

One person is appointed in each boat as an air guard. If an enemy aircraft is sighted, the boats immediately move close to shore for concealment. Troops sit quietly in the boats until all is clear. If the aircraft makes a firing pass, the unit beaches the boats and takes the appropriate defensive actions for an air attack.

Actions taken on enemy contact resemble those taken ashore. The elements caught in the enemy's fire return fire, beach the boats, seek cover, and continue to fire. Other elements beach their boats and maneuver ashore to destroy the enemy. When a patrol is inserted by boat, the landing site must be secured before all elements of the patrol disembark. A suggested technique is to have the lead boat unload its personnel at the landing site while the other boats cover them from a distance. After the site is secured, the other boats are landed on signal. After the boats have landed, the crews either hide the boats or have them removed from the area. In either case, the crews remove any signs of activity on the landing site.

CAPSIZE PROCEDURE

RIGHTING BOAT

During small boat operations, there is always a chance of a boat being capsized (overturned) unexpectedly. In order for a unit to continue its mission, it must right the boat. To do this, the unit must follow this procedure:

The coxswain must first account for his men. He does this by having them count off using the long count method. This will tell him who, if anyone, is injured or missing.

He next has the men hold on to the boat. They then pass their paddles to one man (designated by the coxswain before the operation). This man secures the paddles while the others right the boat.

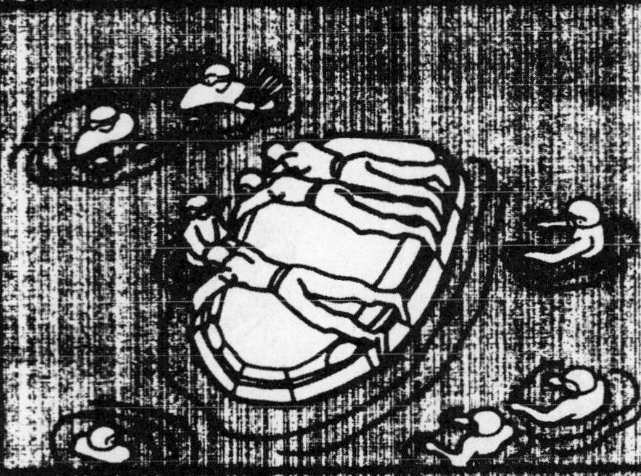

Next, three men are helped onto the boat. These men (all on the same side of the boat) grasp the bowline (which has been secured to one side of the boat), stand up, and prepare to pull the boat over. All but one of the men remaining in the water release the boat and move out to about 3 meters from it. The one man (in the water) holding on prepares to be pulled into the boat once the boat is pulled over.

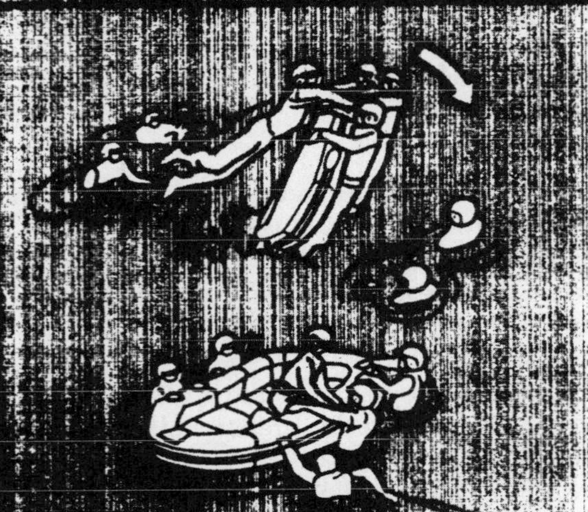

The three men on the boat lean backwards and pull the boat over (upright). This also pulls the one man (in the water) into the boat.

Once the boat is upright, all of the men move to it. The one man in the boat helps the others into the boat. The man with the paddles passes them up to the other crewmembers and then climbs into the boat.

Once the crewmembers are in their positions, the coxswain again has the men count-off using the long count method. The men also check to see that their equipment is accounted for. The coxswain then gives the crew the appropriate orders for continuing the mission.

CHAPTER 9

Defensive Formation

SECTION I. GENERAL

Jungle defensive operations are based on the same fundamentals of the defense used in other type operations. Some of the fundamentals may acquire a special significance in the jungle. The basic factors of observation and fields of fire, cover and concealment, obstacles, key terrain, and avenue of approach should always be considered carefully.

Three defensive formations will be presented here: the perimeter, the triangle, and the "Y". Platoon-size elements will be the primary consideration, although the techniques mentioned are adaptable to larger units. It should be noted that all three defensive postures have definite advantages as well as inherent disadvantages. Units should vary their type of defensive posture in order to avoid establishing a pattern.

SECTION II. FORMATIONS

PERIMETER DEFENSE

The first of the defensive formations is the perimeter. All elements are generally configured in a circular formation, and the terrain is used to the maximum advantage.

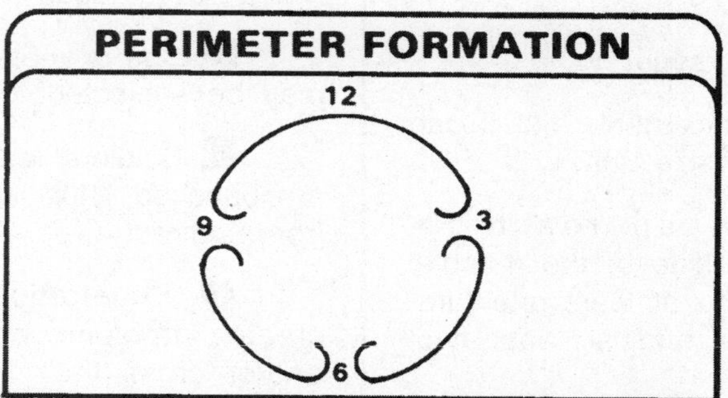

Advantages are:	It is mutually supported by observation/communication, and patrols are easily coordinated.
■ 360-degree security. ■ Centralized control. ■ Quick emplacement, and it can be executed by any size unit. ■ The frontage of the perimeter can be easily adjusted and internally re-inforced.	Disadvantages are: ■ Any penetration creates problems of enfilade, masking, and/or cross fires. ■ It is difficult to achieve final protective fires with the crew-served weapons and, because of the circular configuration, the unit is vulnerable to the entire effects of the bursting radius of an indirect fire weapon.

The basic technique used to establish this defensive formation is the clock system. This involves the platoon using the direction of movement as 12 o'clock, with one squad occupying from 8 to 12, one squad occupying from 8 to 4, and the last squad occupying from 4 to 12. The headquarters element would normally be located in the center of the formation to facilitate control. It is generally suggested that automatic weapons be placed to cover the most likely avenues of approach. At least one machinegun should be kept with the headquarters, under the control of the unit leader, for deployment against a specific threat.

TRIANGLE DEFENSE

The second of the defensive formations is the triangle defense. This formation is a modification of the perimeter.

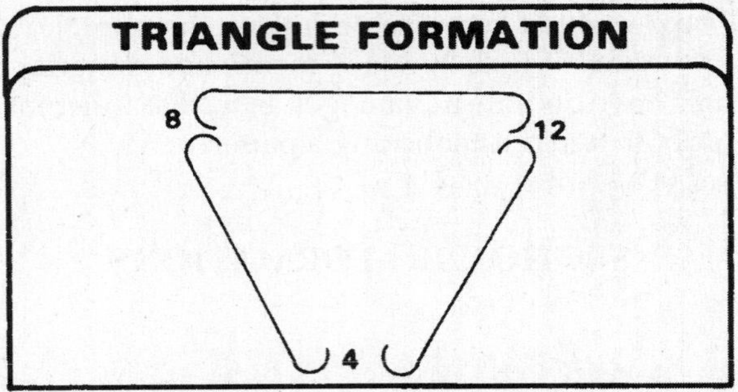

Advantages are:	Disadvantages are:
■ 360-degree security. ■ Quick emplacement, and it can be executed by any size unit. ■ A target approaching perpendicular to any side of the triangle becomes vulnerable to at least one-third of the fighting force and at least two automatic weapons. ■ It is a dual purpose formation in that it may be used as either a defensive or offensive ambush formation.	■ One or more legs of the triangle may be subjected to enfilade fire. ■ Soldiers located at the corners are bunched, thus increasing the danger from indirect fire. ■ Penetration by the enemy creates problems of enfilade, masking, and/or cross fire.

This defensive formation is best established by having the commander move forward with one element and establish a base line. Again, 12 o'clock is used as the direction of movement. The baseline could be established by the first squad, running from 8 to 12. Once this base line is established and the squad is prepared to provide support, the next squad moves forward and occupies the straight line position from 8 to 4; finally, the last squad moves forward and occupies the straight line position from 4 to 12. The headquarters element will normally locate in the center of the formation. If three machine guns are available, one will be placed at each comer in such a manner to allow flexibility in providing final protective fires down either of its two sides. If only two machine guns are available, one may be placed to cover the two sides deemed most vulnerable to attack. The second machine gun should be kept with the headquarters element under control of the unit leader. Firing positions should be prepared at all three comers.

"Y" DEFENSE

The third defensive formation is the "Y". This formation, like the triangle, may be utilized as an offensive formation, usually in an ambush. Depending upon the situation, it can be a very effective defensive formation.

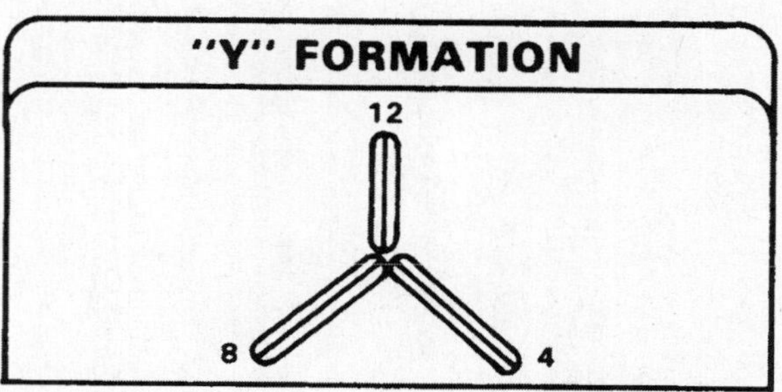

Advantages are:

- **360-degree security.**
- **Centralized control.**
- **Maximum firepower in all directions.**
- **Each penetration by the enemy places him in a new kill zone.**

Disadvantages are:

- **It must be emplaced during daylight to insure that aiming stakes are accurately emplaced, to preclude firing into adjacent positions.**
- **The central point of the "Y" creates bunching, and it increases the danger from indirect fire.**

The recommended technique for emplacement of this formation is for the unit leader to take one element and the headquarters forward and establish the center of the sector. This establishes the 12 o'clock position. The remaining elements stay in security positions. Since all legs of the "Y" are mutually supporting, the commander has the option of having all soldiers on each leg face the same direction, or he may alternate fire teams. Once the decision is made regarding which method is to be used, subsequent legs of the "Y" must conform to the initial one. Once the lead squad is emplaced, the next squad moves forward to the center point and is closely directed into the 8 o'clock position. After the second element is in position, the third element moves forward to the center point and is closely directed into the 4 o'clock position. If three machine guns are available, one is positioned at each leg, with possible final protective fires across the fronts of adjacent legs. If only two are available, they are positioned at the center point to provide fire down the legs. This positioning of two is not preferred because it does not allow for dispersion; plus, the machine guns are bunched and extremely vulnerable to indirect fire.

Combat in the Urban Environment

CHAPTER 1

Urban Combat Skills

Successful combat operations in urban areas depend on the proper employment of the rifle squad. Each member must be skilled in moving, entering buildings, clearing rooms, employing hand grenades, selecting and using fighting positions, navigating in urban areas, and camouflage.

SECTION I. MOVEMENT

Movement in urban areas is the first fundamental skill the soldier must master. Movement techniques must be practiced until they become habitual. To reduce exposure to enemy fire, the soldier avoids open areas, avoids silhouetting himself, and selects his next covered position before movement.

1-1. CROSSING OPEN AREAS

Open areas, such as streets, alleys, and parks, should be avoided. They are natural kill zones for enemy crew-served weapons or snipers. They can be crossed safely if the individual or small-unit leader applies certain fundamentals including using smoke from hand grenades or smoke pots to conceal movement. When employing smoke as an obscurant, keep in mind that thermal sighting systems can see through smoke. Also, when smoke has been thrown in an open area, the enemy may choose to engage with suppressive fires into the smoke cloud.

a. Before moving to another position, the soldier makes a visual reconnaissance, selects the position offering the best cover and concealment, and determines the route he takes to get to that position.

b. The soldier develops a plan for his own movement. He runs the shortest distance between buildings and moves along the far building to the next position, reducing the time he is exposed to enemy fire.

1-2. MOVEMENT PARALLEL TO BUILDINGS

Soldiers and small units may not always be able to use the inside of buildings as routes of advance and must move on the outside of the buildings (Figure 1-1). Smoke, suppressive fires, and cover and concealment should be used to hide movement. The soldier moves parallel to the side of the building (maintaining at least 12 inches of separation between himself and the wall to avoid *rabbit rounds*, ricochets and rubbing or bumping the wall), stays in the shadow, presents a low silhouette, and moves rapidly to his next position (Figure 1-2). If an enemy gunner inside the building fires on a soldier, he exposes himself to fire from other squad members providing overwatch. An enemy gunner farther down the street would have difficulty detecting and engaging the soldier.

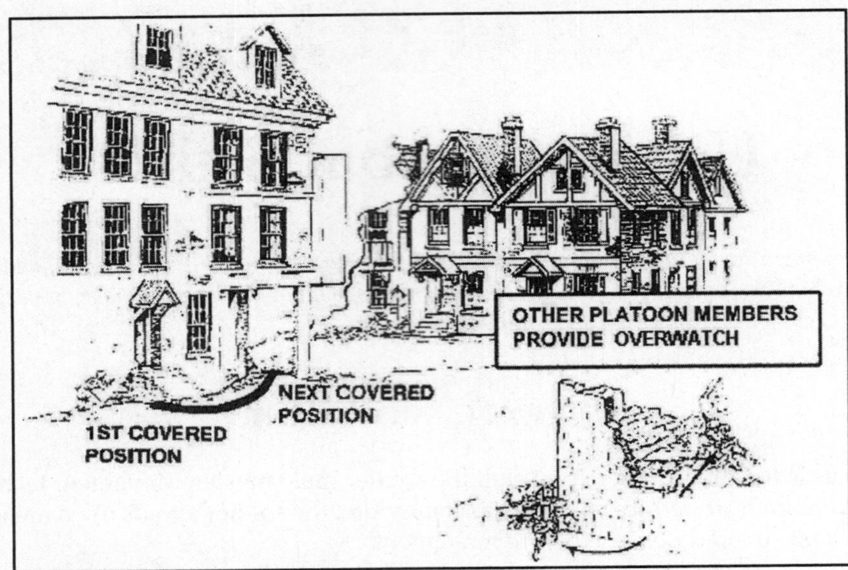

Figure 1-1: Selection of the next position.

Figure 1-2: Soldier moving outside building.

1-3. MOVEMENT PAST WINDOWS

Windows present another hazard to the soldier. The most common mistakes are exposing the head in a first-floor window and not being aware of basement windows.

a. When using the correct technique for passing a first-floor window, the soldier stays below the window level and near the side of the building (Figure 1-3). He makes sure he does not silhouette himself in the window. An enemy gunner inside the building would have to expose himself to covering fires if he tried to engage the soldier.

Figure 1-3: Soldier moving past windows.

b. The same techniques used in passing first-floor windows are used when passing basement windows. A soldier should not walk or run past a basement window, since he presents a good target to an enemy gunner inside the building. The soldier should stay close to the wall of the building and step or jump past the window without exposing his legs (Figure 1-4).

Figure 1-4: Soldier passing basement windows.

1-4. MOVEMENT AROUND CORNERS

The area around a corner must be observed before the soldier moves. The most common mistake a soldier makes at a corner is allowing his weapon to extend beyond the corner exposing his position (this mistake is known as *flagging* your weapon). He should show his head below the height an enemy soldier would expect to see it. The soldier lies flat on the ground and does not extend his weapon beyond the corner of the building. He wears his Kevlar helmet and only exposes his head (at ground level) enough to permit observation (Figure 1-5). Another corner clearing technique that is used when speed is required is the *pie-ing* method. This procedure is done by aiming the weapon beyond the corner into the direction of travel (without flagging) and side-stepping around the corner in a circular fashion with the muzzle as the pivot point (Figure 1-6).

Figure 1-5: Correct technique for looking around a corner.

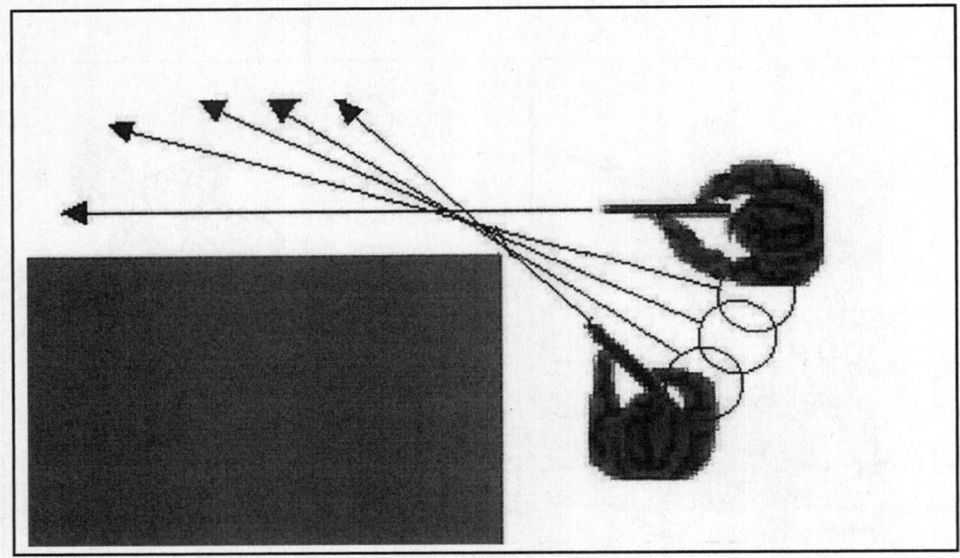

Figure 1-6: *Pie-ing* a corner.

1-5. CROSSING A WALL

Each soldier must learn the correct method of crossing a wall (Figure 1-7). After he has reconnoitered the other side, he rolls over the wall quickly, keeping a low silhouette. Speed of his move and a low silhouette deny the enemy a good target.

Figure 1-7: Soldier crossing a wall.

1-6. USE OF DOORWAYS

Doorways should not be used as entrances or exits since they are normally covered by enemy fire. If a soldier must use a doorway as an exit, he should move quickly to his next position, staying as low as possible to avoid silhouetting himself (Figure 1-8). Preselection of positions, speed, a low silhouette, and the use of covering fires must be emphasized in exiting doorways.

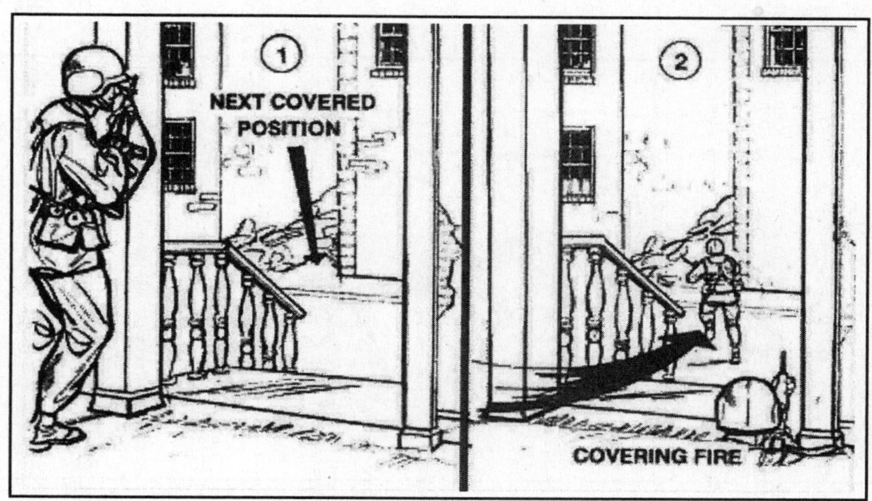

Figure 1-8: Soldier exiting a doorway.

1-7. MOVEMENT BETWEEN POSITIONS

When moving from position to position, each soldier must be careful not to mask his supporting fires. When he reaches his next position, he must be prepared to cover the movement of other members of his fire team or squad. He must use his new position effectively and fire his weapon from either shoulder depending on the position.

a. The most common errors a soldier makes when firing from a position are firing over the top of his cover and silhouetting himself against the building to his rear. Both provide the enemy an easy target. The correct technique for firing from a covered position is to fire around the side of the cover, which reduces exposure to the enemy (Figure 1-9).

Figure 1-9: Soldier firing from a covered position.

b. Another common error is for a right-handed shooter to fire from the right shoulder around the left corner of a building. Firing left-handed around the left corner of a building takes advantage of the cover afforded by the building (Figure 1-10). Right-handed and left-handed soldiers should be trained to adapt cover and concealment to fit their manual orientation. Soldiers should be able to fire from the opposite shoulder.

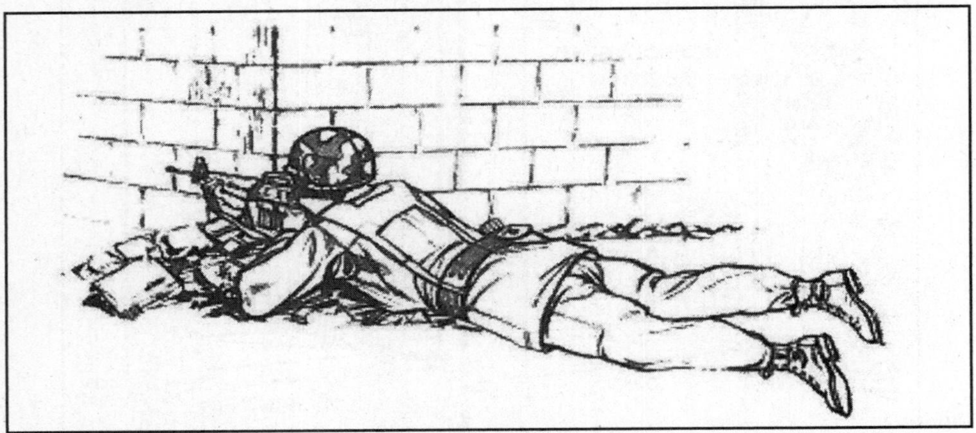

Figure 1-10: Firing left-handed around the corner of a building.

1-8. FIRE TEAM EMPLOYMENT

Moving as a fire team from building to building or between buildings presents a large target for enemy fire (Figure 1-11). When moving from the corner of one building to another, the fire team should move across the open area in a group. Moving from the side of one building to the side of another presents a similar problem and the technique of movement employed is the same. The fire team uses the building as cover. In moving to an adjacent building (Figure 1-12) team members should keep a distance of 3 to 5 meters between themselves and, using a planned signal, make an abrupt flanking movement (on line) across the open area to the next building.

Figure 1-11: Fire team movement.

Figure 1-12: Movement to adjacent building.

SECTION II. ENTRY TECHNIQUES

When entering buildings a soldier must minimize the time he is exposed. Before moving toward the building he must select the entry point. When moving to the entry point the soldier should use smoke to conceal his advance. He must avoid using windows and doors except as a last resort. He should consider the use of demolitions, tank rounds, and other means to make new entrances. If the situation permits he should precede his entry with a grenade, enter immediately after the grenade explodes, and be covered by one of his buddies.

1-9. UPPER BUILDING LEVELS

Although entering a building from any level other than the ground floor is difficult, clearing a building from the top down is the preferred method. Assaulting or defending a building is easier from an upper story. Gravity and the building's floor plan become assets when throwing hand grenades and moving from floor to floor.

a. An enemy who is forced to the top of a building may be cornered and fight desperately or escape over the roof. An enemy who is forced down to ground level may withdraw from the building, thus exposing himself to friendly fires from the outside.

b. Various means, such as ladders, drainpipes, vines, helicopters, or the roofs and windows of adjoining buildings, may be used to reach the top floor or roof of a building. One soldier can climb onto the shoulders of another and reach high enough to pull himself up.

c. Ladders offer the quickest method to access the upper levels of a building (Figure 1-13). Units deploying into an urban environment should be equipped with a lightweight, man-portable, collapsible ladder as referenced in the platoon urban operations kit.

Figure 1-13: Entering using portable ladder

(1) If portable ladders are not available, material to build ladders can be obtained through supply channels. Ladders can also be built with resources available throughout the urban area; for example, lumber can be taken from inside the walls of buildings (Figure 1-14).

Figure 1-14: Getting lumber from inside the walls.

(2) Although ladders do not permit access to the top of some buildings, they do offer security and safety through speed. Ladders can be used to conduct an exterior assault of an upper level if soldiers' exposure to enemy fire can be minimized.

1-10. USE OF GRAPPLING HOOK

The use of a grappling hook and rope to ascend into a building is not recommended. Experimentation and training has determined that using the grappling hook and rope to ascend is extremely difficult for the average soldier, and makes a unit more likely to fail their mission. Grappling hooks are still a viable tool for accomplishing the following tasks:

- Clearing concertina or other tangle wire.
- Clearing obstacles or barricades that may be booby trapped.
- Descending to lower floors.

1-11. SCALING OF WALLS

When required to scale a wall during exposure to enemy fire, all available concealment must be used. Smoke and diversionary measures improve the chances of success. When using smoke for concealment, soldiers must plan for wind direction. They should use suppressive fire, shouting, and distraction devices from other positions to divert the enemy's attention.

a. A soldier scaling an outside wall is vulnerable to enemy fire. Soldiers who are moving from building to building and climbing buildings should be covered by friendly fire. Properly positioned friendly weapons can suppress and eliminate enemy fire. The M203 grenade launcher is effective in suppressing or neutralizing the enemy from rooms inside buildings (Figure 1-15).

Figure 1-15: Employment of M203 grenade launcher for clearing enemy snipers.

b. If a soldier must scale a wall with a rope, he should avoid silhouetting himself in windows that are not cleared and avoid exposing himself to enemy fires from lower windows. He should climb with his weapon slung over the firing shoulder so he can bring it quickly to a firing position. If the ROE permits, the objective window and any lower level windows in the path of the climber should be engaged with grenades (hand or launcher) before the soldier begins his ascent.

c. The soldier enters the objective window with a low silhouette (Figure 1-16). Entry can be head first; however, the preferred method is to hook a leg over the window sill and enter sideways straddling the ledge.

Figure 1-16: Soldier entering the objective window.

1-12. RAPPELLING

Rappelling is an entry technique that soldiers can use to descend from the rooftop of a tall building into a window (Figure 1-17), or through a hole in the floor, in order to descend to the lower floor.

Figure 1-17: Rappelling.

1-13. ENTRY AT LOWER LEVELS

Buildings should be cleared from the top down. However, entering a building at the top may be impossible. Entry at the bottom or lower level is common and may be the only course of action. When entering a building at lower levels, soldiers avoid entering through windows and doors since both can be easily booby trapped and are usually covered by enemy fire. (Specific lower-level entry techniques are shown in Figure 1-18. These techniques are used when soldiers can enter the building without receiving effective enemy fire.)

a. When entering at lower levels, demolitions, artillery, tank fire, antiarmor weapons fire, or similar means can be used to create a new entrance to avoid booby traps. This procedure is preferred if the ROE permit it. Quick entry is then required to take advantage of the effects of the blast and concussion.
b. When the only entry to a building is through a window or door, supporting fire is directed at that location to destroy or drive away enemy forces. The assaulting soldiers should not leave their covered positions before the support by fire element has accomplished this procedure.
c. Before entering, soldiers may throw a cooked off hand grenade into the new entrance to reinforce the effects of the original blast. The type grenade used, fragmentation, concussion, or stun, is based on METT-TC factors and the structural integrity of the building.
   (1) When making a new entrance in a building, soldiers consider the effects of the blast on the building and on adjacent buildings. If there is the possibility of a fire in adjacent building, soldiers coordinate with adjacent units and obtain permission before starting the operation.
   (2) In wooden frame buildings, the blast may cause the building to collapse. In stone, brick, or cement buildings, supporting fires are aimed at the corner of the building or at weak points in the building construction.

> ✍ **NOTE**
> Armored vehicles can be positioned next to a building allowing soldiers to use the vehicle as a platform to enter a room or gain access to a roof.

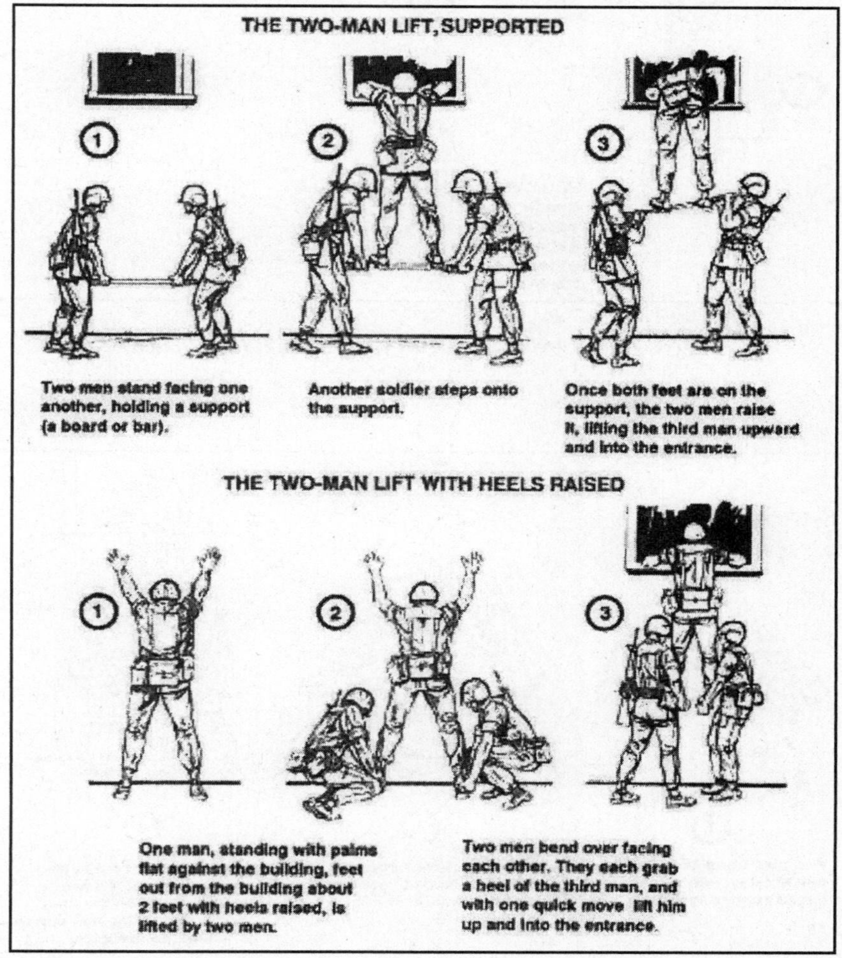

Figure 1-18: Lower-level entry technique.

Figure 1-18: Lower-level entry technique. *(Continued)*

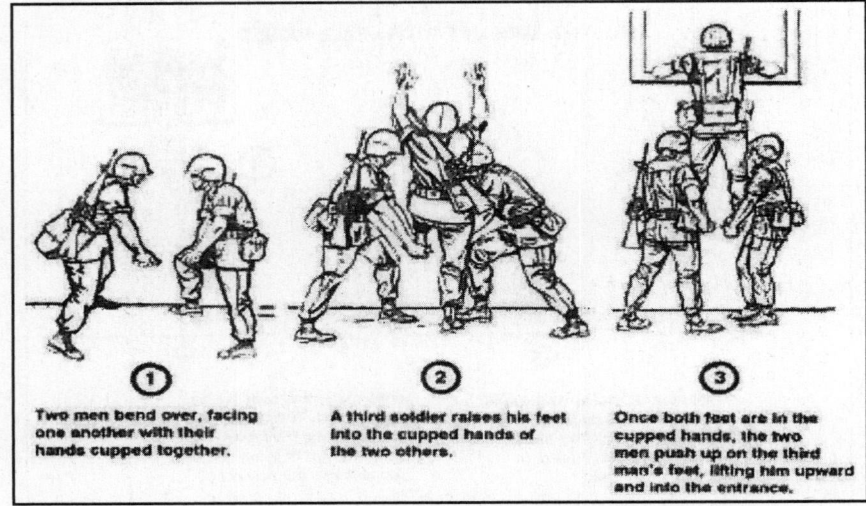

Figure 1-18: Lower-level entry technique. *(Continued)*

1-14. USE OF HAND GRENADES

Combat in urban areas often requires extensive use of hand grenades. Unless the ROE prevent it, use grenades before assaulting defended areas, moving through breaches, or entering unsecured areas. Effective grenade use in urban areas may require throwing overhand or underhand, with both the left and right hand. Normally, the fragmentation grenade should be cooked off for two seconds to prevent the enemy from throwing them back.

a. Three types of hand grenades can be used when assaulting an urban objective: stun, concussion, and fragmentation. METT-TC factors and the type of construction materials used in the objective building influence the type of grenades that can be used.

(1) The M84 stun hand grenade is a *flash-bang* distraction device, which produces a brilliant flash and a loud bang to momentarily surprise and distract an enemy force (Figure 1-19). The M84 is often used under precision conditions and when the ROE demand use of a nonlethal grenade. The use of stun hand grenades under high intensity conditions is usually limited to situations where fragmentation and concussion grenades pose a risk to friendly troops or the structural integrity of the building.

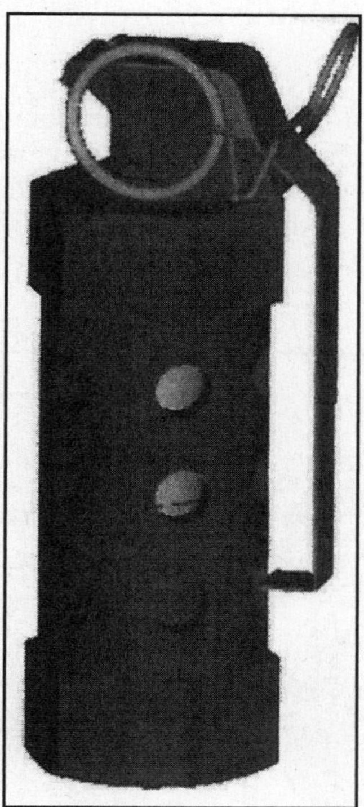

Figure 1-19: M84 stun hand grenade.

(2) The concussion grenade causes injury or death to persons in a room by blast overpressure and propelling debris within the room (Figure 1-20). While the concussion grenade does not discard a dangerous fragmentation from its body, the force of the explosion can create debris fallout that may penetrate thin walls.

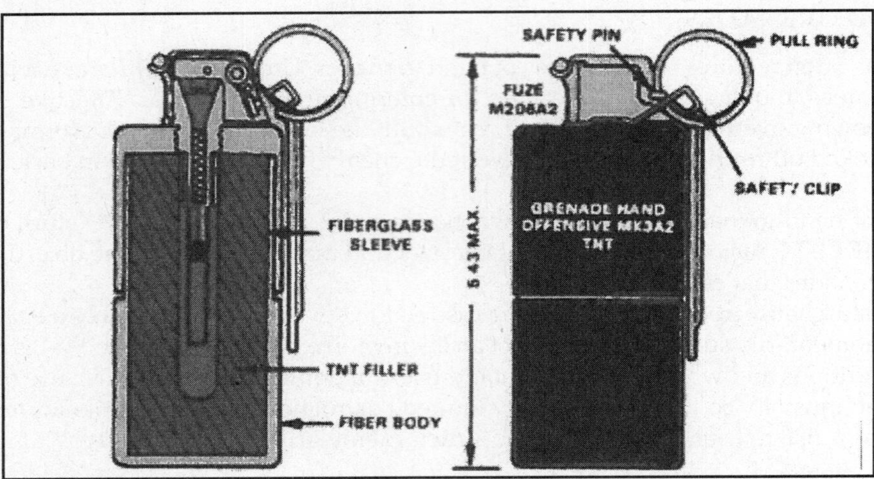

Figure 1-20: MK3A2 (concussion grenade).

(3) The fragmentation grenade (Figure 1-21) produces substantial overpressure when used inside buildings and, coupled with the shrapnel effects, can be extremely dangerous to friendly soldiers. If the walls of a building are made of thin material, such as Sheetrock or thin plywood, soldiers should either lie flat on the floor with their helmet towards the area of detonation, or move away from any wall that might be penetrated by grenade fragments.

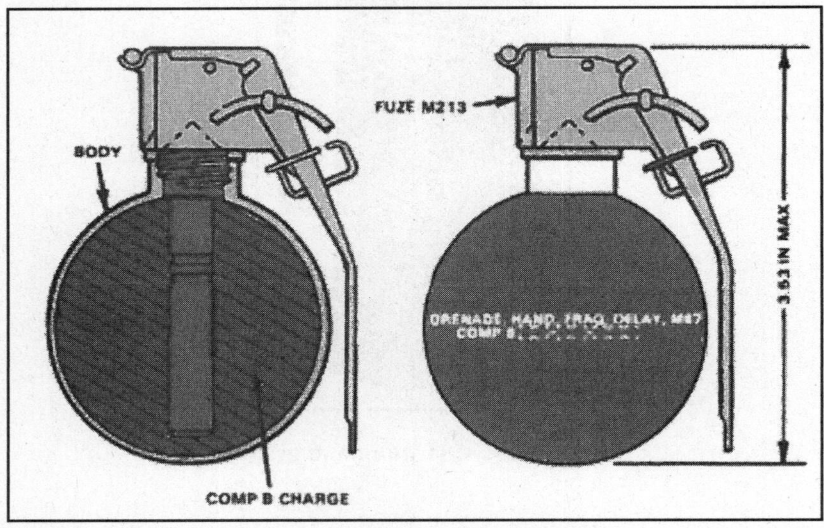

Figure 1-21: Fragmentation grenade.

b. Soldiers should engage upper-level openings with grenades (by hand or launcher) before entering to eliminate enemy that might be near the entrance.

(1) The M203 grenade launcher is the best method for putting a grenade in an upper-story window. The primary round of ammunition used for engaging an urban threat is the M433 high-explosive, dual-purpose cartridge (Figure 1-22). Throwing a hand grenade into an upper-story opening is a task that is difficult to do safely during combat.

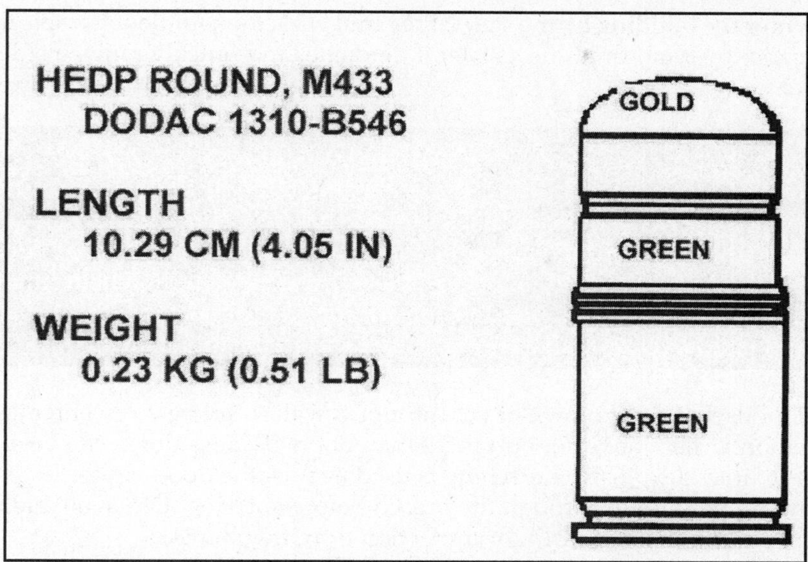

Figure 1-22: 40-mm, tube-launched, high-explosive, dual-purpose (HEDP) grenade.

(2) When a hand grenade must be thrown into an upper-story opening, the thrower should stand close to the building, using it for cover. This technique should only be employed when the window opening is free of glass or screen.

(3) The thrower should allow the grenade to cook off for at least two seconds, and then step out far enough to lob the grenade into the upper-story opening (Figure 1-23). He should keep his weapon in the nonthrowing hand, to be used if needed. The weapon should never be laid outside or inside the building. At the same time, everyone should have a planned area to move to for safety if the grenade does not go through the window but falls back to the ground.

(4) Once the grenade has been thrown into the opening and detonates, assaulting troops must move swiftly to enter the building.

Figure 1-23: Hand grenade thrown through window.

c. If soldiers must enter the building by the stairs, they must first look for booby traps, then engage the stairwell door with a grenade (by hand or launcher), let it detonate, and quickly move inside. They can then use the staircase for cover.

WARNING

1. If stealth is not a factor, after throwing the grenade the soldier must immediately announce *frag out* to indicate that a grenade has been thrown. He then takes cover since the grenade may bounce back or be thrown back, or the enemy may fire at him.
2. When the M203 grenade launcher is used to deliver the grenade into a window or doorway, ensure proper standoff for arming the round. Also, the assaulting element should take cover around a corner or away from the target area.

d. Breachholes and mouseholes are blown or cut through a wall so soldiers can enter a building. (See Chapter 2 for more information.) These are safer entrances than doors because doors can be easily booby trapped and should be avoided, unless explosive breaching is used against the door.
   (1) A grenade should be thrown through the breach before entering. Use available cover, such as the lower corner of the building (Figure 2-24), for protection from fragments.
   (2) Use stun and concussion grenades when engaging through thin walls.

Figure 2-24: Soldier entering through a mousehole.

e. When a door is the only means of entering a building, soldiers must beware of booby traps and fire from enemy soldiers within the room.
   (1) Locked doors can be breached (forced open) using one of the four breaching methods: mechanical, ballistic, explosive, or thermal. If none of these methods are available, soldiers can resort to kicking the door open. This method is the least preferred since it is difficult and tiring to the soldier. It rarely works the first time, and gives any enemy soldiers in the room ample warning and time to shoot through the door. Once the door is breached, a grenade should precede the soldier's entry.
   (2) When opening an unlocked door by hand, the assault team should be sure not to expose themselves to enemy fire through the door. The soldiers should stay close to one side of the doorway to minimize exposure in the open doorframe.
   (3) Once the door is open, a hand grenade should be tossed in. After the grenade explodes, soldiers enter and clear the room IAW the tactics, techniques, and procedures discussed in Section III.

f. Although buildings are best cleared from the top down, this procedure is not always possible. While clearing the bottom floor of a building, soldiers may encounter stairs, which must also be cleared. Once again, grenades play an important role.

(1) To climb stairs, first inspect for booby traps, then toss a grenade to the head of the stairs (Figure 2-25). Soldiers must use voice alerts when throwing grenades.

(2) Using the staircase for cover, soldiers throw the grenade underhand to reduce the risk of it bouncing back and rolling down the stairs.

(3) Once the first grenade has detonated, another grenade should be thrown over and behind the staircase banister and into the hallway, neutralizing any exposed enemy in the hallway.

(4) When the second hand grenade has detonated, soldiers proceed to clear the stairway in accordance with prescribed TTP.

> ✍ **NOTE**
>
> Large quantities of hand grenades are used when clearing buildings. A continuous supply must be available.

Figure 1-25: Soldier tossing grenade up stairway.

> ⚠ **CAUTION**
>
> Throwing fragmentation grenades up a stairway has a high probability for the grenades to roll back down and cause fratricide. Soldiers should avoid clustering at the foot of the stairway and ensure that the structural integrity of the building permits the use of either a fragmentation or concussion grenade.

1-15. INDIVIDUAL WEAPONS CONTROL WHEN MOVING

As in all combat situations, the clearing team members must move tactically and safely. Individuals who are part of a clearing team must move in a standard manner, using practiced techniques known to all.

a. When moving, team members maintain *muzzle awareness* by holding their weapons with the muzzle pointed in the direction of travel. Soldiers keep the butt of the rifle in the pocket of their shoulder, with the muzzle slightly down to allow unobstructed vision. Soldiers keep both eyes open and swing the muzzle as they turn their head so the rifle is always aimed where the soldier is looking. This procedure allows to soldier to see what or who is entering their line of fire.
b. Team members avoid *flagging* (leading) with the weapon when working around windows, doors, corners, or areas where obstacles must be negotiated. Flagging the weapon gives advance warning to anyone looking in the soldier's direction, making it easier for an enemy to grab the weapon.
c. Team members should keep weapons on safe (selector switch on SAFE and index finger outside of trigger guard) until a hostile target is identified and engaged. After a team member clears his sector of all targets, he returns his weapon to the SAFE position.
d. If a soldier's weapon malfunctions during room clearing, he should immediately announce "gun down" and drop to one knee and conduct immediate action to reduce the malfunction. The other members of the team should engage targets in his sector. Once the weapon is operational, he should announce "gun up" and remain in the kneeling position until directed to stand-up by the team leader.

SECTION III. CLEARING

Infantry units often use close combat to enter and clear buildings and rooms. This section describes the TTP for clearing.

1-16. HIGH INTENSITY VERSUS PRECISION CLEARING TECHNIQUES

Precision clearing techniques do not replace other techniques currently being used to clear buildings and rooms during high-intensity combat. Specifically, they do not replace the clearing technique in which a fragmentation or concussion grenade is thrown into a room before the U.S. forces enter. Precision room clearing techniques are used when the tactical situation calls for room-by-room clearing of a relatively intact building in which enemy combatants and noncombatants may be intermixed. They involve increased risk in order to clear a building methodically, rather than using overwhelming firepower to eliminate or neutralize all its inhabitants.

a. From a conceptual standpoint, standard high-intensity room clearing drills can be thought of as a deliberate attack. The task is to seize control of the room with the purpose being the neutralization of the enemy in the room. The fragmentation and or concussion grenades can be thought of as the preparatory fires used before the assault. As in a deliberate attack against any objective, the assaulting elements move into position using covered and concealed routes. The preparatory fires (fragmentation and or concussion grenades) are initiated when soldiers are as close to the objective as they can get without being injured by the fires. The assault element follows the preparatory fires onto the objective as closely as possible. A rapid, violent assault overwhelms and destroys the enemy force and seizes the objective.
b. Compared to the deliberate attack represented by high-intensity room clearing techniques, precision room clearing techniques are more conceptually like a reconnaissance in force or perhaps an infiltration attack. During a reconnaissance in force, the friendly unit seeks to determine the enemy's locations, dispositions, strength, and intentions. Once the enemy is located, the friendly force is fully prepared to engage and destroy it, especially if surprise is achieved. The friendly force retains the options of not employing preparatory fires (fragmentation and or concussion grenades) if they are not called for (the enemy is not in the room) or if they are inappropriate (there are noncombatants present also). The attacking unit may choose to create a diversion (use a stun grenade) to momentarily distract the defender while they enter and seize the objective.
c. The determination of which techniques to employ is up to the leader on the scene and is based on his analysis of the existing METT-TC conditions. The deliberate attack (high-intensity techniques), with its devastating

suppressive and preparatory fires, neutralizes everyone in the room and is less dangerous to the assaulting troops. The reconnaissance in force (precision techniques) conserves ammunition, reduces damage, and minimizes the chance of noncombatant casualties. Unfortunately, even when well-executed, it is very stressful and hazardous for friendly troops.

d. Certain precision room clearing techniques, such as methods of squad and fire team movement, the various firing stances, weapon positioning, and reflexive shooting, are useful for all combat in confined areas. Other techniques, such as entering a room without first neutralizing known enemy occupants by fire or explosives, are appropriate in only some tactical situations.

e. Generally, if a room or building is occupied by an alerted enemy force that is determined to resist, and if most or all noncombatants are clear, overwhelming firepower should be employed to avoid friendly casualties. In such a situation, supporting fires, demolitions, and fragmentation grenades should be used to neutralize a space before friendly troops enter.

f. In some combat situations the use of heavy supporting fires and demolitions would cause unacceptable collateral damage or would unnecessarily slow the unit's movement. In other situations, often during stability and support operations, enemy combatants are so intermixed with noncombatants that U.S. forces cannot, in good conscience, use all available supporting fires. Room-by-room clearing may be necessary. At such times, precision room clearing techniques are most appropriate.

1-17. PRINCIPLES OF PRECISION ROOM CLEARING

Battles that occur at close quarters, such as within a room or hallway, must be planned and executed with care. Units must train, practice, and rehearse precision room clearing techniques until each fire team and squad operates smoothly. Each unit member must understand the principles of precision room clearing: surprise, speed, and controlled violence of action.

a. **Surprise.** Surprise is the key to a successful assault at close quarters. The fire team or squad clearing the room must achieve surprise, if only for seconds, by deceiving, distracting, or startling the enemy. Sometimes stun grenades may be used to achieve surprise. These are more effective against a nonalert, poorly trained enemy than against alert, well-trained soldiers.

b. **Speed.** Speed provides a measure of security to the clearing unit. It allows soldiers to use the first few vital seconds provided by surprise to their maximum advantage. In precision room clearing, speed is not how fast you enter the room, rather it's how fast the threat is eliminated and the room is cleared.

c. **Controlled Violence of Action.** Controlled violence of action eliminates or neutralizes the enemy while giving him the least chance of inflicting friendly casualties. It is not limited to the application of firepower only, but also involves a soldier mind-set of complete domination. Each of the principles of precision room clearing has a synergistic relationship to the others. Controlled violence coupled with speed increases surprise. Hence, successful surprise allows increased speed.

1-18. FUNDAMENTALS OF PRECISION ROOM CLEARING

The ten fundamentals of precision room clearing address actions soldiers take while moving along confined corridors to the room to be cleared, while preparing to enter the room, during room entry and target engagement, and after contact. Team members—

- Move tactically and silently while securing the corridors to the room to be cleared.
- Carry only the minimum amount of equipment. (Rucksacks and loose items carried by soldiers tire them, slow their pace, and cause noise.)
- Arrive undetected at the entry to the room in the correct order of entrance, prepared to enter on a single command.
- Enter quickly and dominate the room. Move immediately to positions that allow complete control of the room and provide unobstructed fields of fire.
- Eliminate all enemy in the room by fast, accurate, and discriminating fires.
- Gain and maintain immediate control of the situation and all personnel in the room.

- Confirm whether enemy casualties are wounded or dead. Disarm, segregate, and treat the wounded. Search all enemy casualties.
- Perform a cursory search of the room. Determine if a detailed search is required.
- Evacuate all wounded and any friendly dead.
- Mark the room as cleared using a simple, clearly identifiable marking in accordance with the unit SOP.
- Maintain security and be prepared to react to more enemy contact at any moment. Do not neglect rear security.

1-19. COMPOSITION OF THE CLEARING TEAM

Precision room clearing techniques are designed to be executed by the standard four-man fire team. Because of the confined spaces typical of building- and room-clearing operations, units larger than squads quickly become unwieldy. When shortages of personnel demand it, room clearing can be conducted with two- or three-man teams, but four-man teams are preferred. Using fewer personnel greatly increases the combat strain and risks.

1-20. BREACHING

An integral part of precision room clearing is the ability to gain access quickly to the rooms to be cleared. Breaching techniques vary based on the type of construction encountered and the types of munitions available to the breaching element. Techniques range from simple mechanical breaching to complex, specialized demolitions.

a. A useful method of breaching is the *shotgun ballistic* breach for forced entry of standard doors. A 12-gauge shotgun loaded with buckshot or slugs can be used to breach most standard doors quickly. Number 9 shot works equally well with reduced collateral damage on the other side of the door. When done properly, the shotgun breach requires only a few seconds. The two standard techniques of shotgun breaching are the *doorknob breach* and the *hinge breach.* When attempting either technique, the gunner is announcing his presence by using the shotgun and is completely exposed to fire through the door. Therefore, exposure time must be minimized and the number 1 man must be ready to gain entry and return fire as soon as possible. While holding the stock of the shotgun in the pocket of his shoulder, the gunner places the muzzle tightly against the door, and aims down at a 45-degree angle.

> ✍ **NOTE**
>
> If the shotgun muzzle is not held tightly against the door, splatter may occur that could affect friendly troops. Also, buckshot and rifled slugs can overpenetrate doors and may kill or wound occupants in the room.

(1) For the doorknob breach, the aim point is a spot halfway between the doorknob and the frame, not at the doorknob itself. The gunner fires two quick shots in the same location, ensuring the second shot is aimed as carefully as the first. Weak locks may fly apart with the first shot, but the gunner should always fire twice. Some locks that appear to be blown apart have parts still connected that can delay entry. If the lock is not defeated by the second shot, the gunner repeats the procedure. Doors may not always open after firing. The gunner should be prepared to kick the door after firing to ensure opening of the entry point.

(2) The hinge breach technique is performed much the same as the doorknob breach, except the gunner aims at the hinges. He fires three shots per hinge—the first at the middle, then at the top and bottom (Figure 1-26). He fires all shots from less than an inch away from the hinge. Because the hinges are often hidden from view, the hinge breach is more difficult. Hinges are generally 8 to 10 inches from the top and bottom of the door; the center hinge is generally 36 inches from the top, centered on the door. Regardless of which technique the gunner uses, immediately after he fires, he kicks the door in or pulls it out. He then pulls the shotgun barrel sharply upward and quickly turns away from the doorway to signal that the breach point has been cleared. This rapid clearing of the doorway allows the following man in the fire team a clear shot at any enemy who may be blocking the immediate breach site.

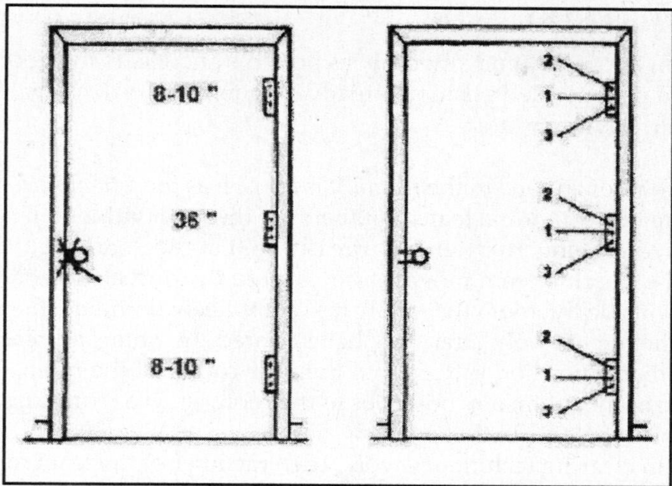

Figure 1-26: Aim points for shotgun breach of a standard door, doorknob target on left and hinge targets on right.

> ✍ **NOTE**
>
> The use of small arms (5.56-mm or 7.62-mm) as a ballistic breach on doorknobs and hinges is unsafe and should only be used as a last resort.

b. Demolitions are often needed to defeat more elaborate barriers or to produce a desired effect to aid the initial entry.

c. Mechanical breaching is planned as a backup to a ballistic or explosive breach. Mechanical breaching is an assumed capability within all units. Taking the time to defeat weak barriers, such as doors or windows, by means of crowbars, saws, sledgehammers, battering rams, axes, or other breaching tools is a decision that must be made based on the conditions of METT-TC.

d. Clearing team members must approach the breach point quickly, quietly, and in standard order. This approach preserves the element of surprise and allows for quick entry and domination of the room. The order of movement to the breach point is determined by the method of breach and intended actions at the breach point. The members of the fire team are assigned numbers 1 through 4, with the team leader normally designated number 2. If one member of the clearing team is armed with the SAW rather than an M16 rifle or carbine, he should be designated number 4.

   (1) ***Ballistic (Shotgun) Breach.*** The order of movement for a shotgun breach has the gunner up front, followed by the number 1 man, number 2 man (team leader), and then the number 3 man. After the door is breached, the gunner moves to the rear of the lineup and assumes the position of the number 4 man.

   (2) ***Explosive (Demolition) Breach.*** The order of movement for an explosive breach without engineer support is number 1, number 2 (team leader), number 3, and then number 4. The number 1 man provides security at the doorway. The number 2 man (team leader) carries the demolition charge and places it. The number 3 man provides security overhead, and the number 4 man provides rear security. After the demolition charge is placed, the team moves to covered positions and prepares to enter in the standard 1, 2, 3, 4 order.

   (3) ***Mechanical Breach.*** A suggested order of movement for a mechanical breach is the initial assault team in order, followed by the breach man or element. At the breach point, the assault team leader brings the breach team forward while the assault team provides local security. After the breach is conducted, the breach team moves aside and provides local security as the assault team enters the breach.

1-21. CONSIDERATIONS FOR ENTRY

The entire team enters the room as quickly and smoothly as possible and clears the doorway immediately. If possible, the team moves from a covered or concealed position already in their entry order. Ideally, the team arrives and passes through the entry point without having to stop.

a. The door is the focal point of anyone in the room. It is known as the *fatal funnel*, because it focuses attention at the precise point where the individual team members are the most vulnerable. Moving into the room quickly reduces the chance anyone being hit by enemy fire directed at the doorway.

b. On the signal to go, the clearing team moves from covered or concealed positions through the door quickly and takes up positions inside the room that allow it to completely dominate the room and eliminate the threat. Team members stop movement only after they have cleared the door and reached their designated point of domination. The first man's position is deep into the near corner of the room. The depth of his movement is determined by the size of the room, any obstacles in the room, such as furniture, and by the number and location of enemy and noncombatants in the room.

c. To make precision room clearing techniques work, each member of the team must know his sector of fire and how his sector overlaps and links with the sectors of the other team members. Team members do not move to the point of domination and then engage their targets. They engage targets as they move to their designated point. However, engagements must not slow movement to their points of domination. Team members may shoot from as short a range as 1 to 2 inches. They engage the most immediate enemy threats first. Examples of immediate threats are enemy personnel who—
   - Are armed and prepared to return fire immediately.
   - Block movement to the position of domination.
   - Are within arm's reach of a clearing team member.
   - Are within 3 to 5 feet of the breach point.

d. Each clearing team member has a designated sector of fire unique to him initially and expands to overlap sectors of the other team members.
   (1) The number 1 and number 2 men are initially concerned with the area directly to their front, then along the wall on either side of the door or entry point. This area is in their path of movement, and it is their primary sector of fire. Their alternate sector of fire is from the wall they are moving toward, back to the opposite far corner.
   (2) The number 3 and number 4 men start at the center of the wall opposite their point of entry and clear to the left if moving toward the left, or to the right if moving toward the right. They stop short of their respective team member (either the number 1 man or the number 2 man).

e. The team members move toward their points of domination, engaging all targets in their sector. Team members must exercise fire control and discriminate between hostile and noncombatant room occupants. Shooting is done without stopping, using reflexive shooting techniques. Because the soldiers are moving and shooting at the same time, they must move using careful hurry. (Figure 1-31 in paragraph 1-23, shows all four team members at their points of domination and their overlapping sectors of fire.)

1-22. TECHNIQUES FOR ENTERING BUILDINGS AND CLEARING ROOMS

Battle Drill 6 is the standard technique used by the four-man fire team when they perform the task, Enter Building/Clear Room. However, ROE may not allow for, nor the enemy situation requires, such aggressive action on the part of the assaulting unit. Based on the aforementioned conditions, commanders may determine to use the following techniques when entering and clearing buildings and rooms.

a. **Situation.** Operating as part of a larger force (during daylight or darkness), the squad is tasked to participate in clearing a building. The platoon leader directs the squad to enter the building or to clear a room. An entry point breach has already been identified, or will be created before initiating the entry.

b. **Special Considerations.** Platoon and squad leaders must consider the task and purpose they have been given and the method they are to use to achieve the desired results.
   (1) To seize or gain control of a building may not always require committing troops into the structure or closing with the enemy. The following steps describe effective techniques to be used when training soldiers to

the toughest possible conditions. These techniques and procedures can be trained, rehearsed, and modified to a specific situation and mission. Before initiating this action the employment of all organic, crew-served, and supporting weapon systems should be directed onto the objective area in order to suppress and neutralize the threat, providing the mission and ROE permit.

(2) When conducting urban operations, soldiers must be equipped at all times with a night vision device or light source to illuminate the immediate area.

> **NOTE**
>
> The following discussion assumes that only the platoon's organic weapons are to support the infantry squad. Urban situations may require precise application of firepower. This situation is especially true of an urban environment where the enemy is mixed with noncombatants. Noncombatants may be found in the room, which can restrict the use of fires and reduce the combat power available to a squad leader. His squad may have to operate with *no fire* areas. Rules of engagement can prohibit the use of certain weapons until a specific hostile action takes place. All soldiers must be aware of the ROE. Leaders must include the specific use of weapons in their planning for precision operations in urban terrain.

c. **Required Actions.** Figures 1-27, 1-28, 1-29, and 1-30 illustrate the required actions for performing this task.

(1) The squad leader designates the assault team and identifies the location of the entry point for them.

(2) The squad leader positions the follow-on assault team to provide overwatch and supporting fires for the initial assault team.

(3) Assault team members move as close to the entry point as possible, using available cover and concealment.

(a) If an explosive breach or a ballistic breach is to be performed by a supporting element, the assault team remains in a covered position until the breach is made. They may provide overwatch and fire support for the breaching element if necessary.

(b) All team members must signal one another that they are ready before the team moves to the entry point.

(c) Team members avoid the use of verbal signals, which may alert the enemy and remove the element of surprise.

(d) Assault team members must move quickly from the covered position to the entry point, minimizing the time they are exposed to enemy fire.

(4) The assault team enters through the breach. Unless a grenade is being thrown prior to entry, the team should avoid stopping outside the point of entry.

(a) The number 2 man may throw a grenade of some type (fragmentation, concussion, stun) into the room before entry.

(b) The use of grenades should be consistent with the ROE and building structure. The grenade should be cooked off before being thrown, if applicable to the type of grenade used.

(c) If stealth is not a factor, the thrower should sound off with a verbal indication that a grenade of some type is being thrown ("frag out," "concussion out," "stun out"). If stealth is a factor, only visual signals are given as the grenade is thrown.

> **CAUTION**
>
> If walls and floors are thin, fragments from fragmentation grenades and debris created by concussion grenades can injure soldiers outside the room. If the structure has been stressed by previous explosive engagements, the use of these grenades could cause it to collapse. Leaders must determine the effectiveness of these types of grenades compared to possibilities of harm to friendly troops.

(5) On the signal to go, or immediately after the grenade detonates, the assault team moves through the entry point (Figure 1-27) and quickly takes up positions inside the room that allow it to completely dominate the room and eliminate the threat (Figure 1-30). Unless restricted or impeded, team members stop movement

only after they have cleared the door and reached their designated point of domination. In addition to dominating the room, all team members are responsible for identifying possible loopholes and mouse-holes in the ceiling, walls and floor.

> ✍ **NOTE**
>
> Where enemy forces may be concentrated and the presence of noncombatants is highly unlikely, the assault team can precede their entry by throwing a fragmentation or concussion grenade (structure dependent) into the room, followed by bursts of automatic small-arms fire by the number one man as he enters.

(a) The first man (rifleman), enters the room and eliminates the immediate threat. He has the option of going left or right, normally moving along the path of least resistance to one of two corners. When using a doorway as the point of entry, the path of least resistance is determined initially based on the way the door opens; if the door opens inward he plans to move away from the hinges. If the door opens outward, he plans to move toward the hinged side. Upon entering, the size of the room, enemy situation, and furniture or other obstacles that hinder or channel movement become factors that influence the number 1 man's direction of movement.

(b) The direction each man moves in should not be preplanned unless the exact room layout is known. Each man should go in a direction opposite the man in front of him (Figure 1-27). Every team member must know the sectors and duties of each position.

(c) As the first man goes through the entry point, he can usually see into the far corner of the room. He eliminates any immediate threat and continues to move along the wall if possible and to the first corner, where he assumes a position of domination facing into the room.

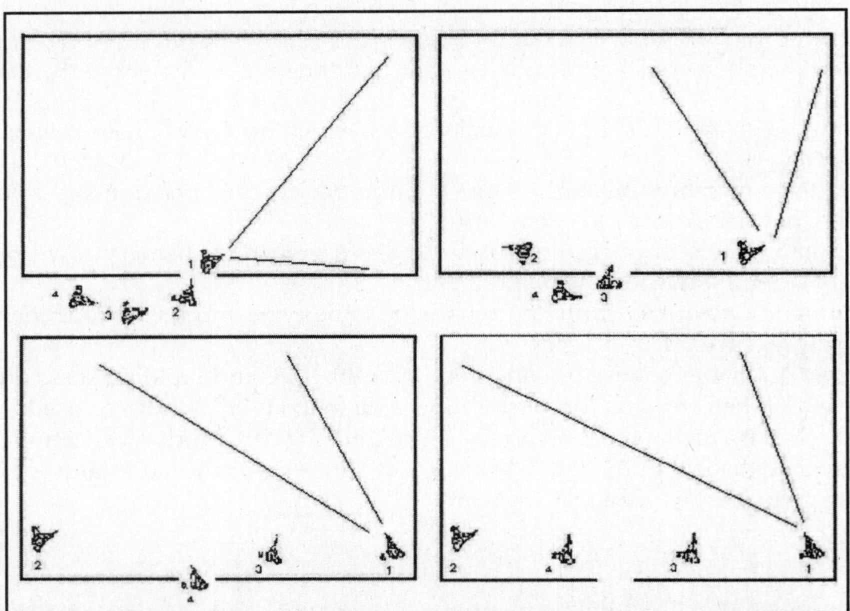

Figure 1-27: First man enters a room.

(6) The second man (team leader), entering almost simultaneously with the first, moves in the opposite direction, following the wall and staying out of the center (Figure 1-28). The second man must clear the entry point, clear the immediate threat area, clear his corner, and move to a dominating position on his side of the room.

(7) The third man (grenadier) simply goes opposite of the second man inside the room at least one meter from the entry point and moves to a position that dominates his sector (Figure 1-29).

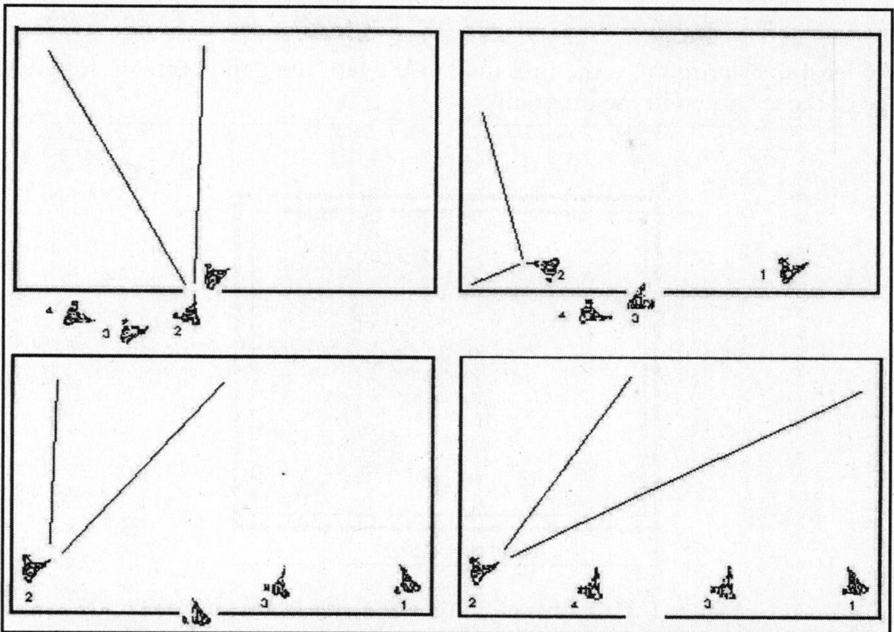

Figure 1-28: Second man enters a room.

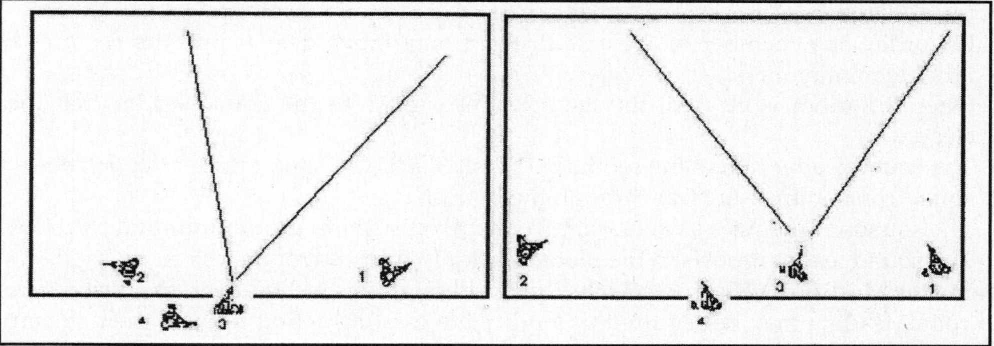

Figure 1-29: Third man enters a room.

(8) The fourth man (SAW gunner) moves opposite of the third man and moves to a position that dominates his sector (Figure 1-30).

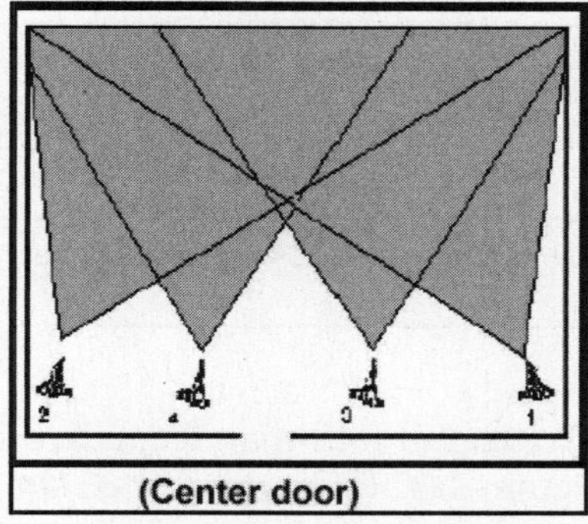

Figure 1-30: Fourth man in a room.

> ✍ **NOTE**
> If the path of least resistance takes the first man to the left, then all points of domination are the mirror image of those shown in the diagrams.

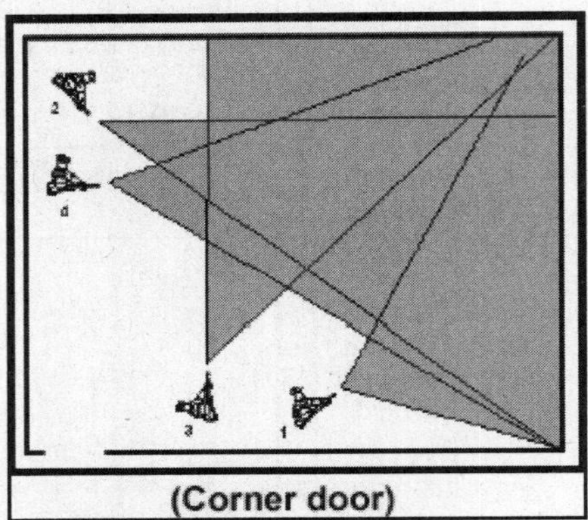

Figure 1-31: Points of domination and sectors of fire.

(9) Points of domination should not be in front of doors or windows so team members are not silhouetted to the outside of the room (Figure 3-31). No movement should mask the fire of any of the other team members.
(10) On order, any member of the assault team may move deeper into the room overwatched by the other team members.
(11) Once the room is cleared, the team leader signals to the squad leader that the room has been cleared.
(12) The squad leader marks the room (IAW unit SOP). The squad leader determines whether or not his squad can continue to clear through the building.
(13) The squad reorganizes as necessary. Leaders redistribute the ammunition.
(14) The squad leader reports to the platoon leader when the room is clear.

d. **Reasons for Modifying the Entry Technique.** Although this technique is an effective procedure for clearing a room, leaders may be required to modify the existing action to meet their current situation. Some example reasons and methods of modifying the technique are shown in Table 1-1.

Table 1-1: Reasons and methods for modifying entry techniques.

REASON	METHOD
Objective rooms are consistently small.	Clear with two or three men.
Shortage of personnel.	Clear in teams of two or three.
Enemy poses no immediate threat.	One or two men search each room to ensure no enemy or noncombatants are present.
No immediate threat, and speed is of the essence	One man visually searches each room.

e. **Three- and Two-Man Teams.** When full four-man teams are not available for room clearing three- and two-man teams can be used. Figures 1-32 (below) and 1-33 show the points of domination and sectors of fire for a three-man clearing team. Figures 1-34 and 1-35 show the same thing for a two-man team. Leaders should use the entry technique *blueprint* when modifying their techniques.

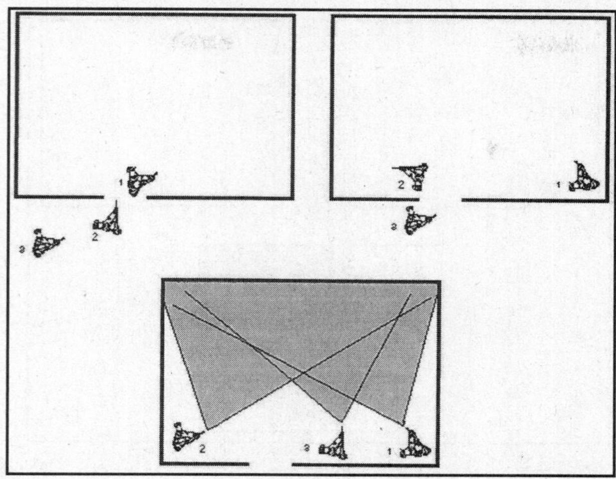

Figure 1-32: Points of domination and sectors of fire (three-man team, center door).

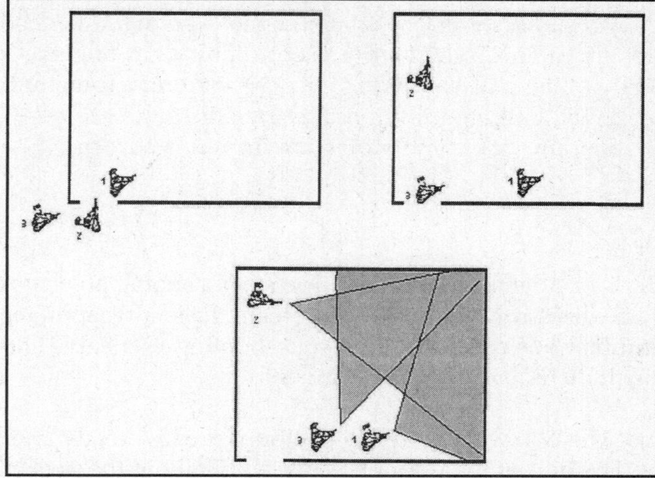

Figure 1-33: Points of domination and sectors of fire (three-man team, corner door).

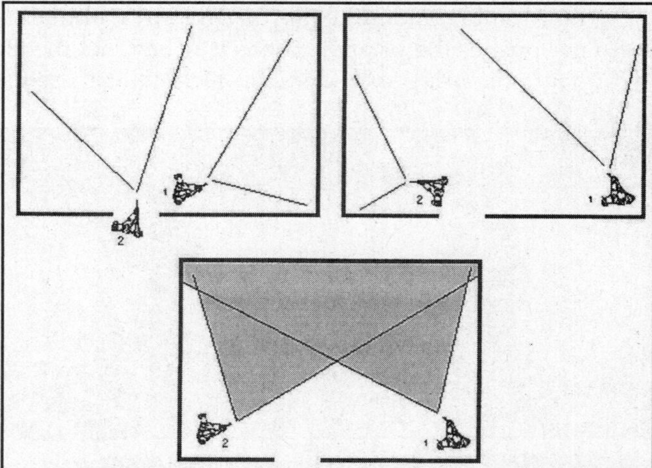

Figure 1-34: Points of domination and sectors of fire (two-man team, center door).

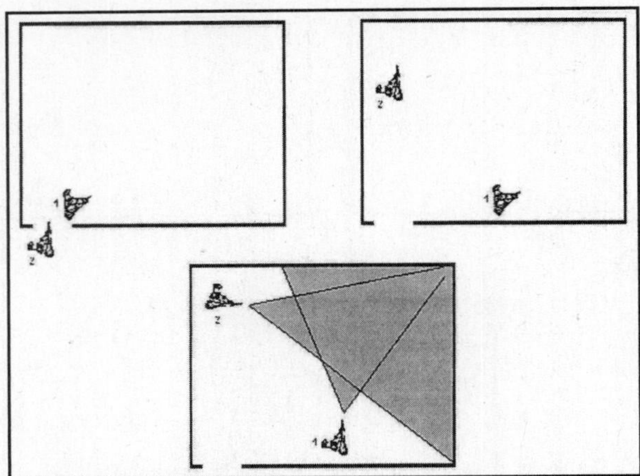

Figure 1-35: Points of domination and sectors of fire (two-man team, corner door).

> ⚠ **CAUTION**
>
> Ricochets are a hazard. All soldiers must be aware of the type of wall construction of the room being cleared. The walls of an enclosed room present many right angles. Combined with hard surfaces such as concrete, a bullet may continue to ricochet around a room until its energy is spent. After hitting threat personnel, ball ammunition may pass through the body and ricochet. Body armor and the Kevlar helmet provide some protection from this hazard.

1-23. REFLEXIVE SHOOTING

Precision room clearing allows little or no margin for error. Too slow a shot at an enemy, too fast a shot at a noncombatant, or inaccurate shots can all be disastrous for the clearing team. Proper weapon ready technique, stance, aiming, shot placement, and trigger manipulations constitute reflexive shooting. Reflexive shooting techniques are used by all members of the fire team, to include M203 and M249 gunners.

a. **Weapon Ready Positions.** The two weapon ready positions are low ready and high ready (Figure 1-36).

(1) ***Low Ready Position.*** The butt of the weapon is placed firmly in the pocket of the shoulder with the barrel pointed down at a 45-degree angle. This position is the safest carry position. It should be used by the clearing team while inside the room, except when actually entering and clearing.

(2) ***High, Ready Position.*** The butt of the weapon is held under the armpit, with the barrel pointed slightly up, keeping the front sight assembly under the line of sight but within the gunner's peripheral vision. To engage a target, the gunner pushes the weapon out as if to bayonet the target. When the weapon leaves the armpit, he slides it up into the firing shoulder. This technique is used when moving in a single file.

Figure 1-36: Ready positions for the M16A2.

b. **Stance.** Feet are about shoulder-width apart. Toes are pointed to the front (direction of movement). The firing side foot is slightly staggered to the rear of the non-firing side foot. Knees are slightly bent and the upper body is leaned slightly forward. Shoulders are square and pulled back, not rolled over or slouched. The head is up and both eyes are open. When engaging targets, the gunner holds the weapon with the butt in the pocket of his shoulder.

c. **Aiming with Iron Sights.** The four aiming techniques all have their place during combat in urban areas, but the aimed quick-kill technique is the one most often used in precision room clearing.
   (1) ***Slow Aimed Fire.*** This technique is the most accurate. It consists of taking up a steady, properly aligned sight picture and squeezing off rounds. It is normally used for engagements beyond 25 meters or when the need for accuracy overrides speed.
   (2) ***Rapid Aimed Fire.*** This technique features an imperfect sight picture in which windage is critical but elevation is of lesser importance. When the front sight post is in line with the target, the gunner squeezes the trigger. This technique is used against targets out to 15 meters and is fairly accurate and very fast.
   (3) ***Aimed Quick Kill.*** This technique consists of using a good spot weld and placing the front sight post flush on top of the rear peep sight. It is used for very quick shots out to 12 meters. Windage is important, but elevation is not critical with relation to the target. This technique is the fastest and most accurate. With practice, soldiers can become deadly shots at close range.
   (4) ***Instinctive Fire.*** This technique is the least desirable. The gunner focuses on the target and points the weapon in the target's general direction, using muscle memory to compensate for lack of aim. This technique should be used only in emergencies.

d. **M68 Close Combat Optic.** The M68 close combat optic (CCO) is an excellent close combat aiming system when used properly. Remember, the M68 is not a telescope sight.
   (1) ***Aimed Fire.*** This technique requires looking through the CCO with both eyes open and focusing on the target. An optical illusion places a red aiming dot in front of the firer. The dot is placed on the target then the target is engaged with fire. The aiming dot does not have to be centered in the optic. The CCO is used in the same manner at all ranges. Therefore, there is no distinction between slow aimed fire, rapid aimed fire, and aimed quick kill techniques.
   (2) ***Instinctive Fire.*** This technique remains the same with the CCO.

e. **Trigger Manipulation.** Rapid, aimed, semiautomatic fire is the most effective method of engaging targets during precision room clearing. As each round is fired from the aimed quick-kill position, the weapon's recoil makes the front sight post move in a small natural arc. The gunner should not fight this recoil. He should let the weapon make the arc and immediately bring the front sight post back onto the target and take another shot. This two-shot combination is known as firing a *controlled pair.* Soldiers must practice a *controlled pair* until it becomes instinctive. Clearing team members continue to fire *controlled pairs* until the target goes down. If there are multiple targets, team members engage with a controlled pair and then return to reengage any enemy left standing or still trying to resist.

f. **Shot Placement.** In precision room clearing, enemy soldiers must be incapacitated immediately. Shots that wound or are mortal but do not incapacitate the target instantaneously are better than misses but may allow the enemy to return fire. While a solid *head-shot* is expected to instantaneously incapacitate the enemy, a target area of 5 by 8 inches may be difficult to hit when moving rapidly in a low crouch position.
   (1) Members of clearing teams should concentrate on achieving solid, well-placed shots (controlled pairs) to the upper chest, then to the head (Figure 1-37). This shot placement increases the first round hit probability and allows for a second round incapacitating shot.
   (2) This engagement technique is more reliable than attempting *head-shots* only and is easy for soldiers to learn, having been taught previously to aim at center of mass.

g. **Reflexive Shooting Techniques During Limited Visibility.** Reflexive shooting techniques are also used during periods of limited visibility.
   (1) ***Visible Illumination.*** When using flashlights or other visible illumination, treat all engagements as day engagements and use the applicable technique as described above. Bright light shone into the enemy's eyes can limit his effectiveness; also, be aware that a flashlight marks your location as well.
   (2) ***AN/PAQ-4 and AN/PEQ-2 Aiming Lights.*** When using IR aiming lights in conjunction with night vision goggles (NVGs), use the instinctive fire technique to point the weapon at the target while activating the aiming light. This technique should place the aiming dot within the field of view of the NVGs and on or near the target. Adjust placement of the aiming dot onto the target and fire. Note that target

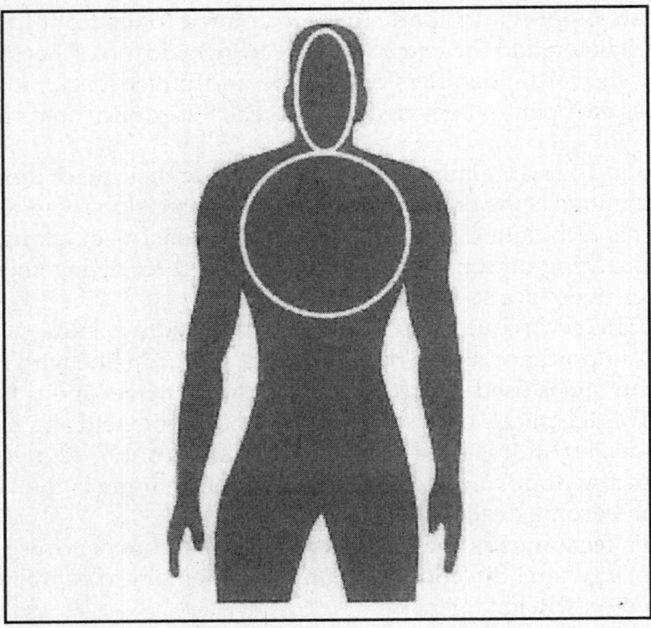

Figure 1-37: Lethal to incapacitating shot placement.

discrimination is more difficult when using NVGs. IR illumination provided by flashlights with IR filters, or the illuminator that is integral with the PEQ-2, can aid in target identification and discrimination. IR illumination is also required inside buildings when there is no ambient light.

(3) ***AN/PAS-13 Thermal Weapons Sight.*** The thermal weapons sight (TWS) offers some distinct advantages over IR viewers. It does not require any ambient light and does not *bloom* out when encountering a sudden light source. However, its weight and bulk are a disadvantage when performing reflexive firing techniques. With the sight in the ON position, the TWS has a power saving feature that turns off the viewer after a period of inactivity. The soldier reactivates the sight by placing his eye against the rubber eyecup. When reactivated, it takes a few seconds for the sight to cool itself down enough to regain an image. This delay is not acceptable for soldiers using TWS while conducting room and building clearing tasks. When performing precision clearing tasks, the TWS must remain in the EMERGENCY setting, which allows it to remain continuously active.

✍ NOTE

The *emergency* setting on the TWS greatly reduces the battery life, which requires more frequent battery changes.

(4) When using the TWS during periods of limited visibility, it is best to use the PAQ-4 aiming light, with the AN/PVS-14 Monocular IWG for reflexive shooting engagements. Use the TWS when the slow aimed fire technique is appropriate. For daytime and high visibility periods, soldiers using the TWS should not be placed on *point*, or be among the numbers 1 through 3 men of a room clearing team. When employed in urban operations, soldiers must be aware that the TWS cannot detect targets through window glass. The TWS is effective in daytime for locating targets hidden in shadows.

3-24. TARGET DISCRIMINATION

Target discrimination is the act of quickly distinguishing between combatant and noncombatant personnel and engaging only the combatants. U.S. forces engage in precision room clearing to apply discriminating combat power and limit unnecessary casualties among noncombatants. Target discrimination is vital in precision room clearing.

If there are no noncombatants then there is less of a need for selective engagements. However, even if an area is known to be free of noncombatants, other soldiers moving through the area may be mistaken as enemy and engaged unless clearing team members are disciplined and well-trained in fire control and target discrimination. Even with well-trained, disciplined soldiers, precision room clearing can result in unintentional casualties among noncombatants. Commanders must recognize this and take steps to relieve the stress it causes soldiers.

3-25. MOVEMENT WITHIN A BUILDING

When operating under precision conditions, movement techniques may be modified based on the room clearing technique being used. The terrain, the enemy situation, visibility, and the likelihood of contact dictate movement techniques.

a. **Individual Movement.** When moving within a building, the soldier avoids silhouetting himself in doors and windows (Figure 1-38). When moving in hallways, he never moves alone—he always moves with at least one other soldier for security. The soldier should try to stay 12 to 18 inches away from walls when moving; rubbing against walls may alert an enemy on the other side, or, if engaged by an enemy, ricochet rounds tend to travel parallel to a wall.

Figure 1-38: Movement within a building.

b. **Hallway Clearing Techniques.** The clearing team must always be alert. Team members provide security at the breach point and to the rear. Inside buildings they provide security laterally down corridors, and upward if near stairs or landings. The two basic techniques for moving down hallways are shown in Figure 1-39. Hallway intersections are dangerous areas and should be approached cautiously (Figures 1-40 and 1-41).

(1) ***Serpentine.*** The serpentine technique is used in narrow hallways. The number 1 man provides security to the front. His sector of fire includes any enemy soldiers who appear at the far end of the hall or from any doorways near the end. The number 2 and number 3 men cover the left and right sides of the number 1 man. Their sectors of fire include any soldiers who appear suddenly from nearby doorways on either side of the hall. The number 4 man, normally carrying the M249, provides rear protection against any enemy soldiers suddenly appearing behind the clearing team.

(2) ***Rolling T.*** The rolling-T technique is used in wide hallways. The number 1 and number 2 men move abreast, covering the opposite side of the hallway from the one they are walking on. The number 3 man covers the far end of the hallway from a position behind the number 1 and number 2 men, firing between them. Once again, the number 4 man provides rear security.

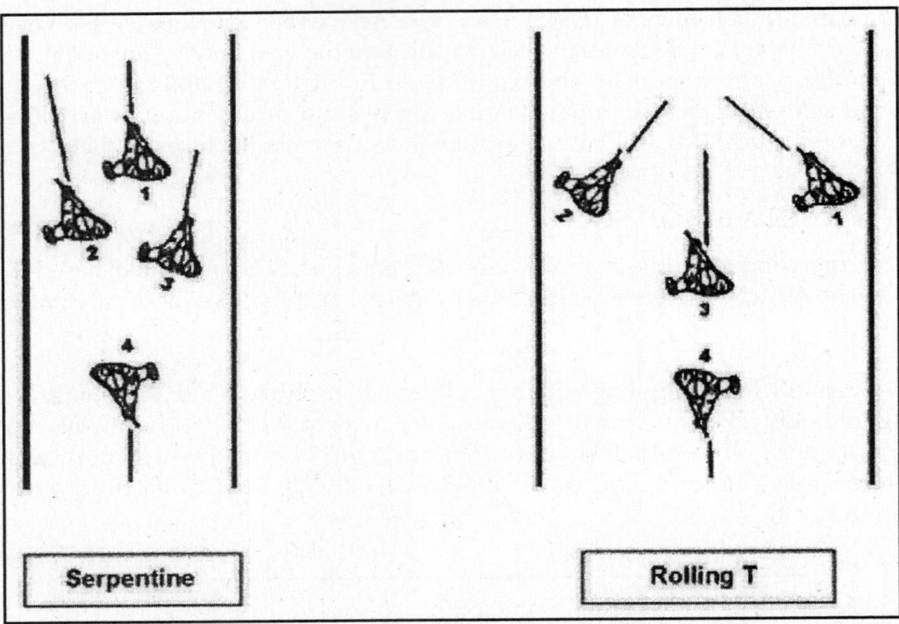

Figure 1-39: Hallway clearing techniques.

(3) ***Clearing "T" Intersections.*** Figure 1-40 depicts the fire team's actions upon reaching a hallway "T" intersection when approaching from the *base* of the "T". The fire team is using the serpentine formation for movement.

- The team configures into a 2-by-2 formation with the numbers 1 and 2 men left, and the 3 and 4 men right. (When clearing a right-hand corner, use the left-handed firing method to minimize exposure.)
- The numbers 1 and 3 men move to the edge of the corner and assume a low crouch or kneeling position. On signal, the numbers 1 and 3 men simultaneously turn left and right, respectively.
- At the same time, the numbers 2 and 4 men step forward and turn left and right, respectively maintaining their (high) position. (Sectors of fire interlock and the *low/high* positions prevent soldiers from firing at another.)
- Once the left and right portions of the hallway are clear, the fire team resumes the movement formation.

Figure 1-41 depicts the fire team's actions upon reaching a hallway "T" intersection when approaching along the *cross* of the "T". The fire team is using the serpentine formation for movement.

- The team configures into a modified 2-by-2 formation with the numbers 1 and 3 men abreast and toward the right side of the hall. The number 2 man moves to the left side of the hall and orients to the front, and the number 4 man shifts to the right side (his left) and maintains rear security. (When clearing a right-hand corner, use the left-handed firing method to minimize exposure.)
- The numbers 1 and 3 men move to the edge of the corner and the number 3 man assumes a low crouch or kneeling position. On signal, the number 3 man turns right around the corner keeping low, the number 1 man steps forward while turning to the right and staying high. (Sectors of fire interlock and the *low/high* positions prevent soldiers from firing at one another.)
- The numbers 2 and 4 men continue to move in the direction of travel. As the number 2 man passes behind the number 1 man, the number 1 man shifts laterally to his left until he reaches the far corner.
- The numbers 2 and 4 men continue to move in the direction of travel. As the number 4 man passes behind the number 3 man, the number 3 man shifts laterally to his left until he reaches the far corner. As the number 3 man begins to shift across the hall, the number 1 man turns into the direction of travel and moves to his position in the formation.
- As the numbers 3 and 4 men reach the far side of the hallway, they too assume their original positions in the serpentine formation, and the fire team continues to move.

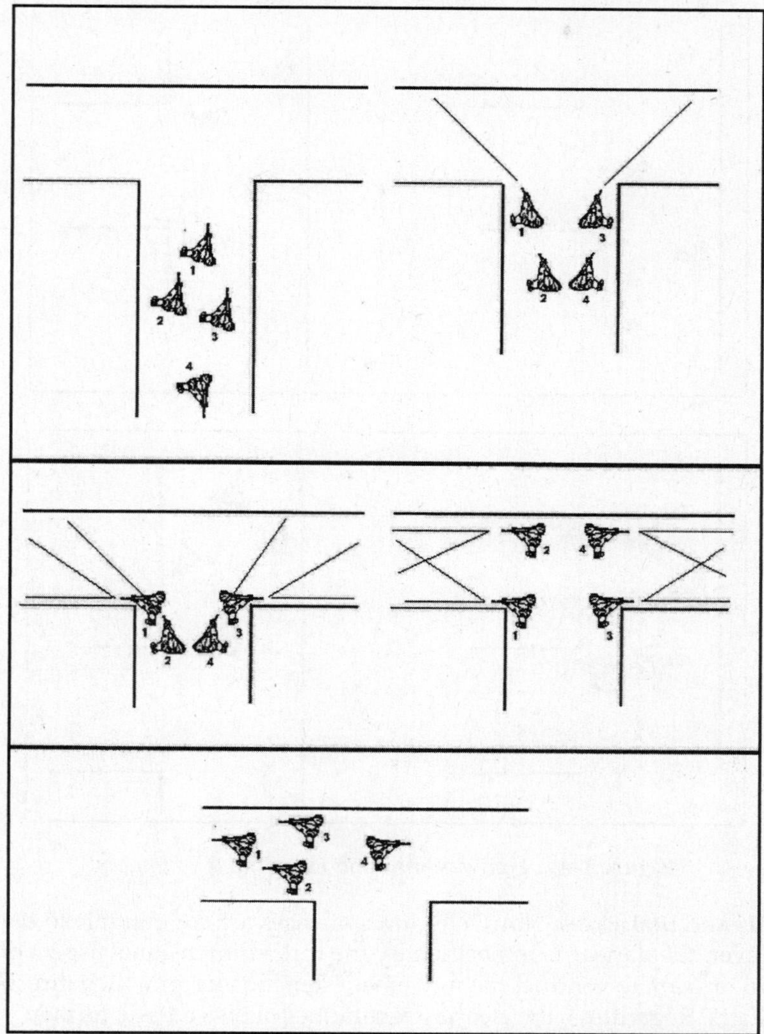

Figure 1-40: T-shaped hallway intersection clearing positions.

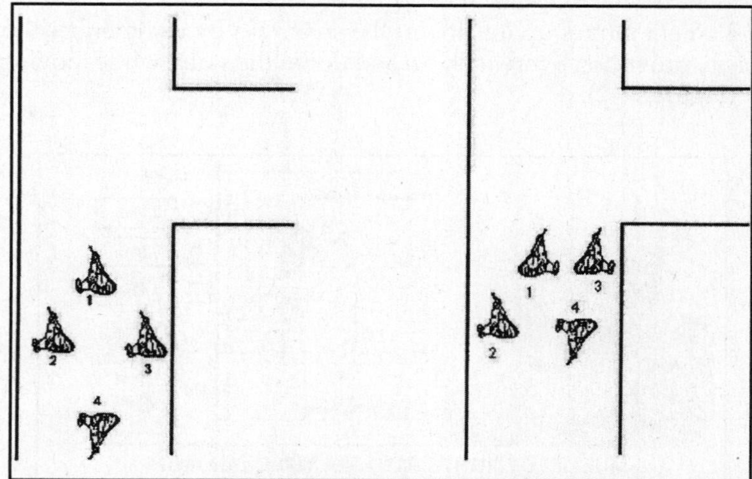

Figure 1-41: Hallway junction clearing.

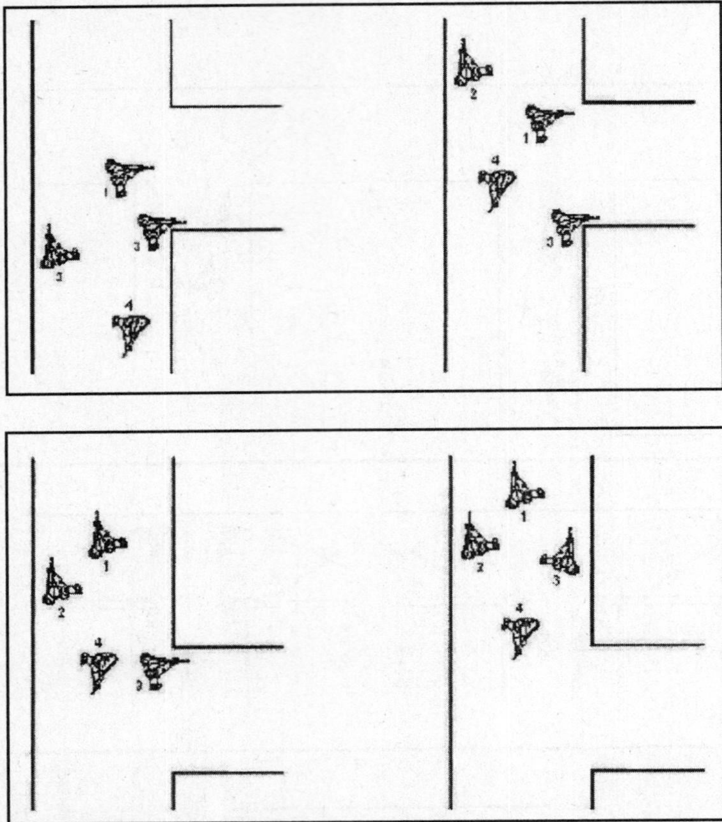

Figure 1-41: Hallway junction clearing. *(Continued)*

c. **Clearing Stairwells and Staircases.** Stairwells and staircases are comparable to doorways in that they create a *fatal funnel*; however, the danger is intensified by the three-dimensional aspect of additional landings. The ability of the squad or team to conduct the movement depends upon which direction they are traveling and the layout of the stairs. Regardless, the clearing technique follows a basic format:

- The squad leader designates an assault element to clear the stairs.
- The squad or team maintains 360-degree, three-dimensional security in the vicinity of the stairs.
- The squad leader then directs the assault team to locate, mark, bypass and or clear any obstacles or booby traps that may be blocking access to the stairs.
- The assault element moves up (or down) the stairways by using either the two-, three-, or four-man flow technique, providing overwatch up and down the stairs while moving. The three-man variation is preferred (Figure 1-42).

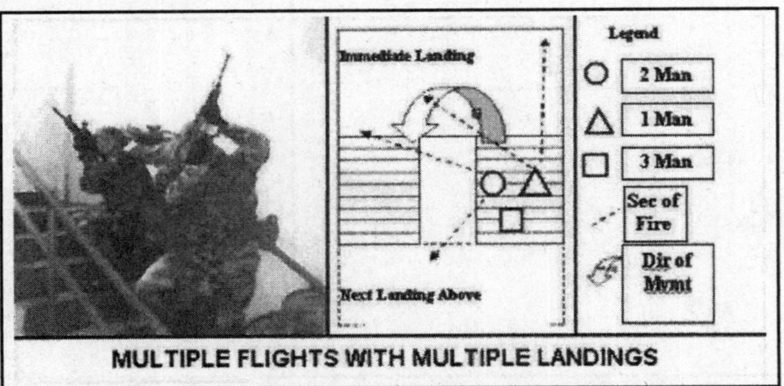

Figure 1-42: ***Three-man flow*** **clearing technique.**

1-26. VERBAL COMMANDS AND SIGNALS

When conducting precision clearing, soldiers are very close to each other as they engage targets. The high volume of noise makes communications extremely difficult. The command and control techniques used during precision combat must consist of terms and actions that soldiers are familiar with and to which they know how to respond.

a. The use of verbal commands and signals within the assault element are extremely important. The soldier must always let others in the assault element know where he is and what he is doing.
b. As an example, terms similar to the ones listed in Table 1-2 should be a part of each soldier's vocabulary IAW unit SOP.

Table 1-2: Verbal commands and signals.

TERM	EXPLANATION
"STATUS!"	Signal by an element leader that requires all members to report whether their sectors are clear and if they are prepared to continue the mission.
"CLEAR!"	Signal given by individuals to report their sector is clear.
"UP!"	Signal given by individuals to report they are ready to continue the mission (weapon loaded, equipment accounted for).
"ROOM CLEAR!"	Signal from team leader to team members, squad leader, and follow-on teams that the room is secure and cleared.
"COMING OUT!"	Signal given by an individual or team that they are about to exit a room.
"COME OUT!"	Reply given by security element or follow-on team that it is safe to exit the room.
"COMING IN!"	Signal given by an individual who is about to enter an occupied room.
"COME IN!"	Reply given by an occupant of a room stating it is safe to enter.
"COMING UP (DOWN)!	Signal given by an individual or team that is about to ascend or descend a stairway.
"COME UP (DOWN)!"	Reply given by security element that it is safe to ascend or descend a stairway.
"MAN DOWN!"	Signal given when an individual has been wounded or injured and cannot continue his mission.
"SHORT ROOM!"	Signal given by either the number 1 man or the number 2 man to indicate a small room, and that all team members should not enter.
"GRENADE!"	A command given by any soldier, when an enemy grenade has been thrown. All soldiers need to take immediate actions. Although difficult, the soldier should identify the location of the grenade, if possible.
"GO LONG!"	A command given by one member of the team to tell another team member to take up security farther into the room or farther down a hallway.
"GUN DOWN"	A signal given when an individual's weapon has malfunctioned and is being corrected.
"GUN UP"	A signal given when an individual has corrected a malfunction and is ready for action.
"RELOADING"	A signal given when an individual is reloading any weapon system. This signal is followed by "GUN UP" when ready.

> ✍ **NOTE**
> The use of loud verbal commands may reveal to the enemy the location and immediate intent of friendly forces. Although code words may be substituted, they can be heard and used by enemy forces if friendly forces use them too loudly.

1-27. SAFETY AND FORCE PROTECTION

Precision clearing is high risk, and even training for it can be hazardous. Only well-trained, disciplined soldiers are able to execute these techniques successfully.

a. Leaders at all levels must enforce safe handling of weapons and demolitions. The concern that individual soldiers not be injured in accidents is essential to mission accomplishment. Unintentional and unsafe weapons fire or detonation of explosives or munitions can jeopardize the mission of the clearing team and subsequently the entire unit.

b. Soldiers engaged in precision clearing should wear all their protective equipment.

   (1) Soft body armor, such as the standard Army-issue Kevlar vest, is effective in preventing death or serious injury from high-velocity fragments that strike the torso area. Although the Kevlar protective vest is effective, flexible, and relatively comfortable, it is not designed to stop bullets. As a rule, soft body armor stops some low-power handgun rounds but not rifle or carbine ammunition.

   (2) Some versions of hard body armor stops almost any round fired at it. They tend to be heavy and stiff, but they have proven effective during precision clearing. If a commander knows his unit is going to conduct lengthy precision room clearing, he requests a special issue of threat level III or IV protective equipment. This equipment is excellent, but soldiers must train and rehearse wearing it before they enter combat. All precision clearing is tiring, and soldiers wearing threat level III or IV protection tire or overheat more quickly.

   (3) The standard Army Kevlar helmet and ballistic protective eyeglasses have also been proven to significantly reduce casualties during precision room clearing.

   (4) Hard plastic knee and elbow protectors are available on special request. They are useful, especially during prolonged search and clear operations. They prevent injury from rubble and broken glass when kneeling or prone.

c. Detailed knowledge of weapons and munitions effects is important to the safety of members of the clearing team, as well as to mission accomplishment. Most interior building wails do not stop rifle fire. Fragments from grenades often penetrate interior walls. Standard home furnishings or office furniture offer little protection from high-velocity rounds. Excessive amounts of demolitions used to breach a wall may knock it down instead, perhaps even bring the roof of the building down also.

> ⚠ **CAUTION**
> Goggles or ballistic eye protection should always be worn to protect soldiers from debris caused by explosives, tools, weapons, grenades, and so forth.

SECTION IV. FIGHTING POSITIONS

Whether a unit is attacking, defending, or conducting retrograde operations, its success or failure depends on the ability of the individual soldier to place accurate fire on the enemy with the least exposure to return fire. Consequently, the soldier must immediately seek and use firing positions properly.

1-28. HASTY FIGHTING POSITION

A hasty fighting position is normally occupied in the attack or the early stages of the defense. It is a position from which the soldier can place fire upon the enemy while using available cover for protection from return fire. The soldier may occupy it voluntarily or he may be forced to occupy it due to enemy fire. In either case, the position lacks preparation before occupation. Some of the more common hasty fighting positions in an urban area are: corners of buildings, behind walls, windows, unprepared loopholes, and the peak of a roof.

a. **Corners of Buildings.** The soldier must be capable of firing his weapon both right- and left-handed to be effective around corners.
   (1) A common error made in firing around corners is firing from the wrong shoulder. This exposes more of the soldier's body to return fire than necessary. By firing from the proper shoulder, the soldier can reduce exposure to enemy fire.
   (2) Another common mistake when firing around corners is firing from the standing position. The soldier exposes himself at the height the enemy would expect a target to appear, and risks exposing the entire length of his body as a target for the enemy.

b. **Walls.** When firing from behind walls, the soldier must fire around cover and not over it (Figure 1-43).

Figure 1-43: Soldier firing around cover.

c. **Windows.** In an urban area, windows provide convenient firing ports. The soldier must avoid firing from the standing position since it exposes most of his body to return fire from the enemy and could silhouette him against a light-colored interior beyond the window. This is an obvious sign of the soldier's position, especially at night when the muzzle flash can easily be observed. In using the proper method of firing from a window (Figure 1-44), the soldier is well back into the room to prevent the muzzle flash from being seen, and he is kneeling to limit exposure and avoid silhouetting himself.

Figure 1-44: Soldier firing from window.

d. **Loopholes.** The soldier may fire through a hole created in the wall and avoid windows (Figure 1-45). He stays back from the loophole so the muzzle of the weapon does not protrude beyond the wall, and the muzzle flash is concealed.

Figure 1-45: Soldier firing from loophole.

e. **Roof.** The peak of a roof provides a vantage point for snipers that increases their field of vision and the ranges at which they can engage targets (Figure 1-46). A chimney, a smokestack, or any other object protruding from the roof of a building can reduce the size of the target exposed and should be used.

Figure 1-46: Soldier firing from peak of a roof.

f. **No Position Available.** When the soldier is subjected to enemy fire and none of the positions mentioned above are available, he must try to expose as little of himself as possible. The soldier can reduce his exposure to the enemy by lying prone as close to a building as possible, on the same side of the open area as the enemy. To engage the soldier, the enemy must then lean out the window and expose himself to return fire.

g. **No Cover Available.** When no cover is available, the soldier can reduce exposure by firing from the prone position, by firing from shadows, and by presenting no silhouette against buildings.

1-29. PREPARED FIGHTING POSITION

A prepared firing position is one built or improved to allow the soldier to engage a particular area, avenue of approach, or enemy position, while reducing his exposure to return fire. Examples of prepared positions include barricaded windows, fortified loopholes, sniper positions, antiarmor positions, and machine gun positions.

a. The natural firing port provided by windows can be improved by barricading the window, leaving a small hole for the soldier's use. Materials torn from the interior walls of the building or any other available material may be used for barricading.

(1) When barricading windows, avoid barricading only the windows that are going to be used as firing ports. The enemy can soon determine that the barricaded windows are fighting positions.

(2) Also avoid neat, square, or rectangular holes that are easily identified by the enemy. A barricaded window should not have a neat, regular firing port. The window should keep its original shape so that the position of the soldier is hard to detect. Firing from the bottom of the window gives the soldier the advantage of the wall because the firing port is less obvious to the enemy. Sandbags are used to reinforce the wall below the window and to increase protection for the soldier. All glass must be removed from the window to prevent injury to the soldier. Lace curtains permit the soldier to see out and prevent the enemy from seeing in. Wet blankets should be placed under weapons to reduce dust. Wire mesh over the window keeps the enemy from throwing in hand grenades.

b. Although windows usually are good fighting positions, they do not always allow the soldier to engage targets in his sector.

(1) To avoid establishing a pattern of always firing from windows, an alternate position is required such as in an interior room and firing through a rubbled outer wall (Figure 1-47), or a prepared loophole (Figure 1-48). The prepared loophole involves cutting or blowing a small hole into the wall to allow the soldier to observe and engage targets in his sector.

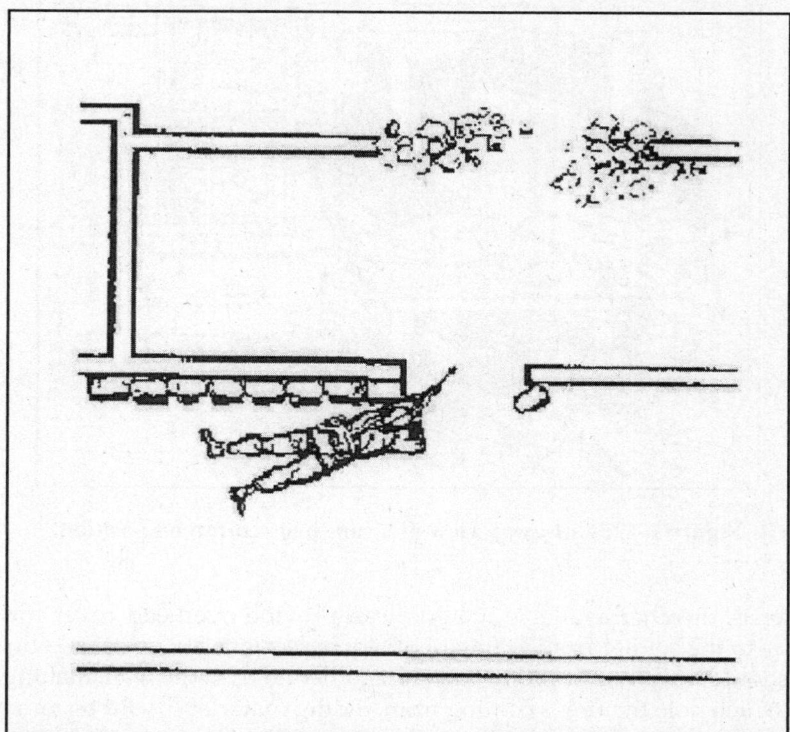

Figure 1-47: Interior room position.

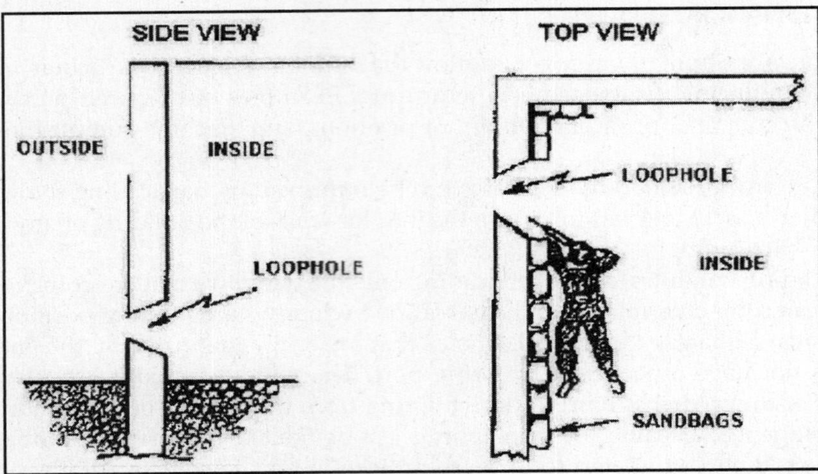

Figure 1-48: Prepared loophole.

(2) Sandbags are used to reinforce the walls below, around, and above the loophole (Figure 1-49). Two layers of sandbags are placed on the floor under the soldier to protect him from an explosion on a lower floor (if the position is on the second floor or higher). A wall of sandbags, rubble, furniture, and so on should be constructed to the rear of the position to protect the soldier from explosions in the room.

Figure 1-49: Cut-away view of a sandbag reinforced position.

(3) A table, bedstead, or other available material can provide overhead cover for the position. This cover prevents injury to the soldier from falling debris or explosions above his position.

(4) The position should be camouflaged by knocking other holes in the wall, making it difficult for the enemy to determine which hole the fire is coming from. Siding material should be removed from the building in several places to make loopholes less noticeable.

(5) Because of the angled firing position associated with loopholes, primary and supplementary positions can be prepared using the same loophole (Figure 1-50). This procedure allows the individual to shift his fire onto a sector that was not previously covered by small arms fire.

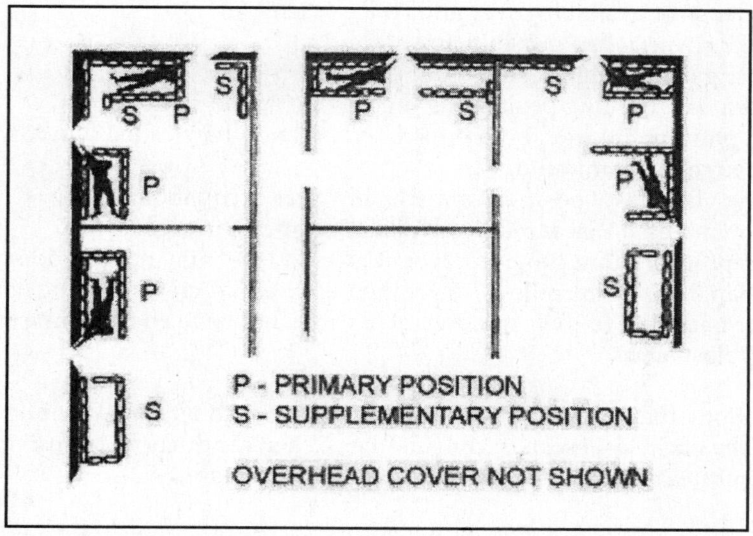

Figure 1-50: Loopholes with primary and supplementary positions.

c. A chimney or other protruding structure provides a base from which a sniper position can be prepared. Part of the roofing material is removed to allow the sniper to fire around the chimney. He should stand inside the building on the beams or on a platform with only his head and shoulders above the roof (behind the chimney). Sandbags placed on the sides of the position protect the sniper's flanks.

d. When the roof has no protruding structure to provide protection, the sniper position should be prepared from underneath on the enemy side of the roof (Figure 1-51). The position is reinforced with sandbags, and a small piece of roofing material should be removed to allow the sniper to engage targets in his sector. The missing

Figure 1-51: Sniper position.

piece of roofing material should be the only sign a position exists. Other pieces of roofing should be removed to deceive the enemy as to the true sniper position. The sniper should be invisible from outside the building and the muzzle flash must be hidden from view.

e. Some considerations for selecting and occupying individual fighting positions are:
   - Make maximum use of available cover and concealment.
   - Avoid firing over cover; when possible, fire around it.
   - Avoid silhouetting against light-colored buildings, the skyline, and so on.
   - Carefully select a new fighting position before leaving an old one.
   - Avoid setting a pattern; fire from both barricaded and non-barricaded windows.
   - Keep exposure time to a minimum.
   - Begin improving your hasty position immediately after occupation.
   - Use construction material that is readily available in an urban area.
   - Remember that positions that provide cover at ground level may not provide cover on higher floors.

f. In attacking an urban area, the recoilless AT weapon and ATGM crews may be hampered in choosing firing positions due to the backblast of their weapons. They may not have enough time to knock out walls in buildings and clear backblast areas.

They should select positions that allow the backblast to escape such as corner windows where the round fired goes out one window and the backblast escapes from another. When conduction defensive operations the corner of a building can be improved with sandbags to create a firing position (Figure 1-52).

Figure 1-52: Corner firing position.

g. The rifle squad during an attack on and in defense of an urban area is often reinforced with attached antitank weapons. The rifle squad leader must be able to choose good firing positions for the antitank weapons under his control.

h. Various principles of employing antitank weapons have universal applications such as: making maximum use of available cover; trying to achieve mutual support; and allowing for the backblast when positioning recoilless weapons, TOWs, Dragons, Javelins, and AT4s.

i. Operating in an urban area presents new considerations. Soldiers must select numerous alternate positions, particularly when the structure does not provide cover from small-arms fire. They must position their weapons in the shadows and within the building.

j. AT4s and Javelins firing from the top of a building can use the chimney for cover (Figure 1-53). The rear of this position should be reinforced with sandbags but should not interfere with backblast area.

Figure 1-53: A recoilless weapon crew firing from a rooftop.

k. When selecting firing positions for recoilless weapons and ATGMs, make maximum use of rubble, corners of buildings, and destroyed vehicles to provide cover for the crew. Recoilless weapons and ATGMs can also be moved along rooftops to obtain a better angle to engage enemy armor. When buildings are elevated, positions can be prepared using a building for overhead cover (Figure 1-54). The backblast under the building must not damage or collapse the building or injure the crew.

Figure 1-54: Prepared positions using a building for overhead cover.

> **✍ NOTE**
> When firing from a slope, ensure that the angle of the launcher relative to the ground or firing platform is not greater than 20 degrees. When firing within a building, ensure the enclosure is at least 10 feet by 15 feet, is clear of debris and loose objects, and has windows, doors, or holes in the walls for the backblast to escape.

l. The machine gun can be emplaced almost anywhere. In the attack, windows and doors offer ready-made firing ports (Figure 1-55). For this reason, the enemy normally has windows and doors under observation and fire, which should be avoided. Any opening in walls created during the fighting may be used. Small explosive charges can create loopholes for machine gun positions (Figure 1-56). Regardless of what openings are used, machine guns should be in the building and in the shadows.

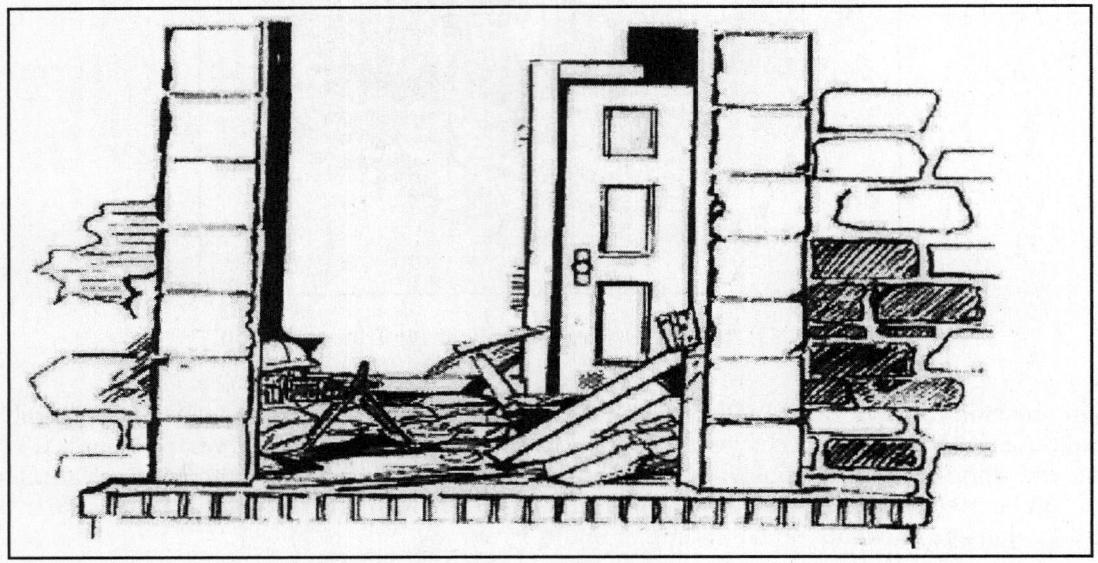

Figure 1-55: Emplacement of machine gun in a doorway.

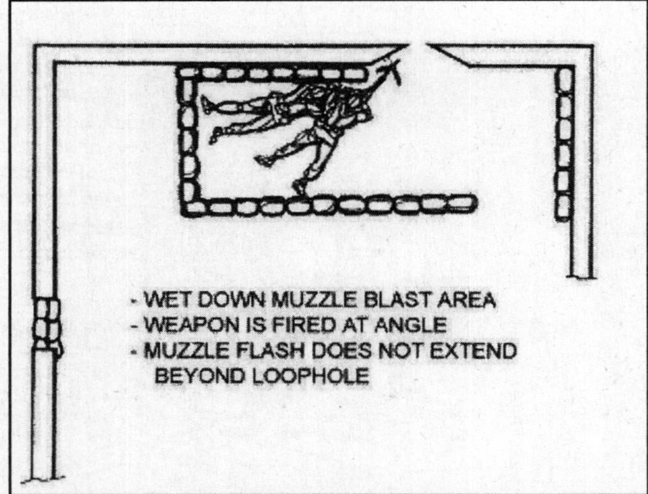

Figure 1-56: Use of a loophole with a machine gun.

m. Upon occupying a building, soldiers board up all windows and doors. By leaving small gaps between the slots, soldiers can use windows and doors as good alternate positions.

n. Loopholes should be used extensively in the defense. They should not be constructed in any logical pattern, nor should they all be at floor or tabletop level. Varying their height and location makes them hard to pinpoint and identify. Dummy loopholes, knocked off shingles, or holes cut that are not intended to be used as firing positions aid in the deception. Loopholes located behind shrubbery, under doorjambs, and under the eaves of a building are hard to detect. In the defense, as in the offense, a firing position can be constructed using the building for overhead cover.

o. Increased fields of fire can be obtained by locating the machine gun in the corner of the building (Figure 1-57), in the cellar (Figure 1-58), or sandbagged under a building (Figure 1-59). Available materials, such as desks, overstuffed chairs, couches, and other items of furniture, should be integrated into the construction of bunkers to add cover and concealment.

Figure 1-57: Corner machine gun bunker.

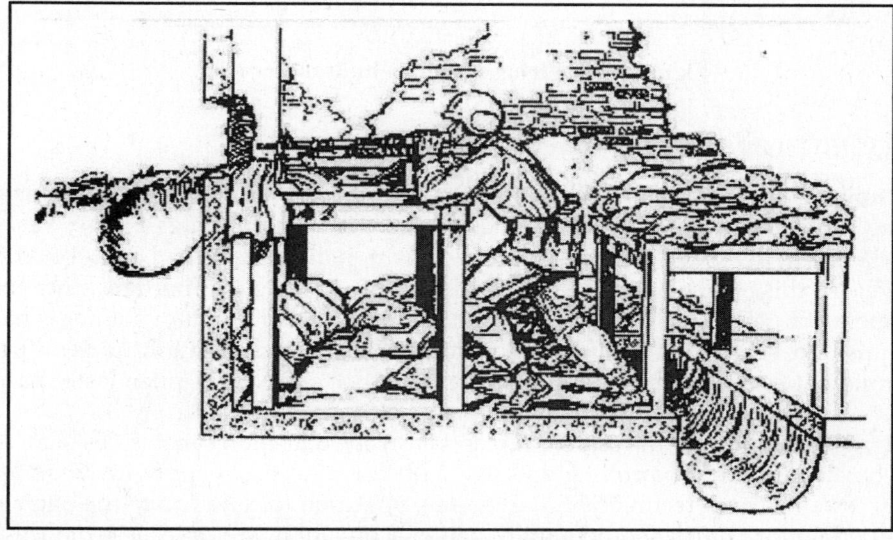

Figure 1-58: Machine gun position in cellar.

Figure 1-59: Sandbagged machine gun emplacement under a building.

p. Although grazing fire is desirable when employing the machine gun, it may not always be practical or possible. Where destroyed vehicles, rubble, and other obstructions restrict the fields of grazing fire, the gun can be elevated to where it can fire over obstacles. Firing from loopholes on the second or third story may be necessary. A firing platform can be built under the roof and a loophole constructed (Figure 1-60). Again, the exact location of the position must be concealed. Camouflage the position by removing patches of shingles, over the entire roof.

Figure 1-60: Firing platform built under roof.

1-30. TARGET ACQUISITION

Urban areas provide unique target acquisition challenges to units. Buildings mask movement and the effects of direct and indirect fires. The rubble from destroyed buildings, along with the buildings themselves, provides cover and concealment for attackers and defenders, making target acquisition difficult. Urban areas often favor the defender's ability to acquire targets so this makes offensive target acquisition extremely important, since the side that fires first may win the engagement. Target acquisition must be continuous, whether a unit or soldier is halted or moving. The six steps of target acquisition, search, detection, location, identification, classification, and confirmation are no different in an urban environment than anywhere else but are usually performed at a much faster pace.

a. **Search.** Using all senses during the search step enhances the detection capabilities of all soldiers on the urban battlefield. The techniques of patrolling and using observation posts apply in urban as well as in wooded or more open terrain. These techniques enable units to search for and locate the enemy. Soldiers searching the urban battlefield for targets should employ target acquisition devices. These devices can include binoculars, image intensification devices, thermal sights, ground surveillance radar (GSR), remote sensors (REMs), platoon early warning systems (PEWS), and field expedient early warning devices. Several types of devices should be used since no single device can meet every need of a unit.

(1) ***Observation.*** Observation duties must be clearly given to squad members to ensure 360 degrees and three-dimensional security as they move. This security continues at the halt. Soldiers soon recognize the sights, smells, sounds and so forth, associated with their urban battlefield and can soon distinguish targets.

(2) ***Movement.*** Stealth should be used when moving in urban areas since there are often short distances between attackers and defenders. Hand and arm signals should be used until contact is made. The unit should stop periodically to look and listen. Routes should be carefully chosen so that buildings and piles of rubble can be used to mask the unit's movement.

(3) ***Movement Techniques.*** Techniques are basically the same as in open terrain (traveling, traveling overwatch, bounding overwatch). When a unit is moving and enemy contact is likely, the unit must use a movement technique with an overwatching element. This principle applies in urban areas as it does in other kinds of terrain except that in urban terrain, the overwatching element must observe both the upper floors of buildings and street level.

(4) ***Observation Posts.*** The military aspects of urban terrain must be considered in selecting observation posts (OPs). OPs can be positioned in the upper floors of buildings, giving soldiers a better vantage point than at street level. Leaders should avoid selecting obvious positions, such as water towers or church steeples that attract the enemy's attention (Figure 1-61).

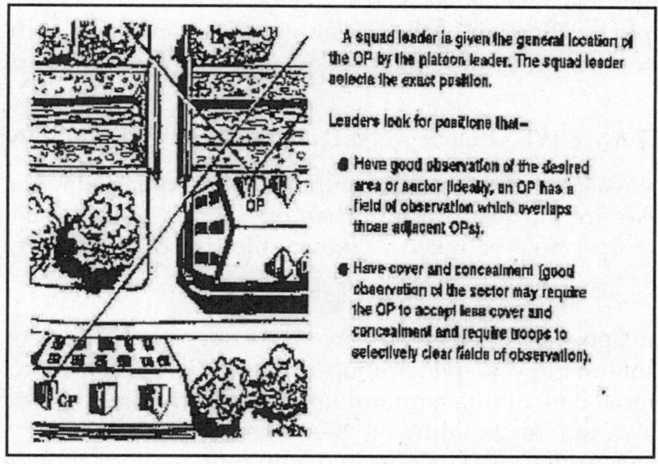

Figure 1-61: Selection of OP location.

b. **Detection.** Personnel, weapons, and vehicles have distinguishing signatures. Soldiers must recognize signatures so they can acquire and identify targets. This is extremely important in the urban battlefield, where one or more senses can be degraded. For example, soldiers operating in an urban area where smoke is used as an obscurant will have their sense of sight degraded, since they may not be able to see through the smoke with the naked eye. Their sense of smell and breathing is also affected. Some considerations are:

- Soldiers must look for targets in areas where they are most likely to be employed. Squad leaders must place OPs where they are most likely to see targets.
- Odors from diesel fuel, gasoline, cooking food, burning tobacco, after-shave lotion, and so forth reveal enemy and friendly locations.
- Running engines, vehicles, and soldiers moving through rubble-covered streets can be heard for great distances. Vehicles driven in urban areas produce more noise than those moving through open terrain. Soldiers moving through rubble on a street or in the halls of a damaged building create more noise than in a wooded area.
- Sounds and smells can aid in acquiring targets at night since they transmit better in the cooler, damper night air.

- Dust and noise created by the firing of some weapons such as a tank main gun can be seen and smelled.
- Irregularly shaped objects that do not conform to the surrounding area stand out.
- Abnormal reflections or flashes from movement of optics or metal can be seen.
- Voices can often be heard at long distances, with the sound reflecting off of structures.
- Shadows can be seen day or night.
- When scanning multistory buildings, soldiers may have to scan up as well as out (three-dimensional scanning).

c. **Location.** In an urban environment, determining the target location can be difficult. The cover and concealment provided by buildings and rubble can provide the enemy with an advantage that is not easily overcome. After the enemy is detected or contact is made, soldiers must visualize the situation from the enemy's viewpoint. This visualization helps the soldier determine where the likely enemy position is. At that point, the suspected enemy position should be suppressed, consistent with the ROE.

d. **Identification.** Being able to identify potential targets as quickly as possible after they are detected gives soldiers the advantage during urban combat. As a minimum, identification must determine if the potential target is friend, foe, or, a noncombatant. Correct identification is the key to preventing fratricide. Soldiers must know and understand the ROE. Soldiers must know what to engage and what not to engage.

e. **Classification.** To determine an appropriate method of dealing with a target, the soldier must determine the danger it represents. It requires quick decisions as targets are observed and occurs virtually simultaneously with identification. Situational awareness is vitally important. Multiple targets must be classified from most dangerous to least dangerous and engaged starting with the most dangerous.

f. **Confirmation.** This rapid verification of the initial identification and classification of the target is the final step of target acquisition. Identification, classification, and confirmation are done simultaneously.

1-31. DEFENSE AGAINST FLAME WEAPONS AND INCENDIARY MUNITIONS

Incendiary ammunition, special weapons, and the ease with which incendiary devices can be constructed from gasoline and other flammables make fire a threat during urban operations. During defensive operations, fighting fire should be a primary concern. Steps must be taken to reduce the risk of a fire that could make a chosen position indefensible.

a. Soldiers should construct positions that do not have large openings. These positions should provide as much built-in cover as possible to prevent penetration by incendiary ammunition. All unnecessary flammable materials should be removed including ammunition boxes, furniture, rugs, newspapers, curtains, and so on. Electricity and gas coming into the building must be shut off.

b. A concrete block building, with concrete floors and a tin roof, is an ideal place for a position. However, most buildings have wooden floors or subfloors, wooden rafters, and wooden inner walls, which require improvement. Inner walls should be removed and replaced with blankets to resemble walls from the outside. Sand should be spread 2 inches deep on floors and in attics to retard fire.

c. All available fire-fighting gear is pre-positioned so it can be used during actual combat. For the individual soldier such gear includes entrenching tools, helmets, sand or earth, and blankets. These items are supplemented with fire extinguishers.

d. Fire is so destructive that it can easily overwhelm personnel regardless of precautions. Soldiers should plan routes of withdrawal so a priority of evacuation from righting positions can be established. This procedure allows soldiers to exit through areas that are free from combustible material and provide cover from enemy direct fire.

e. The confined space and large amounts of combustible material in urban areas can influence the enemy to use flame weapons or incendiary munitions. Two major first-aid considerations are burns and smoke inhalation. These can easily occur in buildings and render the victim combat ineffective. Although there is little defense against flame inhalation and lack of oxygen, smoke inhalation can be reduced by wearing the individual protective mask. Medics and combat lifesavers should be aware of the withdrawal plan and should be prepared to treat and evacuate burn and smoke inhalation casualties.

f. Offensive operations also require plans for fighting fire since the success of the mission can easily be threatened by fire. Poorly planned use of incendiary munitions can make fires so extensive that they become obstacles to offensive operations. The enemy may use fire to cover his withdrawal and to create obstacles and barriers to the attacker. Intentional flame operations, in an urban area, are difficult to control and may undermine mission success.

g. When planning offensive operations, the attacker must consider the effects of all weapons and munitions. Targets are chosen during the initial planning to avoid accidentally destroying critical facilities within the urban area. When planning flame operations in an urban area, priorities must be established to determine which critical installations (hospitals, power stations, radio stations, and historical landmarks) should have primary fire-fighting support.

h. Every soldier participating in the attack must be ready to deal with fire. The normal fire-fighting equipment available includes the entrenching tool, helmet (for carrying sand or water), and blankets (for snuffing out small fires).

1-32. DEFENSE AGAINST ENHANCED FLAME WEAPONS

Combat operations in Afghanistan, Chechnya, and Bosnia saw the increased use of enhanced flame weapons in an urban environment. While these weapons have been in existence for some time, U.S. forces have not had much experience (after Vietman) in the use of and defense against them. Because future threats may use these weapons against U.S. forces, this paragraph explains what enhanced flame weapons are and how to defend against them.

a. **Enhanced Flame Weapons.** These types of weapons primarily rely on blast, flame and concussion to inflict damage, rather than explosively driven projectiles, fragments, or shaped charges. The Russians found these weapons to be especially effective in Chechnya because they produced casualties without fragmentation and shrapnel. As Chechens would "hug" Russian units to negate the use of Russian firepower, Russians would use directed blast weapons against enemy personnel and positions to minimize fratricide due to ricochets, shrapnel, and fragmentation.

(1) ***Types of Enhanced Flame Weapons.*** There are two types of these weapons, though their effects are the same. Fuel air explosives (FAE) are the older generation of blast weapons. FAE rely on distributing fuel in the air and igniting it. Casualties are primarily produced by fuel exploding and burning in the air. The newer generation blast weapons are referred to as volumetric or thermobaric. They throw out explosives from a warhead into a larger volume and use oxygen to ignite as a single event. This technique provides more reliable and controllable effects than FAE. Thermobaric weapons cause a tremendous blast in a confined space, such as a room or small building—the larger the volume of the weapon, the larger the blast effect. Many of these weapons are shoulder fired and are operated by a single gunner (Figure 1-62). Some shoulder fired blast weapons have tandem warheads that consist of a shaped charge followed by a Thermobaric munition (Figure 1-63). Currently, there are no thermobaric weapons in the U.S. inventory, but are under research and development as a possible replacement for the M202A2 (Flash).

(2) ***Effects of Enhanced Flame Weapons.*** These types of weapons are characterized by the production of a powerful fireball (flame temperatures of up to 1,200 degrees centigrade) together with a relatively long duration pressure wave. The fireball, and its associated dust storm, damages exposed skin and eyes over a wider radius than the blast effect. Most physical damage is caused by the heave and the push of the

Figure 1-62: Russian RPO-A SHMEL, a shoulder fired thermobaric weapon.

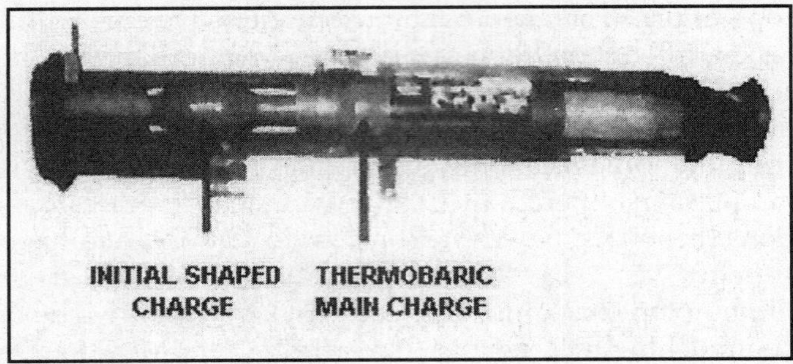

Figure 1-63: Russian RShG-1, tandem warhead.

blast wave. This blast wave can collapse brick or block-built structures. Therefore, internal injuries to vital organs and internal bleeding are common blast effects to personnel. Such weapons are particularly effective against fortified positions such as buildings. Confined spaces enhance the blast effect and, unlike fragments, blast and flame can travel around corners and down passages such as hallways or tunnels. Since blast pressure falls off rapidly in the open, much shorter minimum safety distances are possible and assault troops can be relatively close (to within 40 meters depending on the size of the munition) when many of these weapons are employed.

b. **Defensive Measures.** Using materials that absorb its energy or block its path can reduce the lethality of the blast/flame wave. The best protection is to isolate personnel from the wave; however, this procedure may not be possible in many tactical situations. Balance should be struck between protecting soldiers and not hampering their ability to fight or protect themselves from other threats. The first step is to prevent the munition from entering a structure by providing a physical barrier. If that is not possible, then the next step is to minimize damage from the weapons by weakening and isolating their effect. Another consideration is to make enhanced flame weapon gunners' priority targets for snipers or selected marksmen.

(1) ***Personnel.*** Personal injury can be minimized if soldiers wear a balaclava or similar garment to protect the face, goggles to protect the eyes from flash and flying dust and debris, and leather gloves to protect the hands.

(2) ***Armored Vehicles.*** If vehicles are *buttoned up*, the crew is protected against blast/flame damage; however, antennas, external components, and optics suffer varying degrees of damage. Tandem warheads pose a greater threat to armored vehicles.

c. **Fighting Positions.** Fixed fortifications, such as concrete bunkers or heavy-clad framed buildings, provide good protection against enhanced flame weapons detonating near the outside of the structure. Hastily prepared fighting positions or prepared fighting positions in lighter clad or framed buildings are more susceptible to blast effects. Unframed masonry buildings with concrete floors should be avoided since a falling floor is likely to cause injury to personnel. Fighting from basements or below ground positions or from prepared strong points in heavy-clad framed buildings provide additional protection. To reduce blast effects within a structure, unused openings inside buildings should be sealed to block the blast/flame wave path, while exterior openings should be left open or sealed with panels that blow off, depending on the tactical considerations, allowing the blast energy an exit route. Wet heavy curtains hung over exits, entries, and firing ports help weaken the blast energy.

SECTION V. NAVIGATION IN URBAN AREAS

Urban areas present a different set of challenges involving navigation. Deep in the city core, the normal terrain features depicted on maps may not apply—buildings become the major terrain features and units become tied to streets. Fighting in the city destroys buildings and the rubble blocks streets. Street and road signs are destroyed during the fighting if defenders do not remove them. Operations in subways and sewers present other unique challenges. Maps and photographs are available to help the unit overcome these problems. The global positioning system (GPS) can provide navigation assistance in urban areas.

1-33. MILITARY MAPS

The military city map is a topographical city map delineating streets and showing street names, important buildings, and other urban elements. The scale of a city map can vary from 1:25,000 to 1:50,000 depending on the importance and size of the city, density of detail, and intelligence information.

a. Special maps, prepared by supporting topographic engineers, can assist units in navigating in urban areas. These maps have been designed or modified to give information not covered on a standard map, which includes road and bridge networks, railroads, urban areas, and electric power fields. They can be used to supplement military city maps and topographical maps. Products that can be developed by the National Imagery Mapping Agency (NIMA) can be specifically tailored for the area of operations.
b. Once in the urban area, soldiers use street intersections as reference points much as they use hills and streams in rural terrain. City maps supplement or replace topographic maps as the basis of navigation. These maps enable units moving in the urban area to know where they are and to move to new locations even though streets have been blocked or a key building destroyed.
c. Techniques such as compass reading and pace counting can still be used, especially in a city where street signs and buildings are not visible. The presence of steel and iron in the urban environment may cause inaccurate compass readings. Sewers must be navigated much the same way. City sewer departments maintain maps providing the basic layout of the sewer system. This information includes directions the sewer lines run and distances between manhole covers. Along with basic compass and pace count techniques, such information enables a unit to move through the city sewers.
d. Helicopters can assist units in moving to objectives. An OH-58D assisting with a laser or an IR searchlight can be a useful technique.
e. Operations in an urban area adversely affect the performance of sophisticated electronic devices such as GPS and data distribution systems. These systems function the same as line-of-sight communications equipment. They cannot determine underground locations or positions within a building. These systems must be employed on the tops of buildings, in open areas, and down streets where obstacles do not affect line-of-sight readings.
f. City utility workers are assets to units fighting in urban areas. They can provide maps of sewers and electrical fields, and information about the city, which is especially important with regard to the use of the sewers. Sewers can contain pockets of highly toxic methane gas. City sewer workers know the locations of these danger areas and can advise a unit on how to avoid them.

1-34. GLOBAL POSITIONING SYSTEMS

Most GPS use a triangulation technique using satellites to calculate their position. Preliminary tests have shown that small urban areas, such as villages, do not affect GPS. Large urban areas with a mixture of tall and short buildings cause some degradation of most GPS. This effect may increase as the system is moved into the interior of a large building or taken into subterranean areas.

1-35. AERIAL PHOTOGRAPHS

Current aerial photographs are excellent supplements to military city maps and can be substituted for a map. A topographic map, military map, or city map could be obsolete. A recent aerial photograph shows changes that have taken place since the map was made, which could include destroyed buildings and streets that have been blocked by rubble as well as enemy defensive preparations. More information can be gained by using aerial photographs and maps together than using either one alone. Whenever possible, the aerial photos or satellite imagery should be acquired during the noon hour to minimize the amount of shadowing around structures.

SECTION VI. CAMOUFLAGE

To survive and win in combat in urban areas, a unit must supplement cover and concealment with camouflage. To properly camouflage men, vehicles, and equipment, soldiers must study the surrounding area and make positions look like the local terrain.

1-36. APPLICATION

Only the material needed for camouflaging a position should be used since excess material could reveal the position. Material must be obtained from a wide area. For example, if defending a cinderblock building, do not strip the front, sides, or rear of the building to camouflage a position.

a. Buildings provide numerous concealed positions. Armored vehicles can often find isolated positions under archways or inside small industrial or commercial structures. Thick masonry, stone, or brick walls offer excellent protection from direct fire and provide concealed routes.
b. After camouflage is completed, the soldier inspects positions from the enemy's viewpoint. He makes routine checks to see if the camouflage remains natural looking and actually conceals the position. If it does not look natural, the soldier must rearrange or replace it.
c. Positions must be progressively camouflaged, as they are prepared. Work should continue until all camouflage is complete. When the enemy has air superiority, work may be possible only at night. Shiny or light-colored objects attracting attention from the air must be hidden.
d. Shirts should be worn since exposed skin reflects light and attracts the enemy.
e. Camouflage face paint is issued in three standard, two-tone sticks. When face-paint sticks are not available, burnt cork, charcoal, or lampblack can be used to tone down exposed skin. Mud should be used as a last resort since it dries and peels off, leaving the skin exposed.

1-37. USE OF SHADOWS

Buildings in urban areas throw sharp shadows, which can be used to conceal vehicles and equipment (Figure 1-64). Soldiers should avoid areas not in shadows. Vehicles may have to be moved periodically as shadows shift during the day. Emplacements inside buildings provide better concealment.

a. Soldiers should avoid the lighted areas around windows and loopholes. They are better concealed if they fire from the shadowed interior of a room (Figure 1-65).
b. A lace curtain or piece of cheesecloth provides additional concealment to soldiers in the interior of rooms if curtains are common to the area. Interior lights are prohibited.

Figure 1-64: Use of shadows for concealment.

Figure 1-65: Concealment inside a building.

1-38. COLOR AND TEXTURE

Standard camouflage pattern painting of equipment is not as effective in urban areas as a solid, dull, dark color hidden in shadows. Since repainting vehicles before entering a urban area is not always practical, the lighter sand-colored patterns should be subdued with mud or dirt.

a. The need to break up the silhouette of helmets and individual equipment exists in urban areas as it does elsewhere. Burlap or canvas strips are a more effective camouflage than foliage (Figure 1-66). Predominant colors are normally browns, tans, and grays rather than greens, but each camouflage location should be evaluated.

Figure 1-66: Helmet camouflaged with burlap strips.

b. Weapons emplacements should use a wet blanket (Figure 1-67), canvas, or cloth to keep dust from rising when the weapon is fired.

Figure 1-67: Wet blankets used to keep dust down.

c. Command posts and logistical emplacements are easier to camouflage and better protected if located underground. Antennas can be remoted to upper stories or to higher buildings based on remote capabilities. Field telephone wire should be laid in conduits, in sewers, or through buildings.

d. Soldiers should consider the background to ensure they are not silhouetted or skylined, but blend into their surroundings. To defeat enemy urban camouflage, soldiers should be alert for common camouflage errors such as:
   - Tracks or other evidence of activity.
   - Shine or shadows.
   - An unnatural color or texture.
   - Muzzle flash, smoke, or dust.
   - Unnatural sounds and smells.
   - Movement.

e. Dummy positions can be used effectively to distract the enemy and make him reveal his position by firing.

f. Urban areas afford cover, resources for camouflage, and locations for concealment. The following basic rules of cover, camouflage, and concealment should be adhered to:
   - Use the terrain and alter camouflage habits to suit your surroundings.
   - Employ deceptive camouflage of buildings.
   - Continue to improve positions. Reinforce fighting positions with sandbags or other fragment- and blast-absorbent material.
   - Maintain the natural look of the area.
   - Keep positions hidden by clearing away minimal debris for fields of fire.
   - Choose firing ports in inconspicuous spots when available.

CHAPTER 2

Offensive Operations

"From 1942 to the present, shock units or special assault teams have been used by attackers (and often by defenders) with great success. These assault teams are characterized by integration of combined arms. Assault teams typically contain Infantry with variable combinations of armor, artillery, or engineers."

Technical Memorandum 5–87
Modern Experience in City Combat
U.S. Army Human Engineering Laboratory
March, 1987

SECTION I. OFFENSIVE CONSIDERATIONS

Offensive operations in urban areas are based on offensive doctrine modified to conform to the urban terrain. Urban combat also imposes a number of demands that are different from other field conditions such as combined arms integration, fires, maneuver, and use of special equipment. As with all offensive operations, the commander must retain his ability to fix the enemy and maneuver against him. Offensive UO normally have a slower pace and tempo than operations in other environments. Unlike open terrain, units cannot maneuver quickly, even when mounted. Missions are more methodical. Brigades must be prepared to operate independently or within a division or joint task force (TF). The brigade and its subordinate battalion TFs must also be prepared to conduct different missions simultaneously. For example, a battalion may establish checkpoints in one section of a city and clear enemy in another section simultaneously.

2-1. REASONS FOR ATTACKING URBAN AREAS

Reasons for attacking urban areas include the following:

a. The results of the commander and staff's estimate may preclude bypassing as an option. The mission itself may dictate an attack of an urban area.
b. Cities control key routes of commerce and provide a tactical advantage to the commander who controls them. Control of features, such as bridges, railways, and road networks, can have a significant outcome on future operations. The requirement for a logistics base, especially a port or airfield, may play a pivotal role during a campaign.
c. The political importance of some urban areas may justify the use of time and resources to liberate it. Capturing the city could deal the threat a decisive psychological blow and or lift the moral of the people within the city.
   (1) The tactical situation may require the enemy force to be contained.
   (2) The urban area itself may sit on dominating terrain that would hinder bypassing for combat support (CS) and combat service support (CSS) elements.
   (3) The enemy within that urban area may be able to interdict lines of communications even though the terrain around an urban area may facilitate its bypass.

2-2. REASONS FOR NOT ATTACKING URBAN AREAS

Conversely, reasons for not attacking urban areas include the following:

a. The commander may decide to bypass if he determines no substantial threat exists in the urban area that could interdict his unit's ability to accomplish its mission. The commander's intent may dictate speed as essential to the mission. Since combat in an urban area is time consuming, the commander may choose to bypass the urban area to save time.
b. During the estimate process, the commander and staff may realize a sufficient force is not available to seize and clear the urban area, or enough forces are available to accomplish the mission but cannot be logistically supported. If the tactical situation allows, the commander should avoid attacks on urban areas.
c. The urban area may be declared an *open city* to prevent civilian casualties or to preserve cultural or historical sites. An open city, by the law of land warfare, is a city that cannot be defended or attacked. The defender must immediately evacuate the open city and cannot distribute weapons to the city's inhabitants. The attacker assumes administrative control of the city and must treat its citizens as noncombatants in an occupied country.

2-3. TROOP REQUIREMENTS

Due to the nature of combat in urban areas, more troops are normally needed than in other combat situations. This situation is due to the number of requirements placed upon units, soldier fatigue, controlling civilians, and evacuation of casualties.

a. Because of the need to clear buildings and provide security, the number of troops required to accomplish an offensive mission is much greater. Some forces must be left behind in a building once it has been cleared to prevent enemy forces from repositioning or counterattacking friendly forces. Commanders and staffs need to be keenly aware that attacking units will effectively lose manpower from assault elements as they secure rooms and floors. They must ensure that the proper force ratios exist to conduct the missions assigned to subordinate units.
b. Commanders must also consider soldier fatigue. Fighting in urban areas is physically demanding and quickly tires a force. Commanders must plan for the relief or rotation of their forces before they reach the point of exhaustion. This situation is facilitated through proper task organization and maintenance of adequate reserves.
c. Additional forces may be needed to deal with noncombatants in the urban area. These forces must protect the noncombatants, provide first aid, and prevent them from interfering with the tactical plan.
d. Fighting in an urban area may result in a greater number of friendly casualties. The greater the restrictions on firepower, the less suppressive fire can be used, and the more the individual soldier is exposed to enemy fire. MEDEVAC/CASEVAC must be planned and subordinate units designated to conduct this task.

2-4. FIRES AND MANEUVER

As in other terrain, units conduct penetrations, envelopments, turning movements, and frontal attacks. Unlike open terrain, commanders cannot maneuver their units and attachments quickly due to the close, dense environment. Clearing buildings and looking for antiarmor ambushes, snipers, and booby traps degrade the ability of subordinate units to maneuver. Due to the dense environment and its effects on weapon systems, the synchronization of combat power is one of the commander's main challenges. Offensive operations need to be planned in detail, with subordinate elements given specific instructions and on order missions. Maintaining situational awareness assist in overcoming the inability to maneuver quickly.

a. **Indirect Fires.** The fire support plan may require extensive air and artillery bombardment to precede the ground attack on an urban area. Supporting fire suppresses the defender's fire, restricts his movement, and may destroy his position. However, indirect fire in urban areas with heavily clad construction creates rubble, which can be used for cover but may restrict the movements of attacking troops. For that reason, the artillery preparation should be short and violent. Assaulting troops must follow the artillery fire closely to exploit its effect on the defenders. While the supporting fire suppresses the enemy, maneuver units move near the coordinated fire line (CFL). As the attacking force assaults the objective, fires are lifted or shifted to block enemy withdrawal or to prevent the enemy from reinforcing their position.

(1) Prior coordination is critical to determine the techniques and procedures for communication, target identification, and shifting of fires. Consideration must be given to the noncombatants, houses of worship, medical centers, schools, public services, and historical monuments. The fire support plan can include integrating tanks, Infantry weapons, artillery, and dismounted direct and indirect fires.

(2) Indirect fire is planned to isolate objectives, to prevent reinforcement and resupply, to neutralize known and suspected command and observation posts, and to suppress enemy defenders. Most indirect fires are high-angle in urban terrain.

(3) Mortars are the most responsive indirect fires to hit targets of opportunity at the close ranges typical of combat in urban areas. Forward observers move with the forward units to adjust fire on targets as requested by the supported troops.

b. **Direct-Fires.** Direct-fire is the most effective fire support in urban areas. Once a target can be located in a building, one or two direct-fire rounds can accomplish what entire salvos of indirect fire cannot. The best direct-fire support is provided by Bradley fighting vehicles (BFVs) but can also be provided by tanks and/or howitzers. Tanks and howitzers may create rubble and building and street damage that could restrict movement for the attacking force.

(1) Tanks may support by fire when lead units are seizing a foothold. During the attack of an urban area, tanks overwatch the Infantry's initial assault until an entry into the area has been secured. Tanks are supported by Infantry organic weapons to suppress enemy strongpoints while they move into overwatch positions. Commanders employ tanks to take advantage of the long range of their main gun. This procedure is usually achieved with tanks employed outside the urban area, for the duration of the attack to cover high-speed mounted avenues of approach, especially during the isolation phase. Tanks may also support Infantry in the urban area as an assault and support weapon. In both cases, Infantry must protect tanks.

(2) In house-to-house and street fighting, tanks and/or BFVs move down streets protected by the Infantry, which clears the area of enemy ATGM weapons. Tanks and BFVs in turn support the Infantry by firing their main guns and machine guns to destroy enemy positions. Tanks are the most effective weapon for heavy fire against structures and may be used to clear rubble with dozer blades (Figure 2-1). The BFV can provide sustained, accurate suppressive fires with its 25-mm gun.

Figure 2-1: Tank in direct fire supported by Infantry.

(3) Large-caliber artillery rounds that are shot by direct-fire are effective for destroying targets in buildings. If available, self-propelled 155-mm howitzers can use direct-fire to destroy or neutralize bunkers, heavy fortifications, or enemy positions in reinforced concrete buildings (Figure 2-2). The self-propelled 155-mm can be used to clear or create avenues of approach. The 105-mm artillery can be used in this role but are not the preferred artillery pieces used in offensive UO. When artillery is used in the direct-fire role, it must be close to the Infantry for security against enemy ground attack. Prior coordination must be accomplished so the bulk of the field artillery unit's shells are switched to High Explosive (HE).

Figure 2-2: Artillery in direct-fire role.

(4) Tanks, self-propelled artillery, and BFVs are vulnerable in urban areas because streets and alleys provide ready-made fire lanes for defenders. Motorized traffic is restricted, canalized, and vulnerable to ambush and close-range fire. Tanks are at a further disadvantage because their main guns cannot be depressed sufficiently to fire into basements or elevated to fire into upper floors of buildings at close range (Figure 2-3).

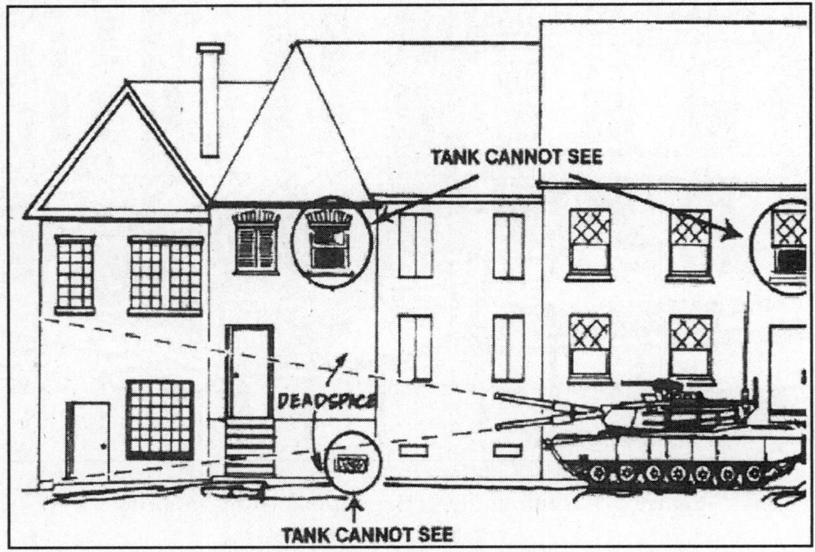

Figure 2-3: Tank dead space.

(5) Direct-fire systems organic to Infantry battalions—mainly ATGMs and recoilless weapons, such as the AT4, are initially employed to support the seizure of a foothold. Then, if necessary, they are brought forward to fight enemy armor within the town. Antitank weapons are not as effective as tank rounds for neutralizing targets behind walls. They neutralize a target only if that target is located directly behind the point of impact. ATGMs are at a greater disadvantage because of their 65-meter arming distance and the possibility of their guiding wires becoming caught on ground clutter. These factors limit employment in close engagements like those in urban areas.

(6) Snipers are a valuable asset during urban operations. They must be equipped with effective observation devices and placed in a key area to be effective. In situations where the ROE permit the use of destructive force, snipers can be used as part of the support element to provide accurate, long-range fires. Depending on the commander's concept, snipers can be employed in the counter-sniper role or assigned priority targets. If a restrictive ROE is in effect, snipers may be used to prevent collateral damage. Snipers can also overwatch breaching operations and call for indirect artillery fires.

c. **Maneuver.** The first phase of the attack should be conducted when visibility is poor. Troops can exploit poor visibility to cross open areas, gain access to rooftops, infiltrate enemy areas, and gain a foothold. If the attack must be made when visibility is good, units should consider using smoke to conceal movement.

(1) The formation used in an attack depends on the width and depth of the zone to be cleared, the character of the area, anticipated enemy resistance, and the formation adopted by the next higher command.

(2) Lead companies may have engineers attached for immediate support. Tasks given to the engineers may include:

- Preparing and using explosives to breach walls and obstacles.
- Finding and exploding mines in place or helping remove them.
- Clearing barricades and rubble.
- Cratering roads and other countermobility measures.

(3) When the unit is involved in clearing, bypassing buildings increases the risk of attack from the rear or flank. A single building may be an objective for a rifle squad, or if the building is large, for a rifle platoon or company. When the commander's concept is based on speed or when conducting a hasty attack, a battalion may be directed not to clear its entire zone.

(4) The reserve should be mobile and prepared for commitment. The reserve can stay close to forward units because of the available cover in urban areas. Battalion reserves normally follow one to two blocks to the rear of the lead company. A company reserve, if available, follows within the same block so it can immediately influence the attack. A unit with a reserve mission may be called upon to perform one or more of the following tasks:

- Attacking from another direction.
- Exploiting an enemy weakness or friendly success.
- Clearing bypassed enemy positions.
- Securing the rear or a flank.
- Maintaining contact with adjacent units.
- Supporting or counterattacking by fire.

(5) The battalion reconnaissance scout platoon is normally employed to reconnoiter the battalion's flanks and rear. Its capability for reconnaissance and security is somewhat reduced in urban areas. The reconnaissance/scout platoon can also help isolate a village or small town. They must be prepared to dismount and enter buildings for reconnaissance or for setting up OPs. Infantry platoons and squads conduct reconnaissance patrols and man OPs to supplement the reconnaissance/scout platoon effort.

(6) Security in an urban area presents special problems. All troops must be alert to an enemy that may appear from the flanks, from above, or from subterranean areas.

d. **Movement.** Moving from building to building or between buildings present a problem to units conducting offensive operations. Historical examples, recent operations in Somalia, and the Russian experience in Grozny have shown that most casualties can be expected during movement from building to building and down streets. Therefore, during mission analysis, commanders and staffs should plan operations in such a manner that allow subordinate elements to take maximum advantage of covered and concealed routes within the urban area. Additionally, commanders and staffs must carefully analyze which buildings must be isolated, suppressed, and obscured, consistent with the ROE, as well as using armored assets as shields for maneuver elements.

(1) In movement down narrow streets, or down wider streets with narrow paths through the debris, Infantry should move ahead of the tanks clearing the buildings on each side. Personnel movement across open areas must be planned with a specific destination in mind. Street intersections should be avoided, since they are normally used as engagement areas. Suppression of enemy positions and smoke to cover Infantry movement should also be included in the fire support plan. When needed, tanks move up to places secured by the Infantry to hit suitable targets. When an area is cleared, the Infantry again moves forward to clear the next area. Tanks and Infantry should use the traveling overwatch movement technique and communicate with tank crews by using arm-and-hand signals and radio.

(2) For movement down wider streets, Infantry platoons normally have a section of attached tanks with one tank on each side of the street. Single tanks should not be employed. Other tanks of the attached tank platoon should move behind the Infantry and fire at targets in the upper stories of buildings. In wide boulevards, commanders may employ a tank platoon secured by one or more Infantry platoons. The Infantry can secure the forward movement of the lead tanks, while the trailing tanks overwatch the movement of the lead units.

(3) If an Infantry unit must travel along streets that are too narrow for mutual tank support, the tanks travel in single file for support. The tanks move and fire to cover each other's approach while the Infantry provides ATGM fire from buildings as necessary.

(4) Tanks may drive inside buildings or behind walls for protection from enemy antitank missile fire where feasible. Buildings are cleared by the Infantry first. Ground floors are checked to ensure they support the tank and there is no basement into which the tank could fall. When moving, all bridges and overpasses are checked for mines, booby traps, and load capacity. Specific Infantry elements are assigned to protect specific tanks.

2-5. LIMITATIONS

Commanders attacking an urban area must recognize some important limitations in the use of available assets.

a. **Indirect Fires.** Normally, the use of indirect fires is much more restricted in urban areas than in open terrain. Consideration must be given to the effects of the indirect fire on the urban area and noncombatants. This procedure is especially true when extremely restrictive ROE are in effect. When indirect fires are authorized, they must be fired in greater mass to achieve the desired effect. When units are performing multiple missions, indirect fire supporting one element can easily cause casualties in adjacent elements. The rubbling caused by massive indirect fires adversely affect a unit's ability to maneuver during the attack.

b. **Noncombatants.** If there are noncombatants intermingled with combatants, the ability to use all available firepower may be restricted.

c. **Night Vision Devices.** Commanders and leaders must consider the effect that city lights, fires, and background illumination have on night vision devices. These elements may limit the effectiveness of night vision goggles (NVGs) and make thermal imagery identification difficult.

d. **Communications.** Communications equipment may not function to its maximum effectiveness because of the density in building construction. Intelligent use of graphic control measures, understanding the commander's intent, and maintaining situational awareness at all levels become more important to mission accomplishment.

SECTION II. MISSION, ENEMY, TERRAIN, TROOPS, TIME, CIVIL FACTORS

The planning, preparation, and conduct of offensive operations in an urban area are the same as all other offensive operations and must be based on the mission, enemy, terrain, troops, time, and civil (METT-TC) factors. Commanders must focus on the synchronization of maneuver forces and the fire support plan to accomplish the assigned mission. Combat support (CS) and combat service support (CSS) play a critical role in the offense.

2-6. MISSION

The commander and staff must receive, analyze, and understand the mission before beginning planning. The conditions of the operation; either precision or high intensity; the ROE; and the desired end-state must be clearly understood and stated. Brigades and battalions may be required to conduct different missions simultaneously. Additional considerations that are specific to offensive operations are discussed below. When conducting this analysis, commanders and staff must consider the higher level commander's intent. For example, a brigade must determine if supporting efforts are needed to shape the battlefield prior to the main effort executing its mission. A battalion must determine if a mission given to them means clearing every building within an area, block by block, or if the seizure of key terrain only requires clearing along the axis of advance.

a. In certain circumstances, subordinate units may secure rather than clear buildings. Normally, clearing means entering and searching each building to kill, capture, or force the withdrawal of the threat in the zone of action or objective area as well as leaving security to prevent reoccupation of cleared buildings. This procedure may not be feasible due to the nature of the mission and should be made clear when orders are issued. Clearing requires a systematic search of every room. Securing means a search of selected areas and preventing the occupation or reoccupation of the area by the threat and questioning of noncombatants, if present.
b. Commanders and staffs must also consider how and where the unit is postured in order to conduct follow-on missions to facilitate higher echelon missions, and influences the missions that are given to subordinate units.
c. When the battalion is involved in clearing operations, bypassing buildings increases the risk of attack from the rear or flank unless planned support isolates and suppresses those buildings.
d. A battle may transition quickly from precision to high intensity conditions. The transition can be caused by enemy actions. Commanders must be prepared to request changes in ROE for certain areas or buildings. Indications of an enemy-forced change of ROE (and a change from precision conditions to high intensity) include:
   - The requirement to breach multiple obstacles.
   - The use of booby traps by the enemy.
   - The requirement to use repetitive explosive breaching to enter a building; and rooms.

2-7. ENEMY

The unique factor the commander must determine to complete the IPB process is the type threat he is attacking—conventional, unconventional or other, such as gangs, factional elements, or organized criminals. The type of threat determines how the unit task-organizes and how combat power is synchronized to accomplish the mission.

2-8. TERRAIN AND WEATHER

Offensive operations must be tailored to the urban environment based on a detailed analysis of each urban terrain setting, its types of urban areas, and existing structural form. Commanders and subordinate leaders must incorporate the following special planning considerations for an urban environment when conducting an offensive operation.

a. Alternates for military maps that do not provide enough detail for urban terrain analysis or reflect the underground sewer system, subways, underground water system, mass transit routes, and utility generation.
b. Natural terrain surrounding the urban area.
c. Key and decisive terrain (stadiums, parks, sports fields, school playgrounds, public buildings, and industrial facilities).
d. Confined spaces limiting observation, fields of fire and maneuver, which also prevents the concentration of fires at critical points.
e. Covered and concealed routes to and within the urban area.
f. Limited ability to employ maximum combat power due to the need to minimize damage and rubbling effects.
g. A greater demand for ammunition and rations, thus imposing unusual strains on logistics elements.
h. Problems with conducting effective reconnaissance during conventional operations. (Reconnaissance by force becomes the most effective reconnaissance means. This method involves probing a defense with successively larger units until the enemy positions are disclosed and successfully attacked. During unconventional operations, the opposite is true. Reconnaissance and security are easily accomplished by both sides and may be difficult to prevent.)

2-9. TROOPS AVAILABLE

Troop density for offensive missions in urban areas can be as much as three to five times greater than for similar missions in open terrain. Urban operations may require unique task organizations. Commanders must consider providing assets where they are needed to accomplish specific tasks. All phases of mission execution must be considered when developing task organization. Changes in task organization may be required to accomplish different tasks during mission execution. Task organizations could very well change as conditions and missions change. For example, high intensity offensive operations probably require different task organizations from precision offensive operations. Likewise, task organizations change as mission transitions from offense to stability and support and vice-versa. (See brigade, battalion, company, and platoon sections [Sections V, VI, VII, VIII] for specific task organizations and troop considerations.)

2-10. TIME AVAILABLE

Combat in urban areas has a slower tempo and an increased use of methodical, synchronized missions. Additionally, a brigade or battalion may find itself planning different operations simultaneously. For example, a task force may have the mission to conduct offensive missions in one part of the brigade's AO and another battalion may be conducting stability missions in yet another part of the brigade's AO. In planning UO, the commander and staff must take these factors into account. Plans must also take into account that more time is required for clearing buildings, blocks, or axes of advance due to the density of urban terrain and that troops tire more quickly because of stress and additional physical exertion caused by the environment. More time must be allowed for thorough reconnaissance and subordinate unit rehearsals. Allocating time for rehearsals is especially important when units are not habitually used to working with each other.

2-11. CIVIL CONSIDERATIONS

The commander and staff must understand the composition, activities, and attitudes of the civilian population, to include the political infrastructure, within the urban area. Various options are available to the commander to control the impact of civilians on the operation such as screening civilians, prohibiting unauthorized movement, diverting or controlling refugee movements, and evacuating. Understanding the urban society requires comprehension of:

- Living conditions.
- Cultural distinctions.
- Ethnicity.
- Factions.
- Religious beliefs.
- Political affiliation and grievances.
- Attitude toward U.S. forces (friendly, hostile, neutral).

SECTION III. COMMAND AND CONTROL

Urban operations require centralized planning and decentralized execution. Therefore the staff must develop a detailed plan that synchronizes the BOS in order to meet the commander's intent and also provide subordinate units with the means to accomplish the mission.

2-12. COMMAND

Subordinate units require mission-type orders that are restrictive in nature. Commanders should use detailed control measures to facilitate decentralized execution. Increased difficulties in command, control, and communications from higher headquarters demand increased responsibility and initiative from subordinate leaders. Understanding of the commander's intent two levels up by all leaders becomes even more important to mission accomplishment in an urban environment.

2-13. CONTROL

Control of the urban battlefield is difficult. In urban areas, radio communications are often less effective than field telephones and messengers. Units often fight without continuous communications, since dependable communications are uncertain. Pyrotechnic signals are hard to see because of buildings and smoke. The high noise level of battles within and around buildings degrades voice alerts. Voice communication can also signal the unit's intention and location to the enemy. Graphic control measures common to other tactical environments are also used in urban combat. These and other control measures ensure coordination throughout the chain of command, enhance the mission, and thus prevent fratricide. Thorough rehearsals and detailed backbriefs also enhance control. It is also important that subordinate leaders clearly understand the commander's intent (two levels up) and the desired mission end state in order to facilitate control. Commanders should consider using the executive officer (XO), the S3, and other staff members to control certain portions of the fight, when the commander's attention needs to be focused elsewhere.

a. **Radio Communications.** Radio communications in urban areas pose special problems to tactical units. Communications equipment may not function properly because of the massive construction of buildings and the environment. In addition to the physical blockage of line of sight transmissions, there is also the interference from commercial power lines, absorption into structures and the presence of large quantities of metal in structures. Leaders should consider these effects when they allocate time to establish communications. Unit SOPs become much more important in urban terrain. The time needed to establish an effective communications system might be greater in urban areas. Leaders should consider the following techniques when planning for radio communications:
   - Emplace radios and retransmission sites on the upper floors of buildings. Radio antennas should blend in with the building structure so as not to be easily identifiable to the enemy.
   - Construct field expedient antennas to enhance capabilities.
   - RTOs should utilize an earpiece to keep their hands free in order to write messages and use their weapon to defend themselves.
   - Use windows and holes in walls to extend antennas for better communications.
   - Open doors and windows to enhance the flow of FM signals.

b. **Other Types of Communications.** Wire laid at street level is easily damaged by rubble and vehicle traffic. Also, the noise of urban combat is much louder than in other areas, making sound or verbal signals difficult to hear.
   - Develop and utilize other nonverbal signals. Use color-coded signaling devices per unit SOP. Marking areas as the unit moves is a key to success.
   - If possible, lay wire through buildings for maximum protection.
   - Use existing telephone systems. Telephones are not always secure even though many telephone cables are underground.
   - Use messengers at all levels since they are the most secure means of communications.

c. **Graphic Control Measures.** The use of detailed graphic control measures is critical to mission accomplishment and fratricide avoidance in urban terrain. Phase lines can be used to report progress or to control the advance of attacking units. Limits of advance should be considered. Principal streets, rivers, and railroad lines are suitable phase lines or limits of advance. Examples are shown below.
   (1) When attacking to seize a foothold, a battalion normally assigns each company a sector or a group of buildings as its first objective. When an objective extends to a street, only the near side of the street is included in the objective area. Key buildings or groups of buildings may be assigned as intermediate objectives. The battalion's final objective may be a group of buildings within the built-up area, key terrain, or nodes, depending on the brigade's mission. To simplify assigning objectives and reporting, all buildings along the route of attack should be identified by letters or numbers (Figure 2-4). Mixing numbers and letters may help differentiate between blocks as an attack progresses.
   (2) Phase lines can be used to report progress or to control the advance of attacking units (Figure 2-5). Phase lines should be on the near side of the street or open area. In systematic clearing, a unit may have the mission to clear its zone of action up to a phase line or limit of advance. In that case, the commander chooses his own objectives when assigning missions to his subordinate units.
   (3) Boundaries are usually set within blocks so that a street is included in the zone. Boundaries must be placed to ensure that both sides of a street are included in the zone of one unit.

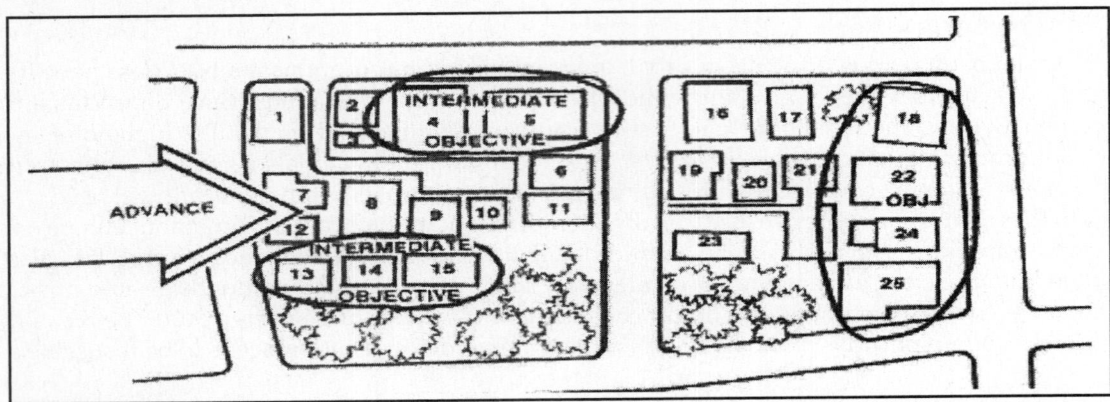

Figure 2-4: Example of a numbering system.

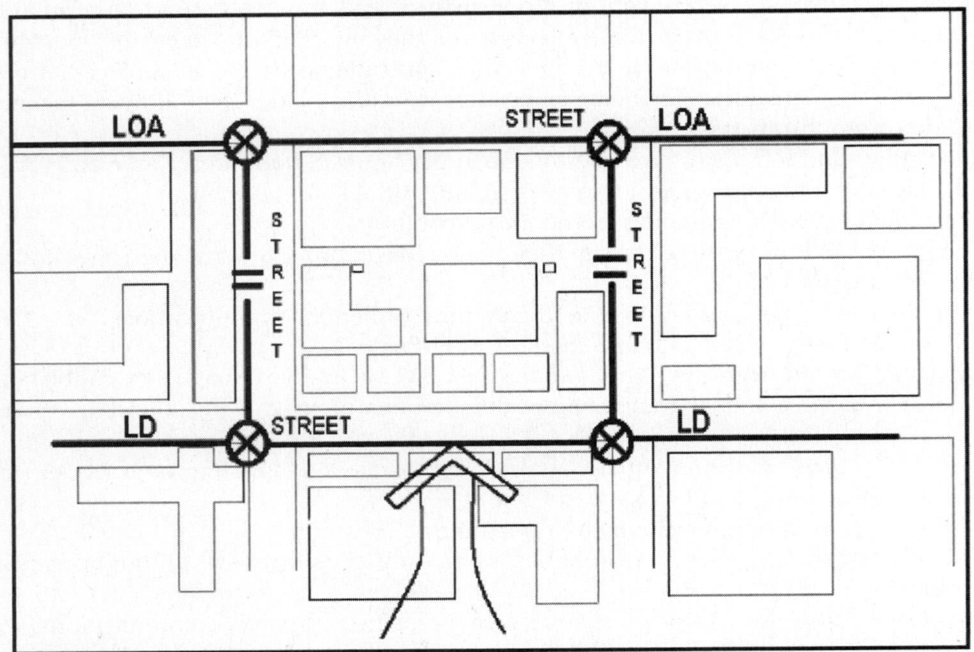

Figure 2-5: Boundaries and phase lines.

(4) Checkpoints and contact points are planned at street corners, buildings, railway crossings, bridges, or any other easily identifiable urban feature.

(5) Forward units may occupy an attack position for last-minute preparation and coordination. The attack position is often behind or inside the last covered and concealed position, such as a large building, before crossing the LD. The LD should be the near side of a street, a rail line, or a row of buildings.

(6) A unit's assigned frontage for the attack of a built-up area depends on the size of buildings and the resistance anticipated. A company normally attacks on a one- to two-block front, and a battalion on a two- to four-block front, based on city blocks averaging 175 meters in width.

2-14. FOCUS ON THE THREAT

During the mission analysis, the plan should focus on the factors of METT-TC. Make the plan enemy-oriented instead of terrain-oriented. Use terrain factors to defeat the threat—do not attack buildings for the sake of seizing buildings, attack buildings to defeat the threat. Considerations include, but are not limited to, the following:

a. Thorough evaluation of the urban area's related terrain and threat may take much longer than other environments. This time factor also affects friendly planning efforts.
b. Determine the threat's location, strength, and capabilities. Develop a plan that defeats his direct and indirect fire systems.
c. Focus the axis of advance on the threat's weaknesses while maintaining adequate force protection measures. When possible employ multiple and supporting axes of advance.
d. Divide the objective area into manageable smaller areas that facilitate battalion TF maneuver.
e. Isolate the objective area and establish a foothold at the point of entry. The location chosen for the foothold must allow for expansion.
f. The brigade and battalion maneuver plans directly affect the company schemes of maneuver. Every company within the brigade must know what enemy targets will be engaged by brigade and battalion assets.

2-15. COMMANDER'S CRITICAL INFORMATION REQUIREMENTS

The commander's critical information requirements (CCIR) directly affect his decisions and dictate the successful execution of tactical operations. The staff must develop the components of CCIR that facilitate the commander's ability to make decisions that impact the plan during urban operations. Logical deductions are that essential elements of friendly information (EEFI) should address the enemy commander's priority intelligence requirements (PIR) and friendly forces information requirements (FFIR) should be items that cause the commander to make decisions that impact the plan. The following are examples of PIR, EEFI, and FFIR that would be more likely to help the commander in an urban environment.

a. **PIR.** These are intelligence requirements that a commander has anticipated and have stated priority in task planning and decision making. Examples include:
   - Where are the threat command posts?
   - What are the most likely threat infiltration routes into the area of operations?
   - What streets and alleys restrict movement of friendly armored and wheeled vehicles?
   - Where are the likely threat strong points and engagement areas?
   - What is the threat air defense capability against Army aviation assets?

b. **EEFI.** These are critical aspects of a friendly operation that, if known by the threat, would subsequently compromise, lead to failure, or limit success of the operation and, therefore, must be protected from detection. Examples include:
   - Is the unit command net vulnerable to intercept, direction finding, and electronic attack?
   - Is the unit vulnerable to HUMINT collection and sabotage by local nationals?
   - Where are the supply routes/LOC most vulnerable to ambush and snipers?
   - Are friendly troop concentrations and movement under threat observation?

c. **FFIR.** This requirement is information the commander and staff need about the friendly forces available for the operation. Examples include:
   - Scouts captured or compromised.
   - Main bridge locations along the ground route that have been blown.
   - OPORD compromised.
   - Loss of cryptographic equipment.
   - Expected personnel and equipment replacements that did not arrive.

2-16. REHEARSALS

After developing a thorough, well-synchronized plan, commanders should require subordinate units to conduct combined arms rehearsals and include all phases of the operation. When conducted properly, combined arms rehearsals identify potential problems in the synchronization of the plan between maneuver, combat support, and combat service support elements. Rehearsals provide a means for units that seldom operate together to train collective skills. Carefully consider where rehearsals are conducted within the brigade AO. It is preferable to conduct rehearsals on urban terrain similar to the objective area.

SECTION IV. OFFENSIVE FRAMEWORK AND TYPES OF ATTACKS

This section discusses the framework that is used and the types of attacks that are conducted during offensive UO.

2-17. OFFENSIVE FRAMEWORK

Figure 2-6 depicts the operational framework of brigade urban offensive operations. The brigade commander's primary responsibility is to set the conditions for tactical success for his subordinate units. Whenever possible, close combat by maneuver units is minimized and brigades attempt to move from assess to transition. At the brigade level and below, offensive operations often take the form of either a hasty or deliberate attack. Both hasty and deliberate attacks are characterized by as much planning, reconnaissance, and coordination as time and the situation permit. Battalions and below conduct those attacks executing the tasks shown in Figure 2-6. The elements of offensive operations are not phases. There is no clear line of distinction that delineates when the brigade moves from one element to another. Properly planned and executed operations involve all four elements. They may be conducted simultaneously or sequentially, depending on the factors of METT-TC. During offensive operations, the brigade commander seeks to:

- Synchronize precision fires (lethal and non-lethal effects) and information operations.
- Isolate decisive points.
- Use superior combat power to destroy high pay-off targets.
- Use close combat, when necessary, against decisive points.

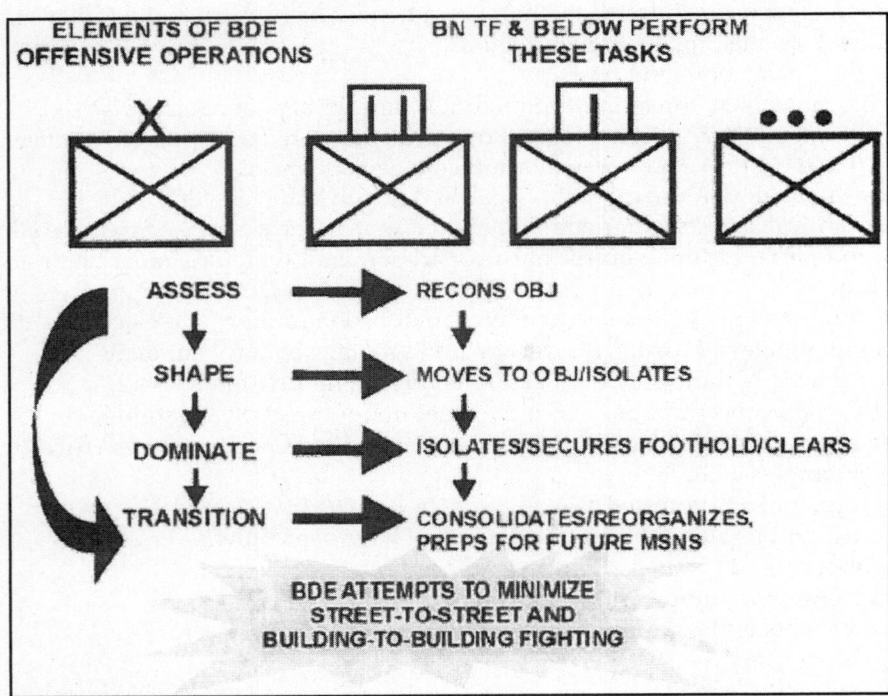

Figure 2-6: Offensive urban operational framework.

2-18. HASTY ATTACK

Battalions and companies conduct hasty attacks as a result of a movement to contact, a meeting engagement, or a chance contact during a movement; after a successful defense or part of a defense; or in a situation where the unit has the opportunity to attack vulnerable enemy forces. When contact is made with the enemy, the commander immediately deploys; suppresses the enemy; attacks through a gap, flank, or weak point; and reports to his higher commander. The preparation for a hasty attack is similar to that of a deliberate attack, but time and resources are limited to what is available. The hasty attack in an urban area differs from a hasty attack in open terrain because the terrain makes command, control, communications, and massing fires to suppress the enemy difficult.

a. In urban areas, incomplete intelligence and concealment may require the maneuver unit to move through, rather than around, the friendly unit fixing the enemy in place. Control and coordination become critical to reduce congestion at the edges of the urban area.
b. On-order missions, be-prepared missions, or fragmentary orders may be given to a force conducting a hasty attack so it can react to a contingency once its objective is secured.

2-19. DELIBERATE ATTACK

A deliberate attack is a fully synchronized operation employing all available assets against the enemy. It is necessary when enemy positions are well prepared, when the urban area is large or severely congested, or when the element of surprise has been lost. Deliberate attacks are characterized by precise planning based on detailed information, thorough reconnaissance, preparation, and rehearsals. The deliberate attack of an urban area is similar to the technique employed in assaulting a strong point. Attacking the enemy's main strength is avoided and combat power is focused on the weakest point of his defense. Battalions and below conduct deliberate attacks of an urban area in the phases shown in Figure 2-7. Detailed descriptions of these phases at the battalion, company, and platoon levels are found in Sections VI, VII, and VIII, respectively.

Phase 1. Reconnoiter the Objective
Phase 2. Move to the Objective
Phase 3. Isolate the Objective
Phase 4. Secure a Foothold
Phase 5. Clear the Objective
Phase 6. Consolidate/Reorganize
Phase 7. Prepare for Future Missions

Figure 2-7: Phases of a deliberate urban attack.

SECTION V. BRIGADE OFFENSIVE OPERATIONS

A brigade may be assigned an objective that lies within an urban area, and may conduct the full range of offensive operations within a single large city or in an AO that contains several small villages and towns.

2-20. TASK ORGANIZATION

Proper task organization is essential for successful execution of offensive UO.

a. During UO, the brigade is often augmented with additional assets, which may include aviation, engineers, signal, smoke and or decontamination, ADA, MI, counterintelligence, MP, public affairs, PSYOP, civil affairs, translators, and LRS assets, when available. The brigade may also receive additional mechanized Infantry or armor. A sample Infantry brigade task organization is shown at Figure 2-8. Actual task organizations are METT-TC dependent. How the brigade commander task-organizes so that the BOS can be synchronized is of critical importance to tactical success.

> ✍ **NOTE**
> The task organization shown in Figure 2-8 would be essentially the same for light, airborne, and air assault Infantry brigades. Heavy brigades would differ based on the composition of their Table of Organization and Equipment (TOE).

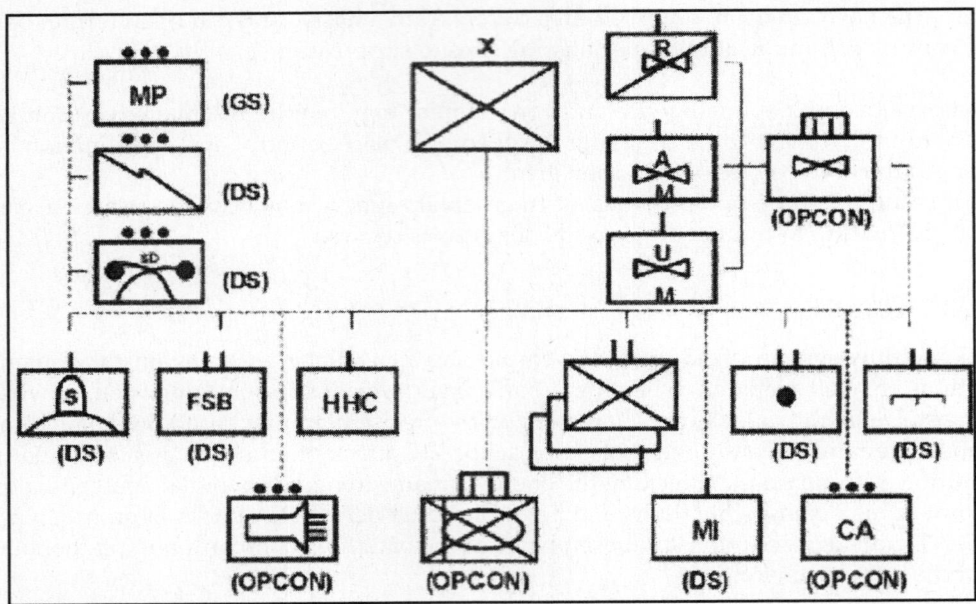

Figure 2-8: Sample UO task organization for an Infantry brigade.

b. Urban operations may require unique task organizations. Figure 2-9 depicts a sample brigade task organization for offensive operations, showing units under brigade control, and subordinate task forces necessary to accomplish decisive and shaping operations, specifically, the main and supporting efforts and the brigade reserve. Commanders must consider providing assets where they are needed to accomplish specific tasks. All phases of mission execution must be considered when developing task organization. Changes in task organization may be required to accomplish different tasks during mission execution. Task organizations could very well change from shape through transition.

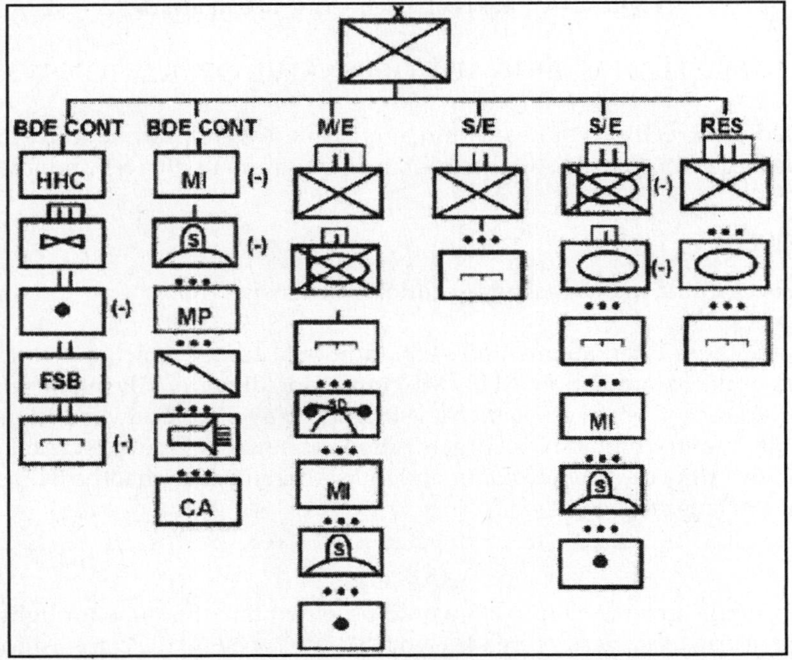

Figure 2-9: Sample brigade task organization for offensive UO.

> ✍ **NOTE**
> Figure 2-9 also depicts two field artillery platoons that have been given DS missions to provide direct fire support to the main and the supporting attacks.

2-21. ASSESS

Brigades primarily assess the urban environment using the military decision-making process (MDMP); intelligence preparation of the battlefield (IPB) acts as a key tool in that process. IPB is combined with the following:

- Division or joint task force (JTF) reconnaissance efforts and other shaping operations.
- Reconnaissance efforts of brigade units.
- Results of previous operations that impact current operations.
  a. An important step in mission analysis is to determine the essential tasks. Combat power is applied precisely at decisive points, and other portions of the urban area are isolated to the extent necessary to ensure they do not adversely influence the UO. Operations are conducted both sequentially and simultaneously, as appropriate. Specific tasks to subordinates may address the full spectrum of Army operations, and the brigade will likely be conducting support, stability, and combat operations simultaneously. The complexity of UO may require simultaneous full spectrum operations down to company level.
  b. The brigade commander and staff must determine, during assessment, whether the shaping efforts of higher headquarters are sufficient for the brigade to accomplish its missions or whether additional shaping efforts are required—for example, isolation of nodes or other key terrain. Additionally, the brigade commander and staff must assess whether the shaping efforts of higher headquarters permit them to move directly to domination and or transition.

2-22. SHAPE

Brigades normally shape the area of operations through isolation. Isolation is defined as a tactical task to seal off (both physically and psychologically) an enemy from his sources of support, to deny an enemy freedom of movement, and prevent an enemy unit from having contact with other enemy forces. During isolation, the brigade commander sets the conditions for tactical success. Implied in this step are the thorough reconnaissance of the objectives and movement of subordinate units to positions of tactical advantage. The brigade commander must carefully determine the extent and the manner in which his forces can isolate the objectives. The factors of METT-TC determine how the brigade will isolate the objective psychologically and physically. Only areas essential to mission success are isolated.

a. **Psychological Isolation of the Objective.** Isolation begins with the efforts of the division and corps psychological and civil affairs operations to influence enemy and civilian actions. The brigade commander should consider using PSYOP teams to broadcast appropriate messages to the threat and to deliver leaflets directing the civilian population to move to a designated safe area. These actions must be coordinated with the overall PSYOP plan for the theater and must not sacrifice surprise. By themselves, PSYOP are seldom decisive. They take time to become effective and often their effects are difficult to measure until after the actual attack, but they have usually proven to be successful. Under some METT-TC conditions, they have achieved results far outweighing the effort put into them.

b. **Sensors and Reconnaissance Units.** One of the more common methods of isolation involves the use of a combination of sensors and reconnaissance units along avenues of approach to detect enemy forces as they attempt to enter or leave the objective area. The brigade can engage these enemy forces with indirect fires, aerial fires, or a combination of the two, consistent with the ROE. This technique may be effective in detecting and stopping large enemy units from entering or leaving, but the cover and concealment the urban area provides make it difficult to totally seal off the urban objective. To be successful, this technique requires skillful reconnaissance units and responsive fires. It may not be possible for the brigade to observe all avenues of approach, and enemy units may escape detection by infiltrating or exfiltrating. It may be difficult to distinguish between enemy and friendly personnel and noncombatants moving in and out of the urban area. Indirect fires may cause unacceptable damage to key parts of the urban area.

c. **Snipers.** In certain situations that require precise fire, snipers can provide an excellent method of assisting in isolating key areas. Skillful application of snipers can provide lethal fire while simultaneously minimizing collateral damage and noncombatant casualties. Snipers can also be used to observe and report enemy activity and to call for and adjust indirect fire.

d. **Combination of Assets.** The most effective method of isolating an urban objective is probably the use of a combination of sensors, reconnaissance elements, and maneuver forces. The brigade can move platoons and companies into positions where they can dominate avenues of approach with observation and direct fires. Smaller urban areas with clearly defined boundaries make this method easier to accomplish. Larger urban areas may prevent a maneuver force from gaining access to a position from which to stop enemy movement into the objective area.

e. **Use of Fires and Smoke.** In some instances, where the ROE permit, indirect and aerial fires may be the only available or appropriate method of isolation. This technique is the most destructive; it demands large amounts of ammunition, and it may only last for short periods of time. Brigade fire planners can improve the effectiveness of this technique by careful selection of high pay-off targets and use of precision munitions. Mortar and light artillery fires falling onto large buildings are not as effective in preventing enemy movement as fires falling into open areas. Targeting them against larger avenues, parks, and other open areas force the enemy to move within buildings. Artillery and aerial fires can be directed against buildings that the enemy is using for movement and observation. This method slows and impedes enemy movement, but not stop it. It can also hinder enemy supply efforts and make it difficult to reinforce units under attack. Targeting obvious choke points, such as bridges or main road junctions, can also assist in the isolation effort. Smoke can be used to isolate the objective from enemy observation, but it is difficult to predict what smoke does in an urban area.

> ✍ **NOTE**
>
> Multiple flat polished surfaces in an urban area may degrade laser use, thereby rendering some weapon systems useless. Close coordination must occur between maneuver and fire support planners in order to obtain the desired effects of laser-guided precision munitions. Also, obscuration rounds may cause uncontrolled fires in the city and must be carefully planned.

2-23. DOMINATE

The brigade uses all combined arms available, consistent with the ROE, to defeat or destroy the enemy at decisive points and achieve the desired end-state of the mission. The brigade seeks to dominate the enemy through well-planned isolation and skillful use of combined arms. The brigade commander seeks to minimize the amount of street to street and house to house fighting that must be performed by battalions.

2-24. TYPES OF OFFENSIVE OPERATIONS

The brigade conducts the same types of offensive operations as it would on open terrain. Techniques that may be more applicable during urban offensive operations are discussed in the following paragraphs. These techniques are applicable to all forms of offensive maneuver and would be determined by METT-TC factors.

a. **Movement to Contact, Search and Attack Technique.** Figure 2-10, depicts a brigade conducting a movement to contact in an urban area using the search and attack technique. This technique is used when knowledge of the enemy is unclear and contact is required. It is normally employed against a weak enemy force that is disorganized and incapable of massing strength against task forces (for example, urban insurgents or gangs). The brigade divides the AO into smaller areas and coordinates the movement of battalions through the brigade AO. In the example shown in Figure 2-10, the enemy is found and fixed during isolation and finished during domination. During a mission of this type, the urban environment makes it difficult for conventional Infantry forces to find, fix, and finish the enemy. For example, movement of units may become canalized due to streets and urban *canyons* created by tall buildings. The application of firepower may become highly restricted based on the ROE. The use of HUMINT in this type of action becomes increasingly more important and can be of great assistance during the *find* portion of the mission. (Table 2-1 shows the advantages and disadvantages of search and attack.)

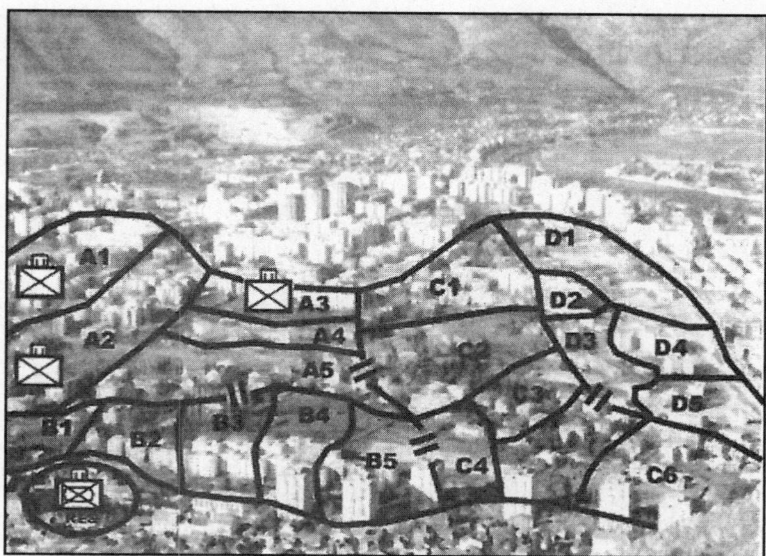

Figure 2-10: Search and attack technique.

Table 2-1: Advantages and disadvantages of search and attack.

TECHNIQUE	ADVANTAGES	DISADVANTAGES
Search and Attack	Requires enemy to fight in multiple directions. Increases maneuver space and flexibility.	Difficult to command and control. Difficult to provide CS and CSS. Difficult to provide for mutual support of maneuver forces. Find/fix/finish forces are challenged/limited.

b. **Attack on a Single Axis.** If the brigade must mass combat power in order to conduct a deliberate attack against an enemy strongpoint, an attack on a single axis may be considered. This technique would be used when the axis of advance is not well defended by the enemy. Figure 2-11 depicts a brigade conducting an attack on a single axis on OBJ GOLD. In the example shown, the lead task force (TF) has the mission of conducting a supporting attack to seize OBJ 22 and facilitate passage of the second the TF through OBJ 22. The second TF conducts the main attack to seize and clear OBJ 21 with an on order mission to seize OBJ 23. A third TF follows in reserve. In the example shown below, the brigade would normally receive assistance in isolating the objective. (Table 2-2 shows the advantages and disadvantages of an attack on a single axis.)

c. **Attack on Multiple Axes.** If enemy defenses are more robust and the brigade commander wishes to force the enemy to fight in multiple directions, an attack on multiple axes can be considered.

(1) Figure 2-12 depicts a brigade conducting the same attack on OBJ GOLD using multiple axes. In this case, a battalion TF (air assault) conducts an air assault on OBJ C and then conducts a supporting attack to seize OBJ D. A second TF conducts a supporting attack to seize OBJ B, with a third conducting the main attack to seize and clear OBJ A. The supporting attacks isolate OBJ A. (Table 2-3 shows the advantages and disadvantages of an attack on multiple axes.) Synchronization of BOS is crucial to ensure the massing of effects at the critical points and to prevent the isolation and piecemeal destruction of smaller elements separated by the structures in the urban area.

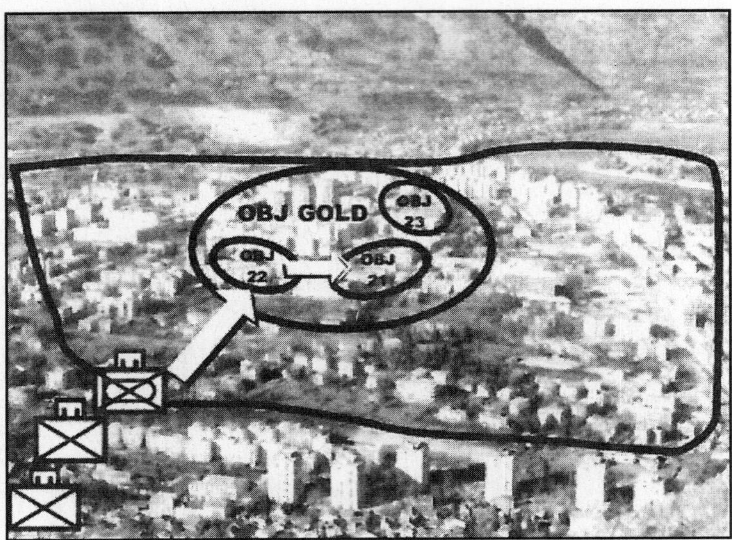

Figure 2-11: Attack on a single axis.

Table 2-2: Advantages and disadvantages of an attack on a single axis.

TECHNIQUE	ADVANTAGES	DISADVANTAGES
Attack on a Single Axis	Facilitates command and control. Limited combat power to the front. Concentrates combat power at a critical point.	Limits manuever. Presents denser target to the enemy. Presents a single threat to the enemy. Reduces flexibility.

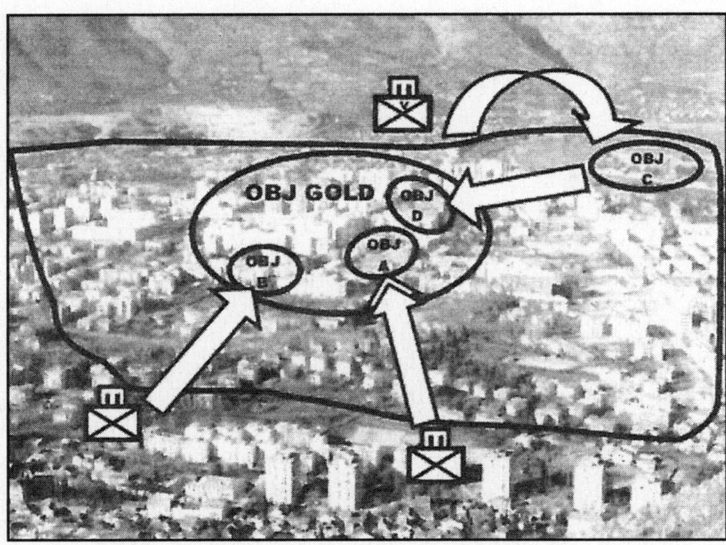

Figure 2-12: Attack on multiple axes.

Table 2-3: Advantages and disadvantages of an attack on multiple axes.

TECHNIQUE	ADVANTAGES	DISADVANTAGES
Attack on Multiple Axes	Better distributes combat power. Requires the enemy to fight in multiple directions. Increases maneuver space and flexibility.	More difficult to command and control. More difficult to provide CS and CSS.

(2) Figure 2-13 depicts an attack on multiple axes on different terrain. In this situation the brigade has the mission to seize OBJ ZULU (OBJs DOG, RAT, and CAT). The brigade commander has decided to attack on multiple axes with two battalion task forces conducting supporting attacks to seize OBJs DOG and RAT in order to isolate OBJ CAT. The brigade main attack seizes and clears OBJ CAT.

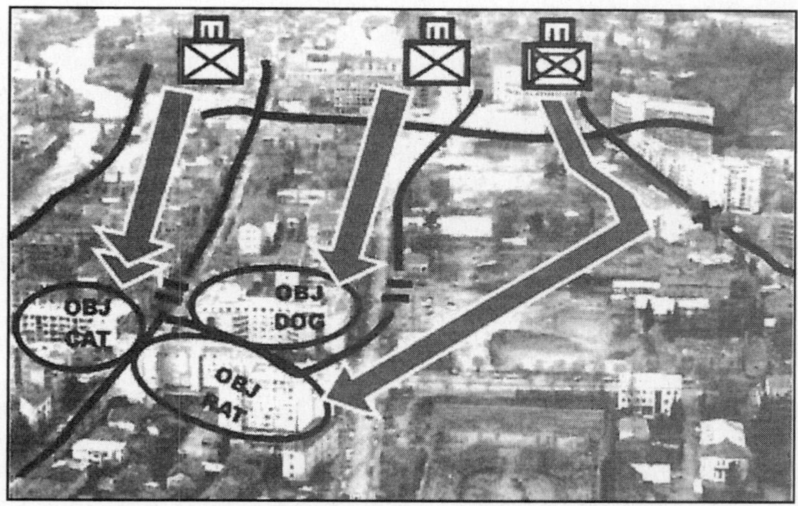

Figure 2-13: Attack on multiple axes, different terrain.

d. **Cordon and Attack.** The brigade may find itself in a position where it may physically isolate a large portion of an urban objective. The brigade commander may also determine that he can force the enemy out of his positions and out into more open areas where he can be engaged by direct and indirect fires. In this case, the cordon and attack technique may be considered. A cordon is a type of isolation. Cordon is a tactical task given to a unit to prevent withdrawal from or reinforcement of a position. Cordon implies seizing or controlling key terrain and or mounted and dismounted avenues of approach. Figure 2-14 depicts a brigade attacking to seize and clear OBJ EAGLE using the cordon and attack technique. One task force (four company teams) cordons OBJ EAGLE by occupying battle positions. (A cordon may also be accomplished using ambushes, roadblocks, checkpoints, OPs, and patrols.) The example in Figure 4-14 shows one TF seizing and clearing OBJ EAGLE and another as the brigade reserve. Skillful application of fires and other combat multipliers may also defeat the enemy when this technique is used and minimize or preclude close combat. (Table 2-4 lists the advantages and disadvantages of cordon and attack.)

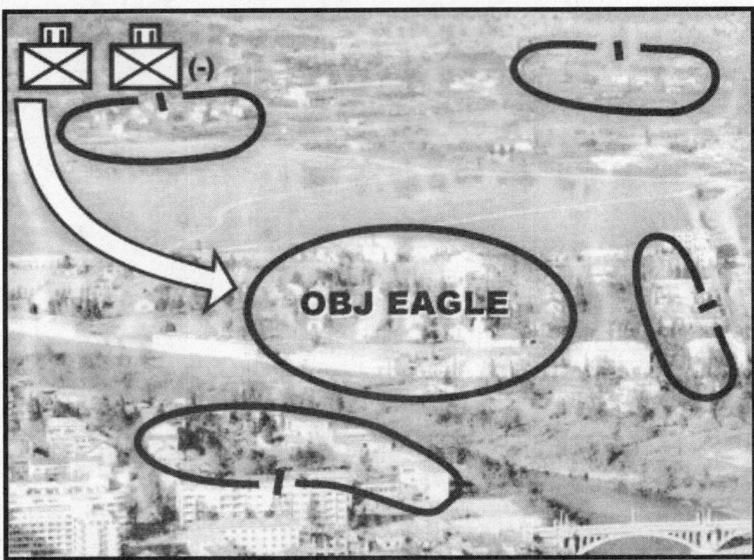

Figure 2-14: Cordon and attack.

> ✍ NOTE
> In the example shown in Figure 2-14, the battle positions are oriented to place fires on the enemy leaving OBJ EAGLE and to prevent his withdrawal from the objective area. The factors of METT-TC determine how the battle positions are oriented and what the mission end-state will be. Additional direct fire control measures, such as TRPs and engagement areas, as well as indirect fire control measures can focus fires and assist in canalizing the enemy into desired areas.

Table 2-4: Advantages and disadvantages of cordon and attack.

TECHNIQUE	ADVANTAGES	DISADVANTAGES
Cordon and Attack	Concentrates combat power. Provides mutual support of maneuver forces.	Sequencing the cordon can be difficult. Considerable combat power can be committed to the cordon.

e. **Fix and Bypass.** A brigade may find itself in a position where it is conducting operations near an urban area that needs to be bypassed. In certain situations the enemy may have to be fixed prior to the brigade's bypassing the urban area. Figure 2-15 depicts a brigade conducting a limited offensive action to fix the enemy with a small force and bypass the urban area with the bulk of the brigade's combat power. If entering the urban area is unavoidable or force protection requirements force the brigade to attack the urban area, the fix and bypass technique may be considered. (Table 2-5 lists the advantages and disadvantages of fix and bypass.) It is preferable to completely avoid the urban area if it is eventually bypassed. During the planning process, routes are chosen so that close combat in the urban area can be avoided. Also, the brigade may be able to fix the enemy with fires and avoid having to enter the urban area.

f. **Multiple Nodal Attacks.** The brigade may be given the mission to attack multiple nodes either simultaneously or sequentially. This mission is characterized by rapid attacks followed by defensive operations. The enemy situation must permit the brigade to divide its forces and seize key nodes. Multiple attacks such as this require precise maneuver and supporting fires. This mission may be given to a brigade before an anticipated

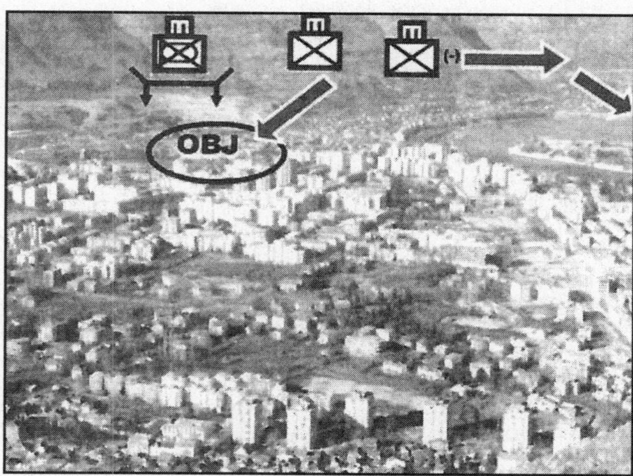

Figure 2-15: Fix and bypass.

Table 2-5: Advantages and disadvantages of fix and bypass.

TECHNIQUE	ADVANTAGES	DISADVANTAGES
Fix and Bypass	Avoids urban area. Facilitates freedom of action.	Requires the brigade to separate, commit, and support part of its force. Fixing force may become isolated and cut off.

stability operation, or to isolate an urban area for other units that are going to conduct offensive operations inside the urban area. Figure 2-16 depicts a brigade conducting multiple nodal attacks. This technique is used to deny the enemy the use of key infrastructure. Use of this technique may also require designated rapid response elements in reserve in the event that enemy forces mass and quickly overwhelm an attacking battalion. The duration of this attack should not exceed the brigade's self-sustainment capability. (Table 2-6 lists the advantages and disadvantages of multiple nodal attacks.)

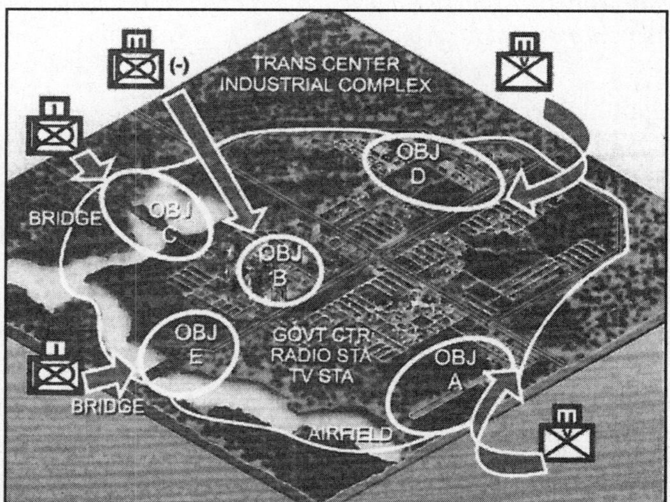

Figure 2-16: Multiple nodal attacks.

Table 2-6: Advantages and disadvantages of multiple nodal attacks.

TECHNIQUE	ADVANTAGES	DISADVANTAGES
Multiple Nodal Attacks	Presents multiple threats to the enemy. Increases maneuver space and flexibility.	Difficult to command and control. Difficult to provide CS and CSS. Difficult to provide for mutual support of maneuver forces. Difficult to sequence.

2-25. TRANSITION

During transition, the brigade continues to use all CS and CSS assets consistent with the mission end-state and ROE to move from offensive operations to stability and or support operations in order to return the urban area back to civilian control. During this step, the roles and use of SOF, CSS, and CS units, such as civil affairs (CA), PSYOP, medical, and MPs become more important with the requirements to maintain order and stabilize the urban area. Subordinate task forces and other brigade units consolidate, reorganize, conduct area protection and logistical missions, and prepare for follow-on missions. The brigade staff prepares to transition from being a *supported* force to being the *supporting* force.

SECTION VI. BATTALION TASK FORCE OFFENSIVE OPERATIONS

The battalion plan of action was as follows: one platoon of Company "F," with a light machine gun section, would stage the initial diversionary attack. It would be supported by two tanks and two tank destroyers, who were instructed to shoot at all or any suspected targets. Observation posts had been manned on a slag pile to support the advance with 81-mm mortar fire... The platoon action was to be the first step... to reduce the town of Aachen.

...the remainder of our zone of action...would be cleared by Companies "F" and "G," who would execute a flanking attack, jumping off abreast of each other through the area secured by the Company "F" platoon... Preparatory fire by medium artillery was to be planned...Mortar observers would accompany each company... Tanks and tank destroyers were assigned to each company...

LTC Darrel M. Daniel
Commander, 2nd Bn, 26th In Rgt
October, 1944, Battle of Aachen

This section discusses tactics, techniques, and procedures (TTP) and considerations that battalion task forces can employ to conduct independent UO or to conduct operations as part of larger brigade UO. The TTP described in this section can apply to all types of battalion task forces, with modifications made for the assets available.

2-26. TASK ORGANIZATION

As with brigade UO, battalion task forces (TF) may require unique task organizations. For example, UO provide one of the few situations where Infantry and armor elements may be effectively task-organized below platoon levels. Battalion commanders must consider providing assets where they are needed to accomplish specific tasks. All phases of mission execution must be considered when developing task organization. Changes in task organization may be required to accomplish different tasks during mission execution. Figure 2-17 depicts a sample task organization for a light Infantry TF conducting an offensive UO that consists of a main effort, two supporting efforts, and a reserve.

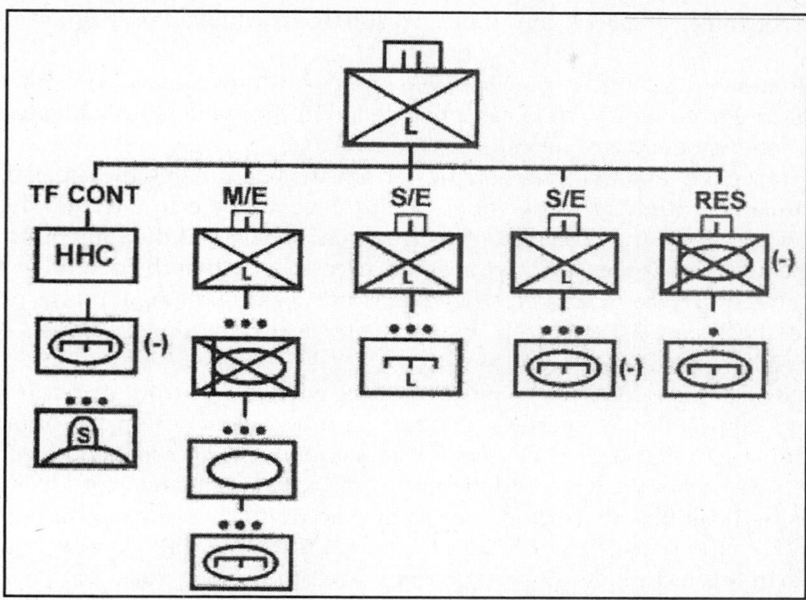

Figure 2-17: Sample offensive task organization.

> ✍ **NOTE**
> The task organization shown may change after the assault when the TF reorganizes for follow-on missions.

2-27. DELIBERATE ATTACK

Because companies or company teams may become isolated during the attack, the TF commander should attach some support elements to ensure the success of his plan. Armored vehicles (tanks, BFVs, self-propelled artillery) attached to light units must have their own logistics packages. Tanks and BFVs can be used to clear or isolate hardened targets protected by buildings or rubble. Engineers can neutralize obstacles hindering the attack. The TF commander plans to conduct a deliberate attack by performing the following actions.

a. **Reconnoiter the Objective.** This method involves making a physical reconnaissance of the objective with battalion assets and those of higher headquarters, as the tactical situation permits. It also involves making a map reconnaissance of the objective and all the terrain that affects the mission, as well as the analysis of aerial imagery, photographs, or any other detailed information about the buildings or other urban terrain the battalion is responsible for. Additionally, any human intelligence (HUMINT) collected by reconnaissance and surveillance units, such as the battalion reconnaissance platoon, snipers, and so forth, should be considered during the planning process.

b. **Move to the Objective.** This method may involve moving through open and or urban terrain. Movement should be made as rapidly as possible without sacrificing security. Movement should be made along covered and concealed routes and can involve moving through buildings, down streets, in subsurface areas, or a combination of all three. Urban movement must take into account the three-dimensional aspect of the urban area.

c. **Isolate the Objective.** Isolation begins with the efforts of SOF units controlled by higher headquarters to influence enemy and civilian actions. The battalion commander should consider using PSYOP teams to broadcast appropriate messages to the threat and to deliver leaflets directing the civilian population to move to a designated safe area, if the units are available to support the battalion. These actions must be coordinated with the overall PSYOP plan for the brigade and must not sacrifice surprise. By themselves, PSYOP are seldom decisive. They take time to become effective and often their effects are difficult to measure until after the actual attack. Under some METT-TC conditions, PSYOP have achieved results far outweighing the effort put into them.

(1) In certain situations that require precise fire, snipers can provide an excellent method of isolating key areas. Skillful application of snipers can provide lethal fire while simultaneously minimizing collateral damage and noncombatant casualties.

(2) Isolating the objective also involves seizing terrain that dominates the area so that the enemy cannot supply, reinforce, or withdraw its defenders. It also includes selecting terrain that provides the ability to place suppressive fire on the objective. (This step may be taken at the same time as securing a foothold.) If isolating the objective is the first step, speed is necessary so that the defender has no time to react. Battalions may be required to isolate an objective as part of brigade operations, or may be required to do so independently (Figure 2-18). Depending on the tactical situation, companies within the battalion may isolate an objective by infiltration and stealth.

(3) Cordon is a tactical task given to a unit to prevent withdrawal from or reinforcement of a position. A cordon is a type of isolation. It implies seizing or controlling key terrain and or mounted and dismounted avenues of approach. Figure 2-18 depicts a brigade attacking to seize and clear OBJ EAGLE using the cordon and attack technique. One battalion TF (four company teams) cordons (isolates) OBJ EAGLE by occupying battle positions. (A cordon may also be accomplished through use of ambushes, roadblocks, checkpoints, OPs, and patrols.) Skillful application of fires and other combat multipliers may also defeat the enemy when this technique is used and minimize or preclude close combat. In the example shown in Figure 2-18, the battle positions are oriented to place fires on the enemy leaving OBJ EAGLE and to prevent his withdrawal from the objective area. The factors of METT-TC determine how the battle positions are oriented and what the mission end-state will be. Additional direct fire control measures, such as TRPs and engagement areas, as well as indirect fire control measures, can focus fires and assist in canalizing the enemy into desired areas.

Figure 2-18: Isolation of an urban area by an Infantry battalion using the cordon technique.

> ✍ **NOTE**
>
> Combat experience and recent rotations at the CTCs have shown that many casualties can be sustained when moving between buildings, down streets, and through open areas to enter a building either to gain a foothold or to clear it. One purpose of isolation at the company and battalion levels must be to dominate the area leading to the points of entry to protect assaulting troops entering the building from effective enemy fire. This technique is accomplished by using direct and indirect fires and obscurants, maintaining situational awareness, and exercising tactical patience prior to movement.

d. **Secure a Foothold.** Securing a foothold involves seizing an intermediate objective that provides cover from enemy fire and a location for attacking troops to enter the urban area. The size of the foothold is METT-TC dependent and is usually a company intermediate objective. In some cases a large building may be assigned as a company intermediate objective (foothold).

(1) As a company attacks to gain a foothold, it should be supported by suppressive fire and smoke. In the example shown in Figure 2-19, the center TF conducts a supporting attack to seize OBJ DOG. (In the brigade scheme of maneuver, the TF on the left conducts the main attack to seize and clear OBJ CAT, and the TF on the right conducts a supporting attack to seize OBJ RAT. The seizure of OBJs RAT and DOG isolates OBJ CAT.) In order to seize OBJ DOG the TF commander determined that two intermediate objectives were necessary.

(2) One company secures a foothold in OBJ Y. As a follow-on mission, the same company seizes OBJ Z and supports the battalion main effort by fire, or facilitates the passage of another company through OBJ Y to seize OBJ Z to support the battalion main effort by fire.

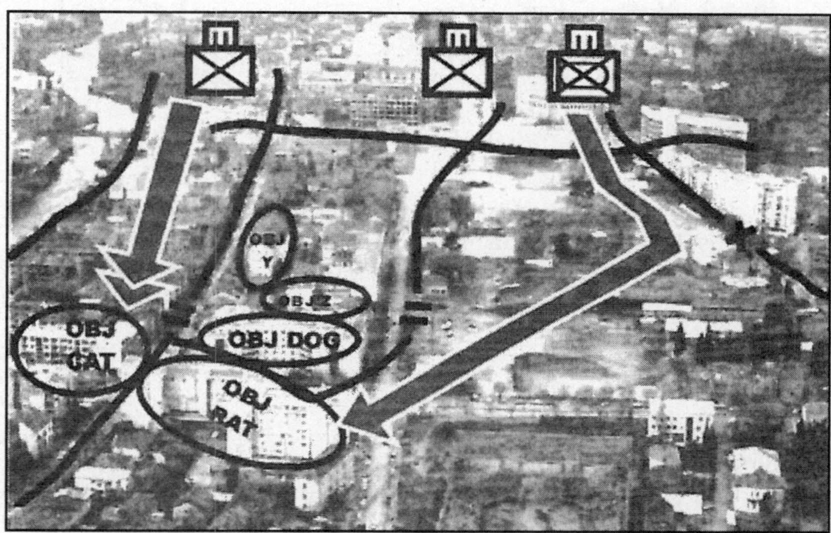

Figure 2-19: Securing a foothold, battalion attack.

e. **Clear an Urban Area.** Before determining to what extent the urban area must be cleared, the factors of METT-TC must be considered. The ROE affect the TTP subordinate units select to move through the urban area and clear individual buildings and rooms. The commander may decide to clear only those parts necessary for the success of his mission if—

- An objective must be seized quickly.
- Enemy resistance is light or fragmented.
- The buildings in the area have large open areas between them. In this case, the commander would clear only those buildings along the approach to his objective, or only those buildings necessary for security.

An Infantry battalion may have a mission to systematically clear an area of all enemy. Through detailed analysis, the commander may anticipate that he will be opposed by strong, organized resistance or will be in areas having strongly constructed buildings close together. Companies may be assigned their own AO within the battalion sector in order to conduct systematic clearing (Figure 2-20).

f. **Consolidate/Reorganize and Prepare for Future Missions.** Consolidation occurs immediately after each action. Reorganization and preparation for future missions occurs after consolidation. Many of these actions occur simultaneously.

(1) Consolidation provides security and facilitates reorganization, and allows the battalion to prepare for counterattack. Rapid consolidation after an engagement is extremely important in an urban environment. The assault force in a cleared building must be quick to consolidate in order to repel enemy counterattacks and to prevent the enemy from infiltrating back into the cleared building. After securing a floor,

Figure 2-20: Systematic clearance within assigned areas.

selected members of the assault force are assigned to cover potential enemy counterattack routes to the building. Priority must be given to securing the direction of attack first.

(2) Reorganization actions (many occurring simultaneously) prepare the unit to continue the mission. The battalion prepares to continue the attack, prepares for future missions, and prepares for the possible transition to stability and support operations.

> **✍ NOTE**
> Friendly force situational awareness is significantly improved in digitally equipped units through the use of Force XXI Battalion Command Brigade and Below (FBCB2) assets.

g. **Transition.** During transition, the battalion continues to use all CS and CSS assets consistent with the mission end-state and ROE to move from offensive operations to stability and or support operations in order to return the urban area to civilian control. During this step, the roles and use of SOF, CS, and CSS units, such as civil affairs (CA), PSYOP, medical, and MPs, become more important with the requirements to maintain order and stabilize the urban area. These assets normally support the battalion's transition efforts under brigade control. The battalion and other brigade units consolidate, reorganize, conduct area protection and logistical missions, and prepare for follow-on missions. The battalion staff, in coordination with the brigade staff, must prepare to transition from being a *supported* force to being the *supporting* force.

2-28. MOVEMENT TO CONTACT

Figure 2-21 depicts a movement to contact in an urban area using the search and attack technique. This technique is used when knowledge of the enemy is unclear and contact is required. It is normally employed against a weak enemy force that is disorganized and incapable of massing strength against the battalion; for example, urban insurgents or gangs. The battalion divides its portion of the AO into smaller areas and coordinates the movement of companies. The battalion can either assign sectors to specific companies or control movement of companies by sequential or alternate bounds within the battalion sector. In the example shown in Figure 2-21 individual companies would find, fix, and finish the enemy (company sectors), or they would find and fix the enemy and the battalion would assign another company the task of finishing the enemy (sequential or alternate bounds). During a mission of this type, the urban environment makes finding, fixing, and finishing the enemy difficult for conventional Infantry forces. For example, movement of units may become canalized due to streets and urban *canyons* created by tall buildings. The application of firepower may become highly restricted based on the ROE. The use of HUMINT in this type of action becomes increasingly more important and can be of great assistance during the *find* portion of the mission.

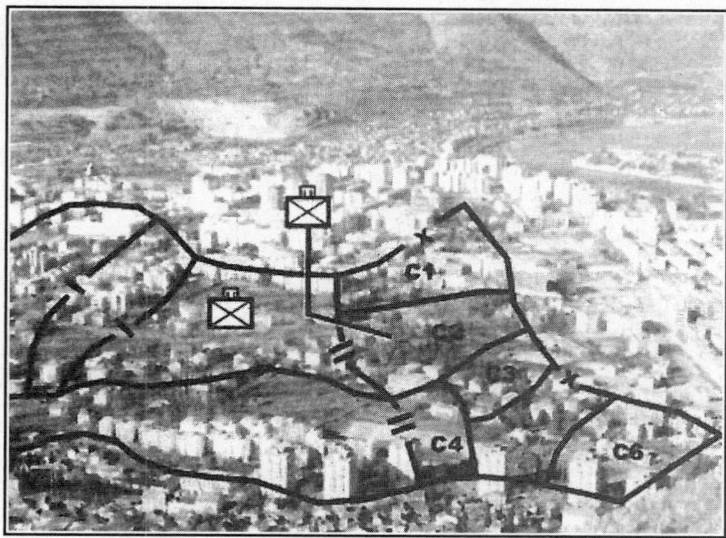

Figure 2-21: Search and attack technique.

2-29. INFILTRATION

The following example describes the actions of an Infantry battalion conducting an infiltration. With some modification, it could also apply to a dismounted mechanized Infantry battalion.

a. The outskirts of an urban area may not be strongly defended. Its defenders may have only a series of antiarmor positions, security elements on the principal approach, or positions blocking the approaches to key features in the town. The strongpoints and reserves are deeper in the urban area.
b. A battalion may be able to seize a part of the urban area by infiltrating platoons and companies between those enemy positions on the outskirts. Moving by stealth on secondary streets by using the cover and concealment of back alleys and buildings, the battalion may be able to seize key street junctions or terrain features, to isolate enemy positions, and to help following units pass into the urban area. Such an infiltration should be performed when visibility is poor and no civilians are in the area. Bypassing enemy strongpoints may result in flank and rear security problems for the infiltrating battalion. Bypassed units may become a counterattack force or cut lines of communications, if not isolated. Planning should include securing all mounted and dismounted avenues of approach from the bypassed enemy strongpoints to ensure their isolation.
c. The Infantry battalion is organized into infiltration companies with appropriate attachments and a reserve consistent with METT-TC. Each company should have an infiltration lane that allows stealthy infiltration by company or smaller size units. Depending on the construction of the urban area and streets, the infiltration lane may be 500 to 1,500 meters wide.
d. The infiltrating companies advance stealthily on foot using available cover and concealment. Mortar and artillery fire can be used to divert the enemy's attention and cover the sound of infiltrating troops.
e. Armored vehicles and antiarmor weapons are positioned to cover likely avenues of approach for enemy armored vehicles. The battalion commander may position antiarmor weapons to cover the likely avenues of approach, if no BFVs or tanks are available. The reconnaissance platoon and antiarmor company screen the battalion's more vulnerable flanks. Also, the antiarmor company can support by fire if the situation provides adequate support by fire positions.
f. As the companies move into the urban area, they secure their own flanks. Security elements may be dropped off along the route to warn of a flank attack. Engineers assist in breaching or bypassing minefields or obstacles encountered. Enemy positions are avoided but reported.
g. The infiltrating companies proceed until they reach their objective. At that time, they consolidate and reorganize and arrange for mutual support. They patrol to their front and flanks, and establish contact with each other. The company commander may establish a limit of advance to reduce chances of enemy contact or to ensure safety from friendly forces.

h. If the infiltration places the enemy in an untenable position and he must withdraw, the rest of the battalion is brought forward for the next phase of the operation. If the enemy does not withdraw, the battalion must clear the urban area before the next phase of the operation (Figure 2-22).

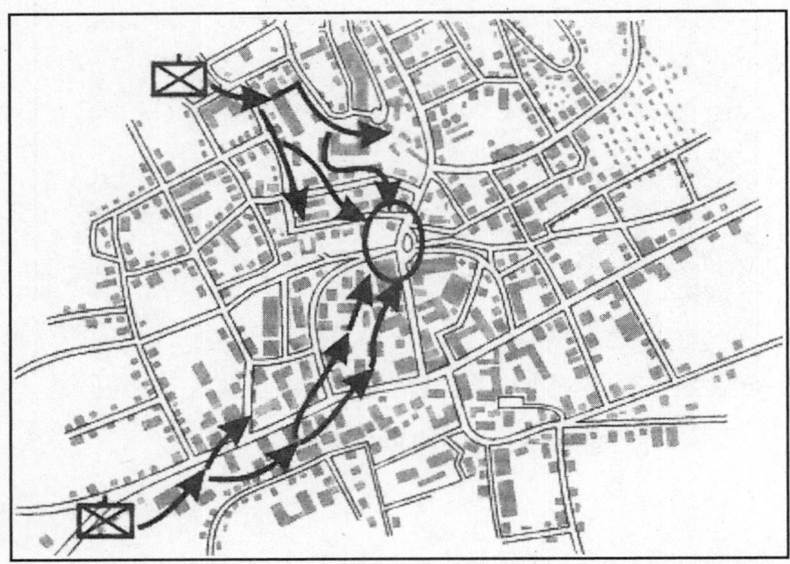

Figure 2-22: Infiltration.

2-30. ATTACK OF A VILLAGE

The battalion may have to conduct either a hasty or deliberate attack of a village that is partially or completely surrounded by open terrain. (Figure 2-23 depicts a TF conducting such an attack.) After the factors of METT-TC have been considered, the tactical tasks discussed in paragraph 2-27 are performed (specifically, reconnoiter the objective, move to the objective, isolate the objective, secure a foothold, clear the objective, consolidate and reorganize, and/or prepare for future missions). In the example shown in Figure 2-23, two companies and or company teams isolate the village, and a company team secures a foothold and enters and clears the village.

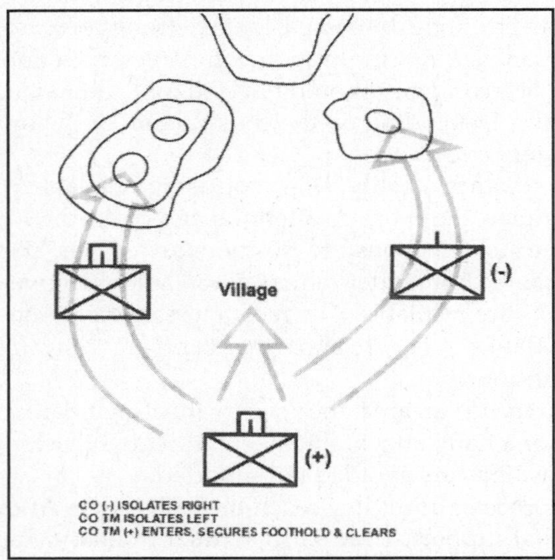

Figure 2-23: Attack of a village.

2-31. ROUTE SECURITY AND CLEARANCE

An Infantry battalion may have to clear buildings to secure a route through a city. How quickly the battalion can clear the buildings depends on enemy resistance and the size and number of the buildings. The battalion deploys companies/company teams IAW with METT-TC factors. Figure 2-24 shows three companies abreast clearing routes in sector. The enemy situation must permit the battalion to deploy its subordinate, units. This mission would not normally be executed against well prepared enemy defenses in depth. In outlying areas, the forward units proceed by bounds from road junction to road junction. Other platoons provide flank security by moving down parallel streets and by probing to the flanks.

a. Depending on the required speed and enemy situation, the Infantry may either move mounted or dismounted. The platoons move down the widest streets, avoiding narrow streets. Each BFV section overwatches the squad to its front, keeping watch on the opposite side of the street. Sections provide their wingman with mutual support. Combat vehicles providing overwatch should be secured by dismounted troops. The rest of the Infantry should stay mounted to maximize speed and shock effect until required to dismount due to the enemy situation or upon reaching the objective.
b. When contact with the enemy is made, tanks support. Supporting fire fixes and isolates enemy positions which dismounted troops maneuver to attack.
c. Phase lines can be used to control the rate of advance of subordinate companies or company teams and other action. At each phase line, the forward companies might reestablish contact, reorganize, and continue clearing (Figure 2-24).

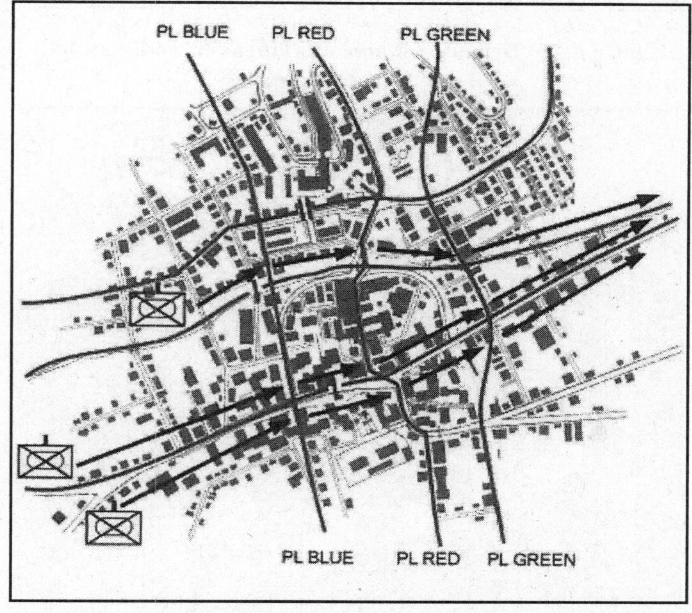

Figure 2-24: Clearing along a route.

2-32. NODAL ATTACK

The battalion may be given the mission to seize key nodes as part of a brigade operation. (See Figures 2-25 and 2-26.) In certain situations, the battalion may be required to seize nodes independently. This mission is characterized by rapid attacks followed by defensive operations. The enemy situation must permit the attacking force to divide its forces and seize key nodes. Multiple attacks, as depicted in Figures 2-25 and 2-26, require precise maneuver and supporting fires. This mission may be given to a battalion before an anticipated stability and or support operation, or to isolate an urban area for other units that will be conducting offensive operations inside the urban area. Figure 2-25 depicts a brigade conducting multiple nodal attacks. Figure 2-26 depicts a battalion TF executing its assigned mission. This technique is used to deny the enemy key infrastructure. Use of this technique may also require designated rapid response elements in reserve in the event that enemy forces mass and quickly overwhelm an attacking battalion. Normally the reserve is planned at brigade level. Battalions executing a nodal attack independently needs to plan for a designated rapid response reserve element. The duration of this attack should not exceed the battalion's self-sustainment capability.

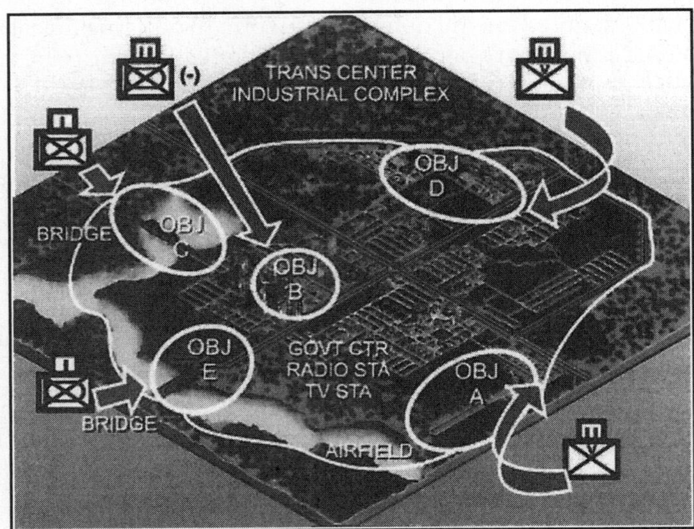

Figure 2-25: Brigade scheme of maneuver, nodal attack.

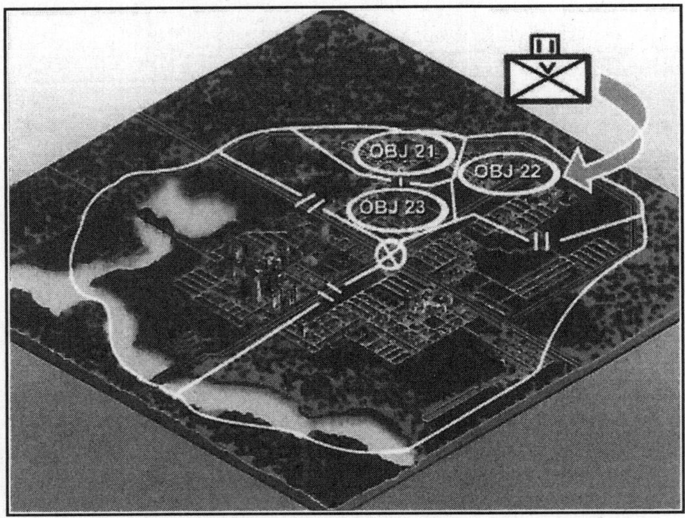

Figure 2-26: Battalion nodal attack.

SECTION VII. COMPANY TEAM ATTACK OF AN URBAN AREA

"We finally reached the front of the company where the lead APC was stopped and learned that the fire was coming from the large hotel on the left side of the street, about 50 meters to the front of the lead platoon. I guided the MK 19 HMMWV up onto a steep sidewalk so the gunner could get an effective shot and told him to watch my M16 tracer rounds and to work the building from top to bottom. I fired several tracers into the hotel; he fired a spotting round into one of the top story windows and then fired the grenade launcher on automatic, hitting every single window in the building. The effects were devastating. Concrete fragments flew everywhere, and one or two Somalis fell out of the building."

CPT Charles P. Ferry
Mogadishu, October 1993
Personal Account of a Rifle Company XO
Infantry Magazine, Sep–Oct 94

This section discusses tactics, techniques, and procedures (TTP) and considerations that company teams can employ to conduct independent UO or to conduct operations as part of larger battalion TF UO, The TTP described in this section can apply to all types of company teams, with modifications made for the assets available.

2-33. TASK ORGANIZATION

The company commander normally task-organizes his company into two elements: an assault element and a support element. The support element may be given a number of tasks that are conducted on order or simultaneously; specifically, support by fire, isolate the objective, and conduct other support functions. The tactical situation dictates whether or not separate elements need to be task-organized in order to conduct these support missions. The mission to breach is METT-TC dependent and may be given to the assault or support element; or a separate element may be formed to conduct this task. If available, engineers are usually task-organized into the element that performs the breach. The size and composition of the elements are determined by METT-TC. If the company is part of a battalion operation, the company could be given the mission to conduct one or more of the tasks mentioned above. If conducting an urban attack independently, the company team performs both assault and support tasks.

a. **Assault Element.** The purpose of the assault element is to kill, capture, or force the withdrawal of the enemy from an urban objective. The assault element of a company team may consist of one or more platoons usually reinforced with engineers, BFVs, and possibly tanks. Building and room clearing are conducted at the platoon and squad level. The assault element must be prepared to breach to gain entry into buildings.

b. **Support Element.** The purpose of the support element is to provide any support that may be required by the assault element. The support element at company level normally consists of the company's organic assets (platoons, mortars, and antitank weapons), attachments, and units that are under the OPCON of the company commander. This assistance includes, but is not limited to, the following:
   - Suppressing and obscuring enemy within the objective buildings and adjacent structures.
   - Isolating the objective buildings with observation and direct or indirect fires to prevent enemy withdrawal, reinforcement, or counterattack.
   - Breaching walls en route to and in the objective structure.
   - Destroying or suppressing enemy positions with direct fire weapons.
   - Securing cleared portions of the objective.
   - Providing squads to assume assault element missions.
   - Providing resupply of ammunition, explosives, and personnel.
   - Evacuating casualties, EPWs, and noncombatants.

c. **Reserves.** Companies fighting in urban terrain may not be able to designate a reserve, based on the number of troops required to conduct offensive operations. A platoon may be detached from the company to form a battalion reserve. The company reserve, if one is designated, should be mobile and prepared for commitment. Because of the available cover in urban areas, the reserve can stay close to forward units. The reserve normally follows within the same block so that it can immediately influence the attack. The size of the reserve is METT-TC dependent, but at company level, the reserve normally consists of a squad, detached from an organic platoon, or attached elements. In addition, the reserve may be called upon to perform one or more of the following tasks based on the commander's priority of commitment:
   - Assuming the mission of the assault element.
   - Clearing bypassed enemy positions.
   - Moving behind the assault element to provide security in cleared buildings, allowing the assault element to continue to move.

d. **Breaching Element.** At the company level, breaching is normally conducted by the assault element. However, a separate breaching element may be created and a platoon may be given this mission and task organized accordingly. The purpose of breaching is to provide the assault element with access to an urban objective. Breaching can be accomplished using explosive, ballistic, thermal, or mechanical methods. Ballistic breaching includes using direct fire weapons; mechanical breaching includes the use of crowbars, axes, saws, sledgehammers, or other mechanical entry devices. Thermal breaching is accomplished through the use of a torch to cut metal items such as door hinges. Attached engineers, or a member of the assault element who has had additional training in mechanical, thermal, ballistic, and explosive breaching techniques, may conduct the breach.

e. **Sample Task Organizations.** Task organization of the company varies based on the factors of METT-TC and the ROE.

(1) ***Light Infantry Task Organization.*** An Infantry company conducting this mission might task-organize as follows:

Assault Two rifle platoons and one rifle platoon (-) reinforced with engineers (attached to the platoons).
Reserve A squad from one of the platoons.
Support The company AT weapons, 60-mm mortar section, and M240 machine guns. (Other support provided by the battalion task force.)

(2) ***Light/Heavy Task Organizations.*** Different METT-TC factors might produce the following light/heavy task organizations:

☞ **EXAMPLE 1**

Assault Two rifle platoons, each reinforced with engineers.
Reserve One rifle platoon.
Support BFV platoon and the company AT weapons and 60-mm mortar section. (Other support provided by the battalion task force.)

☞ **EXAMPLE 2**

Assault Two rifle platoons reinforced with engineers.
Reserve One rifle platoon.
Support One tank platoon. The company AT weapons and 60-mm mortar section.

☞ **EXAMPLE 3**

Assault Two rifle platoons, each with engineers. One tank section OPCON to an Infantry platoon.
Reserve One rifle platoon.
Support A tank section and the company AT weapons under the tank platoon leader's control. The company 60-mm mortar section. (All available direct and indirect fire weapons should be used to isolate objective buildings. Direct fire down streets and indirect fire in open areas between buildings to help in the objective isolation.)

✍ **NOTE**

The company commander may use the company executive officer, tank platoon leader, BFV platoon leader, or first sergeant to control the support element, as the task organization and situation dictate. Based on METT-TC factors, a BFV platoon can perform any of the missions described above (assault, support, reserve). Unit integrity should be maintained at the platoon level. If the tactical situation requires the employment of sections, it should be for a limited duration and distance.

2-34. DELIBERATE ATTACK

At the company level, a deliberate attack of an urban area usually involves the sequential execution of the tactical tasks below.

a. **Reconnoiter the Objective.** This method involves making a physical reconnaissance of the objective with company assets and those of higher headquarters, as the tactical situation permits. It also involves a map reconnaissance of the objective and all the terrain that affects the mission, to include the analysis of aerial imagery, photographs, or any other detailed information about the building or other urban terrain, which the company is responsible for. Additionally, any human intelligence (HUMINT) collected by reconnaissance and surveillance units, such as the battalion reconnaissance platoon, snipers, and so forth, should be considered during the planning process.

b. **Move to the Objective.** This method may involve moving the company tactically through open and or urban terrain. Movement should be made as rapidly as possible without sacrificing security. Movement should be made along covered and concealed routes and can involve moving through buildings, down streets, subsurface areas, or a combination of all three. Urban movement must take into account the three-dimensional aspect of the urban area.

c. **Isolate the Objective.** Isolating the objective involves seizing terrain that dominates the area so that the enemy cannot supply, reinforce, or withdraw its defenders. It also includes selecting terrain that provides the ability to place suppressive fire on the objective. (This step may be taken at the same time as securing a foothold.) If isolating the objective is the first step, speed is necessary so that the defender has no time to react. Companies may be required to isolate an objective as part of a battalion operation or may be required to do so independently. Depending on the tactical situation, an Infantry company may isolate an objective by infiltration and stealth.

d. **Secure a Foothold.** Securing a foothold involves seizing an intermediate objective that provides cover from enemy fire and a location for attacking troops to enter the urban area. The size of the foothold is METT-TC dependent and is usually a company intermediate objective. In some cases a large building may be assigned as a company intermediate objective (foothold). As the company attacks to gain a foothold, it should be supported by suppressive fire and smoke.

e. **Clear an Urban Area.** Before determining to what extent the urban area must be cleared, the factors of METT-TC must be considered. The ROE influence the TTP platoons and squads select as they move through the urban area and clear individual buildings and rooms.

(1) The commander may decide to clear only those parts necessary for the success of his mission if—
- An objective must be seized quickly.
- Enemy resistance is light or fragmented.
- The buildings in the area have large open areas between them. In this case, the commander would clear only those buildings along the approach to his objective, or only those buildings necessary for security. (See Figure 2-27.)

(2) A company may have a mission to systematically clear an area of all enemy. Through detailed analysis, the commander may anticipate that he will be opposed by a strong, organized resistance or will be in areas having strongly constructed buildings close together. Therefore, one or two platoons may attack on a narrow front against the enemy's weakest sector. They move slowly through the area, clearing systematically from room to room and building to building. The other platoon supports the clearing units and is prepared to assume their mission.

Figure 2-27: Clearing selected buildings within sector.

f. **Consolidate/Reorganize and Prepare for Future Missions.** Consolidation occurs immediately after each action. Consolidation is security and allows the company to prepare for counterattack and to facilitate reorganization. It is extremely important in an urban environment that units consolidate and reorganize rapidly after each engagement. The assault force in a cleared building must be quick to consolidate in order to repel enemy counterattacks and to prevent the enemy from infiltrating back into the cleared building. After securing a floor, selected members of the assault force are assigned to cover potential enemy counterattack routes to the building. Priority must be given to securing the direction of attack first. Those soldiers alert the assault force and place a heavy volume of fire on enemy forces approaching the building. Reorganization occurs after consolidation. Reorganization actions prepare the unit to continue the mission; many actions occur at the same time.

(1) ***Consolidation Actions.*** Platoons assume hasty defensive positions after the objective has been seized or cleared. Based upon their specified and implied tasks, assaulting platoons should be prepared to assume an overwatch mission and support an assault on another building, or another assault within the building. Commanders must ensure that platoons guard enemy mouseholes between adjacent buildings, covered routes to the building, underground routes into the basement, and approaches over adjoining roofs.

(2) ***Reorganization Actions.*** After consolidation, the following actions are taken:

- Resupply and redistribute ammunition, equipment, and other necessary items.
- Mark the building to indicate to friendly forces that the building has been cleared.
- Move support or reserve elements into the objective if tactically sound.
- Redistribute personnel and equipment on adjacent structures.
- Treat and evacuate wounded personnel.
- Treat and evacuate wounded EPW and process remainder of EPW.
- Segregate and safeguard civilians.
- Re-establish the chain of command.
- Redistribute personnel on the objective to support the next phase or mission.

(3) ***Prepare for Future Missions.*** The company commander anticipates and prepares for future missions and prepares the company chain of command for transition to defensive and or stability and support missions.

> ✍ **NOTE**
>
> Friendly force situational awareness is significantly improved in digitally equipped units through the use of Force XXI Battle Command Brigade and below (FBCB2) assets.

2-35. ISOLATE AN URBAN OBJECTIVE

Infantry companies isolate an urban objective to prevent reinforcement of, or a counterattack against, the objective and to kill or capture any withdrawing enemy forces. When planning the isolation, commanders must consider three-dimensional and in-depth isolation of the objective (front, flanks, rear, upper stories, rooftops, and subsurface). All available direct and indirect fire weapons, to include attack helicopters and CAS, should be employed, consistent with the ROE. Isolating the objective is a key factor in facilitating the assault and preventing casualties. The company may perform this mission as the support element for a battalion operation, or it may assign the task to its own internal support element for a company attack. In certain situations, companies may be required to isolate an objective or an area for special operations forces or for stability/support operations. When possible, the objective should be isolated using stealth and or rapid movement in order to surprise the enemy. Depending on the tactical situation, companies may use infiltration in order to isolate the objective. Likely tasks include, but are not limited to, the ones described below.

> ✍ **NOTE**
> Combat experience and recent rotations at the CTCs have shown that many casualties can be sustained when moving between buildings, down streets, and through open areas in order to gain entry into a building either to gain a foothold or to clear it. One of the purposes of isolation at the company level must be to dominate the outside area that leads to the point of entry in order to allow assaulting troops to enter the building without receiving effective fire from the enemy. This method is accomplished by the effective use of direct and indirect fires, obscurants, maintaining situational awareness, and exercising tactical patience prior to movement.

a. **Isolating the Objective (Battalion Attack).** A company may isolate the objective as the support element for a battalion operation. When a company is given this mission, the objective is normally a larger structure, a block, or a group of buildings. The company commander task-organizes his platoons and assigns them support by fire positions based on the factors of METT-TC. In addition to isolating the objective, the company (support element) may be given additional tasks that will be conducted on order or at the same time. Examples of these additional tasks include assuming assault element missions, securing cleared buildings, handling noncombatants and EPWs, and CASEVAC.

b. **Isolating the Objective (Company Attack).** When a company conducts an attack, the task organization and tasks given to the company support element is determined by the factors of METT-TC. If the company conducts an attack, the objective can be a building, a block or group of buildings, a traffic circle, or a small village (Figure 2-28). Emphasis must be placed on suppressing or neutralizing the fires on and around the objective. Figure 2-28 depicts an infantry company with tanks assaulting Buildings (BLDG) 41 and 42. In order to secure a foothold and clear BLDGs 41 and 42, the commander has assigned a platoon to support by fire and suppress the enemy squad in BLDG 11 and the medium machine gun in BLDG 21. A tank section suppresses the light machine gun in BLDG 51 and assists in the suppression of BLDG 11. Another platoon supports by fire and suppresses any enemy fire from BLDGs 31, 41, and 42. The company's third platoon, positioned in buildings behind the support element, acts as the assault element to clear BLDGs 41 and 42. In this manner, three-dimensional isolation of the objective (BLDGs 41 and 42) is accomplished.

> ✍ **NOTE**
> All buildings within the support element's sector of fire were numbered to facilitate command and control.

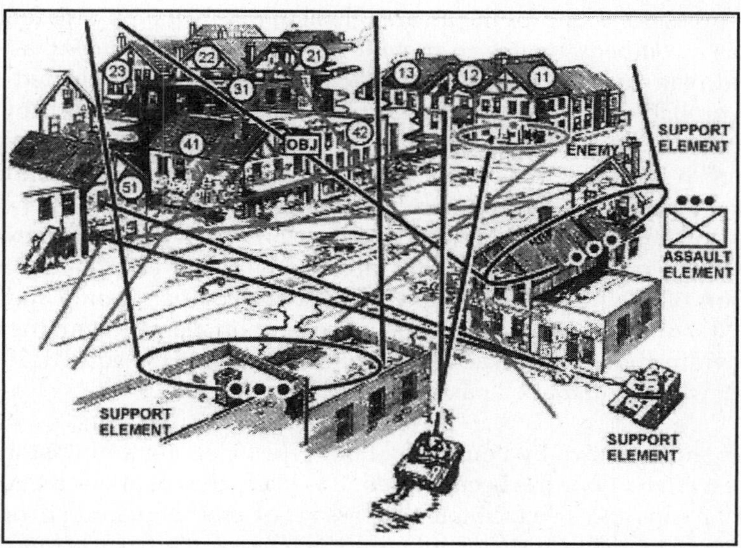

Figure 2-28: Isolating an urban objective.

c. **Tasks.** The company commander isolates the objective with direct and indirect fires before and during the assault element's execution of its mission. The company will—

- Suppress known, likely, and suspected enemy targets, consistent with the ROE, with direct and indirect fire weapons. Under restrictive ROE, suppression may be limited only to actual enemy locations.
- Cover mounted avenues of approach with antiarmor weapons.
- Cover dismounted avenues of approach with automatic weapons.
- Control key terrain near or adjacent to the objective in order to prevent the enemy from reinforcing his positions, withdrawing, or counterattacking.
- Be prepared to move to other locations in order to suppress enemy fires and neutralize enemy positions as the assault element performs its tasks.

(1) Company commanders must give specific instructions to subordinate leaders concerning where to place fires in support of the assault element. For example, from TRP 1 to TRP 2, along the third and second floor windows on the east side of Building 21, shift fires to the west side of the objective from TRP 1 to TRP 4 when the green star cluster is seen, and so on. Once suppressive fires on the objective begin, they normally increase and continue until masked by the advancing assault element. Suppressive fires may or may not be used from the beginning of the assault depending on the ROE. Targets can be marked and identified with tracer rounds; M203 smoke, HE, or illumination rounds; voice and arm-and-hand signals; laser pointers; or similar devices.

(2) The precise well-placed volume of fire, as opposed to a volume of fire, suppresses the enemy. The volume of fire and types of weapons employed is ROE dependent. Once masked, fires are shifted to upper or lower windows and continued until the assault force has entered the building. At that time, fires are shifted to adjacent buildings to prevent enemy withdrawal or reinforcement. If the ROE are restrictive, the use of supporting fires is normally limited to known enemy locations that have engaged the unit.

> ✍ **NOTE**
>
> Care must be taken in urban areas when WP, ILLUM, or tracers are used since urban fires can be caused. Care must also be exercised, if sabot rounds are used by the armored vehicles, based on the its penetration capability. Sabot rounds can penetrate many walls and travel great distances to include passing through multiple buildings, creating unintended damage, casualties, and fratricide.

2-36. ASSAULT A BUILDING

The company conducts this mission as part of the assault element of a battalion task force or independently. (Independently is defined here as a company having to provide its own support element, as opposed to conducting an operation without flank and rear support, such as a raid or ambush.) If it is conducted as the assault element of a battalion task force, it will probably be conducted against a large building defended by a strong enemy force; for example, a reinforced platoon. Company commanders need to clearly understand the specified and implied tasks that are required to accomplish the mission, as well as the brigade/battalion commanders' intent and the desired mission end-state. This procedure allows the company commander to task-organize and issue specific missions to his subordinate elements as to which floors and rooms to clear, seize, or bypass. As an example, Figure 2-29, depicts an Infantry TF assigned the mission of clearing the objectives in its sector (DOG and TAIL). Company B has been given the TF supporting effort of seizing and clearing OBJ TAIL. The company commander has decided to assign an intermediate objective (WING) to 1st platoon. 3d platoon is the support element with the mission of isolating WING (1st and 2d squads) and providing one squad to act as the company reserve (3d squad). 2d platoon has the mission of passing through 1st platoon, which will mark a passage lane and seize TAIL.

a. **Execution.** Platoons should move by bounds by floor when clearing a multistory building. This procedure permits troops to rest after a floor has been cleared. It is likely that platoons are required to leave security on floors and in cleared rooms and also facilitate the passage of another platoon in order to continue the assault. The assault element must quickly and violently execute its assault and subsequent clearing operations. Once momentum has been gained, it is maintained to prevent the enemy from organizing a more determined

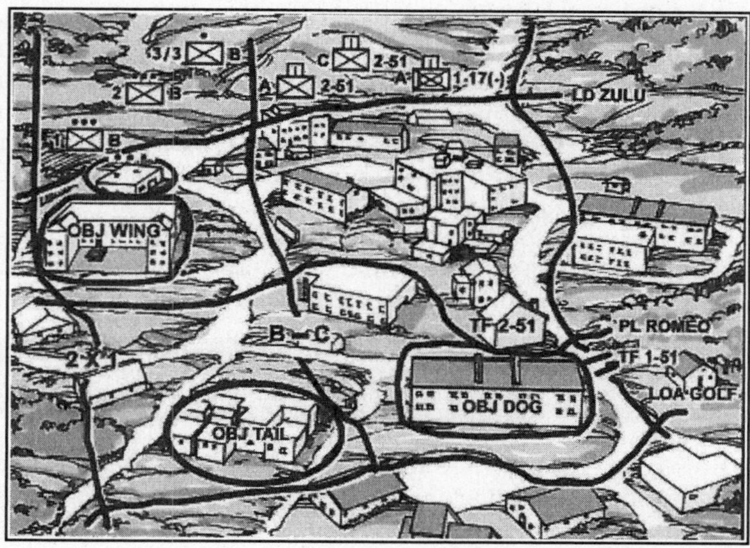

Figure 2-29: Assault of a building.

resistance on other floors or in other rooms. If platoons come across rooms/hallways/stairwells that are barricaded with furniture or where obstacles have been placed, they should first attempt to bypass the barricade or obstacle and maintain the momentum of the attack. If they cannot bypass the barricade or obstacle, security should be placed on it, it should be checked for booby traps, and should then be reduced. Also, sealing doors and floors may be an option in order to maintain momentum. Subordinate leaders should continue the momentum of the assault, yet not allow the operation to become disorganized.

b. **Ammunition and Equipment.** METT-TC factors and the ROE determine how the assault element is equipped and armed. The assault element carries only a fighting load of equipment and as much ammunition as possible, especially grenades (fragmentation, smoke, concussion, and stun consistent with the building construction and the ROE). The support element maintains control of additional ammunition and equipment not immediately needed by the assault element. An often overlooked munition in an urban battle is the light antitank weapon such as the M72 LAW and the AT4. Soldiers can use these for a variety of purposes such as suppressing a manned position or supporting the breaching or assault elements. Resupply should be pushed to the assault element by the support element. Commanders must carefully manage the soldier's load during the assault. Normally, ammunition, water, special assault weapons/equipment, and medical supplies/litters are the only items carried in the assault. Attached or OPCON tank or BFV platoons should also configure their ammunition load to support their mission, consistent with the ROE.

c. **Assault Locations.** The assault may begin from the top or bottom of the building.

(1) ***Top Entry.*** Entry at the top and fighting downward is the preferred method of clearing a building. This method is only feasible, however, when access to an upper floor or rooftop can be gained by ladder; from the windows or roofs of adjoining, secured buildings; or when enemy air defense weapons can be suppressed and troops can be transported to the rooftops by helicopter.

(2) ***Bottom Entry.*** Entry at the bottom is common and may be the only option available. When entering from the bottom, breaching a wall is the preferred method because doors and windows may be booby trapped and covered by fire from inside the structure. If the assault element must enter through a door or window, entry from a rear or flank position is preferred. Under certain situations, the ROE may not permit the use of certain explosives, therefore entry through doors and windows may be the only option available. Armored vehicles can be especially useful in supporting bottom entry.

d. **Breaching.** Squads and platoons will have to conduct breaching. Engineers may be attached to the unit responsible for breaching. Depending on the factors of METT-TC, company commanders may need to designate specific breaching locations or delegate the task to platoon leaders. The ROE also influences whether mechanical, thermal, ballistic, or explosive breaching is used. For example, if BFVs are attached to the company and the ROE permit their use, they can breach the wall by main-gun fire for the initial-entry point.

e. **Assault Tasks.** Once inside the building, the priority tasks are to cover the staircases and to seize rooms that overlook approaches to the building. These actions are required to isolate enemy forces within the building and to prevent reinforcement from the outside. The assault element clears each room on the entry floor and then proceeds to clear the other floors to include the basement. If entry is not made from the top, consideration may be given to rushing / clearing and securing a stairwell and clearing from the top down, if the tactical situation permits. If stairwell use is required, minimize their use and clear them last. If there is a basement, it should be cleared as soon as possible, preferably at the same time as the ground floor. The procedures for clearing a basement are the same as for any room or floor, but important differences do exist. Basements may contain entrances to tunnels such as sewers and communications cable tunnels. These should be cleared and secured to prevent the enemy from infiltrating back into cleared areas.

☠ DANGER
A safety consideration for clearing buildings is the high probability of ricochet.

f. **Suppressive Fires During the Assault.** The support element provides suppressive fire while the assault element is systematically clearing the building. It also provides suppressive fire on adjacent buildings to prevent enemy reinforcements or withdrawal. Suppressive fire may consist of firing at known and suspected enemy locations; or, depending on the ROE, may only include firing at identified targets or returning fire when fired upon. The support element destroys or captures any enemy trying to exit the building. The support element must also deal with civilians displaced by the assault. Armored vehicles are useful in providing heavy, sustained, accurate fire.

g. **Clearing Rooms.** Company commanders must ensure that clearing platoons carry enough room marking equipment and plainly mark cleared rooms from the friendly side IAW unit SOP. Also, if the operation occurs during limited visibility, marking must be visible to friendly units. The support element must understand which markings will be employed and ensure that suppressive fires do not engage cleared rooms and floors. Maintaining situational awareness concerning the location of the assault teams and which rooms / floors have been cleared is imperative and a key command and control function for the company commander. Radios can be consolidated, if necessary, with priority going to the squads and platoons clearing rooms. When exiting cleared buildings friendly troops should notify supporting elements using the radio or other preplanned signals.

2-37. ATTACK OF A BLOCK OR GROUP OF BUILDINGS

A company team normally attacks a block or group of buildings as part of a battalion task force. To attack a block or a group of buildings, a company team may need to be reinforced with BFVs or tanks and engineers, consistent with the ROE and the enemy situation.

a. **Execution.** The execution of this mission is characterized by platoon attacks supported by both direct and indirect fires. Success depends on isolating the enemy positions which often become platoon objectives, suppressing enemy weapons, seizing a foothold in the block, and clearing the block's buildings room by room.

b. **Direct Fire Weapons.** BFVs, tanks, machine guns, and other direct fire support weapons fire on the objective from covered positions, consistent with the ROE. These weapons should not be fired for prolonged periods from one position. The gunners should use a series of positions and displace from one to another to gain better fields of fire and to avoid being targeted by the enemy. Direct fire support tasks can be assigned as follows:
   (1) Machine guns fire along streets and into windows, doors, mouseholes, and other probable enemy positions. ROE may restrict firing only to known enemy locations.
   (2) BFVs, tanks, and antitank weapons fire at enemy tanks and other armored vehicles can also provide a countersniper capability due to their range and target acquisition capability.
   (3) Tanks fire at targets protected by walls and provide protection against enemy tanks, as required.
   (4) BFVs may be used to create breaches with the 25-mm gun and TOW.
   (5) Riflemen engage targets of opportunity.

c. **Obscuration and Assault.** Before an assault, the company commander should employ smoke to conceal the assaulting platoons. He secures their flanks with direct fire weapons and by employment of the reserve, if necessary. Concealed by smoke and supported by direct fire weapons, an assaulting platoon attacks the first isolated building. The assault element utilizes the cover of suppressive fires to gain a foothold. The company commander must closely coordinate the assault with its supporting fire so that the fire is shifted at the last possible moment. The squads and platoons then clear each designated building. After seizing the block, the company consolidates and reorganizes to repel a counterattack or to continue the attack. Periods of limited visibility may provide the best conditions to attack, especially if NVGs provide the company a technological advantage over the threat.

> ✍ **NOTE**
> Obscuration rounds may cause uncontrolled fires in the city and must be carefully planned.

2-38. HASTY ATTACK

A company team may find itself moving to an urban area or conducting a movement to contact with a mission of clearing a village of enemy. The following discussion provides a technique for conducting a hasty attack on a village. The company commander makes a quick assessment of the factors of METT-TC and reacts appropriately to support the higher level commander's intent.

a. **Establish Support.** If attached or OPCON, tanks, BFVs, MK19s or M2HBs mounted on HMMWVs, and TOWs assume support-by-fire positions from which they can fire on the village, prevent the enemy from withdrawing, and destroy any reinforcements (support element functions). If these assets are not available, then the company commander moves Infantry elements into position to accomplish the same tasks. The company's 60-mm mortar and AT sections also provide fire support. Armored vehicles can reposition during the assault, if necessary, to gain better fields of fire and provide better support.

b. **Assault the Village.** The rifle platoons assault from a covered route so as to hit the village at a vulnerable point (Figure 2-30). As the platoons approach the village, smoke is employed to screen their movement and supporting fires are shifted. Once the platoons close on the village, they clear the buildings quickly, consistent with the ROE, and consolidate. The company is then ready to continue operations.

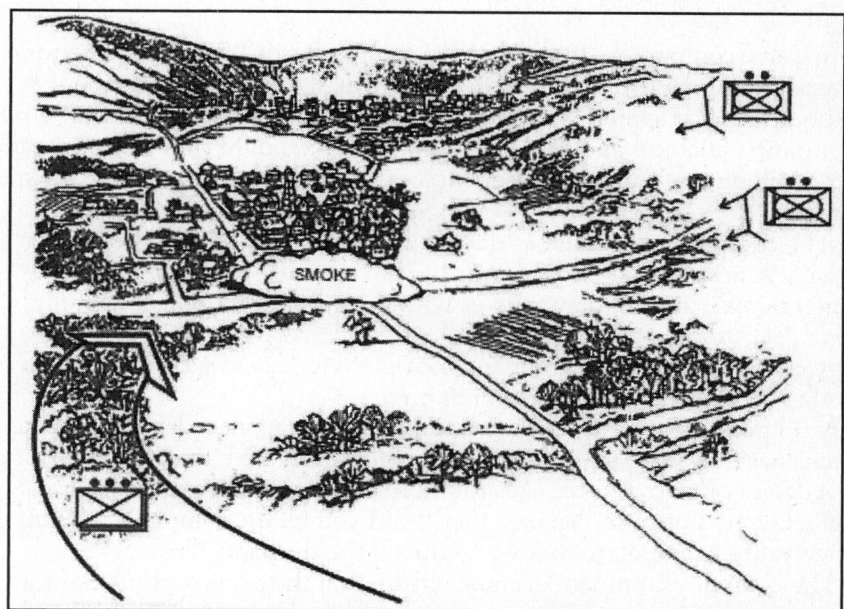

Figure 2-30: Hasty attack of a village.

2-39. MOVEMENT TO CONTACT AND RECONNAISSANCE

In a fast-moving situation, a company team may have to conduct a movement to contact through an urban area to fix enemy forces (Figure 2-31). Similarly, a company team may have to reconnoiter such a route to prepare for a battalion task force attack or other mission. This type of reconnaissance is accomplished with a company team. It is preferable to conduct this mission with tanks and or BFVs. The actual task organization will be determined by the factors of METT-TC.

Figure 2-31: Movement to contact through an urban area.

a. **Tempo.** These operations are characterized by alternating periods of rapid movement to quickly cover distances and much slower movement for security. The speed of movement selected depends on the terrain and enemy situation.
b. **Execution.** An infantry company without support from tanks or BFVs would conduct travelling overwatch or bounding overwatch along urban routes. In open areas where rapid movement is possible due to terrain, a tank section should lead, if available. In closer terrain, the infantry should lead while overwatched by the tanks. Another infantry platoon and the other tank section should move on a parallel street. Artillery fire should be planned along the route. Engineers accompany the lead platoon on the main route to help clear obstacles and mines.
c. **Danger Areas.** The company should cross danger areas (crossroads, bridges, and overpasses, and so forth) by a combination of actions:
   - Between danger areas, the company moves with the infantry mounted, or rapidly on foot, when contact is not likely.
   - When enemy contact is likely, the company moves to clear enemy positions or to secure the danger area. Tanks and other combat vehicles support infantry.
d. **Axis of Advance.** In peripheral areas, this advance should be on one axis with the lead unit well forward and security elements checking side streets as they are reached. In the city core, this operation is conducted as a coordinated movement on two or three axes for more flank security.
e. **Enemy Positions.** Enemy positions can be either destroyed by the company itself or, if the need for speed is great, bypassed, reported, and left to following units if the situation allows.
f. **Coordination.** The company commander must ensure that the actions of platoons and attached or OPCON elements are coordinated. Situational awareness must be maintained in a rapidly moving or changing environment. The company commander reports all information collected to the battalion task force.

2-40. SEIZURE OF KEY URBAN TERRAIN

A traffic circle, bridge or overpass that spans a canal, a building complex, or, in some cases, the population itself are examples of key urban terrain. Therefore, seizing such terrain intact and securing it for friendly use is a likely mission for a company team. The discussion below describes the TTP for seizing and controlling a bridge and seizing a traffic circle.

a. **Seizure of a Bridge.** For this mission (Figure 2-32), a company team should perform the following actions.

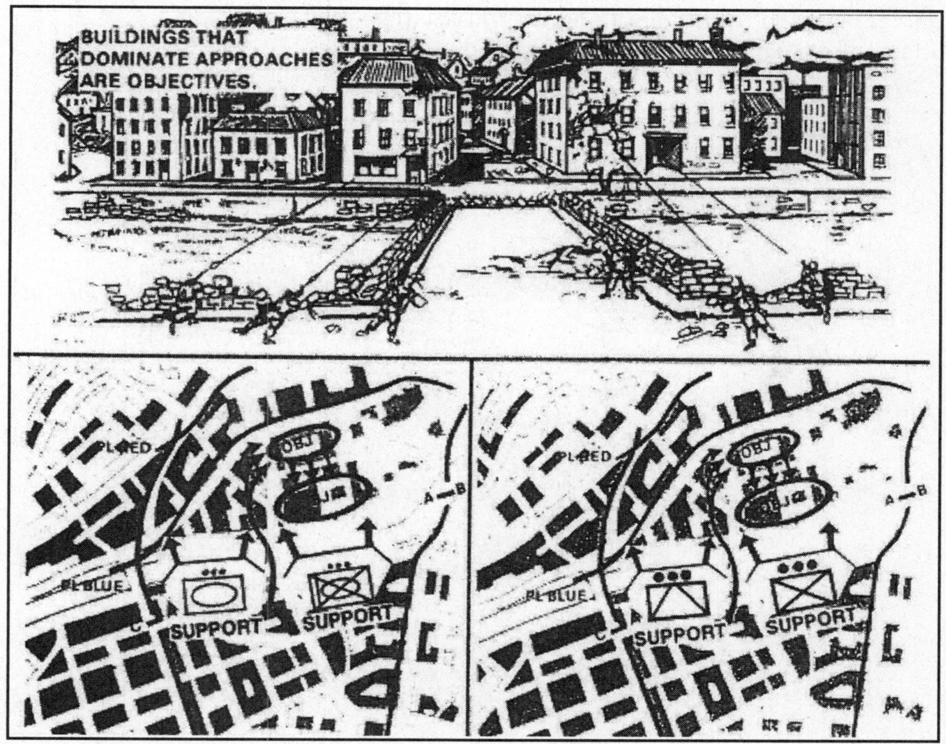

Figure 2-32: Seizure of a bridge.

(1) ***Clear the Near Bank.*** The first step in seizing a bridge is to clear the buildings on the near bank that overwatch the bridge and the terrain on the far side. The commander must find out which buildings dominate the approaches to the bridge. Buildings that permit him to employ anti-tank weapons, machine guns, and riflemen are cleared while supporting fire prevents the enemy from reinforcing his troops on the far bank and keeps enemy demolition parties away from the bridge.

(2) ***Suppress.*** Suppress enemy weapons on the far bank with direct and indirect fire. In suppressing the enemy's positions on the far bank, priority is given to those positions from which the enemy can fire directly down the bridge. Tanks, BFVs, TOWs, and machine guns mounted on HMMWVs are effective in this role. TOWs, Dragons, Javelins, and AT4s can be used against enemy tanks covering the bridge. Use screening smoke to limit enemy observation. All suppression must be consistent with the ROE.

(3) ***Assault.*** Seize a bridgehead (buildings that overwatch and dominate the bridge) on the far bank by an assault across the bridge. The objectives of the assaulting platoons are buildings that dominate the approaches to the bridge on the far side. One or two platoons assault across the bridge using all available cover while concealed by smoke. In addition to a frontal assault across the bridge, other routes should be considered. They are supported by the rest of the company and any attached and OPCON forces. Once on the other side, they call for the shifting of supporting fire and start clearing buildings. When the first buildings are cleared, supporting fire is lifted and or shifted again and the assault continues until all the buildings in the objective area are cleared.

(4) ***Clear the Bridge.*** Secure a perimeter around the bridge so that the engineers can clear any obstacles and remove demolitions from the bridge. The company commander may expand his perimeter to prepare for counterattack. Once the bridge is cleared, tanks, BFVs, and other support vehicles are brought across to the far bank.

b. **Seizure of a Traffic Circle.** A company may have to seize a traffic circle either to secure it for friendly use or to deny it to the enemy (Figure 2-33). This operation consists of seizing and clearing the buildings that control the traffic circle, and bringing direct-fire weapons into position to cover it. After gathering all available intelligence on the terrain, enemy, and population, the commander takes the following steps:

- Isolates the objective.
- Seizes and or clears the buildings along the traffic circle.
- Consolidates and prepares for counterattack.

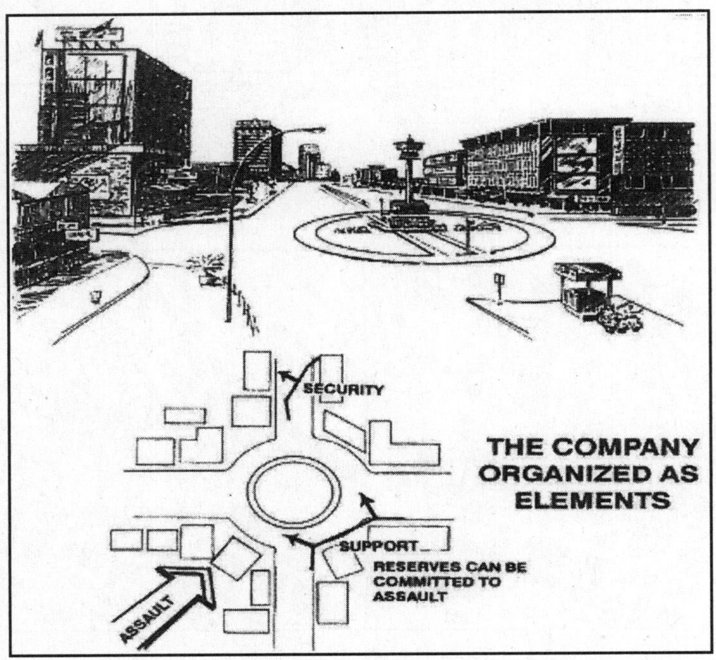

Figure 2-33: Seizure of a traffic circle.

(1) ***Troop Safety.*** Friendly troops should not venture into the traffic circle until it is secure. A traffic circle is a natural kill zone.

(2) ***Task Organization.*** The company should be organized with assault, support, and reserve elements based on the factors of METT-TC and the ROE.

(a) *Assault.* Seizes and or clears the terrain (buildings) that influence the objective. (For example, two rifle platoons, reinforced with engineers.)

(b) *Support.* Isolates the traffic circle and provides security. This element can be mounted (preferred) or dismounted; for example, an infantry platoon with a section of BFVs. Provides direct fire support for the assault element. The element could consist of tanks, BFVs, TOWs, MK 19s, or M2HBs mounted on HMMWVs, occupying a support-by-fire position.

(c) *Reserve.* Reinforces the assault element on order. (Normally a detached squad from one of the rifle platoons.)

(3) ***Flexibility.*** At various stages in this operation, roles may change. For example, the assault element may clear buildings until the support element can no longer support it. Then the reserve can be committed to the assault. It may also occur that one of the assault elements finds itself in a better position to isolate the traffic circle and becomes the support element. At that time, the isolating (support) element would become part of the assault element. The support element may also have to reposition to continue support.

2-41. DIRECT FIRE PLANNING AND CONTROL

One of the company commander's primary responsibilities will be to plan and control direct fires during the attack of an urban objective. The information below applies to a company isolating an objective for either a battalion or company attack. Direct fire support can be very resource intensive. Commanders must ensure that enough ammunition is available to support their fire plans.

a. **Principles of Direct Fire Planning.** A thorough direct fire plan will adhere to the principles stated below.

(1) ***Mass fires.*** Massing of fires is defined by the terminal effect on the enemy, not by the number of systems firing or the number of rounds fired. Mass must not be confused with volume of fires. Massing fires is achieved by placing accurate fires on multiple targets at the same time. This method means firing at enemy targets in or outside of buildings laterally and in depth. The objective is to force the enemy to respond to multiple threats and to kill or suppress enemy soldiers or positions.

(2) ***Leaders control fires.*** Leaders must control fires to simultaneously engage different priority targets. Allowing individual crews to select their own priority target will probably result in multiple systems engaging the same target while leaving other dangerous targets free to engage and possibly maneuver against friendly units.

(3) ***Fire plans must be understood by the soldiers who execute them.*** It is imperative that every soldier understands how to execute his portion of the direct fire plan. This understanding is necessary in order to avoid fratricide. This understanding is also necessary to ensure destruction or suppression of enemy soldiers and positions. A soldier must be able to identify where they are responsible for firing and if there is an enemy to engage. Then he must understand how his fires are to be controlled and directed during the course of the fight. Ensuring terms are commonly understood assists all involved. Exchanging SOPs, chalk talks, terrain models, and rehearsals assist in understanding.

(4) ***Focus fires.*** Focusing fires means accurately directing fires to hit specific targets, points, or areas, and is the most difficult task of controlling fires. The commander focuses fires by clearly conveying instructions (either preplanned or hasty) to direct the fires of the individual platoons on specific targets or areas that support his plan for distribution. Platoons must be able to recognize the point at which to focus their fires. Failure to do so will result in different units/assets in the support element engaging the same targets, while others are not engaged. Recognizable control measures allow the support element to focus fires (see paragraph d). OPORDs and rehearsals must paint the visual picture of how the commander wants the fires focused and what the platoons will see to focus their fires.

(5) ***Distribute fires.*** Distributing fires is the process of engaging different enemy threats simultaneously to avoid overkill by multiple systems engaging the same targets and to degrade the enemy's ability to deal with single threats one at a time. Proper distribution ensures critical targets are engaged first and the enemy is engaged three dimensionally. The following points should be emphasized:

a. Avoid target overkill. Minimize engaging targets that are already destroyed or suppressed.

b. Use each weapon system in its best role. Different weapons systems and ammunition types have specific characteristics that maximize their capability to kill or suppress specific enemy weapons systems at different ranges. For example, an AT 4 can be used to suppress an enemy sniper position, but it will probably not destroy the position itself.

c. Destroy the most dangerous targets first. Proper focus, distribution, and firing first are the keys to maximizing this principle.

d. Concentrate on enemy crew-served weapons and combat vehicles. This method deprives the enemy of his ability to use his fire support weapons against friendly troops.

e. Take the best shots and expose only those weapons systems actually needed to fire in order to maximize the probability of hitting and killing enemy targets, and to protect friendly forces as long as possible.

(6) ***Shift fires.*** Shifting fires is the process of re-focusing weapons systems to change the distribution of fires as targets are destroyed or as the situation changes, for example, the introduction of new forces on the battlefield. At the company level, this method is accomplished by shifting the fires of the support element and focusing them on new targets. This fire may be used to isolate, suppress, prevent counterattack/reinforcement, and so forth.

(7) ***Rehearse the fire plan.*** The most important part of any operation that requires soldiers to shoot their weapons is the fire plan. Every fire plan must be rehearsed; for example, what is the fire plan and how is it executed in each phase: isolation/gaining a foothold, breaching, assault of the building. A rehearsed fire plan enhances execution, prevents fratricide, identifies shortcomings, and works to synchronize the operation.

b. **Questions to Answer.** When the direct fire plan is complete, the commander should be able to answer the following questions:

- How does the fire plan help achieve success at the decisive point?
- What is the company mission and the desired effect of our fires?
- Is the fire plan consistent with the ROE?
- Where are combat vehicles or other dangerous weapons systems?
- Which course of action has the enemy selected?
- What are the PIR to determine the enemy's actions?
- Where are we going to kill or suppress the enemy?
- From where will we engage him?
- Which enemy weapons do we want to engage first?
- How will we initiate fires with each weapon system?
- Which weapons will fire first? What will each engage? What are the engagement criteria?
- What is the desired effect of fires from each unit in the support element?
- How will we distribute the fires of platoons to engage the enemy three dimensionally?
- What will the support element focus their fires on? (How will the support element units know where to engage? Will they be able to see and understand the control measures?)
- How will we mass fires to deal with multiple enemy threats and achieve the desired volume of fire?
- Where will leaders be positioned to control fires; how will we focus fires on new targets?
- How will we deal with likely enemy reactions to our fires?
- Does the plan avoid overkill; use each weapon system in its best role; concentrate on combat vehicles, take the best shots, expose only those friendly weapons needed, destroy the most dangerous targets first?
- Have my fires been massed to achieve suppression, obscuration, and security needs of the breach?
- Will the fires be masked by buildings or assault element movement?

c. **Fire Commands.** Fire commands are verbal orders used to control direct fires. They are standard formats that rapidly and concisely articulate the firing instructions for single or multiple engagements. They can be given over the radio or landline to control fires. At company level fire commands must control the fires of multiple elements with different weapons systems. Fire commands should concentrate on ensuring that the support element is accurately focused and understands its portion of fire distribution. Platoon leaders generally give these commands after the company commander gives the order to initiate fires. A general format includes:

- Alert (call sign).
- Weapon ammunition (optional, METT-TC dependent).
- Target description.
- Location or method to focus fires.
- Control pattern technique (optional, METT-TC dependent).
- Execution (my command, your command, event).

Sample Fire Command:

"Tango 27 (PSG) This is Tango 16 (PL), over"-Alert
"7.62 mm, 40 mm, and AT 4s"-Weapons/ammunition
"Windows and Door"-Target description
"OBJ 4; White; A1, B1, C1"-Location
"Fire"-Execution.

d. **Direction of Assault Technique of Direct Fire Control.** In this technique, the company commander assigns building numbers in a consistent pattern in relation to the direction of assault. In the example shown in Figure 2-34, the commander numbered the buildings consecutively, in a counterclockwise manner. Further, the sides of the buildings were color coded consistently throughout the objective area (WHITE = direction of assault side; GREEN = right side; BLACK = rear side; RED = left side; BLUE = roof). An odd-shaped building is also shown. Note that a *four-sided* concept was retained to minimize confusion. Further designations of WHITE 1, WHITE 2, WHITE 3, and so on from left to right can be added to specify which wall will be engaged. Apertures on the buildings are also labeled consecutively using rows and columns, as shown. In the example, "OBJ 4, WHITE, window A1" is the lower left-hand window on the direction of assault side of OBJ 4. All designations are labeled in relation to the direction of assault.

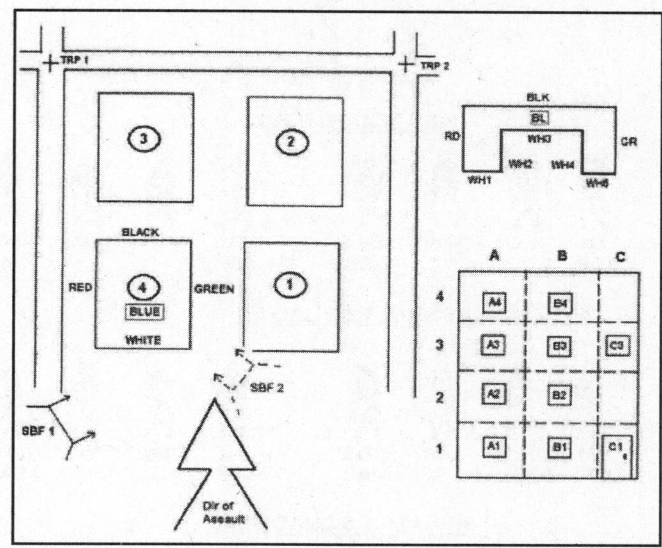

Figure 2-34: Direction of assault technique of direct fire control.

SECTION VIII. PLATOON ATTACK OF AN URBAN AREA

The Infantry platoon will normally conduct offensive tasks as part of a company mission. However, there may be times that the platoon will be required to perform an independent offensive operation in support of the main effort. This section discusses how the platoon conducts the various tasks as part of a company operation or as an independent mission.

2-42. TASK ORGANIZATION (PLATOON ATTACK OF A BUILDING)

The platoon leader will normally organize his platoon into at least two elements: an assault element consisting of two rifle squads, and a support element consisting of the platoon's crew-served weapons and one rifle squad as the support or reserve (Figure 2-35). If engineers are not available, he can designate a breaching team from within either the assault or the support element or, depending on the situation, he may task organize a separate breach element. The size and composition of these elements are determined by the mission given, the number of troops available, the type and size of the objective building, whether the adjacent terrain provides open or covered approaches, and the organization and strength of the enemy defenses. As part of a company operation, the platoon will be part of either the assault element or the support element.

- As part of the company's assault element, the platoon would organize into three assault squads with two assault teams each, and will attach the machine guns to the company support element.
- As the part of the company's support element, the platoon may be organized into three support squads with machine guns and antiarmor weapons attached. The attached machine guns provide the support element with added firepower for increased lethality.

a. **Assault Element.** The purpose of the assault element is to kill, capture, or force the withdrawal of the enemy from an urban objective and to seize key terrain. The assault element of a platoon may consist of one, two, or three squads. Squad leaders will normally organize their two fire teams into two assault teams or, in special circumstances, the squad may be kept as a single assault element.

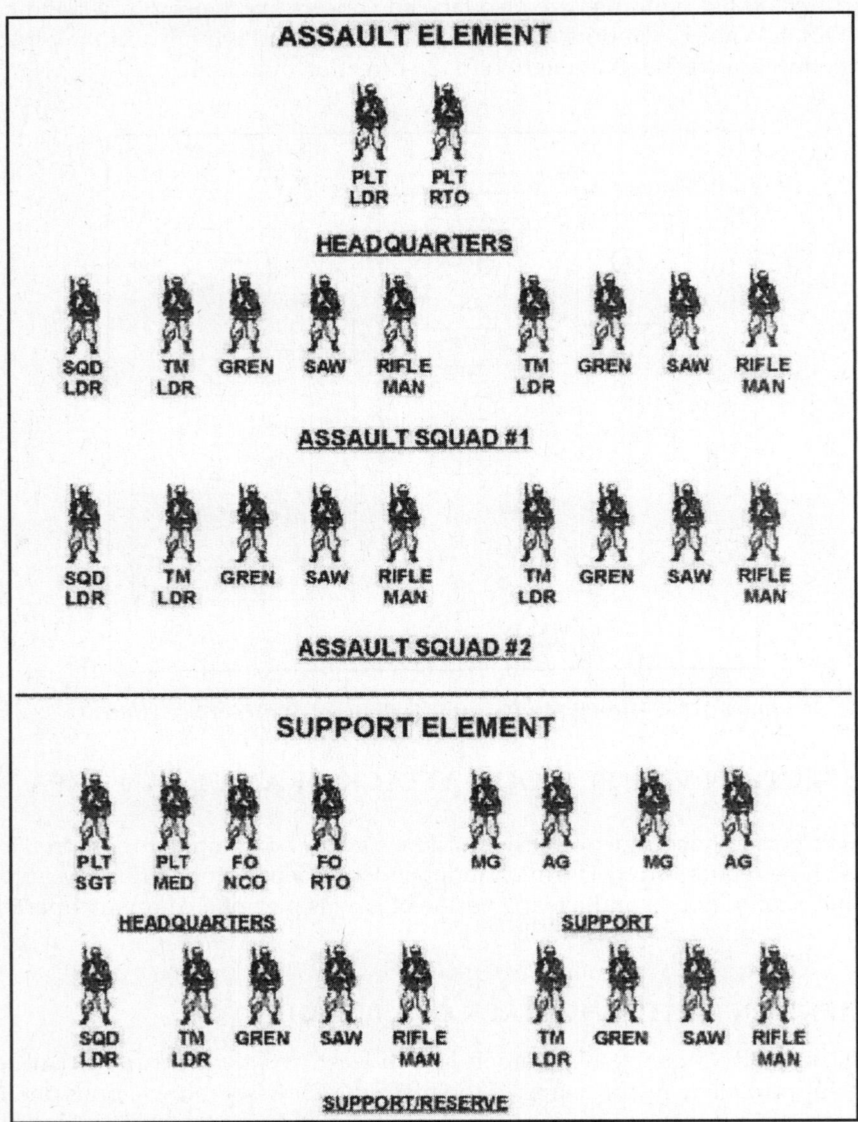

Figure 2-35: Platoon organization.

> ✍ **NOTE**
>
> Clearing techniques are designed to be executed by the standard four-man fire team. This method does not mean that all four members must enter a room to clear it. Because of the confined spaces typical of building/room clearing operations, units larger than squads quickly become awkward and unmanageable. When shortages of personnel demand it, two- and three-man teams can conduct room-clearing operations, but four-man teams are best suited. Using fewer personnel adds to the combat strain and greatly increases the risks to the team. For clearing large open buildings, such as hangars or warehouses, it may be necessary to commit two squads at the same time using a bounding overwatch movement technique to effectively cover the entire structure and provide force protection.

b. **Support Element.** The purpose of the support element (except for the medic) is to provide immediate suppressive fire support to enable the assault element to close with the enemy. Suppressive fires must be closely controlled to avoid excessive expenditure of ammunition and prevent fratricide. The support element is normally controlled by the platoon sergeant or a senior squad leader and normally consists of the platoon's crew-served weapons, light and medium antitank weapons systems, forward observer team, platoon medic, and any personnel not designated as part of the assault element (Figure 2-36). The support element provides both direct and indirect fire support and other assistance to advance the assault element. This support includes, but is not limited to, the following:

- Suppressing enemy weapons systems and obscuring the enemy's observation within the objective building and adjacent structures.
- Isolating the objective building with direct and indirect fires to prevent enemy withdrawal, reinforcement, or counterattack.
- Obscuring enemy observation of obstacles en route to the objective and at the entry point of the objective during breaching operations.
- Destroying or suppressing enemy positions with direct fire weapons.
- Engaging armored vehicles.
- Securing cleared portions of the objective.
- Providing replacements for the assault element.
- Providing the resupply of ammunition and pyrotechnics.
- Bringing up specific equipment that the assault element could not carry in the initial assault.
- Treating and evacuating casualties, prisoners, and civilians.

> ✍ **NOTE**
> The platoon sergeant must be prepared to rapidly evacuate wounded from the objective area to the company casualty collection point (CCP). The use of ground ambulances may be impeded by rubble in the streets, barricades, and demolition of roads; therefore, litter teams could be used extensively. Also, snipers can affect medical evacuation from forward positions.

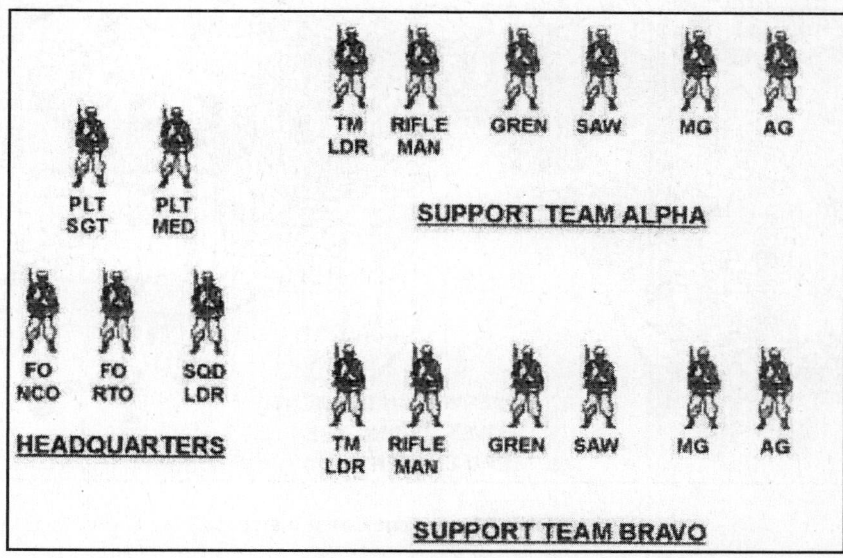

Figure 2-36: Platoon support element with squad integrated.

c. **Breaching Element.** The purpose of the breaching element is to clear and mark lanes through obstacles during movement, providing the assault element with access to an urban objective. The platoon leader organizes the force to ensure breaching elements are designated. One technique is to assign one fire team from the assault element as the breaching element. Alternatively, the breach can be conducted using an attached engineer or any member of the assault or support element who has had additional breach training.

2-43. MOVEMENT IN URBAN TERRAIN

As the lead element for the company when conducting movement, the platoon must be prepared to react to contact.

a. Platoon members must be ready to take cover and return fire immediately. They must also be alert for any signs or indications of the enemy and report promptly.
b. The rate of movement is controlled by the lead element based on the density of the urban terrain and enemy threat. In outlying or lightly defended areas, a mechanized infantry platoon may proceed along streets mounted, but send dismounted squads forward to reconnoiter key terrain (bridges, intersections or structural choke points).
c. Enemy action against the unit may come in the way of an ambush along a street, enfilade fire down the street, sniper fire from upper stories of buildings, or artillery and mortar fire when canalized. For protection from those types of threats, the platoon should move through buildings, along walls and other forms of cover, use tanks, BFV's, as well as indirect and direct fire weapons to overwatch and support movement.
d. The platoon moves using a lead maneuver element (one squad on narrow streets and two squads on wide streets). These squads will move forward along the streets using buildings for cover when possible. They will scout danger areas and close with the enemy. An overwatching element (the rest of the platoon and the supporting weapons) will follow securing the flanks and rear while providing support to the point element. At any time the platoon leader may choose to rotate the point squad with an overwatching squad (Figure 2-37).

Figure 2-37: Movement down a street.

2-44. ATTACKING IN URBAN TERRAIN

As the culminating effort of a planned (deliberate) attack, or a result of a movement to contact, a meeting engagement or a chance contact during movement, the platoon may be required to be part of a company attack or conduct a platoon attack on an urban area or building.

a. The attack involves isolating the building to prevent the reinforcing or withdrawal of its defenders (normally planned at company level); suppressing the enemy with BFVs, tanks, machine gun and mortar fire; entering the building at the least defended point; and clearing the building. There must be close coordination between the isolation/support elements and the assault elements.

b. As the lead element in the company movement formation when a chance contact is made with the enemy (hasty attack), the platoon takes the following actions:

   (1) Forward squad (or squads) will immediately return fire, get down, seek cover and suppress the enemy.

   (2) Those squads not in direct fire contact will provide supporting fire with individual and crew-served weapons (to include tanks and BFVs, if attached). Engage known, then suspected, enemy positions.

   (3) Provide a situation report to the commander.

   (4) The commander will either direct the platoon to establish a support by fire position in order to allow another platoon to assault or, if the threat is small and disorganized, he will direct the platoon in contact to conduct a platoon attack of the enemy position (subparagraph c, below).

c. When conducting a deliberate attack of an urban objective there are three steps that must be considered, planned and coordinated in order to achieve success.

- Isolate the objective.
- Enter the building (secure a foothold).
- Clear the building (room by room, floor by floor).

   (1) Isolation of the objective requires the seizing of dominant terrain in order to cut off enemy routes for reinforcing, supplying, or facilitating the withdrawal of its defenders. The intent is to completely dominate what comes and goes within the objective area and provide early warning for the assault element (Figure 2-38).

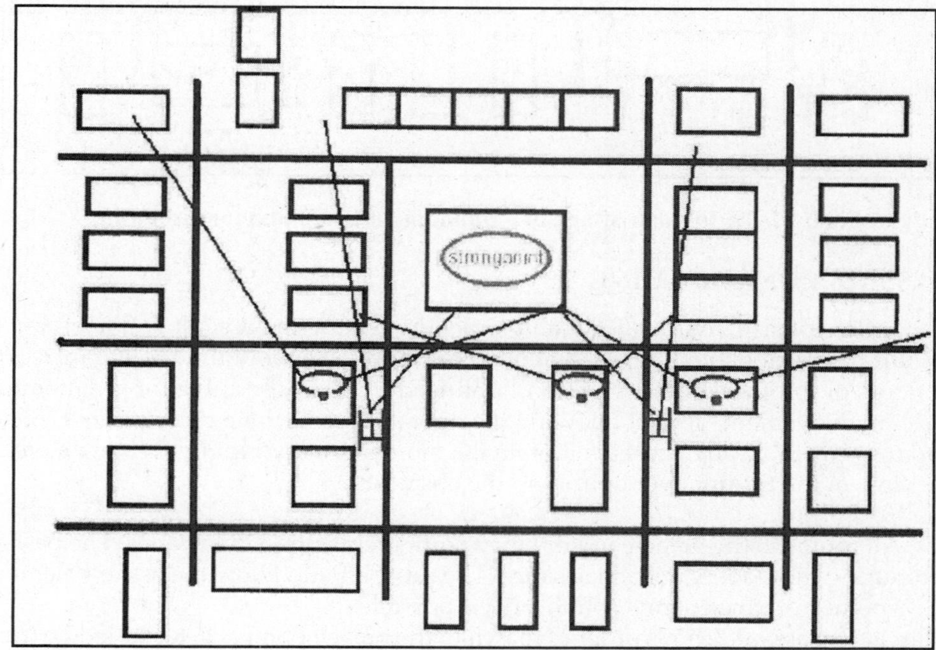

Figure 2-38: Infantry platoon with two tanks as support element, isolating the objective.

   (2) As the assault element for the company, the platoon (or platoons) is responsible for entering and clearing the objective building. This method may involve creating a breach into the building and securing a foothold as well as killing, capturing or forcing the withdrawal of all enemy personnel within the structure. Squads and teams perform room clearing. The squad leader controls the maneuver of the two fire teams as they clear along hallways, stairways, and in rooms. (See Chapter 1.) The platoon leader alternates the squads as required, and maintains momentum, and ensures resupply of ammunition and water.

d. If a platoon is conducting an assault of a building independently, it should be organized with an assault element and a support element (Figure 2-39). The assault element, usually led by the platoon leader, normally consists of two squads with two fire teams each. The support element, usually controlled by the platoon sergeant, normally consists of one rifle squad equipped with antitank weapons, two medium machine gun crews, and attached forward observers. The support element must designate individuals to provide flank and rear security. In addition to its own support element, BFVs, tanks, and other company assets can support the platoon.

NOTE

Isolation of the surrounding area in conducted by the rest of the company.

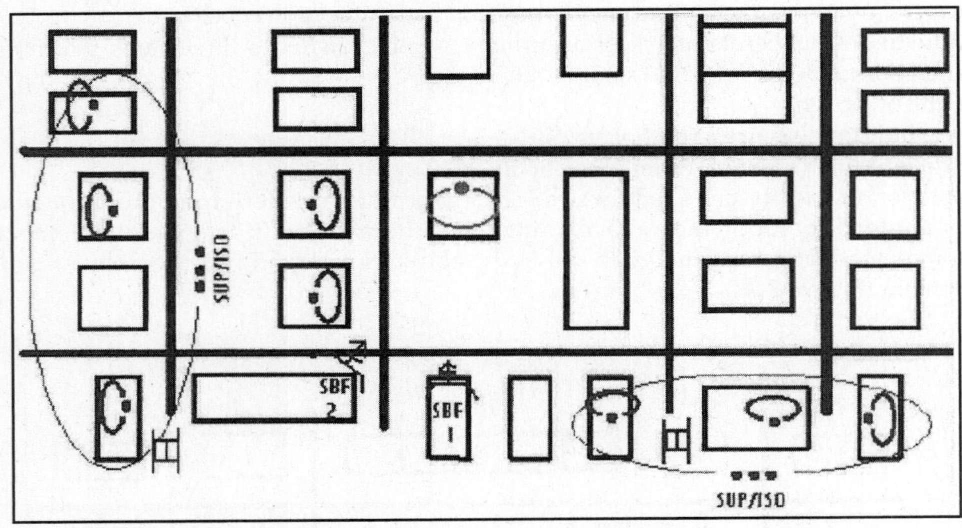

Figure 2-39: Platoon attack of a building with two platoons isolating.

2-45. PLATOON ASSAULT OF A BUILDING

The assault force, regardless of size, must quickly and violently execute the assault and subsequent clearing operations. Once momentum has been gained, it is maintained to deny the enemy time to organize a more determined resistance on other floors or in other rooms. The small unit leaders are responsible for maintaining the momentum of the assault, controlling movement, yet not allowing the operation to become disorganized. Enemy obstacles may slow or stop forward movement. Leaders must maintain the momentum by rapidly creating a breach in the obstacle, or by redirecting the flow of the assault over or around the obstacles.

a. **Approaches.** All routes to the breach and or entry point are planned in advance. The best route is confirmed and selected during the leaders' reconnaissance. The route should allow the assault element to approach the breach (entry) point from the enemy's blind side, if possible.
b. **Order of March.** The assault team's order of march to the breach point is determined by the method of breach and their intended actions at the breach (entry) point. This preparation must be completed prior to or in the last covered and concealed location before reaching the breach (entry) point. Establishing an order of march is done to aid the team leader with C2 and to minimize exposure time in open areas and at the entry point. An order of march technique is to number the assault team 1, 2, 3, and 4. The number 1 man should always be responsible for frontal/door security. If the breach has been conducted prior to their arrival the assault team quickly moves through the breach (entry) point. If a breach has not been made prior to their arrival at the breach (entry) point, and depending on the type of breach to be made, the team leader conducts the breach himself or signals forward the breach man/element. One option is to designate the squad leader as the breach man. If the breach man is part of the assault team, he is normally the last of the four men to enter the building or room. This method allows him to transition from his breaching task to his combat role.

(1) ***Ballistic Breach (Shot Gun).*** A suggested order of movement for a ballistic (shot gun) breach has the gunner up front, followed by the number 1 man, number 2 man, and then the number 3 man (team leader). After the door is breached, the gunner moves to the rear of the lineup and assumes the position of the number 4 man.

(2) ***Explosive Breach.*** A suggested order of movement for an explosive breach without engineer support is; number 1, number 3 (team leader), number 2, and then number 4 man. The number 1 man provides security at the entry point. The number 3 man (team leader) carries the demolition charge and places it. Number 4 provides rear security. After the demolition charge is placed, team members re-form in the original configuration and take cover around a corner or behind other protection. Team members can line up on either or both sides if there is adequate protection from the blast.

(3) ***Mechanical Breach.*** A suggested order of movement for a mechanical breach is the initial assault team in order, followed by the breach man/element. At the breach point the team leader will bring the breach element forward while the assault team provides local security. After the breach is made, the breach element moves aside and provides local security as the assault team enters the breach.

c. **Security.** Because of the three-dimensional threat associated with urban terrain, the assault element must maintain 360-degree security during movement to the breach (entry) point. If the assault element is to stop in the vicinity of the breach (entry) point to wait for the breach element to complete its task, the support element must maintain suppressive fire to protect the assault element.

d. **Assault Locations.** Entry at the top and fighting downward is the preferred method of clearing a building. This method forces the defenders down and out of the building where the support element can engage them. This method is only feasible, however, when access to an upper floor or rooftop can be gained from the windows or roofs of adjoining, secured buildings. Rooftops are treated as danger areas when surrounded by higher buildings from which enemy forces could engage the assault element. Helicopters should land only on those buildings that have a roof structure that can support their weight. If the structure cannot support the helicopter, soldiers can dismount as the helicopter hovers a few feet above the roof. Troops then breach the roof or common walls to gain entrance into the building. (If using explosives on the rooftop, ensure cover is available to the soldiers.) They may use ropes or other means to enter the lower floors through the holes created.

> ✍ **NOTE**
>
> Soldiers should consider the use of devices and techniques that allow them upper level access without using interior stairways. These devices and techniques include, but are not limited to, adjacent rooftops, fire escapes, portable ladders, and various soldier-assisted lifts.

e. **Support Element.** The support element isolates the building with direct and indirect fires to support the assault element's move to the breach point. The support element covers mounted avenues of approach with antiarmor weapons, covers dismounted avenues of approach with automatic weapons, and suppresses enemy fires and neutralizes enemy positions to enable the breach team and assault element to move into position. The location of adjacent units must be considered in the emplacement of supporting fires.

(1) The support element uses smoke to obscure the movement of the breach team and assault element to the building. If possible, the smoke obscuration is maintained until the assault element has entered the building.

(2) Depending upon the ROE, just before the rush of the assault element, the support element increases suppressive fires on the objective and continues until masked by the advancing assault element. Once masked, fires are shifted to upper or lower windows and continued until the assault element has entered the building. At that time, fires are shifted to adjacent buildings to prevent enemy withdrawal or reinforcement.

(3) If the ROE are very restrictive, the use of supporting fires may be restricted to known enemy locations that have engaged the unit.

(4) The support element must also deal with civilians displaced by the assault, EPWs, and casualties.

2-46. CONSOLIDATION AND REORGANIZATION

The squad and platoon will conduct consolidation and reorganization immediately after each action where soldiers are engaged and ammunition is expended. Consolidation is the action taken by the squad or platoon to ensure its security, to prepare for a counterattack by the enemy, and to prepare to continue the mission. Consolidation in an urban environment must be quick in order to repel enemy counterattacks and to prevent the enemy from infiltrating back into cleared buildings or floors. After securing a floor (bottom, middle, or top), selected members of the unit are assigned to cover potential enemy counterattack routes to the building. Priority must be given initially to securing the direction of attack. Security elements alert the unit and place a heavy volume of fire on enemy forces approaching the unit. Reorganization occurs after consolidation. These actions prepare the unit to continue the mission by ensuring key leadership positions are filled and important weapon systems are manned. Many reorganization actions occur simultaneously during the consolidation of the objective.

a. **Consolidation Actions.** Squads assume hasty defensive positions to gain security immediately after the objective has been seized or cleared. Squads that performed missions as assault elements should be prepared to assume an overwatch mission and to support another assault element. Units must guard all avenues of approach leading into their area. These may include:
   - Enemy mouse-holes between adjacent buildings.
   - Covered routes to the building.
   - Underground routes into the basement.
   - Approaches over adjoining roofs.

b. **Reorganization Actions.** After consolidation, leaders ensure the following actions are taken:
   - Resupply and redistribute ammunition.
   - Mark buildings to indicate to friendly forces that they have been cleared.
   - Treat and evacuate wounded personnel. Once the objective area is secure, begin evacuating noncombatants then enemy wounded.
   - Process EPWs.
   - Segregate and safeguard noncombatants.
   - Reestablish the chain of command.

c. **Continuation of the Assault**. If the unit is going to continue with its original mission, its "be prepared/on order" mission, or receives a new mission, it must accomplish the following:
   (1) The momentum must be maintained. Keeping momentum is a critical factor in clearing operations. The enemy is not allowed to move to its next set of prepared positions or to prepare new positions.
   (2) The support element pushes replacements, ammunition, and supplies forward to the assault element.
   (3) Security for cleared areas must be established IAW the OPORD or TACSOP.
   (4) The support element must displace forward to ensure that it is in place to provide support to the assault element, such as isolation of the new objective.

CHAPTER 3

Defensive Operations

"[Captain] Liebschev prepared his defenses with extraordinary thoroughness, choosing only to defend the northern half of the town. The southern half was turned into a nightmare of trapped and mined houses some of which were blown into the streets to form road blocks and others were blown up to clear arcs of fire. All his strong points were linked by what is best described as 'mouse holing' from house to house. All approaches to the defended sector were either heavily mined or under concealed enfilade fire. The main approach into the town square was left attractively unobstructed…The 2nd Canadian Brigade was given the task of clearing a way through the town and was forced to fight its way from house to house on not more than a 250-yard front. Every building, when taken, had to be occupied to stop the Germans infiltrating back into it again after the leading troops had passed on. The fighting was at such close quarters that artillery support was impossible…"

Extracted from *The Battle for Italy*
By General W. G. F. Jackson

SECTION I. DEFENSIVE CONSIDERATIONS

Full spectrum operations require that units be prepared to defend in urban areas. Before making a decision to defend urban areas, commanders at all levels should consider the issues discussed in this chapter.

3-1. REASONS FOR DEFENDING URBAN AREAS

The worldwide increase in urban sprawl has made it virtually impossible for forces conducting operations to avoid cities and towns. For various reasons, these areas must be defended.

a. Certain urban areas contain strategic industrial, transportation, or economic complexes that must be defended. Capitals and cultural centers may be defended for strictly psychological or national morale purposes even when they do not offer a tactical advantage to the defender. Because of the sprawl of such areas, significant combat power is required for their defense. The decision to defend these complexes is made by political authorities or the theater commander.

b. The defenders' need to shift and concentrate combat power, and to move large amounts of supplies over a wide battle area may require retention of vital transportation centers. Since most transportation centers serve large areas, the commander must defend the urban area to control such centers.

c. Most avenues of approach are straddled by small towns every few kilometers and must be controlled by defending forces. These areas can be used as battle positions or strongpoints. Blocked streets covered by mortar and or artillery fire can canalize attacking armor into mined areas or zones covered by antiarmor fire. If an attacker tries to bypass an urban area, he may encounter an array of tank-killing weapons. To clear such an area, the attacker must sacrifice speed and momentum, and expend many resources. A city or town can easily become a major obstacle.

d. A well-trained force defending an urban area can inflict major losses on a numerically superior attacker. The defender can conserve the bulk of his combat power so it is available for use in open terrain. The defenders remaining in urban areas perform an economy-of-force role.

e. Aerial photography, imagery, and sensory devices cannot detect forces deployed in cities. Well-emplaced CPs, reserves, CSS complexes, and combat forces are hard to detect.

3-2. REASONS FOR NOT DEFENDING URBAN AREAS

Reasons for not defending urban areas include the following:

a. The location of the urban area does not support the overall defensive plan. If the urban area is too far forward or back in a unit's defensive sector, is isolated, or is not astride an enemy's expected avenue of approach, the commander may choose not to defend it.
b. Nearby terrain allows the enemy to bypass on covered or concealed routes. Some urban areas, mainly smaller ones, are bypassed by main road and highway systems.
c. Structures within the urban area do not adequately protect the defenders. Extensive areas of lightly built or flammable structures offer little protection. Urban areas near flammable or hazardous industrial areas, such as refineries or chemical plants, should not be defended because of increased danger of fire to the defenders.
d. Dominating terrain is close to the urban area. If the urban area can be dominated by an enemy force occupying this terrain, the commander may choose to defend from there rather than the urban area. This applies mainly to small urban areas such as a village.
e. Better fields of fire exist outside the urban area. The commander may choose to base all or part of his defense on long-range fields of fire outside an urban area. This applies mainly to armor-heavy forces defending sectors with multiple, small, urban areas surrounded by open terrain, such as agricultural areas with villages.
f. The urban area has cultural, religious, or historical significance. The area may have been declared an "open city" in which case, by international law, it is demilitarized and must be neither defended nor attacked. The attacking force must assume civil administrative control and treat the civilians as noncombatants in an occupied country. The defender must immediately evacuate and cannot arm the civilian population. A city can be declared open only before it is attacked. The presence of large numbers of noncombatants, hospitals, or wounded personnel may also affect the commander's decision not to defend an urban area.

3-3. GENERAL CONSIDERATIONS

The basic fundamentals of defense do not change in an urban environment. In urban combat, the defender does possess key advantages over the attacker. The defender can shape the battlefield by maximizing the natural restrictions and obstacles found in the restrictive terrain of the urban environment. U.S. forces may not wish to inflict collateral damage on the urban terrain they are defending but the very nature of conducting an urban defense may lead to high-intensity conditions on the urban battlefield and to extensive collateral damage. Typically, U.S. forces should not expect enemy forces attacking in urban terrain to be bound by restrictive ROE and should therefore not expect to accrue any of the advantages that a defender might have if the attacker is restricted in the application of force.

SECTION II. MISSION, ENEMY, TERRAIN, TROOPS AND TIME AVAILABLE, CIVIL CONSIDERATIONS

The defense of an urban area should be organized around key terrain features, buildings, and areas that preserve the integrity of the defense and provide the defender ease of movement. The defender must organize and plan his defense considering factors of mission, enemy, terrain, troops and time available, and civil considerations (METT-TC). Procedures and principles for planning and organizing the defense of an urban area are the same as for other defensive operations. In developing a defensive plan, the defender considers METT-TC factors with emphasis on fire support, preparation time, work priorities, and control measures. Planning for the defense of an urban area must be detailed and centralized. As in the offense, execution is decentralized as the battle develops, and the enemy forces assault the buildings and rooms. Therefore, it is imperative that all leaders understand the mission end-state and the commanders' intent, two levels up.

3-4. MISSION

Commanders and leaders must receive, analyze, and understand the mission before they begin planning. They may receive the mission as a FRAGO or as a formal OPORD, and must analyze all specified and implied tasks. Depending on mission requirements, an infantry unit at brigade and battalion level must be prepared to defend as part of a larger force or independently; companies and below normally defend as part of a larger force. Mission analysis for defense in urban terrain will essentially be the same as for other defensive operations. Detailed IPB is essential and must include building construction; routes, including underground systems; civilian communications; and utilities. A hasty defense may be conducted in any of the defensive situations described in this chapter, immediately after offensive operations, or when a higher state of security is warranted during stability operations or support operations. The major difference between a hasty defense and a deliberate defense is in the amount of time for preparation. Similar to offensive operations, units must be prepared to transition to offensive or stability and support missions, and back.

3-5. ENEMY

Units must also analyze the type of enemy force they may encounter. If the attacker is mostly dismounted infantry, the greatest danger is allowing him to gain a foothold. If the attacker is mostly armor or mounted motorized infantry, the greatest danger is that he will mass direct fire and destroy the defender's positions. If the threat is primarily asymmetrical, force protection measures must be enhanced.

3-6. TERRAIN AND WEATHER

Specific defensive considerations are discussed in this paragraph. Terrain in urban areas is three-dimensional; the defender must make use of the entire battle space:

- Surface (ground level, for example streets and parks).
- Supersurface (buildings, both interior and exterior).
- Subterranean (subways and sewers).

Analysis of all man-made and natural terrain features is critical when planning to defend in urban terrain. The type of urban area in which it will be operating affects the unit's defensive plan.

a. **Observation and Fields of Fire.** Although concealment and cover will be plentiful, observation will be limited. Attacking forces generally advance by crossing streets and open areas between buildings where they are exposed to fires from concealed positions.

(1) ***Weapons and Range.*** Units must position weapons to obtain maximum effect and mutual supporting fire. This allows for long-range engagements out to the maximum effective ranges. FOs should be well above street level to adjust fires on the enemy at maximum range. Observed fire will be very difficult in densely constructed areas. Fires and FPFs should be preplanned and, if possible and ROE permit, preregistered on the most likely approaches to allow for their rapid shifting to threatened areas.

(2) ***Limited Visibility.*** Units can expect the attacker to use limited visibility conditions to conduct necessary operations to sustain or gain daylight momentum. The following should be considered:

- Unoccupied areas that can be observed and covered by fire during daylight may have to be occupied or patrolled at night.
- Remote sensors and early warning devices should be employed in dead space and on avenues of approach.
- The artificial illumination available in urban terrain should be considered for use during the defense.

Responding to night probes with direct fire weapons should be avoided, as this gives away the location of the positions.

b. **Cover and Concealment.** Battle positions should be prepared using the protective cover of walls, floors, and ceilings. Units will continue to improve positions using materials on hand. Units prepare the terrain for movement between positions and can reduce exposure by—

- Using prepared breaches through buildings.
- Moving through reconnoitered and marked subterranean systems.
- Using trenches.
- Using the concealment offered by smoke and darkness to cross open areas.

c. **Obstacles.** An urban area is by its very nature an obstacle and or an obstruction. The series of man-made structures inherent in urban terrain canalizes and impedes an attack.

d. **Key Terrain.** Key terrain is any place where seizure, retention, or control affords a marked advantage to either enemy or friendly forces. Primary examples of key terrain are ports, airfields, bridges over canals or rivers, building complexes, or parks. Urban areas are unusual in that the population of the area itself may be considered key terrain. The identification of key terrain allows the defender to select his defensive positions and assists in determining the enemy's objectives. A special kind of key terrain is the nodes that are found in urban areas. These include governmental centers, power distribution facilities, and communication hubs. These nodes may have to be protected by the defender from asymmetrical as well as conventional threats.

(1) ***Villages.*** Villages are often on choke points in valleys, dominating the only high-speed avenue of approach through the terrain (Figure 3-1). If the buildings in such a village are well constructed and provide good protection against both direct and indirect fires, a formidable defense can be mounted by placing a company in the town, while controlling close and dominating terrain with other battalion task force elements.

Figure 3-1: Village.

(2) ***Strip Areas.*** Strip areas consist of houses, stores, and factories and are built along roads or down valleys between towns and villages (Figure 3-2). They afford the defender the same advantages as villages. If visibility is good and enough effective fields of fire are available, a unit acting as a security force need occupy only a few strong positions spread out within the strip. This will deceive the enemy, when engaged at long ranges, into thinking the strip is an extensive defensive line. Strip areas often afford covered avenues of withdrawal to the flanks once the attacking force is deployed and before the security force becomes decisively engaged.

Figure 3-2: Strip area.

(3) ***Towns and Small Cities.*** Small forces can gain an advantage in combat power when defending a small city or town (Figure 3-3) that is a choke point if it places tanks, BFVs, TOWs, Javelins, and Dragons on positions dominating critical approaches, when facing a predominantly armored enemy. To deny the enemy the ability to bypass the town or city, the defending force must control key terrain and coordinate with adjacent forces. Reserve forces should be placed where they can quickly reinforce critical areas. Obstacles and minefields assist in slowing and canalizing the attacker.

Figure 3-3: Towns and small cities.

(4) ***Large Cities.*** In large cities, units must consider that the terrain is restrictive due to large buildings that are normally close together (Figure 3-4). This situation requires a higher density of troops and smaller defensive sectors than in natural open terrain. Units occupy defensive frontages about one-third the size of those in open areas.

Figure 3-4: Large cities.

e. **Avenues of Approach.** The defender must not only consider the surface (streets, boulevards, parks) avenues of approach into and out of the urban area, but also supersurface (interior and exterior of buildings) and subterranean avenues of approach. The defender normally has the advantage. He knows the urban area and can move rapidly from position to position through buildings and underground passages. Control of these above- and below-ground avenues of approach becomes more critical when the defense of nodes must be oriented against terrorism and sabotage.

3-7. TIME AVAILABLE

Units must organize and establish priorities of work, depending upon the time available. Many tasks can be accomplished simultaneously, but priorities for preparation should be in accordance with the commander's order. A sample priority of work sequence follows:

- Establish security and communications.
- Assign sectors of responsibility and final protective fires.
- Clear fields of fire.
- Select and prepare initial fighting positions.
- Establish and mark routes between positions.
- Emplace obstacles and mines.
- Improve fighting positions.

3-8. TROOPS AVAILABLE

The defensive employment of troops in urban areas is governed by all METT-TC factors and on the ROE. The defender has a terrain advantage and can resist the attacker with much smaller forces.

SECTION III. DEFENSIVE FRAMEWORK AND ORGANIZATION

This section discusses the defensive framework and organization used during the planning and execution of defensive UO.

3-9. DEFENSIVE FRAMEWORK

Similar to offensive operations, the brigade will be the primary headquarters that will be task-organized to conduct defensive urban operations. The brigade can conduct the full range of defensive operations within a single urban area or in an AO that contains several small towns and cities using the elements shown in the defensive urban operational framework in Figure 3-5. The elements are similar to those in offensive operations in that the brigade commander attempts to set the conditions for tactical success. Isolation of the brigade by the enemy is avoided through security operations; defensive missions are assigned subordinate task forces in order to achieve the commander's intent and desired end-state; and then the brigade transitions to stability and or support operations. During urban defensive operations, the transition to stability and support operations may not be clear to the soldiers conducting the operations. Commanders must offset this tendency with clear mission type orders and updated ROE. Again, as in offensive operations, the elements are not phases. They may occur simultaneously or sequentially. Well planned and executed defensive operations will have all four elements present. During defensive operations the brigade commander seeks to:

- Avoid being isolated by the enemy.
- Defend only the decisive terrain, institutions, or infrastructure.
- Conduct counter or spoiling attacks to retain the initiative.

Battalion TFs and below conducts defensive operations by conducting counterreconnaissance missions and patrols (shaping/avoiding isolation); assigning battle positions or sectors to subordinate units (dominating); and consolidating/reorganizing and preparing for follow-on missions (transitioning).

3-10. COMMAND AND CONTROL

In all defensive situations, commanders should position themselves well forward so that they can control the action. In urban terrain, this is even more critical due to obstacles, poor visibility, difficulty in communication, and intense fighting. Other key leaders may be placed in positions to report to the commander and to make critical, time-sensitive decisions.

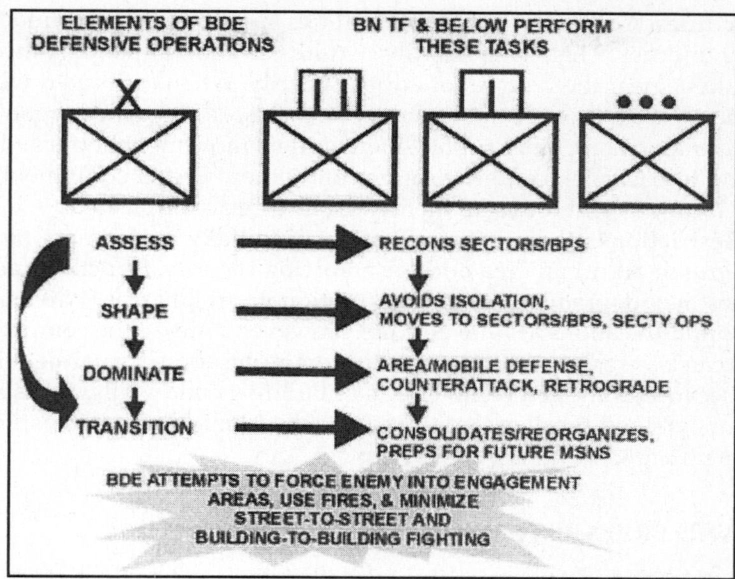

Figure 3-5: Defensive urban operational framework.

a. **Graphic Control Measures.** The use of graphic control measures to synchronize actions become even more important to mission accomplishment in an urban environment (Figure 3-6). Phase lines can be used to report the enemy's location or to control the advance of counterattacking units. Principal streets, rivers, and railroad lines are suitable phase lines, which should be clearly and uniformly marked on the near or far side of the street or open area. Checkpoints aid in reporting locations and controlling movement. Contact points are used to designate specific points where units make physical contact. Target reference points (TRPs) can facilitate fire control. Many of these points can be designated street intersections. These and other control measures ensure coordination throughout the chain of command.

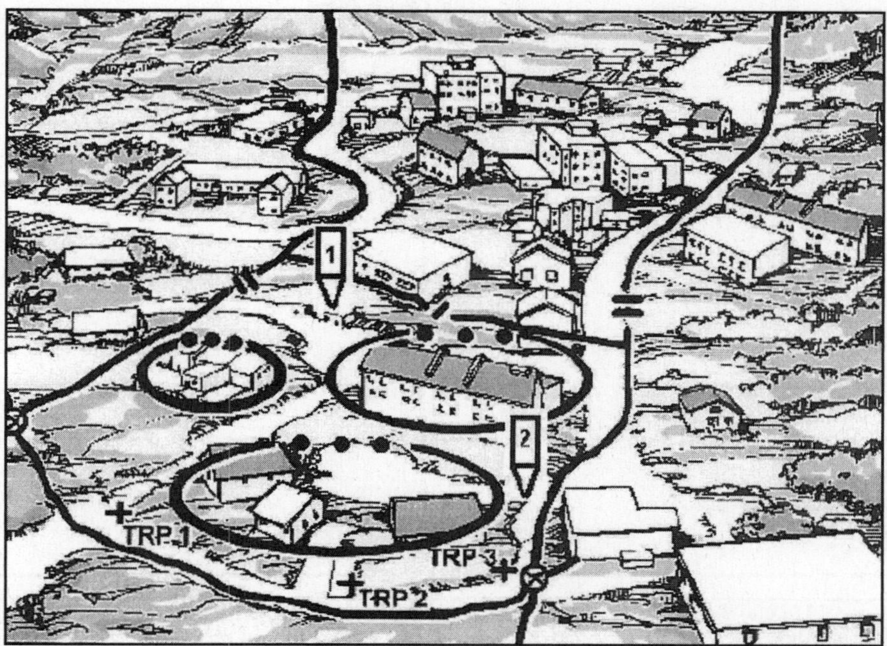

Figure 3-6: Graphic control measures.

b. **Command Post Facilities.** Command post (CP) facilities should be located underground, if possible, or in solidly constructed buildings. Their vulnerability requires all-round security. Since each facility may have to secure itself, it should be near the reserve for added security. When collocated with another unit, command post facilities may not need to provide their own security. Also, a simplified organization for command posts is required for ease of movement. Since rubble often hinders movement of tracked and wheeled vehicles, the CP must be prepared to backpack communications and other needed equipment for operations. Identification of alternate CP locations and routes to them must also be accomplished.

c. **Communications Restrictions.** Radio communications is initially the primary means of communication for controlling the defense of an urban area and for enforcing security. Structures and a high concentration of electrical power lines may degrade radio communication in urban areas. Wire is emplaced and used as the primary means of communications as time permits. However, wire can be compromised if interdicted by the enemy. Messengers can be used as another means of communication. Visual signals may also be used but are often not effective because of the screening effects of buildings and walls. Signals must be planned, widely disseminated, and understood by all assigned and attached units. Increased battle noise makes the effective use of sound signals difficult.

3-11. ORGANIZATION AND PREPARATION OF THE DEFENSE

The defensive organization described in this paragraph will likely be used against a conventional enemy force that may threaten U.S. forces with mechanized and dismounted Infantry supported by other combined arms. This defensive organization may also occur in a brigade area of operation (AO) where there are multiple threats. For example, one part of the AO may require linear features; other parts may require the use of other defensive techniques, such as a perimeter defense, against different types of threats in the same brigade AO. METT-TC factors and the ROE determine how units plan, prepare, and execute the defense. The defense is organized into three areas—the security force area, main battle area, and rear area (Figure 3-7). Units defending in urban areas may have missions in any one of these areas, depending on the nature of the operation. Infantry units are well suited to conduct defensive operations in close urban terrain where engagement ranges will be short, where there is abundant cover and concealment, and where the enemy's assault must be repelled.

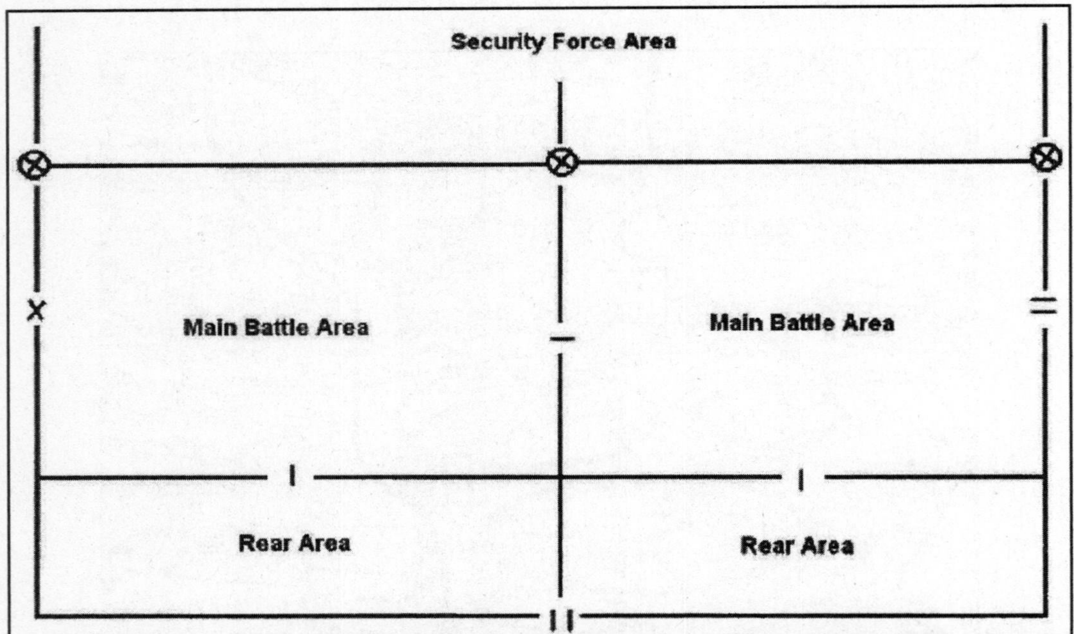

Figure 3-7: Organization of the defense.

a. **Patterns of Defense.** Of the two patterns of defense, area and mobile, the area defense will probably be the pattern most used since many of the reasons for defending on urban terrain are focused on retaining terrain. The mobile defense pattern is more focused on the enemy and the commander may decide to use it based on his estimate of the situation. Many defenses may include a combination of both. In large urban areas, the concept of defensive operations may be mobile and exploit depth, with the defender concentrating on moving forces from key terrain features or buildings to other similar features. The defender must seek to disrupt the enemy throughout all phases of battle.

b. **General Concept of the Defense.** Planning of the defense must be detailed and centralized while execution is decentralized. In an urban area, the defender must take advantage of inherent cover and concealment afforded by the urban terrain. He must also consider restrictions to the attacker's ability to maneuver and observe. By using the terrain and fighting from well-prepared and mutually supporting positions, a defending force can inflict heavy losses on, delay, block, or fix a much larger attacking force. The defense of an urban area should be organized around key terrain features, buildings, and areas that preserve the integrity of the defense and that provide the defender ease of movement. The defender must organize and plan his defense by considering obstacles, avenues of approach, key terrain, observation and fields of fire, cover and concealment, (OCOKA) and the considerations in this paragraph. Detailed knowledge of the terrain by the defender allows him to force an attacker to expend exorbitant amounts of time, supplies, equipment, and manpower.

(1) ***Reconnaissance.*** To obtain the detailed knowledge that they need, the commanders and staffs need to conduct a reconnaissance of the defensive area. The amount of time spent and the level of detail obtained will vary greatly between a deliberate defense and a hasty defense. The defender must identify the following:

- Positions that enable him to place suppressive fires on the enemy.
- Covered and concealed routes for friendly elements to move between positions (subways and sewers).
- Structures that dominate large areas.
- Areas such as parks, boulevards, rivers, highways, and railroads where antiarmor weapons have fields of fire.
- Firing positions for mortars.
- Command locations that offer cover, concealment, and ease of command and control.
- Protected storage areas for supplies.

(2) ***Security Operations.*** The defensive battle normally begins with a combined arms force conducting security operations well forward of the main body. Operations consist of security, reconnaissance, and counterreconnaissance tasks. Counterreconnaissance missions to support these operations employ ambushes, mines, obstacles, deception, security patrols, OPs, indirect fires, camouflage, demonstrations, and other measures to destroy or deceive the enemy's reconnaissance elements. Again, urban areas are well suited for infantry counterreconnaissance operations because of the abundance of cover and concealment that permits infantry to move by stealth.

c. **Main Battle Area.** The decisive battle is usually fought in the main battle area (MBA). Depending on the threat, units can deploy on the forward edges of the urban area or in battle positions in depth. In either case, the defense is made stronger by including forces that are defending on close terrain or on the flanks into the defensive scheme.

(1) ***Size of Battle Positions.*** The size and location of battle positions within the area of operations depends mainly on the type of enemy encountered and the ability to move between positions to block threatened areas. It may be desirable to place small antiarmor elements, secured by infantry, on the forward edges while the main defense is deployed in depth.

(2) ***Considerations.*** Defensive positions on the forward edge of a city or town should:

- Provide early warning of the enemy's advance.
- Engage the enemy at long range.
- Deceive the enemy as to the true location of the defense.

(3) ***Sectors.*** Depending on the factors of METT-TC, units may also assign sectors to defend instead of battle positions. In certain instances, the units may employ both. Sectors would normally be assigned when blocks and streets provide a grid type pattern and boundaries can be clearly delineated.

(4) ***Frontages.*** Infantry units will normally occupy less terrain in urban areas. For example, an infantry company, which might occupy 1,500 to 2,000 meters in open terrain, is usually restricted to a frontage of

300 to 800 meters in urban areas. The density of buildings and rubble and street patterns will dictate the frontage of the unit (Table 3-1).

Table 3-1: Approximate frontages and depths in large urban areas.

UNIT	FRONTAGES	DEPTHS
Battalion or Battalion TF	4 to 8 blocks	3 to 6 blocks
Company or Company Team	2 to 4 blocks	2 to 3 blocks
Platoon	1 to 2 blocks	1 block
NOTE: An average city block has a frontage of about 175 meters. These minimum figures apply in areas of dense, block-type construction; multistory buildings; and underground passages.		

(5) ***Selection of Buildings.*** Buildings that add most to the general plan of defense are chosen for occupation. Mutual support between these positions is vital to prevent the attacker from maneuvering and outflanking positions, making them untenable. Buildings chosen for occupation as defensive positions should:

- Offer good protection.
- Have strong floors to keep the structure from collapsing under the weight of debris.
- Have thick walls.
- Be constructed of nonflammable materials (avoid wood).
- Be strategically located (corner buildings and prominent structures).
- Be adjacent to streets, alleys, vacant lots, and park sites. These buildings usually provide better fields of fire and are more easily tied in with other buildings.
- Be covered by friendly fire and offer good escape routes.

(6) ***Occupation of Positions.*** See paragraph 3-11 and Chapter 1, Section IV.

(7) ***Obstacles.*** Obstacles are easily constructed in an urban area. An urban area itself is an obstacle since it canalizes and impedes an attack. Likely avenues of approach should be blocked by obstacles and covered by fire (Figure 3-8). Units must hinder or prevent enemy maneuver without interfering with its own maneuver elements. Therefore, the battalion usually detonates cratering charges at key street locations on order. Mines are laid on the outskirts of the urban area or the sector and along routes the unit will not use. Barriers and obstacles are normally emplaced in three belts, consistent with the ROE. All avenues of approach (three-dimensional) must be denied. Units must not overlook the use of field-expedient materials, such as cars, light poles, and so on, or the emplacement of command-detonated antipersonnel mines and antitank mines. Commanders must clearly understand the ROE and what they will be permitted to emplace. When necessary, obstacles can be emplaced without mines and covered by fire.

(a) *First Belt.* The first obstacle belt is at the nearest buildings across from and parallel to the main defensive position (MDP). This belt consists of wire and improvised barriers to include: building interiors, subterranean avenues of approach, and exterior areas, such as open areas, danger areas, and dead space. The barriers and obstacles are covered by long-range fires. This belt impedes enemy movement, breaks up and disorganizes attack formations, and inflicts casualties and is protective in nature.

(b) *Second Belt.* The second obstacle belt is placed between the first belt and the MDP buildings, but out of hand grenade range from defensive positions. It impedes movement, canalizes the enemy into the best fields of fire, breaks up attack formations, and inflicts casualties. This belt is not meant to stop enemy soldiers permanently. It should be constructed efficiently to give the most benefit—not to be an impenetrable wall. It consists mainly of wire obstacles, improvised barriers, road craters, and mine fields. It should include command-detonated Claymores. Triple-strand concertina is placed along the machine gun final protective line (FPL), as marked earlier IAW unit SOP, to slow the enemy on the FPL and to allow the machine gun to be used effectively.

(c) *Third Belt.* The third obstacle belt is the defensive position's denial belt. It consists of wire obstacles placed around, through, and in the defensive buildings and close-in mine fields as well as in

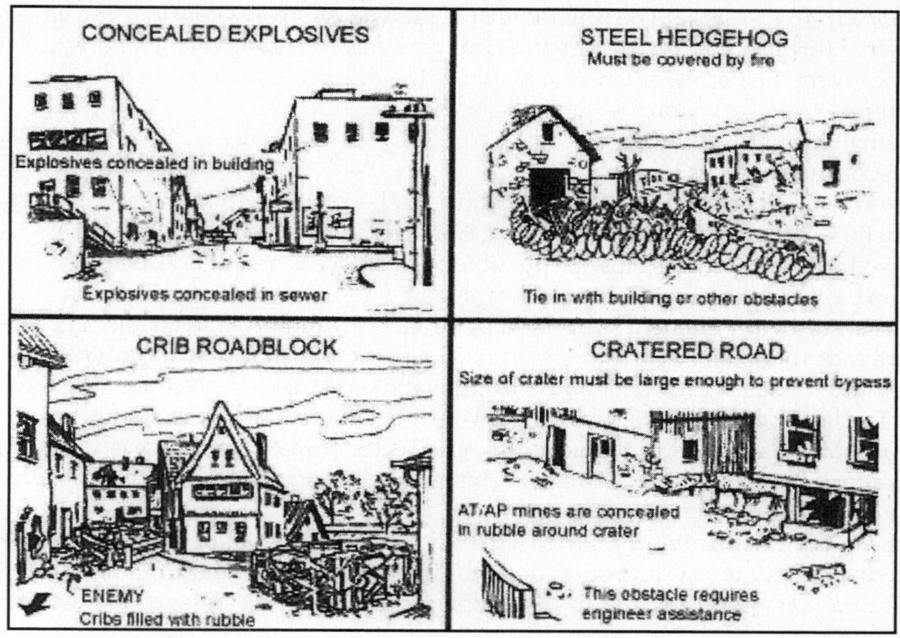

Figure 3-8: Example of urban obstacles.

subterranean accesses. It impedes and complicates the enemy's ability to gain a foothold in the defensive area. Command-detonated Claymores should be used extensively. Claymores should be placed so as not to cause friendly casualties when detonated.

(8) ***Rubbling.*** If they have the authority and the ROE permit, commanders also decide if buildings should be rubbled to increase fields of fire. However, rubbling the buildings too soon or rubbling too many may disclose exact locations and destroy cover from direct fire. Because rubbling may take more resources than are available to units, careful consideration of available resources must be made prior to rubbling. Additionally, care must be taken not to rubble areas that are necessary to support operations, such as MSRs. Buildings are normally rubbled with engineer assistance; engineers will usually employ explosives and engineer equipment to accomplish this task. If available, armored vehicles can be used to rubble buildings.

(9) ***Fire Hazards.*** The defender's detailed knowledge of the terrain permits him to avoid areas that are likely to be fire hazards. All urban areas are vulnerable to fire, especially those with many wooden buildings. The defender can deliberately set fires—

- To disrupt and disorganize the attackers.
- To canalize the attackers into more favorable engagement areas.
- To obscure the attacker's observation.

Likewise, the enemy may cause fires to confuse, disrupt, or constrain friendly forces and efforts. Units should anticipate this possibility and ensure that fire-fighting equipment is on hand when conducting these types of operations. Battalion S4s can move sand and water to buildings. The S5 can coordinate for usage of local fire-fighting equipment. Defensive positions should not be located atop known gas lines, oil storage tanks, or other highly flammable areas.

(10) ***Actions on Contact.*** When enemy forces enter and maneuver to seize initial objectives, the defender should employ all available fires to destroy and suppress the direct-fire weapons that support the ground attack. Tanks and enemy APCs should be engaged as soon as they come within the effective range of antiarmor weapons. As the enemy attack develops, the actions of small-unit leaders assume increased importance. Squad and platoon leaders are often responsible for fighting independent battles. Thus, it is important that all leaders understand their commander's concept of the defense. Situational awareness must be maintained and where the enemy's efforts are likely to result in a gaining a foothold, violent counterattacks must be employed to deny him access into the MBA.

(11) ***Employment of a Reserve.*** The unit defensive plan must always consider the employment of a reserve. The reserve force should be prepared to counterattack to regain key positions, to block enemy penetrations, to protect the flanks, or to assist by fire in the disengagement and withdrawal of positions. During urban combat, a reserve force—
- Normally consists of infantry.
- Must be as mobile as possible.
- May be a company or platoon at battalion level; a squad or platoon at company level.
- May be supported by tanks or other armored vehicles.
- Should be positioned as close as possible to the place where it is anticipated being employed.

(12) ***Counterattacks.*** All elements should be prepared to counterattack. The best counterattack force is a small, infantry-heavy element supported by BFVs and or tanks, if available. They should be prepared to counterattack to regain key positions, to block enemy penetrations, to provide flank protection, and to assist by fire the disengagement and withdrawal of endangered positions. It is especially important for enemy footholds to be repelled violently. When an element is committed to counterattack to reinforce a unit, it may be attached to the unit in whose sector the counterattack is taking place. Otherwise, the counterattack becomes the main effort. This makes coordination easier, especially if the counterattack goes through the unit's positions.

(13) ***Defense During Conditions of Limited Visibility.*** Commanders can expect the attacker to use conditions of limited visibility to conduct operations to sustain or gain daylight momentum.

(a) Commanders should employ the following measures to defend against attacks during limited visibility:
- Defensive positions and crew-served weapons should be shifted from an alternate position or a hasty security position just before dark to deceive the enemy as to the exact location of the primary position.
- Unoccupied areas between units, which can be covered by observed fire during daylight, may have to be occupied, blocked, or patrolled during limited visibility. Early warning devices and obstacles need to be installed.
- Radar, remote sensors, and night observation devices should be emplaced to cover streets and open areas. Thermal imagery devices, such as the one found on the TOW weapon system, are excellent for observation during limited visibility.
- Noise-making devices, tanglefoot tactical wire, and LP/OPs should be positioned on all avenues of approach for early warning and to detect infiltration.
- Artificial illumination should be planned, to include the use of street lamps, stadium lights, pyrotechnics, visible and IR ILLUM, and so forth.
- Indirect fire weapons, grenade launchers, and hand grenades should be used when defenses are probed to avoid disclosure of defensive positions.
- Tank and BFV platoons must know the locations of friendly positions. The use of thermal recognition signals and markers can help decrease the possibility of fratricide.

(b) Commanders should initiate FPFs through the use of a planned signal. Crew-served weapons, armored vehicle-mounted weapons if available, and individual riflemen fire within their assigned sectors. Grenades and command-detonated mines should be used to supplement other fires as the enemy approaches the positions.

(c) Defenders should move to daylight positions before BMNT. Buildings should be marked from the friendly side IAW unit SOP in order to facilitate movement. Armored vehicles can be used to cover the movement of friendly troops.

d. **Rear Area.** Units may be deployed in the rear area to protect CSS elements and to defend high payoff assets, lines of communications, C2 nodes, and other key locations. Units will employ the tactics, techniques, and procedures (TTP) discussed in Sections V, VI, and VII.

3-12. PRIORITIES OF WORK

Priorities of work in during defensive operations in urban areas are the same as other defensive operations. Specific considerations for a defense on urbanized terrain are discussed in this paragraph.

a. **Establish Security.** Units should quickly establish all-round security by placing forces on likely avenues of approaches. The level of security (50 percent, 30 percent, and so forth) is determined by METT-TC factors. The reconnaissance and counterreconnaissance plan should be emphasized. While security is being established, civilians located within the defensive area need to be identified and evacuated.

b. **Assign Areas of Responsibility.** Boundaries define sectors of responsibility. They include areas where units may fire and maneuver without interference or coordination with other units. Responsibility for primary avenues of approach should never be split. In areas of semidetached construction, where observation and movement are less restricted, boundaries should be established along alleys or streets to include both sides of a street in a single sector. Where buildings present a solid front along streets, boundaries may have to extend to one side of the street. Battle positions should also be specifically assigned, as required by METT-TC. Commanders and leaders should specify which buildings comprise the battle positions or strongpoints. Positions should be clearly designated so that no doubt remains as to which elements will have responsibility for occupation or control.

c. **Clear Fields of Fire.** In urban areas, units may need to rubble certain buildings and structures to provide greater protection and fields of fire to the defender (see paragraph 3-11c(8), Rubbling). If the ceiling of a lower-story room can support the weight of the rubble, collapsing the top floor of a building before the battle starts may afford better protection against indirect fires. Rubbling an entire building can increase the fields of fire and create an obstacle to enemy movement. Planning must be extensive so that rubbled buildings will not interfere with planned routes of withdrawal or counterattack. Vehicles may also have to be moved to clear fields of fire.

d. **Select and Prepare Initial Fighting Positions.** Units should select positions in depth. Units should prepare positions as soon as troops arrive and continue preparing as long as positions are occupied. Enemy infiltration or movement sometimes occurs between and behind friendly positions. Therefore, each position must be organized for all-round defense. The defender should also:

(1) Make minimum changes to the outside appearance of buildings where positions are located.

(2) Screen or block windows and other openings to keep the enemy from seeing in and tossing in hand grenades. This must be done so that the enemy cannot tell which openings the defenders are behind.

(3) Remove combustible material to limit the danger of fire. Fires are dangerous to defenders and create smoke that could conceal attacking troops. For these reasons, defenders should remove all flammable materials and stockpile fire-fighting equipment (water, sand, and so forth). The danger of fire also influences the type of ammunition used in the defense. Tracers or incendiary rounds should not be used extensively if threat of fire exists.

(4) Turn off electricity and gas. Both propane and natural gas are explosive. Natural gas is also poisonous, displaces oxygen, and is not filtered by a protective mask. Propane gas, although not poisonous, is heavier than air. If it leaks into an enclosed area, it displaces the oxygen and causes suffocation. Gas mains and electricity should be shut off at the facility that serves the urban area.

(5) Locate positions so as not to establish a pattern. Units should avoid obvious firing locations like towers and buildings prohibited for use by the Law of Land Warfare, such as churches.

(6) Camouflage positions.

(7) Reinforce positions with all materials available such as mattresses, furniture, and so forth. The S4 will have to arrange for as much protective material as possible. Caution should be taken as mattresses and fabric furniture are flammable. Drawers and cabinets should be filled with earth or sand to provide cover. Vehicles, such as trucks or buses can be placed over positions outside buildings. Flammable fluids should be drained. Other flammables, such as seats should be removed, and the gas tank filled with water.

(8) Block stairwells and doorways with wire or other material to prevent enemy movement. Create holes between floors and rooms to allow covered and concealed movement within a building.

(9) Prepare range cards, fire plans, and sector sketches.

(10) Look at how basements may be used. If grazing fire can be achieved from basement widows, emplace machine guns in basements. When basements are not used, they should be sealed to prevent enemy entry.

(11) Cache resupply of ammunition, water, and medical supplies.

e. **Establish Communications.** Commanders should consider the effects of urban areas on communications when they allocate time to establish communications. Line-of-sight limitations affect both visual and radio communications. Wire laid at street level is easily damaged by rubble and vehicle traffic. The noise of urban area combat is much louder than in other areas, making sound signals difficult to hear. Therefore, the time needed to establish an effective communications system in urban terrain may be greater than in other terrain. Units should consider the following techniques when planning for communications:

- Emplace line of sight radios and retransmission sites on the upper floors of buildings.
- Use existing telephone systems. However, telephones are not secure even though many telephone cables are underground.
- Use messengers at all levels since they are the most secure means of communications.
- Lay wire through buildings for maximum protection, if the assets are available.

f. **Emplace Obstacles and Mines.** To save time and resources in preparing the defense, commanders must emphasize using all available materials (automobiles, railcars, rubble) to create obstacles. Civilian construction equipment and materials must be located and inventoried. This equipment can be used with engineer assets or in place of damaged equipment. Coordination must be made with proper civilian officials before use.

(1) Engineers must be able to provide advice and resources as to the employment of obstacles and mines. The principles for employing mines and obstacles do not change in the defense of an urban area; however, techniques do change. For example, burying and concealing mines in streets are hard due to concrete and asphalt. Consider placing mines in sandbags so they cannot be seen and also using fake mines placed in sandbags in order to deceive the enemy.

(2) FASCAM may be effective on the outskirts of an urban area or in parks; however, in a city core, areas may be too restrictive. Mines and obstacles must be emplaced consistent with the ROE. Any antipersonnel mines must be command-detonated. Riot control agents may be employed to control noncombatant access into defensive areas, if permission is granted by the National Command Authority (NCA).

g. **Improve Fighting Positions.** When time permits, all positions, to include supplementary and alternate positions, should be reinforced with sandbags and provided overhead cover. Attached engineers can help in this effort by providing advice and assisting with construction.

h. **Establish and Mark Routes Between Positions.** Reconnaissance by all defending elements will assist in route selection for use by defenders moving between positions. Movement is crucial in fighting in urban areas. Early selection and marking of routes adds to the defender's advantages.

SECTION IV. BRIGADE DEFENSIVE OPERATIONS

This section discusses planning considerations and provides tactics and techniques for the planning of brigade defensive UO.

3-13. DEFENSIVE PLANNING

In planning a defense in an urban area, the brigade staff must identify the following:

- Positions and areas that must be controlled to prevent enemy infiltration.
- Sufficient covered and concealed routes for movement and repositioning of forces.
- Structures and areas that dominate the urban area.
- Areas such as parks and broad streets that provide fields of fire for tanks and antiarmor weapons.
- Position areas for artillery assets.
- C2 locations.
- Protected areas for CSS activities.
- Suitable structures that are defensible and provide protection for defenders.
- Contingency plans in the event that the brigade must conduct breakout operations.
- Plans for rapid reinforcement.

a. Units defending in urban areas must prepare their positions for all around defense. The brigade must employ aggressive security operations that include surveillance of surface and subsurface approaches. The brigade must constantly patrol and use OPs and sensors to maintain effective security. Special measures must be taken to control possible civilian personnel who support the enemy or enemy combatants who have intermixed with the local population. Consideration must also be given to the protection of non-combatants that remain in the AO, and contingency actions in the event that the situation deteriorates and requires their evacuation.

b. Defensive fire support in urban operations must take advantage of the impact of indirect fires on the enemy before he enters the protection of the urban area. Fire support officers at all levels must coordinate and rehearse contingencies that are inherent to nonlinear fire support coordination measures and clearance of fires. Mutually supporting observation plans for daylight and periods of limited visibility must account for the degradation of lasers in well-lit urban areas. The brigade fire support officer also plans and coordinates nonlethal capabilities for the brigade Civil affairs and PSYOP assets should be coordinated with the appropriate command and control warfare/information operations headquarters.

3-14. INTEGRATING THE URBAN AREA INTO THE DEFENSE

The brigade may also integrate villages, strip areas, and small towns into the overall defense, based on higher headquarters' constraints and applicable ROE (Figure 3-9). A defense in an urban area or one that incorporates urban areas normally follows the same sequence of actions. When defending large urban areas, the commander must consider that the terrain is more restrictive due to buildings that are normally close together. This requires a higher density of troops and smaller AOs than in open terrain. The brigade normally assigns task force AOs and may use phase lines, control measures, or other positions to position forces in depth.

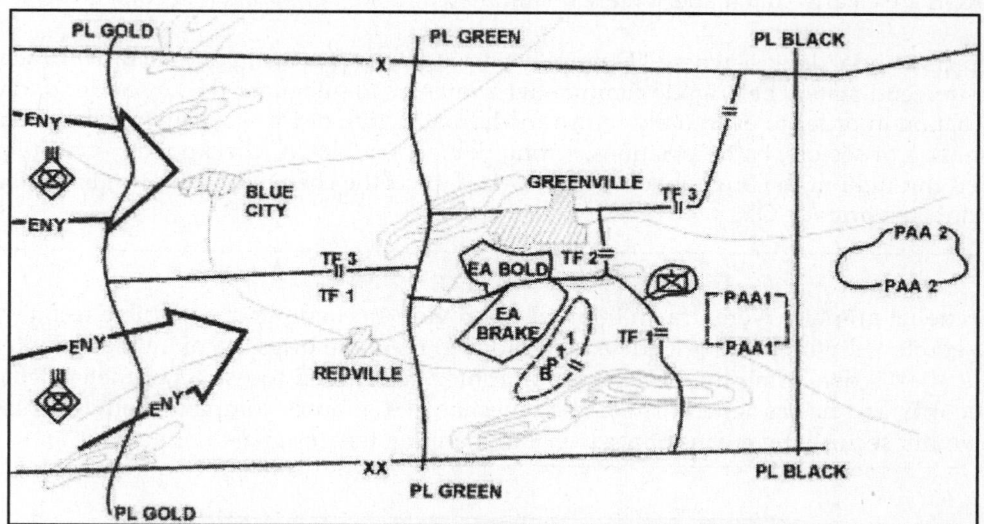

Figure 3-9: Integrating urban areas into a defense.

3-15. NODAL DEFENSE

Figure 3-10 depicts a transitional situation where the brigade moves from an offensive to a defensive or stability operation. The brigade mission may contain METT-TC factors that require varying defensive techniques by the subordinate battalion TFs under the brigade's control. Considerations in a situation such as this include:

a. **Task Organization.** TFs may very well have to be task-organized differently to conduct the specific missions assigned by the brigade commander. The task organization required for the defensive or stability operation will probably be different from the task organization used in an offensive operation.

b. **Symmetrical/Asymmetrical Threats.** The brigade will likely respond to both symmetrical and asymmetrical threats within the area of operations. The defensive techniques chosen by subordinate battalion TFs should be capable of responding to the specific threats in their respective AOs.

c. **Boundary Changes.** Again, based on the commander's intent and the brigade's defensive scheme of maneuver, boundary changes may be required in order to give battalion's more or less maneuver space.

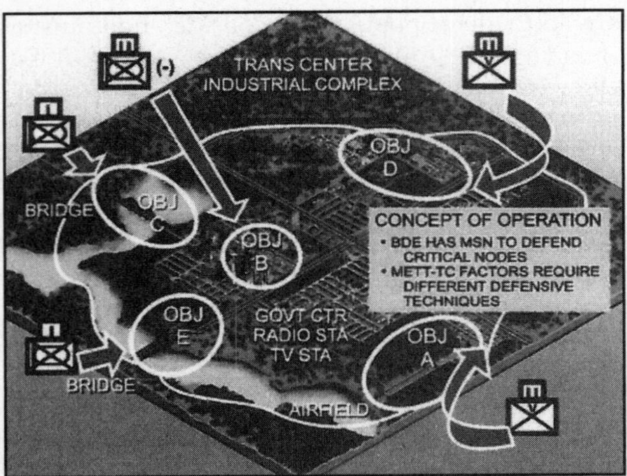

Figure 3-10: Nodal defense, transitional situation.

d. **ROE Modification.** The ROE may require modification based on the type of mission to be conducted. The ROE may become more or less restrictive based on METT-TC factors. Commanders and leaders must insure that the ROE are clearly stated and widely disseminated at the beginning and conclusion of each day.

Figure 3-11 depicts a nodal defense where TFs employ varying defensive techniques in order to achieve the brigade commander's desired end-state. The brigade commander's intent is to safeguard the key nodes that were seized during the offensive action in order to eventually return the infrastructure of this particular urban area back to civilian control. A combination of sectors, battle positions, strong points, roadblocks, checkpoints, security patrols, and OPs could be employed throughout the brigade AO. Figure 3-11 depicts the changed TF task organizations, the extended boundaries, and directed brigade OPs.

> ✍ **NOTE**
>
> TF operational graphics were drawn in order to provide an example of a possible technique that may be employed within the brigade AO in order to meet the brigade commander's intent. For example, the TF defending the transportation center has elected to use a perimeter defense for inner security and has assigned the attached mechanized infantry company team the mission to conduct outer security by means of a screen and manning the designated brigade OP.

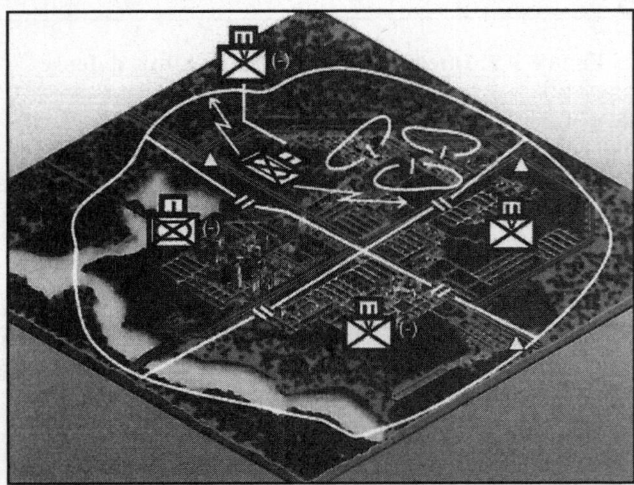

Figure 3-11: Nodal defense, varying defensive techniques.

SECTION V. BATTALION DEFENSIVE OPERATIONS

This section discusses planning considerations and provides tactics and techniques for the planning of battalion TF defensive UO.

3-16. EMPLOYMENT OF COMBAT AND COMBAT SUPPORT ASSETS

This paragraph will concentrate on the employment of combat and combat support assets at the battalion level. Once the battalion has decided where to defend, it should select company battle positions or sectors that block or restrict the enemy's ability to maneuver and control key areas. The battalion needs to plan two levels down at the platoon level where the battle will be fought. The frontage for a platoon is about one to two city blocks long. Platoons can occupy about three small structures or one larger two- or three-story building (Table 3-1 and Figure 3-6), depending on METT-TC factors. Companies may be tasked to detach a platoon to act as the battalion reserve.

a. **Mortar Platoon.** The battalion mortar platoon may be initially positioned forward in support of the security area. After withdrawal of security forces, it is positioned to support the entire battalion. Mortars at the battalion level are employed to maximize the effect of their high-angle fires. They should be used to engage:
- Enemy overwatch positions.
- Enemy infantry before they seize a foothold.
- Targets on rooftops.
- Enemy reinforcements within range.

b. **AT Weapons.** The commander will give the AT platoon missions that support the defensive scheme of maneuver based on the capabilities and limitations of the system and the type of threat that the battalion will face. For example, battalion defending against conventional threats that have armored vehicles will most likely give the AT platoon missions that primarily defend against armored threats. Battalions defending against asymmetrical threats will most likely give the AT platoon missions that will enhance force protection.

c. **Scout Platoon.** Depending on the situation and terrain, the battalion scout platoon may provide a security force forward of the battalion to give early warning of enemy activity. Alternately, the scout platoon may be used to screen a flank or the rear.

d. **Employment of Tanks and BFVs.** The battalion should employ tanks and BFVs to take advantage of their long-range fires and mobility. Urban areas restrict the mobility of tanks and BFVs and make them vulnerable to enemy infantry antiarmor weapons.

(1) When tanks and BFVs are employed in the defense of an urban area, infantry should be positioned to provide security against close antitank fires and to detect targets for the armored vehicles. Tanks and BFVs should be assigned engagement areas in support of the defensive scheme of maneuver. BFVs may be placed along the forward edge of the area in order to engage enemy armored vehicles. Friendly armored vehicles can also be placed in positions to the rear of the buildings and interior courtyards where their weapon systems can provide added rear and flank security. Combat vehicles are assigned primary, alternate, and supplementary positions as well as primary and secondary sectors of fire. They should be positioned in defilade behind rubble and walls or inside buildings for movement into and out of the area. Armored vehicles can also be used for resupply, CASEVAC, and rapid repositioning during the battle. BFVs can also provide a mobile reserve. Tank or BFV elements should be placed OPCON to a light infantry battalion rather than attached. A tank or BFV element attached or OPCON will have to be divided up within the defensive area to take advantage of the fires available to this asset. BFVs and antitank weapons should supplement tank fires. Tanks and BFVs may be—
- Positioned on the edge of the urban area in mutually supporting positions.
- Positioned on key terrain on the flanks of towns and villages.
- Used to cover barricades and obstacles by fire.
- Part of the reserve.

(2) Tanks and BFVs are normally employed as platoons. However, sections may be employed with light infantry platoons or squads based on METT-TC factors and identified engagement areas. This provides tanks and BFVs with the close security of the infantry. Tanks and BFVs provide the commander with a mobile force to respond quickly to enemy threats on different avenues of approach. They can also be effectively employed in counterattacks.

e. **Indirect Fire Support.** Fire planning must be comprehensive due to the proximity of buildings to targets, minimum range restrictions, repositioning requirements, and the ROE. Mortar and artillery fires are planned on top of and immediately around defensive positions for close support.
   (1) ***Artillery.*** Artillery may be used as direct or indirect support. In the defense, artillery fire should be used to—
      - Suppress and blind enemy overwatch elements.
      - Disrupt or destroy an assault.
      - Provide counterbattery fire.
      - Support counterattacks.
      - Provide direct fire when necessary.
   (2) ***Fire Planning.*** Fire planning is conducted for urban areas in much the same manner as it is for other areas, taking into concern the limitations of the restrictive terrain. Consideration should be given to TRPs, covering obstacles, FPFs.
   (3) ***Priorities of Fire.*** The commander should establish priorities of fire based on enemy avenues of approach and threat systems that present the greatest danger to the defense. For example, during the attacker's initial advance, tanks, BMPs, and overwatching elements are the greatest threat to the defense. In certain situations, enemy APCs may provide a larger threat than enemy tanks in an urban area; the APCs carry infantry, which can gain footholds in buildings. Artillery and mortar fires should suppress and destroy enemy ATGMs and overwatch positions and or elements. If enemy formations secure a foothold, priority is shifted to the destruction of enemy forces within the penetration.
   (4) ***Control of Supporting Fires.*** As the enemy attack progresses in the city, fires are increased to separate infantry from supporting tanks and fighting vehicles. During this phase, friendly artillery concentrates on attacking infantry, counterfire missions, and the destruction of reinforcements that are approaching the city.
   (5) ***Support of Counterattacks.*** When initiated, counterattacks are given priority of supporting fires. When artillery is firing the missions as mentioned above, it must remain mobile and be prepared to displace to preplanned positions to avoid enemy counterbattery fire.

f. **Employment of Engineers.** Normally, one engineer platoon or company supports a battalion or battalion task force. Engineers are employed under battalion control or attached to companies. Company commanders may be given an engineer squad to assist them in preparing the defense. The battalion commander and staff must consider engineer tasks that enhance survivability, mobility, and countermobility. The supporting engineers use C4 and other explosives to make firing ports, mouseholes, and demolition obstacles. Based upon priority of work, the battalion tells the attached or OPCON engineer element to assist each of the infantry companies preparing the village for defense and to execute their obstacle plan. The engineers' mission is to tell the infantrymen exactly where to place the demolitions and how much is needed for the desired effect. They assist in preparation of charges. Tasks that engineers can accomplish in the defense of an urban area include:
   - Constructing obstacles and rubbling.
   - Clearing fields of fire.
   - Laying mines.
   - Preparing mobility routes between positions.
   - Preparing fighting positions.

g. **Air Defense Assets.** Air defense assets available to the commander, such as Stinger and Avenger, are normally employed to ensure all-round air defense. These assets are normally controlled at battalion level, however they may be placed under a company commander's control when METT-TC factors warrant that type of use. The lack of good firing positions for long-range air defense missile systems in some urban areas may limit the number of deployed weapons. In the defense, weapons systems may have to be winched or airlifted into positions. Rooftops and parking garages are good firing positions because they normally offer a better line-of-sight. Stingers and Avengers can be assigned the missions of protecting specific positions or of functioning in general support of the battalion.

h. **Battalion Trains/Service Support.** The battalion locates an area where the trains can be positioned near enough to provide support but far enough away to not get in the line of fire. A location is chosen near the main avenue of approach to ease resupply, recovery, and maintenance operations. Company trains are often collocated with the battalion trains. Ammunition expenditure is usually high when fighting in an urban area.

To avoid moving around the village with ammunition resupply during the battle, ammunition should be stockpiled in each occupied platoon and squad position. Platoons should also stockpile firefighting equipment, drinking water, food, and first-aid supplies at each squad position. Other factors the battalion must consider are:

- Resupply.
- Medical evacuation.
- Firefighting.
- Security.

3-17. INTEGRATING URBAN AREAS INTO THE DEFENSE

The battalion may often integrate villages, strip areas, and small towns into the overall defense, based on higher headquarters' constraints and applicable ROE. (See Figure 3-12.) A defense in an urban area, or one that incorporates urban areas, normally follows the same sequence of actions. Specific TTP are discussed in paragraphs 3-18 through 3-21.

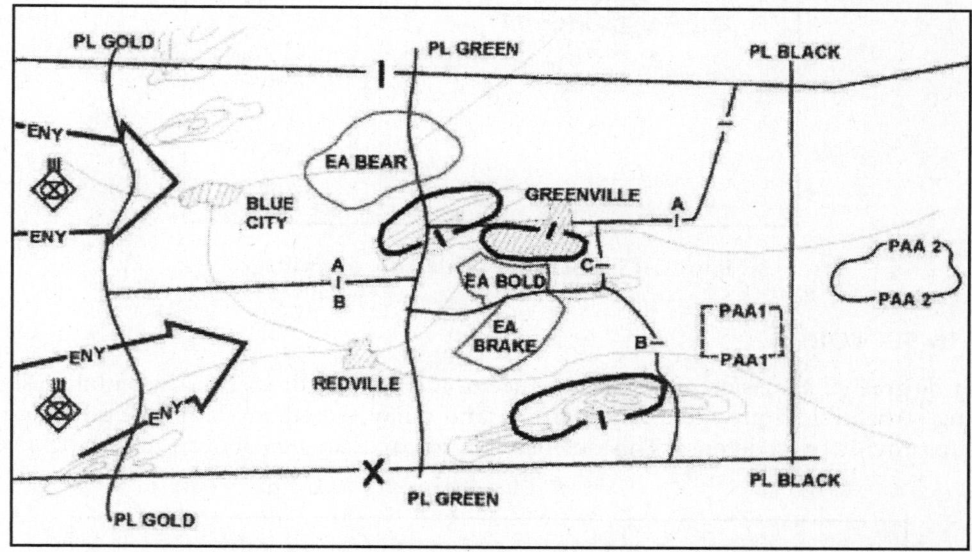

Figure 3-12: Integrating urban areas into the defense.

3-18. DEFENSE OF A VILLAGE

A battalion TF assigned a defensive sector that includes a village may incorporate the village as a strongpoint in its defense. This use of an urban area is most common when the village stands astride a high-speed avenue of approach or when it lies between two difficult obstacles. To incorporate such an area into its defense, the battalion TF must control the high ground on either side of the village to prevent the enemy from firing from those areas into the village.

a. The majority of the TF tanks and BFVs should be employed where maneuver room is the greatest on the key terrain to the flanks of the village. This is also where the TF BFVs should be employed. As the security force withdraws and companies and or teams assume the fight, BFVs can assume support by fire positions.

b. Although the battalion TFs disposition should prevent large enemy forces from threatening the rear and flanks of the village, the danger of small-unit enemy infiltration means the village must be prepared for all-round defense.

c. Engineers required for team mobility operations should stay with the company or company team in the village to provide continuous engineer support if the company team becomes isolated. The TF commander should centrally control engineer support for the rest of the TF. Engineer assets may be in DS of the other companies or company teams. The priority of barrier materials, demolitions, and mines should go to the company or company team in the village.

d. The TF commander should use any key terrain on the village flanks for maneuver to prevent the village's defense from becoming isolated. The strongpoints in the town should provide a firm location where the enemy can be stopped and around which counterattacks can be launched (Figure 3-13).

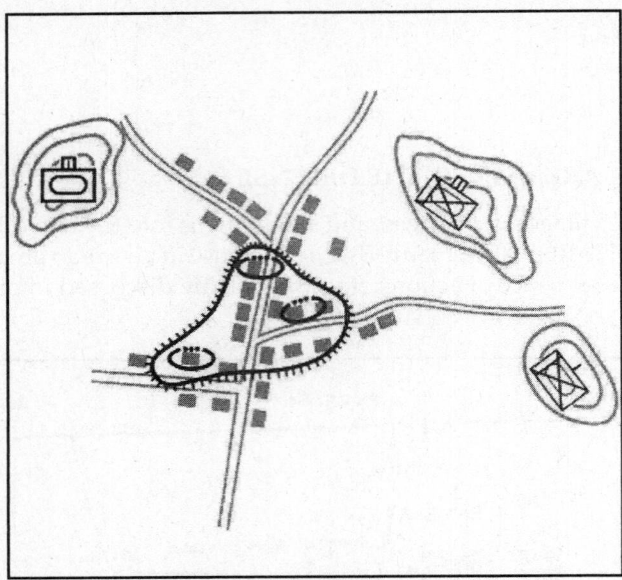

Figure 3-13: Battalion TF defense of a village.

3-19. DEFENSE IN SECTOR

A battalion TF may be given the mission of defending a sector in a city (Figure 3-14). The battalion should take advantage of the outlying structures to provide early warning and delay the enemy and take advantage of the tougher interior buildings to provide fixed defense. This defense should cover an area about 4 to 12 blocks square.

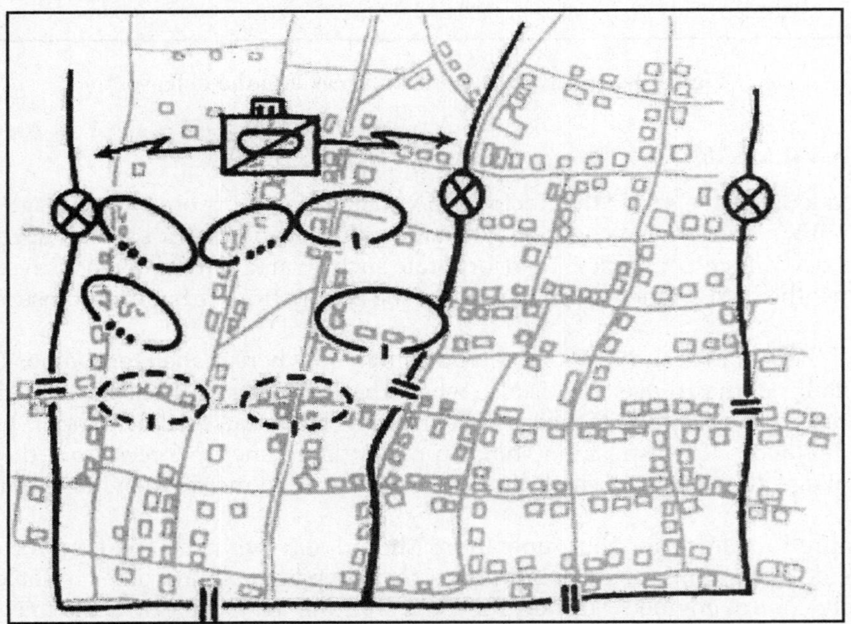

Figure 3-14. Defense in sector.

a. The battalion TF deployment begins with the reconnaissance/scout platoon reconnoitering the urban area to provide an area reconnaissance and location of the enemy. At the edge of the area, where fields of fire are the greatest, the battalion TF should deploy BFVs and other antiarmor weapon systems to provide long-range antiarmor defense.
b. The forward edge of the battle area (FEBA) should include the most formidable buildings in the sector. Forward of the FEBA, the battalion TF should organize a guard force, which could be a reinforced company. The guard force should concentrate on causing the enemy to deploy without engaging the enemy in decisive combat. This can be done through maximum use of ambushes and obstacles and using covered and concealed routes through buildings for disengagement. The guard force inflicts casualties and delays the enemy, but the guard force avoids decisive engagement since buildings beyond the FEBA do not favor the defense. As the action nears the FEBA, the guard force detects the location of the enemy's main attack. Upon reaching the FEBA, the guard force passes through the battalion lines and can be used as a reserve and reinforce other elements of the battalion, or it can counterattack.
c. Defense along the FEBA consists of a series of positions set up similar to that described in the company defense of the village (see paragraph 3-23). Key terrain features such as strong buildings, road junctions, and good firing positions should be the center of the strongpoint defense. Based on METT-TC considerations, the defense in sector may consist of either strongpoints or battle positions. Strongpoints located on or covering decisive terrain are extremely effective in the defense. Buildings should be prepared for defense as outlined in Chapter 1.
d. BFVs should be used to engage threat armored vehicles; to cover obstacles with fire; and to engage in counterattacks with tanks. They can also be used to transport casualties and supplies to and from the fight.
e. The battalion's attached tanks should be used to engage enemy tanks, cover obstacles by fire, and engage in counterattacks. They should be employed in platoons where possible, but in congested areas may be employed in sections.
f. Artillery and mortar fire should be used to suppress and blind enemy overwatch elements, to engage enemy infantry on the approaches to the city, to provide counterbattery fire, and to support counterattacks using both indirect and direct fire.
g. Engineers should be attached to the defending force to help in laying mines and constructing obstacles, clearing fields of fire, and preparing routes to the rear. These routes should also have obstacles. Engineers should help prepare fighting positions in support of the force in strongpoints.

3-20. NODAL DEFENSE

Figure 3-15 depicts a transitional situation where the battalion moves from an offensive to a defensive or stability operation. The brigade mission may contain METT-TC factors that require varying defensive techniques by the subordinate battalions under the brigade's control. Figure 3-16 depicts a nodal defense where battalions employ different defensive techniques in order to achieve the brigade commander's desired end-state. The brigade commander's intent is to safeguard the key nodes that were seized during the offensive action in order to eventually return the infrastructure of this particular urban area back to civilian control. A combination of sectors, battle positions, strong points, roadblocks, checkpoints, security patrols, and OPs could be employed within the TF sector or AO. Figure 3-16 depicts the changed TF task organizations, the extended boundaries, and directed brigade OPs. Considerations in a situation such as this include:

a. **Task Organization.** Companies may have to be task organized differently to conduct the specific missions assigned by the battalion or TF commander. The task organization required for the defensive or stability operation will probably be different from the task organization used in an offensive operation.
b. **Symmetrical/Asymmetrical Threats.** The battalion or TF will likely respond to both symmetrical and asymmetrical threats within the area of operations. The defensive techniques chosen by subordinate companies should allow them to respond to the specific threats in their respective AOs, battle positions, or sectors.
c. **Boundary Changes.** Again, based on the commander's intent and the battalion's or TF's defensive scheme of maneuver, boundary changes may be required in order to give companies more or less maneuver space.
d. **ROE Modification.** The ROE may require modification based on the type of mission to be conducted. The ROE may become more or less restrictive based on METT-TC factors. Commanders and leaders must ensure that the ROE are clearly stated and widely disseminated at the beginning and conclusion of each day.

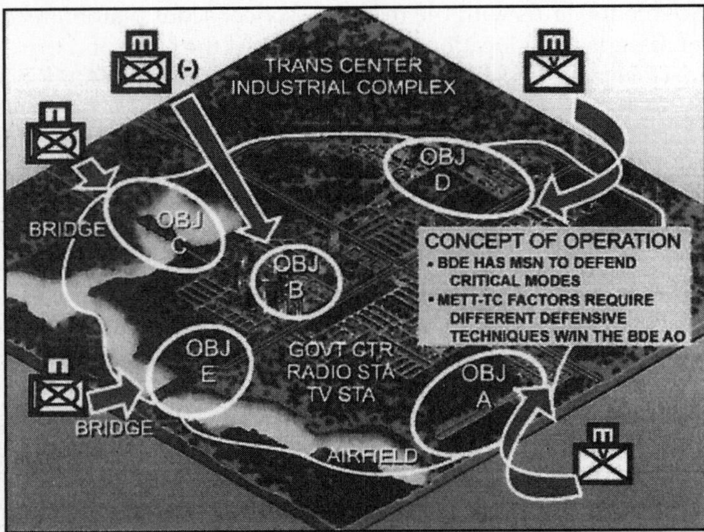

Figure 3-15: Nodal defense, transitional situation.

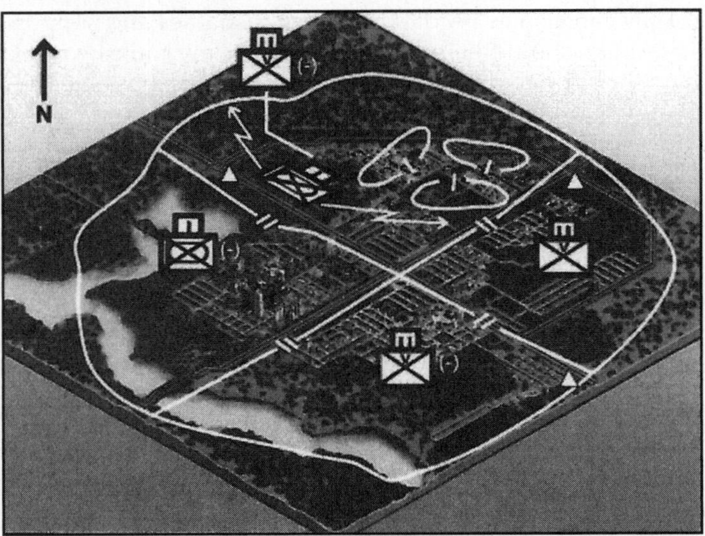

Figure 3-16: Nodal defense, different defensive techniques.

> ✍ **NOTE**
>
> In Figure 3-16, the northern TF defending the transportation center/industrial complex has decided to use a perimeter defense for inner security and has assigned the attached mechanized Infantry company the mission to conduct outer security by means of a screen and manning the designated brigade OP. Other TFs within the brigade AO may be required to use different defensive techniques.

> ✍ **NOTE**
>
> The digital force has the potential to provide accurate threat information that can enhance situational awareness, which facilitates targeting and obstacle placement. JSTARS; GUARDRAIL; unmanned aerial vehicles, if present; and other reconnaissance assets will significantly improve the threat situational awareness and targeting capability of the unit.

3-21. DELAY

The purpose of a delay is to slow the enemy, cause enemy casualties, and stop the enemy (where possible) without becoming decisively engaged or bypassed. The delay can be oriented either on the enemy or on specified terrain such as a key building or manufacturing complex.

a. **Ambushes and Battle Positions.** A delay in an urban area is conducted from a succession of ambushes and battle positions (Figure 3-17). The width of the TF zone depends upon the amount of force available to control the area, the nature of the buildings and obstacles along the street and the length of time that the enemy must be delayed.

(1) ***Ambushes.*** Ambushes are planned on overwatching obstacles and are closely coordinated but they are executed at the lowest levels. The deployment of the TF is realigned at important cross streets. The ambushes can be combined with limited objective attacks on the enemy's flanks. These are usually effective in the edge of open spaces, parks, wide streets, and so on. Tanks and BFVs should execute these along with dismounted Infantry.

(2) ***Battle Positions.*** Battle positions should be placed where heavy weapons, such as tanks, BFVs, antiarmor weapons, and machine guns, will have the best fields of fire. Such locations are normally found at major street intersections, parks, and at the edge of open residential areas. Battle positions should be carefully and deliberately prepared, reinforced by obstacles and demolished buildings, and supported by artillery and mortars. They should be positioned to inflict maximum losses on the enemy and cause him to deploy for a deliberate attack.

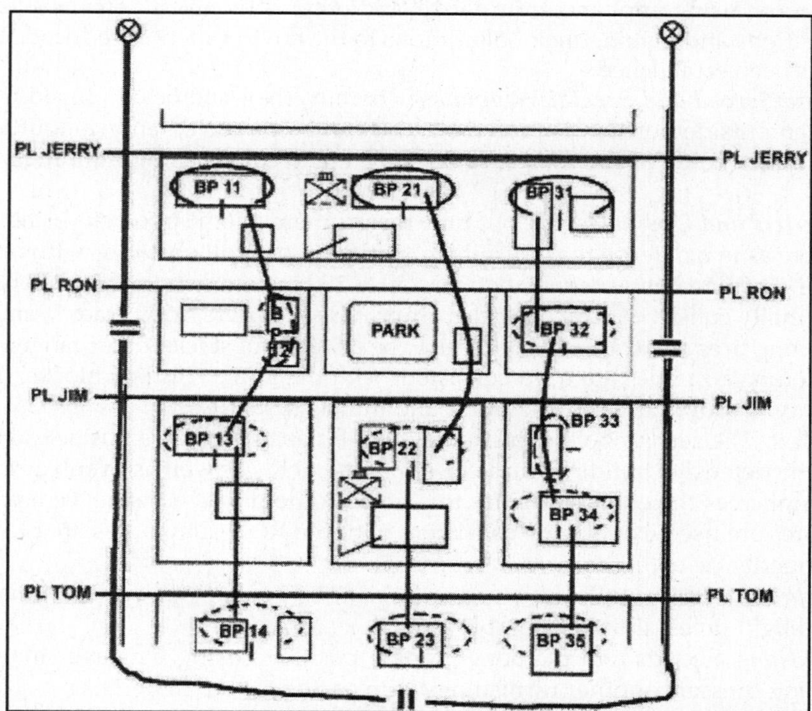

Figure 3-17: Battalion delay in an urban area.

b. **Two Delaying Echelons.** The TF is most effective when deployed in two delaying echelons, alternating between conducting ambushes and fighting from battle positions. As the enemy threatens to overrun a battle position, the company disengages and delays back toward the next battle position. As the company passes through the company to the rear, it establishes another battle position. Smoke and demolitions are used to aid in the disengagement. Security elements on the flank can be employed to prevent the enemy from outflanking the delaying force. A small reserve can be used to react to unexpected enemy action and to conduct continued attacks on the enemy's flank.

c. **Engineers.** The engineer effort should first be centralized to support the preparation of battle positions and then decentralized to support the force committed to ambush.

SECTION VI. COMPANY DEFENSIVE OPERATIONS

This section discusses planning considerations and provides tactics and techniques for the planning of company team defensive UO.

3-22. HASTY DEFENSE

A very likely defensive mission for the Infantry company in urban terrain will be to conduct a hasty defense. This mission is characterized by reduced time for the preparation of the defense. All of the troop-leading procedures are the same. The priorities of work will basically be the same, but many will take place concurrently. Units will be deployed, weapons emplaced, and positions prepared in accordance with the mission analysis and amount of time the company commander has available. Companies must be prepared to conduct a hasty defensive mission as part of stability and support operations.

a. **Occupation and Preparation of Positions.** Preparations for the hasty defense will vary with the time available. The preparations described below will generally take between two to four hours. In a hasty defense, the primary effort is to camouflage and conceal the presence of the hasty fighting positions and provide as much protection as possible for the soldiers manning them. Positions are constructed back from the windows in the shadows of the room using appliances, furniture, and other convenient items and materials. The emphasis on fortifying positions and making major alterations to the environment is reduced. These actions will occur after security has been established.

(1) ***Position Crew-Served and Special Weapons.*** Generally, they will be employed from the inside of buildings, unless an outside position is preferable and can be protected and camouflaged. Armored vehicles can exploit longer fields of fire or a reverse slope engagement using buildings to protect the vehicle's position.

(2) ***Emplace Barriers and Obstacles.*** Lack of time means there will be two belts established and they will not be as extensive as in a defense that permits more time. Cover all obstacles with observation and fire.

(a) *First Belt.* The first belt is usually between 50 to 100 meters from and parallel to the defensive trace. It will normally consist of wire obstacles, improvised barriers, road craters, and minefields. For example, burning tires and trash have proven to be effective obstacles on urban terrain. Antitank and command detonated mines are used consistent with the ROE. This belt blocks, fixes, turns, or canalizes the enemy; disrupts attack formations; and inflicts casualties.

(b) *Second Belt.* The second belt is the denial belt. It consists of wire obstacles placed around, through, and in the defensive buildings and close-in mine fields as well as in subsurface accesses. It impedes and complicates the enemy's ability to gain a foothold in the defensive area. Command detonated Claymores are used extensively consistent with the ROE. Claymores are placed where they will not cause friendly casualties.

(c) *Field-Expedient Obstacles.* Field-expedient obstacles made from available materials, such as rubble, cars and light poles, should be employed.

(3) ***Prepare Positions.*** Squads and platoons prepare positions using whatever materials are available; for example, filling dressers or other furnishings with earth or other materials.

(4) ***Rehearsals.*** Conduct rehearsals with leaders and soldiers concerning the orientation of the defense, unit positions, location of crew served weapons, CASEVAC, resupply, execution of counterattack plans, withdrawal plan, and so on. One of the more important rehearsals to conduct is the synchronization of direct and indirect fires to accomplish the commander's intent.

(5) ***Movement Enhancement.*** There will not be much time to improve movement within the defense. Units should plan to use subsurface and supersurface (through buildings) routes. Priority should be given to removing obstructions to alternate positions and to the counterattack route.

(6) ***Communications.*** Check communications. Communications is initially radio. Plans are made for messengers and routes improved for them. Wire is emplaced as an improvement to the defense as time and the terrain allows.

> ✍ **NOTE**
> The digital force has the potential to provide accurate threat information that can enhance situational awareness, which helps facilitate targeting and obstacle placement. JSTARS; GUARDRAIL; unmanned aerial vehicles, if present; and other reconnaissance assets will significantly improve the threat situational awareness and targeting capability of the unit.

b. **Improving the Defense.** As time permits, the following areas can be given consideration and prioritized in accordance with METT-TC.

- Sleep plan.
- Barrier and obstacle improvement.
- Improvement of primary and alternate positions.
- Preparation of supplementary positions.
- Additional movement enhancement efforts.
- Initiation of patrols.
- Improvement of camouflage.
- Maintenance/refueling.
- Continued rehearsals for counterattack and withdrawal.

3-23. DEFENSE OF A VILLAGE

An Infantry company may be given the mission to defend a village (Figure 3-18). Once the company commander has completed his reconnaissance of the village, he scouts the surrounding terrain and, with the information assembled, he develops his plan for the defense. One of his first decisions is whether to defend with his Infantry on the leading edge of the village or farther back within the confines of the village. Normally, defending on the leading edge will be more effective against an armor heavy force, where the defending company can take advantage of longer range observation and fields of fire. Defending in depth within the village will be more effective against a primarily Infantry heavy force, in order to deny the enemy a foothold. This decision will be based on the factors of METT-TC. This mission is usually characterized with the company defending an urban area that is surrounded by open terrain. The company may need to coordinate with adjacent units to plan for the defense or control of this terrain.

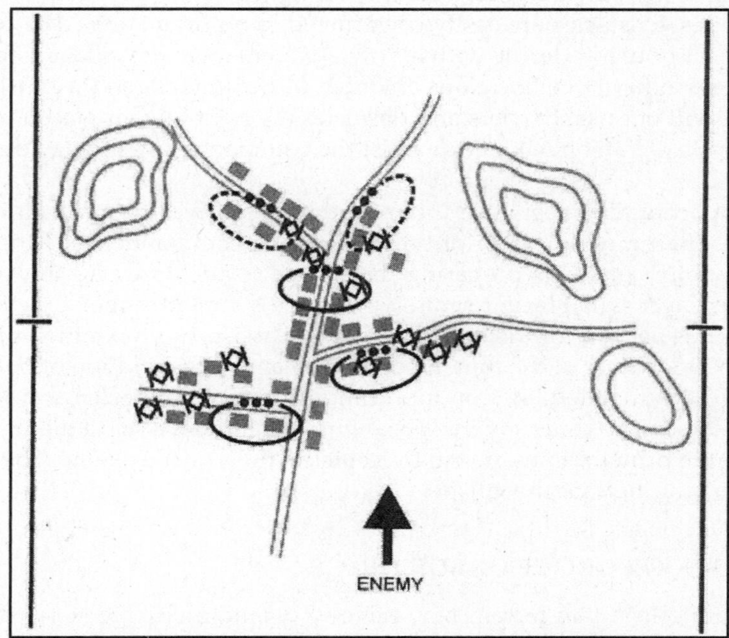

Figure 3-18: Company defense of a village.

a. **Influencing Factors.** Several factors influence the commander's decision. First, he must know the type of enemy that his company defends against. If the threat is mainly Infantry, the greater danger is allowing them to gain a foothold in the village. If the threat is armor or motorized Infantry, the greatest danger is that massive direct fire destroys the company's defensive positions. The company commander must also consider the terrain forward and to the flanks of the village from which the enemy can direct fires against his positions.
b. **Platoon Battle Positions.** Based on the mission analysis, platoons are normally given a small group of buildings in which to prepare their defense, permitting the platoon leader to establish mutually supporting squad-sized positions. This increases the area that the platoon can control and hampers the enemy's ability to isolate or bypass a platoon. A platoon may be responsible for the road through the village. The rest of the company is then positioned to provide all-round security and defense in depth.
c. **Company Mortars and Antitank.** Weapons. A position for the company mortars must be chosen that protects mortars from direct fire and allows for overhead clearance. Antitank weapons are placed where they can engage targets at maximum ranges with alternate firing points. Infantry should protect antitank weapons.
d. **BFVs.** Based on METT-TC considerations, BFVs may be placed along the forward edge of the urban area to engage enemy armored vehicles. Friendly armored vehicles can also be placed in positions to the rear of the buildings and interior courtyards where their weapon systems can provide added rear and flank security. Combat vehicles are assigned primary, alternate, and supplementary positions as well as primary and secondary sectors of fire. They should be positioned in defilade behind rubble and walls or inside buildings for movement into and out of the area. Armored vehicles can also be used for resupply, CASEVAC, and rapid repositioning during the battle. BFVs can also provide a mobile reserve for the company. If a mechanized Infantry platoon is attached, it is controlled through its chain of command. If a mechanized Infantry section is attached, it can be controlled through the senior squad leader.
e. **Tanks.** If a tank platoon is available from the battalion task force, the company commander could place the tanks along the leading edge where rapid fire would complement the antitank weapons. The tank platoon leader should select exact firing positions and recommend engagement areas. If faced by enemy Infantry, the tanks move to alternate positions with the protection of friendly Infantry. These alternate positions allow the tanks to engage to the front as well as the flanks with as little movement as possible. Positions can be selected within buildings and mouseholes can be constructed. After they are withdrawn from the leading edge of the village, the tanks could provide a mobile reserve for the company.
f. **FPFs.** FPFs are planned to address the biggest threat to the company—the enemy's Infantry. When firing an FPF inside an urban area is required, mortars are more effective than artillery. This situation is true due to their higher angle of fall that gives them a greater chance of impacting on the street.
g. **Barriers and Obstacles.** Obstacles are easily constructed in an urban area. The company commander must stop enemy vehicles without interfering with his own movement in the village. Therefore, the company detonates cratering charges at key street locations on order. Mines are laid on the outskirts of the town and along routes the company will not use. Barriers and obstacles are normally emplaced in three belts. If attached or OPCON, the tank or BFV platoon leader can assist the commander by giving advice on where to place anti-vehicular obstacles.
h. **Engineers.** The supporting engineers use C4 and other explosives to make firing ports, mouseholes, and demolition obstacles. Based upon his priority of work, the commander tells the engineer squad leader to assist each of the Infantry platoons preparing the village for defense and to execute the company team's obstacle plan. The engineer squad leader's mission is to tell the Infantrymen exactly where to place the demolitions and how much is needed for the desired effect. He assists in preparation of charges. He also assists in the emplacement and recording of the minefields as well as the preparation of fighting positions.
i. **Communications.** To ensure adequate communications, redundant verbal and nonverbal communications are planned and checked. The company installs a wire net and develops a plan for pyrotechnic signals. Lay backup wire in case the primary lines are cut by vehicles, fires, or the enemy. The commander also plans for the use of messengers throughout the village.

3-24. DEFENSE OF A BLOCK OR GROUP OF BUILDINGS

An Infantry company operating in urban terrain may have to defend a city block or group of buildings in a core periphery or residential area. The company conducts this operation in accordance with the battalion task force's defensive scheme of maneuver. The operation should be coordinated with the action of security forces charged with delaying to the front of the company's position. The defense should take advantage of the protection of buildings that dominate the avenues of approaches into the MBA. This mission differs from defense of a village in that it is more likely to be conducted completely on urban terrain, without surrounding open terrain that characterizes the defense of a village. An Infantry company is particularly well suited for this type of mission, since the fighting will require the enemy to move Infantry into the urban area in order to seize and control key terrain. (See Table 3-1.)

a. **Task and Purpose.** A well-organized company defense in an urban area—
   - Defeats the enemy's attack on the streets and city blocks by using obstacles and fire.
   - Destroys the enemy by ambush and direct fire from prepared positions within defensible buildings.
   - Clears the enemy from footholds or remains in place for a counterattack.

b. **Reconnaissance and Security.** The execution of the mission will be more effective if the terrain is reconnoitered and obstacles and fire lanes are prepared. The LP/OPs should be supplemented by patrols, mainly during periods of limited visibility, and wire communications should be used. Platoons should be given the mission to provide one LP/OP in order to provide spot reports concerning the size, location, direction and rate of movement, and type of enemy assaulting the company sector or battle position.

c. **Task Organization.** METT-TC factors will determine how the company will be task organized to accomplish the mission. A possible task organization might be:
   (1) ***Rifle Platoons.*** Three platoons (one platoon minus a squad) occupy the defensive sector.
   (2) ***Reserve.*** Detached squad from one of the rifle platoons. The reserve should be given priority of commitment missions such as reinforcing the fires of the defense, reacting to a danger on the flank, or counterattacking to throw the enemy from a foothold. The biggest threat to the company is for the enemy to gain a foothold and use it to begin clearing buildings. Any foothold should be counterattacked and the enemy must be quickly and violently expelled.
   (3) ***Fire Support.*** Company 60-mm mortar and antitank weapons.
   (4) ***Company Control.*** An engineer squad, with priority to the company obstacle plan, then reverts to company reserve. Engineers should be controlled at company level. They construct obstacles, prepare access routes, and assist in preparing defensive positions. Additional attachments or OPCON units, such as BFVs and tanks may be placed under company control. For example, a BFV Infantry element can be used to defend a sector or battle position. The BFVs can stay under the control of the platoon sergeant and support by fire and or conduct other missions as determined by the company commander. A platoon or section of tanks attached or OPCON to the company should provide heavy direct-fire support, engage enemy tanks, and support counterattacks. An attached or OPCON tank platoon can initially attack by fire and then revert to a mobile reserve role. The company executive officer can be used to control a reserve with multiple elements.

d. **Execution.** The defensive forces should ambush on the avenues of approach, cover the obstacles by fire, and prepare a strong defense inside the buildings. Counterattack forces should be near the front of the company sector in covered and concealed positions with an on order mission to counterattack. Rehearsals should be conducted both day and night. Counterattack forces should also be given specific instructions of what their actions will be after the enemy assault has been repelled; for example, stay in sector or revert back to reserve status.

3-25. DEFENSE OF KEY URBAN TERRAIN

An Infantry company may have to defend key urban terrain. This defense may be part of defensive operations or may be an adjunct mission to stability and support operations. In many cases, the mission is characterized by an unclear enemy situation and extremely restrictive ROE. The key terrain may be a public utility, such as gas, electrical, or water plants; a communications center, such as radio and or television; transportation center; a traffic circle; and so forth. When assigned a mission of this type, a company commander may often find his company having to defend a piece of terrain that he would rather not have to occupy. Often the facilities previously described are sited for their centrality of location and convenience and not for the defensibility of the terrain.

a. **Task Organization.** The factors of METT-TC will determine the task organization of the company. Figure 3-19, depicts an Infantry rifle company reinforced with an additional rifle platoon to defend the objective (water purification plant). Additional assets will be given to the company commander as they are requested or assigned, based on mission requirements and availability. In the situation depicted in Figure 3-19, the organic weapons of the Infantry company are sufficient to accomplish the mission. The only additional requirement was for another rifle platoon to defend the objective.

b. **Tasks.** In the situation shown in Figure 3-19, the company commander has determined that in order to properly defend the objective, he needs to deploy platoons on the defensible terrain available. Therefore, he is defending urban terrain (left), high ground (top), and low vegetated terrain (right, bottom). Additionally, it may be necessary to perform some of the tasks listed below:
- Provide inner and outer security patrols.
- Conduct counterreconnaissance.
- Establish LP/OPs.
- Establish checkpoints and roadblocks.
- Conduct civilian control and evacuation.
- Conduct coordination with local authorities.
- Prevent collateral damage.
- Supervise specific functions associated with operation of the facility, such as water purification tests, site inspections, and so forth.

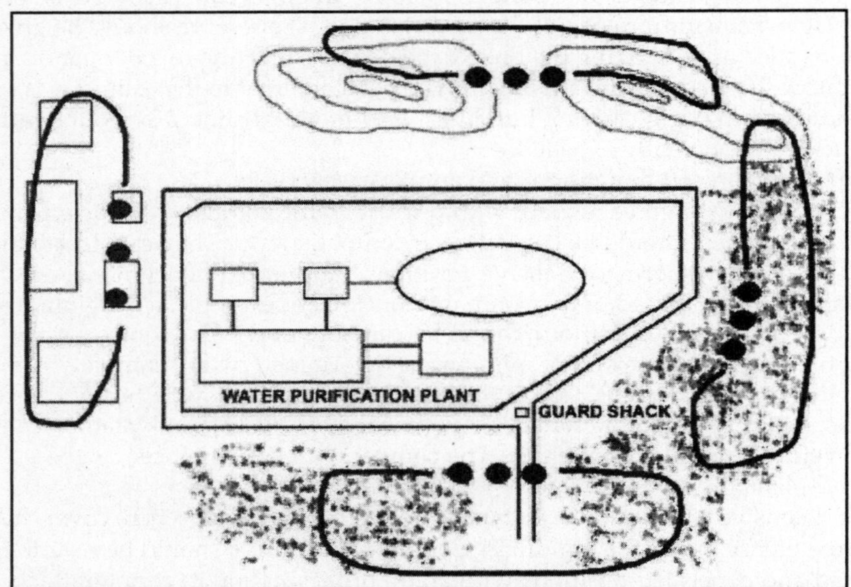

Figure 3-19: Perimeter defense of key terrain.

c. **Execution.** The company commander will normally deploy platoons in a perimeter around the objective in order to dominate key terrain and cover the mounted and dismounted avenues of approach into the objective. Machine guns and antitank weapons will be emplaced to cover the dismounted and mounted avenues of approach into the objective, respectively. Wire obstacles will normally be used to restrict and deny entry into the objective area. Obstacles should be covered by fire and rigged with detection devices and trip flares. Antitank and command-detonated mines will be used consistent with the ROE. The company prepares to defend against a direct attack, such as a raid, or sabotage against key facilities within the objective, for example, water filtration system, pump station, and so forth. The commander makes an assessment as to the overall importance of the key facilities within the objective and prioritizes security requirements. The 60-mm mortar section is positioned to provide 360-degree fire support. The AT section is positioned to engage vehicular targets. If the threat does not require the employment of mortars or AT weapons, these sections are given other tasks.

> ✍ **NOTE**
> IBCT company assets will be positioned using the same considerations.

d. **Other Considerations.** Depending on the mission requirements and threat, the company commander may have to consider the need for the following:
   - Artillery and attack helicopter support.
   - ADA assets to defend against air attack.
   - Engineer assets to construct obstacles.
   - Interpreters to assist in the functioning of the facility and operation of the equipment.
   - MP, civil affairs, and or PSYOP assets for civilian control and liaison/coordination with local police and or authorities.
   - BFVs or tanks to act as a mobile reserve or reaction force, or integrated into the company plan.

e. **Force Protection.** The company may be required to conduct a perimeter defense as part of force protection, such as defending a friendly base camp on urban terrain. The same techniques of establishing a perimeter defense would be used. The company maintains the appropriate level of security (100, 50, 30 percent, and so forth), consistent with the commander's plan and the enemy situation. Additional tasks may include:
   - Setting up roadblocks and checkpoints.
   - Searching individuals and vehicles prior to entry into the camp.
   - Maintaining a presence as a show of force to the population outside the base camp.
   - Conducting inner and outer security patrols.
   - Clearing potential threats from any urban terrain that overwatches the base camp.
   - Conducting ambushes to interdict any enemy forces moving towards the base camp.
   - Restricting access to locations within the base camp. Conducting surveillance of these locations from within or from adjacent structures or positions.
   - Conducting reaction force duties inside and outside the perimeter of the camp.

f. **Defense of a Traffic Circle.** An Infantry company may be assigned the mission of defending a key traffic circle in an urban area, or similar terrain, to prevent the enemy from seizing it or to facilitate movement of the battalion task force or other units (Figure 3-20).

Figure 3-20: Defense of a traffic circle.

(1) The company commander with this mission should analyze enemy avenues of approach into the objective and buildings that dominate those avenues. He should plan direct and indirect fires, consistent with the ROE, on to the traffic circle itself and on the approaches to it. He should also plan for all-round defense of the buildings that dominate the traffic circle to prevent encirclement. The company should prepare as many covered and concealed routes between these buildings as time permits. This makes it easier to mass or shift fires and to execute counterattacks.

(2) Obstacles can also deny the enemy the use of the traffic circle. Obstacle planning, in this case, must take into account whether friendly forces will need to use the traffic circle.

(3) Antitank weapons can fire across the traffic circle if fields of fire are long enough. Tanks should engage enemy armored vehicles and provide heavy direct-fire support for counterattacks. BFVs should engage enemy armored vehicles and provide direct fire to protect obstacles.

3-26. DEFENSE OF AN URBAN STRONGPOINT

A company may be directed to construct a strongpoint as part of a battalion defense (Figure 3-21). In order to do so, it must be augmented with engineer support, more weapons, and CSS resources. A strong point is defended until the unit is formally ordered out of it by the commander directing the defense. Urban areas are easily converted to strongpoints. Stone, brick, or steel buildings provide cover and concealment. Buildings, sewers, and some streets provide covered and concealed routes and can be rubbled to provide obstacles. Also, telephone systems can provide communications.

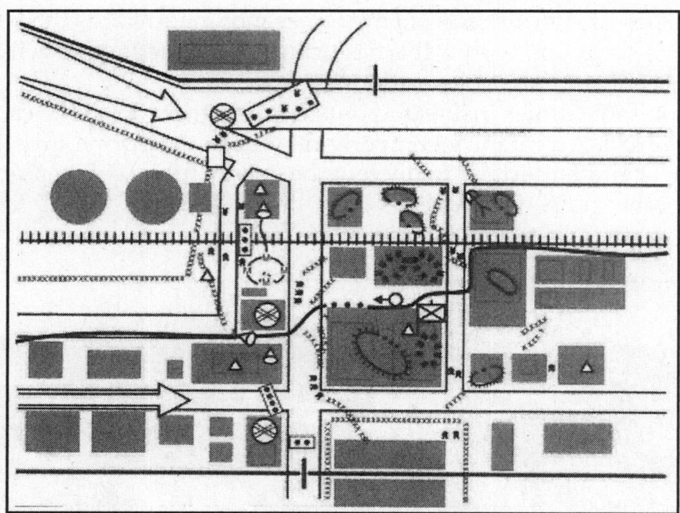

Figure 3-21: Urban strongpoint.

a. The specific positioning of unit in the strongpoint depends on the commander's mission analysis and estimate of the situation. The same considerations for a perimeter defense apply in addition to the following:

(1) Reinforce each individual fighting position (to include alternate and supplementary positions) to withstand small-arms fire, mortar fire, and artillery fragmentation. Stockpile food, water ammunition, pioneer tools, and medical supplies in each fighting position.

(2) Support each individual fighting position with several others. Plan or construct covered and concealed routes between positions and along routes of supply and communication. Use these to support counterattack and maneuver within the strongpoint.

(3) Divide the strongpoint into several independent, but mutually supporting, positions or sectors. If one of the positions or sectors must be evacuated or is overrun, limit the enemy penetration with obstacles and fires and support a counterattack.

(4) Construct obstacles and minefields to disrupt and canalize enemy formations, to reinforce fires, and to protect the strongpoint from the assault. Place the obstacles and mines out as far as friendly units can observe them, within the strongpoint, and at points in between where they will be useful.
(5) Prepare range cards for each position and confirm them by fires. Plan indirect fires in detail and register them. Indirect fires should also be planned for firing directly on the strongpoint using proximity fuses.
(6) Plan and test several means of communication within the strongpoint and to higher headquarters. These are radio, wire, messenger, pyrotechnics, and other signals.
(7) Improve or repair the strongpoint until the unit is relieved or withdrawn. More positions can be built, routes to other positions marked, existing positions improved or repaired, and barriers built or fixed.

b. A strong point may be part of any defensive plan. It may be built to protect vital units or installations, as an anchor around which more mobile units maneuver, or as part of a trap designed to destroy enemy forces that attack it.

3-27. DELAY

The intent of a delay is to slow the enemy, cause casualties, and stop him, where possible, without becoming decisively engaged. This procedure is done by defending, disengaging, moving, and defending again. A company delay is normally conducted as part of the battalion task force's plan. The delay destroys enemy reconnaissance elements forward of the outskirts of the urban area, prevents the penetration of the urban area, and gains and maintains contact with the enemy to determine the strength and location of the main attack by trading space for time. Infantry companies are well suited for this operation, because they can take advantage of the cover and concealment provided by urban terrain and inflict casualties on the enemy at close range. Delays are planned by assigning platoon battle positions, platoon sectors, or both. Figure 3-22 depicts a company delay in urban terrain with the company commander assigning platoon battle positions. Routes are planned to each subsequent battle position or within the sector. Routes also are planned to take advantage of the inherent cover and concealment afforded by urban terrain, such as going through and hugging buildings, using shadows, subsurface areas, and so forth.

Figure 3-22: Company delay in an urban area.

a. The company's sector should be prepared with obstacles to increase the effect of the delay. Engineers prepare obstacles on main routes but avoid some covered and concealed routes that are known by the friendly troops for reinforcement, displacement, and resupply. These routes are destroyed and obstacles are executed when no longer needed.

b. Antiarmor weapon systems, tanks, and BFVs should be positioned on the outskirts of the urban area to destroy the enemy at maximum range. They should be located in defilade positions or in prepared shelters. They fire at visible targets and then fall back or proceed to alternate positions. Platoons should be assigned sectors from 100 to 300 meters (one to two blocks) wide. If available, they should be reinforced with sensors or GSRs, which can be emplaced on the outskirts or on higher ground to attain the maximum range in the assigned AO. Platoons delay by detecting the enemy early and inflicting casualties on him using patrols, OPs, and ambushes and by taking advantage of all obstacles. Each action is followed by a disengagement and withdrawal. Withdrawals occur on covered and concealed routes through buildings or underground. By day, the defense is dispersed; at night, it is more concentrated. Close coordination and maintaining situational awareness are critical aspects of this operation.

SECTION VII. PLATOON DEFENSIVE OPERATIONS

In urban areas, buildings provide cover and concealment, limit fields of observation and fire, and restrict the movement of troops and armored vehicles. This section covers the key planning considerations, weapons selection, preparations, and the construction of a platoon defensive position on urbanized terrain.

3-28. PLANNING THE DEFENSE

Planning the defense begins when the leader receives a mission or determines a requirement to defend such as during consolidation and reorganization after an assault. The leader must use terrain wisely and designate a point of main effort. He chooses defensive positions that force the enemy to make costly attacks or conduct time-consuming maneuvers to avoid them. A position that the enemy can readily avoid has no defensive value unless the enemy can be induced to attack it. The defense, no less than the offense, should achieve surprise. As platoon leaders conduct their troop-leading procedures, they also have to consider civilians, ROE, limited collateral damage, and coordination with adjacent units to eliminate the probability of fratricide. Maneuver, methods, and courses of action in establishing defensive positions in and around urbanized terrain are METT-TC intensive.

a. **Focus.** The squad's and platoon's focus for defending in an urban area is the retention of terrain. As with most defensive scenarios, the squad and platoon will defend as part of the company. The platoon will either be given a sector to defend or a battle position to occupy and the platoon leader must construct his defense within the constraints given to him. See Sections II and III for other planning considerations.

b. **Strongpoint.** One of the most common defensive tasks a platoon will be given during urban operations is to conduct a strongpoint defense of a building, part of a building, or a group of small buildings (see paragraph 3-26 and Figure 3-21). The platoon's defense is normally integrated into the company's mission. The platoon leader organizes the strongpoint defense by positioning personnel and their weapons systems to maximize their capabilities. Supporting fires are incorporated into the overall defensive plan to provide depth to the engagement area.

   (1) The platoon leader organizes the defense into a series of individual, team, and squad fighting positions located to cover avenues of approach and obstacles, and to provide mutual support in order to repel the enemy advance. Snipers should be positioned to support the commander's intent and to allow for the opportunity to engage C2 and key targets.

   (2) Depending on the length of the mission, the platoon should stockpile munitions (especially grenades), food and water, medical supplies, and firefighting equipment.

3-29. PRIORITIES OF WORK AND DEFENSIVE CONSIDERATIONS

A critical platoon- and squad-level defensive task during defensive urban operations is the preparation of fighting positions. General defensive considerations in urban terrain are similar to any other defensive operations. Fighting positions in urban areas are usually constructed inside buildings and are selected based on an analysis of the area in which the building is located, the individual characteristics of the building, and the characteristics of the weapons system.

a. **Priorities of Work.** The priorities of work are the same as those listed in paragraph 3-12. Specific considerations at platoon level are discussed below.

   (1) Select key weapons and crew-served weapon positions to cover likely mounted and dismounted avenues of approach. To cover armored avenues of approach, position antiarmor weapons inside buildings with adequate space and ventilation for backblast (on upper floors, if possible, for long-range shots). Position

machine guns / M249s to cover dismounted avenues of approach. Place them near ground level to increase grazing fires. If ground rubble obstructs grazing fires, place machine guns / M249s in the upper stories of the building. Ensure weapons are mutually supporting and are tied in with adjacent units.

(2) Ensure the position is free of noncombatants. Remove them from the area of operations before occupying the position.

(3) Clear fields of fire. Prepare loopholes, aiming stakes, sector stakes, and TRP markings. Construct positions with overhead cover and camouflage (inside and outside).

(4) Identify and secure subsurface avenues of approach (sewers, basements, stairwells, and rooftops).

(5) Stockpile ammunition, food, fire-fighting equipment, and drinking water.

(6) Construct barriers and emplace obstacles to deny the enemy any access to streets, underground passages, and buildings, and to slow his movement. Integrate barriers and or obstacles with key weapons. Cover all barriers and obstacles by fire (both direct and indirect) and or observation. (See Chapter 8 for more information concerning obstacles.)

(7) Improve and mark movement routes between positions as well as to alternate and supplementary positions. Improve routes by digging trenches, if possible; using sewers and tunnels; creating entry holes; and positioning ropes and ladders for ascending and descending.

b. **Considerations.** The following must be considered when establishing a defensive position:

(1) ***Security.*** The first priority is establishing all-around security. Each position should have at least one soldier providing security during all preparations.

(2) ***Protection.*** Select buildings that provide protection from direct and indirect fires. Reinforced concrete buildings with three or more floors provide suitable protection while buildings constructed of wood, paneling, or other light material must be reinforced to provide sufficient protection. One- and two-story buildings without a strongly constructed cellar are vulnerable to indirect fires and require construction of overhead protection for each fighting position. If possible, use materials gathered from the immediate area to build the overhead cover.

(3) ***Dispersion.*** A platoon position should not be established in a single building when it is possible to occupy two or more buildings that permit mutually supporting fires. A position without mutual support in one building is vulnerable to bypass, isolation, and subsequent destruction from any direction.

(4) ***Concealment.*** Do not select buildings that are obvious defensive positions (easily targeted by the enemy). If the requirements for security and fields of fire dictate the occupation of exposed buildings, the platoon will be required to add reinforcement materials to the building to provide suitable protection to the troops inside.

(5) ***Fields of Fire.*** To prevent isolation, individual and crew-served weapons positions should be mutually supporting and have fields of fire in all directions. When clearing fields of fire, try to maintain the natural appearance of the surrounding area if possible. Removing objects that interfere with the gunner's field of vision may be necessary.

(6) ***Covered Routes.*** Defensive positions should have at least one covered and concealed route that allows resupply, medical evacuation, reinforcement, or withdrawal from the building without being detected, or at least provides protection from direct fire weapons. The route can be established using underground systems, communications trenches, or walls and buildings that allow covered movement.

(7) ***Observation.*** Positions in buildings should permit observation of enemy avenues of approach and adjacent defensive sectors. Upper stories offer the best observation but also attract enemy fire.

(8) ***Fire Hazard.*** If possible, avoid selecting positions in buildings that are obvious fire hazards. If these flammable structures must be occupied, reduce the danger of fire by wetting down the immediate area, laying an inch of sand on the floors, and providing fire extinguishers and fire fighting equipment. Ensure that each defender is familiar with the withdrawal routes and that they have the opportunity to rehearse their withdrawal using these planned routes in the event of fire.

(9) ***Tag Lines.*** Tag lines are a flexible handhold used to guide individuals along a route. Tag lines aid in navigation and movement when operating in confined spaces such as buildings, tunnel systems and caverns where visibility is limited and sense of direction can be lost. When preparing defensive positions inside buildings, tag lines can be run from each fighting position back to the command post, or along an egress route. These lines can be made of rope, string, cable, wire and so forth. The most effective item to be used as a tag line is WD-1A communications wire. Along with serving as a tag line it can be used as a primary means of communication between individual fighting positions and leader's positions.

(10) ***Time.*** Time is the one element in METT-TC that the platoon and its leaders have no control over. The most important factor to consider when planning the use of time is to provide subordinate leaders with two-thirds of all available time. The unit TACSOP provides the leaders with their priorities when time does not allow for detailed planning. The platoon will complete defensive preparation IAW the TACSOP and the commander's operational priorities.

c. **Preparation.** Preparation of the platoon's individual fighting positions will normally be conducted inside the buildings the platoon has been assigned to defend. As with all defensive positions, the leader's first task is to establish security. This will normally be in the form of an observation post located within the protection of the platoon's direct fire weapons. The OP should be manned with at least two personnel. Leaders then assign individual or two-man positions to adequately cover his sector. The squad leader will position himself to best control his squad. The platoon leader will designate the level of security to be maintained. The remaining personnel will continue to work preparing the defense. The leaders will continue to make improvements to the defense as time permits. (The preparation of fighting positions is discussed in detail in Chapter 1.)

d. **Other Typical Tasks.** Additional defensive preparation tasks may be required in basements, on ground floors, and on upper floors.

(1) ***Basements and Ground Floors.*** Basements require preparation similar to that of the ground floor. Any underground system not used by the defender that could provide enemy access to the position must be blocked.

(a) *Doors.* Unused doors should be locked or nailed shut, as well as blocked and reinforced with furniture, sandbags, or other field expedients.

(b) *Hallways.* If not required for the defender's movement, hallways should be blocked with furniture and tactical wire (Figure 3-23).

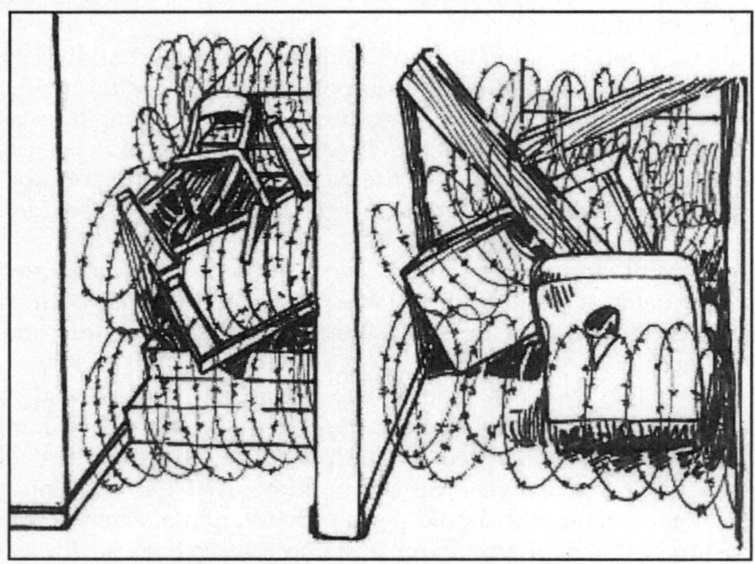

Figure 3-23: Blocking stairs and doorways.

(c) *Stairs.* Unused stairs should be blocked with furniture and tactical wire, or removed. If possible, all stairs should be blocked (Figure 3-23), and ladders should be used to move from floor to floor and then removed.

(d) *Windows.* Remove all glass. Block unused windows with boards or sandbags to prevent observation and access.

(e) *Floors.* Make fighting positions in the floors. If there is no basement, fighting positions can give additional protection from heavy direct fire weapons.

(f) *Ceilings.* Erect support for ceilings that otherwise would not withstand the weight of fortified positions or rubble from upper floors (Figure 3-24).

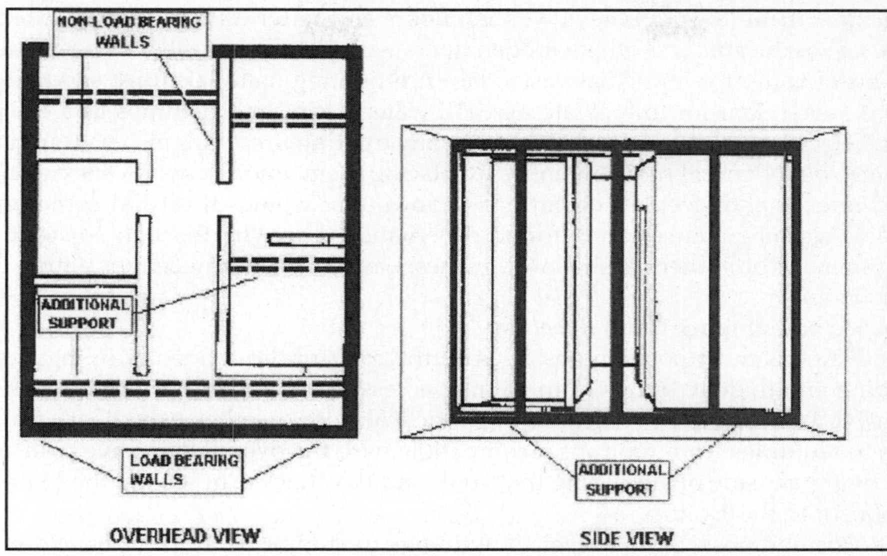

Figure 3-24: Reinforcing ceilings.

(g) *Unoccupied Rooms.* Block rooms not required for defense with tactical wire.

(2) ***Upper Floors.*** Upper floors require the same preparation as ground floors. Windows need not be blocked, but should be covered with wire mesh, canvas, ponchos, or other heavy material, to prevent grenades from being thrown in from the outside. The covering should be loose at the bottom to permit the defender to drop grenades.

(3) ***Interior Routes.*** Routes are required that permit defending fire teams and squads to move within the building (Figure 3-25) to engage enemy forces from any direction. Plan and construct escape routes to permit rapid evacuation of a room or a building. Mouseholes should be made through interior walls to permit movement between rooms. Such holes should be marked to enable defenders to easily locate them during day and night conditions. Brief all personnel as to where the various routes are located. Conduct rehearsals so that everyone becomes familiar with the routes.

Figure 3-25: Movement routes within building.

(4) ***Fire Prevention.*** Buildings that have wooden floors and rafter ceilings require extensive fire prevention measures. Cover the attic and other wooden floors with about one to two inches of sand or dirt, and position buckets of water for immediate use. Place fire-fighting materials (dirt, sand, fire extinguishers, and blankets) on each floor for immediate use. Fill water basins and bathtubs as a reserve for fire fighting. Turn off all electricity and gas. If available, use any existing fire extinguishers found in buildings.

(5) ***Communications.*** Conceal radio antennas by placing them among civilian television antennas, along the sides of chimneys and steeples, or out of windows that would direct FM communications away from enemy early-warning sources and ground observation. Lay wire through adjacent buildings or underground systems or bury them in shallow trenches. Lay wire communications within the building through walls and floors.

(6) ***Rubbling.*** See paragraph 3-11c(8) *Rubbling*.

(7) ***Rooftops.*** Platoons must position obstacles on the roofs of flat-topped buildings to prevent helicopters from landing and to deny troops from gaining access to the building from the roof. Cover rooftops that are accessible from adjacent structures with tactical wire or other expedients and guard them. Block entrances to buildings from rooftops if compatible with the overall defensive plan. Remove or block the structure on the outside of a building that could aid the attacker in scaling the building to gain access to upper floors or to the rooftop.

(8) ***Obstacles.*** Position obstacles adjacent to buildings to stop or delay vehicles and infantry. To save time and resources in preparing the defense, platoon leaders must allow the use of all available materials, such as automobiles, railcars, and rubble, to create obstacles. Vehicles can be tied together by running poles through their windows. Leaders must supervise the construction of obstacles to ensure they are tied to buildings and rubble areas to increase effectiveness, and to canalize the enemy into engagement areas selected by the leader. Direct support engineers can provide advice and resources as to the employment of obstacles and mines.

(9) ***Fields of Fire.*** The field of fire is the area a weapon or group of weapons may cover effectively with fire from a given position. After the defensive positions are selected and the individuals have occupied their assigned positions, they will determine what clearance is necessary to maximize their field of fire. Leaders and individuals must view fields of fire from the fighting position and from the view of the enemy. Only selective clearing will be done to improve the field of fire. If necessary, the position will be relocated to attain the desired field of fire. Within the field of fire leaders will designate for each weapons system a primary and an alternate sector of fire. Each weapons system has unique requirements for its field of fire, and the platoon and squad leaders must ensure these requirements are met. Each position is checked to ensure that the fields of fire provide the maximum opportunity for target engagement and to determine any dead space within the sector of fire.

e. **Antitank Weapons Positions.** Employ antitank weapons in areas that maximize their capabilities in the urban area. The lack of a protective transport could require the weapon to be fired from inside a building, from behind the cover of a building, or from behind the cover of protective terrain. Leaders should make every effort to employ antitank weapons in pairs so that the same target can be engaged from different positions. Another consideration is security for the crew and system. This is necessary to allow the gunner to concentrate on locating and engaging enemy armor.

f. **Sniper Positions.** Snipers give the platoon a force multiplier by providing an overwatch capability and by engaging enemy C2 targets. Snipers normally operate in two-man teams, which provides the shooter with security and another set of eyes for observation and to locate and identify targets. Leaders should allow the snipers to select their own positions for supporting the defense. An effective sniper organization can trouble the enemy far more than its cost in the number of friendly soldiers employed. Snipers deploy in positions where they are not easily detected, and where they can provide the most benefit.

3-30. CONDUCT OF THE DEFENSE

The conduct of the defense in an urban area is similar to the conduct of the defense in any other environments.

a. **Occupy Positions.** After planning and preparing for the defense, the platoon moves to the defensive positions using prescribed movement techniques. To establish the defense the platoon will stop short of the actual site and conduct a reconnaissance to ensure the area is free of enemy or noncombatants, and to identify individual and crew served weapons positions. The platoon then establishes security and begins to occupy positions. Once the platoon has occupied, the priorities of work will be performed as established by the platoon leader.

b. **Locate the Enemy.** The platoon establishes and maintains OPs and conducts security patrols as directed by the commander. OPs, patrols, and individual soldiers look and listen using night vision devises, binoculars, and early warning systems to detect the enemy's approach.

c. **Action on Contact.** Once the enemy is detected, the platoon leader—
   - Alerts the platoon sergeant, squad leaders and forward observer.
   - Reports the situation to the company commander.
   - If possible, calls in OP's.
   - Initiates indirect fire mission when enemy is at maximum range.
   - Initiates long-range direct fires on command.

d. **Fight the Defense.** Determining that the platoon can destroy the enemy from their current positions, the platoon leader—
   - Continues with indirect and direct fire engagements.
   - Controls fires using standard commands, pyrotechnics, and other prearranged signals.
   - Initiates FPF as the enemy closes on the protective wire.

The platoon continues to defend until the enemy is repelled or ordered to disengage.

3-31. CONSOLIDATION AND REORGANIZATION

Once the enemy has been repelled, the order to consolidate and reorganize will be given by the platoon leader.

a. The platoon will—
   - Reestablish security.
   - Reman key weapons.
   - Provide first aid and prepare to evacuate casualties.
   - Repair damaged obstacles and replace mines and early warning devices.
   - Redistribute ammunition and supplies.
   - Relocate key weapons, and adjust positions for mutual support.
   - Reestablish communications.
   - Prepare for a renewed enemy attack.

b. Squad leaders provide ammunition, casualties, and equipment (ACE) report to the platoon leader.

c. The platoon leader—
   - Reestablishes the platoon chain of command.
   - Provides a platoon ACE report to the commander.

d. The platoon sergeant coordinates for resupply and supervises casualty evacuation.

e. The platoon quickly reestablishes OP's, resumes patrolling and continues to improve the defense.

3-32. COUNTERATTACK

A platoon may be given the mission to counterattack in order to retake a defensive position or key point, to destroy or eject an enemy foothold, or to stop an enemy attack by hitting his flank and forcing him to stop his movement and establish a hasty defense.

a. A platoon counterattack is planned at company level to meet each probable enemy penetration. They must be well coordinated and aggressively executed. Counterattacks should be directed at the enemy's flank and supported with direct and indirect fires.

b. If tank support is available, it should be used to spearhead the counterattack. Tanks have the mobility, firepower, and survivability to quickly execute the counterattack mission. Tanks are ideally suited for destroying enemy armor, heavy weapons, and fortifications with their main gun and engaging enemy infantry with their coaxial machine gun. This capability will assist the infantry in executing their part of the mission.

c. The counterattack mission is planned and coordinated as part of the defensive operation.

(1) Considerations for counterattack planning may include, but are not limited to, the following:
- Location of friendly units.
- Location of noncombatants.
- Critical location in the defense that, if threatened, could collapse.
- Size and type of force required to defeat and eject the enemy.
- Where in the defense do we want the enemy to think he is successful?
- Who determines and initiates the execution of the counterattack?

(2) Control measures needed for the conduct of the counterattack include:
- Assembly area or blocking position.
- Start point, route, and release point, if necessary.
- Attack position.
- Line of departure or line of contact.
- Zone of action, direction of attack, and or axis of advance.
- Objective.
- Limit of advance.

3-33. DEFENSE AGAINST ARMOR

Urban terrain is well suited to an infantry's defense against mechanized infantry and armored forces. Mechanized infantry and armored forces will attempt to avoid the dense, canalizing urban areas but may be forced to pass through them. Well-trained infantry can inflict heavy casualties on such forces.

a. Urban areas have certain traits that favor antiarmor operations.
- Rubble in the streets can be used to block enemy vehicles, conceal mines, and cover and conceal defending infantry.
- The buildings restrict and canalize armor maneuver, fields of fire, and communications, reducing the enemy's ability to reinforce.
- Buildings provide cover and concealment for defending infantry.
- Rooftops, alleys, and upper floors provide good firing positions.
- Sewers, drains, and subways provide underground routes for infantry forces.

b. When preparing for antiarmor operations in urban areas leaders should:

(1) ***Choose a good engagement area.*** Enemy tanks should be engaged where most restricted in their ability for mutual support. The best way for infantrymen to engage tanks is one at a time, so they can destroy one tank without being open to the fires of another. Typical locations include narrow streets, turns in the road, "T" intersections, bridges, tunnels, split-level roads, and rubbled areas. Less obvious locations can include using demolitions or mines to create obstacles.

(2) ***Select good weapons positions.*** The best weapons positions are places where the tank is weakest and the infantry is most protected. A tank's ability to see and fire is limited, to the rear and flanks, if the tanks are buttoned up. Figure 3-26, shows the weapons and visual dead space of a buttoned-up tank against targets located at ground level and overhead. The TRPs should be clearly visible through the gunner's sights and resistant to battle damage (for example, large buildings or bridge abatements, but not trees or cars). The leader of the antiarmor operation should specify what type of engagement should be used such as frontal, crossfire, or depth. Frontal fire is the least preferred since it exposes the gunner to the greatest probability of detection and is where armor is the thickest.

(a) The best places to fire on tanks from the dismounted infantry perspectives are at the flanks and rear at ground level or at the top of tanks if the force is in an elevated position in a building. A suitable antiarmor defense might be set up as shown in Figure 3-27.

(b) The best place to engage a tank from a flank is over the second road wheel at close range. This can be done using a corner so the tank cannot traverse the turret to counterattack.

(c) For a safe engagement from an elevated position, infantrymen should engage the tank from a range three times the elevation of the weapons.

Figure 3-26: Tanks cannot fire at close-range, street-level, and overhead targets.

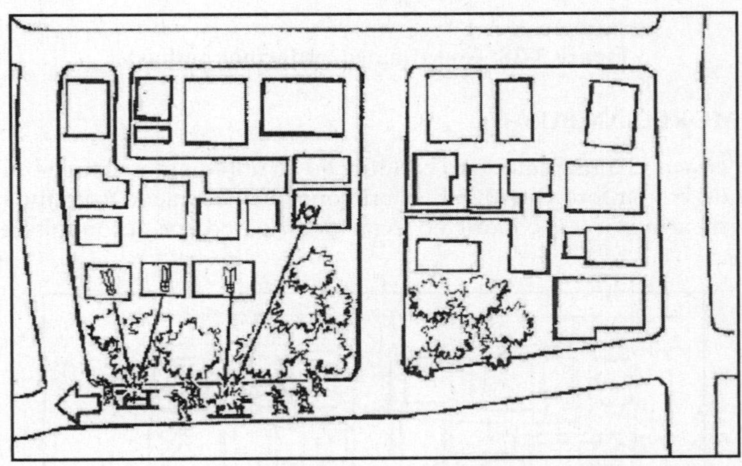

Figure 3-27: A platoon's antiarmor defense.

(d) To engage at a longer range is to risk counterfire since the weapon's position will not be in the tank's overhead dead space. Overhead fire at the rear or flank of the tank is even more effective. Alternate and supplementary positions should be selected to enforce all-round security and to increase flexibility.

(3) ***Coordinate target engagement.*** The first task of the tank-killing force is to force the tanks to button up using all available direct and indirect fire because tanks are most vulnerable when buttoned up. The next task is to coordinate the fires of the antitank weapons so if there is more than one target in the engagement area, all targets are engaged at the same time.

c. Often armored vehicles are accompanied by infantry in built-up areas so antiarmor weapons must be supported by an effective all-round antipersonnel defense (Figure 3-28).

d. At a planned signal (for example, the detonation of a mine) all targets are engaged at the same time. If targets cannot be engaged simultaneously, they are engaged in the order of the most dangerous first. Although tanks present the greatest threat, threat armored personnel carriers (APCs) are also dangerous because their infantry can dismount and destroy friendly antiarmor positions. If the friendly force is not secured by several infantrymen, priority of engagement might be given to threat APCs.

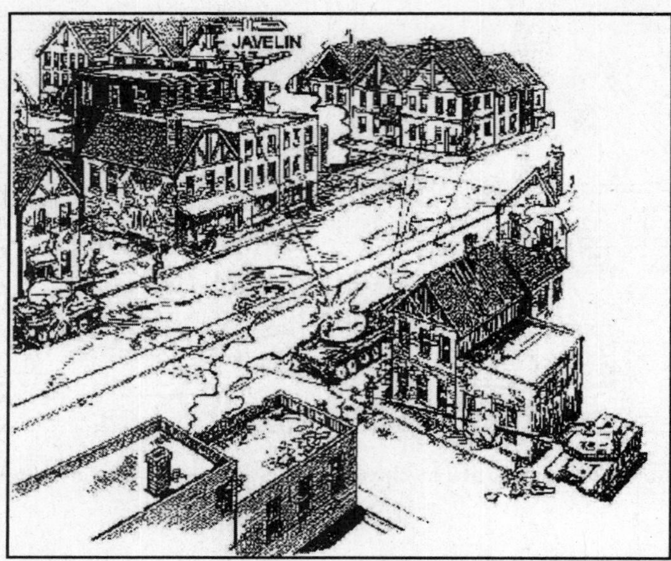

Figure 3-28: Coordinated antiarmor ambush.

3-34. CONDUCT OF ARMORED AMBUSH

A rifle company can use an attached tank platoon to conduct an armored ambush in a built-up area (Figure 3-29). To do so, the tank platoon should be reinforced with a BFV and one or two squads from the rifle company. The ambush can be effective against enemy armor if it is conducted in an area cleared and reconnoitered by friendly forces.

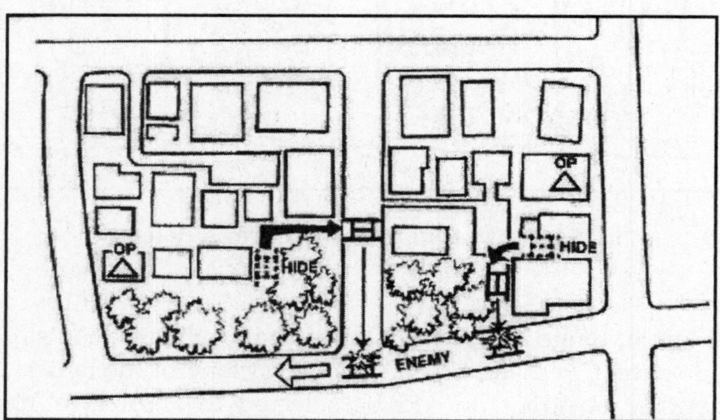

Figure 3-29: Armored ambush.

a. The ambushing tank platoon must know the area. The operation involves maneuver on a road network that is free of obstacles. Obstacles outside the ambush area can be used to canalize and delay the enemy.
b. The ambushing tanks should be located in a hide position about 1,000 meters from the expected enemy avenue of approach. A security post, located at a choke point, observes and reports the approach, speed, security posture, and activity of the enemy. This role is assigned to scouts, if available, or Infantrymen who use the BFV to move from OP to OP; or a series of dismounted OPs are established. When the enemy is reported at a trigger point or TRP, the tank platoon leader knows how much he must move his tanks to execute the ambush.
c. Tanks move quickly from their hide positions to firing positions, taking advantage of all available concealment. They try for flank shots on the approaching enemy at an average range of 300 to 400 meters. These ranges do not expose tanks to the enemy infantry. Once the enemy is engaged, tanks break contact and move to a rally point with close security provided by an infantry squad and moves to a new ambush site.